10,000 Drinks

To my wife Nicole, my children Camryn and Colby, and to all my drinking buddies, past and present.

Library of Congress Cataloging-in-Publication Data

Knorr, Paul.
10,000 drinks / Paul Knorr.
p. cm.
ISBN-13: 978-1-4027-4287-3
ISBN-10: 1-4027-4287-8
1. Bartending. I. Title. II. Title: Ten thousand drinks.

TX951.K54 2007
641.8'74--dc22 2007001784

2 4 6 8 10 9 7 5 3 1

Published by Sterling Publishing Co., Inc.
387 Park Avenue South, New York, NY 10016

Distributed in Canada by Sterling Publishing
c/o Canadian Manda Group, 165 Dufferin Street
Toronto, Ontario, Canada M6K 3H6
Distributed in the United Kingdom by GMC Distribution Services
Castle Place, 166 High Street, Lewes, East Sussex, England BN7 1XU
Distributed in Australia by Capricorn Link (Australia) Pty. Ltd.
P.O. Box 704, Windsor, NSW 2756, Australia

Printed in China

Sterling ISBN-13: 978-1-4027-4287-3
ISBN-10: 1-4027-4287-8

10,000 Drinks

27 Years' Worth of Cocktails!

Recipes and tips for 10,000 alcoholic and nonalcoholic mixed drinks, eye-openers, party starters, pick-me-ups, and thirst-quenching libations

Paul Knorr

New York / London
www.sterlingpublishing.com

Introduction

I'm from New York and here we don't usually serve hamburgers with mustard on them. For a period of time, I lived in Atlanta, where mustard was more common than ketchup. Ordering that most basic of American foods resulted in a completely different taste. The same thing can and does happen with mixed drinks.

This book tries to capture the vast variety of cocktails and mixed drinks that exist in the world today. There are as many different drinks as there are bartenders. A good bartender can take a customer's request to "surprise me" and make up a mixology masterpiece on the spot. In culling my collection of recipes down to just 10,000 for this book, I've tried to include most of the popular favorites—the drinks that people know and love—as well as a selection of more exotic libations that are outside of the norm. Amazingly, I feel like 10,000 barely scratches the surface of all the drinks I could have included.

In organizing this book I've tried to separate the drinks into logical categories, grouping similar drinks together. This resulted in some rather broad categories like "tall drinks" as well as some very focused ones like "Tabasco® shots." Sometimes the drinks are grouped by what's in them as is the case with "coffee drinks" and "champagne drinks;" other times the categories are based on how the drink is made as in "blended and frozen" and "depth charge." Some of my favorite categories are based on how the drinks are consumed, as with "shots" and "mind erasers." Within each category, the drinks are arranged alphabetically to make things easier to find. I hope this breakdown encourages you to browse and explore rather than use this book solely as a reference.

Finally, most of the drinks in this book give measurements in "parts," as in 1 part this and 2 parts that. This serves two purposes. First, it makes the recipes work even if you're metrically challenged, as there's no need to convert between ounces and centiliters. The other reason for listing the proportions is to allow for different glassware. A Cosmopolitan (as an overused example) requires different amounts of ingredients when poured into a cocktail glass than when served over ice in a rocks glass, but proportionally the ingredients are the same. Either way, it's 1 part this and 2 parts that.

Contents

Bartending Tools

Bar Mats

Also known as spill stops, these mats trap spillage and keep the bar neat. They are especially handy during messy tasks such as pouring shots. Don't forget to empty the mats and wash them after each use.

Bar Rags

Always keep at least two bar rags handy to wipe up spills and keep the bar clean.

Bar Spoon

A bar spoon is a small spoon with a very long handle. It has many uses behind the bar. It can be used for stirring cocktails of course, but you can also pour a liqueur over the back of the spoon when layering it on top of another liqueur. You can also use it to scrape the bottom of the blender.

Blender

What bar would be complete without a blender for making fancy frozen drinks? A heavy-duty, multi-speed blender is a good choice.

Boston Shaker

This is a less elegant, but easier, cheaper, and more reliable alternative to the martini shaker. It consists of a metal cup and a pint glass. Place ice and liquids in the cup, perss the glass tightly over the cup to form a seal, shake, and serve. Since a Boston shaker does not have a strainer built in, you will need a separate strainer to hold back the ice as you poor.

Garnish Tray

A nice, neat, covered tray to hold your lemon slices, lime wedges, orange wheels, and cherries.

Ice Scoop

All commercial establishments require a designated scoop for use with ice, and it's wise to use an ice scoop at home as well. Ice is legally considered a food, all the food-handling safety procedures apply. Do not use a use a glass to scoop the ice, or you run the risk of chipping the glass–imagine trying to find a glass chip in an ice bin! Also, keep your hands, used glassware, and any other potentially dirty object out of contact with the ice.

Jigger

A jigger is a measuring device that consists of two metal cups welded bottom to bottom. One of the cups is 1.5 ounces (45 ml) and the other is 1 ounce (30 ml). Some fancier jiggers have handles.

Knife

A good, sharp knife is essential for cutting fruit for garnish. A knife can also serve as a zester and peeler. It can also be used to cut wedges and slices or to make lemon zest or lime twists.

Liquor Pours or Spouts

A liquor pour is used to control the flow of liquor from the bottle. This helps to prevent spilling and splashing and also controls under- or over-pouring. Most pours flow at 1 ounce per second; with a little practice and a liquor pour a bartender can accurately measure an ounce counting.

A "measured pour" has a built-in measurement, and stops the flow after that amount.

Shaker

Also called a "cocktail shaker" or "martini shaker," a shaker has three parts: the cup, the top, and the cap. Place ice in the cup followed by the liquids press the top and the cap on tightly, and shake (away from the customer!). To serve, remove the cap and use the top as a strainer.

Strainer

A strainer fits over the top of a Boston shaker or any other glass and is used to strain the ice from a drink after it's been stirred or shaken. At the top of the previous page, the drawing on the left is of a shaker and the drawing on the right is of a strainer.

Wine Opener

Any bar that serves wine should have a wine opener, whether it be a simple corkscrew, or a fancy "estate" wine opener that mounts on the edge of the bar. The most popular is the "waiter's corkscrew," which is small, easy to use, and folds up so it can be kept in a pocket.

Drink Styles

Aperitif An alcoholic drink taken before a meal, or any of several wines or bitters.

Buck A drink made with an ounce of liquor with lemon juice and ginger ale, and topped with a twist of lemon.

Chaser A beverage you consume after doing a shot of liquor rather than combining them with a spirit in the same glass. The original chaser was the Boiler-maker, which is a shot followed by a beer.

Cobbler A tall summer-style drink that consists of ice, wine or liqueur, and a variety of fruit slices, cherries, berries, and so forth

Collins Tall, cool, punch-like drinks made by combining any basic liquor with sugar, soda water and lime or lemon juice. Serve over ice cubes in a frosted glass. (A Tom Collins is made with Gin, a John Collins with Whiskey, and a Joe Collins with Scotch.)

Cooler A low-alcohol drink consisting of either white or red wine mixed with lemon-lime soda, ginger ale, club soda or a citrus juice.

Dry A term used to describe a lack of sweetness in a wine or liqueur.

Fix A sour drink, usually made with pineapple juice and crushed ice.

Fizz A drink made from liquor, citrus juices, and sugar, shaken with ice and strained into a highball glass to which any carbonated beverage, even champagne, may added.

Flip An eggnog-and-fizz combination that is made with liquor, egg, sugar, and shaved ice, shaken well, and sprinkled with nutmeg.

Frappé A drink made by packing a glass with crushed ice and pouring liqueur over it.

Highball Any liquor served with ice, soda, ginger ale, or another carbonated beverage.

Julep Made with a liquor (traditionally bourbon) and fresh mint leaves (muddled, crushed, or whole), served in a frosted glass with shaved ice and a mint garnish

Lowball A short drink consisting of spirits served with ice alone or with water, or soda in a short glass. A lowball is also known as an on-the-rocks or old-fashioned.

Mist A drink in which a spirit, usually straight, is served in a glass packed with crushed ice.

Neat A straight shot of any spirit taken in a single gulp, usually without any accompaniment. Also called a shooter.

Pick-Me-Up Any concoction designed to allay the effects of overindulgence in alcoholic beverages.

Pousse-Café A sweet, multi-layered after-dinner drink in which each layer is separate and distinct from the others. The layers are achieved by determining the relative heaviness of the component liquids and adding them heaviest to lightest.

Rickey A drink that is a cross between a collins and a sour consisting of lime or lemon juice, club soda, and alcohol. Unlike the collins and sour, it contains no added sugar.

Sangaree A drink made with whiskey, gin, rum, or brandy; with port wine floated on top, or with wine, ale, porter, or stout with a sprinkle of nutmeg.

Shooter A straight shot of spirits taken neat, or a mixture of spirits and other ingredients chilled and strained into a shot glass

Sling Made like sangarees, but with the addition of lemon juice and a twist of lemon peel, and served in an old-fashioned glass.

Smash Small juleps, served in an old-fashioned glass, made from muddled sugar, ice cubes, soda water, and whiskey, gin, rum or brandy.

Sour A drink made by combining lemon juice, ice, sugar, with any basic liquor.

Swizzle Originally a tall rum cooler filled with cracked ice that was "swizzled" with a long stirring rod or spoon rotated rapidly between the palms to produce frost on the glass

Toddy Originally a hot drink made with spirits, sugar, spices such as cinnamon and cloves, and a lemon peel, mixed with hot water and served in a tall glass. Toddys can also be served cold.

Bartending Techniques

Pour ingredients into glass neat (do not chill) Add all of the ingredients to the glass (typically a shot glass) straight from the bottle. Don't chill them if they're not already cold.

Layer in a shot glass Pour each of the ingredients into a shot glass or a pousse-café glass, keeping each ingredient on its own distinct layer. To achieve the layering effect, place a bar spoon upside down against the inner rim of the glass, just above the first ingredient. Gently pour the next ingredient over the back of the spoon to prevent the liquor from entering the glass too quickly and therefore mixing with the previous ingredient. For these types of drinks, the order is important; for best results pour heavier ingredients first.

Layer over ice Fill the glass with ice and gently add each ingredient so they mix as little as possible.

Layer over ice. Drink through a straw. Layer the drink over ice as described above, but fin ish by adding a straw. These types of drinks are meant to be consumed quickly, with the layers of the drink providing different flavors.

Shake with ice and strain Fill the cup of a cocktail or Boston shaker with ice, add the ingredients, and cover it with the lid. Shake it briskly until the outside begins to frost, then take the top lid off (for a cocktail shaker) or remove the pint glass and place the strainer over the cup (for a Boston shaker) and strain the drink into the glass, leaving the ice behind in the shaker. This method is commonly used to create a martini.

Shake with ice and strain over ice Follow instructions to "shake with ice and strain", but strain into a glass filled with ice.

Shake with ice and pour Follow instructions to "shake with ice and strain", but remove the strainer and allow the ice to pour into the glass with the liquid.

Build over ice Fill a glass with ice and add the ingredients, allowing them to mix naturally. This is the method used to create the "sunrise" effect in a Tequila Sunrise.

Build over ice and stir Fill the glass with ice, add the ingredients, stir the drink with a stir stick or a bar spoon.

Build in the glass with no ice

Add the ingredients to the glass without ice. This is typically called for when the ingredients are already cold and should not be diluted with ice. Most champagne or beer-based drinks are created this way.

Build in a heatproof cup or mug

Combine the ingredients in a heatproof container such as a coffee mug or Irish coffee cup, then add the ingredients in the order listed. This method is typically called for with hot drinks, such as an Irish Coffee.

Stir gently with ice and strain

Using a cocktail shaker or a Boston shaker, combine the ingredients and ice. Stir them gently with a bar spoon before straining the mixture into the appropriate glass. Do not shake.

Stir gently with ice

Using a cocktail shaker or a Boston shaker, combine the ingredients and ice. Stir them gently with a bar spoon and pour the ice into the glass with the liquid.

Combine all ingredients in a blender. Blend until smooth.

Place all the ingredients in the blender without adding any ice. Blend everything until smooth. This is the method commonly used for drinks made with ice cream.

Combine all ingredients in a blender with ice. Blend until smooth.

Add ice to the blender and then add all the ingredients. Blend everything until smooth. This is the method commonly used for most frozen drinks.

Shake all but x with ice and strain into the glass. Top with x.

In this case, X is typically club soda or tonic water, but it could also be ginger ale or even champagne. Shake all the ingredients with ice and strain them into a glass, then fill the glass the rest of the way with X. Whether ice should be added to the glass before straining in the liquid depends on the type of drink; if ice would dilute the mixer (champagne, for example) then do not add it.

Stocking a Home Bar

When deciding what to purchase for your home bar, consider the tastes of those who will partake, the space you have available, and, of course, the amount of money you're willing to spend. Based on my experience, you can keep most people happy with a few basic liquors, liqueurs, wine, and a small assortment of beers.

The Basics

Vodka Buy a premium name brand such as Absolut® or Skyy®. Make it more upscale with super-premium vodka, such as Grey Goose®.

Gin Purchase a recognized brand like Tanqueray®, Gordon's®, or Bombay Sapphire®.

Rum Stock at least three different types: a dark (Gosling's Black Seal® or Myers's®), a light (Bacardi®) and a spiced rum (Captain Morgan's®).

Whiskey Good whiskey can be expensive. For some people a basic bottle of Jack Daniel's® might suffice, while others might want an assortment of Irish, Canadian, and American whiskeys.

Bourbon Wild Turkey®, Maker's Mark®, and Jim Beam® are among the biggest names.

Scotch Scotch can also be expensive. Choose according to the tastes of your guests and your budget. Cutty Sark®, Johnnie Walker®, J&B®, and Teachers® are among the most well known. If your guests appreciate a good whiskey, then a single-malt scotch might be called for.

Tequila There are two different types of Tequila drinkers. There's the "Lick it, slam it, suck it" crowd (based on the traditional salt, shot, lime sequence), and there is the 100 percent Blue Agave sipping crowd. To keep both happy, consider a bottle of Jose Cuervo® for the slammers and a more upscale tequila such as Petrón® or XQ® for the sipping crowd.

Liqueurs

There are literally hundreds of different liqueurs and liquors out there in almost every flavor.

Schnapps The single most commonly used schnapps in the United States is Peach Schnapps. It's found in everything from Sex on the Beach to the Woo Woo. After Peach, consider a Melon (Midori®), Apple, Butterscotch, and any other flavors that strike your fancy.

Crèmes The essentials here are Crème de Menthe (Green and/or White) Crème de Cacao (Brown or White), and Crème de Banana.

Brandies Flavored brandies are often a party favorite, especially with older guests. Cherry and Blackberry are most common.

Orange-Flavored Liqueurs
Many different kinds of liqueurs are flavored with orange. They are often lumped together under the name Triple Sec, but this category also includes items such as Grand Mariner®, Blue Curaçao, and Cointreau®.

Others Kahlua®, Jägermeister®, Rumple Minze®, Benedictine®, Frangelico® and Chambord are some staples in any bar.

Wine

When it comes to wine, mild-mannered people become freakish snobs. You'll never please everyone, so it's best to keep it simple with a good bottle of Merlot and a nice Chardonnay. Wine doesn't keep well after it's been opened, so trying to keep a large selection on hand is not really practical. Of course, if you know that your guests like a particular style (say a fine Mad Dog 20/20® or a good vintage Wild Irish Rose®), then base your wine offerings on your guest's tastes.

Beer

Beer, as with wine, depends on the tastes of your guests. For a large party, I'll typically have a lot of Corona® and Coors Light®, and a small selection of others, such as Sam Adams®, Beck's®, Bud®, and a few cans of Guinness®. I know that most of my guests like Corona® or Coors Light®, with the exception of a few.

If you don't know your guests' tastes ahead of time, then you'll need a selection that includes domestic and imported beers as well as at least one brand of light beer. You might also want to consider a non-alcoholic beer.

There is also a trend in the category of "Clear Malts." Zima® was the first, but they now seem to be everywhere: Smirnoff®, Skyy®, and Bacardi® each sell a clear malt flavored beverage. I've tried all three and I like Skyy® Blue the best, but a 12 pack of Skyy® Blue costs more than a case of Corona®!

Mixers

Mixers are almost as important as the liquors themselves. Here are the basics that will satisfy almost any guest. One thing to keep in mind is that sodas will go flat over time, even if the bottle is never opened. This is especially true of club soda and tonic water. As a general rule, if the bottle is more than six months old, consider replacing it.

Cola (Coke® or Pepsi®)
I get whatever is on sale.

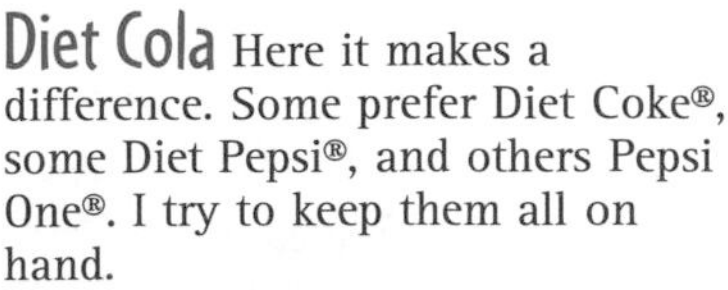

Diet Cola Here it makes a difference. Some prefer Diet Coke®, some Diet Pepsi®, and others Pepsi One®. I try to keep them all on hand.

Sprite® / 7-Up®

Ginger Ale, Tonic Water, and Club Soda Unless you use it all the time, get the small bottles so less is wasted.

Pineapple Juice This is available in little 8-ounce cans and keeps for years, so it's easy to keep it available.

Orange Juice

Cranberry Juice

Grapefruit Juice

Bar Mixes

Lime Juice

Grenadine

Sour Mix You can buy this at most grocery stores in either a bottle or a powder. You can also make your own with lemon juice, sugar, and water.

Margarita Mix Pick your favorite. It beats squeezing limes.

Bloody Mary Mix I've never been asked for a Bloody Mary in my entire career—but you never know.

Glossary of Ingredients

Below is a description of some of the ingredients called for in this book. Several Internet sources were used to produce these definitions, including the Wikipedia Free Encyclopedia (wikipedia.org), the Internet Cocktail Database (cocktaildb.com), and various product and company web sites.

Absinthe A high-percent proof (50 to 75% alcohol by volume) anise-flavored spirit made from several herbs and flowers including the flowers, and leaves of the *Artemisia absinthium*, also called wormwood. Sale of absinthe has been banned since 1915 in most of the world. The usual substitute for Absinthe is Pernod®.

Advocaat A creamy Dutch liqueur made from a blend of brandy, herb extracts, sugar, vanilla, and egg yolks. The drink started in the Dutch colonies in South America, where it was made from avocados; when the drink was brought north, egg yolks were used instead.

Agavero® Liqueur A tequila-based liqueur made from a blend of tequila and damiana flower tea. The liqueur is very sweet with a strong agave flavor.

Alizé® A French brand that offers several varieties of cognac and fruit juice blends. The original flavor of Alize® ("Alize® Gold Passion") is a blend of French cognac and passion fruit juice.

Amaretto An Italian liqueur made from apricot kernels and seeds combined with almond extract steeped in brandy and sweetened with sugar syrup. Amaretto is Italian for "a little bitter."

Amaro Averna® An Italian herbal liqueur based on a secret recipe created in Caltanissetta in 1854. The liqueur has a mild bitter flavor and is used as a digestive in Italy.

Amarula® Crème Liqueur A crème liqueur made in South Africa from the fruit of the marula tree.

Amer Picon® A bittersweet French aperitif made from herbs with a distinct orange flavor. Produced and sold in France, Amer Picon® is rarely exported and is difficult to find. Torani (Amer®) is the version sold in the United States.

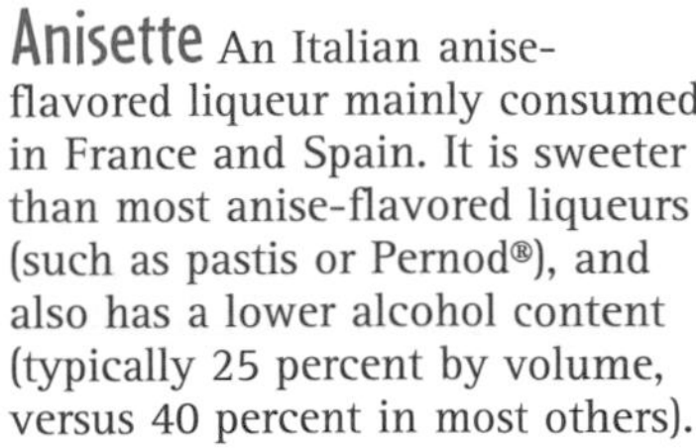

Anisette An Italian anise-flavored liqueur mainly consumed in France and Spain. It is sweeter than most anise-flavored liqueurs (such as pastis or Pernod®), and also has a lower alcohol content (typically 25 percent by volume, versus 40 percent in most others).

Aperol™ An Italian aperitif made by infusing neutral spirits with bitter orange, gentian, rhubarb, and an array of herbs and roots, using a secret recipe that has been unchanged since 1919. It has a sweet, bitter orange–and-herbs taste and a red-orange color.

Applejack An alcoholic beverage produced from apples that originated during the American colonial period. It is made by concentrating hard cider, either by the traditional method of freeze distillation or by true evaporative distillation. The term "applejack" is derived from "jacking," an expression referring to freeze distillation.

Aquavit A caraway-flavored liqueur from Scandinavia. The name comes from *aqua vitae*, Latin for "water of life."

Armagnac A brandy similar to cognac that is produced in the Armagnac region of France. Armangac differs from cognac in that is distilled once instead of twice. The distillation also occurs at a lower temperature, allowing more of the character of the fruit to remain.

B&B® Benedictine® and Brandy.

Bärenjäger® A German neutral spirit-based liqueur that is sweetened and then flavored with honey. The word translates as "bear hunter."

Benedictine® A brandy-based herbal liqueur produced in France. Benedictine® is believed to be the oldest liqueur continuously made, having first been developed by Dom Bernardo Vincelli in 1510 at the Benedictine Abbey of Fécamp in Normandy. Every bottle of Benedictine carries the initials "D.O.M." which stand for *Deo Optimo Maximo*, or, "To God, most good, most great."

Bitters Bitter-tasting herbal flavorings. Originally marketed as patent medicines, the few remaining varieties are principally used as a flavoring in food recipes or in cocktails.

Angostura® Bitters Angostura® was named for the town of Angostura in Venezuela. It contains no angostura bark, a medicinal bark named after the same town. Angostura® Bitters is the most widely distributed bar item in the world.

Curaçao A liqueur flavored with the dried peels of larahas, bitter relatives of oranges grown on the island of Curaçao. The liqueur has an orange flavor and is packaged with coloring added. The most common color is blue, but it also is sold in green, orange, and red colors.

Orange Bitters Made from the rinds of unripe oranges.

Peychaud's® Bitters is associated with New Orleans, Louisiana, and can be difficult to find elsewhere. It has a subtly sweeter taste than the Angostura® brand.

Bourbon An American form of whiskey made from at least 51 percent corn, with the remainder being wheat or rye and malted barley. It is distilled to no more than 160 proof and aged in new, charred white-oak barrels for at least two years. It must be put into the barrels at no more than 125 U.S. proof.

Calvados An apple brandy from the French region of Lower Normandy.

Campari® A branded alcoholic beverage (20 to 24 percent alcohol by volume) introduced in Italy in 1860 by Gaspare Campari. It is a mild bitters-type aperitif, often combined with soda or orange juice or served in mixed drinks.

Chambord® A french liqueur made from small black raspberries.

Champagne A sparkling wine produced only in the Champagne region of France. Champagne is produced by adding sugar to bottled wine, allowing additional fermentation to occur in the bottle that produces carbon dioxide bubbles.

Chartreuse® A famous French liqueur produced by the Carthusian monks, from a formula created in 1605 that contain 130 herbs and spices.

Green Chartreuse® 55 percent alcohol by volume and naturally green in color. The color chartreuse is named after the liqueur.

Yellow Chartreuse® Only 40 percent alcohol by volume, it has a milder and sweeter flavor than the green.

Cherry Heering® A proprietary Danish cherry liqueur with a brandy base. It has been produced since 1818 and sold under several different names, including "Heering," "Peter Heering," and "Cherry Heering."

Clamato® A blend of tomato juice and clam broth that is sold by Motts.

Cognac A type of brandy that is produced only in the cognac region of western France and is universally recognized as the finest and most elegant liqueur in the world. Not a drop of any other wine or brandy is ever allowed to enter a bottle of cognac. The Cognac region is divided into six districts; the cognac of Grand Champagne is considered the best. Cognac is coded on the label by the following letters: V (very), S (superior), O (old), P (pale), E (extra or especial), F (fine), and X (extra). French law states that cognac with 3 stars must be aged at least 1 year to be rated VS and 4 years to be rated VSOP (although 7 to 10 years is more common). By French law the words Extra, Napoleon, Reserve, and Vieille may not appear on the label unless the cognac has been aged at least 5 years.

Cointreau® A fine, colorless, orange-flavored liqueur made from the dried skins of oranges grown on the island of Curaçao in the Dutch West Indies. The generic term for this type of liqueur is curaçao if it is redistilled and clarified, is called *triple sec*.

Courvoisier® A type of cognac. Courvoisier is famous for being the favorite drink of Napoleon.

Crème Liqueurs Crème liqueurs are very sweet with a single flavor that dominates.

Crème de Almond Almond-flavored sweet liqueur.

Crème de Banana Banana-flavored sweet liqueur.

Crème de Cacao (Dark) Chocolate-flavored sweet liqueur that is dark brown in color.

Crème de Cacao (White) Colorless chocolate-flavored sweet liqueur.

Crème de Cassis Black currant-flavored sweet liqueur.

Crème de Coconut Coconut-flavored sweet liqueur.

Crème de Menthe (Green) Mint-flavored sweet liqueur that is green in color.

Crème de Menthe (White) Colorless mint-flavored sweet liqueur.

Crème de Noyaux Sweet liqueur made from fruit pits; has a bitter almond flavor.

Crème de Violette (or Crème Yevette) Sweet liqueur made from and flavored with violets.

Cream Soda A vanilla-flavored carbonated soda.

Cream Sherry A style of sweet sherry created by blending dry sherry with sweet wines. The result is a dark, rich wine with a soft, sweet finish.

Crown Royal® A brand of blended Canadian whiskey.

Drambuie® A famous whiskey liqueur consisting of Highland malt Scotch whiskey, heather honey, and herbs.

Dubonnet® A brand of quinquina, a sweetened fortified apertif wine that contains quinine. It is produced in France and available in two varieties.

Blonde Lighter in color and less sweet

Rouge Red in color and more sweet

Everclear® A brand of grain alcohol that is 95 percnt alcohol by volume (190 proof).

Fernet® Branca An extremely bitter Italian herbal apertif or digestif made from cinchona bark, gentian root, rhubarb, calamus, angelica, myrrh, chamomile, and peppermint. It is often employed as a stomach settler and/or hangover remedy. It's classified as bitters.

Fire Water® A brand of cinnamon-flavored liqueur that is bright red in color.

Frangelico® An Italian brand of hazelnut-flavored liqueur packaged in a distinctive monk-shaped bottle.

Galliano® A sweetish, golden Italian liqueur with an herby, spicy taste.

Gin Gin begins as a neutral spirit. It is then redistilled with or filtered through juniper berries and botanicals such as coriander seeds, cassia bark, orange peels, fennel seeds, anise, caraway, angelica root, licorice, lemon peel, almonds, cinnamon bark, bergamot, and cocoa; it is this secondary process that imparts to each gin its particular taste.

Dry (or London Dry) Gin Most of the gin now produced is London dry, which is light, dry, and perfect for making martinis and other mixed drinks.

Plymouth Gin A sweeter and more mild gin originally produced in Plymouth, England.

Ginger Beer A type of fermented, carbonated beverage, flavored with ginger, lemon, and sugar. Ginger beer reached the height of its popularity in England in the 1900's. It is popular today in Bermuda and is part of the "national drink" of Bermuda, the "Dark and Stormy."

Godiva® Liqueur A neutral spirit–based liqueur flavored with Godiva® brand Belgian chocolate and other flavors. There are currently four types: milk chocolate, original chocolate, white chocolate, and mocha.

Goldschläger® A cinnamon-flavored liqueur produced in Switzerland that includes flakes of real gold in the bottle.

Gosling's Black Seal ® Rum An 80 proof dark rum produced in Bermuda. Along with Ginger Beer, an essential part of Bermuda's "national drink," the "Dark and Stormy."

Grain Alcohol An unaged neutral spirit with a very high alcohol content (greater than 90 percent alcohol by volume, or 180 proof). Grain alcohol cannot be legally sold in many states in the United States.

Grand Marnier® A French brand of aged, orange-flavored liqueur (triple sec) with a brandy base.

Grappa An Italian brandy distilled from the pulpy mass of skins, pits, and stalks left in the wine press after the juice of the grapes has been extracted. Young grappa can be harsh, but it mellows with age.

Grenadine A sweet syrup made from pomegranate juice, containing little or no alcohol.

Guinness® Stout A dry stout made from water, barley malt, hops, and brewers yeast. A proportion of the barley is flaked and roasted to give Guinness® its dark color and characteristic taste. Draught and canned Guinness® both contain nitrogen in addition to the natural CO_2. The nitrogen in the beer is part of what gives Guinness its thick head and "waterfall" settling effect.

Hard Apple Cider (or Hard Cider) Fermented apple cider with an alcohol content similar to beer.

Hennessy® A brand of cognac produced in France.

Hot Damn!® Cinnamon Schnapps A brand of cinnamon-flavored liqueur with a strong cinnamon flavor and a red color.

Hypnotiq® A French fruit liqueur made from vodka, cognac, and tropical fruit juices.

Irish Cream Liqueur A mocha-flavored whiskey and double-cream liqueur, combining Irish whiskey, cream, coffee, chocolate, and other flavors.

Irish Mist® A liqueur produced in Ireland, consisting of Irish whiskey flavored with heather honey.

Jack Daniel's® A whiskey made in Tennessee that is is perhaps the most famous whiskey made in America. The Jack Daniel's distillery in Lynchburg, Tennessee, dates from 1875 and is the oldest registered distillery in the United States. Jack Daniel's® is made according to the sour-mash process, and by the "Lincoln County Process" of filtration through sugar maple charcoal before being aged in charred American oak casks.

Jägermeister® A complex, aromatic liqueur containing 56 herbs, roots, and fruits that has been popular in Germany since its introduction in 1935. In Germany it is frequently consumed warm as an apertif or after-dinner drink. In the United States it is widely popular as a chilled shooter.

KeKe Beach® Liqueur A key lime-flavored cream liqueur with a hint of graham cracker flavor.

Kirschwasser A clear brandy made from double distillation of the fermented juice of black cherries.

Kümmel A sweet, colorless liqueur flavored with caraway seed, cumin, and fennel.

Licor 43® (Cuarenta y Tres) A yellow-colored liqueur from Spain made from 43 ingredients including fruit juices, vanilla, and other aromatic herbs and spices.

Lillet® An aperitif wine from the Bordeaux region of France. Lillet is sold in both red and white.

Limoncello An Italian liqueur made from lemons.

Madeira A fortified wine made in the Madeira Islands of Portugal that is popular as a dessert wine or for cooking.

Malibu® Rum A Jamaican coconut-flavored rum liqueur.

Mandarine Napoléon® Liqueur A liqueur made from mandarin orange-flavored cognac.

Maraschino Liqueur A very sweet, white, cherry liqueur made from the marasca cherry of Dalmatia, Yugoslavia. This liqueur is sometimes used in sours in place of sugar.

Marsala A fortified wine made in the Italian city of Marsala. It is traditionally served chilled with a spicy cheese between the first and second course of a meal or warmed as a dessert wine. It is also used for cooking.

Melon Liqueur A pale green liqueur that tastes of fresh muskmelon or cantaloupe. The most famous brand, Midori®, is Japanese in origin and produced by the Suntory Company in Mexico, France, and Japan.

Mescal A Mexican distilled spirit made from the agave plant. Tequila is a mescal made only from the blue agave plant in the region around Tequila, Jalisco. Spirits labeled "Mescal" are made from other agave plants and are not part of the tequila family.

Metaxa® A strong, sharp-tasting, aromatic Greek brandy.

Muscatel A wine, often fortified, produced from the Muscat variety of grape.

Nassau Royale® A rum-based liqueur with a vanilla flavor.

Ouzo An anise-flavored liqueur from Greece, usually served on the rocks. Ouzo can be used as a substitute for absinthe in many cases.

Parfait Amour A Cordial made of citrus juices, cinnamon, coriander, and brandy.

Passoã® A passion fruit–flavored liqueur produced by Remy Cointreau.

Pastis A semi-sweet anis-flavored liqueur produced to be a substitute for absinthe.

Peach Schnapps A sweet peach-flavored liqueur.

Pernod® A brand of pastis produced by the Pernod-Ricard company.

Pisang Ambon® A Dutch liqueur green in color and flavored with banana.

Pisco A brandy made in the wine producing regions of South America. It is the most popular spirit in Chile and Peru.

Ponche Kuba® A "ponche" is a homemade cream liqueur similar to egg nog that is popular in Caribbean and Latin American countries. Ponche Kuba is a packaged form of this liqueur. It is made from a rum base with cream, eggs, and sugar added. It's flavored with a proprietary blend of spices.

Port A sweet, fortified wine from the Douro Valley in the northern part of Portugal.

Red Bull® A carbonated soft drink with additives and extra caffeine that claims to reduce mental and physical fatigue.

Rock & Rye® A blend of rye whiskey with rock candy and fruit juice.

Rum A liquor made from fermented and distilled sugarcane juice or molasses. Rum has a wide range of flavors, from light and dry like a vodka to very dark and complex like a cognac.

- **Amber Rum** Gold in color and sweeter than a light rum.
- **Añejo Rum** A rum that has been aged in wood for a period of time.
- **Dark Rum** Almost black in color, with a rich and complex flavor.
- **Flavored Rums** Like vodka, rum is now available in a wide array of flavors. Some of the first flavored rums featured vanilla or lemon. Now almost any flavor can be found.
- **Light Rum** Clear in color and dry in flavor.
- **Rum Cream** Cream liqueurs made with a rum base, with cream and flavoring added. The flavors are typically tropical, such as banana, coconut, and pineapple.
- **Spiced Rum** The original flavored rum. Spiced rum consists of an amber rum with vanilla and cinnamon flavor added.

Rumple Minze® A 100 proof (50 percent alcohol by volume) peppermint schnapps produced in Germany.

Safari® A fruit liqueur flavored with mango, papaya, passion fruit, and lime.

Sake A Japanese alcoholic beverage brewed from rice. It is commonly referred to as "rice wine" in the United States, but its method of production is more similar to that of a malt liquor.

Sambuca An Italian liqueur flavored with anis and elderberry, produced in both clear ("white sambuca") and dark blue or purple ("black sambuca") versions.

Schnapps A liqueur distilled from grains, roots, or fruits. Real schnapps has no sugar or flavoring added, as the flavor should originate from the base material. Many syrupy sweet fruit liqueurs are called schnapps, these are not true schnapps because they have both sugar and flavorings added.

Scotch Scotch whiskey is whiskey that is produced in Scotland. In the United States this whiskey is commonly referred to as Scotch. In Scotland, however, it is referred to simply as whiskey.

Sherry A type of wine produced in Spain that is fortified with brandy.

Simple Syrup (or Sugar Syrup) A combination of equal parts sugar and boiling water that, once cool, is used as a sweetener in many mixed drinks.

Sloe Gin A liqueur flavored with sloe berries and blackthorn fruit. It traditionally was made with a gin base with sugar added, most modern versions use a neutral spirit base and add flavorings later.

Sour Mix A syrup made from a blend of sugar and lemon juice. A simple recipe is to mix equal parts of simple syrup and lemon juice.

Southern Comfort® A liqueur with a neutral spirit base and peach and almond flavors.

Stout A beer made with roasted barley or malt. The roasting of the grain gives the beer a darker color and a stronger flavor.

Strega® An Italian herbal liqueur with mint and fennel flavors. Saffron gives it a yellow color. In Italian, strega means *witch*.

Sweetened Lime Juice As the name would imply, lime juice with sugar added.

T.Q. Hot® A brand of tequila flavored with hot peppers.

Tabasco® Sauce A brand of hot pepper sauce made from a blend of tabasco peppers, vinegar, and salt, aged in wood casks.

Tang® An orange-flavored powdered drink mix brand owned by Kraft Foods. It was introduced in 1959 but became popular when NASA gave it to astronauts in the Gemini program in 1965.

Tequila A type of mescal that is made only from the blue agave plant in the region surrounding Tequila, a town in the Mexican state of Jalisco. Tequila is made in many different styles, with the difference between them dependent on how long the distillate has been aged before being bottled.

Añejo Tequila aged between 1 and 3 years.

Gold ("oro" or "joven abocado") Meaning "bottled when young," this is white tequila with coloring added.

Reposado ("rested") Tequila aged at least 1 year.

Silver ("plata" or "banco") This is clear, unaged tequila, with a very strong flavor.

Tequila Rose® A brand of cream liqueur with a tequila base and a strawberry flavor.

Tia Maria® A brand of coffee-flavored liqueur from Jamaica. Tia Maria® is Jamaican rum-based and flavored with spices.

Tonic Water Carbonated water with quinine added. Originally used to prevent malaria, the amount of quinine in bottled tonic water today is only about half the dose given to patients.

Triple Sec A highly popular flavoring agent in many drinks, triple sec is the best known form of curaçao, a liqueur made from the skins of the curaçao orange.

Vermouth A fortified wine flavored with aromatic herbs and spices. There are three common varieties of vermouth.

Dry Vermouth Clear or pale yellow in color and very dry in flavor.

Sweet Vermouth Red in color and sweeter than dry vermouth.

White Vermouth Clear or pale yellow in color, but sweeter than dry vermouth.

Vodka A neutral spirit that can be distilled from almost anything that will ferment (grain, potato, grapes, corn, and beets). It is distilled multiple times, filtered to remove impurities, then diluted with water to bring the alcohol content down before it is bottled. Vodka is sold in a wide variety of flavors from bison grass to watermelon.

Wasabi A member of the cabbage family, its root is ground and used as a very potent Japanese spice.

Whiskey (or Whisky) A beverage distilled from fermented grain and aged in oak casks. The location, grain, type of oak, and length of the aging all affect the flavor of the whiskey. Whiskey is spelled with an "e" in Ireland and the United States and without the "e" everywhere else. There are four major regions where whiskey is produced: Ireland, Scotland, Canada, and the United States. Each has a different style that imparts a distinctive flavor.

Wild Turkey® A brand of Kentucky bourbon whiskey. It is available in both 80 proof and 101 proof versions.

Wine An alcoholic beverage produced by the fermentation of fruit juice, typically grapes. The type of grape, where the grapes were grown, and the way the wine is stored as it ferments affect the taste and color.

Yukon Jack® A Canadian liqueur made from a whiskey base and flavored with honey.

Zima® A colorless alcoholic carbonated malt beverage. It's produced by the Coors company and was introduced in the U.S. in 1994. It was the first of the "clear malt" beverages that now include products like Smirnoff® Ice and Skyy® Blue. These types of beverages are commonly referred to as "clear beer" or "near beer."

Martinis

There are those who claim that anything other than a combination of gin or vodka and vermouth is not and never can be a "martini." For the purposes of this book, a martini is any drink that has "tini" in the name. This is a very broad range of flavors and styles and covers everything from the classic James Bond Martini to the questionable Chocolate Banana Martini.

50-50 Martini

1 part Gin
1 part Dry Vermouth
Cocktail Glass

Mix with ice and strain

Absinthe Martini

2 parts Gin
1/2 part Dry Vermouth
splash Absinthe
Cocktail Glass

Mix with ice and strain

Absinthe-Minded Martini

3 parts Gin
1/2 part Absinthe
1/2 part Grand Marnier®
Cocktail Glass

Mix with ice and strain

Absolute Martini

2 1/2 parts Vodka
1/2 part Triple Sec
Cocktail Glass

Shake with ice and strain

After Eight® Martini

1 1/2 parts Chocolate Mint Liqueur
1 1/2 parts Scotch
1 1/2 parts Cream
Cocktail Glass

Shake with ice and strain

Alizé Martini

2 1/2 parts Alizé®
1 part Vodka
Cocktail Glass

Shake with ice and strain

Almond Joy® Martini

2 parts Coconut-Flavored Rum
splash Frangelico®
1 part Dark Chocolate Liqueur
Cocktail Glass

Shake with ice and strain

Alterna-tini

2 parts Vodka
1/2 part Crème de Cacao (White)
1/4 part Dry Vermouth
1/4 part Sweet Vermouth
Cocktail Glass

Shake with ice and strain

Alterna-tini #2

1/2 part Vodka
1/2 part Red Curaçao
1/2 part Blue Curaçao
1 part Apple Juice

Cocktail Glass

Shake with ice and strain

Apollo XI Martini

2 parts Vodka
splash Vermouth
splash Tang®
fill with Gatorade®

Cocktail Glass

Shake with ice and strain. Serve in a cocktail glass rimmed with Tang® granules.

Apple Cintini

1 1/2 parts Apple-Flavored Vodka
1/2 part Amaretto
1 part Sour Mix

Cocktail Glass

Shake with ice and strain

Apple Martini

1 part Vodka
1 part Sour Apple Schnapps
splash Lime Juice

Cocktail Glass

Shake with ice and strain

Apple Martini #2

3 parts Vodka
1 part Sour Apple Schnapps
splash Pineapple Juice
splash Sour Mix
splash Melon Liqueur

Cocktail Glass

Shake with ice and strain

Applepuckertini

2 parts Sour Apple Schnapps
2 parts Vodka
fill with Mountain Dew®

Collins Glass

Build over ice and stir

Apple-tini

1 part Light Rum
1 part Apple Liqueur
1 part Triple Sec

Cocktail Glass

Shake with ice and strain

Apple-tini #2

2 parts Vodka
1 part Apple Liqueur
splash Lime Juice

Cocktail Glass

Shake with ice and strain

Armada Martini

3 parts Vodka
1 part Cream Sherry

Cocktail Glass

Shake with ice and strain

Austin Fashion Martini

1 1/2 part Vodka
1/2 part Dry Vermouth
splash Blue Curaçao

Cocktail Glass

Shake with ice and strain

B&T's Purple Martini

1 part Vodka
1/2 part Blue Curaçao
splash Cranberry Juice Cocktail
dash Vermouth

Cocktail Glass

Shake with ice and strain

Baby Face Martini
3 parts Raspberry-Flavored Vodka
1/2 part Dry Vermouth
1/4 part Maraschino Liqueur
Cocktail Glass
Shake with ice and strain

Banana Martini
1 part Vodka
1 part Banana Liqueur
Highball Glass
Shake with ice and strain

Bellini-tini
2 parts Vodka
1/2 part Peach Schnapps
1/2 part Peach Puree
dash Bitters
Cocktail Glass
Shake with ice and strain

Berlin Martini
2 parts Vodka
1 part Peach Schnapps
splash Black Sambuca
Cocktail Glass
Shake with ice and strain

Berrytini
3 parts Currant-Flavored Vodka
1/2 part Raspberry Liqueur
Cocktail Glass
Shake with ice and strain

Black and White Martini
3 parts Vanilla-Flavored Vodka
1 part Crème de Cacao (Dark)
Cocktail Glass
Shake with ice and strain

Black Forest Cake Martini
1 1/2 parts Vodka
1 part Crème de Cacao (White)
splash Raspberry Liqueur
Cocktail Glass
Shake with ice and strain

Black Martini
1 part Gin
1/2 part Black Sambuca
Cocktail Glass
Shake with ice and strain

Black Martini #2
1 1/2 parts Vodka
1 part Raspberry Liqueur
1 part Blue Curaçao
Cocktail Glass
Shake with ice and strain

Black Martini #3
2 parts Blackberry Liqueur
1 part Dry Vermouth
Cocktail Glass
Shake with ice and strain

Blood Orange Martini
1 part Campari®
2 parts Orange-Flavored Vodka
1 part Orange Juice
Cocktail Glass
Shake with ice and strain

Bloody Martini
1 Cherry
1 1/2 parts Gin
splash Grenadine
splash Lemon Juice
splash Vermouth
Cocktail Glass
Shake with ice and strain

Blue Jaffa Martini
1 part Vodka
1 part Blue Curaçao
1 part Crème de Cacao (White)
Cocktail Glass

Shake with ice and strain

Blue on Blue Martini
3 parts Vodka
1/2 part Blue Curaçao
Cocktail Glass

Shake with ice and strain

Bond's Martini
3 parts Gin
1 part Vodka
1/2 part Vermouth
Cocktail Glass

Shake (don't stir) with ice and strain

Boomerang Martini
3 parts Gin
1 part Dry Vermouth
1/4 part Maraschino Liqueur
Cocktail Glass

Shake with ice and strain

Bootlegger Martini
1 1/2 parts Gin
1/4 part Southern Comfort®
Cocktail Glass

Shake with ice and strain

Brantini
1 1/2 parts Brandy
splash Dry Vermouth
1 part Gin
twist of Lemon Peel
Old-Fashioned Glass

Shake with ice and strain

Brazen Martini
2 parts Vodka
1/2 part Parfait Amour®
Cocktail Glass

Shake with ice and strain

Broadway Martini
3 parts Gin
1 part Crème de Menthe (White)
Cocktail Glass

Shake with ice and strain

Buckeye Martini
3 parts Gin
1 part Dry Vermouth
Cocktail Glass

Shake with ice and strain

Burnt Martini
2 parts Gin
1 part Whiskey
Cocktail Glass

Shake with ice and strain

Cabaret Martini
2 parts Gin
splash Pernod®
Cocktail Glass

Shake with ice and strain

California Martini
2 parts Vodka
1 part Red Wine
1/4 part Dark Rum
Cocktail Glass

Shake with ice and strain

Campari® Martini
3 parts Vodka
1 part Campari®
Cocktail Glass

Shake with ice and strain

Caramel Apple Martini
2 parts Butterscotch Schnapps
2 parts Sour Apple Schnapps
1 part Vodka
Cocktail Glass
Shake with ice and strain

Caribbean Martini
1 1/2 parts Vanilla-Flavored Vodka
3/4 part Malibu® Rum
splash Pineapple Juice
Cocktail Glass
Shake with ice and strain

Chocolate Banana Martini
2 parts Vodka
1 part Crème de Cacao (White)
1 part 99-Proof Banana Liqueur
Cocktail Glass
Shake with ice and strain

Chocolate Lovers' Martini
1 1/2 parts Irish Cream Liqueur
1 1/2 parts Vodka
1 1/2 parts Crème de Cacao (White)
1 tbsp. Chocolate Syrup
Cocktail Glass
Shake with ice and strain

Chocolate Martini
2 parts Vodka
1/2 part Crème de Cacao (White)
Cocktail Glass
Shake with ice and strain

Chocolate Martini #2
1 1/2 parts Vanilla-Flavored Vodka
1 part Godiva® Liqueur
Cocktail Glass
Shake with ice and strain

Chocolate Rasp Martini
1 1/2 parts Raspberry Vodka
1 part Crème de Cacao (White)
Cocktail Glass
Shake with ice and strain

Christmas Martini
2 parts Vodka
1/2 part Crème de Menthe (White)
1/2 part Dry Vermouth
Cocktail Glass
Shake with ice and strain

Church Lady Martini
2 parts Gin
1 part Orange Juice
1 part Sweet Vermouth
Cocktail Glass
Shake with ice and strain

Citritini
1 1/2 parts Citrus-Flavored Rum
splash Lime Juice
1 1/2 parts Sour Mix
Cocktail Glass
Shake with ice and strain

Cool Yule Martini
3 parts Vodka
1/2 part Crème de Menthe (White)
1/2 part Dry Vermouth
Cocktail Glass
Shake with ice and strain

Copper Illusion Martini
1 part Gin
1/2 part Triple Sec
1/2 part Campari®
Cocktail Glass
Shake with ice and strain

Crantini
$1^1/_2$ parts Vodka
$^1/_2$ part Triple Sec
$^1/_2$ part Vermouth
2 parts Cranberry Juice Cocktail
Cocktail Glass

Shake with ice and strain

Crantini #2
1 part Sweet Vodka
1 part Cointreau®
1 part Cranberry Juice Cocktail
splash Lime Juice
Cocktail Glass

Shake with ice and strain

Crimson Martini
3 parts Gin
$^1/_2$ part Port
$^1/_2$ part Grenadine
Cocktail Glass

Shake with ice and strain

Cuban Martini
3 parts Light Rum
$^1/_2$ part Dry Vermouth
$^1/_2$ part Powdered Sugar
Cocktail Glass

Shake with ice and strain

Dark Chocolate Martini
1 part Vodka
1 part Crème de Cacao (Dark)
Cocktail Glass

Shake with ice and strain

Daydream Martini
2 parts Citrus-Flavored Vodka
1 part Orange Juice
$^1/_2$ part Triple Sec
dash Powdered Sugar
Cocktail Glass

Shake with ice and strain

Dirty Martini
2 parts Gin
1 tbs Dry Vermouth
2 tbs Olive Brine
2 Olives
Cocktail Glass

Shake with ice and strain

Dirty Martini #2
2 parts Gin
1 splash Olive Brine
Cocktail Glass

Shake with ice and strain

Double Fudge Martini
3 parts Vodka
$^1/_2$ part Crème de Cacao (Dark)
$^1/_2$ part Coffee Liqueur
Cocktail Glass

Shake with ice and strain

Emerald Martini
$1^1/_2$ parts Gin
$^1/_2$ part Dry Vermouth
splash Chartreuse®
Cocktail Glass

Shake with ice and strain

Euro-tini
1 part Vodka
$^1/_2$ part Triple Sec
1 part Orange Juice
$^1/_4$ dash Sugar
Cocktail Glass

Shake with ice and strain

Extra Dry Martini
$1^1/_2$ parts Gin
1 drop Vermouth
Cocktail Glass

Shake with ice and strain

Fare Thee Well Martini
2 parts Gin
1/4 part Dry Vermouth
1/4 part Sweet Vermouth
Cocktail Glass
Shake with ice and strain

Fire-tini Hunter
2 parts Pepper-Flavored Vodka
1 part Dry Vermouth
Cocktail Glass
Shake with ice and strain

French Martini
1 part Vodka
1 part Raspberry Liqueur
1 part Grand Marnier®
1 part Pineapple Juice
1 part Sour Mix
Cocktail Glass
Shake with ice and strain

Fretful Martini
3 parts Blue Curaçao
1/2 part Amaretto
Cocktail Glass
Shake with ice and strain

Fuzzy Martini
2 1/2 parts Vodka
1 part Peach Schnapps
splash Orange Juice
Cocktail Glass
Shake with ice and strain

Granny Smith Martini
1 1/2 parts Vanilla-Flavored Vodka
1/2 part Sour Apple Schnapps
1/4 part Melon Liqueur
Cocktail Glass
Shake with ice and strain

Grappatini
1 1/2 parts Grappa
1/2 part Dry Vermouth
Cocktail Glass
Shake with ice and strain

Green Apple Martini
1 1/2 parts Sour Apple Schnapps
1 1/2 parts Vodka
splash Vermouth
Cocktail Glass
Shake with ice and strain

Gumball Martini
2 parts Gin
1 part Vodka
1/2 part Southern Comfort®
1/4 part Dry Vermouth
Cocktail Glass
Shake with ice and strain

Gumdrop Martini
1 part Citrus-Flavored Rum
1/2 part Vodka
1/4 part Dry Vermouth
1/4 part Southern Comfort®
Cocktail Glass
Shake with ice and strain

Harry Denton Martini
1 1/4 parts Gin
1/2 part Green Chartreuse®
Cocktail Glass
Shake with ice and strain

Hawaiian Martini
2 parts Dirty Gin
1/2 part Triple Sec
splash Pineapple Juice
Cocktail Glass
Shake with ice and strain

Honeydew Martini
2 parts Vodka
1/2 part Triple Sec
1/2 part Melon Liqueur
Cocktail Glass

Shake with ice and strain

Hot and Dirty Martini
2 parts Absolut® Peppar Vodka
1/2 part Dry Vermouth
1/2 part Olive Brine
Cocktail Glass

Shake with ice and strain

Hpnotiq® Martini
1 part Cherry-Flavored Vodka
2 parts Hpnotiq® Liqueur
Cocktail Glass

Shake with ice and strain

Imperial Martini
3 parts Gin
1 part Dry Vermouth
1/4 part Maraschino Liqueur
Cocktail Glass

Shake with ice and strain

In and Out Martini
splash Dry Vermouth
3 parts Gin
Cocktail Glass

Pack cocktail glass with ice, add a splash of Dry Vermouth. While glass chills, pour 3 parts of Gin in a shaker with ice. Throw away ice/Vermouth in cocktail glass, then strain in the Gin.

Irish Martini
2 parts Vodka
1/2 part Dry Vermouth
1/4 part Whiskey
Cocktail Glass

Shake with ice and strain

Island Martini
2 parts Dark Rum
1/2 part Dry Vermouth
1/2 part Sweet Vermouth
Cocktail Glass

Shake with ice and strain

Jack London Martini
3 parts Currant-Flavored Vodka
1/2 part Maraschino Liqueur
Cocktail Glass

Shake with ice and strain

Jacktini
1 part Whiskey
1 part Mandarine Napoleon® Liqueur
1/4 part Fresh Lime Juice
Cocktail Glass

Shake with ice and strain

James Bond Martini
1 1/2 parts Gin
1/2 part Vodka
1/4 part Lillet®
Lemon Twist
Cocktail Glass

Shake with ice and strain. The original order that Mr. Bond placed was "Three measures Gordon's®, one of Vodka, half a measure of Kina Lillet®. Shake it very well until it's ice-cold, then add a large thin slice of Lemon Peel." (From *Casino Royale* by Ian Fleming, 1953.)

Jamie's Martini
2 parts Vodka
1 part Orange Juice
1/2 part Triple Sec
dash Powdered Sugar
Cocktail Glass

Shake with ice and strain

Kamitini
1 part Vodka
1/2 part Raspberry Liqueur
1/2 part Vanilla Liqueur
1 part Raspberry Juice
splash Fresh Lime Juice
Cocktail Glass

Shake with ice and strain

Kentucky Martini
3 parts Bourbon
1 part Crème de Cacao (White)
Cocktail Glass

Shake with ice and strain

Kir Martini
1 part Gin
1 part Extra Dry Vermouth
1 part Crème de Cassis
Cocktail Glass

Shake with ice and strain

Leap Year Martini
3 parts Citrus-Flavored Vodka
1/2 part Sweet Vermouth
Cocktail Glass

Shake with ice and strain

Lemon Splash Martini
1 1/2 parts Vodka
1/2 part Triple Sec
1/2 part Amaretto
Cocktail Glass

Shake with ice and strain

Long Kiss Goodnight
1 part Vodka
1 part Vanilla-Flavored Vodka
1 part Crème de Cacao (White)
Cocktail Glass

Shake with ice and strain

Low Tide Martini
3 parts Vodka
1/2 part Dry Vermouth
1/2 part Oyster Juice
Cocktail Glass

Shake with ice and strain

Main Beach Martini
1 1/2 parts Orange Vodka
1/2 part Crème de Cacao (White)
Highball Glass

Shake with ice and strain over ice

Mama's Martini
2 parts Vanilla-Flavored Vodka
1/2 part Apricot Brandy
Cocktail Glass

Shake with ice and strain

Mangotini
1 1/2 parts Vodka
1/2 part Sour Apple Schnapps
1 part Mango Nectar
splash Vermouth
Cocktail Glass

Shake with ice and strain

Margatini
1 1/2 parts Tequila Silver
1/2 part Triple Sec
splash Fresh Lime Juice
Cocktail Glass

Shake with ice and strain

Martian Martini
2 parts Gin
1 part Melon Liqueur
Cocktail Glass

Shake with ice and strain

Martini
2 1/2 parts Gin
1/2 part Dry Vermouth
Cocktail Glass

Shake with ice and strain. Garnish with an olive or a lemon twist. A drier martini uses less (or no) Vermouth. A Vodka martini substitutes Vodka for the Gin. A martini garnished with a cocktail onion instead of an olive is called a Gibson.

Martini Esoterica
2 1/2 parts Gin
1/2 part Dry Vermouth
splash Pernod®
Cocktail Glass

Shake with ice and strain

Martini Oriental
1 1/2 parts Gin
1/2 part Sake
Cocktail Glass

Shake with ice and strain
Garnish with a Lemon Twist

Martini Patton
2 1/2 parts Gin
1/2 part Sake
Cocktail Glass

Shake with ice and strain
Garnish with a Lemon Twist

Martini Colorado
1/2 part Gin
1/2 part Vodka
1 1/2 parts Vermouth
2 dashes Angostura® Bitters
dash salt
Cocktail Glass

Shake with ice and strain
Garnish with two Olives

Martini Milano
2 parts Gin
1/2 part Dry Vermouth
1/2 part Campari®
1/2 part White Wine
Cocktail Glass

Shake with ice and strain

Martinique
1 part Light Rum
1 part Triple Sec
1 part Fresh Lime Juice
1 part Orange Juice
fill with Pineapple Juice
Collins Glass

Shake with ice and strain over ice

Ma-tini
1 part Vodka
1/2 part Blackberry Liqueur
1/2 part Cointreau®
1 part Lemonade
Cocktail Glass

Shake with ice and strain

Mellow Martini
1 1/2 parts Vodka
3/4 part Crème de Banana
splash Lychee Liqueur
2 parts Pineapple Juice
Cocktail Glass

Shake with ice and strain

Melon Martini
2 1/2 parts Vodka
1/2 part Melon Liqueur
Cocktail Glass

Shake with ice and strain

Mexicali Martini
1 part Gold Tequila
1/2 part Grand Marnier®
1/2 part Triple Sec
1/2 part Lime Juice
1/2 part Orange Juice
Cocktail Glass

Shake with ice and strain

Mexico Martini
1 1/2 parts Tequila
1/2 part Dry Vermouth
3 splashes Vanilla Extract
Cocktail Glass

Shake with ice and strain

Milky Way® Martini
1 part Vanilla-Flavored Vodka
1 part Chocolate Liqueur
1 part Irish Ceam Liqueur
Cocktail Glass

Shake with ice and strain

Mint-tini
2 parts Vodka
1 part Crème de Menthe (White)
1/2 part Dry Vermouth
Cocktail Glass

Shake with ice and strain

Mocha Blanca Martini
1 part Vodka
1 part Chocolate Liqueur
1 part Coffee Liqueur
Cocktail Glass

Shake with ice and strain

Mocha Martini
2 1/2 parts Vodka
1/2 part Coffee Liqueur
1 part Crème de Cacao (White)
Cocktail Glass

Shake with ice and strain

Monk's Martini
1 part Vodka
1 part Crème de Menthe (White)
1 part Crème de Banana
1 part Irish Cream Liqueur
Cocktail Glass

Shake with ice and strain

Mortini
2 parts Vodka
splash Amaretto
splash Grenadine
Cocktail Glass

Shake with ice and strain

Mozart Martini
1 part Crème de Cacao (Dark)
1 part Chocolate Liqueur
2 parts Cream
splash Vodka
Cocktail Glass

Shake with ice and strain

Neopolitan Martini
1 part Vanilla-Flavored Vodka
1 part Orange-Flavored Vodka
1/2 part Grand Marnier®
1/2 part Parfait Amour
splash Lime Juice
Cocktail Glass

Shake with ice and strain

New Orleans Martini
2 parts Vanilla-Flavored Vodka
1/2 part Dry Vermouth
1/2 part Pernod®
Cocktail Glass

Shake with ice and strain

Nicotini
1 part Crème de Cacao (Dark)
1/2 part Crème de Banana
1/2 part Apricot Brandy
1/2 part Milk
1/2 part Cream
Cocktail Glass

Shake with ice and strain

Ninja Martini
2 parts Gin
1 part Sweet Vermouth
1 part Sake
Cocktail Glass

Shake with ice and strain

Nutty Martini
3 parts Vodka
1/2 part Frangelico®
Cocktail Glass

Shake with ice and strain

Old Country Martini
1 part Vodka
1 part Kirschwasser
1 part Madeira
Cocktail Glass

Shake with ice and strain

Olorosa Martini
2 parts Sherry
1/2 part Vodka
Cocktail Glass

Shake with ice and strain

Opera Martini
3 parts Gin
1/2 part Maraschino Liqueur
Cocktail Glass

Shake with ice and strain

Orange Martini
3 parts Vodka
1 part Triple Sec
dash Orange Bitters
Cocktail Glass

Shake with ice and strain

Orangetini
1 1/2 parts Orange-Flavored Vodka
1 1/2 parts Triple Sec
Cocktail Glass

Shake with ice and strain

Oyster Martini
3 parts Vodka
1 part Dry Vermouth
Cocktail Glass

Shake with ice and strain
Garnish with an Oyster

Paisley Martini
2 parts Gin
splash Scotch
1/2 part Dry Vermouth
twist of Lemon Peel
Old-Fashioned Glass

Shake with ice and pour

Parisian Martini
2 parts Gin
1 part Dry Vermouth
1/2 part Crème de Cassis
Cocktail Glass

Shake with ice and strain

Park Avenue Martini
2 parts Gin
1/2 part Sweet Vermouth
1/2 part Pineapple Juice
Cocktail Glass

Shake with ice and strain

Parrothead Martini
3 parts Silver Tequila
1 part Triple Sec
Cocktail Glass

Shake with ice and strain

Peach Blossom Martini
2 parts Peach-Flavored Vodka
1/2 part Maraschino Liqueur
Cocktail Glass

Shake with ice and strain

Peach Martini
2 parts Vodka
1 part Peach Schnapps
Cocktail Glass

Shake with ice and strain

Peachtini
2 parts Gin
1 part Peach Schnapps
Cocktail Glass

Shake with ice and strain

Peppar Bayou Martini
1 1/2 parts Absolut® Peppar Vodka
1/4 part Dry Vermouth
Cocktail Glass

Shake with ice and strain

Peppermint Martini
2 parts Gin
1 part Peppermint Schnapps
Cocktail Glass

Shake with ice and strain

Picadilly Martini
2 parts Gin
3/4 part Dry Vermouth
1/2 part Pernod®
splash Grenadine
Cocktail Glass

Shake with ice and strain

Pineapple Martini
1 part Orange-Flavored Vodka
1 part Pineapple-Flavored Rum
1 part Pineapple Juice
Cocktail Glass

Shake with ice and strain

Platinium Blonde
2 parts Rum
1 part Cream
Cocktail Glass

Shake with ice and strain

Pompano Martini
1 part Gin
1/2 part Dry Vermouth
1 part Grapefruit Juice
Cocktail Glass

Shake with ice and strain

Pontberry Martini
2 parts Vodka
1/2 part Blackberry Liqueur
Cocktail Glass

Shake with ice and strain

Pretty Martini
2 parts Vodka
1/2 part Dry Vermouth
1/2 part Amaretto
Cocktail Glass

Shake with ice and strain

Princess Elizabeth Martini
2 parts Sweet Vermouth
1/2 part Dry Vermouth
Cocktail Glass

Shake with ice and strain

Princess Martini
$1^1/_2$ parts Gin
$1^1/_2$ parts Orange Juice
$1^1/_2$ parts Pineapple Juice
splash Lemon-Lime Soda

Highball Glass

Build over ice and stir

Prospector Martini
$1^1/_2$ parts Vanilla-Flavored Vodka
$^3/_4$ part Goldschläger®
$^1/_2$ part Butterscotch Schnapps
splash Vanilla Extract

Cocktail Glass

Shake with ice and strain

Really Dry Martini
3 parts Gin
Dry Vermouth
2 Olives

Cocktail Glass

Place 2 Olives in a chilled glass. Pour Gin in a shaker with ice. Hold an open bottle of Vermouth, lean over the shaker and whisper "Vermouth." Strain the Gin into the glass.

Red Dog Martini
2 parts Vodka
$^1/_2$ part Port
$^1/_2$ part Grenadine

Cocktail Glass

Shake with ice and strain

Red Passion Martini
$1^1/_2$ parts Passion Fruit Liqueur
$^1/_2$ part Campari®

Cocktail Glass

Stir with ice and strain

Red Vodkatini
2 parts Vodka
1 part1Sweet Vermouth
splash Crème de Cassis

Cocktail Glass

Shake with ice and strain

Redhead Martini
$2^1/_2$ parts Vodka
$^1/_2$ part Strawberry Syrup

Collins Glass

Shake with ice and strain

Renaissance Martini
$2^1/_2$ parts Gin
$^1/_2$ part Dry Sherry

Cocktail Glass

Shake with ice and strain

Resolution Martini
2 parts Gin
1 part Apricot Brandy

Cocktail Glass

Shake with ice and strain

Reverse Martini
2 parts Gin
1 part Apple Brandy

Cocktail Glass

Shake with ice and strain

Rontini
1 part Vodka
fill with Mountain Dew®

Highball Glass

Build over ice and stir

Rouge Martini
2 parts Gin
splash Raspberry Liqueur

Cocktail Glass

Shake with ice and strain

Rum Martini
$2^1/_2$ parts Light Rum
splash Dry Vermouth
Lemon Twist
Cocktail Glass
Shake with ice and strain

Rumtini
2 parts Light Rum
$^1/_2$ part Dry Vermouth
Cocktail Glass
Shake with ice and strain

Russian Peachtini
$1^1/_2$ parts Vodka
splash Peach Schnapps
Cocktail Glass
Shake with ice and strain

Saketini
$2^1/_2$ parts Gin
splash Sake
Cocktail Glass
Shake with ice and strain

Salt and Pepper Martini
2 parts Absolut® Peppar Vodka
splash Dry Vermouth
Cocktail Glass
Shake with ice and strain. Serve in a cocktail glass with a salted rim.

Scarlett Martini
$1^1/_2$ parts Southern Comfort®
$1^1/_2$ parts Cranberry Juice Cocktail
Cocktail Glass
Shake with ice and strain

Scotini
2 parts Gin
$^1/_2$ part Scotch
Cocktail Glass
Shake with ice and strain

Sea Blue Martini
2 parts Dry Gin
$^1/_2$ part Blue Curaçao
$^1/_2$ part Triple Sec
Cocktail Glass
Shake with ice and strain

Secret Martini
3 parts Gin
1 part Lillet®
Cocktail Glass
Shake with ice and strain

Shrimptini
3 parts Gin
1 part Dry Vermouth
splash Tabasco® Sauce
Cocktail Glass
Shake with ice and strain. Garnish with a Cocktail Shrimp hanging over the side.

Smoked Martini
1 part Scotch
1 part Vodka
Cocktail Glass
Stir gently with ice and strain

Smokey Martini
$2^1/_2$ parts Gin
$^1/_2$ part Scotch
Cocktail Glass
Stir gently with ice and strain

South Beach Martini
1 part Orange-Flavored Vodka
1 part Citrus-Flavored Vodka
$^1/_2$ part Cointreau®
$^1/_2$ part Lime Juice
Cocktail Glass
Shake with ice and strain

Soviet Martini
2 parts Currant-Flavored Vodka
1/2 part Dry Vermouth
1/2 part Dry Sherry
Cocktail Glass
Shake with ice and strain

Spartinique
1 part Cherry Brandy
1 part Jim Beam®
2/3 part Sour Mix
splash Lemon Juice
Cocktail Glass
Shake with ice and strain

Springtime Martini
2 parts Vodka
1 part Lillet®
Cocktail Glass
Shake with ice and strain

Strawberry Blonde Martini
2 parts Strawberry-Flavored Vodka
1 part Lillet®
Cocktail Glass
Shake with ice and strain

Surfer Martini
1 part Rum
1/2 part Coconut-Flavored Rum
1/2 part Banana Liqueur
1 part Pineapple Juice
Cocktail Glass
Shake with ice and strain

Sweet and Spicy Martini
2 parts Vodka
1/2 part Sweet Vermouth
1/2 part Triple Sec
Cocktail Glass
Shake with ice and strain

Sweet Martini
1 1/2 part Gin
1/2 part Sweet Vermouth
Cocktail Glass
Shake with ice and strain

Tequila Martini
2 1/2 parts Tequila
1/2 part Dry Vermouth
Cocktail Glass
Shake with ice and strain

Third Degree Martini
1 1/2 parts Gin
1/2 part Dry Vermouth
splash Pernod®
Cocktail Glass
Shake with ice and strain

Tiajuanatini
2 parts Silver Tequila
splash Triple Sec
Cocktail Glass
Shake with ice and strain

Tini Rita
1 1/4 parts Vodka
1/4 part Cointreau®
1/4 part Grand Marnier®
splash Lime Juice
splash Sour Mix
Cocktail Glass
Shake with ice and strain

Toffee Martini
1 part Frangelico®
1 part Vanilla Liqueur
1 part Vodka
Cocktail Glass
Shake with ice and strain

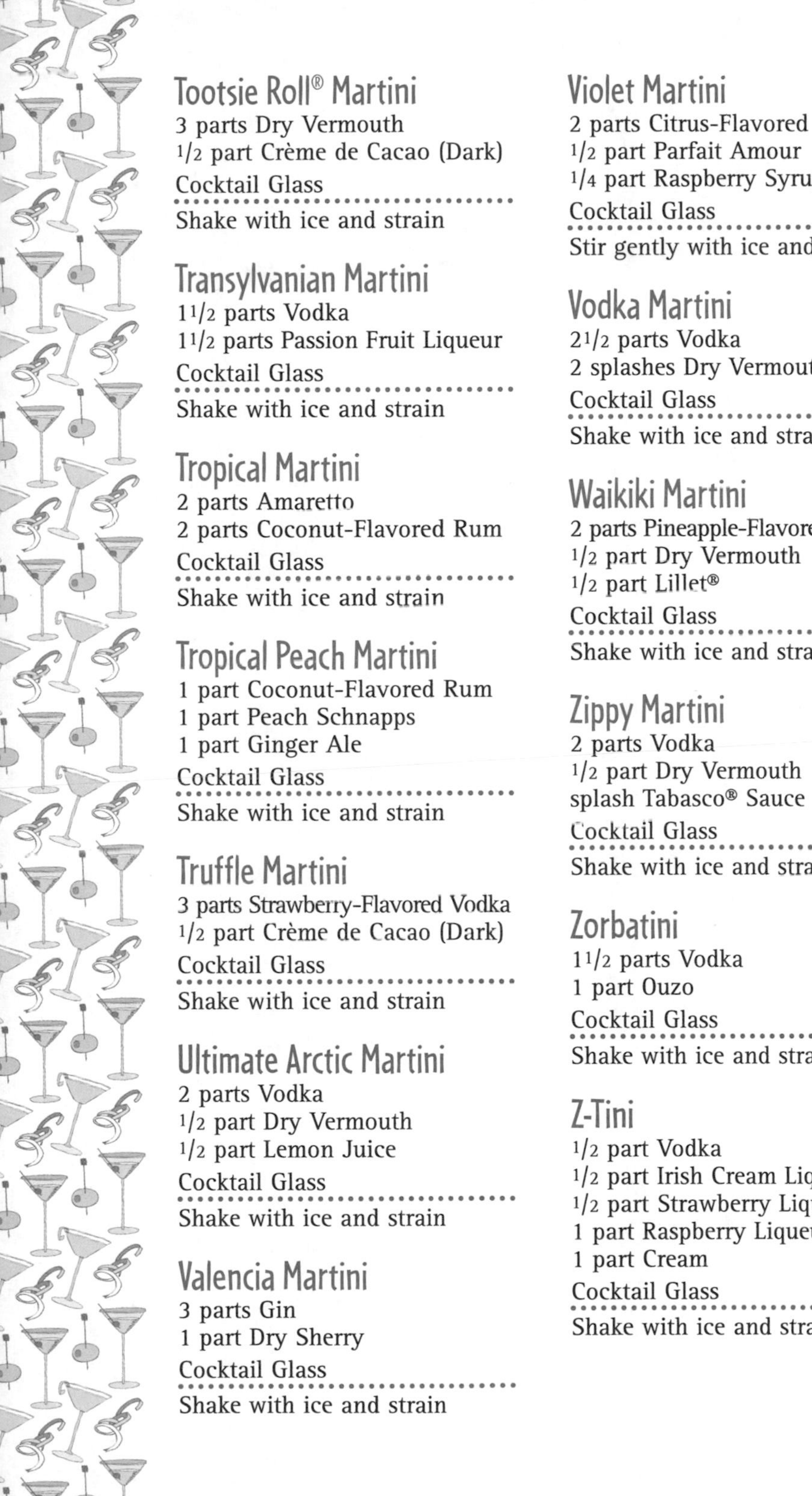

Tootsie Roll® Martini

3 parts Dry Vermouth
1/2 part Crème de Cacao (Dark)
Cocktail Glass

Shake with ice and strain

Transylvanian Martini

1 1/2 parts Vodka
1 1/2 parts Passion Fruit Liqueur
Cocktail Glass

Shake with ice and strain

Tropical Martini

2 parts Amaretto
2 parts Coconut-Flavored Rum
Cocktail Glass

Shake with ice and strain

Tropical Peach Martini

1 part Coconut-Flavored Rum
1 part Peach Schnapps
1 part Ginger Ale
Cocktail Glass

Shake with ice and strain

Truffle Martini

3 parts Strawberry-Flavored Vodka
1/2 part Crème de Cacao (Dark)
Cocktail Glass

Shake with ice and strain

Ultimate Arctic Martini

2 parts Vodka
1/2 part Dry Vermouth
1/2 part Lemon Juice
Cocktail Glass

Shake with ice and strain

Valencia Martini

3 parts Gin
1 part Dry Sherry
Cocktail Glass

Shake with ice and strain

Violet Martini

2 parts Citrus-Flavored Vodka
1/2 part Parfait Amour
1/4 part Raspberry Syrup
Cocktail Glass

Stir gently with ice and strain

Vodka Martini

2 1/2 parts Vodka
2 splashes Dry Vermouth
Cocktail Glass

Shake with ice and strain

Waikiki Martini

2 parts Pineapple-Flavored Vodka
1/2 part Dry Vermouth
1/2 part Lillet®
Cocktail Glass

Shake with ice and strain

Zippy Martini

2 parts Vodka
1/2 part Dry Vermouth
splash Tabasco® Sauce
Cocktail Glass

Shake with ice and strain

Zorbatini

1 1/2 parts Vodka
1 part Ouzo
Cocktail Glass

Shake with ice and strain

Z-Tini

1/2 part Vodka
1/2 part Irish Cream Liqueur
1/2 part Strawberry Liqueur
1 part Raspberry Liqueur
1 part Cream
Cocktail Glass

Shake with ice and strain

Cocktails

What makes a cocktail different from a martini? What makes it different from a run-of-the-mill mixed drink? Here, a cocktail is a mixed drink that is shaken or stirred with ice, strained in a cocktail glass. Additionally, none of the drinks below and with "tini".

1 Randini

2 parts Cranberry Juice Cocktail
3 parts Gin
1 Lime Wedge
1 part Triple Sec
Cocktail Glass

Shake with ice and strain

1001 Nights

1 1/2 parts Crème de Cacao (Dark)
1 1/2 parts Triple Sec
Cocktail Glass

Shake with ice and strain

1-900-Fuk-Meup

2 parts Currant-Flavored Vodka
1 part Grand Marnier®
1 part Raspberry Liqueur
1 part Melon Liqueur
1 part Coconut-Flavored Rum
1 part Amaretto
2 parts Cranberry Juice Cocktail
1 part Pineapple Juice
Cocktail Glass

Shake with ice and strain

20th Century

2 parts Gin
1 part Crème de Cacao (White)
1 part Lillet®
1 part Lemon Juice
Cocktail Glass

Shake with ice and strain into a chilled glass

21 Joc

1 part Vodka
1/2 part Triple Sec
1/2 part Strawberry Liqueur
splash Lime Juice
Cocktail Glass

Shake with ice and strain

22 Park Lane

1 1/2 parts Gin
1/4 part Sweet Vermouth
1/4 part Triple Sec
Cocktail Glass

Shake with ice and strain

2lips

2/3 part Vodka
1/2 part Parfait Amour
splash Crème de Cassis
splash Lime Juice
splash Cranberry Juice Cocktail
Cocktail Glass

Shake with ice and strain

3 Base Hit
1 part Strawberry Liqueur
1 part Orange Liqueur
1 part Crème de Banana
Cocktail Glass

Shake with ice and strain

3 Commandments
1 part Añejo Rum
1 part Citrus Flavored Rum
1 part Orange-Flavored Rum
Cocktail Glass

Shake with ice and strain

3C
1 1/2 parts Cherry Brandy
1 part Cream
3 parts Cranberry Juice Cocktail
Cocktail Glass

Shake with ice and strain

420 Kicker
2 parts Absolut® Peppar Vodka
1 part Peppermint Schnapps
1 part Sour Mix
Cocktail Glass

Shake with ice and strain

43 Amigos
1 part Tequila
1/2 part Licor 43®
1/2 part Triple Sec
1/2 part Lime Juice
Cocktail Glass

Shake with ice and strain

44 Special
1 part Cranberry-Flavored Vodka
1 part Vodka
1 part Peach Schnapps
2 1/2 parts Grape Juice
2 1/2 parts Pineapple Juice
Cocktail Glass

Shake with ice and strain

4th Estate Cocktail
1 part Gin
1 part Dry Vermouth
1 part Sweet Vermouth
splash Absinthe
Cocktail Glass

Shake with ice and strain

4th of July
1 1/2 parts Vodka
1/2 part Blue Curaçao
1/2 part Triple Sec
1/2 part Sour Mix
Cocktail Glass

Shake with ice and strain. Top with splash of grenadine.

5 M
1 part Dark Rum
1/2 part Mandarine Napoléon® Liqueur
1/2 part Crème de Banana
1 part Cream
splash Grenadine
Cocktail Glass

Shake with ice and strain

'57 Chevy
1 part Southern Comfort®
1 part Gin
1 part Vodka
splash Orange Juice
splash Pineapple Juice
splash Grenadine
Cocktail Glass
Shake with ice and strain

73 Bus
3 parts Gin
1 part Triple Sec
1 part Cranberry Juice Cocktail
Cocktail Glass
Shake with ice and strain

7 Kickers
3 parts Pineapple Juice
1 part Blue Curaçao
1 part Peach Schnapps
1/2 part Coconut-Flavored Liqueur
Cocktail Glass
Shake with ice and strain

7th Heaven
1 1/2 parts Gin
1/2 part Maraschino Liqueur
1/2 part Grapefruit Juice
Cocktail Glass
Shake with ice and strain

8th Birthday
3/4 part Raspberry Liqueur
1/4 part Crème de Cacao (Dark)
1 part Vodka
1 part Milk
Cocktail Glass
Shake with ice and strain

9 1/2 Weeks
2 parts Citrus-Flavored Vodka
1/2 part Triple Sec
1 part Orange Juice
splash Strawberry Liqueur
Cocktail Glass
Shake with ice and strain

A.J.
1 1/2 parts Grapefruit Juice
3 dashes Grenadine
1 1/2 parts Apple Brandy
Cocktail Glass
Shake with ice and strain

Abbey in the Hills
2/3 part Vodka
1/2 part Crème de Cacao (White)
1/2 part Irish Cream Liqueur
1/2 part Frangelico®
Cocktail Glass
Shake with ice and strain

Abe's Tropical Night in Hell
2 parts Vodka
2 parts Banana Liqueur
2 parts Godiva® Liqueur
1 part Grenadine
Cocktail Glass
Shake with ice and strain

Absinthe Sour
1 part Absinthe
1 Egg White
1/2 part Sugar
1/2 part Lemon Juice
Cocktail Glass
Shake with ice and strain

Cocktails

Absinthe Special Cocktail
1 1/2 parts Anisette
dash Bitters
dash Sugar
1 part Water
Cocktail Glass

Shake with ice and strain

Absolut® Evergreen
2/3 part Citrus-Flavored Vodka
1/3 part Pisang Ambon® Liqueur
splash Lemon Juice
Cocktail Glass

Mix with ice and strain

Absolut® Northern Style
1 part Vodka
splash Apple Brandy
1/2 part Cream
fill with White Wine
Cocktail Glass

Shake with ice and strain

Absolut® Pissy
2 parts Vodka
1 part Lime Juice
2 parts Pineapple Juice
Cocktail Glass

Shake with ice and strain

Acapulco
1 1/2 parts Tequila
3 parts Pineapple Juice
1 part Grapefruit Juice
Cocktail Glass

Shake with ice and strain

Accidental Tourist
1 1/2 parts Gin
1 part Vanilla-Flavored Vodka
1/2 part Apple Brandy
1/2 part Passion Fruit Liqueur
Cocktail Glass

Shake with ice and strain

Accordion
1 1/2 parts Brandy
1/2 part Sweet Vermouth
1/2 part Dry Vermouth
2 splashes Triple Sec
Cocktail Glass

Shake with ice and strain

Acme
1/2 part Apricot Brandy
1 1/2 parts Light Rum
1/2 part Lime Juice
dash Powdered Sugar
Cocktail Glass

Shake with ice and strain

Acrobat
1 part Gin
2/3 part Apricot Brandy
2/3 part Dry Vermouth
splash Lime Juice
Cocktail Glass

Shake with ice and strain

Across the Stars
1/2 part Light Rum
1/2 part Dark Rum
1/2 part Triple Sec
2/3 part Lemon Juice
2/3 part Pineapple Juice
2/3 part Cranberry Juice Cocktail
Cocktail Glass

Shake with ice and strain

Adam and Eve
1 part Brandy
1 part Gin
1 part Apple-Flavored Liqueur
1 splash Lemon Juice
Cocktail Glass

Shake with ice and strain

Admiral Cocktail
1 1/2 parts Gin
1 part Cherry Liqueur
2 splashes Lime Juice
Cocktail Glass

Shake with ice and strain over ice

Admiralens Lile
1/2 part Apricot Brandy
1/2 part Dark Rum
1 part Crème de Banana
1 part Apple Juice
splash Grenadine
Cocktail Glass

Shake with ice and strain

Admirals Only
1/2 part Citrus-Flavored Vodka
2/3 part Amaretto
2/3 part Grand Marnier®
1 1/2 parts Cranberry Juice Cocktail
Cocktail Glass

Shake with ice and strain

The Admiral's Passion
1 part Passoã®
1 part Lemon-Lime Soda
1 part Orange Juice
Cocktail Glass

Shake with ice and strain

Adriana
1 part Orange Juice
1 part Gin
1/2 part Dry Vermouth
1/2 part Sweet Vermouth
Cocktail Glass

Shake with ice and strain

Adult's Channel
1 part Gin
1/2 part Strawberry Liqueur
splash Vanilla Liqueur
splash Lemon Juice
Cocktail Glass

Shake with ice and strain

Aer Rianta
1/2 part Gin
1/2 part Crème de Banana
1/2 part Sweet Vermouth
1/2 part Lemon Juice
Cocktail Glass

Shake with ice and strain

African Coffee
1 1/2 parts Crème de Cacao (Dark)
1 1/2 parts Hot Coffee
1 1/2 parts Tia Maria®
dash Strawberry Juice
Cocktail Glass

Shake with ice and strain

After 8
1 part Irish Cream Liqueur
1 part Coffee-Flavored Brandy
1 part Crème de Menthe (Green)
Cocktail Glass

Shake with ice and strain

After Dinner Delight
1 part Creme de Menthe (White)
1 part Frangelico®
2 parts Irish Cream Liqueur
Cocktail Glass

Shake with ice and strain

Afterburner
1 part Vodka
1/2 part Triple Sec
1 splash Grapefruit Juice
Cocktail Glass

Shake with ice and strain

Aftermath
2 parts Vodka
1 part Mandarine Napoléon® Liqueur
4 parts Grapefruit Juice
Cocktail Glass
Shake with ice and strain

Afternoon Chat
1 part Jim Beam®
1 part Maraschino Liqueur
1/2 part Peach Schnapps
2 parts Cranberry Juice Cocktail
3 parts Pineapple Juice
Cocktail Glass
Shake with ice and strain

Afternoon Cocktail
1 part Cognac
1 part Maraschino Liqueur
1 part Fernet-Branca®
Cocktail Glass
Shake with ice and strain

Agavemon
1/2 part Tequila Reposado
1 part Melon Liqueur
1/2 part Triple Sec
1 1/2 parts Fresh Lime Juice
Cocktail Glass
Shake with ice and strain

Ahh
1 part Vodka
1 part Parfait Amour
1 part Fruit Juice
Cocktail Glass
Shake with ice and strain

Ahi, Mi Amor!
1 1/2 parts Dark Rum
1/2 part Fresh Lime Juice
1/4 part Parfait Amour
1/2 part Simple Syrup
Cocktail Glass
Shake with ice and strain

Air Mail Special
1 1/2 parts Sweet Vermouth
1/2 part Grappa
Cocktail Glass
Shake with ice and strain

Airbag
1 1/2 parts Silver Tequila
3 parts Grapefruit Juice
1/2 part Mango Juice
splash Lemon Juice
splash Triple Sec
Cocktail Glass
Shake with ice and strain

Airborne Penguin
1 1/2 parts Gin
1 1/2 parts Dry Vermouth
splash Maraschino Liqueur
splash Pernod®
dash Orange Bitters
Cocktail Glass
Shake with ice and strain

Akuna Matata
2/3 part Crème de Banana
2/3 part Coconut-Flavored Liqueur
2/3 part Frangelico®
2/3 part Spiced Rum
3 parts Cream
Cocktail Glass
Shake with ice and strain

Alabama

1 part Brandy
1 part Triple Sec
1/2 part Fresh Lime Juice
1/2 part Sugar
Cocktail Glass

Shake with ice and strain

Alabammy Sammy

1 part Cherry Brandy
1/2 part Sambuca
1 part Sour Mix
2/3 part Ginger Ale
Cocktail Glass

Shake with ice and strain

Aladdin Sane

1 part Citrus-Flavored Vodka
1/2 part Lime
1/2 part Cointreau®
2 parts Fruit Punch
Cocktail Glass

Shake with ice and strain

Alberta Warmer

1/2 part Maraschino Liqueur
1/2 part Dry Vermouth
1 part Canadian Whiskey
1 part Pineapple Juice
Cocktail Glass

Shake with ice and strain

Aleluia

1 part Vodka
1/2 part Peach Schnapps
1/2 part Apricot Brandy
1 part Orange Juice
Cocktail Glass

Shake with ice and strain

Alessandro

1 part Gin
1 part Sambuca
1 part Cream
Cocktail Glass

Shake with ice and strain

Alexandre le Grand

1 1/2 parts Brandy
1/2 part Triple Sec
1/2 part Mandarine Napoléon® Liqueur
splash Galliano®
1 part Cream
Cocktail Glass

Shake with ice and strain. Top with cream.

Alfa Romeo®

2 parts Sweet Vermouth
1/2 part Gin
1 part Maraschino Liqueur
splash Campari®
Cocktail Glass

Shake with ice and strain

Algebra

1 part Light Rum
1/2 part Triple Sec
1/2 part Lemon Juice
Cocktail Glass

Shake with ice and strain

Alien Sky

1 part Light Rum
1 part Cherry Brandy
1/2 part Blue Curaçao
2 parts Orange Juice
3 parts Pineapple Juice
Cocktail Glass

Shake with ice and strain

All Jacked Up
$1/2$ part Jack Daniel's®
1 part Sloe Gin
1 part Melon Liqueur
1 part Pineapple Juice
Cocktail Glass

Shake with ice and strain

All Plucked Up
$1\frac{1}{2}$ parts Añejo Rum
$1\frac{1}{2}$ parts Coconut-Flavored Rum
$1/4$ part Grenadine
1 part Lime Juice
2 parts Orange Juice
3 parts Pineapple Juice
Cocktail Glass

Shake with ice and strain

All Stars
1 part Gin
1 part Triple Sec
1 part Sweet Vermouth
Cocktail Glass

Shake with ice and strain

All White Frappe
1 part Peppermint Schnapps
1 part Crème de Cacao (White)
1 part Anisette
1 part Lemon Juice
Cocktail Glass

Shake with ice and strain

All at Once
1 part Licor 43®
1 part Cherry Brandy
$1/2$ part Apricot Brandy
Cocktail Glass

Shake with ice and strain

Allegheny
1 part Dry Vermouth
1 part Blackberry Brandy
$1/2$ part Lemon Juice
Twist of Lemon Peel
Cocktail Glass

Shake all ingredients (except Lemon Peel) with ice and strain into a cocktail glass. Top with Lemon Peel twist and serve.

Allegro Agitato
1 part Maraschino Liqueur
1 part Grenadine
1 part Grappa
1 part Dry Sherry
Cocktail Glass

Shake with ice and strain

Alleluia
2 parts Tequila Reposado
1 part Maraschino Liqueur
Cocktail Glass

Shake with ice and strain

Alley Shooter
1 part Irish Cream Liqueur
1 part Coffee Liqueur
1 part Frangelico®
1 part Amaretto
1 part Vodka
Cocktail Glass

Shake with ice and strain

Allota Fagina
1 part Butterscotch Schnapps
1 part Irish Cream Liqueur
1 part Coconut-Flavored Rum
Cocktail Glass

Shake with ice and strain

Alma Cocktail
2 parts Crème de Cacao (Dark)
1 part Light Rum
1 part Gin
$^1/_2$ part Cream
Cocktail Glass
Shake with ice and strain

Almodovar
1 part Cherry Brandy
1 part Apricot Brandy
1 part Dry Vermouth
1 part Dry Sherry
Cocktail Glass
Shake with ice and strain

Almond Colada
3 parts Amaretto
$^1/_4$ cup Crème de Coconut
1$^1/_2$ parts Vodka
1 part Chocolate Syrup
Cocktail Glass
Shake with ice and strain

Almond Delight
1$^1/_2$ parts Amaretto
$^1/_2$ part Sambuca
Cocktail Glass
Shake with ice and strain

Almond Eye
1 part Amaretto
1 part Crème de Cacao (Dark)
1 part Cream
Cocktail Glass
Shake with ice and strain

Almond Joy®
$^1/_2$ part Amaretto
$^1/_2$ part Crème de Cacao (White)
2 parts Light Cream
Cocktail Glass
Shake with ice and strain

Almondini
1 part Vodka
1 part Amaretto
Cocktail Glass
Shake with ice and strain

Alphabet
$^1/_2$ part Drambuie®
$^2/_3$ part Apple Brandy
splash Blue Curaçao
splash Chartreuse®
Cocktail Glass
Shake with ice and strain

Amagansett
1$^1/_2$ parts Gin
$^1/_2$ part Dry Vermouth
$^1/_2$ part Pernod®
splash Crème de Menthe (White)
Cocktail Glass
Shake with ice and strain

Amaretto Flip
2 parts Amaretto
1 Egg White
1 part Orange Juice
$^3/_4$ part Cream
Cocktail Glass
Shake with ice and strain

Amaretto Stinger
1$^1/_2$ parts Amaretto
$^3/_4$ part Crème de Menthe (White)
Cocktail Glass
Shake with ice and strain

Amba
1 part Scotch
$^1/_2$ part Dark Rum
1 part Triple Sec
1 part Sweet Vermouth
Cocktail Glass
Shake with ice and strain

Ambaraba
1 part Whiskey
1/2 part Light Rum
1/4 part Triple Sec
1/4 part Sweet Vermouth
Cocktail Glass

Shake with ice and strain

Ambrosia
2 parts Vodka
1/2 part Melon Liqueur
1/4 part Orange Bitters
Cocktail Glass

Stir gently with ice and strain

Ambrous
1 part Apricot Brandy
1 part Apple Brandy
1 part Ginger Ale
splash Lime Juice
Cocktail Glass

Shake with ice and strain

America On Line
1 1/2 parts Jim Beam©
1 1/2 parts Orange Juice
splash Peppermint Liqueur
splash Amaretto
Cocktail Glass

Shake with ice and strain

American Dragon
1 1/2 parts Gin
1/2 part Peppermint Liqueur
1/2 part Kümmel
1/2 part Lemon Juice
dash Orange Bitters
Cocktail Glass

Shake with ice and strain

American Pie
1 part Brandy
1/2 part Dry Vermouth
1/2 part Tawny Port
splash Crème de Menthe (White)
1 part Orange Juice
Cocktail Glass

Shake with ice and strain

Amethyst
1 part Parfait Amour
1/2 part Raspberry Liqueur
1/2 part Vanilla-Flavored Vodka
Cocktail Glass

Shake with ice and strain

Amigo
1 part Dark Rum
1/2 part Crème de Banana
1/2 part Apricot Brandy
1 part Pear Juice
splash Grenadine
Cocktail Glass

Shake with ice and strain

Amer Picon® Cocktail
1 part Sweet Vermouth
1 part Amer Picon®
Cocktail Glass

Shake with ice and strain

Amor Brujo
1 1/2 parts Cherry Brandy
1 1/2 parts Chocolate Liqueur
1 1/2 parts Cream
Cocktail Glass

Shake with ice and strain

Amore Me Amore
1 part Blackberry Liqueur
1 part Currant-Flavored Vodka
1/2 part Frangelico®
1/2 part Lemon Juice
2 parts Raspberry-Flavored Seltzer
Cocktail Glass

Shake with ice and strain

Amsterdam
$1\frac{1}{2}$ parts Gin
$\frac{3}{4}$ part Triple Sec
$\frac{1}{2}$ part Orange Juice
Cocktail Glass
Shake with ice and strain

Anchor's Seagrit
$\frac{1}{2}$ part Dark Rum
1 part Triple Sec
splash Passion Fruit Liqueur
splash Lime Juice
splash Sour Mix
Cocktail Glass
Shake with ice and strain

Andalusia
$\frac{1}{2}$ part Light Rum
$1\frac{1}{2}$ parts Dry Sherry
$\frac{1}{2}$ part Brandy
Cocktail Glass
Shake with ice and strain

Andicuri Special
1 part Light Rum
1 part Crème de Cacao (White)
1 part Cream
splash Coffee
Cocktail Glass
Shake with ice and strain

Angel Face
1 part Gin
$\frac{1}{2}$ part Apricot Brandy
$\frac{1}{2}$ part Apple Brandy
Cocktail Glass
Shake with ice and strain

Angel with Dirty Face
$\frac{2}{3}$ part Cherry Brandy
$1\frac{1}{2}$ parts Scotch
$1\frac{1}{2}$ parts Carpano Punt e Mes Vermouth
Cocktail Glass
Shake with ice and strain

Angelic Cocktail
1 part Bourbon
$\frac{1}{2}$ part Crème de Cacao (White)
$\frac{1}{2}$ part Cream
splash Grenadine
Cocktail Glass
Shake with ice and strain

Angers Rose
1 part Pineapple Juice
$\frac{1}{2}$ part Triple Sec
$\frac{1}{2}$ part Bourbon
splash Campari®
1 Egg White
Cocktail Glass
Shake with ice and strain

Anisette Cocktail
1 part Anisette
1 dash Sugar
splash Water
Cocktail Glass
Shake with ice and strain

Ankle Sprainer
$\frac{1}{2}$ part Cherry Brandy
splash Crème de Banana
splash Pineapple Juice
splash Orange Juice
Cocktail Glass
Shake with ice and strain

Ann Sheridan
1 part Light Rum
$\frac{1}{2}$ part Blue Curaçao
$\frac{1}{2}$ part Lime Juice
Cocktail Glass
Shake with ice and strain

Annabele Special

1 1/2 parts Benedictine®
1 part Dry Vermouth
1 part Lime Juice
Cocktail Glass

Shake with ice and strain

Año

2/3 part Raspberry Liqueur
2/3 part Vodka
2/3 part Dry Vermouth
Cocktail Glass

Shake with ice and strain

Antananarivo

1/2 part Amaretto
1/2 part Crème de Cacao (White)
1/2 part Cherry Brandy
1 part Dark Rum
1 part Cream
Cocktail Glass

Shake with ice and strain

Antidote

1 part Amaretto
1/2 part Triple Sec
1 1/2 parts Scotch
2 parts Orange Juice
1 part Lemon Juice
Cocktail Glass

Shake with ice and strain

Aperitivo

1 1/2 parts Gin
1 part Sambuca
2 dashes Orange Bitters
Cocktail Glass

Shake with ice and strain

Aperol™ '86

1 part Aperol™
1 part Cointreau®
1 part Dry Vermouth
Cocktail Glass

Shake with ice and strain

Aphrodite

1 1/2 parts Parfait Amour
1/2 part Vanilla Liqueur
1 1/2 parts Cream
Cocktail Glass

Shake with ice and strain

Appalachia

1 1/2 parts Scotch
1 part Green Ginger Wine
1 part Orange Juice
Cocktail Glass

Shake with ice and strain

Appian Way

1 1/2 parts Gin
1/2 part Strega®
1/2 part Amaretto
Cocktail Glass

Shake with ice and strain

Apple Bee

1 1/2 parts Sour Apple Schnapps
1/2 part Applejack
1/2 part Cranberry Juice Cocktail
Cocktail Glass

Shake with ice and strain

Apple Daiquiri

1/2 part Apple Juice
1/2 part Lime Juice
1 1/2 parts Light Rum
dash Powdered Sugar
Cocktail Glass

Fill a mixing glass with 4 parts of shaved ice and add all ingredients. Shake and strain into a chilled glass.

Apple Jax
1 part Melon Liqueur
1/2 part Whiskey
1/2 part Apple Liqueur
Cocktail Glass
Shake with ice and strain

Apple Judy
1/2 part Grand Marnier®
1/2 part Vodka
3 parts Apple Juice
Cocktail Glass
Shake with ice and strain

Apple Juice
1 part Coconut-Flavored Rum
1 part Peach Schnapps
1 part Pisang Ambon® Liqueur
1 part Fresh Lime Juice
1 part Apple Juice
Cocktail Glass
Shake with ice and strain

Apple Ordeal
1 part Apricot Brandy
1 part Apple Brandy
1/2 part Coconut Cream
1/2 part Cream
Cocktail Glass
Shake with ice and strain

Apple Pie
3/4 part Sweet Vermouth
3/4 part Rum
splash Apple Brandy
splash Grenadine
splash Lemon Juice
Cocktail Glass
Shake with ice and strain

Apple Stone Sour
2 parts Apricot Brandy
1 part Fresh Lime Juice
splash Orange Juice
dash Sugar
Cocktail Glass
Shake with ice and strain

Applecar
1 part Applejack
1 part Triple Sec
1 part Lemon Juice
Cocktail Glass
Shake with ice and strain

Applejack Manhattan
2 parts Apple Brandy
1/2 part Sweet Vermouth
dash Orange Bitters
Cocktail Glass
Shake with ice and strain

Apples to Oranges
1 part Apple Brandy
1 part Dubonnet® Blonde
1/2 part Triple Sec
Cocktail Glass
Shake with ice and strain

Apricot Blossom
1 part Rum
1/2 part Strawberry Liqueur
1 1/2 parts Apricot Juice
1/2 part Cream
Cocktail Glass
Shake with ice and strain

Apricot Cocktail
1 part Gin
1 1/2 parts Apricot Brandy
1/4 part Lemon Juice
1/2 part Orange Juice
Cocktail Glass
Shake with ice and strain

Apricot Moonshine
2 parts Apricot Brandy
1 part Triple Sec
Cocktail Glass

Shake with ice and strain

Apricot Pie
2 parts Light Rum
1 part Apricot Brandy
1 Egg White
1/2 part Triple Sec
1/2 part Fresh Lime Juice
Cocktail Glass

Shake with ice and strain

April Rain
2 parts Dry Vodka
1/2 part Lime Cordial
1/2 part Vermouth
Cocktail Glass

Shake with ice and strain

Aprishot
2 parts Vodka
1/2 part Apricot Brandy
1 part Pineapple Juice
Cocktail Glass

Shake with ice and strain

Aqua Plunge
1/2 part Blue Curaçao
1 part Aquavit
1/2 part Margarita Mix
1 part Cranberry Juice Cocktail
Cocktail Glass

Shake with ice and strain

Aqueduct
1 1/2 parts Vodka
3/4 part Amaretto
3/4 part Triple Sec
1/2 part Fresh Lime Juice
Cocktail Glass

Shake with ice and strain

Arcadia
1 1/2 parts Gin
1/2 part Galliano®
1/2 part Crème de Banana
1/2 part Grapefruit Juice
Cocktail Glass

Shake with ice and strain

Archimedes
1 1/2 parts Amaretto
1 1/2 parts Orange Juice
1 1/2 parts Cranberry Juice Cocktail
Cocktail Glass

Shake with ice and strain

Arcimboldo Punch
2 parts Light Rum
1 part Dry Vermouth
2 parts Pineapple Juice
1 part Grape Juice
Cocktail Glass

Shake with ice and strain

Arena
1 part Dry Vermouth
1 part Sweet Vermouth
1 part Sherry
dash Bitters
Cocktail Glass

Shake with ice and strain

Ariete
1 part Vodka
1 part Dry Vermouth
1/2 part Dry Sherry
splash Peach Schnapps
splash Blue Curaçao
Cocktail Glass

Shake with ice and strain

Aristocracy
1 part Apricot Brandy
1 part Crème de Banana
1/2 part Crème de Cacao (White)
1/2 part Coconut Cream
Cocktail Glass
Shake with ice and strain

Armagnac Lilie
1 1/2 parts Lillet®
1 part Armagnac
Cocktail Glass
Shake with ice and strain

Armon
1 part Vodka
1/2 part Coffee Liqueur
splash Crème de Menthe (White)
splash Blue Curaçao
Cocktail Glass
Shake with ice and strain

Armour Cocktail
1 3/4 parts Dry Sherry
1 part Sweet Vermouth
Cocktail Glass
Shake with ice and strain

Army Cocktail
1 1/2 parts Gin
1 part Sweet Vermouth
2 dashes Grenadine
Cocktail Glass
Shake with ice and strain

Arnaud
1 part Dry Vermouth
1 part Gin
1 part Crème de Cassis
Cocktail Glass
Shake with ice and strain

Arrowhead
1/2 part Bourbon
1/2 part Dry Vermouth
1/2 part Sweet Vermouth
1 Egg White
Cocktail Glass
Shake with ice and strain

Arsenic and Old Lace
1 part Gin
1/2 part Pastis
splash Dry Vermouth
splash Parfait Amour
Cocktail Glass
Shake with ice and strain

Artificial Satellite
1 part Blue Curaçao
2/3 part Spiced Rum
1/2 part Lime Juice
1 part Pineapple Juice
Cocktail Glass
Shake with ice and strain

Aruba
1 part Gin
1/2 part Blue Curaçao
1 part Lemon Juice
1 Egg
1 splash Amaretto
Cocktail Glass
Shake with ice and strain

Asbach Beauty
3/4 part Brandy
3/4 part Extra Dry Vermouth
splash Crème de Menthe (White)
1 part Port
3/4 part Orange Juice
splash Grenadine
Cocktail Glass
Shake with ice and strain

Asbury Park
$1\frac{1}{2}$ parts Brandy
$\frac{1}{2}$ part Applejack
$\frac{1}{2}$ part Sweet Vermouth
Cocktail Glass
Shake with ice and strain

Ascot
1 part Gin
$\frac{1}{2}$ part Sweet Vermouth
$\frac{1}{2}$ part Dry Vermouth
dash Bitters
1 splash Anisette
Lemon Twist
Cocktail Glass
Shake with ice and strain

Ashcroft
$\frac{1}{2}$ part Peach Schnapps
$\frac{1}{2}$ part Goldschläger®
$\frac{1}{2}$ part Butterscotch Schnapps
$\frac{1}{2}$ part Irish Cream Liqueur
1 part Milk
Cocktail Glass
Shake with ice and strain

Asphalt Jungle
1 part Vodka
$\frac{1}{2}$ part Irish Cream Liqueur
$\frac{1}{2}$ part Lime Juice
Cocktail Glass
Shake with ice and strain

Atahualpa
1 part Peach Schnapps
1 part Cachaça
1 part Pineapple Juice
splash Simple Syrup
Cocktail Glass
Shake with ice and strain

Athenian Night
$1\frac{1}{2}$ parts Gin
$\frac{1}{2}$ part Cherry Brandy
$\frac{1}{2}$ part Madeira
splash Orange Juice
Cocktail Glass
Shake with ice and strain

Atlantis
$1\frac{1}{2}$ parts Citrus-Flavored Vodka
$\frac{1}{2}$ part Blue Curaçao
$\frac{2}{3}$ part Passion Fruit Juice
$\frac{2}{3}$ part Grapefruit Juice
Cocktail Glass
Shake with ice and strain

Atmosphere
1 part Gin
$\frac{2}{3}$ part Passion Fruit Liqueur
$\frac{2}{3}$ part Mandarine Napoléon® Liqueur
splash Simple Syrup
$\frac{1}{2}$ part Lemon Juice
Cocktail Glass
Shake with ice and strain

Atomic Powered
1 part Gin
1 part Dry Vermouth
splash Cherry Brandy
splash Pernod®
Cocktail Glass
Shake with ice and strain

Attention Grabber
$1\frac{1}{2}$ parts Gin
$\frac{1}{2}$ part Dry Vermouth
splash Passion Fruit Liqueur
splash Chartreuse®
dash Orange Bitters
Cocktail Glass
Shake with ice and strain

Aussie Boomerang

1 part Melon Liqueur
1 part Kiwi Schnapps
1 part Cream
Cocktail Glass

Shake with ice and strain

Autumn Buzz

1 part Blue Curaçao
1 part Chambord®
1/2 part Rémy Martin® VSOP
Cocktail Glass

Shake with ice and strain

Aviator

1 part Gin
1/2 part Apricot Brandy
1/2 part Maraschino Liqueur
1 part Lemon Juice
Cocktail Glass

Shake with ice and strain

Aztec Gold

2 parts Gold Tequila
1 part Crème de Banana
1 part Amaretto
1 part Galliano®
Cocktail Glass

Shake with ice and strain

Azteca

1 1/2 parts Light Rum
1 part Coffee Liqueur
1 part Crème de Cacao (White)
dash Blue Curaçao
Cocktail Glass

Shake with ice and strain

Azulejo

1 part Vodka
1/2 part Parfait Amour
1/2 part Triple Sec
splash Pineapple Juice
dash Bitters
Cocktail Glass

Shake with ice and strain

B.M. Slider

1 part Coffee Liqueur
1 part Cream
1 part Southern Comfort®
Cocktail Glass

Shake with ice and strain

B.V.D.

1 part Blackberry Brandy
1 part Gin
1 part Peach Schnapps
1 part Lemon-Lime Soda
1 part Cola
Cocktail Glass

Shake with ice and strain

B-52

1 part Coffee Liqueur
1 part Irish Cream Liqueur
1 part Amaretto
Cocktail Glass

Layer in a cocktail glass

Baby

1 1/2 parts Triple Sec
1 part Cream
dash Bitters
Cocktail Glass

Shake with ice and strain

Baby Aspirin
$1^1/_2$ parts Coconut-Flavored Rum
$^1/_2$ part Orange Juice
$^1/_2$ part Pineapple Juice
$^1/_2$ part Grenadine
$^1/_2$ part Triple Sec
Cocktail Glass
Shake with ice and strain

Baby Doll
2 parts Courvoisier®
$1^1/_2$ parts Grand Marnier®
$^1/_2$ part Lemon Juice
Cocktail Glass
Stir gently with ice and strain

Baby's Bottom
$1^1/_2$ parts Whiskey
$^1/_2$ part Crème de Cacao (White)
$^1/_2$ part Crème de Menthe (White)
Cocktail Glass
Shake with ice and strain

Bacardi® Alexander
$^3/_4$ part Rum
$^1/_2$ part Crème de Cacao (Dark)
$^1/_2$ part Cream
dash Ground Nutmeg
Cocktail Glass
Shake with ice and strain

Bacardi® Special
2 parts Light Rum
$^3/_4$ part Gin
splash Lime Juice
splash Grenadine
dash Sugar
Cocktail Glass
Shake with ice and strain

Bacarra
$1^1/_2$ parts Raspberry Liqueur
$^2/_3$ part Grand Marnier®
$^2/_3$ part Campari®
Cocktail Glass
Shake with ice and strain

Baci da Roma
1 part Coffee Liqueur
$^1/_4$ part Crème de Cacao (White)
$^1/_4$ part Sambuca
1 part Cream
Cocktail Glass
Shake with ice and strain

Back in Black
1 part Blackberry Liqueur
1 part Amaretto
1 part Lychee Liqueur
1 part Cream
splash Anisette
Cocktail Glass
Shake with ice and strain

Back Seater
$^1/_2$ part Apple Brandy
$^1/_2$ part Brandy
$^1/_2$ part Triple Sec
splash Lemon Juice
Cocktail Glass
Shake with ice and strain

Backstreet
$1^1/_2$ parts Light Rum
$^1/_2$ part Applejack
$^1/_2$ part Sweet Vermouth
$^1/_2$ part Cherry Brandy
Cocktail Glass
Shake with ice and strain

Bahama-Americana
1 part Light Rum
1 part Southern Comfort®
1/2 part Crème de Banana
Cocktail Glass
Shake with ice and strain

Bahia
1 part Dry Sherry
1 part Dry Vermouth
1 part Pastis
dash Orange Bitters
Cocktail Glass
Shake with ice and strain

Baileys® Comet
1 part Irish Cream Liqueur
1 part Butterscotch Schnapps
1 part Goldschläger®
1/4 part Sambuca
dash Ground Nutmeg
Cocktail Glass
Shake with ice and strain

Baileys® Cuddler
1 part Irish Cream Liqueur
1/2 part Amaretto
Cocktail Glass
Shake with ice and strain

Baileys® Tropic
1 part Dark Rum
1 part Blue Curaçao
2 parts Pineapple Juice
Cocktail Glass
Shake with ice and strain

Baja Bug
1/2 part Coconut-Flavored Liqueur
splash Sloe Gin
splash Raspberry Liqueur
1 part Pineapple Juice
1 part Cranberry Juice Cocktail
Cocktail Glass
Shake with ice and strain

Bajadera
1 part Blue Curaçao
1 part Tequila Silver
1 part Maraschino Liqueur
Cocktail Glass
Shake with ice and strain

Bali Dream
1 part Light Rum
1 part Dark Rum
1 part Crème de Banana
1 part Passoã®
1/2 part Coconut-Flavored Liqueur
splash Grenadine
splash Orange Juice
Cocktail Glass
Shake with ice and strain

Ballet Russe Cocktail
2 parts Vodka
1/2 part Crème de Cassis
4 splashes Lime Juice
Cocktail Glass
Shake with ice and strain

Balmoral
1 1/2 parts Scotch
1/2 part Sweet Vermouth
1/2 part Dry Vermouth
2 dashes Bitters
Cocktail Glass
Shake with ice and strain

Bam Bam
$1^1/_2$ parts Whiskey
$^1/_2$ part Crème de Cacao (White)
$^1/_2$ part Crème de Menthe (White)
Cocktail Glass
Shake with ice and strain

Banana Baron
$^1/_2$ part Crème de Banana
$^2/_3$ part Maraschino Liqueur
$^1/_2$ part Anisette
Cocktail Glass
Shake with ice and strain

Banana Bird
1 part Cream
2 splashes Crème de Banana
2 splashes Triple Sec
Cocktail Glass
Shake with ice and strain

Banana Boomer
1 part Crème de Banana
1 part Pineapple Juice
1 part Orange Juice
$^1/_2$ part Apricot Brandy
$^1/_2$ part Cherry Brandy
Cocktail Glass
Shake with ice and strain

Banana Cow
1 part Light Rum
1 part Crème de Banana
$1^1/_2$ parts Cream
splash Grenadine
Cocktail Glass
Shake with ice and strain

Banana Girl
1 part Crème de Cacao (White)
1 part Cream
1 part Pisang Ambon® Liqueur
1 part Coconut-Flavored Liqueur
Cocktail Glass
Shake with ice and strain

Banana Irlandese
2 parts Banana Juice
1 part Crème de Cacao (White)
Cocktail Glass
Shake with ice and strain

Banana Mango
$1^1/_2$ parts Light Rum
1 part Crème de Banana
$^1/_2$ part Fresh Lime Juice
$^1/_2$ part Mango Nectar
Cocktail Glass
Shake with ice and strain

Banana Nut
$1^1/_2$ parts Frangelico®
$^1/_2$ part Crème de Banana
1 part Pineapple Juice
Cocktail Glass
Shake with ice and strain

Banana Rum Cream
$1^1/_2$ parts Dark Rum
$^1/_2$ part Crème de Banana
1 part Light Cream
Cocktail Glass
Shake with ice and strain

Banana Split
$^1/_2$ part Vodka
$1^1/_2$ parts Crème de Banana
1 part Crème de Cacao (White)
1 part Light Cream
Cocktail Glass
Shake with ice and strain

Banana Sunrise
1 part Coconut-Flavored Rum
1 part Crème de Banana
1 part Piña Colada Mix
Cocktail Glass
Shake with ice and strain

Bananarama
1/2 part Vodka
1 part Crème de Banana
1/2 part Triple Sec
1 part Light Cream
Cocktail Glass
Shake with ice and strain

Banff Cocktail
1 1/2 parts Canadian Whiskey
1/2 part Grand Marnier®
1/2 part Kirschwasser
dash Bitters
1 Lemon Twist
Cocktail Glass
Shake with ice and strain

Bank Holiday
1 part Orange-Flavored Vodka
1 part Crème de Cacao (White)
1 part Blackberry Liqueur
Cocktail Glass
Shake with ice and strain

Banshee
1 part Crème de Banana
1/2 part Crème de Cacao (White)
1 1/2 parts Light Cream
Cocktail Glass
Shake with ice and strain

Barbados Cocktail
2 parts Light Rum
1/2 part Triple Sec
1 part Pineapple Juice
Cocktail Glass
Shake with ice and strain

Barbancourt Winner
2/3 part Amaretto
2/3 part Dark Rum
2/3 part Pineapple Juice
1 part Cranberry Juice Cocktail
Cocktail Glass
Shake with ice and strain

Barbazul
2/3 part Triple Sec
2/3 part Currant-Flavored Vodka
1 1/2 parts Grapefruit Juice
splash Lime Juice
splash Blue Curaçao
Cocktail Glass
Shake with ice and strain

Bare Cheeks
1 part Vodka
1 part Apple Juice
splash Grenadine
splash Lemon Juice
Cocktail Glass
Shake with ice and strain

Barefoot
1 part Brandy
1/2 part Dry Vermouth
2 splashes Maraschino Liqueur
splash Crème de Menthe (White)
Cocktail Glass
Shake with ice and strain

Barely Legal
2/3 part Amaretto
1/2 part Peach Schnapps
2/3 part Cranberry Juice Cocktail
Cocktail Glass
Shake with ice and strain

Baron Cocktail
1/2 part Dry Vermouth
1 1/2 parts Gin
splash Triple Sec
splash Sweet Vermouth
1 Lemon Wedge
Cocktail Glass

Shake with ice and strain

Barrel of Monkeys
1 part Crème de Banana
1/2 part Coconut-Flavored Liqueur
1 part Light Rum
1 part Cream
Cocktail Glass

Shake with ice and strain

Bartender's Delight
1 part Dry Vermouth
1 part Gordon's® Orange Vodka
1 part Dry Sherry
Cocktail Glass

Shake with ice and strain

Basic Bill
1 1/2 parts Añejo Rum
1/2 part Dubonnet® Rouge
1/2 part Grand Marnier®
2 dashes Bitters
Cocktail Glass

Shake with ice and strain

Basin Street
2 parts Bourbon
1 part Triple Sec
Cocktail Glass

Shake with ice and strain

Bastardly
1/2 part Vodka
1/2 part Blackberry Liqueur
splash Vanilla Liqueur
splash Amaretto
Cocktail Glass

Shake with ice and strain

Battery Charger
1 1/2 parts Vermouth
1 part Jamaican Rum
splash Cherry Brandy
Cocktail Glass

Shake with ice and strain

Bavarian Cherry
1/2 part Kirschwasser
1/2 part Citrus-Flavored Vodka
1/4 part Crème de Cassis
1 Egg White
Cocktail Glass

Shake with ice and strain

Bay Dream
1 part Gin
1/2 part Advocaat
1 1/2 parts Dry Vermouth
dash Angostura® Bitters
1/2 part Lemon Juice
splash Simple Syrup
Cocktail Glass

Shake with ice and strain

BCC
1 1/2 parts Blackberry Liqueur
1 part Triple Sec
1 part Cognac
1 part Grenadine
Cocktail Glass

Shake with ice and strain

Be Bop a Lula
1 part Vanilla Liqueur
1 part Armagnac
1 part Cream
1 part Pineapple Juice
splash Chocolate Mint Liqueur
Cocktail Glass
Shake with ice and strain

Beach Blanket Bop
1/2 part Vodka
1/2 part Coconut-Flavored Liqueur
1/2 part Melon Liqueur
1/2 part Blackberry Liqueur
1 part Pineapple Juice
1/2 part Cranberry Juice Cocktail
Cocktail Glass
Shake with ice and strain

Beachbum
2 parts Rum
3/4 part Triple Sec
3/4 part Fresh Lime Juice
splash Grenadine
Cocktail Glass
Shake with ice and strain

Beachcomber
1 1/2 parts Light Rum
1/2 part Triple Sec
1/2 part Lime Juice
splash Maraschino Cherry Liqueur
dash Granulated Sugar
Cocktail Glass
Shake with ice and strain

Beachcomber's Gold
2 parts Dark Rum
1/2 part Dry Vermouth
1/2 part Sweet Vermouth
Cocktail Glass
Shake with ice and strain

Beadlestone Cocktail
1 1/2 parts Dry Vermouth
1 1/2 parts Scotch
Cocktail Glass
Stir gently with ice and strain

Beals Cocktail
1 1/2 parts Scotch
1/2 part Dry Vermouth
1/2 part Sweet Vermouth
Cocktail Glass
Shake with ice and strain

Beau Rivage
1 part Dry Gin
1 part Light Rum
1 part Dry Vermouth
1 part Orange Juice
1 part Sweet Vermouth
1 part Grenadine
Cocktail Glass
Shake with ice and strain

Beautiful American
1 part Melon Liqueur
1 part Blue Curaçao
1 part Sour Mix
Cocktail Glass
Shake with ice and strain

Beautiful Bateaux
1 part Amaretto
1 part Maraschino Liqueur
3 parts Cranberry Juice Cocktail
2 parts Sour Mix
Cocktail Glass
Shake with ice and strain

Beauty and the Beach
1 1/2 parts Light Rum
1 1/2 parts Southern Comfort®
splash Grand Marnier®
splash Lemon Juice
dash Orange Bitters
Cocktail Glass
Shake with ice and strain

Beauty Gump
1/2 part Blue Curaçao
1/2 part Peach Schnapps
1/2 part Orange-Flavored Vodka
splash Sour Mix
Cocktail Glass
Shake with ice and strain

Bee Stinger
1 1/2 parts Blackberry Brandy
1/2 part Crème de Menthe (White)
Cocktail Glass
Shake with ice and strain

Beeing Frenzy
1 1/2 parts Light Rum
1/2 part Strawberry Liqueur
2/3 part Orange Juice
2/3 part Pineapple Juice
2/3 part Lemon Juice
2/3 part Club Soda
Cocktail Glass
Shake with ice and strain

Bee's Kiss
1 part Rum
splash Cream
splash Honey
Cocktail Glass
Shake with ice and strain

Bee's Knees
1 1/2 parts Rum
1/2 part Triple Sec
1/2 part Orange Juice
1/2 part Powdered Sugar
1/2 part Fresh Lime Juice
Cocktail Glass
Shake with ice and strain

Before Dawn
2 parts Port
1/2 part Amaretto
Cocktail Glass
Shake with ice and strain

Before Midnight
1/2 part Vodka
1/2 part Orange Juice
1/2 part Gin
splash Apricot Brandy
Cocktail Glass
Shake with ice and strain

Beige Blindfold
1 1/2 parts Gin
1/2 part Triple Sec
2 splashes Brandy
2 splashes Lemon Juice
Cocktail Glass
Shake with ice and strain

Bekki's Boobs
1 1/2 parts Melon Liqueur
1 1/2 parts Jamaican Rum
1 part Kiwi Schnapps
Cocktail Glass
Shake with ice and strain

Belching Dragon
1 part Pepper-Flavored Vodka
1 part Cinnamon Schnapps
1 part Vanilla Liqueur
Cocktail Glass

Shake with ice and strain

Belinda
1 part Dark Rum
1/2 part Dry Vermouth
splash Crème de Banana
splash Amaretto
Cocktail Glass

Shake with ice and strain

Bells of St. Mary's
1 1/2 parts Gin
1 part Triple Sec
1 part Apricot Brandy
splash Lemon Juice
Cocktail Glass

Shake with ice and strain

Belmont
2 parts Gin
1/2 part Raspberry Syrup
Cocktail Glass

Shake with ice and strain

Belmont Stakes
1 1/2 parts Vodka
3/4 part Rum
1/2 part Fresh Lime Juice
1/2 part Strawberry
1/4 part Grenadine
Cocktail Glass

Shake with ice and strain

Benedictus
1 part Gin
1 part Benedictine®
1/2 part Maraschino Liqueur
Cocktail Glass

Shake with ice and strain

Bengal Tiger
1 1/2 parts Brandy
1/2 part Maraschino Liqueur
1/2 part Triple Sec
1 part Pineapple Juice
Cocktail Glass

Shake with ice and strain

Bentley
1 1/2 parts Apple Brandy
1 part Dubonnet® Blonde
Twist of Lemon Peel
Cocktail Glass

Stir gently with ice and strain

Bergenline
2 parts Frangelico®
1 part Sweet Vermouth
3/4 part Triple Sec
1 Lime Wedge
Cocktail Glass

Shake with ice and strain

Berimbau
1 1/2 parts Jägermeister®
1/2 part Cachaça
1/4 part Triple Sec
splash Lemon Juice
Cocktail Glass

Shake with ice and strain

Bernardo
2 parts Gin
1/2 part Triple Sec
2 splashes Lemon Juice
2 dashes Bitters
Cocktail Glass
Shake with ice and strain

Berry Deauville
1 part Vodka
1/2 part Blackberry Liqueur
1/2 part Raspberry Liqueur
1/2 part Peach Schnapps
1 1/2 parts Pineapple Juice
Cocktail Glass
Shake with ice and strain

Berry Festival
1 part Vodka
1 part Crème de Cacao (White)
1/2 part Blackberry Liqueur
1 part Cream
Cocktail Glass
Shake with ice and strain

Berry Harry
1 part Light Rum
1 part Blackberry Liqueur
1 part Crème de Cassis
1 part Raspberry Juice
1 part Blackberry Juice
Cocktail Glass
Shake with ice and strain

Berry Patch
1 part Currant-Flavored Vodka
1/4 part Fresh Lime Juice
1/4 part Blackberry
Cocktail Glass
Shake with ice and strain

Beso de Limon
2 parts Crème de Banana
2 parts Dark Rum
1 part Lemon Juice
Cocktail Glass
Shake with ice and strain

Bethlehem
1 part Dark Rum
1/2 part Benedictine®
splash Amaretto
splash Drambuie®
Cocktail Glass
Stir gently with ice and strain

Betsy Ross
1 1/2 parts Brandy
1 1/2 parts Port
splash Triple Sec
Cocktail Glass
Shake with ice and strain

Better than Ever
1 part Vodka
1/2 part Triple Sec
1/2 part Fresh Lime Juice
1/2 part Pear Liqueur
1/2 part Raspberry Syrup
Cocktail Glass
Shake with ice and strain

Beware of the Currant
1 1/2 parts Blue Curaçao
1/2 part Raspberry Liqueur
1 part Currant-Flavored Vodka
1 part Pineapple Juice
Cocktail Glass
Shake with ice and strain

Bianca Castafiore
1 part Amaretto
1 part Sambuca
1 part Galliano®
Cocktail Glass
Shake with ice and strain

Bibe '77
1 part Vodka
1 part Sweet Vermouth
1 part Dry Vermouth
1/2 part Apricot Brandy
splash Amaretto
splash Grenadine
Cocktail Glass
Shake with ice and strain

Big Band Charlie
1 1/2 parts Dark Rum
1/2 part Melon Liqueur
1/2 part Triple Sec
1/2 part Lime Juice
Cocktail Glass
Shake with ice and strain

Big Calm
2/3 part Coconut-Flavored Liqueur
2/3 part Melon Liqueur
2/3 part Amaretto
splash Pineapple Juice
Cocktail Glass
Shake with ice and strain

Bijou
1 1/4 parts Dry Gin
3/4 part Chartreuse®
3/4 part Vermouth
Cocktail Glass
Shake with ice and strain

Bikini
1 part Light Rum
2 parts Vodka
1/2 part Milk
1 dash Sugar
1/2 part Lemon Juice
Lemon Twist
Cocktail Glass
Shake with ice and strain

Bikini Top
1 1/2 parts Vanilla-Flavored Vodka
1 part Blackberry Liqueur
2/3 part Crème de Cacao (White)
Cocktail Glass
Shake with ice and strain

Billy Hamilton
1 part Crème de Cacao (White)
1 part Cognac
1 part Triple Sec
1 Egg White
Cocktail Glass
Shake with ice and strain

Biondina
1 part Triple Sec
1 part Anisette
Cocktail Glass
Shake with ice and strain

Bird of Paradise Cocktail
1 part Silver Tequila
1 part Crème de Cacao (White)
1/2 part Amaretto
2 parts Cream
Cocktail Glass
Shake with ice and strain

Bishop Brandy
1/2 part Triple Sec
1 part Brandy
1/2 part Maraschino Liqueur
dash Orange Bitters
1 part Pineapple Juice
Cocktail Glass
Shake with ice and strain

Bitch Fight
1 part Cointreau®
1 part Peach Schnapps
1 part Cranberry Juice Cocktail
splash Lime Juice
Cocktail Glass
Shake with ice and strain

Bittersweet
1 part Dry Vermouth
1 part Sweet Vermouth
dash Bitters
dash Orange Bitters
Cocktail Glass
Shake with ice and strain

Bittersweet Symphony
1 part Light Rum
3/4 part Crème de Cacao (White)
1/2 part Cherry Brandy
1 part Grapefruit Juice
dash Orange Bitters
Cocktail Glass
Shake with ice and strain

Black and Blue
2 parts Black Death® Vodka
1 part Blue Curaçao
1 part Cranberry Juice Cocktail
Cocktail Glass
Shake with ice and strain

Black Baltimore
2 parts Brandy
1 part Black Sambuca
1 Egg White
Cocktail Glass
Shake with ice and strain

Black Bird
3/4 part Gin
1/4 part Sweet Vermouth
1/4 part Crème de Cassis
splash Pernod®
Cocktail Glass
Shake with ice and strain

Black Bite
1 part Vodka
1 part Blackberry Liqueur
1 part Grapefruit Juice
Cocktail Glass
Shake with ice and strain

Black Cherry
1 part Vodka
1 part Southern Comfort®
1 part Amaretto
1 part Melon Liqueur
1 part Cranberry Juice Cocktail
Cocktail Glass
Shake with ice and strain

Black Devil
2 parts Light Rum
1/2 part Dry Vermouth
1 Black Olive
Cocktail Glass
Stir gently with ice and strain

Black Friday
1 part Gin
1 part Black Vodka
1 part Grapefruit Juice
1 part Fresh Lime Juice
Cocktail Glass
Shake with ice and strain

Black Gin
1 1/2 parts Gin
1/2 part Black Sambuca
splash Sweet Vermouth
Cocktail Glass
Shake with ice and strain

Black Jack
$1^1/_2$ parts Scotch
1 part Coffee Liqueur
$^1/_2$ part Triple Sec
$^1/_2$ part Lemon Juice
Cocktail Glass
Shake with ice and strain

Black Jack #2
2 parts Grand Marnier®
$^1/_2$ part Coffee Liqueur
splash Brandy
Cocktail Glass
Shake with ice and strain

Black Metal
$^1/_2$ part Vodka
$^1/_2$ part Blue Curaçao
$^1/_2$ part Crème de Cassis
$^1/_2$ part Lime Cordial
Cocktail Glass
Shake with ice and strain

Black Monday
1 part Dark Rum
$^1/_2$ part Black Sambuca
1 splash Cherry Brandy
$^1/_2$ part Lemon Juice
Cocktail Glass
Shake with ice and strain

Black Widow
$^3/_4$ part Dark Rum
$^1/_2$ part Southern Comfort®
1 part Sour Mix
Cocktail Glass
Shake with ice and strain

Black Witch
$1^1/_2$ parts Gold Rum
$^1/_4$ part Dark Rum
$^1/_4$ part Apricot Brandy
$^1/_2$ part Pineapple Juice
Cocktail Glass
Shake with ice and strain

Blackberry Cream
$1^1/_2$ parts Blackberry Liqueur
1 part Dry Gin
1 part Cream
1 Egg Yolk
Cocktail Glass
Shake with ice and strain

Blackout
$1^1/_2$ parts Gin
1 part Blackberry Brandy
splash Lime Juice
Cocktail Glass
Shake with ice and strain

Blade Runner
2 parts Jim Beam®
$1^1/_2$ parts Apricot Brandy
$^1/_2$ part Lemon Juice
Cocktail Glass
Shake with ice and strain

Blanca Playa
1 part Crème de Banana
1 part Pineapple Juice
1 part Coconut-Flavored Liqueur
Cocktail Glass
Shake with ice and strain

Blarney Stone Cocktail
2 parts Irish Whiskey
splash Anisette
splash Triple Sec
splash Maraschino Cherry
Twist of Orange Peel
1 Olive
Cocktail Glass
Shake with ice and strain

Blaze of Glory
$1^1/_2$ parts Dark Rum
$^1/_2$ part Grand Marnier®
splash Crème de Cacao (Dark)
Cocktail Glass

Shake with ice and strain

Bledsko Jezero
1 part Vodka
1 part Sweet Vermouth
1 part Maraschino Liqueur
splash Blue Curaçao
Cocktail Glass

Shake with ice and strain

Blenheim
1 part Orange Juice
1 part Apricot Brandy
$^1/_2$ part Grenadine
dash Orange Bitters
Cocktail Glass

Shake with ice and strain

Blimey
2 parts Scotch
$^1/_2$ part Lime Juice
dash Sugar
Cocktail Glass

Shake with ice and strain

Blind Melon
1 part Melon Liqueur
$^1/_2$ part Vodka
$^1/_2$ part Light Rum
$^1/_2$ part Triple Sec
Cocktail Glass

Shake with ice and strain

Blitz
1 part Tequila
1 part Triple Sec
1 part Southern Comfort®
1 part Grenadine
1 part Lemon Juice
1 part Orange Juice
Cocktail Glass

Shake with ice and strain

Blood Shot
1 part Whiskey
1 part Vodka
1 part Apricot Brandy
1 part Sweet Vermouth
2 dashes Bitters
Cocktail Glass

Shake with ice and strain

Blood Transfusion
1 part Orange Liqueur
2 parts Citrus-Flavored Vodka
3 parts Orange Juice
splash Lime Cordial
Cocktail Glass

Shake with ice and strain

Bloody Brain
$1^1/_2$ parts Strawberry Liqueur
$^1/_2$ part Grenadine
$^1/_2$ part Irish Cream Liqueur
Cocktail Glass

Shake all but Irish Cream with ice and strain into the glass. Carefully pour the Irish Cream into the center of the drink.

Bloody Lip
1 part Cherry Brandy
$^1/_2$ part Vodka
$^1/_2$ part Maraschino Liqueur
Cocktail Glass

Shake with ice and strain

Bloody Matador
$1^1/_2$ parts Tequila
3 splashes Maraschino Liqueur
1 splash Grenadine
2 splashes Orange Juice
Cocktail Glass
Shake with ice and strain

Blue Agave
$1^1/_2$ parts Silver Tequila
$^3/_4$ part Cream
$^1/_4$ part Blue Curaçao
$^1/_4$ part Crème de Cacao (White)
Cocktail Glass
Shake with ice and strain

Blue Alexander
1 part Gin
$^1/_2$ part Blue Curaçao
$^1/_2$ part Cream
Cocktail Glass
Shake with ice and strain

Blue and Gold
1 part Vodka
$^1/_2$ part Blueberry Schnapps
$^1/_2$ part Pineapple Juice
Cocktail Glass
Shake with ice and strain

Blue Angel
$^1/_2$ part Blue Curaçao
$^1/_2$ part Brandy
$^1/_2$ part Crème de Cacao (White)
$^1/_2$ part Lemon Juice
$^1/_2$ part Cream
Cocktail Glass
Shake with ice and strain

Blue Bananas
$1^1/_2$ parts Grapefruit Juice
1 part Whiskey
1 part Crème de Banana
1 part Blue Curaçao
1 Egg White
Cocktail Glass
Shake with ice and strain

Blue Bayou
$^2/_3$ part Blue Curaçao
$^1/_2$ part Coffee Liqueur
$1^1/_2$ parts Dark Rum
1 part Orange Juice
1 part Lemon Juice
Cocktail Glass
Shake with ice and strain

Blue Belle Babe
1 part Blue Curaçao
1 part Southern Comfort®
$^1/_2$ part Lime Juice
Cocktail Glass
Shake with ice and strain

Blue Bird
$1^1/_2$ parts Gin
$^1/_2$ part Triple Sec
dash Bitters
Twist of Lemon Peel
1 Cherry
Cocktail Glass
Shake with ice and strain

Blue Buddha
2 parts Vodka
splash Blue Curaçao
splash Sake
splash Grapefruit Juice
$^1/_2$ part Lemon Juice
$^1/_2$ part Lime Juice
splash Simple Syrup
Cocktail Glass
Shake with ice and strain

Blue Bullet
1/2 part Maraschino Liqueur
1/2 part Peach Schnapps
1/2 part Blue Curaçao
Cocktail Glass

Shake with ice and strain

Blue Capri
1 1/2 parts Crème de Cacao (White)
1/2 part Crème de Menthe (Green)
1 part Blue Curaçao
Cocktail Glass

Shake with ice and strain

Blue Carnation
1/2 part Crème de Cacao (White)
1/2 part Blue Curaçao
2 parts Light Cream
Cocktail Glass

Shake with ice and strain

Blue Chili
2 parts Blue Curaçao
1 part Vodka
1/2 part Gin
1/2 part Light Rum
Cocktail Glass

Shake with ice and strain

Blue Cosmopolitan
2 parts Citrus-Flavored Vodka
1 part Blue Curaçao
1/2 part Grapefruit Juice
1/2 part Simple Syrup
Cocktail Glass

Shake with ice and strain

Blue Creole
2 parts Light Rum
1/2 part Goldschläger®
1/2 part Fresh Lime Juice
Cocktail Glass

Shake with ice and strain

Blue Danube
1/2 part Vodka
1/2 part Blue Curaçao
1/2 part Triple Sec
1/2 part Crème de Banana
splash Cream
Cocktail Glass

Shake with ice and strain

Blue Diamond
1 part Blue Curaçao
1 part Dry Gin
1 part Fresh Lime Juice
1 part Cream
Cocktail Glass

Shake with ice and strain

Blue Edisonian
2 parts Campari®
2 parts Brandy
1 part Lemon Juice
Cocktail Glass

Shake with ice and strain

Blue Fox Trot
1 1/2 parts Light Rum
1/2 part Lemon Juice
3 dashes Blue Curaçao
Cocktail Glass

Shake with ice and strain

Blue Grass
2 parts Bourbon
1 part Pineapple Juice
1/2 part Maraschino Liqueur
Cocktail Glass

Shake with ice and strain

Blue Haze
1 part Dark Rum
1/2 part Dry Vermouth
1/2 part Parfait Amour
1/2 part Triple Sec
Cocktail Glass
Shake with ice and strain

Blue Is Beautiful
1 1/2 parts Dry Gin
1 part Blue Curaçao
1/2 part Lime Cordial
Cocktail Glass
Shake with ice and strain

Blue Kontiki
1 part Triple Sec
1 part Grapefruit Juice
splash Blue Curaçao
Cocktail Glass
Shake with ice and strain

Blue Lagoon
1 part Blueberry Schnapps
1 part Blue Curaçao
splash Pineapple Juice
Cocktail Glass
Shake with ice and strain

Blue Light Special
3/4 part Sour Apple Schnapps
1/4 part Vodka
1/4 part Blue Curaçao
splash Pineapple Juice
Cocktail Glass
Shake with ice and strain

Blue Margarita
1 1/2 parts Tequila
1 part Blue Curaçao
1 part Lime Juice
Cocktail Glass
Shake with ice and pour

Blue Marine
1 1/2 parts Vodka
1 part Butterscotch Schnapps
1 part Blue Curaçao
splash Lemonade
Cocktail Glass
Shake with ice and strain

Blue Monday
1 part Vodka
1 part Triple Sec
1 part Blue Curaçao
Cocktail Glass
Shake with ice and strain

Blue Morning
2 parts Vodka
1 part Blue Curaçao
1 part Peach Schnapps
Cocktail Glass
Shake with ice and strain

Blue Ocean
3/4 part Melon Liqueur
1/2 part Anisette
1/2 part Cognac
3/4 part Grapefruit Juice
Cocktail Glass
Shake with ice and strain

Blue Panther
2 parts Vodka
1 part Dry Vermouth
1 part Orange Juice
1 Egg White
1/2 part Crème de Cassis
Cocktail Glass
Shake with ice and strain

Blue Riband
2/3 part Gin
1/2 part Blue Curaçao
2/3 part Triple Sec
Cocktail Glass
Shake with ice and strain

Blue Rocks
1 1/2 parts Peach Schnapps
3/4 part Blue Curaçao
3/4 part Orange Juice
Cocktail Glass
Shake with ice and strain

Blue Shark
1 part Silver Tequila
1 part Vodka
splash Blue Curaçao
Cocktail Glass
Shake with ice and strain

Blue Sky Delight
1 1/2 parts Coconut Liqueur
2/3 part Dark Rum
2/3 part Blue Curaçao
1 part Apple Juice
Cocktail Glass
Shake with ice and strain

Blue Star
1 part Blue Curaçao
1 part Orange Juice
1 part Gin
Cocktail Glass
Shake with ice and strain

Blue Sunrise
1 1/2 parts Rum
1 part Blue Curaçao
1 part Pineapple Juice
1/2 part Parfait Amour
Cocktail Glass
Shake with ice and strain

Blue Tartan
1 1/2 parts Scotch
1/2 part Blue Curaçao
1/2 part Crème de Cacao (White)
Cocktail Glass
Shake with ice and strain

Blue Temptation
1 part Vodka
1 part Blue Curaçao
1 part Pisang Ambon® Liqueur
1/2 part Crème de Banana
2 parts Cream
Cocktail Glass
Shake with ice and strain

Bluebird Tropicale
1 1/2 parts Gin
1/2 part Triple Sec
1/2 part Blue Curaçao
2 dashes Bitters
Cocktail Glass
Shake with ice and strain

Blueblooded
1 1/2 parts Light Rum
1/2 part Blue Curaçao
1 1/2 parts Dark Rum
splash Apricot Juice
Cocktail Glass
Shake with ice and strain

Bluenette
1/2 part Blue Curaçao
1/2 part Coconut-Flavored Liqueur
1/2 part Peach Schnapps
splash Sour Mix
Cocktail Glass
Shake with ice and strain

Blushing Mellow
1 part Vodka
1/2 part Strawberry Liqueur
1/2 part Grenadine
1 1/2 parts Cream
Cocktail Glass

Shake with ice and strain

Blushing Monarch
2/3 part Gin
1/2 part Blue Curaçao
1/2 part Campari®
2/3 part Passion Fruit Juice
Cocktail Glass

Shake with ice and strain

Bobbit
1 part Vodka
1 part Gin
1/2 part Peach Schnapps
1/2 part Campari®
Cocktail Glass

Shake with ice and strain

Boca Chico Banana
1/2 part Vodka
1/2 part Pisang Ambon® Liqucur
1/2 part Coconut-Flavored Liqueur
splash Passion Fruit Nectar
1 part Guava Juice
Cocktail Glass

Shake with ice and strain

Boccie Bounce
1 part Amaretto
1/2 part Orange Juice
1 1/2 parts Cream
Cocktail Glass

Shake with ice and strain

Bodil
1 part Crème de Menthe (White)
1 part Parfait Amour
1 part Crème de Cacao (White)
1 part Cream
Cocktail Glass

Shake with ice and strain

Body Shiver
1 part Gold Tequila
1 part Passion Fruit Liqueur
1 part Melon Liqueur
splash Lemon Juice
Cocktail Glass

Shake with ice and strain

Bodyguard
2 parts Jim Beam®
1 1/2 parts Melon Liqueur
2/3 part Pisang Ambon® Liqueur
splash Lemon Juice
Cocktail Glass

Shake with ice and strain

Bold Gold Monkey
1 part Gold Rum
1 part Vodka
4 parts Orange Juice
splash Grenadine
Cocktail Glass

Shake with ice and strain

Bolo Blast
1/2 part Coconut-Flavored Liqueur
1/2 part Raspberry Liqueur
1/2 part Crème de Banana
1/2 part Blackberry Liqueur
1/2 part Orange-Flavored Vodka
Cocktail Glass

Shake with ice and strain

Bolshoi Punch
1 part Vodka
1/2 part Light Rum
1/4 part Crème de Cassis
1/2 part Lemon Juice
2 splashes Simple Syrup
Cocktail Glass

Shake with ice and strain

Bombar Cocktail
1 1/2 parts Blue Curaçao
1 part Orange-Flavored Vodka
1 part Coconut-Flavored Rum
Cocktail Glass

Shake with ice and strain

Bon Lis
2/3 part Vodka
2/3 part Passion Fruit Liqueur
2 parts Pear Juice
splash Lemon Juice
Cocktail Glass

Shake with ice and strain

Bon Voyage
1 part Gin
1 part Tequila
splash Lemon Juice
splash Blue Curaçao
Cocktail Glass

Shake with ice and strain

Bongo
1 part Citrus-Flavored Vodka
1 part Lychee Liqueur
1 part Pisang Ambon® Liqueur
1 part Fresh Lime Juice
Cocktail Glass

Shake with ice and strain

Buona Sera
1 part Silver Tequila
1/2 part Coffee Liqueur
1/2 part Irish Cream Liqueur
Cocktail Glass

Shake with ice and strain

Booby Trap
2 parts Bourbon
3/4 part Maraschino Liqueur
Cocktail Glass

Shake with ice and strain

Bosom Caresser
1 part Brandy
1/2 part Triple Sec
1 part Madeira
Cocktail Glass

Shake with ice and strain

The Boss' Favorite
2/3 part Gin
1 1/2 parts Apricot Brandy
1/2 part Crème de Cassis
1/2 part Lemon Juice
Cocktail Glass

Shake with ice and strain

Boston Sidecar
3/4 part Light Rum
3/4 part Brandy
3/4 part Triple Sec
1/2 part Lime Juice
Cocktail Glass

Shake with ice and strain

Botogo
1 part Gin
1 part Blue Curaçao
splash Vermouth
1 part Pineapple Juice
Cocktail Glass

Shake with ice and strain

Bounce Heart
1 part Cherry Brandy
1 part Triple Sec
1 part Sweet Vermouth
1 part Lemon Juice
Cocktail Glass
Shake with ice and strain

Bounty Fresh
1 part Light Rum
1 part Coconut-Flavored Liqueur
1/2 part Amaretto
1 1/2 parts Passion Fruit Juice
Cocktail Glass
Shake with ice and strain

Bourbon à la Créme
2 parts Bourbon
1 part Crème de Cacao (Dark)
1/2 part Vanilla Liqueur
Cocktail Glass
Shake with ice and strain

Bourbon Del Mar
1 part Jim Beam®
2/3 part Triple Sec
splash Lime Juice
1 part Sour Mix
Cocktail Glass
Shake with ice and strain

Bourbon Sidecar
2 parts Bourbon
1 part Triple Sec
Cocktail Glass
Shake with ice and strain

Bourbonella
2 parts Bourbon
1 1/2 parts Dry Vermouth
1 1/2 parts Triple Sec
splash Grenadine
Cocktail Glass
Shake with ice and strain

Bourbonnaise
1 1/2 parts Bourbon
1/2 part Crème de Cassis
splash Dry Vermouth
Cocktail Glass
Shake with ice and strain

Boyard Boy
1/2 part Southern Comfort®
1/2 part Melon Liqueur
1/2 part Triple Sec
1 part Sour Mix
1/2 part Orange Juice
splash Passion Fruit Juice
Cocktail Glass
Shake with ice and strain

Boys Don't Cry
2 parts Gin
1/2 part Crème de Cacao (White)
splash Grenadine
1 Egg White
Cocktail Glass
Shake with ice and strain

Brainbow
3/4 part Gin
3/4 part Cherry Brandy
3/4 part Chartreuse®
Cocktail Glass
Shake with ice and strain

Brainwave
1/2 part 151-Proof Rum
1 part Amaretto
1/4 part Irish Cream Liqueur
Cocktail Glass
Shake with ice and strain

Brandy Alexander
1/2 part Brandy
1/2 part Crème de Cacao (Dark)
2 parts Heavy Cream
Cocktail Glass
Shake with ice and strain

Brandy Breezer
2 parts Brandy
1/2 part Triple Sec
1/2 part Maraschino Liqueur
Cocktail Glass

Shake with ice and strain

Brandy Classic
1 1/2 parts Brandy
1/2 part Triple Sec
1/4 part Maraschino Liqueur
1/2 part Lemon Juice
dash Powdered Sugar
Cocktail Glass

Shake with ice and strain

Brandy Elite
1/2 part Apricot Brandy
1/2 part Brandy
1/2 part Grand Marnier®
1/2 part Lemon Juice
Cocktail Glass

Shake with ice and strain

Brandy Rainbow
1 part Apple Brandy
1 part Apricot Brandy
1/2 part Cherry Brandy
Cocktail Glass

Shake with ice and strain

Brave Soldier
1 part Cherry Brandy
1/2 part Passion Fruit Liqueur
1/2 part Southern Comfort®
1/2 part Lemon Juice
1/2 part Sour Mix
Cocktail Glass

Shake with ice and strain

Brazilian Daiquiri
2 parts Dark Rum
1 part Light Rum
1 splash Vanilla Extract
2 dashes Brown Sugar
Cocktail Glass

Shake with ice and strain

Brazilian Night
1 part Blue Curaçao
1 part Vodka
1 part Coconut-Flavored Liqueur
Cocktail Glass

Shake with ice and strain

Briar Rabbit
2/3 part Blackberry Liqueur
2/3 part Sweet Vermouth
2/3 part Dry Vermouth
dash Orange Bitters
dash Angostura® Bitters
Cocktail Glass

Shake with ice and strain

Brisas del Paraíso
1 part Dry Gin
1 part Vodka
1 part Parfait Amour
splash Lemon Juice
Cocktail Glass

Shake with ice and strain

British Comfort
1 1/2 parts Southern Comfort®
1/2 part Gin
1/2 part Lemon Juice
1 part Orange Juice
Cocktail Glass

Shake with ice and strain

Brittany
1 1/2 parts Gin
1 part Orange Juice
1/2 part Amer Picon®
Cocktail Glass

Shake with ice and strain

Broadside
1 part Dark Rum
1/2 part Vodka
1/2 part Cherry Brandy
1/2 part Frangelico®
2 splashes Grenadine
Cocktail Glass

Shake with ice and strain

Broken Parachute
1 part Raspberry Liqueur
1 part Citrus-Flavored Rum
dash Powdered Sugar
Cocktail Glass

Shake with ice and strain

Bronx Ain't So Sweet
1 1/2 parts Gin
1 splash Dry Vermouth
1/2 part Orange Juice
Cocktail Glass

Shake with ice and strain

Bronx Boxer
1/2 part Apricot Brandy
1/2 part Cranberry Juice Cocktail
splash Parfait Amour
Cocktail Glass

Shake with ice and strain

A Brood Bloodbath
2 parts Vodka
1 part Cherry Juice
1 Cherry
splash Orange Juice
Cocktail Glass

Shake with ice and strain

Brooklyn
1 1/2 parts Whiskey
1 part Dry Vermouth
1 part Maraschino Liqueur
Cocktail Glass

Shake with ice and strain

Brown Kitten
1 part Dry Gin
1 part Crème de Cacao (Dark)
1 part Triple Sec
Cocktail Glass

Shake with ice and strain

Brown Velvet
2 parts Cream
1 part Crème de Cacao (Dark)
1 part Triple Sec
Cocktail Glass

Shake with ice and strain

Bubble Gum
1 part Southern Comfort®
1 part Crème de Banana
1 part Grenadine
1 part Milk
Cocktail Glass

Shake with ice and strain

Buca Alma
1 1/2 parts Vodka
1 1/2 parts Sambuca
1 part Amaretto
Cocktail Glass

Shake with ice and strain

Buckle Your Seatbelt
1/2 part Crème de Cassis
1/2 part Grand Marnier®
1/2 part Sour Mix
splash Lemon Juice
Cocktail Glass

Shake with ice and strain

Buddha's Banshee
1/2 part Spiced Rum
1/4 part Crème de Cacao (White)
1/2 part Crème de Banana
3 parts Half and Half
Cocktail Glass

Shake with ice and strain

Buen Viaje
1 part Dry Gin
1 part Dark Rum
splash Grenadine
Cocktail Glass
Shake with ice and strain

Buena Vista
1 1/2 parts Grenadine
1 1/2 parts Dark Rum
1 part Sweet Vermouth
1 part Lime Cordial
Cocktail Glass
Shake with ice and strain

Bull & Bear
1 part Jim Beam®
1 part Peach Schnapps
1 part Pineapple Juice
splash Grenadine
splash Lemon Juice
Cocktail Glass
Shake with ice and strain

Bull Fighter
1 part Triple Sec
1 part Spanish Brandy
1 part Port
splash Crème de Menthe (White)
splash Strawberry Syrup
Cocktail Glass
Shake with ice and strain

Bumbo
2 parts Dark Rum
1 part Lemon Juice
splash Grenadine
dash Ground Nutmeg
Cocktail Glass
Shake with ice and strain

Bunny Bonanza
2 parts Silver Tequila
1 part Apple Brandy
1/2 part Maple Syrup
splash Triple Sec
Cocktail Glass
Shake with ice and strain

Burning North Pole Breeze
1 part Pepper-Flavored Vodka
1 part Peppermint Liqueur
1 part Crème de Menthe (White)
Cocktail Glass
Shake with ice and strain

Burnt Embers
1 1/2 parts Añejo Rum
1/2 part Apricot Brandy
1 part Pineapple Juice
Cocktail Glass
Shake with ice and strain

Butt Tickler
1/2 part Goldschläger®
1/2 part Vanilla Extract
1 part Cranberry Juice Cocktail
1 part Sour Mix
Cocktail Glass
Shake with ice and strain

Butter Nuts
1 part Butterscotch Schnapps
1 part Crème de Cacao (White)
1 part Irish Cream Liqueur
Cocktail Glass
Shake with ice and strain

Butterfly
1 part Vodka
1 part Crème de Banana
1 part Pineapple Juice
1 part Blackberry
Cocktail Glass
Shake with ice and strain

Buttery Nipple

1 part Irish Cream Liqueur
1 part Butterscotch Schnapps
Cocktail Glass

Shake with ice and strain

By the Light of the Moon

1½ parts Coffee Liqueur
1 part Cream
1 part Mandarine Napoléon® Liqueur
½ part Simple Syrup
Cocktail Glass

Shake with ice and strain

Byculla Cocktail

1 part Triple Sec
1 part Dry Sherry
1 part Ginger Liqueur
1 part Port
Cocktail Glass

Shake with ice and strain

Bye Bye Brood

1 part Peppermint Liqueur
1 part Absinthe
Cocktail Glass

Shake with ice and strain

Byrrh Bird

1 part Advocaat
1 part Crème de Banana
1 part Sour Mix
Cocktail Glass

Shake with ice and strain

Caballero

1 part Pisang Ambon® Liqueur
1 part Campari®
Cocktail Glass

Shake with ice and strain

Cable Car

1 part Apricot Brandy
1 part Triple Sec
Cocktail Glass

Shake with ice and strain

Cabo

1½ parts Tequila
fill with Pineapple Juice
splash Lime Juice
Cocktail Glass

Shake with ice and strain

Cactus Bite

2 parts Tequila
2 parts Lemon Juice
2 splashes Triple Sec
2 splashes Drambuie®
dash Sugar
1 dash Bitters
Cocktail Glass

Shake with ice and strain

Cactus Flower

2 parts Silver Tequila
½ part Blue Curaçao
½ part Amaretto
½ part Vanilla Liqueur
½ part Lime Juice
Cocktail Glass

Shake with ice and strain

Cactus Jack

1 part Vodka
½ part Blue Curaçao
1½ parts Pineapple Juice
1½ parts Orange Juice
Cocktail Glass

Shake with ice and strain

Cafe Kirsch Cocktail
$1^1/_2$ parts Dry Gin
1 part Egg White
$^1/_2$ part Cream
splash Anisette
Cocktail Glass
Shake with ice and strain

Cafe Trinidad
1 part Dark Rum
$^1/_2$ part Amer Picon®
$^1/_2$ part Tia Maria®
1 part Cream
Cocktail Glass
Shake with ice and strain

Caleigh
$1^1/_2$ parts Scotch
$^1/_2$ part Blue Curaçao
$^1/_2$ part Crème de Cacao (White)
Cocktail Glass
Shake with ice and strain

California Dream
2 parts Tequila
1 part Sweet Vermouth
$^1/_2$ part Dry Vermouth
Cocktail Glass
Shake with ice and strain

Californian Skateboarder
1 part Light Rum
$^1/_2$ part Maraschino Liqueur
$^1/_2$ part Grenadine
1 part Pineapple Juice
Cocktail Glass
Shake with ice and strain

Calin Cocktail
1 part Anisette
1 part Mandarine Napoléon® Liqueur
1 part Orange Juice
Cocktail Glass
Shake with ice and strain

Calvados Cream
$1^1/_2$ parts Calvados Apple Brandy
1 part Cream
1 Egg White
splash Pineapple Juice
Cocktail Glass
Shake with ice and strain

Camel Cracker
1 part Black Sambuca
$^1/_2$ part Raspberry Liqueur
$^1/_2$ part Irish Cream Liqueur
1 part Milk
Cocktail Glass
Shake with ice and strain

Campay
1 part Campari®
1 part Gin
$^1/_2$ part Simple Syrup
2 parts Grapefruit Juice
Cocktail Glass
Shake with ice and strain

Campeador
1 part Triple Sec
splash Blue Curaçao
splash Amaretto
splash Dry Vermouth
Cocktail Glass
Shake with ice and strain

Campfire Cocktail

$1^1/_2$ parts Melon Liqueur
1 part Sour Mix
splash Lime Juice
dash Powdered Sugar
Cocktail Glass

Shake with ice and strain

Canada

1 part Canadian Whiskey
$^1/_2$ part Triple Sec
$^1/_2$ part Maple Syrup
Cocktail Glass

Shake with ice and strain

Canadian Beauty

$1^1/_2$ parts Canadian Whiskey
$^1/_2$ part Dry Vermouth
$^1/_2$ part Goldschläger®
splash Crème de Menthe (Green)
splash Port
$^1/_2$ part Orange Juice
Cocktail Glass

Shake all but the Port with ice and strain into the glass. Top with the Port.

Canadian Breeze

$1^1/_2$ parts Coconut Liqueur
1 part Blue Curaçao
$1^1/_2$ parts Coconut Cream
1 part Orange Juice
Cocktail Glass

Shake with ice and strain

Canadian Manhattan

3 parts Canadian Whiskey
1 part Sweet Vermouth
Cocktail Glass

Shake with ice and strain
Garnish with a cherry

Candy Apple

1 part Peach Schnapps
1 part Calvados Apple Brandy
$^1/_2$ part Cranberry Juice Cocktail
Cocktail Glass

Shake with ice and strain

Candy from Strangers

$1^1/_2$ parts Vodka
$^1/_2$ part Triple Sec
$^1/_2$ part Amaretto
$^1/_2$ part Dry Vermouth
Cocktail Glass

Shake with ice and strain

Canterbury

1 part Gin
$1^1/_2$ parts Kiwi Schnapps
$^1/_2$ part Strawberry Liqueur
$^1/_2$ part Sour Mix
Cocktail Glass

Shake with ice and strain

Cape of Good Will

$1^1/_2$ parts Light Rum
$^1/_2$ part Apricot Brandy
$^1/_2$ part Lime Juice
1 part Orange Juicc
2 dashes Orange Bitters
Cocktail Glass

Shake with ice and strain

Capitán Cienfuegos

$1^1/_2$ parts Light Rum
$^1/_2$ part Fresh Lime Juice
$^1/_2$ part Honey
splash Vanilla Liqueur
Cocktail Glass

Shake with ice and strain

Cappuccino Cocktail
1 part Vodka
1 part Coffee-Flavored Brandy
1 part Light Cream
Cocktail Glass

Shake with ice and strain

Caprice
1 part Dry Gin
1/2 part Apricot Brandy
splash Dry Vermouth
dash Orange Bitters
Cocktail Glass

Shake with ice and strain

Captain Haddock
1 part Scotch
1 part White Wine
1/2 part Melon Liqueur
1/2 part Lime Juice
Cocktail Glass

Shake with ice and strain

Captain Medellin
1 part Light Rum
1 part Crème de Banana
1 part Orange Juice
splash Sour Mix
Cocktail Glass

Shake with ice and strain

The Captain's Silver Sunrise
1 part Spiced Rum
1 1/2 parts Coconut-Flavored Rum
splash Orange Juice
splash Cranberry Juice Cocktail
Cocktail Glass

Shake with ice and strain

Captive
1 part Gin
splash Cherry Brandy
splash Kirschwasser
Cocktail Glass

Shake with ice and strain

Cara Sposa
1 part Coffee-Flavored Brandy
1 part Triple Sec
1/2 part Light Cream
Cocktail Glass

Shake with ice and strain

Cardicas
2 parts Light Rum
1 part White Port
1 part Cointreau®
Cocktail Glass

Shake with ice and strain

Cardinal
1 1/2 parts Añejo Rum
1/2 part Maraschino Liqueur
splash Triple Sec
splash Grenadine
Cocktail Glass

Shake with ice and strain

Carefree
1 part Cherry Brandy
1 part Apple Juice
1 part Grapefruit Juice
splash Grenadine
Cocktail Glass

Shake with ice and strain

Caribbean Cruise
3/4 part Dark Rum
3/4 part Tia Maria®
3/4 part Coconut Cream
1 part Orange Juice
1 part Pineapple Juice
Cocktail Glass

Shake with ice and strain

Caribbean Kiss
1/2 part Dark Rum
1/2 part Amaretto
1/2 part Coffee Liqueur
1 part Cream
dash Cinnamon
dash Brown Sugar
Cocktail Glass
Shake with ice and strain

Caribbean Shooter
3/4 part Spiced Rum
1/2 part Brandy
1 part Cranberry Juice Cocktail
Cocktail Glass
Shake with ice and strain

Caribbean White
1 part Dark Rum
1/2 part Coconut-Flavored Liqueur
1/2 part Crème de Cacao (Dark)
splash Cream
Cocktail Glass
Shake with ice and strain

Carlton
1 1/2 parts Whiskey
3/4 part Triple Sec
3/4 part Orange Juice
Cocktail Glass
Shake with ice and strain

Carmencita
1 part Silver Tequila
1/2 part Blue Curaçao
1/2 part Amaretto
Cocktail Glass
Shake with ice and strain

The Carnal Instinct
1 part Gin
1/2 part Peach Schnapps
splash Limoncello
1/2 part Lemon Juice
1 1/2 parts Apple Juice
splash Simple Syrup
Cocktail Glass
Shake with ice and strain

Carnegie Melon
1/2 part Coconut-Flavored Liqueur
1/2 part Melon Liqueur
splash Lime Juice
Cocktail Glass
Shake with ice and strain

Carol
2 parts Gin
1/2 part Apricot Brandy
dash Orange Bitters
Cocktail Glass
Shake with ice and strain

Carpe Diem
1 1/2 parts 151-Proof Rum
splash Blue Curaçao
splash Mescal
1/2 part Lemon Juice
1 part Passion Fruit Juice
Cocktail Glass
Shake with ice and strain

Carta Vieja
1 part Peach Schnapps
1 part Light Rum
1/2 part Lime Juice
splash Simple Syrup
Cocktail Glass
Shake with ice and strain

Casanova
2 parts Melon Liqueur
2/3 part Crème de Cacao (White)
1 part Cream
Cocktail Glass
Shake with ice and strain

Castelo dos Mouros
1 1/2 parts Brandy
1/2 part Crème de Cacao (White)
1 part Port
Cocktail Glass
Shake with ice and strain

Catcher in the Rye
1 part Irish Whiskey
1 part Apricot Brandy
splash Coffee Liqueur
splash Lemon Juice
Cocktail Glass
Shake with ice and strain

Catholic Coronation
1 part Vodka
1/2 part Amaretto
1/2 part Butterscotch Schnapps
1/2 part Frangelico®
1/2 part Milk
Cocktail Glass
Shake with ice and strain

Cavalier
1 1/2 parts Tequila
1/2 part Galliano®
1 1/2 parts Orange Juice
1/2 part Cream
Cocktail Glass
Shake with ice and strain

Celebration
1 1/2 parts Rum
1 part Cognac
1 part Cointreau®
1 part Lemon Juice
Cocktail Glass
Shake with ice and strain

Celtic Cheer
1 part Butterscotch Schnapps
1 part Peach Schnapps
1 part Irish Cream Liqueur
Cocktail Glass
Shake with ice and strain

Celtic Twilight
1 part Irish Cream Liqueur
1 part Bushmills® Irish Whiskey
1 part Frangelico®
Cocktail Glass
Shake with ice and strain

Cessna
1 1/2 parts Gin
1/2 part Dubonnet® Blonde
2 splashes Maraschino Liqueur
Cocktail Glass
Shake with ice and strain

C'est Parfait
1 part Parfait Amour
2/3 part Amaretto
splash Blue Curaçao
1 part Vanilla Syrup
1 part Cream
Cocktail Glass
Shake with ice and strain

Chain Lightning
2 parts Gin
1/2 part Triple Sec
2 splashes Lemon Juice
Cocktail Glass
Shake with ice and strain

Champs Elysées Cocktail
1 part Brandy
1/2 part Yellow Chartreuse®
splash Lemon Juice
dash Powdered Sugar
dash Bitters
Cocktail Glass

Shake with ice and strain

Chantilly Lace
11/2 parts Vanilla Liqueur
11/2 parts Maraschino Liqueur
1/2 part Vodka
splash Chocolate Syrup
Cocktail Glass

Shake with ice and strain

Chaos
2/3 part Blackberry Liqueur
11/2 parts Jamaican Rum
2/3 part Lemon Juice
2 parts Raspberry-Flavored Seltzer
Cocktail Glass

Shake with ice and strain

Charger
11/2 parts Dark Rum
1/2 part Cherry Brandy
1/2 part Lemon Juice
dash Sugar
Cocktail Glass

Shake with ice and strain

Charging Rhino
11/2 parts Vodka
1/2 part Dry Vermouth
1/2 part Campari®
Cocktail Glass

Shake with ice and strain

Charmer
11/2 parts Scotch
1 part Blue Curaçao
splash Dry Vermouth
dash Orange Bitters
Cocktail Glass

Shake with ice and strain

Cheesecake
1 part Vanilla-Flavored Vodka
1/2 part Triple Sec
1/2 part Sour Mix
1 part Cream
splash Crème de Cacao (White)
Cocktail Glass

Shake with ice and strain

Chellengae
1 part Vodka
1 part Grand Marnier®
1/2 part Lime Juice
Cocktail Glass

Shake with ice and strain

Cherie
1 part Light Rum
1/2 part Cherry Brandy
1/2 part Triple Sec
1/2 part Lime Juice
Cocktail Glass

Shake with ice and strain

Cherokee
11/2 parts Cognac
1 part Amaretto
1 part Apricot Brandy
splash Grenadine
Cocktail Glass

Shake with ice and strain

Cherried Cream Rum

1 1/2 parts Light Rum
1/2 part Cherry Brandy
1/2 part Light Cream
Cocktail Glass

Shake with ice and strain

Cherry Berry

1 part Vodka
1 part Raspberry Liqueur
1/2 part Cherry Brandy
1/2 part Blackberry Juice
splash Lime Juice
Cocktail Glass

Shake with ice and strain

The Cherry Drop

1 1/2 parts Light Rum
1/2 part Crème de Cacao (White)
1 part Cream
splash Cherry Brandy
Cocktail Glass

Shake with ice and strain

Cherry Flower

1 part Cognac
1 part Cherry Brandy
1 part Triple Sec
1 part Grenadine
Cocktail Glass

Shake with ice and strain

Cherry Kid

1 part Cherry-Flavored Vodka
1 part Amaretto
1 part Cranberry Juice Cocktail
Cocktail Glass

Shake with ice and strain

Cherry Ripe

1 1/2 parts Vodka
1/2 part Cherry Brandy
1/2 part Brandy
Cocktail Glass

Shake with ice and strain

Cherry O

1 part Cream
1 part Coffee Liqueur
1 part Cherry Brandy
Cocktail Glass

Shake with ice and strain

Cheryl

1 part Triple Sec
1 part Raspberry Liqueur
1/2 part Grenadine
1/2 part Sour Mix
Cocktail Glass

Shake with ice and strain

Chicago Style

3/4 part Rum
1/4 part Triple Sec
1/4 part Anisette
1/2 part Sweetened Lime Juice
Cocktail Glass

Shake with ice and strain

Chicken Run

1 part Raspberry Liqueur
1/2 part Triple Sec
1/2 part Mescal
Cocktail Glass

Shake with ice and strain

The Child Prodigy

1 1/2 parts Orange Vodka
1/2 part Vanilla Liqueur
1/2 part Coconut-Flavored Liqueur
2/3 part Mango Juice
2/3 part Cream
Cocktail Glass

Shake with ice and strain

Childhood Memories
1 part Crème de Banana
1 part Blackberry Liqueur
1 part Irish Cream Liqueur
Cocktail Glass
Shake with ice and strain

Chilly Willy
1 part Melon Liqueur
1 part Coconut-Flavored Rum
3/4 part Peach Schnapps
Cocktail Glass
Shake with ice and strain

Chocolate Banana
1 1/4 part Crème de Banana
1 1/4 part Crème de Cacao (White)
splash Milk
Cocktail Glass
Shake with ice and strain

Chocolate Chip
1 1/2 parts Vodka
1 1/2 parts Frangelico®
Cocktail Glass
Shake with ice and strain

Chocolate Club
1 part Dark Rum
1 part Chocolate Mint Liqueur
1 part Cream
splash Crème de Cacao (White)
Cocktail Glass
Shake with ice and strain

Chocolate Cream
1 part Rum
1 part Crème de Cacao (Dark)
1/2 part Crème de Menthe (White)
1 part Cream
Cocktail Glass
Shake with ice and strain

Chocolate Princess
1 part Dark Rum
1 part Milk
1/2 part Crème de Menthe (Green)
1/2 part Crème de Cacao (Dark)
Cocktail Glass
Shake with ice and strain

Chocolate Pudding
1 part Crème de Cacao (White)
1 part Cream
1 part Hazelnut Liqueur
Cocktail Glass
Shake with ice and strain

Chocolate Raspberry Delight
1 1/2 parts Irish Cream Liqueur
1 1/2 parts Raspberry Liqueur
Cocktail Glass
Shake with ice and strain

Chocolate Screwdriver
2 parts Vodka
1 part Crème de Cacao (White)
fill with Orange Juice
Cocktail Glass
Shake with ice and strain

Choker
2 parts Scotch
2 splashes Pernod®
2 dashes Bitters
Cocktail Glass
Shake with ice and strain

Cholla Bay
1 part Tequila
1 dash Sugar
1 part Sour Mix
1/2 part Grenadine
Cocktail Glass
Shake with ice and strain

Chop-Nut
3/4 part Vodka
1 part Crème de Banana
1 part Coconut Liqueur
1/2 part Orange Juice
Cocktail Glass
Shake with ice and strain

Chorus Lady Cocktail
1 part Dry Gin
1 part Dry Vermouth
1 part Sweet Vermouth
1 part Orange Juice
Cocktail Glass
Shake with ice and strain

Christ
1 1/2 parts Bourbon
1/2 part Peach Schnapps
Cocktail Glass
Shake with ice and strain

Churchill
1 1/2 parts Scotch
1/2 part Sweet Vermouth
Cocktail Glass
Shake with ice and strain

Cielo Nublado
1 part Gin
1/2 part Blue Curaçao
1/2 part Parfait Amour
Cocktail Glass
Shake with ice and strain

Cinammon Twist
1 part Vodka
1 part Triple Sec
splash Lemon-Lime Soda
Cocktail Glass
Shake Vodka and Triple Sec with ice and strain. Top with a splash of Lemon-Lime soda and garnish with Cinnamon Candies.

Cinco de Mayo
2 1/2 parts Tequila
1 part Grenadine
1 part Sweetened Lime Juice
Cocktail Glass
Shake with ice and strain

Circus Flyer
2 parts Vodka
2/3 part Crème de Cassis
splash Blue Curaçao
Cocktail Glass
Shake with ice and strain

Citizen Kane
1 part Coffee Liqueur
1 part Irish Whiskey
2 parts Cream
Cocktail Glass
Shake with ice and strain

Citrus Crown
1 1/2 parts Crown Royal® Whiskey
1/2 part Lemon Juice
1 part Orange Juice
Cocktail Glass
Shake with ice and strain

City Slicker
2 parts Brandy
1/2 part Triple Sec
splash Lemon Juice
Cocktail Glass
Shake with ice and strain

The Clan Chieftain
splash Orange Liqueur
1 part Cointreau®
2 parts Scotch
Cocktail Glass
Shake with ice and strain

Claridge
1 part Dry Vermouth
1 part Gin
3/4 part Triple Sec
3/4 part Apricot Brandy
Cocktail Glass
Shake with ice and strain

Clash
1 part Light Rum
1 part Maraschino Liqueur
1 part Crème de Menthe (Green)
1 part Dry Vermouth
Cocktail Glass
Shake with ice and strain

The Classic
1 part Cognac
1/2 part Lemon Juice
1/2 part Maraschino Liqueur
1 part Triple Sec
Cocktail Glass
Shake with ice and strain

Classy Sanctuary
1 part Vodka
1 part Melon Liqueur
1 part Sour Mix
splash Passion Fruit Liqueur
Cocktail Glass
Shake with ice and strain

Cleopatra
1 part Rum
splash Amaretto
1/2 part Lemon Juice
3 dashes Angostura® Bitters
Cocktail Glass
Shake with ice and strain

Climax
1/2 part Vodka
1/2 part Amaretto
1/2 part Crème de Cacao (White)
1/2 part Triple Sec
1/2 part Crème de Banana
1 part Light Cream
Cocktail Glass
Shake with ice and strain

Clipper
1 part Whiskey
1/2 part Simple Syrup
1/2 part Apricot Brandy
splash Campari®
Cocktail Glass
Shake with ice and strain

Cloister
1 1/2 parts Gin
1 part Grapefruit Juice
1/4 part Sugar
Cocktail Glass
Shake with ice and strain

Closing Time
1 part Peppermint Liqueur
1 part Vanilla Liqueur
1 part Cream
Cocktail Glass
Shake with ice and strain

Cloud
1 part Crème de Menthe (Green)
1 part Anisette
1 part Milk
Cocktail Glass
Shake with ice and strain

Clove Cocktail
1 part Sweet Vermouth
1/2 part Sloe Gin
1/2 part Muscatel
Cocktail Glass

Shake with ice and strain

Cocktail DTV
1 part Gin
1 part Cinzano®
1/2 part Grenadine
Cocktail Glass

Shake with ice and strain

Coco Candy Cane
1 part Vodka
1 part Crème de Cacao (White)
1 part Peppermint Schnapps
Cocktail Glass

Shake with ice and strain

Coco Poco
1 part Vodka
1 part Coconut-Flavored Liqueur
1 part Tia Maria®
Cocktail Glass

Shake with ice and strain

Coco Tobacco
1 part Crème de Menthe (Green)
1 part Peach Schnapps
1 part Crème de Banana
Cocktail Glass

Shake with ice and strain

Cocoa Chanel
1 1/2 parts Cognac
1/2 part Chocolate Liqueur
1/2 part Amaretto
1 1/2 parts Coconut Cream
Cocktail Glass

Shake with ice and strain

Coconut Grove
1 part Dark Rum
1/2 part Southern Comfort®
1/2 part Crème de Banana
splash Lime Juice
splash Lemon Juice
Cocktail Glass

Shake with ice and strain

Coconut's Coffee
1 1/2 parts Coconut Liqueur
1/2 part Coffee Liqueur
1/2 part Coconut Cream
Cocktail Glass

Shake with ice and strain

Cocoon
2 parts Jamaican Rum
1/2 part Coconut-Flavored Liqueur
2/3 part Vanilla Liqueur
1 part Cream
Cocktail Glass

Shake with ice and strain

Coffee Alexander
1 part Gin
1 part Coffee Liqueur
1 part Cream
Cocktail Glass

Shake with ice and strain

Cognac Cocktail
2 parts Cognac
dash Powdered Sugar
splash Triple Sec
Cocktail Glass

Shake with ice and strain

Cold Kiss
1 1/2 parts Whiskey
1/2 part Peppermint Schnapps
2 splashes Crème de Cacao (White)
Cocktail Glass

Shake with ice and strain

Cold Plunge
1 part Vodka
1/2 part Triple Sec
1/2 part Apricot Brandy
splash Crème de Banana
Cocktail Glass
Shake with ice and strain

Collection
1 part Vodka
1 part Citrus-Flavored Vodka
1/2 part Blackberry Liqueur
1 part Fresh Lime Juice
Cocktail Glass
Shake with ice and strain

Colonial Retreat
1 part Sloe Gin
1/2 part Apricot Brandy
1/2 part Lime Juice
Cocktail Glass
Shake with ice and strain

Colorado
1 part Cream
1 part Cherry Brandy
1 part Kirschwasser
splash Cherry Juice
Cocktail Glass
Shake with ice and strain

Columbia
1 1/2 parts Light Rum
1/2 part Simple Syrup
1/2 part Kirschwasser
Cocktail Glass
Shake with ice and strain

Combustible Edison
2 parts Brandy
1 part Campari®
1 part Lemon Juice
Cocktail Glass
Shake with ice and strain

Comet Dust
1/2 part Crème de Cacao (Dark)
1/2 part Coconut-Flavored Liqueur
1/2 part Hazelnut Liqueur
2 parts Milk
Cocktail Glass
Shake with ice and strain

Comfort Inn
1/2 part Gin
1 part Apricot Brandy
1 part Apple Brandy
1 part Sour Mix
Cocktail Glass
Shake with ice and strain

Comfortable
1 part Crème de Cacao (Dark)
1 part Southern Comfort®
1 part Lemon Juice
Cocktail Glass
Shake with ice and strain

Compadre
1 1/2 parts Tequila
splash Maraschino Liqueur
1 splash Grenadine
2 dashes Orange Bitters
Cocktail Glass
Shake with ice and strain

Compel to Work
1 part Citrus-Flavored Vodka
1/2 part Orange Liqueur
1 part Grapefruit Juice
1/2 part Lemon Juice
Cocktail Glass
Shake with ice and strain

Complicated Lady

1 part Tequila
1/2 part Apricot Brandy
1/2 part Grand Marnier®
1 part Lime Juice
Cocktail Glass

Shake with ice and strain

Conca d'oro

2 parts Dry Gin
1/2 part Triple Sec
1/2 part Cherry Brandy
1/2 part Maraschino Liqueur
Cocktail Glass

Shake with ice and strain

Concarde

1 part Gin
1 part Apricot Brandy
1/2 part Campari®
1/2 part Grenadine
Cocktail Glass

Shake with ice and strain

Concrete Jungle

2 parts Vodka
1/2 part Apricot Brandy
1/2 part Banana Juice
Cocktail Glass

Shake with ice and strain

Concubine

1 part Cherry Brandy
1 part Amaretto
1 part Cream
Cocktail Glass

Shake with ice and strain

Conquistador

1 part Cognac
1/2 part Crème de Cacao (White)
1/2 part Triple Sec
splash Cream
splash Strawberry Syrup
Cocktail Glass

Shake with ice and strain

Continental

1 3/4 parts Light Rum
splash Crème de Menthe
2 splashes Lime Juice
dash Powdered Sugar
Cocktail Glass

Shake with ice and strain

Contradiction

1 part Vodka
1/2 part Melon Liqueur
1/2 part Coffee Liqueur
1 part Cream
Cocktail Glass

Shake with ice and strain

Control Freak

1 1/2 parts Crème de Menthe (White)
3/4 part Amaretto
1/2 part Crème de Cacao (White)
1/4 part Coffee Liqueur
Cocktail Glass

Shake with ice and strain

Cool Jazz

1 part White Wine
1 part Crème de Banana
1/2 part Fresh Lime Juice
Cocktail Glass

Shake with ice and strain

Cool Summer Breeze
1 part Passion Fruit Liqueur
1 part Vodka
1 part Cranberry Juice Cocktail
1 part Pear Juice
Cocktail Glass
Shake with ice and strain

Copper Rivet
1 part Brandy
1/2 part Dry Vermouth
1/2 part Sweet Vermouth
2 splashes Triple Sec
Cocktail Glass
Shake with ice and strain

Corazón
1 part Cherry Brandy
1 part Coffee-Flavored Brandy
1 part Cherry Juice
1/2 part Brandy
Cocktail Glass
Shake with ice and strain

Corkscrew
1 1/2 parts Light Rum
1/2 part Peach Brandy
1 1/2 parts Dry Vermouth
Cocktail Glass
Shake with ice and strain

Cornhole
1 1/2 parts Irish Cream Liqueur
1 1/2 parts Tequila
splash Dubonnet® Blonde
Cocktail Glass
Shake with ice and strain

Coronado
1 1/2 parts Gin
1/2 part Blue Curaçao
2 parts Pineapple Juice
splash Kirschwasser
Cocktail Glass
Shake with ice and strain

Cortez Chorus
1/2 part Coconut-Flavored Liqueur
2/3 part Amaretto
1/2 part Spiced Rum
2/3 part Orange Juice
2/3 part Pineapple Juice
Cocktail Glass
Shake with ice and strain

Cosmo Katie
2 parts Currant-Flavored Vodka
1 part Grand Marnier®
splash Lime Juice
splash Cranberry Juice Cocktail
Cocktail Glass
Shake with ice and strain

Cosmopolitan
1 1/4 parts Citrus-Flavored Vodka
1/4 part Lime Juice
1/4 part Triple Sec
splash Cranberry Juice Cocktail
Cocktail Glass
Shake with ice and strain

Cosmorita
1 1/2 parts Tequila
1/2 part Triple Sec
1/2 part Lime Juice
1/2 part Cranberry Juice Cocktail
Cocktail Glass
Shake with ice and strain

Cossack Charge
1 1/2 parts Vodka
1/2 part Cognac
1/2 part Cherry Brandy
Cocktail Glass
Shake with ice and strain

Costa del Sol
2 parts Gin
1 part Apricot Brandy
1 part Grand Marnier®
Cocktail Glass
Shake with ice and strain

Cotillion Cocktail
1 part Triple Sec
1 part Orange Juice
1 part Lemon Juice
splash Rum
Cocktail Glass
Shake with ice and strain

Country Club
1 part Whiskey
1/2 part Apricot Brandy
1/2 part Triple Sec
splash Cream
splash Grenadine
Cocktail Glass
Shake with ice and strain

Countryside Garden
1 part Apricot Brandy
2/3 part Dry Vermouth
2/3 part Grape Juice
splash Lemon Juice
Cocktail Glass
Shake with ice and strain

County Fair
1 part Melon Liqueur
1 part Sloe Gin
1 part Sour Mix
Cocktail Glass
Shake with ice and strain

Covadonga
1 part Campari®
1 part Sweet Vermouth
1 part Orange Juice
1/2 part Grenadine
Cocktail Glass
Shake with ice and strain

Coyote Girl
1 1/2 parts Bourbon
1 part Southern Comfort®
1 part Lemon Juice
Cocktail Glass
Shake with ice and strain

Cranberry Blast
1 1/2 parts Peach Schnapps
1/2 part Dark Rum
1/2 part Vodka
1/2 part Scotch
1/2 part Orange Juice
2 parts Cranberry Juice Cocktail
splash Lemon Juice
Cocktail Glass
Shake with ice and strain

Cranberry Kami
1 1/2 parts Vodka
1/2 part Triple Sec
1/2 part Lime Juice
1/2 part Cranberry Juice Cocktail
Cocktail Glass
Shake with ice and strain

Cranium Meltdown
1 part Dark Rum
1 part Coconut-Flavored Liqueur
1 part Pineapple Juice
Cocktail Glass
Shake with ice and strain

Cranmint
3/4 part Raspberry Liqueur
1/2 part Crème de Menthe (White)
1/2 part Citrus-Flavored Vodka
Cocktail Glass

Shake with ice and strain

Crantango Bay
1/2 part Citrus-Flavored Vodka
1 part Blackberry Liqueur
2 parts Cranberry Juice Cocktail
Cocktail Glass

Shake with ice and strain

Cranxious
2/3 part Strawberry Liqueur
1 part Sloe Gin
splash Blue Curaçao
1/2 part Lime Juice
2 parts Cranberry Juice Cocktail
Cocktail Glass

Shake with ice and strain

Crash Landing
1 1/2 parts Vodka
2 splashes Grenadine
1 splash Lime Juice
1 splash Lemon Juice
1 dash Sugar
Cocktail Glass

Shake with ice and strain

Crawford
2 parts Citrus-Flavored Rum
1/2 part Melon Liqueur
1/2 part Blue Curaçao
splash Dry Vermouth
Cocktail Glass

Shake with ice and strain

Crazy Calypso
1 part Peach Schnapps
1 part Orange-Flavored Vodka
splash Sour Mix
Cocktail Glass

Shake with ice and strain

Crazy Fin
2 parts Vodka
1 part Dry Sherry
1 part Cointreau®
1/2 part Lemon Juice
Cocktail Glass

Shake with ice and strain

Crazy Idea
1 part Parfait Amour
1 part Ouzo
Cocktail Glass

Shake with ice and strain

Crazy Janey
1 part Apricot Brandy
1 part Crème de Menthe (White)
1 part Triple Sec
Cocktail Glass

Shake with ice and strain

Creamberry
1 part Strawberry Liqueur
1/2 part Raspberry Liqueur
splash Cream
Cocktail Glass

Shake with ice and strain

Creamsicle®
1 1/2 parts Vanilla Liqueur
1/2 part Grand Marnier®
splash Orange Juice
Cocktail Glass

Shake with ice and strain

Creamy Crispy Crunch
1 part Crème de Cacao (White)
1 part Frangelico®
2 parts Milk
Cocktail Glass
Shake with ice and strain

Creepy Soldier
1 part Coffee-Flavored Brandy
1/2 part Butterscotch Schnapps
2/3 part Hazelnut Liqueur
1 1/2 parts Cream
splash Honey
Cocktail Glass
Shake with ice and strain

Crème de Gin Cocktail
1 1/2 parts Gin
1/2 part Crème de Menthe (White)
2 splashes Lemon Juice
2 splashes Orange Juice
1 Egg White
Cocktail Glass
Shake with ice and strain

Creole Lady
1 1/2 parts Madeira
1 splash Grenadine
Cocktail Glass
Shake with ice and strain

Creole Scream
1 1/2 parts Light Rum
1 part Dry Vermouth
dash Angostura® Bitters
splash Grenadine
Cocktail Glass
Shake with ice and strain

Cricket
3/4 part Light Rum
1/4 part Crème de Cacao (White)
1/4 part Crème de Menthe (Green)
1 part Cream
Cocktail Glass
Shake with ice and strain

Crimson Marsh
1 part Blackberry Liqueur
1/2 part Vanilla Liqueur
1/2 part Hazelnut Liqueur
1 1/2 parts Cream
splash Honey
Cocktail Glass
Shake with ice and strain

Cripple Creek
1 1/2 parts Silver Tequila
1 part Orange Juice
1/2 part Galliano®
Cocktail Glass
Shake with ice and strain

Crista Solar
1 part Vodka
1 part Dry Vermouth
1 part Triple Sec
1 part White Port
dash Bitters
Cocktail Glass
Shake with ice and strain

Cristal Blue
1 1/2 parts Vodka
1 part Parfait Amour
1 part Dry Sherry
dash Bitters
Cocktail Glass
Shake with ice and strain

Cristalle
1 1/2 parts Silver Tequila
1 part Blue Curaçao
1 part Peach Schnapps
1 part Lemon Juice
1 part Simple Syrup
Cocktail Glass
Shake with ice and strain

Crossbow
1 1/2 parts Gin
1 part Crème de Cacao (White)
1 part Triple Sec
Cocktail Glass
Shake with ice and strain

Crouching Tiger
1 1/2 parts Citrus-Flavored Rum
1/2 part 151-Proof Rum
splash Maraschino Liqueur
1 1/2 parts Cranberry Juice Cocktail
Cocktail Glass
Shake with ice and strain

Crown Bomb
1/2 part Coconut-Flavored Liqueur
1/2 part White Wine
1/2 part Amaretto
1/2 part Pineapple Juice
Cocktail Glass
Shake with ice and strain

Crown Jewel
1/2 part Peach Schnapps
1 part Sloe Gin
1 part Orange Juice
1/2 part Sour Mix
Cocktail Glass
Shake with ice and strain

A Crowned Head
2/3 part Blackberry Liqueur
1 part Dry Vermouth
1 1/2 parts Bourbon
splash Lemon Juice
Cocktail Glass
Shake with ice and strain

Cruel Intentions
2 parts Orange-Flavored Vodka
1 part Vanilla Liqueur
splash Vermouth
Cocktail Glass
Shake with ice and strain

Crystal Palace
2 parts Calvados Apple Brandy
1 1/2 parts Grand Marnier®
2/3 part Lemon Juice
Cocktail Glass
Shake with ice and strain

Cuban Cocktail
2 parts Rum
dash Sugar
1/2 part Lime Juice
Cocktail Glass
Shake with ice and strain

Cuban Sidecar
1 1/2 parts Rum
3/4 part Fresh Lime Juice
1/2 part Triple Sec
Cocktail Glass
Shake with ice and strain

Cuban Sour
2 parts Rum
dash Powdered Sugar
2 dashes Lime Juice
Cocktail Glass
Shake with ice and strain

Cuban Special
1 part Light Rum
splash Triple Sec
2 splashes Pineapple Juice
splash Lime Juice
Cocktail Glass

Shake with ice and strain

The Cubano Cocktail
1 1/2 parts Gin
1 1/2 parts Dry Vermouth
splash Pineapple Syrup
Cocktail Glass

Shake with ice and strain

Cumdrop
1 part Coffee Liqueur
1 part Irish Cream Liqueur
1/2 part Crème de Banana
Cocktail Glass

Shake with ice and strain

Cupidon
2/3 part Brandy
1/2 part Raspberry Liqueur
1/2 part Hazelnut Liqueur
1 1/2 parts Cream
Cocktail Glass

Shake with ice and strain

Current Event
1 part Orange Liqueur
2 parts Currant-Flavored Vodka
splash Cranberry Juice Cocktail
Cocktail Glass

Shake with ice and strain

Cyberlady
1 part Cognac
1/2 part Triple Sec
1/2 part Strawberry Liqueur
1 part Orange Juice
splash Lemon Juice
Cocktail Glass

Shake with ice and strain

Czarina
1 part Vodka
3/4 part Apricot Brandy
1/2 part Dry Vermouth
1/2 part Sweet Vermouth
Cocktail Glass

Shake with ice and strain

Daily Mail
2 parts Scotch
dash Sugar
2 splashes Lemon Juice
2 splashes Blue Curaçao
splash Amaretto
Cocktail Glass

Shake with ice and strain

Dainty Taste
1 1/2 parts Gin
1/2 part Passion Fruit Liqueur
1/2 part Limoncello
1 part Guava Juice
1/2 part Lemon Juice
Cocktail Glass

Shake with ice and strain

Daiquiri
1 1/2 parts Light Rum
1/2 part Lime Juice
dash Powdered Sugar
Cocktail Glass

Shake with ice and strain for a basic Daiquri for a frozen Daiquri, blend with ice intil smooth. For a frozen fruit daiquri, add fruit (Strawberry, Banana, Apple, etc.) to the blender as well.

Dallas

1 1/2 parts Passion Fruit Juice
1 part Bourbon
1 part Apricot Brandy
Cocktail Glass

Shake with ice and strain

Danao

1 1/2 parts Light Rum
1/2 part Triple Sec
2 parts Cream
1 part Pineapple Juice
1 part Orange Juice
Cocktail Glass

Shake with ice and strain

Dance with the Devil

2 parts Vodka
1 part Blue Curaçao
1/2 part Sambuca
Cocktail Glass

Shake with ice and strain

Dancin'

1 part Vodka
1 part Dry Vermouth
1 part Whiskey
splash Triple Sec
splash Cherry Brandy
Cocktail Glass

Shake with ice and strain

Dandy

1 1/2 parts Dubonnet® Blonde
1 1/2 parts Rye Whiskey
dash Angostura® Bitters
3 splashes Cointreau®
Cocktail Glass

Shake with ice and strain

Danish Girl

1 part Amaretto
1 part Crème de Cacao (Dark)
1 1/2 parts Milk
Cocktail Glass

Shake with ice and strain

Dante's Inferno

2 parts Brandy
1 part Raspberry Liqueur
1 part Lemon Juice
Cocktail Glass

Shake with ice and strain

Darby

1/2 part Coconut-Flavored Liqueur
2/3 part Amaretto
1 part Dry Sherry
1/2 part Lime Juice
Cocktail Glass

Shake with ice and strain

Daring Apricot

2 parts Vodka
1/2 part Triple Sec
1/2 part Apricot Brandy
1/2 part Fresh Lime Juice
Cocktail Glass

Shake with ice and strain

Dark Quaalude

1 part Coffee Liqueur
1 part Frangelico®
1 part Irish Cream Liqueur
Cocktail Glass

Shake with ice and strain

Dark Star

1 part Scotch
1 part Crème de Cacao (Dark)
splash Cream
Cocktail Glass

Shake with ice and strain

Dawdle in the Snow
$1^1/_2$ parts Vodka
$^1/_2$ part Triple Sec
$1^1/_2$ parts Pear Juice
1 part Cream
Cocktail Glass
Shake with ice and strain

Daydreaming
$1^1/_2$ parts Light Rum
$^1/_2$ part Grenadine
3 parts Grapefruit Juice
2 parts Coconut Cream
Cocktail Glass
Shake with ice and strain

Day-O
$^1/_2$ part Crème de Banana
$^1/_2$ part Strawberry Liqueur
$^1/_2$ part Irish Cream Liqueur
$^1/_2$ part Chocolate Liqueur
Cocktail Glass
Shake with ice and strain

De Rigueur Cocktail
$1^1/_2$ parts Whiskey
1 part Honey
1 part Grape Juice
Cocktail Glass
Shake with ice and strain

Dead Lawyer
1 part Dry Vermouth
1 part Crème de Cacao (White)
1 part Maraschino Liqueur
Cocktail Glass
Shake with ice and strain

Dead Man's Party
$1^1/_2$ parts Gin
$^1/_2$ part Dry Vermouth
$^1/_2$ part Sweet Vermouth
splash Peppermint Liqueur
dash Angostura® Bitters
Cocktail Glass
Shake with ice and strain

Deadly Desires
$^2/_3$ part Cherry Brandy
$^1/_2$ part Coffee Liqueur
$^2/_3$ part Irish Cream Liqueur
Cocktail Glass
Shake with ice and strain

Deanne
1 part Vodka
$^1/_2$ part Sweet Vermouth
$^1/_2$ part Triple Sec
Lemon Twist
Cocktail Glass
Shake with ice and strain

Debut D'etre
$1^1/_2$ parts Maraschino Liqueur
2 parts Rémy Martin® VSOP
1 part Cranberry Juice Cocktail
$^1/_2$ part Lime Juice
splash Passion Fruit Juice
Cocktail Glass
Shake with ice and strain

Debutante
1 part Brandy
1 part Pineapple Juice
$^1/_2$ part Cherry Brandy
Cocktail Glass
Shake with ice and strain

Decadence
1 part Vanilla-Flavored Vodka
1 part Coffee Liqueur
1 part White Chocolate Liqueur
1 part Cherry Cola
1 part Chocolate Milk
Cocktail Glass
Build over ice and stir

Deep Dark Secret
1 1/2 parts Dark Rum
1/2 part Añejo Rum
1/2 part Coffee Liqueur
1/2 part Heavy Cream
Cocktail Glass
Shake with ice and strain

Deep Green Dragon
1 1/2 parts Scotch
1 part Dry Gin
1/2 part Blue Curaçao
Cocktail Glass
Shake with ice and strain

Deep Menace
2/3 part Orange Liqueur
1 part 151-Proof Rum
splash Lime Juice
Cocktail Glass
Shake with ice and strain

Deep Sea Cocktail
1 part Gin
1 part Dry Vermouth
splash Anisette
dash Orange Bitters
Cocktail Glass
Shake with ice and strain

Defy Gravity
2/3 part Melon Liqueur
2/3 part Raspberry Liqueur
2/3 part Pineapple Juice
2/3 part Cranberry Juice Cocktail
Cocktail Glass
Shake with ice and strain

Delicatessen
1 1/2 parts Apricot Brandy
1 1/2 parts Strawberry Juice
1 1/2 parts Cream
Cocktail Glass
Shake with ice and strain

Delilah
1 1/2 parts Gin
1/2 part Cointreau®
1/2 Lemon
Cocktail Glass
Shake with ice and strain

Delta Dawn
2 parts Gin
1 part Coffee Liqueur
1/2 part Lemon Juice
Cocktail Glass
Shake with ice and strain

Demon's Eye
1 1/2 parts Gin
2/3 part Kirschwasser
2/3 part Peppermint Liqueur
splash Lemon Juice
Cocktail Glass
Shake with ice and strain

Derosier
1 part Añejo Rum
1/2 part Crème de Cacao (Dark)
1/2 part Cherry Brandy
1 part Heavy Cream
Cocktail Glass
Shake with ice and strain

Desert Death

$1/2$ part Coconut-Flavored Liqueur
$1/2$ part Melon Liqueur
$1/2$ part 151-Proof Rum
splash Crème de Banana
1 part Cranberry Juice Cocktail
1 part Pineapple Juice
Cocktail Glass
Shake with ice and strain

Desert Tumbler

1 part Gin
1 part Blue Curaçao
1 part Lime Juice
Cocktail Glass
Shake with ice and strain

Desire

1 part Crème de Cacao (Dark)
1 part Coffee Liqueur
$1/2$ part Vodka
Cocktail Glass
Shake with ice and strain

Devil

$1\,1/2$ parts Crème de Menthe (Green)
$1\,1/2$ parts Triple Sec
Cocktail Glass
Shake with ice and strain

Devil with a Blue Dress On

2 parts Gin
splash Blue Curaçao
splash Grenadine
$1/2$ part Lime Juice
Cocktail Glass
Shake with ice and strain

Dewini

1 part Mountain Dew®
1 part Gin
1 part Sweet Vermouth
Cocktail Glass
Stir gently with ice and strain

Diablo

$1\,1/2$ parts Dry White Port
1 part Sweet Vermouth
splash Lemon Juice
Cocktail Glass
Shake with ice and strain

Diabolique

1 part Vodka
splash Crème de Cassis
2 parts Pineapple Juice
Cocktail Glass
Shake with ice and strain

Diamond Head

$1\,1/2$ parts Gin
$1/2$ part Blue Curaçao
2 parts Pineapple Juice
1 splash Vermouth
Cocktail Glass
Shake with ice and strain

Dianne-on-the-Tower

2 parts Light Rum
1 splash Crème de Cacao (Dark)
1 splash Cherry Brandy
Cocktail Glass
Shake with ice and strain

Difficult Drake

$1/2$ part Peppermint Liqueur
$1/2$ part Coffee Liqueur
$2/3$ part Crème de Cacao (White)
Cocktail Glass
Shake with ice and strain

Digging for Gold

1 part Goldschläger®
$1/2$ part Crème de Cacao (Dark)
$1/2$ part Cream
Cocktail Glass
Shake with ice and strain

Dinah Cocktail

$1^1/_2$ parts Whiskey
dash Powdered Sugar
$^1/_4$ part Lemon Juice
Cocktail Glass

Shake with ice and strain

Diplomat

$1^1/_2$ parts Dry Vermouth
$^1/_2$ part Sweet Vermouth
splash Maraschino Cherry Liqueur
2 dashes Bitters
Cocktail Glass

Shake with ice and strain

Dirty Dancer

1 part Crème de Cacao (White)
1 part Cream
$^1/_4$ part Crème de Menthe (White)
Cocktail Glass

Shake with ice and strain

Dirty Maiden

$^1/_2$ part Blackberry Liqueur
$^1/_2$ part Southern Comfort®
splash Lemon Juice
$^1/_2$ part Cranberry Juice Cocktail
Cocktail Glass

Shake with ice and strain

Dirty Panty

1 part Tequila
1 part Sambuca
1 part Irish Cream Liqueur
1 part Tabasco® Sauce
Cocktail Glass

Shake with ice and strain. Top with a sprinkle of Parmesean Cheese.

Dirty Redhead

1 part Crown Royal® Whiskey
1 part Raspberry Liqueur
1 part Southern Comfort®
Cocktail Glass

Shake with ice and strain

Disaronno®

1 part Amaretto
1 part Cognac
$1^1/_2$ parts Cream
Cocktail Glass

Shake with ice and strain

Dive Bomb

$1^1/_2$ parts Dark Rum
$^1/_2$ part Cherry Brandy
$^1/_2$ part Lemon Juice
dash Sugar
Cocktail Glass

Shake with ice and strain

Divine Comedy

1 part Scotch
1 part Dry Vermouth
$^1/_2$ part Triple Sec
$^1/_2$ part Lemon Juice
Cocktail Glass

Shake with ice and strain

Divorzio

$1^1/_2$ parts Brandy
splash Blue Curaçao
$1^1/_2$ parts Grappa
Cocktail Glass

Shake with ice and strain

Dixie Delight

1 part Gin
1 part Southern Comfort®
1 part Dry Vermouth
splash Simple Syrup
3 dashes Pernod®
Cocktail Glass

Shake with ice and strain

Dixie Queen
1 part Southern Comfort®
1/2 part Orange Juice
1/4 part Peach Schnapps
Cocktail Glass

Shake with ice and strain

Do or Die
1/2 part Brandy
1 part Chocolate Liqueur
Cocktail Glass

Shake with ice and strain

Doctor-Patient Relationship
1 1/2 parts Whiskey
1/2 part Triple Sec
dash Powdered Sugar
Cocktail Glass

Shake with ice and strain

Doctor's Orders
1 part Vodka
1 part Amaretto
splash Kiwi Schnapps
1/2 part Lime Juice
Cocktail Glass

Shake with ice and strain

Dodge Special
1 1/2 parts Cointreau®
1 1/2 parts Gin
splash Grape Juice
Cocktail Glass

Shake with ice and strain

Doggy Style
1 part Vodka
splash Coffee-Flavored Brandy
splash Cream
Cocktail Glass

Shake with ice and strain

Dolphin Fin
1 part Vodka
1/2 part Sweet Vermouth
1 part Orange Juice
1/4 part Lemon Juice
2 splashes Grenadine
Cocktail Glass

Shake with ice and strain

Dolphin's Foam
1 part Blue Curaçao
1 part Piña Colada Mix
Cocktail Glass

Shake with ice and strain

Donkey Peppermint
1 1/2 parts Sambuca
1 part Crème de Menthe (White)
1 part Coffee Liqueur
Cocktail Glass

Shake with ice and strain

Donna
1 part Coconut-Flavored Liqueur
1 part Light Rum
1 part Coconut Cream
splash Cream
Cocktail Glass

Shake with ice and strain

Don't Chicken Out
2 parts Light Rum
1/2 part Peach Schnapps
1/2 part Apricot Brandy
splash Simple Syrup
1 part Lemon Juice
Cocktail Glass

Shake with ice and strain

Don't Shoot the Bartender

1/2 part Amaretto
1/2 part Sloe Gin
1/2 part Triple Sec
1/2 part Vanilla-Flavored Vodka
Cocktail Glass

Shake with ice and strain

Doorknob

1 1/2 parts Light Rum
1/2 part Amaretto
splash Lime Juice
splash Lemon Juice
dash Sugar
Cocktail Glass

Shake with ice and strain

The Dope Show

2/3 part Passion Fruit Liqueur
1/2 part Damiana®
splash Lemon Juice
Cocktail Glass

Shake with ice and strain

Dorothy's Orgasm

2/3 part Vodka
splash Butterscotch Schnapps
splash Coffee Liqueur
1/2 part Cream
Cocktail Glass

Shake with ice and strain

Double Apple Barrel

1 part Apple Brandy
1 part Apple Juice
1/2 part Goldschläger®
1/2 part Triple Sec
Cocktail Glass

Shake with ice and strain

Double Trouble

2/3 part Vodka
splash Amaretto
1/2 part Melon Liqueur
1/2 part Cranberry Juice Cocktail
1/2 part Orange Juice
Cocktail Glass

Shake with ice and strain

Dovjenko

1 1/2 parts Vodka
splash Cherry Brandy
1/2 part Chartreuse®
1/2 part Grapefruit Juice
Cocktail Glass

Shake with ice and strain

Down Under

1 part Vodka
2 splashes Brandy
2 splashes Triple Sec
2 splashes Crème de Cassis
Cocktail Glass

Shake with ice and strain

Downhill Skier

1 part Blackberry Liqueur
1 part Crème de Banana
1/2 part Blue Curaçao
1/2 part Sour Mix
Cocktail Glass

Shake with ice and strain

Doyen

1 1/2 parts Gin
1 part Maraschino Liqueur
1/2 part Lime
Cocktail Glass

Shake with ice and strain

Dr. Livingstone
$1\frac{1}{2}$ parts Vodka
1 part Kiwi Schnapps
$\frac{1}{2}$ part Crème de Banana
Cocktail Glass
Shake with ice and strain

Dracula's Breakfast
1 part Melon Liqueur
1 part Campari®
$\frac{1}{2}$ part Brandy
$\frac{1}{2}$ part Pernod®
Cocktail Glass
Shake with ice and strain

Dragon Fire
1 part Pepper-Flavored Vodka
1 part Crème de Menthe (Green)
Cocktail Glass
Shake with ice and strain

Dreaming
1 part Crème de Cacao (White)
1 part Cream
1 part Black Currant Juice
Cocktail Glass
Shake with ice and strain

Droog's Date Cocktail
$1\frac{1}{2}$ parts Light Rum
2 splashes Cherry Brandy
2 splashes Triple Sec
$\frac{1}{2}$ part Lime Juice
Cocktail Glass
Shake with ice and strain

Drop Your Halitosis
$\frac{1}{2}$ part Peppermint Liqueur
splash Sambuca
splash Lemon Juice
splash Simple Syrup
splash Club Soda
Cocktail Glass
Shake with ice and strain

Dry Ice
$\frac{2}{3}$ part Blackberry Liqueur
$\frac{2}{3}$ part Citrus-Flavored Vodka
splash Blue Curaçao
splash Lemon Juice
Cocktail Glass
Shake with ice and strain

Duchess
$1\frac{1}{2}$ parts Anisette
$\frac{1}{2}$ part Sweet Vermouth
$\frac{1}{2}$ part Dry Vermouth
Cocktail Glass
Shake with ice and strain

Dune Buggy
$1\frac{1}{2}$ parts Vodka
$\frac{3}{4}$ part Cherry Brandy
$\frac{1}{2}$ part Lime Juice
dash Powdered Sugar
Cocktail Glass
Shake with ice and strain

Dunhill 71
$\frac{3}{4}$ part Crème de Banana
$\frac{3}{4}$ part Cognac
$\frac{1}{2}$ part Crème de Cacao (Dark)
$\frac{1}{4}$ part Triple Sec
Cocktail Glass
Shake with ice and strain

East India
2 parts Brandy
1 part Triple Sec
1 part Orange Juice
Cocktail Glass
Shake with ice and strain

East India #2
1 1/2 parts Brandy
1/4 part Blue Curaçao
1/4 part Pineapple Juice
dash Bitters
Cocktail Glass
Shake with ice and strain

East of Eden
1 part Amaretto
2/3 part Apricot Brandy
1 part Irish Cream Liqueur
1 part Pineapple Juice
Cocktail Glass
Shake with ice and strain

East Wing
3 parts Vodka
1 part Cherry Brandy
1/2 part Campari®
Cocktail Glass
Shake with ice and strain

Ebony
1 1/2 parts Dark Rum
1/2 part Crème de Cacao (Dark)
Cocktail Glass
Shake with ice and strain

Eclipsed Sun
1 part Crème de Cacao (White)
1 part Crème de Banana
1 1/2 parts Orange Juice
Cocktail Glass
Shake with ice and strain

Eden Eve
1 part Raspberry Liqueur
1 part Vodka
2/3 part Pineapple Juice
2/3 part Cranberry Juice Cocktail
Cocktail Glass
Shake with ice and strain

Edge of Oblivion
1 part Cherry Brandy
2/3 part Triple Sec
1 part Apple Brandy
1/2 part Sour Mix
Cocktail Glass
Shake with ice and strain

Eight Bells
2 parts Dark Rum
1 part Dry Vermouth
1/2 part Lemon Juice
1/2 part Orange Juice
Cocktail Glass
Shake with ice and strain

The Eighth Wonder
1 part Kirschwasser
2/3 part Crème de Cacao (White)
2/3 part Hazelnut Liqueur
1 1/2 parts Cream
Cocktail Glass
Shake with ice and strain

Ekatherina Andreevna
2 parts Vodka
1 part Orange Juice
Cocktail Glass
Shake with ice and strain

El Barbarazo
1 part Jim Beam®
1/2 part Triple Sec
1/2 part Sweet Vermouth
1/2 part Dry Vermouth
Cocktail Glass

Shake with ice and strain

El Chico
1 1/2 parts Light Rum
1/2 part Sweet Vermouth
splash Blue Curaçao
splash Grenadine
Cocktail Glass

Shake with ice and strain

El Cid
1/2 part Gin
1/2 part Melon Liqueur
1/2 part Sweetened Lime Juice
1 part Orange Juice
Cocktail Glass

Shake with ice and strain

El Floridita
1 1/2 parts Light Rum
1/2 part Lime Juice
1/2 part Sweet Vermouth
splash Crème de Cacao (White)
splash Grenadine
Cocktail Glass

Shake with ice and strain

El Metraya
1 part Tia Maria®
1/2 part Rum
2 parts Simple Syrup
Cocktail Glass

Shake with ice and strain

El Pacifico Vasso
1 part Silver Tequila
1/2 part Coconut-Flavored Liqueur
1/2 part Hazelnut Liqueur
1/2 part Lemon Juice
Cocktail Glass

Shake with ice and strain

El Presidente
1 1/4 part Dark Rum
1/2 part Lime Juice
1/2 part Pineapple Juice
1/2 part Grenadine
Cocktail Glass

Shake with ice and strain

El Torro
2 parts Tequila
1 part Coffee Liqueur
Cocktail Glass

Shake with ice and strain

Electric Cafe
1 part Silver Tequila
1 part Lemon Juice
1/2 part Simple Syrup
splash Coffee Liqueur
Cocktail Glass

Shake with ice and strain

Electric Chair
1/2 part Orange Liqueur
1 part Tequila
1/2 part Lemon Juice
splash Tabasco® Sauce
Cocktail Glass

Shake with ice and strain

Elephant Gun
1 part Whiskey
1 part Pineapple Juice
splash Lemon Juice
dash Sugar
Cocktail Glass

Shake with ice and strain

Elevation
1 1/2 parts Coconut Liqueur
1 1/2 parts Crème de Banana
3 parts Pineapple Juice
Cocktail Glass
Shake with ice and strain

Elisa
1 part Dark Rum
1/4 part Apricot Brandy
1/4 part Sparkling White Wine
1/4 part Amaro Averna®
1/4 part Dry Vermouth
Cocktail Glass
Shake with ice and strain

Elysium
1 part Peach Schnapps
1 part Vodka
1 1/2 parts Orange Juice
1 1/2 parts Pineapple Juice
Cocktail Glass
Shake with ice and strain

Emanuelle
1 part Crème de Cacao (White)
1 part Benedictine®
splash Espresso
splash Coconut Cream
Cocktail Glass
Shake with ice and strain

Embassy Royal
1 part Bourbon
1/2 part Sweet Vermouth
splash Orange Juice
Cocktail Glass
Shake with ice and strain

Emerald
1 1/2 parts Gin
1/2 part Crème de Menthe (Green)
1/2 part Crème de Menthe (White)
Cocktail Glass
Shake with ice and strain

Emergency Ward
1 part Kiwi Schnapps
1 part Blue Curaçao
1 part Lime Juice
Cocktail Glass
Shake with ice and strain

Emerson
1 1/2 parts Gin
1 part Sweet Vermouth
1/2 part Lime Juice
splash Maraschino Cherry Juice
Cocktail Glass
Shake with ice and strain

Empire
1 1/2 parts Gin
3/4 part Apricot Brandy
1/2 part Apple Brandy
Cocktail Glass
Shake with ice and strain

Empire Strikes Back
2 parts Tequila Silver
1/2 part Vanilla Liqueur
2/3 part Passion Fruit Juice
2/3 part Cream
Cocktail Glass
Shake with ice and strain

Erotic
1 part Bourbon
splash Crème de Cassis
splash Grenadine
splash Lemon Juice
Cocktail Glass
Shake with ice and strain

Escape
1 part Whiskey
1 part Orange Juice
1 part Apricot Brandy
Cocktail Glass

Shake with ice and strain

Escila
1 part Blue Curaçao
1 part Jamaican Rum
1/2 part Lemon Juice
splash Simple Syrup
Cocktail Glass

Shake with ice and strain

Esperanza
1/2 part Triple Sec
1/2 part Light Rum
1 part Pineapple Juice
1 part Kiwi Liqueur
Cocktail Glass

Shake with ice and strain

Estate Sale
1 part Gin
1 part Blue Curaçao
2/3 part Light Rum
1/2 part Sour Mix
Cocktail Glass

Shake with ice and strain

Estoril
2 parts Port
1 part Grand Marnier®
1/2 part Amaretto
Cocktail Glass

Shake with ice and strain

Estrella Dorado
1 part Dry Gin
1 part Dry Vermouth
1 part Campari®
1 part Cherry Brandy
2 splashes Lemon Juice
Cocktail Glass

Shake with ice and strain

Eva
1 part Vodka
1 part Crème de Menthe (Green)
1 part Simple Syrup
Cocktail Glass

Shake with ice and strain

Evans
1 part Rye Whiskey
1 part Triple Sec
1 part Apricot Brandy
Cocktail Glass

Shake with ice and strain

Evening Delight
2 parts Irish Cream Liqueur
1 part Vodka
Cocktail Glass

Shake with ice and strain

Evergreen
1 1/2 parts Crème de Banana
1/2 part Blue Curaçao
1/2 part Gin
2 parts Grapefruit Juice
Cocktail Glass

Shake with ice and strain

Exploration
1 part Scotch
1 part Dry Sherry
1/2 part Amaretto
Cocktail Glass

Shake with ice and strain

Eyes Wide Shut
1/2 part Southern Comfort®
1/2 part Crown Royal® Whiskey
1/2 part Amaretto
1/2 part Orange Juice
1/2 part Pineapple Juice
1/2 part Cranberry Juice Cocktail
splash Grenadine
Cocktail Glass
Shake with ice and strain

Fade to Black
1 part Coffee Liqueur
1 part Vodka
1/2 part Crème de Menthe (White)
Cocktail Glass
Shake with ice and strain

Fair Sex
1 part Maraschino Liqueur
1 part Gin
1/2 part Cherry Brandy
splash Simple Syrup
Cocktail Glass
Shake with ice and strain

Fairbanks
1 part Apricot Brandy
1 part Gin
splash Grenadine
splash Lemon Juice
1 part Dry Vermouth
Cocktail Glass
Shake with ice and strain

Fairy Belle Cocktail
3/4 part Apricot Brandy
1 1/2 parts Gin
1 splash Grenadine
1 Egg White
Cocktail Glass
Shake with ice and strain

Fairy Queen
1 part Vodka
1/2 part Cream
1/2 part Coffee Liqueur
Cocktail Glass
Shake with ice and strain

The Falcon Chaser
1 part Gin
1/2 part Chambord®
1/2 part Hazelnut Liqueur
splash Coconut-Flavored Liqueur
splash Galliano®
1 1/2 parts Cream
Cocktail Glass
Shake with ice and strain

Fantastico
1 part Dark Rum
1/2 part Triple Sec
1/2 part Apricot Brandy
splash Pineapple Juice
splash Orange Juice
Cocktail Glass
Shake with ice and strain

Far West
1/2 part Brandy
1/2 part Advocaat
1/2 part Dry Vermouth
dash Angostura® Bitters
Cocktail Glass
Shake with ice and strain

Farewell
2/3 part Coffee Liqueur
2/3 part Apricot Brandy
splash Scotch
2/3 part Cream
2/3 part Milk
Cocktail Glass
Shake with ice and strain

Farinelli
1 1/2 parts Vodka
1/2 part Dry Vermouth
1/2 part Campari®
splash Amaretto
Cocktail Glass
Shake with ice and strain

Farmer Giles
2 parts Gin
1/2 part Dry Vermouth
1/2 part Sweet Vermouth
2 dashes Bitters
Lemon Twist
Cocktail Glass
Shake with ice and strain

Fast Punch
1 part Blue Curaçao
splash Apricot Brandy
splash Lime Juice
splash Pineapple Juice
Cocktail Glass
Shake with ice and strain

Fat Friar
3/4 part Apple Brandy
3/4 part Benedictine®
1/4 part Triple Sec
1/4 part Lemon Juice
Cocktail Glass
Shake with ice and strain

Favorite
1 part Sweet Vermouth
1/2 part Triple Sec
1/2 part Maraschino Liqueur
dash Orange Bitters
Cocktail Glass
Shake with ice and strain

Feliz Natal
1 part Port
1 part Amaretto
2 parts Crème de Cacao (White)
1 part Cherry Brandy
1/2 part Brandy
Cocktail Glass
Stir gently with ice and strain

Femina
1 1/2 parts Brandy
1 1/2 parts Triple Sec
1/2 part Orange Juice
Cocktail Glass
Shake with ice and strain

Ferndale Fruit
1 part Sloe Gin
1 part Blackberry Liqueur
1 part Sour Mix
Cocktail Glass
Shake with ice and strain

Fernet Jacque
1 1/2 parts Gin
1/2 part Fernet-Branca®
splash Maraschino Liqueur
splash Sweet Vermouth
Cocktail Glass
Shake with ice and strain

Feroux
1/2 part Apricot Brandy
1 part Crème de Banana
2/3 part Cachaça
1/2 part Lemon Juice
Cocktail Glass
Shake with ice and strain

Festival Flavor

1/2 part Coconut-Flavored Liqueur
1/2 part Melon Liqueur
1/2 part Blackberry Liqueur
1 1/2 parts Cranberry Juice Cocktail
Cocktail Glass

Shake with ice and strain

The Fifth Element

1 1/2 parts Jim Beam®
1/2 part Kirschwasser
1/2 part Vanilla Liqueur
splash Amaretto
1 part Cream
Cocktail Glass

Shake with ice and strain

Fifty-Fifty

1 1/2 parts Vanilla Liqueur
1 1/2 parts Orange Juice
Cocktail Glass

Shake with ice and strain

Fig Newton

1/2 part Vodka
1/2 part Grand Marnier®
1/4 part Crème de Almond
splash Orange Juice
splash Lemon Juice
Cocktail Glass

Shake with ice and strain

Final Storm

2 parts Tequila Silver
2/3 part Passion Fruit Liqueur
1 1/2 parts Guava Juice
Cocktail Glass

Shake with ice and strain

Fire and Ice

1 1/2 parts Pepper-Flavored Vodka
2 splashes Dry Vermouth
Cocktail Glass

Shake with ice and strain

Fire Island Sunrise

1 part Rum
1 part Vodka
1/2 part Orange Juice
1/2 part Lemonade
splash Cranberry Juice Cocktail
Cocktail Glass

Shake with ice and strain

Firehammer

1 1/2 parts Vodka
1/2 part Amaretto
1/2 part Triple Sec
splash Lemon Juice
Cocktail Glass

Shake with ice and strain

Firing Line

1 part Jim Beam®
1/2 part Coffee Liqueur
splash Crème de Cacao (White)
splash Galliano®
2 parts Cream
Cocktail Glass

Shake with ice and strain

Fish Lips

1 1/2 parts Vodka
1/2 part Kirschwasser
1/2 part Triple Sec
1/2 part Grapefruit Juice
Cocktail Glass

Shake with ice and strain

Fjord
1 part Brandy
1 part Orange Juice
1/2 part Grenadine
1/2 part Fresh Lime Juice
1/2 part Aquavit
Cocktail Glass
Shake with ice and strain

Flame of Love
1 1/2 parts Vodka
1/2 part Dry Sherry
Cocktail Glass
Shake with ice and strain

Flamingo Shooter
1/2 part Southern Comfort®
1/2 part Amaretto
1/2 part Crème de Banana
1 part Milk
splash Grenadine
Cocktail Glass
Shake with ice and strain

A Flash of Mellow
1/2 part Pisang Ambon® Liqueur
1/2 part Melon Liqueur
2 parts Light Rum
2/3 part Lemon Juice
splash Honey
Cocktail Glass
Shake with ice and strain

Fleet Street
1 1/2 parts Gin
1/2 part Sweet Vermouth
splash Dry Vermouth
splash Triple Sec
splash Lemon Juice
Cocktail Glass
Shake with ice and strain

Flipside Beach Bomber
1 part Vodka
1/2 part Triple Sec
1/2 part Grapefruit Juice
1/2 part Orange Juice
1/2 part Apricot Brandy
Cocktail Glass
Shake with ice and strain

Florida Beach Breeze
1 part Vodka
1/2 part Crème de Cacao (White)
1/2 part Crème de Banana
1 part Orange Juice
Cocktail Glass
Shake with ice and strain

Florida Keys Cocktail
2/3 part Light Rum
1/2 part Grand Marnier®
1/2 part Lime Juice
1 part Passion Fruit Liqueur
Cocktail Glass
Shake with ice and strain

Florida Rain
1/2 part Gin
2 splashes Kirschwasser
2 splashes Triple Sec
1 part Orange Juice
splash Lemon Juice
Cocktail Glass
Shake with ice and strain

Flower of Nippon
1 part Light Rum
1 part Banana Liqueur
splash Cointreau®
splash Lime Juice
splash Grenadine
Cocktail Glass
Shake with ice and strain

Flower of the Orient
1 part Cream Sherry
1 part Tia Maria®
1 part Cream
1/2 part Passion Fruit Juice
Cocktail Glass
Shake with ice and strain

Flowerdance
1 part Gin
1 part Peach Juice
1 part Lychee Liqueur
1/2 part Lime Juice
Cocktail Glass
Shake with ice and strain

Fluffy Ruffles Cocktail
1 1/2 parts Rum
1 1/2 parts Sweet Vermouth
Cocktail Glass
Shake with ice and strain

Flying Dutchman
3 parts Gin
splash Blue Curaçao
dash Orange Bitters
Cocktail Glass
Shake with ice and strain

Flying Fancy
1 part Crème de Cacao (White)
1 part Amaretto
1 part Melon Liqueur
Cocktail Glass
Shake with ice and strain

Flying Grasshopper
1 part Vodka
1 part Crème de Menthe (Green)
1 part Crème de Cacao (White)
Cocktail Glass
Shake with ice and strain

Flying Horse
1 1/2 parts Vodka
1 part Cream
1 part Cherry Brandy
Cocktail Glass
Shake with ice and strain

Focal Point
1 1/2 parts Melon Liqueur
1 part Light Rum
1/2 part Lemon Juice
splash Grenadine
Cocktail Glass
Shake with ice and strain

Fog at Bowling Green
1 part Peppermint Liqueur
1 part Vodka
1 part Cream
Cocktail Glass
Shake with ice and strain

Foggy Afternoon
1 part Vodka
1/2 part Apricot Brandy
1/2 part Triple Sec
splash Crème de Banana
splash Lemon Juice
1 Maraschino Cherry
Cocktail Glass
Shake with ice and strain

Foiled Plan
1 part Irish Whiskey
2/3 part Triple Sec
2/3 part Frangelico®
2/3 part Cranberry Juice Cocktail
Cocktail Glass
Shake with ice and strain

Fondling Fool
$1^1/_2$ parts Brandy
1 part Madeira
$^1/_2$ part Triple Sec
Cocktail Glass
Shake with ice and strain

Fontainebleau Special
1 part Brandy
1 part Anisette
$^1/_2$ part Dry Vermouth
Cocktail Glass
Shake with ice and strain

Forbidden Smoke
1 part Gin
splash Grenadine
Cocktail Glass
Shake with ice and strain

Foreign Dignitary
$1^1/_2$ parts Brandy
$^1/_2$ part Raspberry Liqueur
1 part Lime Juice
Cocktail Glass
Shake with ice and strain

Formal Wear
1 part Vodka
1 part Blackberry Liqueur
$^2/_3$ part Cranberry Juice Cocktail
$^2/_3$ part Orange Juice
Cocktail Glass
Shake with ice and strain

Fort Lauderdale
2 parts Light Rum
1 part Orange Juice
1 part Fresh Lime Juice
$^1/_2$ part Sweet Vermouth
Cocktail Glass
Shake with ice and strain

Four Flush
1 part Light Rum
1 part Dry Vermouth
1 part Grenadine
1 part Maraschino Liqueur
Cocktail Glass
Shake with ice and strain

The Four-Hundred Blows
1 part Vodka
$^2/_3$ part Lime Juice
$^1/_2$ part Simple Syrup
Cocktail Glass
Shake with ice and strain

Fox and Hounds
1 part Pernod®
1 part Lemon Juice
splash Sugar
1 Egg White
Cocktail Glass
Shake with ice and strain

Fox Trot
$1^1/_4$ parts Dark Rum
splash Blue Curaçao
1 part Lemon Juice
dash Sugar
Cocktail Glass
Shake with ice and strain

Foxy Lady
$^1/_2$ part Amaretto
$^1/_2$ part Crème de Cacao (Dark)
2 parts Light Cream
Cocktail Glass
Shake with ice and strain

Francis Anne

1 part Scotch
1 part Dry Vermouth
1 part Cherry Brandy
Cocktail Glass

Shake with ice and strain

Frankenjack Cocktail

1 part Gin
3/4 part Dry Vermouth
1/2 part Apricot Brandy
splash Triple Sec
1 Maraschino Cherry
Cocktail Glass

Shake with ice and strain

Free Fly

1 1/2 parts Vodka
1/2 part Parfait Amour
1/4 part Triple Sec
1/4 part Sweet Vermouth
splash Kiwi Juice
Cocktail Glass

Shake with ice and strain

French Acquisition

1 part Scotch
1 part Sweet Vermouth
1 part Dry Vermouth
splash Orange Liqueur
Cocktail Glass

Shake with ice and strain

French Advance

2/3 part Gin
2/3 part Blackberry Liqueur
1/2 part Sweet Vermouth
splash Grenadine
splash Pernod®
Cocktail Glass

Shake with ice and strain

French Cosmopolitan

1 part Citrus-Flavored Vodka
1/2 part Grand Marnier®
1/2 part Sour Mix
1/2 part Cranberry Juice Cocktail
1/4 part Lime Juice
splash Grenadine
Cocktail Glass

Shake all but Grenadine with ice and strain into the glass. Place a few drops of Grenadine in the center of the drink.

French Daiquiri

1 part Light Rum
1/2 part Lime Juice
dash Powdered Sugar
splash Crème de Cassis
Cocktail Glass

Shake with ice and strain

French Sidecar

1 1/2 parts Dry Gin
1/2 part Triple Sec
splash Lemon Juice
Cocktail Glass

Shake with ice and strain

French Tear

2/3 part Grand Marnier®
2/3 part Spiced Rum
2 parts Pineapple Juice
Cocktail Glass

Shake with ice and strain

French Tickler

1 part B&B®
1 part Grand Marnier®
1 part Courvoisier®
1 Maraschino Cherry
Cocktail Glass

Shake with ice and strain

Cocktails

French Vineyard
2/3 part Raspberry Liqueur
splash Vanilla Liqueur
2/3 part Plum Brandy
2/3 part Port
1 part Cream
Cocktail Glass
Shake with ice and strain

Friar Tuck
1 part Frangelico®
1 part Crème de Cacao (White)
2 parts Cream
Cocktail Glass
Shake with ice and strain

Friendly Alien
1 1/2 parts Vodka
1/2 part Coconut-Flavored Liqueur
1/2 part Mango Schnapps
1/2 part Lemon Juice
1 part Pineapple Juice
Cocktail Glass
Shake with ice and strain

Frightleberry Murzenquest
1 part Vodka
1/2 part Galliano®
1/2 part Triple Sec
1/2 part Lime Juice
1 splash Maraschino Liqueur
dash Bitters
Cocktail Glass
Shake with ice and strain

Frisco
2 parts Rye Whiskey
1/4 part Benedictine®
3/4 part Lemon Juice
Cocktail Glass
Shake with ice and strain

Frisky Intern
1 part Raspberry Liqueur
1 part Jim Beam®
1 part Cream
splash Vanilla Extract
Cocktail Glass
Shake with ice and strain

Frog's Tongue
1 1/2 parts Vodka
1/2 part Scotch
Cocktail Glass
Shake with ice and strain

Froot Loops
1 1/2 parts Sour Apple Schnapps
2 parts Orange Juice
Cocktail Glass
Shake with ice and strain

Frosty Dawn
1/2 part Light Rum
1/2 part Orange Juice
1/4 part Maraschino Liqueur
1/4 part Ginger Liqueur
Cocktail Glass
Shake with ice and pour

Froupe
1 1/2 parts Brandy
1 1/2 parts Sweet Vermouth
Cocktail Glass
Shake with ice and strain

Frozen Blackcurrant
1 part Pineapple Juice
1 part Crème de Cassis
1/2 part Brandy
Cocktail Glass
Shake with ice and strain

Frozen Pussy
1 part Irish Cream Liqueur
1 part Strawberry Liqueur
1/2 part Grenadine
Cocktail Glass
Shake with ice and strain

Fruhling
1 part Gin
splash Orange Liqueur
splash Grenadine
splash Lemon Juice
Cocktail Glass
Shake with ice and strain

Fruit Dangereux
1 part Melon Liqueur
splash Lemon Juice
splash Simple Syrup
Cocktail Glass
Shake with ice and strain

Fuck Me by the Pool
1 part Tropical Punch Schnapps
1 part Peach Schnapps
2 parts Orange Juice
Cocktail Glass
Shake with ice and strain

Fuck Me to Death
1/2 part Brandy
1/2 part Scotch
1/2 part Vodka
1/2 part Coconut-Flavored Liqueur
Cocktail Glass
Shake with ice and strain

Funky Doctor
1/2 part Peppermint Liqueur
1 1/2 parts Light Rum
1/2 part Mandarine Napoléon® Liqueur
splash Vanilla Liqueur
Cocktail Glass
Shake with ice and strain

Fuschia
1 part Peach Schnapps
1 1/2 parts Vodka
splash Passion Fruit Juice
Cocktail Glass
Shake with ice and strain

Fuzzy Pucker
1 1/2 parts Peach Schnapps
1 part Grapefruit Juice
Cocktail Glass
Shake with ice and strain

Galactic Trader
1 part Vodka
splash Apricot Brandy
1/2 part Blue Curaçao
1/2 part Lime Juice
Cocktail Glass
Shake with ice and strain

Galviston
1 part Amaretto
1 part Orange Juice
1 part Milk
1/2 part Cream
Cocktail Glass
Shake with ice and strain

Galway Gray
$1^1/_2$ parts Vodka
1 part Crème de Cacao (White)
1 part Cointreau®
$^1/_2$ part Lime Juice
splash Cream
Cocktail Glass
Shake with ice and strain

Garden Party
$1^1/_2$ parts Spiced Rum
1 part Carrot Juice
$^2/_3$ part Triple Sec
$^2/_3$ part Tomato Juice
splash Tabasco® Sauce
Cocktail Glass
Shake with ice and strain

Gareth Glowworm
$1^1/_2$ parts Light Rum
$^1/_2$ part Crème de Cacao (White)
1 part Heavy Cream
splash Cherry Brandy
Cocktail Glass
Shake with ice and strain

Gaslight Girl
2 parts Vodka
splash Orange Liqueur
splash Grenadine
1 part Gold Tequila
Cocktail Glass
Shake with ice and strain

Gatorade
$1^1/_2$ parts Vodka
$1^1/_2$ parts Rum
$1^1/_2$ parts Orange Liqueur
1 part Sour Mix
$^1/_2$ part Orange Juice
Cocktail Glass
Shake with ice and strain

Gay Scorpion
1 part Light Rum
splash Peach Schnapps
splash Grenadine
2 parts Pineapple Juice
splash Cream
Cocktail Glass
Shake with ice and strain

Gazette
$1^1/_2$ parts Brandy
splash Lemon Juice
splash Simple Syrup
1 part Sweet Vermouth
Cocktail Glass
Shake with ice and strain

Genesis
$^2/_3$ part Blue Curaçao
$1^1/_2$ parts Limoncello
$^2/_3$ part Mandarine Napoléon® Liqueur
$^2/_3$ part Lemon Juice
$^1/_2$ part Simple Syrup
Cocktail Glass
Shake with ice and strain

Geneva Convention
2 parts Vodka
$^1/_2$ part Goldschläger®
$^1/_2$ part Grain Alcohol
Cocktail Glass
Shake with ice and strain

Geneva Summit
1 part Southern Comfort®
1 part Vodka
$^1/_2$ part Orange Juice
$^1/_2$ part Lime Juice
splash Peppermint Schnapps
splash Lemon-Lime Soda
Cocktail Glass
Shake with ice and strain

Gentle Touch
$1\frac{1}{2}$ parts Citrus-Flavored Rum
$\frac{1}{2}$ part Cointreau®
$\frac{1}{2}$ part Apricot Brandy
splash Grenadine
1 part Lemon Juice
Cocktail Glass
Shake with ice and strain

Georgia Cruise
1 part Cherry Brandy
splash Grenadine
1 part Apple Brandy
1 part Sour Mix
Cocktail Glass
Shake with ice and strain

German Chocolate Cake
$\frac{1}{2}$ part Coconut-Flavored Rum
$\frac{1}{2}$ part Crème de Cacao (Dark)
2 parts Cream
splash Frangelico®
Cocktail Glass
Shake with ice and strain

Ghetto Gold
1 part Dark Rum
1 part Goldschläger®
$\frac{1}{2}$ part Vanilla Liqueur
Cocktail Glass
Shake with ice and strain

Ghostbuster
1 part Vodka
$\frac{1}{2}$ part Irish Cream Liqueur
$\frac{1}{2}$ part Coffee Liqueur
Cocktail Glass
Shake with ice and strain

Gimlet
$1\frac{1}{2}$ parts Gin
1 part Lime Juice
dash Powdered Sugar
Cocktail Glass
Shake with ice and strain

Gimme Some
$\frac{1}{2}$ part Coconut-Flavored Liqueur
1 part Vanilla-Flavored Vodka
1 part Chocolate Liqueur
splash Sweet Vermouth
Cocktail Glass
Shake with ice and strain

Gin and Berry It
$1\frac{1}{2}$ parts Gin
splash Maraschino Liqueur
2 splashes Raspberry Syrup
splash Lemon Juice
Cocktail Glass
Shake with ice and strain

Gin Blue Devil
1 part Gin
splash Blue Curaçao
dash Powdered Sugar
splash Maraschino Liqueur
Cocktail Glass
Shake with ice and strain

Gin Rummy
1 part Gin
$\frac{1}{4}$ part Dry Vermouth
$\frac{1}{4}$ part Sweet Vermouth
Cocktail Glass
Shake with ice and strain

Ginny
1 part Gin
1/2 part Dry Vermouth
1/2 part Apricot Brandy
Cocktail Glass
Shake with ice and strain

Glacier
1 part Blackberry Liqueur
1/2 part Crème de Cacao (White)
1/2 part Light Rum
Cocktail Glass
Shake with ice and strain

Glacier Mint
1 1/2 parts Vodka
1/2 part Lemon-Flavored Vodka
1/2 part Crème de Menthe (Green)
Cocktail Glass
Shake with ice and strain

Gladness
1 1/2 parts Vodka
1/2 part Green Chartreuse®
splash Triple Sec
Cocktail Glass
Shake with ice and strain

Glasgow
2 parts Scotch
1 part Amaretto
1/2 part Dry Vermouth
Cocktail Glass
Shake with ice and strain

Glaucoma
1 part Vodka
1 part Rum
1 part Gin
1/2 part Coffee Liqueur
splash Lemon Juice
dash Sugar
Cocktail Glass
Shake with ice and strain

A Glint in Your Life
1/2 part Vanilla Liqueur
1 1/2 parts Plum Brandy
1/2 part Sweetened Lime Juice
splash Lemon Juice
Cocktail Glass
Shake with ice and strain

Gloom Raiser
2 parts Gin
3/4 part Dry Vermouth
2 splashes Pernod®
2 splashes Grenadine
Cocktail Glass
Shake with ice and strain

Gloria
1/2 part Brandy
1/2 part Campari®
1/2 part Scotch
1/4 part Amaretto
1/4 part Dry Vermouth
Cocktail Glass
Shake with ice and strain

Glory Box
1 part Gin
1 part Grand Marnier®
1 part Dry Vermouth
Cocktail Glass
Shake with ice and strain

Gnome Depot
2/3 part Melon Liqueur
2 parts Orange-Flavored Vodka
splash Dry Vermouth
Cocktail Glass
Shake with ice and strain

Go Kucha
1/2 part Triple Sec
1/2 part Frangelico®
1/2 part Light Rum
1/2 part Apricot Juice
1 1/2 parts Pineapple Juice
Cocktail Glass
Shake with ice and strain

Godfather Dada
2 parts Amaretto
2 parts Grand Marnier®
3 parts Ketel One® Vodka
Orange Twist
Cocktail Glass
Shake with ice and strain

Going Nuts
1/2 part Amaretto
1 1/2 parts Frangelico®
2 parts Cream
Cocktail Glass
Shake with ice and strain

Gold Card
1 part Brandy
1/2 part Benedictine®
1/4 part Chartreuse®
Cocktail Glass
Shake with ice and strain

Gold Zest
1 part Passion Fruit Liqueur
1/2 part Crème de Noyaux
1 part Cachaça
1 1/2 parts Lemon Juice
Cocktail Glass
Shake with ice and strain

Golden Bird
1 1/2 parts Orange Juice
1 part Light Rum
1 part Pineapple Juice
1 part Mandarine Napoléon® Liqueur
1/2 part Crème de Banana
Cocktail Glass
Shake with ice and strain

Golden Dream
1 part Galliano®
1/2 part Triple Sec
2 splashes Orange Juice
2 splashes Light Cream
Cocktail Glass
Shake with ice and strain

Golden Ermine Cocktail
1 1/2 parts Dry Gin
1 part Dry Vermouth
1/2 part Sweet Vermouth
Cocktail Glass
Shake with ice and strain

Golden Flute
1/2 part Blue Curaçao
splash Peach Schnapps
2 parts Vodka
splash Campari®
Cocktail Glass
Shake with ice and strain

Golden Glow
2 parts Orange Juice
2 parts Bourbon
1 part Dark Rum
1/4 part Simple Syrup
splash Grenadine
Cocktail Glass
Shake with ice and strain

Golden Purple
$1^1/_2$ parts Gin
1 part Parfait Amour
1 part Goldschläger®
Cocktail Glass
Shake with ice and strain

Goldfish
1 part Gin
1 part Goldschläger®
$^1/_2$ part Triple Sec
$^1/_2$ part Orange Juice
Cocktail Glass
Shake with ice and strain

Goldilocks' Cosmo
2 parts Vodka
$^1/_4$ part Lime Juice
$^1/_4$ part Triple Sec
splash White Cranberry Juice
Cocktail Glass
Shake with ice and strain

Goldmine
2 parts Gin
1 part Pineapple Juice
$^1/_2$ part Maraschino Liqueur
Cocktail Glass
Shake with ice and strain

Gonzo Gonzales
1 part Gin
$^1/_2$ part Crème de Banana
$^1/_2$ part Grapefruit Juice
Cocktail Glass
Shake with ice and strain

Good Morning Jamaica
1 part Dark Rum
2 parts Coffee Liqueur
$^1/_2$ part Lime Juice
Cocktail Glass
Shake with ice and strain

Good Morning Mexico
1 part Tequila
2 parts Coffee Liqueur
$^1/_2$ part Lime Juice
Cocktail Glass
Shake with ice and strain

Goody-Goody
$^1/_2$ part Brandy
$^1/_2$ part Crème de Cacao (White)
$^2/_3$ part Sloe Gin
1 part Milk
Cocktail Glass
Shake with ice and strain

Gotham
1 part Crème de Cassis
2 parts Rémy Martin® VSOP
1 part Lime Juice
Cocktail Glass
Shake with ice and strain

Governing Body
$^2/_3$ part Gin
$^1/_2$ part Sweet Vermouth
$^2/_3$ part Dry Vermouth
splash Triple Sec
splash Pernod®
Cocktail Glass
Shake with ice and strain

Grand Apple
$^1/_2$ part Cognac
$^1/_2$ part Grand Marnier®
1 part Apple Brandy
Cocktail Glass
Shake with ice and strain

Grand Casino

2/3 part Peach Schnapps
2/3 part Dry Vermouth
splash Blue Curaçao
splash Crème de Cacao (White)
Cocktail Glass

Shake with ice and strain

Grand Gate

1 part Coffee Liqueur
1 part Amaretto
splash Goldschläger®
1 part Milk
Cocktail Glass

Shake with ice and strain

Grand Occasion

1/2 part Crème de Cacao (White)
1/2 part Grand Marnier®
2 splashes Lemon Juice
1 1/2 parts Light Rum
Cocktail Glass

Shake with ice and strain

Grape Ape

1 part Vodka
1/2 part Crème de Cacao (White)
1 part Grape Juice (red)
Cocktail Glass

Shake with ice and strain

Grape Popsicle®

1/2 part Raspberry Liqueur
1/2 part Southern Comfort®
2/3 part Cranberry Juice Cocktail
splash Sour Mix
Cocktail Glass

Shake with ice and strain

Grapeshot

1/2 part Blue Curaçao
1 1/2 parts Tequila
1 part Grape Juice
Cocktail Glass

Shake with ice and strain

Grappa Strega

1 part Grappa
1 part Strega®
splash Lemon Juice
splash Orange Juice
Cocktail Glass

Shake with ice and strain

Grasshopper

1 part Crème de Menthe (Green)
1 part Crème de Cacao (White)
1 part Light Cream
Cocktail Glass

Shake with ice and strain

Great Dane

2 parts Gin
1 part Cherry Brandy
1/2 part Dry Vermouth
1/2 part Kirschwasser
Cocktail Glass

Shake with ice and strain

Greek Cherry Tree

1 part Light Rum
1 part Cherry Brandy
1/2 part Grenadine
splash Grapefruit Juice
Cocktail Glass

Shake with ice and strain

Green and Gold
1 part Gin
2/3 part Peppermint Liqueur
splash Goldschläger®
1/2 part Vermouth
2/3 part Pineapple Juice
Cocktail Glass

Shake with ice and strain

Green Apple Tequini
1 part Apple Liqueur
2 parts Silver Tequila
splash Fresh Lime Juice
splash Melon Liqueur
Cocktail Glass

Shake with ice and strain

Green Bay
1 1/2 parts Gin
1/2 part Green Chartreuse®
1/2 part Chartreuse®
Cocktail Glass

Shake with ice and strain

Green Bracer
1 part Peppermint Liqueur
1 part Irish Cream Liqueur
1/2 part Crème de Cacao (White)
1/2 part Peach Schnapps
Cocktail Glass

Shake with ice and strain

Green Cat
1 1/2 parts Kiwi Schnapps
1 part Rum
Cocktail Glass

Shake with ice and strain

Green Cubed
2/3 part Melon Liqueur
splash Peppermint Liqueur
splash Green Chartreuse®
splash Lime Juice
Cocktail Glass

Shake with ice and strain

Green Hope
1 1/2 parts Vodka
1/2 part Blue Curaçao
1/2 part Crème de Banana
Cocktail Glass

Shake with ice and strain

Green Iguana
2 parts Tequila Silver
1 part Melon Liqueur
1 part Lime Cordial
Cocktail Glass

Shake with ice and strain

Green Ireland
1 1/2 parts Crème de Menthe (Green)
1 1/2 parts Whiskey
Cocktail Glass

Shake with ice and strain

Green Kryptonite
2 parts Vodka
splash Lime Juice
1 part Melon Liqueur
Cocktail Glass

Shake with ice and strain

The Green Mile
1 part Melon Liqueur
1/2 part Coconut-Flavored Rum
1/2 part Cointreau®
1 part Pineapple Juice
Cocktail Glass

Shake with ice and strain

Green Mist
1 part Scotch
1 part Crème de Menthe (White)
1/2 part Lemon Juice
Cocktail Glass
Shake with ice and strain

Green Scarab
1 1/2 parts Gin
splash Peppermint Liqueur
1 1/2 parts Absinthe
Cocktail Glass
Shake with ice and strain

Green Whip
1 1/2 parts Maraschino Liqueur
1 1/2 parts Melon Liqueur
splash Lime Juice
Cocktail Glass
Shake with ice and strain

Green Wood
1 1/2 parts Apple Liqueur
1 1/2 parts Parfait Amour
Cocktail Glass
Shake with ice and strain

Greenbriar Cocktail
2 parts Sherry
1 part Dry Vermouth
Cocktail Glass
Shake with ice and strain

Greensleeves
1 part Cream
1 part Crème de Cacao (White)
1 part Crème de Menthe (White)
Cocktail Glass
Shake with ice and strain

Greta Garbo
2 parts Light Rum
1 part Fresh Lime Juice
1/2 part Simple Syrup
1/4 part Maraschino Liqueur
Cocktail Glass
Shake with ice and strain

Grouse to Death
1 1/2 parts Scotch
1/2 part Blackberry Liqueur
dash Angostura® Bitters
1/2 part Lemon Juice
splash Vanilla Syrup
Cocktail Glass
Shake with ice and strain

Grumpy Dwarf
1 1/2 parts Gin
1/2 part Orange Liqueur
splash Dry Vermouth
splash Plum Brandy
Cocktail Glass
Shake with ice and strain

Guacamayo
1/2 part Coffee Liqueur
splash Calvados Apple Brandy
splash Cream
splash Coconut Cream
Cocktail Glass
Shake with ice and strain

Guadalupe
1 1/2 parts Silver Tequila
1/2 part Vanilla Liqueur
1 part Cream
Cocktail Glass
Shake with ice and strain

Guantanamera
1 part Light Rum
1/2 part Cream
1/2 part Coffee
1/2 part Coconut Cream
Cocktail Glass

Shake with ice and strain

Guapasipati
1 1/2 parts Vodka
1/2 part Dry Vermouth
1/4 part Crème de Banana
splash Orange Juice
splash Grenadine
Cocktail Glass

Shake with ice and strain

Guerilla
1/2 part Triple Sec
1 part Tequila
splash Tabasco® Sauce
Cocktail Glass

Shake with ice and strain

Gun Barrel
1/2 part Currant-Flavored Vodka
1/2 part Triple Sec
splash Cranberry Juice Cocktail
Cocktail Glass

Shake with ice and strain

Gun Shot
1/2 part Blue Curaçao
splash Coconut-Flavored Liqueur
splash Peach Schnapps
splash Sour Mix
Cocktail Glass

Shake with ice and strain

Gypsy Dream Cream
1/2 part Blackberry Liqueur
1/2 part Raspberry Liqueur
1/2 part Irish Cream Liqueur
2 parts Milk
Cocktail Glass

Shake with ice and strain

H&H Cocktail
2 parts Dry Gin
1 part Lillet®
splash Triple Sec
Cocktail Glass

Shake with ice and strain

Haidin-Haidin
2 parts Light Rum
1/2 part Dry Vermouth
dash Bitters
1 Lemon Twist
Cocktail Glass

Shake with ice and strain

Hair of the Dog
1 part Scotch
1/2 part Cream
1/2 part Honey
Cocktail Glass

Shake with ice and strain

Hairy Armpit
1 part Ouzo
2 parts Grapefruit Juice
Cocktail Glass

Build over ice and stir

Half Note
1 1/2 parts Gin
2/3 part Melon Liqueur
2/3 part Lime Juice
Cocktail Glass

Shake with ice and strain

Half on Orange
1/2 part Blue Curaçao
2 parts Chocolate Liqueur
1/2 part Light Rum
Cocktail Glass
Shake with ice and strain

Halloween in Tijuana
2 parts Absinthe
1 part Grand Marnier®
1 part Lime Juice
Cocktail Glass
Shake with ice and strain

Hammer and Tongs
2 parts Light Rum
2 splashes Lime Juice
splash Grenadine
1/2 part Cream
Cocktail Glass
Shake with ice and strain

Hammerhead
1 part Amaretto
1 part Blue Curaçao
1 part Gold Rum
splash Southern Comfort®
Cocktail Glass
Shake with ice and strain

Happy Daddy
1/2 part Gin
1/2 part Crème de Cassis
1/2 part Crème de Banana
splash Cream
splash Mango Juice
Cocktail Glass
Shake with ice and strain

Harper's Ferry
1/2 part Blue Curaçao
1/2 part Light Rum
1/2 part Southern Comfort®
1 1/2 parts Dry Vermouth
Cocktail Glass
Shake with ice and strain

Harry's Pick Me Up Cocktail
2 parts Brandy
1/2 part Grenadine
Cocktail Glass
Shake with ice and strain

Harvey Wallpaper Hanger
2 parts Vodka
1 part Galliano®
Cocktail Glass
Shake with ice and strain

Hasty
1 1/2 parts Gin
1/2 part Dry Vermouth
1/2 part Grenadine
splash Pastis
Cocktail Glass
Shake with ice and strain

Hat Trick
1 part Dark Rum
1 part Light Rum
1 part Sweet Vermouth
Cocktail Glass
Shake with ice and strain

Haute Couture
1 1/2 parts Brandy
1 1/2 parts Crème de Cacao (Dark)
Cocktail Glass
Shake with ice and strain

Havana Special
1 part Triple Sec
1 part Light Rum
1 part Pineapple Juice
1 part Fresh Lime Juice
Cocktail Glass

Shake with ice and strain

Hawaiian Comfort
1 part Southern Comfort®
1 part Amaretto
2 parts Sour Mix
1 part Pineapple Juice
1 part Grenadine
Cocktail Glass

Shake with ice and strain

Head over Heels
2 parts Aquavit
splash Raspberry Liqueur
splash Lemon Juice
splash Simple Syrup
Cocktail Glass

Shake with ice and strain

Headlights
1 part Vodka
1/2 part Chartreuse®
2 splashes Galliano®
2 splashes Blue Curaçao
splash Lemon Juice
Cocktail Glass

Shake with ice and strain

Healthy Hiatus
1 1/2 parts Amaretto
1/2 part Apricot Brandy
1/2 part Dry Vermouth
1 part Sour Mix
Cocktail Glass

Shake with ice and strain

Heaven and Hell
1 1/2 parts Scotch
1 part Coffee Liqueur
1/2 part Maraschino Liqueur
Cocktail Glass

Shake with ice and strain

Heavenly Opera
1 part Apricot Brandy
1/2 part Dry Vermouth
1 part Irish Whiskey
splash Lemon Juice
1/2 part Sour Mix
Cocktail Glass

Shake with ice and strain

Heavy Fuel
1 part Bourbon
1 part Maraschino Liqueur
splash Peppermint Liqueur
Cocktail Glass

Shake with ice and strain

Heberts Alexander
2 parts Brandy
1/2 part Crème de Cacao (Dark)
1/2 part Frangelico®
1 part Cream
Cocktail Glass

Shake with ice and strain

Hello Nurse
1 1/2 parts Vodka
1/2 part Amaretto
1/2 part Coconut Cream
1/2 part Light Cream
Cocktail Glass

Shake with ice and strain

Hemingway Special
2 parts Light Rum
1 part Grapefruit Juice
1/2 part Fresh Lime Juice
1/4 part Maraschino Liqueur
Cocktail Glass

Shake with ice and strain

Hep Cat
3 parts Currant-Flavored Vodka
1/2 part Dry Vermouth
splash Sweet Vermouth
Cocktail Glass

Shake with ice and strain

Her Name in Lights
1 part Vodka
1/2 part Chartreuse®
2 splashes Galliano®
2 splashes Blue Curaçao
1/2 part Lemon Juice
1 Maraschino Cherry
Cocktail Glass

Shake with ice and strain

Herbie
1 part Dark Rum
2/3 part Strawberry Liqueur
splash Grenadine
splash Cream
Cocktail Glass

Shake with ice and strain

Heretic
1 part Calvados Apple Brandy
1/2 part Pear Brandy
splash Blackberry Liqueur
Cocktail Glass

Shake with ice and strain

Hibernian Special
1 part Blue Curaçao
1 part Triple Sec
1 part Gin
Cocktail Glass

Shake with ice and strain

Hidden Allies
2/3 part Amaretto
1 part Triple Sec
1 part Rémy Martin® VSOP
1/2 part Grapefruit Juice
Cocktail Glass

Shake with ice and strain

High Fashion
2 parts Vodka
1 part Scotch
1 part Triple Sec
Cocktail Glass

Shake with ice and strain

Highland Victory
1 part Scotch
2/3 part Orange Liqueur
1/2 part Dry Vermouth
1/2 part Grapefruit Juice
Cocktail Glass

Shake with ice and strain

Hippo in a Tutu
2 parts Currant-Flavored Vodka
1/2 part Raspberry Liqueur
1/2 part Blue Curaçao
Cocktail Glass

Shake with ice and strain

Hokkaido Cocktail
1 1/2 parts Gin
1/2 part Triple Sec
1 part Sake
Cocktail Glass

Shake with ice and strain

Hole in One

$1^3/4$ parts Scotch
$^3/4$ part Dry Vermouth
splash Lemon Juice
dash Orange Bitters
Cocktail Glass
Shake with ice and strain

Hollywood Shooter

3 parts Vodka
1 part Pineapple Juice
Cocktail Glass
Shake with ice and strain

Holy Grail

1 part Vodka
1 part Campari®
$^1/2$ part Apricot Brandy
$1^1/2$ parts Orange Juice
1 Egg White
Cocktail Glass
Shake with ice and strain

Homecoming

$^3/4$ part Gin
$^3/4$ part Apricot Brandy
$^3/4$ part Dry Vermouth
splash Lemon Juice
Cocktail Glass
Shake with ice and strain

Honey Blossom

$1^1/2$ parts Raspberry Liqueur
1 part Citrus-Flavored Rum
$^1/2$ part Honey
$^1/2$ part Sour Mix
Cocktail Glass
Shake with ice and strain

Honeymoon

$^3/4$ part Benedictine®
$^3/4$ part Apple Brandy
1 part Lemon Juice
2 splashes Triple Sec
Cocktail Glass
Shake with ice and strain

Honolulu Hammer

$1^1/2$ parts Vodka
$^1/2$ part Amaretto
splash Pineapple Juice
splash Grenadine
Cocktail Glass
Shake with ice and strain

Honolulu with Fruit

2 parts Gin
$^3/4$ part Fresh Lime Juice
$^1/2$ part Orange Juice
$^1/2$ part Pineapple
dash Sugar
Cocktail Glass
Shake with ice and strain

Hoochie Mama

$1^1/2$ parts Vodka
1 part Crème de Menthe (White)
$^1/2$ part Chocolate Syrup
Cocktail Glass
Shake with ice and strain

Hope and Peace

$1^1/2$ parts Dark Rum
$^1/2$ part Pisang Ambon® Liqueur
$^1/2$ part Kiwi Schnapps
2 parts Cream
Cocktail Glass
Shake with ice and strain

Hop-Scotch
1 part Scotch
1/2 part Dry Vermouth
1/2 part Triple Sec
splash Blue Curaçao
Cocktail Glass

Shake with ice and strain

Horizon
1 1/2 parts Dark Rum
1 part Anisette
1 part Grenadine
Cocktail Glass

Shake with ice and strain

Hornet Stinger
1 part Vodka
1/2 part Melon Liqueur
dash Powdered Sugar
splash Lime Juice
Cocktail Glass

Shake with ice and strain

Horse and Jockey
1 part Añejo Rum
1 part Southern Comfort®
1/2 part Sweet Vermouth
2 dashes Bitters
Cocktail Glass

Shake with ice and strain

Horse Power
1 1/2 parts Whiskey
1 part Mandarine Napoléon® Liqueur
splash Campari®
Cocktail Glass

Shake with ice and strain

Hot Cherry
1 1/2 parts Cherry Brandy
1 part Silver Tequila
Cocktail Glass

Shake with ice and strain

Hot Lava
1 1/4 parts Pepper-Flavored Vodka
1/4 part Amaretto
Cocktail Glass

Shake with ice and strain

Hot Property
1 1/2 parts Brandy
1/2 part Grenadine
splash Anisette
splash Sambuca
1/2 part Lemon Juice
Cocktail Glass

Shake with ice and strain

Hot Roasted Nuts
1 part Coffee Liqueur
1 part Cinnamon Schnapps
1 part Frangelico®
Cocktail Glass

Shake with ice and strain

Hot Winter Night
1 1/2 parts Spiced Rum
splash Vanilla Liqueur
splash Goldschläger®
splash Lemon Juice
Cocktail Glass

Shake with ice and strain

Hotel Plaza Cocktail
1 part Dry Vermouth
1 part Sweet Vermouth
1 part Gin
Cocktail Glass

Shake with ice and strain

Houla Houla
2 parts Gin
1 part Orange Juice
1/4 part Triple Sec
Cocktail Glass

Shake with ice and strain

House of Usher
$1^1/_2$ parts Brandy
splash Triple Sec
splash Pineapple Juice
splash Maraschino Liqueur
Cocktail Glass
Shake with ice and strain

Hudson Bay
$^1/_2$ part Cherry Brandy
1 part Gin
splash 151-Proof Rum
2 splashes Orange Juice
splash Lime Juice
Cocktail Glass
Shake with ice and strain

Humjob
$1^1/_2$ parts Light Rum
$^1/_4$ part Crème de Cacao (Dark)
$^1/_4$ part Cherry Brandy
Cocktail Glass
Shake with ice and strain

The Hunt Master
1 part Jägermeister®
$^1/_2$ part Peppermint Liqueur
$^1/_2$ part Goldschläger®
splash Coconut-Flavored Liqueur
Cocktail Glass
Shake with ice and strain

Hunter
$1^1/_2$ parts Bourbon
1 part Cherry Brandy
Cocktail Glass
Shake with ice and strain

Hunting Man
$1^1/_2$ parts Sloe Gin
$^1/_2$ part Raspberry Liqueur
$^1/_2$ part Frangelico®
$^2/_3$ part Lemon Juice
$1^1/_2$ parts Blackberry Juice
Cocktail Glass
Shake with ice and strain

Hurlyburly
$1^1/_4$ parts Citrus-Flavored Vodka
$^1/_2$ part Cointreau®
$^1/_2$ part Orange Juice
$^1/_2$ part Cranberry Juice Cocktail
1 part Sour Mix
Cocktail Glass
Shake with ice and strain

Hurricane
1 part Light Rum
1 part Dark Rum
1 part Passion Fruit Nectar
2 splashes Lime Juice
Cocktail Glass
Shake with ice and strain

Hyde and Seek
2 parts Passion Fruit Liqueur
$^1/_2$ part Coffee Liqueur
Cocktail Glass
Shake with ice and strain

I Love Lucy
1 part Vodka
$^1/_2$ part Fresh Lime Juice
$^1/_4$ part Parfait Amour
$^1/_4$ part Triple Sec
Cocktail Glass
Shake with ice and strain

I Love You
1 part Dark Rum
1 part Apricot Brandy
1/2 part Peach Schnapps
splash Amaretto
splash Orange Juice
Cocktail Glass

Shake with ice and strain

I See Nothing
1 part Brandy
1 part Dry Vermouth
splash Triple Sec
dash Orange Bitters
splash Maraschino Liqueur
splash Pernod®
Cocktail Glass

Shake with ice and strain

Ice Crystals
1 1/2 parts Vodka
1/2 part Lemon-Flavored Vodka
1/2 part Crème de Menthe (Green)
Cocktail Glass

Shake with ice and strain

Iffy Stiffy
1 part Jim Beam®
1 part Cherry Brandy
1/2 part Dry Vermouth
1/2 part Orange Juice
splash Lime Juice
Cocktail Glass

Shake with ice and strain

Ignition Key
1/2 part Grenadine
1 1/2 parts Light Rum
1/2 part Lime Juice
Cocktail Glass

Shake with ice and strain

Iguana
1/2 part Vodka
1/2 part Tequila
1/4 part Coffee-Flavored Vodka
1 1/2 parts Sour Mix
1/2 Lime Slice
Cocktail Glass

Shake with ice and strain

Immaculata
1 1/2 parts Light Rum
1/2 part Amaretto
1/2 part Lime Juice
splash Lemon Juice
dash Sugar
Cocktail Glass

Shake with ice and strain

In a Nutshell
1 part Amaretto
1/2 part Vanilla-Flavored Vodka
1/2 part Frangelico®
2 parts Cream
Cocktail Glass

Shake with ice and strain

In Mint Condition
1 part Crème de Menthe (White)
1 part Triple Sec
1 part Apricot Brandy
Cocktail Glass

Shake with ice and strain

In the Attic
1 part Gin
1/2 part Cherry Brandy
1/2 part Benedictine®
splash Lemon Juice
Cocktail Glass

Shake with ice and strain

In Trance as Mission
1 part Triple Sec
1 part Brandy
1 part Lemon Juice
Cocktail Glass

Shake with ice and strain

Inca
1 part Dry Gin
1/2 part Dry Vermouth
1/2 part Sweet Vermouth
1/2 part Dry Sherry
dash Orange Bitters
Cocktail Glass

Shake with ice and strain

Indecent Proposal
1 part Gold Tequila
1/2 part Grand Marnier®
1/2 part Cointreau®
1 part Lemon Juice
1 part Lime Juice
Cocktail Glass

Shake with ice and strain

Independence
2/3 part Melon Liqueur
1/2 part Amaretto
2/3 part Peach Schnapps
1/2 part Lime Juice
fill with Cranberry Juice Cocktail
Cocktail Glass

Shake with ice and strain

Indy Blanket
1 1/2 parts Cognac
1 part Rum
3/4 part Triple Sec
3/4 part Simple Syrup
1/2 part Lemon Juice
Cocktail Glass

Shake with ice and strain

Ink Street Cocktail
1 1/2 parts Whiskey
1 1/2 parts Orange Juice
Cocktail Glass

Shake with ice and strain

Inside Out
1 part Peppermint Liqueur
1 part Plum Brandy
2 parts Pear Juice
Cocktail Glass

Shake with ice and strain

Intermezzo
1 part Crème de Cacao (White)
1 part Advocaat
1/2 part Milk
1/2 part Vanilla Liqueur
Cocktail Glass

Shake with ice and strain

International Cocktail
1 1/2 parts Cognac
1 part Triple Sec
1 part Anisette
1/2 part Vodka
Cocktail Glass

Shake with ice and strain

Intimacy
1/2 part Strawberry Liqueur
splash Crème de Cassis
2/3 part Dark Rum
splash Simple Syrup
splash Lime Juice
Cocktail Glass

Shake with ice and strain

Intimate Confession
1/2 part Coconut Liqueur
1/2 part Frangelico®
2 parts White Port
splash Honey
1 part Cream
Cocktail Glass
Shake with ice and strain

Intrigue Cocktail
1 part Crème de Banana
1/2 part Coffee
1/2 part Dry Vermouth
Cocktail Glass
Shake with ice and strain

Irish
2 dashes Blue Curaçao
dash Cherry Liqueur
1 1/2 parts Rye Whiskey
2 splashes Pernod®
Cocktail Glass
Shake with ice and strain

Irish Blessing
1 part Irish Cream Liqueur
1 part Irish Whiskey
Cocktail Glass
Shake with ice and strain

Irish Eyes
2 parts Crème de Menthe (Green)
2 parts Heavy Cream
1 part Irish Whiskey
Cocktail Glass
Shake with ice and strain

Irish Kilt
2 parts Whiskey
1 part Scotch
1/2 part Sugar
dash Orange Bitters
Cocktail Glass
Shake with ice and strain

Irish Rose
2 parts Whiskey
1/2 part Grenadine
Cocktail Glass
Shake with ice and strain

Irish Shillelagh
3 parts Irish Whiskey
1 part Sloe Gin
1 part Light Rum
1 part Lemon Juice
dash Powdered Sugar
Cocktail Glass
Shake with ice and strain

Irish Whiskey
2 parts Irish Whiskey
splash Triple Sec
splash Anisette
splash Maraschino Liqueur
dash Bitters
1 Olive
Cocktail Glass
Shake with ice and strain

Isla Tropical
1 part Dark Rum
1/2 part Dry Gin
1/2 part Crème de Banana
1/2 part Pineapple Juice
splash Grenadine
Cocktail Glass
Shake with ice and strain

Island Nation
1/2 part Triple Sec
1/2 part Vodka
1/2 part Peppermint Liqueur
1 1/2 parts Pineapple Juice
Cocktail Glass
Shake with ice and strain

Cocktails

Italian Delight
1 part Amaretto
1/2 part Orange Juice
1 1/2 parts Cream
1 Maraschino Cherry
Cocktail Glass

Shake with ice and strain

It's Now or Never
1 part Vodka
splash Apricot Brandy
splash Campari®
splash Limoncello
Cocktail Glass

Shake with ice and strain

Jack Pine Cocktail
1 part Dry Gin
1 part Dry Vermouth
1 part Orange Juice
1/2 part Pineapple Juice
Cocktail Glass

Shake with ice and strain

Jack Sour
2 parts Jack Daniel's®
splash Cherry Juice
2 parts Sour Mix
2 Maraschino Cherries
1 Orange Wedge
Cocktail Glass

Shake with ice and strain

Jack Withers
3/4 part Gin
1/2 part Orange Juice
3/4 part Dry Vermouth
3/4 part Sweet Vermouth
Cocktail Glass

Shake with ice and strain

Jackie O's Rose
2 parts Light Rum
1/2 part Lime Juice
dash Cointreau®
dash Powdered Sugar
Cocktail Glass

Shake with ice and strain

Jack-of-All-Trades
2/3 part Peach Schnapps
1 1/2 parts Whiskey
splash Limoncello
splash Almond Syrup
Cocktail Glass

Shake with ice and strain

Jaded Dreams
1 1/2 parts Light Rum
2 splashes Crème de Menthe (Green)
splash Triple Sec
splash Lime Juice
dash Sugar
Cocktail Glass

Shake with ice and strain

Jamaica Hoop
1 part Crème de Cacao (White)
1 part Cream
1 part Coconut-Flavored Liqueur
Cocktail Glass

Shake with ice and strain

Jamaican Breakfast
1/2 part Coffee-Flavored Brandy
1/2 part Vanilla Liqueur
1 part Jamaican Rum
2 parts Cream
splash Caramel syrup
Cocktail Glass

Shake with ice and strain

Jamaican Cocktail
1 part Dark Rum
1/2 part Coffee Liqueur
1 part Lime Juice
dash Bitters
Cocktail Glass

Shake with ice and strain

Jamaican Creamsicle®
1 part Rum Crème Liqueur
1 part Half and Half
1 part Orange Juice
1 splash Vanilla Extract
Cocktail Glass

Shake with ice and strain

Jamaican Fever
2/3 part Passion Fruit Liqueur
1 1/2 parts Jamaican Rum
1 1/2 parts Guava Juice
1/2 part Cranberry Juice Cocktail
1/2 part Lemon Juice
Cocktail Glass

Shake with ice and strain

Jamaican Green Sunrise
1 1/2 parts Light Rum
1 part Orange Juice
1/2 part Blue Curaçao
1/2 part Pineapple-Flavored Vodka
Cocktail Glass

Shake with ice and strain

Jamaican Renegade
1/2 part Sloe Gin
1/2 part Crème de Banana
splash Lime Juice
splash Coconut Cream
Cocktail Glass

Shake with ice and strain

Jamaican Russian Handshake
2 parts Vodka
1/2 part Grenadine
2/3 part Spiced Rum
2/3 part Lemon Juice
Cocktail Glass

Shake with ice and strain

Jamaican Tennis Beads
1 part Vodka
1 part Coconut-Flavored Rum
1 part Raspberry Liqueur
1 part Crème de Banana
1 part Pineapple Juice
1 part Half and Half
Cocktail Glass

Shake with ice and strain

James the Second Comes First
2 parts Scotch
1/2 part Tawny Port
1/2 part Dry Vermouth
dash Bitters
Cocktail Glass

Shake with ice and strain

Japanese Cocktail
2 parts Brandy
splash Amaretto
1/2 part Lime Juice
dash Bitters
Cocktail Glass

Shake with ice and strain

Japanese Slipper
1 part Melon Liqueur
1 part Cointreau®
1 part Lemon Juice
Cocktail Glass

Shake with ice and strain

Jasmine
$1^1/_2$ parts Gin
$^1/_4$ part Cointreau®
$^1/_4$ part Campari®
$^3/_4$ part Lemon Juice
Cocktail Glass
Shake with ice and strain

Jazz
2 parts Gin
1 part Crème de Cassis
$^1/_2$ part Lime Juice
Cocktail Glass
Shake with ice and strain

Je T'adore
$^1/_2$ part Crème de Cacao (White)
1 part Rémy Martin® VSOP
$^1/_2$ part Benedictine®
2 parts Cream
Cocktail Glass
Shake with ice and strain

Jelly Belly
1 part Blackberry Liqueur
1 part Peppermint Liqueur
$^1/_2$ part Bourbon
Cocktail Glass
Shake with ice and strain

Jersey Lightening
2 parts Apple Brandy
1 part Sweet Vermouth
1 part Fresh Lime Juice
Cocktail Glass
Shake with ice and strain

Jerusalem Love Cream
$1^1/_2$ parts Guava Juice
$1^1/_2$ parts Vanilla-Flavored Vodka
$^1/_2$ part Lychee Syrup
Cocktail Glass
Shake with ice and strain

Jet Black
$1^1/_2$ parts Gin
2 splashes Sweet Vermouth
splash Black Sambuca
Cocktail Glass
Shake with ice and strain

Jewel of the Nile
$1^1/_2$ parts Gin
$^1/_2$ part Green Chartreuse®
$^1/_2$ part Chartreuse®
Cocktail Glass
Shake with ice and strain

Joan Miró
1 part Dubonnet® Blonde
1 part Grand Marnier®
1 part Scotch
Cocktail Glass
Shake with ice and strain

Jockey's Choice Manhattan
$2^1/_2$ parts Bourbon
$^3/_4$ part Sweet Vermouth
2 dashes Angostura® Bitters
Cocktail Glass
Shake with ice and strain

Johan
1 part Peppermint Liqueur
1 part Crème de Cacao (White)
splash Benedictine®
splash Cream
Cocktail Glass
Shake with ice and strain

John Doe
1 part Gin
splash Apricot Brandy
splash Calvados Apple Brandy
1 part Lemon Juice
Cocktail Glass
Shake with ice and strain

John Wood Cocktail
1 1/2 parts Dry Vermouth
1 part Whiskey
Cocktail Glass
Shake with ice and strain

Johnnie Mack Cocktail
2 parts Sloe Gin
1 part Triple Sec
Cocktail Glass
Shake with ice and strain

Johnny Appleseed
1 part Cherry Brandy
2 parts Apple Juice
1 part Grapefruit Juice
Cocktail Glass
Shake with ice and strain

Jolly Roger
1 part Dark Rum
1 part Banana Liqueur
2 parts Lemon Juice
Cocktail Glass
Shake with ice and strain

Joshua Tree
1 part Peach Schnapps
1 part Brandy
1 part Orange Juice
1/2 part Cranberry Juice Cocktail
Cocktail Glass
Shake with ice and strain

Josie & the Pussycats
1 part Cranberry-Flavored Vodka
1 part Triple Sec
1/2 part Currant-Flavored Vodka
1/2 part Citrus-Flavored Vodka
dash Angostura® Bitters
Cocktail Glass
Shake with ice and strain

Joulouville
1 part Gin
1/2 part Apple Brandy
splash Sweet Vermouth
1/2 part Lemon Juice
2 splashes Grenadine
Cocktail Glass
Shake with ice and strain

Joy Division
1 1/2 parts Coconut Liqueur
1/2 part Chocolate Liqueur
1 1/2 parts Frangelico®
1/2 part Cream
Cocktail Glass
Shake with ice and strain

Joy Jumper
1 1/2 parts Vodka
2 splashes Kümmel
splash Lime Juice
splash Lemon Juice
dash Sugar
1 Lemon Twist
Cocktail Glass
Shake with ice and strain

Judgette
1 part Dry Gin
1 part Dry Vermouth
1 part Peach Schnapps
splash Lime Juice
Cocktail Glass
Shake with ice and strain

Julia
1 part Pineapple Juice
1 part Dark Rum
1/2 part Blue Curaçao
1/2 part Parfait Amour
splash Simple Syrup
Cocktail Glass
Shake with ice and strain

Juliet
1 part Tequila Silver
1 part Pisang Ambon® Liqueur
1 part Pineapple Juice
splash Grenadine
Cocktail Glass

Shake with ice and strain

Jump for Joy
1 part Peach Schnapps
1 part Melon Liqueur
1/2 part Sour Mix
Cocktail Glass

Shake with ice and strain

Jumping Bean
1 1/2 parts Tequila
1/2 part Sambuca
3 Coffee Beans
Cocktail Glass

Shake with ice and strain. Top with Coffee Beans.

Juniper Blend
1 part Cherry Liqueur
1 part Gin
splash Dry Vermouth
Cocktail Glass

Shake with ice and strain

Jupiter Cocktail
2 parts Dry Gin
1 part Dry Vermouth
1/2 part Parfait Amour
1/2 part Orange Juice
Cocktail Glass

Shake with ice and strain

Just So Presto
1 1/2 parts Apricot Brandy
1/2 part Lemon Juice
1 part Orange Juice
Cocktail Glass

Shake with ice and strain

Kabut
1 1/2 parts Vanilla Liqueur
1 part Blue Curaçao
1/2 part Vodka
Cocktail Glass

Shake with ice and strain

Kahlodster
1 part Coffee Liqueur
1 part Vodka
1 part Jägermeister®
Cocktail Glass

Shake with ice and strain

Kama-Kura
1 1/2 parts Crème de Banana
1 1/2 parts Pineapple Juice
Cocktail Glass

Shake with ice and strain

Kangaroo
1 1/2 parts Vodka
3/4 part Dry Vermouth
Cocktail Glass

Shake with ice and strain

Kashmir
1 part Vodka
1 part Crème de Cacao (White)
2 splashes Grenadine
2 splashes Lemon Juice
Cocktail Glass

Shake with ice and strain

KC Rum
1 part Light Rum
1 part Coffee Liqueur
1 part Cream
Cocktail Glass

Shake with ice and strain

Kempinsky Fizz
2 parts Vodka
1 part Crème de Cassis
Cocktail Glass

Shake with ice and strain

Kentucky Mint
1 1/2 parts Bourbon
1/2 part Crème de Cacao (White)
1/2 part Crème de Menthe (White)
Cocktail Glass

Shake with ice and strain

Key Club Cocktail
2 parts Gin
1/2 part Light Rum
1/2 part Fresh Lime Juice
1/2 part Fernet-Branca®
Cocktail Glass

Shake with ice and strain

Kharamazov
1 part Coffee Liqueur
1 part Vodka
1 part Blue Curaçao
splash Orange Juice
Cocktail Glass

Shake with ice and strain

A Kick in the Bollocks
1 part Rum
1 part Peach Schnapps
1/2 part Coconut Cream
1 part Cream
1 part Orange Juice
Cocktail Glass

Shake with ice and strain

Kick in the Pants
1 part Triple Sec
1 part Cognac
1 part Bourbon
Cocktail Glass

Shake with ice and strain

Kicking Cow
1 part Rye Whiskey
1 part Maple Syrup
1 part Cream
Cocktail Glass

Shake with ice and strain

Kidney Machine
2/3 part Triple Sec
1 1/2 parts Dubonnet® Blonde
2/3 part Rémy Martin® VSOP
Cocktail Glass

Shake with ice and strain

Killer Whale
1 1/2 parts Blue Curaçao
splash Orange-Flavored Vodka
1 part Orange Juice
splash Pineapple Juice
dash Sugar
Cocktail Glass

Shake with ice and strain

Kilt Club
2/3 part Citrus-Flavored Vodka
1 part Kiwi Schnapps
1 part Drambuie®
1/2 part Pineapple Juice
Cocktail Glass

Shake with ice and strain

King Kooba
2 parts Dark Rum
1/2 part Brandy
1/2 part Triple Sec
1/2 part Lemon Juice
Cocktail Glass

Shake with ice and strain

King of Kingston
1 part Gin
1/2 part Crème de Banana
splash Grenadine
1 part Cream
1 part Pineapple Juice
splash Grapefruit Juice
Cocktail Glass
Shake with ice and strain

Kings Club
2 parts Bourbon
1/2 part Grenadine
1/2 part Fernet-Branca®
Cocktail Glass
Shake with ice and strain

Kinky Cherry
1/2 part Vodka
2 parts Cherry Brandy
1/2 part Jim Beam®
1/2 part Sweet Vermouth
1/2 part Lemon Juice
Cocktail Glass
Shake with ice and strain

Kiss and Tell
1 part Calvados Apple Brandy
1 part Sloe Gin
splash Lemon Juice
1 Egg White
Cocktail Glass
Shake with ice and strain

Kiss My Monkey
1 1/2 parts Passion Fruit Liqueur
1/2 part Crème de Banana
1/2 part Dry Vermouth
Cocktail Glass
Shake with ice and strain

Kiss the Boys Goodbye
3/4 part Brandy
3/4 part Sloe Gin
1 Lemon
1/2 Egg White
Cocktail Glass
Shake with ice and strain

Kissing Game
1 part Kiwi Schnapps
1 part Triple Sec
splash Lime Juice
Cocktail Glass
Shake with ice and strain

Kiwillingly
1 part Kiwi Schnapps
1/2 part Safari®
1 part Cachaça
1 part Lemon-Lime Soda
Cocktail Glass
Shake with ice and strain

Klondike
1 1/2 parts Irish Cream Liqueur
1 1/2 parts Yukon Jack®
Cocktail Glass
Shake with ice and strain

Knight-Errant
1 1/2 parts Gin
1/2 part Crème de Cassis
1 part Dry Sherry
Cocktail Glass
Shake with ice and strain

Koh-i-Noor
1 part Gin
1 part Maraschino Liqueur
1/2 part Crème de Menthe (White)
Cocktail Glass
Shake with ice and strain

Koko Smile
1 part Light Rum
1 part Peach Schnapps
1/2 part Kiwi Schnapps
1 part Cranberry Juice Cocktail
Cocktail Glass
Shake with ice and strain

Kriki
1 part Crème de Cacao (White)
1 part Crème de Menthe (Green)
1 part Cream
Cocktail Glass
Shake with ice and strain

Kuala Lumpur
1 1/2 parts Vodka
2/3 part Pisang Ambon® Liqueur
1 part Coconut-Flavored Liqueur
fill with Orange Juice
splash Cream
Cocktail Glass
Shake with ice and strain

Kulio Drink
1/2 part Whiskey
1/2 part Gin
1 part Triple Sec
1 part Lemon Juice
Cocktail Glass
Shake with ice and strain

Kyoto
1 1/2 parts Gin
1/2 part Apricot Brandy
1/2 part Triple Sec
1/2 part Dry Vermouth
Cocktail Glass
Shake with ice and strain

LA Cocktail
1 1/2 parts Whiskey
splash Sweet Vermouth
1 Egg White
dash Sugar
Cocktail Glass
Shake with ice and strain

La Carré
1 1/2 parts Vodka
2 splashes Dry Vermouth
2 splashes Kümmel
Cocktail Glass
Shake with ice and strain

La Fontaine Des Anges
1 part Jim Beam®
1/2 part Orange Liqueur
1/2 part Lemon Juice
1 part Orange Juice
Cocktail Glass
Shake with ice and strain

La Habana Affair
1 part Light Rum
1 part Sweet Vermouth
1 part Maraschino Liqueur
Cocktail Glass
Shake with ice and strain

La Jolla
1 1/2 parts Brandy
1/2 part Crème de Banana
2 splashes Lemon Juice
splash Orange Juice
Cocktail Glass
Shake with ice and strain

La Manga
1 part Vodka
1 part Apricot Brandy
1 part Licor 43®
splash Grenadine
Cocktail Glass
Shake with ice and strain

La Vida Loca
1 part Crème de Banana
1 part Cherry Brandy
1 part Melon Liqueur
1 part Coconut-Flavored Liqueur
Cocktail Glass
Shake with ice and strain

Labanga
1 part Triple Sec
1 part Melon Liqueur
1/2 part Green Chartreuse®
1/2 part Sour Mix
splash Maraschino Liqueur
Cocktail Glass
Shake with ice and strain

Ladbroke Treaty
2/3 part Gin
2/3 part Blackberry Liqueur
1/2 part Chartreuse®
splash Lemon Juice
1 part Pineapple Juice
Cocktail Glass
Shake with ice and strain

Ladies' Night
1 part Vodka
1/2 part Peach Schnapps
1/2 part Triple Sec
1/2 part Lemon Juice
Cocktail Glass
Shake with ice and strain

Lady 52
1 part Coffee Liqueur
1 part Irish Cream Liqueur
1 1/2 parts Cream
1/2 part Cointreau®
Cocktail Glass
Shake with ice and strain

Lady Bird
splash Coffee-Flavored Brandy
splash Crème de Cacao (White)
splash Vanilla Liqueur
2 parts Strawberry Juice
1 1/2 parts Cream
Cocktail Glass
Shake with ice and strain

Lady Diana
2 parts Gin
1 1/2 parts Campari®
1 part Fresh Lime Juice
1/2 part Simple Syrup
Cocktail Glass
Shake with ice and strain

Lady Finger
1 part Cherry Brandy
1 part Gin
1/2 part Kirschwasser
Cocktail Glass
Shake with ice and strain

Lady Liberty in a Thong
1 1/2 parts Dark Rum
1 part Coffee-Flavoured Brandy
2 splashes Lemon Juice
Cocktail Glass
Shake with ice and strain

Lady Man
1/2 part Peach Schnapps
1 part Vodka
splash Grenadine
splash Lemon Juice
splash Papaya Juice
Cocktail Glass

Shake with ice and strain

Lady Scarlett
1 part Gin
1 part Cointreau®
1/2 part Dry Vermouth
1/2 part Lime Juice
dash Bitters
Cocktail Glass

Shake with ice and strain

Laguna Cocktail
2 parts Brandy
1/4 part Vodka
1/4 part Vermouth
splash Campari®
dash Bitters
Cocktail Glass

Shake with ice and strain

L'Ambassadeur
1 1/2 parts Orange-Flavored Gin
1/2 part Crème de Banana
1/2 part Dry Vermouth
splash Lemon Juice
Cocktail Glass

Shake with ice and strain

Lambino
2/3 part Raspberry Liqueur
splash Blackberry Liqueur
1 part Crème de Cacao (White)
1 part Milk
Cocktail Glass

Shake with ice and strain

L'amour le Night
3/4 part Blue Curaçao
3/4 part Cream
3/4 part Amaretto
3/4 part Kirschwasser
Cocktail Glass

Shake with ice and strain

Landed Gentry
1 1/2 parts Dark Rum
1/2 part Tia Maria®
1 part Heavy Cream
Cocktail Glass

Shake with ice and strain

Lascivious Cream
1 1/2 parts Crème de Cacao (White)
1 1/2 parts Melon Liquer
Cocktail Glass

Shake with ice and strain

The Last Judgment
2 parts Brandy
1/2 part Amaretto
1/2 part Blue Curaçao
1 part Cream
Cocktail Glass

Shake with ice and strain

Last Tango
1 1/2 parts Gin
1/2 part Triple Sec
1 part Orange Juice
Cocktail Glass

Shake with ice and strain

The Last Warrior
2 parts Dark Rum
1/2 part Vanilla Liqueur
1/2 part Blackberry Liqueur
1 part Cream
Cocktail Glass

Shake with ice and strain

Latin Manhattan

1 part Dark Rum
1 part Sweet Vermouth
1 part Dry Vermouth
dash Bitters
Cocktail Glass

Shake with ice and strain

Lawhill Cocktail

1½ parts Whiskey
¾ part Dry Vermouth
¼ splash Anisette
¼ splash Maraschino Cherry
dash Bitters
Cocktail Glass

Shake with ice and strain

La-Z-Boy® Comfortable

1 part Amaretto
1 part Apricot Brandy
1 part Southern Comfort®
splash Sour Mix
Cocktail Glass

Shake with ice and strain

Le Cavalier Mysterieux

1 part Calvados Apple Brandy
⅔ part Irish Cream Liqueur
½ part Hazelnut Liqueur
splash Amaretto
1 part Cream
Cocktail Glass

Shake with ice and strain

Le Marseillaise

1 part Gin
1 part Blue Curaçao
½ part Pastis
splash Fresh Lime Juice
Cocktail Glass

Shake with ice and strain

Lele Free

⅔ part Amaretto
⅔ part Crème de Cacao (Dark)
½ part Amaretto
1 part Milk
Cocktail Glass

Shake with ice and strain

Lemon Lance

1 part Vanilla Liqueur
1 part Limoncello
splash Citrus-Flavored Vodka
splash Bacardi® Limón Rum
Cocktail Glass

Shake with ice and strain

Lemonade Claret

1½ parts Bourbon
½ part Sweet Vermouth
½ part Dry Vermouth
½ part Campari®
Cocktail Glass

Shake with ice and strain

L'enclume

1 part Gin
1 part Kirschwasser
½ part Rémy Martin® VSOP
½ part Grand Marnier®
Cocktail Glass

Shake with ice and strain

Les Fleurs du Mal

1½ parts Kirschwasser
1½ parts Dubonnet® Blonde
Cocktail Glass

Shake with ice and strain

Let's Party

1 part Melon Liqueur
½ part Pineapple Juice
splash Coconut Cream
splash Sour Mix
Cocktail Glass

Shake with ice and strain

Lexus
2 parts Brandy
1/2 part Triple Sec
1/2 part Vanilla Liqueur
Cocktail Glass

Shake with ice and strain

Licorice Stick
1 part Black Sambuca
1 part Vodka
1/2 part Crème de Cacao (White)
Cocktail Glass

Shake with ice and strain

Life Saver
1 part Light Rum
1 part Pineapple Juice
1/4 part Fresh Lime Juice
splash Blue Curaçao
splash Triple Sec
splash Simple Syrup
Cocktail Glass

Shake with ice and strain

Lifeline
1 part Light Rum
1/2 part Apricot Brandy
1/2 part Brandy
1/2 part Sweet Vermouth
1/2 part Triple Sec
Cocktail Glass

Shake with ice and strain

Light Blue Something
1 1/2 parts Rum
1 part Blue Curaçao
1 part Light Cream
Cocktail Glass

Shake with ice and strain

Light Saber
1/2 part Vodka
1/2 part 151-Proof Rum
1 part Crème de Banana
1/2 part Triple Sec
1/2 part Vanilla Liqueur
Cocktail Glass

Shake with ice and strain

Light Years
1 1/2 parts Drambuie®
1/2 part Blue Curaçao
1 part Cream
Cocktail Glass

Shake with ice and strain

Lightning
1 part Blue Curaçao
1 part Citrus-Flavored Vodka
splash Crème de Cassis
splash Lime Juice
Cocktail Glass

Shake with ice and strain

Lilith
1 part Kirschwasser
1 part Grand Marnier®
1 part Campari®
Cocktail Glass

Stir gently with ice and strain

Lillet® Pad
1 part Gin
splash Advocaat
1 1/2 parts Lillet®
Cocktail Glass

Shake with ice and strain

Lime Light
2 parts Vodka
1/2 part Melon Liqueur
1/2 part Grapefruit Juice
Cocktail Glass

Shake with ice and strain

The Limey

$2^1/_2$ parts Vodka
$^1/_2$ part Blue Curaçao
$^1/_2$ part Lime Juice
Cocktail Glass
Shake with ice and strain

Lino Ventura

1 part Irish Whiskey
$^1/_2$ part Frangelico®
$^1/_2$ part Benedictine®
splash Vanilla Liqueur
Cocktail Glass
Shake with ice and strain

Liquid Art

2 parts Crème de Cassis
1 part Apricot Brandy
$^1/_2$ part Lemon Juice
Cocktail Glass
Shake with ice and strain

Liquid Coma

$1^1/_2$ parts Dark Rum
$^1/_2$ part Southern Comfort®
$^1/_2$ part Crème de Cacao (Dark)
Cocktail Glass
Shake with ice and strain

Liquid Gold

1 part Vodka
$^1/_2$ part Galliano®
$^1/_2$ part Crème de Cacao (White)
1 part Cream
Cocktail Glass
Shake with ice and strain

Liquid Prozac

1 part Apricot Brandy
$^1/_2$ part Orange Juice
$^1/_2$ part Pineapple Juice
splash Amaretto
splash Lemon Juice
Cocktail Glass
Shake with ice and strain

Little Rascal

1 part Gin
$^1/_2$ part Crème de Cassis
splash Peppermint Liqueur
$^1/_2$ part Lemon Juice
$^1/_2$ part Water
Cocktail Glass
Shake with ice and strain

Liveliness

$^1/_2$ part Blue Curaçao
$1^1/_2$ parts Irish Whiskey
$^1/_2$ part Orange Juice
$^1/_2$ part Pineapple Juice
Cocktail Glass
Shake with ice and strain

Living Monument

$^1/_2$ part Amaretto
$^1/_2$ part Drambuie®
$^1/_2$ part Chocolate Liqueur
$1^1/_2$ parts Milk
Cocktail Glass
Shake with ice and strain

Lola

1 part Rum
$^1/_2$ part Crème de Cacao (White)
$^1/_2$ part Orange Juice
$^1/_2$ part Mandarine Napoléon® Liqueur
$^1/_2$ part Crème
Cocktail Glass
Shake with ice and strain

Lola Flores
1 part Gin
1 part Raspberry Liqueur
1 part Dry Sherry
Cocktail Glass
Shake with ice and strain

London Bridges
2 parts Gin
1/2 part Blue Curaçao
1/2 part Lime Cordial
1 part Lemon Juice
Cocktail Glass
Shake with ice and strain

London Kamikaze
1 part Gin
1 part Triple Sec
1/2 part Sweetened Lime Juice
Cocktail Glass
Shake with ice and strain

Loop
1 part Apricot Brandy
1 part Sweet Vermouth
1 part Gin
splash Whiskey
Cocktail Glass
Shake with ice and strain

Lopez
2/3 part Gin
2/3 part Crème de Cassis
1/2 part Peach Schnapps
1/2 part Sour Mix
Cocktail Glass
Shake with ice and strain

Lord Suffolk Cocktail
2 parts Dry Gin
1/2 part Sweet Vermouth
1/2 part Maraschino Liqueur
Cocktail Glass
Shake with ice and strain

Lorraine Cocktail
1 3/4 parts Kirschwasser
1/2 part Benedictine®
2 splashes Lime Juice
Cocktail Glass
Shake with ice and strain

Louisiana Sour
1 1/2 parts Bourbon
1/2 part Triple Sec
1/2 part Passion Fruit Nectar
1 part Pineapple Juice
Cocktail Glass
Shake with ice and strain

Louisville Cocktail
1 1/2 parts Whiskey
1/2 part Triple Sec
1/2 part Dry Sherry
2 dashes Orange Bitters
Cocktail Glass
Shake with ice and strain

Louisville Slugger
1 part Blackberry Brandy
1 part Dry Vermouth
1/2 part Lemon Juice
Cocktail Glass
Shake with ice and strain

Love Boat
1 part Vodka
1 part Coconut Cream
1 part Pineapple Juice
splash Blue Curaçao
Cocktail Glass
Shake with ice and strain

Love Bull

1/2 part Tequila Reposado
1/2 part Parfait Amour
1 part Lychee Liqueur
1 part Fresh Lime Juice
Cocktail Glass
Shake with ice and strain

Love Cocktail

2 parts Sloe Gin
splash Raspberry Juice
splash Lemon Juice
1 Egg White
Cocktail Glass
Shake with ice and strain

The Love Doctor

2 parts Vodka
1 part Crème de Cacao (White)
1/2 part Raspberry Liqueur
Cocktail Glass
Shake with ice and strain

Love Heart

1 part Vodka
1/2 part Orange Juice
1/2 part Passion Fruit
splash Peach Schnapps
Cocktail Glass
Shake with ice and strain

Love Story

1 part Whiskey
1/2 part Triple Sec
1/2 part Melon Liqueur
1/2 part Fresh Lime Juice
Cocktail Glass
Shake with ice and strain

Love Supreme

2/3 part Crème de Banana
splash Crème de Cacao (White)
splash Coffee Liqueur
splash Butterscotch Schnapps
splash Galliano®
1 part Cream
Cocktail Glass
Shake with ice and strain

Lovers Cocktail

2 parts Sloe Gin
1 Egg White
splash Lemon Juice
splash Raspberry Juice
Cocktail Glass
Shake with ice and strain

Lover's Kiss

1/2 part Amaretto
1/2 part Cherry Brandy
1/2 part Crème de Cacao (Dark)
1 part Cream
Cocktail Glass
Shake with ice and strain

LPR (Liquid Pants Remover)

1 part Dark Rum
1 part Vodka
1 part Tequila
1 part Southern Comfort®
1 part Amaretto
Cocktail Glass
Shake with ice and strain

Lucid

1 1/2 parts Cachaça
1 part Peppermint Liqueur
splash Dry Sherry
splash Simple Syrup
Cocktail Glass
Shake with ice and strain

Lucky Lady

1 part Dark Rum
1/2 part Crème de Cacao (White)
1/2 part Sambuca
1 part Cream
Cocktail Glass
Shake with ice and strain

Lugger

1 part Apple Brandy
1 part Brandy
1 part Apricot Brandy
Cocktail Glass
Shake with ice and strain

A Luke Skywalker

2 parts Blue Curaçao
1 part Gin
2 parts Dry Vermouth
splash Lemon Juice
Cocktail Glass
Shake with ice and strain

Luna City

1 part Sloe Gin
1 part Passion Fruit Liqueur
1 part Cranberry Juice Cocktail
splash Sour Mix
Cocktail Glass
Shake with ice and strain

Lunar Landing

1 1/2 parts Light Rum
3/4 part Brandy
2 splashes Grenadine
splash Lemon Juice
Cocktail Glass
Shake with ice and strain

Luxury

1 part Dry Gin
1 part Crème de Banana
1 part Sweet Vermouth
1 part Fresh Lime Juice
1 part Pimm's® No. 1 Cup
dash Bitters
Cocktail Glass
Shake with ice and strain

Lylyblue

1 part Vodka
1 part Fresh Lime Juice
1 part Lychee Liqueur
splash Blue Curaçao
Cocktail Glass
Shake with ice and strain

Lysogenenis

1 part Light Rum
1/2 part Crème de Cacao (Dark)
2/3 part Milk
splash Blue Curaçao
Cocktail Glass
Shake with ice and strain

Ma Bonnie Wee Hen

1 1/2 parts Scotch
1/2 part Cream Sherry
1/2 part Orange Juice
1/2 part Lemon Juice
splash Grenadine
Cocktail Glass
Shake with ice and strain

Mac Daddy

2 parts Gin
1/2 part Maraschino Liqueur
1 part Pineapple Juice
Cocktail Glass
Shake with ice and strain

Macaroni Cocktail
1 1/2 parts Absinthe
1 1/2 parts Sweet Vermouth
Cocktail Glass

Shake with ice and strain

Macaroon
2 parts Vodka
1/2 part Amaretto
1/2 part Crème de Cacao (Dark)
Cocktail Glass

Shake with ice and strain

Macbeth
2 parts Scotch
2 splashes Blue Curaçao
2 splashes Amaretto
1/2 part Lemon Juice
1 splash Sugar
Cocktail Glass

Shake with ice and strain

Machiavelli
1 part Crème de Banana
splash Galliano®
splash Anisette
1 part Lemon Juice
Cocktail Glass

Shake with ice and strain

Machintoch
1 part Vodka
1/2 part Blackberry Liqueur
1/2 part Apple Brandy
2 parts Cream
Cocktail Glass

Shake with ice and strain

Macubo
2 parts Whiskey
3/4 part Blue Curaçao
1/2 part Simple Syrup
1/4 part Maraschino Liqueur
Cocktail Glass

Shake with ice and strain

Madam Delight
1 part Blackberry Liqueur
1 part Amaretto
1/2 part Orange Juice
1/2 part Milk
Cocktail Glass

Shake with ice and strain

Madame Butterfly
1 part Apple Brandy
1 part Gin
1/2 part Blue Curaçao
1/2 part Dry Vermouth
Cocktail Glass

Shake with ice and strain

Madeira Cocktail
1 1/2 parts Rye Whiskey
1 1/2 parts Triple Sec
splash Grenadine
splash Lemon Juice
Cocktail Glass

Shake with ice and strain

Magic Star
3/4 part Crème de Cacao (White)
3/4 part Pisang Ambon® Liqueur
1/2 part Cream
1/2 part Kiwi Schnapps
splash Grenadine
Cocktail Glass

Shake with ice and strain

Magician
1/4 part Cointreau®
1 1/2 parts Gin
1/4 part Grand Marnier®
splash Dry Vermouth
1/2 part Lillet®
Cocktail Glass

Shake with ice and strain

Mah-Jonng
1/2 part Cointreau®
1 part Gin
1/2 part Dark Rum
Cocktail Glass

Shake with ice and strain

Mahukona
2 parts Light Rum
1/2 part Triple Sec
1/4 part Amaretto
dash Orange Bitters
Cocktail Glass

Shake with ice and strain

Maiden's Dream
1 part Gin
1 part Pernod®
1 part Grenadine
Cocktail Glass

Shake with ice and strain

Majestic
1 part Gin
1 part Grapefruit Juice
1/2 part Crème de Banana
Cocktail Glass

Shake with ice and strain

Majoba
1 part Dark Rum
1/2 part Triple Sec
1/4 part Crème de Cacao (Dark)
1/4 part Crème de Banana
splash Pineapple Juice
Cocktail Glass

Shake with ice and strain

Major Tom
1 1/2 parts Vodka
1/2 part Triple Sec
1/2 part Kirschwasser
1/2 part Grapefruit Juice
Cocktail Glass

Shake with ice and strain

Malibu Wave
1 part Tequila
1/2 part Triple Sec
1 1/2 parts Sour Mix
splash Blue Curaçao
Cocktail Glass

Shake with ice and strain

Malmaison
2 parts Light Rum
1/2 part Cream Sherry
2 splashes Lemon Juice
Cocktail Glass

Shake with ice and strain

Maltese Skies
1 part Orange Juice
1 part Dark Rum
1/2 part Parfait Amour
1/2 part Passion Fruit
Cocktail Glass

Shake with ice and strain

Mama Mia
1 1/2 parts Vodka
1 part Amaretto
1/2 part Cream
Cocktail Glass

Shake with ice and strain

Man Eater
1 1/2 parts Brandy
1/2 part Southern Comfort®
dash Orange Bitters
Cocktail Glass

Shake with ice and strain

Manana
$1^1/_2$ parts Light Rum
$^1/_2$ part Apricot Brandy
$^1/_2$ part Grenadine
Cocktail Glass

Shake with ice and strain

Mandarin Dream
2 parts Orange-Flavored Vodka
splash Orange Juice
splash Cranberry Juice Cocktail
Cocktail Glass

Shake with ice and strain

Mandarin Metropolitan
$1^1/_2$ parts Orange-Flavored Vodka
1 part Cranberry Juice Cocktail
$^1/_2$ part Sweetened Lime Juice
Cocktail Glass

Shake with ice and strain

Manhasset
$1^1/_2$ parts Whiskey
splash Sweet Vermouth
splash Dry Vermouth
2 splashes Lemon Juice
Cocktail Glass

Shake with ice and strain

Manhattan South
1 part Gin
$^1/_2$ part Southern Comfort®
$^1/_2$ part Dry Vermouth
dash Angostura® Bitters
Cocktail Glass

Shake with ice and strain

Manhattan (Perfect)
$1^1/_2$ parts Whiskey
$^1/_2$ part Dry Vermouth
$^1/_2$ part Sweet Vermouth
Cocktail Glass

Shake with ice and strain

Maple Leaf
1 part Canadian Club® Rye
$^1/_4$ part Lemon Juice
splash Maple Syrup
Cocktail Glass

Shake with ice and strain

Maraca
$1^1/_2$ parts Tequila
$^1/_2$ part Lemon Juice
2 splashes Grenadine
1 part Pineapple Juice
Cocktail Glass

Shake with ice and strain

Mardi Gras
$1^1/_2$ parts Light Rum
$^1/_2$ part Fresh Lime Juice
$^1/_4$ part Crème de Banana
$^1/_4$ part Southern Comfort®
Cocktail Glass

Shake with ice and strain

Mariachi-Loco
$1^1/_2$ parts Sour Mix
1 part Passion Fruit
$^1/_2$ part Tequila Reposado
Cocktail Glass

Shake with ice and strain

Marina
$1^1/_2$ parts Dry Gin
1 part Dry Vermouth
2 dashes Parfait Amour
splash Lemon Juice
Cocktail Glass

Shake with ice and strain

Mariposa
1 part Light Rum
1/2 part Brandy
splash Grenadine
2 splashes Orange Juice
2 splashes Lemon Juice
Cocktail Glass

Shake with ice and strain

Marital Bliss
1 part Light Rum
1 part Apricot Brandy
1 part Melon Liqueur
Cocktail Glass

Shake with ice and strain

Marmalade Cocktail
2 parts Gin
1 part Lemon Juice
2 splashes Orange Marmalade
Cocktail Glass

Shake with ice and strain

Martinez Cocktail
1 part Gin
1 part Dry Vermouth
1/4 splash Triple Sec
dash Orange Bitters
Cocktail Glass

Stir gently with ice and strain

Massive Attack
2 parts Tequila Silver
1/2 part Cherry Brandy
1/2 part Galliano®
1/2 part Lemon Juice
Cocktail Glass

Shake with ice and strain

Matrix
1 part Light Rum
1/2 part Triple Sec
1/2 part Passion Fruit
1/2 part Lime Cordial
splash Grenadine
Cocktail Glass

Shake with ice and strain

Maurice Cocktail
1 part Gin
1/2 part Sweet Vermouth
1/2 part Dry Vermouth
1/2 part Orange Juice
dash Bitters
Cocktail Glass

Shake with ice and strain

Max the Silent
1 part Añejo Rum
1/2 part Brandy
1/2 part Applejack
splash Anisette
Cocktail Glass

Shake with ice and strain

Maxim
1 1/2 parts Gin
1 part Dry Vermouth
splash Crème de Cacao (White)
Cocktail Glass

Shake with ice and strain

Mazatlan Morning
1 part Blackberry Liqueur
1 part Tequila Silver
splash Lime Juice
1 part Lemon-Lime Soda
1/2 part Honey
Cocktail Glass

Shake with ice and strain over ice

McDuff
1 1/2 parts Scotch
1/2 part Triple Sec
2 dashes Bitters
Cocktail Glass
Shake with ice and strain

Me Amigo de la Canaria
1/2 part Lychee Liqueur
2/3 part Lemon Juice
2/3 part Mango Juice
1 part Passion Fruit Juice
Cocktail Glass
Shake with ice and strain

Medical Solution
1 1/2 parts Vodka
1/2 part Parfait Amour
1 part Cream
Cocktail Glass
Shake with ice and strain

Mediterranean Delight
2 parts Gin
1/2 part Crème de Banana
1/2 part Grapefruit Juice
Cocktail Glass
Shake with ice and strain

Mellon Collie and the Infinite Gladness
1 part Light Rum
1/2 part Melon Liqueur
1/2 part Coconut-Flavored Rum
1/2 part Chocolate Syrup
1 part Cream
Cocktail Glass
Shake with ice and strain

Melon Heaven
1 part Vodka
1 part Melon Liqueur
1/2 part Triple Sec
1/2 part Lime Juice
Cocktail Glass
Shake with ice and strain

Melon Lychee
1 1/2 parts Melon Liqueur
1/2 part Lychee Liqueur
1 part Grapefruit Juice
Cocktail Glass
Shake with ice and strain

Melrose Beauty
1 part Vodka
1/2 part Raspberry Liqueur
1/2 part Cranberry Juice Cocktail
splash Pineapple Juice
splash Lemon Juice
splash Lime Juice
Cocktail Glass
Shake with ice and strain

Memphis Belle Cocktail
1 1/2 parts Brandy
3/4 part Southern Comfort®
1/2 part Lemon Juice
4 dashes Bitters
Cocktail Glass
Shake with ice and strain

Ménage à Trois
1 part Dark Rum
1 part Triple Sec
1 part Light Cream
Cocktail Glass
Shake with ice and strain

Mentholated Cognac
1 part Peppermint Liqueur
1 part Rémy Martin® VSOP
1 part Dry Vermouth
Cocktail Glass
Shake with ice and strain

Merchant Prince

2/3 part Vodka
1 part Cherry Brandy
2/3 part Drambuie®
2/3 part Vanilla Liqueur
Cocktail Glass

Shake with ice and strain

Merletto

1 part Crème de Cacao (White)
1 part Advocaat
1 part Coffee
Cocktail Glass

Shake with ice and strain

Mermaid

1 part Aquavit
1/2 part Dry Vermouth
1/2 part Cherry Brandy
splash Egg White
splash Lime Cordial
Cocktail Glass

Shake with ice and strain

Merry Widow Cocktail

1 1/2 parts Dry Vermouth
1 1/2 parts Gin
splash Benedictine®
splash Anisette
dash Bitters
Lemon Twist
Cocktail Glass

Shake with ice and strain

Meteorite

1 1/2 parts Vodka
1/2 part Triple Sec
1/2 part Cherry Brandy
2/3 part Dry Vermouth
Cocktail Glass

Shake with ice and strain

Metropolitan

2 parts Brandy
1/2 part Sweet Vermouth
dash Bitters
dash Sugar
Cocktail Glass

Shake with ice and strain

Mets Manhattan

1 1/2 parts Whiskey
1/4 part Sweet Vermouth
1/4 part Strawberry Liqueur
Cocktail Glass

Shake with ice and strain

Mexican Bee Sting

1 1/2 parts Tequila
splash Pernod®
splash Crème de Menthe (White)
Cocktail Glass

Shake with ice and strain

Mexican Clover Club

1 1/2 parts Tequila Silver
1/2 part Grenadine
1/2 part Simple Syrup
1 Egg White
Cocktail Glass

Shake with ice and strain

Mexican Sheets

2/3 part Tequila Silver
2/3 part Triple Sec
1 part Peach Schnapps
1/2 part Sour Mix
splash Lime Juice
Cocktail Glass

Shake with ice and strain

Mexican Snowball

2/3 part Crème de Cacao (Dark)
2/3 part Tequila Silver
2/3 part Cream
2/3 part Coconut Cream
Cocktail Glass

Shake with ice and strain

Mexican Surfer

2 parts Coconut-Flavored Rum
2 parts Tequila
Cocktail Glass

Shake with ice and strain

Mexico City Ambulance

1 part Tequila Silver
1 part Melon Liqueur
1/2 part Sour Mix
1/2 part Grapefruit Juice
Cocktail Glass

Shake with ice and strain

Mezzanine

2 parts Brandy
splash Blue Curaçao
splash Kirschwasser
splash Maraschino Liqueur
splash Dark Rum
Cocktail Glass

Shake with ice and strain

Mi Casa, Su Casa

splash Raspberry Liqueur
1/2 part Grand Marnier®
1/2 part Gold Tequila
splash Lime Juice
Cocktail Glass

Shake with ice and strain

Mia Vida

1 part Tequila Reposado
1/2 part Cream
1/2 part Crème de Cacao (Dark)
Cocktail Glass

Shake with ice and strain

Miami Beach Cocktail

1 part Dry Vermouth
1 part Scotch
1 part Grapefruit Juice
Cocktail Glass

Shake with ice and strain

Miami Special

1 part Light Rum
1/4 part Crème de Menthe (White)
3/4 part Lemon Juice
Cocktail Glass

Shake with ice and strain

Mickie Walker Cocktail

2 parts Scotch
1 part Sweet Vermouth
splash Grenadine
Cocktail Glass

Shake with ice and strain

Midnight Cap

2 parts Apricot Brandy
1/2 part Blue Curaçao
1/2 part Lemon Juice
Cocktail Glass

Shake with ice and strain

Midnight Delight

1 1/2 parts Vodka
1 part Crème de Cacao (White)
1 part Chocolate Mint Liqueur
Cocktail Glass

Shake with ice and strain

Midnight Joy
1 1/2 parts Crème de Cacao (White)
1 1/2 parts Black Sambuca
Cocktail Glass
Shake with ice and strain

Midnight Rhapsody
1/2 part Crème de Cacao (Dark)
1/2 part Whiskey
1/4 part Crème de Menthe (White)
1/4 part Vanilla-Flavored Vodka
1 part Cream
Cocktail Glass
Shake with ice and strain

Midnight Sun
2 parts Vodka
1 part Cointreau®
1 part Apricot Brandy
1 part Grenadine
1/2 part Lemon Juice
Cocktail Glass
Shake with ice and strain

Midsummernight's Dreamer
2/3 part Blackberry Liqueur
1 part Sloe Gin
1/2 part Lemon Juice
1/2 part Cherry Syrup
Cocktail Glass
Shake with ice and strain

MILF
1/2 part Irish Cream Liqueur
1/2 part Frangelico®
1/2 part Light Rum
1 part Cream
Cocktail Glass
Shake with ice and strain

Miller's Special
2 parts Gin
1/2 part Lychee Liqueur
splash Crème de Cassis
splash Lime Juice
Cocktail Glass
Shake with ice and strain

Millionaire Cocktail
1 1/2 parts Whiskey
1/2 part Triple Sec
splash Grenadine
1 Egg White
Cocktail Glass
Shake with ice and strain

Mintzerac
2/3 part Vodka
1 part Peppermint Liqueur
1/2 part Melon Liqueur
1/2 part Lime Juice
Cocktail Glass
Shake with ice and strain

Mirage
1 part Melon Liqueur
1 part Pineapple Juice
1/2 part Lemon Juice
1/2 part Strawberry Juice
Cocktail Glass
Shake with ice and strain

Mirror Conspiracy
2 parts Light Rum
1/2 part Amer Picon®
splash Cherry Brandy
splash Pear Liqueur
Cocktail Glass
Shake with ice and strain

Miss Belle
$1^1/_2$ parts Dark Rum
$^1/_2$ part Grand Marnier®
2 splashes Crème de Cacao (Dark)
Cocktail Glass

Shake with ice and strain

Mississippi Steamboat
1 part Amaretto
1 part Brandy
1 part Pineapple Juice
splash Lime Juice
Cocktail Glass

Shake with ice and strain

Missouri Mule
$1^1/_2$ parts Bourbon
1 part Crème de Cassis
Cocktail Glass

Shake with ice and strain

Missouri Rattlesnake
1 part Southern Comfort®
1 part Triple Sec
$^1/_2$ part Grenadine
1 part Orange Juice
Cocktail Glass

Shake with ice and strain

Mocha Mint
1 part Coffee-Flavored Brandy
1 part Crème de Menthe (White)
1 part Crème de Cacao (White)
Cocktail Glass

Shake with ice and strain

Mockingbird
$1^1/_2$ parts Tequila
1 part Lime Juice
2 splashes Crème de Menthe (White)
Cocktail Glass

Shake with ice and strain

Modern Castle
1 part Melon Liqueur
$^1/_2$ part Peppermint Liqueur
1 part Irish Cream Liqueur
1 part Milk
Cocktail Glass

Shake with ice and strain

Moll Flanders Cocktail
$1^1/_2$ parts Gin
1 part Sloe Gin
1 part Dry Vermouth
Cocktail Glass

Shake with ice and strain

Molokini
1 part Kiwi Schnapps
1 part Blue Curaçao
splash Lime Juice
Cocktail Glass

Shake with ice and strain

Mon Amour
$1^1/_2$ parts Gin
$^1/_2$ part Orange Juice
$^1/_4$ part Sake
Cocktail Glass

Shake with ice and strain

Mon Cherie
1 part Crème de Cacao (White)
1 part Cream
1 part Cherry Brandy
Cocktail Glass

Shake with ice and strain

Monkey Gland Cocktail
2 parts Gin
splash Benedictine®
$^1/_2$ part Orange Juice
splash Grenadine
Cocktail Glass

Shake with ice and strain

Montmarte
2 parts Gin
1/2 part Triple Sec
1/2 part Sweet Vermouth
Cocktail Glass

Shake with ice and strain

Montreal after Dark
1 1/2 parts Crème de Cacao (White)
1 1/2 parts Whiskey
splash Cream
Cocktail Glass

Shake with ice and strain

Moo Moo Land
1 part Light Rum
1 part Crème de Banana
1/4 part Grenadine
1 1/2 parts Cream
Cocktail Glass

Shake with ice and strain

Moon Quake Shake
1 part Coffee-Flavored Brandy
1 1/2 parts Dark Rum
2 splashes Lemon Juice
Cocktail Glass

Shake with ice and strain

Moonglow
1 1/2 parts Crème de Menthe (White)
1 1/2 parts Brandy
Cocktail Glass

Shake with ice and strain

Moonlight
1 part Cream
1 part Cognac
1 part Chocolate Mint Liqueur
splash Mandarine Napoléon® Liqueur
Cocktail Glass

Shake with ice and strain

Moonshine Bells
1 1/2 parts Triple Sec
1 part Fresh Lime Juice
1 part Triple Sec
splash Blackcurrant Juice
Cocktail Glass

Shake with ice and strain

Moose River Hummer
1 part Galliano®
1 part 151-Proof Rum
1 part Rye Whiskey
1 part Rumple Minze®
Cocktail Glass

Shake with ice and strain

Morgan's Mountain
1 1/2 parts Spiced Rum
1/2 part Crème de Cacao (White)
1 part Heavy Cream
splash Coffee Liqueur
Cocktail Glass

Shake with ice and strain

Morituri te Salutant
1/2 part Cherry Brandy
1/2 part Dry Vermouth
1/2 part Campari®
1 1/2 parts Light Rum
Cocktail Glass

Shake with ice and strain

Mortal Kombat®
2/3 part Lychee Liqueur
2 parts Sake
1/2 part Lemon Juice
splash Tabasco® Sauce
Cocktail Glass

Shake with ice and strain

Mother Russia
$1^1/_2$ parts Vodka
$^1/_2$ part Maraschino Liqueur
$^1/_2$ part Coconut-Flavored Rum
1 part Cream
$^1/_2$ part Egg White
Cocktail Glass

Shake with ice and strain

Mother Tongue
1 part Crème de Banana
1 part Red Curaçao
$^1/_4$ part Light Rum
splash Simple Syrup
Cocktail Glass

Shake with ice and strain

Mounds Bar Cocktail
$1^1/_2$ parts Chocolate-Flavored Vodka
$1^1/_2$ parts Coconut-Flavored Rum
Cocktail Glass

Shake with ice and strain

Mousse Cherry
1 part Vodka
1 part Grapefruit Juice
$^1/_2$ part Cherry Brandy
Cocktail Glass

Shake with ice and strain

Mozart
$1^1/_2$ parts Añejo Rum
$^1/_2$ part Sweet Vermouth
splash Triple Sec
2 dashes Orange Bitters
1 Lemon Twist
Cocktail Glass

Shake with ice and strain

Mr. Manhattan Cocktail
2 parts Gin
dash Powdered Sugar
$^1/_2$ part Mineral Water
splash Orange Juice
4 Mint Leaves
Cocktail Glass

Muddle the Mint with the Water and Sugar in the bottom of a shaker. Add Gin and Orange Juice. Shake with ice and strain.

Muddy River
1 part Coffee Liqueur
1 part Coconut-Flavored Rum
1 part Light Cream
Cocktail Glass

Shake with ice and strain

Mulata
2 parts Light Rum
$^1/_2$ part Crème de Cacao (Dark)
$^1/_4$ part Sugar
Cocktail Glass

Shake with ice and strain

Mule's Hind Leg
$^3/_4$ part Gin
$^3/_4$ part Brandy
$^3/_4$ part Benedictine®
$^3/_4$ part Simple Syrup
Cocktail Glass

Shake with ice and strain

Multi-Colored Smurf®
$^1/_2$ part Blueberry Schnapps
$^1/_2$ part Apricot Brandy
$^1/_2$ part Vodka
$^1/_2$ part Mango Nectar
1 part Orange Juice
Cocktail Glass

Shake with ice and strain

Muse
1 part Blackberry Liqueur
1 part Advocaat
1 part Apple Brandy
Cocktail Glass

Shake with ice and strain

Mutiny
1 1/2 parts Dark Rum
1/2 part Dubonnet® Rouge
2 dashes Bitters
Cocktail Glass

Shake with ice and strain

Mystic
1 1/2 parts Sloe Gin
1/2 part Triple Sec
2/3 part Lemon Juice
splash Honey
1 part Apple Juice
Cocktail Glass

Shake with ice and strain

Mysticism
1 part Scotch
1/2 part Triple Sec
1/2 part Sweetened Lime Juice
splash Lemon Juice
Cocktail Glass

Shake with ice and strain

Nachtmar
1 part Peach Schnapps
1 part Jägermeister®
1 part Cranberry Juice Cocktail
Cocktail Glass

Shake with ice and strain

Naked Lady
1 part Light Rum
1 part Sweet Vermouth
splash Apricot Brandy
splash Lemon Juice
splash Grenadine
Cocktail Glass

Shake with ice and strain

Naked Pear
1/2 part Apple-Flavored Vodka
1/2 part Melon Liqueur
1/2 part Triple Sec
1 part Pineapple Juice
splash Sour Mix
Cocktail Glass

Shake with ice and strain

Napoleon
2 parts Gin
splash Blue Curaçao
splash Dubonnet® Blonde
Cocktail Glass

Shake with ice and strain

Nasty
1 1/4 parts Vodka
3/4 part Coffee Liqueur
3/4 part Wild Turkey® Bourbon
3/4 part Crème de Cacao (Dark)
1/2 part Cream
Cocktail Glass

Shake with ice and strain

National Cocktail
2 parts Rum
3 splashes Apricot Brandy
1/2 part Pineapple Juice
3 splashes Lime Juice
Cocktail Glass

Shake with ice and strain

Nature
1 part Tequila Reposado
1 part Peach Schnapps
1 part Cream
Cocktail Glass

Shake with ice and strain

Naughty Farmer
1 part Sloe Gin
1 part Kirschwasser
1 part Cream
splash Amaretto
Cocktail Glass

Shake with ice and strain

Navy Cocktail
1 1/2 parts Light Rum
1 part Orange Juice
1 part Dry Vermouth
Cocktail Glass

Shake with ice and strain

Negroni
2 parts Gin
3/4 part Campari®
1/2 part Dry Vermouth
Cocktail Glass

Shake with ice and strain. Garnish with an Orange Twist.

NeO
1 part Jim Beam®
1 part Crème de Cassis
1/2 part Cinzano®
splash Apple Juice
Cocktail Glass

Shake with ice and strain

Neon Lights
1 1/2 parts Tequila Silver
1/2 part Melon Liqueur
1/2 part Blue Curaçao
1/2 part Lime Juice
Cocktail Glass

Shake with ice and strain

Neopolitan Cocktail
1 1/2 parts Cranberry-Flavored Vodka
1/2 part Cointreau®
splash Raspberry Liqueur
splash Lime Juice
Cocktail Glass

Shake with ice and strain

Neptune's Pond
1 1/2 parts Vodka
1 1/2 parts Dubonnet® Blonde
Cocktail Glass

Shake with ice and strain

Network Special
1 1/2 parts Light Rum
1/2 part Coffee-Flavored Brandy
1 splash 151-Proof Rum
1/4 part Crème
Cocktail Glass

Shake with ice and strain

New Gold Dream
1 1/2 parts Goldschläger®
1 part Galliano®
1/2 part Cream
Cocktail Glass

Shake with ice and strain

New Mexico
1 part Mescal
1/2 part Blue Curaçao
1/2 part Triple Sec
1/2 part Grand Marnier®
1/2 part Lemon Juice
Cocktail Glass

Shake with ice and strain

New Orleans Cocktail

2 parts Bourbon
1/2 part Pernod®
splash Simple Syrup
splash Anisette
dash Orange Bitters
Old Fashioned Glass

Shake with ice and strain over ice

New Orleans Hooker

1 part Southern Comfort®
1 part Blackberry Liqueur
splash Vanilla Liqueur
Cocktail Glass

Shake with ice and strain

New Wave

1 part Peach
1 part Pineapple Juice
1 part Cream
Cocktail Glass

Shake with ice and strain

New York Lemonade

1 part Citrus-Flavored Vodka
1/2 part Grand Marnier®
1/2 part Lemon Juice
1 part Club Soda
Cocktail Glass

Stir gently with ice and strain

Newport Chocolate

2/3 part Crème de Cacao (White)
2/3 part Chocolate Mint Liqueur
2/3 part Irish Cream Liqueur
1 part Milk
Cocktail Glass

Shake with ice and strain

Nicky Finn

1 part Apricot Brandy
1 part Cointreau®
1 part Lemon Juice
splash Pernod®
Cocktail Glass

Shake with ice and strain

A Night in Corfu

1 part Banana Liqueur
1 part Light Rum
splash Grenadine
1 part Lemon Juice
splash Milk
Cocktail Glass

Shake with ice and strain over ice

Night Light

1 1/2 parts Rum
1 part Triple Sec
1 Egg Yolk
Cocktail Glass

Shake with ice and strain

Night Stars

1 part Brandy
1/2 part Whiskey
1/2 part Triple Sec
splash Crème de Banana
splash Apple Juice
Cocktail Glass

Shake with ice and strain

Nightmare

1 1/2 parts Gin
1/2 part Cherry Brandy
1/2 part Madeira
splash Orange Juice
Cocktail Glass

Shake with ice and strain

Nineteen and Single
2/3 part Raspberry Liqueur
2/3 part Blackberry Liqueur
1 part Irish Cream Liqueur
1 part Milk
Cocktail Glass

Shake with ice and strain

Nineteen Twenty
1 part Dry Vermouth
1 part Gin
1 part Kirschwasser
splash Pastis
Cocktail Glass

Shake with ice and strain

Nineteenth Hole
1 1/2 parts Gin
1 part Dry Vermouth
splash Sweet Vermouth
dash Bitters
Cocktail Glass

Shake with ice and strain

Ninotchka Cocktail
1 1/2 parts Vodka
1/2 part Crème de Cacao (White)
1/2 part Lemon Juice
Cocktail Glass

Shake with ice and strain

Nitro Cocktail
1 1/2 parts Vodka
3/4 part Scotch
1 part Cranberry Juice Cocktail
1 part Orange Juice
Collins Glass

Build over ice and stir

Nocturnal
1 1/2 parts Crème de Cacao (Dark)
1 1/2 parts Cream
Cocktail Glass

Shake with ice and strain

Nomad
1 part Cointreau®
1 part Melon Liqueur
1 part Lemon Juice
Cocktail Glass

Shake with ice and strain

Nordic Sea
1 part Dry Gin
1 part Kiwi Schnapps
1/2 part Blue Curaçao
splash Pineapple Juice
Cocktail Glass

Shake with ice and strain

North Pole Cocktail
1 part Gin
1/2 part Maraschino Liqueur
1/2 part Lemon Juice
1 Egg White
Cocktail Glass

Shake with ice and strain

Northern Exposure
1 1/2 parts Gin
1 part Apricot Brandy
1 part Triple Sec
2 splashes Lemon Juice
Cocktail Glass

Shake with ice and strain

Nostromo
1 part Limoncello
1/2 part Apricot Brandy
1/2 part Mandarine Napoléon® Liqueur
1/2 part Lemon Juice
1/2 part Simple Syrup
Cocktail Glass

Shake with ice and strain

Nostromo's Chaser
1 part Armagnac
1/2 part Vanilla Liqueur
1/2 part Gin
splash Crème de Noyaux
dash Orange Bitters
Cocktail Glass

Stir gently with ice and strain

Notre Dame
1 part Calvados Apple Brandy
1/2 part Blue Curaçao
splash Lemon Juice
Cocktail Glass

Shake with ice and strain

Nougat Ice Cream
1 part Cream
1 part Hazelnut Liqueur
1 part Vanilla Liqueur
Cocktail Glass

Shake with ice and strain

Nuts and Berries
1 part Frangelico®
1 part Raspberry Liqueur
1 part Light Cream
Cocktail Glass

Shake with ice and strain

Nutty Stinger
1 1/2 parts Amaretto
1 1/2 parts Crème de Menthe (White)
Cocktail Glass

Shake with ice and strain

Oakland Cocktail
1 part Vodka
1 part Dry Vermouth
1 part Orange Juice
Cocktail Glass

Shake with ice and strain

Obsession
1 part Vodka
1/2 part Passion Fruit Liqueur
1/2 part Pisang Ambon® Liqueur
1 part Orange Juice
Cocktail Glass

Shake with ice and strain

Obsidian
1 part Dark Rum
1/2 part Blackberry Liqueur
1/2 part Black Sambuca
1/2 part Lemon Juice
splash Cherry Brandy
Cocktail Glass

Shake with ice and strain

Ocean Drive
1 1/2 parts Coconut-Flavored Rum
3/4 part Blue Curaçao
splash Orange Juice
splash Pineapple Juice
splash Cranberry Juice Cocktail
Cocktail Glass

Shake with ice and strain

Oceanographer
1/2 part Light Rum
1/2 part Peach Schnapps
1/2 part Apple Brandy
1/2 part Cranberry Juice Cocktail
1/2 part Orange Juice
1/2 part Pineapple Juice
Cocktail Glass

Shake with ice and strain

Odin's Juice
1 1/2 parts Coconut-Flavored Rum
1/2 part Spiced Rum
splash Grenadine
splash Orange Juice
splash Pineapple Juice
Cocktail Glass

Shake with ice and strain

Off-White
1 part Vodka
1 part Amaretto
1 part Coconut-Flavored Liqueur
1 part Vanilla Liqueur
Cocktail Glass
Shake with ice and strain

Old Car
1 part Vodka
1/2 part Apricot Brandy
1/2 part Triple Sec
1/4 part Grapefruit Juice
Cocktail Glass
Shake with ice and strain

Old Etonion
1 part Gin
1 part Lillet®
2 splashes Crème de Noyaux
2 dashes Orange Bitters
Cocktail Glass
Shake with ice and strain

Old San Juan Cocktail
1 1/2 parts Dark Rum
1/4 part Grenadine
1/4 part Pineapple Juice
Cocktail Glass
Shake with ice and strain

Old Switzerland
1 part Amaretto
splash Crème de Cacao (White)
splash Chocolate Syrup
Cocktail Glass
Shake with ice and strain

Olden Times
1 1/2 parts Scotch
1 1/2 parts Carpano Punt e Mes®
1/2 part Cherry Brandy
Cocktail Glass
Shake with ice and strain

Ole
2 parts Tequila Silver
1 part Coffee
1/2 part Simple Syrup
Cocktail Glass
Shake with ice and strain

Olive in an Olive
1 1/2 parts Gold Tequila
1 1/2 parts Sweet Vermouth
splash Blue Curaçao
1 Olive
Cocktail Glass
Shake with ice and strain

Omen of Fire
1 part Orange Liqueur
1 part Kirschwasser
1 part Apricot Brandy
Cocktail Glass
Shake with ice and strain

On the Loose
1 part Light Rum
1 part Triple Sec
1 part Cherry Brandy
splash Banana Juice
Cocktail Glass
Shake with ice and strain

On Top of the Sheets
1/2 part Triple Sec
1 part Rémy Martin® VSOP
splash Limoncello
splash Lime Juice
1/2 part Simple Syrup
Cocktail Glass
Shake with ice and strain

Oompa Loompa
1/2 part Vodka
1/2 part Chocolate Mint Liqueur
1/2 part Banana Liqueur
1 1/2 parts Light Cream
Cocktail Glass
Shake with ice and strain

Opa Cocktail
1 1/2 parts Gin
1 part Orange Juice
1/2 part Powdered Sugar
splash Orange Flower Water
Cocktail Glass
Shake with ice and strain

Opal
1 1/2 parts Vodka
1 part Crème de Banana
splash Campari®
splash Grenadine
Cocktail Glass
Shake with ice and strain

Openheim
2 parts Bourbon
1/2 part Dry Vermouth
1/2 part Grenadine
Cocktail Glass
Shake with ice and strain

Opening Night
1 1/2 parts Whiskey
1/2 part Dry Vermouth
1/2 part Strawberry Liqueur
Cocktail Glass
Shake with ice and strain

Ophelia
1 1/2 parts Aquavit
1 1/2 parts Orange Juice
1/2 part Lime Cordial
Cocktail Glass
Shake with ice and strain

Opium
1 part Vodka
1 part Amaretto
1 part Peach Schnapps
Cocktail Glass
Shake with ice and strain

Orange Bloom
1 part Gin
1/2 part Cointreau®
1/2 part Sweet Vermouth
Cocktail Glass
Shake with ice and strain

Orange Bomb
1 part Mandarine Napoléon® Liqueur
1/2 part Chocolate Liqueur
1/2 part Irish Cream Liqueur
1/2 part Half and Half
Cocktail Glass
Shake with ice and strain

Orange Cadillac
1/2 part Galliano®
1/2 part Crème de Cacao (White)
1 part Cream
1 part Orange Juice
Cocktail Glass
Shake with ice and strain

Orange Kamikaze
1 1/2 parts Vodka
1/2 part Triple Sec
1/2 part Orange Juice
Cocktail Glass
Shake with ice and strain

Orange Lion
1 part Orange-Flavored Vodka
1 part Peach Schnapps
1 part Orange Juice
Cocktail Glass
Shake with ice and strain

Orcabessa
1 part Peach Schnapps
splash Vodka
splash Orange Juice
splash Sour Mix
Cocktail Glass
Shake with ice and strain

Orchidea Nera
1 part Coffee
1 part Cognac
1 part Whiskey
Cocktail Glass
Shake with ice and strain

Orgasm
1/2 part Crème de Cacao (White)
1/2 part Amaretto
1/2 part Triple Sec
1/2 part Vodka
1 part Light Cream
Cocktail Glass
Shake with ice and strain

Orlof
1/2 part Triple Sec
1/2 part Melon Liqueur
1 part Brandy
1 part Sour Mix
Cocktail Glass
Shake with ice and strain

Osaka Dry
3 parts Vodka
1/2 part Sake
Cocktail Glass
Shake with ice and strain

Ostwind Cocktail
1 part Vodka
1 part Dry Vermouth
1 part Sweet Vermouth
1/2 part Rum
Cocktail Glass
Shake with ice and strain

Outlandish Coffee
1 part Vanilla Liqueur
1/2 part Chocolate Liqueur
1 part Cream
1 part Coffee Liqueur
Cocktail Glass
Shake with ice and strain

Pacific Fleet
1/2 part Peach Schnapps
1/2 part Kiwi Schnapps
1/2 part Vodka
1/2 part Light Rum
1 part Cranberry Juice Cocktail
Cocktail Glass
Shake with ice and strain

Pacifist
3/4 part Light Rum
3/4 part Brandy
1/4 part Lemon Juice
2 splashes Raspberry Syrup
Cocktail Glass
Shake with ice and strain

Paddy Cocktail
1 1/2 parts Irish Whiskey
1 1/2 parts Sweet Vermouth
dash Bitters
Cocktail Glass
Shake with ice and strain

Paddy's Special
1 part Cognac
1/2 part Fresh Lime Juice
1/4 part Crème de Banana
splash Triple Sec
Cocktail Glass

Shake with ice and strain

Pagoda
1 part Vodka
1 part Mandarine Napoléon® Liqueur
1 part Pineapple Juice
Cocktail Glass

Shake with ice and strain

Pale Face
2 parts Gin
2/3 part Crème de Banana
1/2 part Cream
Cocktail Glass

Shake with ice and strain

Palmetto Cocktail
1 1/2 parts Light Rum
1 1/2 parts Dry Vermouth
2 dashes Bitters
Cocktail Glass

Shake with ice and strain over ice

Palooka
1 part Apricot Brandy
1 part Apple Brandy
1/2 part Sour Mix
2/3 part Cranberry Juice Cocktail
Cocktail Glass

Shake with ice and strain

Panama Cocktail
1 part Brandy
1 part Light Cream
1 part Crème de Cacao (White)
Cocktail Glass

Shake with ice and strain

Pancho Villa
1 part Gin
1 part Light Rum
1/2 part Apricot Brandy
splash Cherry Liqueur
splash Pineapple Juice
Cocktail Glass

Shake with ice and strain

Pandora's Box
1 part Gin
1 part Calvados Apple Brandy
1 part White Wine
splash Blue Curaçao
splash Frangelico®
Cocktail Glass

Shake with ice and strain over ice

Pantomime
1 1/2 parts Dry Vermouth
splash Grenadine
splash Amaretto
1 Egg White
Cocktail Glass

Shake with ice and strain

Panty Delight
1 1/2 parts Gin
1/2 part Dry Vermouth
dash Orange Bitters
Cocktail Glass

Shake with ice and strain

Paradise Cocktail
1 part Apricot Brandy
3/4 part Gin
1/2 part Orange Juice
Cocktail Glass

Shake with ice and strain

Parallel Universe
1 part Cointreau®
1 part Light Rum
1 part Grapefruit Juice
Cocktail Glass
Shake with ice and strain

Parfait Cheer
1 1/2 parts Crème de Cassis
1 1/2 parts Parfait Amour
splash Lemon Juice
Cocktail Glass
Shake with ice and strain

Paris Opera
1 part Blue Curaçao
1 part Grapefruit Juice
1 part Light Rum
Cocktail Glass
Shake with ice and strain

Parisian
1 part Dry Vermouth
1 part Gin
1/4 part Crème de Cassis
Cocktail Glass
Shake with ice and strain

Parisian Peggy
1 1/2 parts Cherry Brandy
2/3 part Crème de Cacao (White)
1 part Cream
Cocktail Glass
Shake with ice and strain

Park Lane
1 1/2 parts Dry Gin
1 part Apricot Brandy
1 1/2 parts Orange Juice
1/2 part Grenadine
Cocktail Glass
Shake with ice and strain

Parrotti
1 part Vodka
1/2 part Apricot Brandy
splash Lychee Liqueur
splash Grenadine
splash Lime Juice
Cocktail Glass
Shake with ice and strain

Passion Girl
1/2 part Apricot Brandy
1/2 part Bourbon
1/2 part Passion Fruit Liqueur
1/2 part Dark Rum
splash Amaretto
Cocktail Glass
Shake with ice and strain

Passionate Affair
1 part Orange Liqueur
1 part Aquavit
1 part Passion Fruit Juice
Cocktail Glass
Shake with ice and strain

Passionate Sunset
1 part Passion Fruit
1/2 part Orange Juice
1/2 part Grenadine
1/2 part Tequila Reposado
Cocktail Glass
Shake with ice and strain

Passport to Joy
1/2 part Frangelico®
1/2 part Strawberry Liqueur
1/2 part Melon Liqueur
1 1/2 parts Cream
Cocktail Glass
Shake with ice and strain

Patchanka
1 part Light Rum
splash Coconut-Flavored Liqueur
splash Passonã®
1 part Pineapple Juice
Cocktail Glass
Shake with ice and strain

Pauline Cocktail
1 part Rum
1 part Lemon Juice
Cocktail Glass
Shake with ice and strain

Pavarotti
1 1/2 parts Amaretto
1/2 part Brandy
1/2 part Crème de Cacao (White)
Cocktail Glass
Shake with ice and strain

Peace
2 parts Dark Rum
splash Triple Sec
1/2 part Orange Juice
1/2 part Lime Juice
dash Sugar
Cocktail Glass
Shake with ice and strain

Peach Bunny
1 part Peach Brandy
1 part Crème de Cacao (White)
1 part Light Cream
Cocktail Glass
Shake with ice and strain

Peach Me Tender
1 part Jack Daniel's®
1 part Peach Schnapps
1/2 part Limoncello
1/2 part Amaretto
splash Grenadine
Cocktail Glass
Shake with ice and strain

Peach Slider
1 part Peach Schnapps
1/2 part Amaretto
1/2 part Vanilla Liqueur
1 part Cream
Cocktail Glass
Shake with ice and strain

Peach Valley
2 parts Peach Schnapps
2/3 part Raspberry Juice
1 part Lime Juice
Cocktail Glass
Shake with ice and strain

Peachtree Square
1 part Vodka
1 part Peach Schnapps
1/2 part Crème de Cacao (White)
1/2 part Cream
Cocktail Glass
Shake with ice and strain

Peagreen
1 part Vodka
1 part Peppermint Liqueur
1 part Cream
Cocktail Glass
Shake with ice and strain

Peanut Butter Cup
1/2 part Vodka
1/2 part Frangelico®
1/2 part Crème de Cacao (White)
2 parts Light Cream
Cocktail Glass
Shake with ice and strain

Pear Drop
1 1/2 parts Citrus-Flavored Vodka
1 1/2 parts Lychee Liqueur
Cocktail Glass

Shake with ice and strain

Pearls from Jamacia
1/2 part Amaretto
1/2 part Crème de Banana
1/2 part Maraschino Liqueur
1/2 part Melon Liqueur
splash Grenadine
splash Cranberry Juice Cocktail
Cocktail Glass

Shake with ice and strain

Peccati Mei
1 part Triple Sec
1 part Campari®
1 part Grappa
Cocktail Glass

Shake with ice and strain

Pedi Cocktail
2 parts Vodka
splash Triple Sec
2/3 part Campari®
Cocktail Glass

Shake with ice and strain

Peking Express
1 part Gin
1 part Triple Sec
1 Egg White
1/2 part Crème de Menthe (White)
Cocktail Glass

Shake with ice and strain

Pendennis Club Cocktail
1 1/2 parts Gin
3/4 part Brandy
1/2 part Lime Juice
splash Simple Syrup
dash Bitters
Cocktail Glass

Shake with ice and strain

Pendragon
2/3 part Blackberry Liqueur
1/2 part Kirschwasser
1 1/2 parts Armagnac
1 part Cream
Cocktail Glass

Shake with ice and strain

Pepper Perfect
1/2 part Vanilla Liqueur
1/2 part Pepper-Flavored Vodka
1/2 part Lemon-Lime Soda
1 part Cranberry Juice Cocktail
Cocktail Glass

Shake with ice and strain

Peppermint Twist
1 part Peppermint Schnapps
1 part Coffee Liqueur
1 part Crème de Cacao (Dark)
Cocktail Glass

Shake with ice and strain

Peregrine's Peril
1 part Dark Rum
1/2 part Crème de Banana
1/2 part Southern Comfort®
splash Lemon Juice
splash Lime Juice
Cocktail Glass

Shake with ice and strain

Perfect Cocktail
1 1/2 parts Gin
splash Sweet Vermouth
splash Dry Vermouth
dash Bitters
Cocktail Glass
Shake with ice and strain

Perfect Lady
1 part Gin
1 1/2 parts Peach Schnapps
1 Egg White
Cocktail Glass
Shake with ice and strain

Perfect Manhattan
1/2 part Sweet Vermouth
1/2 part Dry Vermouth
dash Bitters
1 Lemon Twist
Cocktail Glass
Shake with ice and strain

Pernod® Cocktail
2 parts Pernod®
3 dashes Angostura® Bitters
3 splashes Simple Syrup
1/2 part Water
Cocktail Glass
Shake with ice and strain

Perpetual Motion
1 part Amaretto
2/3 part Triple Sec
1/2 part Passion Fruit Liqueur
splash Southern Comfort®
1/2 part Sour Mix
Cocktail Glass
Shake with ice and strain

Persian Delight
1 part Vodka
1/2 part Crème de Cacao (White)
1/2 part Lychee Liqueur
1/4 part Maraschino Liqueur
1/4 part Sweetened Lime Juice
Cocktail Glass
Shake with ice and strain

Peruvian White
1 1/2 parts Cointreau®
2/3 part Pisco
splash Peppermint Liqueur
splash Lime Juice
Cocktail Glass
Shake with ice and strain

Peto Cocktail
1 1/2 parts Dry Gin
1 part Dry Vermouth
1 part Orange Juice
1 part Sweet Vermouth
splash Maraschino Liqueur
Cocktail Glass
Shake with ice and strain

Petticoat
1 part Vanilla-Flavored Vodka
1/2 part Crème de Cacao (White)
1/2 part Chocolate Liqueur
1 part Cream
splash Galliano®
Cocktail Glass
Shake with ice and strain

Pheromone
1 part Dark Rum
1/2 part Crème de Menthe (White)
1/2 part Cream
1/2 part Crème de Cacao (Dark)
1/2 part 151-Proof Rum
Cocktail Glass
Shake with ice and strain

Phoebe Snow
1 1/2 parts Dubonnet® Blonde
1 1/2 parts Brandy
splash Anisette
Cocktail Glass
Shake with ice and strain

Picasso
2 1/2 parts Cognac
1/2 part Simple Syrup
Cocktail Glass
Shake with ice and strain

Piccadilly Cocktail
1 1/2 parts Gin
3/4 part Dry Vermouth
1/4 splash Anisette
1/4 splash Grenadine
Cocktail Glass
Shake with ice and strain

Pickens' Punch
1 part Crème de Menthe (White)
1 part Peach Schnapps
1 part Cherry Brandy
Cocktail Glass
Shake with ice and strain

Pie in the Sky
2 parts Light Rum
1 part Pineapple Juice
dash Powdered Sugar
Cocktail Glass
Shake with ice and strain

Piedra Putamadre
1 part Tequila
1 part Fernet-Branca®
1 part Anisette
Cocktail Glass
Shake with ice and strain

Pierced Hooter
1/2 part Peach Schnapps
1 1/2 parts Bacardi® Limón Rum
1/2 part Cranberry Juice Cocktail
1/2 part Orange Juice
Cocktail Glass
Shake with ice and strain

Pilot Boat
1 1/2 parts Dark Rum
1 part Banana Liqueur
2 parts Lime Juice
Cocktail Glass
Shake with ice and strain

Pimm's® Flower
1 1/2 parts Orange Juice
1 part Pimm's® No. 1 Cup
1 part Gin
1/2 part Grenadine
Cocktail Glass
Shake with ice and strain

Pimp Cocktail
2 parts Vodka
1 part Blue Curaçao
1 part Peach Schnapps
fill with Orange Juice
Cocktail Glass
Build over ice and stir

Pineapple Reef
1 part Coconut-Flavored Liqueur
1 part Spiced Rum
1 1/2 parts Pineapple Juice
Cocktail Glass
Shake with ice and strain

Pineapple Rum Cassis
1 part Light Rum
1/2 part Crème de Cassis
1 part Pineapple Juice
Cocktail Glass
Shake with ice and strain

Pink Baby Cocktail
1 1/2 parts Gin
2/3 part Grenadine
1 Egg White
2/3 part Lemon Syrup
Cocktail Glass
Shake with ice and strain

Pink Creole
1 1/2 parts Light Rum
2 splashes Lime Juice
splash Grenadine
splash Light Cream
Cocktail Glass
Shake with ice and strain

Pink Fluid
1 1/2 parts Vodka
1/2 part Crème de Cacao (White)
1/2 part Strawberry Syrup
Cocktail Glass
Shake with ice and strain

Pink Mink
1 part Vodka
1 part Rum
1 part Strawberry Liqueur
Cocktail Glass
Shake with ice and strain

Pink 'n' Tart
1 1/2 parts Rum
1/2 part Lemon Juice
1/2 part Lime Juice
splash Grenadine
Cocktail Glass
Shake with ice and strain

Pink Panther
1 part Amaretto
1/2 part Vodka
splash Grenadine
2 parts Light Cream
Cocktail Glass
Shake with ice and strain

Pink Pussycat Cocktail
1 1/2 parts Gin
3/4 part Grenadine
1 Egg White
Cocktail Glass
Shake with ice and strain

Pink Slip
1 part Crème de Cacao (White)
1 part Crème de Noyaux
1 part Cream
Cocktail Glass
Shake with ice and strain

Pink Teddy
1 part Vodka
1 part Passion Fruit Liqueur
1/2 part Lychee Liqueur
1/2 part Cream
splash Grenadine
Cocktail Glass
Shake with ice and strain

Pipe and Smoke
1 1/2 parts Drambuie®
1/2 part Coconut-Flavored Liqueur
1/2 part Cherry Brandy
1 part Lemon Juice
Cocktail Glass
Shake with ice and strain

Piranha
1 1/2 parts Vodka
1 1/2 parts Crème de Cacao (Dark)
Cocktail Glass
Shake with ice and strain

Pirate Cocktail
1 1/2 parts Rum
1/2 part Sweet Vermouth
2 dashes Angostura® Bitters
Cocktail Glass

Shake with ice and strain

Pirate's Gold
1 1/2 parts Dark Rum
1 part Dry Vermouth
2 dashes Orange Bitters
Cocktail Glass

Shake with ice and strain

Pisa
1 part Amaretto
1 part Cream
splash Apricot Brandy
splash Orange Juice
Cocktail Glass

Shake with ice and strain

Pixy Stix® Cocktail
1 1/2 parts Light Rum
1/2 part Apricot Brandy
2 splashes Lime Juice
2 splashes Lemon Juice
dash Sugar
Cocktail Glass

Shake with ice and strain

Plankton
1 1/2 parts Light Rum
1/2 part Galliano®
splash Crème de Cacao (White)
Cocktail Glass

Shake with ice and strain

Play It Again Sam
2 parts Light Rum
splash Triple Sec
splash Maraschino Liqueur
splash Lime Juice
Cocktail Glass

Shake with ice and strain

Playa del Mar
1 part Tequila Silver
1 part Pineapple Juice
1/2 part Fresh Lime Juice
1/2 part Strawberry
splash Simple Syrup
Cocktail Glass

Shake with ice and strain

Playmate
1 part Brandy
1/2 part Apricot Brandy
1/2 part Mandarine Napoléon® Liqueur
1 part Orange Juice
1/2 Egg White
Cocktail Glass

Shake with ice and strain

Plaza Cocktail
3/4 part Gin
3/4 part Dry Vermouth
3/4 part Sweet Vermouth
Cocktail Glass

Shake with ice and strain

Police Brutality
2/3 part Light Rum
2/3 part Crème de Banana
1/2 part Galliano®
1 1/2 parts Pineapple Juice
Cocktail Glass

Shake with ice and strain

Polish Sidecar
2 parts Gin
1 part Blackberry Liqueur
Cocktail Glass

Shake with ice and strain

Polly's Cocktail
2 parts Scotch
1/2 part Pineapple Juice
1/2 part Triple Sec
Cocktail Glass

Shake with ice and strain

Polyanthus
1 part Blackberry Liqueur
1 part Chocolate Liqueur
1 part Cream
Cocktail Glass

Shake with ice and strain

Polynesian Cocktail
1 1/2 parts Vodka
3/4 part Cherry Brandy
1/2 part Lime Juice
dash Powdered Sugar
Cocktail Glass

Shake with ice and strain

Polynesian Sour
2 parts Light Rum
1/2 part Orange Juice
1/2 part Guava Juice
Cocktail Glass

Shake with ice and strain

Ponce de Leon
1 1/2 parts Light Rum
1/2 part Grapefruit Juice
1/2 part Mango Juice
Cocktail Glass

Shake with ice and strain

Ponche Orinoco
1 part Light Rum
1/2 part Apricot Brandy
1/4 part Vodka
1/4 part Orange Juice
splash Grenadine
dash Bitters
Cocktail Glass

Shake with ice and strain

Pool Table Sex
1 part Peach Schnapps
1 part Triple Sec
1 part Raspberry Liqueur
1 part Melon Liqueur
1 part Grapefruit Juice
Cocktail Glass

Shake with ice and strain

Popstar
1 part Dark Rum
1 part Strawberry Liqueur
splash Vanilla Liqueur
splash Cream
Cocktail Glass

Shake with ice and strain

Pornography
1 1/2 parts Passion Fruit Liqueur
1 part Campari®
1 part Lime Juice
Cocktail Glass

Shake with ice and strain

Port Royal
1 part Spiced Rum
1/2 part Crème de Banana
splash Crème de Cacao (White)
2 parts Cream
Cocktail Glass

Shake with ice and strain

Potemkin
3 parts Vodka
splash Benedictine®
Cocktail Glass
Shake with ice and strain

Potpourri
1 1/2 parts Vodka
1/2 part Cherry Brandy
1/2 part Brandy
Cocktail Glass
Shake with ice and strain

Potted President
2/3 part Blackberry Liqueur
2/3 part Raspberry Liqueur
2/3 part Sambuca
1 part Sour Mix
Cocktail Glass
Shake with ice and strain

Power-Line
1 part Brandy
1 part Crème de Banana
1 part Orange Juice
splash Cream
Cocktail Glass
Shake with ice and strain

Prankster
1 part Crème de Banana
1 part Fresh Lime Juice
1 part Sour Mix
Cocktail Glass
Shake with ice and strain

Prelude
1 part Dry Vermouth
1/2 part Peach Schnapps
1/4 part Gin
3/4 part Peach Juice
1/4 part Honey
splash Strawberry Juice
Cocktail Glass
Shake with ice and strain

Presto Cocktail
1 1/2 parts Brandy
1/2 part Sweet Vermouth
2 splashes Orange Juice
1/4 splash Anisette
Cocktail Glass
Shake with ice and strain

Prestwick
2 parts Light Rum
1 part Crème de Cassis
1 part Crème de Noyaux
1 part Orange Juice
1 part Cranberry Juice Cocktail
1 part Pineapple Juice
Cocktail Glass
Shake with ice and strain

Pretty Angel
1 part Crème de Banana
1/2 part Crème de Menthe (White)
1/2 part Cream
1/2 part Dark Rum
splash Grenadine
Cocktail Glass
Shake with ice and strain

Primo Amore
1 part Apricot Brandy
1 part Cognac
1/2 part Orange Juice
splash Grenadine
Cocktail Glass
Shake with ice and strain

Prince Regent
1 part Apricot Brandy
1 part Crème de Cacao (White)
1 part Chocolate Milk
Cocktail Glass
Shake with ice and strain

Prince's Smile
1 part Gin
1/2 part Apple Brandy
1/2 part Apricot Brandy
1/4 splash Lemon Juice
Cocktail Glass
Shake with ice and strain

Princeton Cocktail
1 part Gin
1 part Dry Vermouth
1/2 part Lime Juice
Cocktail Glass
Shake with ice and strain

Private Meeting
1 1/2 parts Gin
1/2 part Peach Schnapps
1/2 part Mandarine Napoléon® Liqueur
dash Orange Bitters
Cocktail Glass
Stir gently with ice and strain

Prohibition
1 part Gin
1 part Lillet®
splash Apricot Brandy
2 splashes Orange Juice
Cocktail Glass
Shake with ice and strain

Proserpine's Revenge
1 1/2 parts Crème de Menthe (White)
1 1/2 parts Cognac
Cocktail Glass
Shake with ice and strain

Psycho Therapy
1 part Vodka
1 part Rémy Martin® VSOP
1 part Scotch
Cocktail Glass
Shake with ice and strain

Pulmonia
1 part Gold Tequila
2/3 part Blue Curaçao
2/3 part Maraschino Liqueur
1 part Sour Mix
Cocktail Glass
Shake with ice and strain

Pulsar
1 part Blue Curaçao
1/2 part Crème de Cassis
splash Vodka
splash Lime Juice
Cocktail Glass
Shake with ice and strain

Punisher
1 1/2 parts Scotch
1 part Crème de Cacao (Dark)
1/2 part Coffee Liqueur
Cocktail Glass
Shake with ice and strain

Pure Delight
1 part Raspberry Liqueur
1 part Grand Marnier®
1 part Irish Cream Liqueur
Cocktail Glass
Shake with ice and strain

Puropi
2 parts Tequila Silver
3/4 part Crème de Cassis
1/2 part Crème de Menthe (Green)
Cocktail Glass
Shake with ice and strain

Purple Bunny
$1^1/_2$ parts Cherry Brandy
$^1/_2$ part Crème de Cacao (White)
$^1/_2$ part Cream
Cocktail Glass
Shake with ice and strain

Purple Kiss
$1^1/_4$ parts Gin
$^3/_4$ part Lemon Juice
$^3/_4$ part Crème de Noyaux
splash Cherry Brandy
Cocktail Glass
Shake with ice and strain

Purple Mask
1 part Vodka
$^1/_2$ part Crème de Cacao (White)
1 part Grape Juice (red)
Cocktail Glass
Shake with ice and strain

Purple Turtle
$^1/_2$ part Blue Curaçao
1 part Coconut-Flavored Rum
1 part Triple Sec
1 part Cranberry Juice Cocktail
Cocktail Glass
Shake with ice and strain

Pursuit Plane
$1^1/_2$ parts Vodka
$^2/_3$ part Vanilla Liqueur
$^2/_3$ part Butterscotch Schnapps
Cocktail Glass
Shake with ice and strain

Pussy Supreme
$^3/_4$ part Irish Cream Liqueur
$^3/_4$ part Blue Curaçao
2 parts Half and Half
Cocktail Glass
Shake with ice and strain

Quattro
1 part Amaretto
1 part Whiskey
$^1/_2$ part Dry Vermouth
$^1/_2$ part Crème de Cassis
Cocktail Glass
Shake with ice and strain

Quebec Cocktail
$1^1/_2$ parts Canadian Whiskey
$^1/_2$ part Cherry Liqueur
$^1/_2$ part Dry Vermouth
$^1/_2$ part Amer Picon®
Cocktail Glass
Shake with ice and strain

Queen of Scots
2 parts Scotch
splash Chartreuse®
splash Blue Curaçao
dash Sugar
2 splashes Water
splash Lemon Juice
Cocktail Glass
Shake with ice and strain

Quentin
$1^1/_2$ parts Dark Rum
$^1/_2$ part Coffee Liqueur
1 part Light Cream
pinch Ground Nutmeg
Cocktail Glass
Shake with ice and strain

Quick-Fire
1 part Chocolate Mint Liqueur
1 part Light Rum
$^1/_2$ part Cream
splash 151-Proof Rum
Cocktail Glass
Shake with ice and strain

Quicksand

1 part Vodka
2/3 part Coffee Liqueur
splash Vanilla Liqueur
Cocktail Glass

Shake with ice and strain

Quiet Sunday

1 part Vodka
1 part Orange Juice
1/2 part Amaretto
1/2 part Grenadine
Cocktail Glass

Shake with ice and strain

R&B Cocktail

1 part Jack Daniel's®
1/2 part Triple Sec
1/2 part Brandy
fill with Cola
splash Grenadine
Cocktail Glass

Build over ice and stir

Rad Fuck

3/4 part Raspberry Liqueur
3/4 part Amaretto
1/2 part Pineapple Juice
1/2 part Sour Mix
splash Lemon-Lime Soda
Cocktail Glass

Stir gently with ice and strain

Radioactivity

1 part Vodka
1/2 part Lychee Liqueur
1/2 part Pisang Ambon® Liqueur
1 part Lemon Juice
Cocktail Glass

Shake with ice and strain

Ragtime

1 part Coffee Liqueur
1 part Brandy
1 part Half and Half
Cocktail Glass

Shake with ice and strain

Ramasi

1/2 part Vodka
1/2 part Triple Sec
1/2 part Amaretto
1 part Sour Mix
1/2 part Pineapple Juice
Cocktail Glass

Shake with ice and strain

Ramos Fizz

2 parts Gin
1 1/2 parts Cream
1/2 part Lemon Juice
1/2 part Lime Juice
2 drops Orange Flower Water
dash Powdered Sugar
fill with Club Soda
Cocktail Glass

Shake all but Club Soda with ice and strain into the glass. Top with Club Soda.

Randini

2 parts Cranberry Juice Cocktail
3 parts Gin
1 Lime Wedge
1 part Triple Sec
1 part Vodka
Cocktail Glass

Shake with ice and strain

Ranger Cocktail

1 part Light Rum
1 part Gin
1 part Lemon Juice
dash Sugar
Cocktail Glass

Shake with ice and strain

Rapture of Rum

$1^1/_2$ parts Coconut-Flavored Rum
$^1/_2$ part Orange Liqueur
$^1/_2$ part Lime Juice
dash Powdered Sugar
Cocktail Glass

Shake with ice and strain

Raquel

1 part Vodka
$^1/_2$ part Blue Curaçao
$^1/_2$ part Parfait Amour
$^1/_2$ part Cherry Brandy
splash Cream
Cocktail Glass

Shake with ice and strain

Rasp Royale

1 part Vodka
$^1/_2$ part Raspberry Liqueur
$^1/_2$ part Coffee Liqueur
$^1/_2$ part Irish Cream Liqueur
Cocktail Glass

Shake with ice and strain

Raspberry Blush

1 part Dark Rum
$^1/_2$ part Dry Vermouth
1 part Lime Juice
2 splashes Raspberry Syrup
Cocktail Glass

Shake with ice and strain

Rattlesnake Cocktail

$1^1/_2$ parts Whiskey
splash Lemon Juice
splash Anisette
dash Powdered Sugar
1 Egg White
Cocktail Glass

Shake with ice and strain

Razzberi Kazi

1 part Raspberry-Flavored Vodka
1 part Triple Sec
1 part Sour Mix
$^1/_2$ part Grenadine
Cocktail Glass

Shake with ice and strain

Razzmopolitan

$1^1/_2$ parts Vodka
$^3/_4$ part Raspberry Liqueur
$^1/_2$ part Fresh Lime Juice
splash Cranberry Juice Cocktail
Cocktail Glass

Shake with ice and strain

Rebel Roar

1 part Crème de Banana
1 part Triple Sec
1 part Grape Juice (white)
Cocktail Glass

Shake with ice and strain

Recession Depression

$1^1/_2$ parts Citrus-Flavored Vodka
$^1/_2$ part Triple Sec
$^1/_2$ part Lemon Juice
2 splashes Sweetened Lime Juice
Cocktail Glass

Shake with ice and strain

Red Apple

1 part Vodka
1 part Apple Juice
2 splashes Lemon Juice
splash Grenadine
Cocktail Glass

Shake with ice and strain

Red Cloud
$1^1/_2$ parts Gin
$^1/_2$ part Apricot Brandy
2 splashes Lemon Juice
splash Grenadine
Cocktail Glass
Shake with ice and strain

Red Delight
1 part Peach Schnapps
1 part Coconut-Flavored Rum
1 part Cream
1 part Strawberry Syrup
2 parts Mango Juice
Cocktail Glass
Shake with ice and strain

Red Finnish
2 parts Orange Juice
1 part Vermouth
$^3/_4$ part Red Curaçao
Cocktail Glass
Shake with ice and strain

Red Gaze
$^1/_2$ part Sloe Gin
$^1/_2$ part Crème de Cassis
splash Lemon Juice
splash Lemon-Lime Soda
Cocktail Glass
Shake with ice and strain

Red Jobber
2 parts Coconut-Flavored Rum
1 part Crème de Banana
1 part Strawberry Liqueur
1 part Jägermeister®
splash Grenadine
Cocktail Glass
Shake with ice and strain

Red Knocker
1 part Sloe Gin
1 part Passion Fruit Liqueur
1 part Apple Juice
splash Sour Mix
Cocktail Glass
Shake with ice and strain

Red Light
1 part Gin
$^1/_2$ part Sloe Gin
$^1/_2$ part Dry Vermouth
Cocktail Glass
Shake with ice and strain

Red Lion Cocktail
1 part Gin
1 part Grand Marnier®
$^1/_2$ part Lemon Juice
$^1/_2$ part Orange Juice
Cocktail Glass
Shake with ice and strain

Red Panties
$1^1/_2$ parts Vodka
1 part Peach Schnapps
splash Grenadine
1 part Orange Juice
Cocktail Glass
Shake with ice and strain

Red Russian
1 part Vodka
$^1/_2$ part Crème de Cacao (White)
1 part Cranberry Juice Cocktail
Cocktail Glass
Shake with ice and strain

Red Sonja
1 part Vodka
1 part Raspberry Liqueur
1 part Cranberry Juice Cocktail
Cocktail Glass
Shake with ice and strain

Red Tulip

2/3 part Gin
splash Triple Sec
splash Apricot Brandy
1/2 part Dry Vermouth
1/2 part Sweet Vermouth
Cocktail Glass
Shake with ice and strain

Red Viking

1 part Maraschino Liqueur
1 part Aquavit
1/2 part Grenadine
Cocktail Glass
Shake with ice and strain

Red Whiskey

1 part Whiskey
1 part Sloe Gin
1/2 part Lemon Juice
Cocktail Glass
Shake with ice and strain

Redcoat

1 1/2 parts Light Rum
1/2 part Vodka
1/2 part Apricot Brandy
1/2 part Lime Juice
splash Grenadine
Cocktail Glass
Shake with ice and strain

Redheaded Slut

1 part Jack Daniel's®
1 part Peach Schnapps
1 part Cranberry Juice Cocktail
Cocktail Glass
Shake with ice and strain

Reformation

1 1/2 parts Parfait Amour
1 part Cherry Brandy
1/2 part Scotch
Cocktail Glass
Shake with ice and strain

Remote Control

1 part Galliano®
1/2 part Cointreau®
1 part Orange Juice
1/2 part Cream
Cocktail Glass
Shake with ice and strain

Renaissance Cocktail

1 1/2 parts Gin
1/2 part Dry Sherry
1/2 part Light Cream
dash Ground Nutmeg
Cocktail Glass
Shake with ice and strain

Renton

1 part Sloe Gin
1 part Crème de Cassis
1 part Milk
Cocktail Glass
Shake with ice and strain

Reunion

1 part Light Rum
1/2 part Cherry Brandy
1/2 part Triple Sec
1/4 part Lime Juice
Cocktail Glass
Shake with ice and strain

Reve Satin
1 part Blackberry Liqueur
1 part Strawberry Liqueur
1 part Cream
Cocktail Glass

Shake with ice and strain

Rhapsody in Blue
1 part Blue Curaçao
1 part Grappa
1 part Amaretto
Cocktail Glass

Shake with ice and strain

Rheingold
1 part Dry Gin
1/2 part Dry Vermouth
1/2 part Campari®
Cocktail Glass

Shake with ice and strain

Rhett Butler
1 1/2 parts Southern Comfort®
1/2 part Triple Sec
1/2 part Fresh Lime Juice
Cocktail Glass

Shake with ice and strain

Riley
1 part Dark Rum
1/2 part Cointreau®
1/2 part Lemon Juice
1/2 part Orange Juice
1/2 part Lime Juice
splash Crème de Cassis
splash Raspberry Syrup
Cocktail Glass

Shake with ice and strain

Rin Tin Tin
1 part Cherry Brandy
1 part Sour Mix
1 part Cranberry Juice Cocktail
Cocktail Glass

Shake with ice and strain

Rio Grande
1 1/2 parts Tequila Silver
3/4 part Peach Schnapps
1/2 part Fresh Lime Juice
Cocktail Glass

Shake with ice and strain

Ripe Reagents
1/2 part Peppermint Liqueur
1 part Triple Sec
1 part Light Rum
1/2 part Lime Juice
dash Powdered Sugar
Cocktail Glass

Shake with ice and strain

Risky Business
1 1/2 parts Vodka
splash Raspberry Liqueur
splash Lime Juice
splash Blackberry Juice
Cocktail Glass

Shake with ice and strain

Roadster
1/2 part Crème de Cacao (White)
1/2 part Crème de Banana
1/2 part Raspberry Liqueur
1 part Orange Juice
1 part Cream
Cocktail Glass

Shake with ice and strain

Roberta
1 part Vodka
1 part Dry Vermouth
1 part Cherry Brandy
splash Crème de Banana
splash Campari®
Cocktail Glass

Shake with ice and strain

Robson Cocktail
1 part Dark Rum
splash Grenadine
2 splashes Lemon Juice
1 part Orange Juice
Cocktail Glass
Shake with ice and strain

Rocket Radium
1 1/2 parts Peppermint Liqueur
1 1/2 parts Ouzo
Cocktail Glass
Shake with ice and strain

Rococo
1 part Cherry Vodka
1/2 part Triple Sec
1 part Orange Juice
Cocktail Glass
Shake with ice and strain

Roller Coaster
1 part Gin
1 part Brandy
1/2 part Crème de Menthe (Green)
1/2 part Lemonade
splash Fresh Lime Juice
Cocktail Glass
Shake with ice and strain

Rolling Thunder
1 1/2 parts Light Rum
1/2 part Vodka
1/2 part Apricot Brandy
1/4 part Lime Juice
1/4 part Grenadine
Cocktail Glass
Shake with ice and strain

Roma Citta Aperta
1 part Grappa
1 part Triple Sec
1/2 part Apricot Brandy
1/2 part Campari®
Cocktail Glass
Shake with ice and strain

Romance Cocktail
1/4 part Brandy
1/4 part Blue Curaçao
1/2 part Amer Picon®
1/2 part Dry Vermouth
1/2 part Sweet Vermouth
Cocktail Glass
Shake with ice and strain

Rome under the Snow
1/2 part Crème de Cassis
1/2 part Plum Brandy
2/3 part Grappa
2 parts Cream
Cocktail Glass
Shake with ice and strain

Ronrico
1 part Passion Fruit Liqueur
2/3 part Dark Rum
2/3 part Coffee Liqueur
splash Coconut Cream
splash Milk
splash Pineapple Juice
Cocktail Glass
Shake with ice and strain

Rook Yah
1/2 part Peppermint Liqueur
1 part Triple Sec
1/2 part Jägermeister®
1 1/2 parts Cranberry Juice Cocktail
Cocktail Glass
Shake with ice and strain

Rose

2 parts Dry Gin
1/2 part Cherry Brandy
splash Sweet Vermouth
Cocktail Glass
Shake with ice and strain

Rose Bird

1 part Cognac
1/2 part Crème de Banana
1/2 part Apricot Brandy
splash Orange Juice
Cocktail Glass
Shake with ice and strain

Rose Hall

1 part Orange Juice
1/2 part Banana Liqueur
splash Lime Juice
Cocktail Glass
Shake with ice and strain

Rose of Warsaw

1 1/2 parts Polish Vodka
1 part Cherry Liqueur
1/2 part Cointreau®
dash Bitters
Cocktail Glass
Shake with ice and strain

Rose Walk

1 part Maraschino Liqueur
1 part Brandy
1 part Dry Vermouth
1/2 part Sour Mix
Cocktail Glass
Shake with ice and strain

Roseanne

1 part Coffee-Flavored Brandy
splash Brandy
splash Irish Cream Liqueur
splash Frangelico®
Cocktail Glass
Shake with ice and strain

Roselin

1 1/2 parts Dark Rum
1/4 part Triple Sec
1/4 part Mandarine Napoléon® Liqueur
splash Pineapple Juice
splash Grenadine
dash Bitters
Cocktail Glass
Shake with ice and strain

Rosie Mcgann

1 part Peppermint Liqueur
1 part Irish Whiskey
1 part Sour Mix
Cocktail Glass
Shake with ice and strain

Roy Howard Cocktail

1 part Lillet®
1 part Brandy
1 part Orange Juice
splash Grenadine
Cocktail Glass
Shake with ice and strain

Royal Clover Club Cocktail

1 1/2 parts Gin
1/2 part Lemon Juice
2 splashes Grenadine
1 Egg Yolk
Cocktail Glass
Shake with ice and strain over ice

Royal Cocktail
1½ parts Gin
½ part Lemon Juice
dash Powdered Sugar
1 Whole Egg
Cocktail Glass
Shake with ice and strain

Royal Mounted Police
2 parts Canadian Whiskey
½ part Blue Curaçao
½ part Dry Sherry
Cocktail Glass
Shake with ice and strain

Royal Passion
1½ parts Vodka
¾ part Raspberry Liqueur
½ part Passion Fruit Juice
Cocktail Glass
Shake with ice and strain

Royal Wedding
1 part Apricot Brandy
1 part Grand Marnier®
½ part Lime Juice
Cocktail Glass
Shake with ice and strain

Rubaiyat
2 parts Gin
1 part Cointreau®
splash Orange Juice
Cocktail Glass
Shake with ice and strain

Ruben's
1½ parts Whiskey
1 part Apricot Brandy
splash Lemon Juice
splash Simple Syrup
Cocktail Glass
Shake with ice and strain

Ruby in the Rough
1½ parts Gin
½ part Cherry Brandy
splash Sweet Vermouth
Cocktail Glass
Shake with ice and strain

Ruby Red Lips
1½ parts Gin
½ part Sloe Gin
½ part Dry Vermouth
splash Grenadine
Cocktail Glass
Shake with ice and strain

Rude Cosmopolitan
1½ parts Tequila Silver
¾ part Triple Sec
½ part Fresh Lime Juice
Cocktail Glass
Shake with ice and strain

Rum Blossom
1½ parts Dark Rum
1 part Orange Juice
½ part Sugar
Cocktail Glass
Shake with ice and strain

Rum Flare
1 part Rum
½ part Brandy
½ part Triple Sec
½ part Lemon Juice
Cocktail Glass
Shake with ice and strain

Rum Rummy
$1\frac{1}{2}$ parts Light Rum
1 part Orange Juice
1 part Fresh Lime Juice
dash Orange Bitters
splash Simple Syrup
Cocktail Glass

Shake with ice and strain

Rumba
2 parts Dark Rum
$\frac{1}{2}$ part Crème de Cacao (Dark)
splash Grenadine
Cocktail Glass

Shake with ice and strain

Rummer
$1\frac{1}{2}$ parts Dark Rum
$\frac{1}{2}$ part Amaretto
$\frac{1}{2}$ part Triple Sec
$\frac{1}{2}$ part Lemon Juice
Cocktail Glass

Shake with ice and strain

Runaway Bay
$1\frac{1}{2}$ parts Spiced Rum
$\frac{2}{3}$ part Blue Curaçao
splash Pernod®
$\frac{2}{3}$ part Lime Juice
Cocktail Glass

Shake with ice and strain

Rushkin
1 part Vodka
1 part Raspberry Liqueur
$\frac{1}{2}$ part Blackberry Liqueur
$\frac{1}{2}$ part Lime Juice
$\frac{1}{2}$ part Sour Mix
Cocktail Glass

Shake with ice and strain

Russian Armpit
$\frac{1}{2}$ part Orange-Flavored Vodka
$\frac{1}{2}$ part Citrus-Flavored Vodka
1 part Crème de Banana
1 part Mango Juice
Cocktail Glass

Shake with ice and strain

Russian Cocktail
1 part Vodka
1 part Gin
1 part Crème de Cacao (White)
Cocktail Glass

Shake with ice and strain

Russian Haze
1 part Vodka
$\frac{1}{2}$ part Frangelico®
$\frac{1}{2}$ part Irish Cream Liqueur
Cocktail Glass

Shake with ice and strain

Russian Peach
1 part Vodka
$\frac{1}{2}$ part Peach Schnapps
$\frac{1}{2}$ part Crème de Cassis
1 part Orange Juice
Cocktail Glass

Shake with ice and strain

Russian Smooth Side
1 part Vodka
$\frac{1}{2}$ part Orange Liqueur
$\frac{1}{2}$ part Mandarine Napoléon® Liqueur
$\frac{1}{2}$ part Lemon Juice
1 part Orange Juice
Cocktail Glass

Shake with ice and strain

Russian Twilight
1 part Vodka
1 part Crème de Cacao (White)
1 part Cream
Cocktail Glass

Shake with ice and strain

Russin' About
$1^1/_2$ parts Vodka
$^1/_2$ part Irish Cream Liqueur
$^1/_2$ part Tia Maria®
$^1/_4$ part Frangelico®
Cocktail Glass

Shake with ice and strain

Rye Lane
1 part Triple Sec
1 part Orange Juice
1 part Rye Whiskey
Cocktail Glass

Shake with ice and strain

Rye Whiskey Cocktail
2 parts Rye Whiskey
dash Powdered Sugar
dash Bitters
Cocktail Glass

Shake with ice and strain

Sacrifice
1 part Gin
1 part Calvados Apple Brandy
1 part Dry Vermouth
splash Cherry Brandy
Cocktail Glass

Shake with ice and strain

Safe and Sound
1 part Crème de Cacao (White)
1 part Calvados Apple Brandy
1 part Cream
Cocktail Glass

Shake with ice and strain

Saigon Sling
1 part Gin
$^1/_2$ part Sloe Gin
1 part Cherry Brandy
$^1/_2$ part Crème de Cassis
$^1/_2$ part Lime Juice
Cocktail Glass

Shake with ice and strain

Sail Away
1 part Vodka
$^1/_2$ part Peach Liqueur
$^1/_2$ part Melon Liqueur
1 part Fresh Lime Juice
Cocktail Glass

Shake with ice and strain

Sake Cocktail
1 part Melon Liqueur
1 part Sake
1 part Citrus-Flavored Vodka
Cocktail Glass

Shake with ice and strain

Sake to Me
2 parts Orange-Flavored Vodka
$^1/_2$ part Blue Curaçao
splash Sake
Cocktail Glass

Shake with ice and strain

Salamander
$1^1/_2$ parts Melon Liqueur
$1^1/_2$ parts Pisang Ambon® Liqueur
1 part Lemon Juice
Cocktail Glass

Shake with ice and strain

Salem
1 part Vodka
1 part Crème de Menthe (Green)
1/2 part Dry Vermouth
1/2 part Triple Sec
Cocktail Glass
Shake with ice and strain

Samarkanda
2 parts Passoã®
2/3 part Lemon Juice
1 part Orange Juice
Cocktail Glass
Shake with ice and strain

Sammy
1/2 part Black Sambuca
1/2 part Blackberry Brandy
1/2 part Amaretto
1 1/2 parts Light Cream
Cocktail Glass
Shake with ice and strain

Samurai
2 parts Sake
3/4 part Fresh Lime Juice
1/2 part Triple Sec
1/4 part Sour Mix
Cocktail Glass
Shake with ice and strain

San Francisco Cocktail
1 part Sweet Vermouth
1 part Dry Vermouth
1 part Sloe Gin
dash Orange Bitters
Cocktail Glass
Shake with ice and strain

San Juan Cocktail
1 part Light Rum
1/4 part 151-Proof Rum
1 part Grapefruit Juice
1/2 part Lemon Juice
1/4 part Coconut Cream
Cocktail Glass
Shake with ice and strain

San Sebastian
1 part Gin
splash Rum
splash Triple Sec
2 splashes Grapefruit Juice
2 splashes Lemon Juice
Cocktail Glass
Shake with ice and strain

Sangria
2 parts Orange-Flavored Vodka
1/2 part Red Wine
splash Cherry Brandy
1/2 part Orange Juice
splash Lemon Juice
splash Lime Juice
Cocktail Glass
Shake with ice and strain

Sands of Nevada
1 1/2 parts Gin
2/3 part Blue Curaçao
2/3 part Grapefruit Juice
splash Lemon Juice
Cocktail Glass
Shake with ice and strain

Sante Fe
1 1/2 parts Brandy
1/2 part Grapefruit Juice
1/2 part Cinzano®
Cocktail Glass
Shake with ice and strain

Santo Domingo
1 part Cream
1 part Dark Rum
1/2 part Amaretto
1/2 part Coffee Liqueur
Cocktail Glass
Shake with ice and strain

Saratoga Cocktail
2 parts Brandy
splash Pineapple Juice
splash Lemon Juice
splash Maraschino Liqueur
2 dashes Bitters
Cocktail Glass
Shake with ice and strain

Saratoga Party
1 1/2 parts Vodka
splash Grenadine
dash Angostura® Bitters
splash Club Soda
Cocktail Glass
Shake with ice and strain

Sarteano
1 part Galliano®
1 part Orange Liqueur
1 part Triple Sec
1 part Crème de Cassis
splash Lime Cordial
splash Lemon Juice
Cocktail Glass
Shake with ice and strain

Satan's Whiskers
1/2 part Gin
1/2 part Sweet Vermouth
1/2 part Dry Vermouth
1/4 part Grand Marnier®
1 part Orange Juice
dash Orange Bitters
Cocktail Glass
Shake with ice and strain

Satin Doll
1 part Brandy
1/2 part Triple Sec
1/2 part Pineapple Juice
Cocktail Glass
Shake with ice and strain

Satin Glow
1 1/2 parts Gin
splash Crème de Banana
2/3 part Orange Juice
splash Pineapple Juice
Cocktail Glass
Shake with ice and strain

Savannah
1 part Gin
splash Crème de Cacao (White)
splash Orange Juice
1 Egg White
Cocktail Glass
Shake with ice and strain

Save Ferris
1 part Kiwi Schnapps
1 part Scotch
1 part Cream
Cocktail Glass
Shake with ice and strain

Save the Planet
1 part Vodka
1 part Melon Liqueur
1/2 part Blue Curaçao
2 splashes Green Chartreuse®
Cocktail Glass
Shake with ice and strain

Savoy Hotel Cocktail
1 part Crème de Cacao (White)
1 part Brandy
1 part Benedictine®
Cocktail Glass
Shake with ice and strain

Saxon Cocktail
1 3/4 part Light Rum
splash Grenadine
1/2 part Lime Juice
Cocktail Glass
Shake with ice and strain

Sayonara
1 part Vodka
1/2 part Dry Vermouth
1/4 part Triple Sec
1/4 part Apricot Brandy
splash Papaya Juice
Cocktail Glass
Shake with ice and strain

Scallywag
3 parts Light Rum
1 part Blue Curaçao
1 part Galliano®
1 part Lime Juice
Cocktail Glass
Shake with ice and strain

Scanex
2 parts Vodka
1 part Cranberry Liqueur
1 part Lemon Juice
1 part Grenadine
1 part Sugar
Cocktail Glass
Shake with ice and strain

Scarabeus
1 part Gin
1 part Blue Curaçao
1/2 part Crème de Banana
1/2 part Coconut-Flavored Liqueur
Cocktail Glass
Shake with ice and strain

Scarlet Lady
1 1/2 parts Vodka
1/4 part Coffee Liqueur
1/4 part Cherry Brandy
Cocktail Glass
Shake with ice and strain

Scarlett Fever
1 1/2 parts Citrus-Flavored Vodka
1/2 part Amaretto
1 part Cranberry Juice Cocktail
Cocktail Glass
Shake with ice and strain

Schnapple
1 part Gin
1/2 part Grenadine
1 part Sweet Vermouth
1/2 part Apple Brandy
Cocktail Glass
Shake with ice and strain

Scooter
1 part Brandy
1 part Amaretto
1 part Light Cream
Cocktail Glass
Shake with ice and strain

Scotch Bishop Cocktail

1 part Scotch
1/2 part Dry Vermouth
splash Triple Sec
2 splashes Orange Juice
dash Powdered Sugar
Cocktail Glass

Shake with ice and strain

Scotch Citrus

11/2 parts Scotch
1 part Grand Marnier®
1 part Lemon Juice
2 splashes Grenadine
Cocktail Glass

Shake with ice and strain

Scratch and Win

1 part Peach Schnapps
1 part Sambuca
1 part Cranberry Juice Cocktail
Cocktail Glass

Shake with ice and strain

Screaming Banana Banshee

1/2 part Banana Liqueur
1/2 part Vodka
1/2 part Crème de Cacao (White)
11/2 parts Cream
Cocktail Glass

Shake with ice and strain

Screaming Orgasm

1 part Vodka
1 part Amaretto
1 part Crème de Cacao (White)
1 part Triple Sec
2 parts Cream
Cocktail Glass

Shake with ice and strain

Screaming Viking

2 parts Vodka
1 part Dry Vermouth
1 part Lime Juice
Cocktail Glass

Shake with ice and strain

Screech Owl

11/2 parts Brandy
splash Orange Liqueur
1 part Blue Curaçao
1/2 part Strawberry Juice
1 part Lemon Juice
Cocktail Glass

Shake with ice and strain

Screwed and Tattooed

2 parts Tequila Silver
1 part Melon Liqueur
1 part Absinthe
1 part Lemon Juice
Cocktail Glass

Shake with ice and strain

Scuttle for Liberty

11/2 parts Vodka
1/2 part Lychee Liqueur
2/3 part Pineapple Juice
2/3 part Mango Juice
2/3 part Lemon Juice
Cocktail Glass

Shake with ice and strain

Sea Foam

1 part Light Rum
1/2 part Triple Sec
splash Peppermint Liqueur
dash Powdered Sugar
1/2 part Lime Juice
Cocktail Glass

Shake with ice and strain

Sea Spray
$1^1/_2$ parts Gin
$^1/_2$ part Melon Liqueur
$^1/_2$ part Pineapple Juice
Cocktail Glass
Shake with ice and strain

Seaweed
$1^1/_2$ parts Pineapple-Flavored Vodka
$1^1/_2$ parts Melon Liqueur
$^1/_4$ part Strawberry Liqueur
$^1/_4$ part Pineapple Juice
Cocktail Glass
Shake with ice and strain

Seether
$1^1/_2$ parts Vodka
$^1/_2$ part Cherry Brandy
1 part Orange Juice
dash Orange Bitters
Cocktail Glass
Shake with ice and strain

Self Starter
2 parts Gin
1 part Dry Vermouth
$^1/_2$ part Apricot Brandy
$^1/_4$ part Pernod®
Cocktail Glass
Shake with ice and strain

Semen de Burro
$1^1/_2$ parts Coconut-Flavored Rum
$^1/_2$ part Lemon Juice
1 part Crème de Coconut
Cocktail Glass
Shake with ice and strain

Sensation Cocktail
$1^1/_2$ parts Gin
$^1/_4$ part Lemon Juice
splash Maraschino Cherry Juice
Cocktail Glass
Shake with ice and strain

Sensitivity
1 part Amaretto
$1^1/_2$ parts Calvados Apple Brandy
splash Green Chartreuse®
splash Cream
Cocktail Glass
Shake with ice and strain

Sensual Healing
1 part Vanilla Liqueur
1 part Mandarine Napoléon® Liqueur
1 part Cream
Cocktail Glass
Shake with ice and strain

Seppuku
$1^1/_2$ parts Gin
splash Melon Liqueur
splash Lychee Liqueur
splash Lemon Juice
1 part Grapefruit Juice
Cocktail Glass
Shake with ice and strain

Serpentine
1 part Light Rum
$^1/_2$ part Brandy
$^1/_2$ part Sweet Vermouth
$^1/_2$ part Lemon Juice
dash Sugar
Cocktail Glass
Shake with ice and strain

Seventh Heaven Cocktail

$1^1/_2$ parts Vodka
2 splashes Grapefruit Juice
2 splashes Maraschino Cherry Juice
Cocktail Glass

Shake with ice and strain

Sex Apple

2 parts Vodka
splash Goldschläger®
$^1/_2$ part Apple Liqueur
1 part Apple Juice
Cocktail Glass

Shake with ice and strain

Sex on the Beach (West Coast)

1 part Melon Liqueur
2 parts Pineapple Juice
Cocktail Glass

Shake with ice and strain

Sex on the Space Station

1 part Melon Liqueur
1 part Blue Curaçao
1 part Sour Mix
splash Lime Juice
Cocktail Glass

Shake with ice and strain

Sex on the Table

1 part Cognac
$^1/_2$ part Kirschwasser
$^1/_2$ part Banana Juice
1 part Pineapple Juice
dash Orange Bitters
Cocktail Glass

Shake with ice and strain

Sexual

1 part Crème de Menthe (Green)
1 part Maraschino Liqueur
$^1/_2$ part Brandy
$^1/_2$ part Gin
Cocktail Glass

Shake with ice and strain

Sexy

1 part Dry Gin
1 part Triple Sec
1 part Apricot Brandy
splash Grapefruit Juice
Cocktail Glass

Shake with ice and strain

Sexy Mountain

1 part Strawberry Liqueur
1 part Gin
$^1/_2$ part Cream
$^1/_2$ part Strawberry Puree
Cocktail Glass

Shake with ice and strain

Shaker

$1^1/_2$ parts Tequila
$^1/_2$ part Lemon Juice
splash Grenadine
1 part Pineapple Juice
Cocktail Glass

Shake with ice and strain

Shakkah Venue

$^2/_3$ part Jamaican Rum
$^2/_3$ part Lemon Juice
$^1/_2$ part Melon Liqueur
$^1/_2$ part Pisang Ambon® Liqueur
splash Coconut Liqueur
$1^1/_2$ parts Pineapple Juice
Cocktail Glass

Shake with ice and strain

Shamrock Cocktail
1 1/2 parts Irish Whiskey
1 part Sweet Vermouth
1/2 part Crème de Menthe (Green)
1/2 part Green Chartreuse®
Cocktail Glass
Shake with ice and strain

Shamrocker
1 part Maraschino Liqueur
1 part Irish Whiskey
2/3 part Sweet Vermouth
2/3 part Club Soda
Cocktail Glass
Shake with ice and strain

Shark's Breath
1/2 part Vodka
1/2 part Gin
1/2 part Light Rum
1/2 part Blue Curaçao
1/4 part Fresh Lime Juice
Cocktail Glass
Shake with ice and strain

Sharp Soul
1 part Melon Liqueur
1 part Apple Brandy
1 part Sour Mix
splash Lime Juice
Cocktail Glass
Shake with ice and strain

Sheer Elegance
1 1/2 parts Amaretto
1 1/2 parts Blackberry Liqueur
1/2 part Vodka
Cocktail Glass
Shake with ice and strain

Sheriff's Shield
1 part Dark Rum
1/2 part Mandarine Napoléon® Liqueur
1/2 part Peach Schnapps
1 part Cream
splash Galliano®
Cocktail Glass
Shake with ice and strain

Shining Star
1 part Gin
1 part Dry Vermouth
1/2 part Passion Fruit Liqueur
1 part Grapefruit Juice
Cocktail Glass
Shake with ice and strain

Ship Cocktail
1 1/2 parts Sherry
splash Jim Beam®
splash Dark Rum
splash Plum Wine
dash Powdered Sugar
Cocktail Glass
Shake with ice and strain

Shiver
1 part Vodka
1 part Crème de Banana
1/2 part Parfait Amour
Cocktail Glass
Shake with ice and strain

Shompy
1/2 part Tequila Silver
1/2 part Orange Bitters
1 part Apricot Brandy
splash Campari®
dash Bitters
Cocktail Glass
Shake with ice and strain

Shooting Star
1 part Apricot Brandy
1 part Sweet Vermouth
dash Angostura® Bitters
Cocktail Glass

Shake with ice and strain

Short Girl
1/2 part Vodka
1/4 part Coconut-Flavored Rum
1/4 part Peach Schnapps
1 part Orange Juice
1 part Pineapple Juice
splash Cranberry Juice Cocktail
Cocktail Glass

Shake with ice and strain

Shot in the Dark
2 parts Bacardi® Limón Rum
1/2 part Dry Vermouth
1/2 part Cherry Brandy
dash Orange Bitters
Cocktail Glass

Shake with ice and strain

Shotgun Wedding
1 part Gin
1 part Dubonnet® Blonde
2 splashes Cherry Brandy
2 splashes Orange Juice
Cocktail Glass

Shake with ice and strain

Showbiz
1 part Vodka
1 part Grapefruit Juice
1 part Crème de Cassis
Cocktail Glass

Shake with ice and strain

Shrek
1/2 part Kiwi Schnapps
1/2 part Melon Liqueur
1/2 part Vanilla Liqueur
1/2 part Absinthe
1 1/2 parts Cream
Cocktail Glass

Shake with ice and strain

Shut Out
1/2 part Blackberry Liqueur
1/2 part Southern Comfort®
1/2 part Sour Mix
1 part Cranberry Juice Cocktail
Cocktail Glass

Shake with ice and strain

Siberian Express
1 part Dry Vermouth
1/2 part Coffee
1/4 part Simple Syrup
1 part Cold Espresso
Cocktail Glass

Shake with ice and strain

Siberian Surprise
1 part Vodka
1 part Peach Schnapps
1/2 part Coconut-Flavored Liqueur
1/2 part Sour Mix
Cocktail Glass

Shake with ice and strain

Side Kick
2 parts Gin
1/2 part Cointreau®
1/2 part Crème de Cacao (White)
splash Lemon Juice
Cocktail Glass

Shake with ice and strain

Siesta
1 1/2 parts Tequila
3/4 part Lime Juice
1/2 part Sloe Gin
Cocktail Glass

Shake with ice and strain

Silent Broadsider
1 1/2 parts Light Rum
1/2 part Anisette
1/2 part Lemon Juice
splash Grenadine
Cocktail Glass

Shake with ice and strain

Silk Stocking
1 1/2 parts Tequila
1/2 part Crème de Cacao (Dark)
1/2 part Raspberry Liqueur
1 part Cream
Cocktail Glass

Shake with ice and strain

Silver Bullet
1 part Kümmel
1 part Gin
2 splashes Lemon Juice
Cocktail Glass

Shake with ice and strain

Silver Cherries Jubilee
1 1/2 parts Gin
1 1/2 parts Crème de Banana
1/2 part Cherry Brandy
1 1/2 parts Cream
Cocktail Glass

Shake with ice and strain

Silver Cocktail
1 part Gin
1 part Dry Vermouth
splash Simple Syrup
splash Maraschino Liqueur
2 dashes Orange Bitters
Cocktail Glass

Shake with ice and strain

Silver Dollar
1 part Crème de Banana
1 part Crème de Menthe (White)
1 part Light Cream
Cocktail Glass

Shake with ice and strain

Silver Star
1 part Bourbon
1/2 part Dry Vermouth
splash Cherry Brandy
Cocktail Glass

Shake with ice and strain

Silver Streak Cocktail
1 1/2 parts Gin
1 1/2 parts Kümmel
Cocktail Glass

Shake with ice and strain

Simple Charm
1 part Cognac
1 part Coffee Liqueur
1 part Amaretto
1/2 part Cream
Cocktail Glass

Shake with ice and strain

Singapore
1 part Goldschläger®
1 part Gin
1/2 part Sour Mix
1/2 part Blueberry Schnapps
Cocktail Glass

Shake with ice and strain

Singing in the Rain
1 part Passion Fruit Liqueur
1 part Sloe Gin
1 part Mango Juice
Cocktail Glass
Shake with ice and strain

Sintra
1 part Melon Liqueur
2/3 part Orange-Flavored Vodka
1 part Cream
Cocktail Glass
Shake with ice and strain

Sir Knight
2 parts Cognac
1/2 part Cointreau®
1/2 part Chartreuse®
dash Angostura® Bitters
Cocktail Glass
Shake with ice and strain

Sister Moonshine
1 part Vodka
1 part Dry Vermouth
1/2 part Apricot Brandy
1/2 part Grapefruit Juice
Cocktail Glass
Shake with ice and strain

Sister Soul
1 1/2 parts Sloe Gin
2/3 part Sweet Vermouth
splash Blue Curaçao
dash Angostura® Bitters
Cocktail Glass
Shake with ice and strain

Sizilia
1 part Bourbon
1 part Crème de Banana
1 part Cherry Brandy
1/2 part Passion Fruit Juice
Cocktail Glass
Shake with ice and strain

Skippy Cosmo
1 part Vodka
1/2 part Cointreau®
1/4 part Grenadine
Cocktail Glass
Shake with ice and strain

Slaughtering the Slothman
1 part Grand Marnier®
1 part Triple Sec
1 part Lemon Juice
splash Grenadine
Cocktail Glass
Shake with ice and strain

Sledge Hammer
1/2 part Lemon Juice
1/2 part Fruit-Flavored Liqueur
1/2 part Blue Curaçao
1/2 part Grand Marnier®
1/2 part Simple Syrup
Cocktail Glass
Shake with ice and strain

Sleepwalker
1 1/2 parts Orange-Flavored Vodka
1/2 part Blue Curaçao
1/2 part Chocolate Liqueur
1 part Cream
Cocktail Glass
Shake with ice and strain

Slick Willy
1 part Light Rum
1 part Brandy
1 part Triple Sec
splash Lemon Juice
Cocktail Glass
Shake with ice and strain

Slocommotion
2 parts Gin
1/2 part Sloe Gin
1 part Cranberry Juice Cocktail
1/2 part Lime Cordial
Cocktail Glass
Shake with ice and strain

Sloe Advance
1 part Sloe Gin
2 parts Gin
1/2 part Lychee Liqueur
dash Peychaud's® Bitters
Cocktail Glass
Shake with ice and strain

Smile Cocktail
1 part Gin
1 part Grenadine
splash Lemon Juice
Cocktail Glass
Shake with ice and strain

Smiling Ivy
1 part Peach Schnapps
1 part Light Rum
1 part Pineapple Juice
1 Egg White
Cocktail Glass
Shake with ice and strain

Smokescreen
1 part Dark Rum
1 part Cherry Brandy
1/4 part Lime Juice
Cocktail Glass
Shake with ice and strain

Smooth Canadian
1 part Whiskey
1/2 part Triple Sec
1/2 part Lime Syrup
1 part Cherry Juice
Cocktail Glass
Shake with ice and strain

Smooth Grand
2/3 part Vodka
2/3 part Amaretto
2/3 part Root Beer Schnapps
1 part Cream
Cocktail Glass
Shake with ice and strain

Smurf® Cum
1 1/2 parts Light Rum
1/2 part Crème de Cacao (White)
1/2 part Blue Curaçao
1 part Cream
Cocktail Glass
Shake with ice and strain

Snake in the Grass
1 part Gin
1 part Cointreau®
1/2 part Dry Vermouth
1/2 part Lemon Juice
Cocktail Glass
Shake with ice and strain

Snake in the Pants

1 part Light Rum
1/2 part Brandy
1/2 part Sweet Vermouth
1/2 part Lemon Juice
dash Sugar
Cocktail Glass

Shake with ice and strain

Snow Fox

3/4 part Vanilla Liqueur
3/4 part Crème de Cacao (White)
1/2 part Coconut Cream
1/2 part Cream
1/2 part Milk
Cocktail Glass

Shake with ice and strain

Snow Job

2 parts Pear Liqueur
1 part Cream
dash Cinnamon
Cocktail Glass

Shake with ice and strain

Snow Ski

1 1/2 parts Blackberry Liqueur
1 part Peppermint Liqueur
Cocktail Glass

Shake with ice and strain

Snow Slip

1 part Vanilla Liqueur
1 part Melon Liqueur
1 part Orange Juice
Cocktail Glass

Shake with ice and strain

Snyder

1/2 part Dry Vermouth
1 1/2 parts Gin
1/2 part Triple Sec
Cocktail Glass

Shake with ice and strain

So-So Cocktail

1 part Gin
1 part Dry Vermouth
1/2 part Apple Brandy
1/2 part Grenadine
Cocktail Glass

Shake with ice and strain

Society Cocktail

3/4 part Dry Vermouth
1 1/2 parts Gin
splash Grenadine
Cocktail Glass

Shake with ice and strain

Sogno d'autunno

1 1/2 parts Vodka
1/2 part Crème de Banana
1/2 part Dark Rum
splash Blue Curaçao
splash Lime Juice
Cocktail Glass

Shake with ice and strain

Son of Sam

1 1/2 parts Light Rum
1/2 part Apricot Brandy
1/4 part Lemon Juice
2 splashes Grenadine
dash Sugar
Cocktail Glass

Shake with ice and strain

Sonora Cocktail
$1^1/_2$ parts Light Rum
$1^1/_2$ parts Calvados Apple Brandy
splash Apricot Brandy
Cocktail Glass

Shake with ice and strain

Soother Cocktail
1 part Apple Brandy
1 part Brandy
1 part Triple Sec
1 part Lemon Juice
dash Powdered Sugar
Cocktail Glass

Shake with ice and strain

Sophisticated Lady
$1^1/_2$ parts Gin
$^2/_3$ part Maraschino Liqueur
$^2/_3$ part Raspberry Liqueur
splash Lemon Juice
Cocktail Glass

Shake with ice and strain

Soul Bossa Nova
1 part Vodka
$^1/_2$ part Crème de Cacao (White)
splash Grenadine
Cocktail Glass

Shake with ice and strain

Sound of Silence
$1^1/_2$ parts Vodka
$^1/_2$ part Lychee Liqueur
$^1/_2$ part Lemon Juice
$^1/_2$ part Simple Syrup
splash Orange Juice
Cocktail Glass

Shake with ice and strain

Sound the Retreat
$^1/_2$ part Crème de Banana
1 part Brandy
$^2/_3$ part Grand Marnier®
1 part Sour Mix
Cocktail Glass

Shake with ice and strain

Sour Apple Cosmopolitan
$^1/_2$ part Sour Apple-Flavored Schnapps
$1^1/_2$ parts Vodka
1 part Cranberry Juice Cocktail
splash Lime Juice
Cocktail Glass

Shake with ice and strain

Sour French Kiss
1 part Crème de Banana
1 part Kiwi Schnapps
1 part Sour Mix
Cocktail Glass

Shake with ice and strain

Sour Strawberry
1 part Scotch
1 part Sour Mix
1 part Strawberry Liqueur
Cocktail Glass

Shake with ice and strain

South Beach Cosmopolitan
2 parts Citrus-Flavored Vodka
$^1/_2$ part Raspberry Liqueur
$^1/_2$ part Cranberry Juice Cocktail
Cocktail Glass

Shake with ice and strain

South Freshness

1 1/2 parts Southern Comfort®
splash Brandy
splash Peppermint Liqueur
splash Grenadine
1/2 part Lemon Juice
1 part Passion Fruit Juice
Cocktail Glass

Shake with ice and strain

South Park

1 1/2 parts Southern Comfort®
1/2 part Apricot Brandy
splash Simple Syrup
1 part Pear Juice
1/2 part Lemon Juice
Cocktail Glass

Shake with ice and strain

South Seas Aperitif

1 part Melon Liqueur
1/2 part Crème de Banana
1/2 part Coconut-Flavored Liqueur
1/2 part Fresh Lime Juice
Cocktail Glass

Shake with ice and strain

Southern Bride

1 1/2 parts Gin
1 part Grapefruit Juice
splash Maraschino Cherry Juice
Cocktail Glass

Shake with ice and strain

Southern Comfort® Cocktail

1 3/4 parts Southern Comfort®
3/4 part Orange Liqueur
1/2 part Lime Juice
Cocktail Glass

Shake with ice and strain

Southern Comfort® Manhattan

2 parts Southern Comfort®
1 part Sweet Vermouth
2 dashes Bitters
splash Grenadine
Cocktail Glass

Shake with ice and strain

Southern Fortune Teller

1 part Southern Comfort®
2/3 part Crème de Cassis
1/2 part Amaretto
1/2 part Cream
Cocktail Glass

Shake with ice and strain

Southern Life

1/2 part Vodka
1/2 part Kiwi Schnapps
1/2 part Southern Comfort®
1/2 part Cranberry Juice Cocktail
1 part Orange Juice
Cocktail Glass

Shake with ice and strain

Southern Sparkler

1 part Southern Comfort®
1 part Grapefruit Juice
1 part Pineapple Juice
splash Carbonated Water
Cocktail Glass

Stir gently with ice and strain

Southern Sunrise

1 part Southern Comfort®
1/2 part Grenadine
1/2 part Lemon Juice
1 part Orange Juice
Cocktail Glass

Shake with ice and strain

Southern Twist
1 part Passion Fruit Liqueur
1 part Southern Comfort®
1 part Cranberry Juice Cocktail
Cocktail Glass

Shake with ice and strain

Southwest One
1 part Vodka
1 part Orange Juice
1 part Campari®
Cocktail Glass

Shake with ice and strain

SpA
1 1/2 parts Apricot Brandy
1 1/2 parts Dry Vermouth
Cocktail Glass

Shake with ice and strain

Space
1 1/2 parts Gin
1 part Frangelico®
Cocktail Glass

Shake with ice and strain

Space Age
1 part Light Rum
1/2 part Triple Sec
1/2 part Kiwi Schnapps
1 1/2 parts Orange Juice
Cocktail Glass

Shake with ice and strain

Space Truckin'
1 1/2 parts Kiwi Schnapps
1 part Blue Curaçao
1/2 part Lemon Juice
Cocktail Glass

Shake with ice and strain

Spanish Bombs
1 1/2 parts Brandy
1 1/2 parts Dry Sherry
1/2 part Galliano®
Cocktail Glass

Shake with ice and strain

Spanish Eyes
2/3 part Blue Curaçao
1 part Licor 43®
splash Orange Juice
splash Cream
Cocktail Glass

Shake with ice and strain

Spanish Kiss
1 part Brandy
1/2 part Crème de Banana
1/2 part Coffee Liqueur
2/3 part Cream
Cocktail Glass

Shake with ice and strain

Spanish Moss
1/2 part Tequila Silver
3/4 part Coffee Liqueur
1/2 part Crème de Menthe (Green)
Cocktail Glass

Shake with ice and strain

Spark in the Night
1 1/2 parts Dark Rum
1/2 part Coffee Liqueur
2 splashes Lime Juice
Cocktail Glass

Shake with ice and strain

Special
1 part Rye Whiskey
splash Apricot Brandy
1 part Lemon Juice
dash Sugar
Cocktail Glass

Shake with ice and strain

Spellbinder
2 parts Citrus-Flavored Vodka
2/3 part Melon Liqueur
splash Blue Curaçao
Cocktail Glass

Shake with ice and strain

Spencer Cocktail
1 1/2 parts Gin
3/4 part Apricot Brandy
splash Orange Juice
dash Bitters
Cocktail Glass

Shake with ice and strain

Sphinx
1 part Gin
splash Dry Vermouth
splash Sweet Vermouth
Cocktail Glass

Shake with ice and strain

Spin Cycle
1 part Gin
1 part Orange-Flavored Vodka
1/2 part Blue Curaçao
1/2 part Mandarine Napoléon® Liqueur
Cocktail Glass

Stir gently with ice and strain

Spinal Tap
1/2 part Apricot Brandy
1 part Apple Brandy
splash Orange Juice
Cocktail Glass

Shake with ice and strain

Spinward Cocktail
1 part Jim Beam®
1 part Irish Cream Liqueur
1 part Peppermint Liqueur
splash Crème de Cacao (White)
Cocktail Glass

Shake with ice and strain

Spirit Wind
1 part Spiced Rum
1 part Passion Fruit Liqueur
1 part Cranberry Juice Cocktail
Cocktail Glass

Shake with ice and strain

Spitball
2 parts Gin
1/2 part Dry Vermouth
2 splashes Maraschino Liqueur
Cocktail Glass

Shake with ice and strain

Spring Feeling Cocktail
1 part Gin
1/2 part Green Chartreuse®
2 splashes Lemon Juice
Cocktail Glass

Shake with ice and strain

Sprint
1 1/2 parts Grappa
1 1/2 parts Amaro Averna®
1/2 part Grand Marnier®
Cocktail Glass

Shake with ice and strain

Spruce
2/3 part Peppermint Liqueur
1 part Brandy
1/2 part Dry Vermouth
1/2 part Sour Mix
Cocktail Glass
Shake with ice and strain

Spy's Dream
splash Melon Liqueur
1 part Currant-Flavored Vodka
1 part Bacardi® Limón Rum
splash Lime Cordial
Cocktail Glass
Shake with ice and strain

Srap Shrinker
1 part Cranberry-Flavored Vodka
1/2 part Raspberry Liqueur
splash Orange Liqueur
1/2 part Lemon Juice
2/3 part Grapefruit Juice
Cocktail Glass
Shake with ice and strain

Ssimo Suprize
1 part Citrus-Flavored Vodka
1 part Melon Liqueur
1/2 part Kiwi Schnapps
1/2 part Lemon Syrup
Cocktail Glass
Shake with ice and strain

St. Mark Cocktail
1 part Gin
1 part Dry Vermouth
splash Cherry Brandy
splash Vermouth
Cocktail Glass
Shake with ice and strain

St. Ignes
2 parts Dark Rum
1 part Passion Fruit Liqueur
splash Amaretto
1 part Pineapple Juice
1 part Lime Juice
Cocktail Glass
Shake with ice and strain

St. Vincent
1 part Vodka
1 part Apricot Brandy
1 part Licor 43®
splash Grenadine
Cocktail Glass
Shake with ice and strain

Stanley Cocktail
1 part Light Rum
3 parts Gin
1 part Lemon Juice
splash Grenadine
Cocktail Glass
Shake with ice and strain

Star Cocktail
1 part Sweet Vermouth
1 part Apple Brandy
dash Bitters
Cocktail Glass
Shake with ice and strain

Star Legend
1 part Vodka
1/4 part Apricot Brandy
1/4 part Campari®
1/4 part Raspberry Liqueur
1/2 part Orange Juice
splash Blue Curaçao
Cocktail Glass
Shake with ice and strain

Star of Love
1 part Vodka
1 part Crème de Cacao (Dark)
splash Frangelico®
1 part Cream
Cocktail Glass
Shake with ice and strain

Star System
1½ parts Peach Schnapps
½ part Vanilla-Flavored Vodka
1 part Orange Juice
1 part Cream
Cocktail Glass
Shake with ice and strain

Starry Night
1 part Blue Curaçao
1 part Cinnamon Schnapps
1 part Rumple Minze®
Cocktail Glass
Shake with ice and strain

Stratosphere
2 parts Light Rum
1 part Brandy
1 part Cherry Brandy
1 part Simple Syrup
Cocktail Glass
Shake with ice and strain

Statue of Liberty
1½ parts Apricot Brandy
½ part Light Rum
splash Simple Syrup
Cocktail Glass
Shake with ice and strain

Steamboat Gin
1½ parts Gin
¾ part Southern Comfort®
½ part Grapefruit Juice
½ part Lemon Juice
Cocktail Glass
Shake with ice and strain

Steamboat Queen
1 part Whiskey
1 part Gin
½ part Apricot Brandy
dash Bitters
splash Lemon Juice
Cocktail Glass
Shake with ice and strain

Stella's Stinger
1½ parts Tequila
splash Pernod®
splash Crème de Menthe (White)
Cocktail Glass
Shake with ice and strain

Step by Step
1 part Light Rum
1 part Blue Curaçao
1 part Lemon Juice
1 part Mango Juice
1 part Passion Fruit Juice
1 part Kiwi Syrup
Cocktail Glass
Shake with ice and strain

Sterlitamak
1½ parts Cherry Brandy
1½ parts Vodka
splash Dubonnet® Blonde
splash Lemon Juice
Cocktail Glass
Shake with ice and strain

Stolen Sorrow
1 part Cherry Brandy
2/3 part Gin
splash Passoã®
2/3 part Grapefruit Juice
splash Lemon Juice
Cocktail Glass

Shake with ice and strain

Stone Cocktail
1 part Dry Sherry
1/2 part Sweet Vermouth
1/2 part Light Rum
Cocktail Glass

Shake with ice and strain

Stonehenge Collins
2 1/2 parts Gin
1/2 part Simple Syrup
splash Crème de Menthe (White)
Cocktail Glass

Shake with ice and strain

Stoner on Acid
1 part Coconut-Flavored Rum
1 part Alizé®
1 part Jägermeister®
Cocktail Glass

Shake with ice and strain

Stork Club Cocktail
1 1/2 parts Gin
splash Triple Sec
splash Lime Juice
dash Angostura® Bitters
Cocktail Glass

Shake with ice and strain

Stovocor
1 part Jim Beam®
1 part Triple Sec
2/3 part Sloe Gin
1/2 part Lemon Juice
Cocktail Glass

Shake with ice and strain

Strange Brew
1 1/2 parts Gin
splash Crème de Cacao (White)
dash Angostura® Bitters
splash Lemon Juice
Cocktail Glass

Shake with ice and strain

Stranger in Town
1 1/2 parts Light Rum
1/2 part Sweet Vermouth
1/2 part Calvados Apple Brandy
1/2 part Cherry Brandy
Cocktail Glass

Shake with ice and strain

Strapple
1 1/2 parts Sloe Gin
splash Strawberry Liqueur
splash Cider
splash Lemon Juice
Cocktail Glass

Shake with ice and strain

Strawberry Girl
1 part Vodka
1 part Strawberry Liqueur
1 part Crème de Cacao (White)
Cocktail Glass

Shake with ice and strain

Strawsmopolitan
2 parts Strawberry-Flavored Vodka
1 part Cointreau®
splash Lime Juice
splash Cranberry Juice Cocktail
Cocktail Glass

Shake with ice and strain

Stress Buster
1/2 part Dry Gin
1/2 part Dry Vermouth
1/4 part Triple Sec
1/4 part Apricot Brandy
splash Peach Schnapps
Cocktail Glass

Shake with ice and strain

Strike!
1/2 part Triple Sec
2/3 part Vodka
2/3 part Passoã®
Cocktail Glass

Shake with ice and strain

Stupid Cupid
2 parts Citrus-Flavored Vodka
1/2 part Sloe Gin
splash Sour Mix
Cocktail Glass

Shake with ice and strain

Suavitas
1/2 part Strawberry Liqueur
1/2 part Frangelico®
1/2 part Galliano®
splash Melon Liqueur
1 1/2 parts Cream
Cocktail Glass

Shake with ice and strain

Sucubus
1 1/2 parts Gin
splash Calvados Apple Brandy
2/3 part White Wine
Cocktail Glass

Shake with ice and strain

Suffragette City
1 1/2 parts Light Rum
1/2 part Grand Marnier®
1/2 part Lime Juice
splash Grenadine
Cocktail Glass

Shake with ice and strain

Sugar Daddy
2 parts Gin
2 splashes Maraschino Liqueur
1 part Pineapple Juice
dash Bitters
Cocktail Glass

Shake with ice and strain

Sugar Kiss
1 part Dark Rum
splash Strawberry Liqueur
splash Grenadine
1 part Pineapple Juice
Cocktail Glass

Shake with ice and strain

Summer Dreams
1 part Midori®
1 part Orange Juice
1 part Lemon Juice
Cocktail Glass

Shake with ice and strain

Summer Night Dream
2 parts Vodka
1 part Kirschwasser
Cocktail Glass

Shake with ice and strain

Sun Chaser
1 part Blue Curaçao
1 part Grand Marnier®
1 part Lemon Juice
splash Root Beer Schnapps
Cocktail Glass

Shake with ice and strain

Sun Ray
1 part Maraschino Liqueur
1 part Amaretto
splash Citrus-Flavored Vodka
Cocktail Glass

Shake with ice and strain

Sunburnt Senorita
2 parts Southern Comfort®
3/4 part Fresh Lime Juice
1/4 part Simple Syrup
Cocktail Glass

Shake with ice and strain

Sunny Coco
1 part Coconut-Flavored Liqueur
1 part Pineapple
1 part Orange Juice
splash Coconut Cream
Cocktail Glass

Shake with ice and strain

Sunny River
1 part Apricot Brandy
1 part Banana Puree
1 part Orange Juice
splash Lemon Juice
Cocktail Glass

Shake with ice and strain

Sunny Sour
2 parts Dark Rum
1/4 part Lemon Juice
dash Powdered Sugar
Cocktail Glass

Shake with ice and strain

Sunset Beach
1 part Vodka
1 part Melon Liqueur
1 part Coconut-Flavored Liqueur
1 part Apricot Juice
Cocktail Glass

Shake with ice and strain

Sunshine Cocktail
1 1/2 parts Gin
3/4 part Sweet Vermouth
dash Bitters
Cocktail Glass

Shake with ice and strain

Super Hero Respite
2/3 part Vodka
1/2 part Crème de Cacao (White)
1/2 part Raspberry Liqueur
1 part Milk
Cocktail Glass

Shake with ice and strain

Super Whites
1 part Triple Sec
1 part Coconut-Flavored Liqueur
1 part Goldschläger®
Cocktail Glass

Shake with ice and strain

Supernova
$1^1/_2$ parts Light Rum
$^3/_4$ part Apple Brandy
2 splashes Sweet Vermouth
Cocktail Glass

Shake with ice and strain

Surf Rider
1 part Vodka
1 part Sweet Vermouth
$^1/_2$ part Lemon Juice
splash Grenadine
splash Orange Juice
Cocktail Glass

Shake with ice and strain

Surfing into the Waves
1 part Raspberry Liqueur
1 part Melon liqueur
1 part Coconut-Flavored Liqueur
1 part Lemon Juice
2 parts Cranberry Juice Cocktail
Cocktail Glass

Shake with ice and strain

Surreal Deal
1 part Apple Brandy
$^1/_2$ part Brandy
$^1/_2$ part Triple Sec
$^1/_4$ part Lemon Juice
dash Powdered Sugar
Cocktail Glass

Shake with ice and strain

Suspended Animation
1 part Melon Liqueur
1 part Grand Marnier®
splash Lime Juice
Cocktail Glass

Shake with ice and strain

Swallow
1 part Crème de Cacao (Dark)
1 part Crème de Banana
1 part Banana Purée
splash Scotch
Cocktail Glass

Shake with ice and strain

Swamp Water
1 part Vodka
1 part Blue Curaçao
1 part Galliano®
Cocktail Glass

Shake with ice and strain

Swat with a Finger
$^1/_2$ part Mescal
splash Melon Liqueur
splash Lemon Juice
splash Orange Juice
$^1/_2$ part Club Soda
Cocktail Glass

Shake with ice and strain

Sweaty Balls
1 part Gin
1 part Apricot Brandy
1 part Dry Vermouth
splash Lemon Juice
Cocktail Glass

Shake with ice and strain

Swedish Chef
1 part Gin
1 part Grape Juice (red)
1 part Swedish Punch
Cocktail Glass

Shake with ice and strain

Swedish Lady
1 part Vodka
1/2 part Strawberry Liqueur
1 part Simple Syrup
1/2 part Cream
Cocktail Glass

Shake with ice and strain

Sweet Anne
1 part Apricot Brandy
splash Peach Schnapps
2/3 part Orange Juice
splash Lemon Juice
Cocktail Glass

Shake with ice and strain

Sweet Box
1 part Goldschläger®
1 part Coffee Liqueur
1 part Irish Cream Liqueur
1 part 151-Proof Rum
1 part Jägermeister®
Cocktail Glass

Shake with ice and strain

Sweet Charge
1 1/2 parts Dry Vermouth
1/2 part Southern Comfort®
2 splashes Light Rum
2 splashes Triple Sec
Cocktail Glass

Shake with ice and strain

Sweet Cherry Cocktail
1 part Scotch
1 part Cherry Brandy
1/2 part Sweet Vermouth
1/2 part Orange Juice
Cocktail Glass

Shake with ice and strain

Sweet Dream Cocktail
1 1/2 parts Vodka
1/2 part Coconut Cream
1 part Orange Juice
1/2 part Powdered Sugar
splash Coconut Liqueur
Cocktail Glass

Shake with ice and strain

Sweet Dumbo
1 1/2 parts Blue Curaçao
1/2 part Light Rum
1/2 part Crème de Menthe (White)
1 part Cream
Cocktail Glass

Shake with ice and strain

Sweet Harmony
1 part Melon Liqueur
1 part Kiwi Juice
1 part Maraschino Liqueur
Cocktail Glass

Shake with ice and strain

Sweet Heart
1 part Parfait Amour
1/2 part Amaretto
1/2 part Vanilla Syrup
1/2 part Cream
1 part Blue Curaçao
Cocktail Glass

Shake with ice and strain

Sweet Jamaica
1 1/2 parts Dark Rum
1/2 part Pineapple Juice
1/4 part Fresh Lime Juice
splash Maraschino Liqueur
Cocktail Glass

Shake with ice and strain

Sweet Maria
1 part Vodka
1 part Amaretto
1 part Light Cream
Cocktail Glass
Shake with ice and strain

Sweet Melody
1/2 part Vanilla Liqueur
1/2 part Raspberry Liqueur
1/2 part Irish Cream Liqueur
2/3 part Plum Brandy
1 part Cream
Cocktail Glass
Shake with ice and strain

A Sweet Peach
2 parts Vanilla-Flavored Vodka
1 part Peach Schnapps
1/2 part Sour Mix
1/2 part Orange Juice
Cocktail Glass
Shake with ice and strain

Sweet Talk
1 part Raspberry Liqueur
1 part Brandy
1 part Cream
Cocktail Glass
Shake with ice and strain

Sweet William
1 part Apricot Brandy
1 part Pear Brandy
1 part Cream
Cocktail Glass
Shake with ice and strain

Swinging Spartan
2/3 part Gin
2/3 part Cherry Brandy
1/2 part Crème de Cassis
1/2 part Dry Vermouth
splash Lemon Juice
Cocktail Glass
Shake with ice and strain

Swiss Miss
1 part Vodka
1 part Crème de Cacao (White)
1/2 part Butterscotch Schnapps
1/2 part Frangelico®
Cocktail Glass
Shake with ice and strain

Sword Fish
1 part Melon Liqueur
1/2 part Dark Rum
1/2 part Light Rum
1/2 part Lemon Juice
fill with Club Soda
Cocktail Glass
Shake all but Club Soda with ice and strain into the glass. Top with Club Soda.

TNT Cocktail
1 part Cognac
1 part Absinthe
1/2 part Cointreau®
dash Bitters
Cocktail Glass
Stir gently with ice and strain

Tadpole
1 part Kiwi Schnapps
1 part Tequila Silver
1 part Sour Mix
Cocktail Glass
Shake with ice and strain

Tahiti Beach Hut

1½ parts Coconut-Flavored Liqueur
½ part Melon Liqueur
splash Cranberry Juice Cocktail
splash Pineapple Juice
⅔ part Sour Mix
Cocktail Glass

Shake with ice and strain

Tailhook

2 parts Gin
⅔ part Maraschino Liqueur
splash Vanilla Liqueur
1 part Lemon Juice
Cocktail Glass

Shake with ice and strain

Tailspin Cocktail

1 part Gin
1 part Sweet Vermouth
1 part Green Chartreuse®
dash Orange Bitters
Cocktail Glass

Shake with ice and strain

Tales of the Future

3 parts Jägermeister®
1 part Melon Liqueur
1 part Raspberry Liqueur
1 part Pineapple Juice
splash Cranberry Juice Cocktail
Cocktail Glass

Shake with ice and strain

Tanqarita

1½ parts Gin
3 parts Margarita Mix
splash Triple Sec
Cocktail Glass

Shake with ice and strain

Tantric

2 parts Vodka
1 part Passion Fruit Liqueur
splash Cranberry Juice Cocktail
splash Pineapple Juice
Cocktail Glass

Shake with ice and strain

Tap Dance

1 part Vodka
½ part Amaretto
½ part Peach Schnapps
1 part Orange Juice
Cocktail Glass

Shake with ice and strain

Tara Reed

½ part Peppermint Liqueur
1 part Light Rum
dash Powdered Sugar
½ part Lime Juice
splash Lemon Juice
Cocktail Glass

Shake with ice and strain

Tartantula

1½ parts Scotch
1 part Sweet Vermouth
½ part Benedictine®
Cocktail Glass

Shake with ice and strain

Taste of Paradise

1 part Crème de Cacao (Dark)
1 part Coconut-Flavored Liqueur
1 part Coffee Liqueur
Cocktail Glass

Shake with ice and strain

Tasty Trinidad
1 part Citrus Flavored Vodka
1 part Blue Curaçao
1/2 part Sour mix
1/2 part Orange Juice
Cocktail Glass

Shake with ice and strain

Tattoo You
1 part Peach Schnapps
1 part Cranberry-Flavored Vodka
1 part Orange Juice
Cocktail Glass

Shake with ice and strain

Tattooed Love Goddess
1 part Vodka
1 part Vanilla Liqueur
1 part Chocolate Liqueur
splash Cream
Cocktail Glass

Shake with ice and strain

Taxi Driver
1 1/2 parts Gin
1/2 part Crème de Banana
1 part Lemon Juice
splash Simple Syrup
Cocktail Glass

Shake with ice and strain

Tea Break
2 parts Dark Rum
1 part Cold Tea
splash Lemon Juice
splash Grenadine
Cocktail Glass

Stir gently with ice and strain

Teenage Lobotomy
1 1/2 parts Jim Beam®
1 1/2 parts Vodka
splash Blue Curaçao
Cocktail Glass

Shake with ice and strain

Temperature Rise
1/2 part Peach Schnapps
1/2 part Amaretto
1/2 part Dark Rum
1 1/2 parts Cranberry Juice Cocktail
Cocktail Glass

Shake with ice and strain

Temptations
1 part Light Rum
1/2 part Fresh Lime Juice
1/2 part Raspberry Liqueur
splash Grenadine
Cocktail Glass

Shake with ice and strain

Tenderness
2/3 part Vodka
1/2 part Passoã®
splash Grand Marnier®
splash Crème de Cassis
splash Lemon Juice
Cocktail Glass

Shake with ice and strain

Tennessee Rye
2 parts Rye Whiskey
1 part Maraschino Liqueur
Cocktail Glass

Shake with ice and strain

Tequila Mockingbird

1 1/2 parts Tequila
3/4 part Crème de Menthe (Green)
splash Lime Juice
Cocktail Glass

Shake with ice and strain

Tequila Pink

1 1/2 parts Tequila
1 part Dry Vermouth
splash Grenadine
Cocktail Glass

Shake with ice and strain

Tequila Stinger

2 parts Tequila
1/2 part Crème de Menthe (White)
Cocktail Glass

Shake with ice and strain

Tequilini

2 1/2 parts Casa Noble Crystal
splash Dry Vermouth
splash Lime Juice
Cocktail Glass

Shake with ice and strain

Tequini

3 parts Tequila
1 part Dry Vermouth
dash Bitters
Cocktail Glass

Shake with ice and strain

Terre Brulee

1 part Brandy
1/2 part Blackberry Liqueur
1/2 part Vanilla Liqueur
1 part Cream
Cocktail Glass

Shake with ice and strain

Tesary

1 part Tequila Silver
1/2 part Coffee Liqueur
1/2 part Licor 43®
1 part Tomato Juice
Cocktail Glass

Shake with ice and strain

Thanksgiving Special

1 part Apricot Brandy
1 part Dry Vermouth
1 part Gin
splash Lemon Juice
Cocktail Glass

Shake with ice and strain

Thirst Quencher

splash Gin
splash Triple Sec
1 part Passoã®
1 part Strawberry Liqueur
fill with Club Soda
Cocktail Glass

Shake with ice and strain

Thirsty Vampire

1/2 part Grenadine
2 parts Cranberry Juice Cocktail
1/2 part Lemon Juice
Cocktail Glass

Shake with ice and strain

Thorns and More

1 part Gin
1/2 part Parfait Amour
1 part Orange Juice
splash Lime Juice
splash Cranberry Juice Cocktail
Cocktail Glass

Shake with ice and strain

Three Count
1 part Vodka
1/2 part Cherry Brandy
1/4 part Crème de Banana
2 splashes Campari®
Cocktail Glass

Shake with ice and strain

Three Mile Island
3/4 part Vodka
3/4 part Midori®
1/4 part Lime Juice
2 parts Apple Juice
Cocktail Glass

Shake with ice and strain

Three Miller Cocktail
1 1/2 parts Light Rum
3/4 part Brandy
splash Lemon Juice
splash Grenadine
Cocktail Glass

Shake with ice and strain

Three Stripes
1 part Gin
1/2 part Orange Juice
1/2 part Dry Vermouth
Cocktail Glass

Shake with ice and strain

Thriller
1 1/2 parts Scotch
1 part Green Ginger Wine
1 part Orange Juice
Cocktail Glass

Shake with ice and strain

Thug Heaven
2 parts Alizé®
2 parts Vodka
Cocktail Glass

Shake with ice and strain

Thunderbolt
3/4 part Gin
3/4 part Apricot Brandy
2 splashes Grenadine
1/4 part Lemon Juice
Cocktail Glass

Shake with ice and strain

Tiera del Fuego
1 part Dark Rum
1 part Tia Maria®
Cocktail Glass

Shake with ice and strain

Tiki Torch
1 1/2 parts White Wine
1/4 part Pineapple Juice
3 splashes Maraschino Liqueur
Cocktail Glass

Shake with ice and strain

Tikini
1 part Vodka
1/2 part Raspberry Liqueur
1/2 part Blue Curaçao
splash Cranberry Juice Cocktail
splash Pear Juice
splash Lime Juice
Cocktail Glass

Shake with ice and strain

Tilt-a-Whirl®
1 1/2 parts Dark Rum
1/2 part Cherry Brandy
1/2 part Sweet Vermouth
1/4 part Lemon Juice
dash Sugar
Cocktail Glass

Shake with ice and strain

Time Killer
2 parts Tequila
1 part Crème de Cacao (Dark)
1 part Heavy Cream
dash Cocoa Powder
Cocktail Glass
Shake with ice and strain

Time Warp
1 1/2 parts Light Rum
1/2 part Grand Marnier®
1/4 part Lime Juice
2 splashes Grenadine
Cocktail Glass
Shake with ice and strain

Timeless
2 parts Scotch
1/2 part Triple Sec
1/2 part Grapefruit Juice
Cocktail Glass
Shake with ice and strain

Tireless
1/2 part Vanilla Liqueur
1/2 part Coconut-Flavored Liqueur
1/2 part Butterscotch Schnapps
1/2 part Crème de Banana
1 part Cream
Cocktail Glass
Shake with ice and strain

Titanic
1 1/2 parts Vodka
1/2 part Dry Vermouth
1/2 part Galliano®
1/2 part Blue Curaçao
Cocktail Glass
Shake with ice and strain

Titi Pink
2/3 part Passion Fruit Liqueur
2 parts Vanilla-Flavored Vodka
splash Cranberry Juice Cocktail
splash Orange Juice
Cocktail Glass
Shake with ice and strain

Toad Cocktail
2/3 part Ginger-Flavored Brandy
1/2 part Triple Sec
2/3 part Lemon Juice
Cocktail Glass
Shake with ice and strain

Tobago Buca
1 part Melon Liqueur
1/2 part Peach Schnapps
1 part Sambuca
2/3 part Milk
Cocktail Glass
Shake with ice and strain

Todos Diaz
1 part Cherry Brandy
1 part Gold Tequila
1 part Ginger Ale
splash Lemon Juice
Cocktail Glass
Shake with ice and strain

Tojo
1 part Triple Sec
1 part Apricot Brandy
1 part Gin
splash Lemon Juice
Cocktail Glass
Shake with ice and strain

Tokyo Cosmo
1 1/2 parts Vodka
1 1/2 parts Sake
1/4 part Pineapple Juice
Cocktail Glass
Shake with ice and strain

Tomb Raider
1 1/2 parts Peach Schnapps
1/2 part Dark Rum
1 1/2 parts Kiwi Juice
splash Lemon Juice
Cocktail Glass
Shake with ice and strain

Top Hat
1 1/2 parts Gin
1 part Apricot Brandy
splash Grenadine
Cocktail Glass
Shake with ice and strain

Top of the Hill
1 1/2 parts Orange Juice
1 1/2 parts Sweet Vermouth
splash Pineapple Juice
dash Orange Bitters
Cocktail Glass
Shake with ice and strain

Topaz
2 parts Scotch
1 part Butterscotch Schnapps
2 splashes Galliano®
Cocktail Glass
Shake with ice and strain

Topps
1 part Crème de Banana
1 part Maraschino Liqueur
1 part Melon Liqueur
1 part Vodka
1 part Sour Mix
1 part Orange Juice
Cocktail Glass
Shake with ice and strain

Tornado
1 1/2 parts Gin
1/2 part Maraschino Liqueur
1 part Orange Juice
Cocktail Glass
Shake with ice and strain

Toronto Orgy
1 part Vodka
1/2 part Coffee Liqueur
1/2 part Irish Cream Liqueur
1/2 part Grand Marnier®
Cocktail Glass
Shake with ice and strain

Torridora Cocktail
1 1/2 parts Light Rum
splash 151-Proof Rum
1/2 part Coffee-Flavored Brandy
splash Cream
Cocktail Glass
Shake with ice and strain

Total Eclipse
1 part Dark Rum
1 part Cranberry Juice Cocktail
1/2 part Lime Juice
1/2 part Passion Fruit Juice
Cocktail Glass
Shake with ice and strain

Tovarich
$1^1/_2$ parts Vodka
$^3/_4$ part Kümmel
2 splashes Lime Juice
Cocktail Glass
Shake with ice and strain

Train Stopper
1 part Vodka
1 part Blackberry Liqueur
splash Crème de Cassis
splash Simple Syrup
$^1/_2$ part Lemon Juice
Cocktail Glass
Shake with ice and strain

Tranquility Cove
1 part Vodka
1 part Peach Schnapps
$^2/_3$ part Cranberry Juice Cocktail
$^2/_3$ part Orange Juice
Cocktail Glass
Shake with ice and strain

Traveling Trocadero
$^2/_3$ part Citrus-Flavored Vodka
1 part Peppermint Liqueur
$^1/_2$ part Pineapple Juice
splash Lime Juice
Cocktail Glass
Shake with ice and strain

Treachery
$^2/_3$ part Goldschläger®
$1^1/_2$ parts Apple Liqueur
$^2/_3$ part Cream
Cocktail Glass
Shake with ice and strain

Tresserhorn
1 part Blue Curaçao
1 part Orange-Flavored Vodka
1 part Absinthe
1 part Sour Mix
Cocktail Glass
Shake with ice and strain

Tribute to Erwin
1 part Lychee Liqueur
1 part Passoã®
1 part Pineapple Juice
Cocktail Glass
Shake with ice and strain

Trick Pony
$1^1/_2$ parts Vodka
splash Crème de Cassis
splash Amaretto
Cocktail Glass
Shake with ice and strain

Trifecta
$1^1/_2$ parts Light Rum
$^1/_4$ part Dubonnet® Blonde
2 splashes Lemon Juice
Cocktail Glass
Shake with ice and strain

Trinidad Cocktail
2 parts Light Rum
2 splashes Lime Juice
dash Sugar
dash Bitters
Cocktail Glass
Shake with ice and strain

Trinity Cocktail
1 part Gin
1 part Dry Vermouth
1 part Sweet Vermouth
Cocktail Glass

Stir gently with ice and strain

Triple Back Flip
1 part Gin
splash Orange Liqueur
splash Grenadine
1/2 part Lemon Juice
1 Egg Yolk
Cocktail Glass

Shake with ice and strain

Triplet
1 part Dry Vermouth
1 part Gin
1 part Peach Brandy
2 splashes Lemon Juice
Cocktail Glass

Shake with ice and strain

Trocadero
1 part Dry Vermouth
1 part Sweet Vermouth
1 part Grenadine
dash Orange Bitters
Cocktail Glass

Shake with ice and strain

Trojan Horse
3/4 part Brandy
3/4 part Dubonnet® Blonde
2 splashes Maraschino Liqueur
1/2 part Lime Juice
Cocktail Glass

Shake with ice and strain

Tropical Cachaça
1 part Cachaça
1 part Coffee Liqueur
1/2 part Pineapple Juice
1/2 part Mango Juice
Cocktail Glass

Shake with ice and strain

Tropical Cream
1 part Melon Liqueur
1 part Peach Liqueur
1 part Light Rum
1 part Coconut Liqueur
1 part Frangelico®
1 part Cream
1 part Orange Juice
Cocktail Glass

Shake with ice and strain

Tropical Dream
1 part Coconut-Flavored Rum
1 part Blue Curaçao
1 part Pineapple Juice
Cocktail Glass

Shake with ice and strain

Tropical Gaze
1 part Vodka
1 part Melon Liqueur
2/3 part Cranberry Juice Cocktail
2/3 part Pineapple Juice
Cocktail Glass

Shake with ice and strain

Tropical Lullaby
1/2 part Irish Cream Liqueur
3/4 part Butterscotch Schnapps
3/4 part Malibu® Rum
3/4 part Pineapple Juice
Cocktail Glass

Shake with ice and strain

Troubled Water

1 part Gin
1/2 part Blue Curaçao
1/2 part Simple Syrup
1/2 part Grapefruit Juice
Cocktail Glass
Shake with ice and strain

Tulip Cocktail

1 part Apple Brandy
1/2 part Sweet Vermouth
1/2 part Lemon Juice
1/2 part Apricot Brandy
Cocktail Glass
Shake with ice and strain

Turf Cocktail

1 part Dry Vermouth
1 part Gin
splash Anisette
2 dashes Bitters
Cocktail Glass
Shake with ice and strain

Tuscaloosa

1 1/2 parts Whiskey
3/4 part Sweet Vermouth
2 splashes Benedictine®
Cocktail Glass
Shake with ice and strain

Tuttosi

1 part Whiskey
1/2 part Brandy
1/2 part Sweet Vermouth
1/4 part Mandarine Napoléon® Liqueur
Cocktail Glass
Shake with ice and strain

Tuxedo

3 parts Sherry
1/2 part Anisette
splash Maraschino Liqueur
2 dashes Angostura® Bitters
Cocktail Glass
Shake with ice and strain

Tweety®

2/3 part Kiwi Schnapps
2/3 part Pear Brandy
2/3 part Orange Juice
splash Lemon Juice
Cocktail Glass
Shake with ice and strain

Tweety® Bird

1 1/2 parts Light Rum
1 part Lime Juice
1/2 part Galliano®
1/2 part Grand Marnier®
Cocktail Glass
Shake with ice and strain

Twenny

1 part Vodka
1 part Coffee Liqueur
1 part Triple Sec
splash Apricot Brandy
Cocktail Glass
Shake with ice and strain

Twenty Thousand Leagues

1 1/2 parts Gin
1 part Dry Vermouth
splash Pernod®
2 dashes Orange Bitters
Cocktail Glass
Shake with ice and strain

Twizzler®
2 parts Vodka
1 part Strawberry Liqueur
splash Grenadine
Cocktail Glass
Shake with ice and strain

Twizzler® Twist
1 part Cherry Brandy
1/2 part Strawberry Liqueur
splash Grenadine
1 part Anisette
1/2 part Milk
Cocktail Glass
Shake with ice and strain

Two Drink Minimum
1 part Coffee-Flavored Brandy
1 part Crème de Cacao (White)
1 part Light Cream
Cocktail Glass
Shake with ice and strain

Two Sheets to the Wind
1 part Dark Rum
1 part Brandy
1 part Orange Liqueur
1 part Lime Juice
Cocktail Glass
Shake with ice and strain

Ultimate Challenger
2/3 part Peach Schnapps
1 part Cream
Cocktail Glass
Shake with ice and strain

Ultra Violet
2 parts Vodka
1/2 part Parfait Amour
Cocktail Glass
Shake with ice and strain

Ultrasonic
1 1/2 parts Triple Sec
1 1/2 parts Mandarine Napoléon® Liqueur
1 part Lemon Juice
1/2 part Simple Syrup
Cocktail Glass
Shake with ice and strain

Unfaithful
1/2 part Blackberry Liqueur
1/2 part Chambord®
2 parts Red Wine
splash Carpano Punt e Mes®
splash Lemon Juice
Cocktail Glass
Stir gently with ice and strain

Unicorn Horn
1 part Raspberry Liqueur
1/2 part Southern Comfort®
2/3 part Grand Marnier®
1/2 part Lemon Juice
Cocktail Glass
Shake with ice and strain

Unisphere
1 1/2 parts Coconut-Flavored Rum
1/2 part Grenadine
splash Pernod®
Cocktail Glass
Shake with ice and strain

United
$2/3$ part Apricot Brandy
$2/3$ part Dry Vermouth
$2/3$ part Apple Brandy
$1/2$ part Sour Mix
Cocktail Glass
Shake with ice and strain

Unlimited
$1\,1/2$ parts Apricot Brandy
$1\,1/2$ parts Passion Fruit
1 part Parfait Amour
Cocktail Glass
Shake with ice and strain

Uranus
$1\,1/2$ parts Vodka
$1/2$ part Pisang Ambon® Liqueur
$1/2$ part Passion Fruit Liqueur
Cocktail Glass
Shake with ice and strain

Uvula
2 parts Brandy
2 splashes Maraschino Liqueur
$1/4$ part Pineapple Juice
splash Lemon Juice
Cocktail Glass
Shake with ice and strain

Valize
1 part Alizé®
1 part Vodka
Cocktail Glass
Shake with ice and strain

Valkyrie
$1\,1/2$ parts Vodka
splash Peppermint Liqueur
$1/2$ part Jägermeister®
1 part Cream
Cocktail Glass
Shake with ice and strain

Valle Rojo
1 part Whiskey
1 part Dry Gin
1 part Triple Sec
splash Orange Juice
splash Grenadine
Cocktail Glass
Shake with ice and strain

Vampire
1 part Vodka
1 part Raspberry Liqueur
$1/2$ part Sweetened Lime Juice
$1/2$ part Cranberry Juice Cocktail
Cocktail Glass
Shake with ice and strain

Van Dusen Cocktail
2 parts Gin
1 part Dry Vermouth
splash Grand Marnier®
Cocktail Glass
Shake with ice and strain

Vancouver
$1\,1/2$ parts Canadian Whiskey
$1/2$ part Cherry Brandy
$1/2$ part Orange Juice
$1/2$ part Lemon Juice
Cocktail Glass
Shake with ice and strain

Vanilla 43
$3/4$ part Licor 43®
$1\,1/4$ part Vanilla-Flavored Vodka
1 part Pineapple Juice
Cocktail Glass
Shake with ice and strain

Vanilla Cream
1 part Vanilla Liqueur
$1\,1/2$ parts Pineapple Juice
1 part Cream
Cocktail Glass
Shake with ice and strain

Vanishing Cream
1 part Crème de Cacao (White)
1 part Chocolate Liqueur
1 part Cream
splash Vodka
Cocktail Glass

Shake with ice and strain

Vanity Fair
1 part Kirschwasser
1 part Amaretto
1 part Maraschino Liqueur
Cocktail Glass

Shake with ice and strain

Velocity Cocktail
1 part Gin
2 parts Sweet Vermouth
splash Orange Juice
Cocktail Glass

Shake with ice and strain

Velvet Elvis
2 parts Vodka
splash Amaretto
splash Chocolate Liqueur
1/2 part Pear Liqueur
Cocktail Glass

Shake with ice and strain

Velvet Kiss
1 part Gordon's® Gin
1/2 part Crème de Banana
1/2 part Pineapple Juice
1 part Heavy Cream
splash Grenadine
Cocktail Glass

Shake with ice and strain

Velvet Orchid
1 part Crème de Cacao (White)
1 part Dry Vermouth
splash Blackberry Syrup
Cocktail Glass

Shake with ice and strain

Velvet Orgasm
1 part Strawberry Liqueur
1 part Crème de Cassis
1 1/2 parts Cream
Cocktail Glass

Shake with ice and strain

Veneto
1 1/2 parts Brandy
1 part Sugar
1 Egg White
1/4 part Sambuca
Cocktail Glass

Shake with ice and strain

Venice
1 part Scotch
1 part Cherry Brandy
1 part Sherry
Cocktail Glass

Shake with ice and strain

Veracruz
2 parts Tequila Silver
splash Crème de Menthe (White)
Cocktail Glass

Shake with ice and strain

Verboten
3 parts Gin
1 part Passion Fruit Liqueur
1 part Lemon Juice
1 part Orange Juice
Cocktail Glass

Shake with ice and strain

Vermouth Triple Sec
1 part Dry Vermouth
1 part Gin
1/2 part Triple Sec
Cocktail Glass

Shake with ice and strain

Vero Beach
1 part Apricot Brandy
1 part Orange Juice
Cocktail Glass

Shake with ice and strain

Veruska
1 part Vodka
1/2 part Campari®
1/4 part Crème de Banana
splash Sweetened Lime Juice
Cocktail Glass

Shake with ice and strain

Vespa
2 parts Sweet Vermouth
3/4 part Gin
1/4 part Dry Vermouth
Cocktail Glass

Shake with ice and strain

VHS
1 1/2 parts Vanilla Liqueur
1 part Scotch
1 part Frangelico®
Cocktail Glass

Stir gently with ice and strain

Via Veneto
1 3/4 parts Brandy
2 splashes Sambuca
2 splashes Lemon Juice
1 1/2 parts Simple Syrup
1/2 Egg White
Cocktail Glass

Shake with ice and strain

Vicious Kiss
3 parts Citrus-Flavored Vodka
2 splashes Maraschino Cherry Juice
2 splashes Lime Juice
Cocktail Glass

Stir gently with ice and strain

Victor, Victoria
1 1/2 parts Dry Vermouth
1/2 part Gin
1/2 part Cherry Brandy
Cocktail Glass

Shake with ice and strain

Villa Beata
1/2 part Coffee Liqueur
1/2 part Coconut Liqueur
1 part Dark Rum
splash Cream
Cocktail Glass

Shake with ice and strain

Vintage 84
1 part Light Rum
1/2 part Pineapple Juice
1/2 part Orange Juice
1 part Apricot Brandy
splash Grenadine
Cocktail Glass

Shake with ice and strain

Violetta Cocktail
1 part Advocaat
1 part Cream
1 part Crème de Cassis
Cocktail Glass

Shake with ice and strain

Violetta Comfort
1 part Vodka
1 part Parfait Amour
1 part Southern Comfort®
splash Fresh Lime Juice
Cocktail Glass

Shake with ice and strain

VIP

1 part Gin
1 part Pimm's® No. 1 Cup
1 part Pineapple Juice
splash Dry Vermouth
Cocktail Glass

Shake with ice and strain

Virgin

1 part Gin
1/2 part Crème de Menthe (White)
1 part Passion Fruit Juice
Cocktail Glass

Shake with ice and strain

Virgin's Blood

2 parts Vodka
1 part Red Curaçao
1 part Strawberry
Cocktail Glass

Stir gently with ice and strain

Visigothic

1 part Goldschläger®
1 part Jägermeister®
2 parts Cream
Cocktail Glass

Shake with ice and strain

Vixen

2 parts Frangelico®
1/2 part Grenadine
1/2 part Coffee Liqueur
Cocktail Glass

Shake with ice and strain

Vodka Gibson

2 parts Vodka
1/2 part Dry Vermouth
Cocktail Glass

Shake with ice and strain. Garnish with a pearl onion.

Vodka Grasshopper

1 part Vodka
1 part Crème de Menthe (Green)
1 part Crème de Cacao (White)
Cocktail Glass

Shake with ice and strain

Vodka Stinger

1 1/2 parts Vodka
1 1/2 parts Crème de Menthe (White)
Cocktail Glass

Shake with ice and strain

Volatile

2 parts Irish Cream Liqueur
1/2 part Amaretto
1/2 part Chocolate Liqueur
Cocktail Glass

Shake with ice and strain

Volga

1 part Vodka
1 part Pineapple Juice
1 part Orange Juice
splash Grenadine
Cocktail Glass

Shake with ice and strain

Voodoo Cocktail

1 part Peach Schnapps
1 part Vodka
1 part Cream
Cocktail Glass

Shake with ice and strain

Voodoo Lady
1 part Triple Sec
1 part Cognac
1/2 part Lemon Juice
Cocktail Glass
Shake with ice and strain

Voodoo Pigalle
1 part Absinthe
2/3 part Melon Liqueur
2/3 part Green Chartreuse®
splash Lemon Juice
Cocktail Glass
Shake with ice and strain

Vorhees Special
1 part Vodka
1 part Coconut-Flavored Rum
1 part Sambuca
1 part Orange Juice
splash Banana Liqueur
splash Tabasco® Sauce
Cocktail Glass
Shake with ice and strain

Vulgar Vulcan
1 part Coconut-Flavored Liqueur
1/2 part Amaretto
1 part Orange Juice
1 part Cream
Cocktail Glass
Shake with ice and strain

Waikiki Beachcomber
1 part Triple Sec
1 part Gin
2 splashes Pineapple Juice
Cocktail Glass
Shake with ice and strain

Wakeumup
1 1/2 parts Gin
2/3 part Triple Sec
2/3 part Lillet®
splash Pastis
2/3 part Lemon Juice
Cocktail Glass
Shake with ice and strain

Waldorf Cocktail
2 parts Bourbon
1 part Pernod®
1/2 part Sweet Vermouth
Cocktail Glass
Shake with ice and strain

Walk the Dinosaur
1 1/2 parts Apricot Brandy
1 part Lemon Juice
dash Powdered Sugar
dash Angostura® Bitters
Cocktail Glass
Shake with ice and strain

Wall Street
1 part Crème de Cacao (White)
1 part Whiskey
1 part Sweet Vermouth
splash Dry Vermouth
2 dashes Bitters
Cocktail Glass
Shake with ice and strain

Walters
1 1/2 parts Scotch
2 splashes Lemon Juice
2 splashes Orange Juice
Cocktail Glass
Shake with ice and strain

Warsaw Cocktail
1 1/2 parts Vodka
1/2 part Dry Vermouth
1/2 part Blackberry Brandy
splash Lemon Juice
Cocktail Glass

Shake with ice and strain

Wasting Day
1 1/2 parts Spiced Rum
1/2 part Vanilla Liqueur
1/2 part Grand Marnier®
splash Butterscotch Schnapps
1 part Cream
Cocktail Glass

Shake with ice and strain

Watchdog
1 1/2 parts Citrus-Flavored Vodka
splash Maraschino Liqueur
1 part Lemon Juice
Cocktail Glass

Shake with ice and strain

Waterbury Cocktail
1 1/2 parts Brandy
splash Grenadine
1/4 part Lemon Juice
dash Powdered Sugar
1 Egg White
Cocktail Glass

Shake with ice and strain

Webster Cocktail
1 part Gin
1/2 part Dry Vermouth
splash Apricot Brandy
1/2 part Lime Juice
Cocktail Glass

Shake with ice and strain

Wedding Bells Cocktail
1 part Orange Juice
1 part Gin
1/2 part Cherry Brandy
Cocktail Glass

Shake with ice and strain

Wedding Wish
1 part Gin
1 part Crème de Cassis
1/2 part Sour Mix
splash Lemon Juice
Cocktail Glass

Shake with ice and strain

Weekender
1 part Gin
1 part Triple Sec
1 part Dry Vermouth
1 part Sweet Vermouth
splash Pernod®
Cocktail Glass

Shake with ice and strain

Weep No More Cocktail
1 part Dubonnet® Blonde
1 part Brandy
splash Maraschino Liqueur
1/2 part Lime Juice
Cocktail Glass

Shake with ice and strain

Wellington Rose
1 1/2 parts Maraschino Liqueur
1/2 part Ginger Liqueur
1/2 part Grenadine
2/3 part Lime Juice
fill with Club Soda
Cocktail Glass

Shake all but Club Soda with ice and strain into the glass. Top with Club Soda.

Wembeldorf

1 part Vodka
1 part Apricot Brandy
1/2 part Lime Juice
1/2 part Sour Mix
1/2 part Pineapple Juice
Cocktail Glass

Shake with ice and strain

West of Eden

1 1/2 parts Peach Schnapps
1 part Scotch
1 part Coconut-Flavored Liqueur
splash Cream
Cocktail Glass

Shake with ice and strain

Westbrook Cocktail

2 parts Gin
1/2 part Sweet Vermouth
splash Scotch
dash Powdered Sugar
Cocktail Glass

Shake with ice and strain

Western

1 part Cognac
1 part Lime Cordial
1/2 part Triple Sec
1/2 part Maraschino Liqueur
Cocktail Glass

Shake with ice and strain

Western Regiment

1 part Amaretto
1/2 part Coffee-Flavored Brandy
2 parts Milk
Cocktail Glass

Shake with ice and strain

Western World

1 1/2 parts Drambuie®
1 part Crème de Banana
1/2 part Lemon Juice
Cocktail Glass

Shake with ice and strain

Westminster

1 part Dry Vermouth
1 part Rye Whiskey
splash Triple Sec
Cocktail Glass

Shake with ice and strain

Wet Dream Cocktail

1 part Gin
1 part Apricot Brandy
1/2 part Grenadine
splash Lemon Juice
Cocktail Glass

Shake with ice and strain

When a Man Loves Woman

1 part Passion Fruit Liqueur
1 part Irish Whiskey
splash Passion Fruit Juice
splash Strawberry Syrup
Cocktail Glass

Shake with ice and strain

Whimsy

1 part Mandarine Napoléon® Liqueur
1/2 part Amaretto
1/2 part Pisang Ambon® Liqueur
1 part Cream
Cocktail Glass

Shake with ice and strain

Whip Crack
1 part Triple Sec
1 part Advocaat
1 part Sour Mix
Cocktail Glass
Shake with ice and strain

Whiplash
1 1/2 parts Brandy
1/2 part Sweet Vermouth
1/2 part Dry Vermouth
2 splashes Triple Sec
Cocktail Glass
Shake with ice and strain

Whirl Hound
1 part Sloe Gin
1 part Triple Sec
1/2 part Sweet Vermouth
1/2 part Dry Vermouth
1/2 part Lemon Juice
Cocktail Glass
Shake with ice and strain

Whiskey Tango Foxtrot
1 part Jim Beam®
1/2 part Amaretto
1/2 part Pernod®
1 part Pineapple Juice
Cocktail Glass
Shake with ice and strain

Whisper Cocktail
1 part Scotch
1 part Dry Vermouth
1 part Sweet Vermouth
Cocktail Glass
Shake with ice and strain

Whispers of the Frost
1 part Blended Scotch Whisky
1 part Cream Sherry
1 part Port
dash Powdered Sugar
Cocktail Glass
Shake with ice and strain

Whistling Dixie
1 part Crème de Menthe (White)
1 part Triple Sec
dash Powdered Sugar
Cocktail Glass
Shake with ice and strain

White Castle
1 part Dry Gin
1 part Dry Vermouth
1 part Triple Sec
splash Fresh Lime Juice
Cocktail Glass
Shake with ice and strain

White Chocolate Stinger
1 part Crème de Cacao (White)
1 part Crème de Menthe (White)
1 part Vodka
Cocktail Glass
Shake with ice and strain

White Cocktail
2 parts Gin
1/2 part Anisette
dash Orange Bitters
Cocktail Glass
Shake with ice and strain

White Commie
1 part Brandy
1 part Coffee Liqueur
1 part Cream
Cocktail Glass
Shake with ice and strain

White Elephant

$1^1/_2$ parts Gin
1 part Sweet Vermouth
1 Egg White
Cocktail Glass

Shake with ice and strain

White Flush Cocktail

$1^1/_2$ parts Gin
1 part Maraschino Liqueur
1 part Milk
Cocktail Glass

Shake with ice and strain

White Goose

1 part Dry Vermouth
1 part Grenadine
1 part Raspberry Liqueur
Cocktail Glass

Shake with ice and strain

White House

1 part Coconut-Flavored Liqueur
1 part Chocolate Liqueur
1 part Cream
splash Vodka
Cocktail Glass

Shake with ice and strain

White Knight

1 part Scotch
1 part Coffee Liqueur
1 part Cream
Cocktail Glass

Shake with ice and strain

White Lightning Cocktail

1 part Crème de Cacao (White)
1 part Light Rum
1 part Cream
Cocktail Glass

Shake with ice and strain

White Lily Cocktail

1 part Light Rum
1 part Gin
1 part Triple Sec
splash Anisette
Cocktail Glass

Shake with ice and strain

White Lion Cocktail

$1^1/_2$ parts Light Rum
$^1/_2$ part Lemon Juice
splash Grenadine
dash Powdered Sugar
2 dashes Bitters
Cocktail Glass

Shake with ice and strain

White Oak

1 part Light Rum
$^1/_2$ part Crème de Cacao (White)
$^1/_2$ part Jim Beam®
$^1/_2$ part Cream
Cocktail Glass

Shake with ice and strain

White Rose Cocktail

$^3/_4$ part Gin
$^1/_2$ part Maraschino Liqueur
2 splashes Orange Juice
1 Lime Slice
1 Egg White
Cocktail Glass

Shake with ice and strain

White Satin
1 part Galliano®
1 part Tia Maria®
1 part Cream
Cocktail Glass

Shake with ice and strain

White Snow
1 part Cream
1 part Passion Fruit Juice
1/2 part Crème de Cacao (White)
Cocktail Glass

Shake with ice and strain

White Spider
1 1/2 parts Vodka
1/2 part Crème de Menthe (White)
Cocktail Glass

Shake with ice and strain

White Way Cocktail
2 parts Gin
1 part Crème de Menthe (White)
Cocktail Glass

Shake with ice and strain

White Wing
2 parts Gin
1 part Crème de Menthe (White)
Cocktail Glass

Shake with ice and strain

Whitney
2 parts Light Rum
1 part Red Wine
splash Lemon Juice
Cocktail Glass

Shake with ice and strain

Whizz Bang
1 part Scotch
1/2 part Dry Vermouth
splash Grenadine
splash Pernod®
dash Orange Bitters
Cocktail Glass

Shake with ice and strain

Whizz Doodle Cocktail
1 part Gin
1 part Scotch
1 part Crème de Cacao (White)
1 part Cream
Cocktail Glass

Shake with ice and strain

Who Knows
2 parts Tequila
1 part Triple Sec
1/2 part Amaretto
Cocktail Glass

Shake with ice and strain

Whore
1 part Vodka
1 part Triple Sec
1/2 part Lemon Juice
Cocktail Glass

Shake with ice and strain

Who's That Girl?
2 parts Gin
2/3 part Apricot Brandy
2/3 part Apple Brandy
splash Lemon Juice
Cocktail Glass

Shake with ice and strain

Who's Ya Daddy

2 parts Cognac
1 part Coffee Liqueur
Cocktail Glass
Shake with ice and strain

Wicked Tasty Treat

2 parts Cinnamon-Flavored Vodka
1 part Amaretto
1 part Coffee Liqueur
1 part Irish Cream Liqueur
1 part Cream
Cocktail Glass
Shake with ice and strain

Wide-Awake

$1^1/_2$ parts Fernet-Branca®
$1^1/_2$ parts Chartreuse®
$^1/_2$ part Peppermint Liqueur
Cocktail Glass
Shake with ice and strain

Wild Cherry

1 part Vodka
1 part Crème de Cacao (White)
$^1/_2$ part Coffee
$^1/_2$ part Frangelico®
Cocktail Glass
Shake with ice and strain

Wild Flower

1 part Apple Brandy
1 part Bacardi® Limón Rum
splash Apricot Brandy
splash Cranberry Juice Cocktail
Cocktail Glass
Shake with ice and strain

Wild Rose

$1^1/_2$ parts Light Rum
1 part Coconut-Flavored Liqueur
splash Grenadine
splash Lemon Juice
Cocktail Glass
Shake with ice and strain

Wild West

$1^1/_2$ parts Brandy
dash Sugar
1 Egg Yolk
Cocktail Glass
Shake with ice and strain

Will Rogers

$1^1/_2$ parts Gin
$^1/_2$ part Dry Vermouth
splash Triple Sec
2 splashes Orange Juice
Cocktail Glass
Shake with ice and strain

Willem Van Oranje

1 part Brandy
$^1/_2$ part Triple Sec
3 dashes Orange Bitters
Cocktail Glass
Shake with ice and strain

Wilson Cocktail

1 part Gin
2 splashes Orange Juice
2 splashes Dry Vermouth
Cocktail Glass
Shake with ice and strain

Windy Road

1 part Coffee Liqueur
$^1/_2$ part Apricot Brandy
$1^1/_2$ parts Cream
Cocktail Glass
Shake with ice and strain

A Winter in Armagnac

$^1/_2$ part Blackberry Liqueur
$^1/_2$ part Strawberry Liqueur
1 part Armagnac
2 parts Cream
Cocktail Glass
Shake with ice and strain

A Winter in Green Park
1 part Melon Liqueur
1/2 part Maraschino Liqueur
splash Coconut-Flavored Liqueur
1/2 part Limoncello
2 parts Cream
Cocktail Glass
Shake with ice and strain

Wintergreen Breathmint
1 part Peppermint Liqueur
1/2 part Melon Liqueur
1/2 part Anisette
splash Chocolate Mint Liqueur
1/2 part Lime Juice
Cocktail Glass
Shake with ice and strain

Witch of Venice
1 1/2 parts Vodka
1/2 part Strega®
2 splashes Crème de Banana
1 part Orange Juice
Cocktail Glass
Shake with ice and strain

Witchery
2 parts Brandy
1/2 part Vanilla Liqueur
1/2 part Chocolate Liqueur
Cocktail Glass
Shake with ice and strain

Wizardry
1 1/2 parts Kirschwasser
1 part Dry Vermouth
1 part Mandarine Napoléon® Liqueur
Cocktail Glass
Shake with ice and strain

Wolf Hound
1 1/2 parts Canadian Whiskey
1/2 part Cherry Brandy
1/2 part Apricot Brandy
1/2 part Lemon Juice
Cocktail Glass
Shake with ice and strain

Wolf's Milk
1 part Peach Schnapps
1 part Crème de Noyaux
1 part Milk
Cocktail Glass
Shake with ice and strain

Womanizer
1 1/2 parts Gin
1/2 part Parfait Amour
1/2 part Cherry Brandy
1/2 part Lime Cordial
Cocktail Glass
Shake with ice and strain

Wong Tong Cocktail
1 part Vodka
1/2 part Gin
1/2 part Dry Vermouth
1 part Lemonade
Cocktail Glass
Shake with ice and strain

Woodcrest Club
1 1/2 parts Gin
3/4 part Sweet Vermouth
2 splashes Pineapple Juice
2 splashes Grenadine
1 Egg White
Cocktail Glass
Shake with ice and strain

Woodstock
1 1/2 parts Gin
splash Maple Syrup
1 part Lemon Juice
dash Orange Bitters
Cocktail Glass
Shake with ice and strain

Woodward
2 parts Rye Whiskey
1/2 part Dry Vermouth
1/2 part Grapefruit Juice
Cocktail Glass
Shake with ice and strain

Works of God
1 part Vodka
1 part Strawberry Liqueur
1 part Cream
Cocktail Glass
Shake with ice and strain

World Trade Center
1/2 part Apricot Brandy
1 1/2 parts Canadian Whiskey
1 part Sweet Vermouth
Cocktail Glass
Shake with ice and strain

Wormwood
1 1/2 parts Scotch
1/2 part Apricot Brandy
1/2 part Campari®
1/2 part Grand Marnier®
Cocktail Glass
Shake with ice and strain

Wyoming Swing
1 part Dry Vermouth
1 part SweetVermouth
1 part Orange Juice
1/2 part Simple Syrup
Cocktail Glass
Shake with ice and strain

X Files
1 part Licor 43®
1/2 part Peach Schnapps
splash Limoncello
dash Bitters
splash Lemon Juice
Cocktail Glass
Stir gently with ice and strain

Xango
1 1/2 parts Light Rum
1/2 part Triple Sec
1 part Grapefruit Juice
Cocktail Glass
Shake with ice and strain

Xanthia Cocktail
1 part Gin
1 part Cherry Brandy
1 part Chartreuse®
Cocktail Glass
Shake with ice and strain

X-Rays
2 parts Light Rum
1/2 part Blue Curaçao
1/2 part Grapefruit Juice
Cocktail Glass
Shake with ice and strain

XYZ Cocktail
2 parts Light Rum
1/2 part Triple Sec
1/2 part Lemon Juice
Cocktail Glass
Shake with ice and strain

Y B Normal?
1 part Brandy
1/2 part Chartreuse®
1/4 part Lemon Juice
dash Powdered Sugar
Cocktail Glass
Shake with ice and strain

Yankee Yodeler
1 part Blue Curaçao
1/2 part Maraschino Liqueur
1/2 part Grapefruit Juice
Cocktail Glass
Shake with ice and strain

Yellow Jade
3 parts Gin
1 part Blackberry Liqueur
1 part Crème de Banana
1 part Cream
Cocktail Glass
Shake with ice and strain

Yellow Sea
1/2 part Dark Rum
1/2 part Maraschino Liqueur
splash Simple Syrup
Cocktail Glass
Shake with ice and strain

Yokohama Cocktail
1 part Gin
1 part Vodka
1 part Grenadine
1 part Orange Juice
Cocktail Glass
Shake with ice and strain

Yolanda
2 parts Sweet Vermouth
1 part Gin
1 part Brandy
1 part Anisette
splash Grenadine
Cocktail Glass
Shake with ice and strain

Yoshi
1 part Chocolate Mint Liqueur
splash Goldschläger®
splash Vanilla Liqueur
splash Benedictine®
Cocktail Glass
Shake with ice and strain

You and Me
2 parts Dry Gin
1 part Dry Vermouth
dash Orange Bitters
Cocktail Glass
Shake with ice and strain

Yukon Cocktail
1 1/2 parts Canadian Whiskey
1/2 part Sugar
1/4 part Triple Sec
Cocktail Glass
Shake with ice and strain

Yuma
1 part Vodka
1 part Triple Sec
1/2 part Apricot Brandy
1/2 part Cognac
Cocktail Glass
Shake with ice and strain

Zabao
1 part Light Rum
1/2 part Dry Vermouth
1/2 part Pineapple Juice
1/2 part Grenadine
Cocktail Glass
Shake with ice and strain

Zabriski Point
1 part Vodka
splash Vanilla Liqueur
splash Apple Brandy
1 1/2 parts Apple Juice
Cocktail Glass
Shake with ice and strain

Zagoo Bears
1 part Peach Schnapps
1/2 part Sloe Gin
1/2 part Guava Juice
1 part Pineapple Juice
splash Lychee Syrup
Cocktail Glass
Shake with ice and strain

Zamba
1 1/2 parts Rum
1 part Sweet Vermouth
Cocktail Glass
Shake with ice and strain

Zanzibar Cocktail
1/2 part Gin
1 1/2 parts Dry Vermouth
dash Orange Bitters
1/2 part Lemon Juice
splash Simple Syrup
Cocktail Glass
Shake with ice and strain

Zara
2/3 part Gin
2/3 part Maraschino Liqueur
splash Sweet Vermouth
splash Lemon Juice
Cocktail Glass
Shake with ice and strain

Zazie
1 part Triple Sec
1 part Gin
1 part Dry Vermouth
splash Orange Juice
Cocktail Glass
Shake with ice and strain

Zephyr
1 part Vodka
1 part Blue Curaçao
1/2 part Parfait Amour
splash Lemon Juice
Cocktail Glass
Shake with ice and strain

Zero
1 1/2 parts Blue Curaçao
1 part Crème de Cacao (White)
1 part Vodka
Cocktail Glass
Shake with ice and strain

Zero Hour
1 part Brandy
1/2 part Triple Sec
1/2 part Strawberry Liqueur
1 part Orange Juice
Cocktail Glass
Shake with ice and strain

Ziga
1 part Gin
1 part Amaretto
1/2 part Dry Vermouth
1/2 part Lemon Juice
Cocktail Glass
Shake with ice and strain

Zip Fastener
1 part Dark Rum
1 part Triple Sec
1/2 part Coffee
Cocktail Glass
Shake with ice and strain

Zoot
1 part Gin
1 part Jack Daniel's®
fill with Lemon-Lime Soda
Cocktail Glass
Build over ice

Zorba
1 part Whiskey
1 Sweet Vermouth
splash Triple Sec
Cocktail Glass
Shake with ice and strain

Shots & Shooters

Served in small glasses and consumed in a single gulp, shots are much easier to define than martinis or cocktails. In this book, the broad category of "shots" has been refined ever so slightly to "shots," "layered shots," "flaming shots," and "Tabasco® shots."

10 Lb. Sledgehammer

1 part Tequila
1 part Jack Daniel's®
Shot Glass

Pour ingredients into glass neat (do not chill)

24 Seven

2 parts Melon Liqueur
1 part Green Chartreuse®
4 parts Pineapple Juice
1/2 part Sweetened Lime Juice
Shot Glass

Shake with ice and strain

252

1 part 151-Proof Rum
1 part Wild Turkey® 101
Shot Glass

Pour ingredients into glass neat (do not chill)

3 Wise Men

1 part Jack Daniel's®
1 part Johnnie Walker® Black Label
1 part Jim Beam®
Shot Glass

Pour ingredients into glass neat (do not chill)

40 Skit and a Bent Jant

1 part Blue Curaçao
1 part Jägermeister®
1 part Citrus-Flavored Vodka
1 part Peach Schnapps
1 part Cranberry Juice Cocktail
1 part Pineapple Juice
splash Lime Juice
Shot Glass

Shake with ice and strain

49er Gold Rush

1 part Goldschläger®
1 part Tequila
Shot Glass

Shake with ice and strain

649

Various Ingredients (see below)
Shot Glass

Stand facing the bar and count off the bottles: 6th from right, 4th from left, and 9th from right. Pour equal parts of each into a shot glass neat (do not chill).

8 Ball

4 parts Coconut-Flavored Rum
4 parts Peach Schnapps
4 parts Raspberry Liqueur
4 parts Vodka
splash Lemon-Lime Soda
1 1/2 parts Cranberry Juice Cocktail
1 1/2 parts Sour Mix
splash Grenadine
Shot Glass

Shake with ice and strain

8 Seconds

1 part Jägermeister®
1 part Goldschläger®
1 part Hot Damn!® Cinnamon Schnapps
1 part Rumple Minze®
Shot Glass

Shake with ice and strain

911

1 part 100-Proof Peppermint Schnapps
1 part 100-Proof Cinnamon Schnapps
Shot Glass

Pour ingredients into glass neat (do not chill)

Absohot

1/2 part Absolut® Peppar Vodka
splash Hot Sauce
1 Beer
Shot Glass

Mix Vodka and Hot Sauce in a shot glass. Serve with beer chaser.

Absolut® Antifreeze

1 part Melon Liqueur
2 parts Absolut® Citron Vodka
2 parts Lemon-Lime Soda
Shot Glass

Shake with ice and strain

Absolut® Asshole

2 parts Vodka
1 part Sour Apple Schnapps
Shot Glass

Shake with ice and strain

Absolut® Hunter

2 parts Vodka
1 part Jägermeister®
Shot Glass

Shake with ice and strain

Absolut® Passion

2 parts Vodka
1 part Passion Fruit Juice
Shot Glass

Shake with ice and strain

Absolut® Pepparmint

1 part Absolut® Peppar Vodka
splash Peppermint Schnapps
Shot Glass

Shake with ice and strain

Absolut® Testa Rossa

1 part Vodka
1/2 part Campari®
Shot Glass

Shake with ice and strain

Absolutely Fruity

1 part Vodka
1 part 99-proof Banana Liqueur
1 part Watermelon Schnapps
Shot Glass

Shake with ice and strain

Absolutely Screwed

1 part Orange-Flavored Vodka
1 part Orange Juice
Shot Glass

Shake with ice and strain

Acid Cookie

1 part Irish Cream Liqueur
1 part Butterscotch Schnapps
1 part Hot Damn!® Cinnamon Schnapps
splash 151-Proof Rum
Shot Glass

Shake with ice and strain

The Action Contraction

1 part Banana Liqueur
1 part Peppermint Schnapps
1 part Sambuca
splash Lemon Juice
Shot Glass

Shake with ice and strain

Adam Bomb

1 part Sour Apple Schnapps
1 part Goldschläger®
Shot Glass

Shake with ice and strain

Adios, Motherfucker

1 part Vodka
1 part Gin
1 part Rum
1 part Tequila
1 part Triple Sec
2 partsSour Mix
splash Cola
splash Blue Curaçao
Shot Glass

Shake with ice and strain. *Note: Because this recipe includes many ingredients, it's easier to make in volume, about 6 shots.

Adult Lit

1 part Dry Gin
1 part Vodka
1 part Triple Sec
1 part Light Rum
Shot Glass

Shake with ice and strain

Affair Shot

1 part Strawberry Liqueur
1 part Orange Juice
Shot Glass

Shake with ice and strain

After Eight® Shooter

1 part Crème de Cacao (White)
1 part Crème de Menthe (White)
1 part Vodka
Shot Glass

Shake with ice and strain

Afterburner

1 part After Shock® Cinnamon Schnapps
1 part 151-Proof Rum
Shot Glass

Pour ingredients into glass neat (do not chill)

Afterburner #2
1 part Pepper-Flavored Vodka
1 part Coffee
1 part Goldschläger®
Shot Glass

Pour ingredients into glass neat (do not chill)

Airhead
1 1/2 parts Peach Schnapps
fill with Cranberry Juice Cocktail
Shot Glass

Shake with ice and strain

Alabama Slammer
1 part Coffee Liqueur
1 part Tequila
1 part Lemon-Lime Soda
Shot Glass

Shake with ice and strain

Alabama Slammer #2
1 part Southern Comfort®
1 part Jack Daniel's®
1 part Amaretto
splash Orange Juice
splash Grenadine
Shot Glass

Shake with ice and strain

Alaskan Oil Slick
1 part Blue Curaçao
1 part Peppermint Schnapps
splash Jägermeister®
Shot Glass

Chill Blue Curaçao and Strain into shot glass. Float Jägermeister® on top.

Alaskan Pipeline
1 part Yukon Jack®
1 part Amaretto
Shot Glass

Shake with ice and strain

Alcoholic Peppermint Pattie
1 part Rumple Minze®
1/2 part Chocolate Syrup
Shot Glass

Pour Chocolate Syrup into your mouth, followed by a shot of Rumple Minze®. Shake it around and swallow.

Alice from Dallas Shooter
1 part Coffee Liqueur
1 part Mandarine Napoléon® Liqueur
1 part Tequila Reposado
Shot Glass

Shake with ice and strain

Alien
1 part Blue Curaçao
splash Irish Cream Liqueur
Shot Glass

Pour the Blue Curaçao into a chilled shot glass, then pour the Irish Cream into the center

Alien Secretion
1 part Vodka
1 part Melon Liqueur
1 part Coconut-Flavored Rum
1 part Pineapple Juice
Shot Glass

Shake with ice and strain

Almond Cookie
1 part Amaretto
1 part Butterscotch Schnapps
Shot Glass

Shake with ice and strain

Alpine Breeze
1 part Pineapple Juice
1 part Grenadine
1/2 part Crème de Menthe (White)
1/2 part Dark Rum
Shot Glass

Shake with ice and strain

Amaretto Chill
1 part Vodka
1 part Amaretto
1 part Lemonade
1 part Pineapple Juice
Shot Glass

Shake with ice and strain

Amaretto Kamikaze
1 part Vodka
1 part Amaretto
fill with Sour Mix
Shot Glass

Shake with ice and strain

Amaretto Lemondrop
1 part Vodka
1 part Amaretto
fill with Lemonade
Shot Glass

Build over ice and stir

Amaretto Pie
1 part Amaretto
1 part Orange Juice
1 part Pineapple Juice
Shot Glass

Shake with ice and strain

Amaretto Slammer
1 part Amaretto
1 part Lemon-Lime Soda
Shot Glass

Combine in a shot glass. Cover with your hand, slam on the bar, and drink.

Amaretto Slammer #2
1 part Amaretto
1 part Cherry-Flavored Schnapps
Shot Glass

Shake with ice and strain over ice

Amaretto Sourball
1 part Vodka
1 part Amaretto
1 part Lemonade
1 part Orange Juice
Shot Glass

Shake with ice and strain

Amaretto Sweet Tart
1 part Vodka
1 part Amaretto
1 part Cherry Juice
1 part Wild Berry Schnapps
fill with Lemonade
Shot Glass

Shake with ice and strain

Amenie Mama
3 parts Irish Whiskey
1 part Amaretto
Shot Glass

Shake with ice and strain

American Apple Pie
1 part Cinnamon Schnapps
1 part Apple Juice
Shot Glass
Shake with ice and strain

American Dream
1 part Coffee Liqueur
1 part Amaretto
1 part Frangelico®
1 part Crème de Cacao (Dark)
Shot Glass
Shake with ice and strain

Anabolic Steriods
2 parts Triple Sec
2 parts Melon Liqueur
1 part Blue Curaçao
Shot Glass
Shake with ice and strain

Andies
1 part Crème de Cacao (Dark)
1 part Crème de Menthe (White)
Shot Glass
Shake with ice and strain

Angel Wing
1 part Crème de Cacao (White)
1 part Brandy
Shot Glass
Shake with ice and strain

Angel's Lips
1 part Irish Cream Liqueur
2 parts Benedictine®
Shot Glass
Shake with ice and strain

Angel's Rush Shooter
1 part Cream
1 part Frangelico®
Shot Glass
Shake with ice and strain

The Angry German
1 part Amaretto
1 part Black Haus® Blackberry Schnapps
1 part Jägermeister®
2 parts Lime Juice
dash Salt
Shot Glass
Shake with ice and strain

Anita
1 part Apricot Brandy
1 part Maraschino Liqueur
1 part Grenadine
1 part Campari®
1 part Cream
Shot Glass
Shake with ice and strain. *Note: Because this recipe includes many ingredients, it's easier to make in volume, about 6 shots.

Anonymous
1 part Southern Comfort®
1 part Raspberry Liqueur
1 part Sour Mix
Shot Glass
Shake with ice and strain

Anti Freeze
1 part Crème de Menthe (Green)
1 part Vodka
Shot Glass
Shake with ice and strain

Apple and Cinnamon Joy
1 part Sour Apple Schnapps
splash Goldschläger®
Shot Glass
Pour ingredients into glass neat (do not chill)

Apple and Spice Shooter
1 part Sour Apple Schnapps
1 part Spiced Rum
Shot Glass

Shake with ice and strain

Apple Cobbler
1 part Sour Apple Schnapps
1 part Goldschläger®
1 part Irish Cream Liqueur
Shot Glass

Shake with ice and strain

Apple Fucker
1 part Sour Apple Schnapps
1 part Vodka
Shot Glass

Shake with ice and strain

Apple Jolly Rancher®
1 part Melon Liqueur
1 part Sour Mix
1 part Crown Royal® Whiskey
Shot Glass

Shake with ice and strain

Apple Kamihuzi
1 part Tequila
1 part Sour Apple Schnapps
splash Sour Mix
Shot Glass

Shake with ice and strain

Apple Kamikaze
1 part Vodka
1 part Sour Apple Schnapps
splash Sour Mix
Shot Glass

Shake with ice and strain

Apple Lemondrop
1 part Vodka
1 part Sour Apple Schnapps
splash Lemonade
Shot Glass

Shake with ice and strain

Apple Mule
1 part Amaretto
1 part Jack Daniel's®
1 1/2 parts Lime Juice
2 parts Orange Juice
1 part Southern Comfort®
1 part Triple Sec
Shot Glass

Shake with ice and strain. *Note: Because this recipe includes many ingredients, it's easier to make in volume, about 6 shots.

Apple Pie Shot
1 part Irish Mist
1 part Cinnamon Schnapps
1 part Frangelico®
1 part Amaretto
Shot Glass

Shake with ice and strain

Applecake
1 part Licor 43®
1 part Apple Brandy
1 part Milk
Shot Glass

Shake with ice and strain

Arctic Brain Freeze
1 part Amaretto
1 part Melon Liqueur
Shot Glass

Shake with ice and strain

Arizona Antifreeze
1 part Vodka
1 part Melon Liqueur
1 part Sour Mix
Shot Glass

Shake with ice and strain

Arizona Twister

1 part Vodka
1 part Coconut-Flavored Rum
1 part Tequila
splash Orange Juice
splash Pineapple Juice
splash Crème de Coconut
splash Grenadine
Shot Glass

Shake with ice and strain. *Note: Because this recipe includes many ingredients, it's easier to make in volume, about 6 shots.

Arkansas Rattler

1 part Cinnamon Schnapps
1 part Tequila
Shot Glass

Pour ingredients into glass neat (do not chill)

Army Green

1 part Goldschläger®
1 part Jägermeister®
1 part Tequila
Shot Glass

Shake with ice and strain

Arturros' Burning Mindtwister

1 part Scotch
1 part Tequila
Shot Glass

Shake with ice and strain

Astronaut Shooter

1 part Vodka (chilled)
1 Lemon Wedge
dash Sugar
dash Instant Coffee Granules
Shot Glass

Coat the lemon with sugar on one side and instant coffee on the other, suck lemon and drink the chilled vodka

The Atomic Shot

1 part Tequila Silver
1 part Goldschläger®
1 part Absolut® Peppar Vodka
splash Club Soda
Shot Glass

Shake with ice and strain

Auburn Headbanger

1 part Jägermeister®
1 part Goldschläger®
Shot Glass

Shake with ice and strain

Avalanche Shot

1 part Crème de Cacao (Dark)
1 part Coffee Liqueur
1 part Southern Comfort®
Shot Glass

Shake with ice and strain

Awwwwwww

1 part Gold Rum
1 part Triple Sec
dash Bitters
Shot Glass

Pour ingredients into glass neat (do not chill)

Azurra

1 part Light Rum
splash Blue Curaçao
splash Crème de Cacao (White)
Shot Glass

Shake with ice and strain

B-2 Bomber

1 part Rum
1 part Southern Comfort®
1 part Lemon-Lime Soda
1 part Gatorade®
Shot Glass

Shake with ice and strain

B-52

1 part Amaretto
2 parts Irish Cream Liqueur
1 part Rum
Shot Glass

Pour the Amaretto, then the Irish Cream Liqueur, and then, carefully, the Rum. Light the shot on fire and drink it with a straw, or slap it to extinguish the flame and then drink.

B-54

1 part Irish Cream Liqueur
1 part Crème de Menthe (Green)
1 part Grand Marnier®
1 part Coffee Liqueur
Shot Glass

Shake with ice and strain

Back Shot

1 part Vodka
1 part Raspberry Liqueur
2 parts Sour Mix
Shot Glass

Shake with ice and strain

Back Street Romeo

2 parts Whiskey
1 part Irish Cream Liqueur
Shot Glass

Shake with ice and strain

Backdraft Shooter

1 part Rum
1 part Cinnamon Schnapps
Shot Glass

Pour ingredients into glass neat (do not chill)

Bald Eagle Shooter

1 part Crème de Menthe (White)
1 part Tequila Reposado
Shot Glass

Shake with ice and strain

Ball and Chain

1 part Rumple Minze®
1 part Goldschläger®
splash Jägermeister®
Shot Glass

Shake with ice and strain

Ball Hooter

1 part Tequila
1 part Peppermint Schnapps
Shot Glass

Shake with ice and strain

Banamon

1 part Pisang Ambon® Liqueur
1/2 part Amaretto
1/2 part Ginger Ale
Shot Glass

Stir gently with ice and strain

Banana Boat Shooter

1 part Crème de Menthe (White)
1 part Coffee
1 part Ponche Kuba®
Shot Glass

Shake with ice and strain

Banana Boomer Shooter

1 part Vodka
1 part Crème de Banana
Shot Glass

Shake with ice and strain

Banana Cream Pie

1 part Banana Liqueur
1 part Crème de Cacao (White)
1 part Vodka
1 part Half and Half
Shot Glass

Shake with ice and strain

Banana Lemon Surprise
1 part Banana Liqueur
3 parts Lemon Juice
Shot Glass

Shake with ice and strain

Banana Licorice
1 part Banana Liqueur
1/2 part Cherry Brandy
1/2 part Sambuca
Shot Glass

Shake with ice and strain

Banana Popsicle® Shooter
1 part Vodka
1 part Crème de Banana
1 part Orange Juice
Shot Glass

Shake with ice and strain

Banana Slug
3 parts 99-Proof Banana Liqueur
1 part Pineapple Juice
Shot Glass

Shake with ice and strain

Banana Split Shooter
1 part Banana Liqueur
1 part Vodka
Shot Glass

Shake with ice and strain

Banana Sweet Tart
1 part Vodka
1 part Banana Liqueur
1 part Cherry Juice
fill with Lemonade
Shot Glass

Shake with ice and strain

Bananas and Cream
1 part Coffee Liqueur
1 part Irish Cream Liqueur
1 part 99-Proof Banana Liqueur
Shot Glass

Shake with ice and strain

Banderas
1 part Tomato Juice
1 part Silver Tequila
1 part Lime Juice
Shot Glass

Line up the shots to represent the Mexican flag: Tomato (red), Tequila (white), and Lime (green). Consume quickly in order.

Banshee Shooter
1 part Crème de Cacao (White)
1 part Cream
1 part Crème de Banana
Shot Glass

Shake with ice and strain

Barbados Blast
1 part Dark Rum
1 part Triple Sec
1 part Ginger Liqueur
Shot Glass

Shake with ice and strain

Barbed Wire
1 part Goldschläger®
1 part Sambuca
Shot Glass

Shake with ice and strain

Barbie® Shot
1 part Coconut-Flavored Rum
1 part Vodka
1 part Cranberry Juice Cocktail
1 part Orange Juice
Shot Glass

Shake with ice and strain

Bare Ass
1 part Amaretto
splash Peach Schnapps
1/2 part Pineapple Juice
Shot Glass

Shake with ice and strain

Barfing Sensations
1 part Blackberry Liqueur
1 part Peach Schnapps
1 part Vodka
1 part Apple Brandy
1 part Raspberry Liqueur
Shot Glass

Shake with ice and strain. *Note: Because this recipe includes many ingredients, it's easier to make in volume, about 6 shots.

Barney® on Acid
1 part Blue Curaçao
1 part Jägermeister®
splash Cranberry Juice Cocktail
Shot Glass

Shake with ice and strain

Bartender's Wet Dream
1 part Grenadine
1 part Coffee Liqueur
1 part Irish Cream Liqueur
Shot Glass

Shake with ice and strain. Top with whipped cream

Bayou Juice
1 part Coconut-Flavored Rum
1 part Spiced Rum
1 part Amaretto
1 part Cranberry Juice Cocktail
1 part Pineapple Juice
Shot Glass

Shake with ice and strain

Bazooka® Bubble Gum
1 part Southern Comfort®
1 part Banana Liqueur
1 part Cream
1 part Grenadine
Shot Glass

Shake with ice and strain

Bazooka Joe®
1 part Banana Liqueur
1 part Blue Curaçao
1 part Grand Marnier®
Shot Glass

Shake with ice and strain

Bazooka Moe
1 part Blue Curaçao
1 part Crème de Banana
Shot Glass

Shake with ice and strain

Bear Dozer
1 part Tequila
1 part Whiskey
1 part Cherry Brandy
Shot Glass

Shake with ice and strain

Bearded Boy
1 part Southern Comfort®
1 part Vodka
1 part Water
splash Grain Alcohol
Shot Glass

Shake with ice and strain

Beaver Dam
1 part Vodka
1 part Peach Schnapps
1 part Gatorade®
Shot Glass

Shake with ice and strain

Beavis and Butt-head®

1 part Sour Apple Schnapps
1 part Cinnamon Schnapps
Shot Glass

Shake with ice and strain

A Bedrock

1 part Sambuca
1 part Coffee Liqueur
splash Milk
Shot Glass

Shake with ice and strain

Belfast Car Bomb

1 pint Guinness® Stout
1 part Irish Cream Liqueur
1 part Scotch
Shot Glass

Drop a shot glass filled with scotch into a pint of Guiness and float an ounce of Irish Cream Liqueur on top.

Bend Me Over Shooter

1 part Crown Royal® Whiskey
1 part Amaretto
1 part Sour Mix
Shot Glass

Shake with ice and strain

Beowulf

1 part Blue Curaçao
1 part Vodka
Shot Glass

Shake with ice and strain

The Berry Kix®

2 parts Currant-Flavored Vodka
1 part Sour Mix
Shot Glass

Shake with ice and strain

Berube's Death

1 part Cinnamon Schnapps
1 part Black Sambuca
1 part Jägermeister®
1 part Rumple Minze®
Shot Glass

Shake with ice and strain

Betty Come Back

2 parts Tequila Silver
1 part Triple Sec
1 part Parfait Amour
Shot Glass

Shake with ice and strain

The Bianca Pop

1 part Coconut-Flavored Rum
1 part Amaretto
Shot Glass

Shake with ice and strain

Big Baller

2 parts Vodka
1 part Gin
1 part Triple Sec
splash Lemon Juice
Shot Glass

Shake with ice and strain

Big Pine Puss

1 part Spiced Rum
$1/2$ part Banana Liqueur
splash Lime Juice
splash Grenadine
splash Cranberry Juice Cocktail
Shot Glass

Shake with ice and strain

Big Red

1 part Irish Cream Liqueur
1 part Goldschläger®
Shot Glass

Shake with ice and strain

Big Roller
1 part Amaretto
1 part Coffee
1 part Crème de Banana
Shot Glass

Shake with ice and strain

Big Time
1 part Cognac
1 part Pernod®
Shot Glass

Shake with ice and strain

Big Unit
2 parts Tequila
1 part Blue Curaçao
Shot Glass

Shake with ice and strain

The Big V
1 part Vodka
1 part Crème de Cacao (White)
1 part Blue Curaçao
1 part Sour Mix
Shot Glass

Shake with ice and strain

Biglower
2 parts Dark Rum
1 part Crème de Cacao (Dark)
1 part Amaretto
Shot Glass

Shake with ice and strain

Billy Bad Ass
1 part 151-Proof Rum
1 part Tequila
1 part Jägermeister®
Shot Glass

Shake with ice and strain

Bird Shit
1 part Blackberry Brandy
splash Tequila
splash Milk
Shot Glass

Fill shot glass about 3/4 full with Blackberry Brandy. Float the Tequila on top of brandy. Pour in a little bit of milk for effect.

Bite of the Iguana
1 part Tequila
1 part Triple Sec
1/2 part Vodka
2 parts Orange Juice
2 parts Sour Mix
Shot Glass

Shake with ice and strain

Black and Blue Shark
2 parts Jack Daniel's®
1 part Gold Tequila
1 part Vodka
1 part Blue Curaçao
Shot Glass

Shake with ice and strain

Black Apple
1 part Blackberry Liqueur
1 part Sour Apple Schnapps
splash Lemon-Lime Soda
splash Sour Mix
Shot Glass

Shake with ice and strain

Black Blood
2 parts Blue Curaçao
1 part Jägermeister®
1 part Ruby Red Grapefruit Juice
Shot Glass

Shake with ice and strain

Black Death

1 part Jack Daniel's®
1 part Tequila
Shot Glass

Shake with ice and strain

Black Death #2

3 parts Vodka
1 part Soy Sauce
Shot Glass

Shake with ice and strain

Black Forest Cake

1 part Cherry Brandy
1 part Coffee Liqueur
1 part Irish Cream Liqueur
Shot Glass

Shake with ice and strain

Black Gold Shooter

1 part Black Sambuca
1 part Cinnamon Schnapps
Shot Glass

Shake with ice and strain

Black Hole

1 part Jägermeister®
1 part Rumple Minze®
Shot Glass

Shake with ice and strain

Black Orgasm

1 part Vodka
1 part Sloe Gin
1 part Blue Curaçao
1 part Peach Schnapps
Shot Glass

Shake with ice and strain

Black Pepper

1 part Pepper-Flavored Vodka
splash Blackberry Brandy
Shot Glass

Shake with ice and strain

Blackberry Sourball

1 part Vodka
1 part Blackberry Liqueur
splash Lemonade
splash Orange Juice
Shot Glass

Shake with ice and strain

Blazing Saddle

3 parts Blackberry Brandy
1 part 151-Proof Rum
Shot Glass

Shake with ice and strain

Bleacher Creature

1 part Butterscotch Schnapps
1 part 151-Proof Rum
Shot Glass

Pour ingredients into glass neat (do not chill)

Bleedin' Hell

1 part Vodka
1 part Strawberry Liqueur
1 part Lemonade
Shot Glass

Shake with ice and strain

Bliss

1 part Vanilla Liqueur
1 part Vanilla-Flavored Vodka
1 part Vanilla Cola
splash Honey
Shot Glass

Shake with ice and strain

Blister
1 part 151-Proof Rum
1 part Wild Turkey® Bourbon
1 part Blue Curaçao
splash Pineapple Juice
splash Orange Juice
Shot Glass

Shake with ice and strain

Blister in the Sun
2 parts Canadian Whiskey
1 part Raspberry Liqueur
1 part Orange Juice
1 part Lemon Juice
1 part Lemon-Lime Soda
Shot Glass

Shake with ice and strain. *Note: Because this recipe includes many ingredients, it's easier to make in volume, about 6 shots.

Blood Bath
1 part Tequila Silver
1 part Strawberry Liqueur
Shot Glass

Shake with ice and strain

Blood Test
1 part Tequila Reposado
1 part Grenadine
Shot Glass

Shake with ice and strain

Blue Balls
2 parts Blue Curaçao
2 parts Coconut-Flavored Rum
1 part Peach Schnapps
splash Sour Mix
splash Lemon-Lime Soda
Shot Glass

Shake with ice and strain. *Note: Because this recipe includes many ingredients, it's easier to make in volume, about 6 shots.

Blue Balls Shot
1 part Blue Curaçao
1 part Dr. McGillicuddy's® Mentholmint Schnapps
Shot Glass

Shake with ice and strain

Blue Banana
1 part Crème de Banana
1 part Blue Curaçao
Shot Glass

Shake with ice and strain

Blue Bastard
2 parts Triple Sec
1 part Blueberry Schnapps
splash Lime Juice
splash Simple Syrup
Shot Glass

Shake with ice and strain

Blue Caboose
1 part Irish Cream Liqueur
1 part Whiskey
1 part Amaretto
Shot Glass

Shake with ice and strain

Blue Ghost
1 part Banana Liqueur
1 part Blue Curaçao
1 part Coconut-Flavored Rum
1 part Vodka
1 part Crème de Cacao (White)
1 part Light Rum
1 part Triple Sec
4 parts Cream
Shot Glass

Shake with ice and strain. *Note: Because this recipe includes many ingredients, it's easier to make in volume, about 6 shots.

Blue Marlin

1 part Light Rum
1/2 part Blue Curaçao
1 part Lime Juice
Shot Glass

Shake with ice and strain

Blue Meanie

1 part Blue Curaçao
1 part Vodka
1 part Sour Mix
Shot Glass

Shake with ice and strain

Blue Motherfucker

1 part Blue Curaçao
1 part 151-Proof Rum
Shot Glass

Pour ingredients into glass neat (do not chill)

Blue Peach

1 part Peach Schnapps
1 part Blue Curaçao
Shot Glass

Shake with ice and strain

Blue Polarbear

1 part Vodka
1 part Avalanche® Peppermint Schnapps
Shot Glass

Shake with ice and strain

Blue Razzberry Kamikaze

2 parts Raspberry Vodka
1 part Blue Curaçao
splash Lime Cordial
Shot Glass

Shake with ice and strain

Blue Slammer

1 part Blue Curaçao
1 part Sambuca
1 part Vodka
splash Lemon Juice
Shot Glass

Pour ingredients into glass neat (do not chill)

Blue Smurf® Piss

1 part Jägermeister®
1 part 151-Proof Rum
1 part Rumple Minze®
1 part Goldschläger®
1 part Blue Curaçao
Shot Glass

Shake with ice and strain into shot glass. *Note: Because this recipe includes many ingredients, it's easier to make in volume, about 6 shots.

Blue Spruce

1 part Maple Syrup
1 part Vodka
Shot Glass

Pour ingredients into glass neat (do not chill).

Blurricane

1 part Blue Curaçao
1 part Rumple Minze®
1 part Goldschläger®
1 part Jägermeister®
1 part Wild Turkey® Bourbon
1 part Ouzo
Shot Glass

Shake with ice and strain. *Note: Because this recipe includes many ingredients, it's easier to make in volume, about 6 shots.

Body Bag

1 part 151-Proof Rum
1 part Goldschläger®
1 part Jägermeister®
1 part Rumple Minze®
Shot Glass

Pour ingredients into glass neat (do not chill)

Body Shot

1 part Vodka
dash Sugar
1 Lemon Wedge
Shot Glass

Using a partner, lick his or her neck, then pour the Sugar onto the moistened shot. Place the wedge of Lemon in his or her mouth with the skin pointed inward. Lick the Sugar from his or her neck, shoot the Vodka, then suck the Lemon from his or her mouth (while gently holding back of the neck).

Bomb

1 part Coffee Liqueur
1 part Goldschläger®
1 part Irish Cream Liqueur
Shot Glass

Shake with ice and strain

A Bomb

1 part Vodka
1 part Coffee
1/2 part Cold Coffee
Shot Glass

Shake with ice and strain

Bomb #2

1 part Sour Apple Schnapps
1 part Peach Schnapps
1 part Banana Liqueur
1 part Pineapple Juice
1 part Lemon-Lime Soda
Shot Glass

Mix with ice and strain. *Note: Because this recipe includes many ingredients, it's easier to make in volume, about 6 shots.

Bombshell

2 parts Irish Cream Liqueur
1 part Cointreau®
splash Aquavit
Shot Glass

Shake with ice and strain

Bong Water

1 part Melon Liqueur
1 part Orange Juice
1 part Jägermeister®
Shot Glass

Shake with ice and strain

Bonnies Berry's

1 part Vodka
1 part Amaretto
1 part Raspberry Liqueur
Shot Glass

Shake with ice and strain

Boogers in the Grass

1 part Melon Liqueur
1 part Peach Schnapps
splash Irish Cream Liqueur
Shot Glass

Shake all but Irish Cream with ice and strain into the glass. Place a few drops of Irish Cream in the center of the drink.

Boom Box

1 part Vodka
1 part White Wine
1 part Hot Coffee
Shot Glass

Pour ingredients into glass neat (do not chill)

Boomer
1 part Tequila
1 part Triple Sec
1 part Crème de Banana
1 part Orange Juice
1 part Sour Mix
Shot Glass

Shake with ice and strain

Boomerang Shot
1 part Jägermeister®
1 part Yukon Jack®
Shot Glass

Shake with ice and strain

Booster Shot
1 part Cherry Brandy
1 part Chocolate Liqueur
1 part Lemon-Lime Soda
Shot Glass

Shake with ice and strain into a chilled shot glass

Boot to the Head
1 part Drambuie®
1 part Jack Daniel's®
1 part Tequila Silver
Shot Glass

Shake with ice and strain

The Bootlegger
1 part Jack Daniel's®
1 part Southern Comfort®
1 part Sambuca
Shot Glass

Shake with ice and strain

Border Conflict Shooter
2 parts Vodka
2 parts Crème de Menthe (White)
1 part Grenadine
Shot Glass

Shake with ice and strain

Bottle Cap
1 part Butterscotch Schnapps
1 part Raspberry Liqueur
1 part Lime Juice
Shot Glass

Shake with ice and strain

Brain Damage
1 part 151-Proof Rum
1 part Amaretto
splash Irish Cream Liqueur
Shot Glass

Shake all but Irish Cream with ice and strain into the glass. Place a few drops of Irish Cream in the center of the drink.

Brain Eraser
1 part Jägermeister®
1 part Peppermint Schnapps
Shot Glass

Shake with ice and strain

Brain Hemorrhage
1 part Peach Schnapps
1 part Irish Cream Liqueur
splash Grenadine
Shot Glass

Shake all but Grenadine with ice and strain into the glass. Place a few drops of Grenadine in the center of the drink.

Braindead
1 part Vodka
1 part Sour Mix
1 part Triple Sec
Shot Glass

Shake with ice and strain

Brainmaster
2 parts Light Rum
1 part Coconut-Flavored Liqueur
1 part Crème de Cacao (White)
splash Apricot Syrup
Shot Glass

Shake with ice and strain

Brass Balls
1 part Grand Marnier®
1 part Peach Schnapps
1 part Pineapple Juice
Shot Glass

Shake with ice and strain

Brave Bull Shooter
1 part Tequila
1 part Coffee Liqueur
Shot Glass

Pour ingredients into glass neat (do not chill)

Braveheart
1 part Vodka
splash Blue Curaçao
Shot Glass

Shake with ice and strain

Breast Milk
1 part Chocolate Liqueur
1 part Irish Cream Liqueur
1 part Butterscotch Schnapps
splash Half and Half
Shot Glass

Shake with ice and strain

Breath Freshener
1 part Vodka
2 parts Peppermint Schnapps
Shot Glass

Shake with ice and strain

Breathalizer
1 part Peppermint Schnapps
1 part Light Rum
Shot Glass

Shake with ice and strain

Brody's Icy Alien
1 part Rum
1 part Melon Liqueur
1 part Rumple Minze®
splash Cream
Shot Glass

Shake with ice and strain

Brown Lion
1 part Crème de Cacao (Dark)
1 part Coffee Liqueur
Shot Glass

Shake with ice and strain

Bruised Heart
1 part Vodka
1 part Raspberry Liqueur
1 part Peach Schnapps
1 part Cranberry Juice Cocktail
Shot Glass

Shake with ice and strain

Bubba Hubba Boom Boom
1 part Crème de Cacao (White)
1 part Crème de Menthe (White)
Shot Glass

Shake with ice and strain

Bubble Gum
1 part Melon Liqueur
1 part Vodka
1 part Crème de Banana
1 part Orange Juice
Shot Glass

Shake with ice and strain

Buca Bear
1 part Butterscotch Schnapps
1 part Sambuca
Shot Glass

Shake with ice and strain

Bull Shot Shooter
1 part Tequila Silver
1 part Coffee
1 part Dark Rum
Shot Glass

Shake with ice and strain

Bull's Milk
1 part Brandy
1 part Dark Rum
1 part Cream
Shot Glass

Shake with ice and strain

Buonasera Shooter
1 part Amaretto
1 part Coffee
1 part Vanilla Rum
Shot Glass

Shake with ice and strain

Buried under an Avalanche
1 part Ouzo
1 part Rumple Minze®
Shot Glass

Shake with ice and strain

Burning Cherry
1 part George Dickel Whiskey
1 part Irish Cream Liqueur
1 part Jim Beam®
splash Grenadine
Shot Glass

Pour ingredients into glass neat (do not chill)

Burning Worm
1 part Mescal
1 part Goldschläger®
Shot Glass

Pour ingredients into glass neat (do not chill)

Busted Cherry
1 part Coffee Liqueur
1 part Cherry Brandy
Shot Glass

Shake with ice and strain

Butterball
1 part Coffee Liqueur
1 part Irish Cream Liqueur
splash Butterscotch Schnapps
Shot Glass

Pour ingredients into glass neat (do not chill)

Butterfucker
1 part Jägermeister®
1 part Butterscotch Schnapps
1 part Irish Cream Liqueur
Shot Glass

Shake with ice and strain

Butternut Rum Lifesaver
1 part Irish Cream Liqueur
1 part Butterscotch Schnapps
1 part Coconut-Flavored Rum
1 part Pineapple Juice
Shot Glass

Shake with ice and strain

Buttery Nipple
1 part Sambuca
1 part Butterscotch Schnapps
Shot Glass

Shake with ice and strain

Buzzard's Breath
1 part Crème de Menthe (White)
1 part Amaretto
1 part Coffee Liqueur
Shot Glass
Shake with ice and strain

Buzzard's Breath #2
1 part Amaretto
1 part Peppermint Schnapps
1 part Coffee Liqueur
Shot Glass
Shake with ice and strain

Cactus Jack Shooter
1 part Coffee
1 part Light Rum
Shot Glass
Shake with ice and strain

Cactus Thorn
2 parts Tequila
1 part Crème de Menthe (Green)
1 part Lime Juice
Shot Glass
Shake with ice and strain

California Surfer
1 part Jägermeister®
1 part Coconut-Flavored Rum
2 parts Pineapple Juice
Shot Glass
Shake with ice and strain

Camel Driver
1 part Sambuca
1 part Irish Cream Liqueur
Shot Glass
Shake with ice and strain

Canadian Hunter
1 part Yukon Jack®
1 part Wild Turkey® 101
Shot Glass
Shake with ice and strain

Canadian Moose
1 part Coffee Liqueur
1 part Irish Cream Liqueur
1 part Crown Royal® Whiskey
Shot Glass
Shake with ice and strain

Canadian Snakebite
1 part Crème de Menthe (White)
1 part Canadian Whiskey
Shot Glass
Shake with ice and strain

Candy Apple
1 part Crown Royal® Whiskey
1 part Sour Applc Schnapps
splash Cranberry Juice Cocktail
Shot Glass
Shake with ice and strain

Candy Killer with a Kiss
1 part Ouzo
1 part Jägermeister®
1 part Goldschläger®
Shot Glass
Shake with ice and strain

Captain Louie
1 part Spiced Rum
1 part Coffee Liqueur
splash Vanilla Extract
Shot Glass
Pour ingredients into glass neat (do not chill)

Caramilk
2 parts Crème de Cacao (White)
1 part Crème de Banana
1 part Coffee Liqueur
Shot Glass
Shake with ice and strain

Carolina Vagina
2 parts Coconut-Flavored Rum
1 part Irish Cream Liqueur
1 part Coffee Liqueur
splash Grenadine
Shot Glass

Shake with ice and strain

Catfish
3 parts Bourbon
1 part Peach Schnapps
Shot Glass

Shake with ice and strain

Cattle Prod
1 part Butterscotch Schnapps
1 part Crown Royal® Whiskey
Shot Glass

Pour ingredients into glass neat (do not chill)

Cayman Shooter
1 part Crème de Banana
1 part Melon Liqueur
1 part Irish Cream Liqueur
Shot Glass

Shake with ice and strain

Champerelle
1 part Triple Sec
1 part Anisette
1 part Cognac
Shot Glass

Shake with ice and strain

Chariot of Fire
1 part Vodka
1 part Sambuca
Shot Glass

Shake with ice and strain

Che Guevara
1 part Goldschläger®
1 part Tequila
1 part Jägermeister®
Shot Glass

Shake with ice and strain

Cheesecake
1 part Cranberry Juice Cocktail
1 part Vanilla Liqueur
Shot Glass

Shake with ice and strain

Cherry Blow Pop®
1 part Southern Comfort®
1 part Amaretto
1 part Grenadine
Shot Glass

Shake with ice and strain

Cherry Bomb
1 part Vodka
1 part Crème de Cacao (White)
1 part Grenadine
Shot Glass

Shake with ice and strain

Cherry Bomb #2
2 parts Vodka
1 part Goldschläger®
1 part Light Rum
1 Maraschino Cherry
Shot Glass

Shake with ice and strain

Cherry LifeSaver®
1 part Southern Comfort®
1 part Amaretto
2 parts Sour Mix
splash Grenadine
Shot Glass

Shake with ice and strain

Cherry Ripe Shooter

1 part Kirschwasser
1 part Coconut-Flavored Rum
1 part Irish Cream Liqueur
Shot Glass

Shake with ice and strain

Chi Phi

1 part Peach Schnapps
1 part Southern Comfort®
Shot Glass

Shake with ice and strain

Chicken Drop

1 part Jägermeister®
1 part Peach Schnapps
1 part Orange Juice
Shot Glass

Shake with ice and strain

Chick-Lit

1 part Dr. McGillicuddy's® Mentholmint Schnapps
1 part Southern Comfort®
Shot Glass

Shake with ice and strain

Chilly Girl

1 part Melon Liqueur
1 part Gin
1 part Cream
Shot Glass

Shake with ice and strain

Chinese Mandarin

1 part Mandarine Napoléon® Liqueur
1 part Lychee Liqueur
Shot Glass

Shake with ice and strain

Chip Shot

1 part Spiced Rum
1 part Cranberry Juice Cocktail
1 part Pineapple Juice
Shot Glass

Shake with ice and strain

Chiquita

1 part Vodka
2 parts Crème de Banana
1 part Milk
Shot Glass

Shake with ice and strain

Chocolate Banana Shot

1 part Crème de Cacao (White)
1 part Crème de Banana
Shot Glass

Shake with ice and strain

Chocolate Cake

1 part Frangelico®
1 part Vodka
1 Lemon Wedge
dash Sugar
Shot Glass

Shake Frangelico® and Vodka with ice and strain into a shot glass. Moisten hand and sprinkle Sugar onto it, drink the shot, lick the Sugar and suck the Lemon.

Chocolate Chip Shooter

1 part Swiss Chocolate Almond Liqueur
1 part Crème de Cacao (White)
1 part Irish Cream Liqueur
Shot Glass

Shake with ice and strain

Chocolate-Covered Cherry
1 part Coffee Liqueur
1 part Amaretto
1 part Crème de Cacao (White)
splash Grenadine
Shot Glass
Shake with ice and strain

Chocolate Heaven
1 part Irish Cream Liqueur
1 part Coffee Liqueur
1 part Chocolate Liqueur
splash Caramel Syrup
Shot Glass
Shake with ice and strain

Chocolate Valentine
1 part Vanilla-Flavored Vodka
1 part Crème de Cacao (Dark)
1 part Cherry Juice
splash Cream
splash Club Soda
Shot Glass
Shake with ice and strain. *Note: Because this recipe includes many ingredients, it's easier to make in volume, about 6 shots.

Christmas Cheer
1 part Peppermint Schnapps
1 part Egg Nog
Shot Glass
Shake with ice and strain

Chunky Snakebite
1 part Tequila
1 part Salsa
Shot Glass
Pour ingredients into glass neat (do not chill)

Cinnamon Apple Pie
3 parts Sour Apple Schnapps
1 part Cinnamon Schnapps
Shot Glass
Shake with ice and strain

Cinnamon Roll
1 part Irish Cream Liqueur
1 part Cinnamon Schnapps
Shot Glass
Shake with ice and strain

Citron My Face
2 parts Citrus-Flavored Vodka
1 part Grand Marnier®
1 part Sour Mix
Shot Glass
Shake with ice and strain

Citron Sour
1 part Citrus-Flavored Vodka
1 part Lime Juice
Shot Glass
Shake with ice and strain

Closed Casket
2 parts Jägermeister®
2 parts 151-Proof Rum
1 part Fire Water®
1 part Rumple Minze®
Shot Glass
Shake with ice and strain

Cobra Bite
3 parts Yukon Jack®
1 part Lime Cordial
1 part Peppermint Schnapps
Shot Glass
Shake with ice and strain

Cocaine
1 part Vodka
1 part Raspberry Liqueur
1 part Grapefruit Juice
Shot Glass

Shake with ice and strain

Cockroach
1 part Coffee Liqueur
1 part Drambuie®
Shot Glass

Shake with ice and strain

Cockteaser
1 part Triple Sec
1 part Peach Schnapps
1 part Melon Liqueur
Shot Glass

Shake with ice and strain

Coco Bongo
1 part Crème de Cacao (White)
1 part Coconut-Flavored Liqueur
1 part Cream
Shot Glass

Shake with ice and strain

Coconut Cream Pie
1 part Coconut-Flavored Rum
top with Whipped Cream
Shot Glass

Fill a shot glass with chilled Coconut-Flavored Rum and top it with Whipped Cream. Drink without using your hands.

Coma
1 part Grand Marnier®
1 part Coffee Liqueur
1 part Sambuca
Shot Glass

Shake with ice and strain

Cool Cougar
1 part Jack Daniel's®
1 part Peppermint Schnapps
Shot Glass

Shake with ice and strain

Copper Camel
1 part Irish Cream Liqueur
1 part Butterscotch Schnapps
Shot Glass

Shake with ice and strain

Copper Cowboy
1 part Butterscotch Schnapps
1 part Coffee Liqueur
Shot Glass

Shake with ice and strain

Cordless Screwdriver
1 part Vodka
1 Orange Wedge
dash Sugar
Shot Glass

Shake the Vodka with ice and strain into a shot glass. Dip the Orange Wedge in the Sugar, drink the shot, and suck on the Orange.

Cornholio's Revenge
1 part Coconut-Flavored Rum
1 part Banana Liqueur
1 part Cherry Brandy
Shot Glass

Shake with ice and strain

Cortisone
1 part Coffee Liqueur
1 part Rum
splash Vanilla Liqueur
Shot Glass

Shake with ice and strain

Cough Drop
1 part Crème de Menthe (White)
1 part Blackberry Liqueur
Shot Glass

Shake with ice and strain

Cough Syrup
1 part Vodka
1 part Blue Curaçao
1 part Crème de Menthe (White)
Shot Glass

Shake with ice and strain

Cowboy Cocksucker
1 part Butterscotch Schnapps
1 part Irish Cream Liqueur
Shot Glass

Shake with ice and strain

Cowgirl
2 parts Butterscotch Schnapps
1 part Irish Cream Liqueur
Shot Glass

Shake with ice and strain

Crackhouse
1 part Blackberry Liqueur
1 part Cranberry Juice Cocktail
Shot Glass

Shake with ice and strain

Cranapple® Blast
1 part Sour Apple Schnapps
1 part Cranberry Juice Cocktail
1 part Vodka
Shot Glass

Shake with ice and strain

Cranberry Zamboni®
1 part Cranberry Liqueur
1 part Wild Spirit Liqueur
Shot Glass

Shake with ice and strain

Crash Test Dummy Shots
1 part Tequila
1 part Triple Sec
3 parts Margarita Mix
Shot Glass

Shake with ice and strain

Crazy Coco
1 part Coconut-Flavored Liqueur
1 part Irish Cream Liqueur
Shot Glass

Shake with ice and strain

Crazy Noggie
1 part Light Rum
1 part Vodka
1 part Southern Comfort®
1 part Amaretto
Shot Glass

Shake with ice and strain

Cream Hash
1 part Dark Rum
1 part Chocolate Liqueur
Shot Glass

Shake with ice and strain

Cream Soda Slammer
1 part Spiced Rum
1 part Lemon-Lime Soda
Shot Glass

Pour ingredients into glass neat (do not chill)

Creamy Jonny

1 part Irish Cream Liqueur
1 part Raspberry Liqueur
1 part Milk
splash Grenadine
Shot Glass

Shake with ice and strain

Creamy Nuts

1 part Crème de Banana
1 part Frangelico®
Shot Glass

Shake with ice and strain

Creamy Snatch

1 part Butterscotch Schnapps
1 part Coffee Liqueur
2 parts Half and Half
Shot Glass

Shake with ice and strain

Crimson Tide

1 part Vodka
1 part Coconut-Flavored Rum
1 part Raspberry Liqueur
1 part Southern Comfort®
1 part 151-Proof Rum
1 part Cranberry Juice Cocktail
1 part Lemon-Lime Soda
Shot Glass

Shake with ice and strain. *Note: Because this recipe includes many ingredients, it's easier to make in volume, about 6 shots.

Crispy Crunch

1 part Frangelico®
1 part Crème de Cacao (White)
Shot Glass

Shake with ice and strain

Crocket

2 parts Cherry Liqueur
1 part Grenadine
1 part Sour Mix
Shot Glass

Shake with ice and strain

Crowbar

1 part Crown Royal® Whiskey
1 part 151-Proof Rum
1 part Tequila
Shot Glass

Shake with ice and strain

Cruz Azul

1 part 151-Proof Rum
1 part Citrus-Flavored Rum
1 part Citrus-Flavored Vodka
1 part Rumple Minze®
1 part Blue Curaçao
Shot Glass

Shake with ice and strain. *Note: Because this recipe includes many ingredients, it's easier to make in volume, about 6 shots.

Crystal Virgin

1 part Yukon Jack®
1 part Amaretto
2 parts Cranberry Juice Cocktail
Shot Glass

Shake with ice and strain

Cucacaracha

1 part Vodka
1 part Coffee Liqueur
1 part Tequila
Shot Glass

Shake with ice and strain

Cum in a Pond

1 part Blue Curaçao
1 part Vodka
splash Irish Cream Liqueur
Shot Glass

Shake all but Irish Cream with ice and strain into the glass. Place a few drops of Irish Cream in the center of the drink.

Cum Shot

1 part Butterscotch Schnapps
1 part Irish Cream Liqueur
Shot Glass

Shake with ice and strain

Curly Tail Twist

splash 151-Proof Rum
1 part Jägermeister®
1 part Root Beer Schnapps
Shot Glass

Shake with ice and strain

Curtain Call

1 part Jägermeister®
1 part Melon Liqueur
1 part Jack Daniel's®
Shot Glass

Shake with ice and strain

D O A

1 part Crème de Cacao (White)
1 part Peach Schnapps
1 part Frangelico®
Shot Glass

Shake with ice and strain

Daddy's Milk

1 part Crème de Cacao (Dark)
1 part Crème de Cacao (White)
1 part Frangelico®
splash Cream
Shot Glass

Shake with ice and strain

Dakota

1 part Jim Beam®
1 part Tequila
Shot Glass

Pour ingredients into glass neat (do not chill)

Dallas Stars

1 part Crème de Menthe (White)
1 part Goldschläger®
Shot Glass

Shake with ice and strain

Damned if You Do

1 part Whiskey
1 part Cinnamon Schnapps
Shot Glass

Pour ingredients into glass neat (do not chill)

Dangerous Grandma

1 part Coffee Liqueur
1/2 part Whiskey
splash Amaretto
Shot Glass

Pour ingredients into glass neat (do not chill)

Dark Angel

1 part Maraschino Liqueur
1 part Blackberry Liqueur
1 part Advocaat
Shot Glass

Shake with ice and strain

Dark Nightmare

2 parts Coffee Liqueur
1 part Goldschläger®
1 part Milk
Shot Glass

Shake with ice and strain

D-Day

1 part 151-Proof Rum
1 part Citrus-Flavored Vodka
1 part Crème de Banana
1 part Raspberry Liqueur
1 part Orange Juice

Shot Glass

Shake with ice and strain. *Note: Because this recipe includes many ingredients, it's easier to make in volume, about 6 shots.

Dead Bird

1 part Jägermeister®
1 part Wild Turkey® Bourbon

Shot Glass

Shake with ice and strain

Dead End

1 part Amaretto
1 part Coffee Liqueur
1 part Grain Alcohol
1 part Irish Cream Liqueur

Shot Glass

Shake with ice and strain

Dead Frog

1 part Coffee Liqueur
1 part Irish Cream Liqueur
1 part Crème de Menthe (White)

Shot Glass

Shake with ice and strain

Dead Green Frog

1 part Rumple Minze®
1 part Coffee Liqueur
1 part Crème de Menthe (Green)
1 part Irish Cream Liqueur
1 part Vodka

Shot Glass

Shake with ice and strain

Dear Sperm

1 part Jägermeister®
1 part Irish Cream Liqueur

Shot Glass

Shake with ice and strain

Death from Within

1 part Spiced Rum
1 part Dark Rum
1 part Vodka

Shot Glass

Shake with ice and strain

Death Row

1 part Jack Daniel's®
1 part 151-Proof Rum

Shot Glass

Shake with ice and strain

Death Wish

1 part Wild Turkey® 101
1 part Rumple Minze®
1 part Jägermeister®

Shot Glass

Shake with ice and strain

Deep Blue Something

1 part Blue Curaçao
1 part Peach Schnapps
1 part Sour Mix
1 part Lemonade
1 part Pineapple Juice

Shot Glass

Shake with ice and strain. *Note: Because this recipe includes many ingredients, it's easier to make in volume, about 6 shots.

The Demon Knight

1 part Peppermint Schnapps
1 part Vodka
1 part Fruit Punch

Shot Glass

Shake with ice and strain

Desert Skies
1 part Apricot Brandy
1 part Rum Crème Liqueur
1 part Coffee Liqueur
Shot Glass

Shake with ice and strain

Detox
1 part Peach Schnapps
1 part Vodka
1 part Cranberry Juice Cocktail
Shot Glass

Shake with ice and strain

Devastating Body Rocker
1 part Blackberry Brandy
1 part Gin
Shot Glass

Shake with ice and strain

Devil's Kiss
1 part Dark Rum
1 part Coffee Liqueur
1 part Grand Marnier®
Shot Glass

Shake with ice and strain

Devil's Mouthwash
1 part Black Sambuca
1 part Southern Comfort®
Shot Glass

Shake with ice and strain

Diamond Cutter
1 part 151-Proof Rum
1 part Spiced Rum
1 part Grenadine
Shot Glass

Shake with ice and strain

Diesel Fuel
1 part Rum
1 part Jägermeister®
Shot Glass

Shake with ice and strain

Dirtiest Ernie
1 part 151-Proof Rum
1 part Grain Alcohol
1 part Rumple Minze®
Shot Glass

Shake with ice and strain

Dirty Diaper
1 part Vodka
1 part Amaretto
1 part Southern Comfort®
1 part Melon Liqueur
1 part Raspberry Liqueur
1 part Orange Juice
Shot Glass

Shake with ice and strain. *Note: Because this recipe includes many ingredients, it's easier to make in volume, about 6 shots.

Dirty Girl Scout Cookie
1 part Coffee Liqueur
1 part Irish Cream Liqueur
1 part Crème de Menthe (White)
Shot Glass

Shake with ice and strain

Dirty Irish Whiskey
1 part Irish Cream Liqueur
1 part Irish Whiskey
Shot Glass

Shake with ice and strain

The Dirty Leprechaun
1 part Jägermeister®
1 part Irish Cream Liqueur
1 part Midori®
Shot Glass

Shake with ice and strain

Dirty Navel
1 part Crème de Cacao (White)
1 part Triple Sec
Shot Glass
Shake with ice and strain

Dirty Rotten Scoundrel
1 part Vodka
1 part Melon Liqueur
Shot Glass
Shake with ice and strain

Disney® on Ice
1 part Peppermint Schnapps
1 part Grenadine
1 part 151-Proof Rum
splash Lemon Juice
Shot Glass
Shake with ice and strain

Dizzy Damage
1 part Jägermeister®
1 part Rumple Minze®
1 part Goldschläger®
Shot Glass
Shake with ice and strain

The Doc's Medicine
1 part Scotch
1 part Tequila
Shot Glass
Shake with ice and strain

Dolt Bolt
1 part Grain Alcohol
1 part Rumple Minze®
1 part Goldschläger®
Shot Glass
Shake with ice and strain

Dominator
2 parts Crème de Menthe (White)
1 part Coffee
1 part Triple Sec
Shot Glass
Shake with ice and strain

Don't Thrust Me
1 part Goldschläger®
1 part Butterscotch Schnapps
1 part 151-Proof Rum
Shot Glass
Shake with ice and strain

Double Berry Blast
1 part Blueberry Schnapps
1 part Strawberry Liqueur
Shot Glass
Shake with ice and strain

Double Chocolate
1 part Chocolate Liqueur
1 part Crème de Cacao (Dark)
Shot Glass
Shake with ice and strain

Double Gold
1 part Goldschläger®
1 part Gold Tequila
Shot Glass
Shake with ice and strain

Double Homicide
1 part Jägermeister®
1 part Goldschläger®
1 part Orange Juice
Shot Glass
Shake with ice and strain

The Double Team
1 part Amaretto
1 part Rum
Shot Glass

Shake with ice and strain

Doublemint® Blowjob
1 part Coffee Liqueur
1 part Peppermint Schnapps
2 parts Cream
Shot Glass

Shake with ice and strain

Doucet Devil
1 part Amaretto
1 part Southern Comfort®
1 part Crème de Banana
Shot Glass

Shake with ice and strain

Down the Street
1 part Vodka
1 part Grand Marnier®
1 part Raspberry Liqueur
1 part Orange Juice
Shot Glass

Shake with ice and strain

Downinone
2 parts Blavod® Black Vodka
1 part Triple Sec
1 part Gold Rum
Shot Glass

Shake with ice and strain

Dr. Banana
1 part Tequila
1 part Crème de Banana
Shot Glass

Shake with ice and strain

Dragon's Breath
1 part Fire Water®
1 part 151-Proof Rum
Shot Glass

Pour ingredients into glass neat (do not chill)

Drunk Irish Monk
1 part Irish Cream Liqueur
1 part Frangelico®
1 part Brandy
Shot Glass

Shake with ice and strain

Dublin Doubler
1 part Irish Whiskey
1 part Irish Cream Liqueur
Shot Glass

Shake with ice and strain

Duck Call Shooter
1 part 151-Proof Rum
1 part Coconut-Flavored Rum
splash Cranberry Juice Cocktail
splash Pineapple Juice
Shot Glass

Shake with ice and strain

Duck Fuck
2 parts Gin
1 part Vodka
1 part Beer
Shot Glass

Shake with ice and strain

Dumbfuck
1 part Cinnamon Schnapps
1 part Canadian Whiskey
Shot Glass

Shake with ice and strain

Earth Tremor
1 part Gin
1 part Scotch
1 part Pernod®
Shot Glass

Shake with ice and strain

Earthquake Shooter
1 part Sambuca
1 part Amaretto
1 part Southern Comfort®
Shot Glass

Shake with ice and strain

El Diablillo
3 parts Tequila Silver
1 part Crème de Cassis
Shot Glass

Shake with ice and strain

Electric Banana
1 part Tequila Silver
1 part Crème de Banana
1 part Lime Cordial
Shot Glass

Shake with ice and strain

Electric Kamikaze
1 part Triple Sec
1 part Vodka
1 part Blue Curaçao
1 part Lime Juice
Shot Glass

Shake with ice and strain

Electric Smurf®
1 part Coconut-Flavored Rum
1 part Blue Curaçao
Shot Glass

Shake with ice and strain

Elvis Presley
1 part Vodka
1 part Frangelico®
1 part Crème de Banana
splash Irish Cream Liqueur
Shot Glass

Shake with ice and strain

Embryo
1 part Peppermint Schnapps
splash Cream
splash Grenadine
Shot Glass

Place a few drops of Cream and a few drops of Grenadine in the center of a shot of Peppermint Schnapps

Emerald Rocket
1 part Vodka
1 part Coffee Liqueur
1 part Melon Liqueur
1 part Irish Cream Liqueur
Shot Glass

Shake with ice and strain

The End of the World
1 part 151-Proof Rum
1 part Wild Turkey® 101
1 part Vodka
Shot Glass

Pour ingredients into glass neat (do not chill)

Epidural
1 part Grain Alcohol
1 part Vodka
1 part Coconut-Flavored Rum
1 part Coconut Crème
Shot Glass

Shake with ice and strain

The Equalizer

1 part Peach Schnapps
1 part Pineapple Juice
1 part Orange Juice
Shot Glass

Shake with ice and strain

Erect Nipple

1 part Tequila Silver
1 part Sambuca
Shot Glass

Shake with ice and strain

Explosive

2 parts Tequila Reposado
1 part Triple Sec
Shot Glass

Shake with ice and strain

Extended Jail Sentence

1 part Jack Daniel's®
1 part Southern Comfort®
1 part Tequila
splash Pineapple Juice
Shot Glass

Shake with ice and strain

Eyeball

1 part Irish Cream Liqueur
splash Blue Curaçao
splash Grenadine
Shot Glass

Put a splash of Grenadine in the bottom of a shot glass, then top with Irish Cream Liqueur. Place a small splash of Blue Curaçao in the center for the iris.

F-69

1 part Dark Rum
1 part Coffee Liqueur
1 part Amaretto
2 parts Irish Cream Liqueur
Shot Glass

Shake with ice and strain

Fat Box

1 part Crème de Banana
1 part Blue Curaçao
1 part Coconut-Flavored Rum
1 part Pineapple Juice
Shot Glass

Shake with ice and strain

Fat Cat

2 parts Irish Cream Liqueur
1 part Amaretto
1 part Banana Liqueur
Shot Glass

Shake with ice and strain

Favorite Shooter

1 part Triple Sec
1 part Vanilla Liqueur
Shot Glass

Shake with ice and strain

Fiery Kiss

1 part Cinnamon Schnapps
splash Honey
Shot Glass

Shake with ice and strain

Fifth Avenue

1 part Crème de Cacao (Dark)
1 part Apricot Brandy
Shot Glass

Shake with ice and strain

Fig

1 part Coconut-Flavored Rum
1 part Pineapple Juice
1 part Cranberry Juice Cocktail
Shot Glass

Shake with ice and strain

Finger Me Good
1 part Butterscotch Schnapps
3 parts Crown Royal® Whiskey
Shot Glass
Pour ingredients into glass neat (do not chill)

Fire and Ice
1 part Cinnamon Schnapps
1 part Irish Cream Liqueur
Shot Glass
Shake with ice and strain

Fireball
1 part Coffee Liqueur
1 part Ouzo
Shot Glass
Shake with ice and strain

Firetruck
1 part Jägermeister®
1 part Ginger Ale
Shot Glass
Pour ingredients into glass neat (do not chill)

Five Star General
1 part Jägermeister®
1 part 151-Proof Rum
1 part Rumple Minze®
1 part Goldschläger®
1 part Tequila
Shot Glass
Shake with ice and strain. *Note: Because this recipe includes many ingredients, it's easier to make in volume, about 6 shots.

Flamethrower
1 part Vodka
2 parts Cinnamon Schnapps
Shot Glass
Shake with ice and strain

Flaming Cocaine
1 part Cinnamon Schnapps
1 part Vodka
splash Cranberry Juice Cocktail
Shot Glass
Shake with ice and strain

Flaming Squeegee
1 part Rum
1 part Vodka
1 part Lemon Juice
1 part Orange Juice
Shot Glass
Shake with ice and strain

Flashfire
1 part Cinnamon Schnapps
1 part Southern Comfort®
1 part Wild Turkey® 101
Shot Glass
Pour ingredients into glass neat (do not chill)

Flat Tire
2 parts Tequila
1 part Black Sambuca
Shot Glass
Shake with ice and strain

Flooze Booze
1 part Jägermeister®
1 part Root Beer Schnapps
Shot Glass
Shake with ice and strain

Flügel
1 part Cranberry-Flavored Vodka
1 part Red Bull® Energy Drink
Shot Glass
Pour ingredients into glass neat (do not chill)

Flukeman
1 part Irish Cream Liqueur
1 part Melon Liqueur
Shot Glass

Pour ingredients into glass neat (do not chill)

Fog
3 parts Vodka
1 part Fresh Lime Juice
Shot Glass

Shake with ice and strain

The Four Horsemen
1 part Jägermeister®
1 part Tequila
1 part Sambuca
1 part Rum
Shot Glass

Pour ingredients into glass neat (do not chill)

The Four Horsemen #2
1 part Jack Daniel's®
1 part Sambuca
1 part Jägermeister®
1 part Rumple Minze®
Shot Glass

Shake with ice and strain

Foxy Lady #2
1 part Amaretto
1 part Crème de Banana
1 part Cream
Shot Glass

Shake with ice and strain

Freaking Shot
1 part Raspberry Liqueur
1 part Vodka
1 part Cranberry Juice Cocktail
Shot Glass

Shake with ice and strain

Freddy Krueger®
1 part Sambuca
1 part Jägermeister®
1 part Vodka
Shot Glass

Shake with ice and strain

Freebase
1 part Coffee Liqueur
1 part Light Rum
1 part 151-Proof Rum
Shot Glass

Shake with ice and strain

Freight Train
1 part Tequila
1 part Irish Cream Liqueur
Shot Glass

Shake with ice and strain

French Toast
1 part Irish Cream Liqueur
1 part Cinnamon Schnapps
1 part Butterscotch Schnapps
Shot Glass

Shake with ice and strain

Frigid Alaskan Nipple
1 part Butterscotch Schnapps
1 part Rumple Minze®
2 parts Vodka
Shot Glass

Shake with ice and strain

Frog in a Blender
2 parts Tequila
1 part Sloe Gin
splash Sweet Vermouth
Shot Glass

Shake with ice and strain

Fruit Loop®
1 part Amaretto
1 part Blue Curaçao
1 part Grenadine
1 part Milk
Shot Glass

Shake with ice and strain

Fruit of the Loom®
1 part Banana Liqueur
1 part Melon Liqueur
1 part Cherry Brandy
1 part Coconut-Flavored Rum
Shot Glass

Shake with ice and strain

Fruit Salad
1 part Sour Apple Schnapps
1 part Cherry-Flavored Schnapps
1 part Grape-Flavored Schnapps
splash Orange Juice
Shot Glass

Shake with ice and strain

Fruit Tongue Fuck
1 part Citrus-Flavored Rum
1 part Light Rum
1 part Dark Rum
1 part Peach Schnapps
Shot Glass

Shake with ice and strain

Fruity Fairy
1 part Peach Schnapps
1 part Grenadine
1 part Melon Liqueur
Shot Glass

Shake with ice and strain

Fruity Pebbles®
1 part Vodka
1 part Blue Curaçao
1 part Milk
splash Grenadine
Shot Glass

Shake with ice and strain

Fuck Me Running
1 part Jack Daniel's®
1 part Peach Schnapps
1 part Blackberry Brandy
Shot Glass

Shake with ice and strain

Fuck Me Up
1 part Coffee Liqueur
1 part Irish Cream Liqueur
1 part Banana Liqueur
Shot Glass

Shake with ice and strain

Fucking Hot
1 part Pepper-Flavored Vodka
1 part Cinnamon Schnapps
Shot Glass

Pour ingredients into glass neat (do not chill)

Funky Chicken
1 part Tequila
1 part Wild Turkey® Bourbon
Shot Glass

Shake with ice and strain

Fuzzy Irishman
1 part Raspberry Liqueur
1 part Butterscotch Schnapps
1 part Irish Cream Liqueur
Shot Glass

Pour ingredients into glass neat (do not chill)

Fuzzy Logic
1 part Coffee Liqueur
1 part Peach Schnapps
2 parts Cream
Shot Glass
Shake with ice and strain

Fuzzy Melon Shooter
1 part Peach Schnapps
1 part Pineapple Juice
1 part Orange Juice
1 part Melon Liqueur
splash Blue Curaçao
Shot Glass
Shake with ice and strain. *Note: Because this recipe includes many ingredients, it's easier to make in volume, about 6 shots.

Fuzzy Monkey
1 part Vodka
1 part Peach Schnapps
1 part Crème de Banana
1 part Orange Juice
Shot Glass
Shake with ice and strain

Fuzzy Monkey #2
3 parts Crème de Banana
2 parts Orange Juice
1 part Peach Schnapps
Shot Glass
Shake with ice and strain

Fuzzy Nutted Banana
1 part Peach Schnapps
1 part Amaretto
1 part Banana Liqueur
1 part Orange Juice
splash Grenadine
Shot Glass
Shake with ice and strain. *Note: Because this recipe includes many ingredients, it's easier to make in volume, about 6 shots.

Fuzzy Pirate
1 part Dark Rum
1 part Peach Schnapps
splash Triple Sec
Shot Glass
Shake with ice and strain

Fuzzy Russian
1 part Vodka
1 part Peach Schnapps
Shot Glass
Shake with ice and strain

Fuzzy Smurf®
1 part Blue Curaçao
1 part Peach Schnapps
Shot Glass
Shake with ice and strain

G Spot
1 part Southern Comfort®
1 part Raspberry Liqueur
1 part Orange Juice
Shot Glass
Shake with ice and strain

G. T. O.
1 part Vodka
1 part Rum
1 part Gin
1 part Southern Comfort®
1 part Amaretto
1 part Grenadine
4 parts Orange Juice
Shot Glass
Shake with ice and strain. *Note: Because this recipe includes many ingredients, it's easier to make in volume, about 6 shots.

Galactic Ale

2 parts Vodka
2 parts Blue Curaçao
1 part Lime Juice
splash Blackberry Liqueur
Shot Glass

Shake with ice and strain

Gasoline

1 part Southern Comfort®
1 part Tequila
Shot Glass

Shake with ice and strain

Gator Cum

1 part Vodka
1 part Crème de Cacao (Dark)
1 part Frangelico®
Shot Glass

Shake with ice and strain

Gator Tail

1 part Melon Liqueur
1 part Rum
1 part Pineapple Juice
1 part Coconut-Flavored Rum
Shot Glass

Shake with ice and strain

Geiger Counter

1 part 151-Proof Rum
1 part Jägermeister®
Shot Glass

Pour ingredients into glass neat (do not chill)

Gentle Bull Shot

1 part Coffee
1 part Tequila Reposado
splash Cream
Shot Glass

Shake with ice and strain

German Burrito

1 part Tequila
1 part Jägermeister®
Shot Glass

Shake with ice and strain

German Death

1 part Jägermeister®
1 parts Rumple Minze®
Shot Glass

Shake with ice and strain

German Fruit Cup

1 part Rum
1 part Blackberry Liqueur
1 part Blue Curaçao
1 part Grenadine
1 part Honey
Shot Glass

Shake with ice and strain. *Note: Because this recipe includes many ingredients, it's easier to make in volume, about 6 shots.

Gestapo

1 part Rumple Minze®
1 part Jägermeister®
Shot Glass

Shake with ice and strain

Getaway Car

3 parts Peach Schnapps
1 part Citrus-Flavored Vodka
Shot Glass

Shake with ice and strain

Ghetto Blaster

1 part Coffee Liqueur
1 part Sambuca
1 part Tequila
1 part Rye Whiskey
Shot Glass

Shake with ice and strain

Ghostbuster
1 part Vodka
1 part Melon Liqueur
1 part Pineapple Juice
1 part Orange Juice
Shot Glass

Shake with ice and strain

Gila Monster
1 part Jägermeister®
1 part Tequila
1 part Orange Juice
Shot Glass

Shake with ice and strain

Gilligan
1 part Coconut-Flavored Rum
1 part Watermelon Schnapps
Shot Glass

Shake with ice and strain

Gin and Bear It
2 parts Gin
1 part Beer
Shot Glass

Pour ingredients into glass neat (do not chill)

Gingerbread Man
1 part Goldschläger®
1 part Irish Cream Liqueur
1 part Butterscotch Schnapps
1 part Vodka
Shot Glass

Shake with ice and strain

The Girl Mom Warned You About
1 part Grenadine
1 part Triple Sec
1 part Rum
1 part Melon Liqueur
1 part Blue Curaçao
Shot Glass

Shake with ice and strain. *Note: Because this recipe includes many ingredients, it's easier to make in volume, about 6 shots.

Girl Scout Cookie
1 part Coffee Liqueur
1 part Milk
1 part Rumple Minze®
Shot Glass

Shake with ice and strain

Gladiator's Stinger
3 parts Brandy
2 parts Crème de Menthe (White)
1 part Sambuca
Shot Glass

Shake with ice and strain

Glitterbox
1 part Black Sambuca
1 part Coffee Liqueur
Shot Glass

Shake with ice and strain

Godhead
1 part Rum
1 part Vodka
1 part Raspberry Liqueur
splash Lime Juice
splash 151-Proof Rum
Shot Glass

Shake with ice and strain

Godzilla®

2 parts Tequila Silver
1 part Orange Bitters
Shot Glass

Shake with ice and strain

Gold Baron

3 parts Rumple Minze®
1 part Goldschläger®
Shot Glass

Shake with ice and strain

Gold Fever

1 part Goldschläger®
1 part Gold Tequila
Shot Glass

Shake with ice and strain

Golddigger

1 part Jack Daniel's®
1 part Goldschläger®
Shot Glass

Pour ingredients into glass neat (do not chill)

Golden Comfort

1 part Goldschläger®
1 part Southern Comfort®
1 part Jägermeister®
Shot Glass

Shake with ice and strain

Golden Russian

1 part Vodka
1 part Galliano®
Shot Glass

Shake with ice and strain

Golden Sensation

2 parts Amaretto
2 parts Coffee Liqueur
1 part Crème de Banana
1 part Crème de Cacao (Dark)
1 part Goldschläger®
Shot Glass

Shake with ice and strain. *Note: Because this recipe includes many ingredients, it's easier to make in volume, about 6 shots.

Good and Plenty

1 part Sambuca
1 part Tequila
Shot Glass

Shake with ice and strain

Goody Two Shoes

2 parts Passion Fruit Liqueur
1 part Pineapple Juice
1 part Blue Curaçao
Shot Glass

Shake with ice and strain

Gorilla Fart

1 part Rum
1 part Wild Turkey® Bourbon
Shot Glass

Shake with ice and strain

Grab My Coconuts

1 part Dark Rum
1 part Coconut-Flavored Liqueur
2 parts Pineapple Juice
Shot Glass

Shake with ice and strain

The Graduate

3 parts Southern Comfort®
2 parts Pineapple Juice
1 part Amaretto
Shot Glass

Shake with ice and strain

Grandma's Candy
1 part Blue Curaçao
1 part Sambuca
Shot Glass

Shake with ice and strain

Grandpa Is Alive
2 parts Amaretto
1 part Vodka
Shot Glass

Shake with ice and strain

Grape KoolAid®
1 part Blue Curaçao
1 part Southern Comfort®
1 part Raspberry Liqueur
1 part Pineapple Juice
1 part Sour Mix
2 parts Cranberry Juice Cocktail
Shot Glass

Shake with ice and strain. *Note: Because this recipe includes many ingredients, it's easier to make in volume, about 6 shots.

Grapevine Special
1 part Brandy
1 part Apricot Brandy
1 part Banana Liqueur
1 part Cherry Liqueur
1 part Grand Marnier®
Shot Glass

Shake with ice and strain. *Note: Because this recipe includes many ingredients, it's easier to make in volume, about 6 shots.

Grasshopper Shot
1 part Brandy
1 part Blue Curaçao
Shot Glass

Shake with ice and strain

Grave Digger
1 part 151-Proof Rum
1 part Jim Beam®
Shot Glass

Shake with ice and strain

Grazysurfer
1 part Dark Rum
1 part Goldschläger®
1 part Sambuca
Shot Glass

Pour ingredients into glass neat (do not chill)

Greek Fire
3 parts Brandy
1 part Ouzo
Shot Glass

Shake with ice and strain

Greek Lightning
1 part Ouzo
1 part Vodka
1 part Raspberry Liqueur
Shot Glass

Shake with ice and strain

Greek Revolution
1 part Grenadine
1 part Ouzo
Shot Glass

Shake with ice and strain

The Greek Way
2 parts Ouzo
1 part Metaxa®
Shot Glass

Shake with ice and strai

Green Aftermath
1 part Peppermint Schnapps
1 part Mountain Dew®
Shot Glass

Pour ingredients into glass neat (do not chill)

Green Apple Kamikazi
1 part Melon Liqueur
1 part Vodka
1 part Sour Mix
splash Lime Juice
Shot Glass

Shake with ice and strain

Green Apple Toffee
1 part Vodka
1 part Butterscotch Schnapps
1 part Sour Apple Schnapps
Shot Glass

Shake with ice and strain

Green Booger
1 part Irish Cream Liqueur
1 part Crème de Menthe (White)
splash Lime Juice
Shot Glass

Shake with ice and strain

Green Cookie Monster®
2 parts Gin
1 part Melon Liqueur
1 part Rum
Shot Glass

Shake with ice and strain

Green Fly Shooter
1 part Crème de Menthe (Green)
1 part Melon Liqueur
Shot Glass

Shake with ice and strain

Green Gecko
1 part Crème de Menthe (White)
1 part Triple Sec
splash Limoncello
Shot Glass

Shake with ice and strain

Green Gummy Bear
1 part Orange-Flavored Vodka
1 part Melon Liqueur
splash Lemon-Lime Soda
Shot Glass

Shake with ice and strain

Green Jolly Rancher®
1 part Melon Liqueur
1 part Southern Comfort®
splash Sour Mix
Shot Glass

Shake with ice and strain

Green Lizard on the Beach
2 parts Crème de Banana
1 part Blue Curaçao
splash Orange Juice
Shot Glass

Shake with ice and strain

Green Motherfucker
1 part 151-Proof Rum
1 part Crème de Menthe (Green)
Shot Glass

Shake with ice and strain

Green Sneaker
2 parts Vodka
1 part Melon Liqueur
1 part Cointreau®
splash Cream
Shot Glass

Shake with ice and strain

Green Thing
1 part Coconut-Flavored Rum
1 part Melon Liqueur
2 parts Pineapple Juice
Shot Glass

Shake with ice and strain

Green Voodoo
1 part Melon Liqueur
1 part Malibu® Rum
1 part Lemon-Lime Soda
splash Triple Sec
splash Sour Mix
Shot Glass

Shake with ice and strain

Grenade
1 part Vodka
1 part Triple Sec
1 part Grenadine
Shot Glass

Shake with ice and strain

Greyhound
1 part Cointreau®
1 part Drambuie®
Shot Glass

Shake with ice and strain

Gross One
1 part Vodka
1 part Gin
1 part Jack Daniel's®
1 part Amaretto
1 part Sambuca
Shot Glass

Shake with ice and strain. *Note: Because this recipe includes many ingredients, it's easier to make in volume, about 6 shots.

Ground Zero
1 part Peppermint Schnapps
1 part Vodka
1 part Coffee Liqueur
Shot Glass

Shake with ice and strain

Gumball Hummer
1 part Raspberry Liqueur
1 part Banana Liqueur
1 part Grapefruit Juice
Shot Glass

Shake with ice and strain

Haggis
1 part Bourbon
1 part Cognac
1 part Southern Comfort®
Shot Glass

Shake with ice and strain

Hail Caesar
1 part Melon Liqueur
1 part Crème de Banana
1 part Sour Mix
Shot Glass

Shake with ice and strain

Halloween Shooter
1 part Licor 43®
1 part Sambuca
Shot Glass

Shake with ice and strain

Hangin' Around
1 part Tequila Silver
1 part Triple Sec
1 part Grenadine
Shot Glass

Shake with ice and strain

Happy Camper
1 part Amaretto
1 part Frangelico®
1 part Coffee Liqueur
Shot Glass
Shake with ice and strain

Happy Irish
1 part Crème de Menthe (White)
1 part Sambuca
Shot Glass
Shake with ice and strain

Happy Juice
1 part Lemon Juice
1 part Vodka
Shot Glass
Shake with ice and strain

Happy Tooth
1 part Coffee Liqueur
1 part Sambuca
Shot Glass
Shake with ice and strain

Harley Davidson®
1 part Yukon Jack®
1 part Jack Daniel's®
Shot Glass
Shake with ice and strain

Harley Oil
2 parts Jägermeister®
1 part Coffee Liqueur
Shot Glass
Shake with ice and strain

Harsh
1 part Tequila
1 part Jägermeister®
Shot Glass
Shake with ice and strain

Hawaiian Punch® from Hell
1 part Vodka
1 part Southern Comfort®
1 part Amaretto
splash Orange Juice
splash Lemon-Lime Soda
splash Grenadine
Shot Glass
Shake with ice and strain. *Note: Because this recipe includes many ingredients, it's easier to make in volume, about 6 shots.

Hawoo-Woo
1 part Vodka
1 part Peach Schnapps
1 part Cranberry Juice Cocktail
1 part Pineapple Juice
Shot Glass
Shake with ice and strain

Head in the Sand
1 part Crème de Menthe (White)
1 part Brandy
1 part Tequila Silver
1 part Grenadine
Shot Glass
Shake with ice and strain

Head Rush
1 part Peach Schnapps
1 part Pear Liqueur
1 part Sambuca
Shot Glass
Shake with ice and strain

Heavenly Orgasm
2 parts Frangelico®
1 part Amaretto
1 part Irish Cream Liqueur
Shot Glass
Shake with ice and strain

Heilig
1 part Vodka
1 part Blueberry Schnapps
1 part Cranberry Juice Cocktail
Shot Glass

Shake with ice and strain

Helicopter
1 part Green Chartreuse®
1 part 151-Proof Rum
Shot Glass

Pour ingredients into glass neat (do not chill)

Hellraiser
1 part Melon Liqueur
1 part Black Sambuca
1 part Strawberry Liqueur
Shot Glass

Shake with ice and strain

Hell's Eye
1 part Canadian Whiskey
2 parts Coffee Liqueur
1 part Milk
Shot Glass

Shake with ice and strain

Hemorrhaging Brain
2 parts Strawberry Liqueur
1 part Irish Cream Liqueur
splash Grenadine
Shot Glass

Shake all but Grenadine with ice and strain into the glass. Place a few drops of Grenadine in the center of the drink.

Herman's Special
1 part Vodka
1 part Brandy
3 parts Peach Schnapps
splash Raspberry Liqueur
Shot Glass

Shake with ice and strain

Heroin
1 part Black Sambuca
1 part Grand Marnier®
Shot Glass

Shake with ice and strain

Hide the Banana
1 part Amaretto
1 part Melon Liqueur
1 part Citrus-Flavored Vodka
Shot Glass

Shake with ice and strain

Hit and Run
1 part Anisette
1 part Gin
Shot Glass

Shake with ice and strain

Hole-in-One Shooter
3 parts Melon Liqueur
1 part Apple Brandy
splash Half and Half
Shot Glass

Shake with ice and strain

Honey Bear
1 part Cream
1 part Coffee Liqueur
1 part Frangelico®
1 part Honey
Shot Glass

Shake with ice and strain

Honey-Dew-Me
1 part Bärenjäger®
1 part Melon Liqueur
2 parts Orange Juice
Shot Glass

Shake with ice and strain

Honeysuckle Shooter
2 parts Light Rum
1 part Simple Syrup
1 part Sour Mix
Shot Glass

Shake with ice and strain

Honolulu Action
1 part Grenadine
1 part Melon Liqueur
1 part Blue Curaçao
1 part Irish Cream Liqueur
1 part Tequila
1 part Vodka
1 part 151-Proof Rum
top with Whipped Cream
Shot Glass

Shake with ice and strain. *Note: Because this recipe includes many ingredients, it's easier to make in volume, about 6 shots.

Honolulu Hammer Shooter
2 parts Vodka
1 part Amaretto
1 part Pineapple Juice
Shot Glass

Shake with ice and strain

Hooter
1 part Citrus-Flavored Vodka
1 part Amaretto
1 part Orange Juice
1 part Grenadine
Shot Glass

Shake with ice and strain

Hornet
2 parts Sloe Gin
1 part Peppermint Schnapps
Shot Glass

Shake with ice and strain

Horny Bastard
1 part Vodka
1 part Caramel Liqueur
splash Grenadine
Shot Glass

Shake with ice and strain

Horny Bull
1 part Tequila
1 part Rum
Shot Glass

Shake with ice and strain

Horny Girl Scout
1 part Coffee Liqueur
1 part Peppermint Schnapps
Shot Glass

Shake with ice and strain

Horny Monkey
1 part Banana Liqueur
1 part Black Sambuca
Shot Glass

Shake with ice and strain

Horny Southerner
2 parts Southern Comfort®
2 parts Melon Liqueur
1 part Sour Mix
1 part Lemon-Lime Soda
Shot Glass

Shake with ice and strain

Horsemen of the Apocalypse
1 part Jack Daniel's®
1 part Jim Beam®
1 part Tequila
1 part Spiced Rum
Shot Glass

Pour ingredients into glass neat (do not chill)

Hot Afternoon
1 part Peach Schnapps
1 part Coffee Liqueur
Shot Glass

Shake with ice and strain

Hot Apple Pie
1 part Irish Cream Liqueur
1 part Goldschläger®
Shot Glass

Shake with ice and strain

Hot Beach Shooter
1 part Hot Coffee
1 part Peach
1 part Coconut-Flavored Rum
Shot Glass

Pour ingredients into glass neat (do not chill)

Hot Bomb
3 parts Tequila
1 part Cinnamon Schnapps
Shot Glass

Shake with ice and strain

Hot Brown Lizard
1 part Cinnamon Schnapps
1 part Melon Liqueur
Shot Glass

Pour ingredients into glass neat (do not chill)

Hot Damn
1 part Whiskey
1 part Orange Juice
1 part Rum
1 part Vodka
Shot Glass

Shake with ice and strain

Hot Doctor
1 part Hot Damn® Cinnamon Schnapps
1 part Dr. McGillicuddy's® Mentholmint Schnapps
Shot Glass

Shake with ice and strain

Hot Fuck
1 part Hot Damn!® Cinnamon Schnapps
1 part Jägermeister®
Shot Glass

Shake with ice and strain

Hot Fusion
1 part Melon Liqueur
1 part Absolut® Peppar Vodka
Shot Glass

Shake with ice and strain

Hot Georgia Peach
1 part Hot Damn!®Cinnamon Schnapps
1 part Peach Schnapps
Shot Glass

Shake with ice and strain

Hot José
1 part Hot Damn!®Cinnamon Schnapps
1 part Tequila
Shot Glass

Shake with ice and strain

Hot Peach Pie
1 part 151-Proof Rum
1 part Peach Schnapps
Shot Glass

Shake with ice and strain

Hot Stuff

1 part Amaretto
1 part Hot Coffee
Shot Glass

Pour ingredients into glass neat (do not chill)

Hot Tamale

3 parts Goldschläger®
1 part Tequila Silver
Shot Glass

Shake with ice and strain

Hot to Trot

1 part Cinnamon Schnapps
1 part Tequila
splash Lime Juice
Shot Glass

Shake with ice and strain

Hot Wet Pussy

1 part 151-Proof Rum
1 part Melon Liqueur
1 part Peach Schnapps
1 part Lemon-Lime Soda
2 parts Pineapple Juice
Shot Glass

Shake with ice and strain

Howling Coyote

1 part Chambord®
3 parts Tequila
Shot Glass

Shake with ice and strain

Hunting Party

1 part Tequila Reposado
1 part Jack Daniel's®
1 part Jim Beam®
1 part Whiskey
1 part Wild Turkey® Bourbon
Shot Glass

Shake with ice and strain. *Note: Because this recipe includes many ingredients, it's easier to make in volume, about 6 shots.

Hyper Monkey

1 part Banana Liqueur
1 part Coffee Liqueur
Shot Glass

Shake with ice and strain

I Love Rosa

1 part Jack Daniel's®
1 part Amaretto
1 part Cola
Shot Glass

Pour ingredients into glass neat (do not chill)

Ice Blue Kamikaze

1 part Rumple Minze®
1 part Vodka
1 part Lemon-Lime Soda
Shot Glass

Pour ingredients into glass neat (do not chill)

Ice Bolts

1 part Coffee Liqueur
1 part Tonic Water
Shot Glass

Pour ingredients into glass neat (do not chill)

Ice Cream Shot

1 part Vanilla Liqueur
1 part Irish Cream Liqueur
Shot Glass

Shake with ice and strain

Iceberg Shooter

1 part Crème de Menthe (White)
1 part Citrus-Flavored Vodka
Shot Glass

Shake with ice and strain

Iced Blues
1 part Blackberry Liqueur
1 part Blue Curaçao
Shot Glass

Shake with ice and strain

Icy after Eight
2 parts Vodka
1 part Chocolate Syrup
1 part Crème de Menthe (Green)
Shot Glass

Shake with ice and strain

Iguana #2
1 part Vodka
1 part Tequila
1 part Coffee Liqueur
Shot Glass

Shake with ice and strain

Illusion
1 part Coconut-Flavored Rum
1 part Melon Liqueur
1 part Vodka
1 part Cointreau®
splash Pineapple Juice
Shot Glass

Shake with ice and strain

Immaculate Ingestion
1 part Coffee Liqueur
1 part Peppermint Schnapps
1 part Vodka
Shot Glass

Shake with ice and strain

In the Navy
1 part Crème de Cacao (White)
1 part Crème de Menthe (White)
Shot Glass

Shake with ice and strain

Ink Spot
3 parts Blackberry Liqueur
1 part Crème de Menthe (White)
Shot Glass

Shake with ice and strain

International Incident
1 part Vodka
1 part Coffee Liqueur
1 part Amaretto
1 part Frangelico®
2 parts Irish Cream Liqueur
Shot Glass

Shake with ice and strain

Into the Blue
1 part Blue Curaçao
1 part Pineapple Juice
1 part Coffee Liqueur
Shot Glass

Shake with ice and strain

Irish Brogue
3 parts Whiskey
1 part Irish Mist®
Shot Glass

Shake with ice and strain

Irish Bulldog #2
1 part Irish Cream Liqueur
1 part Vodka
Shot Glass

Shake with ice and strain

Irish Hammer
1 part Jack Daniel's®
1 part Irish Mist®
1 part Irish Cream Liqueur
Shot Glass

Shake with ice and strain

Irish Kiss
1 part Irish Cream Liqueur
1 part Rumple Minze®
Shot Glass

Shake with ice and strain

Irish Kiss Shot
1 part Whiskey
1 part Irish Mist®
Shot Glass

Shake with ice and strain

Irish Melon Ball
1 part Irish Whiskey
1 part Melon Liqueur
Shot Glass

Shake with ice and strain

Irish Pirate
1 part Spiced Rum
1 part Irish Mist®
Shot Glass

Shake with ice and strain

Irish Potato Famine
1 part Vodka
1 part Irish Whiskey
1 part Irish Cream Liqueur
Shot Glass

Shake with ice and strain

Irish Quaalude
1 part Crème de Cacao (White)
1 part Frangelico®
1 part Citrus-Flavored Vodka
Shot Glass

Shake with ice and strain

Irish Setter
2 parts Irish Mist®
2 parts Frangelico®
1 part Crème de Menthe (White)
1 part Brandy
Shot Glass

Shake with ice and strain

Irish Slammer
3 parts Crème de Banana
1 part Whiskey
Shot Glass

Shake with ice and strain

Iron Cross
1 part Crème de Menthe (White)
1 part Apricot Brandy
Shot Glass

Shake with ice and strain

Italian Ecstasy
1 part Grappa
1 part Frangelico®
1 part Cream
1 part Espresso
Shot Glass

Shake with ice and strain

Italian Orgasm
1 part Vodka
1 part Amaretto
1 part Irish Cream Liqueur
1 part Frangelico®
Shot Glass

Shake with ice and strain

Italian Russian
1 part Vodka
1 part Sambuca
Shot Glass

Shake with ice and strain

Italian Spear
1 part Crème de Menthe (White)
1 part Amaretto
Shot Glass

Shake with ice and strain

Italian Stallion
2 parts Sambuca
1 part Amaretto
1 part Frangelico®
Shot Glass

Shake with ice and strain

Italian Stallion Shooter
1 part Galliano®
1 part Cream
1 part Crème de Banana
Shot Glass

Shake with ice and strain

Jack and Jill
1 part Jack Daniel's®
1 part Root Beer Schnapps
Shot Glass

Shake with ice and strain

Jack Ass
2 parts Cinnamon Schnapps
1 part Yukon Jack®
Shot Glass

Shake with ice and strain

Jack in the Box
1 part Coffee Liqueur
1 part Jack Daniel's®
1 part Cream de Banana
Shot Glass

Shake with ice and strain

Jackhammer
1 part Jack Daniel's®
1 part Tequila
Shot Glass

Pour ingredients into glass neat (do not chill)

Jackhammer#2
1 part Jack Daniel's®
1 part Tequila
Shot Glass

Shake with ice and strain

Jackson 5
1 part Jim Beam®
1 part Jack Daniel's®
1 part Rye Whiskey
1 part Tequila
1 part Jägermeister®
Shot Glass

Shake with ice and strain. *Note: Because this recipe includes many ingredients, it's easier to make in volume, about 6 shots.

Jäger® Barrel
1 part Jägermeister®
1 part Root Beer Schnapps
1 part Cola
Shot Glass

Shake with ice and strain

Jäger® Mint
1 part Jägermeister®
1 part Peppermint Schnapps
Shot Glass

Shake with ice and strain

Jäger® Oatmeal Cookie
1 part Jägermeister®
1 part Coffee Liqueur
1 part Irish Cream Liqueur
1 part Butterscotch Schnapps
Shot Glass

Shake with ice and strain

Jäger® Shake
1 part Jägermeister®
1 part Crème de Cacao (White)
splash Half and Half
Shot Glass

Shake with ice and strain

Jäger® Baby
1 part Irish Cream Liqueur
1 part Jägermeister®
Shot Glass

Pour ingredients into glass neat (do not chill)

Jägerita
1 part Jägermeister®
1 part Tequila
1 part Lime Juice
Shot Glass

Shake with ice and strain

Jägershock
1 part After Shock® Cinnamon Schnapps
1 part Jägermeister®
Shot Glass

Shake with ice and strain

Jamaica Dust
1 part Southern Comfort®
1 part Tia Maria®
1 part Pineapple Juice
Shot Glass

Shake with ice and strain

Jamaican Bobsled
1 part Vodka
1 part Banana Liqueur
Shot Glass

Shake with ice and strain

Jamaican Dust Buster®
1 part Rum
1 part Coffee Liqueur
2 parts Pineapple Juice
Shot Glass

Shake with ice and strain

Jamaican Lemondrop
1 part Dark Rum
1 part Triple Sec
1 part Lemonade
Shot Glass

Shake with ice and strain

Jamaican Quaalude
1 part Coconut-Flavored Rum
1 part Frangelico®
1 part Irish Cream Liqueur
1 part Milk
Shot Glass

Shake with ice and strain

Jamaican Wind
1 part Coffee Liqueur
3 parts Dark Rum
Shot Glass

Shake with ice and strain

Jambalaya
1 part Peach Schnapps
1 part Southern Comfort®
1 part Sour Mix
splash Grenadine
Shot Glass

Shake with ice and strain

Jamboree
1 part Vodka
1 part Wild Berry Schnapps
1 part Cranberry Juice Cocktail
Shot Glass

Shake with ice and strain

Jealous Queen
1 part Triple Sec
2 parts Vodka
dash Bitters
dash Salt
Shot Glass

Shake with ice and strain

Jedi® Mind Probe

1 part Irish Cream Liqueur
1 part Butterscotch Schnapps
1 part Jägermeister®
Shot Glass

Pour ingredients into glass neat (do not chill)

Jell-O® Shots

1 package instant Jell-O® (see flavor combinations)
1 part Hot Water
1 part Liqueur (see flavor combinations)
Shot Glass

Basic Recipe: Dissolve Jell-O® in hot water. Add liqueur. Pour into small paper cups and chill. Serve after the Jell-O® has set.
Flavor Combinations:
Cape Cods–Cranberry Jell-O®/Vodka
Gimlets–Lime Jell-O®/Gin
Lemonheads–Lemon Jell-O®/Vodka
Coco Blue–Blue Raspberry Jell-O®/Coconut Rum
Coco Islands–Island Pineapple Jell-O®/Coconut Rum
Margaritas–Lime Jell-O®/Tequila
Melon Sours–Lime Jell-O®/Melon Liqueur

Jelly Bean

1 part Blackberry Brandy
1 part Peppermint Schnapps
Shot Glass

Shake with ice and strain

Jelly Bean #2

1 part Coffee Liqueur
1 part Anisette
1 part 151-Proof Rum
Shot Glass

Shake with ice and strain

Jelly Fish

1 part Crème de Cacao (White)
1 part Amaretto
1 part Irish Cream Liqueur
2 splashes Grenadine
Shot Glass

Shake all but Grenadine with ice and strain into the glass. Place a few drops of Grenadine in the center of the drink.

Jet Fuel

1 part Grand Marnier®
1 part Southern Comfort®
Shot Glass

Shake with ice and strain

Jive-Aid

1 part Vodka
1 part Sloe Gin
1 part Cherry Liqueur
1 part Watermelon Schnapps
splash Lemon-Lime Soda
splash Sour Mix
Shot Glass

Shake with ice and strain

Jogger

1 part Citrus-Flavored Vodka
1 part Vodka
1 part Orange Juice
1 part Galliano®
Shot Glass

Shake with ice and strain

Johnny on the Beach

3 parts Vodka
2 parts Melon Liqueur
2 parts Blackberry Liqueur
1 part Pineapple Juice
1 part Orange Juice
1 part Grapefruit Juice
1 part Cranberry Juice Cocktail
Shot Glass

Shake with ice and strain. *Note: Because this recipe includes many ingredients, it's easier to make in volume, about 6 shots.

Jonny Appleseed
1 part Vodka
1 part Raspberry Liqueur
1 part Melon Liqueur
1 part Peach Schnapps
1 part Pineapple Juice
Shot Glass

Shake with ice and strain. *Note: Because this recipe includes many ingredients, it's easier to make in volume, about 6 shots.

Jonny G Spot
1 part Vodka
1 part Blue Curaçao
1 part Orange Juice
Shot Glass

Shake with ice and strain

José Flame-O
1 part Tequila
1 part Fire Water®
Shot Glass

Pour ingredients into glass neat (do not chill)

José Pache Sombrero
1 part Jack Daniel's®
1 part Brandy
1 part Tequila
Shot Glass

Pour ingredients into glass neat (do not chill)

Judgment Day
1 part Coffee Liqueur
1 part Jägermeister®
1 part Rumple Minze®
splash 151-Proof Rum
splash Grain Alcohol
Shot Glass

Shake with ice and strain. *Note: Because this recipe includes many ingredients, it's easier to make in volume, about 6 shots.

Juicy Fruit®
2 parts Raspberry Liqueur
1 part Triple Sec
1 part Melon Liqueur
Shot Glass

Shake with ice and strain

Juicy Lips
1 part Vodka
1 part Crème de Banana
1 part Pineapple Juice
Shot Glass

Shake with ice and strain

Juicy Pussy
1 part Irish Cream Liqueur
1 part Peach Schnapps
1 part Pineapple Juice
Shot Glass

Shake with ice and strain

Juicy Volkheimer
1 part Vodka
1 part Coconut-Flavored Rum
Shot Glass

Shake with ice and strain

Junior Mint®
1 part Peppermint Schnapps
1 part Crème de Cacao (Dark)
Shot Glass

Shake with ice and strain

Just Shoot Me
1 part Jim Beam®
1 part Jack Daniel's®
1 part Johnnie Walker® Red Label
1 part Tequila
1 part Jägermeister®
1 part 151-Proof Rum
Shot Glass

Shake with ice and strain. *Note: Because this recipe includes many ingredients, it's easier to make in volume, about 6 shots.

Kaisermeister
1 part Jägermeister®
1 part Root Beer Schnapps
Shot Glass
Shake with ice and strain

Kalabreeze
1 part Cherry Brandy
1 part Apricot Brandy
1 part Triple Sec
Shot Glass
Shake with ice and strain

Kamihuzi
1 part Tequila
1 part Triple Sec
1 part Sour Mix
Shot Glass
Shake with ice and strain

Kamikaze
1 part Vodka
1 part Triple Sec
1 part Lime Juice
Shot Glass
Shake with ice and strain

Kare Bear
1 part Amaretto
1 part Blue Curaçao
1 part Banana Liqueur
Shot Glass
Shake with ice and strain

Ke Largo
1 part KeKe Beach® Key Lime Cream Liqueur
1 part Melon Liqueur
Shot Glass
Shake with ice and strain

Keith Jackson
1 part Amaretto
1 part Southern Comfort®
1 part Peach Schnapps
1 part Sour Mix
1 part Lemon-Lime Soda
Shot Glass
Shake with ice and strain

Keremiki
1 part 151-Proof Rum
1 part Goldschläger®
1 part Rumple Minze®
Shot Glass
Shake with ice and strain

Kermit's Belly Button
1 part Peach Schnapps
1 part Blue Curaçao
1 part Orange Juice
Shot Glass
Shake with ice and strain

Key Lime Pie
2 parts Licor 43®
2 parts Half and Half
1 part Lime Juice
Shot Glass
Shake with ice and strain

Key Lime Shooter
2 parts Licor 43®
1 part Light Rum
1 part Sour Mix
splash Sweetened Lime Juice
splash Half and Half
Shot Glass
Shake with ice and strain

Key West Shooter
1 part Vodka
1 part Melon Liqueur
1 part Orange Juice
1 part Pineapple Juice
Shot Glass

Shake with ice and strain

Kick Me in the Jimmy
1 part Jägermeister®
1 part Jack Daniel's®
1 part Tequila
1 part Fire Water®
Shot Glass

Shake with ice and strain

Kickstand
1 part Amaretto
1 part Southern Comfort®
1 part Coffee Liqueur
1 part Irish Cream Liqueur
Shot Glass

Shake with ice and strain

Killer Bee
1 part Jägermeister®
1 part Bärenjäger®
Shot Glass

Shake with ice and strain

Killer Crawdad
1 part Goldschläger®
1 part Cherry Brandy
Shot Glass

Shake with ice and strain

Killer Kool-Aid®
2 parts Vodka
1 part Amaretto
1 part Melon Liqueur
1 part Cranberry Juice Cocktail
Shot Glass

Shake with ice and strain

Killer Oreos®
1 part Jägermeister®
1 part Coffee Liqueur
1 part Irish Cream Liqueur
Shot Glass

Shake with ice and strain

Killer Sniff
1 part Sambuca
1 part Blue Curaçao
Shot Glass

Shake with ice and strain

Killing Spree
1 part Passion Fruit Liqueur
1 part Advocaat
Shot Glass

Shake with ice and strain

Kimber Krush
1 part Vanilla-Flavored Vodka
1 part Rumple Minze®
1 part Irish Cream Liqueur
1 part Raspberry Liqueur
Shot Glass

Shake with ice and strain

King's Ransom
1 part Goldschläger®
1 part Crown Royal® Whiskey
Shot Glass

Shake with ice and strain

Kish Wacker
1 part Irish Cream Liqueur
1 part Crème de Cacao (Dark)
1 part Vodka
1 part Coffee Liqueur
Shot Glass

Shake with ice and strain

Kitty

1 part Crème de Banana
1 part Triple Sec
1 part Jim Beam®
1 part Lemon Juice
Shot Glass

Shake with ice and strain

Kiwiki

1 part Vodka
1 part Kiwi Schnapps
1 part Triple Sec
Shot Glass

Shake with ice and strain

Klingon® Disrupter

1 part Jim Beam®
1 part Mescal
1 part Cinnamon Schnapps
Shot Glass

Shake with ice and strain

Klondyke

1 part Irish Cream Liqueur
1 part Jägermeister®
Shot Glass

Shake with ice and strain

Kool-Aid®

1 part Vodka
1 part Amaretto
1 part Melon Liqueur
1 part Raspberry Liqueur
Shot Glass

Shake with ice and strain

Krazy Kat

1 part Coffee Liqueur
1 part Crème de Banana
1 part Coconut-Flavored Liqueur
Shot Glass

Shake with ice and strain

Kremlin Shooter

1 part Vodka
splash Grenadine
Shot Glass

Shake with ice and strain

Kriaura

1 part Wild Berry Schnapps
1 part Lemon-Lime Soda
1 part Cranberry Juice Cocktail
Shot Glass

Shake with ice and strain

Kris Kringle

1 part Crème de Noyaux
1 part Root Beer Schnapps
1 part Half and Half
Shot Glass

Shake with ice and strain

Kurant Shooter

1 part Melon Liqueur
1 part Currant-Flavored Vodka
2 parts Pineapple Juice
Shot Glass

Shake with ice and strain

Kurant Stinger

1 part Bärenjäger®
1 part Currant-Flavored Vodka
Shot Glass

Shake with ice and strain

La Pussy

1 part Light Rum
1 part Cointreau®
1 part Brandy
1 part Sour Apple Schnapps
Shot Glass

Shake with ice and strain

The Lady in Red
1 part Peppermint Schnapps
1 part Peach Schnapps
1 part Vodka
1 part Grenadine
Shot Glass

Shake with ice and strain

Lady Killer Shooter
1 part Coffee
1 part Melon Liqueur
1 part Frangelico®
Shot Glass

Shake with ice and strain

Land Rover®
1 part Spiced Rum
1 part Coffee Liqueur
1 part Irish Cream Liqueur
Shot Glass

Shake with ice and strain

Landmine
1 part 151-Proof Rum
1 part Jägermeister®
Shot Glass

Shake with ice and strain

Laserbeam
1 part Amaretto
1 part Grand Marnier®
1 part Melon Liqueur
1 part Pineapple Juice
1 part Southern Comfort®
Shot Glass

Shake with ice and strain. *Note: Because this recipe includes many ingredients, it's easier to make in volume, about 6 shots.

The Last Stop
1 part Maraschino Liqueur
1 part Blackberry Liqueur
splash Absinthe
Shot Glass

Shake with ice and strain

Lay Down and Shut Up!
1 part Jägermeister®
1 part Cinnamon Schnapps
1 part Coffee Liqueur
splash Cream
Shot Glass

Shake with ice and strain

Lazer Beam
1 part Amaretto
1 part Peach Schnapps
1 part Orange Juice
Shot Glass

Shake with ice and strain

Leather Whip
1 part Tequila
1 part Triple Sec
1 part Jack Daniel's®
1 part Peach Schnapps
Shot Glass

Shake with ice and strain

Lemon Drop Shooter
1 part Vodka
1 Lemon Wedge
dash Sugar
Shot Glass

Shake the Vodka with ice and strain into a shot glass. Pour the Sugar onto the Lemon Wedge. Drink the shot and bite down on the Lemon Wedge.

Lemon Meringue
1 part Vodka
1 part Lemon Juice
Shot Glass

Shake with ice and strain. Top with Whipped Cream.

Leprechaun Shooter
1 part Blue Curaçao
1 part Peach Schnapps
1 part Orange Juice
Shot Glass

Shake with ice and strain

Leprechaun's Gold
1 part Goldschläger®
1 part Irish Cream Liqueur
Shot Glass

Shake with ice and strain

Lethal Injection
1 part Rum
1 part Coconut-Flavored Rum
1 part Dark Rum
1 part Amaretto
1 part Orange Juice
1 part Pineapple Juice
Shot Glass

Shake with ice and strain

Levite Pepper Slammer
1 part Southern Comfort®
2 parts Dr Pepper®
Shot Glass

Build in the glass with no ice

Lewinsky Blowjob
1 part Amaretto
2 parts Cola
splash 151-Proof Rum
Shot Glass

Shake with ice and strain. Top with whipped cream and drink without using your hands.

Life Preserver
1 part Blue Curaçao
1 part Vodka
1 piece Cheerio's® cereal
Shot Glass

Shake the Vodka and Blue Curaçao with ice and strain. Float the Cheerio in the center of the shot.

Light Green Panties
1 part Crème de Menthe (Green)
1 part Vodka
1 part Irish Cream Liqueur
splash Grenadine
Shot Glass

Shake all but Grenadine with ice and strain into the glass. Place a few drops of Grenadine in the center of the drink.

Light Headed
1 part Blue Curaçao
1 part Coconut-Flavored Liqueur
1 part Strawberry Liqueur
Shot Glass

Shake with ice and strain

Lime Lizard
1 part Vodka
1 part Rum
1 part Lime Juice
1 part Grenadine
Shot Glass

Shake with ice and strain

Liplock
1 part Dark Rum
1 part Coconut-Flavored Rum
1 part Grenadine
1 part Pineapple Juice
1 part Orange Juice
Shot Glass

Shake with ice and strain. *Note: Because this recipe includes many ingredients, it's easier to make in volume, about 6 shots.

Lipstick Lesbian
1 part Raspberry-Flavored Vodka
1 part Watermelon Schnapps
1 part Cranberry Juice Cocktail
1 part Sour Mix
Shot Glass

Shake with ice and strain

Liquid Asphalt

1 part Sambuca
1 part Jägermeister®
Shot Glass

Shake with ice and strain

Liquid Candy Cane

1 part Vodka
2 parts Cherry Liqueur
2 parts Peppermint Schnapps
Shot Glass

Shake with ice and strain

Liquid Cocaine

1 part Grand Marnier®
1 part Southern Comfort®
1 part Vodka
1 part Amaretto
1 part Pineapple Juice
Shot Glass

Shake with ice and strain. *Note: Because this recipe includes many ingredients, it's easier to make in volume, about 6 shots.

Liquid Crack

1 part Jägermeister®
1 part Rumple Minze®
1 part 151-Proof Rum
1 part Goldschläger®
Shot Glass

Shake with ice and strain

Liquid Heroin

1 part Vodka
1 part Rumple Minze®
1 part Jägermeister®
Shot Glass

Shake with ice and strain

Liquid Mentos®

1 part Blue Curaçao
1 part Peach Schnapps
1 part Banana Liqueur
Shot Glass

Shake with ice and strain

Liquid Nitrogen

1 part Sambuca
1 part Ouzo
Shot Glass

Shake with ice and strain

Liquid Quaalude

1 part Jägermeister®
3 parts Irish Cream Liqueur
Shot Glass

Shake with ice and strain

Liquid Rocher®

2 parts Crème de Cacao (White)
1 part Frangelico®
1 part Vanilla Liqueur
Shot Glass

Shake with ice and strain

Liquid Screw

1 part Coconut-Flavored Rum
1 part Peach Schnapps
1 part Vodka
1 part Lemon-Lime Soda
Shot Glass

Shake with ice and strain

Liquid Valium

1 part Jack Daniel's®
1 part Amaretto
1 part Tequila
1 part Triple Sec
Shot Glass

Shake with ice and strain

Lit City
1 part Jägermeister®
1 part Butterscotch Schnapps
1 part Irish Cream Liqueur
1 part Goldschläger®
Shot Glass

Shake with ice and strain

Little Bitch
1 part Southern Comfort®
1 part Amaretto
1 part Cranberry Juice Cocktail
1 part Orange Juice
Shot Glass

Shake with ice and strain

A Little Green Man from Mars
1 Green Maraschino Cherry
1 part Jägermeister®
1 part Rumple Minze®
Shot Glass

Remove stem from the Green Maraschino Cherry and drop the cherry in the glass. Pour equal parts Jägermeister and Rumple Minze.

A Little Nervous
1 part Vodka
1 part Peach Schnapps
1 part Blackberry Liqueur
Shot Glass

Shake with ice and strain

A Little Piece of Hell
1 part Cinnamon Schnapps
1 part Simple Syrup
Shot Glass

Shake with ice and strain

Lobotomy
1 part Amaretto
1 part Raspberry Liqueur
1 part Pineapple Juice
Shot Glass

Shake with ice and strain

London Pummel
1 part Gin
1 part Tonic Water
splash Lime Juice
Shot Glass

Build in a shot glass

Long Island Shooter
1 part Tequila Silver
1 part Vodka
1 part Light Rum
1 part Gin
1 part Triple Sec
1 part Cola
1 part Sour Mix
Shot Glass

Shake with ice and strain

Love in the Snow
1 part Crème de Cacao (White)
1 part Amaretto
1 part Pisang Ambon® Liqueur
Shot Glass

Shake with ice and strain

Love Is in the Air
1 part Amaretto
1 part Crème de Banana
1 part Coconut-Flavored Liqueur
Shot Glass

Shake with ice and strain

Love Shack Shooter

2 parts Dark Rum
1 part Lemon-Lime Soda
1 part Orange Juice
splash Grenadine
Shot Glass

Shake with ice and strain

Luna Rossa

1 part Peach Schnapps
1 part Campari®
1 part Limoncello
Shot Glass

Shake with ice and strain

M&M®

1 part Amaretto
1 part Coffee Liqueur
Shot Glass

Shake with ice and strain

M O Shooter

1 part Cream
1 part Amaretto
Shot Glass

Shake with ice and strain

Mad Cow

1 part Coffee Liqueur
1 part Cream
1 part 151-Proof Rum
Shot Glass

Shake with ice and strain

Mad Hatter

1 part Vodka
1 part Peach Schnapps
1 part Lemonade
1 part Cola
Shot Glass

Shake with ice and strain

Mad Melon Shooter

1 part Watermelon Schnapps
1 part Vodka
Shot Glass

Shake with ice and strain

Mad Scientist

1 part Blueberry Schnapps
1 part Raspberry Liqueur
splash Irish Cream Liqueur
Shot Glass

Shake with ice and strain

Madman's Return

1 part Triple Sec
1 part Goldschläger®
1 part Cachaça
1 part Gin
Shot Glass

Shake with ice and strain

Mage's Fire

2 parts Vodka
1 part Cinnamon Schnapps
1 part Blue Curaçao
Shot Glass

Shake with ice and strain

Magic Potion

1 part Coffee Liqueur
1 part Amaretto
1 part Crème de Cacao (Dark)
Shot Glass

Shake with ice and strain

Maiden's Prayer Shooter

1 part Gin
1 part Lillet
1 part Calvados Apple Brandy
Shot Glass

Shake with ice and strain

Masconivich Shooter
1 part Brandy
1 part Triple Sec
1 part Cognac
Shot Glass

Shake with ice and strain

Mattikaze
1 part Vodka
1 part Lime Juice
1 part Triple Sec
1 part Peach Schnapps
Shot Glass

Shake with ice and strain

Max Factor®
1 part Raspberry Liqueur
1 part Cranberry Juice Cocktail
1 part Triple Sec
Shot Glass

Shake with ice and strain

Mean Machine
1 part Crème de Menthe (White)
1 part Triple Sec
Shot Glass

Shake with ice and strain

Meat and Potatoes
1 part Potato Vodka
1 Pepperoni Slice
Shot Glass

Shake the Vodka with ice and strain into a shot glass. Garnish with a slice of Pepperoni.

Melaretto
1 part Melon Liqueur
1 part Amaretto
Shot Glass

Shake with ice and strain

Melon Ball Shooter
2 parts Melon Liqueur
1 part Vodka
1 part Orange Juice
Shot Glass

Shake with ice and strain

Melon Cheer
1 part Melon Liqueur
1 part Strawberry Liqueur
1 part Sour Mix
Shot Glass

Shake with ice and strain

Melon Kamikaze
1 part Vodka
1 part Melon Liqueur
1 part Sour Mix
Shot Glass

Shake with ice and strain

Melonoma
2 parts Vodka
1 part Melon Liqueur
Shot Glass

Shake with ice and strain

Memory Loss
1 part Vodka
1 part Raspberry Liqueur
1 part Banana Liqueur
1 part Cranberry Juice Cocktail
1 part Orange Juice
Shot Glass

Shake with ice and strain. *Note: Because this recipe includes many ingredients, it's easier to make in volume, about 6 shots.

Menstrual Mint
1 part Gin
1 part Grenadine
1 part Tequila
Shot Glass

Shake with ice and strain

Merry Kay

2 parts Jim Beam®
1 part Blue Curaçao
Shot Glass

Shake with ice and strain

Mexican Apple

1 part Apple Liqueur
1 part Tequila Silver
Shot Glass

Shake with ice and strain

Mexican Cherry Bomb

1 part Coffee Liqueur
1 part Cream
1 part Grenadine
Shot Glass

Shake with ice and strain

Mexican Glow Worm

1 part Melon Liqueur
1 part Gold Tequila
Shot Glass

Shake with ice and strain

Mexican Inca

1 part Tequila Silver
1 part Coffee
1 part Grenadine
Shot Glass

Shake with ice and strain

Mexican Kamikaze

2 parts Tequila
1 part Vodka
1 part Lemon Juice
1 part Lime Juice
Shot Glass

Shake with ice and strain

Mexican Killer

1 part Gold Tequila
1 part Peach Schnapps
1 part Sweetened Lime Juice
Shot Glass

Shake with ice and strain

Mexican Melon

1 part Tequila Silver
1 part Melon Liqueur
Shot Glass

Shake with ice and strain

Mexican Mountie

1 part Tequila
1 part Yukon Jack®
Shot Glass

Shake with ice and strain

Mexican Mouthwash

1 part Tequila
1 part Rumple Minze®
Shot Glass

Shake with ice and strain

Mexican Pebble

1 part Blue Curaçao
1 part Gold Tequila
1 part Raspberry Liqueur
1 part Lemon-Lime Soda
Shot Glass

Shake with ice and strain

Mexican Shake

1 part Tequila
1 part Coffee Liqueur
1 part Cola
1 part Cream
Shot Glass

Shake with ice and strain

Mexican Snowshoe
1 part Peppermint Schnapps
1 part Tequila
Shot Glass
Shake with ice and strain

Mexican Stand-Off
1 part Vodka
1 part Tequila
1 part Passoã®
Shot Glass
Shake with ice and strain

Mexican Thanksgiving
1 part Tequila
1 part Wild Turkey® Bourbon
Shot Glass
Shake with ice and strain

Mexican Water
1 part Crown Royal® Whiskey
1 part Tequila Reposado
1 part Vodka
Shot Glass
Shake with ice and strain

Midnight Matinee
1 part Peach Schnapps
1 part Passion Fruit Liqueur
1 part Lemon Juice
Shot Glass
Shake with ice and strain

Milano Shooter
1 part Crème de Menthe (White)
1 part Fernet-Branca®
1 part Sambuca
Shot Glass
Shake with ice and strain

Mild Jizz
1 part Vodka
1 part Melon Liqueur
1 part Coconut-Flavored Rum
1 part Lemon-Lime Soda
Shot Glass
Shake with ice and strain

Milky Nooky
1 part Peppermint Schnapps
1 part Irish Cream Liqueur
1 part Jägermeister®
Shot Glass
Shake with ice and strain

Milky Way®
1 part Amaretto
1 part Crème de Cacao (Dark)
1 part Cream
Shot Glass
Shake with ice and strain

Milky Way®#2
3 parts Irish Cream Liqueur
2 parts Root Beer Schnapps
1 part Goldschläger®
Shot Glass
Shake with ice and strain

Mind Collapse
1 part Crème de Menthe (White)
1 part Whiskey
Shot Glass
Shake with ice and strain

Mind Game
1 part Pernod®
1 part Blue Curaçao
2 parts Milk
Shot Glass
Shake with ice and strain

Mind Probe
1 part 151-Proof Rum
1 part Sambuca
1 part Jägermeister®
Shot Glass

Shake with ice and strain

Mini Margarita
1 part Tequila Silver
1 part Triple Sec
1 part Sour Mix
Shot Glass

Shake with ice and strain

Mint Chocolate
2 parts Crème de Menthe (Green)
1 part Coffee Liqueur
1 part Irish Cream Liqueur
Shot Glass

Shake with ice and strain

Mint Desire
1 part Rumple Minze®
1 part Coconut Cream
2 parts Cream
Shot Glass

Shake with ice and strain

Mint Julep Shot
2 parts Bourbon
1 part Crème de Menthe (Green)
Shot Glass

Shake with ice and strain

Mintarita
1 part Crème de Menthe (White)
1 part Tequila Silver
Shot Glass

Shake with ice and strain

Misconavitch
1 part Cointreau®
3 parts Grand Marnier®
Shot Glass

Shake with ice and strain

Misdemeanor
1 part Butterscotch Schnapps
1 part Crown Royal® Whiskey
Shot Glass

Shake with ice and strain

Misty Blue Cumming
1 part Vodka
1 part Sloe Gin
1 part Blue Curaçao
1 part Peach Schnapps
Shot Glass

Shake with ice and strain

Mongolian Clusterfuck
1 part Jägermeister®
1 part Goldschläger®
1 part Rumple Minze®
Shot Glass

Shake with ice and strain

Monkey Brain
3 parts Coffee Liqueur
1 part Advocaat
splash Grenadine
Shot Glass

Shake all but Grenadine with ice and strain into the glass. Place a few drops of Grenadine in the center of the drink.

Monkey Poop Shooter
1 part Vodka
1 part Crème de Banana
1 part Pineapple Juice
1 part Orange Juice
1 part Lime Cordial
Shot Glass

Shake with ice and strain. *Note: Because this recipe includes many ingredients, it's easier to make in volume, about 6 shots.

Monkey Pussy
1 part Irish Cream Liqueur
1 part Banana Liqueur
1 part Crown Royal® Whiskey
1 part Raspberry Liqueur
Shot Glass

Shake with ice and strain

Monsoon
1 part Currant-Flavored Vodka
1 part Amaretto
1 part Coffee Liqueur
1 part Frangelico®
Shot Glass

Shake with ice and strain

Montana Stump Puller
2 parts Canadian Whiskey
1 part Crème de Cacao (White)
Shot Glass

Shake with ice and strain

Moose Fart
1 part Vodka
1 part Bourbon
1 part Coffee Liqueur
1 part Irish Cream Liqueur
Shot Glass

Shake with ice and strain

Moranguito
1 part Absinthe
1 part Tequila
1 part Grenadine
Shot Glass

Shake with ice and strain

Morgan's Wench
1 part Spiced Rum
1 part Amaretto
1 part Crème de Cacao (Dark)
Shot Glass

Shake with ice and strain

Morning Wood
1 part Vodka
1 part Peach Schnapps
1 part Orange Juice
1 part Sour Mix
1 part Raspberry Liqueur
Shot Glass

Shake with ice and strain. *Note: Because this recipe includes many ingredients, it's easier to make in volume, about 6 shots.

Mother Load
1 part Vodka
1 part Blackberry Liqueur
1 part Coconut-Flavored Rum
Shot Glass

Shake with ice and strain

Mother Pucker Shooter
1 part Vodka
1 part Sour Apple Schnapps
splash Lemon-Lime Soda
splash Club Soda
Shot Glass

Shake with ice and strain

Mouth Wash
1 part Crème de Menthe (White)
1 part Vodka
1 part Blue Curaçao
Shot Glass
Shake with ice and strain

Mouthwatering
1 part Amaretto
1 part Melon Liqueur
Shot Glass
Shake with ice and strain

Mr. Bean
1 part Anisette
1 part Blackberry Liqueur
Shot Glass
Shake with ice and strain

Mr. G
1 part Licor 43®
1 part Vodka
2 parts Grenadine
Shot Glass
Shake with ice and strain

Mud Slide Shooter
1 part Vodka
1 part Coffee Liqueur
1 part Irish Cream Liqueur
Shot Glass
Shake with ice and strain

Muddy Water
1 part Vodka
1 part Coffee Liqueur
1 part Irish Cream Liqueur
Shot Glass
Shake with ice and strain

Mudguppy
1 part Amaretto
1 part Irish Cream Liqueur
2 parts Bourbon
Shot Glass
Shake with ice and strain

Muff Dive
1 part Vodka
1 part Peach Schnapps
1 part Cranberry Juice Cocktail
Shot Glass
Shake with ice and strain

Mussolini
1 part Goldschläger®
1 part Jägermeister®
1 part Sambuca
Shot Glass
Shake with ice and strain

Mutated Mother's Milk
1 part Jägermeister®
1 part Irish Cream Liqueur
1 part Peppermint Schnapps
Shot Glass
Shake with ice and strain

MVP's Strawberry Bomb
1 part Tequila Rose®
1 part Vodka
1 part Strawberry Liqueur
Shot Glass
Shake with ice and strain

My Johnson Is Ten Inches Long
2 parts Malibu® Rum
2 parts Raspberry Liqueur
2 parts Melon Liqueur
1 part Sour Mix
1 part Cranberry Juice Cocktail
Shot Glass
Shake with ice and strain

Nalgas de Oro
1 part Raspberry Liqueur
1 part Vanilla Liqueur
1 part 151-Proof Rum
1 part Grand Marnier®
Shot Glass

Shake with ice and strain

Nasty Stewardess
1 part Licor 43®
2 parts Tonic Water
2 parts Orange Bitters
Shot Glass

Build in the glass with no ice

Natural Disaster
1 part Cinnamon Schnapps
1 part Peppermint Schnapps
Shot Glass

Shake with ice and strain

Naughty Angel
3 parts Chocolate Liqueur
1 part 151-Proof Rum
Shot Glass

Shake with ice and strain

Navy Seal
1 part Crown Royal® Whiskey
1 part Rum
Shot Glass

Shake with ice and strain

Neon Bull Frog
1 part Vodka
1 part Blue Curaçao
1 part Melon Liqueur
1 part Sour Mix
Shot Glass

Shake with ice and strain

Neon Cactus
1 part Cactus Juice Schnapps
1 part Margarita Mix
Shot Glass

Shake with ice and strain

Neon Lizard
1 part Blue Curaçao
1 part Melon Liqueur
Shot Glass

Shake with ice and strain

Nerd
1 part Cream
1 part Black Sambuca
1 part Strawberry Liqueur
Shot Glass

Shake with ice and strain

Nero's Delight
1 part Vodka
1 part Sambuca
Shot Glass

Shake with ice and strain

Neuronium
1 part Crème de Menthe (White)
1 part Vodka
splash Grenadine
Shot Glass

Shake all but Grenadine with ice and strain into the glass. Place a few drops of Grenadine in the center of the drink.

Never a Seven
2 parts Jack Daniel's®
1 part Tequila
1 part Rum
1 part Goldschläger®
1 part Hot Sauce
Shot Glass

Shake with ice and strain

New England Kamikaze
2 parts Grand Marnier®
1 part Sour Mix
Shot Glass

Shake with ice and strain

New York Slammer
1 part Amaretto
1 part Orange Juice
1 part Southern Comfort®
1 part Triple Sec
1 part Sloe Gin
Shot Glass

Shake with ice and strain

A Night at Naughty Nikki's
1 part Vodka
2 parts Lemon-Lime Soda
Skittles
Shot Glass

Place the Skittles, or other fruity chewy candy, in the bottom of a shot glass, then pour Lemon-Lime Soda and Vodka.

Night Flight Shooter
1 part Amaretto
1 part Peach Schnapps
1 part Blackberry Liqueur
Shot Glass

Shake with ice and strain

Ninja
3 parts Frangelico®
1 part Melon Liqueur
Shot Glass

Shake with ice and strain

Nitro
1 part Sambuca
1 part Goldschläger®
1 part Brandy
Shot Glass

Shake with ice and strain

No Name
1 part Amaretto
1 part Whiskey
1 part Sour Mix
Shot Glass

Shake with ice and strain

Norwegian Pastry
1 part Crème de Cacao (Dark)
1 part Coffee
1 part Aquavit
1 part Vanilla Liqueur
Shot Glass

Shake with ice and strain

Nuclear Accelerator
1 part Citrus-Flavored Vodka
1 part Crème de Menthe (White)
Shot Glass

Shake with ice and strain

Nuclear Holocaust
1 part Blue Curaçao
1 part Peach Schnapps
1 part Crème de Banana
1 part Dark Rum
Shot Glass

Shake with ice and strain

Nuclear Kamikaze
3 parts Vodka
1 part Lime Juice
1 part Triple Sec
2 parts Melon Liqueur
Shot Glass

Shake with ice and strain

Nuclear Waste
2 parts Vodka
1 part Melon Liqueur
1 part Triple Sec
splash Lime Juice
Shot Glass

Shake with ice and strain

Nuts 'n' Holly
1 part Drambuie®
1 part Irish Cream Liqueur
1 part Frangelico®
1 part Amaretto
Shot Glass

Shake with ice and strain

Nutty Aruban
1 part Frangelico®
1 part Ponche Kuba®
Shot Glass

Shake with ice and strain

Nutty Jamaican
1 part Dark Rum
1 part Frangelico®
Shot Glass

Shake with ice and strain

Nutty Mexican
1 part Tequila Silver
1 part Frangelico®
Shot Glass

Shake with ice and strain

Nutty Orange
1 part Amaretto
1 part Triple Sec
Shot Glass

Shake with ice and strain

Nutty Professor
1 part Grand Marnier®
1 part Frangelico®
1 part Irish Cream Liqueur
Shot Glass

Shake with ice and strain

Nymphomaniac
3 parts Spiced Rum
1 part Peach Schnapps
1 part Coconut-Flavored Rum
Shot Glass

Shake with ice and strain

Oatmeal Cookie
2 parts Cinnamon Schnapps
1 part Irish Cream Liqueur
1 part Coffee Liqueur
1 part Frangelico®
1 part Cream
Shot Glass

Shake with ice and strain

Obly Gooh
2 parts Crème de Menthe (White)
1 part Brandy
Shot Glass

Shake with ice and strain

An Offer You Can't Refuse
1 part Amaretto
1 part Sambuca
Shot Glass

Shake with ice and strain

Oil Slick
1 part Jägermeister®
1 part Rumple Minze®
Shot Glass

Pour ingredients into glass neat (do not chill)

Old Crusty
1 part 151-Proof Rum
1 part Wild Turkey® Bourbon
Shot Glass

Shake with ice and strain

Open Grave

1 part Jägermeister®
1 part Rumple Minze®
1 part Irish Cream Liqueur
Shot Glass

Shake with ice and strain

Opera House Special

1 part Tequila
1 part Gin
1 part Light Rum
1 part Vodka
1 part Pineapple Juice
1 part Orange Juice
1 part Sour Mix
Shot Glass

Shake with ice and strain. *Note: Because this recipe includes many ingredients, it's easier to make in volume, about 6 shots.

Oral Sex

1 part Amaretto
1 part Irish Cream Liqueur
Shot Glass

Shake with ice and strain

Orange Crisis

2 parts Light Rum
2 parts Peach Schnapps
1 part Triple Sec
1 part Apricot Brandy
1 part Cream
splash Grenadine
Shot Glass

Shake with ice and strain. *Note: Because this recipe includes many ingredients, it's easier to make in volume, about 6 shots.

Orange Crush Shooter

1 part Vodka
1 part Triple Sec
1 part Club Soda
Shot Glass

Stir gently with ice and strain

Orange Monk

3 parts Frangelico®
1 part Grand Marnier®
Shot Glass

Pour ingredients into glass neat (do not chill)

Orgasm #1

1 part Amaretto
1 part Coffee Liqueur
1 part Light Cream
Shot Glass

Shake with ice and strain

Orgasm #2

1 part Vodka
1 part Amaretto
1 part Coffee Liqueur
1 part Irish Cream Liqueur
Shot Glass

Shake with ice and strain

Orgasm #3

3 parts Southern Comfort®
2 parts Pineapple Juice
1 part Amaretto
Shot Glass

Shake with ice and strain

Otter Pop

2 parts Light Rum
2 parts Blue Curaçao
1 part Sour Mix
1 part Lemon-Lime Soda
Shot Glass

Shake with ice and strain

Paddington Bear Surprise

1 part Bacardi® Limón Rum
1 part Coffee Liqueur
2 splashes Orange Marmalade
dash Brown Sugar
Shot Glass

Combine all ingredients in a blender with no ice. Blend until smooth.

Paddy's Day Special
1 part Crème de Menthe (Green)
1 part Triple Sec
1 part Melon Liqueur
Shot Glass

Build in the glass with no ice

Paint Ball
1 part Banana Liqueur
1 part Blue Curaçao
1 part Irish Cream Liqueur
1 part Southern Comfort®
1 part Triple Sec
Shot Glass

Shake with ice and strain. *Note: Because this recipe includes many ingredients, it's easier to make in volume, about 6 shots.

Paintbox
1 part Banana Liqueur
1 part Blue Curaçao
1 part Cherry Liqueur
Shot Glass

Shake with ice and strain

Pamoyo
1 part Gin
1 part Lemon-Lime Soda
1 part Grape Juice (Red)
Shot Glass

Shake with ice and strain

Pancake
1 part Cinnamon Schnapps
1 part Irish Cream Liqueur
1 part Cream
Shot Glass

Shake with ice and strain

Pancho Villa Shooter
1 part Tequila Silver
1 part Amaretto
1 part 151-Proof Rum
Shot Glass

Shake with ice and strain

Pants on Fire
1 part Vodka
1 part Strawberry Liqueur
1 part Banana Liqueur
1 part Grapefruit Juice
1 part Orange Juice
Shot Glass

Shake with ice and strain. *Note: Because this recipe includes many ingredients, it's easier to make in volume, about 6 shots.

Panty Burner Shooter
1 part Advocaat
1 part Coffee
1 part Frangelico®
Shot Glass

Shake with ice and strain

Panty Quiver
1 part Jägermeister®
1 part Blackberry Brandy
Shot Glass

Shake with ice and strain

Panty Raid
2 parts Citrus-Flavored Vodka
1 part Chambord®
splash Lemon-Lime Soda
splash Pineapple Juice
Shot Glass

Shake with ice and strain

Paralyzer Shooter
1 part Vodka
1 part Coffee Liqueur
1 part Cola
1 part Milk
Shot Glass
Shake with ice and strain

Paranoia
2 parts Amaretto
1 part Orange Juice
Shot Glass
Shake with ice and strain

Party Animal
1 part Parfait Amour
1 part Coconut-Flavored Liqueur
1 part Orange Juice
Shot Glass
Shake with ice and strain

Passion Killer Shooter
1 part Tequila Silver
1 part Melon Liqueur
1 part Passion Fruit Liqueur
Shot Glass
Shake with ice and strain

Passion Slam
1 part Passion Fruit Liqueur
1 part Kiwi Schnapps
1 part Lime Juice
Shot Glass
Shake with ice and strain

Passout
1 part Amaretto
1 part Licor 43®
1 part Southern Comfort®
1 part Triple Sec
1 part Jack Daniel's®
Shot Glass
Shake with ice and strain. *Note: Because this recipe includes many ingredients, it's easier to make in volume, about 6 shots.

PB&J
1 part Vodka
1 part Raspberry Liqueur
1 part Frangelico®
Shot Glass
Shake with ice and strain

Peach Death
1 part Vodka
1 part Peach Schnapps
1 part Amaretto
Shot Glass
Shake with ice and strain

Peach Nehi
1 part Vodka
1 part Peach Schnapps
1 part Cherry Liqueur
1 part Sour Mix
1 part Pineapple Juice
1 part Lemon-Lime Soda
Shot Glass
Shake with ice and strain. *Note: Because this recipe includes many ingredients, it's easier to make in volume, about 6 shots.

Peaches and Cream Shot
3 parts Peach Schnapps
2 parts Cream
1 part 151-Proof Rum
Shot Glass
Shake with ice and strain

Peachfuzz
1 part Peach Schnapps
1 part Cranberry Juice Cocktail
Shot Glass
Shake with ice and strain

Pearl Diver

1 part Melon Liqueur
1 part Pineapple Juice
1 part Coconut-Flavored Rum
Shot Glass

Shake with ice and strain

Pearl Harbor

1 part Vodka
1 part Melon Liqueur
1 part Orange Juice
Shot Glass

Shake with ice and strain

Pearl Necklace

1 part Tequila Rose®
1 part Irish Cream Liqueur
Shot Glass

Shake with ice and strain

Pecker Head

1 part Southern Comfort®
1 part Amaretto
1 part Pineapple
Shot Glass

Shake with ice and strain

Pecker Wrecker

1 part Blackberry Brandy
1 part Crème de Noyaux
1 part 151-Proof Rum
1 part Pineapple Juice
1 part Cranberry Juice Cocktail
Shot Glass

Shake with ice and strain. *Note: Because this recipe includes many ingredients, it's easier to make in volume, about 6 shots.

Pedra

1 part Tequila
1 part Vodka
1 part Dark Rum
1 part Irish Cream Liqueur
1 part Grenadine
1 part Absinthe
Shot Glass

Shake with ice and strain. *Note: Because this recipe includes many ingredients, it's easier to make in volume, about 6 shots.

Pee Gee

1 part Cinnamon Schnapps
1 part Orange Juice
1 part Vodka
Shot Glass

Shake with ice and strain

Penthouse

1 part Tequila
1 part Bacardi® Limón Rum
1 part Lime Juice
Shot Glass

Shake with ice and strain

Peppermint

3 parts Pepper-Flavored Vodka
1 part Crème de Menthe (White)
Shot Glass

Shake with ice and strain

Peppermint Bonbon

4 parts Peppermint Schnapps
1 part Chocolate Syrup
Shot Glass

Shake with ice and strain

Peppermint Pattie®

1 part Coffee Liqueur
1 part Peppermint Schnapps
1 part Half and Half
Shot Glass

Shake with ice and strain

Peppermint Rose
1 part Peppermint Schnapps
1 part Tequila Rose®
Shot Glass
Shake with ice and strain

Peschino
1 part Peach Schnapps
1 part Strawberry Liqueur
Shot Glass
Shake with ice and strain

Petronius
2 parts Jim Beam®
1 part Vanilla Liqueur
1 part Peppermint Liqueur
Shot Glass
Shake with ice and strain

Pez®
1 part Spiced Rum
1 part Raspberry Liqueur
1 part Sour Mix
Shot Glass
Shake with ice and strain

Photon Torpedo
1 part After Shock® Cinnamon Schnapps
1 part Vodka
Shot Glass
Shake with ice and strain

A Piece of Ass
1 part Amaretto
1 part Southern Comfort®
Shot Glass
Shake with ice and strain

Pierced Fuzzy Navel
2 parts Peach Schnapps
1 part Vodka
1 part Orange Juice
Shot Glass
Shake with ice and strain

Pierced Nipple
1 part Sambuca
1 part Irish Cream Liqueur
Shot Glass
Shake with ice and strain

Pigskin Shot
1 part Vodka
1 part Melon Liqueur
1 part Sour Mix
Shot Glass
Shake with ice and strain

Piña Crana Kazi
2 parts Vodka
1 part Triple Sec
1 part Pineapple Juice
Shot Glass
Shake with ice and strain

Pineapple Bomb
1 part Southern Comfort®
1 part Triple Sec
1 part Pineapple Juice
Shot Glass
Shake with ice and strain

Pineapple Upside-Down Cake
1 part Irish Cream Liqueur
1 part Vodka
1 part Butterscotch Schnapps
1 part Pineapple Juice
Shot Glass
Shake with ice and strain

Pineberry
1 part Cranberry-Flavored Vodka
1 part Pineapple-Flavored Vodka
Shot Glass
Shake with ice and strain

Pink Belly

1 part Jim Beam®
1 part Amaretto
1 part Sloe Gin
1 part Irish Cream Liqueur
1 part Lemon-Lime Soda
Shot Glass

Shake with ice and strain. *Note: Because this recipe includes many ingredients, it's easier to make in volume, about 6 shots.

Pink Cadillac

2 parts Vodka
1 part Cherry Juice
1 part Lemonade
1 part Orange Juice
Shot Glass

Shake with ice and strain

Pink Cod Shooter

1 part Tequila Reposado
1 part Sour Mix
Shot Glass

Shake with ice and strain

Pink Cotton Candy

1 part Vodka
1 part Amaretto
splash Grenadine
Shot Glass

Shake with ice and strain

Pink Danger

1 part Butterscotch Schnapps
2 parts Vodka
3 parts Fruit Punch
Shot Glass

Shake with ice and strain

Pink Floyd

1 part Vodka
1 part Peach Schnapps
1 part Cranberry Juice Cocktail
1 part Grapefruit Juice
Shot Glass

Shake with ice and strain

Pink Lemonade Shooter

1 part Vodka
1 part Sour Mix
1 part Cranberry Juice Cocktail
Shot Glass

Shake with ice and strain

Pink Nipple Shooter

3 parts Currant-Flavored Vodka
1 part Sambuca
Shot Glass

Shake with ice and strain

Pink Ranger

2 parts Vodka
1 part Coconut-Flavored Rum
1 part Peach Schnapps
1 part Cranberry Juice Cocktail
1 part Pineapple Juice
Shot Glass

Shake with ice and strain

Pinkeye

1 part Vodka
1 part Cranberry Juice Cocktail
1 part Sour Mix
Shot Glass

Shake with ice and strain

Pinky

3 parts Rumple Minze®
1 part Fire Water®
Shot Glass

Shake with ice and strain

Pissed Off Mexican

1 part Cinnamon Schnapps
1 part Tequila Silver
Shot Glass

Shake with ice and strain

Pistol Shot

1 part Triple Sec
1 part Apricot Brandy
1 part Cherry Brandy
Shot Glass

Shake with ice and strain

Pit Bull and Crank Shooter

1 part Rum
1 part Tequila
1 part Jägermeister®
1 part Seagram's® Crown 7 Whiskey
1 part Peppermint Schnapps
Shot Glass

Shake with ice and strain* Note: Because this recipe includes many ingredients, it's easier to make in volume, about 6 shots.

Pixy Stix®

2 parts Southern Comfort®
1 part Amaretto
Shot Glass

Shake with ice and strain

Pleading Insanity

1 part Tequila Silver
1 part Vodka
1 part Dark Rum
Shot Glass

Shake with ice and strain

Poco Loco Boom

1 part Vodka
1 part Tia Maria®
1 part Coconut Cream
Shot Glass

Shake with ice and strain

Point-Blank

1 part Brandy
1 part Crème de Banana
1 part Apricot Brandy
1 part Cherry Brandy
Shot Glass

Shake with ice and strain

Poison Apple

1 part Apple Brandy
1 part Vodka
Shot Glass

Shake with ice and strain

Poison Ivy

1 part Cinnamon Schnapps
1 part Coffee Liqueur
Shot Glass

Shake with ice and strain

Poison Milk

1 part Jägermeister®
1 part Irish Cream Liqueur
Shot Glass

Shake with ice and strain

Polar Bear Shot

1 part Crème de Cacao (White)
1 part Peppermint Schnapps
Shot Glass

Shake with ice and strain

Poop Shoot

2 parts Sambuca
1 part Fruit Punch
Shot Glass

Shake with ice and strain

Popper
1 part Vodka
3 parts Lemon-Lime Soda
Shot Glass
Build in the glass with no ice

Porto Covo
1 part Vodka
1 part Absinthe
1 part Coconut-Flavored Liqueur
1 part Banana Liqueur
Shot Glass
Shake with ice and strain

Pouce Coupe Puddle
2 parts Irish Cream Liqueur
1 part Peach Schnapps
1 part Crème de Menthe (White)
Shot Glass
Shake with ice and strain

Power Drill
1 part Vodka
1 part Orange Juice
1 part Beer
Shot Glass
Build in the glass with no ice

Power Shot
2 parts Vodka
1 part Absolut® Peppar Vodka
dash Wasabi
Shot Glass
Build in the glass with no ice

Prestone
1 part Melon Liqueur
2 parts Citrus-Flavored Vodka
2 parts Lemon-Lime Soda
Shot Glass
Shake with ice and strain

Protein Smoothie
1 part Scotch
1 part Cream
1 part Clamato® Juice
Shot Glass
Shake with ice and strain

Prozac®
1 part Crown Royal® Whiskey
1 part Melon Liqueur
1 part Lemon-Lime Soda
Shot Glass
Shake with ice and strain

Pucker Sucker
1 part Sour Apple Schnapps
1 part Coffee Liqueur
1 part Orange Juice
Shot Glass
Shake with ice and strain

Puerto Rican Monkey Fuck
2 parts Coffee Liqueur
2 parts Crème de Banana
1 part 151-Proof Rum
Shot Glass
Shake with ice and strain

Puke
1 part Jack Daniel's®
1 part Jim Beam®
1 part Yukon Jack®
1 part Vodka
1 part Tequila
Shot Glass
Shake with ice and strain

Pumpkin Pie
2 parts Coffee Liqueur
1 part Irish Cream Liqueur
1 part Goldschläger®
Shot Glass
Shake with ice and strain

Puppy's Nose
1 part Peppermint Schnapps
1 part Tia Maria®
1 part Irish Cream Liqueur
Shot Glass

Build in the glass with no ice

Purple Alaskan
1 part Amaretto
1 part Jack Daniel's®
1 part Orange Juice
1 part Southern Comfort®
1 part Raspberry Liqueur
Shot Glass

Shake with ice and strain. *Note: Because this recipe includes many ingredients, it's easier to make in volume, about 6 shots.

Purple Elastic Thunder Fuck
1 part Vodka
1 part Crown Royal® Whiskey
1 part Southern Comfort®
1 part Amaretto
1 part Raspberry Liqueur
1 part Pineapple Juice
1 part Cranberry Juice Cocktail
Shot Glass

Shake with ice and strain. *Note: Because this recipe includes many ingredients, it's easier to make in volume, about 6 shots.

Purple Haze #1
1 part Citrus-Flavored Vodka
1 part Raspberry Liqueur
1 part Lemon-Lime Soda
Shot Glass

Shake with ice and strain

Purple Haze #2
1 part Amaretto
1 part Root Beer Schnapps
1 part Milk
1 part Grape Soda
Shot Glass

Shake with ice and strain

Purple Helmeted Warrior
1 part Gin
1 part Southern Comfort®
1 part Peach Schnapps
1 part Blue Curaçao
1 part Lime Juice
1 part Grenadine
1 part Lemon-Lime Soda
Shot Glass

Shake with ice and strain. *Note: Because this recipe includes many ingredients, it's easier to make in volume, about 6 shots.

Purple Nipple
3 parts Melon Liqueur
1 part Jägermeister®
2 parts Cranberry Juice Cocktail
1 part Orange Juice
Shot Glass

Shake with ice and strain

Purple Panther
3 parts Sour Apple–Flavored Vodka
1 part Blue Curaçao
Shot Glass

Shake with ice and strain

Purple Penis
2 parts Vodka
1 part Blue Curaçao
1 part Raspberry Liqueur
Shot Glass

Shake with ice and strain

Purple Rain Shooter
3 parts Cranberry-Flavored Vodka
1 part Blue Curaçao
Shot Glass

Shake with ice and strain

Purple Viper
1 part Sloe Gin
1 part Vodka
2 parts Raspberry Liqueur
Shot Glass

Shake with ice and strain

Purple Wind
1 part Raspberry Liqueur
2 parts Sake
Shot Glass

Shake with ice and strain

Pussy in Fight
1 part Gin
1 part Frangelico®
Shot Glass

Shake with ice and strain

Pussy Juice
1 part Goldschläger®
1 part Vodka
1 part Vegetable Juice Blend
Shot Glass

Shake with ice and strain

Quaalude
1 part Vodka
1 part Coffee Liqueur
1 part Irish Cream Liqueur
1 part Amaretto
1 part Frangelico®
Shot Glass

Shake with ice and strain. *Note: Because this recipe includes many ingredients, it's easier to make in volume, about 6 shots.

Quick Fuck
1 part Coffee Liqueur
1 part Melon Liqueur
1 part Irish Cream Liqueur
Shot Glass

Shake with ice and strain

Quick Silver
1 part Anisette
1 part Triple Sec
1 part Tequila
Shot Glass

Shake with ice and strain

Quicksand Shooter
1 part Black Sambuca
3 parts Orange Juice
Shot Glass

Shake with ice and strain

Rabbit Punch
1 part Campari®
1 part Crème de Cacao (Dark)
1 part Coconut-Flavored Rum
2 parts Irish Cream Liqueur
Shot Glass

Shake with ice and strain

Raging Indian
1 part Vodka
1 part Coffee Liqueur
1 part Orange Juice
1 part Mango Nectar
Shot Glass

Shake with ice and strain

Raija
1 part Vanilla Liqueur
1 part Coffee Liqueur
1 part Orange Juice
1 part Mango Juice
Shot Glass

Shake with ice and strain

Rambo Shot
1 part Jägermeister®
1 part Rumple Minze®
Shot Glass

Shake with ice and strain

Raspberry Beret
1 part Vodka
1 part Raspberry Liqueur
1 part Cream
Shot Glass

Shake with ice and strain

Rat Shooter
3 parts Green Chartreuse®
1 part Rumple Minze®
Shot Glass

Build in the glass with no ice

Ray of Light
1 part Crème de Cacao (White)
1 part Galliano®
1 part Grand Marnier®
Shot Glass

Shake with ice and strain

Razor Blade
1 part Jägermeister®
1 part 151-Proof Rum
Shot Glass

Shake with ice and strain

Ready Set Go
1 part Crème de Banana
1 part Melon Liqueur
1 part Strawberry Liqueur
Shot Glass

Shake with ice and strain

A Real Strong Dirty Rotten Scoundrel
1 part Cranberry-Flavored Vodka
1/2 part Melon Liqueur
Shot Glass

Shake with ice and strain

Rebel Jester
2 parts Kiwi Schnapps
1 part Goldschläger®
Shot Glass

Shake with ice and strain

Reboot
1 part Crème de Menthe (Green)
1 part Cachaça
2 parts Absolut® Peppar Vodka
Shot Glass

Shake with ice and strain

Red Baron Shooter
2 parts Crown Royal® Whiskey
1 part Amaretto
1 part Cranberry Juice Cocktail
Shot Glass

Shake with ice and strain

Red Beard
2 parts Spiced Rum
2 parts Coconut-Flavored Rum
1 part Grenadine
1 part Lemon-Lime Soda
Shot Glass

Shake with ice and strain

Red Death
1 part Vodka
1 part Fire Water®
1 part Yukon Jack®
1 part 151-Proof Rum
Shot Glass

Shake with ice and strain

Red Devil Shooter
1 part Vodka
1 part Southern Comfort®
1 part Amaretto
1 part Triple Sec
1 part Grenadine
1 part Orange Juice
1 part Sour Mix
Shot Glass

Shake with ice and strain. *Note: Because this recipe includes many ingredients, it's easier to make in volume, about 6 shots.

Red Dragon's Breath
1 part Cinnamon Schnapps
1 part Whiskey
Shot Glass

Shake with ice and strain

Red-Eyed Hell
1 part Triple Sec
1 part Vodka
1 part 151-Proof Rum
2 parts Vegetable Juice Blend
Shot Glass

Build in the glass with no ice

Red Frog Roadkill
1 part Raspberry Liqueur
1 part Amaretto
1 part Jim Beam®
2 parts Cranberry Juice Cocktail
Shot Glass

Shake with ice and strain

Red-Headed Princess
1 part Jägermeister®
1 part Peach Schnapps
2 parts Cranberry Juice Cocktail
Shot Glass

Shake with ice and strain

Red-Headed Vamp
1 part Raspberry Liqueur
1 part Jägermeister®
1 part Cranberry Juice Cocktail
Shot Glass

Shake with ice and strain

Red-Line
1 part Tequila Silver
1 part Sambuca
splash Crème de Cassis
Shot Glass

Shake with ice and strain

Red Lobster
1 part Amaretto
1 part Southern Comfort®
1 part Cranberry Juice Cocktail
Shot Glass

Shake with ice and strain

Red Monster
1 part Tequila
1 part Orange Juice
Shot Glass

Shake with ice and strain

Red Mosquito
1 part Vodka
1 part Hot Damn!® Cinnamon Schnapps
Shot Glass

Shake with ice and strain

Red Royal Shot
1 part Crown Royal® Whiskey
1 part Amaretto
Shot Glass

Shake with ice and strain

Red Snapper Shooter
2 parts Canadian Whiskey
1 part Amaretto
Shot Glass

Shake with ice and strain

Redneck Killer

1 part Jack Daniel's®
1 part Jim Beam®
1 part Wild Turkey® 101
Shot Glass

Build in the glass with no ice

Regulator

1 part Crown Royal® Whiskey
1 part Melon Liqueur
3 parts Cranberry Juice Cocktail
Shot Glass

Shake with ice and strain

Republica das Bananas

1 part Tequila Silver
1 part Rum
1 part Crème de Banana
Shot Glass

Shake with ice and strain

Retribution

1 part Rumple Minze®
1 part Tequila
1 part Jägermeister®
1 part Fire Water®
Shot Glass

Shake with ice and strain

Roadkill Shot

1 part Tequila
1 part Hot Damn!® Cinnamon Schnapps
1 part Whiskey
Shot Glass

Shake with ice and strain

Roadrunner Punch

1 part Coconut-Flavored Rum
1 part Blue Curaçao
1 part Peach Schnapps
1 part Fruit Punch
Shot Glass

Shake with ice and strain

Roasted Toasted Almond Shooter

1 part Amaretto
1 part Coffee Liqueur
1 part Cream
1 part Vodka
Shot Glass

Shake with ice and strain

Robot

2 parts Jack Daniel's®
1 part Vodka
1 part Grenadine
Shot Glass

Shake with ice and strain

Rocket Fuel

2 parts 151-Proof Rum
1 part Vodka
1 part Blue Curaçao
Shot Glass

Shake with ice and strain

Rocket Pop

2 parts Bacardi® Limón Rum
1 part Lemon-Lime Soda
1 part Cranberry Juice Cocktail
1 part Sour Mix
Shot Glass

Shake with ice and strain

Rocky Mountain

2 parts Southern Comfort®
2 parts Amaretto
1 part Lime Juice
Shot Glass

Shake with ice and strain

Rocky Mountain Bear Fucker

1 part Tequila
1 part Jack Daniel's®
1 part Southern Comfort®
Shot Glass

Shake with ice and strain

Romulan Ale Shooter

1 part Vodka
1 part Tropical Punch Schnapps
1 part Cactus Juice Schnapps
Shot Glass

Shake with ice and strain

Roommate Killer

1 part Jägermeister®
1 part Rumple Minze®
Shot Glass

Shake with ice and strain

Rooster Piss

1 part Jack Daniel's®
1 part Cinnamon Schnapps
Shot Glass

Shake with ice and strain

Rooster Tail

1 part Tequila
1 part Orange Juice
dash Salt
Shot Glass

Shake with ice and strain

Rosso di Sera

1 part Vodka
1 part Strawberry Liqueur
1 part Triple Sec
Shot Glass

Shake with ice and strain

Rosy Cheeks

1 part Strawberry Liqueur
1 part Melon Liqueur
1 part Sour Mix
Shot Glass

Shake with ice and strain

Rott Gut

1 part Cinnamon Schnapps
1 part Vodka
Shot Glass

Shake with ice and strain

Rotten Apple

1 part Jägermeister®
1 part Sour Apple Schnapps
Shot Glass

Shake with ice and strain

Rotten Pussy

2 parts Midori®
1 part Amaretto
1 part Southern Comfort®
1 part Coconut-Flavored Rum
1 part Sour Mix
1 part Pineapple Juice
Shot Glass

Shake with ice and strain

Royal

1 part Vodka
1 part Crème de Banana
1 part Blue Curaçao
1 part Lemon Juice
Shot Glass

Shake with ice and strain

Royal Apple
1 part Crown Royal® Whiskey
1 part Sour Apple Schnapps
2 parts Cranberry Juice Cocktail
Shot Glass

Shake with ice and strain

Royal Bitch
1 part Frangelico®
1 part Crown Royal® Whiskey
Shot Glass

Shake with ice and strain

Royal Flush
1 part Crown Royal® Whiskey
1 part Peach Schnapps
2 parts Cranberry Juice Cocktail
2 parts Orange Juice
splash Club Soda
Shot Glass

Shake all but Club Soda with ice and strain into the glass. Top with Club Soda.

Royal Fuck
1 part Crown Royal® Whiskey
1 part Chambord®
1 part Peach Schnapps
1 part Pineapple-Flavored Vodka
1 part Cranberry Juice Cocktail
Shot Glass

Shake with ice and strain

Royal Scandal
1 part Crown Royal® Whiskey
1 part Southern Comfort®
1 part Amaretto
1 part Sour Mix
1 part Pineapple Juice
Shot Glass

Shake with ice and strain. *Note: Because this recipe includes many ingredients, it's easier to make in volume, about 6 shots.

Royal Shock
1 part After Shock® Cinnamon Schnapps
2 parts Crown Royal® Whiskey
Shot Glass

Build in the glass with no ice

Royal Sicilian Kiss
2 parts Amaretto
1 part Crown Royal® Whiskey
1 part Southern Comfort®
Shot Glass

Shake with ice and strain

Rubber Biscuit
1 part Crown Royal® Whiskey
1 part Butterscotch Schnapps
Shot Glass

Shake with ice and strain

Ruby Red
2 parts Vodka
2 parts Cranberry Juice Cocktail
1 part Sour Mix
Shot Glass

Shake with ice and strain

Rug Burn
1 part Irish Cream Liqueur
1 part Coffee Liqueur
1 part Irish Whiskey
Shot Glass

Shake with ice and strain

Rum Bubblegum
1 part Crème de Banana
1 part Irish Cream Liqueur
1 part Light Rum
Shot Glass

Shake with ice and strain

Rum Runner Shooter

1 part Dark Rum
1 part Spiced Rum
1 part Coconut-Flavored Rum
1 part Crème de Banana
1 part Blackberry Liqueur
1 part Grenadine
1 part Sour Mix
1 part Orange Juice
Shot Glass

Shake with ice and strain. *Note: Because this recipe includes many ingredients, it's easier to make in volume, about 6 shots.

Rumka

1 part Vodka
1 part Spiced Rum
Shot Glass

Shake with ice and strain

Russian Ballet

3 parts Vodka
1 part Crème de Cassis
Shot Glass

Shake with ice and strain

Russian Kamikaze

2 parts Vodka
1 part Raspberry Liqueur
Shot Glass

Shake with ice and strain

Russian Quaalude Shooter

1 part Vodka
1 part Frangelico®
1 part Irish Cream Liqueur
1 part Coffee Liqueur
1 part Cream
Shot Glass

Shake with ice and strain. *Note: Because this recipe includes many ingredients, it's easier to make in volume, about 6 shots.

Russian Roulette

1 part Vodka
1 part Galliano®
1 part 151-Proof Rum
Shot Glass

Shake with ice and strain

Russian Tongue

1 part Goldschläger®
1 part Rumple Minze®
1 part Vodka
Shot Glass

Shake with ice and strain

Rusted Throat

1 part Light Rum
1 part Orange Juice
1 part Passion Fruit Nectar
1 part 151-Proof Rum
Shot Glass

Shake with ice and strain

Rusty Halo

1 part Vodka
1 part Amaretto
1 part Banana Liqueur
1 part Melon Liqueur
Shot Glass

Shake with ice and strain

Rusty Navel

1 part Tequila
1 part Amaretto
Shot Glass

Shake with ice and strain

Rythym & Blues

1 part Jack Daniel's®
1 part Blueberry Schnapps
Shot Glass

Shake with ice and strain

S.H.I.T.
1 part Sambuca
2 parts Crème Liqueur
2 parts Irish Mist®
1 part Tequila
Shot Glass
Shake with ice and strain

Saikkosen Special
1 part Cointreau®
2 parts Crème de Cassis
2 parts Tia Maria®
Shot Glass
Shake with ice and strain

Sambuca Slide
2 parts Sambuca
1 part Vodka
1 part Light Cream
Shot Glass
Shake with ice and strain

Sambuca Surprise
1 part Crème de Cacao (White)
1 part Crème de Menthe (White)
1 part Sambuca
Shot Glass
Shake with ice and strain

Sammy Slammer
2 parts Southern Comfort®
1 part Vanilla Liqueur
1 part Peach Schnapps
Shot Glass
Shake with ice and strain

A Sample
1 part Grain Alcohol
1 part Gatorade®
Shot Glass
Shake with ice and strain

Sand Bag
1 part Tequila
1 part Jägermeister®
dash Salt
Shot Glass
Shake with ice and strain

Sandblaster
1 part Light Rum
1 part Fresh Lime Juice
2 parts Cola
Shot Glass
Stir gently with ice and strain

Sandy Beach
1 part Irish Cream Liqueur
1 part Butterscotch Schnapps
1 part Amaretto
1 part Cream
Shot Glass
Shake with ice and strain

Saratoga Trunk
1 part Tequila Silver
1 part Tia Maria®
1 part Goldschläger®
Shot Glass
Shake with ice and strain

Satan's Mouthwash
1 part Jack Daniel's®
1 part Sambuca
Shot Glass
Shake with ice and strain

Saturnus
1 part Crème de Banana
1 part Gin
1 part Dry Vermouth
2 parts Orange Juice
Shot Glass
Shake with ice and strain

Scarlet O'Hara Shooter
2 parts Southern Comfort®
1 part Sour Mix
1 part Grenadine
Shot Glass

Shake with ice and strain

Schwimmer
2 parts Sambuca
1 part Coffee Liqueur
1 part Irish Cream Liqueur
1 part Butterscotch Schnapps
1 part Jägermeister®
Shot Glass

Shake with ice and strain. *Note: Because this recipe includes many ingredients, it's easier to make in volume, about 6 shots.

Scooby Shooter
2 parts Coconut-Flavored Rum
2 parts Peach Schnapps
2 parts Melon Liqueur
1 part Vodka
1 part Orange Juice
1 part Pineapple Juice
Shot Glass

Shake with ice and strain. *Note: Because this recipe includes many ingredients, it's easier to make in volume, about 6 shots.

Scorpion Shooter
2 parts Vodka
1 part Blackberry Liqueur
Shot Glass

Shake with ice and strain

Scorpion Suicide
2 parts Cherry Brandy
1 part Whiskey
1 part Pernod®
Shot Glass

Shake with ice and strain

Screamer
1 part Gin
1 part Rum
1 part Tequila
1 part Triple Sec
1 part Vodka
Shot Glass

Shake with ice and strain. *Note: Because this recipe includes many ingredients, it's easier to make in volume, about 6 shots.

Screaming Blue Messiah
1 part Goldschläger®
1 part Blue Curaçao
Shot Glass

Shake with ice and strain

Screaming Blue Viking
1 part Yukon Jack®
1 part Rumple Minze®
1 part Blue Curaçao
Shot Glass

Shake with ice and strain

Screaming Green Monster
1 part Coconut-Flavored Rum
1 part Midori®
1 part 151-Proof Rum
1 part Pineapple Juice
1 part Lemon-Lime Soda
Shot Glass

Shake with ice and strain. *Note: Because this recipe includes many ingredients, it's easier to make in volume, about 6 shots.

Screaming Moose
1 part Jägermeister®
1 part Coffee Liqueur
1 part Irish Cream Liqueur
Shot Glass

Shake with ice and strain

Screaming Orgasm
1 part Cream
1 part Vodka
1 part Amaretto
1 part Crème de Banana
Shot Glass
Shake with ice and strain

Screaming Peach
1 part Peach Schnapps
1 part Melon Liqueur
1 part Grenadine
2 parts Pineapple Juice
Shot Glass
Shake with ice and strain

Screaming Purple Jesus
1 part Vodka
1 part Grape Juice (Red)
Shot Glass
Shake with ice and strain

Screaming Yoda®
1 part Melon Liqueur
1 part Jägermeister®
1 part Orange Juice
Shot Glass
Shake with ice and strain

Screw 'n' Mail
1 part Crème de Banana
1 part Cherry Brandy
1 part Chocolate Mint Liqueur
Shot Glass
Shake with ice and strain

Second Childhood
1 part Crème de Menthe (White)
1 part Vodka
Shot Glass
Shake with ice and strain

Secret Heart
1 part Crème de Cacao (White)
1 part Amaretto
1 part Strawberry Liqueur
Shot Glass
Shake with ice and strain

Seeing Stars
1 part Crème de Menthe (White)
1 part Coffee
1 part Crème de Banana
Shot Glass
Shake with ice and strain

Señor Freak
1 part Tequila Reposado
1 part Light Rum
1 part Vodka
1 part Lemon-Lime Soda
Shot Glass
Shake with ice and strain

Sensei on the Rocks
1 part Coffee Liqueur
1 part Coconut-Flavored Rum
1 part Jack Daniel's®
Shot Glass
Shake with ice and strain

Seven Twenty-Seven
1 part Vodka
1 part Coconut-Flavored Liqueur
Shot Glass
Shake with ice and strain

Sex in the Parking Lot
1 part Raspberry Liqueur
1 part Vodka
1 part Sour Apple Schnapps
Shot Glass
Shake with ice and strain

Sex Machine
1 part Coffee Liqueur
1 part Irish Cream Liqueur
1 part Milk
Shot Glass

Shake with ice and strain

Sex on Acid
2 parts Jägermeister®
1 part Melon Liqueur
1 part Blackberry Liqueur
1 part Pineapple Juice
1 part Cranberry Juice Cocktail
Shot Glass

Shake with ice and strain. *Note: Because this recipe includes many ingredients, it's easier to make in volume, about 6 shots.

Sex on a Pool Table
1 part Peach Schnapps
1 part Vodka
1 part Pineapple Juice
1 part Sour Mix
1 part Melon Liqueur
Shot Glass

Shake with ice and strain. *Note: Because this recipe includes many ingredients, it's easier to make in volume, about 6 shots.

Sex on the Beach Shooter
1 part Vodka
1 part Peach Schnapps
1 part Orange Juice
Shot Glass

Shake with ice and strain

Sex on the Lake
2 parts Crème de Banana
2 parts Crème de Cacao (Dark)
1 part Light Rum
1 part Cream
Shot Glass

Shake with ice and strain

Sex under the Moonlight
2 parts Vodka
1 part Coffee
1 part Port
1 part Cream
Shot Glass

Shake with ice and strain

Sex up against the Wall
2 parts Currant-Flavored Vodka
1 part Pineapple Juice
1 part Sour Mix
Shot Glass

Shake with ice and strain

Sex with an Alligator
1 part Jägermeister®
1 part Melon Liqueur
1 part Raspberry Liqueur
1 part Pineapple Juice
Shot Glass

Shake with ice and strain

Sexual Stimulation
2 parts Rum
1 part Crème de Menthe (Green)
1 part Crème de Banana
1 part Passion Fruit Nectar
Shot Glass

Shake with ice and strain

Sexy Alligator
2 parts Coconut-Flavored Rum
2 parts Melon Liqueur
1 part Jägermeister®
1 part Raspberry Liqueur
1 part Pineapple Juice
Shot Glass

Shake with ice and strain

Shag Later
2 parts After Shock® Cinnamon Schnapps
1 part Canadian Whiskey
1 part Root Beer
splash Chocolate Syrup
Shot Glass

Shake with ice and strain

Shake That Ass
1 part Blue Curaçao
1 part Banana Liqueur
1 part Sour Mix
1 part Orange Juice
Shot Glass

Shake with ice and strain

Shampoo
1 part Irish Cream Liqueur
1 part Butterscotch Schnapps
Shot Glass

Shake with ice and strain

Shape Shifter
1 part Crème de Menthe (Green)
1 part Orange Juice
dash Wasabi
Shot Glass

Build in the glass with no ice

Shark Bite Shooter
1 part Dark Rum
1 part Grenadine
2 parts Orange Juice
Shot Glass

Shake with ice and strain

Shazam Shooter
1 part Sour Apple Schnapps
1 part Raspberry Liqueur
1 part Cranberry Juice Cocktail
Shot Glass

Shake with ice and strain

Shipwreck Shooter
2 parts Rum
1 part Crème de Banana
1 part Strawberry Liqueur
1 part Sour Mix
Shot Glass

Shake with ice and strain

Shit Kicker
1 part Rye Whiskey
1 part Crème de Menthe (Green)
1 part Grenadine
Shot Glass

Shake with ice and strain

Shit Stain
1 part Crème de Cacao (Dark)
1 part Jägermeister®
1 part Vodka
Shot Glass

Shake with ice and strain

Shogun Shooter
3 parts Citrus-Flavored Vodka
1 part Melon Liqueur
Shot Glass

Shake with ice and strain

Short Vodka
1 part Triple Sec
1 part Orange-Flavored Vodka
Shot Glass

Shake with ice and strain

Shot from Hell
1 part Jägermeister®
2 parts Peppermint Schnapps
Shot Glass

Shake with ice and strain

Shot in the Back
3 parts Vodka
1 part Goldschläger®
dash Wasabi
Shot Glass

Pour ingredients into glass neat (do not chill)

Shot-Gun
1 part Jim Beam®
1 part Jack Daniel's®
1 part Wild Turkey® Bourbon
Shot Glass

Shake with ice and strain

Shot-o-Happiness
2 parts Goldschläger®
2 parts Raspberry Liqueur
1 part Pineapple Juice
1 part Sour Mix
1 part Lemon-Lime Soda
Shot Glass

Shake with ice and strain

Shrewsbury Slammer
1 part Southern Comfort®
1 part Peach Schnapps
2 parts Apple Cider
Shot Glass

Shake with ice and strain

Siberian Gold
2 part Vodka
2 part Goldschläger®
1 part Blue Curaçao
Shot Glass

Shake with ice and strain

Siberian Toolkit
4 parts Vodka
1 part Whiskey
Shot Glass

Shake with ice and strain

Siberian Walrus
2 parts Blue Curaçao
1 part Light Rum
1 part Vodka
1 part Jack Daniel's®
1 part Kirschwasser
1 part Orange Juice
Shot Glass

Shake with ice and strain. *Note: Because this recipe includes many ingredients, it's easier to make in volume, about 6 shots.

Sicilian Sunset
1 part Southern Comfort®
1 part Amaretto
1 part Grenadine
2 parts Orange Juice
Shot Glass

Shake with ice and strain

Silk Panties
1 part Peach Schnapps
3 parts Vodka
Shot Glass

Shake with ice and strain

Silver Bullet Shooter
2 parts Peppermint Schnapps
1 part Vodka
Shot Glass

Shake with ice and strain

Silver Devil
1 part Tequila
1 part Peppermint Schnapps
Shot Glass

Shake with ice and strain

Silver Nipple
4 parts Sambuca
1 part Vodka
Shot Glass

Shake with ice and strain

Silver Spider
1 part Vodka
1 part Rum
1 part Triple Sec
1 part Crème de Cacao (White)
Shot Glass
Shake with ice and strain

Silver Wilson
1 part Kiwi Schnapps
1 part Passion Fruit Liqueur
1 part Sour Mix
Shot Glass
Shake with ice and strain

Simple Green
1 part Blue Curaçao
1 part Galliano®
1 part Jägermeister®
Shot Glass
Shake with ice and strain

Simpson Bronco
4 parts Sambuca
1 part Grenadine
1 part Orange Juice
Shot Glass
Shake with ice and strain

Singles Night
1 part Coffee Liqueur
1 part Crème de Banana
1 part Cointreau®
1 part Irish Cream Liqueur
Shot Glass
Shake with ice and strain

Sing-Sing
1 part Blue Curaçao
1 part Cream
1 part Crème de Banana
1 part Frangelico®
Shot Glass
Shake with ice and strain

Sit Down and Shut Up
1 part Blackberry Liqueur
1 part Peppermint Liqueur
1 part Southern Comfort®
Shot Glass
Shake with ice and strain

Sit on My Face Sammy
1 part Crown Royal® Whiskey
1 part Frangelico®
1 part Irish Cream Liqueur
Shot Glass
Shake with ice and strain

Sivitri
1 part Lychee Liqueur
1 part Absinthe
Shot Glass
Shake with ice and strain

Skandia Iceberg
1 part Crème de Menthe (White)
1 part Vodka
Shot Glass
Shake with ice and strain

Skid Mark
1 part Coffee Liqueur
1 part Jägermeister®
1 part Rumple Minze®
Shot Glass
Shake with ice and strain

Skittles®
1 part Vodka
1 part Southern Comfort®
1 part Melon Liqueur
1 part Pineapple Juice
1 part Sour Mix
Shot Glass
Shake with ice and strain

Skull
1 part Coffee Liqueur
1 part Irish Cream Liqueur
1 part Whiskey
Shot Glass
Shake with ice and strain

Sky Pilot
1 part Vodka
1 part Irish Cream Liqueur
1 part Peppermint Schnapps
Shot Glass
Shake with ice and strain

Slam Dunk Shooter
2 parts Tequila Reposado
1 part Lime Cordial
1 part Club Soda
Shot Glass
Shake all but Club Soda with ice and strain into the glass. Top with Club Soda.

Slammer
1 part Vodka
1 part Lemon-Lime Soda
Shot Glass
Build in the glass with no ice

Slap Shot
2 parts Southern Comfort®
1 part Peppermint Schnapps
Shot Glass
Shake with ice and strain

Slice of Apple Pie
3 parts Vodka
1 part Apple Juice
Shot Glass
Shake with ice and strain

Slick and Sleezy
1 part Salsa
5 parts Vodka
Shot Glass
Build in the glass with no ice

Slickster
2 parts Southern Comfort®
1 part Peach Schnapps
1 part Lemon-Lime Soda
Shot Glass
Stir gently with ice and strain

Slippery Cricket
1 part Vodka
1 part Blue Hawaiian Schnapps
1 part Tropical Punch Schnapps
Shot Glass
Shake with ice and strain

Slippery Nipple
1 part Coffee Liqueur
1 part Irish Cream Liqueur
1 part Peppermint Schnapps
Shot Glass
Shake with ice and strain

Slippery Saddle
1 part Vodka
1 part Licor 43®
1 part Orange Juice
Shot Glass
Shake with ice and strain

Sloe Southern Fuck
1 part Sloe Gin
1 part Southern Comfort®
1 part Sour Mix
1 part Lemon-Lime Soda
Shot Glass
Build in the glass with no ice

Sloppy Bagina
1 part Vodka
1 part Irish Cream Liqueur
2 parts 151-Proof Rum
splash Lime Juice
Shot Glass

Shake with ice and strain

Small Bomb
1 part Vodka
1 part Triple Sec
1 part Grenadine
Shot Glass

Shake with ice and strain

Smartie®
1 part Grape-Flavored Schnapps
1 part Melon Liqueur
Shot Glass

Shake with ice and strain

Smashing Pumpkin
1 part Coffee Liqueur
1 part Irish Cream Liqueur
1 part Goldschläger®
Shot Glass

Shake with ice and strain

Smeraldo
3 parts Gin
3 parts Fruit Punch
2 parts Blue Curaçao
1 part Cointreau®
1 part Peach Nectar
Shot Glass

Shake with ice and strain

Smiles
1 part Crème de Menthe (White)
1 part Amaretto
1 part Whiskey
1 part Lemon-Lime Soda
Shot Glass

Build in the glass with no ice

Smooth and Sweet
2 parts Amaretto
2 parts Blackberry Liqueur
1 part Pineapple Juice
Shot Glass

Shake with ice and strain

Smooth Dog
3 parts Amaretto
1 part Lemon-Lime Soda
Shot Glass

Build in the glass with no ice

Smoothie
1 part Crown Royal® Whiskey
1 part Amaretto
1 part Triple Sec
1 part Sour Mix
1 part Lemon-Lime Soda
Shot Glass

Shake with ice and strain

Smurf® Fart
1 part Blue Curaçao
2 parts Blueberry Schnapps
1 part Cream
Shot Glass

Shake with ice and strain

Smurf® Pee
1 part 151-Proof Rum
1 part Blue Curaçao
1 part Jägermeister®
1 part Rumple Minze®
Shot Glass

Shake with ice and strain

Shots & Shooters

Snakebite
1 part Tequila
1 part Southern Comfort®
Shot Glass

Shake with ice and strain

Sneeker
1 part Raspberry Liqueur
1 part Coconut-Flavored Rum
1 part 151-Proof Rum
1 part Midori®
1 part Cranberry Juice Cocktail
1 part Lemon-Lime Soda
Shot Glass

Shake with ice and strain. *Note: Because this recipe includes many ingredients, it's easier to make in volume, about 6 shots.

Snickers®
1 part Crème de Cacao (Dark)
1 part Frangelico®
Shot Glass

Shake with ice and strain

Snoopy® Dog
2 parts Vodka
1 part Grenadine
1 part Amaretto
1 part Crème de Banana
Shot Glass

Shake with ice and strain

Snot Rocket
1 part Apple Brandy
1 part Sour Apple Schnapps
1 part Vodka
Shot Glass

Shake with ice and strain

Snotty Toddy
1 part Midori®
1 part 151-Proof Rum
1 part Orange Juice
Shot Glass

Shake with ice and strain

Snow Drop Shooter
1 part Crème de Cacao (White)
1 part Vodka
1 part Triple Sec
Shot Glass

Shake with ice and strain

Snow Melter
1 part Sambuca
1 part Crème de Cacao (White)
1 part Rum
Shot Glass

Shake with ice and strain

Snow Shoe
1 part Vodka
1 part Peppermint Schnapps
Shot Glass

Shake with ice and strain

Snowball
1 part Jack Daniel's®
1 part Rumple Minze®
Shot Glass

Shake with ice and strain

Snowsnake Juice
1 part Bourbon
1 part Peppermint Schnapps
Shot Glass

Pour ingredients into glass neat (do not chill)

SoCo Slammer
1 part Southern Comfort®
2 parts Cola
Shot Glass

Build in the glass with no ice

SoCo & Lime
1 part Southern Comfort®
splash Lime Juice
Shot Glass

Shake with ice and strain

SoCo Peach and Lime
2 parts Peach Schnapps
2 parts Southern Comfort®
1 part Lime Juice
Shot Glass

Shake with ice and strain

Solar Flare
1 part Vodka
1 part Triple Sec
Shot Glass

Shake with ice and strain

Solaris
1 part Spiced Rum
1 part Grenadine
dash Sugar
Shot Glass

Shake with ice and strain

Solo Shot
1 part Peach Schnapps
1 part Raspberry Liqueur
3 parts Cranberry Juice Cocktail
Shot Glass

Shake with ice and strain

Son of a Peach
1 part Vodka
1 part Peach Schnapps
1 part Honey
Shot Glass

Shake with ice and strain

Songbird
1 part Tequila Silver
1 part Vodka
1 part Crème de Banana
Shot Glass

Shake with ice and strain

Soother
2 parts Amaretto
2 parts Melon Liqueur
1 part Vodka
1 part Sour Mix
Shot Glass

Shake with ice and strain

Soul Taker
1 part Vodka
1 part Tequila
1 part Amaretto
Shot Glass

Shake with ice and strain

Sour Grapes
1 part Vodka
1 part Raspberry Liqueur
1 part Sour Mix
Shot Glass

Shake with ice and strain

Sour Jack
1 part Jack Daniel's®
1 part Raspberry Liqueur
Shot Glass

Shake with ice and strain

Sourball
1 part Vodka
1 part Lemonade
1 part Orange Juice
Shot Glass

Shake with ice and strain

Southern Beamy Brain Damage

1 part Southern Comfort®
1 part Jim Beam®
1 part Tia Maria®
splash Grenadine
Shot Glass

Shake all but Grenadine with ice and strain into the glass. Place a few drops of Grenadine in the center of the drink.

Southern Bitch

1 part Southern Comfort®
1 part Amaretto
1 part Peach Schnapps
1 part Pineapple Juice
1 part Orange Juice
Shot Glass

Shake with ice and strain. *Note: Because this recipe includes many ingredients, it's easier to make in volume, about 6 shots.

Southern Bondage

1 part Southern Comfort®
1 part Amaretto
1 part Peach Schnapps
1 part Triple Sec
1 part Cranberry Juice Cocktail
1 part Sour Mix
Shot Glass

Shake with ice and strain. *Note: Because this recipe includes many ingredients, it's easier to make in volume, about 6 shots.

Southern Chase

1 part Galliano®
1 part Southern Comfort®
1 part Jim Beam®
Shot Glass

Shake with ice and strain

Southern Comfort® Kamikaze

3 parts Southern Comfort®
2 parts Triple Sec
1 part Lime Juice
Shot Glass

Shake with ice and strain

Southern Comfort® Pink

1 part Light Rum
1 part Southern Comfort®
1 part Grapefruit Juice
1 part Grenadine
Shot Glass

Shake with ice and strain

Southern Fruity Passion

1 part Southern Comfort®
1 part Triple Sec
1 part Grenadine
Shot Glass

Shake with ice and strain

Southern Ireland

1 part Irish Cream Liqueur
1 part Southern Comfort®
Shot Glass

Shake with ice and strain

Southern Peach

2 parts Peach Schnapps
1 part Southern Comfort®
Shot Glass

Shake with ice and strain

Southern Pink Flamingo

1 part Southern Comfort®
1 part Coconut-Flavored Rum
1 part Pineapple Juice
splash Grenadine
splash Lemon Juice
Shot Glass

Shake with ice and strain

Southern Pride

2 parts Southern Comfort®
1 part Peach Schnapps
Shot Glass

Shake with ice and strain

Southern Slammer

1 part Peach Schnapps
1 part Vanilla Liqueur
1 part Southern Comfort®
Shot Glass

Shake with ice and strain

Southern Smile

1 part Southern Comfort®
1 part Amaretto
1 part Cranberry Juice Cocktail
Shot Glass

Shake with ice and strain

Southpaw

1 part Brandy
1 part Orange Juice
1 part Lemon-Lime Soda
Shot Glass

Build in the glass with no ice

Space Odyssey

1 part 151-Proof Rum
1 part Coconut-Flavored Rum
1 part Pineapple Juice
Shot Glass

Shake with ice and strain

Spanish Moss Shooter

2 parts Coffee Liqueur
1 part Crème de Menthe (Green)
1 part Tequila Silver
Shot Glass

Shake with ice and strain

Sparato Milano

2 parts Sambuca
1 part Amaretto
1 part Cherry Brandy
Shot Glass

Shake with ice and strain

Sparkplug

1 part 151-Proof Rum
1 part Rumple Minze®
Shot Glass

Pour ingredients into glass neat (do not chill)

Speedy Gonzales® Shooter

1 part Amaretto
1 part Irish Cream Liqueur
Shot Glass

Shake with ice and strain

Sperm

1 part Tequila
1 part Vodka
splash Cream
Shot Glass

Shake all but Cream with ice and strain into the glass. Place a few drops of Cream in the center of the drink.

Sperm Bank Shooter

1 part Tequila Reposado
splash Irish Cream Liqueur
Shot Glass

Pour the Tequila into the shot glass. Place a few drops of Irish Cream Liqueur in the center of the drink.

Sperm Whale

3 parts Rye Whiskey
3 parts Southern Comfort®
1 part Cream
Shot Glass

Shake with ice and strain

Spice Cake
1 part Irish Cream Liqueur
1 part Amaretto
1 part Cinnamon Schnapps
Shot Glass

Shake with ice and strain

Spiced Apple
1 part Apple Brandy
1 part Goldschläger®
2 parts Spiced Rum
Shot Glass

Shake with ice and strain

Spiced Jolly Roger
1 part Goldschläger®
1 part Spiced Rum
Shot Glass

Shake with ice and strain

Spindle
1 part Amaretto
1 part Crown Royal® Whiskey
1 part Peach Schnapps
Shot Glass

Shake with ice and strain

Spiritwalker
1 part Jägermeister®
1 part Rumple Minze®
1 part 151-Proof Rum
1 part Fire Water®
Shot Glass

Shake with ice and strain

Spitfire
1 part Jack Daniel's®
1 part Rum
1 part Vodka
Shot Glass

Shake with ice and strain

Sprawling Dubinsky
1 part Johnnie Walker® Red Label
1 part Johnnie Walker® Black Label
1 part Citrus-Flavored Vodka
splash Amaretto
Shot Glass

Shake with ice and strain

Spy Catcher
2 parts Whiskey
1 part Sambuca
Shot Glass

Shake with ice and strain

Squirrel's Fantasy
2 parts Amaretto
1 part Frangelico®
1 part Club Soda
Shot Glass

Build in the glass with no ice

Squished Smurf®
2 parts Peach Schnapps
1 part Irish Cream Liqueur
1 part Blue Curaçao
splash Grenadine
Shot Glass

Build in the glass with no ice

Squishy
1 part Raspberry Liqueur
1 part Amaretto
1 part Vodka
Shot Glass

Shake with ice and strain

SR-71

1 part Amaretto
1 part Irish Cream Liqueur
Shot Glass

Shake with ice and strain

St. Clement's Shooter

1 part Triple Sec
1 part Mandarine Napoléon® Liqueur
Shot Glass

Shake with ice and strain

St. Deliah

1 part Crème de Banana
1 part Raspberry Liqueur
Shot Glass

Shake with ice and strain

Stabilizer

1 part 151-Proof Rum
1 part Rumple Minze®
Shot Glass

Shake with ice and strain

Stained Blue Dress

1 part Vodka
1 part Blue Curaçao
splash Irish Cream Liqueur
Shot Glass

Shake all but Irish Cream with ice and strain into the glass. Place a few drops of Irish Cream in the center of the drink.

Star Wars® II

2 parts Southern Comfort®
1 part Orange Juice
Shot Glass

Shake with ice and strain

Starburst Shooter

2 parts Dark Rum
1 part Pineapple Juice
1 part Vermouth
Shot Glass

Shake with ice and strain

Stardust

1 part Citrus-Flavored Vodka
1 part Peach Schnapps
1 part Blue Curaçao
1 part Sour Mix
1 part Pineapple Juice
1 part Grenadine
Shot Glass

Shake with ice and strain. *Note: Because this recipe includes many ingredients, it's easier to make in volume, about 6 shots.

Start Me Up

2 parts Vodka
1 part Tequila
1 part Currant-Flavored Vodka
1 part Dark Rum
Shot Glass

Shake with ice and strain

Steel Shooter

2 parts Cinnamon Schnapps
2 parts Vanilla Liqueur
1 part Whiskey
Shot Glass

Shake with ice and strain

Stevie Ray Vaughan

1 part Jack Daniel's®
1 part Southern Comfort®
1 part Triple Sec
1 part Sour Mix
4 parts Orange Juice
Shot Glass

Shake with ice and strain

Stevie Wonder
1 part Coffee Liqueur
1 part Crème de Cacao (Dark)
1 part Amaretto
1 part Galliano®
Shot Glass

Shake with ice and strain

Stiff Dick
1 part Butterscotch Schnapps
1 part Irish Cream Liqueur
Shot Glass

Shake with ice and strain

Stiletto Shooter
1 part Coffee Liqueur
1 part Peppermint Schnapps
1 part Tequila
Shot Glass

Shake with ice and strain

Stinky Weasel
1 part Tequila
1 part 151-Proof Rum
1 part Lemon Juice
2 dashes Sugar
Shot Glass

Shake with ice and strain

Stop Lights
3 parts Vodka
splash Midori®
splash Orange Juice
splash Cranberry Juice Cocktail
Shot Glass

Shake Vodka with ice and strain equal parts into three shot glasses. Top the first glass with Melon Liqueur, the second with Orange Juice, and the third one with Cranberry Juice. Drink all three shots rapidly and in order.

Stormtrooper®
1 part Peppermint Schnapps
1 part Jägermeister®
Shot Glass

Shake with ice and strain

Straight Jacket
2 parts Cinnamon Schnapps
1 part Passoã®
1 part Orange Juice
Shot Glass

Shake with ice and strain

Stranded in Tijuana
1 part Sloe Gin
1 part Tequila Reposado
1 part 151-Proof Rum
Shot Glass

Shake with ice and strain

Strawberry Bliss Bomb
1 part Crème de Cacao (White)
1 part Strawberry Liqueur
1 part Coconut-Flavored Liqueur
Shot Glass

Shake with ice and strain

Strawberry Lemondrop
1 part Vodka
1 part Strawberry Liqueur
fill with Lemonade
Shot Glass

Build over ice and stir

Strawberry Lips
1 part Strawberry Liqueur
1 part Coconut-Flavored Liqueur
1 part Cream
Shot Glass

Shake with ice and strain

Stroke
3 parts Banana Liqueur
1 part Irish Cream Liqueur
splash Grenadine
Shot Glass

Shake all but Grenadine with ice and strain into the glass. Place a few drops of Grenadine in the center of the drink.

Strong Bad
1 part Southern Comfort®
1 part Vanilla-Flavored Vodka
1 part Tonic Water
Shot Glass

Build in the glass with no ice

Stumble Fuck
1 part Jägermeister®
1 part Rumple Minze®
1 part Cinnamon Schnapps
Shot Glass

Shake with ice and strain

Stumpfucker
1 part Jägermeister®
1 part Rumple Minze®
1 part 151-Proof Rum
Shot Glass

Shake with ice and strain

Sublime
1 part Amaretto
1 part Banana Liqueur
1 part Crème de Cacao (White)
Shot Glass

Shake with ice and strain

Suicide Stop Light
1 part Midori®
1 part Vodka
1 part After Shock® Cinnamon Schnapps
splash Orange Juice
Shot Glass

Fill the first of three shot glasses with Midori®, the second one with 1 part Vodka and 1 part Orange Juice, and the last one with After Shock. Drink all three rapidly and in order.

Sun Scorcher
3 parts Butterscotch Schnapps
1 part Vodka
Shot Glass

Shake with ice and strain

Sunny Mexico
1 part Galliano®
1 part Tequila
Shot Glass

Shake with ice and strain

Sunset at the Beach
2 parts Cranberry-Flavored Vodka
1 part Melon Liqueur
1 part Raspberry Liqueur
2 parts Pineapple Juice
Shot Glass

Shake with ice and strain

Super Dave
1 part Spiced Rum
1 part Coconut-Flavored Rum
1 part Pineapple Juice
1 part Cola
Shot Glass

Shake with ice and strain

Supermodel

3 parts Bacardi® Limón Rum
1 part Melon Liqueur
1 part Blue Curaçao
Shot Glass

Shake with ice and strain

Surfer on Acid

1 part Jägermeister®
1 part Coconut-Flavored Rum
1 part Pineapple Juice
Shot Glass

Shake with ice and strain

Susu

2 parts Vodka
1 part Irish Cream Liqueur
1 part Crème de Cacao (Dark)
1 part Coffee Liqueur
1 part Grenadine
2 parts Milk
Shot Glass

Shake with ice and strain. *Note: Because this recipe includes many ingredients, it's easier to make in volume, about 6 shots.

Swamp Thing

1 part Coffee Liqueur
1 part Irish Cream Liqueur
1 part Crème de Menthe (White)
Shot Glass

Shake with ice and strain

Swan Song

1 part Southern Comfort®
1 part Whiskey
1 part Amaretto
1 part Dark Rum
1 part Orange Juice
1 part Cranberry Juice Cocktail
1 part Lime Juice
Shot Glass

Shake with ice and strain. *Note: Because this recipe includes many ingredients, it's easier to make in volume, about 6 shots.

Swedish Color

1 part Banana Liqueur
1 part Blue Curaçao
1 part Vodka
Shot Glass

Shake with ice and strain

Sweet and Sour Pussy

1 part Raspberry Liqueur
1 part Cherry Whiskey
Shot Glass

Shake with ice and strain

Sweet Indulgence

1 part Crème de Cacao (Dark)
1 part Cherry Brandy
1 part Cream
Shot Glass

Shake with ice and strain

Sweet Jesus

1 part 151-Proof Rum
1 part Southern Comfort®
Shot Glass

Shake with ice and strain

Sweet Lips
1 part 151-Proof Rum
1 part Whiskey
1 part Tequila Reposado
Shot Glass

Shake with ice and strain

Sweet Pickle
1 part Vodka
1 part Rumple Minze®
1 part Melon Liqueur
Shot Glass

Shake with ice and strain

Sweet Pigeon
1 part Citrus-Flavored Vodka
2 parts Crème de Cacao (White)
1 part Blue Curaçao
2 parts Cream
Shot Glass

Shake with ice and strain

Sweet Shit
1 part Vodka
1 part Amaretto
1 part Irish Cream Liqueur
1 part Coffee Liqueur
2 parts Chocolate Syrup
Shot Glass

Shake with ice and strain. *Note: Because this recipe includes many ingredients, it's easier to make in volume, about 6 shots.

Sweet Sting
1 part Goldschläger®
1 part Cream
Shot Glass

Shake with ice and strain

Sweet Tart
1 part Raspberry Liqueur
1 part Sour Mix
1 part Southern Comfort®
Shot Glass

Shake with ice and strain

Sweet Tits
1 part Strawberry Liqueur
1 part Apricot Brandy
1 part Pineapple Juice
Shot Glass

Shake with ice and strain

Swell Sex
1 part Vodka
1 part Coconut-Flavored Rum
1 part Melon Liqueur
1 part Cream
1 part Pineapple Juice
Shot Glass

Shake with ice and strain

Swift Kick in the Balls
1 part Rum
1 part Vodka
1 part Lemon Juice
Shot Glass

Shake with ice and strain

Swiss Peach
1 part Peach Schnapps
1 part Crème de Cacao (White)
Shot Glass

Shake with ice and strain

Tablazo
1 part Vodka
1 part Ginger Ale
Shot Glass

Build in the glass with no ice

Tainted Heart
1 part Cinnamon Schnapps
1 part Chocolate Liqueur
Shot Glass

Shake with ice and strain

Take It and Vomit
1 part Vodka
1 part Peach Schnapps
1 part Blue Curaçao
1 part Grenadine
1 part Orange Juice
Shot Glass

Shake with ice and strain

Tangaroa
3 parts Vodka
1 part Vanilla Liqueur
Shot Glass

Shake with ice and strain

Tank Force
1 part Blue Curaçao
1 part Orange Juice
1 part Goldschläger®
Shot Glass

Shake with ice and strain

Tartan Special
1 part Glayva®
1 part Drambuie®
1 part Irish Cream Liqueur
Shot Glass

Shake with ice and strain

Tarzan® Scream
2 parts Vodka
2 parts 151-Proof Rum
1 part Caramel Syrup
splash Cream
Shot Glass

Shake with ice and strain. Top with Cream.

T-Bone
1 part 151-Proof Rum
splash Steak Sauce
Shot Glass

Build in the glass with no ice

Tear Drop
3 parts Pepper-Flavored Vodka
1 part Triple Sec
Shot Glass

Shake with ice and strain

Teen Wolf
1 part Advocaat
1 part Kirschwasser
Shot Glass

Shake with ice and strain

Temptation Island
1 part Coconut-Flavored Liqueur
1 part Frangelico®
1 part Peach Schnapps
Shot Glass

Shake with ice and strain

Ten Snakes in a Lawnmower
1 part 151-Proof Rum
1 part Raspberry Liqueur
1 part Southern Comfort®
1 part Melon Liqueur
Shot Glass

Shake with ice and strain

Tequila Headfuck

1 part Irish Cream Liqueur
2 parts Tequila
Shot Glass

Shake with ice and strain

Tequila Lemondrop

1 part Tequila
1 part Triple Sec
1 part Lemonade
Shot Glass

Shake with ice and strain

Tequila Pickle Shooter

1 part Tequila
1 part Pickle Juice
Shot Glass

Build in the glass with no ice

Tequila Popper

1 part Tequila Silver
1 part Lemon-Lime Soda
Shot Glass

Build in the glass with no ice. Place your hand or a napkin over the glass and slam it down on the bar. Drink while it's still fizzing.

Tequila Rose

1 part Tequila
1 part Triple Sec
1 part Cherry Juice
2 parts Sour Mix
Shot Glass

Shake with ice and strain

Tequila Shot

1 part Tequila
1 Lemon Wedge
dash Salt
Shot Glass

Rub the lemon on the flesh between the thumb and forefinger of your left hand, cover the spot with salt, then hold the Lemon between your thumb and forefinger. Lick the Salt, shoot the Tequila, and suck the Lemon.

Tequila Slammer

1 part Tequila
1 part Lemon-Lime Soda
Shot Glass

Build in the glass with no ice

Terminator

1 part Jägermeister®
1 part Southern Comfort®
Shot Glass

Shake with ice and strain

Tetanus Shot

1 part Irish Cream Liqueur
1 part Cherry Brandy
1 part Peach Schnapps
Shot Glass

Shake with ice and strain

Texas Antifreeze

1 part Coconut-Flavored Rum
1 part Citrus-Flavored Vodka
1 part Melon Liqueur
Shot Glass

Shake with ice and strain

Texas Rattlesnake

1 part Yukon Jack®
1 part Cherry Brandy
1 part Southern Comfort®
1 part Sour Mix
Shot Glass

Shake with ice and strain

TGV

1 part Tequila
1 part Gin
1 part Vodka
Shot Glass

Build in the glass with no ice

Third and Goal

1 part Peach Schnapps
1 part Grand Marnier®
1 part Sour Mix
Shot Glass

Shake with ice and strain

Third Reich

1 part Jägermeister®
1 part Rumple Minze®
1 part Goldschläger®
Shot Glass

Shake with ice and strain

Thong

2 parts Vodka
1 part Triple Sec
1 part Cream
1 part Orange Juice
1 part Crème de Noyaux
1 part Grenadine
Shot Glass

Shake with ice and strain. *Note: Because this recipe includes many ingredients, it's easier to make in volume, about 6 shots.

Thorazine®

1 part Jägermeister®
1 part Rumple Minze®
1 part 151-Proof Rum
Shot Glass

Shake with ice and strain

Thorny Situation

1 part Coconut-Flavored Liqueur
1 part Frangelico®
1 part Sour Mix
Shot Glass

Shake with ice and strain

Three Day Weekend

1 part Jägermeister®
1 part Malibu® Rum
1 part Pineapple Juice
1 part Grenadine
Shot Glass

Shake with ice and strain

Three Leaf Clover

1 part Whiskey
1 part Irish Mist®
Shot Glass

Shake with ice and strain

Three-Legged Monkey

2 parts Bourbon
1 part Cola
1 part Lemon Juice
Shot Glass

Shake with ice and strain

Three Sheets to the Wind

1 part Jägermeister®
1 part Rumple Minze®
1 part Tequila
Shot Glass

Shake with ice and strain

Three Stages of Friendship

1 part Jack Daniel's®
1 part Tequila
1 part 151-Proof Rum
Shot Glass

Shake with ice and strain

Three Wise Men

1 part Jack Daniel's®
1 part Johnnie Walker® Black Label
1 part Jim Beam®
Shot Glass

Shake with ice and strain

Three Wise Men #2

1 part Jägermeister®
1 part Goldschläger®
1 part Rumple Minze®
Shot Glass

Build in the glass with no ice

Three Wise Men on a Farm

1 part Jack Daniel's®
1 part Jim Beam®
1 part Yukon Jack®
1 part Wild Turkey® Bourbon
Shot Glass

Pour ingredients into glass neat (do not chill)

The Three Wise Men and Their Mexican Porter

1 part Jack Daniel's®
1 part Rye Whiskey
1 part Scotch
1 part Tequila
Shot Glass

Build in the glass with no ice

Thumb Press

2 parts Vodka
2 parts Midori®
1 part 151-Proof Rum
splash Grenadine
Shot Glass

Shake with ice and strain

Thumbs Up

1 part Crème de Banana
1 part Cherry Brandy
1 part Mango Schnapps
Shot Glass

Shake with ice and strain

Thumper

1 part Cognac
1 part Amer Picon®
Shot Glass

Shake with ice and strain

Thunder and Lightning

1 part Rumple Minze®
1 part 151-Proof Rum
Shot Glass

Shake with ice and strain

Thunder Cloud Shooter

1 part Amaretto
1 part Irish Mist®
1 part 151-Proof Rum
Shot Glass

Shake with ice and strain

Thundercloud

2 parts Coffee Liqueur
1 part Southern Comfort®
1 part Peppermint Schnapps
1 part Rum
splash Cream
Shot Glass

Shake all but Cream with ice and strain into the glass. Place a few drops of Cream in the center of the drink.

Thursday Shooter

1 part Blue Curaçao
1 part Peach Schnapps
1 part Pineapple Juice
Shot Glass

Shake with ice and strain

Tic Tac® Shooter

1 part Crème de Menthe (White)
1 part Ouzo
Shot Glass

Shake with ice and strain

Tidy Bowl

4 parts Blue Curaçao
1 part Dr. McGillicuddy's® Mentholmint Schnapps
1 part Irish Cream Liqueur
Shot Glass

Shake with ice and strain

Tie Me to the Bedpost

1 part Midori®
1 part Citrus-Flavored Vodka
1 part Coconut-Flavored Rum
1 part Sour Mix
Shot Glass

Shake with ice and strain

Time Bomb

1 part Blue Curaçao
1 part Melon Liqueur
Shot Glass

Shake with ice and strain

Tip Energizer

1 part Passion Fruit Liqueur
1 part Blue Curaçao
1 part Lime Juice
Shot Glass

Shake with ice and strain

Tiramisu

1 part Coffee Liqueur
1 part Chocolate Mint Liqueur
Shot Glass

Shake with ice and strain

Tired Pussy

3 parts Coconut-Flavored Rum
1 part Pineapple Juice
1 part Cranberry Juice Cocktail
Shot Glass

Shake with ice and strain

TKO

1 part Tequila
1 part Coffee Liqueur
1 part Ouzo
Shot Glass

Shake with ice and strain

Toffee Apple

1 part Vodka
1 part Butterscotch Schnapps
1 part Apple Brandy
Shot Glass

Shake with ice and strain

Tokyo Rose

1 part Vodka
1 part Sake
1 part Melon Liqueur
Shot Glass

Shake with ice and strain

Tongue Twister

2 parts Dark Rum
1 part Triple Sec
1 part Coconut-Flavored Liqueur
Shot Glass

Shake with ice and strain

Toolkit
1 part Crème de Cacao (White)
1 part Irish Cream Liqueur
1 part Amaretto
1 part Coffee Liqueur
Shot Glass

Shake with ice and strain

Tootsie Roll®
1 part Coffee Liqueur
1 part Orange Juice
Shot Glass

Shake with ice and strain

Top Banana Shooter
1 part Crème de Cacao (White)
1 part Vodka
1 part Coffee
1 part Crème de Banana
Shot Glass

Shake with ice and strain

Toro
1 part Spiced Rum
1 part Vodka
1 part Sour Mix
Shot Glass

Shake with ice and strain

To the Moon
1 part Coffee Liqueur
1 part Amaretto
1 part Irish Cream Liqueur
1 part 151-Proof Rum
Shot Glass

Shake with ice and strain

Toxic Jelly Bean
2 parts Jägermeister®
1 part Ouzo
1 part Blackberry Brandy
Shot Glass

Shake with ice and strain

Toxic Refuse
1 part Vodka
1 part Triple Sec
1 part Midori®
splash Lime Juice
Shot Glass

Shake with ice and strain

Traffic Light
1 part Orange Juice
1 part Peach Schnapps
1 part Grenadine
1 part Blue Curaçao
1 part Vodka
Shot Glass

Shake with ice and strain. *Note: Because this recipe includes many ingredients, it's easier to make in volume, about 6 shots.

Transmission Overhaul
1 part Vodka
1 part Amaretto
1 part Southern Comfort®
1 part Mountain Dew®
1 part Orange Juice
1 part Grenadine
Shot Glass

Stir gently with ice and strain. *Note: Because this recipe includes many ingredients, it's easier to make in volume, about 6 shots.

Tree Frog
1 part Citrus-Flavored Vodka
1 part Blue Hawaiian Schnapps
2 parts Grapefruit Juice
Shot Glass
Shake with ice and strain

Triplesex
1 part Vodka
1 part Triple Sec
1 part Sour Mix
1 part Pineapple Juice
Shot Glass
Shake with ice and strain

Tropical Hooter
1 part Citrus-Flavored Vodka
1 part Raspberry Liqueur
1 part Watermelon Schnapps
1 part Lemon-Lime Soda
Shot Glass
Shake with ice and strain

Tropical Passion
1 part Rum
1 part Peach Schnapps
1 part Sloe Gin
1 part Triple Sec
splash Orange Juice
Shot Glass
Shake with ice and strain

Tropical Waterfall
1 part Wild Berry Schnapps
1 part Orange Juice
Shot Glass
Shake with ice and strain

True Canadian
1 part Vodka
1 part Maple Syrup
Shot Glass
Shake with ice and strain

Tub Thumper
1 part Apricot Brandy
1 part Irish Cream Liqueur
1 part Whiskey
Shot Glass
Shake with ice and strain

Tubboocki
2 parts Galliano®
1 part Sambuca
1 part Wild Turkey® Bourbon
Shot Glass
Build in the glass with no ice

Turkey Shoot
3 parts Wild Turkey® Bourbon
1 part Anisette
Shot Glass
Shake with ice and strain

Turkeyball
1 part Wild Turkey® Bourbon
1 part Amaretto
1 part Pineapple Juice
Shot Glass
Shake with ice and strain

Turn Up the Volume
1 part Citrus-Flavored Vodka
1 part Blue Curaçao
1 part Peach Schnapps
Shot Glass
Shake with ice and strain

Twin Sisters
1 part Light Rum
1 part Spiced Rum
splash Cola
splash Sweetened Lime Juice
Shot Glass

Shake with ice and strain

Twisted Jack
1 part Amaretto
1 part Jack Daniel's®
1 part Sour Mix
1 part Southern Comfort®
1 part Raspberry Liqueur
Shot Glass

Shake with ice and strain

Twister Shooter
1 part Vodka
1 part Cherry Brandy
1 part Ouzo
Shot Glass

Shake with ice and strain

T-Zone
1 part Sloe Gin
1 part 151-Proof Rum
Shot Glass

Shake with ice and strain

U-2
1 part Crème de Menthe (White)
1 part Melon Liqueur
Shot Glass

Shake with ice and strain

Uarapito
2 parts Dark Rum
1 part Grenadine
1 part Apple Juice
Shot Glass

Shake with ice and strain

Unabomber
1 part Gin
1 part Vodka
1 part Triple Sec
1 part Lime Juice
Shot Glass

Shake with ice and strain

The Undertaker
1 part Triple Sec
1 part 151-Proof Rum
Shot Glass

Shake with ice and strain

Under Water
1 part Blue Curaçao
1 part Irish Cream Liqueur
1 part Peach Schnapps
Shot Glass

Shake with ice and strain

Undertow
1 part Blue Curaçao
1 part Raspberry Liqueur
Shot Glass

Shake with ice and strain

Unholy Water
1 part Gin
1 part Spiced Rum
1 part Tequila Silver
1 part Vodka
Shot Glass

Shake with ice and strain

Universal Shooter
1 part Grapefruit Juice
1 part Sweet Vermouth
1 part Maraschino Liqueur
Shot Glass

Shake with ice and strain

Up Chuck

1 part 151-Proof Rum
1 part Tequila
1 part Jägermeister®
Shot Glass

Pour ingredients into glass neat (do not chill)

Upside Down Apple Pie Shot

1 part Apple Juice
1 part Cinnamon Schnapps
1 part Vodka
Whipped Cream
Shot Glass

Shake all but the Whipped Cream with ice and strain into a shot glass. Sit facing away from the bar and lean your head back onto the bar. Pour the shot into your mouth followed by a squirt of Whipped Cream and then sit up quickly. A towel might be handy.

Upside Down Kamikaze

2 parts Triple Sec
2 parts Vodka
1 part Lime Juice
Whipped Cream
Shot Glass

Shake with ice and strain into a shot glass. Sit facing away from the bar and lean your head back onto the bar. Pour the shot into your mouth followed by a squirt of Whipped Cream and then sit up quickly. A towel might be handy.

Upside Down Margarita

2 parts Tequila
2 parts Lime Juice
1 part Triple Sec
Whipped Cream
Shot Glass

Shake with ice and strain into a shot glass. Sit facing away from the bar and lean your head back onto the bar. Pour the shot into your mouth followed by a squirt of Whipped Cream and then sit up quickly. A towel might be handy.

Upside Down Oatmeal Cookie

1 part Irish Cream Liqueur
1 part Goldschläger®
Whipped Cream
Shot Glass

Shake with ice and strain into a shot glass. Sit facing away from the bar and lean your head back onto the bar. Pour the shot into your mouth followed by a squirt of Whipped Cream and then sit up quickly. A towel might be handy.

Urban Cowboy

1 part Grand Marnier®
1 part Jack Daniel's®
1 part Southern Comfort®
Shot Glass

Shake with ice and strain

Urine Sample Shooter

1 part Galliano®
1 part Midori®
1 part Vodka
Shot Glass

Shake with ice and strain

Valium®

1 part Rye Whiskey
1 part Peach Schnapps
1 part Cranberry Juice Cocktail
Shot Glass

Shake with ice and strain

Vampire Slayer

2 parts Southern Comfort®
1 part Cognac
1 part Rum
1 part Scotch
1 part Jägermeister®
Shot Glass

Shake with ice and strain. *Note: Because this recipe includes many ingredients, it's easier to make in volume, about 6 shots.

Vanilla Ice

1 part Vanilla Liqueur
2 parts Blueberry Schnapps
Shot Glass

Shake with ice and strain

Vanilla Jack

2 parts Jack Daniel's®
splash Vanilla Extract
fill with Root Beer
Shot Glass

Build over ice and stir

Vanilla Milkshake

1 part Crème de Cacao (Dark)
2 parts Milk
2 parts Vanilla-Flavored Vodka
Shot Glass

Shake with ice and strain

Varadero Especial

1 part Maraschino Liqueur
1 part Grapefruit Juice
Shot Glass

Shake with ice and strain

Varicose Veins

1 part Irish Cream Liqueur
1 part Crème de Menthe (White)
Shot Glass

Shake with ice and strain

Vegas Blowjob

2 parts Rum
2 parts Jägermeister®
1 part Banana Liqueur
1 part Orange Juice
1 part Pineapple Juice
Shot Glass

Shake with ice and strain. *Note: Because this recipe includes many ingredients, it's easier to make in volume, about 6 shots.

Viagra® Shooter

1 part Vodka
1 part Blue Curaçao
1 part Irish Cream Liqueur
Shot Glass

Shake with ice and strain

Vibrator

1 part After Shock® Cinnamon Schnapps
1 part Avalanche® Peppermint Schnapps
1 part Spiced Rum
splash Ginger Ale
Shot Glass

Build in the glass with no ice

Victoria's Shot
2 parts Vodka
2 parts Passion Fruit Liqueur
1 part Pineapple Juice
splash Lime Juice
pinch Powdered Sugar
Shot Glass

Shake with ice and strain

Vigor
1 part Peach Schnapps
1 part Crème de Cassis
1 part Cranberry Juice Cocktail
1 part Lemon Juice
Shot Glass

Shake with ice and strain

Viking Funeral
1 part Rumple Minze®
1 part Jägermeister®
1 part Goldschläger®
Shot Glass

Shake with ice and strain

Village
1 part Vodka
1 part Passion Fruit Liqueur
1 part Pineapple Juice
1 part Aperol™
Shot Glass

Shake with ice and strain

Vine Climber
2 parts Vodka
2 parts Melon Liqueur
1 part Sour Mix
Shot Glass

Shake with ice and strain

Violent Fuck
1 part Grain Alcohol
1 part Cola
Shot Glass

Build in the glass with no ice

Viper
1 part Vodka
1 part Amaretto
1 part Malibu® Rum
1 part Midori®
1 part Pineapple Juice
Shot Glass

Shake with ice and strain

Virgin Breaker
1 part Vodka
1 part Whiskey
1 part Sambuca
1 part Orange Juice
1 part Grenadine
Shot Glass

Shake with ice and strain. *Note: Because this recipe includes many ingredients, it's easier to make in volume, about 6 shots.

Virgin Pussy
1 part Watermelon Schnapps
1 part Cinnamon Schnapps
Shot Glass

Shake with ice and strain

Virulent Death
1 part Blue Curaçao
1 part Yukon Jack®
1 part Galliano®
Shot Glass

Shake with ice and strain

Vodka Passion
1 part Orange-Flavored Vodka
1 part Passion Fruit Juice
Shot Glass

Shake with ice and strain

Volvo®
1 part Cointreau®
1 part Grand Marnier®
1 part Vodka
1 part Cognac
1 part Apricot Brandy
Shot Glass

Shake with ice and strain. *Note: Because this recipe includes many ingredients, it's easier to make in volume, about 6 shots.

Voodoo Doll
1 part Vodka
1 part Raspberry Liqueur
Shot Glass

Shake with ice and strain

Vulcan Death Grip
1 part Goldschläger®
1 part Rum
Shot Glass

Shake with ice and strain

Vulcan Mind Meld
1 part Ouzo
1 part 151-Proof Rum
Shot Glass

Shake with ice and strain

Waffle
1 part Vodka
1 part Butterscotch Schnapps
1 part Orange Juice
Shot Glass

Shake with ice and strain

Wahoo
1 part 151-Proof Rum
1 part Amaretto
1 part Pineapple Juice
Shot Glass

Shake with ice and strain

Wak-Wak
1 part Crème de Cassis
1 part Absinthe
Shot Glass

Shake with ice and strain

Waltzing Matilda Shooter
2 parts Light Rum
1 part Blue Curaçao
1 part Pineapple Juice
Shot Glass

Shake with ice and strain

Wandering Minstrel Shooter
1 part Crème de Menthe (White)
1 part Brandy
1 part Vodka
1 part Coffee
Shot Glass

Shake with ice and strain

Warm and Fuzzy
1 part Triple Sec
1 part Southern Comfort®
1 part Cherry Brandy
Shot Glass

Shake with ice and strain

Warm Carrot Cake
1 part Butterscotch Schnapps
1 part Cinnamon Schnapps
1 part Irish Cream Liqueur
Shot Glass

Shake with ice and strain

A Warm Glass of Shut the Hell Up

1 part Cinnamon Schnapps
1 part Peach Schnapps
1 part Southern Comfort®
Shot Glass

Pour ingredients into glass neat (do not chill)

Warm Leatherette

3 parts Black Sambuca
2 parts Amaretto
1 part Grenadine
Shot Glass

Shake with ice and strain

Warp Core Breach

1 part Goldschläger®
1 part Tequila
1 part Jack Daniel's®
Shot Glass

Shake with ice and strain

Washington Red Apple

1 part Canadian Whiskey
1 part Sour Apple Schnapps
1 part Vodka
1 part Cranberry Juice Cocktail
Shot Glass

Shake with ice and strain

Water Moccasin

1 part Crown Royal® Whiskey
1 part Peach Schnapps
1 part Sour Mix
Shot Glass

Shake with ice and strain

Waterloo

2 parts Mandarine Napoléon® Liqueur
2 parts Spiced Rum
1 part Orange Juice
Shot Glass

Shake with ice and strain

Watermelon Shot

1 part Vodka
1 part Amaretto
1 part Southern Comfort®
1 part Orange Juice
Shot Glass

Shake with ice and strain

Wayne's World

2 parts Jägermeister®
1 part Sambuca
Shot Glass

Shake with ice and strain

Weasel Water

1 part Crème de Banana
1 part Cream
Shot Glass

Shake with ice and strain

Wedgie

2 parts Coffee Liqueur
1 part Crème de Cacao (Dark)
1 part Whiskey
Shot Glass

Shake with ice and strain

Weekend on the Beach

1 part Canadian Whiskey
1 part Sour Apple Schnapps
1 part Peach Schnapps
1 part Sour Mix
Shot Glass

Shake with ice and strain

Wench
1 part Amaretto
1 part Spiced Rum
Shot Glass

Shake with ice and strain

Werther's®
1 part Irish Cream Liqueur
1 part Butterscotch Schnapps
1 part Bourbon
Shot Glass

Shakc with ice and strain

West Side Special
1 part Southern Comfort®
1 part Peppermint Schnapps
Shot Glass

Shake with ice and strain

Wet Back
1 part Coffee Liqueur
1 part Tequila
Shot Glass

Shake with ice and strain

Wet Dream
1 part Southern Comfort®
1 part Coconut-Flavored Rum
1 part Cranberry Juice Cocktail
1 part Pineapple Juice
1 part Lemon-Lime Soda
Shot Glass

Shake with ice and strain

Wet Muff
1 part Butterscotch Schnapps
2 parts Cointreau®
2 parts Tia Maria®
1 part Pineapple Juice
Shot Glass

Shake with ice and strain

Whip Me Baby
1 part Triple Sec
1 part Dry Vermouth
1 part Rémy Martin® VSOP
Shot Glass

Shake with ice and strain

Whipper Snapper
1 part Melon Liqueur
1 part Apple Brandy
1 part Cranberry Juice Cocktail
Shot Glass

Shake with ice and strain

Whisker Biscuit
1 part 151-Proof Rum
1 part Banana Liqueur
1 part Coconut-Flavored Rum
1 part Grenadine
2 parts Pineapple Juice
Shot Glass

Shake with ice and strain. *Note: Because this recipe includes many ingredients, it's easier to make in volume, about 6 shots.

White Cap
1 part Vodka
1 part Cream
1 part Coffee
1 part Port
Shot Glass

Shake with ice and strain

White Cloud
1 part Milk
1 part Peppermint Schnapps
Shot Glass

Shake with ice and strain

White Death
1 part Crème de Cacao (White)
1 part Vodka
1 part Raspberry Liqueur
Shot Glass

Shake with ice and strain

White Knuckle Ride
2 parts Coffee
1 part Vodka
Shot Glass

Shake with ice and strain

White Mess
1 part Light Rum
1 part Crème de Cassis
1 part Root Beer Schnapps
1 part Coconut-Flavored Rum
1 part Heavy Cream
Shot Glass

Shake with ice and strain. *Note: Because this recipe includes many ingredients, it's easier to make in volume, about 6 shots.

White Orbit
1 part Crème de Cacao (White)
1 part Melon Liqueur
1 part Glayva®
1 part Cream
Shot Glass

Shake with ice and strain

White Satin Shooter
2 parts Tia Maria®
1 part Cream
1 part Frangelico®
Shot Glass

Shake with ice and strain

Wicked Snowshoe
1 part Canadian Whiskey
1 part Goldschläger®
1 part Peppermint Schnapps
1 part Wild Turkey® 101
Shot Glass

Shake with ice and strain

Wicked Stepmother
2 parts Pepper-Flavored Vodka
1 part Amaretto
Shot Glass

Shake with ice and strain

Widget
3 parts Peach Schnapps
1 part Gin
Shot Glass

Shake with ice and strain

Widow Maker
1 part Vodka
1 part Jägermeister®
1 part Coffee Liqueur
splash Grenadine
Shot Glass

Shake with ice and strain

Wild Berry Pop-Tart®
1 part Wild Berry Schnapps
1 part Vodka
1 part Strawberry Liqueur
Shot Glass

Shake with ice and strain

Wild Child
1 part Sour Apple Schnapps
1 part Vodka
1 part Lemon-Lime Soda
Shot Glass

Build in the glass with no ice

Wild Peppertini
1 part Wild Turkey® Bourbon
1 part Peppermint Schnapps
Shot Glass
Shake with ice and strain

Wild Thing Shooter
2 parts Vodka
1 part Apricot Brandy
1 part Lemon-Lime Soda
Shot Glass
Build in the glass with no ice

Windex® Shooter
1 part Blue Curaçao
1 part Vodka
Shot Glass
Shake with ice and strain

Windy
1 part Vodka
1 part Blue Curaçao
1 part Pineapple Juice
1 part Sour Mix
Shot Glass
Shake with ice and strain

Winter Green Dragon
2 parts Green Chartreuse®
1 part 151-Proof Rum
1 part Rumple Minze®
Shot Glass
Shake with ice and strain

Wolf Pussy
1 part Bourbon
1 part Cinnamon Schnapps
Shot Glass
Pour ingredients into glass neat (do not chill)

Wonka
1 part Cherry Brandy
1 part Amaretto
1 part Sour Mix
Shot Glass
Shake with ice and strain

Woo Woo Shooter
1 part Vodka
1 part Peach Schnapps
1 part Cranberry Juice Cocktail
Shot Glass
Shake with ice and strain

Woof
1 part Blue Curaçao
1 part Amaretto
1 part Parfait Amour
Shot Glass
Shake with ice and strain

Woo-Shoo
2 parts Cranberry-Flavored Vodka
1 part Peach Schnapps
Shot Glass
Shake with ice and strain

X
2 parts Amaretto
2 parts Wild Berry Schnapps
1 part Sour Mix
1 part Cola
Shot Glass
Shake with ice and strain

Xaibalba
1 part Vodka
1 part Butterscotch Schnapps
1 part Vanilla Liqueur
1 part Chocolate Syrup
Shot Glass
Shake with ice and strain

Y2K Shot
1 part Vodka
1 part Melon Liqueur
1 part Raspberry Liqueur
Shot Glass

Shake with ice and strain

Yak Milk
1 part Crème de Cacao (Dark)
1 part Coconut-Flavored Rum
Shot Glass

Shake with ice and strain

Yaps
1 part Yukon Jack®
1 part Sour Apple Schnapps
Shot Glass

Shake with ice and strain

Yellow Bow Tie
2 parts Vodka
2 parts Amaretto
1 part Triple Sec
1 part Fresh Lime Juice
Shot Glass

Shake with ice and strain

Yellow Cake
1 part Vanilla-Flavored Vodka
1 part Triple Sec
1 part Pineapple Juice
Shot Glass

Shake with ice and strain

Yellow Nutter
1 part Lemon-Lime Soda
1 part Bacardi® Limón Rum
1 part Sour Mix
dash Sugar
Shot Glass

Shake with ice and strain

Yellow Snow
3 parts Pineapple-Flavored Vodka
1 part Pineapple Juice
Shot Glass

Shake with ice and strain

Ying Yang
1 part Jägermeister®
1 part Rumple Minze®
Shot Glass

Shake with ice and strain

Yoda®
1 part Vodka
1 part Blue Curaçao
1 part Sour Mix
1 part Midori®
2 parts Sour Apple Schnapps
Shot Glass

Shake with ice and strain

Yooha
3 parts Whiskey
1 part Yoo-Hoo® Chocolate Drink
Shot Glass

Shake with ice and strain

Yukon Snakebite
3 parts Yukon Jack®
1 part Lime Juice
Shot Glass

Shake with ice and strain

Z Street Slammer
2 parts Crème de Banana
2 parts Pineapple Juice
1 part Grenadine
Shot Glass

Shake with ice and strain

Zeke's Suprise

1 part Grand Marnier®
1 part Scotch
1 part Peppermint Schnapps
Shot Glass

Shake with ice and strain

Zenmeister

1 part Jägermeister®
1 part Root Beer
Shot Glass

Stir gently with ice and strain

Zoo Station

1 part Amaretto
1 part Coffee Liqueur
1 part Irish Cream Liqueur
1 part Banana Liqueur
2 parts Cream
Shot Glass

Shake with ice and strain

Zool

1 part Peach Schnapps
1 part Vodka
1 part Amaretto
Shot Glass

Shake with ice and strain

Zoot Suit Riot

1 part Apricot Brandy
1 part Blackberry Liqueur
1 part Cranberry Juice Cocktail
1 part Southern Comfort®
Shot Glass

Shake with ice and strain

Layered Shots

Creating a layered effect in a shot takes a steady hand and lots of practice. With the back of a bar spoon, a knowledge of which liqueurs are heavier than others, and nerves of steel, you can create art in a very small glass.

4 Horsemen

1 part Goldschläger®
1 part Jägermeister®
1 part Rumple Minze©
1 part 151-Proof Rum
Shot Glass

Layer in a shot glass

10 W 40

1 part Black Sambuca
1 part Goldschläger®
Shot Glass

Layer in a shot glass

50-50 Bar

1 part Irish Cream Liqueur
1 part Coffee Liqueur
splash 151-Proof Rum
Shot Glass

Layer in a shot glass

69er in a Pool

1 part Vodka
1 part 151-Proof Rum
splash Lemon Juice
splash Tabasco® Sauce
Shot Glass

Layer in a shot glass

401

1 part Coffee Liqueur
1 part Crème de Banana
1 part Irish Cream Liqueur
1 part Yukon Jack®
Shot Glass

Layer in a shot glass

A.T.B. (Ask The Barman)

1 part Melon Liqueur
1 part Grenadine
1 part Blue Curaçao
1 part Amaretto
1 part Irish Cream Liqueur
Shot Glass

Layer in a shot glass

ABC

1 part Amaretto
1 part Irish Cream Liqueur
1 part Cognac
Shot Glass

Layer in a shot glass

Adios Motherfucker

1 part Coffee Liqueur
1 part Tequila
Shot Glass

Layer in a shot glass

Advosarry

3 parts Maraschino Liqueur
2 parts Advocaat
Shot Glass

Layer in a shot glass

Aequitas

1 part After Shock® Cinnamon Schnapps
1 part 151-Proof Rum
1 part Jägermeister®
1 part Rumple Minze®
Shot Glass

Layer in a shot glass

After Dark

1 part Coffee Liqueur
1 part Irish Cream Liqueur
1 part Licor 43®
Shot Glass

Layer in a shot glass

After Eight®

1 part Coffee Liqueur
1 part Crème de Menthe (White)
1 part Irish Cream Liqueur
Shot Glass

Layer in a shot glass

After Five

1 part Coffee Liqueur
1 part Peppermint Schnapps
1 part Irish Cream Liqueur
Shot Glass

Layer in a shot glass

After Five #2

1 part Irish Cream Liqueur
1 part Peppermint Schnapps
1 part Coffee Liqueur
Shot Glass

Layer in a shot glass

Afterlanche

1 part After Shock® Cinnamon Schnapps
1 part Avalanche® Peppermint Schnapps
Shot Glass

Layer in a shot glass

Alaskan Oil Spill

1 part Blue Curaçao
1 part Rumple Minze®
splash Jägermeister®
Shot Glass

Shake Blue Curaçao and Rumple Minze® together with ice and strain into a shot glass. Layer the Jägermeister® on top.

Alien Nipple

2 parts Butterscotch Schnapps
1 part Irish Cream Liqueur
1 part Melon Liqueur
Shot Glass

Layer in a shot glass

Alligator Bite

1 part Jägermeister®
1 part Raspberry Liqueur
1 part Vodka
splash Orange Juice
1 part Melon Liqueur
Shot Glass

Layer in a shot glass

Alligator on the Rag

2 parts Melon Liqueur
1 part Raspberry Liqueur
1 part Jägermeister®
Shot Glass

Layer in a shot glass

Almond Joy

1 part Amaretto
1 part Irish Cream Liqueur
1 part Swiss Chocolate Almond Liqueur
Shot Glass

Layer in a shot glass

Altered State
1 part Golden Pear Liqueur
1 part Irish Cream Liqueur
1 part Coffee Liqueur
Shot Glass

Layer in a shot glass

American Flag
1 part Grenadine
1 part Crème de Cacao (White)
1 part Blue Curaçao
Shot Glass

Layer in a shot glass

Amoco Shot
1 part 151-Proof Rum
1 part Grain Alcohol
splash Coffee Liqueur
Shot Glass

Layer in a shot glass

Amy Girl
1 part Banana Liqueur
1 part Butterscotch Schnapps
1 part Frangelico®
Shot Glass

Layer in a shot glass

Andy
1 part Cola
1 part Beer
Shot Glass

Layer in a shot glass

Angel Bliss
3 parts Bourbon
1 part Blue Curaçao
1 part 151-Proof Rum
Shot Glass

Layer in a shot glass

Angel's Delight
1 part Grenadine
1 part Triple Sec
1 part Sloe Gin
1 part Light Cream
Pousse-Café Glass

Layer in a Pousse-Café glass

Angel's Kiss
1 part Coffee Liqueur
1 part Swiss Chocolate Almond Liqueur
splash Irish Cream Liqueur
Shot Glass

Layer in a shot glass

Angel's Tit
1 part Crème de Cacao (White)
1 part Maraschino Liqueur
1 part Heavy Cream
1 Maraschino Cherry
Shot Glass

Layer in a shot glass

Angel's Wing
1 part Crème de Cacao (White)
1 part Brandy
splash Light Cream
Pousse-Café Glass

Layer in a shot glass

Apache
1 part Coffee Liqueur
1 part Irish Cream Liqueur
1 part Melon Liqueur
Shot Glass

Layer in a shot glass

Apple Pie
1 part Vodka
1 part Apple Juice
Shot Glass

Layer in a shot glass

Apple Slammer
1 part Sour Apple Schnapps
1 part Lemon-Lime Soda
Shot Glass

Layer in a shot glass. Cover with your hand, slam down against the bar, and drink while it fizzes.

Aquafresh
1 part After Shock® Cinnamon Schnapps
1 part Rumple Minze®
1 part Avalanche® Peppermint Schnapps
Shot Glass

Layer in a shot glass

Astropop
1 part Grenadine
1 part Amaretto
1 part Rumple Minze®
Shot Glass

Layer in a shot glass

Aunt Jemima®
1 part Brandy
1 part Crème de Cacao (White)
1 part Benedictine®
Pousse-Café Glass

Layer in a pousse-café glass

B and B
1 part Brandy
1 part Benedictine®
Cordial Glass

Layer in a cordial glass

B.B.C.
1 part Benedictine®
1 part Irish Cream Liqueur
1 part Cointreau®
Shot Glass

Layer in a shot glass

B.B.G.
1 part Benedictine®
1 part Irish Cream Liqueur
1 part Grand Marnier®
Shot Glass

Layer in a shot glass

B-52
1 part Grand Marnier®
1 part Coffee Liqueur
1 part Irish Cream Liqueur
Shot Glass

Layer in a shot glass

Baby Beer
3 parts Licor 43®
1 part Cream
Shot Glass

Layer in a shot glass

Baby Guinness®
3 parts Coffee Liqueur
1 part Irish Cream Liqueur
Shot Glass

Layer in a shot glass

Backfire
1 part Coffee Liqueur
1 part Irish Cream Liqueur
1 part Vodka
Shot Glass

Layer in a shot glass

Bad Sting
1 part Grenadine
1 part Anisette
1 part Grand Marnier®
1 part Tequila
Shot Glass

Layer in a shot glass

Baghdad Café
1 part Coffee Liqueur
1 part Tia Maria®
splash San Marco Cream
Shot Glass

Layer in a shot glass

Baileys® Chocolate-Covered Cherry
1 part Coffee Liqueur
1 part Grenadine
1 part Irish Cream Liqueur
Shot Glass

Layer in a shot glass

Baileys® Comet
1 part Irish Cream Liqueur
1 part Goldschläger®
splash 151-Proof Rum
Shot Glass

Layer in a shot glass

Baker's Delite
3 parts Crème de Cacao (White)
1 part Peach Schnapps
Shot Glass

Layer in a shot glass

Ballistic Missile
1 part Amaretto
1 part Grand Marnier®
1 part Pineapple Juice
Shot Glass

Layer in a shot glass

Banana Cream Pie
1 part Coffee Liqueur
1 part Licor 43®
1 part 99-Proof Banana Liqueur
Shot Glass

Layer in a shot glass

Banana Drop
1 part Crème de Banana
1 part Irish Cream Liqueur
1/2 part Cream
1/2 part Chocolate Mint Liqueur
Shot Glass

Layer in a shot glass

Banana Slip
1 part Crème de Banana
1 part Irish Cream Liqueur
Cordial Glass

Layer in a cordial glass

Battered, Bruised, and Bleeding
1 part Grenadine
1 part Melon Liqueur
1 part Blue Curaçao
Shot Glass

Layer in a shot glass

Bazooka Joe®
1 part Parfait Amour
1 part Crème de Banana
1 part Irish Cream Liqueur
Shot Glass

Layer in a shot glass

B.B. Grand
1 part Irish Cream Liqueur
1 part Banana Liqueur
1 part Grand Marnier®
Shot Glass

Layer in a shot glass

Beam Me Up Scotty
1 part Coffee Liqueur
1 part Banana Liqueur
1 part Irish Cream Liqueur
Shot Glass

Layer in a shot glass

Beauty and the Beast

3 parts Jägermeister®
1 part Tequila Rose®
Shot Glass

Layer in a shot glass

Belfast Car Bomb

1 part Coffee Liqueur
splash Irish Cream Liqueur
splash Irish Whiskey
1/2 pint Guinness® Stout
Shot Glass

Layer Coffee Liqueur, Irish Cream Liqueur, and Irish Whiskey in a shot glass. Drop the shot into a 1/2 filled pint of Guiness® and drink all at once.

Bellevue Gangbang

1 part Cinnamon Schnapps
1 part Black Sambuca
Shot Glass

Layer in a shot glass

Bertie Bichberg

1 part Vodka
1 part Crème de Banana
1 Maraschino Cherry
Shot Glass

Layer in a shot glass

Beverly Hills

1 part Swiss Chocolate Almond Liqueur
1 part Irish Cream Liqueur
1 part Grand Marnier®
Shot Glass

Layer in a shot glass

Big 'O'

1 part Peppermint Schnapps
1 part Irish Cream Liqueur
Shot Glass

Layer in a shot glass

Bipple

1 part Butterscotch Schnapps
1 part Irish Cream Liqueur
Shot Glass

Layer in a shot glass

Bit-O-Honey® Shot

1 part Apple Brandy
1 part Frangelico®
Shot Glass

Layer in a shot glass

Black Army

1 part Galliano®
1 part Jägermeister®
Shot Glass

Layer in a shot glass

Blackberry Blossom

1 part Blackberry Liqueur
1 part Irish Cream Liqueur
Shot Glass

Layer in a shot glass

Black Bitch

3 parts Black Sambuca
3 parts Irish Cream Liqueur
2 parts 151-Proof Rum
Shot Glass

Layer in a shot glass

Black Bullet

1 part Peppermint Schnapps
1 part Jägermeister®
Shot Glass

Layer in a shot glass

Black Dragon

1 part Crème de Menthe (White)
1 part Coffee Liqueur
1 part Scotch
Shot Glass

Layer in a shot glass

Black Knight
1 part Coffee Liqueur
1 part Irish Cream Liqueur
1 part Sambuca
splash Advocaat
splash Grenadine
Shot Glass

Layer in a shot glass

Black Magic Cream
1 part Coffee Liqueur
1 part Crème de Cacao (White)
1 part Amarula® Crème Liqueur
Shot Glass

Layer in a shot glass

Black Rain
1 part Black Sambuca
2 parts Champagne
Shot Glass

Layer in a shot glass

Black Sand
1 part Coffee Liqueur
1 part Sambuca
1 part Amaretto
Shot Glass

Layer in a shot glass

Black Tie
1 part Drambuie®
1 part Scotch
1 part Amaretto
Shot Glass

Layer in a shot glass

Black Unicorn
1 part Coffee Liqueur
1 part Butterscotch Schnapps
1 part Irish Cream Liqueur
Shot Glass

Layer in a shot glass

Black Wolf
1 part Black Sambuca
1 part Green Chartreuse
splash Tabasco® Sauce
Shot Glass

Layer in a shot glass

Blackforest
1 part Coffee Liqueur
1 part Grand Marnier®
1 part Cherry Whiskey
Shot Glass

Layer in a shot glass

Blaster
1 part Banana Liqueur
1 part Triple Sec
1 part Coffee Liqueur
Shot Glass

Layer in a shot glass

Bleacher's Twist
1 part Coffee Liqueur
1 part Raspberry Liqueur
1 part Irish Cream Liqueur
Shot Glass

Layer in a shot glass

Blood Clot
2 parts Southern Comfort®
1 part Grenadine
Shot Glass

Layer in a shot glass

Blood of Satan
1 part Jägermeister®
1 part Goldschläger®
1 part Irish Whiskey
1 part Jack Daniel's®
Shot Glass

Layer in a shot glass

Bloodeye

1/2 part Raspberry Liqueur
1 part Citrus-Flavored Vodka
1/2 part Cranberry Liqueur
Shot Glass

Layer in a shot glass

Bloody Frog Cum

1 part Grenadine
splash 151-Proof Rum
1 part Melon Liqueur
splash Irish Cream Liqueur
Shot Glass

Layer in a shot glass

Bloody Psycho

splash Orange Liqueur
splash 151-Proof Rum
1 part Irish Cream Liqueur
Shot Glass

Layer in a shot glass

Blow in the Jaw

splash Goldschläger®
splash Calvados Apple Brandy
1 part Spiced Rum
Shot Glass

Layer in a shot glass

Blow Job

1 part Irish Cream Liqueur
1 part Coffee Liqueur
Shot Glass

Layer in a shot glass. Top with Whipped Cream. Drink without using your hands.

Blue Ice Breathe

1 part Citrus-Flavored Vodka
1 part Blue Curaçao
1 part Bitter Lemon
Shot Glass

Layer in a shot glass

Blue Kisok

2 parts Blue Curaçao
1 part Vodka
splash Lime Juice
fill with Lemon-Lime Soda
Shot Glass

Layer in a shot glass

Blue Moon Shooter

1 part Amaretto
1 part Irish Cream Liqueur
1 part Blue Curaçao
Shot Glass

Layer in a shot glass

Blue Neon

3 parts Goldschläger®
1 part Rum
splash Blue Curaçao
Shot Glass

Layer in a shot glass

Bob Marley

1 part Melon Liqueur
1 part Jägermeister®
1 part Goldschläger®
Shot Glass

Layer in a shot glass

Bonfire

1 part Irish Cream Liqueur
splash Goldschläger®
dash Cinnamon
Shot Glass

Layer in a shot glass

Bonono

1 part Banana Liqueur
1 part Triple Sec
1 part Grand Marnier®
Shot Glass

Layer in a shot glass

Bonsai Pipeline
1 part Wild Turkey® 101
1 part Melon Liqueur
splash 151-Proof Rum
Shot Glass

Layer in a shot glass

Bottom Bouncer
1 part Irish Cream Liqueur
1 part Butterscotch Schnapps
Shot Glass

Layer in a shot glass

Brain Teaser
2 parts Sambuca
2 parts Irish Cream Liqueur
1 part Advocaat
Shot Glass

Layer in a shot glass

Branded Nipple
1 part Butterscotch Schnapps
1 part Irish Cream Liqueur
1 part Goldschläger®
splash 151-Proof Rum
Shot Glass

Layer in a shot glass

Break
1 part Coffee Liqueur
1 part Crème de Banana
1 part Anisette
Shot Glass

Layer in a shot glass

Brimful Rainbow
1 part Blue Curaçao
1 part Amaretto
1 part Grenadine
1 part Melon Liqueur
Shot Glass

Layer in a shot glass

Brush Fire
1 part Tequila
splash Tabasco® Sauce
Shot Glass

Layer in a shot glass

Buckshot
1 part Tequila
1 part Jack Daniel's®
1 part Irish Cream Liqueur
dash Ground Pepper
Shot Glass

Layer in a shot glass

Bulgaria United
1 part Grenadine
1 part Crème de Menthe (Green)
1 part Vodka
Shot Glass

Layer in a shot glass

Bumble Bee
1 part Irish Cream Liqueur
1 part Coffee Liqueur
1 part Sambuca
Shot Glass

Layer in a shot glass

Butter Baby
1 part Butterscotch Schnapps
1 part Irish Cream Liqueur
Shot Glass

Layer in a shot glass

Buttery Jäger Ripple
1 part Jägermeister®
1 part Irish Cream Liqueur
1 part Butterscotch Schnapps
Shot Glass

Layer in a shot glass

Buttery Nipple with a Cherry Kiss
1 part Butterscotch Schnapps
1 part Irish Cream Liqueur
splash Cherry Liqueur
Shot Glass

Layer in a shot glass

Camel Hump
2 parts Butterscotch Schnapps
1 part Irish Cream Liqueur
Shot Glass

Layer in a shot glass

Camel's Snot
1 part Red Wine
1 part Irish Cream Liqueur
Shot Glass

Layer in a shot glass

Candy Cane
1 part Grenadine
1 part Crème de Menthe (White)
1 part Peppermint Schnapps
Shot Glass

Layer in a shot glass

Candy Corn
1 part Licor 43®
1 part Blue Curaçao
1 part Cream
Shot Glass

Layer in a shot glass

Candy Raccoon
1 part Cinnamon Schnapps
1 part Black Sambuca
Shot Glass

Layer in a shot glass

Care Bear®
1 part Raspberry Liqueur
1 part Chocolate Liqueur
Shot Glass

Layer in a shot glass

Cement Mixer
2 parts Irish Cream Liqueur
1 part Sweetened Lime Juice
Shot Glass

Layer in a shot glass. Shake liquid in your mouth before you swallow.

Cerebellum
4 parts Vodka
1 part Grenadine
1 part Irish Cream Liqueur
Shot Glass

Layer in a shot glass

Cerebral Hemorrage
1 part Strawberry Liqueur
splash Irish Cream Liqueur
splash Grenadine
Shot Glass

Layer in a shot glass

Channel 64
1 part Crème de Banana
1 part Irish Cream Liqueur
1 part Advocaat
Shot Glass

Layer in a shot glass

Chastity Belt
1 part Tia Maria®
1 part Frangelico®
1 part Irish Cream Liqueur
1 part Cream
Shot Glass

Layer in a shot glass

Chill Out Shock
1 part Butterscotch Schnapps
1 part Espresso
Shot Glass

Layer in a shot glass

China White
3 parts Crème de Cacao (White)
1 part Irish Cream Liqueur
dash Cinnamon
Shot Glass

Layer in a shot glass

Chocolate Almond
1 part Amaretto
1 part Crème de Cacao (Dark)
1 part Irish Cream Liqueur
Shot Glass

Layer in a shot glass

Chocolate Cherry Bomb
1 part Crème de Cacao (White)
1 part Cream
1 part Grenadine
Shot Glass

Layer in a shot glass

Chocolate Chimp
1 part Crème de Cacao (White)
1 part Coffee Liqueur
1 part Crème de Banana
Shot Glass

Layer in a shot glass

Chocolate Sundae
1 part Irish Cream Liqueur
1 part Crème de Cacao (White)
1 part Coffee Liqueur
Shot Glass

Layer in a shot glass. Top with Whipped Cream.

Chocorange
2 parts Crème de Cacao (Dark)
1 part Raspberry Liqueur
1 part Grand Marnier®
Shot Glass

Layer in a shot glass

Christmas Shots
1 part Melon Liqueur
1 part Raspberry Liqueur
Shot Glass

Layer in a shot glass

Christmas Tree
1 part Crème de Menthe (White)
1 part Grenadine
1 part Irish Cream Liqueur
Shot Glass

Layer in a shot glass

Cinn's Stop Light
1 part Melon Liqueur
1 part Grenadine
1 part Irish Cream Liqueur
Shot Glass

Layer in a shot glass

City Hot Shot
1 part Blue Curaçao
1 part Triple Sec
1 part Grenadine
Shot Glass

Layer in a shot glass

Clear Layered Shot
1 part Lemon-Lime Soda
1 part Grain Alcohol
1 part Grenadine
Shot Glass

Layer in a shot glass. The Grenadine will settle in the middle.

Cobra
1 part Irish Cream Liqueur
1 part Jägermeister®
1 part Rumple Minze®
Shot Glass

Layer in a shot glass

Cock-Sucking Cowboy
2 parts Butterscotch Schnapps
1 part Irish Cream Liqueur
Shot Glass

Layer in a shot glass

The Colombian
1 part Coffee Liqueur
1 part Amaretto
1 part Hennessy®
Shot Glass

Layer in a shot glass

Concrete
1 part Vodka
1 part Irish Cream Liqueur
Shot Glass

Layer in a shot glass.

Cypress
1 part Crème de Cacao (White)
1 part Light Cream
Shot Glass

Layer in a shot glass

Cyrano
1 part Irish Cream Liqueur
1 part Grand Marnier®
splash Raspberry Liqueur
Shot Glass

Layer in a shot glass

Dagger
1 part Tequila
1 part Crème de Cacao (White)
1 part Peach Schnapps
Shot Glass

Layer in a shot glass

Dancin' Cowboy
1 part Banana Liqueur
1 part Coffee Liqueur
1 part Irish Cream Liqueur
Shot Glass

Layer in a shot glass

Dancing Mexican
2 parts Tequila
1 part Milk
Shot Glass

Layer in a shot glass

Decadence
1 part Coffee Liqueur
1 part Frangelico®
1 part Irish Cream Liqueur
Shot Glass

Layer in a shot glass

Desert Water
1 part Tabasco® Sauce
fill with Tequila
Shot Glass

Layer in a shot glass

Dirty Bird
1 part Tequila Reposado
1 part Wild Turkey® 101
Shot Glass

Layer in a shot glass

Dirty Nipple
1 part Sambuca
1 part Irish Cream Liqueur
Shot Glass

Layer in a shot glass

Dirty Oatmeal
1 part Jägermeister®
1 part Irish Cream Liqueur
Shot Glass

Layer in a shot glass

Dog Bowl
1 part Amarula® Crème Liqueur
1 part Banana Liqueur
1 part Frangelico®
Shot Glass

Layer in a shot glass

Don Quixote
1 part Guinness® Stout
1 part Tequila
Shot Glass

Layer in a shot glass

Dragon Slayer
1 part Green Chartreuse®
1 part Tequila
Shot Glass

Layer in a shot glass

Dragoon
1 part Black Sambuca
1 part Coffee Liqueur
1 part Irish Cream Liqueur
Pousse-Café Glass

Shake with ice and strain

Duck Shit Inn
1 part Coffee Liqueur
1 part Melon Liqueur
1 part Irish Cream Liqueur
1 part Tequila
Shot Glass

Layer in a shot glass

E.T.
1 part Melon Liqueur
1 part Irish Cream Liqueur
1 part Vodka
Shot Glass

Layer in a shot glass

El Revolto
1 part Peppermint Schnapps
1 part Irish Cream Liqueur
1 part Cointreau®
Shot Glass

Layer in a shot glass

Electric Banana
1 part Tequila
1 part Banana Liqueur
Shot Glass

Layer in a shot glass

Eliphino
1 part Sambuca
1 part Grand Marnier®
Shot Glass

Layer in a shot glass

Eskimo Kiss
1 part Chocolate Liqueur
1 part Cherry Liqueur
1 part Amaretto
Shot Glass

Layer in a shot glass. Top with Whipped Cream.

Face Off
1 part Grenadine
1 part Crème de Menthe (White)
1 part Parfait Amour
1 part Sambuca
Shot Glass

Layer in a shot glass

Fahrenheit 5,000
1 part Firewater®
1 part Absolut® Peppar Vodka
3 splashes Tabasco® Sauce
Shot Glass

Layer in a shot glass

Feather Duster
1 part Whiskey
splash Blackberry Liqueur
Shot Glass

Layer in a shot glass

Ferrari® Shooter
1 part Sambuca
1 part Tia Maria®
Shot Glass

Layer in a shot glass

Fifth Avenue
1 part Crème de Cacao (Dark)
1 part Apricot Brandy
splash Light Cream
Shot Glass

Layer in a shot glass

Fightin' Irish Gold Shot
1 part Irish Cream Liqueur
1 part Goldschläger®
Shot Glass

Layer in a shot glass

Fisherman's Wharf
1 part Grand Marnier®
1 part Courvoisier©
1 part Amaretto
Shot Glass

Layer in a shot glass

The Flag
1 part Grenadine
1 part Maraschino Liqueur
1 part Chartreuse®
Shot Glass

Layer in a shot glass

Flamboyance
1/2 part Apricot Brandy
1 part Vodka
splash Grand Marnier®
Shot Glass

Layer in a shot glass

Flame Thrower
2 parts Crème de Cacao (White)
1 part Benedictine®
1 part Brandy
Shot Glass

Layer in a shot glass

Flaming Diamond
1 part Strawberry Liqueur
1 part Peppermint Schnapps
1 part Grand Marnier®
Shot Glass

Layer in a shot glass

Flatliner
1 part Sambuca
splash Tabasco® Sauce
1 part Tequila
Shot Glass

Layer in a shot glass

Flying Monkey
1 part Coffee Liqueur
1 part Banana Liqueur
1 part Irish Cream Liqueur
Shot Glass

Layer in a shot glass

Fool's Gold
1 part Coffee Liqueur
1 part Goldschläger®
1 part Jägermeister®
Shot Glass

Layer in a shot glass

Fourth of July
1 part Grenadine
1 part Cream
1 part Blue Curaçao
Shot Glass

Layer in a shot glass

Francis Drake
1 part Coffee Liqueur
1 part Spiced Rum
Shot Glass

Layer in a shot glass

Freddie's Naughty Neopolitan
1 part Coffee Liqueur
1 part Crème de Cacao (White)
1 part Tequila Rose®
Pousse-Café Glass

Layer in a pousse-café glass

French Kiss
1 part Amaretto
1 part Crème de Cacao (White)
1 part Irish Cream Liqueur
Shot Glass

Layer in a shot glass

French Pousse-Café
1 part Cognac
1 part Grenadine
1 part Maraschino Liqueur
Shot Glass

Layer in a shot glass

Frozen Bird
1 part Wild Turkey® Bourbon
1 part Rumple Minze®
Shot Glass

Layer in a shot glass

Full Moon
1 part Amaretto
1 part Grand Marnier®
Shot Glass

Layer in a shot glass

German Blowjob
1 part Irish Cream Liqueur
1 part Jägermeister®
1 part Rumple Minze®
Shot Glass

Layer in a shot glass. Top with Whipped Cream and drink without using your hands.

Gingerbread
1 part Irish Cream Liqueur
1 part Goldschläger®
1 part Butterscotch Schnapps
Shot Glass

Layer in a shot glass

Godfather Shooter
1 part Amaretto
1 part Scotch
Shot Glass

Layer in a shot glass

Gold Rush
1 part Swiss Chocolate Almond Liqueur
1 part Vodka
1 part Yukon Jack®
Shot Glass

Layer in a shot glass

Golden Flash
1 part Sambuca
1 part Triple Sec
1 part Amaretto
Shot Glass

Layer in a shot glass

Golden Night
1 part Swiss Chocolate Almond Liqueur
1 part Irish Cream Liqueur
1 part Frangelico®
Shot Glass

Layer in a shot glass

Golden Nipple
1 part Goldschläger®
1 part Butterscotch Schnapps
1 part Irish Cream Liqueur
Shot Glass

Layer in a shot glass

Gone in 60 Seconds
1 part Strawberry Liqueur
1 part Vanilla Liqueur
1 part Cream
Shot Glass

Layer in a shot glass

Gorilla Snot
1 part Port
1 part Irish Cream Liqueur
Shot Glass

Layer in a shot glass

Grand Baileys®
1 part Irish Cream Liqueur
1 part Grand Marnier®
Shot Glass

Layer in a shot glass

Grand Slam
1 part Crème de Banana
1 part Irish Cream Liqueur
1 part Grand Marnier®
Shot Glass

Layer in a shot glass

Great Balls of Fire
1 part Goldschläger®
1 part Cinnamon Schnapps
1 part Cherry Brandy
Shot Glass

Layer in shot glass

Great White North
1 part Coffee Liqueur
1 part Irish Cream Liqueur
1 part Anisette
Shot Glass

Layer in a shot glass

Green Emerald
1 part Crème de Menthe (White)
1 part Swiss Chocolate Almond Liqueur
Shot Glass

Layer in a shot glass

Green Monkey
1 part Banana Liqueur
1 part Crème de Menthe (White)
Shot Glass

Layer in a shot glass

Green with Envy
1 part Crème de Menthe (Green)
1 part Sambuca
1 part Irish Cream Liqueur
Shot Glass

Layer in a shot glass

Guillotine
1 part Butterscotch Schnapps
1 part Irish Cream Liqueur
1 part After Shock® Peppermint Schnapps
Shot Glass

Layer in a shot glass

Guilty Conscience
1 part Melon Liqueur
splash Grenadine
1 part Gold Tequila
Shot Glass

Layer in a shot glass

Hard On
1 part Coffee Liqueur
1 part Amaretto
1 part Irish Cream Liqueur
Shot Glass

Layer in a shot glass

Hard Rocka
1 part Vodka
1 part Melon Liqueur
1 part Irish Cream Liqueur
Shot Glass

Layer in a shot glass

Heartbreaker
1 part Amaretto
1 part Irish Cream Liqueur
1 part Peach Schnapps
Shot Glass

Layer in a shot glass

Hot Jizz
1 part Melon Liqueur
1 part Hot Damm!® Cinnamon Schnapps
1 part Grain Alcohol
1 part Lemon-Lime Soda
Shot Glass

Layer in a shot glass

Icarus
1 part Crème de Cacao (White)
1 part Irish Cream Liqueur
1 part Plum Brandy
Shot Glass

Layer in a shot glass

Ilicit Affair
1 part Irish Cream Liqueur
1 part Peppermint Schnapps
Shot Glass

Layer in a shot glass. Top with Whipped Cream.

Inhaler
1 part Courvoisier®
1 part Amaretto
Shot Glass

Layer in a shot glass

Innocent Eyes
1 part Coffee Liqueur
1 part Sambuca
1 part Irish Cream Liqueur
Shot Glass

Layer in a shot glass

Irish Flag
1 part Irish Cream Liqueur
1 part Crème de Menthe (Green)
1 part Brandy
Shot Glass

Layer in a shot glass

Layered Shots

Irish Gold
1 part Irish Cream Liqueur
1 part Goldschläger®
Shot Glass
Layer in a shot glass

Irish Headlock
1 part Brandy
1 part Amaretto
1 part Irish Whiskey
1 part Irish Cream Liqueur
Shot Glass
Layer in a shot glass

Irish Monk
1 part Frangelico®
1 part Peppermint Schnapps
1 part Irish Cream Liqueur
Shot Glass
Layer in a shot glass

Jedi® Mind Trick
1 part Goldschläger®
splash Irish Cream Liqueur
splash Melon Liqueur
splash 151-Proof Rum
Shot Glass
Layer in a shot glass

Joe Hazelwood
1 part Rumple Minze®
1 part Jägermeister®
Shot Glass
Layer in a shot glass

Kahbula
1 part Coffee Liqueur
1 part Irish Cream Liqueur
1 part Tequila Reposado
Shot Glass
Layer in a shot glass

Kilted Black Leprechaun
1 part Irish Cream Liqueur
1 part Coconut-Flavored Rum
1 part Drambuie®
Shot Glass
Layer in a shot glass

King Alphonse
1 part Crème de Cacao (Dark)
1 part Coffee Liqueur
1 part Cream
Shot Glass
Layer in a shot glass

Kokopa
1 part Coffee Liqueur
1 part Peppermint Schnapps
Shot Glass
Layer in a shot glass

Kuba Lollipop
1 part Peppermint Liqueur
1 part Ponche Kuba®
Shot Glass
Layer in a shot glass

L.A.P.D. Nightshift
1 part Grenadine
1 part Blue Curaçao
1 part Tequila
Shot Glass
Layer in a shot glass

Landslide
1 part Irish Cream Liqueur
1 part Apricot Brandy
1 part Banana Liqueur
1 part Coffee Liqueur
Shot Glass
Layer in a shot glass

Late Bloomer

1 part Triple Sec
1 part Apricot Brandy
1 part Rum
Shot Glass

Layer in a shot glass

Lava Lamp

1 part Coffee Liqueur
1 part Strawberry Liqueur
1 part Frangelico®
1 part Irish Cream Liqueur
splash Advocaat
Shot Glass

In a shot glass, pour the Coffee Liqueur, Strawberry Liqueur, and Frangelico®. Layer the Irish Cream Liqueur and place 2 to 3 drops of Advocaat in the center.

Layer Cake

1 part Crème de Cacao (Dark)
1 part Apricot Brandy
1 part Heavy Cream
Shot Glass

Layer in a shot glass

Leather and Lace

1 part Swiss Chocolate Almond Liqueur
1 part Peach Schnapps
Shot Glass

Layer in a shot glass

Lewd Lewinsky

1 part Jägermeister®
1 part Cream
Shot Glass

Layer in a shot glass

Liberace

1 part Coffee Liqueur
1 part Milk
1 part 151-Proof Rum
Shot Glass

Layer in a shot glass

Lickity Clit

1 part Irish Cream Liqueur
1 part Butterscotch Schnapps
Shot Glass

Layer in a shot glass

Licorice Heart

1 part Strawberry Liqueur
1 part Sambuca
1 part Irish Cream Liqueur
Shot Glass

Layer in a shot glass

Lizard Slime

3 parts Jose Cuervo© Mistico
1 part Melon Liqueur
Shot Glass

Layer in a shot glass

Lonestar

1 part Parfait Amour
1 part Cherry Liqueur
1 part Rum
Shot Glass

Layer in a shot glass

LSD

1 part Cherry Brandy
1 part Vodka
1 part Passoã®
Shot Glass

Layer in a shot glass

Lube Job

1 part Vodka
1 part Irish Cream Liqueur
Shot Glass

Layer in a shot glass

Machine Shot
1 part 151-Proof Rum
splash Mountain Dew®
Shot Glass

Layer in a shot glass

Marijuana Milkshake
1 part Crème de Cacao (White)
1 part Melon Liqueur
1 part Milk
Shot Glass

Layer in a shot glass

Martian Hard On
1 part Crème de Cacao (White)
1 part Melon Liqueur
1 part Irish Cream Liqueur
Shot Glass

Layer in a shot glass

Meet the Parents
1 part Raspberry Liqueur
1 part Coconut Liqueur
2 parts Cream
Shot Glass

Layer in a shot glass

Melon Pousse-Café
1 part Crème de Almond
1 part Crème de Cacao (White)
1 part Melon Liqueur
Shot Glass

Layer in a shot glass

Menage á Trois Shooter
1 part Coffee Liqueur
1 part Frangelico®
1 part Grand Marnier®
Shot Glass

Layer in a shot glass

Mexican Berry
1 part Coffee Liqueur
1 part Strawberry Liqueur
1 part Tequila
Shot Glass

Layer in a shot glass

Mexican Flag
1 part Grenadine
1 part Crème de Menthe (Green)
1 part Tequila
Shot Glass

Layer in a shot glass

Mexican Motherfucker
1 part Tequila
1 part Irish Cream Liqueur
1 part Frangelico®
1 part Coffee Liqueur
Shot Glass

Layer in a shot glass

Midnight Madness
1 part Triple Sec
1 part Coffee Liqueur
1 part Brandy
Shot Glass

Layer in a shot glass

Miles of Smiles
1 part Amaretto
1 part Peppermint Schnapps
1 part Rye Whiskey
Shot Glass

Layer in a shot glass

Milk of Amnesia
1 part Jägermeister®
1 part Irish Cream Liqueur
Shot Glass

Layer in a shot glass

Mini Guinness®

3 parts Coffee Liqueur
1 part Irish Cream Liqueur
Shot Glass

Layer in a shot glass

Model T

1 part Coffee Liqueur
1 part Crème de Banana
1 part Swiss Chocolate Almond Liqueur
Shot Glass

Layer in a shot glass

Moist and Pink

1 part Sambuca
1 part Tequila Rose®
Shot Glass

Layer in a shot glass

Mom's Apple Pie

3 parts Sour Apple Schnapps
1 part Cinnamon Schnapps
Shot Glass

Layer in a shot glass

Monkey Balls

3 parts Tequila Rose®
1 part 99-Proof Banana Liqueur
Shot Glass

Layer in a shot glass

Mushroom

1 part Grenadine
1 part Irish Cream Liqueur
1 part Melon Liqueur
Shot Glass

Layer in a shot glass

Napalm Death

1 part Cointreau®
1 part Coffee Liqueur
1 part Drambuie®
1 part Irish Cream Liqueur
Shot Glass

Layer in a shot glass

Necrophiliac

1 part Blue Curaçao
1 part Advocaat
Shot Glass

Layer in a shot glass

Nipple on Fire

1 part Firewater®
1 part Butterscotch Schnapps
1 part Irish Cream Liqueur
Shot Glass

Layer in a shot glass

Norwegian Orgasm

1 part Irish Cream Liqueur
1 part Crème de Menthe (White)
Shot Glass

Layer in a shot glass

Nose Opener

3 parts Cinnamon Schnapps
1 part Irish Cream Liqueur
Shot Glass

Layer in a shot glass

Nude Bomb

1 part Coffee Liqueur
1 part Amaretto
1 part Crème de Banana
Shot Glass

Layer in a shot glass

Nutty Buddy
1 part Frangelico®
1 part Swiss Chocolate Almond Liqueur
1 part Peppermint Schnapps
Shot Glass

Layer in a shot glass

Nutty Irishman
1 part Frangelico®
1 part Irish Cream Liqueur
Shot Glass

Layer in a shot glass

Okanagan
1 part Apricot Brandy
1 part Strawberry Liqueur
1 part Blueberry Schnapps
Shot Glass

Layer in a shot glass

Old Glory
1 part Grenadine
1 part Heavy Cream
1 part Blue Curaçao
Shot Glass

Layer in a shot glass

Oreo® Cookie
1 part Coffee Liqueur
1 part Crème de Cacao (White)
1 part Irish Cream Liqueur
splash Vodka
Shot Glass

Layer in a shot glass

P.D.C.
1 part Crème de Menthe (White)
2 parts Black Sambuca
2 parts Green Chartreuse®
1 part Irish Cream Liqueur
Shot Glass

Layer in a shot glass

Pasedena Lady
1 part Swiss Chocolate Almond Liqueur
1 part Amaretto
1 part Brandy
Shot Glass

Layer in a shot glass

Passion Maker
1 part Raspberry Liqueur
1 part Irish Cream Liqueur
Shot Glass

Layer in a shot glass

The Patriot
1 part Blue Curaçao
1 part Crème de Cacao (White)
1 part Grenadine
Shot Glass

Layer in a shot glass

Patriotic Blow
1 part Sloe Gin
1 part Blue Curaçao
1 part Cream
Shot Glass

Layer in a shot glass

Penalty Shot
1 part Crème de Menthe (White)
1 part Tia Maria®
1 part Peppermint Schnapps
Shot Glass

Layer in a shot glass

Peruvian Jungle Fuck
1 part Chocolate Banana Liqueur
1 part Cafe Orange Liqueur
1 part Half and Half
Shot Glass

Layer in a shot glass

Pipeline
1 part Tequila
1 part Vodka
Shot Glass

Layer in a shot glass

Placenta
1 part Amaretto
1 part Irish Cream Liqueur
splash Grenadine
Shot Glass

Layer the Amaretto then the Irish Cream in a shot glass. Place a few drops of Grenadine in the center of the drink.

Pleasure Dome
1 part Brandy
1 part Crème de Cacao (White)
1 part Benedictine®
Shot Glass

Layer in a shot glass

Port and Starboard
1 part Grenadine
1 part Crème de Menthe (Green)
Shot Glass

Layer in a shot glass

Pousse-Café
1 part Crème de Menthe (White)
1 part Crème Yvette®
1 part Grenadine
1 part Chartreuse®
Shot Glass

Layer in a shot glass

Pousse-Café American
1 part Red Curaçao
1 part Cognac
1 part Maraschino Liqueur
Shot Glass

Layer in a shot glass

Primordial
1 part Melon Liqueur
1 part Black Sambuca
Shot Glass

Layer in a shot glass

Pumping Station
1 part Coffee Liqueur
1 part Amaretto
1 part 151-Proof Rum
Shot Glass

Layer in a shot glass

Quick Karlo
1 part Amaretto
1 part Whiskey
Shot Glass

Layer in a shot glass

Quick Tango
1 part Coffee Liqueur
1 part Irish Cream Liqueur
1 part Melon Liqueur
Shot Glass

Layer in a shot glass

Race War
1 part Crème de Cacao (White)
1 part Irish Cream Liqueur
1 part Vodka
Shot Glass

Layer in a shot glass

Raging Bull
1 part Coffee Liqueur
1 part Sambuca
1 part Tequila
Shot Glass

Layer in a shot glass

Raider
1 part Irish Cream Liqueur
1 part Grand Marnier®
1 part Cointreau®
Shot Glass

Layer in a shot glass

Rainbow Cocktail
1 part Blue Curaçao
1 part Crème de Menthe (Green)
1 part Cognac
1 part Maraschino Liqueur
1 part Blackberry Liqueur
1 part Crème de Cassis
Shot Glass

Layer in a shot glass

Raspberry's Romance
1 part Raspberry Liqueur
1 part Coffee Liqueur
1 part Irish Cream Liqueur
Shot Glass

Layer in a shot glass

Rattlesnake
1 part Irish Cream Liqueur
1 part Coffee Liqueur
1 part Crème de Cacao (White)
Shot Glass

Layer in a shot glass

Red, White, and Blue
1 part Cinnamon Schnapps
1 part Goldschläger®
1 part Peppermint Schnapps
Shot Glass

Layer in a shot glass

The Red and Black
1 part Coffee Liqueur
1 part Grenadine
Shot Glass

Layer in a shot glass

Redback Shooter
2 parts Sambuca
1 part Advocaat
Shot Glass

Layer in a shot glass

Redhead's Nipple
1 part Vanilla Liqueur
1 part Irish Cream Liqueur
Shot Glass

Layer in a shot glass

Return of the Yeti
1 part Lychee Liqueur
1 part Parfait Amour
1 part Goldschläger®
Shot Glass

Layer in a shot glass

Rhino
1 part Coffee Liqueur
1 part Amarula® Crème Liqueur
1 part Cointreau®
Shot Glass

Layer in a shot glass

Rhubarb and Custard
1 part Advocaat
1 part Raspberry Liqueur
Shot Glass

Layer in a shot glass

Rock Lobster
1 part Irish Cream Liqueur
1 part Amaretto
1 part Crème de Cacao (White)
Shot Glass

Layer in a shot glass

Rock 'n' Roll
1 part Chocolate Mint Liqueur
1 part Vodka
Shot Glass

Layer in a shot glass

Roly Poly Shooter
1 part Triple Sec
1 part Irish Cream Liqueur
1 part Peach Liqueur
Shot Glass

Layer in a shot glass

Roy Hob Special
1 part Jack Daniel's®
1 part Irish Cream Liqueur
1 part Peppermint Schnapps
Shot Glass

Layer in a shot glass

Rum Roller
1 part Frangelico®
1 part Dark Rum
1 part Espresso
Shot Glass

Layer in a shot glass

Runny Nose
1 part Coffee Liqueur
1 part Irish Cream Liqueur
1 part Cherry Advocaat
Shot Glass

Layer in a shot glass

Russian Candy
1 part Vodka
1 part Peach Schnapps
1 part Grenadine
Shot Glass

Layer in a shot glass

Rusty Spike
1 part Drambuie®
1 part Scotch
Shot Glass

Layer in a shot glass

Saipa
1 part Banana Liqueur
1 part Vodka
Shot Glass

Layer in a shot glass

Santa Shot
1 part Grenadine
1 part Crème de Menthe (Green)
1 part Peppermint Schnapps
Shot Glass

Layer in a shot glass

Savoy Hotel
1 part Benedictine®
1 part Brandy
1 part Crème de Cacao (White)
Shot Glass

Layer in a shot glass

Screaming Lizard
1 part Tequila
1 part Chartreuse®
Shot Glass

Layer in a shot glass

Sea Monkey
2 parts Goldschläger®
1 part Blue Curaçao
Shot Glass

Layer in a shot glass

Seduction
1 part Frangelico®
1 part Crème de Banana
1 part Irish Cream Liqueur
Shot Glass

Layer in a shot glass

Shamrock Shooter
1 part Crème de Menthe (White)
1 part Crème de Cacao (White)
1 part Irish Cream Liqueur
Shot Glass

Layer in a shot glass

Shorty Sex House
2 parts Ouzo
2 parts Crème de Menthe (Green)
1 part Passion Fruit Nectar
Shot Glass

Layer in a shot glass

Silver Thread
1 part Banana Liqueur
1 part Irish Cream Liqueur
1 part Peppermint Schnapps
Shot Glass

Layer in a shot glass

Sleigh Ride
1 part Grenadine
1 part Green Chartreuse®
1 part Tequila Silver
Shot Glass

Layer in a shot glass

Slippery Sin
1 part Coconut-Flavored Liqueur
1 part Irish Cream Liqueur
Shot Glass

Layer in a shot glass

Snap Shot
1 part Peppermint Schnapps
1 part Irish Cream Liqueur
Shot Glass

Layer in a shot glass

Snow Cap
1 part Irish Cream Liqueur
1 part Tequila
Shot Glass

Layer in a shot glass

Soft Porn
1 part Crème de Cassis
1 part Raspberry Liqueur
1 part Irish Cream Liqueur
Shot Glass

Layer in a shot glass

Solar Plexus
2 parts Vodka
1 part Cherry Brandy
1 part Campari®
Shot Glass

Layer in a shot glass

Southern Belle
1 part Brandy
1 part Crème de Cacao (White)
1 part Benedictine®
Shot Glass

Layer in a shot glass

Southern Rattler
1 part Crème de Banana
1 part Southern Comfort®
1 part Gold Tequila
Shot Glass

Layer in a shot glass

Spot Shooter
1 part Vodka
1 part Coffee
splash Irish Cream Liqueur
Shot Glass

Layer in a shot glass. Place a few drops of Irish Cream in the center of the drink.

Spring Fever
1 part Drambuie®
1 part Swiss Chocolate Almond Liqueur
Shot Glass

Layer in a shot glass

Springbok
3 parts Crème de Menthe (White)
2 parts Amarula® Crème Liqueur
1 part Cream
Shot Glass

Layer in a shot glass

Stars and Stripes
1 part Blue Curaçao
1 part Heavy Cream
1 part Grenadine
Shot Glass

Layer in a shot glass

Stinky Beaver
1 part Jägermeister®
1 part Goldschläger®
Pousse-Café Glass

Shake with ice and strain

Storm
1 part Light Rum
1 part Blue Curaçao
1 part Irish Cream Liqueur
Shot Glass

Layer in a shot glass

Storm Cloud
2 parts Rum
1 part Tequila
1 part Amaretto
Shot Glass

Layer in a shot glass

Strawberry Freddo
1 part Irish Cream Liqueur
1 part Coffee Liqueur
1 part Strawberry Liqueur
Shot Glass

Layer in a shot glass

Strawberry Kiss
1 part Coffee Liqueur
1 part Strawberry Liqueur
1 part Irish Cream Liqueur
Shot Glass

Layer in a shot glass

Street Car
1 part Crème de Cacao (Dark)
1 part Irish Cream Liqueur
1 part Apricot Brandy
Shot Glass

Layer in a shot glass

Summer Fling
1 part Blue Curaçao
1 part Irish Cream Liqueur
Shot Glass

Layer in a shot glass

Sun and Surf
1 part Coffee Liqueur
1 part Grand Marnier®
1 part Tequila
Shot Glass

Layer in a shot glass

Sunrise Shooter
1 part Parfait Amour
1 part Grenadine
1 part Chartreuse®
1 part Cointreau®
Shot Glass

Layer in a shot glass

Sweet Bull
2 parts Tequila Reposado
2 parts Lychee Liqueur
1 part Grenadine
Shot Glass

Layer in a shot glass

Sweet Burning Eruption
1 part Triple Sec
1 part Butterscotch Schnapps
1 part Irish Cream Liqueur
splash Grenadine
Shot Glass

Layer all but Grenadine in a shot glass. Place a few drops of Grenadine in the center of the drink.

Swiss and Whoosh
1 part Tia Maria®
1 part Frangelico®
1 part Irish Cream Liqueur
Shot Glass

Layer in a shot glass

Swiss Hiker
1 part Swiss Chocolate Almond Liqueur
1 part Crème de Banana
1 part Irish Cream Liqueur
Shot Glass

Layer in a shot glass

T-52
1 part Coffee Liqueur
1 part Tequila Rose®
1 part Grand Marnier®
Shot Glass

Layer in a shot glass

Tampa Pond Scum
1 part Peach Schnapps
1 part Melon Liqueur
1 part Rum
1 part Milk
Shot Glass

Layer in a shot glass

Technical Knock Out
1 part Ouzo
1 part Coffee Liqueur
1 part Tequila
Shot Glass

Layer in a shot glass

Tequila Knockout
3 parts Tequila Silver
1 part Grenadine
Shot Glass

Layer in a shot glass

Texas Chainsaw Massacre
1 part Strawberry Liqueur
1 part Vodka
Shot Glass

Layer in a shot glass

Texas Thunderstorm
1 part Amaretto
splash 151-Proof Rum
splash Irish Cream Liqueur
Shot Glass

Layer in a shot glass

Thin Blue Line
1 part Vodka
1 part Triple Sec
splash Blue Curaçao
Shot Glass

Layer the Triple Sec on top of the Vodka then gently drip the Blue Curaçao. It will settle between the Vodka and Triple Sec, forming a thin blue line.

Thorny Rose
1 part Tequila Rose®
1 part Peppermint Schnapps
1 part Coffee Liqueur
Shot Glass

Layer in a shot glass

Three's Company
1 part Courvoisier®
1 part Grand Marnier®
1 part Coffee Liqueur
Shot Glass

Layer in a shot glass

Tiger Tail
1 part Tia Maria®
1 part Grand Marnier®
1 part Peppermint Schnapps
Shot Glass

Layer in a shot glass

Toronto Maple Leafs

1 part Blue Curaçao
1 part Irish Cream Liqueur
Shot Glass

Layer in a shot glass

Trap Door

1 part Swiss Chocolate Almond Liqueur
1 part Rum Crème Liqueur
Shot Glass

Layer in a shot glass

Trial of the Century

1 part Jägermeister®
1 part Goldschläger®
1 part Grenadine
Shot Glass

Layer in a shot glass

Tricolore

1 part Crème de Menthe (White)
1 part Apricot Brandy
1 part Maraschino Liqueur
Shot Glass

Layer in a shot glass

Triple Irish Shooter

1 part Irish Whiskey
1 part Irish Cream Liqueur
1 part Irish Mist®
Shot Glass

Layer in a shot glass

Uncle Sam

1 part After Shock® Cinnamon Schnapps
1 part Avalanche® Peppermint Schnapps
1 part Rumple Minze®
Shot Glass

Layer in a shot glass

Undertaker

1 part Jägermeister®
1 part Cointreau®
1 part 151-Proof Rum
Shot Glass

Layer in a shot glass

V-2 Schnieder

1 part Coffee Liqueur
1 part Irish Cream Liqueur
1 part Frangelico®
Shot Glass

Layer in a shot glass

Vibrator

2 parts Southern Comfort®
1 part Irish Cream Liqueur
Shot Glass

Layer in a shot glass

Vice Versa

1 part Pisang Ambon® Liqueur
1 part Passion Fruit Liqueur
1 part Green Chartreuse®
Shot Glass

Layer in a shot glass

Well-Greased Dwarf

1 part Crème de Cacao (White)
1 part Sambuca
1 part Irish Cream Liqueur
Shot Glass

Layer in a shot glass

Wet Kiss

1 part Amaretto
1 part Sour Mix
1 part Watermelon Schnapps
Shot Glass

Layer in a shot glass

Whick

1 part Sambuca
1 part Black Sambuca
Shot Glass

Layer in a shot glass

Whipster
1 part Crème de Cacao (White)
1 part Apricot Brandy
1 part Triple Sec
Shot Glass

Layer in a shot glass

Whistle Stop
1 part Grand Marnier®
1 part Jack Daniel's®
Shot Glass

Layer in a shot glass

Whistling Gypsy
1 part Tia Maria®
1 part Irish Cream Liqueur
1 part Vodka
Shot Glass

Layer in a shot glass

White Lightning
1 part Tequila
1 part Crème de Cacao (White)
Shot Glass

Layer in a shot glass

White Tornado
3 parts Sambuca
1 part Tequila Rose®
Shot Glass

Layer in a shot glass

Windsurfer
1 part Coffee Liqueur
1 part Triple Sec
1 part Yukon Jack®
Shot Glass

Layer in a shot glass

Winter Break
1 part Peach Schnapps
1 part Banana Liqueur
1 part Southern Comfort®
Shot Glass

Layer in a shot glass

Wobble Walker
1 part Crème de Banana
2 parts Irish Cream Liqueur
1 part 151-Proof Rum
Shot Glass

Layer in a shot glass

Yankee's Pousse-Café
1 part Brandy
1 part Red Curaçao
1 part Grenadine
1 part Maraschino Liqueur
1 part Vanilla Liqueur
Shot Glass

Layer in a shot glass

Zipper Shooter
1 part Grand Marnier®
1 part Tequila
1 part Irish Cream Liqueur
Shot Glass

Layer in a shot glass

Zowie
1 part Banana Liqueur
1 part Irish Cream Liqueur
1 part Coconut Flavored Rum
Shot Glass

Layer in a shot glass

Flaming Shots

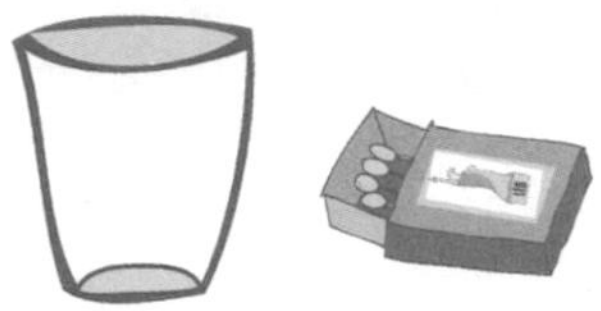

Flaming shots can be dramatic and entertaining, the entertainment factor is greatly reduced if some simple safety rules are not followed:

- Never lift or move the shot while it's lit. A flaming alcohol spill can be very dangerous.
- Always extinguish the flame before consuming the shot.
- Use an inverted empty glass or metal cup to extinguish the flame. An empty shot glass or a jigger work well. Never use your hand.

A.S.S. on Flames

1 part Amaretto
1 part Sour Apple Schnapps
1 part Southern Comfort®
splash 151-Proof Rum
Shot Glass

Layer in a shot glass. Light the Rum with a lighter or match. Extinguish by placing an empty shot glass over the shot. Always extinguish the flame before consuming.

Burning Africa

1 part Jägermeister®
1 part 151-Proof Rum
Shot Glass

Layer in a shot glass. Light the Rum with a lighter or match. Extinguish by placing an empty shot glass over the shot. Always extinguish the flame before consuming.

Concord

1 part Coffee Liqueur
1 part Irish Cream Liqueur
splash 151-Proof Rum
Shot Glass

Layer in a shot glass. Light the Rum with a lighter or match. Extinguish by placing an empty shot glass over the shot. Always extinguish the flame before consuming.

Everybody's Irish

2 parts Whiskey
1/2 part Crème de Menthe (Green)
Shot Glass

Pour ingredients into a glass neat (do not chill). Light the Whiskey with a lighter or a match. Extinguish by placing an empty shot glass over the shot. Always extinguish the flame before consuming.

Feel the Burn

1 part Coffee Liqueur
1 part Irish Cream Liqueur
1 part Ouzo
1 part Wild Turkey® Bourbon
1 part 151-Proof Rum
Shot Glass

Pour ingredients into glass neat (do not chill). Light the Rum with a lighter or match. Extinguish by placing an empty shot glass over the shot. Always extinguish the flame before consuming.

Fiery Balls of Death

1 part 151-Proof Rum
1 part Triple Sec
Shot Glass

Pour ingredients into glass neat (do not chill). Light the Rum with a lighter or match. Extinguish by placing an empty shot glass over the shot. Always extinguish the flame before consuming.

Fiery Blue Mustang

1 part Banana Liqueur
1 part Blue Curaçao
1 part 151-Proof Rum
Shot Glass

Pour ingredients into glass neat (do not chill). Light the Rum with a lighter or match. Extinguish by placing an empty shot glass over the shot. Always extinguish the flame before consuming.

Flambe

1 part Grenadine
1 part Crème de Menthe (White)
1 part Vodka
1 part 151-Proof Rum
Shot Glass

Layer in a shot glass. Light the Rum with a lighter or match. Extinguish by placing an empty shot glass over the shot. Always extinguish the flame before consuming.

Flaming Armadillo

1 part Tequila
1 part Amaretto
1 part Rum
Shot Glass

Pour ingredients into glass neat (do not chill). Light the Rum with a lighter or match. Extinguish by placing an empty shot glass over the shot. Always extinguish the flame before consuming.

Flaming Blazer

1 part Crème de Cacao (White)
1 part Southern Comfort®
1 part 151-Proof Rum
Shot Glass

Pour ingredients into glass neat (do not chill). Light the Rum with a lighter or match. Extinguish by placing an empty shot glass over the shot. Always extinguish the flame before consuming.

Flaming Blue

1 part Anisette
1 part Dry Vermouth
1 part 151-Proof Rum
Shot Glass

Pour ingredients into glass neat (do not chill). Light the Rum with a lighter or match. Extinguish by placing an empty shot glass over the shot. Always extinguish the flame before consuming.

Flaming Blue Fuck

3 parts Sambuca
1 part Blue Curaçao
Shot Glass

Pour ingredients into glass neat (do not chill). Light the Sambuca with a lighter or match. Extinguish by placing an empty shot glass over the shot. Always extinguish the flame before consuming.

Flaming Blue Jesus

1 part Peppermint Schnapps
1 part Southern Comfort®
1 part Tequila
2 parts 151-Proof Rum
Shot Glass

Pour ingredients into glass neat (do not chill). Light the Rum with a lighter or match. Extinguish by placing an empty shot glass over the shot. Always extinguish the flame before consuming.

Flaming Courage

1 part Cinnamon Schnapps
1 part Peppermint Schnapps
1 part Melon Liqueur
splash 151-Proof Rum
Shot Glass

Pour ingredients into glass neat (do not chill). Light the Rum with a lighter or match. Extinguish by placing an empty shot glass over the shot. Always extinguish the flame before consuming.

Flaming Dragon

1 part Green Chartreuse®
1 part 151-Proof Rum
Shot Glass

Pour ingredients into glass neat (do not chill). Light the Rum with a lighter or match. Extinguish by placing an empty shot glass over the shot. Always extinguish the flame before consuming.

Flaming Dragon Snot

1 part Crème de Menthe (White)
1 part Irish Cream Liqueur
1 part 151-Proof Rum
Shot Glass

Pour ingredients into glass neat (do not chill). Light the Rum with a lighter or match. Extinguish by placing an empty shot glass over the shot. Always extinguish the flame before consuming.

Flaming Fart

1 part Cinnamon Schnapps
1 part 151-Proof Rum
Shot Glass

Pour ingredients into glass neat (do not chill). Light the Rum with a lighter or match. Extinguish by placing an empty shot glass over the shot. Always extinguish the flame before consuming.

Flaming Fruit Trees

1 part Peach Schnapps
1 part Banana Liqueur
1 part 151-Proof Rum
Shot Glass

Pour ingredients into glass neat (do not chill). Light the Rum with a lighter or match. Extinguish by placing an empty shot glass over the shot. Always extinguish the flame before consuming.

Flaming Giraffe

2 parts Coffee Liqueur
1 parts Butterscotch Schnapps
1 parts 151-Proof Rum
Shot Glass

Pour ingredients into glass neat (do not chill). Light the Rum with a lighter or match. Extinguish by placing an empty shot glass over the shot. Always extinguish the flame before consuming.

Flaming Glacier

1 part Cinnamon Schnapps
1 part Rumple Minze®
Shot Glass

Pour ingredients into glass neat (do not chill). Light the Schnapps with a lighter or match. Extinguish by placing an empty shot glass over the shot. Always extinguish the flame before consuming.

Flaming Gorilla

1 part Peppermint Schnapps
1 part Coffee Liqueur
1 part 151-Proof Rum
Shot Glass

Pour ingredients into glass neat (do not chill). Light the Rum with a lighter or match. Extinguish by placing an empty shot glass over the shot. Always extinguish the flame before consuming.

Flaming Gorilla Titties

1 part 151-Proof Rum
1 part Coffee Liqueur
Shot Glass

Pour ingredients into glass neat (do not chill). Light the Rum with a lighter or match. Extinguish by placing an empty shot glass over the shot. Always extinguish the flame before consuming.

Flaming Jesus

1 part Vodka
1 part Lime Juice
1 part Grenadine
1 part 151-Proof Rum
Shot Glass

Pour ingredients into glass neat (do not chill). Light the Rum with a lighter or match. Extinguish by placing an empty shot glass over the shot. Always extinguish the flame before consuming.

Flaming Licorice

1 part Jägermeister®
1 part Sambuca
1 part 151-Proof Rum
Shot Glass

Pour ingredients into glass neat (do not chill). Light the Rum with a lighter or match. Extinguish by placing an empty shot glass over the shot. Always extinguish the flame before consuming.

Flaming Nazi

1 part Goldschläger®
1 part Rumple Minze®
1 part 151-Proof Rum
Shot Glass

Pour ingredients into glass neat (do not chill). Light the Rum with a lighter or match. Extinguish by placing an empty shot glass over the shot. Always extinguish the flame before consuming.

Flaming Rasta

1 part Amaretto
1 part Grenadine
1 part 151-Proof Rum
Shot Glass

Layer in a shot glass. Light the Rum with a lighter or match. Extinguish by placing an empty shot glass over the shot. Always extinguish the flame before consuming.

Freakin' Flamin' Fruit

1 part Melon Liqueur
1 part Crème de Banana
1 part Golden Pear Liqueur
1 part 151-Proof Rum
Shot Glass

Pour ingredients into glass neat (do not chill). Light the Rum with a lighter or match. Extinguish by placing an empty shot glass over the shot. Always extinguish the flame before consuming.

Green Lizard

4 parts Green Chartreuse®
1 part 151-Proof Rum
Shot Glass

Layer in a shot glass. Light the Rum with a lighter or match. Extinguish by placing an empty shot glass over the shot. Always extinguish the flame before consuming.

Harbor Light
1 part Coffee Liqueur
1 part Irish Cream Liqueur
1 part 151-Proof Rum
Shot Glass

Layer in a shot glass. Light the Rum with a lighter or match. Extinguish by placing an empty shot glass over the shot. Always extinguish the flame before consuming.

Lighthouse
1 part Coffee Liqueur
1 part Irish Cream Liqueur
1 part 151-Proof Rum
Shot Glass

Layer in a shot glass. Light the Rum with a lighter or match. Extinguish by placing an empty shot glass over the shot. Always extinguish the flame before consuming.

Morphine Drip
1 part Amaretto
1 part Butterscotch Schnapps
splash 151-Proof Rum
Shot Glass

Pour ingredients into glass neat (do not chill). Light the Rum with a lighter or match. Extinguish by placing an empty shot glass over the shot. Always extinguish the flame before consuming.

Napalm
1 part Cinnamon Schnapps
1 part Fire & Ice®
1 part 151-Proof Rum
Shot Glass

Pour ingredients into glass neat (do not chill). Light the Rum with a lighter or match. Extinguish by placing an empty shot glass over the shot. Always extinguish the flame before consuming.

Napalm Crematorium
1 part Cinnamon Schnapps
1 part Rumple Minze®
1 part 151-Proof Rum
Shot Glass

Layer in a shot glass. Light the Rum with a lighter or match. Extinguish by placing an empty shot glass over the shot. Always extinguish the flame before consuming.

Pyro
1 part Vodka
1 part Fire Water®
splash 151-Proof Rum
Shot Glass

Build in the glass with no ice. Light the Rum with a lighter or match. Extinguish by placing an empty shot glass over the shot. Always extinguish the flame before consuming.

Rock Star

1 part Cinnamon Schnapps
1 part Sloe Gin
1 part Triple Sec
1 part Jägermeister®
1 part 151-Proof Rum
Shot Glass

Build in the glass with no ice. Light the Rum with a lighter or match. Extinguish by placing an empty shot glass over the shot. Always extinguish the flame before consuming.

Southern Bound Meteor

Maraschino Cherry
1 part Southern Comfort®
1 part Goldschläger®
splash 151-Proof Rum
Shot Glass

Remove the stem from a cherry and drop it in a shot glass. Pour in the Southern Comfort® and Goldschläger®. Top with a splash of 151-Proof Rum. Light the Rum with a lighter or match. Extinguish by placing an empty shot glass over the shot. Always extinguish the flame before consuming.

Thriller Shooter

1 part Strawberry Liqueur
1 part Dark Rum
Shot Glass

Build in the glass with no ice. Light the Rum with a lighter or match. Extinguish by placing an empty shot glass over the shot. Always extinguish the flame before consuming.

Vesuvius

3 parts Crème de Cacao (Dark)
1 part Green Chartreuse®
Shot Glass

Layer in a shot glass. Light the Chartreuse with a lighter or match. Extinguish by placing an empty shot glass over the shot. Always extinguish the flame before consuming.

Tabasco® Shots

This group of shots is meant to induce pain. These are not for you. They are for your "friends," or for the loud obnoxious guy at the other end of the bar.

911 Ouch

1 part Cinnamon Schnapps
1 part 100-Proof Peppermint Schnapps
splash Tabasco® Sauce

Shot Glass

Pour ingredients into glass neat (do not chill)

Absolution

1 part Vodka
dash Tabasco® Sauce

Shot Glass

Pour ingredients into glass neat (do not chill)

Abuse Machine

1 part Tequila
1/2 part Whiskey
1/2 part Sambuca
splash Tabasco® Sauce
splash Worcestershire Sauce

Shot Glass

Shake with ice and strain

Afterburner

splash Tabasco® Sauce
1 part Tequila Silver
dash Salt
1 Lime slice

Shot Glass

Pour enough Tabasco® Sauce into the shot glass to cover the bottom completely. Fill the rest of the shot glass with Tequila. Lick your hand and pour some Salt on it. Lick the Salt, slam the shot, then suck the Lime.

Afterburner #2

1 part Vodka
1/2 part Tabasco® Sauce

Shot Glass

Pour ingredients into glass neat (do not chill)

Anus Burner

1 Jalapeño Pepper Slice
1 part Tequila
splash Tabasco® Sauce

Shot Glass

Place slice of Jalapeño in shot glass. Add Tequila and enough Tabasco® to make deep red in color.

The Antichrist
1 part Grain Alcohol
1 part 151 Proof Rum
1 part Absolut® Peppar Vodka
3 splashes Tabasco® Sauce
Shot Glass

Shake with ice and strain

Aqua del Fuego
1 part Tequila
1 part Tabasco® Sauce
Shot Glass

Pour ingredients into glass neat (do not chill)

Bloody Chicken
1 part Wild Turkey® Bourbon
1/2 part Tequila
1/4 splash Tabasco® Sauce
Shot Glass

Pour ingredients into glass neat (do not chill)

Brave Bull
1 part Tequila
1 part Tabasco® Sauce
Shot Glass

Pour ingredients into glass neat (do not chill)

Buffalo Ball Sweat
3 parts Yukon Jack®
3 splashes Tabasco® Sauce
Shot Glass

Pour ingredients into glass neat (do not chill)

Buffalo Piss
1 part Tequila
1 part Tabasco® Sauce
Shot Glass

Pour ingredients into glass neat (do not chill)

Burn in Hell and Pray for Snow!
2 parts Rum
2 parts Whiskey
1 part Tabasco® Sauce
12 Hot Peppers
Shot Glass

Combine all ingredients in a blender with ice. Blend until smooth. Pour into shot glasses and top with a splash of Irish Cream.

Burning Angel
1 part Vodka
1 part Jägermeister®
splash Tabasco® Sauce
dash Salt
Shot Glass

Pour ingredients into glass neat (do not chill)

Chuck Wagon
1 part Jägermeister®
1/2 splash Tabasco® Sauce
Shot Glass

Pour ingredients into glass neat (do not chill)

Dead Dog
1 part Bourbon
1 part Beer
3 splashes Tabasco® Sauce
Shot Glass

Pour ingredients into glass neat (do not chill)

Death by Fire

1 part Peppermint Schnapps
1 part Cinnamon Schnapps
1 part Tabasco® Sauce

Shot Glass

Pour ingredients into glass neat (do not chill)

Devil Drink

1 part Irish Cream Liqueur
1 part Sambuca
1 part Vodka
3 splashes Tabasco® Sauce

Shot Glass

Pour ingredients into glass neat (do not chill)

Diablo!

1 part 151-Proof Rum
splash Tabasco® Sauce

Shot Glass

Pour ingredients into glass neat (do not chill)

Estonian Forest Fire

1 part Vodka
6 splashes Tabasco® Sauce
1 Kiwi Slice

Shot Glass

Combine the Tabasco® with a shot of Vodka. Chase it with a slice of Kiwi.

Fence Jumper

1 part Tequila
1 part Rum
splash Tabasco® Sauce

Shot Glass

Pour ingredients into glass neat (do not chill)

Firecracker Shot

2 parts Tequila
1 part Tabasco® Sauce

Shot Glass

Pour ingredients into glass neat (do not chill)

Fire in the Hole

1 1/2 parts Ouzo
3 splashes Tabasco® Sauce

Shot Glass

Pour ingredients into glass neat (do not chill)

Fireball

1 part Fire Water®
splash Tabasco® Sauce

Shot Glass

Pour ingredients into glass neat (do not chill)

Fireball #2

1 part Sambuca
1 part Tequila
splash Tabasco® Sauce

Shot Glass

Pour ingredients into glass neat (do not chill)

Fireball #3

1 part Cinnamon Schnapps
splash Tabasco® Sauce

Shot Glass

Pour ingredients into glass neat (do not chill)

Fireball Shooter

1 part Cinnamon Schnapps
1 part 151-Proof Rum
2 splashes Tabasco® Sauce

Shot Glass

Pour ingredients into glass neat (do not chill)

Fist Fuck

1 part Tabasco® Sauce
1 part Tequila

Shot Glass

Pour ingredients into glass neat (do not chill)

Galaxy
1 part Sambuca
1 part Tequila
3 splashes Tabasco® Sauce
Shot Glass

Pour ingredients into glass neat (do not chill)

Great White Shark
1 part Jack Daniel's®
1 part Tequila
splash Tabasco® Sauce
Shot Glass

Pour ingredients into glass neat (do not chill)

Green Chilli
1 part Cinnamon Schnapps
2 splashes Tabasco® Sauce
Shot Glass

Shake with ice and strain

Gut Bomb
1 part Rum
splash Tabasco® Sauce
Shot Glass

Pour ingredients into glass neat (do not chill)

Hellfire
2 parts Rye Whiskey
1 part Tabasco® Sauce
Shot Glass

Pour ingredients into glass neat (do not chill)

Hell's Gate
2 parts Brandy
1 part Tabasco® Sauce
dash Wasabi
splash Butterscotch Schnapps
Shot Glass

Pour ingredients into glass neat (do not chill)

Hot Bitch
1 part Vodka
1 part Whiskey
1 part Gin
splash Tabasco® Sauce
Shot Glass

Pour ingredients into glass neat (do not chill)

Hot Shot
1 part Vodka
1 part Peppermint Schnapps
splash Tabasco® Sauce
Shot Glass

Shake with ice and strain

Hot Shot #2
1 part Crème de Menthe (White)
1 part Vodka
splash Tabasco® Sauce
Shot Glass

Shake with ice and strain

Hot Spot
1 part Vodka
1 part Tequila
1 part Tabasco® Sauce
Shot Glass

Pour ingredients into glass neat (do not chill)

Incinerator
2 parts Black Sambuca
1 part 151-Proof Rum
splash Tabasco® Sauce
Shot Glass

Pour ingredients into glass neat (do not chill)

Ironman
1 part Green Chartreuse®
1 part Sambuca
1 part Scotch
3 parts Tabasco® Sauce
1 part Tequila
Shot Glass

Pour ingredients into glass neat (do not chill)

Jaw Breaker
1 part Goldschläger®
splash Tabasco® Sauce
Shot Glass

Pour ingredients into glass neat (do not chill)

Kentucky Hot Tub
1 part Jim Beam®
1 part Cointreau®
1 part Blue Curaçao
splash Tabasco® Sauce
Shot Glass

Shake with ice and strain

Kickstarter
1 part Jack Daniel's®
1 part Fire Water®
splash Tabasco® Sauce
Shot Glass

Build in the glass with no ice

Labia Licker
1 part Rum
splash Tabasco® Sauce
Shot Glass

Build in the glass with no ice

Lava
1 part Fire Water®
1 part Grain Alcohol
2 splashes Tabasco® Sauce
Shot Glass

Pour ingredients into glass neat (do not chill)

Leggs
1 part Tequila
1 part Jägermeister®
splash Tabasco® Sauce
Shot Glass

Pour ingredients into glass neat (do not chill)

Louisiana Shooter
1 part Tequila
1 Raw Oyster
1/4 splash Horseradish
splash Tabasco® Sauce
Shot Glass

Pour ingredients into glass neat (do not chill)

Mad Dog
1 part Vodka
1 part Cherry Juice
splash Tabasco® Sauce
Shot Glass

Shake with ice and strain

Mexican Jumping Bean
1 part Tequila
splash Tabasco® Sauce
splash Worcestershire Sauce
Shot Glass

Pour ingredients into glass neat (do not chill)

Mexican Missile
1 part Tequila Silver
splash Tabasco® Sauce
Shot Glass

Shake with ice and strain

Monkey Fart
1 part Vodka
1 part Coffee Liqueur
splash Tabasco® Sauce
Shot Glass

Pour ingredients into glass neat (do not chill)

Napalm Taco
1 part Jägermeister®
1 part Tequila
1 part Tabasco® Sauce
Shot Glass

Shake with ice and strain

Oklahoma Rattler
1 part Tequila Silver
splash Tabasco® Sauce
Shot Glass

Pour ingredients into glass neat (do not chill)

Oyster Shot
1 Raw Oyster
1 part Tequila
splash Tabasco® Sauce
Shot Glass

Build in the glass with no ice

Prairie Dog
1 part 151-Proof Rum
3 splashes Tabasco® Sauce
Shot Glass

Pour ingredients into glass neat (do not chill)

Prairie Fire
1 part Tequila
5 splashes Tabasco® Sauce
Shot Glass

Pour ingredients into glass neat (do not chill)

Psycho Tsunami
1 part Tequila Reposado
1 part Blue Curaçao
1 part Fresh Lime Juice
splash Tabasco® Sauce
Shot Glass

Build in the glass with no ice

Red Hot
1 part Cinnamon Schnapps
splash Tabasco® Sauce
Shot Glass

Build in the glass with no ice

Roswell
1 part Tabasco® Sauce
1 part Tequila Reposado
1 part Red Bull® Energy Drink
Shot Glass

Build in the glass with no ice

Russian Bloody Mary
1 part Vodka
splash Tabasco® Sauce
Shot Glass

Build in the glass with no ice

Satan's Piss
1 part 151-Proof Rum
3 splashes Tabasco® Sauce
Shot Glass

Pour ingredients into glass neat (do not chill)

Satan's Revenge
1 part Tequila
1 part Jack Daniel's®
1 part Goldschläger®
splash Tabasco® Sauce
Shot Glass

Pour ingredients into glass neat (do not chill)

Satan's Spawn
1 part Fire Water®
4 splashes Tabasco® Sauce
Shot Glass

Pour ingredients into glass neat (do not chill)

Scratchy Asshole
2 parts Jägermeister®
2 parts Peach Schnapps
1 part Tabasco® Sauce
1 part Lemon-Lime Soda
Shot Glass

Shake with ice and strain

Sharpshooter
1 part Ouzo
1 part Vodka
splash Tabasco® Sauce
Shot Glass

Pour ingredients into glass neat (do not chill)

Shot of Hell
1 part Vodka
splash Tabasco® Sauce
Shot Glass

Pour ingredients into glass neat (do not chill)

Shot of Respect
1 part Tequila
1 part 151-Proof Rum
1 splash Tabasco® Sauce
Shot Glass

Pour ingredients into glass neat (do not chill)

Square Furnace
1 part Jim Beam®
1 part Tequila
1 part Irish Cream Liqueur
1 part 151-Proof Rum
1 part Tabasco® Sauce
Shot Glass

Shake with ice and strain

Stomachache
1 part Jägermeister®
2 splashes Tabasco® Sauce
Shot Glass

Pour ingredients into glass neat (do not chill)

Sweaty Goat's Ass
3 parts Tequila Silver
splash Tabasco® Sauce
1 part Cream
Shot Glass

Build in the glass with no ice

Sweaty Irishman
1 part Irish Whiskey
1 part Cinnamon Schnapps
splash Tabasco® Sauce
Shot Glass

Build in the glass with no ice

Sweaty Lumberjack
1 part 151-Proof Rum
1 part Tabasco® Sauce
1 part Tequila
Shot Glass

Build in the glass with no ice

Sweaty Melon
1 part Watermelon Schnapps
1 part Vodka
splash Tabasco® Sauce
Shot Glass

Build in the glass with no ice

Sweaty Mexican Lumberjack
3 parts Yukon Jack®
1 part Tequila
splash Tabasco® Sauce
Shot Glass

Build in the glass with no ice

T2
1 part Tequila
1 part Tabasco® Sauce
dash Black Pepper
Shot Glass

Pour ingredients into glass neat (do not chill)

Tenement Fire
1 part Vodka
splash Tabasco® Sauce
Shot Glass

Build in the glass with no ice

Tequila Fire
1 part Tequila
1/2 splash Tabasco® Sauce
Shot Glass

Build in the glass with no ice

Texas Prairie Fire
1 part Tequila
splash Lime Juice
splash Tabasco® Sauce
Shot Glass

Build in the glass with no ice

Texas Roadkill
1 part Wild Turkey® Bourbon
1 part Vodka
1 part Gin
1 part 151-Proof Rum
splash Tabasco® Sauce
Shot Glass

Shake with ice and strain

Toby Wallbanger
1 part Melon Liqueur
1 part Banana Liqueur
1 part Tequila
1 part Gin
1 part Dark Rum
dash Bitters
splash Tabasco® Sauce
Shot Glass

Shake with ice and strain.
*Note: Because this recipe includes many ingredients, it's easier to make in volume, about 6 shots.

Triple Red
1 part Sloe Gin
1 part Amaretto
splash Tabasco® Sauce
Shot Glass

Build in the glass with no ice

Zhivago's Revenge
1 part Cinnamon Schnapps
1 part Pepper-Flavored Vodka
1 part Tabasco® Sauce
Shot Glass

Shake with ice and strain

Classic Drinks

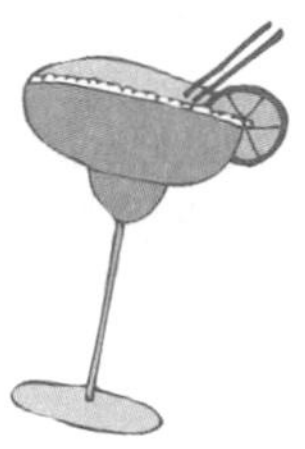

I consider classic drinks to be those that have withstood the test of time–drinks that were invented long ago but are still known today. Many of these recipes have changed over the years as components became scarce (Peychaud's® Bitters), discontinued (Crème Yvette®), or outlawed (Absinthe). Each of the recipes below can be found in a modern-day bartender's guide. What makes them unique is that they can also be found in bartender guides dating to before 1940.

Abbey Cocktail

1 1/2 parts Gin
dash Orange Bitters
1/2 part Orange Juice
1 Maraschino Cherry

Cocktail Glass

Shake all ingredients (except for the cherry) with ice and strain into a cocktail glass. Top with Maraschino Cherry.

Absinthe Cocktail

1 1/2 parts Absinthe
1 Egg White
dash Sugar

Cocktail Glass

Shake with ice and strain

Absinthe Drip

1 1/2 parts Absinthe
1 Sugar Cube
2 parts Water

Highball Glass

Fill a highball glass with crushed ice. Using a french drip spoon, (or other slotted spoon), drizzle Absinthe over the sugar cube so it disolves into the glass. Add water and stir.

Absinthe Flip

1 part Absinthe
1 part Cointreau®
2 splashes Lemon Juice
1 Egg
dash Sugar

Cocktail Glass

Shake with ice and strain

Adonis

2 parts Dry Sherry
1 part Sweet Vermouth
dash Orange Bitters

Collins Glass

Stir with ice and strain over ice

Affinity

1 1/2 parts Scotch
1 part Sweet Vermouth
1 part Dry Vermouth
2 dashes Orange Bitters

Cocktail Glass

Shake with ice and strain

Affinity #2

1 part Dry Vermouth
1 part Sweet Vermouth
1/2 part Crème de Violette
Shot Glass

Shake with ice and strain

Affinity Perfect

1 part Scotch
1/4 part Dry Vermouth
1/4 part Sweet Vermouth
Cocktail Glass

Shake with ice and strain

After Dinner Cocktail

1 1/2 parts Apricot Brandy
1 1/2 parts Blue Curaçao
2 parts Lime Juice
Old-Fashioned Glass

Shake with ice and strain over ice

After Dinner Cocktail

1 part Apricot Brandy
1 part Triple Sec
1 Lime Wedge
Cocktail Glass

Shake with ice and strain

After Dinner Cocktail #2

1 part Prunella Brandy
1 part Cherry Brandy
splash Lemon Juice
Cocktail Glass

Shake with ice and strain

After Supper Cocktail

1 part Triple Sec
1 part Apricot Brandy
splash Lemon Juice
Cocktail Glass

Shake with ice and strain

Alaska

3 parts Gin
1 part Chartreuse®
Highball Glass

Build over ice and stir

Alaska

2 dashes Orange Bitters
2 parts Gin
1 part Yellow Chartreuse®
Highball Glass

Build over ice and stir

Alaska #1

2 parts London Dry Gin
1/2 part Green Chartreuse®
1/2 part Dry Sherry
Cocktail Glass

Shake with ice and strain

Alexander

1/2 part Gin
1/2 part Crème de Cacao (White)
2 parts Light Cream
dash Ground Nutmeg
Cocktail Glass

Shake all ingredients (except Nutmeg) with ice and strain into a cocktail glass. Top with Ground Nutmeg.

Alexander Special

1 part Brandy
1 part Cream
1 part Coffee
Cocktail Glass

Shake with ice and strain

Alexander's Brother

1 part Gin
1 part Crème de Cacao (White)
1 part Cream
Cocktail Glass

Shake with ice and strain

Alfonso No. 2
1 part Dry Vermouth
1 part Sweet Vermouth
1 part Gin
1 part Mandarine Napoléon® Liqueur

Cocktail Glass

Shake with ice and strain

Alfonso Special
2 parts Grand Marnier®
1 part Dry Gin
1 part Dry Vermouth
2 splashes Sweet Vermouth
dash Angostura® Bitters

Cocktail Glass

Shake with ice and strain

Allie's Cocktail
1 part Dry Vermouth
1 part Gin
splash Kümmel

Cocktail Glass

Shake with ice and strain

Amer Picon® Cocktail
1½ part Amer Picon®
splash Grenadine
1 Lime Wedge

Cocktail Glass

Shake with ice and strain

Amer Picon® Cocktail #2
1 part Amer Picon®
1 part Sweet Vermouth

Cocktail Glass

Shake with ice and strain

Amer Picon® Cooler
1½ parts Amer Picon®
1 part Gin
½ part Cherry Heering®
splash Lemon Juice
fill with Club Soda

Highball Glass

Build over ice and stir

Amer Picon® Punch
2½ parts Amer Picon®
splash Grenadine
fill with Club Soda
1 part Brandy

Old-Fashioned Glass

Build over ice and stir. Float Brandy on top.

American Beauty
1 part Brandy
½ part Dry Vermouth
splash Crème de Menthe (White)
1 part Orange Juice
splash Grenadine
½ part Tawny Port

Cocktail Glass

Shake with ice and strain

American Beauty Special
1 part Triple Sec
1 part Cognac
1 part Rum

Cocktail Glass

Shake with ice and strain

Angel's Kiss
1 part Crème de Cacao (White)
1 part Sloe Gin
1 part Brandy
1 part Light Cream

Pousse-Café Glass

Layer in a pousse-café glass

Apparent Cocktail
2 parts Dry Gin
splash Pernod®

Cocktail Glass

Shake with ice and strain

Appetizer
2 parts Gin
1 part Orange Juice

Cocktail Glass

Shake with ice and strain

Apple Pie
1 part Light Rum
1/2 part Sweet Vermouth
splash Applejack
splash Lemon Juice
splash Grenadine
Cocktail Glass
Shake with ice and strain

Applejack
1 part Jack Daniel's®
2 parts Apple Liqueur
1 part Sour Mix
1 part Club Soda
Old-Fashioned Glass
Build over ice and stir

Astoria
2 parts Gin
1 part Campari®
1 part Vermouth
2 Olives
dash Orange Bitters
Cocktail Glass
Shake with ice and strain

Aviation
1 1/2 parts Gin
1/2 part Lemon Juice
splash Maraschino Cherry Juice
splash Brandy
Cocktail Glass
Shake with ice and strain

Aviation #2
2 parts Gin
splash Lemon Juice
4 splashes Maraschino Cherry Juice
Cocktail Glass
Shake with ice and strain

Bacardi® Cocktail
1 1/2 parts Bacardi® Light Rum
splash Grenadine
1/2 part Lime Juice
Cocktail Glass
Shake with ice and strain

Bacardi® Cocktail #2
1 part Rum
1 part Sour Mix
splash Grenadine
Cocktail Glass
Shake with ice and strain

Bachelor's Bait Cocktail
1 1/2 parts Gin
splash Grenadine
1 Egg White
dash Orange Bitters
Cocktail Glass
Shake with ice and strain

Baltimore Bracer
1 part Brandy
1 part Anisette
1 Egg White
Cocktail Glass
Shake with ice and strain

Bamboo
1 part Dry Vermouth
1 part Dry Sherry
Cocktail Glass
Shake with ice and strain

Bamboo
1 part Dry Vermouth
2 parts Dry Sherry
dash Orange Bitters
Cocktail Glass
Shake with ice and strain

Barbary Coast
1 part Scotch
1 part Gin
1 part Rum
1 part Crème de Cacao (White)
1 part Light Cream
Cocktail Glass

Shake with ice and strain

Barbary Coast #2
1 part Scotch
1 part Gin
1 part Light Rum
3/4 part Crème de Cacao (White)
Highball Glass

Shake with ice and strain

Beauty Spot
1 part Dry Gin
1 part Dry Vermouth
1 part Orange Juice
1 part Sweet Vermouth
1 part Grenadine
Cocktail Glass

Shake with ice and strain

Beauty Spot Cocktail
splash Grenadine
1 part Gin
1/2 part Sweet Vermouth
1/2 part Dry Vermouth
splash Orange Juice
Cocktail Glass

Pour a splash of Grenadine in a cocktail glass. Shake remaining ingredients with ice and strain into glass.

Belmont Cocktail
2 parts Gin
splash Raspberry Syrup
3/4 part Light Cream
Cocktail Glass

Shake with ice and strain

Belmont Cocktail #2
2 parts Gin
3/4 part Cream
1/2 part Grenadine
Cocktail Glass

Shake with ice and strain

Bennett Cocktail
1 1/2 parts Gin
1/2 Lime
dash Powdered Sugar
2 dashes Orange Bitters
Cocktail Glass

Shake with ice and strain

Bermuda Rose
1 1/4 parts Gin
splash Apricot Brandy
splash Grenadine
Cocktail Glass

Shake with ice and strain

Between the Sheets
1 part Brandy
1 part Light Rum
1 part Triple Sec
1 part Lemon Juice
Cocktail Glass

Shake with ice and strain

Between the Sheets #2
1 part Cognac
1 part Crème de Cacao (Dark)
1 part Cream
dash Angostura® Bitters
dash Sugar
Cocktail Glass

Shake with ice and strain

Between the Sheets #3
1 part Brandy
1 part Triple Sec
1 part Rum
Cocktail Glass

Shake with ice and strain

Black Eye
$1^1/_2$ parts Vodka
$^1/_2$ part Blackberry Brandy
Cocktail Glass
Shake with ice and strain

Black Hawk
1 part Whiskey
1 part Sloe Gin
Cocktail Glass
Shake with ice and strain

Black Hawk Collins
1 part Whiskey
$^1/_2$ part Crème de Cassis
2 parts Sour mix
Collins Glass
Shake with ice and strain over ice

Block and Fall
1 part Cognac
1 part Cointreau®
1 part Apple Brandy
$^1/_2$ part Pernod®
Cocktail Glass
Shake with ice and strain

Blood and Sand
1 part Scotch
1 part Orange Juice
1 part Cherry Brandy
1 part Sweet Vermouth
Cocktail Glass
Shake with ice and strain

Bloodhound
2 parts Gin
1 part Dry Vermouth
1 part Sweet Vermouth
Cocktail Glass
Shake with ice and strain

Blue Devil
1 part Vodka
1 part Blue Curaçao
fill with Sweet & Sour Mix
splash Cherry Juice
Highball Glass
Build over ice and stir

Blue Devil #2
$1^1/_4$ parts Gin
$^1/_2$ part Blue Curaçao
$^1/_2$ part Sour mix
Cocktail Glass
Combine all ingredients in a blender with ice. Blend until smooth.

Blue Moon
1 part Rum
1 part Blue Curaçao
fill with Pineapple Juice
Highball Glass
Shake with ice and pour

Blue Moon Cocktail
$1^1/_2$ parts Citrus-Flavored Vodka
1 part Vanilla-Flavored Vodka
1 part Blue Curaçao
Cocktail Glass
Shake with ice and strain

Bobby Burns
1 part Scotch
1 part Dry Vermouth
1 part Sweet Vermouth
splash Benedictine®
Cocktail Glass
Shake with ice and strain

Bohemian Martini
1 part Anisette
1 part Vodka
Cocktail Glass
Shake with ice and strain

Bolero
2 parts Light Rum
1 part Apple Brandy
splash Sweet Vermouth

Cocktail Glass

Shake with ice and strain

Bolero #2
1 part Dark Rum
1/2 part Apple Brandy
2 splashes Sweet Vermouth

Cocktail Glass

Shake with ice and strain

Bombay
1 part Brandy
1/2 part Dry Vermouth
1/2 part Sweet Vermouth
1/2 part Triple Sec
splash Pernod®

Old-Fashioned Glass

Build over ice and stir

Booster
2 parts Brandy
1/2 part Blue Curaçao
1 Egg White

Cocktail Glass

Shake with ice and strain

Boston Cocktail
1 part Gin
1 part Apricot Brandy
splash Grenadine
splash Lemon Juice

Cocktail Glass

Shake with ice and strain

Boston Cooler
2 parts Rum
1/2 part Lemon Juice
dash Sugar
fill with Club Soda

Collins Glass

Shake all but club soda with ice and strain into the glass. Top with club soda.

Boxcar
1 1/2 parts Gin
1 part Triple Sec
splash Lemon Juice
splash Grenadine
1 Egg White

Whiskey Sour Glass

Shake with ice and strain

Brainstorm
2 parts Scotch
1/2 part Benedictine®
splash Sweet Vermouth

Cocktail Glass

Shake with ice and strain

Brainstorm Cocktail
2 parts Whiskey
splash Dry Vermouth

Cocktail Glass

Shake with ice and strain

Brandy Fizz
2 parts Brandy
dash Powdered Sugar
1/2 part Lemon Juice
fill with Club Soda

Highball Glass

Shake all but Club Soda with ice and strain into the glass. Top with Club Soda.

Brandy Flip
1 1/2 parts Brandy
dash Powdered Sugar
1 Whole Egg
2 splashes Light Cream
dash Ground Nutmeg

Whiskey Sour Glass

Shake all but Nutmeg with ice and strain into the glass. Top with Ground Nutmeg.

Brandy Gump
1 part Brandy
1 part Lemon Juice
splash Grenadine

Cocktail Glass

Shake with ice and strain

Brandy Rickey
1 1/2 parts Brandy
splash Lime Juice
fill with Club Soda

Highball Glass

Shake all but Club Soda with ice and strain into the glass. Top with Club Soda.

Brandy Stinger
1 1/2 parts Brandy
1/2 part Crème de Menthe (White)

Cocktail Glass

Shake with ice and strain

Brazil
1 part Dry Vermouth
1 part Dry Sherry
splash Absinthe

Cocktail Glass

Shake with ice and strain

Brazil #2
1 part Dry Sherry
1 part Dry Vermouth
splash Anisette
dash Bitters

Cocktail Glass

Shake with ice and strain

Broken Spur
1 part Gin
1 1/2 parts Port
1 part Sweet Vermouth
fill with Club Soda

Old-Fashioned Glass

Shake all but Club Soda with ice and strain into the glass. Top with Club Soda.

Broken Spur #2
1 part Sweet Vermouth
2 parts Port
splash Triple Sec

Cocktail Glass

Shake with ice and strain

Bronx
1 part Gin
1/2 part Dry Vermouth
1/2 part Sweet Vermouth
1 part Orange Juice

Cocktail Glass

Shake with ice and strain

Bronx #2
1 part Gin
1 part Sweet Vermouth
1 part Orange Juice
1/2 Lime

Cocktail Glass

Shake with ice and strain

Brown Cocktail
1 part Light Rum
1 part Gin
1 part Dry Vermouth

Cocktail Glass

Shake with ice and strain

Bulldog Cocktail
1 1/2 parts Cherry Brandy
1 part Gin
1/2 part Lime Juice

Cocktail Glass

Shake with ice and strain

Bulldog Highball
2 parts Gin
1/2 part Orange Juice
fill with Ginger Ale

Highball Glass

Build over ice and stir

Button Hook
1 part Crème de Menthe (White)
1 part Brandy
1 part Apricot Brandy
Cocktail Glass
Shake with ice and strain

Button Hook Cocktail
1 part Brandy
1 part Apricot Brandy
1 part Anisette
1 part Crème de Menthe (White)
Cocktail Glass
Shake with ice and strain

Cabaret
$1^1/_2$ parts Gin
splash Dry Vermouth
splash Benedictine®
2 dashes Bitters
Cocktail Glass
Stir gently with ice and strain. Top with a Cherry.

Café de Paris
2 parts Gin
$^1/_2$ part Anisette
1 Egg White
1 part Heavy Cream
Whiskey Sour Glass
Shake with ice and strain over ice

Cameron's Kick Cocktail
1 part Scotch
1 part Irish Whiskey
splash Lemon Juice
2 dashes Orange Bitters
Cocktail Glass
Shake with ice and strain

Canadian Cocktail
$1^1/_2$ parts Canadian Whiskey
$^1/_2$ part Triple Sec
dash Bitters
dash Powdered Sugar
Cocktail Glass
Shake with ice and strain

Caruso
$1^1/_2$ parts Gin
1 part Dry Vermouth
$^1/_2$ part Crème de Menthe (Green)
Cocktail Glass
Build over ice and stir

Caruso Blanco
$1^1/_2$ parts Gin
1 part Dry Vermouth
1 part Crème de Menthe (White)
Cocktail Glass
Build over ice and stir

Casino
$1^1/_2$ parts Dry Gin
1 part Maraschino Liqueur
dash Orange Bitters
Cocktail Glass
Shake with ice and strain

Casino #2
2 parts Gin
splash Maraschino Cherry Juice
splash Lemon Juice
2 dashes Orange Bitters
Cocktail Glass
Shake with ice and strain

Castle Dip Cocktail
1 part Crème de Menthe (White)
1 part Apple Brandy
Cocktail Glass
Shake with ice and strain

Catastrophe

1 part Goldschläger®
splash Strawberry Liqueur
splash Cranberry-Flavored Vodka
Highball Glass

Build over ice and stir

Champagne Cocktail

1 Sugar Cube
2 dashes Bitters
fill with Champagne
Champagne Flute

Soak the sugar cube with bitters. Place the cube in the bottom of a Champagne Flute. Fill with Champagne.

Chelsea Sidecar

1 1/2 parts Gin
1/2 part Triple Sec
2 splashes Lemon Juice
Cocktail Glass

Shake with ice and strain

Cherry Blossom

1 1/2 parts Brandy
1/2 part Cherry Brandy
2 splashes Lemon Juice
splash Grenadine
splash Triple Sec
1 Maraschino Cherry
Cocktail Glass

Shake with ice and strain into the glass. Top with Maraschino Cherry.

Cherry Blossom #2

1 part Cognac
1/2 part Kirschwasser
splash Triple Sec
splash Grenadine
Champagne Flute

Shake with ice and strain

Classic Cocktail

2 parts Brandy
1/2 part Triple Sec
1/2 part Maraschino Liqueur
Cocktail Glass

Shake with ice and pour

Clover Club

1 part Gin
4 splashes Grenadine
2 parts Lemon Juice
1 Egg White
Highball Glass

Shake with ice and strain

Club Cocktail

2 parts Gin
1 part Sweet Vermouth
Cocktail Glass

Shake with ice and strain

Cold Duck

2 parts Brandy
1 part Peppermint Schnapps
1 part Sweet Vermouth
Cocktail Glass

Shake with ice and strain

Colonial Cocktail

1 1/2 parts Gin
1/2 part Grapefruit Juice
1 splash Maraschino Liqueur
Cocktail Glass

Shake with ice and strain

Commodore

1 1/2 parts Bourbon
1/2 part Simple Syrup
Cocktail Glass

Shake with ice and strain

Commodore
$1^1/_2$ parts Whiskey
$^1/_4$ part Lemon Juice
dash Powdered Sugar
2 dashes Orange Bitters
Cocktail Glass
Shake with ice and strain

Cornell Cocktail
$1^1/_2$ parts Gin
splash Lemon Juice
splash Cherry Juice
1 Egg White
Cocktail Glass
Shake with ice and strain

Coronation Cocktail
1 part Gin
1 part Dry Vermouth
1 part Dubonnet® Blonde
Cocktail Glass
Shake with ice and strain

Coronation Cocktail #2
1 part Dry Vermouth
1 part Sherry
splash Maraschino Liqueur
Cocktail Glass
Shake with ice and strain

Coronation Cocktail #3
2 parts Brandy
splash Triple Sec
splash Crème de Menthe (White)
Cocktail Glass
Shake with ice and strain

Corpse Reviver
2 parts Cognac
1 part Calvados Apple Brandy
1 part Sweet Vermouth
Cocktail Glass
Shake with ice and strain

Cowboy Cocktail
$1^1/_2$ parts Whiskey
splash Light Cream
Cocktail Glass
Shake with ice and strain

Creole Cocktail
1 part Coconut-Flavored Rum
$^3/_4$ part Vodka
1 part Orange Juice
splash Grenadine
Cocktail Glass
Shake with ice and strain

Crystal Slipper Cocktail
$1^1/_2$ parts Gin
$^1/_2$ part Blue Curaçao
2 dashes Orange Bitters
Cocktail Glass
Shake with ice and strain

Cuban
1 part Cognac
1 part Apricot Brandy
Cocktail Glass
Shake with ice and strain

Cupid
2 parts Gin
1 part Dry Vermouth
1 part Sweet Vermouth
Cocktail Glass
Shake with ice and strain

Damn the Weather
1 part Gin
$^1/_2$ part Orange Juice
$^1/_4$ part Triple Sec
$^1/_2$ part Sweet Vermouth
Highball Glass
Shake with ice and pour

Deauville Cocktail
1 part Apple Brandy
1 part Brandy
1 part Triple Sec
1/2 part Lemon Juice
Cocktail Glass
Shake with ice and strain

Delmonico
1 part Dry Vermouth
1 part Sweet Vermouth
1 part Brandy
1/2 part Gin
Cocktail Glass
Shake with ice and strain

Dempsey Cocktail
1 part Apple Brandy
1 part Gin
splash Anisette
splash Grenadine
Cocktail Glass
Shake with ice and strain

Depth Bomb
1 part Apple Brandy
1 part Brandy
splash Lemon Juice
splash Grenadine
Old-Fashioned Glass
Shake with ice and pour

Devil's Cocktail
1 part Brandy
1 part Dry Vermouth
3 splashes Blue Curaçao
2 dashes Bitters
Cocktail Glass
Shake with ice and strain

Devil's Cocktail #2
2 parts Port
1 part Dry Vermouth
Cocktail Glass
Shake with ice and strain

Diana
1 part Brandy
3 parts Crème de Menthe (White)
Highball Glass
Build over ice and stir

Diana #2
2 parts Peppermint Schnapps
3 splashes Cognac
White Wine Glass
Build over ice and stir

Diana #3
2 parts Crème de Cacao (White)
1 part Brandy
Cocktail Glass
Build over ice and stir

Dixie Cocktail
1/2 part Dry Vermouth
1 part Gin
1/2 part Orange Juice
2 splashes Anisette
Cocktail Glass
Shake with ice and strain

Dixie Whiskey
2 parts Bourbon
1/2 part Crème de Menthe (White)
splash Triple Sec
dash Powdered Sugar
Cocktail Glass
Shake with ice and strain

Dolores
1 part Brandy
1 part Cherry Brandy
1 part Crème de Cacao (White)
Cocktail Glass
Shake with ice and strain

Dream Cocktail
2 parts Brandy
1 part Triple Sec
splash Anisette

Cocktail Glass

Shake with ice and strain

Dubarry Cocktail
2 parts Gin
1 part Dry Vermouth
splash Anisette
dash Bitters

Cocktail Glass

Shake with ice and strain

Dubonnet® Cocktail
2 parts Dubonnet® Blonde
1 part Gin
dash Bitters
1 Lemon Twist

Cocktail Glass

Shake with ice and strain

Earthquake
1 part Vodka
1 part Amaretto
1 part Southern Comfort®
1/2 part Sweetened Lime Juice

Cocktail Glass

Shake with ice and strain

Earthquake #2
1 part Gin
1 part Whiskey
1 part Pernod®

Cocktail Glass

Shake with ice and strain

Eclipse
1 part Gin
1 1/2 parts Sloe Gin
1/2 part Grenadine

Old-Fashioned Glass

Shake with ice and strain over ice

Eclipse #2
1 part Vodka
splash Crème de Cacao (White)
splash Strawberry Liqueur
1 part Cream

Highball Glass

Shake with ice and strain over ice

Elk Cocktail
1 part Port
1 part Whiskey
1 Egg White
dash Powdered Sugar

White Wine Glass

Shake with ice and strain

Emerald Isle
1 part Vodka
2 parts Melon Liqueur
fill with Mountain Dew®

Highball Glass

Build over ice and stir

English Rose
2 parts Dry Gin
1 part Dry Vermouth
1 part Apricot Brandy
splash Grenadine

Cocktail Glass

Shake with ice and strain

Ethel Cocktail
1 part Crème de Menthe (White)
1 part Triple Sec
1 part Apricot Brandy

Cocktail Glass

Shake with ice and strain

Ethel Duffy Cocktail
1 part Crème de Menthe (White)
1 part Apricot Brandy
1 part Triple Sec

Cocktail Glass

Shake with ice and strain

Eye Opener
1 Egg Yolk
1 part Light Rum
1/2 part Crème de Cacao (White)
1/2 part Triple Sec
1/2 part Sambuca
Cocktail Glass
Shake with ice and strain

Fair and Warmer Cocktail
2 parts Light Rum
1 part Sweet Vermouth
splash Triple Sec
Cocktail Glass
Shake with ice and strain

Fallen Angel
1 1/2 parts Gin
1/2 part Lemon Juice
splash Crème de Menthe (White)
dash Bitters
Cocktail Glass
Shake with ice and strain

Fallen Angel Cocktail
1 1/2 parts Gin
1 part Lemon Juice
1/2 part Lime Juice
dash Angostura® Bitters
2 splashes Crème de Menthe (White)
Highball Glass
Shake with ice and strain over ice

Fancy Bourbon
1 part Triple Sec
dash Sugar
2 dashes Bitters
1 Lemon Twist
Cocktail Glass
Shake with ice and strain

Fancy Brandy
2 parts Brandy
splash Triple Sec
dash Powdered Sugar
dash Bitters
1 Lemon Twist
Cocktail Glass
Shake with ice and strain

Fancy Brandy #2
2 parts Brandy
1/2 part Triple Sec
1/2 part Powdered Sugar
Cocktail Glass
Shake with ice and strain

Fancy Gin
2 parts Gin
splash Triple Sec
splash Powdered Sugar
dash Bitters
1 Lemon Twist
Cocktail Glass
Shake with ice and strain

Fancy Scotch
2 parts Scotch
splash Triple Sec
dash Sugar
2 dashes Bitters
1 Lemon Twist
Cocktail Glass
Shake with ice and strain

Fancy Whiskey
2 parts Whiskey
splash Triple Sec
dash Powdered Sugar
dash Bitters
1 Lemon Twist
Cocktail Glass
Shake with ice and strain

Farmer's Martini

3 parts Gin
1/2 part Dry Vermouth
1/2 part Sweet Vermouth
dash Bitters

Cocktail Glass

Shake with ice and strain

Fine and Dandy

2 parts Gin
1 part Triple Sec
1 part Lemon Juice
dash Angostura® Bitters

Coupette Glass

Combine all ingredients in a blender with ice. Blend until smooth.

Five Fifteeen Cocktail

1 part Dry Vermouth
1 part Triple Sec
1 part Cream

Cocktail Glass

Shake with ice and strain

Flamingo Cocktail

1/2 part Apricot Brandy
1 1/2 parts Gin
1/2 part Lime Juice
splash Grenadine

Cocktail Glass

Shake with ice and strain

Flying Scotsman

1 part Scotch
1 part Sweet Vermouth
splash Simple Syrup
dash Angostura® Bitters

Highball Glass

Shake with ice and strain over ice

Fox River Cocktail

1 1/2 parts Rye Whiskey
1/2 part Crème de Cacao (Dark)
2 dashes Orange Bitters

Highball Glass

Shake with ice and strain over ice

Frackenjack Cocktail

1 part Gin
1/2 part Triple Sec
1/2 part Apricot Brandy
1/2 part Sweet Vermouth

Cocktail Glass

Shake with ice and strain

French Rose

2 parts Gin
1/2 part Cherry Liqueur

Cocktail Glass

Shake with ice and strain

Froth Blower

1 Egg White
1 1/2 parts Gin
splash Grenadine

Highball Glass

Shake with ice and strain

Gilroy Cocktail

3/4 part Cherry Brandy
3/4 part Gin
1/2 part Dry Vermouth
1/4 part Lemon Juice
dash Orange Bitters

Cocktail Glass

Shake with ice and strain

Gin & Tonic

1 1/2 parts Gin
fill with Tonic Water

Highball Glass

Build over ice and stir

Gin Alexander
1 part Gin
1 part Crème de Cacao (White)
1 part Cream
Highball Glass

Build over ice and stir

Gin Buck
$1^1/_2$ parts Gin
$^1/_2$ part Lemon Juice
fill with Ginger Ale
Old-Fashioned Glass

Build over ice and stir

Gin Fix
$2^1/_2$ parts Gin
dash Powdered Sugar
$^1/_2$ part Lemon Juice
1 Lemon Slice
splash Water
Highball Glass

Shake with ice and strain over ice

Gin Fizz
2 parts Gin
$^1/_2$ part Lemon Juice
dash Powdered Sugar
fill with Carbonated Water
Highball Glass

Build over ice and stir

Gin Rickey
$1^1/_2$ parts Gin
$^1/_2$ part Lime Juice
fill with Carbonated Water
1 Lime Wedge
Highball Glass

Build over ice and stir

Gin Sidecar
$1^1/_2$ parts Dry Gin
1 part Triple Sec
Cocktail Glass

Shake with ice and strain

Gin Sling
2 parts Gin
$^1/_2$ part Lemon Juice
dash Powdered Sugar
splash Water
1 Orange Twist
Old-Fashioned Glass

Shake with ice and strain over ice

Gin Stinger
2 parts Vodka
1 part Crème de Cacao (White)
1 part Crème de Menthe (Green)
Cocktail Glass

Shake with ice and strain

Gin Swizzle
2 parts Gin
$^1/_2$ part Lime Juice
dash Powdered Sugar
2 dashes Bitters
fill with Carbonated Water
Collins Glass

Build over ice and stir

Gin Toddy
2 parts Gin
2 splashes Water
dash Powdered Sugar
1 Lemon Twist
Old-Fashioned Glass

Build over ice and stir

Golden Dawn
1 part Apple Brandy
$^1/_2$ part Apricot Brandy
$^1/_2$ part Gin
1 part Orange Juice
splash Grenadine
Old-Fashioned Glass

Build over ice and stir

Golden Gate
1 part Brandy
1 part Triple Sec
1 part Light Rum
Cocktail Glass

Shake with ice and strain

Good Times
1 part Canadian Whiseky
1 part Dry Vermouth
splash Lemon Juice
Cocktail Glass

Shake with ice and strain

Grapefruit Cocktail
1 part Gin
1 part Grapefruit Juice
splash Maraschino Cherry Juice
Cocktail Glass

Shake with ice and strain

Green Dragon
1 parts Pernod®
1 parts Milk
1 parts Heavy Cream
1/2 part Simple Syrup
White Wine Glass

Shake with ice and strain

Green Dragon #2
1 1/2 parts Gin
1 part Crème de Menthe (Green)
Cocktail Glass

Shake with ice and strain

Green Dragon #3
2 parts Gin
1/2 part Crème de Menthe (White)
1 part Jägermeister®
Cocktail Glass

Shake with ice and strain

Green Room
1 1/2 parts Dry Vermouth
1/2 part Brandy
splash Triple Sec
Cocktail Glass

Shake with ice and strain

Grenadine Cocktail
1 part Grenadine
1 part Orange Juice
1 part Pineapple Juice
Highball Glass

Shake with ice and pour

Guard's Room
2 parts Dry Gin
1 part Dry Vermouth
splash Triple Sec
Cocktail Glass

Shake with ice and strain

Gypsy Martini
3 parts Gin
3/4 part Sweet Vermouth
Cocktail Glass

Shake with ice and strain

Harlem
2 parts Dry Gin
1 part Pineapple Juice
splash Maraschino Liqueur
Cocktail Glass

Shake with ice and strain

Harry Lauder
3/4 part Sweet Vermouth
3/4 part Scotch
1/2 part Simple Syrup
Cocktail Glass

Shake with ice and strain

Harvard Cocktail
2 parts Brandy
1 part Sweet Vermouth
splash Grenadine
2 splashes Lemon Juice
dash Bitters
Cocktail Glass

Shake with ice and strain

Havana
1 part Vodka
1 part Banana Juice
1 part Wild Berry–Flavored Schnapps
2 parts Lemonade
1 part Orange Juice
Highball Glass

Build over ice and stir

Havana Club
1 1/2 parts Light Rum
1/2 part Dry Vermouth
Cocktail Glass

Shake with ice and strain

Havana Cocktail
1 part Light Rum
2 parts Pineapple Juice
splash Lemon Juice
Cocktail Glass

Shake with ice and strain

Havana Martini
1 1/2 parts Light Rum
1/2 part Lime Cordial
1/4 part Sugar
Cocktail Glass

Shake with ice and strain

Hawaiian Cocktail
2 parts Gin
1/2 part Triple Sec
2 splashes Pineapple Juice
Cocktail Glass

Shake with ice and strain

Hoffman House
1 1/2 parts Gin
1/2 part Dry Vermouth
2 dashes Orange Bitters
Cocktail Glass

Shake with ice and strain

Holland House Cocktail
2 parts Dry Gin
1 part Dry Vermouth
splash Maraschino Liqueur
splash Pineapple Juice
Cocktail Glass

Shake with ice and strain

Honeymoon Cocktail
3/4 part Apple Brandy
3/4 part Benedictine®
splash Triple Sec
1/2 part Lemon Juice
Cocktail Glass

Shake with ice and strain

Honolulu Cocktail
1 1/2 parts Gin
splash Orange Juice
splash Pineapple Juice
splash Lemon Juice
dash Sugar
Cocktail Glass

Shake with ice and strain

Honolulu Cocktail #2
1 part Gin
1 part Maraschino Liqueur
1 part Benedictine®
Cocktail Glass

Shake with ice and strain

Hurricane Cocktail
1 1/4 parts Brandy
3/4 part Pernod®
3/4 part Vodka
Cocktail Glass

Shake with ice and strain

Imperial
1 part Dry Gin
1 part Dry Vermouth
1/2 part Maraschino Liqueur
dash Bitters
Cocktail Glass

Shake with ice and strain

Income Tax Cocktail
1 part Gin
2 splashes Sweet Vermouth
2 splashes Dry Vermouth
1/2 part Orange Juice
dash Bitters
Cocktail Glass

Shake with ice and strain

Jack Rose
1 1/2 part Apple Brandy
1/2 part Grenadine
3/4 part Sour Mix
Highball Glass

Shake with ice and strain over ice

Jack Rose Cocktail
1 1/2 parts Apple Brandy
splash Grenadine
1/2 part Lime Juice
Cocktail Glass

Shake with ice and strain

Jewel Cocktail
1 part Gin
1 part Sweet Vermouth
1 part Green Chartreuse®
dash Orange Bitters
Cocktail Glass

Shake with ice and strain

Jockey Club
1 1/2 parts Gin
1/2 part Lemon Juice
splash Crème de Cacao (White)
dash Angostura® Bitters
Cocktail Glass

Shake with ice and strain

Journalist
2 parts Gin
1 part Dry Vermouth
1 part Sweet Vermouth
1 part Triple Sec
splash Lemon Juice
dash Bitters
Cocktail Glass

Shake with ice and strain

Kentucky Colonel
1 1/2 parts Bourbon
1/2 part Benedictine®
1 Lemon Twist
Cocktail Glass

Shake with ice and strain

Kiss in the Dark
1 part Gin
1 part Cherry Brandy
1 part Vermouth
Cocktail Glass

Shake with ice and strain

Knickerbocker Cocktail
2 parts Dry Gin
1 part Dry Vermouth
splash Sweet Vermouth
Cocktail Glass

Shake with ice and strain

Classic Drinks

Knickerbocker Special
2 parts Light Rum
splash Triple Sec
splash Orange Juice
splash Lemon Juice
splash Raspberry Syrup
1 Pineapple Slice
Cocktail Glass
Shake with ice and strain

Knockout Cocktail
1 part Gin
1 part Dry Vermouth
1/2 part Crème de Menthe (White)
1/2 part Pastis
Cocktail Glass
Shake with ice and strain

Kretchma Cocktail
1 part Vodka
1 part Crème de Cacao (White)
splash Grenadine
1/2 part Lemon Juice
Cocktail Glass
Shake with ice and strain

Ladies Cocktail
1 1/2 parts Whiskey
splash Anisette
dash Bitters
Cocktail Glass
Shake with ice and strain

Leap Year
1 1/2 parts Gin
1/2 part Grand Marnier®
splash Lemon Juice
1/2 part Sweet Vermouth
Cocktail Glass
Shake with ice and strain

Leave It to Me
1 part Gin
1/2 part Dry Vermouth
1/2 part Apricot Brandy
splash Grenadine
splash Lemon Juice
Cocktail Glass
Shake with ice and strain

Liberal
1 part Whiskey
1 part Sweet Vermouth
3 splashes Amer Picon®
2 dashes Bitters
Old-Fashioned Glass
Shake with ice and strain over ice

Liberty Cocktail
1 1/2 parts Apple Brandy
1/4 part Light Rum
splash Simple Syrup
Cocktail Glass
Shake with ice and strain

Little Devil Cocktail
1 part Light Rum
2 splashes Triple Sec
1 part Gin
1/4 part Lemon Juice
Cocktail Glass
Shake with ice and strain

London Martini
3 parts Gin
dash Powdered Sugar
1/4 part Maraschino Liqueur
Cocktail Glass
Shake with ice and strain

Lone Tree Cocktail
1 part Dry Gin
1 part Dry Vermouth
1 part Sweet Vermouth
Cocktail Glass
Shake with ice and strain

Los Angeles Cocktail
$1^1/_2$ part Whiskey
$^1/_4$ part Sweet Vermouth
$^1/_2$ part Lemon Juice
dash Powdered Sugar
1 Egg
Whiskey Sour Glass

Shake with ice and strain

Mabel Moon
1 part Melon Liqueur
$^1/_2$ part Maraschino Liqueur
$^1/_2$ part Orange Juice
1 part Sour mix
Cocktail Glass

Shake with ice and strain

Magnolia Blossom
1 part Gin
$^1/_2$ part Lemon Juice
$1^1/_2$ parts Cream
2 splashes Grenadine
Highball Glass

Shake with ice and strain over ice

Maiden's Blush
$1^1/_2$ parts Gin
$^1/_2$ part Triple Sec
splash Cherry Brandy
1 part Lemon Juice
splash Maraschino Cherry Juice
Cocktail Glass

Shake with ice and strain

Maiden's Prayer
$1^1/_2$ parts Gin
1 part Lemon Juice
$^1/_2$ part Triple Sec
Cocktail Glass

Shake with ice and strain

Manhattan
2 parts Whiskey
1 part Sweet Vermouth
dash Bitters
1 Maraschino Cherry
Cocktail Glass

Shake with ice and strain

Marconi
$1^1/_2$ parts Gin
1 part Dry Vermouth
dash Bitters
Cocktail Glass

Shake with ice and strain

Marconi Wireless
$1^1/_2$ parts Apple Brandy
$^1/_2$ part Sweet Vermouth
2 dashes Orange Bitters
Cocktail Glass

Shake with ice and strain

Merry Widow
1 part Gin
1 part Dubonnet® Blonde
Cocktail Glass

Shake with ice and strain

Miami
$1^1/_2$ parts Light Rum
$^1/_2$ part Crème de Menthe (White)
splash Lemon Juice
Cocktail Glass

Shake with ice and strain

Miami Cocktail
$1^1/_2$ parts Rum
$^1/_2$ part Crème de Menthe (White)
splash Lime Juice
Cocktail Glass

Shake with ice and strain

Miami Cocktail #2
2 parts Rum
3/4 part Cointreau®
4 splashes Lemon Juice

Cocktail Glass

Shake with ice and strain

Millionaire
3 splashes Blue Curaçao
1/2 Egg White
splash Grenadine
1/2 part Pernod®

Cocktail Glass

Shake with ice and strain

Minnehaha Cocktail
1 part Dry Gin
1 part Orange Juice
1 part Sweet Vermouth

Cocktail Glass

Shake with ice and strain

Modern Cocktail
1 1/2 parts Scotch
splash Dark Rum
splash Anisette
splash Lemon Juice
dash Orange Bitters

Cocktail Glass

Shake with ice and strain

Monte Cristo Cocktail
1 part Cointreau®
1 part Lemon-Flavored Vodka

Old-Fashioned Glass

Shake with ice and strain over ice

Morning
1 part Brandy
1 part Dry Vermouth
2 dashes Orange Bitters
splash Blue Curaçao
splash Cherry Liqueur
splash Pernod®

Highball Glass

Shake with ice and strain over ice

Morning After
1 part Crème de Cacao (White)
1 part Dark Rum
1/2 part Coffee Liqueur
1/2 part Cream

Coupette Glass

Shake with ice and strain

Moulin Rouge
2 parts Sloe Gin
1 part Sweet Vermouth
dash Bitters

Cocktail Glass

Shake with ice and strain

Mountain Cocktail
1 1/2 parts Whiskey
splash Dry Vermouth
splash Sweet Vermouth
splash Lemon Juice
1 Egg White

Cocktail Glass

Shake with ice and strain

Nevada Cocktail
1 1/2 parts Light Rum
1 part Grapefruit Juice
1/2 part Lime Juice
3 dashes Powdered Sugar
dash Bitters

Cocktail Glass

Shake with ice and strain

New York Cocktail
$1^1/_2$ parts Whiskey
splash Grenadine
$^1/_2$ part Lemon Juice
dash Powdered Sugar

Cocktail Glass

Shake with ice and strain

Nightcap Cocktail
1 part Brandy
1 part Triple Sec
1 part Amer Picon®
1 Egg Yolk

Cocktail Glass

Shake with ice and strain

Oasis
1 part Melon liqueur
1 part Coconut Flavored Rum
$^1/_2$ part Pisang Ambon® Liqueur
2 parts Lemon Juice
splash Cream

Highball Glass

Shake with ice and strain over ice

Old Fashioned
2 parts Rye Whiskey
2 dashes Angostura® Bitters
dash Sugar
splash Water
1 Maraschino Cherry
1 Lemon Twist
1 Orange Slice

Old-Fashioned Glass

Build over ice and stir

Old Pal Cocktail
$1^1/_4$ parts Whiskey
$^1/_2$ part Sweet Vermouth
$^1/_2$ part Grenadine

Cocktail Glass

Shake with ice and strain

Opera
$1^1/_2$ parts Gin
$^1/_2$ part Cherry Liqueur
$^1/_2$ part Dubonnet® Blonde

Cocktail Glass

Shake with ice and strain

Orange Blossom
2 parts Gin
1 part Orange Juice
dash Sugar

Cocktail Glass

Shake with ice and strain

Orange Blossom #2
$1^1/_2$ parts Gin
$^1/_2$ part Orange Juice
2 splashes Blue Curaçao
2 splashes Lemon Juice
splash Orange Flower Water
splash Simple Syrup

Old-Fashioned Glass

Shake with ice and strain over ice

Oriental
1 part Rye Whiskey
$^1/_4$ part Cointreau®
$^1/_4$ part Sweet Vermouth
$^1/_2$ part Lime Juice

Cocktail Glass

Shake with ice and strain

Pall Mall
$1^1/_2$ parts Gin
$^1/_2$ part Dry Vermouth
$^1/_2$ part Sweet Vermouth
$^1/_2$ part Crème de Menthe (White)

Old-Fashioned Glass

Shake with ice and strain over ice

Pall Mall Martini
2 parts Vodka
$1/2$ part Crème de Menthe (White)
$1/2$ part Dry Vermouth
$1/2$ part Sweet Vermouth
Cocktail Glass
Shake with ice and strain

Palm Beach Cocktail
2 parts Gin
splash Sweet Vermouth
2 splashes Grapefruit Juice
Cocktail Glass
Shake with ice and strain

Pan American
1 part Rye Whiskey
$1/2$ part Simple Syrup
Old-Fashioned Glass
Shake with ice and strain over ice

Panama
1 part Crème de Cacao (White)
1 part Heavy Cream
Cocktail Glass
Shake with ice and strain

Paradise
1 part Apricot Brandy
$3/4$ part Gin
$3/4$ part Orange Juice
Highball Glass
Shake with ice and pour

Parisian Blonde
1 part Jamaican Rum
1 part Triple Sec
$1/2$ part Light Cream
Cocktail Glass
Shake with ice and strain

Peter Pan Cocktail
1 part Dry Vermouth
1 part Gin
1 part Orange Juice
2 dashes Bitters
Cocktail Glass
Shake with ice and strain

Pick Me Up
1 part Sweet Vermouth
1 part Cherry Brandy
$1/4$ part Gin
Highball Glass
Shake with ice and strain over ice

Pierre Special
1 part Vodka
1 part Coconut-Flavored Rum
$1/2$ part Passion Fruit Liqueur
$1/2$ part Lime Cordial
Old-Fashioned Glass
Shake with ice and strain

Ping Pong
1 part Melon Liqueur
$1\,1/2$ parts White Wine
fill with Lemon-Lime Soda
Highball Glass
Build over ice and stir

Pink Elephant
1 part Vodka
1 part Galliano®
1 part Crème de Noyaux
1 part Orange Juice
1 part Cream
splash Grenadine
Champagne Flute
Shake with ice and strain

Pink Lady
$1^1/_2$ parts Gin
splash Grenadine
splash Light Cream
1 Egg White
Cocktail Glass

Shake with ice and strain

Pink Whiskers
1 part Apricot Brandy
1 part Port
$^1/_2$ part Dry Vermouth
splash Crème de Menthe (White)
splash Grenadine
fill with Orange Juice
Highball Glass

Shake with ice and strain over ice

Planter's Cocktail
$1^1/_2$ parts Rum
dash Powdered Sugar
$^1/_4$ part Lemon Juice
Cocktail Glass

Shake with ice and strain

Plaza
1 part Gin
2 splashes Pineapple Juice
1 part Dry Vermouth
1 part Sweet Vermouth
Cocktail Glass

Shake with ice and strain

Poker Cocktail
1 part Light Rum
1 part Sweet Vermouth
Cocktail Glass

Shake with ice and strain

Pollyanna
$1^1/_2$ parts Gin
2 splashes Sweet Vermouth
2 splashes Grenadine
Highball Glass

Shake with ice and strain over ice

Polo
$1^1/_2$ parts Gin
2 splashes Grapefruit Juice
2 splashes Orange Juice
Highball Glass

Shake with ice and strain over ice

Polo #2
1 part Gin
$^1/_2$ part Lemon Juice
$^1/_2$ part Orange Juice
Cocktail Glass

Shake with ice and strain

Poppy
$1^1/_2$ parts Dry Gin
1 part Crème de Cacao (White)
Cocktail Glass

Shake with ice and strain

Preakness Cocktail
2 parts Whiskey
1 part Sweet Vermouth
splash Benedictine®
dash Bitters
Cocktail Glass

Shake with ice and strain

Presidente Cocktail
$1^1/_2$ parts Light Rum
$^1/_2$ part Dry Vermouth
$^1/_2$ part Blue Curaçao
splash Grenadine
Cocktail Glass

Shake with ice and strain

Princeton
2 parts Gin
1 part Port
4 dashes Orange Bitters
Cocktail Glass
Shake with ice and strain

Quaker Cocktail
1 part Brandy
1/2 part Rum
1/2 part Lemon Juice
splash Raspberry Syrup
Cocktail Glass
Shake with ice and strain

Queen Elizabeth
1 1/2 parts Gin
1/2 part Dry Vermouth
splash Benedictine®
Cocktail Glass
Shake with ice and strain

Racquet Club Cocktail
2 parts Gin
1 part Dry Vermouth
dash Orange Bitters
Cocktail Glass
Shake with ice and strain

Ritz Bar Fizz
splash Grenadine
1 part Pineapple Juice
1 part Grapefruit Juice
fill with Champagne
Highball Glass
Build over ice

Rob Roy
2 parts Scotch
1/2 part Sweet Vermouth
dash Orange Bitters
Collins Glass
Shake with ice and strain

Rock and Rye Cocktail
1 part Rock & Rye
1 part White Port
2 splashes Dry Vermouth
Cocktail Glass
Shake with ice and strain

Royal Smile
1 1/2 parts Gin
1 part Grenadine
splash Lemon Juice
Cocktail Glass
Shake with ice and strain

Rum Daisy
2 parts Dark Rum
1 part Lemon Juice
dash Sugar
splash Grenadine
Old-Fashioned Glass
Shake with ice and strain over ice

Rum Fix
2 1/2 parts Light Rum
1/2 part Lemon Juice
dash Powdered Sugar
splash Water
Highball Glass
Shake with ice and strain

Rum Fizz
1 part Dark Rum
1/2 part Apricot Brandy
1/2 part Sour mix
fill with Club Soda
Collins Glass
Shake all but Club Soda with ice and strain into the glass. Top with Club Soda.

Rum Rickey
1 1/2 parts Light Rum
1/2 part Lime Juice
fill with Carbonated Water
Highball Glass
Build over ice and stir

Rum Stinger

$1^1/_2$ parts Dark Rum
1 part Crème de Menthe (White)

Cocktail Glass

Shake with ice and strain

Rum Swizzle

2 parts Dark Rum
$^1/_2$ part Lemon Juice
dash Powdered Sugar
2 dashes Bitters
fill with Carbonated Water

Collins Glass

Shake all but Carbonated Water with ice and strain into the glass. Top with Carbonated Water.

Rum Toddy

2 parts Rum
1 Sugar Cube
1 Lemon Slice
dash Ground Nutmeg
fill with Boiling Water

Irish Coffee Cup

Build in a heat-proof cup or mug

Russian

1 part Crème de Cacao (White)
1 part Gin
1 part Vodka

Cocktail Glass

Shake with ice and strain

Salome Cocktail

1 part Gin
1 part Dry Vermouth
1 part Dubonnet® Blonde

Cocktail Glass

Shake with ice and strain

Santiago

$1^1/_2$ parts Light Rum
splash Grenadine
dash Powdered Sugar
splash Lime Juice

Cocktail Glass

Shake with ice and strain

Saratoga

2 parts Brandy
2 splashes Cherry Liqueur
2 dashes Angostura® Bitters
1 part Pineapple Juice

Cocktail Glass

Shake with ice and strain

Saucy Sue

2 parts Apple Brandy
splash Apricot Brandy
splash Pernod®

Cocktail Glass

Shake with ice and strain

Savoy Tango

$1^1/_2$ parts Apple Brandy
1 part Sloe Gin

Cocktail Glass

Shake with ice and strain

Saxon

$1^3/_4$ parts Rum
splash Lime Juice
splash Grenadine

Cocktail Glass

Shake with ice and strain

Sazerac Cocktail
1½ parts Irish Whiskey
splash Absinthe
dash Sugar
2 dashes Peychauds® Bitters
2 dashes Angostura® Bitters
1 Lemon Twist

Old-Fashioned Glass

Chill an old-fashioned glass by filling with crushed ice. In another glass mix the Sugar with the Bitters, dissolving the sugar. Add some ice, stirring to chill. Remove the ice from the old-fashioned glass and pour in the Absinthe, coating the entire inside of the glass. Remove the excess Absinthe. Add the Irish Whiskey and the Bitters/Sugar mixture. Garnish with a Lemon Twist.

September Morn
2 parts Light Rum
½ part Lime Juice
splash Grenadine
1 Egg White

Cocktail Glass

Shake with ice and strain

Seventh Heaven
2 parts Canadian Whiskey
2 parts Amaretto
1 part Pineapple Juice
1 part Lemon-Lime Soda

Collins Glass

Build over ice and stir

Sevilla
1 part Dark Rum
1 part Sweet Vermouth

Old-Fashioned Glass

Shake with ice and strain over ice

Sevilla Cocktail
1 part Light Rum
1 part Port
dash Powdered Sugar
1 Whole Egg

Whiskey Sour Glass

Shake with ice and strain over ice

Shamrock
1½ parts Irish Whiskey
½ part Dry Vermouth
splash Crème de Menthe (Green)

Cocktail Glass

Shake with ice and strain

Shamrock #2
1½ parts Irish Whiskey
½ part Coffee Liqueur
½ part Irish Cream Liqueur

Cocktail Glass

Shake with ice and strain

Shanghai Cocktail
1½ parts Dark Rum
1 part Lemon Juice
splash Anisette
splash Grenadine

Cocktail Glass

Shake with ice and strain

Sherry Cocktail
1 part Gin
1 part Cream Sherry

Cocktail Glass

Shake with ice and strain

Shriner Cocktail
1 part Sloe Gin
1 part Brandy
splash Simple Syrup
2 dashes Bitters

Cocktail Glass

Shake with ice and strain

Sidecar
1 part Brandy
$1^1/_2$ part Lemon Juice
$^1/_2$ part Triple Sec
Old-Fashioned Glass

Shake with ice and strain over ice

Silver King
1 part Gin
1 part Lemon Juice
splash Simple Syrup
2 dashes Orange Bitters
1 Egg White
Highball Glass

Shake with ice and strain

Sir Walter Cocktail
$1^1/_2$ parts Brandy
$^1/_2$ part Rum
splash Grenadine
splash Lime Juice
splash Blue Curaçao
Old-Fashioned Glass

Shake with ice and strain over ice

Sky Rocket
1 part Apricot Brandy
1 part Campari®
1 part Dark Rum
1 part Spiced Rum
2 parts Guava Juice
Cocktail Glass

Shake with ice and strain

Sloe Gin Cocktail
2 parts Sloe Gin
splash Dry Vermouth
dash Orange Bitters
Cocktail Glass

Shake with ice and strain

Sloppy Joe
1 part Brandy
1 part Port
2 splashes Triple Sec
splash Grenadine
1 part Pineapple Juice
Cocktail Glass

Shake with ice and strain

Smile
1 part Melon Liqueur
1 part Apple Brandy
Shot Glass

Shake with ice and strain

Smiler Cocktail
1 part Gin
$^1/_2$ part Dry Vermouth
$^1/_2$ part Sweet Vermouth
splash Orange Juice
dash Bitters
Cocktail Glass

Shake with ice and strain

Snowball
$1^1/_2$ parts Gin
$^1/_2$ part Anisette
$^1/_2$ part Light Cream
Cocktail Glass

Shake with ice and strain

Soul Kiss
1 part Dubonnet® Blonde
$^1/_2$ part Sweet Vermouth
$^1/_2$ part Dry Vermouth
1 part Orange Juice
Cocktail Glass

Shake with ice and strain

Southside
$1^1/_2$ parts Gin
$^1/_2$ part Lemon Juice
dash Powdered Sugar
Cocktail Glass

Shake with ice and strain

Southside
$2^1/_2$ parts Gin
$^1/_2$ part Simple Syrup
Cocktail Glass
Shake with ice and strain

St. Patrick's Day
1 part Crème de Menthe (Green)
1 part Green Chartreuse®
1 part Irish Whiskey
dash Bitters
Cocktail Glass
Shake with ice and strain

Stinger
$1^1/_2$ parts Brandy
$^1/_2$ part Crème de Menthe (White)
Cocktail Glass
Shake with ice and strain

Sunshine
$1^1/_2$ parts Vodka
$^1/_2$ part Triple Sec
fill with Grapefruit Juice
Old-Fashioned Glass
Build over ice and stir

Swiss Family Cocktail
2 parts Whiskey
1 part Dry Vermouth
splash Anisette
2 dashes Bitters
Cocktail Glass
Shake with ice and strain

Tailspin
2 parts Gin
$1^1/_2$ parts Sweet Vermouth
dash Orange Bitters
Cocktail Glass
Shake with ice and strain

Tango
$1^1/_2$ parts Gin
$^1/_2$ part Dry Vermouth
$^1/_2$ part Sweet Vermouth
1 part Orange Juice
splash Blue Curaçao
Old-Fashioned Glass
Shake with ice and strain over ice

Temptation Cocktail
$1^1/_2$ parts Whiskey
splash Dubonnet® Blonde
splash Triple Sec
splash Anisette
Cocktail Glass
Shake with ice and strain

Third Rail
2 parts Dry Vermouth
splash Blue Curaçao
splash Crème de Menthe (White)
Old-Fashioned Glass
Shake with ice and strain over ice

Thunder Cocktail
2 parts Brandy
1 part Egg Yolk
$^1/_2$ part Powdered Sugar
splash Tabasco® Sauce
Cocktail Glass
Shake with ice and strain

Thunderclap
1 part Whiskey
1 part Brandy
1 part Gin
Cocktail Glass
Shake with ice and strain

Tipperary Cocktail
1 part Rye Whiskey
1 part Sweet Vermouth
1 part Green Chartreuse®
Cocktail Glass
Shake with ice and strain

TnT
2 parts Brandy
1 part Triple Sec
splash Pastis
Cocktail Glass
Stir gently with ice and strain

Tropical Cocktail
1 part Dry Vermouth
1 part Crème de Cacao (White)
1 part Maraschino Liqueur
dash Bitters
Cocktail Glass
Shake with ice and strain

Turf
1 part Dry Vermouth
1 part Gin
1/2 part Pernod®
Cocktail Glass
Shake with ice and strain

Twin Six
1 part Gin
1/2 part Sweet Vermouth
2 splashes Grenadine
1/2 part Orange Juice
1 Egg White
Cocktail Glass
Shake with ice and strain

Ulysses
1 part Brandy
1 part Dry Vermouth
1 part Cherry Brandy
Cocktail Glass
Shake with ice and strain

Union Jack Cocktail
2 parts Gin
1 part Sloe Gin
splash Grenadine
Cocktail Glass
Shake with ice and strain

Up to Date Cocktail
1 part Sherry
1 part Canadian Whiskey
dash Angostura® Bitters
splash Grand Marnier®
Cocktail Glass
Shake with ice and strain

Valencia Cocktail
2 parts Apricot Brandy
1 part Orange Juice
2 dashes Orange Bitters
Old-Fashioned Glass
Shake with ice and strain over ice

Vanderbilt
2 parts Brandy
1 part Cherry Liqueur
splash Simple Syrup
2 dashes Angostura® Bitters
Cocktail Glass
Shake with ice and strain

Vermouth Cocktail
1 part Sweet Vermouth
1 part Dry Vermouth
dash Orange Bitters
Cocktail Glass
Shake with ice and strain

Virgin Cocktail
1 part Crème de Menthe (White)
1 part Dry Gin
1 part Triple Sec
Cocktail Glass
Stir gently with ice and strain

Waldorf
3/4 part Pernod®
1/2 part Sweet Vermouth
dash Bitters
Cocktail Glass
Shake with ice and strain

Wallick Cocktail
1 part Gin
1 part Dry Vermouth
splash Triple Sec
Cocktail Glass
Shake with ice and strain

Ward Eight
2 parts Whiskey
1/2 part Lemon Juice
splash Grenadine
dash Powdered Sugar
Red Wine Glass
Shake with ice and strain over ice

Warday's Cocktail
1 part Gin
1 part Sweet Vermouth
splash Chartreuse®
1 part Apple Brandy
Cocktail Glass
Shake with ice and strain over ice

Washington
1 part Dry Vermouth
1 part Brandy
splash Simple Syrup
2 dashes Angostura® Bitters
Cocktail Glass
Shake with ice and strain

Waterbury
2 1/2 parts Brandy
1/2 part Lemon Juice
splash Simple Syrup
1 Egg White
splash Grenadine
Old-Fashioned Glass
Shake with ice and strain over ice

Wedding Belle
1 part Gin
1 part Dubonnet® Blonde
1/2 part Cherry Brandy
1 part Orange Juice
Cocktail Glass
Shake with ice and strain

Wedding Bells
1 1/2 parts Gin
1/2 part Orange Juice
1/2 part Kirschwasser
Old-Fashioned Glass
Shake with ice and strain over ice

Weep No More
1 part Dubonnet® Blonde
1 part Brandy
1 part Lime Juice
splash Maraschino Liqueur
Old-Fashioned Glass
Shake with ice and strain over ice

Western Rose Cocktail
1 part Gin
1 part Apricot Brandy
1/2 part Dry Vermouth
splash Lemon Juice
Cocktail Glass
Shake with ice and strain

Whip
$1^1/_2$ parts Brandy
$^1/_2$ part Dry Vermouth
$^1/_2$ part Sweet Vermouth
splash Triple Sec
splash Anisette

Cocktail Glass

Shake with ice and strain

Whiskey Cocktail
2 parts Whiskey
splash Simple Syrup
dash Bitters

Cocktail Glass

Shake with ice and strain

Whiskey Sour
$1^1/_2$ parts Whiskey
fill with Sour Mix

Old-Fashioned Glass

Shake with ice and strain over ice

White Cargo
2 parts Gin
$^1/_2$ part Maraschino Liqueur
splash White Wine
1 scoop Ice Cream

White Wine Glass

Combine all ingredients in a blender with ice. Blend until smooth.

White Lady
$1^1/_2$ parts Gin
splash Light Cream
dash Powdered Sugar
1 Egg White

Cocktail Glass

Shake with ice and strain

White Rose
$1^1/_2$ parts Gin
$^1/_2$ part Lime Juice
$^1/_2$ part Maraschino Liqueur
splash Simple Syrup
$^1/_2$ Egg White
fill with Orange Juice

Old-Fashioned Glass

Shake with ice and pour

White Way
1 part Brandy
1 part Pernod®
1 part Anisette

Old-Fashioned Glass

Shake with ice and strain over ice

Widow's Dream
2 parts Benedictine®
fill with Heavy Cream

Highball Glass

Shake with ice and pour

Widow's Kiss Cocktail
2 parts Calvados Apple Brandy
$^1/_2$ part Chartreuse®
$^1/_2$ part Benedictine®

Cocktail Glass

Shake with ice and strain

X.Y.Z. Cocktail
1 part Light Rum
$^1/_2$ part Triple Sec
2 splashes Lemon Juice

Cocktail Glass

Shake with ice and strain

Xanthia
1 part Gin
1 part Cherry Brandy
$^1/_2$ part Chartreuse®

Old-Fashioned Glass

Shake with ice and strain over ice

Yale Cocktail
1/2 part Dry Vermouth
1 1/2 part Gin
splash Blue Curaçao
dash Bitters
Cocktail Glass

Shake with ice and strain

Yellow Parrot
1 part Apricot Brandy
1 part Pernod®
1/2 part Chartreuse®
Old-Fashioned Glass

Shake with ice and strain over ice

Yellow Rattler
1 part Gin
1/2 part Sweet Vermouth
1/2 part Dry Vermouth
1/2 part Orange Juice
Cocktail Glass

Shake with ice and strain

Zanzibar
1 part Gin
2 parts Dry Vermouth
1/2 part Lemon Juice
splash Simple Syrup
dash Orange Bitters
Highball Glass

Shake with ice and strain over ice

Zaza Cocktail
2 parts Gin
1 part Dubonnet® Blonde
Cocktail Glass

Shake with ice and strain

Zazarac Cocktail
1 part Canadian Whiskey
1/2 part Anisette
1/2 part Light Rum
splash Absinthe
1/2 part Simple Syrup
Cocktail Glass

Shake with ice and strain

Coffee Drinks

Most of these drinks are served hot and are made by combining coffee with a liqueur or liquor. The classic example of this type of drink is the Irish Coffee, which combines coffee with Irish Whiskey.

Alaskan Coffee

3 parts Coffee
1 1/2 parts Brandy
2 parts Vanilla Ice Cream

Irish Coffee Cup

Build in a heat-proof cup or mug. Float Ice Cream on top.

All-Canadian Coffee

3/4 part Whipped Cream
1/3 part Maple Syrup
1 part Rye Whiskey
3 parts Coffee

Irish Coffee Cup

Combine Whipped Cream with 4 teaspoons Maple Syrup until it forms soft mounds; set aside. Divide remaining Maple Syrup and Whiskey among 4 Irish coffee cups. Pour in coffee and top with Whipped Cream.

Almond Chocolate Coffee

3/4 part Amaretto
1/2 part Crème de Cacao (Dark)
fill with Coffee

Irish Coffee Cup

Build in a heat-proof cup or mug. order into coffee cup. Top with Whipped Cream and Chocolate Shavings.

Amaretto Café

1 part Coffee
1 part Amaretto

Irish Coffee Cup

Fill coffee mug or cup with hot coffee. Stir in Amaretto. Top with Whipped Cream.

Anatole Coffee

1 part Courvoisier®
1 part Tia Maria®
1 part Frangelico®
fill with Coffee

Irish Coffee Cup

Build in a heat-proof cup or mug. Top with Whipped Cream and Chocolate Shavings.

Anders

1 part Amaretto
1/2 part Brandy
1/2 part Coffee Liqueur
fill with Coffee

Irish Coffee Cup

Build in a heat-proof cup or mug

Anise Almond Coffee

1 part Amaretto
1 part Crème de Cacao (Dark)
1 part Sambuca
fill with Coffee

Irish Coffee Cup

Build in a heat-proof cup or mug

Apocolypse
1 part Peppermint Schnapps
3/4 part Vodka
1/2 part Coffee Liqueur
1/2 part Old Grand-Dad®
1 part Crème de Menthe (White)
3/4 part Southern Comfort®
fill with Hot Cocoa

Irish Coffee Cup

Build in a heat-proof cup or mug

Aqualung
2 parts Coffee Liqueur
fill with Espresso
splash Chocolate Syrup

Irish Coffee Cup

Build in a heat-proof cup or mug

Baileys® Cup of Coffee
1 part Baileys® Irish Cream Liqueur
1 part Coffee

Irish Coffee Cup

Build in a heat-proof cup or mug

Belgian Coffee
1 part Triple Sec
1 part Irish Cream Liqueur
fill with Coffee

Irish Coffee Cup

Build in a heat-proof cup or mug

Berliner Mélange
2 parts Cherry Brandy
1/2 part Simple Syrup
fill with Coffee

Irish Coffee Cup

Build in a heat-proof cup or mug

Berries 'n' Cream Coffee
1 part Irish Cream Liqueur
1 part Raspberry Liqueur
fill with Coffee

Irish Coffee Cup

Build in a heat-proof cup or mug. Top with Whipped Cream

Black Gold
1 part Triple Sec
1 part Amaretto
1 part Irish Cream Liqueur
1 part Frangelico®
splash Cinnamon Schnapps
fill with Coffee

Irish Coffee Cup

Build in a heat-proof cup or mug

Black Maria
1 part Light Rum
1 part Coffee-Flavored Brandy
2 dashes Powdered Sugar
fill with Strong Black Coffee

Irish Coffee Cup

Build in a heat-proof cup or mug

Black Rose
2 parts Dark Rum
1/2 part Simple Syrup
fill with Coffee

Irish Coffee Cup

Build in a heat-proof cup or mug

Blackjack
1 1/2 parts Kirschwasser
1/2 part Cherry Brandy
1/2 part Simple Syrup
fill with Coffee

Irish Coffee Cup

Build in a heat-proof cup or mug

Boston-Baked Brandy

1 1/2 parts Brandy
3/4 part Triple Sec
1 part Hot Coffee
1 part Hot Cocoa
splash Honey

Irish Coffee Cup

Build in a heat-proof cup or mug

Boston Caribbean Coffee

1 part Crème de Cacao (Dark)
1 part Dark Rum
fill with Coffee

Irish Coffee Cup

Build in a heat-proof cup or mug

Bounce

1 1/2 parts Coconut-Flavored Liqueur
1/2 part Almond Syrup
fill with Coffee

Irish Coffee Cup

Build in a heat-proof cup or mug

Breathtaking

1 part Amaretto
splash Frangelico®
fill with Coffee

Irish Coffee Cup

Build in a heat-proof cup or mug

Buie Coffee

1 part Drambuie®
1/2 part Crème de Cacao (Dark)
2 parts Cream
fill with Black Coffee

Irish Coffee Cup

Build in a heat-proof cup or mug

Butternut Coffee

1 part Butterscotch Schnapps
1 part Amaretto
fill with Coffee

Irish Coffee Cup

Build in a heat-proof cup or mug

Café Alpine

1 part Peppermint Schnapps
fill with Coffee

Irish Coffee Cup

Build in a heat-proof cup or mug

Café Amaretto

1 part Amaretto
1 part Coffee Liqueur
fill with Coffee

Irish Coffee Cup

Build in a heat-proof cup or mug

Café Boom Boom

1 part Frangelico®
1 part Irish Cream Liqueur
fill with Coffee

Irish Coffee Cup

Build in a heat-proof cup or mug

Café Caribbean

1 part Rum
1 part Amaretto
fill with Coffee
dash Sugar

Irish Coffee Cup

Build in a heat-proof cup or mug. Top with Whipped Cream.

Café Curatao

$1^1/_2$ parts Triple Sec
$^1/_2$ dash Powdered Sugar
fill with Hot Coffee

Irish Coffee Cup

Build in a heat-proof cup or mug. Top with Whipped Cream.

Café Di Limoni

1 part Limoncello
fill with Coffee

Irish Coffee Cup

Build in a heat-proof cup or mug

Café French

1 part Triple Sec
1 part Amaretto
$^1/_2$ part Irish Cream Liqueur
fill with Coffee

Irish Coffee Cup

Build in a heat-proof cup or mug

Café Gates

1 part Brandy
1 part Crème de Cacao (Dark)
fill with Coffee

Irish Coffee Cup

Build in a heat-proof cup or mug

Café Grog

$1^1/_2$ parts Dark Rum
1 part Brandy
fill with Coffee

Irish Coffee Cup

Build in a heat-proof cup or mug

Café Jeavons

1 part Dark Rum
1 part Cognac
splash Coconut Cream
$^1/_2$ part Vanilla Ice Cream
fill with Black Coffee
dash Cinnamon
1 Orange Peel

Irish Coffee Cup

Build in a heat-proof cup or mug

Café Joy

1 part Frangelico®
1 part Coconut-Flavored Rum
1 part Irish Cream Liqueur
fill with Coffee

Irish Coffee Cup

Build in a heat-proof cup or mug

Café King Royale

1 part Coffee-Flavored Brandy
splash Galliano®
splash Grand Marnier®
fill with Coffee

Irish Coffee Cup

Build in a heat-proof cup or mug

Café L'Orange

$^1/_2$ part Cognac
$^1/_2$ part Cointreau®
1 part Grand Marnier®
fill with Coffee

Irish Coffee Cup

Build in a heat-proof cup or mug

Café Mazatlan
1 part Dark Rum
1 part Coffee Liqueur
fill with Coffee
dash Brown Sugar

Irish Coffee Cup

Build in a heat-proof cup or mug. Top with Whipped Cream.

Café Nelson
3/4 part Frangelico®
4 parts Coffee

Irish Coffee Cup

Build in a heat-proof cup or mug

Café Oscar
1 part Amaretto
1 part Crème de Cacao (Dark)
fill with Coffee

Irish Coffee Cup

Build in a heat-proof cup or mug

Café Romano
1 part Sambuca
fill with Coffee

Irish Coffee Cup

Build in a heat-proof cup or mug

Café Royale
1 Sugar Cube
1 part Brandy
1 part Coffee Liqueur
fill with Coffee

Irish Coffee Cup

Soak the sugar cube in Brandy. Place the coffee liqueur in a heat-proof cup or mug and fill with coffee. Place the Brandy-soaked sugar in a teaspoon. Hold the teaspoon above the Coffee and ignite the Brandy on the sugar. Hold it until flame burns out and drop contents into the cup.

Café Seattle
1 part Irish Cream Liqueur
1 part Absolut® Vodka
1 part Chocolate Syrup
fill with Coffee

Irish Coffee Cup

Build in a heat-proof cup or mug

Café Sonia
3/4 part Metaxa®
1/2 part Amaretto
1/2 part Tia Maria®
splash Heavy Cream
splash Vanilla Extract
fill with Coffee

Irish Coffee Cup

Build in a heat-proof cup or mug

Café Toledo
1 part Coffee Liqueur
1/2 part Chocolate Syrup
fill with Coffee

Irish Coffee Cup

Build in a heat-proof cup or mug

Café Wellington
Whipped Cream
dash Instant Coffee
2 splashes Coconut Cream
1 part Light Rum
fill with Coffee

Irish Coffee Cup

Blend Whipped Cream with Instant Coffee until stiff peaks form. In a heat-proof cup or mug add Coconut Cream and Rum and stir well while filling the cup with coffee. Top with prepared Whipped Cream.

Café Zurich
1 part Sambuca
1 part Cognac
1/2 part Amaretto
splash Honey
fill with Coffee

Irish Coffee Cup

Build in a heat-proof cup or mug

Calypso
1 part Rum
1 part Tia Maria®
fill with Coffee

Irish Coffee Cup

Build in a heat-proof cup or mug

Candle in the Window
2 parts Light Rum
splash Crème de Cacao (Dark)
splash Cherry Brandy
fill with Black Coffee

Irish Coffee Cup

Build in a heat-proof cup or mug

Cappuccino Sausalito
1/2 part Amaretto
1/2 part Coffee Liqueur
1 part Coffee
1 part Hot Cocoa

Irish Coffee Cup

Build in a heat-proof cup or mug

Capriccio
1 Sugar Cube
1/2 part Brandy
1/2 part Coffee Liqueur
1 part Amaretto
fill with Coffee

Irish Coffee Cup

Build in a heat-proof cup or mug

Caracof
1 1/2 parts Coffee Liqueur
1 part Caramel syrup
fill with Hot Cocoa

Irish Coffee Cup

Build in a heat-proof cup or mug

Caribbean Coffee
2 parts Dark Rum
dash Sugar
2 parts Cream
fill with Black Coffee

Irish Coffee Cup

Build in a heat-proof cup or mug

Charro
1 part Tequila
1 part Evaporated Milk
fill with Coffee

Irish Coffee Cup

Build in a heat-proof cup or mug

Chocolate Coffee Kiss
1 part Coffee Liqueur
1 part Irish Cream Liqueur
splash Crème de Cacao (Dark)
splash Grand Marnier®
1 part Chocolate Syrup
fill with Coffee

Irish Coffee Cup

Build in a heat-proof cup or mug

Chocolate Strawberry
1 part Tequila Rose®
1/2 part Chocolate Liqueur
fill with Coffee

Irish Coffee Cup

Build in a heat-proof cup or mug

Chump
$1^1/_2$ parts Dark Rum
$^1/_2$ part Tia Maria®
1 part Light Cream
fill with Coffee

Irish Coffee Cup

Build in a heat-proof cup or mug

Co-Co-Mo
2 parts Coconut-Flavored Rum
1 part Hot Cocoa
1 part Coffee

Irish Coffee Cup

Build in a heat-proof cup or mug

Coffee 43
1 part Licor 43®
fill with Coffee

Irish Coffee Cup

Build in a heat-proof cup or mug

Coffee Fling
1 part Scotch
splash Lemon Juice
fill with Coffee

Irish Coffee Cup

Build in a heat-proof cup or mug

Coffee Nudge
$^3/_4$ part Crème de Cacao (Dark)
$^3/_4$ part Coffee Liqueur
$^1/_2$ part Brandy
fill with Coffee

Irish Coffee Cup

Build in a heat-proof cup or mug

Coffee Royale
$1^1/_2$ parts Brandy
fill with Coffee

Irish Coffee Cup

Build in a heat-proof cup or mug

Comforting Coffee
1 part Southern Comfort®
2 splashes Crème de Cacao (Dark)
2 parts Cream
fill with Black Coffee

Irish Coffee Cup

Build in a heat-proof cup or mug

Cossack
1 part Vodka
1 part Coffee Liqueur
1 part Godiva® Liqueur
fill with Warm Milk

Irish Coffee Cup

Build in a heat-proof cup or mug

Dangerous Minds
1 part Vodka
1 part Crème de Cacao (Dark)
fill with Coffee

Irish Coffee Cup

Build in a heat-proof cup or mug

Doublemint
1 part Dr. McGillicuddy's® Mentholmint Schnapps
fill with Coffee
splash Crème de Menthe (Green)

Irish Coffee Cup

Build in a heat-proof cup or mug

Dutch Coffee

1½ parts Chocolate Mint Liqueur
fill with Coffee

Irish Coffee Cup

Build in a heat-proof cup or mug

Finals Night

2 parts Tequila
½ part Crème de Cacao (Dark)
½ part Lemon Juice
fill with Coffee

Irish Coffee Cup

Build in a heat-proof cup or mug

French Coffee

1 Sugar Cube
1 part Grand Marnier®
fill with Coffee

Irish Coffee Cup

Build in a heat-proof cup or mug

Fritzes Coffee

1 part Frangelico®
1 part Irish Cream Liqueur
fill with Coffee

Irish Coffee Cup

Build in a heat-proof cup or mug

Fuzzy Asshole

1 part Coffee
1 part Peach Schnapps

Irish Coffee Cup

Build in a heat-proof cup or mug

Fuzzy Dick

1 part Coffee Liqueur
1 part Grand Marnier®
fill with Coffee

Irish Coffee Cup

Build in a heat-proof cup or mug

Galliano® Hotshot

1 part Galliano®
fill with Coffee

Irish Coffee Cup

Build in a heat-proof cup or mug

Good Golly

1½ parts Dark Rum
½ part Galliano®
2 splashes Crème de Cacao (Dark)
1 part Heavy Cream
fill with Black Coffee

Irish Coffee Cup

Build over ice and stir

Guapo

1 part Irish Cream Liqueur
1 part Coffee Liqueur
2 splashes Butterscotch Schnapps
fill with Coffee

Irish Coffee Cup

Build in a heat-proof cup or mug

Handicapper's Choice

1 part Irish Whiskey
1 part Amaretto
fill with Coffee

Irish Coffee Cup

Build in a heat-proof cup or mug

Heart Warmer
1 part Vanilla Liqueur
1 part Peppermint Liqueur
1 part Amaretto
fill with Coffee

Irish Coffee Cup

Build in a heat-proof cup or mug

HenryIII Coffee
1 part Brandy
1 part Coffee
1 part Mandarine Napoléon® Liqueur
fill with Coffee

Irish Coffee Cup

Build in a heat-proof cup or mug

Hot Bush
1 part Irish Whiskey
1 part Irish Cream Liqueur
fill with Coffee

Irish Coffee Cup

Build in a heat-proof cup or mug

Hot Butterscotch Cocoa
1 part Butterscotch Schnapps
1 part Coffee Liqueur
fill with Hot Cocoa

Irish Coffee Cup

Build in a heat-proof cup or mug

Hot Coconut
1 part Coconut-Flavored Liqueur
1/2 part Simple Syrup
fill with Coffee

Irish Coffee Cup

Build in a heat-proof cup or mug

Hot Irish Nut
1 part Irish Cream Liqueur
1 part Frangelico®
1 part Amaretto
fill with Coffee

Irish Coffee Cup

Build in a heat-proof cup or mug

Hot Kiss
1 part Irish Whiskey
1/2 part Crème de Cacao (White)
fill with Coffee

Irish Coffee Cup

Build in a heat-proof cup or mug

Hot Mollifier
1 1/2 parts Dark Rum
1/2 part Tia Maria®
2 parts Heavy Cream
fill with Coffee

Irish Coffee Cup

Build in a heat-proof cup or mug

Hot Piper
2 parts Tequila
1/2 part Crème de Cacao (Dark)
2 splashes Lemon Juice
fill with Black Coffee

Irish Coffee Cup

Build in a heat-proof cup or mug

Hot Pleasure
1 part Bourbon
1/2 part Amaretto
splash Cream
dash Brown Sugar
fill with Coffee

Irish Coffee Cup

Build in a heat-proof cup or mug

Hot Siberian Almond
1 part Cream
1 part Amaretto
1/2 part Vodka
fill with Coffee

Irish Coffee Cup

Build in a heat-proof cup or mug

Irish '49
Whipped Cream
1 part Irish Mist®
dash Sugar
fill with Coffee

Irish Coffee Cup

Build in a heat-proof cup or mug. Top with whipped cream.

Irish Coffee
1 1/2 parts Irish Whiskey
dash Sugar
fill with Coffee

Irish Coffee Cup

Build in a heat-proof cup or mug

Irish Coffee #2
1 part Irish Whiskey
dash Sugar
2 parts Cream
fill with Black Coffee

Irish Coffee Cup

Build in a heat-proof cup or mug

An Irish Kiss
1 part Irish Cream Liqueur
1 part Coffee Liqueur
fill with Coffee

Irish Coffee Cup

Build in a heat-proof cup or mug

Italian Amaretto Coffee
1 1/2 parts Amaretto
1/2 part Cream
fill with Coffee
Whipped Cream

Irish Coffee Cup

Build in a heat-proof cup or mug. Top with Whipped Cream.

Italian Coffee
1 1/2 part Amaretto
fill with Coffee

Irish Coffee Cup

Build in a heat-proof cup or mug

Jamaica Me Hot
3/4 part Dark Rum
3/4 part Coffee Liqueur
1 part Milk
1 part Coffee

Irish Coffee Cup

Build in a heat-proof cup or mug

Jamaican Coffee #1
1 part Brandy
1 part Rum
fill with Coffee

Irish Coffee Cup

Build in a heat-proof cup or mug

Jamaican Coffee #2

1½ parts Rum
½ part Coffee Liqueur
fill with Coffee

Irish Coffee Cup

Build in a heat-proof cup or mug

Jamaican Coffee #3

1 part Cognac
1 part Tia Maria®
1 part Dark Rum
fill with Coffee
dash Cinnamon
dash Ginger

Irish Coffee Cup

Build in a heat-proof cup or mug

Javameister

1½ parts Jägermeister®
fill with Black Coffee

Irish Coffee Cup

Build in a heat-proof cup or mug

Jungle Coffee

1 part Southern Comfort®
1 part Brandy
1 part Crème de Cacao (Dark)
1 part Crème de Banana
fill with Coffee

Irish Coffee Cup

Build in a heat-proof cup or mug

Kentucky Coffee

1 part Bourbon
fill with Coffee

Irish Coffee Cup

Build in a heat-proof cup or mug. Top with Whipped Cream.

Keoke Coffee

1 part Rum
1 part Brandy
1 part Coffee Liqueur
fill with Coffee

Irish Coffee Cup

Build in a heat-proof cup or mug

Keoke Coffee #2

1 part Coffee Liqueur
1 part Amaretto
fill with Coffee

Irish Coffee Cup

Build in a heat-proof cup or mug. Top with Whipped Cream.

Kong Coffee

1 part Whiskey
1 part Crème de Banana
fill with Coffee

Irish Coffee Cup

Build in a heat-proof cup or mug. Top with Whipped Cream.

Last Dance

1 part Vanilla Liqueur
1 part Almond Syrup
1 part Milk
fill with Coffee

Irish Coffee Cup

Build in a heat-proof cup or mug

Lebanese Coffee

2 parts Apricot Brandy
1 part Coffee Liqueur
fill with Coffee

Irish Coffee Cup

Build in a heat-proof cup or mug

Lift

1 part Amaretto
1 part Drambuie®
1 part Tia Maria®
fill with Coffee

Irish Coffee Cup

Build in a heat-proof cup or mug

Liquid Speedball

1½ parts Vodka
1 part Espresso
fill with Black Coffee
dash Cinnamon

Irish Coffee Cup

Build in a heat-proof cup or mug

Loco Cocoa Mocha

¾ part Coffee Liqueur
2 parts Heavy Cream
fill with Coffee
dash Hot Chocolate Mix

Irish Coffee Cup

Build in a heat-proof cup or mug

Mexican Coffee

1 part Coffee Liqueur
1 part Cream
fill with Coffee

Irish Coffee Cup

Build in a heat-proof cup or mug

Mexitaly Coffee

1 part Coffee Liqueur
1 part Amaretto
fill with Coffee

Irish Coffee Cup

Build in a heat-proof cup or mug

Midnight in Malibu

2 parts Coconut-Flavored Rum
fill with Coffee

Irish Coffee Cup

Build in a heat-proof cup or mug. Top with Whipped Cream.

Millionaire's Coffee

1 part Irish Cream Liqueur
1 part Coffee Liqueur
1 part Frangelico®
fill with Coffee

Irish Coffee Cup

Build in a heat-proof cup or mug

Mocha Almond Fudge

1 part Amaretto
1 part Coffee Liqueur
1 part Crème de Cacao (White)
fill with Coffee

Irish Coffee Cup

Build in a heat-proof cup or mug

Mocha Nut

1½ parts Frangelico®
½ part Crème de Cacao (White)
2 parts Cream
fill with Coffee

Irish Coffee Cup

Build in a heat-proof cup or mug

Monastery Coffee

2 parts Benedictine®
2 parts Heavy Cream
fill with Black Coffee
dash Sugar

Irish Coffee Cup

Build in a heat-proof cup or mug

Monte Cristo
1 part Coffee Liqueur
1/2 part Grand Marnier®
fill with Coffee

Irish Coffee Cup

Build in a heat-proof cup or mug. Top with Whipped Cream.

Morley's Driver
1 1/2 parts Dark Rum
1/2 part Cherry Brandy
2 splashes Crème de Cacao (Dark)
fill with Coffee

Irish Coffee Cup

Build in a heat-proof cup or mug. Top with Heavy Cream.

My Passion in a Cup
1 1/2 parts Butterscotch Schnapps
1 part Chocolate Syrup
fill with Coffee

Irish Coffee Cup

Build in a heat-proof cup or mug

Newport Coffee
3/4 part Crème de Menthe (White)
fill with Coffee

Irish Coffee Cup

Build in a heat-proof cup or mug. Top with Whipped Cream.

Night Train
1 part Vodka
1 part Frangelico®
1/2 part Simple Syrup
fill with Coffee

Irish Coffee Cup

Build in a heat-proof cup or mug

Nikki Coffee
1 part Irish Cream Liqueur
1 part Butterscotch Schnapps
fill with Coffee

Irish Coffee Cup

Build in a heat-proof cup or mug

Nudge
1 part Coffee Liqueur
1 part Crème de Cacao (White)
1 part Vodka
fill with Coffee

Irish Coffee Cup

Build in a heat-proof cup or mug

Nutty Irish Coffee
1 part Irish Cream Liqueur
1 part Frangelico®
splash Chocolate Syrup
fill with Coffee

Irish Coffee Cup

Build in a heat-proof cup or mug

Old Town
1 part Rum
1/2 part Tia Maria®
1/2 part Brown Sugar
fill with Coffee

Irish Coffee Cup

Build in a heat-proof cup or mug

Oslo Coffee
1/2 part Goldschläger®
fill with Coffee

Irish Coffee Cup

Build in a heat-proof cup or mug

Ostrich Shit

1 part Peppermint Schnapps
2 dashes Sugar
fill with Coffee

Irish Coffee Cup

Build in a heat-proof cup or mug

Peach Truffle

1 part Peach Schnapps
1 part Crème de Cacao (White)
fill with Coffee

Irish Coffee Cup

Build in a heat-proof cup or mug

Peppermint Coffee

1 part Crème de Menthe (Green)
1 part Cream
1/2 part Crème de Cacao (White)
fill with Coffee

Irish Coffee Cup

Build in a heat-proof cup or mug

Pike's Peak

1 part Peppermint Schnapps
1 part Coffee Liqueur
fill with Coffee

Irish Coffee Cup

Build in a heat-proof cup or mug

Psycho Joe

1 part Coffee Liqueur
1 part Peppermint Schnapps
fill with Coffee

Irish Coffee Cup

Build in a heat-proof cup or mug

Puppet Master

1 part Whiskey
1/2 part Coffee Liqueur
fill with Coffee

Irish Coffee Cup

Build in a heat-proof cup or mug

Randy's Special

1 part Irish Cream Liqueur
1 part Frangelico®
1 part Amaretto
fill with Coffee

Irish Coffee Cup

Build in a heat-proof cup or mug

Raspberry Cappuccino

2 parts Raspberry Liqueur
fill with Espresso

Irish Coffee Cup

Build in a heat-proof cup or mug

Razzmatazz

1 part Blackberry Liqueur
1/2 part Crème de Cassis
1/2 part Coffee Liqueur
fill with Coffee

Irish Coffee Cup

Build in a heat-proof cup or mug

Rhode Island Iced Coffee

1 part Coffee Liqueur
1 part Vodka
1/2 part Brandy
2 parts Cream

Old-Fashioned Glass

Shake with ice and strain over ice

Roman Coffee
1 part Galliano®
fill with Coffee
Irish Coffee Cup

Build in a heat-proof cup or mug

Saturday Morning Special
1 part Rum
2 splashes Chocolate Syrup
fill with Coffee
Irish Coffee Cup

Build in a heat-proof cup or mug

Schuylkill Pudding
1 1/2 parts Dark Rum
1/2 part Cherry Brandy
1/4 part Crème de Cacao (Dark)
fill with Coffee
Irish Coffee Cup

Build in a heat-proof cup or mug

Scottish Coffee
1 1/2 parts Drambuie®
fill with Coffee
Irish Coffee Cup

Build in a heat-proof cup or mug

Secret Place
1 1/2 parts Dark Rum
1/2 part Cherry Brandy
2 splashes Crème de Cacao (Dark)
fill with Coffee
Irish Coffee Cup

Build in a heat-proof cup or mug

Sly Ol' Bastad
1 part Cream
1 part Amaretto
fill with Coffee
Top with Guinness® Stout
Irish Coffee Cup

Build in a heat-proof cup or mug

Snowball
1 part Cinnamon Schnapps
1 part Coffee Liqueur
fill with Coffee
Irish Coffee Cup

Build in a heat-proof cup or mug

Sorrento Café
1 part Limoncello
1 part Grand Marnier®
fill with Coffee
Irish Coffee Cup

Build in a heat-proof cup or mug

Southfork Coffee
1/2 part Crème de Cacao (Dark)
2 parts Heavy Cream
fill with Black Coffee
Irish Coffee Cup

Build in a heat-proof cup or mug

Sudden Struck
1 part Crème de Cacao (Dark)
1/2 part Sambuca
fill with Coffee
Irish Coffee Cup

Build in a heat-proof cup or mug

Super Coffee
1 parts Brandy
1 parts Coffee Liqueur
fill with Coffee

Irish Coffee Cup

Build in a heat-proof cup or mug. Top with Whipped Cream.

Swedish Coffee
1 part Aquavit
fill with Coffee
dash Sugar

Irish Coffee Cup

Build in a heat-proof cup or mug

Tennessee Mud
1 part Amaretto
1 part Whiskey
fill with Coffee

Irish Coffee Cup

Build in a heat-proof cup or mug

To Die For
1 part Whiskey
1/4 part Crème de Cacao (Dark)
fill with Coffee

Irish Coffee Cup

Build in a heat-proof cup or mug

Torrence Coffee
1 part Crème de Menthe (White)
1 part Irish Cream Liqueur
fill with Coffee

Irish Coffee Cup

Build in a heat-proof cup or mug

Triple Irish Coffee
1 part Irish Whiskey
1 part Irish Cream Liqueur
1 part Irish Mist®
fill with Coffee

Irish Coffee Cup

Build in a heat-proof cup or mug. Top with Whipped Cream.

Tropical Clarkson
1 1/2 parts Coffee Liqueur
fill with Hot Cocoa

Irish Coffee Cup

Build in a heat-proof cup or mug

Ukrainian Coffee
1 part Coffee Liqueur
1/2 part Amaretto
1/2 part Mandarine Napoléon® Liqueur
fill with Coffee

Irish Coffee Cup

Build in a heat-proof cup or mug

Vanilla 49
1 part Vanilla Liqueur
fill with Coffee

Irish Coffee Cup

Build in a heat-proof cup or mug. Top with Heavy Cream.

Venetian Coffee
1 part Brandy
1 Sugar Cube
fill with Coffee

Irish Coffee Cup

Build in a heat-proof cup or mug. Top with Whipped Cream.

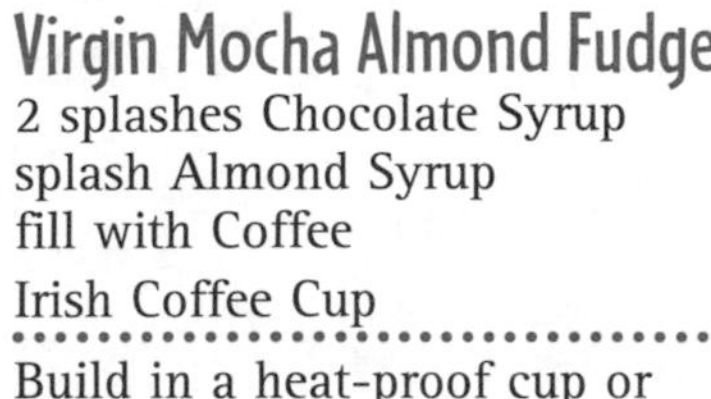

Virgin Mocha Almond Fudge

2 splashes Chocolate Syrup
splash Almond Syrup
fill with Coffee

Irish Coffee Cup

Build in a heat-proof cup or mug

Warm Feelings

1 part Crème de Cacao (Dark)
1 part Dark Rum
fill with Coffee

Irish Coffee Cup

Build in a heat-proof cup or mug

Zorro

1 part Sambuca
1 part Irish Cream Liqueur
1 part Crème de Menthe (White)
fill with Coffee

Irish Coffee Cup

Build in a heat-proof cup or mug

Other Hot Drinks

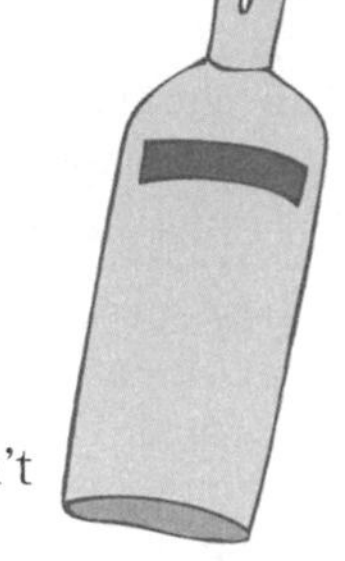

What do you call drinks that are served hot but don't contain coffee? How about "Other Hot Drinks"?

5 P.M.

1 part Dark Rum
1/2 part Cointreau®
fill with Hot Tea
splash Milk

Irish Coffee Cup

Build in a heat-proof cup or mug

A.D.M. (After Dinner Mint)

1/2 part Crème de Menthe (White)
3/4 part Southern Comfort®
1/2 part Vodka
fill with Hot Cocoa

Irish Coffee Cup

Build in a heat-proof cup or mug

Aberdeen Angus

1/2 part Lime Juice
1/2 part Heather Honey
fill with Boiling Water
2 parts Scotch
1 part Drambuie®

Irish Coffee Cup

Pour Lime Juice and Honey into a heat-proof mug. Add a little boiling water and stir until the Honey is dissolved. Add Scotch. Warm Drambuie® ladle over hot water, ignite, and pour into mug while burning. Fill with boiling water and stir.

Adult Hot Chocolate

1 1/2 parts Peppermint Schnapps
1 part Hot Cocoa

Irish Coffee Cup

Build in a heat-proof cup or mug. Top with Whipped Cream.

After Dinner Mint Julep

3/4 part Crème de Menthe (White)
1 part Southern Comfort®
1/2 part Whiskey
fill with Hot Cocoa

Irish Coffee Cup

Combine in a heat-proof cup or mug. If desired, garnish with Whipped Cream and an Andes® Mint.

After Walk

2 parts Citrus-Flavored Vodka
1 part Vanilla Syrup
1 part Brown Sugar
fill with Club Soda

Irish Coffee Cup

Combine in an Irish Coffee Cup and warm it in the microwave until hot

Alhambra Royale

1 part Hot Cocoa
1 Orange Peel
1 1/2 parts Cognac
Irish Coffee Cup

Fill heat-proof cup nearly full of Hot Cocoa and add Orange Peel. Warm Cognac in a ladle over hot water, ignite, and pour into cup of Hot Cocoa while burning. Stir well and top with Whipped Cream.

Almond Hot Chocolate

1 part Dark Rum
1 part Amaretto
fill with Hot Cocoa
Irish Coffee Cup

Build in a heat-proof cup or mug

American Grog

1 1/2 parts Rum
dash Powdered Sugar
1/2 part Lemon Juice
fill with Hot water
Irish Coffee Cup

Build in a heat-proof cup or mug

Apple Skag

1 part Sour Apple–Flavored Schnapps
1 part Apple Brandy
fill with Apple Juice (heated)
Irish Coffee Cup

Build in a heat-proof cup or mug

Apple Toddy

1 1/2 parts Apple Brandy
fill with Hot Apple Cider
Irish Coffee Cup

Build in a heat-proof cup or mug

Aprihot

1 part Apricot Brandy
1 part Boiling Water
Irish Coffee Cup

Build in a heat-proof cup or mug

Bacardi® Fireside

1 1/2 parts Dark Rum
dash Sugar
fill with Hot Tea
1 Lemon Slice
Irish Coffee Cup

Build in a heat-proof cup or mug

Back Burner

2 parts Tequila
1/2 part Galliano®
fill with Cold Hot Chocolate
Irish Coffee Cup

Shake with ice and strain over ice. *Note: This may not be a hot drink, but it will still warm you up.

Barn Burner

1 1/2 parts Southern Comfort®
fill with Hot Apple Cider
1 Cinnamon Stick
1 Lemon Twist
Irish Coffee Cup

Build in a heat-proof cup or mug

Beam of Chocolate

3 parts Jim Beam®
fill with Hot Cocoa
Irish Coffee Cup

Build in a heat-proof cup or mug

Bedroom Farce
1 part Dark Rum
2 splashes Galliano®
fill with Hot Cocoa

Irish Coffee Cup

Build in a heat-proof cup or mug. Top with Whipped Cream and Chocolate Shavings.

Black Flag
2 parts Dark Rum
1/2 part Molasses
splash Honey
fill with Boiling Water

Irish Coffee Cup

Build in a heat-proof cup or mug

Blueberry Tea
1 part Amaretto
1/2 part Grand Marnier®
fill with Black Currant Tea

Irish Coffee Cup

Build in a heat-proof cup or mug

Bun Warmer
1 part Apricot Brandy
1 part Southern Comfort®
fill with Hot Apple Cider

Irish Coffee Cup

Build in a heat-proof cup or mug

Butter Cup
2 parts Butterscotch Schnapps
fill with Hot Cocoa

Irish Coffee Cup

Build in a heat-proof cup or mug

Butter Milk
1 part Butterscotch Schnapps
fill with Warm Milk

Irish Coffee Cup

Build over ice and stir

Butterscotch Benchwarmer
2 parts Butterscotch Schnapps
fill with Hot Milk
splash Honey

Irish Coffee Cup

Build in a heat-proof cup or mug

Café Mocha
1 part Crème de Cacao (Dark)
1 part Cream
fill with Espresso

Irish Coffee Cup

Build in a heat-proof cup or mug

Cappuccino
1 part Brandy
fill with Cappucino

Irish Coffee Cup

Build in a heat-proof cup or mug

Caribbean Hot Chocolate
1 1/2 parts Dark Rum
1/2 part Crème de Cacao (Dark)
fill with Hot Cocoa

Irish Coffee Cup

Build in a heat-proof cup or mug

Chill Out
1 part Coconut-Flavored Liqueur
1 part Amaretto
fill with Hot Cocoa

Irish Coffee Cup

Build in a heat-proof cup or mug

Chocolate Nemesis

1 part Godiva® Liqueur
1 part Irish Cream Liqueur
fill with Hot Cocoa

Irish Coffee Cup

Build in a heat-proof cup or mug

Chocolate Raspberry Dream

1 part Crème de Cacao (White)
1 part Vodka
1 part Raspberry Liqueur
fill with Hot Cocoa

Irish Coffee Cup

Build in a heat-proof cup or mug

Chocolingus

1 part Rum
2 parts Godiva® Liqueur
3 dashes Hot Chocolate Mix
fill with Hot Milk

Irish Coffee Cup

Build in a heat-proof cup or mug

Cocomeister

1 1/2 parts Jägermeister®
fill with Hot Cocoa

Irish Coffee Cup

Build in a heat-proof cup or mug

Cure for What Ails Ya

2 parts Brandy
1 part Honey
fill with Hot Tea

Irish Coffee Cup

Build in a heat-proof cup or mug

Dark Continent

2 parts Dark Rum
1 part Cream
1/2 part Crème de Cacao (Dark)
fill with Hot Cocoa

Irish Coffee Cup

Build in a heat-proof cup or mug

Dreamy Winter Delight

2 parts Irish Cream Liqueur
fill with Hot Cocoa

Irish Coffee Cup

Build in a heat-proof cup or mug

Fireside Chat

1 part Vanilla Liqueur
1 part Dark Rum
fill with Hot Tea

Irish Coffee Cup

Build in a heat-proof cup or mug

First Frost

2 parts Cherry Brandy
splash Goldschläger®
fill with Hot Apple Cider
dash Powdered Sugar

Irish Coffee Cup

Build in a heat-proof cup or mug

Frenchman

1 part Dark Rum
1/2 part Triple Sec
splash Honey
fill with Hot Tea

Irish Coffee Cup

Build in a heat-proof cup or mug

Fuzzy Nut

1 part Peach Schnapps
1 part Amaretto
fill with Hot Cocoa

Irish Coffee Cup

Build in a heat-proof cup or mug

Girl Scout® Thin Mint Cookie

1 part Crème de Menthe (White)
fill with Hot Cocoa

Irish Coffee Cup

Build in a heat-proof cup or mug

Golden Apple Cider

1 part Goldschläger®
fill with Hot Apple Cider

Irish Coffee Cup

Build in a heat-proof cup or mug

Golden Grog

1 part Rye Whiskey
1 part Dark Rum
1 part Cointreau®
splash Amaretto
fill with Boiling Water
1 Cinnamon Stick
1 Lemon Slice

Irish Coffee Cup

Build in a heat-proof cup or mug

Gunfire

1 part Dark Rum
fill with Hot Tea

Irish Coffee Cup

Build in a heat-proof cup or mug

Heat Wave

1 part Dark Rum
1/2 part Triple Sec
1/2 part Rock & Rye
splash Lemon Juice
fill with Boiling Water

Irish Coffee Cup

Build in a heat-proof cup or mug

Hershey® Squirts

1 1/2 parts Whiskey
fill with Hot Cocoa

Irish Coffee Cup

Build in a heat-proof cup or mug

Homemade Heaven

1 1/2 parts Vanilla Liqueur
2/3 part Goldschläger®
fill with Hot Cocoa

Irish Coffee Cup

Build in a heat-proof cup or mug

Hot Brandy Toddy

2 parts Brandy
1 Sugar Cube
fill with Boiling Water

Irish Coffee Cup

Build in a heat-proof cup or mug

Hot Buttered Rum

2 parts Dark Rum
dash Brown Sugar
fill with Boiling Water
dash Ground Cloves
dash Butter

Irish Coffee Cup

Build in a heat-proof cup or mug

Hot Buttery Goose Nipples
1 part Butterscotch Schnapps
1 part Irish Cream Liqueur
fill with Hot Cocoa

Irish Coffee Cup

Build in a heat-proof cup or mug

Hot Chocolate Almond
2 parts Amaretto
1/2 part Butterscotch Schnapps
fill with Hot Cocoa

Irish Coffee Cup

Build in a heat-proof cup or mug

Hot Chocolate Butternut
2 parts Butterscotch Schnapps
1/2 part Amaretto
fill with Hot Cocoa

Irish Coffee Cup

Build in a heat-proof cup or mug

Hot Chocolate Monk
1 part Tuaca®
1 part Frangelico®
fill with Hot Cocoa

Irish Coffee Cup

Build in a heat-proof cup or mug

Hot Cinnamon Roll
1 1/2 parts Cinnamon Schnapps
fill with Hot Apple Cider

Irish Coffee Cup

Build in a heat-proof cup or mug

Hot Dick
1 part Irish Cream Liqueur
1 part Grand Marnier®
fill with Espresso

Irish Coffee Cup

Build in a heat-proof cup or mug. Top with Whipped Cream.

Hot Gin Toddy
2 parts Gin
1 Sugar Cube
fill with Boiling Water

Irish Coffee Cup

Build in a heat-proof cup or mug

Hot Girl Scout®
1 part Crème de Menthe (White)
fill with Hot Cocoa

Irish Coffee Cup

Build in a heat-proof cup or mug

Hot Irish Chocolate
1 part Whiskey
fill with Hot Cocoa

Irish Coffee Cup

Build in a heat-proof cup or mug

Hot Peppermint Pattie®
1 part Peppermint Schnapps
fill with Hot Cocoa

Irish Coffee Cup

Build in a heat-proof cup or mug

Hot Zultry Zoe
$1^1/_2$ parts Tequila
$^1/_2$ part Galliano®
2 parts Heavy Cream
fill with Hot Cocoa
Irish Coffee Cup

Build in a heat-proof cup or mug

Indian Summer
1 part Rum
fill with Hot Apple Cider
dash Cinnamon
Irish Coffee Cup

Build in a heat-proof cup or mug

Jersey Toddy
3 parts Applejack
splash Honey
2 dashes Bitters
fill with Boiling Water
Irish Coffee Cup

Build in a heat-proof cup or mug

Kirchoff's Rule
1 part Irish Cream Liqueur
$^1/_2$ part Godiva® Liqueur
$^1/_2$ part Amaretto
fill with Hot Cocoa
Irish Coffee Cup

Build in a heat-proof cup or mug. Top with Whipped Cream.

Kurant Tea
1 part Currant-Flavored Vodka
fill with Hot Tea
Irish Coffee Cup

Build in a heat-proof cup or mug

Long Island Hot Tea
1 part Pepper-Flavored Vodka
1 part Tequila
1 part Rum
1 part Gin
1 part Triple Sec
fill with Hot Tea
splash Cola
Collins Glass

Build in a heat-proof cup or mug

Mexican Hot Chocolate
$1^1/_2$ parts Tequila
$^1/_2$ part Coffee Liqueur
2 parts Cream
fill with Hot Cocoa
Irish Coffee Cup

Build in a heat-proof cup or mug

Nightgown
$^1/_2$ part Chocolate Mint Liqueur
$1^1/_2$ parts Butterscotch Schnapps
fill with Hot Cocoa
Irish Coffee Cup

Build in a heat-proof cup or mug

Peppermint Hot Chocolate
1 part Rumple Minze®
fill with Hot Cocoa
Irish Coffee Cup

Build in a heat-proof cup or mug

Ponche de Leche
$1^1/_2$ parts Light Rum
$^1/_2$ part Cognac
$^1/_2$ part Triple Sec
dash Powdered Sugar
fill with Hot Milk
Irish Coffee Cup

Build in a heat-proof cup or mug

Raspberry Truffle
1 part Raspberry Liqueur
1 part Crème de Cacao (White)
fill with Hot Milk

Irish Coffee Cup

Build in a heat-proof cup or mug

Royal Hot Chocolate
1 part Raspberry Liqueur
1 part Crème de Cacao (White)
fill with Hot Cocoa

Irish Coffee Cup

Build in a heat-proof cup or mug

Rummy
1 part Dark Rum
splash Honey
dash Brown Sugar
fill with Hot Water

Irish Coffee Cup

Build in a heat-proof cup or mug

Shocking Chocolate
1 part Cinnamon Schnapps
fill with Hot Cocoa

Irish Coffee Cup

Build in a heat-proof cup or mug

Siperia
1 part Vodka
1 part Goldschläger®
1/2 part Raspberry Syrup
fill with Hot Tea

Irish Coffee Cup

Build in a heat-proof cup or mug

Ski Lift
1 part Peach Schnapps
1/2 part CocoRibe®
fill with Hot Cocoa
dash Cinnamon

Irish Coffee Cup

Build in a heat-proof cup or mug. Top with Whipped Cream.

Skier's Toddy
1 part Coffee Liqueur
1 part Triple Sec
fill with Hot Cocoa

Irish Coffee Cup

Build in a heat-proof cup or mug. Top with Marshmallows.

Snow Bunny
1 1/2 parts Triple Sec
fill with Hot Cocoa

Irish Coffee Cup

Build in a heat-proof cup or mug

Snow Warmer
2 parts Rumple Minze®
fill with Hot Cocoa

Irish Coffee Cup

Build in a heat-proof cup or mug

Snowball Melted
1 part Brandy
1 part Peppermint Schnapps
1 part Crème de Cacao (White)
fill with Hot Cocoa

Irish Coffee Cup

Build in a heat-proof cup or mug

Snowplow
1 part Irish Cream Liqueur
1 part Coconut-Flavored Rum
1/2 part Crème de Cacao (White)
dash Cinnamon
fill with Hot Cocoa

Irish Coffee Cup

Build in a heat-proof cup or mug

Snuggler
1 1/2 parts Peppermint Schnapps
fill with Hot Cocoa

Irish Coffee Cup

Build in a heat-proof cup or mug

Spicey Scot
1 part Butterscotch Schnapps
1 part Spiced Rum
fill with Hot Cocoa

Irish Coffee Cup

Build in a heat-proof cup or mug

Squire Racine
1 1/2 parts Dark Rum
1/2 part Southern Comfort®
fill with Hot Malted Milk

Irish Coffee Cup

Build in a heat-proof cup or mug

Tantalus
1 1/2 parts Triple Sec
1/2 part Peach Schnapps
1/2 part Vanilla Liqueur
fill with Hot Apple Juice

Irish Coffee Cup

Build in a heat-proof cup or mug

Tea & Sympathy
1 part Grand Marnier®
fill with Hot Tea

Irish Coffee Cup

Build in a heat-proof cup or mug

Tea Off
1/2 part Amaretto
splash Goldschläger®
splash Peppermint Liqueur
fill with Hot Tea
splash Honey

Irish Coffee Cup

Build in a heat-proof cup or mug

Tropical Heat
1 part Cinnamon Schnapps
fill with Hot Apple Cider

Irish Coffee Cup

Build in a heat-proof cup or mug

Vacuum Bottle
1 part Peppermint Liqueur
1 part Chocolate Liqueur
fill with Hot Cocoa

Irish Coffee Cup

Build in a heat-proof cup or mug

Voyager
1 part Spiced Rum
1/4 part Crème de Banana
fill with Hot Apple Cider

Irish Coffee Cup

Build in a heat-proof cup or mug

Warm Woolly Sheep
1 part Scotch
1 1/2 shot Drambuie®
fill with Warm Milk

Irish Coffee Cup

Build in a heat-proof cup or mug

Whiskey-All-In
2 parts Whiskey
dash Sugar
2 splashes Lemon Juice
fill with Boiling Water
dash Ground Cloves

Irish Coffee Cup

Build in a heat-proof cup or mug

White Ape
1 1/2 parts Irish Cream Liqueur
dash Cinnamon
fill with Hot Cocoa

Irish Coffee Cup

Build in a heat-proof cup or mug

White Hot Chocolate
1 part Crème de Cacao (White)
fill with Hot Cocoa

Irish Coffee Cup

Build in a heat-proof cup or mug

Wooly Mitten
1 1/2 parts Southern Comfort®
1 part Peppermint Schnapps
1 1/2 parts Irish Cream Liqueur
fill with Hot Cocoa

Irish Coffee Cup

Build in a heat-proof cup or mug. Top with Whipped Cream.

Zultry Zoe
2 parts Tequila
1/2 part Galliano®
fill with Hot Cocoa

Irish Coffee Cup

Build in a heat-proof cup or mug

Champagne Drinks

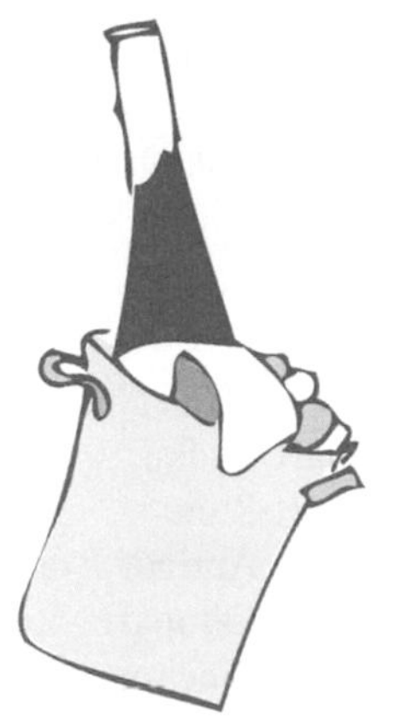

If you combine the elegance of champagne with a combination of juices and liqueurs the result is a collection of effervescent libations sure to please the discerning palate.

7 Miles

1 part Pear Juice
1 part Grenadine
dash Orange Bitters
fill with Champagne
Champagne Flute

Shake all but Champange with ice and strain into the glass. Top with ice-cold Champagne

78 Camaro

1 part Yukon Jack®
1 part Rum
1 part Apricot Brandy
1 1/2 parts Pineapple Juice
fill with Champagne
Highball Glass

Shake all but Champagne with ice and strain into a highball glass. Fill with Champagne.

Absent-Minded

1 part Peach Schnapps
1 part Absinthe
1 part Champagne
1 part Orange Juice
splash Raspberry Juice
Cocktail Glass

Shake with ice and strain

Absinthe Groseille

1 part Absinthe
2/3 part Cointreau®
2 part Champagne
2/3 part Black Currant Juice
splash Crème de Cassis
Cocktail Glass

Shake with ice and strain

Absinth Kir

splash Crème de Cassis
splash Absinthe
fill with Champagne
Highball Glass

Build over ice and stir

Absolut® Champagne

1 part Vodka
splash Cream
fill with Champagne
Collins Glass

Build in the glass with no ice

Absolution

1 part Vodka
fill with Champagne
Champagne Flute

Build in the glass with no ice

Adol-Mari

1/2 part Vodka
1/2 part Rum
1/2 part Apricot Brandy
1/2 part Campari®
1/2 part Pineapple Juice
fill with Champagne
Champagne Flute

Build in the glass with no ice

Adria Look

1 part Blue Curaçao
1 part Dry Gin
fill with Champagne
Champagne Flute

Build in the glass with no ice

Adria Wixcey

3/4 parts Dry Vermouth
1/4 part Sugar
fill with Champagne
Champagne Flute

Build in the glass with no ice

Always Together

1 part Amaretto
1 part Brandy
fill with Champagne
Champagne Flute

Build in the glass with no ice

Ambrosia

1 part Applejack
1 part Brandy
splash Triple Sec
splash Lemon Juice
fill with Champagne
Highball Glass

Shake all but Champagne with ice and strain over ice. Top with Champagne.

American Flyer

2 parts Light Rum
1 part Fresh Lime Juice
dash Sugar
fill with Champagne
Champagne Flute

Shake all but Champagne with ice. Strain and top with Champagne.

American Rose

1 part Cognac
1/2 part Peach Puree
splash Grenadine
splash Pastis
fill with Champagne
Champagne Flute

Shake all but Champagne with ice, strain and top with Champagne

American Rose #2

1 1/2 parts Brandy
1/2 part Grenadine
1/2 part Pastis
fill with Champagne
Champagne Flute

Shake all but Champagne with ice, strain and top with Champagne

Amy Jane
1/2 part Vodka
1 part Blue Curaçao
1 part Melon Liqueur
2 parts Pineapple Juice
fill with Champagne
Collins Glass

Build over ice and stir

Anadulsa
1 part Cherry Brandy
2 1/2 parts Champagne
1 part Cranberry Juice Cocktail
Highball Glass

Build over ice and stir

Apricot Velvet
1 part Vodka
1 part Apricot Brandy
fill with Champagne
Highball Glass

Build over ice and stir

Aqua Marina
1 part Vodka
1/2 part Crème de Menthe (Green)
fill with Champagne
Champagne Flute

Build in the glass with no ice

Arctic Kiss
2 parts Cranberry-Flavored Vodka
fill with Champagne
Champagne Flute

Build in the glass with no ice

Arise My Love
splash Crème de Menthe (Green)
fill with Champagne
Champagne Flute

Build in the glass with no ice

Aruban Angel
1 part Dry Gin
1 part Apricot Brandy
1 part Cherry Brandy
fill with Champagne
White Wine Glass

Shake all but Champagne with ice and strain into glass. Top with Champagne.

Atheist's Best
2 parts Vodka
1 part Cherry Juice
1 part Lemon Juice
fill with Champagne
Champagne Flute

Shake all but Champagne with ice and strain into glass. Top with Champagne.

Austrian Airlines
1 part Vodka
1 part Apricot Brandy
fill with Champagne
Champagne Flute

Build in the glass with no ice

Axis Kiss
splash Amaretto
splash Crème de Cassis
fill with Champagne
Champagne Flute

Build in the glass with no ice

Balalaika Cocktail
2 parts Vodka
1 part Champagne
1 part Orange Juice
Cocktail Glass

Shake with ice and strain

Bartini
1 part Blue Curaçao
2 parts Champagne
1 part Papaya Juice
Cocktail Glass

Shake with ice and strain

Be Back Soon
1 part Vodka
1/2 part Mandarine Napoléon® Liqueur
1/2 part Strawberry Liqueur
1 part Fresh Lime Juice
fill with Champagne
Collins Glass

Build over ice and stir

Bellini
3 parts Peach Puree
splash Lemon Juice
splash Maraschino Liqueur
fill with Champagne
Red Wine Glass

Build in the glass with no ice

Bellini #2
1 part Peach Schnapps
fill with Champagne
Champagne Flute

Build in the glass with no ice

Bentley's Bubbles
1 part Blackberry Liqueur
1 part Cranberry Juice Cocktail
1 part Orange Juice
fill with Champagne
Highball Glass

Build over ice

Beverly Hills Iced Tea
1 part Vodka
1 part Triple Sec
1 part Gin
3 dashes Sugar
fill with Champagne
Collins Glass

Build over ice and stir

Big Flirt
1 part Vodka
1 part Champagne
1/2 part Raspberry Liqueur
1 1/2 parts Pineapple Juice
1/2 part Strawberry Puree
Collins Glass

Combine all ingredients in a blender with ice. Blend until smooth.

Bitchass
1 part Tequila
1 part Brandy
1 part Champagne
1 part Strawberry Liqueur
Highball Glass

Build over ice and stir

Black Pearl
1 part Coffee Liqueur
1 part Cognac
fill with Champagne
Champagne Flute

Build in the glass with no ice

Black Velvet

1 part Chilled Stout
1 part Chilled Champagne
Champagne Flute

Build in the glass with no ice

Blow Blue Bubbles

1 part Blueberry Schnapps
fill with Champagne
Champagne Flute

Build in a glass with no ice

Blue Gecko

1 part Blue Curaçao
1 part Crème de Cacao (White)
fill with Champagne
Champagne Flute

Build in the glass with no ice

Blue Parisian

1/4 part Blue Curaçao
splash Triple Sec
splash Fresh Lime Juice
dash Sugar
fill with Champagne
Champagne Flute

Build in the glass with no ice

Blue Tahoe

1 part Blue Curaçao
1 part Tequila
1 part Lime Juice
fill with Champagne
1 Lemon Slice
1 Orange Slice
1 Cherry
Collins Glass

Build over ice and stir

Bonecrusher

1 part Champagne
1/2 part Triple Sec
1/2 part Tequila
1/2 part Vodka
1/2 part Gin
fill with Sour Mix
splash Grenadine
Highball Glass

Build over ice and stir

Bubblebath

1 part Gin
1 part Campari®
1 part Strawberry Liqueur
2 parts Orange Juice
fill with Champagne
Champagne Flute

Shake all but Champagne with ice and strain into glass. Top with Champagne.

Bubbles 'n' Bells

1 1/2 parts Raspberry Liqueur
fill with Champagne
splash Drambuie®
Highball Glass

Build over ice and stir

Bubblin' Blue

1 part Vodka
1 part Blue Curaçao
fill with Champagne
splash Cranberry Juice Cocktail
splash Sour Mix
Highball Glass

Build over ice and stir

Buzz Bomb
1 part Vodka
1 part Cointreau®
1 part Cognac
1 part Benedictine®
1 part Lime Juice
splash Champagne
Highball Glass

Build over ice and stir

Cameron Diaz
2 parts Vodka
2 parts Orange Juice
1 part Campari®
fill with Champagne
dash Orange Bitters
Collins Glass

Build over ice and stir

Camp Champ
1 part Campari®
1 part Orange
fill with Champagne
White Wine Glass

Build over ice

Cara Bonita
1 part Light Rum
1 part Blue Curaçao
1 part Pineapple Juice
2 splashes Lemon Juice
fill with Champagne
Champagne Flute

Shake all but Champagne with ice and strain into the glass. Top with Champagne.

Caribbean Champagne
splash Rum
fill with Champagne
splash Crème de Banana
Champagne Flute

Build in the glass with no ice

Cha Cha Cha L'Amour
1/2 part Chambord®
splash Chartreuse®
fill with Champagne
Highball Glass

Build over ice and stir

Champagne Berry
1 part Raspberry Liqueur
1 part Kirschwasser
fill with Champagne
Cocktail Glass

Build over ice

Champagne Bibaly
1 Sugar Cube
dash Bitters
fill with Champagne
Champagne Flute

Soak the Sugar Cube with Bitters. Place the cube in the bottom of the glass and fill with Champagne.

Champagne Blitz
1 part Crème de Menthe (White)
fill with Champagne
Champagne Flute

Build in the glass with no ice

Champagne Gem
splash Crème de Menthe (Green)
fill with Champagne
Champagne Flute

Build in the glass with no ice

Champagne Polonaise
1/2 part Blackberry Liqueur
splash Brandy
fill with Champagne
Champagne Flute

Build in the glass with no ice

Champagne Royale
splash Raspberry Liqueur
fill with Champagne
Champagne Flute

Build in the glass with no ice

Champagne Smiler
1 part Cherry Brandy
splash Lemon Juice
fill with Champagne
Champagne Flute

Build in the glass with no ice

A Christmas Ball
3 parts Champagne
1 part Raspberry Liqueur
1 part Triple Sec
Whiskey Sour Glass

Build over ice

Citrus Champagne
1 part Orange Juice
1 part Mandarine Napoléon® Liqueur
dash Orange Bitters
fill with Champagne
Champagne Flute

Build in the glass with no ice

Count Currey
1 part Gin
dash Powdered Sugar
fill with Champagne
Champagne Flute

Build in the glass with no ice

Cristal Fizz
1/2 part Pear Liqueur
dash Triple Sec
fill with Champagne
Champagne Flute

Build in the glass with no ice

Danube Valley
1 part Apricot Brandy
1 part Apricot Juice
fill with Champagne
White Wine Glass

Build in the glass with no ice

Death in the Afternoon
1 1/2 part Pernod
fill with Champagne
Champagne Flute

Build in the glass with no ice

Deep Blue
1 part Blue Curaçao
1/2 part Amer Picon®
fill with Champagne
Champagne Flute

Build in the glass with no ice

Deep River
1/2 part Blue Curaçao
3 parts Champagne
2/3 part Mango Juice
2/3 part Passion Fruit Juice
Highball Glass

Build over ice and stir

Delta Force
1/2 part Blackberry Liqueur
1/2 part Vanilla Liqueur
fill with Champagne
1/2 part Lemon Juice
1 1/2 parts Apple Juice
Highball Glass

Build over ice and stir

Diamond Fizz
2 parts Gin
1/2 part Lemon Juice
dash Powdered Sugar
fill with Champagne
Highball Glass

Build over ice and stir

Down in the Caribbean
splash Dark Rum
splash Mango Juice
splash Passion Fruit Nectar
splash Lemon Juice
fill with Champagne
Collins Glass
Build over ice and stir

Emerald Eunuch
1 part Blue Curaçao
fill with Champagne
Champagne Flute
Build in the glass with no ice

Erotica
1 part Gin
1/4 part Lemon Juice
2 dashes Sugar
fill with Champagne
Champagne Flute
Build in the glass with no ice

Fantasy
1 part Champagne
1 part Grapefruit Juice
1 part Aperol™
1/2 part Goldschläger®
Champagne Flute
Fill in a champagne glass

Finesse
1 part Kiwi Schnapps
1/2 part Coconut-Flavored Liqueur
fill with Champagne
Champagne Flute
Build in the glass with no ice

First Love
1 part Gin
dash Powdered Sugar
2 splashes Cherry Heering®
fill with Champagne
Highball Glass
Build over ice and stir

Fizzgig
1 part Blue Curaçao
1 part Amaretto
2 splashes Lemon Juice
fill with Champagne
Champagne Flute
Build in the glass with no ice

Flaming Fire
1 1/2 parts Strawberry Liqueur
1/2 part Vodka
1/2 part Strawberry Juice
fill with Champagne
Champagne Flute
Build in the glass with no ice

Fleur de Savane
1/2 part Lychee Liqueur
3 parts Champagne
splash Lemon Juice
1 part Passion Fruit Juice
splash Kiwi Syrup
Cocktail Glass
Shake with ice and strain

Flirtini
1 part Orange-Flavored Vodka
1 part Pineapple Juice
fill with Champagne
Champagne Flute
Build in the glass with no ice

Flirtini #2

1/2 part Vodka
1/2 part Triple Sec
splash Pineapple Juice
splash Fresh Lime Juice
fill with Champagne
Cocktail Glass

Shake all but Champagne with ice and strain into the glass. Top with Champagne.

Flirtini #3

1 part Vodka
1 part Champagne
1/2 part Maraschino Liqueur
2 parts Pineapple Juice
Cocktail Glass

Shake all but Champagne with ice and strain into the glass. Top with Champagne.

Forty-Seven-Eleven

1 part Blue Curaçao
1 1/2 parts Pineapple Juice
1 1/2 parts Orange Juice
fill with Champagne
Coupette Glass

Shake all but Champagne with ice and strain into the glass. Fill with Champagne.

Fraise de Champagne

1 part Strawberry Liqueur
1/2 part Cognac
fill with Champagne
Champagne Flute

Build in the glass with no ice

Fraise Royale

1 part Strawberry Liqueur
1 part Raspberry Liqueur
fill with Champagne
Champagne Flute

Build in the glass with no ice

Freedom

1/2 part Coconut-Flavored Liqueur
2/3 part Melon Liqueur
2/3 part Pineapple Juice
fill with Champagne
Highball Glass

Build over ice and stir

French 125

2 parts Sour Mix
1 part Brandy
fill with Champagne
Collins Glass

Build over ice and stir

French 25

1 part Tequila Reposado
splash Maple Syrup
fill with Champagne
Collins Glass

Build over ice and stir

French 75

1 1/2 parts Gin
2 dashes Powdered Sugar
1 1/2 parts Lemon Juice
fill with Champagne
1 Orange Slice
1 Maraschino Cherry
Collins Glass

Build over ice and stir

French 85

1 1/2 parts Brandy
1 part Lemon Juice
dash Powdered Sugar
fill with Champagne
Collins Glass

Build over ice and stir

French Foam
1/2 part Brandy
1/2 part Kirschwasser
1 1/2 parts Simple Syrup
3 dashes Bitters
fill with Champagne
1 scoop Orange Sorbet
Collins Glass

Build over ice

French Lover
1/2 part Peach Schnapps
2/3 part Plum Brandy
fill with Champagne
Highball Glass

Build over ice and stir

French Pirate
1/2 part Blue Curaçao
1 part Dark Rum
fill with Champagne
Champagne Flute

Build in the glass with no ice

Friar Delight
1 part Triple Sec
1/2 part Currant-Flavored Vodka
2 parts Champagne
1 part Pineapple Juice
Highball Glass

Build over ice and stir

Fruity Bubbles
1 part Apricot Brandy
1 part Banana Liqueur
fill with Champagne
Champagne Flute

Build in the glass with no ice

Funny People
1 part Raspberry Liqueur
1 part Apricot Brandy
fill with Champagne
Highball Glass

Build over ice and stir

Gatita Mimosa
1 part Scotch
1 part Triple Sec
fill with Champagne
Champagne Flute

Build in the glass with no ice

Girlie Martini
1 splash Dry Vermouth
4 parts Vodka
3 parts Champagne
splash Maraschino Liqueur
Cocktail Glass

Shake with ice and strain

Glory
splash Crème de Cassis
splash Kiwi Schnapps
fill with Champagne
splash Lime Juice
Highball Glass

Build over ice and stir

Golden Bear
1 part Rum
1 part Vodka
1 part Champagne
1 part Orange Juice
Old-Fashioned Glass

Build over ice and stir

Golden Lady

1 part Triple Sec
1 part Orange Juice
1 part Cognac
fill with Champagne
Champagne Flute

Shake all but Champagne with ice and strain into the glass. Top with Champagne.

A Goodnight Kiss

dash Bitters
1 Sugar Cube
fill with Champagne
splash Campari®
Champagne Flute

Put dash of Bitters on Sugar Cube and drop it in flute. Add the Champagne and the splash of Campari®.

Grand Champagner

1 part Orange Juice
1 part Triple Sec
fill with Champagne
Champagne Flute

Build in the glass with no ice

Green Eagle

1 part Blue Curaçao
1 part Orange Juice
fill with Champagne
Highball Glass

Build in the glass with no ice

Grimosa

1 part Tequila
2 parts Orange Juice
fill with Champagne
Collins Glass

Build over ice and stir

Guadalajara

1/2 part Kiwi Schnapps
1 part Tequila
fill with Champagne
1/2 part Lime Juice
Highball Glass

Build over ice and stir

Hair Spray

1 part Gin
splash Blue Curaçao
splash Pernod®
fill with Champagne
Champagne Flute

Build in the glass with no ice

Happy Birthday

3 parts Blackberry Liqueur
1 part Light Rum
1 part Pineapple Juice
1 part Triple Sec
1 part Peach Juice
fill with Champagne
Champagne Flute

Build in the glass with no ice

Happy Hollander

1 part Mango Juice
1/4 part Maraschino Liqueur
dash Powdered Sugar
fill with Champagne
Champagne Flute

Build in the glass with no ice

Happy New Year

1 part Orange Juice
1 part Port
1/2 part Brandy
fill with Champagne
Champagne Flute

Build in the glass with no ice

Hard Day
2 parts Amaretto
fill with Champagne
splash Lemon Juice
Highball Glass

Build over ice and stir

Harlem Mugger
1 part Vodka
1 part Gin
1 part Light Rum
1 part Tequila
fill with Champagne
splash Cranberry Juice Cocktail
Collins Glass

Build over ice

Harvard Graduation
1 part Melon Liqueur
fill with Champagne
1/2 part Lime Juice
Highball Glass

Build over ice and stir

Head Case
1 part Blue Curaçao
splash Crème de Cassis
fill with Champagne
Champagne Flute

Build in the glass with no ice

Heather Blush
1 part Scotch
1 part Strawberry Liqueur
fill with Champagne
Champagne Flute

Build in the glass with no ice

Hemingway
1 part Anisette
fill with Champagne
Champagne Flute

Build in the glass with no ice

High Heels
1 part Kirschwasser
1/2 part Vanilla Liqueur
fill with Champagne
Champagne Flute

Build in the glass with no ice

Honeydew
1 part Melon Liqueur
1 part Lemonade
1 part Champagne
Highball Glass

Build over ice and stir

Hour of a Star
1 1/2 part Orange Juice
1 1/2 part Southern Comfort®
1 part Champagne
Cocktail Glass

Shake all but Champagne with ice and strain into the glass. Top with Champagne.

Ichirose
1/2 part Vodka
1/2 part Peach Schnapps
1/2 part Blackberry Liqueur
1/2 part Raspberry Liqueur
1 1/2 parts Champagne
1 part Sour Mix
Highball Glass

Build over ice and stir

Indiana Jones®
1 part Tequila
1 part Whiskey
fill with Champagne
Highball Glass

Build over ice and stir

Irish Lady
1 part Melon Liqueur
1 part Orange Juice
fill with Champagne

Champagne Flute

Build in the glass with no ice

Jacuzzi®
1/2 part Gin
1 part Passion Fruit Liqueur
2 parts Orange Juice
fill with Champagne

Champagne Flute

Build in the glass with no ice

Jadranka
1 part Blue Curaçao
1 part Dry Gin
1 part Maraschino Liqueur
fill with Champagne

Champagne Flute

Build in the glass with no ice

Jäger Royale
1 1/2 parts Jägermeister®
fill with Champagne

Champagne Flute

Build in the glass with no ice

Ja-Mora
1 part Vodka
1 part Orange Juice
1 part Apple Juice
fill with Champagne

Champagne Flute

Build in the glass with no ice

Kings Peg
1 part Cognac
fill with Champagne

Champagne Flute

Build in the glass with no ice

Kir Empereur
1 part Pastis
1 part Raspberry Liqueur
fill with Champagne

Champagne Flute

Build in the glass with no ice

Kir Royale
splash Crème de Cassis
fill with Champagne

Champagne Flute

Build in the glass with no ice

Kordulas Special
1 Sugar Cube
dash Bitters
fill with Champagne

Champagne Flute

Soak the Sugar Cube with Bitters. Place the Cube in the bottom of the glass and fill with Champagne.

L'Aiglon
1 part Mandarine Napoléon® Liqueur
fill with Champagne

Champagne Flute

Build in the glass with no ice

Leaping Lizard
1 part Blue Curaçao
1 part Crème de Cacao (White)
fill with Champagne

Champagne Flute

Build in the glass with no ice

Lemon Celebration

1 part Raspberry Liqueur
1 part Bacardi® Limón Rum
fill with Champagne
Cocktail Glass

Stir gently with ice and strain

Lemon Mimosa

1/2 part Lemon Juice
dash Powdered Sugar
fill with Champagne
White Wine Glass

Build in the glass with no ice

Liberty Blue Champagne

splash Blue Curaçao
splash Grand Marnier®
1/2 part Lemon Juice
1 part Vodka
fill with Champagne
Champagne Flute

Build in the glass with no ice

Lion

1/2 part Silver Tequila
1/2 part Peach Schnapps
1 part Passion Fruit Juice
splash Grenadine
fill with Champagne
Champagne Flute

Shake all but Champagne with ice and strain into the glass. Top with Champagne.

Lolala

1/2 part Gin
1/2 part Parfait Amour
2 parts Champagne
2 parts Apple Juice
Highball Glass

Build over ice and stir

London Sunset

1 part Brandy
1 part Cherry Brandy
fill with Champagne
Champagne Flute

Build in the glass with no ice

Lost Temple

splash Blue Curaçao
1/2 part Armagnac
1 1/2 parts Orange Juice
fill with Champagne
Highball Glass

Build over ice

Lozana

1 part Bourbon
1/2 part Strawberry Liqueur
1/2 part Crème de Menthe (White)
fill with Champagne
Champagne Flute

Build in the glass with no ice

Lush

1 part Vodka
fill with Champagne
Champagne Flute

Build in the glass with no ice

Luxury Cocktail

1 part Brandy
fill with Chilled Champagne
2 dashes Orange Bitters
Champagne Flute

Build in the glass with no ice

Lychee Lover

1 part Lychee Liqueur
1 part Crème de Cassis
fill with Champagne
Highball Glass

Build over ice

Magnolia
2/3 part Maraschino Liqueur
1/2 part Tequila Silver
1 part Apple Juice
fill with Champagne
Highball Glass

Build over ice and stir

Manaus Nights
1 part Passion Fruit Liqueur
1 part Cachaça
fill with Champagne
Champagne Flute

Build in the glass with no ice

Mauve Sunset
splash Parfait Amour
fill with Champagne
Champagne Flute

Build in the glass with no ice

Metropolis
1 part Vodka
1/2 part Strawberry Liqueur
fill with Champagne
Champagne Flute

Build in the glass with no ice

Mexican Firewater
2 parts Tequila Reposado
1 part Coffee Liqueur
fill with Champagne
Old-Fashioned Glass

Build over ice and stir

Millennium Cocktail
1/2 part Melon Liqueur
1/2 part Gin
1 part Champagne
2/3 parts Mango Juice
splash Lemon Syrup
Cocktail Glass

Shake with ice and strain

Mimosa
2 parts Orange Juice
fill with Champagne
Champagne Flute

Build in the glass with no ice

Mimosa-Super
1 1/2 parts Orange Juice
1/2 part Triple Sec
fill with Champagne
Champagne Flute

Build in the glass with no ice

Mint Champagne
1 part Crème de Menthe (Green)
1 part Orange Juice
1 part Gin
fill with Champagne
Champagne Flute

Build in the glass with no ice

Money Talk
1/2 part Passion Fruit Liqueur
1/2 part Dark Rum
2/3 parts Orange Juice
fill with Champagne
Cocktail Glass

Build in the glass with no ice

Monte Carlo Imperial
1 1/2 parts Gin
1/2 part Crème de Menthe (White)
splash Lemon Juice
fill with Champagne
Highball Glass

Build over ice and stir

Morning Champagne
1/2 part Apricot Brandy
fill with Champagne
Champagne Flute

Build in the glass with no ice

Morning Kiss
3/4 part Brandy
3/4 part Gin
1 part Orange Juice
fill with Champagne
White Wine Glass

Shake all but Champagne with ice and strain into the glass. Top with Champagne.

Mortal's Nectar
1 part Brandy
1/2 part Raspberry Liqueur
1 part Apple Brandy
1 part Champagne
Cocktail Glass

Shake with ice and strain

Moscow Mimosa
3 parts Orange Juice
1/2 part Vodka
fill with Champagne
Champagne Flute

Build in the glass with no ice

My Sister-in-Law
1 part Scotch
1/2 part Triple Sec
fill with Champagne
Champagne Flute

Build in the glass with no ice

Night and Day
1 part Cognac
1/2 part Apricot Brandy
1 1/2 parts Orange Juice
fill with Champagne
White Wine Glass

Build over ice

Night Flight
1 part Amaretto
1 part Peach Schnapps
1 part Blackberry Liqueur
2 parts Orange Juice
fill with Champagne
Champagne Flute

Shake all but Champagne with ice and strain into the glass. Top with Champagne.

Noblesse
1 1/2 parts Champagne
2/3 part Dark Rum
2/3 part Pear Syrup
splash Melon Liqueur
Cocktail Glass

Stir gently with ice and strain

Norma Jean
1 part Blue Curaçao
fill with Champagne
Champagne Flute

Build in the glass with no ice

The Odyssey
1/2 part Lychee Liqueur
1 1/2 parts Vodka
2 1/2 parts Champagne
dash Peychauds® Bitters
Highball Glass

Build over ice and stir

Ohio

1 part Whiskey
1/2 part Triple Sec
1/2 part Sweet Vermouth
fill with Champagne
dash Bitters
Champagne Flute

Build over ice and stir

Operation Greenpeace

1 part Melon Liqueur
1 part Passion Fruit Juice
fill with Champagne
Highball Glass

Build over ice and stir

Original Sin

1 part Brandy
1 part Cherry Heering®
1/2 shot Triple Sec
splash Sour Mix
splash Grenadine
fill with Champagne
Brandy Snifter

Build over ice and stir

Oriole

1 part Peach Schnapps
1 part Champagne
1 part Orange Juice
1 part Pineapple Juice
Highball Glass

Build over ice and stir

Pamperito

3/4 part Pineapple Juice
1/2 part Gin
1/4 part Triple Sec
splash Lemon Juice
fill with Champagne
Champagne Flute

Build in the glass with no ice

Paradise

1 part Raspberry Liqueur
fill with Champagne
Champagne Flute

Build in the glass with no ice

Paris, Texas

1 part Bourbon
1 part Blackberry Liqueur
fill with Champagne
Champagne Flute

Build in the glass with no ice

Passat

1 part Triple Sec
1 part Apricot Brandy
1 1/2 parts Passion Fruit Juice
splash Orange Juice
fill with Champagne
Champagne Flute

Shake all but Champagne with ice and strain into the glass. Top with Champagne.

Peach Mimosa

1/2 part Peach Schnapps
1 part Orange Juice
fill with Champagne
Champagne Flute

Build in the glass with no ice

Peach Treat

1 part Peach Brandy
2 parts Orange Juice
fill with Chilled Champagne
Collins Glass

Build over ice and stir

Peppermint Peace

1 part Crème de Cacao (White)
1 part Crème de Menthe (White)
fill with Champagne
Champagne Flute

Build in the glass with no ice

Pilot House Fizz

1 part Vodka
1 part Grand Marnier®
splash Sweetened Lime Juice
dash Orange Bitters
fill with Champagne
White Wine Glass

Build over ice and stir

Pimm's® Royal

1 1/2 parts Pimm's® No. 1 Cup
fill with Champagne
Champagne Flute

Build in the glass with no ice

Pink California Sunshine

1/2 part Crème de Cassis
1 part Pink Champagne
1 part Orange Juice
Cocktail Glass

Build over ice

Pink Chevrolet

1 part Strawberry Liqueur
fill with Champagne
Champagne Flute

Build in the glass with no ice

Pink Millenium

1 part Citrus-Flavored Vodka
1 part Cranberry Juice Cocktail
splash Simple Syrup
fill with Champagne
Champagne Flute

Shake all but Champagne with ice and strain into the glass. Top with Champagne.

Pink Tail

1 part Triple Sec
1 part Strawberry Liqueur
1 part Orange Juice
1 part Grape Juice (white)
fill with Champagne
Champagne Flute

Shake all but Champagne with ice and strain into the glass. Top with Champagne.

Player's Passion

1 part Alizé®
1 part Cognac
fill with Champagne
Highball Glass

Build over ice and stir

Poinsettia

1/2 part Triple Sec
3 parts Champagne
Champagne Flute

Build in the glass with no ice

Poinsettia #2

1/2 part Triple Sec
1 part Champagne
1 part Cranberry Juice Cocktail
Highball Glass

Build over ice and stir

Prince of Wales

1 part Cognac
1/2 part Triple Sec
dash Bitters
fill with Champagne
Champagne Flute

Shake all but Champagne with ice and strain into the glass. Top with Champagne.

Qi Spring Punch

1 part Vodka
1 part Strawberry Liqueur
fill with Champagne
Champagne Flute

Build in the glass with no ice

Que Pasion

1 part Southern Comfort®
1 part Passion Fruit Liqueur
fill with Champagne
Champagne Flute

Build in the glass with no ice

Ray Gun

1 part Blue Curaçao
fill with Champagne
Champagne Flute

Build in the glass with no ice

Recife Royal

1 part Passion Fruit Liqueur
splash Crème de Cacao (White)
1 part Orange Juice
1 part Champagne
Champagne Flute

Shake all but Champagne with ice and strain into the glass. Top with Champagne.

Red Kiss

1 part Dark Rum
1 part Cherry Brandy
1 part Pineapple Juice
fill with Champagne
Champagne Flute

Build in the glass with no ice

Ritz Cocktail

1 part Triple Sec
1 part Orange Juice
1 part Cognac
fill with Champagne
Champagne Flute

Shake all but Champagne with ice and strain into the glass. Top with Champagne.

Romy

1 1/2 parts Advocaat
fill with Champagne
Champagne Flute

Build in the glass with no ice

Rosanna

1 1/2 parts Orange Juice
1 part Cinzano®
1/2 part Triple Sec
fill with Champagne
Champagne Flute

Shake all but Champagne with ice and strain into the glass. Top with Champagne.

Roses Are Red

1 1/2 parts Parfait Amour
1/2 part Grenadine
fill with Champagne
Champagne Flute

Shake all but Champagne with ice and strain into the glass. Top with Champagne.

Rototo

1 part Cognac
1 part Triple Sec
1 part Maraschino Liqueur
fill with Champagne
Champagne Flute

Build in the glass with no ice

Royal Bill

1/2 part Pear Brandy
fill with Champagne
Champagne Flute

Build in the glass with no ice

Royal Screw

1 part Cognac
1 part Orange Juice
fill with Champagne
Highball Glass

Build over ice and stir

Royal Starboard

1 part Raspberry Liqueur
1 part Blackberry Liqueur
3 parts Cranberry Juice Cocktail
fill with Champagne
Highball Glass

Build over ice and stir

Rue Royal

1 part Strawberry Liqueur
1/2 part Cognac
fill with Champagne
Champagne Flute

Build in the glass with no ice

Russian Spring Punch

2 parts Vodka
1/2 part Crème de Cassis
dash Powdered Sugar
fill with Champagne
Collins Glass

Shake all but Champagne with ice and strain into the glass. Top with Champagne.

Rusty Betty

1 part Grand Marnier®
1/2 part Raspberry Liqueur
2 parts Pineapple Juice
fill with Champagne
Collins Glass

Build over ice and stir

Saiki

1 part Champagne
splash Crème de Banana
splash Frangelico®
1/2 part Orange Juice
splash Lemon Juice
Highball Glass

Build over ice and stir

Saint Germain

1 part Cherry Brandy
1 part Champagne
Highball Glass

Build over ice and stir

Saint Royal

1 part Strawberry Liqueur
1 part Strawberry Puree
1 part Vanilla-Flavored Vodka
fill with Champagne
Champagne Flute

Shake all but Champagne with ice and strain into the glass. Top with Champagne.

San Remo

1 part Triple Sec
1 part Apricot Brandy
1 part Grapefruit Juice
1 part Champagne
White Wine Glass

Build over ice

Savoy 90

1 part Amaretto
splash Orange Flower Water
fill with Champagne
Champagne Flute

Build in the glass with no ice

Scotch Royale

1 Sugar Cube
$1\frac{1}{2}$ parts Scotch
dash Bitters
fill with Champagne
Champagne Flute

Place sugar cube in a Champagne Flute and add Scotch and Bitters. Fill with Champagne.

Sea of Love

1 part Coconut-Flavored Liqueur
1 part Strawberry Puree
$\frac{1}{2}$ part Rum
fill with Champagne
Hurricane Glass

Shake all but Champagne with ice and strain into the glass. Top with Champagne.

Seelbach Cocktail

1 part Bourbon
$\frac{1}{2}$ part Triple Sec
7 dashes Peychaud's® Bitters
7 dashes Angostura® Bitters
fill with Champagne
Champagne Flute

Shake all but Champagne with ice and strain into the glass. Top with Champagne.

Sexy Seville

1 part Peach Schnapps
1 part Cranberry Juice Cocktail
fill with Champagne
Highball Glass

Build over ice and stir

Shake

1 part Apricot Brandy
$\frac{1}{2}$ part Kirschwasser
fill with Champagne
Champagne Flute

Build in the glass with no ice

Silvester Royal

1 part Passion Fruit Liqueur
1 part Cachaça
$1\frac{1}{2}$ parts Orange Juice
fill with Champagne
Champagne Flute

Shake all but Champagne with ice and strain into the glass. Top with Champagne.

Singapore Fizz

1 part Gin
$\frac{1}{2}$ part Cherry Brandy
splash Simple Syrup
fill with Champagne
Champagne Flute

Shake all but Champagne with ice and strain into the glass. Top with Champagne.

Sinus Dream

1 part Blue Curaçao
1 part Vodka
1 part Advocaat
fill with Champagne
White Wine Glass

Shake all but Champagne with ice and strain into the glass. Top with Champagne.

Sir Henry

1 part Peach Schnapps
1 part Orange Juice
fill with Champagne
Collins Glass

Shake all but Champagne with ice and strain into the glass. Top with Champagne.

Southern Bubbles

$^{1}/_{2}$ part Southern Comfort®
fill with Champagne
Champagne Flute

Build in the glass with no ice

Space Journey

1 part Vodka
$^{1}/_{2}$ part Cherry Brandy
fill with Champagne
Champagne Flute

Build in the glass with no ice

Sparkling Kiwi

$1^{1}/_{2}$ parts Kiwi Schnapps
fill with Champagne
Champagne Flute

Build in the glass with no ice

Sparkling Strawberry

1 part Remy Martin® VSOP
splash Cherry Brandy
$1^{1}/_{2}$ parts Pineapple Juice
splash Strawberry Syrup
fill with Champagne
Collins Glass

Build over ice and stir

Sparks

1 part Pepper-Flavored Vodka
fill with Champagne
Champagne Flute

Build in the glass with no ice

Spotlight

1 part Cherry Brandy
splash Dry Gin
splash Dry Vermouth
splash Campari®
fill with Champagne
Champagne Flute

Shake all but Champagne with ice and strain into the glass. Top with Champagne.

Spring into Summer

$^{1}/_{2}$ part Apricot Brandy
splash Crème de Menthe (Green)
fill with Champagne
Champagne Flute

Build in the glass with no ice

Spring Sun

1 part Triple Sec
1 part Orange Juice
fill with Champagne
Champagne Flute

Build in the glass with no ice

Spring Time

1 part Gordon's® Orange Vodka
1 part Lychee Liqueur
splash Fresh Lime Juice
fill with Champagne
Champagne Flute

Build in the glass with no ice

Stockholm 75

1 part Citrus-Flavored Vodka
1 part Simple Syrup
1 part Lemon Juice
fill with Champagne
Champagne Flute

Shake all but Champagne with ice and strain into the glass. Top with Champagne.

Storm's a Brewing

1 part Cherry Brandy
1/2 part Kiwi Schnapps
1 part Orange Juice
1 part Pineapple Juice
1 part Sour Mix
fill with Champagne
Highball Glass

Build over ice and stir

Strawberry Blonde Champagne

2 parts Strawberry Liqueur
1 part Irish Mist®
fill with Champagne
Champagne Flute

Shake all but Champagne with ice and strain into the glass. Top with Champagne.

Sunny Side

1 part Vodka
1/2 part Grenadine
1/2 part Raspberry Liqueur
fill with Champagne
Champagne Flute

Shake all but Champagne with ice and strain into the glass. Top with Champagne.

Sunset in a Glass

2 parts Peach Schnapps
1 part Cranberry Juice Cocktail
splash Orange Juice
fill with Champagne
Champagne Flute

Shake all but Champagne with ice and strain into the glass. Top with Champagne.

Sunshine Smile

1 part Vodka
1 part Orange Juice
fill with Champagne
Champagne Flute

Shake all but Champagne with ice and strain into the glass. Top with Champagne.

Sweet Thing

1 part Melon Liqueur
1 part Peach Schnapps
fill with Champagne
Champagne Flute

Shake all but Champagne with ice and strain into the glass. Top with Champagne.

Sweetest Taboo

splash Blue Curaçao
1 1/2 parts Orange Juice
fill with Champagne
Champagne Flute

Shake all but Champagne with ice and strain into the glass. Top with Champagne.

Tahiti

1 part Dry Gin
1 part Triple Sec
fill with Champagne
White Wine Glass

Build in the glass with no ice

Think I Love You

1 part Strawberry Puree
1 part Pineapple Juice
1/2 part Red Curaçao
1/2 part Simple Syrup
fill with Champagne
Champagne Flute

Shake all but Champagne with ice and strain into the glass. Top with Champagne.

Titiani
2 parts Grape Juice (red)
splash Grenadine
fill with Champagne
Champagne Flute

Build in the glass with no ice

Torque Wrench
1 part Champagne
1 part Orange Juice
1 part Melon Liqueur
Shot Glass

Build in the glass with no ice

Tropical Bellini
1 part Peach Schnapps
1 part Peach Sorbet
1 part Pineapple Juice
fill with Champagne
Collins Glass

Shake all but Champagne with ice and strain into the glass. Top with Champagne.

Tropical Champagne
1/2 part Dark Rum
1 part Passion Fruit Liqueur
1 1/2 parts Pineapple Juice
fill with Champagne
Champagne Flute

Shake all but Champagne with ice and strain into the glass. Top with Champagne.

True Lies
1 part Triple Sec
1 part Strawberry Syrup
fill with Champagne
Champagne Flute

Build in the glass with no ice

Tryst & Shout
1 1/2 parts Amaretto
2 parts Sour Mix
fill with Champagne
Champagne Flute

Shake all but Champagne with ice and strain into the glass. Top with Champagne.

The Twist
3/4 parts Vermouth
1/2 part Crème de Menthe (White)
1 scoop Orange Sorbet
fill with Champagne
Champagne Flute

Shake all but Champagne with ice and strain into the glass. Top with Champagne.

Typhoon
1 part Gin
1/2 part Anisette
1 part Lime Juice
fill with Champagne
Collins Glass

Shake all but Champagne with ice and strain into the glass. Top with Champagne.

Ultra-Marine
1/2 part Blue Curaçao
fill with Champagne
Champagne Flute

Build in the glass with no ice

Uptown Girl
1 1/2 parts Maraschino Liqueur
fill with Champagne
Coupette Glass

Build in the glass with no ice

Champagne Drinks

Valencia Fizz

1 part Apricot Brandy
1 part Orange Juice
fill with Champagne
Champagne Flute

Shake all but Champagne with ice and strain into the glass. Top with Champagne.

Virginia Asshole

1 part Blue Curaçao
1 part Vodka
fill with Champagne
Hurricane Glass

Build over ice and stir

Volcano Fizz

1 part Raspberry Liqueur
1 part Blue Curaçao
fill with Champagne
Champagne Flute

Build in the glass with no ice

Wayamata

1 part Dark Rum
1/2 part Strawberry juice
1/4 part Triple Sec
fill with Champagne
Champagne Flute

Shake all but Champagne with ice and strain into the glass. Top with Champagne.

Weirdness

1 part Peach Schnapps
1 part Crème de Banana
fill with Champagne
Highball Glass

Build over ice and stir

Wings of Tenderness

1 part Vodka
1 part Campari®
fill with Champagne
Champagne Flute

Shake all but Champagne with ice and strain into the glass. Top with Champagne.

Winter 42

1 1/2 part Vodka
1 part Light Rum
dash Bitters
fill with Champagne
Coupette Glass

Shake all but Champagne with ice and strain into the glass. Top with Champagne.

Y2K

1 part Vodka
1 part Melon Liqueur
1/2 part Melon Puree
1/2 part Simple Syrup
fill with Champagne
Champagne Flute

Shake all but Champagne with ice and strain into the glass. Top with Champagne.

Yellow Cat

1 part Orange Juice
1 part Dry Vermouth
1 part Coconut-Flavored Liqueur
fill with Champagne
Champagne Flute

Shake all but Champagne with ice and strain into the glass. Top with Champagne.

Wine-Based Drinks

This collection of drinks falls somewhere between the wine cooler and a wicked hangover.

8th Wonder

2 parts White Wine
1 part Brandy
1 part Triple Sec
1 part Maraschino Liqueur
1 part Sour Mix
White Wine Glass

Shake with ice and strain over ice

Adler's OJ

1 part Red Wine
3 parts Orange Juice
3 parts Orange Soda
Collins Glass

Build over ice and stir

Amaretto Flirt

3 parts Sparkling White Wine
1 part Amaretto
1 part Orange Juice
Champagne Flute

Build in the glass with no ice

Amaretto Sangria

2 parts Amaretto
1 part Red Wine
1 part Orange Juice
1 part Pineapple Juice
Highball Glass

Build over ice and stir

Amaretto Wine Cooler

2 parts Amaretto
1 part White Wine
1 part Lemon-Lime Soda
Highball Glass

Build over ice and stir

Amaretto Wine Fizz

2 parts Amaretto
1 part Sour Mix
1 part Orange Juice
1 part White Wine
1 part Lemon-Lime Soda
Highball Glass

Build over ice and stir

Anime Sailor

1 part Light Rum
1 part Advocaat
1/2 part Galliano®
3/4 part Lemon Juice
fill with White Wine
Collins Glass

Build over ice and stir

Apple Wine Cooler

2 parts Sour Apple–Flavored Schnapps
1 part Wine
1 part Lemon-Lime Soda
Highball Glass

Build over ice and stir

Apple Wine Spritzer

2 parts Sour Apple–Flavored Schnapps
1 part White Wine
1 part Club Soda
Highball Glass

Build over ice and stir

Balalaika Magika

1/2 part Creme de Menthe (White)
1 part Lemonade
fill with White Wine
White Wine Glass

Build over ice

Balaton

1 part Apricot Brandy
1 part Peach Schnapps
fill with Sparkling White Wine
White Wine Glass

Shake all but Wine with ice and strain into glass. Top with Sparkling Wine.

Balla Balla

1 part Dry Gin
1 part Triple Sec
1 part Campari®
fill with Sparkling White Wine
White Wine Glass

Build over ice

Balthazar

1/2 part Vanilla Liqueur
1/2 part Lemon Juice
2 parts Raspberry-Flavored Seltzer
3 parts Red Wine
Collins Glass

Build over ice and stir

Bambi

1 part Cola
1 part Red Wine
Collins Glass

Build over ice and stir

Beach Cooler

1 part Vodka
1 part Red Wine
1 part Cola
1 part Orange Juice
1 part Passion Fruit
Collins Glass

Build over ice and stir

Beach Peach

1 part Apricot Brandy
2 parts Peach Wine
2 parts Orange Juice
Highball Glass

Shake with ice and strain

Bermuda Blanc

1 part Light Rum
1 part Lime Cordial
fill with White Wine
White Wine Glass

Build over ice and stir

Bernetto

1 part Currant-Flavored Vodka
1/2 part Blackberry Liqueur
1/2 part Vanilla Liqueur
fill with Sparkling Wine
Highball Glass

Build over ice and stir

Berry Wine Cooler

1 part Blackberry Liqueur
4 parts White Wine
2 parts Pineapple Juice
1 part Cranberry Juice Cocktail
1 part Club Soda
Highball Glass

Build over ice and stir

Better Breezer
1/2 part Scotch
1 part Crème de Cassis
1/2 part Orange Liqueur
3 parts Sparkling Wine
Highball Glass
Build over ice and stir

The Big Shamble
splash Vanilla Liqueur
1/2 part Chambord®
1/2 part Hazelnut Liqueur
2 parts Red Wine
2 parts Raspberry-Flavored Seltzer
1/2 part Lemon Juice
Highball Glass
Build over ice and stir

Bishop
1/4 part Lemon Juice
1/2 part Orange Juice
dash Powdered Sugar
fill with Red Wine
Highball Glass
Shake all but Wine with ice and strain into the glass. Top with Red Wine.

Blackberry Wine Cooler
2 parts Blackberry Liqueur
1 part White Wine
1 part Lemon-Lime Soda
Highball Glass
Build over ice and stir

Bloody Pepper
1 part Red Wine
1 part Dr Pepper®
Red Wine Glass
Build over ice and stir

Boston Bottle Rocket
1 part White Wine
1/2 part Lemon Juice
dash Sugar
fill with Orange Juice
Old-Fashioned Glass
Shake with ice and pour

Burgundy Bishop
1 part Light Rum
1/4 part Lemon Juice
dash Powdered Sugar
fill with Red Wine
Highball Glass
Shake all but Wine with ice and strain into the glass. Top with Red Wine.

Butterfly
1 part Sweet Vermouth
1 part Dry Vermouth
1/2 part Orange Juice
1/2 part Red Wine
Old-Fashioned Glass
Shake with ice and strain

Cactus Berry
1 1/4 parts Tequila
1 1/4 parts Red Wine
1 part Triple Sec
fill with Sour Mix
splash Lemon-Lime Soda
splash Lime Juice
Coupette Glass
Shake with ice and strain

Calimocho
1 part Red Wine
1 part Cola
Highball Glass
Build over ice and stir

Captain with a Skirt
2 parts Spiced Rum
2 parts White Wine
fill with Cola
1 Lime Slice
Collins Glass

Build over ice and stir

Cliffhanger
1 part Vanilla Liqueur
1/2 part Passion Fruit Liqueur
fill with White Wine
Champagne Flute

Build in the glass with no ice

Cocomacoque
1 1/2 parts Light Rum
2 parts Red Wine
1/2 part Lemon Juice
2 parts Pineapple Juice
2 parts Orange Juice
Collins Glass

Shake with ice and pour

Czar
1 part Vodka
1 part Grand Marnier®
1/2 part Lime Juice
fill with Dry Sparkling White Wine
dash Orange Bitters
Highball Glass

Build over ice and stir

Damn Yankees
1 part Triple Sec
2 parts White Wine
1 1/2 parts Lemon-Lime Soda
1 part Pineapple Juice
Highball Glass

Build over ice and stir

Dog Day Cooler
1 1/2 parts Gin
1 part Orange Juice
1 part Red Wine
1 part Lime Cordial
Old-Fashioned Glass

Shake with ice and pour

Fernando
1 1/2 parts Triple Sec
1 1/2 parts Strawberry Liqueur
1 part White Wine
1 part Orange Juice
Collins Glass

Shake with ice and strain over ice

A Fruity Fuck Face
4 parts Vodka
2 parts Rum
1 part White Wine
3 parts Orange Juice
Old-Fashioned Glass

Build over ice and stir

Green Pineapple
1 1/2 parts Pineapple Juice
1 part Blue Curaçao
fill with Sparkling White Wine
White Wine Glass

Build over ice and stir

Hillary Wallbanger
4 parts Dry White Wine
1/2 part Galliano®
fill with Orange Juice
Collins Glass

Build over ice and stir

Imperial Czar
$1\frac{1}{2}$ parts White Wine
1/2 part Vodka
1/2 part Triple Sec
1/4 part Lime Cordial
2 dashes Orange Bitters
White Wine Glass

Shake with ice and strain

Italian Perfume
1 part Brandy
1 part Amaretto
fill with White Wine
White Wine Glass

Build over ice and stir

Kalimotxo
1 part Red Wine
1 part Cola
Collins Glass

Build over ice and stir

Laguna
1/2 part Blue Curaçao
1 part Pineapple Juice
1 part Sparkling White Wine
Collins Glass

Build over ice and stir

Lemon Wine Cooler
1 part White Wine
1 part Lemonade
1 part Lemon-Lime Soda
Highball Glass

Build over ice and stir

May Day
$1\frac{1}{2}$ parts Bourbon
splash Kirschwasser
splash Strawberry Liqueur
fill with Red Wine
Highball Glass

Build over ice and stir

My Best Friend's Girl
1 part Peach Schnapps
1 part White Wine
1 part Club Soda
Highball Glass

Shake with ice and pour

Paparazzi
1/2 part Dark Rum
1/4 part Fresh Lime Juice
1 part Pineapple Juice
fill with Sparkling White Wine
White Wine Glass

Build over ice and stir

Peach Bottom
1 part Peach Schnapps
1 part Vodka
fill with White Wine
splash Lemon Juice
Beer Mug

Build over ice and stir

Peep Hole
1 part Orange Juice
1 part Brandy
1/2 part Simple Syrup
fill with White Zinfandel Wine
Collins Glass

Build over ice and stir

Queen Charlotte
2 parts Red Wine
1 part Grenadine
fill with Lemon-Lime Soda
Collins Glass

Build over ice and stir

Quick Thrill
1/2 part Dark Rum
1 part Red Wine
1 part Cola
White Wine Glass

Build over ice and stir

Red Rover

1 part Dark Rum
1/2 part Raspberry Syrup
1 part Red Wine
1 part Club Soda
Collins Glass

Build over ice and stir

Red Wine Cobbler

1 part Orange Juice
1 part Maraschino Liqueur
1 part Fresh Lime Juice
fill with Red Wine
Collins Glass

Build over ice and stir

Red Wine Cooler

2 parts Red Wine
1 part Lemon-Lime Soda
1 part Ginger Ale
Highball Glass

Build over ice and stir

Regal Fizz

1 part Cherry Brandy
1 part Kirschwasser
fill with Sparkling White Wine
Highball Glass

Build over ice and stir

Regatta

1 part Vodka
1 part Triple Sec
fill with Sparkling White Wine
Highball Glass

Build over ice and stir

Rembrandt

1 part Apricot Brandy
fill with White Wine
White Wine Glass

Build in the glass with no ice

Rhine Cooler

1 part Lime Juice
1 part White Wine
1 part Club Soda
dash Sugar
Collins Glass

Build over ice and stir

Royal Peach Freeze

1/2 part Lime Juice
2 parts Orange Juice
2 parts Peach Schnapps
1 1/2 parts Dry Sparkling White Wine
Coupette Glass

Combine all ingredients in a blender with ice. Blend until smooth.

Sangre de Toro

splash Apricot Brandy
fill with Red Wine
Highball Glass

Build over ice and stir

Smurf® Juice

splash Blue Curaçao
1 part White Wine
1 part Ginger Ale
Collins Glass

Build over ice and stir

Smut

1 part Peach Schnapps
1 part Red Wine
1 part Cola
1 part Orange Juice
Beer Mug

Build over ice and stir

Sparkling Wine Polonaise
1/2 part Blackberry Liqueur
splash Cognac
fill with Dry Sparkling White Wine
White Wine Glass

Build in the glass with no ice

Stab in the Back
1/2 part Brandy
1 1/2 parts Orange Juice
2 parts Dry White Wine
2 parts Club Soda
Highball Glass

Build over ice and stir

Sunny Sex
1 part Coconut-Flavored Rum
1 part Fire Water®
1/2 part Vodka
1/2 part Red Wine
1 part Orange Juice
Coupette Glass

Shake with ice and pour

Sunset Horizon
2/3 part Gin
2/3 part Cherry Liqueur
2 parts Vegetable Juice Blend
fill with White Wine
White Wine Glass

Build over ice and stir

Talisman
1/2 part Crème de Cassis
3 parts White Wine
1 part Strawberry Juice
splash Orange Juice
Old-Fashioned Glass

Shake with ice and strain over ice

Teacher's Pet
2/3 part Advocaat
2/3 part Calvados Apple Brandy
3 parts White Wine
1 part Lemon-Lime Soda
Highball Glass

Shake with ice and strain over ice

Urbinos
1 part Cognac
1/2 part Red Curacao
fill with White Wine
White Wine Glass

Build over ice and stir

Webmaster Wine
1 1/2 parts Blackberry Liqueur
1 part White Wine
1 part Lemon-Lime Soda
1 part Cranberry Juice Cocktail
Highball Glass

Build over ice and stir

White Wine Cooler
2 parts White Wine
1 part Lemon-Lime Soda
1 part Ginger Ale
Highball Glass

Build over ice and stir

White Wine Spritzer
1 part White Wine
1 part Club Soda
White Wine Glass

Build over ice and stir

Wine & Coke
1 part Red Wine
1 part Cola
Highball Glass

Build over ice and stir

Wine Cooler

1 part White Wine
2 parts Lemon-Lime Soda
Highball Glass

Build over ice and stir

Wine Spritzer

3 parts White Wine
1 part Club Soda
White Wine Glass

Build over ice and stir

Yellow-Bellied Chupacabra

1 part Red Wine
1 part Tequila
splash Sweet Vermouth
Brandy Snifter

Build in the glass with no ice

Mind Eraser Drinks

This category of drink is like a combination of a layered shot and a mixed drink. The liquor, liqueur, and mixer are layered over ice in an old-fashioned or small rocks glass. The drink is then consumed quickly through a straw.

B-28

1 part Irish Cream Liqueur
1 part Coffee Liqueur
1 part Amaretto
1 part Butterscotch Schnapps
Whiskey Sour Glass

Layer over ice. Drink through a straw.

Blue Knickers

1 part Vodka
1 part Blue Curaçao
1 part Galliano®
splash Cream
Old-Fashioned Glass

Layer over ice. Drink through a straw.

Brain Drain

1 part Coffee Liqueur
1 part Cola
1 part Vodka
Highball Glass

Layer over ice. Drink through a straw.

Brain Eraser

1/2 part Amaretto
1/2 part Coffee Liqueur
1 part Vodka
fill with Club Soda
Highball Glass

Layer over ice. Drink through a straw.

Brain Eraser #2

1 part Goldschläger®
1 part Coffee Liqueur
1 part Vodka
Old-Fashioned Glass

Layer over ice. Drink through a straw.

Brainteaser

1 part Sambuca
1 part Cream
splash Advocaat
Whiskey Sour Glass

Layer over ice. Drink through a straw.

Cookie Monster

1 part Coffee Liqueur
1 part Irish Cream Liqueur
1 part 151-Proof Rum
Whiskey Sour Glass

Layer over ice. Drink through a straw.

Derailer

1 part Vodka
1 part Gold Tequila
1 part Coffee Liqueur
Highball Glass

Layer over ice. Drink through a straw.

Disco Ball

1 part Melon Liqueur
1 part Goldschläger®
Old-Fashioned Glass

Layer over ice. Drink through a straw.

Fat Cat Cooler

1 part Citrus-Flavored Rum
1 part Cranberry Juice Cocktail
2 parts Lemon-Lime Soda
Highball Glass

Layer over ice. Drink through a straw.

Felching Banana

1 part Vodka
1 part Irish Cream Liqueur
1 part Crème de Cacao (Dark)
splash Banana Liqueur
Old-Fashioned Glass

Layer over ice. Drink through a straw.

Fin 'n' Tonic

1 part Gin
1 part Peppermint Schnapps
1 part Tonic Water
Highball Glass

Layer over ice. Drink through a straw.

Flaming Cockroach

1 part Coffee Liqueur
1 part 151-Proof Rum
1 part Tequila
Highball Glass

Layer over ice. Drink through a straw.

Flaming Pisser

1 part 151-Proof Rum
1 part Lemon-Lime Soda
1 part Lime Juice
Highball Glass

Layer over ice. Drink through a straw.

The Forehead

1 part Coffee Liqueur
1 part Irish Cream Liqueur
1 part Water
Highball Glass

Layer over ice. Drink through a straw.

French Kiss Shooter

1 1/2 parts Vodka
1 part Fresh Lime Juice
1/2 part Grapefruit Juice
1/4 part Triple Sec
Old-Fashioned Glass

Layer over ice. Drink through a straw.

Frog

1 part Gin
1 part Triple Sec
1 part Sour Mix
Highball Glass

Layer over ice. Drink through a straw.

Glenndog

1 part Amaretto
1 part Drambuie®
1 part Tequila
1/2 part Ouzo
Highball Glass

Layer over ice. Drink through a straw.

Green Russian
1 part Vodka
1 part Melon Liqueur
Highball Glass

Layer over ice. Drink through a straw.

Heavy Hairy Testicle
1 part Crème de Cacao (White)
1 part Amaretto
1 part Milk
Highball Glass

Layer over ice. Drink through a straw.

High Jamaican Wind
1 part Rum
1 part Coffee Liqueur
fill with Cream
Highball Glass

Layer over ice. Drink through a straw.

Innocent Girl
1 part Goldschläger®
1 part Vanilla Liqueur
1 part Apple Liqueur
Highball Glass

Layer over ice. Drink through a straw.

Jäger Eraser
1 part Jägermeister®
1 part Vodka
fill with Club Soda
Whiskey Sour Glass

Layer over ice. Drink through a straw.

Jäger Float
1 part Cola
1 part Irish Cream Liqueur
1 part Jägermeister®
Whiskey Sour Glass

Layer over ice. Drink through a straw.

Kick in the Face
1 part Rum
1 part Lemon Juice
1 part Club Soda
Highball Glass

Layer over ice. Drink through a straw.

Knickerbocker
1 part Amaretto
1 part Citrus-Flavored Vodka
1 part Crème de Menthe (White)
Old-Fashioned Glass

Layer over ice. Drink through a straw.

Lactating Green Monkey
1 part Crème de Menthe (White)
1 part Coffee Liqueur
1 part Milk
Highball Glass

Layer over ice. Drink through a straw.

Lakokarocha
1 part Coffee Liqueur
1 part Tequila
1 part Club Soda
Highball Glass

Layer over ice. Drink through a straw.

Macedonian Haircut
1 part Black Sambuca
1 part Ouzo
1 part Jägermeister®
Highball Glass

Layer over ice. Drink through a straw.

Milwaukee Stop Light
1 part Cinnamon Schnapps
1 part Jägermeister®
1 part Goldschläger®
Highball Glass

Layer over ice. Drink through a straw.

Mind Blanker
1 part Vodka
1 part Coffee
1 part Lemon-Lime Soda
Whiskey Sour Glass

Layer over ice. Drink through a straw.

Mind Eraser
1 part Vodka
1 part Coffee Liqueur
1 part Club Soda
Whiskey Sour Glass

Layer over ice. Drink through a straw.

Mind Fuck
1 part Melon Liqueur
1 part Rum
1 part Tequila
Highball Glass

Layer over ice. Drink through a straw.

Neuralizer
1 part Sour Mix
1 part Whiskey
1 part Ginger Ale
Highball Glass

Layer over ice. Drink through a straw.

Nurse
1 part Absolut® Vodka
1 part Licor 43®
1 part Club Soda
Highball Glass

Layer over ice. Drink through a straw.

Paralyzer
1 part Vodka
1 part Coffee Liqueur
1 part Cream
1 part Cola
Highball Glass

Layer over ice. Drink through a straw.

Peachaholic Popper
1 part Peach Schnapps
1 part Club Soda
1 part Milk
Highball Glass

Layer over ice. Drink through a straw.

Purple Haze
1 part Raspberry Liqueur
1 part Citrus-Flavored Vodka
1 part Lemon-Lime Soda
Collins Glass

Layer over ice. Drink through a straw.

Purple Jumping Jesus

1 part Rum

1 part Peppermint Schnapps

1 part Jägermeister®

Highball Glass

Layer over ice. Drink through a straw.

Purple Mexican

1 part Vodka

1 part Tequila

1 part Grand Marnier®

Highball Glass

Layer over ice. Drink through a straw.

Raspberry Felch

1 part Irish Cream Liqueur

1 part Crème de Cacao (Dark)

1 part Raspberry-Flavored Vodka

Old-Fashioned Glass

Layer over ice. Drink through a straw.

Reptile

1 part Whiskey

1 part Mountain Dew®

1 part Orange Juice

Highball Glass

Layer over ice. Drink through a straw.

Separator

1 part Brandy

1 part Coffee Liqueur

1 part Cream

Old-Fashioned Glass

Layer over ice. Drink through a straw.

Southampton Slam

1 part Crème de Menthe (Green)

1 part Anisette

1 part Club Soda

Highball Glass

Layer over ice. Drink through a straw.

Summer Night

1 part Orange Juice

2 parts Red Wine

1 part Hard Apple Cider

Highball Glass

Layer over ice. Drink through a straw.

Traffic Light

1 part Crème de Menthe (Green)

1 part Cherry Brandy

1 part Triple Sec

Old-Fashioned Glass

Layer over ice. Drink through a straw.

Yellow Snow Slammer

1 part Cream

1 part Vodka

3 parts Pineapple Juice

Highball Glass

Layer over ice. Drink through a straw.

Zebra

1 part Black Sambuca

1 part Tequila Silver

Highball Glass

Layer over ice. Drink through a straw.

Zipper

1 part Cream

1 part Triple Sec

1 part Tequila

Old-Fashioned Glass

Layer over ice. Drink through a straw.

"Depth Charge" or "Bomber" Drinks

Take a mug of beer and drop a shot of liquor into it and you have a "Depth Charge" drink. Drop a shot into an energy drink such as Red Bull® and you have a "Bomber".

110 in the Shade

1 shot Tequila
fill with Lager Beer
Shot Glass, Beer Mug

Fill a shot glass with Tequila. Fill a beer mug with Lager. Drop the shot into the Beer and drink quickly.

Beton

1 part Scotch
1 part Vodka
1 pint Beer
Shot Glass, Beer Mug

Place the Scotch and Vodka in a shot glass and drop the into the Beer. Drink quickly.

Bomber

1 shot Tequila
1 pint Beer
Shot Glass, Collins Glass

Fill a shot glass with Tequila. Fill a Collins glass with Beer. Drop the shot into the Beer and drink quickly.

Car Bomb

1 part Irish Whiskey
1 part Irish Cream Liqueur
1/2 pint Guinness® Stout
Shot Glass, Beer Mug

Layer the Whiskey and Irish Cream in a shot glass. Drop the shot into the Beer and drink quickly.

Dive Bomber

1 shot Amaretto
1 part Root Beer Schnapps
1 pint Beer
Shot Glass, Beer Mug

Fill shot glass with Amaretto and Root Beer Schnapps. Drop the shot into the Beer and drink quickly.

Dr Pepper®

3 parts Amaretto
1 part 151-Proof Rum
1 pint Lager Beer
Shot Glass, Beer Mug

Fill a shot glass with Amaretto and 151-Proof Rum. Drop the shot into the Beer and drink quickly.

Dr Pepper® #2

1 part 151-Proof Rum

1 part Amaretto

1 pint Beer

Shot Glass, Beer Mug

Fill a shot glass with 151-Proof Rum and Amaretto. Drop the shot into the Beer and drink quickly.

Drunk Driver

1 shot Jägermeister®

1 pint Guinness® Stout

Shot Glass, Beer Mug

Fill a shot glass with Jägermeister® and beer mug with Beer. Drop the shot into the beer and drink quickly.

Flaming Cornholio

1 part Jack Daniel's®

4 parts Orange Juice

1 shot Cinnamon Schnapps

Shot Glass, Beer Mug

Combine Jack Daniel's® and Orange Juice in a Beer mug. Drop a shot of Cinnamon Schnapps into the glass and drink quickly.

Flaming Depth Charge

1 shot 151-Proof Rum

Beer

Shot Glass, Beer Mug

Fill a beer mug with Beer and a shot glass with 151-Proof Rum. Light the Rum and drop the shot into the beer. Drink quickly.

Flaming Dr Pepper®

3 parts Raspberry Liqueur

1 part 151-Proof Rum

Beer

Shot Glass, Beer Mug

Combine the Raspberry Liqueur and the 151-Proof Rum in a shot glass. Light the Rum and drop the shot into the beer. Drink quickly.

Flaming Dr. Pepper® #2

3 parts Amaretto

1 part 151-Proof Rum

Beer

Shot Glass, Beer Mug

Combine the Amaretto and the 151-Proof Rum in a shot glass. Light the Rum and drop the shot into the Beer. Drink quickly.

Fuzzy Iranian

1 shot Peach Schnapps

Beer

Shot Glass, Beer Mug

Fill a shot glass with Peach Schnapps and a beer mug with Beer. Drop the shot into the Beer and drink quickly.

Green Bastard

1 part Sour Apple–Flavored Schnapps

1 part Blue Curaçao

Beer

Shot Glass, Beer Mug

Combine Apple Schnapps and Blue Curaçao in a shot glass. Drop the shot into a pint of Beer and drink quickly

Hairball

1 shot Irish Whiskey
1 part Hard Apple Cider
1 part Guinness® Stout

Shot Glass, Collins Glass

Fill a shot glass with Irish Whiskey. Fill a Collins glass with Hard Cider and Guinness®. Drop the shot into the glass and drink quickly.

Irish Car Bomb

1 pint Guinness® Stout
1 part Irish Whiskey
1 part Coffee Liqueur
1 part Irish Cream Liqueur

Shot Glass, Beer Mug

Fill a mug with Guinness® and a shot glass with the Liqueurs. Drop the shot into the Beer and drink quickly.

Lunch Box

1 part Beer
1 part Orange Juice
1 shot Amaretto

Shot Glass, Beer Mug

Fill a beer mug with Beer and Orange Juice. Fill a shot glass with Amaretto. Drop the shot into the Beer mug and drink quickly.

Melon Squishy

1 shot Melon Liqueur
1 part Pineapple Juice
1 part Orange Juice

Shot Glass, Collins Glass

Fill a shot glass with Melon Liqueur and a beer mug with Pineapple Juice and Orange Juice. Drop the shot into the mug and drink quickly.

Mexican Hillbilly

1 shot Jack Daniel's®
Corona® Beer

Shot Glass, Beer Mug

Fill a shot glass with Jack Daniel's®. Fill a beer mug with Corona®. Drop the shot into the Beer and drink quickly.

Minty Cum Shot

1 shot Peppermint Schnapps
fill with Mountain Dew®

Shot Glass, Beer Mug

Fill a shot glass with Peppermint Schnapps. Fill a beer mug with Mountain Dew®. Drop the shot into the mug and drink quickly.

Mountain Dew®

1 shot Melon Liqueur
1 part Beer
1 part Lemon-Lime Soda

Shot Glass, Beer Mug

Fill a shot glass with Melon Liqueur. Fill a beer mug with Beer and Lemon-Lime Soda. Drop the shot into the mug and drink quickly.

Pap Smear

1 shot Smirnoff® Vodka
Pabst® Blue Ribbon Beer

Shot Glass, Beer Mug

Fill a shot glass with chilled Vodka. Fill a beer mug with Beer. Drop the shot into the Beer and drink quickly.

Peppermint Depth Charge

1 shot Peppermint Schnapps

Beer

Shot Glass, Beer Mug

Fill a shot glass with Peppermint Schnapps. Fill a beer mug with Beer. Drop the shot into the Beer and drink quickly.

Root Beer Barrel

1 shot Root Beer Schnapps

Beer

Root Beer Mug

Fill a shot glass with Root Beer Schnapps. Fill a beer mug with Beer. Drop the shot into the Beer and drink quickly.

Russian Boilermaker

1 shot Vodka

Beer

Shot Glass, Beer Mug

Fill a shot glass with chilled Vodka. Fill a beer mug with Beer. Drop the shot into the Beer and drink quickly.

Sake Bomb

1 shot Sake

Beer

Shot Glass, Beer Mug

Fill a shot glass with Sake. Fill a beer mug with Beer. Drop the shot into the Beer and drink quickly.

Sambuca Depth Charge

1 shot Sambuca

Beer

Shot Glass, Beer Mug

Fill a shot glass with Sambuca. Fill a beer mug with Beer. Drop the shot into the Beer and drink quickly.

Samuel Jackson

1 shot 151-Proof Rum

Samuel Adams® Beer

Shot Glass, Beer Mug

Fill a shot glass with 151-Proof Rum. Fill a beer mug with Beer. Drop the shot into the Beer and drink quickly.

School Bus

1 shot Amaretto

1 part Beer

1 part Orange Juice

Shot Glass, Beer Mug

Fill a shot glass with chilled Amaretto. Combine the Beer and the Orange Juice in a beer mug. Drop the shot into the mug and drink quickly.

Sergeant Pepper

1 part Amaretto

1 part Beer

1 part Cola

Shot Glass, Beer Mug

Fill a shot glass with Amaretto. Fill a beer mug with Beer and Cola. Drop the shot into the mug and drink quickly.

Shoot the Root

1 shot Root Beer Schnapps

Beer

Shot Glass, Beer Mug

Fill a shot glass with Root Beer Schnapps. Fill a beer mug with Beer. Drop the shot into the Beer and drink quickly.

Strawberry

1 shot Strawberry Liqueur

Beer

Shot Glass, Beer Mug

Fill a shot glass with Strawberry Liqueur and a beer mug with Beer. Drop the shot into the Beer and drink quickly.

Strawberry #2

1 shot Strawberry-Flavored Vodka

Beer

Shot Glass, Beer Mug

Fill a shot glass with Strawberry Liqueur and a beer mug with Beer. Drop the shot into the Beer and drink quickly.

Submarine

1 shot Jägermeister®

Beer

Shot Glass, Beer Mug

Fill a shot glass with Jägermeister. Fill a beer mug with Beer. Drop the shot into the Beer and drink quickly.

Tennessee Boilermaker

1 shot Whiskey

Beer

Shot Glass, Beer Mug

Fill a shot glass with Whiskey and a beer mug with Beer. Drop the shot into the Beer and drink quickly.

Tiajuana Car Bomb

1 shot Tequila

Beer

Shot Glass, Beer Mug

Fill a shot glass with Tequila and a beer mug with Beer. Drop the shot into the Beer and drink quickly.

Triple H

1 part Hennessy®

1 part Hypnotiq®

Heineken®

Shot Glass, Beer Mug

Fill a shot glass with Hennesy® and Hypnotiq® and a beer mug with Heineken®. Drop the shot into the Beer and drink quickly.

Whore in a Bucket

1 shot Southern Comfort®

Cranberry Juice Cocktail

Shot Glass, Beer Mug

Fill a shot glass with Southern Comfort® and a beer mug with Cranberry Juice. Drop the shot into the Cranberry Juice and drink quickly.

Wisconsin Lunch Box

1 shot Amaretto

1 part Orange Juice

2 parts Beer

Shot Glass, Beer Mug

Fill a shot glass with Amaretto and a beer mug with Orange Juice and Beer. Drop the shot into the Beer and drink quickly.

Beer Drinks

Take the goodness of beer (ginger, root or otherwise) and mess with it.

101 Degrees in the Shade

1 part Absolut® Peppar Vodka
1 part Beer
1 part Tomato Juice
Tabasco® Sauce
Collins Glass

Build over ice and stir. Add Tabasco® to taste

3-Week Vacation

1 part Raspberry Liqueur
1/2 part Cranberry Juice Cocktail
1/2 part Pineapple Juice
fill with Beer
Highball Glass

Build over ice and stir

666

1 part Banana Liqueur
1 part Blue Curaçao
fill with Beer
Collins Glass

Build over ice and stir

Aaron

1 part Beer
1 part Lemonade
Beer Mug

Build in the mug with no ice

Abre Piernas

2 parts Lemon-Lime Soda
1 part Melon Liqueur
1 part Tequila
1 part White Wine
fill with Beer
Collins Glass

Build over ice and stir

Absolut® Beast

1 can Beer
1 part Absolut® Citron Vodka

Open the can of Beer, drink a little, and pour in the Vodka

Adam's Lunch Box

1½ parts Amaretto
2 parts Beer
3 parts Orange Juice
Beer Mug

Build in the glass with no ice

Aespec

1 part Beer
1 part Gin
Beer Mug

Build in the glass with no ice

AJ's Bubbling Brew

1 part Tequila
1 part Southern Comfort®
1 part 100-Proof Peppermint Schnapps
1 part 151-Proof Rum
fill with Beer
Beer Mug

Carefully pour the Tequila, Southern Comfort®, Peppermint Schnapps, and Rum into the glass and light on fire. Quickly add the Beer, stir, and watch it bubble froth.

Ambassador
1 1/2 parts Rum
1 part Limeade
1 part Ginger Beer
Highball Glass

Build over ice and stir

Anus on Fire
1 part Jack Daniel's®
1 part Sloe Gin
1 part Southern Comfort®
1 part Jägermeister®
fill with Beer
Beer Mug

Build over ice and stir

Apple Cider Slider
1 part Sour Apple Schnapps
fill with Beer
Beer Mug

Pour the Schnapps in a Beer mug and fill with Beer

Asphalt
1 1/2 parts Blackberry Liqueur
1 part Chocolate Syrup
fill with Dark Beer
Beer Mug

Build in the glass with no ice

Bad-Ass Brew
1 part Vodka
1 1/2 parts Beer
2 parts Tomato Juice
dash Salt
Collins Glass

Build in the glass with no ice

Baked Apple
1 part Cinnamon Schnapps
fill with Hard Apple Cider
Beer Mug

Pour the Schnapps into the mug first, then add the Cider. Serve cold.

Baltimore Zoo
1 part Light Rum
1 part Gin
1 part Vodka
1/2 part Triple Sec
1 part Sour Mix
splash Grenadine
splash Beer
Highball Glass

Build over ice and stir

BB's Margarita
1 part Beer
1 part Tequila Reposado
1 part Frozen Limeade Concentrate
3 splashes Margarita Mix
Pitcher

Combine all ingredients in a blender with ice. Blend until smooth.

Beer Bloody Mary
splash Worcestershire Sauce
dash Salt
dash Pepper
splash Lime Juice
fill with Beer
Beer Mug

Build in the glass with no ice

Beer Breezer
2 parts Vodka
splash Tabasco® Sauce
dash Celery Salt
fill with Beer
Beer Mug

Build in the glass with no ice

Beer Buster
1 1/2 parts 100-Proof Vodka
fill with Beer
splash Tabasco® Sauce
Beer Mug

Build in the glass with no ice

Beer Garden
1 part Vodka
1 part Triple Sec
1 part Lychee Liqueur
1 part Vanilla Liqueur
fill with Beer
Beer Mug

Shake all but Beer with ice and strain into the glass. Top with Beer.

Beer Panache
splash Simple Syrup
1 part Lemon-Lime Soda
1 part Beer
Collins Glass

Build in the glass with no ice

Beer-a-Lade
1 part Beer
1 part Gatorade®
splash Maple Syrup
splash Tabasco® Sauce
Beer Mug

Build in the glass with no ice and stir

Beeraquirilla
1/2 part Tequila
1/2 part Light Rum
4 parts Beer
2 parts Strawberry Daiquiri Mix
2 parts Margarita Mix
Margarita Glass

Combine all ingredients in a blender with ice. Blend until smooth.

Beerdriver
2 parts Vodka
1 part Orange Juice
1 part Beer
Beer Mug

Build in the glass with no ice

Big Belly
1 part Crème de Cassis
1/2 part Blackberry Liqueur
1/2 part Lemon Juice
fill with Beer
Collins Glass

Shake all but Beer with ice and strain into a glass. Top with Beer.

Bionic Beaver
1 part Vodka
1 part Southern Comfort®
1 part Sloe Gin
1 part Gin
splash Grenadine
fill with Beer
Beer Mug

Build over ice and stir

Black & Tan
1 part Bass® Pale Ale
1 part Guinness® Stout
Beer Mug

Layer in a beer mug or pint glass

Black and Brown
1 part Root Beer
1 part Guinness® Stout
Beer Mug

Layer in a Beer mug or pint glass

Black Beerd
1 part Blackberry Liqueur
fill with Beer
Beer Mug

Build in the glass with no ice

Black Cow
2 scoops Vanilla Ice Cream
fill with Root Beer
Beer Mug

Build in the glass with no ice

Black Velvet
1 part Rum
fill with Lager
Beer Mug

Build in the glass with no ice

Black Velvet (England)
1 part Guinness® Stout
1 part Hard Apple Cider
Beer Mug

Build in the glass with no ice

Bloody Brew
1 1/2 parts Vodka
1 part Beer
1 part Tomato Juice
dash Salt
Collins Glass

Build over ice and stir

Bloody Mary's White Trash Lover
1 part Tomato Juice
1 part Beer
dash Salt
1/4 part Lemon Juice
Beer Mug

Build over ice and stir

Blue Bear
1 part Blue Curaçao
fill with Beer
Beer Mug

Build in the glass with no ice

Bluebeer
fill with Beer
splash Blue Curaçao
Beer Mug

Build in the glass with no ice

Boilermaker
1 shot Whiskey
Beer
Shot Glass, Beer Mug

Fill shot glass with Whiskey. Drop full shot into mug of beer and drink immediately.

British Snakebite
1 part Beer
1 part Hard Cider
Beer Mug

Build in the glass with no ice

Brooklyn Zoo
1 part Rum
1 part Vodka
1 part Gin
splash Pineapple Juice
splash Raspberry Liqueur
splash Sour Mix
fill with Beer
Collins Glass

Build over ice and stir

Brutus
1 part Beer
2 parts Clamato® Juice
dash Celery Salt
Collins Glass

Build over ice and stir

Butter Beer
1 part Butterscotch Schnapps
fill with Beer
Beer Mug

Build in the glass with no ice

Clara

1 part Beer
1 part Lemon-Lime Soda
Highball Glass

Build over ice and stir

Concussion

1 part Beer
1 part Grain Alcohol
1 part Jack Daniel's®
dash Sugar
Old-Fashioned Glass

Shake with ice and strain

Cranberry

1 part Cranberry Juice Cocktail
fill with Beer
Beer Mug

Build in the glass with no ice

Cream de Spooge

1 part Beer
1 part Cream Soda
Beer Mug

Build in the glass with no ice

Dark & Stormy

2 parts Gosling's Black Seal® Rum
fill with Ginger Beer
Old-Fashioned Glass

Build over ice

Dead Penis

1 part Light Rum
1 part Tequila
1/2 part Scotch
1/2 part Dark Rum
1/2 part Vodka
fill with Stout
Beer Mug

Build in the glass with no ice

Death Star

1 part Irish Cream Liqueur
1 1/2 parts Drambuie®
1 part Gin
2 parts Jägermeister®
fill with Beer
splash Crème de Menthe (Green)
Beer Mug

Build in the glass with no ice

Euthanasia

1 part Southern Comfort®
1 part Jack Daniel's®
fill with Beer
Beer Mug

Build in the glass with no ice

The Field Camp

1 part Blue Curaçao
1 part Whiskey
1 part Cola
fill with Beer
Hurricane Glass

Build over ice and stir

Flaming Dr Pepper®

1 part Amaretto
1 part Rum
1 pint Beer
Beer Mug

Fill a shot glass with Amaretto and Rum, and a beer mug with beer. Light the Rum with a match or lighter and drop the flaming shot into the Beer. Drink quickly.

Flaming Orgasm

1 shot 151-Proof Rum
Beer
Beer Mug

Fill a shot glass with Rum and a beer mug with Beer. Light the Rum with a match or lighter and drop it into the Beer. Drink quickly.

A Furlong Too Late

1 part Light Rum
2 parts Ginger Beer
1 Lemon Twist
Highball Glass

Build over ice and stir

German Car Bomb

1 shot Jägermeister®
Heineken®
Beer Mug

Drop a shot of Jägermeister® into a Beer mug filled with Heineken®. Drink quickly.

Ginger Mule

1 1/2 parts Citrus-Flavored Vodka
splash Parfait Amour
fill with Ginger Beer
splash Lime Juice
Collins Glass

Build over ice and stir

Graveyard

1 part Triple Sec
1 part Light Rum
1 part Vodka
1 part Gin
1 part Tequila
1 part Scotch
2 parts Lager
2 parts Stout
Beer Mug

Shake all the liquor with ice and strain into a beer mug. Top with Lager and Stout.

Graveyard Light

1 part Triple Sec
1 part Light Rum
1 part Vodka
1 part Gin
1 part Tequila
2 parts Lager
2 parts Stout
Beer Mug

Shake all the liquor with ice and strain into a Beer mug. Top with Lager beer and Stout.

Green Goblin

1 part Hard Apple Cider
1 part Lager
splash Blue Curaçao
Beer Mug

Build over ice and stir

Guinness® Shandy

1 part Guinness® Stout
1 part Lemonade
Beer Mug

Build in the glass with no ice

Hard Eight

1 1/2 parts Dark Rum
1/2 part Lime Juice
2 dashes Bitters
fill with Ginger Beer
Collins Glass

Build over ice and stir

Head Fake Jake

1 1/2 parts Beer
1 part Applejack
1/2 part Melon Liqueur
1/2 part Sour Mix
2 scoops Ice Cream
Coupette Glass

Combine all ingredients in a blender with ice. Blend until smooth.

Hop, Skip, and Go Naked

1 part Vodka
1 part Gin
1/2 part Lime Juice
fill with Beer
Collins Glass

Build over ice and stir

Horse Jizz

1 part Beer
1 part Milk
Beer Mug

Build in the glass with no ice

Jägerbeer Bomb

1 shot Jägermeister®
Draft Beer
Beer Mug

Drop a shot of Jägermeister® into a mug full of beer. Drink quickly.

Jalisco Cooler

1 1/2 parts Tequila Reposado
1/2 part Fresh Lime Juice
1/2 part Vanilla Liqueur
fill with Beer
Collins Glass

Build over ice and stir

Jamaica Mule

2 parts Light Rum
1 part Fresh Lime Juice
1/2 part Ginger Liqueur
splash 151-Proof Rum
fill with Ginger Beer
Collins Glass

Build over ice and stir

Järngrogg

2 parts Vodka
fill with Beer
Beer Mug

Build in the glass with no ice

Lager & Lime

fill with Lager
splash Lime Juice
Beer Mug

Build in the glass with no ice

Li'l Amick

1 part Gin
1/2 part Lime Juice
fill with Beer
Beer Mug

Build over ice

Mead

1 1/2 parts Irish Mist®
fill with Beer
Beer Mug

Build in the glass with no ice

Mexican Iced Tea

1 1/2 parts Tequila
fill with Beer
splash Lime Juice
Cocktail Glass

Build in the glass with no ice

Michelada

1 Lemon
2 splashes Worcestershire Sauce
splash Soy Sauce
splash Tabasco® Sauce
dash Salt
fill with Beer
Collins Glass

Build over ice and stir

Miner's Lung

2 parts Vodka
fill with Guinness® Stout
Beer Mug

Build in the glass with no ice

Monaco
1 part Beer
1 part Lemonade
splash Grenadine
Beer Mug

Build in the glass with no ice

Moscow Mule
1½ parts Vodka
1 part Lime Juice
fill with Ginger Beer
1 Lime Wedge
Highball Glass

Build over ice

Mosquito
1½ parts Raspberry Liqueur
1 part Hard Cider
1 part Beer
Beer Mug

Build in the glass with no ice

Mule
1¼ parts Vodka
fill with Ginger Beer
splash Lime Juice
Highball Glass

Build over ice and stir

Musegg
1 part Orange Juice
1 part Apricot Brandy
1 part Triple Sec
fill with Beer
Collins Glass

Build over ice and stir

North Coast Dr Pepper®
1 part Amaretto
1 part Root Beer Schnapps
1 part 151-Proof Rum
fill with Beer
Beer Mug

Pour the Amaretto, Schnapps and Rum into a shot glass. Fill a beer mug ¾ full of Beer. Light the shot with a match or lighter and drop it into the Beer. Drink quickly.

Nuthugger
1 part 151-Proof Rum
1 part Vodka
1 part Lime Juice
fill with Beer
Beer Mug

Build in the glass with no ice

Oyster Shooter
2 splashes Tabasco® Sauce
splash Horseradish
splash Cocktail Sauce
fill with Beer
1 Raw Oyster
Whiskey Sour Glass

Mix all except the Oyster in a whiskey sour glass. Drop in the Oyster and drink.

Ozone
1½ parts Amaretto
splash Beer
fill with Sour Mix
splash Lemon-Lime Soda
Old-Fashioned Glass

Build over ice and stir

Pickled Beer

1 part Pickle Juice
2 parts Beer
Beer Mug

Build in the glass with no ice

Pink Kangaroo

1 part Tequila
2 parts Vodka
2 parts Hard Apple Cider
1 part Cranberry Juice Cocktail
1 part Orange Juice
Beer Mug

Build over ice and stir

Pond Water

1 part Beer
1 part Cola
Beer Mug

Build in the glass with no ice

Poor Man's Mimosa

1 part Beer
1 part Orange Juice
Highball Glass

Build over ice and stir

Pukemeister General

1 part Tequila
1 part Rumple Minze®
1 part Hard Apple Cider
1 part Beer
Beer Mug

Build in the glass with no ice

Purple Velvet

2 parts Port
fill with Guinness® Stout
Beer Mug

Build in the glass with no ice

Rabid Pitbull

2 parts Jack Daniel's®
2 dashes Bitters
1 part Lemon-Lime Soda
1 part Beer
Collins Glass

Build over ice and stir

Red Horn

1 part RedRum®
fill with Hard Apple Cider
Beer Mug

Build in the glass with no ice

Redeye

1 part Rye Whiskey
1 part Beer
1 part Cola
Collins Glass

Build over ice and stir

Refajo

1 part Beer
1 part Cola
Highball Glass

Build over ice and stir

Rude Awakening

1 part Jack Daniel's®
1 part Vodka
1 part Cinnamon Schnapps
1 part Orange Juice
1 part Beer
Beer Mug

Build over ice and stir

Schnider

2 parts Peach Schnapps
fill with Hard Cider
Beer Mug

Build over ice and stir

Shady
1 part Beer
1 part Lemonade
Beer Mug

Build in the glass with no ice

Shady Grove
1½ parts Gin
Juice of half a Lemon
dash Powdered Sugar
fill with Ginger Beer
Highball Glass

Build over ice and stir

Shandy
1 part Beer
1 part Ginger Ale
Beer Mug

Build in the glass with no ice

Shanty
1 part Lemon-Lime Soda
1 part Beer
Collins Glass

Build in the glass with no ice

Sip and Get Funky
1 part Gin
½ part Grenadine
½ part Lemon-Lime Soda
fill with Beer
Collins Glass

Build over ice and stir

Skip and Go Naked
1 part Gin
1 part Apricot Brandy
1 part Cherry juice
½ part Sour Mix
fill with Beer
Highball Glass

Build over ice and stir

Skip, Run, and Go Naked
2 parts Tequila
dash Bitters
fill with Beer
Collins Glass

Build over ice and stir

Sloppy Seconds
1 part Rum
splash Lime Juice
fill with Beer
Beer Mug

Build in the glass with no ice

Snakebite
1 part Lager
1 part Hard Cider
Beer Mug

Build in the glass with no ice

Snake Venom
1 part Lager
1 part Hard Apple Cider
1 part Pernod®
Beer Mug

Build in the glass with no ice

St. Paddy's Day Beer
2 parts Melon Liqueur
fill with Beer
Hurricane Glass

Build in the glass with no ice

Stiff Pounder
1 part Jägermeister®
fill with Beer
Beer Mug

Build in the glass with no ice

Stone Cold Stunner
1 part Vodka
1 part Beer
fill with Grapefruit Juice
Collins Glass

Build over ice and stir

Strip and Go Naked
2 parts Vodka
1 part Beer
1 part Lemonade
Collins Glass

Build over ice and stir

Sweaty Mexican
1 1/2 parts Tequila
splash 151-Proof Rum
fill with Beer
Beer Mug

Build in the glass with no ice

Toolbox Puker
1 part Rum
1 part Vodka
fill with Beer
Beer Mug

Build in the glass with no ice

Tractor
1 part Tia Maria®
1 part Guinness® Stout
1 part Hard Apple Cider
Beer Mug

Build in the glass with no ice

Tropical Fart
1 part Coconut-Flavored Rum
1 part Peach Schnapps
1 part Orange Juice
1 part Pineapple Juice
splash Beer
Collins Glass

Build over ice and stir

Urine Sample with Gonorrhea
1 part Tequila
1 part Beer
splashes Tabasco® Sauce
Highball Glass

Build in the glass with no ice

V8® Beer
2 parts Beer
1 part V8® Vegetable Juice Blend
Beer Mug

Build in the glass with no ice

Valley
2 parts Dark Rum
3 parts Apple Juice
1 part Beer
Collins Glass

Build over ice and stir

Vancouver in the Morning
1 part Vodka
1 part Pink Lemonade
1 part Beer
Collins Glass

Shake with ice and strain over ice

Wild Brew Yonder
1 part Vodka
1/2 part Blue Curaçao
fill with Beer
Highball Glass

Build in the glass with no ice

Yellow
1/2 part Lemon Juice
fill with Beer
Beer Mug

Build in the glass with no ice

X-Rated Drinks

What makes a drink X-Rated? According to the Supreme Court, you'll know it when you see it.

69

1 part Licor 43®
5 parts 7-Up®
1 part Seagram's® 7 Crown Whiskey
5 Cubes of Ice

Highball Glass

Build over ice. 1 + 43 + 5 + 7 + 1 + 7 + 5 = 69.

69er

1 part Light Rum
1 part Peach Schnapps
1 part Cola

Highball Glass

Build over ice

Absolut® Royal Fuck

1 part Crown Royal® Whiskey
1/2 part Currant-Flavored Vodka
1/2 part Peach Schnapps
splash Cranberry Juice Cocktail
splash Pineapple Juice

Whiskey Sour Glass

Shake with ice and strain over ice

Absolut® Sex

1 part Currant-Flavored Vodka
1/2 part Cranberry Juice Cocktail
1/2 part Melon Liqueur
2 parts Lemon-Lime Soda

Highball Glass

Build over ice and stir

Adios Motherfucker

1 part Gin
1 part Light Rum
1 part Triple Sec
1 part Vodka
fill with Sour Mix

Collins Glass

Build over ice and stir

American Clusterfuck

1 part Light Rum
1 part Dark Rum
1 part Tequila
1 part Vodka
1 part Cranberry Juice Cocktail
splash Tropical Punch Schnapps

Collins Glass

Build over ice. in Top with a splash of Tropical Punch Schnapps.

Apple Screw
1 part Apple Liqueur
1 part Vodka
fill with Orange Juice

Highball Glass

Build over ice and stir

Ass
2 parts Vodka
1 part Lemon-Lime Soda
1 part Orange Juice
splash Grenadine

Highball Glass

Build over ice and stir

Assmaster 5000+
1 1/2 parts Rum
1 part Grain Alcohol
1 1/2 parts Grenadine
1 part Triple Sec
fill with Orange Juice

Highball Glass

Build over ice and stir

Bag of Filth
1 part Pernod®
1 part Tia Maria®

Old-Fashioned Glass

Shake with ice and pour

Bald Pussy
1 part Citrus-Flavored Vodka
1 part Vodka
1 part Triple Sec
1 1/2 parts Blueberry Schnapps
1 1/2 parts Melon Liqueur
splash Lime Juice
splash Lemon-Lime Soda

Highball Glass

Build over ice and stir

Ballbreaker
2 parts Vodka
1 part Dry Vermouth
1 part Tequila Silver
1 part Raspberry Syrup
2 parts Vegetable Juice Blend

Old-Fashioned Glass

Shake with ice and pour

Banana Assmaster
1 part Vodka
2 parts Milk
1 Banana
4 scoops Ice Cream

Collins Glass

Combine all ingredients in a blender with ice. Blend until smooth.

Bare-Naked Lady
1 part Dark Rum
1 part Apple Brandy
3 parts Sour Mix
2 parts Orange Juice

Collins Glass

Shake with ice and pour

Better than Sex
1 part Frangelico®
1 part Crème Liqueur
1/2 part Grand Marnier®
1 part Coffee Liqueur
fill with Cream

Collins Glass

Shake with ice and pour

Bishop's Nipple

1 part Orange-Flavored Vodka
1 part Raspberry Liqueur
1 part Lime Cordial
fill with Lemon-Lime Soda

Collins Glass

Build over ice and stir

Bitch Ass

1 1/2 parts Coconut-Flavored Rum
1 1/2 parts Vanilla-Flavored Vodka
splash Cranberry Juice Cocktail
1 part Orange Juice
1 part Pineapple Juice

Hurricane Glass

Build over ice and stir

Blue Motherfucker

1 part Blue Curaçao
1 part Gin
1 part Light Rum
1 part Tequila Silver
1 part Vodka
splash Lemon-Lime Soda
splash Sour Mix

Collins Glass

Build over ice and stir

Blue Screw

1 1/2 parts Orange-Flavored Vodka
1 part Blue Curaçao
fill with Orange Juice

Highball Glass

Build over ice and stir

Breast Caresser

1 1/2 parts Brandy
1 part Madeira
1/2 part Triple Sec

Highball Glass

Shake with ice and pour

Breast Milk on Acid

1/2 part Coconut-Flavored Rum
3/4 part Jägermeister®
1/2 part Melon Liqueur
1 part Sour Mix
splash Orange Juice

Old-Fashioned Glass

Shake with ice and strain

British Clusterfuck

1 part Gin
1 part Irish Cream Liqueur
1 part Scotch

Collins Glass

Shake with ice and pour

Bunny Fucker

1 part Tequila
1 part Lemon-Lime Soda
1 part Orange Juice
splash Grenadine

Collins Glass

Build over ice and stir

Butt Munch

2 parts Brandy
1/2 dash Cinnamon
1 part Coffee Liqueur
1 part Milk

Coupette Glass

Combine all ingredients in a blender with ice. Blend until smooth.

Butt Naked
1 part Amaretto
1 part Southern Comfort®
fill with Cranberry Juice Cocktail
Old-Fashioned Glass
Build over ice and stir

Buttcrack
1 part RedRum®
1 part Citrus-Flavored Vodka
Collins Glass
Pour ingredients into glass neat (do not chill)

Buttery Nipple (Frozen)
1 part Irish Cream Liqueur
1 part Butterscotch Ice Cream topping
2 scoops Ice Cream
Coupette Glass
Combine all ingredients in a blender. Blend until smooth.

Chicken Fucker
2 parts Coconut-Flavored Rum
1 part Amaretto
1 part Peach Schnapps
fill with Orange Juice
Highball Glass
Build over ice and stir

Clusterfuck
1 part Southern Comfort®
1 part Vodka
splash Grenadine
1 part Orange Juice
1 part Pineapple Juice
Highball Glass
Build over ice and stir

Colorado Motherfucker
1 part Tequila
1 part Coffee Liqueur
fill with Milk
splash Cola
Highball Glass
Build over ice and stir

Comfortable Screw
1 part Vodka
1 part Southern Comfort®
fill with Orange Juice
Highball Glass
Shake with ice and pour

Comfortable Screw Up Against a Fuzzy Wall
1/2 part Vodka
3/4 part Southern Comfort®
1/2 part Peach Schnapps
1/4 part Galliano®
fill with Orange Juice
Highball Glass
Shake with ice and pour

Comfortable Screw Up Against a Wall
3/4 part Vodka
3/4 part Southern Comfort®
1/4 part Galliano®
fill with Orange Juice
Highball Glass
Shake with ice and pour

Cool Summer Sex
1 part Currant-Flavored Vodka
1 part Melon Liqueur
1 part Fresh Lime Juice
fill with Lemon-Lime Soda
Collins Glass
Build over ice and stir

Cuban Screw

1 1/2 parts Rum
fill with Orange Juice
Highball Glass

Build over ice and stir

Cum Fuck Me Punch

1 part Amaretto
1/2 part Southern Comfort®
1/2 part Vodka
1 part Pineapple Juice
1 part Orange Juice
1 part Sour Mix
1 part Grenadine
Collins Glass

Build over ice and stir

Cum in a Bucket

2 parts Crème de Cacao (White)
2 parts Cream
1 part Milk
Old-Fashioned Glass

Shake with ice and pour

Cybersex Orgasm

1 part Peach Schnapps
1 part Amaretto
2 parts Cranberry Juice Cocktail
1 part Grenadine
3 parts Orange Juice
Collins Glass

Shake with ice and pour

Deep Sea Sex

1 part Melon Liqueur
1 part Blue Curaçao
1 part Amaretto
splash Sour mix
splash Lemon-Lime Soda
Highball Glass

Shake with ice and pour

Dick Hard

1 part Vodka
1 part Gin
1 part Light Rum
fill with Lemon-Lime Soda
1 Lime Wedge
Highball Glass

Build over ice and stir

Dickey Wallbanger

1 part Tequila Silver
1 part Vodka
fill with Orange Juice
Old-Fashioned Glass

Build over ice and stir

Dirty Screwdriver

1 1/2 parts Vodka
fill with Orange Juice
2 splashes Cinnamon Schnapps
Highball Glass

Build over ice and stir

Fluffy Fucknut

1 part Peach Schnapps
1 part Frangelico®
1 part Amaretto
splash Grenadine
fill with Milk
Highball Glass

Shake with ice and pour

French Nipple

1 part Coffee Liqueur
1 part Amaretto
1 part Vodka
fill with Milk
Collins Glass

Combine all ingredients in a blender with ice. Blend until smooth.

French Screw
1 part Vodka
1 part Raspberry Liqueur
fill with Orange Juice

Highball Glass

Build over ice and stir

Frog Cum
1 part Vodka
1 part Melon Liqueur
1 part Lemonade
1 part Club Soda

Old-Fashioned Glass

Build over ice and stir

Frosted Breast
1/2 part Crème de Banana
2/3 part Blue Curaçao
1/2 part Hazelnut Liqueur
fill with Milk

Highball Glass

Shake with ice and pour

Frozen Nipples
fill with Butterscotch Schnapps
3 scoops Vanilla Ice Cream

Hurricane Glass

Combine all ingredients in a blender. Blend until smooth.

Fruity Fuck
1/2 part Vodka
1 part Melon Liqueur
2 parts Orange Juice
2 parts Pineapple Juice
1 part Passion Fruit Liqueur
1/2 part Lime Juice

Collins Glass

Shake with ice and pour

Fuck in the Graveyard
1 part Vodka
1 part Rum
1 part Blueberry Schnapps
1 part Sour Apple Schnapps
1 part Blue Curaçao
1 part Raspberry Liqueur
fill with Cranberry Juice Cocktail
splash Orange Juice

Highball Glass

Shake with ice and pour

Fuck Me Hard
1 part Vodka
1 part Triple Sec
1 part Amaretto
2 parts Raspberry Liqueur
1 part Southern Comfort®
splash Cranberry Juice Cocktail
splash Orange Juice

Old-Fashioned Glass

Shake with ice and pour

Fuck Me Rough
1 part Raspberry Liqueur
1 part Crème de Banana
1 part Irish Cream Liqueur
fill with Cream

Collins Glass

Shake with ice and pour

Fuck You
1 part Tequila
1 part Jack Daniel's®
1 part Wild Turkey® Bourbon
1 part Goldschläger®
1 part Rum
1 part Blueberry Schnapps

Highball Glass

Shake with ice and strain over ice

Fuck Your Buddy

1 part Amaretto
1 part Coconut-Flavored Rum
1/2 part Crown Royal® Whiskey
1/2 part Jack Daniel's®
splash Grenadine
fill with Pineapple Juice

Highball Glass

Shake with ice and strain over ice

Fuzzy Ass

2 parts Citrus-Flavored Vodka
1 1/2 parts Peach Schnapps
1 part Sour Mix
splash Grenadine
1 part Triple Sec
fill with Lemon-Lime Soda

Collins Glass

Build over ice and stir

Fuzzy Cum(fort)

1/2 part Peach Schnapps
1 1/2 parts Southern Comfort®
fill with Lemon-Lime Soda

Old-Fashioned Glass

Build over ice and stir

Fuzzy Fucker

1 part Peach Schnapps
1 part Vodka
1 part Southern Comfort®
2 parts Orange Juice

Highball Glass

Build over ice and stir

Fuzzy Nipple

1 1/2 parts Vodka
1 1/2 parts Peach Schnapps
splash Triple Sec
fill with Orange Juice

Highball Glass

Build over ice and stir

Fuzzy Screw

1 part Vodka
1 part Peach Schnapps
fill with Orange Juice

Highball Glass

Build over ice and stir

Fuzzy Screw Up Against a Wall

1 part Vodka
1 part Peach Schnapps
splash Galliano®
fill with Orange Juice

Highball Glass

Build over ice and stir

Getting Naked

1 part Blue Curaçao
1 part Peach Schnapps
1 part Rum
fill with Orange Juice

Old-Fashioned Glass

Shake with ice and pour

Golden Mountain Screw

1 part Banana Liqueur
2 parts Vodka
fill with Mountain Dew®

Highball Glass

Build over ice and stir

Golden Screw
1 $1/2$ parts Vodka
dash Angostura® Bitters
fill with Orange Juice

Highball Glass

Shake with ice and strain over ice

Good as Sex
1 part Blue Curaçao
1 part Pisang Ambon® Liqueur
1 part Passoã
$3/4$ part Orange-Flavored Vodka
fill with Lemonade

Collins Glass

Shake with ice and pour

Green Pussy
1 part Light Rum
1 part Melon Liqueur
1 part Sour Mix

Old-Fashioned Glass

Build over ice and stir

Gulf Coast Sex on the Beach
2 parts Dark Rum
1 part Crème de Banana
1 part Melon Liqueur
fill with Pineapple Juice

Collins Glass

Build over ice and stir

Hard Fuck
1 part Melon Liqueur
1 part Vodka
1 part Blue Curaçao
1 part Blueberries
fill with Orange Juice

Highball Glass

Build over ice and stir

Hawaiian Screw
1 part Vodka
1 part Rum
1 part Orange Juice
1 part Pineapple Juice

Highball Glass

Build over ice and stir

Heavenly Sex
2 parts Spiced Rum
2 parts Amaretto
splash Chocolate Syrup
$1/2$ part Grenadine

Highball Glass

Shake with ice and strain over ice

Hot Pussy
$1/2$ part Cinnamon Schnapps
2 Tabasco® Sauce
1 part Alizé®

Highball Glass

Shake with ice and strain over ice

How Many Smurfs® Does It Take to Screw In a Light Bulb?
1 part Blue Curaçao
1 part Jägermeister®
fill with Zima®

Collins Glass

Two, but I don't know how they get in there. . . Build over ice and stir.

Italian Screw
1 $1/2$ parts Vodka
1 part Galliano®
fill with Orange Juice

Highball Glass

Build over ice and stir

Jamaican Screw
2 parts Coconut-Flavored Rum
fill with Orange Juice

Highball Glass

Build over ice and stir

Let's Get Drunk and Screw
2 parts Vodka
1 part Raspberry Liqueur
fill with Cranberry Juice Cocktail

Collins Glass

Build over ice and stir

Liquid Panty Remover
1 part 151-Proof Rum
1/2 part Coconut-Flavored Rum
1 part Raspberry Liqueur
1 part Cranberry Juice Cocktail
1 part Orange Juice
1 part Pineapple Juice
1 part Lemon-Lime Soda

Hurricane Glass

Build over ice and stir

Mexican Screw
1 1/2 parts Tequila
fill with Orange Juice

Highball Glass

Build over ice and stir

Mindfuck
1 part Jack Daniel's®
1 part Cactus Juice Schnapps
fill with Cola

Highball Glass

Build over ice and stir

Mongolian Motherfucker
1 part Citrus-Flavored Vodka
1 part Coconut-Flavored Rum
1/2 part Blue Curaçao
1/2 part Peach Schnapps
splash Melon Liqueur
splash Grand Marnier®
splash Banana Liqueur
splash Orange Juice
splash Pineapple Juice
splash Lemonade
splash Piña Colada Mix

Highball Glass

Shake with ice and strain over ice

Mountain Fuck
2 parts Cinnamon Schnapps
fill with Mountain Dew®

Beer Mug

Build over ice and stir

Mountain Screw
2 parts Vodka
fill with Mountain Dew®

Collins Glass

Build over ice and stir

Mountain Sex
1 part Mountain Dew®
1 part Triple Sec

Old-Fashioned Glass

Build over ice and stir

Mud Fuck
2 parts Vodka
1/2 part Chocolate Syrup
2 parts Dr Pepper®
1 part Milk

Coupette Glass

Combine all ingredients in a blender with ice. Blend until smooth.

Naked in Blackberries
3 parts Blackberry Liqueur
fill with Iced Tea

Beer Mug

Build over ice and stir

Naked Pretzel
3/4 part Vodka
1 part Melon Liqueur
1/2 part Crème de Cassis
fill with Pineapple Juice

Old-Fashioned Glass

Shake with ice and strain over ice

Naked Sunburn
1 part Melon Liqueur
1 part Coconut-Flavored Rum
1 part Crème de Noyaux
1 part Cranberry Juice Cocktail
1 part Pineapple Juice
splash Lemon-Lime Soda
splash Sour mix

Hurricane Glass

Build over ice and stir

Naked Twister
1 part Melon Liqueur
1/2 part Vodka
1/2 part Tuaca®
fill with Pineapple Juice
splash Lemon-Lime Soda

Beer Mug

Build over ice and stir

Oral Sex on the Beach
1 part Melon Liqueur
1 part Raspberry Liqueur
1/2 part Vodka
fill with Orange Juice

Highball Glass

Shake with ice and strain over ice

Passion Pussy
1 1/2 parts Passion Fruit Liqueur
2 parts Heavy Cream
splash Grenadine

Highball Glass

Shake with ice and pour

Passionate Kiss
1 part Southern Comfort®
1 part Peach Schnapps
1 part Raspberry Liqueur
fill with Pineapple Juice

Coupette Glass

Shake with ice and pour

Passionate Screw
2 parts Vodka
1 part Orange Juice
2 dashes Bitters

Collins Glass

Shake with ice and strain

Peppermint Screw
1 part Gin
3/4 part Pisang Ambon® Liqueur
splash Peppermint Liqueur
1/2 part Sour Mix

Highball Glass

Shake with ice and pour

Perfect Screw
1 1/4 part Peach Schnapps
1/4 part Vodka
fill with Orange Juice

Highball Glass

Shake with ice and pour

Piece of Ass
1 part Amaretto
1 part Southern Comfort®
splash Lime Juice
fill with Lemon-Lime Soda
Collins Glass
Build over ice and stir

Pink Nipple
2 parts Raspberry Liqueur
fill with Cream
splash Grenadine
Hurricane Glass
Shake with ice and pour

Pink Pussy
1 part Campari®
1/2 part Peach Brandy
fill with Lemon-Lime Soda
Highball Glass
Build over ice and stir

Purple Alaskan Thunderfuck
1 part Jack Daniel's®
1 part Southern Comfort®
1/2 part Raspberry Liqueur
1/2 part Amaretto
1 part Orange Juice
1 part Pineapple Juice
Collins Glass
Shake with ice and strain over ice

Pussy on Your Face
1 part Melon Liqueur
3/4 part Strawberry-Flavored Vodka
3/4 part Banana Liqueur
1 part Sour Mix
1 part Orange Juice
1 part Pineapple Juice
Hurricane Glass
Build over ice and stir

Raspberry Screw
1 part Vodka
1 part Raspberry Liqueur
1 part Orange Juice
1 part Lemon-Lime Soda
Collins Glass
Build over ice and stir

Red Hot Lover
2 parts Vodka
2 parts Peach Schnapps
splash Grenadine
1 part Strawberry Juice
1 part Orange Juice
Hurricane Glass
Shake with ice and pour

Red Hot Passion
1 part Amaretto
1 part Bourbon
1 part Southern Comfort®
1 part Sloe Gin
1 part Triple Sec
1 part Pineapple Juice
1 part Orange Juice
Old-Fashioned Glass
Shake with ice and strain over ice

Red Raw Ass
3 parts Gin
1 part Triple Sec
1 part Strawberry Daiquiri Mix
splash Lime Juice
fill with Pineapple Juice
Highball Glass
Shake with ice and pour

Russian Pussy
1 part Vodka
1 part Crème de Cacao (White)
Old-Fashioned Glass
Shake with ice and strain over ice

Rusty Screw

$1^1/_2$ parts Scotch
$^1/_2$ splash Grand Marnier®
Brandy Snifter

Build in the glass with no ice

Sand in Your Ass

1 part Rum
1 part Coconut-Flavored Rum
splash Blue Curaçao
fill with Pineapple Juice
Highball Glass

Shake with ice and pour

Sand in Your Butt

1 part Southern Comfort®
1 part Melon Liqueur
fill with Pineapple Juice
Old-Fashioned Glass

Shake with ice and pour

Sand in Your Crack

$^1/_2$ part Vodka
$^1/_2$ part Blue Curaçao
$^1/_2$ part Melon Liqueur
4 parts Pineapple Juice
Coupette Glass

Combine all ingredients in a blender with ice. Blend until smooth.

Screaming Multiple Climax

2 parts Vodka
1 part Crème de Cacao (White)
1 part Amaretto
1 part Frangelico®
1 part Crème de Banana
fill with Cream
Hurricane Glass

Shake with ice and pour

Screaming Nipple Twister

2 parts Vodka
fill with Dr Pepper®
1 scoop Ice Cream
Collins Glass

Build over ice and stir

Screw You

1 part Vodka
1 part Coffee Liqueur
1 part Strawberry Liqueur
Highball Glass

Combine all ingredients in a blender with ice. Blend until smooth.

Screwed Banana

1 part Banana Liqueur
1 part Peach Schnapps
fill with Orange Juice
Highball Glass

Build over ice and stir

Screwed Driver

$1^1/_2$ parts Orange-Flavored Vodka
fill with Lemonade
splash Cranberry Juice Cocktail
Old-Fashioned Glass

Build over ice and stir

Screwed Strawberry Stripper

1 part Vodka
2 parts Strawberry Liqueur
fill with Orange Juice
Collins Glass

Build over ice and stir

Sex

1 part Coffee Liqueur
1 part Grand Marnier®
Old-Fashioned Glass

Shake with ice and pour

Sex and Candy

1 part Peach Schnapps
1 part Lemon-Lime Soda
Collins Glass

Build over ice and stir

Sex Appeal

1 part Light Rum
1 part Coconut-Flavored Rum
1 part Melon Liqueur
1 part Peach Schnapps
1 part Blue Curaçao
fill with Sour Mix
splash Lemonade
Collins Glass

Build over ice and stir

Sex by the Lake

1 part Vodka
1 part Peach Schnapps
1 part Pineapple Juice
1 part Orange Juice
Collins Glass

Build over ice and stir

Sex in a Bubblegum Factory

1 part Crème de Banana
1 part Blue Curaçao
1 part Apricot Brandy
1 part Rum
fill with Lemon-Lime Soda
Highball Glass

Build over ice and stir

Sex in a Jacuzzi

2 parts Vodka
1 part Cranberry Juice Cocktail
1 part Orange Juice
1 part Pineapple Juice
fill with Lemon-Lime Soda
splash Raspberry Liqueur
splash Orange Soda
Highball Glass

Build over ice and stir

Sex in a Tent

1 part Coconut-Flavored Rum
1 part Spiced Rum
fill with Mountain Dew®
Collins Glass

Build over ice and stir

Sex in a Tree

1 1/4 parts Midori®
1 part Banana Liqueur
1 part Coconut-Flavored Rum
fill with Pineapple Juice
Collins Glass

Build over ice and stir

Sex in the City

2 parts Blue Curaçao
1 1/2 parts Peach Schnapps
1 1/2 parts Vodka
1 part Pineapple Juice
1 part Raspberry Juice
Collins Glass

Shake with ice and pour

Sex in the Desert

1 part Tequila
1 part Triple Sec
1 part Cherry Juice
1 part Margarita Mix
1 part Cranberry Juice Cocktail
Highball Glass

Shake with ice and pour

Sex in the Forest

1 part Coconut-Flavored Rum
1 part Peach Schnapps
splash Vodka
splash Crème de Menthe (White)
fill Lemon-Lime Soda
splash Cream
Highball Glass

Build over ice and stir

Sex in the Jungle

1 1/2 parts Vodka
1 part Blue Curaçao
1 part Melon Liqueur
1 part Coconut-Flavored Rum
1 part Fresh Lime Juice
1 part Pineapple Juice
1 part Orange Juice

Hurricane Glass

Shake with ice and pour

Sex in the Shower

1 part Blue Curaçao
1 part Triple Sec
1 part Butterscotch Schnapps
fill with Orange Juice

Champagne Flute

Shake with ice and strain

Sex in the Sun

1/2 part Coconut-Flavored Rum
1/2 part Light Rum
1/2 part Galliano®
1/2 part Melon Liqueur
1 part Lemon Juice
1 part Orange Juice

Coupette Glass

Shake with ice and pour

Sex, Lies, and Video Poker

1 part Spiced Rum
1 part Amaretto
1 part Whiskey
1 part Orange Juice
1 part Pineapple Juice
1 part Cranberry Juice Cocktail
1 part Grenadine

Highball Glass

Shake with ice and strain over ice

Sex on an Arizona Beach

1 part Vodka
1 part Peach Schnapps
splash Grapefruit Juice
splash Lime Juice
splash Grenadine

Old-Fashioned Glass

Shake with ice and strain over ice

Sex on Daytona Beach

1 part Vodka
1 part Peach Schnapps
1/2 part Grenadine
1/4 part Heavy Cream
fill with Pineapple Juice

Highball Glass

Shake with ice and pour

Sex on Malibu Beach

1/2 part Vodka
1/2 part Coconut-Flavored Rum
1/2 part Peach Schnapps
1 part Cranberry Juice Cocktail
1 part Orange Juice
splash Grenadine

Highball Glass

Shake with ice and pour

Sex on My Face

1 part Yukon Jack®
1 part Coconut-Flavored Rum
1 part Southern Comfort®
1 part Banana Liqueur
splash Cranberry Juice Cocktail
splash Pineapple Juice
splash Orange Juice

Highball Glass

Shake with ice and pour

Sex on the Beach

1 part Vodka
1 part Peach Schnapps
1 part Cranberry Juice Cocktail
1 part Orange Juice

Highball Glass

Shake with ice and pour

Sex on the Beach (Southern Style)

1 part Peach Schnapps
1 part Sour Apple Schnapps
1 part Cranberry Juice Cocktail
1 part Pineapple Juice

Highball Glass

Shake with ice and strain over ice

Sex on the Beach in Winter

1 part Vodka
1 part Peach Schnapps
1/2 part Coconut Crème
1 part Cranberry Juice Cocktail
1 part Pineapple Juice

Coupette Glass

Combine all ingredients in a blender with ice. Blend until smooth.

Sex on the Beach with a California Blonde

1 part Vodka
1/2 part Midori®
1/2 part Raspberry Liqueur
1 part Pineapple Juice
1 part Cranberry Juice Cocktail

Collins Glass

Shake with ice and pour

Sex on the Beach with a Friend

1 part Crème de Cassis
1 part Midori®
1 part Pineapple Juice
1 part Vodka

Highball Glass

Shake with ice and pour

Sex on the Boat

1 part Spiced Rum
1/2 part Crème de Banana
fill with Orange Juice

Highball Glass

Shake with ice and pour

Sex on the Brain

1 part Peach Schnapps
1 part Vodka
1 part Midori®
1 part Pineapple Juice
1 part Orange Juice
splash Sloe Gin

Hurricane Glass

Shake with ice and pour

Sex on the Farm

1/4 part Vodka
1/4 part Amaretto
1/4 part Peach Schnapps
1/4 part Coconut-Flavored Rum
1/4 part Midori®
splash Grenadine
1 part Orange Juice
1 part Pineapple Juice

Collins Glass

Shake with ice and pour

Sex on the Grass

1 part Vodka
1 part Peach Schnapps
1/2 part Southern Comfort®
1/2 part Blue Curaçao
1 part Melon Liqueur

Highball Glass

Shake with ice and pour

Sex on the Sidewalk

1 part Melon Liqueur
1 part Raspberry Liqueur
1 part Cranberry Juice Cocktail

Highball Glass

Shake with ice and strain

Sex on the Sofa

1 part Vodka
1 part Peach Schnapps
fill with Orange Juice

Old-Fashioned Glass

Shake with ice and strain over ice

Sex under the Boardwalk

1 part Peach Schnapps
1 part Raspberry Liqueur
1 part Midori®

Old-Fashioned Glass

Shake with ice and strain over ice

Sex under the Sun

1 part Light Rum
1/2 part Dark Rum
1 part Orange Juice
1 part Pineapple Juice
splash Grenadine

Collins Glass

Build over ice and stir

Sex Wax

1 part Coconut Cream
1 part Rum
1/2 part Southern Comfort®
1 part Orange Juice
1 part Pineapple Juice

Collins Glass

Shake with ice and pour

Sex with a Virgin

2 parts Butterscotch Schnapps
1 part Crème de Menthe (White)
1 1/2 parts Irish Cream Liqueur
2 scoops Ice Cream

Coupette Glass

Combine all ingredients in a blender with ice. Blend until smooth.

Sex with the Bartender

1 part Light Rum
1 part Strawberry Liqueur
splash Cranberry Juice Cocktail
fill with Orange Juice

Collins Glass

Shake with ice and pour

Sex with the Captain

1 1/2 parts Spiced Rum
1 part Amaretto
1 part Peach Schnapps
1 part Cranberry Juice Cocktail
1 part Orange Juice

Highball Glass

Shake with ice and pour

Sexual Deviant

1 part Citrus-Flavored Vodka
3/4 part Melon Liqueur
1/2 part Raspberry Liqueur
2 parts Orange Juice
2 parts Pineapple Juice
1 part Margarita Mix

Highball Glass

Shake with ice and strain over ice

Sexual Harrassment

$1/2$ part Crown Royal® Whiskey
$1/2$ part Amaretto
$1/2$ part Sloe Gin
1 part Orange Juice
1 part Pineapple Juice

Highball Glass

Shake with ice and strain over ice

Sexual Longing

1 part Melon Liqueur
1 part Jägermeister®
fill with Pineapple Juice

Highball Glass

Shake with ice and strain over ice

Sexual Peak

$1/2$ part Amaretto
$1/2$ part Vodka
$1/4$ part Peach Schnapps
1 part Orange Juice
1 part Pineapple Juice
splash Sour Mix

Collins Glass

Shake with ice and pour

Sexual Trance

1 part Citrus-Flavored Vodka
1/2 part Midori®
1/2 part Raspberry Liqueur
1 part Orange Juice
1 part Pineapple Juice
splash Sour mix

Collins Glass

Shake with ice and pour

Sexy Blue-Eyed Boy

1 part Blue Curaçao
1 part Vodka
1 part Crème de Cacao (Dark)
1 part Rum Cream Liqueur
1 scoop Ice Cream

Coupette Glass

Combine all ingredients in a blender with ice. Blend until smooth.

Sexy Green Frogs

1 part Vodka
1 part Triple Sec
1 part Melon Liqueur
fill with Lemon-Lime Soda

Highball Glass

Build over ice and stir

Sexy Motherfucker

$1/2$ part Melon Liqueur
$1/2$ part Raspberry Liqueur
$1/2$ part Light Rum
1 part Pineapple Juice
1 part Orange Juice

Collins Glass

Shake with ice and strain over ice

Shag in the Sand

$1\,1/2$ parts Southern Comfort®
$1\,1/2$ parts Sloe Gin
1 part Vodka
1 part Maraschino Liqueur
$1/2$ part Red Curacao
fill with Orange Juice

Hurricane Glass

Shake with ice and strain over ice

Sicilian Sex

1 part Amaretto
$1\,1/2$ parts Southern Comfort®
fill with Cranberry Juice Cocktail

Highball Glass

Build over ice and stir

Silky Screw
1 part Gin
1 part Sloe Gin
1/2 part Crème de Cassis
1/2 part Cream
2 parts Orange Juice

Coupette Glass

Combine all ingredients in a blender with ice. Blend until smooth.

Slippery Dick
1 1/2 parts Butterscotch Schnapps
2 parts Irish Cream Liqueur
fill with Half and Half

Collins Glass

Shake with ice and pour

Slow Comfortable Fuzzy Screw
1 part Vodka
1 part Sloe Gin
1 part Southern Comfort®
1 part Peach Schnapps
fill with Orange Juice

Highball Glass

Build over ice and stir

Slow Comfortable Screw
1 part Sloe Gin
1/2 part Southern Comfort®
fill with Orange Juice

Collins Glass

Build over ice and stir.

Slow Comfortable Screw 151 Times in the Dark
1 part Vodka
1 part Sloe Gin
1 part Southern Comfort®
1 part Galliano®
1 part Tequila
1 part Dark Rum
splash 151-Proof Rum
fill with Orange Juice

Collins Glass

Build over ice and stir

Slow Comfortable Screw Up Against the Wall
1 part Sloe Gin
1 part Southern Comfort®
1 part Vodka
splash Galliano®
fill with Orange Juice

Highball Glass

Slow Comfortable Screw Up Against the Wall with a Bang
3/4 part Sloe Gin
3/4 part Southern Comfort®
1/2 part 151-Proof Rum
1/2 part Galliano®
fill with Orange Juice

Collins Glass

Build over ice and stir

Slow Comfortable Screw Between the Sheets
1 part Sloe Gin
1 part Southern Comfort®
1 part Vodka
1 part Triple Sec
fill with Orange Juice

Collins Glass

Build over ice and stir

Slow Comfortable Screw Mexican Style

1 part Sloe Gin
1 part Southern Comfort®
1 part Galliano®
1 part Sauza® Tequila
fill with Orange Juice

Highball Glass

Build over ice and stir

Slow Comfortable Screw on a Dogbox

1 part Southern Comfort®
1 part Jack Daniel's®
1 part Sloe Gin
splash Grenadine
fill with Orange Juice

Collins Glass

Build over ice and stir

Slow Comfortable Screw Up Against a Fuzzy Wall

1 part Vodka
1 part Southern Comfort®
1 part Sloe Gin
1 part Peach Schnapps
1/2 part Galliano®
fill with Orange Juice

Highball Glass

Build over ice and stir

Slow Fuzzy Screw

1 part Vodka
1 part Sloe Gin
1 part Peach Schnapps
fill with Orange Juice

Highball Glass

Build over ice and stir

Slow Fuzzy Screw Up Against the Wall

1 part Vodka
1 part Sloe Gin
1 part Peach Schnapps
fill with Orange Juice
splash Galliano®

Highball Glass

Build over ice and stir

Slow Passionate Screw

2 parts Sloe Gin
1 part Orange Juice
1 part Passion Fruit Juice

Highball Glass

Build over ice and stir

Slow Screw

1 part Sloe Gin
fill with Orange Juice

Highball Glass

Build over ice and stir

Slow Screw Mildly Comfortable, Slightly Wild

1 part Vodka
1 part Sloe Gin
3/4 part Bourbon
3/4 part Southern Comfort®
1 part Lemonade
1 part Orange Juice

Hurricane Glass

Shake with ice and pour

Slow Screw Up Against the Wall

1 part Vodka
1 part Sloe Gin
fill with Orange Juice
splash Galliano®

Highball Glass

Build over ice and stir

Smooth and Sexy
1 part Passion Fruit
1 part Safari®
1/2 part Amaretto
1/2 part Blackberry Juice
fill with Orange Juice

Collins Glass

Shake with ice and pour

Soapy Tits
1 part Rumple Minze®
1 part Goldschläger®
1 part Cinnamon Schnapps
fill Lemon-Lime Soda

Beer Mug

Build over ice and stir

Southern Sex
2 parts Southern Comfort®
fill Lemonade

Highball Glass

Build over ice and stir

Stop and Go Naked
2 parts Triple Sec
1 part Silver Tequila
1 part Vodka
1 part Light Rum
1 part Gin

Old-Fashioned Glass

Shake with ice and pour

Sweet Sex
1 part Raspberry-Flavored Vodka
1 part 99-Proof Banana Liqueur
1 part Coconut-Flavored Rum
1 part Tequila Rose®
1 part Watermelon Schnapps
splash Grenadine
fill with Orange Juice

Hurricane Glass

Shake with ice and pour

A Thumb in the Ass
1 part Butterscotch Schnapps
1 part Cinnamon Schnapps
1 part Peach Schnapps
1 part Peppermint Schnapps
1 part Blueberry Schnapps

Highball Glass

Shake with ice and strain over ice

Thunderfuck
1 part Vodka
1 part Amaretto
1 part Melon Liqueur
1 part Rum
1 part Sour Mix
1 part Orange Juice

Highball Glass

Shake with ice and strain

Tropical Screw
1 part Vodka
1/2 part Triple Sec

Highball Glass

Build over ice and stir

Tropical Sex
1 part Coconut-Flavored Rum
1 part Midori®
fill with Pineapple Juice

Highball Glass

Combine all ingredients in a blender with ice. Blend until smooth.

Twenty-Dollar Blowjob
3/4 part Vodka
3/4 part Southern Comfort®
3/4 part Peach Schnapps
2 parts Cranberry Juice Cocktail
2 parts Sour Mix
1/2 part Orange Juice

Collins Glass

Build over ice and stir

Twisted Asshole
1 part Vodka
1 part Melon Liqueur
1/2 part Peach Schnapps
splash Blue Curaçao
1 part Pineapple Juice
1 part Orange Juice
Collins Glass
Shake with ice and pour

Twisted Screw
2 parts Vodka
fill with Orange Juice
splash Banana Juice
Highball Glass
Build over ice and stir

Virgin Sex on the Beach
1 part Peach Nectar
1/2 part Grenadine
1 part Orange Juice
1 part Cranberry Juice Cocktail
Highball Glass
Build over ice and stir

Wet Pussy
1 part Raspberry Liqueur
2 parts Irish Cream Liqueur
fill with Milk
Collins Glass
Shake with ice and pour

Wild Screw
1 part Vodka
1 part Bourbon
fill with Orange Juice
Collins Glass
Build over ice and stir

Wild Sex
1 part Dark Rum
1 part Peach Schnapps
1/2 part Grenadine
1 part Pineapple Juice
1 part Orange Juice
1 part Coconut-Flavored Liqueur
Hurricane Glass
Shake with ice and pour

Wild Squirrel Sex
1/2 part Lemon-Flavored Vodka
1/2 part Strawberry-Flavored Vodka
1/2 part Orange-Flavored Vodka
1/2 part Raspberry-Flavored Vodka
1 part Amaretto
1 part Sour Mix
1 part Cranberry Juice Cocktail
splash Grenadine
Beer Mug
Build over ice and stir

Tiki or Island Drinks

Here are some colorful, fruity, tropical drinks that will help you pretend you're on the beach even in mid-January.

2-Tonga

1 part Cranberry-Flavored Vodka
1 1/2 parts Red Curacao
1 1/2 parts Mango Schnapps
4 parts Orange Juice
1 part Fresh Lime Juice

Hurricane Glass

Shake with ice and strain over ice

Acapulco Beach

2 parts Gold Tequila
2/3 part Peach Schnapps
2/3 part Blue Curaçao
1 part Papaya Juice
2 parts Pineapple Juice

Collins Glass

Shake with ice and strain over ice

Admiral's Grog

2 parts Gosling's Seal® Black Rum
1 Lime Wedge

Whiskey Sour Glass

Pour Rum over ice and squeeze the Lime in

Aloha

1 part Dark Rum
1 1/2 parts Myers's® Rum Crème Liqueur
1/2 part Sweetened Lime Juice
2 parts Pineapple Juice
2 parts Orange Juice
1 part Coco López®
1 scoop Vanilla Ice Cream
1 Pineapple Slice

Collins Glass

Combine all ingredients in a blender with ice. Blend until smooth.

Amaretto Paradise

1 part Amaretto
1 part Coconut-Flavored Rum
1 part Melon Liqueur
fill with Pineapple Juice

Hurricane Glass

Build over ice and stir

Amaretto Rum Punch

1 part Rum
1 part Amaretto
1 part Cherry Juice
1 part Orange Juice
1 part Pineapple Juice

Highball Glass

Build over ice and stir

Ambros Lighthouse

2 parts Vodka
1 part Parfait Amour
1 part Coconut-Flavored Liqueur
fill with Banana Juice

Hurricane Glass

Build over ice and stir

Anchors Away

1 part Vodka
1 part Amaretto
1 part Blackberry Liqueur
fill with Orange Juice

Hurricane Glass

Combine all ingredients in a blender with ice. Blend until smooth.

Apple Swizzle

1 1/2 parts Apple Brandy
1 part Rum
3/4 part Fresh Lime Juice
dash Powdered Sugar

Old-Fashioned Glass

Build over ice and stir

Aruba Rum Punch

1 part Dark Rum
1 part Light Rum
1 part Orange Juice
1 part Pineapple Juice
1/2 part Sour Mix
splash Grenadine
2 dashes Bitters

Hurricane Glass

Shake with ice and pour

Avery Island

1 part Melon Liqueur
1 part Dark Rum
1/2 part Guava Juice
1/2 part Lime Juice

Highball Glass

Build over ice and stir

Bacardi® Spice on the Beach

1 1/2 parts Spiced Rum
1 part Peach Schnapps
fill with Orange Juice

Collins Glass

Build over ice and stir

Bahama Mama

1 1/2 parts Rum
1 part Coconut-Flavored Rum
1/2 part Cherry Heering®
1/2 part Lemon Juice
2 parts Orange Juice
2 parts Pineapple Juice
splash Grenadine

Hurricane Glass

Build over ice and stir

Bahamian Goombay Smash

3/4 part Coconut-Flavored Rum
1 1/4 parts Dark Rum
1/4 part Triple Sec
1/4 part Lemon Juice
3 parts Pineapple Juice
dash Simple Syrup

Hurricane Glass

Shake with ice and pour

Balmy Beach

1 1/2 parts Peach Schnapps
1 part Spiced Rum
1/2 part Lemon Juice
fill with Orange Juice

Collins Glass

Build over ice and stir

Banana Banshee (Frozen)

1 part Crème de Cacao (White)
1 part Crème de Banana
2 scoops Vanilla Ice Cream

Collins Glass

Combine all ingredients in a blender with ice. Blend until smooth.

Banana Barbados

3/4 part Mount Gay® Eclipse Rum
1/2 part Crème de Banana
2 parts Sour Mix
2 scoops Vanilla Ice Cream

Coupette Glass

Combine all ingredients in a blender with ice. Blend until smooth.

Banana Boat

1 part Light Rum
1 part Brandy
1 part Crème de Banana
2 scoops Vanilla Ice Cream

White Wine Glass

Combine all ingredients in a blender with ice. Blend until smooth.

Banana Bunch

2 parts Crème de Banana
1 part Maple Syrup
3 parts Cream
1 part Kiwi Juice
1 part Banana Puree

Coupette Glass

Combine all ingredients in a blender with ice. Blend until smooth.

Banana Chi Chi

1 part Vodka
1 part Cherry Juice
1 part Banana Juice
fill with Piña Colada Mix
splash Orange Juice

Highball Glass

Combine all ingredients in a blender with ice. Blend until smooth.

Banana Colada

1 part Dark Rum
1 part Light Rum
1 Banana
1 part Coconut Crème
4 parts Pineapple Juice

Collins Glass

Combine all ingredients in a blender with ice. Blend until smooth.

Banana Milk Punch

1 part Crème de Banana
1 part Dark Rum
1 part Cream
fill with Milk
splash Simple Syrup

Collins Glass

Build over ice and stir

Banana Punch

2 parts Vodka
1 1/2 splashes Banana Liqueur
1/2 part Lime Juice
fill with Carbonated Water

Collins Glass

Build over ice and stir

Banana Rum Punch

1 part Rum
1 part Banana Liqueur
1 part Cherry Juice
1 part Orange Juice
1 part Pineapple Juice

Highball Glass

Build over ice and stir

Banana Surfer

2 parts Milk
1 part Frangelico®
1 part Banana Puree
1 part Crème de Cacao (White)

Coupette Glass

Combine all ingredients in a blender with ice. Blend until smooth.

Bandung Exotic
2 parts Crème de Menthe (Green)
1 part Crème de Banana
1 part Cherry Brandy
fill with Ginger Ale

Hurricane Glass

Shake all but Ginger Ale with ice and strain into a shot glass. Top with Ginger Ale.

Barbados Planter's Punch
3 parts Sparkling Water
3 parts Dark Rum
1 part Fresh Lime Juice
dash Powdered Sugar
dash Orange Bitters

Collins Glass

Shake with ice and strain over ice

Barrier Reef
1 part Gin
1 part Cointreau®
1 scoop Vanilla Ice Cream

Pitcher

Combine all ingredients in a blender. Blend until smooth.

Baywatch
1 part Vodka
1 part Galliano®
fill with Orange Juice
splash Cream

Hurricane Glass

Build over ice and stir

Beach Blanket Bingo
1 part Cranberry Juice Cocktail
1 part Grape Juice (Red)

Highball Glass

Build over ice and stir

Beach Bum
1 1/2 parts Vodka
1 part Apple Juice
1 part Banana Liqueur
2 parts Pineapple Juice
fill with Fruit Punch

Collins Glass

Shake with ice and pour

Beach Cruiser
1 1/4 parts Spiced Rum
1 part Pineapple Juice
1 part Cranberry Juice Cocktail

Collins Glass

Build over ice and stir

Beach Dream
1 part KeKe Beach® Key Lime Cream Liqueur
1 part Melon Liqueur
1 part Lime Cordial
1/2 part Coconut-Flavored Liqueur
1/2 part Grenadine
4 parts Orange Juice
3 parts Pineapple Juice

Hurricane Glass

Combine all ingredients in a blender with ice. Blend until smooth.

Beach Party
1 1/4 parts Rum
1 part Pineapple Juice
1 part Orange Juice
1 part Grenadine

Collins Glass

Combine all ingredients in a blender with ice. Blend until smooth.

Beach Sunday
2 parts Peach-Flavored Vodka
1 part Chambord®
3 parts Cranberry Juice Cocktail

Highball Glass

Build over ice and stir

Beach Sweet
2 parts Vodka
1 part Apricot Brandy
1/2 part Fresh Lime Juice
3 parts Banana Juice

Old-Fashioned Glass

Combine all ingredients in a blender with ice. Blend until smooth.

Beachcomber
1 part Vodka
1 1/2 parts Light Rum
6 Strawberries
1 Banana
1/2 part Coconut Cream
splash Lime Juice
1/2 part Grenadine

Highball Glass

Combine all ingredients in a blender with ice. Blend until smooth.

Beachside
1 part Vodka
1 part Melon Liqueur
1 part Strawberry Daiquiri Mix
1 part Orange Juice
1 part Pineapple Juice

Highball Glass

Shake with ice and strain over ice

Beauty on the Beach
1 part Light Rum
1 part Southern Comfort®
splash Grand Marnier®
splash Lemon Juice
dash Orange Bitters

Collins Glass

Shake with ice and strain over ice

Bender's Sling
1 1/2 parts Gin
1 part Lemonade
1 part Orange Juice
1 Orange Slice
1 Maraschino Cherry

Collins Glass

Build over ice and stir

Bermuda Rum Swizzle
2 parts Gosling's Black Seal® Rum
2 parts Light Rum
1/4 part Lime Juice
2 parts Pineapple Juice
2 parts Orange Juice
1/2 part Grenadine
3 dashes Angostura® Bitters

Pitcher, Glasses

Fill a pitcher 1/3 full with crushed ice. Add all ingredients and stir or shake vigorously until a frothing head appears. Strain into glasses.

Berry Buster
1 1/2 parts Currant-Flavored Vodka
1/2 part Raspberry Liqueur
2 parts Cranberry Juice Cocktail

Coupette Glass

Shake with ice and strain over ice

Berry Me in the Sand

1 part Vodka
1/2 part Blackberry Liqueur
1/2 part Triple Sec
fill with Orange Juice

Highball Glass

Build over ice and stir

Blackberry Rum Punch

1 part Rum
1 part Blackberry Liqueur
1 part Cherry Juice
1 part Orange Juice
1 part Pineapple Juice

Highball Glass

Shake with ice and pour

Black Magic

1 1/2 parts Vodka
3/4 part Coffee Liqueur
splash Lemon Juice

Old-Fashioned Glass

Build over ice and stir

Blue Hawaiian

1 part Light Rum
2 parts Pineapple Juice
1 part Blue Curaçao
1 part Coconut-Flavored Liqueur

Highball Glass

Combine all ingredients in a blender with ice. Blend until smooth.

Blue Jeep® Island

1 part Triple Sec
1 part Raspberry Liqueur
fill with Lemon-Lime Soda

Highball Glass

Build over ice and stir

Bolduc on the Beach

1 part Vodka
1 part Orange Juice
1 part Grapefruit Juice

Highball Glass

Shake with ice and pour

Bora-Bora Island

1 part Jamaican Rum
1 part Coffee Liqueur
1 part Coconut-Cream
1/2 part Crème de Banana
1/2 part Coconut-Flavored Liqueur
1 1/2 parts Cream
1 1/2 parts Banana Juice
1/2 part Almond Syrup

Hurricane Glass

Combine all ingredients in a blender with ice. Blend until smooth.

Cannon Beach

1 part Blackberry Liqueur
1 part Dark Rum
3 parts Pineapple Juice
2 parts Club Soda

Collins Glass

Build over ice and stir

Caribbean Beach Party

1 part Rum
1 part Cherry Juice
1 part Banana Juice
1 part Piña Colada Mix
1 part Pineapple Juice
1 part Cranberry Juice Cocktail

Highball Glass

Build over ice and stir

Caribbean Punch
2 parts Dark Rum
3/4 part Crème de Banana
1 part Pineapple Juice
1 part Orange Juice
1/4 part Sweetened Lime Juice

Highball Glass

Shake with ice and pour

Cherry Sling
2 parts Cherry Brandy
1/2 part Lemon Juice
1 Lemon Twist

Old-Fashioned Glass

Build over ice and stir

Club Tropicana
1 part Coconut-Flavored Rum
1 part Blue Curaçao
1/2 part Triple Sec
1 part Pineapple Juicc
1 part Lemon-Lime Soda
splash Grenadine
1 Maraschino Cherry

Hurricane Glass

Build over ice and stir

Cocoa Beach
1 part Vodka
1 part Blue Curaçao
2 parts Piña Colada Mix
1 part Lemonade
1 part Pineapple Juice

Hurricane Glass

Shake with ice and strain over ice

Cuban Crime of Passion
1 part Spiced Rum
1 part Light Rum
1 part Coconut-Flavored Rum
1 part Triple Sec
2 parts Pineapple Juice

Hurricane Glass

Shake with ice and pour

A Day at the Beach
1 part Coconut-Flavored Rum
1/2 part Amaretto
4 parts Orange Juice
1/2 part Grenadine

Highball Glass

Shake with ice and strain over ice

Daytona Beach
1 part Vodka
1 part Cherry Juice
1 part Wild Berry Schnapps
2 parts Lemonade
1 part Orange Juice

Highball Glass

Shake with ice and pour

Down Home Punch
1 part Whiskey
1 part Pcach Schnapps
2 parts Orange Juice
1 part Lemon-Lime Soda
1 part Sour Mix
splash Grenadine

Collins Glass

Build over ice and stir

El Niño
1 part Vodka
1 part Peach Schnapps
1/2 part Blue Curaçao
2 parts Pineapple Juice
2 parts Orange Juice
splash Club Soda

Hurricane Glass

Shake all but Club Soda with ice and strain into the glass over ice. Top with Club Soda.

Flirting with the Sandpiper
1 1/2 parts Light Rum
1/2 part Cherry Brandy
3 parts Orange Juice
2 dashes Orange Bitters

Highball Glass

Shake with ice and pour

Florida Punch

1 part Dark Rum
1/4 part Cognac
1 part Grapefruit Juice
1 part Orange Juice

Highball Glass

Shake with ice and strain over ice

Fog Cutter

1 1/2 parts Light Rum
1/2 part Gin
1/2 part Brandy
1 part Orange Juice
3 splashes Lemon Juice
2 splashes Amaretto

Collins Glass

Shake with ice and strain over ice

Fruity Punch

1/2 part Coconut-Flavored Rum
1/2 part Light Rum
1/2 part Triple Sec
1 1/2 parts Pineapple Juice
splash Grenadine

Highball Glass

Shake with ice and pour

Fun on the Beach

1 part Vodka
1 part Melon Liqueur
splash Raspberry Liqueur
1 part Pineapple Juice
1 part Cranberry Juice Cocktail

Highball Glass

Build over ice and stir

Gay Bartender

1 1/2 parts Coconut-Flavored Rum
1/2 part Blue Curaçao
1/2 part Grand Marnier®
1/2 part Raspberry Liqueur
1 part Apple Juice
1 part Cranberry Juice Cocktail
1 part Orange Juice
1/2 part Strawberry Liqueur

Parfait Glass

Shake with ice and strain over ice

Gilligan's Island®

1 part Vodka
1 part Peach Schnapps
3 parts Orange Juice
3 parts Cranberry Juice Cocktail

Collins Glass

Shake with ice and strain over ice

Gilligan's Island® Retreat

1 part Melon Liqueur
1 part Coconut-Flavored Rum
1 part Banana Liqueur
1 part Amaretto
1 part Spiced Rum
1 Sour Mix
fill with Pineapple Juice
1 part Cherry Juice

Highball Glass

Shake with ice and pour

Gin Beachball

1 1/2 parts Gin
1 part Grapefruit Juice
1 part Orange Juice

Collins Glass

Build over ice and stir

Golden Pony
1 part Scotch
1 part Orange Juice
1 part Apricot Brandy

Coupette Glass

Shake with ice and pour

Gringo Swizzle
2 parts Tequila Silver
2 parts Ginger Ale
1 part Pineapple Juice
1 part Orange Juice
1 part Fresh Lime Juice
1/2 part Crème de Cassis

Old-Fashioned Glass

Shake with ice and strain over ice

Grog
2 parts Dark Rum
3 parts Water

Old-Fashioned Glass

Build in the glass with no ice

Hairy Slut
2 parts Rum
1 part Triple Sec
2 parts Pineapple Juice

Coupette Glass

Shake with ice and pour

Hawaiian Island Sunset
1 part Amaretto
1 part Coconut-Flavored Rum
1 part Peach Schnapps
splash Grenadine
2 parts Lemonade
fill with Pineapple Juice
1 1/2 parts Mango Schnapps

Highball Glass

Build over ice and stir

Hawaiian Kisses
1 1/2 parts Light Rum
1 part Blue Curaçao
1 part Triple Sec
fill with Orange Juice

Hurricane Glass

Build over ice and stir

Hawaiian Punch
1/2 part Vodka
1/2 part Southern Comfort®
1/2 part Amaretto
1/2 part Sloe Gin
1 part Orange Juice
1 part Pineapple Juice

Hurricane Glass

Build over ice and stir

Hawaiian Surf City
1 part Vodka
1 part Wild Berry Schnapps
1 part Peach Nectar
2 parts Lemonade
1 part Pineapple Juice

Highball Glass

Build over ice and stir

Heat Wave
1 1/4 parts Coconut-Flavored Rum
1/2 part Peach Schnapps
1 part Pineapple Juice
1 part Orange Juice
1/2 part Grenadine

Parfait Glass

Build over ice and stir

Hoi Punch
2 parts Vodka
1/2 part Crème de Cassis
1/2 part Light Rum
fill with Lemon Juice
1 1/2 parts Simple Syrup

Collins Glass

Shake with ice and strain over ice

Hurricane

4 parts Dark Rum
2 splashes Lime Juice
fill with Hawaiian Punch®
1 part 151-Proof Rum

Hurricane Glass

Shake with ice and pour

Hurricane Leah

1/4 part Light Rum
1/4 part Gin
1/4 part Vodka
1/4 part Tequila
1/4 part Blue Curaçao
splash Cherry Brandy
1 part Sour Mix
1 part Orange Juice

Hurricane Glass

Shake with ice and strain over ice

Hurricane (New Orleans Style)

1 part Light Rum
1 part 151-Proof Rum
1 part Orange Juice
1 part Pineapple Juice
1/2 part Grenadine

Hurricane Glass

Shake with ice and pour

Iceberg Vacation

1 1/2 parts Blue Curaçao
1 1/2 parts Vodka
1 part Cream
1 part Crème de Menthe (White)
1 part Fresh Lime Juice
fill with Lemon-Lime Soda

Hurricane Glass

Build over ice and stir

Island Breeze

1 1/4 parts Coconut-Flavored Rum
fill with Cranberry Juice Cocktail

Collins Glass

Build over ice and stir

Island Hideaway

1 part Dark Rum
1 part Passion Fruit Liqueur
1 part Pineapple Juice
1 part Orange Juice

Collins Glass

Build over ice and stir

Island Jack

3/4 part Banana Liqueur
3/4 part Malibu® Rum
1/2 part Jack Daniel's®
1 part Pineapple Juice
1 part Sour Mix
2 parts Cola

Collins Glass

Build over ice and stir

Island Oasis

1/2 part Coconut-Flavored Liqueur
1/2 part Crème de Banana
2/3 part Spiced Rum
2/3 part Dark Rum
3 parts Piña Colada Mix
2 parts Strawberry Puree

Collins Glass

Combine all ingredients in a blender with ice. Blend until smooth.

Island Punch

1 part Light Rum
splash Grenadine
1 part Orange Juice
1 part Pineapple Juice
2 Maraschino Cherries

Collins Glass

Build over ice and stir

Island Toy
1 part Spiced Rum
1/4 part Peach Schnapps
1/4 part Lime Juice
fill with Pineapple Juice

Highball Glass

Build over ice and stir

Islander
2 parts Gosling's Black Seal® Rum
fill with Pineapple Juice

Collins Glass

Build over ice and stir

Italian Surfer
1 part Coconut-Flavored Rum
1 part Amaretto
fill with Pineapple Juice
splash Cranberry Juice Cocktail

Highball Glass

Build over ice

Jamaican 10-Speed
1 1/2 parts Coconut-Flavored Rum
1/2 part Banana Liqueur
1 part Melon Liqueur
1 part Cream
fill with Pineapple Juice

Hurricane Glass

Shake with ice and strain over ice

Jamaican Punch
3/4 part Spiced Rum
3/4 part Coconut-Flavored Rum
3/4 part Banana Liqueur
1 part Orange Juice
1 part Pineapple Juice
splash Grenadine

Collins Glass

Shake with ice and strain over ice

Jamaican Surfer
1 part Coconut-Flavored Rum
1/2 part Tia Maria®
1 part Cream

Old-Fashioned Glass

Shake with ice and strain over ice

Jamaican Zombie
2 1/2 parts Light Rum
1 part Dark Rum
1 part Apricot Brandy
1 part Lime Juice
1 part Pineapple Juice
1 part Orange Juice

Collins Glass

Shake with ice and strain over ice

Kangeroo Jumper
1 part Vodka
1 part Rum
1 part Coconut Crème
1/2 part Blue Curaçao
fill with Passion Fruit Juice

Coupette Glass

Shake with ice and strain over ice

Kon Tiki
2 parts Scotch
1 part Dark Rum
1 part Cointreau®

Highball Glass

Shake with ice and strain over ice

Las Brisas
2 parts Rum
1 part Coconut Cream
1 part Pineapple Juice
1 part Orange Juice

Hurricane Glass

Shake with ice and strain over ice

Lazy Licker
1 part Tequila Reposado
1/2 part Blue Curaçao
1/4 part Peach Schnapps
2 parts Sour Mix
fill with Cola

Coupette Glass

Shake all but Cola with ice and strain into the glass. Top with Cola.

Loch Lomond
1 part Scotch
1/2 part Peach Schnapps
1 part Blue Curaçao
fill with Grapefruit Juice
1/2 part Lemon Juice

Parfait Glass

Shake with ice and strain over ice

London Fog
1 1/2 parts Gin
1/4 part Pernod®

Highball Glass

Shake with ice and strain over ice

Long Island Sunset
1 part Spiced Rum
1 part Peach Schnapps
1 part Sour Mix
1 part Cranberry Juice Cocktail

Highball Glass

Shake with ice and pour

Lost in Paradise
1 1/2 parts Light Rum
1 part Blue Curaçao
1 part Triple Sec
3 parts Orange Juice
1 part Pineapple Juice

Hurricane Glass

Shake with ice and strain over ice

Mai Tai
1 1/2 parts Light Rum
1 part Dark Rum
1/2 part Amaretto
1/2 part Triple Sec
1/2 part Sour Mix
fill with Pineapple Juice
splash 151-Proof Rum

Collins Glass

Shake with ice and strain over ice. Top with splash of 151-Proof Rum.

Malibu Beach
1 part Vodka
1 part Coconut-Flavored Rum
1 part Orange Juice
1 part Pineapple Juice

Highball Glass

Build over ice and stir

Marco Island Rum Runner
3/4 part Crème de Banana
3/4 part Blackberry Brandy
3/4 part Light Rum
2 parts Sour Mix
fill with Orange Juice
splash Grenadine

Collins Glass

Build over ice and stir

Maui Sunset
1 part Light Rum
1 1/2 parts Apricot Brandy
1 1/2 parts Triple Sec
fill with Pineapple Juice

Hurricane Glass

Build over ice

Melon Chiquita® Punch
1 1/2 parts Crème de Banana
1 1/2 parts Melon Liqueur
1 part Pineapple Juice
1 part Milk

Collins Glass

Shake with ice and strain over ice

Mississippi Planters' Punch
1 part Brandy
1/2 part Light Rum
1/2 part Lemon Juice
dash Powdered Sugar
fill with Carbonated Water

Collins Glass

Shake all but Carbonated Water with ice and strain into the glass. Top with Carbonated Water.

Monkey Island
1 1/2 parts Light Rum
1 part Crème de Banana
1 part Pisang Ambon® Liqueur
1/2 part Simple Syrup
fill with Pineapple Juice

Collins Glass

Shake with ice and pour

Monster on the Beach
1 1/2 parts Tequila
2 parts Cranberry Juice Cocktail
splash Lime Juice
splash Grenadine

Highball Glass

Shake with ice and pour

Myrtle Beach
1 part Vodka
1 part Blue Curaçao
1 part Piña Colada Mix
1 part Lemonade
1 part Orange Juice

Highball Glass

Shake with ice and strain over ice

Navy Grog
1 part Light Rum
1 part Dark Rum
1 part Spiced Rum
1 part Orange Juice
2 parts Pineapple Juice
1 part Guava Juice
1 part Lime Juice

Collins Glass

Shake with ice and pour

Nutty Surfer
1 part Coconut-Flavored Rum
1 part Frangelico®
1 part Cream

Old-Fashioned Glass

Shake with ice and strain over ice

Orgasm on the Beach
1 part Light Rum
1 part Coconut-Flavored Rum
1/2 part Blue Curaçao
1/2 part Raspberry Liqueur
fill with Pineapple Juice

Collins Glass

Shake with ice and pour

The Original Hurricane
1/2 part Amaretto
1/2 part Dark Rum
1/2 part Gin
1/2 part Light Rum
2 parts Grapefruit Juice
2 parts Orange Juice
2 parts Pineapple Juice
1/4 part Grenadine

Hurricane Glass

Shake with ice and pour

Oslo Breeze
1 part Vodka
1 part Aquavit
dash Orange Bitters
fill with Cider

Coupette Glass

Build over ice and stir

Pacific Sunshine
1 part Tequila
1 part Blue Curaçao
1 part Sour Mix
dash Bitters

Parfait Glass

Shake with ice and strain over ice

Palm Island
1 part Passion Fruit Liqueur
1 part Melon Liqueur
1/2 part Dark Rum
1/2 part Coconut Crème
2 parts Orange Juice
2 parts Grape Juice (white)
2 parts Pineapple Juice

Coupette Glass

Combine all ingredients in a blender with ice. Blend until smooth.

Panama Punch
1 part Rum
1 part Piña Colada Mix
1 part Banana Juice
1 part Orange Juice
1 part Pineapple Juice

Highball Glass

Build over ice and stir

Paradise Island
1 part Gin
1/2 part Triple Sec
1/2 part Peach Schnapps
splash Fresh Lime Juice
fill with Pineapple Juice

Old-Fashioned Glass

Shake with ice and pour

Peach on Malibu Beach
1 part Coconut-Flavored Rum
1 part Peach Schnapps
1 part Orange Juice
1 part Pineapple Juice
1 part Cranberry Juice Cocktail

Highball Glass

Build over ice and stir

Peach on the Beach
1 1/2 parts Vodka
1/2 part Peach Schnapps
fill with Pineapple Juice

Highball Glass

Shake with ice and pour

Puerto Rican Punch
3/4 part Vodka
3/4 part Gin
3/4 part Sloe Gin
3/4 part Peach Schnapps
1 part Orange Juice
1 part Pineapple Juice
splash Grenadine

Hurricane Glass

Build over ice and stir

Rio Bamba
1 part Vodka
1 part Gin
1/2 part Passion Fruit Liqueur
1/2 part Peach Schnapps
1/2 part Cream
1 part Pineapple Juice
1 part Orange Juice

Hurricane Glass

Shake with ice and pour

Rockaway Beach
1½ parts Light Rum
½ part Dark Rum
½ part Tequila
splash Crème de Noyaux
½ part Cranberry Juice Cocktail
½ part Pineapple Juice
1 part Orange Juice

Highball Glass

Shake with ice and strain over ice

Rum Dinger
1 part Coconut-Flavored Rum
1 part Melon Liqueur
1 part Orange Juice
1 part Pineapple Juice

Hurricane Glass

Shake with ice and pour

Rum Punch
1½ parts Rum
1 part Orange Juice
1 part Pineapple Juice
1 part Cranberry Juice Cocktail

Highball Glass

Build over ice and stir

Rum Relaxer
1½ parts Light Rum
1 part Pineapple Juice
½ part Grenadine
fill with Lemon-Lime Soda

Parfait Glass

Shake all but Lemon-Lime Soda with ice and strain into the glass. Top with Lemon-Lime Soda.

Sammy Special
1 part Coconut-Flavored Rum
1 part Light Rum
1 part Pineapple Juice
1 part Orange Juice

Hurricane Glass

Shake with ice and pour

Sandbar Sleeper
1 part Vodka
1 part Irish Crème Liqueur
1 part Coffee Liqueur
1 part Frangelico®
½ part Milk

Highball Glass

Shake with ice and strain over ice

Sandcastle
2 parts Citrus-Flavored Vodka
1 part Grenadine
fill with Pineapple Juice

Collins Glass

Shake with ice and pour

Sandpiper
1 part Light Rum
1 part Cherry Brandy
½ part Grapefruit Juice
1 part Orange Juice

Highball Glass

Shake with ice and strain

Sanibel Island
1 part Bacardi® Limón Rum
1 part Orange-Flavored Vodka
1 part Sour Mix
1 part Cranberry Juice Cocktail
1 part Lemon-Lime Soda

Highball Glass

Shake with ice and pour

Scotch Bounty
1 part Scotch
1 part Coconut-Flavored Rum
1 part Crème de Cacao (White)
½ part Grenadine
fill with Orange Juice

Parfait Glass

Shake with ice and pour

Sewer Water
1 part 151-Proof Rum
1/2 part Gin
3/4 part Melon Liqueur
splash Pineapple Juice
splash Lime Juice
splash Grenadine

Parfait Glass

Shake with ice and pour

Shit on the Beach
2 parts Irish Crème Liqueur
1 part Dark Rum
1 part Chocolate Milk
1 part Milk

Highball Glass

Shake with ice and pour

Singapore Sling
1 1/2 parts Gin
1/2 part Cherry Heering®
1/4 part Cointreau®
1/4 part Benedictine®
1/2 part Lime Juice
1/3 part Grenadine
dash Bitters
fill with Pineapple Juice

Collins Glass

Shake with ice and strain over ice

South Padre Island
1 part Vodka
3/4 part Peach Schnapps
1 part Sour Mix
fill with Cranberry Juice Cocktail
splash Orange Juice
splash Pineapple Juice

Hurricane Glass

Build over ice

Spanish Planter's Punch
2 parts Light Rum
2 parts Pineapple Juice
1 part Triple Sec
1/2 part Maraschino Liqueur
splash Dark Rum

Highball Glass

Shake with ice and strain over ice

Spice on the Beach
1 1/2 parts Spiced Rum
1 part Peach Schnapps
1 part Orange Juice
1 part Cranberry Juice Cocktail

Highball Glass

Build over ice and stir

Suede Vixen
1 1/2 parts Crème de Cacao (White)
1 1/2 parts Frangelico®
1 part Triple Sec
fill with Cream

Coupette Glass

Shake with ice and pour

Sun of a Beach
1 part Gin
1 part Midori®
fill with Orange Juice

Highball Glass

Build over ice and stir

Sunny Beach
1 part Gin
1 part Apricot Brandy
1/2 part Cherry Brandy
1/2 part Grenadine
fill with Orange Juice

Old-Fashioned Glass

Shake with ice and strain over ice

Sunrise Sling
1 part Dry Gin
1 part Blue Curaçao
1 part Apricot Brandy
fill with Lemonade

Collins Glass

Shake with ice and strain over ice

Sunset at the Beach
1½ parts Cranberry-Flavored Vodka
½ part Melon Liqueur
½ part Raspberry Liqueur
3 parts Pineapple Juice
fill with Lemon-Lime Soda

Collins Glass

Shake all but Lemon-Lime soda with ice and strain into the glass. Top with Lemon-Lime soda.

Sunset on the Beach
½ part Vodka
1 part Peach Schnapps
1 part Melon Liqueur
1 part Coconut Cream
1 part Sour Mix
fill with Orange Juice

Hurricane Glass

Shake with ice and strain over ice

Surfin' Safari
1½ parts Light Rum
½ part Safari®
splash Grenadine
fill with Mango Juice

Highball Glass

Build over ice and stir

Surfside
1 part Peach Schnapps
1 part Crème de Banana
1 part Orange Juice
1 part Dark Rum
1 part Southern Comfort®
splash Grenadine

White Wine Glass

Shake with ice and strain over ice

Survivor Island
1 part Sloe Gin
1 part Melon Liqueur
1 part Currant-Flavored Vodka
fill with Orange Juice

Highball Glass

Shake with ice and strain over ice

Tahitian Surfer
½ part Amaretto
½ part Blue Curaçao
1 part Spiced Rum
½ part Lime Juice
fill with Apple Juice

Highball Glass

Shake with ice and pour

Thunder Cloud
½ part Crème de Noyaux
½ part Blue Curaçao
½ part Amaretto
¾ part Vodka
2 parts Sour Mix
fill with Lemon-Lime Soda

Hurricane Glass

Build over ice and stir

Trinidad Swizzle
1 part Dark Rum
1 part Grand Marnier®
¼ part Lime Juice
2 splashes Grenadine
½ part Mango Nectar

Highball Glass

Shake with ice and strain over ice

Tropical Blend

1 part Crème de Banana
1 part Melon Liqueur
1 part Pineapple Juice
1 part Coconut Cream

Hurricane Glass

Combine all ingredients in a blender with ice. Blend until smooth.

Tropical Delight

1 1/2 parts Rum
3/4 part Pineapple Juice
3/4 part Coconut Cream
1 scoop Vanilla Ice Cream
1 scoop Orange Sorbet
1/2 Banana

White Wine Glass

Combine all ingredients in a blender. Blend until smooth.

Tropical Flower

1 1/2 parts Light Rum
1 1/2 parts Passion Fruit Liqueur
1 part Lychee Liqueur
2 parts Passion Fruit Juice
1/2 Banana

Hurricane Glass

Combine all ingredients in a blender with ice. Blend until smooth.

Tropical Kick

1 part Coconut-Flavored Rum
1 part Pineapple-Flavored Vodka
1 part Light Rum
1/2 part Tropical Punch Schnapps
1/2 part Raspberry Liqueur
fill with Pineapple Juice

Hurricane Glass

Shake with ice and pour

Tropical Nat

2 parts Spiced Rum
1 part Vodka
1 part Orange Juice
1 part Cranberry Juice Cocktail
splash Pineapple Juice

Hurricane Glass

Build over ice

Tropical Oasis

2 parts Pineapple Juice
2 parts Papaya Juice
1 part Peach Juice
3 scoops Orange Sorbet

White Wine Glass

Combine all ingredients in a blender. Blend until smooth.

Tropical Paradise

1 1/4 parts Spiced Rum
2 parts Orange Juice
2 parts Coconut-Flavored Liqueur
1/4 part Grenadine
1/2 Banana

Hurricane Glass

Combine all ingredients in a blender with ice. Blend until smooth.

Tropical Punch

1 part Rum
1 part Banana Liqueur
2 dashes Brown Sugar
1 part Lemonade
1 part Orange Juice
1 part Pineapple Juice

Highball Glass

Shake with ice and pour

Tropical Toucan
$1^1/_2$ parts Light Rum
$^1/_2$ part Crème de Banana
1 part Pineapple Juice
1 part Orange Juice

Hurricane Glass

Shake with ice and pour

Tung Shing Dragon Scorpion Bowl
2 parts Vodka
2 parts Gin
2 parts Rum
1 part 151-Proof Rum
3 parts Grenadine
3 parts Pineapple Juice
3 parts Orange Juice

Scorpion Bowl

Shake with ice and strain over ice into a Scorpion Bowl. This is a drink for two or more people.

Tuxedo Beach
1 part Blue Curaçao
1 part Dark Rum
$^1/_2$ part Coconut-Flavored Liqueur
splash Sour Mix
splash Pineapple Juice

Highball Glass

Shake with ice and strain over ice

Virgin Islands Rum Punch
2 parts Rum
dash Bitters
dash Sugar
$^1/_2$ part Grenadine
1 part Orange Juice
1 part Grapefruit Juice

Highball Glass

Shake with ice and strain over ice

Waikiki Hawaiian
$1^1/_2$ parts Light Rum
$1^1/_2$ parts Dark Rum
1 part Blue Curaçao
1 part Pineapple Juice
1 part Orange Juice

Hurricane Glass

Shake with ice and pour

Waikiki Tiki
$1^1/_2$ parts Light Rum
1 part Orange Juice
1 part Pineapple Juice

Highball Glass

Shake with ice and pour

Walking Zombie
$^1/_2$ part Amaretto
2 parts Pineapple Juice
2 parts Fresh Lime Juice
2 parts Guava Juice
2 parts Orange Juice
1 part Grenadine

Collins Glass

Shake with ice and pour

Wiki Waki
1 part Light Rum
1 part Amaretto
$^1/_2$ part Tequila Silver
$^1/_2$ part Vodka
$^1/_2$ part Triple Sec
1 part Pineapple Juice
1 part Orange Juice

Hurricane Glass

Shake with ice and pour

Wiki Waki Woo

1/2 part Vodka
1/2 part Rum
1/2 part 151-Proof Rum
1/2 part Tequila
1/2 part Triple Sec
1 part Amaretto
1 part Orange Juice
1 part Pineapple Juice
1 part Cranberry Juice Cocktail

Hurricane Glass

Shake with ice and pour

Wild Thang

1/2 part Gin
1/2 part Light Rum
1/2 part Dark Rum
1/2 part Triple Sec
1/2 part Maraschino Liqueur
1/2 part Papaya Juice
1 part Pineapple Juice
1 part Orange Juice
splash 151-Proof Rum

Hurricane Glass

Build over ice and stir

Winter Tropic

2 parts Vodka
1 part Cranberry Juice Cocktail
1 part Strawberry Daiquiri Mix

Hurricane Glass

Build over ice and stir

Yellow Parakeet

1 part Midori®
1/2 part Banana Liqueur
1/2 part Light Rum
2 parts Orange Juice
1 part Pineapple Juice
splash Sour Mix

Hurricane Glass

Build over ice and stir

Yo Ho

1 part Vodka
1 1/2 parts Amaretto
1 1/2 parts Grapefruit Juice
splash Amaretto
1 Banana

Collins Glass

Combine all ingredients in a blender with ice. Blend until smooth.

Zombie

1 part Light Rum
1/2 part Amaretto
1/2 part Triple Sec
1 part Sour Mix
1 part Orange Juice
Top with 151-Proof Rum

Collins Glass

Shake with ice and pour, top with 151 proof rum

Zombies in the Night

1 part Vodka
1 part Apricot Brandy
1 part Wild Berry Schnapps
1 part Orange Juice
1 part Pineapple Juice

Highball Glass

Shake with ice and pour

A Zubb Hurricane

1 part Dark Rum
1 part Light Rum
1 part Triple Sec
1 part Pineapple Juice
1 part Grenadine

Hurricane Glass

Build over ice and stir

Coolers

Start with a liquor, add a liqueur or some juice for flavor, and fill the glass with soda.

10 Toes

3 parts Hypnotiq®
fill with Lemon-Lime Soda
Collins Glass

Build over ice

3001

1 part Vodka
1 part Blue Curaçao
splash Lime Juice
fill with Lemon-Lime Soda
Collins Glass

Mix with ice

491

1 part Light Rum
1 part Gin
1 part Apricot Brandy
fill with Ginger Ale
Highball Glass

Mix with ice

Absolut® Limousine

2 parts Citrus-Flavored Vodka
1 part Lime Juice
fill with Tonic Water
Collins Glass

Build over ice and stir

Absolutely Screwed Up

1 part Citrus-Flavored Vodka
1 part Orange Juice
1 part Triple Sec
fill with Ginger Ale
Collins Glass

Build over ice and stir

Albemarle

1 part Club Soda
2 parts Gin
1 1/2 parts Lemon Juice
splash Raspberry Syrup
1/2 part Powdered Sugar
Collins Glass

Shake all but Club Soda with ice and strain into a glass filled with ice. Top with Club Soda.

Algo Especial

1 1/2 parts Dark Rum
1/2 part Crème de Cacao (White)
1/2 part Dry Gin
fill with Tonic Water
splash Grenadine
Collins Glass

Shake with ice and strain over ice. Top with a splash of Grenadine.

Alien Secretion
1 part Melon Liqueur
1 part Vodka
2 parts Pineapple Juice
fill with Club Soda
Collins Glass

Build over ice and stir

Almond Eye
1 part Brandy
1 part Gin
1 part Amaretto
1/2 part Grenadine
fill with Club Soda
Collins Glass

Build over ice and stir

Amaretto Collins
2 parts Amaretto
1/2 part Simple Syrup
fill with Club Soda
Collins Glass

Build over ice and stir

Amaretto Cooler
11/2 parts Amaretto
11/2 parts Vanilla-Flavored Vodka
fill with Cola
Highball Glass

Build over ice and stir

Amaretto Rose
11/2 parts Amaretto
1/2 part Lime Juice
fill with Club Soda
Collins Glass

Build over ice and stir

Amaretto Spritzer
2 parts Amaretto
fill with Club Soda
Collins Glass

Build over ice and stir

Amber Amour
11/2 parts Amaretto
1/2 part Sour Mix
fill with Club Soda
Collins Glass

Build over ice and stir

American Cobbler
1 part Southern Comfort®
1/2 part Peach Schnapps
1/2 part Lemon Juice
1/2 part Simple Syrup
fill with Ginger Ale
Collins Glass

Build over ice and stir

Americano
1 part Sweet Vermouth
1 part Campari®
1 Lemon Twist
fill with Club Soda
Highball Glass

Build over ice and stir

An Arif
11/2 parts Rum
1/2 part Peach Schnapps
2 parts Orange Juice
1 part Cranberry Juice Cocktail
fill with Ginger Ale
splash Lemon Juice
Collins Glass

Build over ice and stir

Angel of Mercy
11/2 parts Blue Curaçao
2/3 part Orange Liqueur
2/3 part Lime Juice
fill with Ginger Ale
Highball Glass

Build over ice and stir

Annie
1 part Vodka
1 part Cranberry Liqueur
1/2 part Cream
splash Lime Juice
fill with Club Soda
Collins Glass

Build over ice and stir

Apple Blow
1 1/2 parts Applejack
1 Lemon Wedge
1 Egg White
dash Powdered Sugar
1 part Apple Juice
fill with Club Soda
Collins Glass

Shake all but Club Soda with ice and pour. Top with Club Soda.

Apple Brandy Cooler
2 parts Apple Brandy
fill with Lemon-Lime Soda
Highball Glass

Build over ice and stir

Apple Core
1 1/2 parts Light Rum
1/2 part Applejack
1/2 part Sour Apple Schnapps
1/2 part Sweetened Lime Juice
fill with Club Soda
Collins Glass

Build over ice and stir

Appled Rum Cooler
1 1/2 parts Añejo Rum
1/2 part Applejack
splash Lime Juice
fill with Club Soda
Old-Fashioned Glass

Shake all but Club Soda with ice and strain over ice into the glass. Top with Club Soda.

Apribon
1 1/2 parts Jim Beam®
splash Apricot Brandy
dash Angostura® Bitters
fill with Club Soda
splash Grapefruit Juice
splash Lemon Juice
Collins Glass

Build over ice and stir

Apricot Breeze
1 part Vodka
3 parts Apricot Nectar
fill with Tonic Water
Hurricane Glass

Build over ice and stir

Apricot Collins
1/2 part Apricot Brandy
1 1/2 parts Gin
splash Lemon Juice
fill with Club Soda
Highball Glass

Build over ice and stir

Apricot Fizz
2 parts Apricot Brandy
dash Powdered Sugar
1/2 part Lemon Juice
1/2 part Lime Juice
fill with Club Soda
Highball Glass

Shake all but Club Soda with ice and strain into the glass over ice. Top with Club Soda.

April Shower
1 1/2 parts Brandy
2 parts Orange Juice
fill with Club Soda
White Wine Glass

Build over ice and stir

Aquafresh
1 1/2 parts Vodka
1/2 part Crème de Menthe (Green)
fill with Club Soda
Old-Fashioned Glass

Build over ice and stir

Aquarium
1 part Rum
1 part Blue Curaçao
1/2 part Grapefruit Juice
fill with Tonic Water
Collins Glass

Build over ice and stir

Arawack Slap
1/2 part Light Rum
1/2 part Dark Rum
1 part Triple Sec
1/2 part Sour Mix
1/2 part Pineapple Juice
fill with Ginger Ale
Highball Glass

Build over ice and stir

Arcturian Sunrise
1 part Blue Curaçao
1 part Blackberry Liqueur
1/2 part Grenadine
fill with Club Soda
Collins Glass

Build over ice

Arsenic
1 part Tequila Silver
1/2 part Passion Fruit Liqueur
splash Peach Schnapps
dash Orange Bitters
2/3 part Lemon Juice
2/3 part Peach Puree
fill with Club Soda
Collins Glass

Shake all but Club Soda with ice and strain into the glass. Top with Club Soda.

Aunt Flo
1 1/2 parts Sloe Gin
1/2 part Orange Juice
1/4 part Lemon Juice
1 Egg White
dash Powdered Sugar
fill with Club Soda
Highball Glass

Shake all but Club Soda with ice and strain into the glass. Top with Club Soda.

Auto da Fe
1 1/2 parts Vodka
splash Lime Juice
fill with Club Soda
Collins Glass

Build over ice and stir

Axelrod's Sweet Concoction
1 part Amaretto
1 part Peach Schnapps
1/2 part Dry Vermouth
fill with Club Soda
Highball Glass

Build over ice and stir

Top with Club Soda.

Baby Doc
1 part Gin
1/2 part Crème de Cacao (White)
1 part Pineapple Juice
1 part Kiwi Juice
fill with Tonic Water
Collins Glass

Build over ice and stir

Back Bay Balm
1 1/2 parts Gin
3 parts Cranberry Juice Cocktail
1/2 part Lemon Juice
3 dashes Orange Bitters
fill with Club Soda
Collins Glass

Shake all but Club Soda with ice and strain into the glass. Top with Club Soda.

Back Wash
1/2 part Kiwi Schnapps
1/2 part Grand Marnier®
1 1/2 parts Mescal
splash Lemon Syrup
2/3 part Lemon Juice
fill with Club Soda
Collins Glass

Shake all but Club Soda with ice and strain into the glass. Top with Club Soda.

Backstage Pass
1 part Orange-Flavored Vodka
1/2 part Triple Sec
1/2 part Cherry Brandy
1 part Citrus-Flavored Rum
2 parts Orange Juice
fill with Club Soda
Highball Glass

Shake all but Club Soda with ice and strain into the glass.

Bahama Highball
2 parts Gin
splash Vermouth
fill with Ginger Ale
1 Lemon Twist
Highball Glass

Build over ice and stir

Banana Balm
1 1/2 parts Vodka
1/2 part Banana Liqueur
splash Lime Juice
fill with Club Soda
Collins Glass

Shake all but Club Soda with ice and strain into the glass. Top with Club Soda.

Banana Cooler
2 parts Banana Liqueur
1 part Orange Juice
1 part Lemon-Lime Soda
Highball Glass

Build over ice and stir

Banker's Doom
1 part Whiskey
1 part Vodka
1 part Melon Liqueur
fill with Club Soda
Collins Glass

Shake all but Club Soda with ice and strain into the glass. Top with Club Soda.

Barramundy
1 part Vodka
1/2 part Blackberry Liqueur
1/2 part Raspberry Liqueur
fill with Club Soda
1 part Cranberry Juice Cocktail
Highball Glass

Build over ice and stir

Bayard Fizz

2 parts Gin
1/2 part Maraschino Liqueur
1/2 part Fresh Lime Juice
1/2 part Raspberry Syrup
fill with Club Soda
Collins Glass

Shake all but Club Soda with ice and strain into the glass. Top with Club Soda.

Beach Ball Cooler

1 1/2 parts Vodka
1 part Lime
1/2 part Crème de Cacao (White)
fill with Ginger Ale
Collins Glass

Shake all but Ginger Ale with ice and strain into the glass. Top with Ginger Ale.

Beach Beauty

1 1/2 parts Vodka
1 1/2 parts Orange Juice
1 part Crème de Banana
splash Grenadine
fill with Tonic Water
Collins Glass

Build over ice and stir

Beady Little Eyes

1 1/2 parts Light Rum
1 part Orange Juice
1/4 part Lemon Juice
fill with Ginger Ale
Collins Glass

Build over ice and stir

Beasley

1 part Brandy
1 part Tequila
1 part Triple Sec
1 part Vodka
2 parts Vanilla Liqueur
1/2 part Lemon Juice
fill with Tonic Water
Collins Glass

Shake all but Club Soda with ice and strain into the glass. Top with Club Soda.

Bee

1 part Vodka
1 part Banana Liqueur
fill with Ginger Ale
Highball Glass

Build over ice and stir

Beefeater® Sunrise

1 part Dry Gin
splash Crème de Banana
fill with Tonic Water
splash Grenadine
Collins Glass

Build over ice

Bermuda Cooler

1 part Brandy
1 part Dry Gin
fill with Ginger Ale
dash Orange Bitters
Collins Glass

Build over ice and stir

Bermuda Highball

1 part Brandy
1 part Dry Vermouth
1 part Gin
fill with Ginger Ale
Collins Glass

Build over ice and stir

Big Dipper
1 part Dark Rum
1 part Brandy
splash Lime Juice
dash Sugar
splash Cointreau®
fill with Club Soda
Old-Fashioned Glass

Shake all but Club Soda with ice and strain into the glass. Top with Club Soda.

Big Ol' Girl
1 part Triple Sec
1 part Vodka
splash Lime Juice
fill with Club Soda
Collins Glass

Build over ice and stir

Billie Holiday
1 part Vodka
fill with Ginger Ale
splash Grenadine
Collins Glass

Build over ice and stir

Billy Taylor
2 parts Gin
1/2 part Lime Juice
fill with Club Soda
Collins Glass

Build over ice and stir

Bingo
1 part Vodka
1 part Mandarine Napoléon® Liqueur
1 part Apricot Brandy
fill with Club Soda
Collins Glass

Build over ice and stir

Bitter Tears
1 1/2 parts Gin
1 part Maraschino Liqueur
splash Peppermint Liqueur
splash Lemon Juice
fill with Tonic Water
Highball Glass

Build over ice and stir

Black Betty
1 part Peach Schnapps
1 part Blackberry Liqueur
1 part Fresh Lime Juice
fill with Club Soda
Collins Glass

Build over ice and stir

Blue Ice Mountain
2 parts Blue Curaçao
1 part Vodka
fill with Club Soda
Highball Glass

Build over ice and stir

Blue in the Face
1 part Vodka
1 part Gin
1 part Light Rum
1 part Blue Curaçao
splash Sugar
fill with Tonic Water
Whiskey Sour Glass

Build over ice and stir

Blue Rose
1 part Blue Curaçao
1 part Blavod® Black Vodka
1 part Currant-Flavored Vodka
fill with Tonic Water
Collins Glass

Build over ice and stir

Blue Water

$1^{1}/_{2}$ parts Vodka
$^{1}/_{4}$ part Blue Curaçao
fill with Club Soda
Highball Glass

Build over ice and stir

Blueberry Kick

1 part Vodka
2 parts Blueberry Schnapps
splash Cream
fill with Club Soda
Collins Glass

Build over ice and stir

Blues Club

1 part Blueberry Schnapps
1 part Orange Juice
fill with Club Soda
Highball Glass

Build over ice and stir

Bomba

1 part Spiced Rum
1 part Light Rum
fill with Ginger Ale
splash Lime Juice
Highball Glass

Build over ice and stir

Bonanza Fresh

$1^{1}/_{2}$ parts Gin
$^{2}/_{3}$ part Lychee Liqueur
$^{1}/_{2}$ part Sake
$^{1}/_{2}$ part Mango Schnapps
splash Orange Bitters
fill with Club Soda
splash Lemon Juice
Collins Glass

Build over ice and stir

Bongofizz

2 parts Gin
$^{1}/_{2}$ part Maraschino Liqueur
$^{1}/_{2}$ part Fresh Lime Juice
$^{1}/_{2}$ part Raspberry Syrup
fill with Club Soda
Collins Glass

Shake all but Club Soda with ice and strain into the glass. Top with Club Soda.

Bonne Chance

1 part Cognac
1 part Triple Sec
fill with Club Soda
Collins Glass

Build over ice and stir

The Bottom Line

$1^{1}/_{2}$ parts Vodka
$^{1}/_{2}$ part Lime Juice
fill with Tonic Water
Highball Glass

Build over ice and stir

Bourbon Rumbo

1 part Bourbon
1 part Dark Rum
1 part Dry Vermouth
1 part Simple Syrup
fill with Club Soda
Collins Glass

Shake all but Club Soda with ice and strain into the glass. Top with Club Soda.

Branded Nuts

$1^{1}/_{2}$ parts Apricot Brandy
splash Blue Curaçao
splash Amaretto
splash Orange Liqueur
splash Frangelico®
fill with Club Soda
Collins Glass

Shake all but Club Soda with ice and strain into the glass. Top with Club Soda.

Brandy Cobbler
2 parts Brandy
splash Sugar
1 Lemon Slice
fill with Club Soda
Old-Fashioned Glass

Shake all but Club Soda with ice and strain into the glass. Top with Club Soda.

Brighton Punch
$1\frac{1}{2}$ parts Bourbon
1 part Brandy
1 part Orange Juice
fill with Club Soda
Collins Glass

Build over ice and stir

Bronx Cheer
2 parts Apricot Brandy
1 part Raspberry Syrup
fill with Club Soda
Collins Glass

Build over ice and stir

Buck Jones
$1\frac{1}{2}$ parts Light Rum
1 part Sweet Sherry
splash Lime Juice
fill with Ginger Ale
Highball Glass

Build over ice and stir

Buckhead Root Beer
$1\frac{1}{2}$ parts Jägermeister®
fill with Club Soda
Highball Glass

Build over ice and stir

Bulldog
$1\frac{1}{2}$ parts Gin
fill with Ginger Ale
splash Orange Juice
Highball Glass

Build over ice and stir

Bull's Eye
1 part Brandy
2 parts Hard Apple Cider
fill with Ginger Ale
Highball Glass

Build over ice and stir

Cablegram
2 parts Whiskey
$\frac{1}{2}$ part Lemon Juice
dash Powdered Sugar
fill with Ginger Ale
Highball Glass

Build over ice and stir

Café Cabana
1 part Coffee Liqueur
fill with Club Soda
Collins Glass

Build over ice and stir

Cagnes Sur Mer
$1\frac{1}{2}$ parts Gin
$\frac{1}{2}$ part Blue Curaçao
$\frac{1}{2}$ part Passion Fruit Nectar
splash Lemon Juice
2 parts Orange Juice
fill with Club Soda
Collins Glass

Build over ice and stir

California Lemonade
2 parts Whiskey
$\frac{1}{2}$ part Lemon Juice
$\frac{1}{2}$ part Lime Juice
dash Powdered Sugar
splash Grenadine
fill with Club Soda
Collins Glass

Shake all but Club Soda with ice and strain into the glass. Top with Club Soda.

California Lemonade #2

1 1/2 parts Rum
3 parts Lemon Juice
2 dashes Sugar
dash Bitters
fill with Club Soda
Collins Glass

Build over ice and stir

Calypso Cooler

1/2 part Spiced Rum
1/2 part Peach Schnapps
splash Dark Rum
2 parts Orange Juice
1 part Grenadine
1 part Lime Juice
fill with Lemon-Lime Soda
Collins Glass

Build over ice and stir

Campari® and Soda

2 parts Campari®
fill with Club Soda
Highball Glass

Build over ice and stir

Canal Street Daisy

1 part Bourbon
1 part Orange Juice
fill with Club Soda
Collins Glass

Build over ice and stir

Candy Isle

1 part Goldschläger®
1 part Amaretto
fill with Club Soda
splash Vanilla Liqueur
Highball Glass

Build over ice and stir

Cannonballer

1/2 part Melon Liqueur
1/2 part Crème de Banana
2 parts Cranberry Juice Cocktail
fill with Club Soda
Highball Glass

Build over ice and stir

Cantaloupe Dizzy

1 part Vodka
1 part Melon Liqueur
1 part Peach Schnapps
fill with Club Soda
Parfait Glass

Build over ice and stir

Captain Collins

1 part Bourbon
splash Grenadine
fill with Club Soda
Collins Glass

Build over ice and stir

Captain's Table

2 parts Gin
1/2 part Campari®
splash Grenadine
1 part Orange Juice
fill with Ginger Ale
Collins Glass

Build over ice and stir

Carat Fizz

1 part Crème de Cacao (White)
1 part Campari®
fill with Tonic Water
Collins Glass

Build over ice and stir

Caribbean Sling
2 parts Light Rum
1 part Triple Sec
splash Simple Syrup
fill with Club Soda
Collins Glass

Build over ice and stir

Carthusian Cooler
1 part Bourbon
fill with Club Soda
Collins Glass

Build over ice and stir

Cherry Cobbler
1 1/2 parts Gin
3/4 part Cherry Brandy
dash Powdered Sugar
fill with Club Soda
Old-Fashioned Glass

Build over ice and stir

Cherry Cooler
2 parts Cherry Vodka
1 Lemon Slice
fill with Cola
Collins Glass

Build over ice and stir

Chevy® Subbourbon
2 parts Jim Beam®
splash Blue Curaçao
dash Angostura® Bitters
fill with Club Soda
Collins Glass

Build over ice and stir

Chicago Fizz
1 part Light Rum
1 part Port
1/2 part Lemon Juice
dash Powdered Sugar
1 Egg White
fill with Club Soda
Highball Glass

Build over ice and stir

Chilton
1 part Vodka
splash Margarita Mix
fill with Club Soda
Highball Glass

Build over ice and stir

Chit Chat
1 part Gin
1/2 part Strawberry Liqueur
splash Limoncello
splash Lemon Juice
fill with Tonic Water
Collins Glass

Build over ice and stir

Cielo
1 1/4 parts Vodka
3/4 part Crème de Cassis
2 dashes Bitters
fill with Ginger Ale
Collins Glass

Build over ice and stir

Cinnamon Road
1 part Wild Turkey® Bourbon
1 part Apple Liqueur
1 part Goldschläger®
fill with Ginger Ale
Collins Glass

Build over ice and stir

Citron Cooler

$1^1/_2$ parts Citrus-Flavored Vodka
$^1/_2$ part Lime Cordial
fill with Tonic Water
Collins Glass

Build over ice and stir

City Coral

1 part Dry Gin
$^1/_2$ part Melon Liqueur
splash Blue Curaçao
splash Grapefruit Juice
fill with Tonic Water
Collins Glass

Build over ice and stir

Clear Distinction

1 part Dry Gin
1 part Light Rum
1 part Triple Sec
fill with Club Soda
Collins Glass

Build over ice and stir

Cloud Reader

$1^1/_2$ parts Crème de Cassis
1 part Lime Juice
2 parts Orange Juice
fill with Ginger Ale
Collins Glass

Shake with ice and strain over ice

Clouseau

1 part Vodka
1 part Coffee Liqueur
fill with Ginger Ale
Highball Glass

Build over ice and stir

Clown

1 part Light Rum
1 part Melon Liqueur
1 part Grenadine
fill with Tonic Water
Highball Glass

Build over ice and stir

Coconut Cooler

2 parts Coconut-Flavored Rum
1 part Orange Juice
1 part Lemon-Lime Soda
Highball Glass

Build over ice and stir

Color Blind

2 parts Gin
1 part Triple Sec
$^1/_2$ part Blue Curaçao
splash Lime Juice
fill with Tonic Water
Collins Glass

Build over ice and stir

Cool Blue

1 part Blue Curaçao
1 part Anisette
fill with Club Soda
Collins Glass

Build over ice and stir

Cosmic South

1 part Southern Comfort®
$^1/_2$ part Lychee Liqueur
$^1/_2$ part Peach Schnapps
$^1/_2$ part Lemon Juice
fill with Club Soda
Collins Glass

Build over ice and stir

Cotton Panties
1 part Vodka
2 parts Peach Schnapps
1 part Half and Half
fill with Tonic Water
Collins Glass

Build over ice and stir

Cotton Picker's Punch
$1\frac{1}{2}$ parts Dark Rum
1 part Fresh Lime Juice
$\frac{3}{4}$ part Whiskey
$\frac{1}{2}$ part Apricot Brandy
$\frac{1}{2}$ part Simple Syrup
fill with Club Soda
Collins Glass

Build over ice and stir

Country Club Cooler
2 parts Dry Vermouth
fill with Club Soda
splash Grenadine
Collins Glass

Build over ice

Cream Fizz
2 parts Gin
dash Powdered Sugar
$\frac{1}{2}$ part Lemon Juice
splash Light Cream
fill with Club Soda
Highball Glass

Shake all but Club Soda with ice and strain into the glass. Top with Club Soda.

Cream Puff
2 parts Light Rum
1 part Light Cream
dash Powdered Sugar
fill with Club Soda
Highball Glass

Shake all but Club Soda with ice and strain into the glass. Top with Club Soda.

Crocodile
1 part Citrus-Flavored Rum
2 parts Melon Liqueur
fill with Club Soda
Collins Glass

Build over ice and stir

Crowning Glory
$\frac{3}{4}$ part Bourbon
$\frac{1}{2}$ part Peach Schnapps
1 part Orange Juice
fill with Club Soda
Old-Fashioned Glass

Build over ice and stir

Crystal Iceberg
$1\frac{1}{2}$ parts Southern Comfort®
1 part Sour Apple Schnapps
2 parts Sour Mix
fill with Ginger Ale
splash Grenadine
Collins Glass

Build over ice and stir

Cuban Cooler
2 parts Light Rum
fill with Ginger Ale
Collins Glass

Build over ice and stir

Cuernavaca Collins
1 part Tequila Silver
1 part Fresh Lime Juice
1 part Gin
fill with Club Soda
Collins Glass

Build over ice and stir

Curaçao Cooler
1 part Rum
1 part Triple Sec
1 part Fresh Lime Juice
fill with Club Soda
Collins Glass

Build over ice and stir

Dancing Leprechaun
$1\frac{1}{2}$ parts Irish Whiskey
fill with Ginger Ale
Collins Glass

Build over ice and stir

Dead Bastard
1 part Brandy
1 part Gin
1 part Rum
$\frac{1}{2}$ part Lime Juice
dash Bitters
fill with Ginger Ale
Collins Glass

Build over ice and stir

Derby Fizz
2 parts Scotch
splash Triple Sec
$\frac{1}{2}$ part Lemon Juice
dash Powdered Sugar
1 Whole Egg
fill with Club Soda
Highball Glass

Shake all but Club Soda with ice and strain into the glass. Top with Club Soda.

Desert Healer
$1\frac{1}{2}$ parts Dry Gin
1 part Orange Juice
1 part Cherry Brandy
fill with Ginger Ale
Collins Glass

Build over ice and stir

Diamond Ale
$1\frac{1}{2}$ parts Gin
1 part Blue Curaçao
$\frac{1}{2}$ part Coconut Cream
fill with Ginger Ale
Collins Glass

Build over ice and stir

Dragonfly
$1\frac{1}{2}$ parts Gin
fill with Ginger Ale
1 Lime Wedge
Highball Glass

Build over ice and stir

Dry Hole
1 part Light Rum
$\frac{1}{2}$ part Apricot Brandy
$\frac{1}{2}$ part Cointreau®
$\frac{1}{2}$ part Lemon Juice
fill with Club Soda
Collins Glass

Shake all but Club Soda with ice and strain into the glass. Top with Club Soda.

Dusty Dog
2 parts Vodka
$\frac{1}{2}$ part Crème de Cassis
splash Lemon Juice
fill with Ginger Ale
Highball Glass

Build over ice and stir

Elephant's Eye
1 part Dark Rum
1 part Dry Vermouth
1 part Triple Sec
1 part Fresh Lime Juice
fill with Tonic Water
Collins Glass

Build over ice and stir

Empire Builder
2 parts Apricot Brandy
1 part Lemon Juice
fill with Club Soda
Highball Glass

Build over ice and stir

English Highball

1 part Brandy
1 part Gin
1 part Dry Vermouth
fill with Ginger Ale
Collins Glass

Build over ice and stir

Eye of the Tiger

$1^1/_2$ parts Southern Comfort®
$^2/_3$ part Raspberry Liqueur
$^1/_2$ part Apple Liqueur
fill with Club Soda
Collins Glass

Build over ice and stir

Fat Man's Cooler

2 parts Light Rum
$^1/_2$ part Blue Curaçao
$^1/_2$ part Fresh Lime Juice
fill with Ginger Ale
Collins Glass

Build over ice and stir

The Feminist

1 part Amaretto
1 part Coffee Liqueur
1 part Peppermint Schnapps
1 part Rum
fill with Ginger Ale
Highball Glass

Build over ice and stir

Fidel Castro

$1^1/_2$ parts Dark Rum
$^1/_2$ part Lime Juice
fill with Ginger Ale
Collins Glass

Build over ice and stir

Filthy Mind

$1^1/_2$ parts Gin
$^1/_2$ part Vanilla Liqueur
1 part Cranberry Juice Cocktail
$^1/_2$ part Lemon Juice
fill with Club Soda
Collins Glass

Shake all but Club Soda with ice and strain into the glass. Top with Club Soda.

Flaming Soda

1 part Vodka
$^1/_2$ part Melon Liqueur
$^1/_2$ part Triple Sec
fill with Club Soda
Highball Glass

Build over ice and stir

Flashing Fizz

$1^1/_2$ parts Brandy
1 part Crème de Cassis
fill with Club Soda
Collins Glass

Build over ice and stir

Floradora Cooler

2 parts Dry Gin
splash Grenadine
dash Powdered Sugar
$^1/_2$ part Lime Juice
fill with Club Soda
Collins Glass

Build over ice and stir

Florida Fizz

$1^1/_2$ parts Southern Comfort®
2 parts Orange Juice
fill with Club Soda
Collins Glass

Build over ice and stir

Flower Power
1 part Peach Schnapps
1 part Coconut-Flavored Liqueur
fill with Club Soda
Collins Glass

Build over ice and stir

Flying High
1 part Vodka
1 part Fresh Lime Juice
1/2 part Crème de Banana
fill with Orange Soda
Collins Glass

Build over ice and stir

Fraise Fizz
2 parts Gin
1 part Strawberry Liqueur
1/4 part Powdered Sugar
fill with Club Soda
Collins Glass

Build over ice and stir

Free Bird
1 1/2 parts Canadian Whiskey
fill with Ginger Ale
splash Blue Curaçao
Highball Glass

Build over ice

French Colonial
1 1/2 parts Dark Rum
1 part Triple Sec
1 part Crème de Cassis
fill with Tonic Water
Collins Glass

Build over ice and stir

French Summer
1 part Raspberry Liqueur
fill with Club Soda
White Wine Glass

Build over ice and stir

Frontal Lobotomy
1/2 part Jack Daniel's®
1/2 part Tequila
1/2 part Vodka
1 part Jägermeister®
fill with Club Soda
Collins Glass

Shake all but Club Soda with ice and strain into the glass. Top with Club Soda.

Fuzzy Charlie
1 1/4 parts Dark Rum
1/2 part Crème de Banana
1/2 part Crème de Coconut
2 parts Pineapple Juice
fill with Ginger Ale
Collins Glass

Build over ice and stir

Fuzzy Feeling
1 part Orange-Flavored Vodka
2/3 part Blackberry Liqueur
1/2 part Lemon Juice
fill with Club Soda
Highball Glass

Build over ice and stir

Gables Collins
1 1/2 parts Vodka
1 part Crème de Noyaux
1 part Pineapple Juice
1 part Lemon Juice
fill with Club Soda
1 Lemon Slice
Collins Glass

Shake all but Club Soda with ice and strain into the glass. Top with Club Soda.

General Lee
2 parts Gin
splash Anisette
dash Sugar
1 part Lime Juice
fill with Ginger Ale
Collins Glass

Build over ice and stir

Geting
1 part Vodka
1/2 part Banana Liqueur
fill with Ginger Ale
Highball Glass

Build over ice and stir

Gilded Lei
2/3 part Coconut-Flavored Liqueur
1 part Parfait Amour
1/2 part Light Rum
fill with Club Soda
Highball Glass

Build over ice and stir

Gin and Pink
2 parts Gin
fill with Tonic Water
2 dashes Bitters
1 Lemon Twist
Highball Glass

Build over ice and stir

Gin Chiller
1 1/2 parts Gin
fill with Ginger Ale
1 Lime Wedge
Highball Glass

Build over ice and stir

Ginger 'n' Spice
1 1/2 parts Spiced Rum
fill with Ginger Ale
Collins Glass

Build over ice and stir

Ginger Rum
2 parts Light Rum
fill with Ginger Ale
Highball Glass

Build over ice and stir

Ginger Scotch
2 parts Scotch
fill with Ginger Ale
Highball Glass

Build over ice and stir

Gin-Ger-Ale
2 parts Gin
fill with Ginger Ale
Highball Glass

Build over ice and stir

Gingervitas
1 part Citrus-Flavored Vodka
1 part Dry Vermouth
fill with Ginger Ale
Collins Glass

Build over ice and stir

Ginny Cooler
1 part Dry Gin
1 part Sweet Vermouth
1 part Grenadine
fill with Tonic Water
Collins Glass

Build over ice and stir

The Glen Ridge
2 parts Irish Whiskey
fill with Ginger Ale
Collins Glass

Build over ice and stir

Golden Fizz
1 1/2 parts Gin
1/2 part Lemon Juice
1/2 part Sugar
1 Egg Yolk
fill with Club Soda
Highball Glass

Shake all but Club Soda with ice and strain into the glass. Top with Club Soda.

Golden Friendship
1 part Amaretto
1 part Sweet Vermouth
1 part Light Rum
fill with Ginger Ale
Collins Glass

Build over ice and stir

Golden Pirate
3 parts Dark Rum
fill with Ginger Ale
Collins Glass

Build over ice and stir

Gospodin
1 part Vodka
2/3 part Apricot Brandy
fill with Club Soda
Collins Glass

Build over ice and stir

Grand Master
2 parts Scotch
1/2 part Peppermint Schnapps
fill with Club Soda
1 Lemon Twist
Highball Glass

Build over ice and stir

Grandma Happy Bottoms
3 parts Maraschino Liqueur
fill with Club Soda
Highball Glass

Build over ice and stir

The Grass Skirt
1 part Peppermint Liqueur
1 part Light Rum
1/2 part Lime Cordial
fill with Club Soda
Highball Glass

Build over ice and stir

Grass Snake
2/3 part Kiwi Schnapps
1 1/2 parts Light Rum
1/2 part Limoncello
2/3 part Lemon Juice
fill with Club Soda
Collins Glass

Build over ice and stir

Greek Buck
1 1/2 parts Brandy
splash Ouzo
2 splashes Lemon Juice
fill with Ginger Ale
Collins Glass

Build over ice and stir

Green Dinosaur

1 part Rum
1 part Vodka
1 part Tequila
1 part Gin
1 part Melon Liqueur
splash Lemon Juice
fill with Club Soda
Highball Glass

Build over ice and stir

Green Grass

1 1/2 parts Gin
1 part Crème de Menthe (White)
fill with Tonic Water
Collins Glass

Build over ice and stir

Green Highlands

1 part Blue Curaçao
1 part Scotch
2 dashes Orange Bitters
fill with Club Soda
Collins Glass

Build over ice and stir

Green Shark

1 1/2 parts Dark Rum
1 part Blue Curaçao
1/2 part Fresh Lime Juice
fill with Club Soda
Collins Glass

Shake all but Club Soda with ice and strain into the glass. Top with Club Soda.

Green Star

1 part Rum
1/2 part Blue Curaçao
1/2 part Mandarine Napoléon® Liqueur
1/2 part Grapefruit Juice
1 part Pineapple Juice
fill with Tonic Water
Collins Glass

Build over ice and stir

Guava Cooler

2 parts Light Rum
1 1/2 parts Guava Juice
1 part Pineapple Juice
1 part Maraschino Liqueur
1/2 part Simple Syrup
fill with Club Soda
Collins Glass

Shake all but Club Soda with ice and strain into the glass. Top with Club Soda.

Guinness® Cooler

1 part Coffee Liqueur
1 part Triple Sec
fill with Guinness® Stout
Collins Glass

Build in the glass with no ice

Gumball

1 part Blue Curaçao
1/2 part Vodka
1/2 part Crème de Banana
fill with Ginger Ale
Collins Glass

Build over ice and stir

Hackensack Lemonade

2 parts Canadian Whiskey
1 part Triple Sec
1 part Lime Juice
1 part Lemon Juice
dash Powdered Sugar
fill with Club Soda
Collins Glass

Shake all but Club Soda with ice and strain into the glass. Top with Club Soda.

Hard Hat

1 1/2 parts Light Rum
1 1/2 parts Lime Cordial
1/2 part Sugar
1/4 part Grenadine
fill with Club Soda
Collins Glass

Shake all but Club Soda with ice and strain into the glass. Top with Club Soda.

Harvard Cooler

2 parts Apple Brandy
dash Powdered Sugar
fill with Club Soda
1 Orange Twist
1 Lemon Twist
Collins Glass

Build over ice and stir

Hasty Heart

1 1/2 parts Gin
1 1/2 parts Crème de Cassis
1/2 part Sour Mix
fill with Ginger Ale
splash Lemon Juice
Collins Glass

Build over ice and stir

Headhunter

2 parts Gin
1 part Crème de Menthe (White)
fill with Ginger Ale
Collins Glass

Build over ice and stir

Headless Horseman

2 parts Vodka
3 dashes Bitters
fill with Ginger Ale
1 Orange Slice
Collins Glass

Build over ice and stir

Hedgerow Sling

2 parts Sloe Gin
1/2 part Blackberry Liqueur
1/4 part Simple Syrup
fill with Club Soda
Collins Glass

Shake all but Club Soda with ice and strain into the glass. Top with Club Soda.

Hidden Dragon

2/3 part Melon Liqueur
2/3 part Pisang Ambon® Liqueur
1/2 part Sake
fill with Club Soda
Collins Glass

Shake all but Club Soda with ice and strain into the glass. Top with Club Soda.

High and Dry

1 part Canadian Whiskey
fill with Ginger Ale
dash Bitters
Highball Glass

Build over ice and stir

High Valley Sneeker

1 part Vodka
1/2 part Banana Liqueur
1/2 part Jägermeister®
fill with Ginger Ale
Highball Glass

Build over ice and stir

Highland Cooler

2 parts Scotch
dash Powdered Sugar
fill with Carbonated Water
1 Orange Twist
1 Lemon Twist
Collins Glass

Build over ice and stir

Hillbilly Buttkicker
1 part Southern Comfort®
1 part Gin
1 part Vodka
1 part Orange Juice
fill with Ginger Ale
1 part Grenadine
Collins Glass

Build over ice and stir

Hippie
1 part Gin
1 part Peach Schnapps
1/2 part Sweet Vermouth
splash Grenadine
fill with Ginger Ale
Old-Fashioned Glass

Build over ice and stir

Holy Water
2 parts Vodka
1 part Triple Sec
1 part Light Rum
fill with Tonic Water
splash Grenadine
Old-Fashioned Glass

Build over ice and stir

Honolulu
1 1/2 parts Peach Schnapps
1 1/2 parts Crème de Banana
1/2 part Peppermint Extract
fill with Club Soda
Collins Glass

Build over ice and stir

Houdini
1 part Raspberry Liqueur
2 parts Southern Comfort®
fill with Ginger Ale
Highball Glass

Build over ice and stir

Hudson
1 part Peach Schnapps
1/2 part Gin
fill with Club Soda
Highball Glass

Build over ice and stir

Imperial Fizz
1/2 part Light Rum
1 1/2 parts Whiskey
1/2 part Lemon Juice
dash Powdered Sugar
fill with Club Soda
Highball Glass

Shake all but Club Soda with ice and strain into the glass. Top with Club Soda.

Incognito
1 1/2 parts Vodka
1 part Apricot Brandy
fill with Ginger Ale
Collins Glass

Build over ice and stir

Indian Sun
1 1/2 parts Gin
2/3 part Campari®
2/3 part Lemon Juice
fill with Ginger Ale
splash Grenadine
Collins Glass

Build over ice and stir

Indira
1/2 part Blue Curaçao
1 1/2 parts Campari®
1 1/2 parts Dry Vermouth
fill with Club Soda
Highball Glass

Build over ice and stir

Intellectual
2 parts Jim Beam®
fill with Ginger Ale
Collins Glass

Build over ice and stir

Invisible Man
2 parts Gin
1/2 part Triple Sec
1/2 part Brandy
2 splashes Orange Juice
fill with Ginger Ale
Highball Glass

Build over ice and stir

Irish Highball
2 parts Irish Whiskey
fill with Ginger Ale
Old-Fashioned Glass

Build over ice and stir

Island Soda
2 parts Vodka
1/2 part Banana Liqueur
2 parts Pineapple Juice
fill with Ginger Ale
Collins Glass

Build over ice and stir

Italian Cooler
1 1/2 parts Sweet Vermouth
splash Grenadine
fill with Sparkling Water
Collins Glass

Build over ice and stir

Jack & Ginger
2 parts Jack Daniel's®
fill with Ginger Ale
Collins Glass

Build over ice and stir

Jackhammer Fizz
1 1/2 parts Whiskey
1 part Powdered Sugar
fill with Club Soda
Highball Glass

Shake all but Club Soda with ice and strain into the glass. Top with Club Soda.

Jäger Tonic
1 1/2 parts Jägermeister®
fill with Tonic Water
Highball Glass

Build over ice and stir

Jamaica Cooler
2 parts Dark Rum
1/2 part Lemon Juice
dash Powdered Sugar
2 dashes Orange Bitters
fill with Lemon-Lime Soda
Collins Glass

Build over ice and stir

Jamaican Collins
2 parts Dark Rum
1 1/2 parts Pineapple Juice
dash Sugar
fill with Club Soda
Collins Glass

Shake all but Club Soda with ice and strain into the glass. Top with Club Soda.

Japanese Fizz
1 1/2 parts Whiskey
1/2 part Lemon Juice
dash Powdered Sugar
2 splashes Port
1 Egg White
fill with Club Soda
Highball Glass

Shake all but Club Soda with ice and strain into the glass. Top with Club Soda.

Jealous Husband

1/2 part Vodka
2/3 part Peach Schnapps
2/3 part Triple Sec
3 part Cranberry Juice Cocktail
fill with Ginger Ale
Highball Glass

Build over ice and stir

Johnny Cat

1 part Gin
1 part Dry Vermouth
1/2 part Triple Sec
splash Grenadine
fill with Club Soda
Red Wine Glass

Shake all but Club Soda with ice and strain into the glass. Top with Club Soda.

Joumbaba

1 1/2 parts Tequila
2 parts Grapefruit Juice
fill with Tonic Water
Highball Glass

Build over ice and stir

Joy Ride

1 1/2 parts Citrus-Flavored Vodka
1 part Campari®
3 parts Sour Mix
1 part Sugar
fill with Club Soda
Hurricane Glass

Shake all but Club Soda with ice and strain over ice into the glass. Top with Club Soda.

Kentucky Tea

2 parts Bourbon
1 part Triple Sec
1/2 part Sugar
fill with Ginger Ale
Collins Glass

Shake all but Ginger Ale with ice and strain into the glass. Top with Ginger Ale.

Kirsch and Cassis

2 parts Crème de Cassis
1 part Kirschwasser
fill with Club Soda
White Wine Glass

Build over ice and stir

Kiwi Light

1 part Kiwi Schnapps
fill with Tonic Water
Highball Glass

Build over ice and stir

Kurant Collins

2 parts Currant-Flavored Vodka
1 part Lemon Juice
dash Powdered Sugar
fill with Club Soda
Collins Glass

Shake all but Club Soda with ice and strain into the glass. Top with Club Soda.

L.A. Iced Tea

1 part Vodka
1 part Triple Sec
1 part Melon Liqueur
1 part Gin
1 part Rum
fill with Club Soda
Collins Glass

Shake all but Club Soda with ice and strain into the glass. Top with Club Soda.

La Coppa de la Passion
$1^{1}/_{2}$ parts Dark Rum
$^{1}/_{2}$ part Passion Fruit Liqueur
$^{1}/_{2}$ part Mango Schnapps
$1^{1}/_{2}$ parts Banana Puree
$^{1}/_{2}$ part Lemon Juice
fill with Club Soda
Collins Glass

Shake all but Club Soda with ice and strain into the glass. Top with Club Soda.

Lappland
1 part Vodka
1 part Apricot Brandy
1 part Sour Mix
fill with Ginger Ale
Collins Glass

Build over ice and stir

Leap Frog
$1^{1}/_{2}$ parts Gin
splash Lemon Juice
fill with Ginger Ale
Highball Glass

Build over ice and stir

Lei Lani
$1^{1}/_{4}$ parts Dark Rum
$^{1}/_{2}$ part Lemon Juice
$^{1}/_{2}$ part Pineapple Juice
$^{1}/_{2}$ part Papaya Juice
1 part Orange Juice
splash Grenadine
fill with Club Soda
Collins Glass

Shake all but Club Soda with ice and strain into the glass. Top with Club Soda.

Leprechaun
2 parts Irish Whiskey
fill with Tonic Water
Old-Fashioned Glass

Build over ice and stir

Lilac Cooler
1 part Triple Sec
1 part Cognac
1 part Sweet Vermouth
fill with Ginger Ale
Collins Glass

Build over ice and stir

Lili
1 Lime Twist
dash Sugar
Juice from half a Lime
1 part Vodka
1 part Triple Sec
fill with Club Soda
Collins Glass

Muddle the Lime, Sugar, and Lime Juice in the bottom of a collins glass. Fill the glass with ice and add the Vodka and Triple Sec. Fill with Club Soda.

Lisbonne
1 part Tequila Silver
$^{1}/_{2}$ part Blue Curaçao
$^{1}/_{2}$ part Maraschino Liqueur
fill with Tonic Water
Collins Glass

Build over ice and stir

Loch Ness Monster
$1^{1}/_{2}$ parts Scotch
splash Peppermint Schnapps
fill with Club Soda
Highball Glass

Build over ice and stir

Lone Tree Cooler

2 parts Gin
splash Dry Vermouth
dash Powdered Sugar
fill with Club Soda
Collins Glass

Shake all but Club Soda with ice and strain into the glass. Top with Club Soda.

Long Joe

1 part Apricot Brandy
1/2 part Sweet Vermouth
1/2 part Gin
fill with Ginger Ale
Collins Glass

Build over ice and stir

Long Vodka

2 parts Vodka
1/2 part Lime Juice
4 dashes Angostura® Bitters
fill with Tonic Water
Collins Glass

Build over ice and stir

Lost Heart

1 1/2 parts Crème de Cassis
2/3 part Sweet Vermouth
2 parts Lemon Juice
splash Amaretto
fill with Club Soda
Highball Glass

Shake all but Club Soda with ice and strain into the glass. Top with Club Soda.

Love 'n' Fizz

1 part Gin
1 part Lime Cordial
1/2 part Mango Nectar
splash Grenadine
splash Crème de Menthe (White)
fill with Club Soda
Collins Glass

Shake all but Club Soda with ice and strain into the glass. Top with Club Soda.

Love Bond

2/3 part Melon Liqueur
2 parts Dark Rum
1 1/2 parts Melon Purée
2/3 part Lemon Juice
1/2 part Honey
fill with Club Soda
Collins Glass

Shake all but Club Soda with ice and strain into the glass. Top with Club Soda.

Love in an Elevator

2 parts Gin
1 part Blue Curaçao
fill with Club Soda
Collins Glass

Build over ice and stir

Lycheeto

1 part Light Rum
1 part Lychee Liqueur
1 part Simple Syrup
1/2 part Crème de Menthe (Green)
fill with Club Soda
Collins Glass

Shake all but Club Soda with ice and strain into the glass. Top with Club Soda.

Machete
1 part Vodka
2 parts Pineapple Juice
fill with Tonic Water
Collins Glass

Build over ice and stir

Maestro
1 1/2 parts Añejo Rum
1/2 part Cream Sherry
1/2 part Lime Juice
fill with Ginger Ale
1 Lemon Twist
Collins Glass

Shake all but Ginger Ale with ice and strain into the glass. Top with Ginger Ale.

Magic Trace
3/4 part Dry Gin
1/2 part Lemon Syrup
splash Triple Sec
splash Strawberry Juice
fill with Tonic Water
Collins Glass

Build over ice and stir

Magnolia Maiden
1 part Mandarine Napoléon® Liqueur
1 part Bourbon
splash Simple Syrup
fill with Club Soda
Old-Fashioned Glass

Build over ice and stir

Maktak Special
1 1/2 parts Dark Rum
1/2 part Cream Sherry
1/2 part Lime Juice
fill with Ginger Ale
Collins Glass

Build over ice and stir

Mamie Gilroy
2 parts Scotch
1/2 part Lime Juice
fill with Ginger Ale
Collins Glass

Build over ice and stir

Man o' War
1 part Gin
2 parts Rum
1 part Grenadine
1 part Lime Juice
fill with Tonic Water
Highball Glass

Build over ice and stir

Mandarin Delight
1 1/2 parts Orange-Flavored Vodka
fill Tonic Water
1 Lime Wedge
Collins Glass

Build over ice and stir

Margue Collins
1 1/2 parts Tequila Silver
1/2 part Simple Syrup
splash Lime Juice
fill with Club Soda
Collins Glass

Shake all but Club Soda with ice and strain into the glass. Top with Club Soda.

Mark Pilkinton
1 1/2 parts Vodka
3/4 part Triple Sec
1 part Sour Mix
fill with Raspberry Ginger Ale
Highball Glass

Build over ice and stir

Mayan Whore
1½ parts Tequila
1 part Coffee Liqueur
1 part Pineapple Juice
fill with Club Soda
splash Grenadine
Collins Glass

Build over ice

Melba Tonic
2 parts Vodka
½ part Peach Schnapps
½ part Grenadine
½ part Simple Syrup
fill with Tonic Water
Collins Glass

Build over ice and stir

Melon Patch
1 part Melon Liqueur
½ part Triple Sec
½ part Vodka
fill with Club Soda
Highball Glass

Shake all but Club Soda with ice and strain into the glass. Top with Club Soda.

Mexican Bike Race
2 parts Tequila
splash Campari®
fill with Ginger Ale
Highball Glass

Build over ice and stir

Mexican Mule
1½ parts Tequila Reposado
¼ part Sugar
splash Fresh Lime Juice
fill with Ginger Ale
Collins Glass

Build over ice and stir

Midnight in the Garden
1 part Amaretto
1 part Peach Schnapps
splash Orange Juice
fill with Club Soda
Collins Glass

Shake all but Club Soda with ice and strain into the glass. Top with Club Soda.

Mint Fizz
2 parts Crème de Menthe (White)
fill with Tonic Water
Collins Glass

Build over ice and stir

Mistletoe Warm Up
1 part Peppermint Liqueur
3 parts Grapefruit Juice
splash Lime Juice
½ part Simple Syrup
fill with Club Soda
Highball Glass

Shake all but Club Soda with ice and strain into the glass. Top with Club Soda.

Monkey Spanker
3 parts Jack Daniel's®
fill with Ginger Ale
Beer Mug

Build over ice and stir

Montgomery
1 part Vodka
¼ part Grenadine
2 parts Sour Mix
fill with Ginger Ale
Collins Glass

Build over ice and stir

Morning Fizz

$1^{1}/_{2}$ parts Vodka
1 part Simple Syrup
3 parts Grapefruit Juice
fill with Club Soda
White Wine Glass

Shake all but Club Soda with ice and strain into the glass. Top with Club Soda.

Mudskipper

1 part Dry Gin
fill with Ginger Ale
splash Chocolate Syrup
Collins Glass

Build over ice and stir

Nadir

1 part Gin
$^{1}/_{2}$ part Cherry Liqueur
$^{1}/_{2}$ part Grenadine
splash Pineapple Juice
splash Lemon Juice
splash Simple Syrup
fill with Club Soda
Highball Glass

Shake all but Club Soda with ice and strain into the glass. Top with Club Soda.

Naked Truth

$^{2}/_{3}$ part Vodka
1 part Melon Liqueur
1 part Lemon Juice
dash Powdered Sugar
fill with Club Soda
Collins Glass

Shake all but Club Soda with ice and strain into the glass. Top with Club Soda.

Napoli

1 part Vodka
1 part Campari®
$^{1}/_{2}$ part Dry Vermouth
splash Sweet Vermouth
fill with Club Soda
Highball Glass

Shake all but Club Soda with ice and strain into the glass. Top with Club Soda.

Near the Cataclysm

$1^{1}/_{2}$ parts Melon Liqueur
$^{1}/_{2}$ part Orange Liqueur
$^{1}/_{2}$ part Lychee Liqueur
$^{2}/_{3}$ part Lemon Juice
fill with Club Soda
Highball Glass

Shake all but Club Soda with ice and strain into the glass. Top with Club Soda.

New Orleans Buck

$1^{1}/_{2}$ parts Light Rum
1 part Orange Juice
$^{1}/_{2}$ part Lemon Juice
fill with Ginger Ale
Collins Glass

Build over ice and stir

Newport Cooler

2 parts Gin
$^{1}/_{2}$ part Brandy
$^{1}/_{2}$ part Peach Liqueur
splash Fresh Lime Juice
fill with Ginger Ale
Collins Glass

Build over ice and stir

Night Fever

1 part Blue Curaçao
1 part Vodka
1/2 part Cachaca
fill with Club Soda
Collins Glass

Shake all but Club Soda with ice and strain into the glass. Top with Club Soda.

Nirvana

1 1/2 parts Orange-Flavored Vodka
1/2 part Melon Liqueur
1/2 part Passion Fruit Liqueur
splash Lime Cordial
fill with Club Soda
Champagne Flute

Shake all but Club Soda with ice and strain into the glass. Top with Club Soda.

Northside Special

1 1/4 parts Dark Rum
2 parts Orange Juice
1/2 part Lemon Juice
fill with Club Soda
Collins Glass

Build over ice and stir

Notre Belle Epoque

1/2 part Blue Curaçao
2 1/2 parts White Wine
2/3 part Plum Brandy
2/3 part Lemon Juice
fill with Club Soda
Highball Glass

Shake all but Club Soda with ice and strain into the glass. Top with Club Soda.

November Sea Breeze

1 1/2 parts Fresh Lime Juice
2 parts Apple Juice
fill with Club Soda
Collins Glass

Build over ice and stir

Nuclear Fizz

3/4 part Vodka
1/2 part Melon Liqueur
1/2 part Triple Sec
splash Lime Juice
fill with Club Soda
Collins Glass

Shake all but Club Soda with ice and strain into the glass. Top with Club Soda.

Nutty Ginger

1 part Amaretto
1 part Frangelico®
fill with Ginger Ale
Highball Glass

Build over ice and stir

One over Par

1 part Rum
1 part Grapefruit Juice
1 part Orange Juice
1 part Pineapple Juice
fill with Club Soda
Collins Glass

Build over ice and stir

Oral Intruder

1 part Coconut-Flavored Rum
1 part Melon Liqueur
1 part Sour Mix
fill with Ginger Ale
splash Lime Juice
Highball Glass

Build over ice and stir

Orange Fizz

2 parts Gin
2 splashes Triple Sec
2 parts Lemon Juice
1/2 part Orange Juice
2 dashes Orange Bitters
dash Sugar
fill with Club Soda
Collins Glass

Shake all but Club Soda with ice and strain into the glass. Top with Club Soda.

Oregon Coastline

1 part Amaretto
1 part Passion Fruit Juice
1 part Lime Juice
fill with Club Soda
Highball Glass

Build over ice and stir

Oscar

1 part Gin
1/2 part Blue Curaçao
1/2 part Orange Juice
fill with Tonic Water
Collins Glass

Build over ice and stir

Pacific Exchange

1 1/2 parts Vodka
1/2 part Raspberry Liqueur
2/3 part Plum Brandy
2/3 part Lemon Juice
fill with Club Soda
Highball Glass

Shake all but Club Soda with ice and strain into the glass. Top with Club Soda.

Paddlesteamer

1 part Vodka
1 part Southern Comfort®
2 parts Orange Juice
fill with Ginger Ale
Collins Glass

Shake all but Ginger Ale with ice and strain into the glass. Top with Ginger Ale.

Painter's Delight

1 part Gin
1 part Blue Curaçao
splash Pernod®
1/2 part Lemon Juice
fill with Club Soda
Highball Glass

Shake all but Club Soda with ice and strain into the glass. Top with Club Soda.

Palmetto Cooler

1 part Bourbon
1 part Apricot Brandy
1 part Dry Vermouth
fill with Club Soda
Collins Glass

Build over ice and stir

Passione al Limone

1 1/2 parts Vodka
1/2 part Passion Fruit Liqueur
1/2 part Simple Syrup
fill with Club Soda
Collins Glass

Shake all but Club Soda with ice and strain into the glass. Top with Club Soda.

Password to Paradise

2 parts Gin
dash Powdered Sugar
splash Passion Fruit Nectar
fill with Club Soda
Collins Glass

Shake all but Club Soda with ice and strain into the glass. Top with Club Soda.

Peabody
2 parts Gin
1/2 part Campari®
2 splashes Grenadine
1 part Orange Juice
fill with Ginger Ale
Collins Glass

Build over ice and stir

Peach Temptation
1 1/2 parts Gin
1 part Peach Schnapps
1 part Triple Sec
2 parts Lemon Juice
fill with Club Soda
Collins Glass

Shake all but Club Soda with ice and strain into the glass. Top with Club Soda.

Peachy Comfort
1 part Southern Comfort®
1 part Peach Schnapps
fill with Ginger Ale
Collins Glass

Build over ice and stir

Peek in Pandora's Box
1 part Scotch
1 part Mandarine Napoléon® Liqueur
splash Campari®
splash Strega®
fill with Ginger Ale
Old-Fashioned Glass

Shake with ice and strain over ice

Peyton Place
1 1/2 parts Sloe Gin
1 part Gin
1/2 part Simple Syrup
2 parts Grapefruit Juice
fill with Club Soda
Collins Glass

Shake all but Club Soda with ice and strain into the glass. Top with Club Soda.

Phat Louie
2 parts Vanilla-Flavored Vodka
1/2 part Grenadine
fill with Ginger Ale
Collins Glass

Build over ice and stir

Pierre Collins
2 parts Brandy
1/2 part Sugar
1/2 part Lime Cordial
fill with Club Soda
Collins Glass

Shake all but Club Soda with ice and strain into the glass. Top with Club Soda.

Pigs in Space
1 part Dark Rum
fill with Ginger Ale
Collins Glass

Build over ice and stir

Pimm's Rangoon
1 1/2 parts Pimm's® No. 1 Cup
fill with Ginger Ale
1 Lemon Twist
1 Cucumber Slice
Highball Glass

Build over ice and stir

Pink Cream Fizz

2 parts Gin
1 part Lemon Juice
dash Sugar
1 part Light Cream
splash Grenadine
fill with Club Soda
Collins Glass

Shake all but Club Soda with ice and strain into the glass. Top with Club Soda.

Pisco Collins

2 parts Pisco
1 1/2 parts Lime Cordial
1/2 part Sugar
fill with Club Soda
Collins Glass

Shake all but Club Soda with ice and strain into the glass. Top with Club Soda.

Planter's Punch

1 1/2 parts Dark Rum
1 1/2 parts Light Rum
1/2 part Lemon Juice
1/2 part Lime Juice
1 part Orange Juice
fill with Club Soda
Collins Glass

Shake all but Club Soda with ice and strain into the glass. Top with Club Soda.

Playboy Cooler

1 part Gold Rum
1 part Coffee Liqueur
2 splashes Lemon Juice
fill with Pineapple Juice
splash Cola
Collins Glass

Build over ice and stir

Plugged on Fruit

1 part Orange-Flavored Vodka
1 part Blue Curaçao
1 part Peach Schnapps
1 part Lime Juice
1 part Lemon Juice
fill with Club Soda
Highball Glass

Shake all but Club Soda with ice and strain into the glass. Top with Club Soda.

Polar Attraction

2 parts Brandy
fill with Tonic Water
Collins Glass

Build over ice and stir

Pond Scum

1 part Vodka
fill with Club Soda
1/2 part Irish Cream Liqueur
Highball Glass

Build over ice. Top with Irish Cream Liqueur.

Port Arms

2 parts Port
1 part Brandy
1/2 part Triple Sec
1 part Orange Juice
fill with Club Soda
Collins Glass

Build over ice and stir

Princess Morgan

3/4 part Spiced Rum
1/4 part Crème de Banana
2 1/2 parts Orange Juice
fill with Club Soda
Highball Glass

Build over ice and stir

Province Town
1 part Vodka
1/2 part Citrus-Flavored Vodka
2 parts Grapefruit Juice
2 parts Cranberry Juice Cocktail
fill with Club Soda
Collins Glass

Shake all but Club Soda with ice and strain into the glass. Top with Club Soda.

Rabbit's Revenge
1 part Bourbon
1 part Pineapple Juice
1/2 part Grenadine
fill with Tonic Water
Collins Glass

Shake all but Tonic Water with ice and strain into the glass. Top with Tonic Water.

Rail Splitter
splash Simple Syrup
splash Lemon Juice
fill with Ginger Ale
Collins Glass

Build over ice and stir

Rangoon Ruby
2 parts Vodka
2 parts Cranberry Juice Cocktail
1/2 part Lime Juice
fill with Club Soda
Highball Glass

Build over ice and stir

Raspberry Watkins
1 1/2 parts Vodka
1/2 part Raspberry Liqueur
1/4 part Lime Cordial
splash Grenadine
fill with Club Soda
Collins Glass

Shake all but Club Soda with ice and strain into the glass. Top with Club Soda.

Red Bait
1 part Sloe Gin
1/2 part Dark Rum
1/2 part Fresh Lime Juice
1 part Guava Juice
fill with Tonic Water
Collins Glass

Build over ice and stir

Red Devil's Poison
1 1/2 parts Citrus-Flavored Vodka
1/2 part Parfait Amour
1 part Lemon Juice
fill with Tonic Water
Collins Glass

Build over ice and stir

Red Mystery
1 1/2 parts Pastis
1/2 part Grenadine
fill with Club Soda
Collins Glass

Build over ice and stir

Red Rock West
1 part Crème de Cassis
1 part Raspberry Liqueur
1 part Vodka
fill with Club Soda
Highball Glass

Build over ice and stir

Red Tonic
2 parts Vodka
1 part Grenadine
1 part Lemon Juice
fill with Tonic Water
Highball Glass

Build over ice and stir

Remsen Cooler
2 parts Gin
dash Powdered Sugar
fill with Club Soda
Collins Glass

Build over ice and stir

Rhapsody
2 parts Tequila Silver
1 part Passion Fruit Liqueur
1 1/2 parts Kiwi Schnapps
1/2 part Lemon Juice
fill with Club Soda
Highball Glass

Shake all but Club Soda with ice and strain into the glass. Top with Club Soda.

Rocky Mountain Cooler
1 1/2 parts Peach Schnapps
4 parts Pineapple Juice
fill with Lemon-Lime Soda
Collins Glass

Build over ice and stir

Roman Cooler
2 parts Gin
1 part Sambuca
1/2 part Simple Syrup
1/4 part Sweet Vermouth
fill with Tonic Water
Collins Glass

Shake all but Tonic Water with ice and strain into the glass. Top with Tonic Water.

Roman Punch
1/2 part Dark Rum
1/2 part Cognac
splash Port
1 part Raspberry Syrup
1 part Lemon Juice
fill with Club Soda
Collins Glass

Shake all but Club Soda with ice and strain into the glass. Top with Club Soda.

Royal Air Class
1 1/2 parts Gin
1/2 part Lychee Liqueur
1/2 part Lemon Juice
1/2 part Grenadine
fill with Tonic Water
Highball Glass

Shake all but Tonic Water with ice and strain into the glass. Top with Tonic Water.

Royal Eagle
1 1/2 parts Currant-Flavored Vodka
1/2 part Blackberry Liqueur
1/2 part Kirschwasser
2/3 part Lemon Juice
fill with Ginger Ale
Highball Glass

Shake all but Ginger Ale with ice and strain into the glass. Top with Ginger Ale.

Royalty Fizz
2 parts Gin
splash Blue Curaçao
1 part Lemon Juice
dash Sugar
1 Egg
fill with Club Soda
Collins Glass

Shake all but Club Soda with ice and strain into the glass. Top with Club Soda.

Ruddy Scotch
1 part Peach Schnapps
1 part Whiskey
splash Cranberry Juice Cocktail
splash Raspberry Juice
fill with Ginger Ale
Highball Glass

Build over ice and stir

Rumbubble
2 parts Rum
1 1/2 parts Triple Sec
splash Cinnamon Schnapps
fill with Club Soda
Collins Glass

Build over ice and stir

Rum Cobbler
2 parts Dark Rum
dash Sugar
fill with Club Soda
Old-Fashioned Glass

Build over ice and stir

Salute
1/2 part Gin
1/2 part Crème de Cassis
1 1/2 parts Dry Vermouth
1 part Sweet Vermouth
1/2 part Campari®
fill with Club Soda
Champagne Flute

Shake all but Club Soda with ice and strain into the glass. Top with Club Soda.

Sambuca Blitz
1 1/2 parts Sambuca
1 1/2 parts Crème de Cassis
1 part Dry Vermouth
fill with Club Soda
Collins Glass

Build over ice and stir

San Juan Sling
1 part Light Rum
1 part Cherry Brandy
1 part Fresh Lime Juice
fill with Club Soda
Collins Glass

Shake all but Club Soda with ice and strain into the glass. Top with Club Soda.

Santa Cruz
2 parts Dark Rum
1/2 part Cherry Brandy
1 part Fresh Lime Juice
1/2 part Simple Syrup
fill with Club Soda
Collins Glass

Shake all but Club Soda with ice and strain into the glass. Top with Club Soda.

Saratoga Cooler
2 parts Brandy
splash Pineapple Juice
splash Lemon Juice
splash Maraschino Cherry Juice
fill with Ginger Ale
Collins Glass

Build over ice and stir

Satin Slave
2/3 part Light Rum
2/3 part Sloe Gin
1/2 part Apricot Brandy
1 part Sour Mix
fill with Ginger Ale
Highball Glass

Build over ice and stir

Schnapp Pop
1 1/2 parts Wild Berry-Flavored Schnapps
fill with Club Soda
Collins Glass

Build over ice and stir

Scotch Collins
2 parts Scotch
1 part Lemon Juice
dash Sugar
splash Grenadine
fill with Club Soda
Collins Glass

Shake all but Club Soda with ice and strain into the glass. Top with Club Soda.

Scottish Pirate

1 part Scotch
1/2 part Orange Liqueur
1/2 part Crème de Cassis
3 parts Sour Mix
fill with Club Soda
Highball Glass

Shake all but Club Soda with ice and strain into the glass. Top with Club Soda.

Scummy Nut Sack

1 part Southern Comfort®
1 part Amaretto
1 part Banana Liqueur
1 part Crème de Menthe (White)
1 part Tequila
1 part Peppermint Schnapps
fill with Club Soda
Collins Glass

Shake all but Club Soda with ice and strain into the glass. Top with Club Soda.

Sea Fizz

1 1/2 parts Absinthe
1/2 part Lemon Juice
dash Sugar
1 Egg White
fill with Tonic Water
Highball Glass

Shake all but tonic water with ice and strain into the glass. Top with tonic water.

Sea Story

1 part Blue Curaçao
1 part Triple Sec
fill with Tonic Water
Collins Glass

Build over ice and stir

Seadoo

1 part Vodka
splash Cranberry Juice Cocktail
fill with Club Soda
Collins Glass

Build over ice and stir

Seersucker

2 parts Light Rum
1 part Orange Juice
2 splashes Grenadine
fill with Tonic Water
Highball Glass

Build over ice and stir

Sehangat Senyuman

1 1/2 parts Crème de Menthe (Green)
1 part Brandy
fill with Club Soda
Collins Glass

Build over ice and stir

Seth Allen

3 parts Spiced Rum
fill with Ginger Ale
Collins Glass

Build over ice and stir

Seven Seas

1 1/2 parts Pisang Ambon® Liqueur
1 part Gin
splash Crème de Banana
fill with Tonic Water
Collins Glass

Build over ice and stir

Shady Grove Cooler

2 parts Gin
1 part Fresh Lime Juice
1/2 part Sugar
fill with Ginger Ale
Collins Glass

Shake all but Ginger Ale with ice and strain into the glass. Top with Ginger Ale.

Sharky Punch

1 1/2 parts Apple Brandy
1/2 part Rye Whiskey
splash Simple Syrup
fill with Club Soda
Highball Glass

Shake all but Club Soda with ice and strain into the glass. Top with Club Soda.

Shetland Skye

1 part Sambuca
1 part Amaretto
splash Cherry Brandy
3 parts Orange Juice
fill with Club Soda
Highball Glass

Build over ice and stir

Ship of Fools

1 part Amaretto
1 part Dark Rum
1 part Orange Juice
splash Lemon Juice
fill with Ginger Ale
Highball Glass

Build over ice and stir

Short Dog Cooler

2 parts Peach Schnapps
1 part Lemon-Lime Soda
2 parts Pineapple Juice
Highball Glass

Build over ice and stir

Shotgun Lou

1 1/2 parts Brandy
2 1/2 parts Milk
dash Brown Sugar
fill with Ginger Ale
Highball Glass

Shake all but Ginger Ale with ice and strain into the glass. Top with Ginger Ale.

Show Tune

1 part Spiced Rum
1/4 part Amaretto
3 parts Grapefruit Juice
splash Grenadine
fill with Club Soda
Collins Glass

Shake all but Club Soda with ice and strain into the glass. Top with Club Soda.

Sienna

3/4 part Spiced Rum
1/2 part Amaretto
2 parts Orange Juice
fill with Ginger Ale
White Wine Glass

Build over ice and stir

Sign of the Times

2 parts Amaretto
1 part Crème de Banana
fill with Tonic Water
Highball Glass

Build over ice and stir

Silly Kentucky

1 1/2 parts Jim Beam®
1/2 part Orange Liqueur
splash Apricot Brandy
splash Limoncello
2/3 part Lemon Juice
fill with Club Soda
Collins Glass

Shake all but Club Soda with ice and strain into the glass. Top with Club Soda.

Silver Fizz

2 parts Gin
1/2 part Lemon Juice
dash Powdered Sugar
1 Egg White
fill with Club Soda
Highball Glass

Shake all but Club Soda with ice and strain into the glass. Top with Club Soda.

Sister Starseeker

2 parts Light Rum
1 part Lemon Juice
splash Grenadine
fill with Tonic Water
Highball Glass

Build over ice and stir

Skyscraper

1 1/2 parts Gin
1/2 part Crème de Menthe (Green)
1/2 part Triple Sec
1/2 part Fresh Lime Juice
splash Simple Syrup
fill with Club Soda
Collins Glass

Shake all but Club Soda with ice and strain into the glass. Top with Club Soda.

Sleepwalker on the Roof

1 1/2 parts Dark Rum
1/2 part Orange Liqueur
1/2 part Passion Fruit Liqueur
2/3 part Lemon Juice
fill with Ginger Ale
Highball Glass

Shake with ice and strain over ice

(S)limey Coconut

1 part Coconut-Flavored Liqueur
3/4 part Fresh Lime Juice
fill with Lemon-Lime Soda
Collins Glass

Shake with ice and strain in the glass over ice cubes

Sloe Gin Sin

1 part Sloe Gin
1 part Orange Liqueur
1 1/2 parts Sour Mix
fill with Club Soda
Highball Glass

Build over ice and stir

Smith & Kearns

1 part Cream
1 part Coffee
fill with Club Soda
Old-Fashioned Glass

Build over ice and stir

Smoke on the Water

1 part Tequila Reposado
1/2 part Pisang Ambon® Liqueur
1/2 part Blue Curaçao
1 part Pineapple Juice
fill with Club Soda
Old-Fashioned Glass

Shake all but Club Soda with ice and strain into the glass. Top with Club Soda.

Smurf®-o-Tonic

1 part Gin
1 part Blue Curaçao
fill with Tonic Water
Highball Glass

Build over ice and stir

Southern Ginger

2 parts Bourbon
1/2 part Ginger Liqueur
fill with Ginger Ale
Collins Glass

Build over ice and stir

South-of-the-Border Iced Tea

1 part Vodka
1 part Coffee Liqueur
fill with Club Soda
Collins Glass

Build over ice and stir

Soviet Sunset

1 part Lemon-Flavored Vodka
1 part Triple Sec
1 part Sweetened Lime Juice
fill with Club Soda
Highball Glass

Build over ice and stir

Sparkling Southern Apple

1 part Southern Comfort®
1 part Sour Apple Schnapps
fill with Club Soda
Collins Glass

Build over ice and stir

Split Beaver

1 part Gin
1 part Peach Schnapps
fill with Tonic Water
Highball Glass

Build over ice and stir

Spring Field

2/3 part Pear Liqueur
1/2 part Rémy Martin® VSOP
splash Kirschwasser
1/2 part Simple Syrup
fill with Club Soda
Collins Glass

Shake all but Club Soda with ice and strain into the glass. Top with Club Soda.

Spritzer

1 1/2 parts Vodka
fill with Club Soda
Highball Glass

Build over ice and stir

Squeeze My Lemon

1 1/2 parts Gin
1/2 part Lemon Juice
fill with Ginger Ale
Highball Glass

Build over ice and stir

Star Gazer

1 1/2 parts Dark Rum
1/2 part Blue Curaçao
1/2 part Triple Sec
1/2 part Simple Syrup
fill with Club Soda
Collins Glass

Shake all but Club Soda with ice and strain into the glass. Top with Club Soda.

Starseeker

2 parts Light Rum
1 part Orange Juice
splash Grenadine
fill with Tonic Water
Highball Glass

Shake all but Tonic Water with ice and strain into the glass. Top with Tonic Water.

Steeplejack

1 1/2 parts Apple Brandy
splash Fresh Lime Juice
fill with Club Soda
Collins Glass

Build over ice and stir

Stork Club Cooler

2 parts Gin
dash Sugar
fill with Club Soda
Collins Glass

Build over ice and stir

Stranded in the Rain

2 parts Tequila Reposado
2/3 part Lychee Liqueur
2/3 part Lemon Juice
1/2 part Lime Juice
fill with Club Soda
Highball Glass

Build over ice and stir

Strawberry Shortcake Cooler

2 parts Strawberry Liqueur
1/4 part Grenadine
fill with Lemon-Lime Soda
splash Cream
Collins Glass

Build over ice and stir

Submarine Cooler

1 1/2 parts Gin
1 part Ginger Ale
fill with Tonic Water
Highball Glass

Build over ice and stir

Suisesse

1 part Pernod®
1 part Lemon Juice
1 Egg White
fill with Club Soda
Old-Fashioned Glass

Shake all but Club Soda with ice and strain into the glass. Top with Club Soda.

Summer Light

3 parts White Wine
1 1/2 parts Dry Vermouth
fill with Club Soda
Collins Glass

Build over ice and stir

Summer Scotch

1 part Scotch
3 splashes Crème de Menthe (White)
fill with Club Soda
Highball Glass

Build over ice and stir

Sun 'n Shade

2 parts Gosling's Black Seal® Rum
fill with Tonic Water
splash Lime Juice
Collins Glass

Build over ice and stir

Sunken Ship

2/3 part Crème de Banana
2/3 part Blackberry Liqueur
1/2 part Light Rum
1 1/2 parts Sour Mix
fill with Ginger Ale
Highball Glass

Build over ice and stir

Sunnier Sour

1 1/4 parts Dark Rum
1/4 part Lemon Juice
dash Powdered Sugar
1 1/2 parts Grapefruit Juice
fill with Club Soda
Highball Glass

Shake all but Club Soda with ice and strain into the glass. Top with Club Soda.

Superfly
2 parts Gin
1 part Lime Juice
fill with Ginger Ale
Highball Glass

Build over ice and stir

Surfboard Popper
1 part Kiwi Schnapps
1 part Passion Fruit Liqueur
fill with Ginger Ale
Highball Glass

Build over ice and stir

Swashbuckler
1 1/2 parts Spiced Rum
1 part Cola
fill with Club Soda
1/4 part Lime Juice
Collins Glass

Build over ice and stir

Sweet Concoction
1 1/2 parts Amaretto
1 1/2 parts Peach Schnapps
1 part Dry Vermouth
fill with Club Soda
Highball Glass

Build over ice and stir

Sweet Ginger
1 part Rum
1 part Amaretto
1/2 part Sweet Vermouth
fill with Ginger Ale
Highball Glass

Build over ice and stir

Sweet Summer
2 parts Raspberry-Flavored Vodka
fill with Ginger Ale
splash Cranberry Juice Cocktail
Collins Glass

Build over ice and stir

Sweet Tart Cooler
1 part Vodka
1 part Cherry Juice
1 part Wild Berry Schnapps
1 part Lemonade
1 part Orange Juice
1 part Lemon-Lime Soda
Highball Glass

Build over ice and stir

TNT
1 1/2 parts Tequila
fill with Tonic Water
Highball Glass

Build over ice and stir

Tall Islander
2 parts Light Rum
3 parts Pineapple Juice
3 splashes Lime Juice
splash Simple Syrup
fill with Club Soda
Collins Glass

Shake all but Club Soda with ice and strain into the glass. Top with Club Soda.

Tapico
1 1/2 parts Tequila Silver
1 part Crème de Cassis
1 part Banana Juice
fill with Tonic Water
Collins Glass

Shake all but Tonic Water with ice and strain into the glass. Top with Tonic Water.

Tartan Swizzle

2 parts Scotch
1 1/2 parts Lime Juice
dash Sugar
dash Bitters
fill with Club Soda
Collins Glass

Shake all but Club Soda with ice and strain into the glass. Top with Club Soda.

Tenderberry

1 part Cream
1 part Grenadine
6 Strawberries
fill with Ginger Ale
Collins Glass

Combine all ingredients except the Ginger Ale in a blender and blend until smooth. Pour into a collins glass and top with Ginger Ale.

Tequila Cooler

2 parts Tequila
fill with Lemon-Lime Soda
Highball Glass

Build over ice and stir

Tequila Fizz

2 parts Tequila
2 splashes Lemon Juice
3/4 part Grenadine
1 Egg White
fill with Ginger Ale
Collins Glass

Shake all but Ginger Ale with ice and strain into the glass. Top with Ginger Ale.

Tequila Press

2 parts Tequila
1/2 part Simple Syrup
splash Lime Juice
fill with Club Soda
Collins Glass

Build over ice and stir

Test Drive

1/2 part Amaretto
1 part Banana Liqueur
fill with Tonic Water
Highball Glass

Build over ice and stir

Texas Fizz

1 1/2 parts Gin
1 part Orange Juice
dash Powdered Sugar
1/4 part Grenadine
fill with Club Soda
Collins Glass

Shake all but Club Soda with ice and strain into the glass. Top with Club Soda.

Thermometer

2 parts Vodka
1 part Cranberry Juice Cocktail
fill with Club Soda
Highball Glass

Build over ice and stir

Tijuana Iced Tea

2 parts Tequila
1 part Coffee Liqueur
fill with Club Soda
Collins Glass

Build over ice and stir

Tonic Twist

1 part Apricot Brandy
1 part Sweet Vermouth
fill with Tonic Water
Collins Glass

Build over ice and stir

Tonica

2 parts Strawberry Liqueur
1 part Lemon Juice
fill with Tonic Water
Highball Glass

Build over ice and stir

Trade Winds

1 1/2 parts Dark Rum
1/2 part Fresh Lime Juice
1/2 part Plum Brandy
1/2 part Simple Syrup
fill with Club Soda
Collins Glass

Shake all but Club Soda with ice and strain into the glass. Top with Club Soda.

Triad

1/2 part Añejo Rum
1/2 part Sweet Vermouth
1/2 part Amaretto
fill with Ginger Ale
Highball Glass

Build over ice and stir

Trinidad

1 part Light Rum
1 part Dark Rum
1 part Fresh Lime Juice
splash Triple Sec
dash Brown Sugar
fill with Club Soda
Collins Glass

Shake all but Club Soda with ice and strain into the glass. Top with Club Soda.

Triple Fizz

1 1/2 parts Gin
splash Triple Sec
splash Dry Vermouth
fill with Club Soda
Highball Glass

Build over ice and stir

Triple Iceberg

1 1/2 parts Triple Sec
fill with Club Soda
Collins Glass

Build over ice and stir

Tropical Rain

2 parts Dark Rum
2/3 part Grand Marnier®
2/3 part Lemon Juice
splash Blue Curaçao
fill with Club Soda
Collins Glass

Shake all but Club Soda with ice and strain into the glass. Top with Club Soda.

TV Special

2 parts Gin
1 part Triple Sec
1 part Pineapple Juice
fill with Club Soda
Collins Glass

Shake all but Club Soda with ice and strain into the glass. Top with Club Soda.

Twinkie® Star

1 1/2 parts Cherry Brandy
fill with Tonic Water
Collins Glass

Build over ice and stir

Urine

2 parts Gin
1 part Lime Juice
fill with Club Soda
Highball Glass

Build over ice and stir

Valencia Lady

2 parts Vodka
splash Blue Curaçao
splash Cranberry Juice Cocktail
fill with Club Soda
Highball Glass

Build over ice and stir

Velvet Tongue

1 part Southern Comfort®
1 part Canadian Club® Classic
fill with Ginger Ale
Highball Glass

Build over ice and stir

Venus on the Rocks

1 part Amaretto
2 parts Peach Schnapps
fill with Club Soda
Old-Fashioned Glass

Build over ice and stir

Vermouth Sparkle

2 parts Dry Vermouth
splash Sweet Vermouth
splash Grenadine
fill with Ginger Ale
Collins Glass

Build over ice and stir

Very Berry Tonic

1 part Currant-Flavored Vodka
1/2 part Raspberry Liqueur
fill with Tonic Water
Collins Glass

Build over ice and stir

Victoria's Dream

2/3 part Peach Schnapps
1/2 part Strawberry Liqueur
1/2 part Irish Cream Liqueur
splash Milk
fill with Club Soda
Highball Glass

Shake all but Club Soda with ice and strain into the glass. Top with Club Soda.

Victory

2 parts Pernod®
1 part Grenadine
fill with Club Soda
Old-Fashioned Glass

Build over ice and stir

Viktor

2 parts Currant-Flavored Vodka
1 part Lime Juice
fill with Ginger Ale
Highball Glass

Build over ice and stir

Violetta

1/2 part Parfait Amour
1/2 part Anisette
1 part Pineapple Juice
splash Grenadine
fill with Club Soda
Collins Glass

Shake all but Club Soda with ice and strain into the glass. Top with Club Soda.

Virtual Reality

1 part Gin
1 part Calvados Apple Brandy
1/2 part Grenadine
1/2 part Lemon Juice
fill with Club Soda
Highball Glass

Shake all but Club Soda with ice and strain into the glass. Top with Club Soda.

Viva Zapata
2 parts Tequila Reposado
1/2 part Kiwi Liqueur
1/2 part Fresh Lime Juice
1/4 part Simple Syrup
fill with Club Soda
Collins Glass

Shake all but Club Soda with ice and strain into the glass. Top with Club Soda.

Vodka Cooler
2 parts Vodka
dash Powdered Sugar
fill with Carbonated Water
Collins Glass

Build over ice and stir

Vodka Highball
2 parts Vodka
1/2 part Dry Vermouth
fill with Ginger Ale
Old-Fashioned Glass

Build over ice and stir

Vodka Rickey
2 parts Vodka
1/2 part Sweetened Lime Juice
fill with Club Soda
Highball Glass

Build over ice and stir

Walk the Dog
2 parts Rye Whiskey
fill with Club Soda
Highball Glass

Build over ice and stir

Wasp
1 part Vodka
1 part Banana Liqueur
fill with Ginger Ale
Collins Glass

Build over ice and stir

Whirlaway
1 part Blue Curaçao
dash Bitters
fill with Club Soda
Highball Glass

Build over ice and stir

Whirlpool
1 part Dark Rum
1/2 part Strawberry Liqueur
fill with Ginger Ale
Old-Fashioned Glass

Build over ice and stir

Whiskey Cooler
2 parts Whiskey
fill with Lemon-Lime Soda
Highball Glass

Build over ice and stir

White Cactus
1 part Tequila Silver
1/2 part Lime Cordial
fill with Club Soda
Old-Fashioned Glass

Build over ice and stir

Wild at Heart
1 part Brandy
1 part Vodka
1 part Triple Sec
1 part Gin
fill with Ginger Ale
Collins Glass

Build over ice and stir

Wild Kiwi
1 part Light Rum
1 1/2 parts Kiwi Schnapps
fill with Tonic Water
Collins Glass

Build over ice and stir

Wild-Eyed Rose

2 1/2 parts Whiskey
1 part Grenadine
1/2 part Fresh Lime Juice
fill with Club Soda
Collins Glass

Build over ice and stir

Wrench

1 part Canadian Whiskey
fill with Ginger Ale
splash Orange Juice
Highball Glass

Build over ice and stir

Yazoo

2 parts Coconut-Flavored Liqueur
2 parts Safari®
fill with Club Soda
Collins Glass

Build over ice and stir

Yellow Seersucker

2 parts Light Rum
1 part Lemon Juice
2 splashes Grenadine
fill with Tonic Water
Highball Glass

Shake all but Tonic Water with ice and strain into the glass. Top with Tonic Water.

Yodel

1 part Fernet-Branca®
1 part Orange Juice
fill with Club Soda
Old-Fashioned Glass

Build over ice and stir

Yukon Icee

2 parts Yukon Jack®
fill with Ginger Ale
Collins Glass

Build over ice and stir

Zanzibar Cooler

2 parts Vodka
1 part Peach Liqueur
dash Brown Sugar
fill with Ginger Ale
Collins Glass

Build over ice and stir

Zenith

2 1/2 parts Gin
1 part Pineapple Juice
fill with Club Soda
Old-Fashioned Glass

Build over ice and stir

Tall Drinks

Drinks that are served in a tall glass that don't fit into any other category fall into this "catch-all" category of tall drinks.

007

1 part Orange-Flavored Vodka
1 part Lemon-Lime Soda
1 part Orange Juice
Collins Glass

Mix with ice

187 Urge

1 part Jack Daniel's®
1 part Vodka
fill with Dr Pepper®
Collins Glass

Mix with ice

2001

1/2 part Apricot Brandy
1/2 part Crème de Cassis
2 parts Pineapple Juice
1 part Rum
Collins Glass

Mix with ice

319 Special

1 part Vodka
1 part Orange Juice
1 part Lemon-Lime Soda
splash Lime Juice
Collins Glass

Mix with ice

.357 Magnum

1 part Vodka
1 part Spiced Rum
fill with Lemon-Lime Soda
1 1/2 parts Amaretto
Collins Glass

Mix with ice and float Amaretto on top

3 A.M. on a School Night

2 parts Wild Turkey® Bourbon
fill with Fruit Punch
Collins Glass

Mix with ice

435 French

1 part Citrus-Flavored Rum
2 parts Lemon-Lime Soda
2 parts Cranberry-Raspberry Juice
Collins Glass

Mix with ice

The 5th Element

1/2 part 151-Proof Rum
1/2 part Southern Comfort®
1/2 part Vodka
1 part Pineapple Juice
1 part Lemon-Lime Soda
Beer Mug

Build over ice and stir

Tall Drinks

50/50

2 1/2 parts Vanilla-Flavored Vodka
splash Grand Marnier®
fill with Orange Juice
Collins Glass

Build over ice and stir

500 Proof

1/2 part Vodka
1/2 part Southern Comfort®
1/2 part Bourbon
1/2 part 151-Proof Rum
1 part Orange Juice
1/2 part Simple Syrup
Collins Glass

Shake with ice and strain over ice

501 Blues

1 part Lemon-Lime Soda
1 part Blue Curaçao
1 part Blueberry Schnapps
1/2 part Club Soda
Collins Glass

Shake with ice and strain over ice

'57 Chevy® (In Ohio)

1 part Amaretto
1 part Sloe Gin
1 part Southern Comfort®
splash Grapefruit Juice
fill with Cranberry Juice Cocktail
Hurricane Glass

Shake with ice and strain over ice

'57 T-Bird with Florida Plates

1 part Vodka
1 part Amaretto
1 part Grand Marnier®
fill with Orange Juice
Collins Glass

Build over ice and stir

612 Delight

1 part Vodka
1 part Diet Lemonade
fill with Cola
Collins Glass

Build over ice and stir

7&7

2 parts Seagram's® 7 Whiskey
fill with 7-Up®
Collins Glass

Build over ice

A&W Ryebeer

1 part A & W® Root Beer
1 part Crown Royal® Whiskey
Beer Mug

Mix with ice

A Capella

1 part Blue Curaçao
1 part Grapefruit Juice
1/2 part Fresh Lime Juice
fill with Tonic Water
Collins Glass

Shake all but Tonic with ice and strain into a Collins Glass filled with ice. Fill with Tonic.

Aaron Insanity

1 part Jägermeister®
1/4 part Triple Sec
1/2 part Cachaça
fill with Lemonade
Collins Glass

Build over ice and stir

The Abba
2 parts Citrus-Flavored Vodka
fill with Lemon-Lime Soda
Collins Glass

Build over ice and stir

Abbie Dabbie
2 parts Vodka
2 parts Melon Liqueur
3 parts Apple Juice
Collins Glass

Build over ice and stir

Abe Froman
3 parts Vodka
1/2 part Grenadine
fill with Lemonade
Collins Glass

Build over ice and stir

A-Bomb
2 parts Tequila
1 part Vodka
3 parts Root Beer Schnapps
fill with Root Beer
1 scoop Ice Cream
Beer Mug

Combine all but Ice Cream in a large beer mug over ice and stir. Top with a scoop of Ice Cream and drizzle Root Beer Schnapps over the top.

Absinthe Curaçao Frappé
1 part Blue Curaçao
2 parts Absinthe
1 part Orange Juice
splash Lemon Juice
Collins Glass

Shake with ice and strain over ice

Abso Bloody Lutly
1 1/2 parts Absolut® Vodka
4 parts Tomato Juice
splash Worchestershire Sauce
dash Horseradish
Collins Glass

Shake with ice and strain over ice

Absolut® Apple
1 part Absolut® Vodka
1 part Sour Apple Schnapps
3 parts Lemon-Lime Soda
3 parts Apple Juice
Collins Glass

Build over ice and stir

Absolut® Can Dew
2 parts Vodka
1 part Blue Curaçao
1/2 parts Mountain Dew®
Collins Glass

Build over ice and stir

Absolut® Hollywood
1 1/2 parts Vodka
1 part Raspberry Liqueur
fill with Pineapple Juice
Collins Glass

Build over ice and stir

Absolut® Lemonade
1 part Citrus-Flavored Vodka
1 part Amaretto
splash Sour Mix
splash Lemon-Lime Soda
Collins Glass

Build over ice and stir

Absolut® Nothing
1 part Vodka
fill with Lemon-Lime Soda
Collins Glass

Build over ice and stir

Absolut® Orgasm

2 parts Vodka
1 part Triple Sec
fill with Lemon-Lime Soda
1 part Sour Mix
Collins Glass

Build over ice and stir

Absolut® Power Juice

2 parts Vodka
2 parts Peach Schnapps
1 part Raspberry Liqueur
1 part Lemonade
Collins Glass

Build over ice and stir

Absolut® Russian

1 part Vodka
3 parts Tonic Water
splash Currant Syrup
Collins Glass

Build over ice and stir

Absolut® Slut

1 part Vodka
2 parts Orange Juice
2 parts Pineapple Juice
Collins Glass

Build over ice and stir

Absolut® Stress

1/2 part Vodka
1/2 part Coconut-Flavored Rum
1/2 part Peach Schnapps
1 part Orange Juice
1 part Pineapple Juice
1 part Cranberry Juice Cocktail
Collins Glass

Build over ice and stir

Absolut® Summer

1 1/2 parts Citrus-Flavored Vodka
2/3 part Blue Curaçao
3 parts Grapefruit Juice
3 parts Orange Juice
Collins Glass

Build over ice and stir

Absolut® Summertime

1 1/2 parts Citrus-Flavored Vodka
3/4 part Sour Mix
1/2 part Lemon-Lime Soda
3 parts Club Soda
1 Lemon Wedge
Collins Glass

Shake with ice and strain over ice

Absolut® Viking

1 part Currant-Flavored Vodka
1 part Crème de Cassis
fill with Ginger Ale
Collins Glass

Build over ice and stir

Absolutly Horny

1 part 99-proof Banana Liqueur
1 part Crown Royal® Whiskey
1 part Peach Schnapps
1 part Vodka
1 1/2 parts Cranberry Juice Cocktail
1 1/2 parts Pineapple Juice
Collins Glass

Build over ice and stir

Acapulco Blue

1 1/2 parts Tequila Silver
3/4 part Blue Curaçao
1/2 part Simple Syrup
fill with Lemon-Lime Soda
Collins Glass

Build over ice and stir

Acapulco Blue #2

1 1/2 parts Tequila Silver
2/3 part Blue Curaçao
1/2 part Simple Syrup
1 1/2 parts Lemon Juice
Collins Glass

Shake with ice and strain over ice

Acapulco Gold

1/2 part Tequila Silver
1/2 part Rum
1/2 part Crème de Cacao (Dark)
1/2 part Grapefruit Juice
1 part Pineapple Juice
Collins Glass

Build over ice and stir

Ace

1 part Vodka
1 part Rum
2 parts Pineapple Juice
2 parts Orange Juice
1 part Fresh Lime Juice
1/2 part Grenadine
1/2 part Sugar
Hurricane Glass

Shake with ice and strain over ice

Acid Banana

1/2 part Crème de Banana
1/2 part Pisang Ambon® Liqueur
1/2 part Sour Apple Schnapps
3 parts Lemon-Lime Soda
1 part Grape Juice (White)
Collins Glass

Shake with ice and strain over ice

Adam's Bomb

2 parts Gin
1 part Jägermeister®
3 parts Gatorade®
4 parts Orange Juice
4 parts Club Soda
Collins Glass

Build over ice and stir

Adam's Hawaiian Monster

1 part Rum
1 part Banana Liqueur
1 part Peach Schnapps
fill with Pineapple Juice
Collins Glass

Build over ice and stir

Addington

1 part Dry Vermouth
1 part Sweet Vermouth
fill with Club Soda
Collins Glass

Build over ice and stir

Adelle's Delight

1 part Apple Juice
1 part Hard Apple Cider
1 part Ginger Ale
fill with Rum
Collins Glass

Build over ice and stir

Adios

1 part Dry Gin
1 part Vodka
1 part Rum
1 part Blue Curaçao
1 part Sour Mix
fill with Lemonade
Collins Glass

Build over ice and stir

Adios Mother

1 part Vodka
1 part Gin
1 part Light Rum
1 part Blue Curaçao
2 parts Sour Mix
fill with Lemon-Lime Soda
Hurricane Glass

Build over ice and stir

Adrienne's Dream

2 parts Brandy
1/2 part Crème de Cacao (White)
1/2 part Peppermint Schnapps
1 1/2 parts Club Soda
1/2 part Lemon Juice
dash Sugar
Collins Glass

Shake with ice and strain over ice

Adult Kool-Aid®

1 part Amaretto
1 part Grenadine
1 part Melon Liqueur
2 parts Pineapple Juice
1 1/2 parts Sour Mix
Collins Glass

Build over ice and stir

African Knight

1 part Orange Liqueur
1 part Dark Rum
2 parts Banana Puree
splash Lime Juice
2 parts Mango Juice
Collins Glass

Shake with ice and strain

African Queen

2 parts Crème de Banana
1 part Triple Sec
fill with Orange Juice
Collins Glass

Build over ice and stir

After Party

1 part Vodka
2 parts Pineapple Juice
2 parts Cranberry Juice Cocktail
2 parts Ginger Ale
dash Sugar
Collins Glass

Build over ice and stir

Aftershock

1 part Drambuie®
1 part Coconut-Flavored Rum
1 part Cherry Brandy
fill with Lemonade
Collins Glass

Shake with ice and strain over ice

Agavalada

1 1/2 parts Agavero®
1 part Jamaican Rum
fill with Pineapple Juice
3/4 part Crème de Coconut
1 Pineapple Slice
1 Maraschino Cherry
Collins Glass

Shake with ice and strain over ice

Agave's Cup

1 3/4 parts Tequila Silver
3/4 part Crème de Menthe (Green)
1 part Sour Mix
2 parts Club Soda
Collins Glass

Build over ice and stir

Agent Orange

1 part Vodka
1 part Rum
1 part Gin
1 part Southern Comfort®
1 part Yukon Jack®
1 part Sour Apple Schnapps
1 part Melon Liqueur
fill with Orange Juice
splash Grenadine
Collins Glass

Build over ice and stir

Agent G

1 part Vodka
1 part Rum
1 part Gin
1 part Southern Comfort®
1 part Yukon Jack®
2 parts Grenadine
fill with Grapefruit Juice
Collins Glass

Build over ice and stir

Aggie Punch

2 parts Tequila
splash Lime Juice
fill with Apple-Cranberry Juice
Collins Glass

Build over ice and stir

AK-47

1 part Sour Apple Schnapps
1 part Rum
1 part Sambuca
1 part Tequila
1 part Tia Maria®
Collins Glass

Build over ice and stir

Alabama Riot

2 parts Southern Comfort®
1 part Peppermint Schnapps
1 part Vodka
fill with Fruit Punch
1 part Lime Juice
Collins Glass

Shake with ice and strain over ice

Alabama Slammer

1 part Southern Comfort®
1 part Amaretto
1 part Grenadine
6 parts Orange Juice
6 parts Pineapple Juice
Collins Glass

Shake with ice and strain over ice

Alamo Splash

1 1/2 parts Tequila
1 part Orange Juice
1/2 part Pineapple Juice
splash Lemon-Lime Soda
Collins Glass

Shake with ice and strain over ice

Alaska White

2 parts Tequila
2 parts Vodka
1 part Gin
1 part Sambuca
fill with Lemon-Lime Soda
Collins Glass

Build over ice and stir

Albemarle Fizz

2 parts Gin
splash Raspberry Liqueur
1/2 part Raspberry Syrup
3 parts Sparkling Water
Collins Glass

Shake with ice, strain over ice, and top with Sparkling Water

Alcudia
2 parts Pineapple Juice
1 part Cream
1 part Crème de Banana
1/2 part Amaretto
1/2 part Grenadine
Hurricane Glass

Shake with ice and strain over ice

Aleluia
2 parts Tequila Silver
1 part Blue Curaçao
1 part Maraschino Liqueur
Collins Glass

Shake with ice and strain over ice

Alexandra
1 Tia Maria®
1 Cream
1 Rum
1 Coconut Cream
Collins Glass

Build over ice and stir

Alex's Super Stinger
1 part Honey
3 parts Rum
3 parts Vodka
fill with Apple Juice
Collins Glass

Build over ice and stir

Ali Baba
1 part Crème de Cacao (White)
1 part Peppermint Liqueur
1 part Frangelico®
1 part Cream
Collins Glass

Shake with ice and strain

Alice Milkshake
2 parts Pineapple Juice
2 parts Orange Juice
1/2 part Cream
1/2 part Cherry Syrup
Collins Glass

Build over ice and stir

Alien Urine
1 part Coconut-Flavored Rum
1/2 part Melon Liqueur
1/2 part Peach Schnapps
1 part Sour Mix
1 part Orange Juice
Collins Glass

Shake with ice and strain over ice

All Night Long
1/2 part Vodka
1/2 part Coconut-Flavored Rum
1/2 part Coffee Liqueur
1/2 part Crème de Cacao (White)
4 parts Pineapple Juice
2 parts Sour Mix
Hurricane Glass

Shake with ice and strain over ice

Almond Soda
2 parts Amaretto
fill with Cream Soda
Collins Glass

Build over ice and stir

Almost Alcoholic
3 parts Orange Juice
1 1/2 parts Light Rum
1 part Blue Curaçao
1 part Pisang Ambon® Liqueur
Hurricane Glass

Shake with ice and strain over ice

Almost Heaven

1 part Currant-Flavored Vodka
3 part Amaretto
3 part Raspberry Liqueur
splash Pineapple Juice
splash Cranberry Juice Cocktail
Collins Glass

Shake with ice and strain over ice

Aloha Joe

1 part Dark Rum
1 part Peach Schnapps
1/2 part Almond Syrup
splash Goldschläger®
fill with Passion Fruit Juice
Collins Glass

Build over ice and stir

Amando IV

1 1/2 parts Citrus-Flavored Vodka
2/3 part Blue Curaçao
2 parts Orange Juice
1 part Lemon Juice
splash Simple Syrup
Collins Glass

Shake with ice and strain over ice

Amaretto Backflip

1 part Amaretto
2 parts Lemon-Lime Soda
2 parts Lemonade
splash Sour Mix
Collins Glass

Build over ice and stir

Amaretto Cheesecake

2 parts Amaretto
1 part Chocolate Syrup
fill with Milk
Collins Glass

Build in the glass with no ice and stir

Amaretto Fizz

3 parts Orange Juice
2 parts Lemonade
1 1/2 parts Amaretto
fill with Lemon-Lime Soda
Collins Glass

Build over ice and stir

Amaretto Stiletto

2 parts Amaretto
1 part Vodka
1 part Lemon-Lime Soda
1 part Lime Juice
1 part Sour Mix
Collins Glass

Build over ice and stir

Amaretto Stone Sweet

1 1/2 parts Amaretto
1 part Cherry Syrup
2 parts Orange Juice
fill with Lemon-Lime Soda
Collins Glass

Build over ice and stir

Amaretto Vodka Collins

1 part Vodka
1 part Amarctto
1/2 Sour Mix
fill with Lemon-Lime Soda
Collins Glass

Build over ice and stir

Amarissimo

2 parts Dry Gin
1 part Triple Sec
2 parts Orange Juice
dash Bitters
Collins Glass

Shake with ice and strain over ice

Amarita
2 parts Amaretto
fill with Margarita Mix
Collins Glass

Shake with ice and strain over ice

Amaya
1 part Vodka
1 part Apricot Brandy
1/2 part Grenadine
1/2 part Passion Fruit Nectar
2 parts Orange Juice
Hurricane Glass

Shake with ice and strain over ice

Amazing Pepper
2 parts Amaretto
1 part Vodka
fill with Cola
Collins Glass

Build over ice and stir

Ambulance
2 parts Vodka
1 part Coffee Liqueur
1 1/2 parts Coffee
fill with Cola
Collins Glass

Build over ice and stir

Amelia Airhart
2 parts Gin
1 part Apricot Brandy
splash Triple Sec
splash Grenadine
1/2 part Lemon Juice
1/2 part Orange Juice
dash Sugar
Collins Glass

Build over ice and stir

Amigos Para Siempre
1 part Citrus-Flavored Rum
1 part Coconut-Flavored Liqueur
splash Grenadine
splash Cream
fill with Pineapple Juice
Collins Glass

Shake with ice and strain over ice

Amor a la Mexicana
1 1/2 parts Coffee Liqueur
1/2 part Tequila Silver
1/4 part Vanilla Liqueur
1/4 part Simple Syrup
fill with Milk
Collins Glass

Build over ice and stir

Amore Mio
1 1/2 parts Dark Rum
1/2 part Maraschino Liqueur
fill with Orange Juice
splash Grenadine
Collins Glass

Build over ice and stir

Amorosae
1 part Parfait Amour
1 part Vodka
splash Crème de Cassis
splash Lime Juice
fill with Lemon-Lime Soda
Collins Glass

Shake with ice and strain over ice

Amy's Tattoo
1/2 part Dark Rum
1/2 part Light Rum
2 parts Pineapple Juice
2 parts Orange Juice
splash Grenadine
Collins Glass

Shake with ice and pour

Anamer
1 part Dark Rum
1/2 part Triple Sec
1/2 part Apricot Brandy
fill with Pineapple Juice
Collins Glass

Build over ice and stir

Ananas Exotic
1 part Light Rum
1/2 part Cherry Brandy
fill with Pineapple Juice
Collins Glass

Build over ice and stir

Anastavia
1 part Vodka
splash Triple Sec
splash Grenadine
1 part Orange Juice
splash Lemon Juice
Collins Glass

Shake with ice and pour

Andees Candees Magical Mix
2 parts Prepared Mudslide Mix
1 part Peppermint Schnapps
fill with Milk
Collins Glass

Build over ice and stir

Andersson
1 part Vodka
1 part Melon Liqueur
fill with Milk
Collins Glass

Build over ice and stir

Andes® Mint
1 1/2 parts Peppermint Schnapps
fill with Cola
Collins Glass

Build over ice and stir

Andrea
1 1/2 parts Blue Curaçao
fill with Orange Juice
splash Amaretto
Collins Glass

Shake with ice and strain over ice

Andy Pandy
1 part Vodka
1 part Peach Schnapps
1 part Blue Curaçao
1 part Lemonade
1 part Orange Juice
Collins Glass

Build over ice and stir

Angel Affinity
2 parts Raspberry Liqueur
1/2 part Blackberry Liqueur
2 parts Coconut Cream
fill with Milk
Collins Glass

Blend ingredients with crushed ice

Angel's Milk
4 parts Raspberry Liqueur
2 parts Peach Juice
1 Egg
1/2 part Amaretto
Collins Glass

Shake with ice and pour

Angry Chameleon
2 parts Light Rum
2 tsp Cherry Kool-Aid® granules
fill with Mountain Dew®
Beer Mug

Dissolve Kool-Aid® in Rum and add Mountain Dew®

Anna's Wish
1 part Dark Rum
1/2 part Triple Sec
fill with Pineapple Juice
Collins Glass

Build over ice and stir

Anne's Black Rose
1 part 100-Proof Blackberry Schnapps
fill with Sour Mix
splash Cherry Juice
Collins Glass

Build over ice and stir

Anon
2 parts Light Rum
1 part Melon Liqueur
1 part Coconut-Flavored Liqueur
1 part Apple Brandy
1 part Pineapple Juice
1 part Apple Juice
Collins Glass

Build over ice and stir

Anti-Acrtic
1 1/2 parts Citrus-Flavored Vodka
1/2 part Triple Sec
fill with Iced Tea
Collins Glass

Shake with ice and pour

Anu
1 part Apricot Brandy
1/2 part Dry Vermouth
1/2 part Triple Sec
fill with Lemonade
Collins Glass

Build over ice and stir

Aphrodite's Love Potion
1 1/2 parts Metaxa®
dash Angostura® Bitters
fill with Pineapple Juice
1 Maraschino Cherry
1 Orange Slice
Collins Glass

Shake with ice and strain over ice

Apple Cider Surprise
2 parts Vodka
1 part Apple Juice
1 part Ginger Ale
Collins Glass

Build over ice and stir

Apple Cola
1 part Triple Sec
1 part Apple Liqueur
fill with Cola
Collins Glass

Build over ice and stir

Apple Knocker

$1^1/_2$ parts Vodka
splash Lemon Juice
splash Strawberry Liqueur
fill with Apple Cider
Collins Glass

Shake with ice and strain over ice

Apple Rancher

$^1/_2$ part Blue Curaçao
$^2/_3$ part Melon Liqueur
$^2/_3$ part Peach Schnapps
fill with Sour Mix
splash Orange Juice
Collins Glass

Shake with ice and pour

Apple to the 3rd Power

1 part Rum
1 part Cranberry Liqueur
2 parts Lemon-Lime Soda
$1^1/_2$ parts Apple Juice
Collins Glass

Build over ice and stir

Apple-Dew

1 part Apple Liqueur
1 part Vodka
fill with Mountain Dew®
Collins Glass

Build over ice and stir

Applehawk

2 parts Apple Brandy
fill with Grape Soda
splash Simple Syrup
Collins Glass

Build over ice and stir

Apple-Snake Nuts

1 part Vodka
1 part Amaretto
1 part Sour Apple Schnapps
1 part Triple Sec
splash Sweetened Lime Juice
Collins Glass

Shake with ice and pour

Apricanza

1 part Vodka
$^1/_2$ part Apricot Brandy
fill with Lemon-Lime Soda
splash Grenadine
Collins Glass

Build over ice and stir

Apricot Anise Collins

$^1/_2$ part Apricot Brandy
$1^1/_2$ parts Gin
2 splashes Anisette
1 part Lemon Juice
fill with Carbonated Water
1 Lemon Slice
Collins Glass

Build over ice and stir

Apricot Brandy Sour

1 part Apricot Brandy
1 part Lemon Juice
fill with Orange Juice
Collins Glass

Shake with ice and pour

Apricot Dandy

2 parts Light Rum
1 part Crème de Banana
1 part Apricot Brandy
splash Grenadine
splash Apricot Juice
Collins Glass

Shake with ice and pour

Apricot Fiesta
1 part Cherry Brandy
3 parts Grapefruit Juice
2 parts Orange Juice
splash Simple Syrup
Collins Glass
Shake with ice and pour

Apricot Girl
1 1/2 parts Rum
1 part Triple Sec
fill with Apricot Juice
1 Egg White
Collins Glass
Shake with ice and pour

April's Apple
1 part Sour Apple Schnapps
1 part Grenadine
fill with Lemonade
Collins Glass
Build over ice and stir

Aquamarine
1 part Vodka
1/2 part Peach Schnapps
splash Blue Curaçao
splash Triple Sec
fill with Apple Juice
Collins Glass
Build over ice and stir

Arbogast
1 part Vodka
1/2 part Rumple Minze®
1/2 part Coffee Liqueur
1/2 part Irish Cream Liqueur
fill with Milk
Collins Glass
Shake with ice and pour

Arcadian Lovemaker
1 part Citrus-Flavored Vodka
1 part Sloe Gin
1 part Southern Comfort®
1 part Orange Juice
Collins Glass
Shake with ice and pour

Arctic
1 part Blue Curaçao
1/2 part Crème de Menthe (White)
1/2 part Triple Sec
splash Lime Juice
fill with Lemon-Lime Soda
Collins Glass
Build over ice and stir

Arctic Circle
2 parts Vodka
1 part Lime Juice
3 parts Ginger Ale
Collins Glass
Build over ice and stir

Arctic Sunset
1 part Rye Whiskey
1 part Peppermint Schnapps
fill with Cranberry Juice Cocktail
2 parts Orange Juice
Collins Glass
Build over ice

Arriba Arriba
1 1/2 parts Dark Rum
1 part Crème de Banana
fill with Lemon-Lime Soda
Collins Glass
Build over ice and stir

Ashtray
1 part Vodka
1 part Blavod® Black Vodka
1 1/2 parts Blackberry Liqueur
2 parts Milk
2 parts Blackberry Juice
Collins Glass

Shake with ice and pour

Assassin
1 part Lemon-Flavored Rum
1 part Citrus-Flavored Vodka
1 part Lemon-Lime Soda
1 part Orange Juice
Collins Glass

Build over ice and stir

ASU Girls
1 1/2 parts Vodka
1/2 part Peach Schnapps
fill with Pineapple Juice
Collins Glass

Build over ice and stir

Atlantico
1 part Blue Curaçao
2 parts Grapefruit Juice
2 parts Passion Fruit Juice
1 1/2 parts Banana Juice
Collins Glass

Build over ice and stir

Atomic Dog
1 part Light Rum
1/2 part Melon Liqueur
1/2 part Coconut-Flavored Liqueur
fill with Pineapple Juice
Collins Glass

Shake with ice and pour

Atomic Kool-Aid®
1/2 part Melon Liqueur
1/2 part Vodka
1/2 part Amaretto
splash Grenadine
1 part Orange Juice
1 part Pineapple Juice
Collins Glass

Shake with ice and pour

Atomic Lokade
1 part Vodka
1/2 part Blue Curaçao
1/2 part Triple Sec
fill with Lemonade
Collins Glass

Build over ice and stir

Atomic Shit
1 part Vodka
1 part Grapefruit Juice
fill with Lemonade
splash Jack Daniel's®
Collins Glass

Build over ice and stir

Attitude
1 part Amaretto
1 part Southern Comfort®
1 part Lemon-Flavored Vodka
1 part Melon Liqueur
1/2 part Sloe Gin
fill with Orange Juice
splash Cranberry Juice Cocktail
Hurricane Glass

Shake with ice and pour

Attitude Adjustment
1 part Vodka
1 part Gin
1 part Triple Sec
1 part Amaretto
1 part Peach Schnapps
1 part Sour Mix
splash Cranberry Juice Cocktail
Collins Glass

Shake with ice and strain over ice

Authentic Shut the Hell Up
1 part 151-Proof Rum
1 part Southern Comfort®
1 part Tequila
fill with Cranberry Juice Cocktail
Collins Glass

Shake with ice and pour

Autumn Day
1 part Rum
1 part Orange Juice
1 part Grape Juice (Red)
Collins Glass

Build over ice and stir

Avalon
3 parts Vodka
1 part Pisang Ambon® Liqueur
1 1/2 parts Lemon Juice
fill with Apple Juice
Collins Glass

Build over ice and stir

Aviator Fuel
1 part Vodka
1 part Lemonade
1 part Lemon-Lime Soda
Collins Glass

Build over ice and stir

Azteken Punch
1 1/2 parts Pineapple Juice
1 part Vodka
1 part Crème de Cacao (Dark)
fill with Orange Juice
Collins Glass

Build over ice and stir

Azurro
1 1/2 parts Pineapple Juice
1 1/2 parts Passion Fruit Juice
1 part Blue Curaçao
1 part Pisang Ambon® Liqueur
1 part Safari®
Collins Glass

Shake with ice and strain over ice

Bacardi® Gold
1 1/2 parts Dark Rum
fill with Cola
1 Lemon Slice
Collins Glass

Build over ice and stir

Bac Bug
1/2 part Light Rum
1/2 part Crème de Banana
1/2 part Coconut-Flavored Rum
1 1/2 parts Sour Mix
fill with Pineapple Juice
Collins Glass

Shake with ice and strain over ice

Bacio & Kiss
1 part Vodka
splash Lychee Liqueur
splash Peach Schnapps
2 parts Grapefruit Juice
2 parts Cranberry Juice Cocktail
Collins Glass

Shake with ice and strain over ice

Bad Attitude
1/2 part Rum
1/2 part Vodka
1/2 part Gin
1/2 part Tequila
1/2 part Triple Sec
1 part Amaretto
1 part Pineapple Juice
1 part Orange Juice
1 part Cranberry Juice Cocktail
splash Grenadine
Collins Glass

Build over ice and stir

Bad North Disaster
1 part Tequila
1 part Triple Sec
fill with Lemon-Lime Soda
splash Lime Juice
splash Lemon Juice
Beer Mug

Build over ice and stir

Bahama Mama
1/2 part Coffee-Flavored Vodka
1 part Dark Rum
1 part Coconut-Flavored Rum
1 part Lemon Juice
fill with Pineapple Juice
splash 151-Proof Rum
Collins Glass

Build over ice and stir

Bahama Todd
1 part Light Rum
1 part Dark Rum
1 part Spiced Rum
1 part Coconut-Flavored Rum
1 part 151-Proof Rum
1 part Blue Curaçao
fill with Pineapple Juice
Collins Glass

Shake with ice and pour

Bahia
1 part Light Rum
1 part Pineapple Juice
1 part Coconut Cream
3/4 part Triple Sec
Collins Glass

Shake with ice and pour

Bahia de Plata
1 part Dark Rum
1 part Vodka
1 part Triple Sec
fill with Pineapple Juice
splash Grenadine
Collins Glass

Build over ice and stir

Baja Mar
1 1/2 parts Dark Rum
1/4 part Vodka
1/4 part Crème de Banana
fill with Orange Juice
splash Grenadine
Collins Glass

Build over ice and stir

Ballet Russe
1 1/2 parts Vodka
1/2 part Crème de Cassis
3 parts Sour Mix
Collins Glass

Shake with ice and pour

Balmy Days
3/4 part Coffee Liqueur
1 part Spiced Rum
fill with Fruit Juice
Collins Glass

Build over ice and stir

Balou
1 part Pisang Ambon® Liqueur
1 part Dry Gin
1 part Apricot Brandy
2 parts Orange Juice
Collins Glass

Shake with ice and strain over ice

Baltic
1 part Vodka
1/2 part Passion Fruit Juice
splash Blue Curaçao
fill with Orange Juice
Collins Glass

Build over ice and stir

Baltic Murder Mystery
1 part Vodka
1 part Crème de Cassis
fill with Lemon-Lime Soda
Collins Glass

Build over ice and stir

Baltic Sea Breeze
1 1/2 parts Grapefruit Juice
1 part Apple Liqueur
1 part Cranberry-Flavored Vodka
1/2 part Melon Liqueur
Collins Glass

Build over ice and stir

Baltimore Egg Nog
1 part Jamaican Rum
1 part Brandy
1 part Madeira
1 Whole Egg
dash Powdered Sugar
1 part Milk
Collins Glass

Shake with ice and strain

Baltimore Zoo
1 part Vodka
1 part Rum
1 part Tequila
1 part Triple Sec
1 part Sweetened Lime Juice
1 part Grenadine
1 part Sour Mix
1 part Root Beer
1 part 151-Proof Rum
Collins Glass

Build over ice and stir

Bam-Bam Special
1 part Rumple Minze®
1 part Cola
Collins Glass

Build over ice and stir

Bambola Hawaiana
1 part Rum
1 part Grape Juice (White)
1/2 part Cherry Brandy
1 part Pineapple Juice
1/2 part Grenadine
1/2 part Vanilla Syrup
Collins Glass

Build over ice and stir

Bamby
1 part Dark Rum
1 part Vodka
1 part Crème de Menthe (Green)
1 part Crème de Banana
fill with Pineapple Juice
Collins Glass

Build over ice and stir

Banana Coffee
2 parts Banana Juice
1 1/2 parts Orange Juice
1 part Coffee
1 part Crème de Banana
1 part Cognac
Collins Glass

Shake with ice and strain over ice

Banana Cool

1 part Blue Curaçao
1 part Crème de Banana
fill with Orange Juice
Collins Glass

Build over ice and stir

Banana Rama

1 part Vodka
1 part Banana Liqueur
1/2 part Coconut-Flavored Rum
fill with Milk
Collins Glass

Build over ice and stir

Bananarita

1 part Crème de Banana
2 parts Gold Tequila
splash Blue Curaçao
splash Lime Juice
splash Banana Juice
Margarita Glass

Shake with ice and strain over ice

Bananes Royalle

1 1/2 parts Crème de Banana
1/2 part Light Rum
fill with Pineapple Juice
Collins Glass

Build over ice and stir

Banoffee Milkshake

1 part Banana Liqueur
1 part Butterscotch Schnapps
fill with Milk
Collins Glass

Shake with ice and pour

The Bantam

2 parts Jack Daniel's®
1 part Coconut-Flavored Rum
fill with Cola
Collins Glass

Build over ice and stir

Barbarian

2 splashes Grenadine
splash Lime Juice
1 part Tequila
1 part Pineapple Juice
Collins Glass

Build over ice and stir

Barbie®

1 part Gin
1 part Vodka
fill with Lime Soda
splash Grenadine
Collins Glass

Build over ice and stir

Barbisonia

1 part Dark Rum
1/2 part Cherry Brandy
1/2 part Ponche Kuba®
fill with Orange Juice
splash Grenadine
Collins Glass

Build over ice and stir

Baretto Juice

1 part Light Rum
3/4 part Amaretto
fill with Pineapple Juice
Collins Glass

Build over ice and stir

Barlin McNabbsmith
4 parts Jack Daniel's®
3 parts Scotch
2 parts Molasses
1 part Bitters
Collins Glass

Shake with ice and strain over ice

Barney's® Revenge
1 part Vodka
1 part Blue Curaçao
splash Apricot Brandy
fill with Raspberry-Flavored Seltzer
Collins Glass

Build over ice and stir

Barnstormer
1 1/2 parts Whiskey
1/2 part Peppermint Schnapps
2 splashes Crème de Cacao (Dark)
1/2 part Lemon Juice
Collins Glass

Build over ice and stir

Baron Samedi
1 1/2 parts Dry Gin
1/2 part Cherry Brandy
3 parts Ginger Ale
2 parts Orange Juice
Collins Glass

Build over ice and stir

Barracuda
2 parts Vodka
2 parts Grapefruit Juice
1 part Tonic Water
Collins Glass

Build over ice and stir

Bartender in a Cup
2 parts Vodka
1 part Triple Sec
1 part Pineapple Juice
1 part Orange Juice
1 part Sour Mix
1 part Grenadine
Collins Glass

Shake with ice and pour

Barton's
1 1/2 parts Calvados Apple Brandy
splash Gin
splash Orange Liqueur
splash Scotch
2 parts Ginger Ale
Collins Glass

Shake with ice and strain over ice

Baseball Pleasure
2 parts Vodka
1 1/2 parts Whiskey
1 1/2 parts Amaretto
fill with Orange Juice
Collins Glass

Build over ice and stir

Bay of Passion
1 part Vodka
2 parts Pineapple Juice
1 part Passion Fruit Liqueur
Collins Glass

Build over ice and stir

Bayou Backwater
2 parts Southern Comfort®
fill with Lemonade
Collins Glass

Build over ice and stir

Bayou Self
1 part Spiced Rum
1 part Butterscotch Schnapps
fill with Pineapple Juice
splash Grenadine
Collins Glass

Build over ice and stir

Bazooka Bull
1 part Blue Curaçao
1 part Crème de Banana
fill with Red Bull® Energy Drink
Collins Glass

Build over ice and stir

B-Bob
1½ parts Peach Schnapps
1 part Dark Rum
1 part Grenadine
1 part Fresh Lime Juice
fill with Orange Juice
Hurricane Glass

Build over ice and stir

Beakers Blue
1 part Citrus-Flavored Rum
1 part Blue Curaçao
1 part Triple Sec
splash Lemon-Lime Soda
splash Sour Mix
Hurricane Glass

Shake with ice and pour

Beam & Cream
1½ parts Jim Beam®
fill with Cream Soda
Collins Glass

Build over ice and stir

Beam Me Up
1 part Jim Beam®
1 part Amaretto
fill with Cola
Collins Glass

Build over ice and stir

Bean's Blast
1 part Blackberry Liqueur
2 parts Coffee Liqueur
1½ parts Cognac
fill with Milk
Collins Glass

Build over ice and stir

The Beatle
1 part Scotch
fill with Cola
Collins Glass

Build over ice and stir

Beatle Juice
½ part Gin
½ part Tequila Reposado
½ part Light Rum
½ part Vodka
1 part Melon Liqueur
splash Grenadine
fill with Sour Mix
top with Lemon-Lime Soda
Hurricane Glass

Shake all but Soda with ice and strain into a shot glass. Top with Soda.

Beekers Fruit
1 part Jack Daniel's®
1 part Vodka
1 part Sloe Gin
1 part Pineapple Juice
1 part Passion Fruit Nectar
Collins Glass

Shake with ice and pour

Beekers Poison
1 part Spiced Rum
1 part Triple Sec
1 part Lemon Juice
fill with Cola
Collins Glass

Build over ice and stir

Beep
1 part Vodka
3 parts Orange Juice
fill with Lemon-Lime Soda
Collins Glass

Build over ice and stir

Beer Nuts
1 part Frangelico®
1 part Root Beer Schnapps
Collins Glass

Shake with ice and pour

Beetlejuice
1 part Vodka
1 part Melon Liqueur
1 part Blue Curaçao
1 part Raspberry Liqueur
1 part Cranberry Juice Cocktail
fill with Sour Mix
Collins Glass

Build over ice and stir

Before the Kiss
1/2 part Vodka
1/2 part Triple Sec
1 part Melon Liqueur
1 part Pear Syrup
fill with Apple Juice
Collins Glass

Shake all but Apple Juice with ice and strain into the glass. Top with Apple Juice.

Bejia Flor
1 1/2 parts Vodka
1/4 part Parfait Amour
1/4 part Southern Comfort®
splash Crème de Banana
splash Apricot Brandy
fill with Lemon-Lime Soda
Collins Glass

Build over ice

Bella
1 part Coconut-Flavored Rum
1 part Sour Apple Schnapps
1 part Spiced Rum
splash Grenadine
fill with Pineapple Juice
Hurricane Glass

Shake with ice and pour

Belladonna
1 part Light Rum
1 part Dark Rum
1 part Cranberry Juice Cocktail
1 part Pineapple Juice
1 part Orange Juice
Collins Glass

Build over ice and stir

Bent Bum
1 1/2 parts Gin
1 1/2 parts Vodka
1 part Orange Juice
1 part Grapefruit Juice
splash Cola
Collins Glass

Build over ice and stir

Berlin Wall
1 part Goldschläger®
1 part Rumple Minze®
1 part Jägermeister®
Collins Glass

Shake with ice and strain

Berry Blast
2 parts Rye Whiskey
1 part Cola
1 part Cranberry Juice Cocktail
Collins Glass

Build over ice and stir

Berry Lemonade
1 part Vodka
splash Strawberry Liqueur
fill with Lemonade
Collins Glass

Build over ice and stir

Berrynice
1 part Strawberry Liqueur
1/2 part Peach Schnapps
1/2 part Melon Liqueur
1/2 part Coconut Cream
splash Simple Syrup
1/2 part Cream
2 parts Fruit Juice
Collins Glass

Shake with ice and pour

Berta's Special
2 parts Tequila Silver
1 Egg White
1 part Fresh Lime Juice
1/2 part Honey
3 parts Club Soda
Collins Glass

Shake all but Club Soda with ice and strain into the glass. Top with Club Soda.

Best Year
1 part Vodka
1/2 part Blue Curaçao
1/2 part Licor 43
1/2 part Lime Juice
fill with Pineapple Juice
Collins Glass

Shake with ice and pour

Betsy
1 part Whiskey
1 part Triple Sec
1/2 part Crème de Banana
fill with Passion Fruit Juice
Collins Glass

Build over ice and stir

Bette Davis Eyes
1 part Vodka
1/2 part Blue Curaçao
1/2 part Coconut-Flavored Liqueur
fill with Lemon-Lime Soda
Collins Glass

Build over ice and stir

The Betty Ford
1 1/2 parts Citrus-Flavored Vodka
fill with Lemon-Lime Soda
1/2 part Grenadine
Collins Glass

Build over ice

Big Apple
2 parts Vodka
fill with Apple Juice
splash Crème de Menthe (White)
Collins Glass

Build over ice and stir

Big Hawaiian
3/4 part Rum
3/4 part Coconut-Flavored Rum
1/2 part Melon Liqueur
fill with Pineapple Juice
splash Grenadine
Collins Glass

Build over ice and stir

A Big Pink Dink
1 part Coconut-Flavored Rum
fill with Milk
splash Grenadine
Hurricane Glass

Build over ice and stir

The Big Robowski
1 part Jack Daniel's®
1 part Southern Comfort®
1 part Goldschläger®
1 part Dark Rum
1 part Amaretto
fill with Cola
Beer Mug

Build over ice and stir

Bikini Bomber
1 1/2 parts Dry Gin
1/2 part Blue Curaçao
1/2 part Triple Sec
fill with Grapefruit Juice
Collins Glass

Shake with ice and pour

Bill's Tropical Depression
1 part Coconut-Flavored Rum
1 part Raspberry Liqueur
1/2 part Crème de Banana
fill with Pineapple Juice
splash Orange Juice
splash Cranberry Juice Cocktail
Collins Glass

Build over ice and stir

Billy Belly Bomber
1 part Vodka
3 parts Pineapple Juice
splash Lemon Juice
Collins Glass

Build over ice and stir

Bine's Brain Blower
1 part Amaretto
1 part Brandy
2 parts Cream
1 part Jägermeister®
Collins Glass

Shake all but Jägermeister® with ice and strain into the glass. Top with Jägermeister®.

Bingo Bongo
1 1/2 parts Dark Rum
1/2 part Triple Sec
2 parts Pineapple Juice
1 part Guava Juice
1/2 part Fresh Lime Juice
1/2 part Passion Fruit
Collins Glass

Build over ice and stir

Birdy Num-Num
1 part Coconut-Flavored Rum
1 part Pineapple Juice
Collins Glass

Build over ice and stir

Bitch's Brew
1 part 151-Proof Rum
1 part Whiskey
1 part Brandy
2 parts Dr Pepper®
1 part Ginger Ale
splash Lime Juice
Beer Mug

Build over ice and stir

Bitter Bourbon Lemonade
2 parts Bourbon
1 part Fresh Lime Juice
1/2 part Grenadine
1/2 part Simple Syrup
Collins Glass

Build over ice and stir

Bitter Kraut

1 part Jägermeister®
1 part Campari®
1 part Club Soda
2 dashes Bitters
Collins Glass

Build over ice and stir

Bitter Sweet Symphon-Tea

1½ parts Citrus-Flavored Vodka
splash Orange Liqueur
fill with Iced Tea
splash Lemon Juice
Collins Glass

Shake with ice and strain over ice

Black Bottom

¼ part Brandy
¼ part Cointreau®
¼ part Blackberry Brandy
splash Gin
1 part Lemon Juice
1 part Orange Juice
Collins Glass

Shake with ice and pour

Black Butterfly

1 part Blackberry Brandy
1 part Cranberry Juice Cocktail
2 parts Lemon-Lime Soda
Hurricane Glass

Build over ice and stir

Black Cow

1 part Coffee Liqueur
1 part Half and Half
1½ parts Cola
Collins Glass

Build over ice and stir

Black Forest

1 part Crème de Cacao (White)
1 part Cherry Liqueur
1 part Kirschwasser
1 part Cream
Collins Glass

Shake with ice and pour

Black Jacket

1 part Coffee Liqueur
splash Vodka
splash Crème de Noyaux
⅔ part Cream
Collins Glass

Shake with ice and pour

Black Temple

2 parts Blackberry Liqueur
1 part Lemon-Lime Soda
1 part Ginger Ale
splash Grenadine
Hurricane Glass

Build over ice and stir

Black-Eyed Susan

1 part Vodka
1 part Light Rum
1 part Triple Sec
splash Lime Juice
1 part Pineapple Juice
1 part Orange Juice
Collins Glass

Shake with ice and strain over ice

Blanqita

1½ parts Coffee Liqueur
1 part Anisette
fill with Pineapple Juice
Collins Glass

Build over ice and stir

Blast-Off
1 part Vodka
1/2 part Cointreau®
1/2 part Galliano®
4 parts Orange Juice
2 parts Pineapple Juice
Collins Glass

Build over ice and stir

Bleach
1 part Light Rum
1/2 part Apricot Brandy
1/2 part Peach Schnapps
1/2 part Blue Curaçao
fill with Red Bull® Energy Drink
splash Lemon Juice
Collins Glass

Build over ice and stir

Bleeker
1 part Vodka
1/2 part Lillet®
1/2 part Triple Sec
1 Egg White
Collins Glass

Shake with ice and pour

Blind White Russian
3/4 part Irish Cream Liqueur
3/4 part Godiva® Liqueur
3/4 part Coffee Liqueur
1/2 part Butterscotch Schnapps
fill with Milk
Collins Glass

Shake with ice and pour

Blinkert
1 part Cherry Brandy
1 part Sloe Gin
1/2 part Whiskey
fill with Lemonade
Collins Glass

Build over ice and stir

Bloody Caesar
1 1/2 parts Vodka
fill with Clamato® Juice
1 dash Tabasco® Sauce
2 dashes Worcestershire Sauce
1 Lime Wedge
1 Celery Stick
dash Salt
dash Pepper
Collins Glass

Build over ice and stir

Bloody Maru
2 parts Sake
2 splashes Worcestershire Sauce
splash Tabasco® Sauce
dash horseradish
splash Lime Juice
Collins Glass

Build over ice and stir

Blue Aegean
1 part Blue Curaçao
1 part Vodka
1 part Triple Sec
fill with Pineapple Juice
Collins Glass

Build over ice and stir

Blue Breeze
1 part Light Rum
1 part Orange Juice
1 part Sour Mix
1/2 part Blue Curaçao
1/4 part Coconut-Flavored Rum
fill with Pineapple Juice
Collins Glass

Build over ice and stir

Blue Bunny
1 part Rum
1 part Vodka
splash Sour Mix
splash Blue Curaçao
Collins Glass

Shake with ice and strain

Blue Cobra
1 part Blue Curaçao
1 1/2 parts Coconut Liqueur
1 1/2 parts Pineapple Juice
3 parts Tonic Water
Collins Glass

Build over ice and stir

Blue Cruncher
1 part Gin
1 part Blue Curaçao
1 1/2 parts Sour Mix
fill with Lemon-Lime Soda
Collins Glass

Build over ice and stir

Blue Fairy
1 part Blue Curaçao
1 part Absinthe
splash Lime Juice
1 part Grapefruit Juice
Collins Glass

Shake with ice and pour

Blue Harbor
1 part Rum
1 part Lime Syrup
1/2 part Blue Curaçao
1/2 part Triple Sec
fill with Lemon-Lime Soda
Collins Glass

Build over ice and stir

Blue Heaven
1 part Rum
1 part Amaretto
1 part Blue Curaçao
fill with Pineapple Juice
Collins Glass

Shake with ice and pour

Blue Horizon
1 part Spiced Rum
1 part 151-Proof Rum
1 part Blue Curaçao
splash Grenadine
fill with Orange Juice
Collins Glass

Build over ice and stir

Blue Ice with Wings
1 part Vodka
3/4 part Blue Curaçao
1/2 part Coconut-Flavored Liqueur
1/2 part Sour Mix
fill with Red Bull® Energy Drink
Hurricane Glass

Build over ice and stir

Blue Jeans
1 part Vodka
1 part Blue Curaçao
1 part Grapefruit Juice
1 part Pineapple Juice
Collins Glass

Build over ice and stir

Blue Malibu®

1/2 part Gin
1/2 part Rum
1/2 part Vodka
1/2 part Blue Curaçao
2 parts Sour Mix
splash Lemon-Lime Soda
Collins Glass

Build over ice and stir

Blue Mouth

1 part Dry Vermouth
1/2 part Southern Comfort®
fill with Orange Juice
splash Blue Curaçao
Collins Glass

Build over ice

Blue Nerfherder

1 part Tequila
1 part Blue Curaçao
fill with Lemonade
Collins Glass

Build over ice and stir

Blue Nuke

1 part Vodka
1 part 151-Proof Rum
1 part Gin
1 part Blue Curaçao
1 part Blueberry Schnapps
fill with Sour Mix
Collins Glass

Build over ice and stir

Blue Owl

1/2 part Vodka
1 part Blue Curaçao
1 part Crème de Banana
splash Cherry Brandy
fill with Lemonade
Collins Glass

Shake with ice and pour

Blue Paradiso

1 1/2 parts Blue Curaçao
1 1/2 parts Orange-Flavored Vodka
1/2 parts Coconut-Flavored Rum
fill with Pineapple Juice
Hurricane Glass

Shake with ice and pour

Blue Passion

3/4 part Spiced Rum
1/2 part Blue Curaçao
fill with Sour Mix
Collins Glass

Shake with ice and pour

Blue Pussycat

2 parts Scotch
1 part Blue Curaçao
fill with Orange Juice
Collins Glass

Build over ice and stir

The Blues

1 part Vodka
1 part Coconut-Flavored Rum
3/4 part Blue Curaçao
1/2 part Triple Sec
fill with Pineapple Juice
Collins Glass

Shake with ice and strain over ice

Blue Shadow

1 1/2 parts Rum
1 part Parfait Amour
fill with Lemon-Lime Soda
Collins Glass

Build over ice and stir

Blue Sky

1 part Blue Curaçao
fill with Milk
Collins Glass

Shake with ice and pour

Blue Spider

2 parts Cranberry-Flavored Vodka
fill with Red Bull® Energy Drink
Collins Glass

Build over ice and stir

Blue Suede Juice

1 part Citrus-Flavored Vodka
1/4 part Blue Curaçao
3/4 part Triple Sec
fill with Sour Mix
splash Lemon-Lime Soda
Collins Glass

Build over ice and stir

Blue Sweden

1 part Blue Curaçao
1 part Vodka
1 part Crème de Banana
fill with Orange Juice
Collins Glass

Build over ice and stir

Blue Wave

1 part Gin
1 part Rum
1/2 parts Blue Curaçao
1 part Fresh Lime Juice
fill with Pineapple Juice
Hurricane Glass

Build over ice and stir

Blue with You

1 part Citrus-Flavored Rum
1 part Blue Curaçao
1 part Lychee Liqueur
1 part Pernod®
fill with Pineapple Juice
Hurricane Glass

Shake with ice and pour

Blueberry Hill

1/2 part Vodka
1/2 part Raspberry Liqueur
1/4 part Blackberry Liqueur
1 part Sour Mix
splash Peach Schnapps
fill with Lemonade
Collins Glass

Build over ice and stir

Boardwalk Breeze

1 1/2 parts Coconut-Flavored Rum
1 1/2 parts Amaretto
1 part Orange Juice
1 part Pineapple Juice
splash Grenadine
Hurricane Glass

Shake with ice and pour

Boca Chica

1/2 part Vodka
splash Pisang Ambon® Liqueur
splash Coconut-Flavored Liqueur
1 part Guava Juice
splash Passion Fruit Nectar
Collins Glass

Shake with ice and strain over ice

Bodega Blues
1 part Melon Liqueur
1 part Vodka
1 part Peach Schnapps
1 part Orange Juice
1 part Passion Fruit Juice
Collins Glass

Build over ice and stir

Bog Ale
1 1/2 parts Gin
3 parts Cranberry Juice Cocktail
fill with Ginger Ale
1 Lime Slice
Collins Glass

Build over ice and stir

Bolster
1 part Sake
1/2 part Peach Schnapps
fill with Orange Juice
splash Cherry Brandy
Collins Glass

Build over ice and stir

Bonaire Punch
1/2 part Coconut-Flavored Liqueur
1 part Dark Rum
1 part Ponche Kuba®
fill with Pineapple Juice
Collins Glass

Build over ice and stir

Bongo Drum
1 part Rum
1/4 part Blackberry Brandy
fill with Pineapple Juice
Collins Glass

Build over ice and stir

Bonneti
1 part Scotch
1 part Crème de Cacao (White)
1 part Caramel Syrup
splash Cream
Collins Glass

Shake with ice and pour

Booda's Black Brew
1 part Coconut-Flavored Rum
3/4 part Blue Curaçao
3/4 part Raspberry Liqueur
1/2 part Grenadine
fill with Cranberry Juice Cocktail
Hurricane Glass

Build over ice and stir

Boogie Beck
1 part Vodka
1 part Amaretto
1 part Southern Comfort®
1/2 part Fresh Lime Juice
1 part Pineapple Juice
1 part Orange Juice
Collins Glass

Build over ice and stir

Boot Blaster
1 part Light Rum
1 part Gin
1 part Vodka
1 part Triple Sec
fill with Lemonade
splash Cola
Collins Glass

Build over ice and stir

Bootlegger Tea
3/4 part Vodka
3/4 part Rum
3/4 part Triple Sec
1 part Sour Mix
1 part Lemon-Lime Soda
splash Grenadine
Collins Glass

Build over ice and stir

Bootyshaker
1 part Dark Rum
1 part Crème de Banana
1 part Fresh Lime Juice
1/2 part Triple Sec
Collins Glass

Shake with ice and pour

Borisov
1 part Jack Daniel's®
1 part Vodka
1/2 part Brandy
1/2 part Campari®
1/2 part Cognac
fill with Red Bull® Energy Drink
Collins Glass

Build over ice and stir

Bossa Nova
3/4 part Dark Rum
1/4 part Apricot Brandy
1/4 part Galliano®
fill with Pineapple Juice
splash Lemon Juice
Collins Glass

Build over ice and stir

Bottleneck
1 part Vodka
1 part Parfait Amour
1 part Crème de Banana
1 part Melon Liqueur
splash Fresh Lime Juice
fill with Lemon-Lime Soda
Collins Glass

Build over ice and stir

Bowl Hugger
1 part Tequila
1 part Gin
1 part Rum
1 part Triple Sec
splash Sweetened Lime Juice
1 part Orange Juice
1 part Pineapple Juice
1 part Sour Mix
Collins Glass

Build over ice and stir

Brain Candy
1 part Vodka
1 part Crème de Menthe (White)
fill with Mountain Dew®
Collins Glass

Build over ice and stir

Brainwash
1 part Gin
1 part Vodka
1 part Jägermeister®
1 part Blue Curaçao
fill with Pineapple Juice
Collins Glass

Shake with ice and pour

Brandy Egg Nog

2 parts Brandy
1 Whole Egg
dash Powdered Sugar
dash Ground Nutmeg
fill with Milk
Collins Glass

Shake all but Milk with ice and strain into the glass. Top with Milk.

Break the Rules

1 part Gin
1/2 part Kiwi Schnapps
1/2 part Melon Liqueur
fill with Orange Juice
Collins Glass

Build over ice and stir

Breezy Spring

1 1/2 parts Gin
1 part Coconut-Flavored Liqueur
fill with Grapefruit Juice
Collins Glass

Build over ice and stir

Brewer Street Rascal

1 part Mandarine Napoléon® Liqueur
1/2 part Vermouth
3 parts Grapefruit Juice
1 Egg White
Collins Glass

Shake with ice and pour

Bridge to the Moon

1 part Currant-Flavored Vodka
1 part Apple Liqueur
1 part Passion Fruit Liqueur
fill with Lemon-Lime Soda
Collins Glass

Build over ice and stir

Bridget in the Buff

2 parts Vodka
1 1/2 parts Raspberry Liqueur
fill with Lemon-Lime Soda
splash Sour Mix
Collins Glass

Build over ice and stir

Brief Bikini

1 1/2 parts Triple Sec
fill with Lemonade
Collins Glass

Build over ice and stir

Brittle Fracture

2 parts Root Beer Schnapps
fill with Lemon-Lime Soda
Beer Mug

Build over ice and stir

Broken-Down Golf Cart

1 part Vodka
1 part Melon Liqueur
1 part Amaretto
fill with Cranberry Juice Cocktail
Collins Glass

Shake with ice and pour

Brown Derby

1 1/4 parts Vodka
fill with Cola
Collins Glass

Build over ice and stir

Bubba Collins

2 parts Scotch
1 part Sour Mix
fill with Cola
Collins Glass

Build over ice and stir

Bubblicious®
2/3 part Crème de Cacao (White)
1/2 part Vanilla-Flavored Vodka
2/3 part Southern Comfort®
1/2 part Sour Mix
1 part Pineapple Juice
1 part Orange Juice
Collins Glass

Shake with ice and pour

Buena Carmencita
1 part Crème de Banana
1 part Brandy
fill with Milk
Collins Glass

Build over ice and stir

Bueno
1 part Coconut-Flavored Liqueur
1 part Passoã®
2 parts Orange Juice
2 parts Pineapple Juice
splash Lemon Juice
Collins Glass

Shake with ice and pour

Buenos Noches
2 parts Tequila
1 part Crème de Banana
1/2 part Lemon Juice
Collins Glass

Shake with ice and pour

Bugix
1 1/2 parts Vodka
1/2 part Crème de Banana
1 part Pineapple Juice
1 part Strawberry Juice
Hurricane Glass

Shake with ice and pour

Bull Blaster
1 part Jägermeister®
fill with Red Bull® Energy Drink
Collins Glass

Build over ice and stir

Bull Frog
1 1/2 parts Whiskey
fill with Lemonade
Collins Glass

Build over ice and stir

Bullpup
1 part Rum
1 part Orange Juice
1 part Ginger Ale
Collins Glass

Build over ice and stir

Burning Bitch!
1 part Vodka
1 part Irish Cream Liqueur
1/2 part Lemon Juice
splash Maraschino Cherry Juice
Collins Glass

Shake with ice and pour

Burning Embers
1 1/2 parts Tequila Silver
1 part Spiced Rum
1/2 part Worcestershire Sauce
dash Wasabi
fill with Tomato Juice
Collins Glass

Build over ice and stir

Buster Cherry
1 1/2 parts Whiskey
1/2 part Cherry Brandy
1 part Orange Juice
1 part Lemon Juice
Collins Glass

Shake with ice and strain over ice

But I Know the Owner
1 1/2 parts Spiced Rum
1/2 part Amaretto
1 part Orange Juice
1 part Pineapple Juice
Collins Glass

Build over ice and stir

Butcherblock
1 1/2 parts Tequila
1 1/2 parts Coffee Liqueur
fill with Half and Half
Collins Glass

Build over ice and stir

Butter Cream
1 1/2 parts Butterscotch Schnapps
fill with Cream Soda
Collins Glass

Build over ice and stir

Buzz Lightyear
1 part Vodka
1 part Melon Liqueur
fill with Orange Juice
Collins Glass

Build over ice and stir

Bye-Bye Honey
1 part Citrus-Flavored Rum
1 part Orange-Flavored Vodka
2 parts Blue Curaçao
1 part Orange Juice
fill with Lemon-Lime Soda
Collins Glass

Build over ice and stir

Bye-Bye New York
1 part Vodka
1 part Dark Rum
1 part Hazelnut Syrup
fill with Orange Juice
Collins Glass

Build over ice and stir

C.O.P.
1 part Coconut-Flavored Liqueur
1 part Triple Sec
1/2 part Fresh Lime Juice
fill with Pineapple Juice
Collins Glass

Build over ice and stir

Caballo
1 1/2 parts Tequila Silver
1 part Amaretto
fill with Grapefruit Juice
Collins Glass

Build over ice and stir

Caballo Viejo
1 part Dark Rum
1 part Apricot Brandy
1/2 part Dry Gin
fill with Pineapple Juice
Collins Glass

Build over ice and stir

Cactus Breeze

1 part Vodka
1 part Cranberry Juice Cocktail
1 part Pineapple Juice
1 part Sour Mix
Collins Glass

Build over ice and stir

Cactus Cafe

1 part Tequila Silver
2 parts Coffee Liqueur
fill with Lemonade
Collins Glass

Build over ice and stir

Cactus Juice

1 1/2 parts Tequila
1 part Amaretto
fill with Sour Mix
Collins Glass

Build over ice and stir

Caesar

1 part Vodka
4 parts Clamato® Juice
splash Tabasco® Sauce
splash Worcestershire Sauce
Collins Glass

Build over ice and stir

Calico Jack

2 parts Dark Rum
1/2 part Coconut-Flavored Liqueur
1 1/2 parts Pineapple Juice
1 part Orange Juice
1/2 part Fresh Lime Juice
Collins Glass

Build over ice and stir

California Coastline

1 part Peach Schnapps
1 part Coconut-Flavored Rum
1/2 part Blue Curaçao
1 part Pineapple Juice
1 part Sour Mix
Collins Glass

Build over ice and stir

California Dreaming

1/2 part Vodka
1/2 part Coffee Liqueur
1/2 part Vanilla Liqueur
2 parts Sour Mix
1 1/2 parts Cola
Collins Glass

Build over ice and stir

California Gold Rush

2 parts Vodka
1 1/2 parts Goldschläger®
fill with Lemon-Lime Soda
Collins Glass

Build over ice and stir

California Monkey

1 1/2 parts Coconut-Flavored Rum
1/2 part Crème de Banana
fill with Cola
Collins Glass

Build over ice and stir

California Rattlesnake

1/2 part Malibu® Rum
1/2 part Southern Comfort®
1/2 part Amaretto
splash Sour Mix
splash Lemon-Lime Soda
splash Grenadine
Collins Glass

Build over ice and stir

California Root Beer

1 part Galliano®
1 part Triple Sec
1 part Coffee Liqueur
1 part Cola
1 part Ginger Ale
Beer Mug

Build over ice and stir

California Screwdriver

1½ parts Grand Marnier®
2 parts Vodka
1 part Club Soda
1 part Orange Juice
Collins Glass

Build over ice and stir

Call Girl

½ part Light Rum
½ part Dark Rum
½ part Coconut-Flavored Rum
½ part Melon Liqueur
½ part Crème de Banana
1 part Pineapple Juice
1 part Orange Juice
Collins Glass

Shake with ice and pour

Campari® Punch

1 part Campari®
1 part Triple Sec
1 part Grapefruit Juice
1 part Orange Juice
Collins Glass

Build over ice and stir

Campechuela

1 part Dark Rum
2 parts Orange Juice
3 parts Cranberry Juice Cocktail
splash Cherry Brandy
Collins Glass

Build over ice and stir

Camurai

1 part Vodka
½ part Blue Curaçao
½ part Coconut Cream
fill with Sparkling Water
Collins Glass

Build over ice and stir

Candy

1¼ parts 151-Proof Rum
1 part Amaretto
fill with Dr Pepper®
Collins Glass

Build over ice and stir

Cantagallo

1 part Gin
splash Blue Curaçao
splash Amaretto
½ part Sweet Vermouth
splash Papaya Juice
Collins Glass

Shake with ice and pour

Cape Cod Crush

2½ parts Southern Comfort®
fill with Cranberry Juice Cocktail
Collins Glass

Build over ice and stir

Cape Cod Sour Squishy

1 part Light Rum
½ part Sour Apple Schnapps
1 part Cranberry Juice Cocktail
1 part Sour Mix
fill with Lemon-Lime Soda
Collins Glass

Build over ice and stir

Cape Driver (or Screw Codder)

1 part Vodka
1 part Cranberry Juice Cocktail
1 part Orange Juice
Collins Glass

Build over ice and stir

Cape May

1 1/2 parts Gin
1/2 part Cherry Brandy
1 part Orange Juice
1 part Ginger Ale
Collins Glass

Build over ice and stir

Captain Billy's Kool-Aid®

1 part Southern Comfort®
1 part Amaretto
1 part Lemon-Lime Soda
fill with Cranberry Juice Cocktail
Collins Glass

Build over ice and stir

Captain Hawk

1 part Light Rum
1/2 part Amaretto
1/2 parts Crème de Banana
splash Passion Fruit Liqueur
1 part Orange Juice
1 part Pineapple Juice
Collins Glass

Shake with ice and strain over ice

Captain Hook

1 part Gin
1/2 part Amaretto
1/2 part Strawberry Liqueur
1 part Orange Juice
1 part Peach Juice
Collins Glass

Shake with ice and strain over ice

Captain Kirsch

1 part Vodka
1 part Kirschwasser
1 part Black Currant Syrup
fill with Lemonade
Collins Glass

Build over ice and stir

Captain's Cruiser

1 1/4 part Coconut-Flavored Rum
3 parts Orange Juice
2 parts Pineapple Juice
Collins Glass

Shake with ice and strain over ice

Captain's Crush

2 parts Spiced Rum
1 part Amaretto
3 parts Pineapple Juice
Collins Glass

Shake with ice and strain over ice

Caputo Special

1 part Gin
1 part Vodka
1 part Tequila
1 part Blue Curaçao
1 part Peach Schnapps
fill with Lemon-Lime Soda
splash Lime Juice
Collins Glass

Build over ice and stir

Carabinieri
1 part Tequila
3/4 part Galliano®
1/2 part Cointreau®
splash Sweetened Lime Juice
3 parts Orange Juice
1 Egg Yolk
Collins Glass

Shake with ice and strain over ice

Caribbean Breeze
2 parts Coconut-Flavored Rum
1 part Vodka
fill with Orange Juice
splash Grenadine
Collins Glass

Build over ice and stir

Caribbean Queen
1 1/2 parts Watermelon Schnapps
1/2 part Coconut-Flavored Rum
1 1/2 parts Triple Sec
1 part Orange Juice
1 part Lemonade
splash Lemon Juice
Collins Glass

Build over ice and stir

Caribbean Screwdriver
1/2 part Peach Schnapps
1/2 part Crème de Banana
1/2 part Coconut-Flavored Rum
2 parts Orange Juice
1 part Pineapple Juice
splash Cream
Collins Glass

Build over ice and stir

Caribbean Smuggler
3/4 part Dark Rum
1/2 part Triple Sec
1 part Orange Juice
1 part Margarita Mix
1/2 part Simple Syrup
fill with Lemon-Lime Soda
Hurricane Glass

Shake all but Soda with ice and strain into the glass. Top with Soda.

Carlin
1 part Citrus-Flavored Vodka
1 part Triple Sec
3 parts Fresh Lime Juice
Collins Glass

Shake with ice and pour

Carman's Dance
1 part Vodka
1 part Gin
1 part Cranberry Juice Cocktail
1 1/2 parts Strawberry Daiquiri Mix
fill with Orange Juice
Mason Jar

Build over ice and stir

Casco Bay Lemonade
1 1/2 parts Citrus-Flavored Vodka
fill with Sour Mix
splash Cranberry Juice Cocktail
splash Lemon-Lime Soda
Collins Glass

Build over ice and stir

Catalina Margarita
1 1/2 parts Tequila
1 part Peach Schnapps
1 part Blue Curaçao
fill with Sour Mix
Margarita Glass

Shake with ice and pour

Catuche
1 part Dark Rum
1/2 part Dry Gin
1/2 part Triple Sec
fill with Orange Juice
Collins Glass
Build over ice and stir

Cave Blue
1 1/2 parts Blue Curaçao
1 part Vodka
fill with Pineapple Juice
Collins Glass
Build over ice and stir

Cervino
1 part Vodka
1/2 part Coffee Liqueur
1/2 part Coconut-Flavored Liqueur
fill with Pineapple Juice
Collins Glass
Build over ice and stir

Change of Heart
1 part Light Rum
1 part Crème de Banana
1 part Red Curaçao
dash Sugar
fill with Cola
Collins Glass
Build over ice and stir

Chapman
1 part Gin
1 part Rum
1/2 part Blue Curaçao
fill with Lemon-Lime Soda
Collins Glass
Build over ice and stir

Charlott
2 parts Triple Sec
1 part Crème de Banana
1 part Pineapple Juice
1 part Orange Juice
Collins Glass
Build over ice and stir

Cherry Cough Syrup
1 part Vodka
1 part Peach Schnapps
1 part Triple Sec
1 part Grenadine
Collins Glass
Build over ice and stir

Cherry Spice
1 part Cherry Brandy
1 part Spiced Rum
fill with Cola
Collins Glass
Build over ice and stir

Cherry-Bucko
1 part Cherry Brandy
1/2 part Vodka
1/2 part Lemon Juice
1/2 part Lime Juice
fill with Lemonade
Collins Glass
Build over ice and stir

China Blue
1 1/2 parts Blue Curaçao
3/4 part Lychee Liqueur
fill with Grapefruit Juice
Collins Glass
Build over ice and stir

Chippendale
$1/2$ part Light Rum
$1 1/2$ parts Pineapple Juice
splash Blue Curaçao
splash Crème de Cacao (Dark)
splash Lime Cordial
Collins Glass

Shake with ice and pour

Chocolate Banana Splitter
2 parts Crème de Banana
1 part Crème de Cacao (Dark)
2 parts Irish Cream Liqueur
1 part Frangelico®
1 part Cherry Syrup
3 parts Cream
Collins Glass

Shake with ice and pour

Chocolate Monk
1 part Frangelico®
1 part Créme de Cacao (Dark)
1 part Coffee Liqueur
1 part Irish Cream Liqueur
Collins Glass

Shake with ice and strain

Cinco de Rob-O
$2 1/2$ parts Tequila
$1 1/2$ parts Triple Sec
1 part Sour Mix
1 part Ginger Ale
Beer Mug

Build over ice and stir

Cinderella
1 part Cream
1 part Grenadine
1 part Pineapple Juice
1 part Orange Juice
Collins Glass

Shake with ice and strain over ice

Citrus Breeze
$1 1/2$ parts Citrus-Flavored Vodka
1 part Cranberry Juice Cocktail
1 part Grapefruit Juice
Collins Glass

Build over ice and stir

Citrus Smack
$1 1/2$ parts Rum
$1 1/2$ parts Triple Sec
1 part Sour Mix
fill with Grapefruit Juice
Collins Glass

Build over ice and stir

Classic Jack
2 parts Jack Daniel's®
fill with Cola
1 Lime Wedge
Collins Glass

Build over ice and stir

Club Coke
$1 1/2$ parts Vodka
$1/2$ part Peach Schnapps
2 parts Orange Juice
fill with Cola
Collins Glass

Build over ice and stir

Coco Cherry
1 part Cherry Brandy
$2/3$ part Coconut-Flavored Liqueur
3 parts Milk
3 parts Cherry Juice
Collins Glass

Shake with ice and pour

Coco Flirt
2 parts Coconut-Flavored Liqueur
1/2 part Blue Curaçao
fill with Orange Juice
Collins Glass
Build over ice and stir

Coconut Almond Margarita
1 1/4 part Tequila
2 1/2 parts Sour Mix
1/2 part Crème de Coconut
1/4 part Amaretto
1/2 part Lime Juice
Margarita Glass
Shake with ice and pour

Coconut Bra
1 part Coconut-Flavored Rum
1 part Raspberry Liqueur
splash Lemon-Lime Soda
fill with Sour Mix
Collins Glass
Build over ice and stir

Cocoskiss
1 1/2 parts Coconut Liqueur
1 part Light Rum
1 part Passion Fruit Nectar
1 part Pineapple Juice
1 part Orange Juice
Collins Glass
Build over ice and stir

Coffee Orange
1 1/2 parts Coffee Liqueur
fill with Orange Juice
Collins Glass
Build over ice and stir

Cokaretto
1 part Amaretto
fill with Cola
Collins Glass
Build over ice and stir

Cold Kentucky
1 part Amaretto
1 part Southern Comfort®
splash Orange Juice
fill with Pineapple Juice
Collins Glass
Build over ice and stir

Collins
1 1/2 parts Vodka
3 parts Sour Mix
1 part Club Soda
Collins Glass
Build over ice and stir

Colorado Crush
1 part Rum
1 part Amaretto
1 part Sloe Gin
fill with Iced Tea
Collins Glass
Build over ice and stir

Colt Cruiser
1 part Dark Rum
1 part Amaretto
1 part Crème de Banana
fill with Lemonade
Collins Glass
Build over ice and stir

Cool by the Pool
1 part Light Rum
3/4 part Coconut-Flavored Rum
1/4 part Lime Cordial
2 parts Pineapple Juice
2 parts Orange Juice
splash Grenadine
Collins Glass
Build over ice and stir

Cool Carlos

1 1/2 parts Dark Rum
1 part Blue Curaçao
2 parts Cranberry Juice Cocktail
2 parts Pineapple Juice
splash Sour Mix
Collins Glass

Build over ice and stir

Copabanana

2 parts Rum
1/2 part Crème de Banana
1/2 part Apricot Brandy
1 part Pineapple Juice
1 part Orange Juice
Collins Glass

Build over ice and stir

Coral Sea

1 part Light Rum
1 part Pineapple Juice
1 part Coconut Cream
splash Blue Curaçao
Collins Glass

Shake with ice and strain over ice

Costa Dorada

1 part Vodka
1 part Spiced Rum
1/2 part Strawberry Liqueur
fill with Lemon-Lime Soda
Collins Glass

Build over ice and stir

Costanza

1 1/2 parts Vodka
1/2 part Peach Schnapps
1/2 part Grenadine
fill with Carrot Juice
Collins Glass

Build over ice and stir

Cow Puncher

1 part Dark Rum
1 part Crème de Cacao (White)
fill with Milk
Collins Glass

Build over ice and stir

Cowgirl's Prayer

2 parts Tequila Silver
1 part Fresh Lime Juice
fill with Lemonade
Collins Glass

Build over ice and stir

Cran Daddy

1 part Vanilla-Flavored Vodka
1 part Lemon-Lime Soda
1 part Cranberry Juice Cocktail
Hurricane Glass

Build over ice and stir

Cranberry Kiss

3/4 part Spiced Rum
1/2 part Peppermint Schnapps
1 part Collins Mix
1 part Cranberry Juice Cocktail
Collins Glass

Shake with ice and pour

Cranberry Margarita

1 1/2 parts Tequila
1 part Lime Juice
1 1/2 parts Triple Sec
1 1/2 parts Sour Mix
2 parts Cranberry Juice Cocktail
Margarita Glass

Shake with ice and pour

Crawling up the Wall

1 1/2 parts Scotch
1/2 part Raspberry Liqueur
1/2 part Lemon Juice
1 part Apple Juice
1 part Raspberry-Flavored Seltzer
Collins Glass

Build over ice and stir

Crazy Coconut

1 1/2 parts Coconut Liqueur
1 part Crème de Banana
1/2 part Blue Curaçao
1 part Grapefruit Juice
1 part Pineapple Juice
Collins Glass

Shake with ice and pour

Creamsicle®

1 1/2 parts Vanilla-Flavored Vodka
1 1/2 parts Milk
fill with Orange Juice
Collins Glass

Shake with ice and strain over ice

Creamy Avalanche

1/4 part Rum
1/4 part Coconut-Flavored Rum
1/4 part Coffee Liqueur
1/4 part Irish Cream Liqueur
1/4 part Frangelico®
1 part Half and Half
1 part Cola
Hurricane Glass

Shake with ice and pour

Creamy Dream

1 part Coffee Liqueur
1 part Crème de Cacao (White)
1 part Crème de Menthe (White)
1 part Irish Cream Liqueur
fill with Milk
Collins Glass

Shake with ice and pour

Crimson Flow

2 parts Cranberry Liqueur
fill with Cranberry Juice Cocktail
splash Grenadine
Collins Glass

Build over ice and stir

Croc Punch

1 part Melon Liqueur
1 part Crème de Banana
1 part Vodka
1 part Parfait Amour
fill with Lemon-Lime Soda
splash Lime Juice
Hurricane Glass

Build over ice and stir

Crossing the Line

2 parts Cherry Brandy
1 part Dry Gin
fill with Apple Juice
Collins Glass

Build over ice and stir

Cruiser

1 1/4 parts Coconut-Flavored Rum
1 part Orange Juice
1 part Pineapple Juice
Collins Glass

Build over ice and stir

Crystal Cranberry
1 part Vodka
1/4 part Bourbon
1/4 part Gin
1/4 part Amaretto
1 part Orange Juice
1 part Cranberry Juice Cocktail
Collins Glass
Build over ice and stir

Cuban Planter's
2 parts Light Rum
4 parts Orange Juice
1 part Strawberry Puree
1/2 part Fresh Lime Juice
Collins Glass
Shake with ice and pour

Curbfeeler
1 part Peach Schnapps
1 part Light Rum
1 part Vodka
fill with Iced Tea
Collins Glass
Build over ice and stir

Cyclone
1 part Amaretto
1 part Grenadine
fill with Orange Juice
Collins Glass
Shake with ice and pour

D J Special
1 part Vodka
1 part Triple Sec
1 part Amaretto
1 part Southern Comfort®
1 part Sloe Gin
fill with Pineapple Juice
Collins Glass
Build over ice and stir

D.P.R.
1 part Vodka
1 part Triple Sec
fill with Cranberry Juice Cocktail
splash Club Soda
Collins Glass
Build over ice and stir

Daily Double
1 part Southern Comfort®
1 part Amaretto
1 part Orange Juice
1 part Cranberry Juice Cocktail
Collins Glass
Shake with ice and strain over ice

Dallas
1 part Blue Curaçao
1 part Crème de Banana
1 part Coconut Cream
fill with Pineapple Juice
Collins Glass
Shake with ice and pour

Damn Gumby®
1 part Melon Liqueur
1 part Vodka
fill with Hard Apple Cider
Beer Mug
Build in the glass with no ice

Darth Maul®
1 part Gin
1 part Light Rum
1 part Tequila Silver
1 part Vodka
1 part Triple Sec
1 part Jägermeister®
2 splashes Grenadine
fill with Sour Mix
Collins Glass
Shake with ice and pour

Darth Vader®

1/2 part Vodka
1/2 part Gin
1/2 part Light Rum
1/2 part Tequila Silver
1/2 part Triple Sec
1 part Jägermeister®
fill with Sour Mix
Collins Glass

Shake with ice and pour

Death from Above

1 part 151-Proof Rum
1 part Gin
fill with Cola
Collins Glass

Build over ice and stir

Debutante

1 part Tequila Silver
2/3 part Peach Schnapps
splash Peppermint Liqueur
1/2 part Lemon Juice
Collins Glass

Shake with ice and strain

Deep Blue Sea

2 parts Vodka
2 parts Blue Curaçao
1 part Passion Fruit Juice
1 part Grapefruit Juice
Collins Glass

Shake with ice and strain over ice

Delkozak

2 parts Vodka
1 part Grapefruit Juice
1 part Lemon Juice
1 part Lime Juice
1 part Orange Juice
Collins Glass

Build over ice and stir

Derby Daze

1 part Vodka
1 part Kiwi Schnapps
1 part Blackberry Liqueur
Hurricane Glass

Shake with ice and strain over ice

Desert Rose

1 1/2 parts Raspberry Liqueur
2 parts Orange Juice
2 parts Mango Juice
2 parts Pineapple Juice
Collins Glass

Shake with ice and pour

Desert Sunrise

3/4 part Vodka
1 part Orange Juice
1 part Pineapple Juice
splash Grenadine
Collins Glass

Build over ice

Devil in Miss Jones

1 1/2 parts Brandy
1/2 part Triple Sec
2 splashes Crème de Noyaux
2 splashes Grenadine
Collins Glass

Shake with ice and strain over ice

Dew Me

1 part Jack Daniel's®
1 part Southern Comfort®
splash Lemon Juice
fill with Mountain Dew®
Collins Glass

Build over ice and stir

Dewin' the Captain
$1^1/_2$ parts Spiced Rum
fill with Mountain Dew®
Collins Glass

Build over ice and stir

Dewrunrum
$1^1/_2$ parts 151-Proof Rum
fill with Mountain Dew®
Collins Glass

Build over ice and stir

Diamond-Studded Screwdriver
$1^1/_2$ parts Vodka
fill with Orange Soda
Collins Glass

Build over ice and stir

Diaz
$1^1/_2$ parts Vanilla-Flavored Vodka
2 parts Apple Juice
2 parts Ginger Ale
Collins Glass

Build over ice and stir

Diego Garcia
1 part Light Rum
1 part Mandarine Napoléon® Liqueur
1 part Dark Rum
$^1/_2$ part Triple Sec
fill with Pineapple Juice
Collins Glass

Build over ice and stir

Dirty Mop
$^1/_2$ part Blavod® Black Vodka
$^1/_2$ part Blue Curaçao
$^1/_2$ part Passoã®
$1^1/_2$ parts Orange Juice
$1^1/_2$ parts Cranberry Juice Cocktail
Collins Glass

Build over ice and stir

Diva
$1^1/_2$ parts Vodka
$^1/_2$ part Lime Juice
splash Maraschino Cherry Juice
fill with Lemon-Lime Soda
Collins Glass

Build over ice and stir

Dixieland Tea
2 parts Whiskey
$^1/_2$ part Amaretto
fill with Iced Tea
Mason Jar

Build over ice and stir

Dizzy Tart
1 part 151-Proof Rum
1 part Crème de Banana
1 part Coconut-Flavored Liqueur
splash Grenadine
1 part Orange Juice
1 part Pineapple Juice
1 part Papaya Juice
Hurricane Glass

Shake with ice and pour

Dog Biscuit
$^1/_2$ part Cinnamon Schnapps
$^1/_2$ part Root Beer Schnapps
fill with Lemon-Lime Soda
splash Irish Cream Liqueur
Collins Glass

Build over ice and stir

Dominican Goddess

1 1/2 parts Light Rum
1/2 part Pink Grapefruit Juice
fill with Lemon-Lime Soda
Collins Glass

Build over ice and stir

Don Frederico

1 part Dark Rum
1/2 part Grenadine
fill with Orange Juice
splash Apricot Brandy
Collins Glass

Build over ice and stir

Donkey Ride

1 part Tequila Reposado
1/2 part Blue Curaçao
1/2 part Triple Sec
1 part Pineapple Juice
1 part Orange Juice
Hurricane Glass

Shake with ice and pour

Dorothy

1 part Dark Rum
1/2 part Amaretto
1/2 part Crème de Banana
fill with Pineapple Juice
splash Coconut Cream
Collins Glass

Build over ice and stir

Double Vision

1 part Currant-Flavored Vodka
1 part Citrus-Flavored Vodka
fill with Apple Juice
Collins Glass

Build over ice and stir

Downshift

2 parts Tequila
2 parts Fruit Punch
1 part Lemon-Lime Soda
splash 151-Proof Rum
Hurricane Glass

Build over ice and stir

Dragon Piss

3/4 part Butterscotch Schnapps
1 part Cinnamon Schnapps
fill with Mountain Dew®
Collins Glass

Build over ice and stir

Drink of the Year

1 part Vodka
1/2 part Triple Sec
1/2 part Raspberry Syrup
splash Blue Curaçao
Collins Glass

Shake with ice and pour

Dumpster™ Juice

1 part Vodka
1 part Light Rum
1 part Raspberry Liqueur
1 part Melon Liqueur
1 part Cranberry Juice Cocktail
1 part Orange Juice
1 part Pineapple Juice
Collins Glass

Shake with ice and pour

Early Riser

1 part Melon Liqueur
1 part Tequila Silver
fill with Orange Juice
Collins Glass

Shake with ice and strain over ice

El Cerro

1 part Light Rum
1 part Dark Rum
$1^1/_2$ parts Pineapple Juice
splash Triple Sec
splash Grenadine
Collins Glass

Build over ice and stir

El Dorado

2 parts Tequila Silver
$1^1/_2$ parts Pineapple Juice
$1^1/_2$ parts Orange Juice
$1^1/_2$ parts Banana Juice
splash Triple Sec
splash Crème de Banana
Collins Glass

Shake with ice and strain over ice

El Gringo Loco

$1^1/_2$ parts Tequila
$^1/_2$ part Cherry Brandy
2 splashes Lemon Juice
2 splashes Lime Juice
Collins Glass

Shake with ice and strain over ice

Ecstasy

1 part Blue Curaçao
1 part Melon Liqueur
1 part Fresh Lime Juice
fill with Cranberry Juice Cocktail
Collins Glass

Shake with ice and pour

Electric Lemonade

$1^1/_4$ part Vodka
$^1/_2$ part Blue Curaçao
2 parts Sour Mix
splash Lemon-Lime Soda
Collins Glass

Build over ice and stir

Electric Lizard

1 part Melon Liqueur
1 part Vodka
fill with Sour Mix
Collins Glass

Build over ice and stir

Electric Margarita

$1^1/_2$ parts Tequila
$^1/_2$ part Blue Curaçao
$^1/_2$ part Sweetened Lime Juice
Margarita Glass

Shake with ice and pour

Electric Popsicle

2 parts Melon Liqueur
2 parts Blue Curaçao
fill with Lemon-Lime Soda
1 Lime Slice
Collins Glass

Build over ice and stir

Electric Screwdriver

1 part Southern Comfort®
2 parts Amaretto
fill with Orange Juice
Collins Glass

Build over ice and stir

Electric Tea
1 part Vodka
1 part Gin
1 part Light Rum
1 part Tequila
1 part Blue Curaçao
2 parts Sour Mix
1 1/2 parts Lemon-Lime Soda
Collins Glass

Shake with ice and pour

Eliana
1 1/2 parts Dry Gin
1 part Grapefruit Juice
1 part Pineapple Juice
1/2 part Fresh Lime Juice
1/2 part Raspberry Liqueur
Collins Glass

Build over ice and stir

Eliminator
1 part Wild Turkey® 101
1 part Tequila
fill with Orange Soda
Collins Glass

Build over ice and stir

Emerald Caribbean
3/4 part Coconut-Flavored Rum
1/2 part Melon Liqueur
1/4 part Crème de Banana
3/4 part Blue Curaçao
2 parts Pineapple Juice
1 part Orange Juice
Collins Glass

Shake with ice and pour

Emerald Lily
1 part Vodka
1 part Rum
1/2 part Crème de Menthe (Green)
1/2 part Fresh Lime Juice
fill with Pineapple Juice
Hurricane Glass

Build over ice and stir

Esclava
1 1/2 parts Dark Rum
1 part Triple Sec
1 part Coconut-Flavored Liqueur
fill with Pineapple Juice
splash Grenadine
Collins Glass

Build over ice and stir

Excitabull
1 part Vodka
1 part Peach Schnapps
fill with Red Bull® Energy Drink
splash Cranberry Juice Cocktail
Collins Glass

Build over ice and stir

Exciting Night in Georgia
1 part Peach Schnapps
1/2 part Apricot Brandy
1 part Southern Comfort®
fill with Cranberry Juice Cocktail
Collins Glass

Build over ice and stir

Executive Gimlet
1 1/2 parts Jim Beam®
1 part Triple Sec
1/2 part Lemon Juice
1/2 part Lime Juice
Collins Glass

Shake with ice and strain

Eye
1 part Vodka
2/3 part Passion Fruit Liqueur
2/3 part Triple Sec
2 parts Passion Fruit Juice
1 part Orange Juice
Collins Glass

Shake with ice and pour

Fantastico
1 1/2 parts Dark Rum
1/2 part Crème de Banana
splash Lemon Juice
fill with Pineapple Juice
Collins Glass

Build over ice and stir

Fatality
1 part Rum
1 part Blue Curaçao
1 part Peach Schnapps
1 part Sour Mix
Collins Glass

Shake with ice and strain

Father's Milk
3 parts Tia Maria®
2 parts Crème de Banana
1 part Crème de Menthe (Green)
fill with Milk
Hurricane Glass

Shake with ice and pour

Femme Fatale
2 parts Light Rum
1 part Amaretto
1/2 part Blue Curaçao
fill with Pineapple Juice
Collins Glass

Shake with ice and pour

Field of Green
1 part Sloe Gin
1 part Amaretto
fill with Lemon-Lime Soda
Collins Glass

Build over ice and stir

Fino Mint
1/2 part Vodka
2/3 part Coffee Liqueur
1/2 part Peppermint Liqueur
fill with Milk
Collins Glass

Shake with ice and strain over ice

Fire Eater
1 part Triple Sec
1 part Tequila Silver
1 part Orange Juice
1 part Cranberry Juice Cocktail
Collins Glass

Build over ice and stir

Fire in the Hills
2/3 part Melon Liqueur
1 part Spiced Rum
2 parts Orange Juice
2 parts Pineapple Juice
1 part Cranberry Juice Cocktail
Collins Glass

Build over ice and stir

First Sight
1 part Blue Curaçao
1 part Vodka
1 part Tequila Reposado
fill with Lemon-Lime Soda
Collins Glass

Build over ice and stir

Flaming Jesse (Tropical Sunshine)
1 part Coconut-Flavored Rum
1/2 part Vodka
1/2 part Irish Cream Liqueur
fill with Orange Juice
Collins Glass

Build over ice and stir

Flaming Scotsman
1 part Melon Liqueur
1 part Coconut-Flavored Rum
1 part Raspberry Liqueur
fill with Sour Mix
Collins Glass

Shake with ice and pour

Florida Daiquiri
$1\frac{1}{2}$ parts Light Rum
1 part Orange Juice
2 splashes Lime Juice
dash Sugar
Collins Glass

Shake with ice and pour

Florida Sunrise
$1\frac{1}{4}$ part Light Rum
$\frac{1}{2}$ part Grenadine
fill with Orange Juice
Collins Glass

Build over ice

Flubber
1 part Sambuca
2 parts Vodka
fill with Orange Juice
Collins Glass

Build over ice and stir

Flying Bull
1 part Dark Rum
1 part Light Rum
1 part Red Bull® Energy Drink
1 part Orange Juice
Collins Glass

Build over ice and stir

Flying Kangaroo
$1\frac{1}{2}$ parts Pineapple Juice
1 part Vodka
1 part Light Rum
1 part Orange Juice
$\frac{1}{2}$ part Cream
$\frac{1}{2}$ part Coconut-Flavored Liqueur
Collins Glass

Shake with ice and strain over ice

Flying Meister
1 part Jägermeister®
fill with Red Bull® Energy Drink
Collins Glass

Build over ice and stir

Forest Funk
$1\frac{1}{2}$ parts Citrus-Flavored Vodka
$\frac{3}{4}$ part Peach Schnapps
fill with Grapefruit Juice
Collins Glass

Build over ice and stir

Forest Nymph
$1\frac{1}{2}$ parts Gin
$\frac{1}{2}$ part Blue Curaçao
2 parts Pineapple Juice
2 parts Mango Juice
Collins Glass

Build over ice and stir

Forever Yours
$1\frac{1}{2}$ parts Vodka
1 part Passion Fruit Liqueur
1 part Fresh Lime Juice
fill with Orange Juice
Collins Glass

Shake with ice and pour

Free Fall
1 part Scotch
2/3 part Coconut-Flavored Liqueur
fill with Pineapple Juice
splash Passion Fruit Juice
splash Lemon Juice
Collins Glass

Shake with ice and pour

French Margarita
1/2 part Tequila Silver
1/4 part Triple Sec
2 parts Passion Fruit Liqueur
2 parts Lime Cordial
Margarita Glass

Shake with ice and pour

Frenchy
1 1/2 parts Cognac
1 part Crème de Banana
1/2 part Strawberry Syrup
2 parts Pineapple Juice
2 parts Orange Juice
Collins Glass

Shake with ice and strain over ice

Frequency
2/3 part Passion Fruit Liqueur
1/2 part Lemon Juice
2/3 part Papaya Juice
fill with Sparkling Water
Collins Glass

Build over ice and stir

Fresh
1 part Citrus-Flavored Vodka
1 part Amaretto
1 1/2 parts Orange Juice
fill with Apple Cider
Collins Glass

Build over ice and stir

Fresh Coconut
1 1/2 parts Coconut-Flavored Rum
fill with Grapefruit Juice
3 splashes Grenadine
3 splashes Lemon-Lime Soda
Collins Glass

Build over ice and stir

Freshness
1 part Light Rum
1/2 part Amaretto
1/2 part Crème de Banana
fill with Lemonade
Collins Glass

Build over ice and stir

Froggy Potion
1 part Rum
1 part Vodka
1 part Gin
1 part Tequila
fill with Orange Juice
splash Cola
Collins Glass

Build over ice and stir

Frosty Death
2 parts Peppermint Schnapps
1 part Vodka
Collins Glass

Shake with ice and strain

Frosty Rain
1 part Vodka
1 part Parfait Amour
1 part Triple Sec
fill with Lemonade
splash Crème de Banana
Collins Glass

Build over ice and stir

Fruit Collins
1 part Strawberry Liqueur
1 part Gin
splash Simple Syrup
1 part Lemon Juice
Collins Glass

Shake with ice and strain over ice

Fruit Lush
1 1/2 parts Light Rum
1 1/2 parts Peach Schnapps
1 1/2 parts Wild Berry Schnapps
1/2 part Crème de Banana
2 1/2 parts Pineapple Juice
fill with Lemon-Lime Soda
Collins Glass

Build over ice and stir

Fruit Tickler
1 part Peach Schnapps
2/3 part Melon Liqueur
2/3 part Vodka
1 part Orange Juice
1 part Cranberry Juice Cocktail
fill with Lemon-Lime Soda
Collins Glass

Build over ice and stir

Fruit Tingle
1 part Blue Curaçao
1 part Raspberry Liqueur
fill with Lemonade
Collins Glass

Build over ice and stir

Fruity Bitch
1 1/2 parts Vodka
1 1/2 parts Triple Sec
1 part Peach Schnapps
fill with Fruit Punch
splash Cola
Collins Glass

Build over ice and stir

Fubar
1 part Gin
2 parts Rum
2 parts Tequila
2 parts Vodka
fill with Apple Cider
Collins Glass

Build over ice and stir

Funkmaster 2000
1 part Peach Schnapps
2 parts Vodka
fill with Cranberry Juice Cocktail
Collins Glass

Build over ice and stir

Funky Cold Medina
1/2 part Blue Curaçao
1/2 part Melon Liqueur
1/2 part Peach Schnapps
1 part Cranberry Juice Cocktail
1 part Orange Juice
1 part Pineapple Juice
Collins Glass

Shake with ice and pour

Funky Filly
3/4 part Vodka
3/4 part Melon Liqueur
3/4 part Cherry Liqueur
3/4 part Triple Sec
2 parts Cranberry Juice Cocktail
2 parts Lemon-Lime Soda
1 1/2 parts Lime Juice
Hurricane Glass

Build over ice and stir

Funny Duck
1 part Coconut-Flavored Liqueur
splash Grenadine
splash Cream
fill with Pineapple Juice
Collins Glass

Shake with ice and pour

Furry Reggae
1 part Coconut-Flavored Liqueur
1/2 part Vodka
1/2 part Peach Schnapps
fill with Orange Juice
Collins Glass

Build over ice and stir

The Future Is Bright
3/4 part Red Curaçao
3/4 part Triple Sec
1/2 part Blue Curaçao
fill with Orange Juice
Collins Glass

Shake with ice and pour

Fuzzy Almond
1 1/2 parts Amaretto
1 1/2 parts Light Rum
1 part Cranberry Juice Cocktail
1 part Club Soda
Collins Glass

Build over ice and stir

Fuzzy Charlie
3/4 part Spiced Rum
3/4 part Peach Schnapps
2 parts Piña Colada Mix
fill with Orange Juice
Collins Glass

Shake with ice and pour

Fuzzy Hippo
1 part Peach Schnapps
1 part Vodka
2 parts Hypnotiq®
splash Lemon-Lime Soda
fill with Pineapple Juice
Hurricane Glass

Build over ice and stir

Fuzzy Pierced Navel
1 part Tequila
1 1/2 parts Peach Schnapps
fill with Orange Juice
Collins Glass

Shake with ice and pour

Fuzzy Prick
2 parts Peach Schnapps
fill with Pineapple Juice
Collins Glass

Build over ice and stir

A Fuzzy Thing
2 parts Citrus-Flavored Vodka
1 part Triple Sec
1 1/2 parts Peach Schnapps
splash Orange Juice
splash Pineapple Juice
splash Sour Mix
Collins Glass

Build over ice and stir

G String
2 parts Vodka
1 part Blue Curaçao
1 part Blackberry Liqueur
2 parts Lemonade
2 parts Lime Juice
2 parts Sour Mix
Collins Glass

Shake with ice and pour

Gadfly
1 part Crème de Banana
1 part Melon Liqueur
1 part Coconut-Flavored Liqueur
1 part Vanilla Liqueur
fill with Pineapple Juice
Collins Glass

Build over ice and stir

Gatsby
1 part Southern Comfort®
splash Lime Juice
fill with Lemonade
Collins Glass

Build over ice and stir

Geisha Cup
1 1/2 parts Gin
1 part Apricot Brandy
1 Maraschino Cherry
2 parts Grapefruit Juice
2 parts Orange Juice
Collins Glass

Build over ice and stir

Gekko
1 part Vodka
1 part Crème de Cassis
2 parts Grapefruit Juice
fill with Ginger Ale
Collins Glass

Build over ice and stir

The General
1 1/2 parts Cherry Brandy
1/2 part Grenadine
1 part Cranberry Juice Cocktail
1 part Carbonated Water
Collins Glass

Build over ice and stir

Generation X
1 part Tequila
1 part Jim Beam®
1 part Triple Sec
1 part Blue Curaçao
1 part Melon Liqueur
fill with Zima®
Hurricane Glass

Build over ice and stir

Geng Green Xu
1 part Gin
1 part Green Chartreuse®
1 part Vodka
1 part Lemon-Lime Soda
splash Lemon Juice
Collins Glass

Build over ice and stir

Gentle Ben
1 part Gin
1 part Vodka
1 part Tequila
fill with Orange Juice
1 Orange Slice
1 Maraschino Cherry
Collins Glass

Build over ice and stir

Genuine Risk
1/2 part Vodka
1/2 part Coffee Liqueur
1/2 part Amaretto
1/2 part Coconut-Flavored Liqueur
1/2 part Frangelico®
3 parts Cream
Collins Glass

Build over ice and stir

German Tower
1 part Triple Sec
1 part Gold Tequila
1/2 part Jägermeister®
fill with Sour Mix
1/2 part Lime Juice
Collins Glass

Shake with ice and strain over ice

Get Fruity
1 part Limoncello
1 part Melon Liqueur
1 part Tropical Punch-Flavored Schnapps
fill with Lemon-Lime Soda
Collins Glass

Build over ice and stir

Get'cha Laid
1 part Vodka
2 parts Peach Schnapps
1 part Cranberry Juice Cocktail
1 part Orange Juice
Collins Glass

Build over ice and stir

Gettin' Loose
1 1/2 parts Amaretto
2 parts Vodka
fill with Lemon-Lime Soda
Collins Glass

Build over ice and stir

Gibbs
1 part Vodka
1 part Watermelon Schnapps
fill with Lemon-Lime Soda
Collins Glass

Build over ice and stir

Gideon's Green Dinosaur
1 part Dark Rum
1 part Vodka
1 part Triple Sec
1 part Tequila
1 part Melon Liqueur
fill with Mountain Dew®
Collins Glass

Build over ice and stir

Gigantic White
1 part Irish Cream Liqueur
3 parts Piña Colada Mix
fill with Milk
splash Sloe Gin
Collins Glass

Shake all but Sloe Gin with ice and strain into the glass. Top with Sloe Gin.

Gilligan
1 part Light Rum
1/2 part Crème de Banana
1/2 part Lemon Juice
1 part Orange Juice
1 part Pineapple Juice
Collins Glass

Build over ice and stir

Gin Breeze
1 1/2 parts Gin
1 part Grapefruit Juice
fill with Cranberry Juice Cocktail
Collins Glass

Build over ice and stir

Giraffe
1 part Melon Liqueur
1 part Vodka
fill with Pineapple Juice
splash Cranberry Juice Cocktail
Hurricane Glass

Build over ice and stir

Glass Tower
1 part Vodka
1 part Peach Schnapps
1 part Rum
1 part Triple Sec
1/2 part Sambuca
fill with Lemon-Lime Soda
Collins Glass

Build over ice and stir

The Gobbler

2 parts Wild Turkey® 101
fill with Lemon-Lime Soda
Collins Glass

Build over ice and stir

Golden Blizzard

1 part Goldschläger®
1 part Peppermint Schnapps
fill with Egg Nog
Collins Glass

Shake with ice and pour

Golden Girl

1 part Apricot Brandy
1 part Vodka
fill with Orange Juice
Collins Glass

Shake with ice and pour

Golden Margarita

2 parts Tequila
1 part Simple Syrup
2 parts Sweetened Lime Juice
1/4 part Grand Marnier®
1/4 part Cointreau®
1/4 part Blue Curaçao
Margarita Glass

Shake with ice and strain over ice

Golden Moment

1 part Orange-Flavored Vodka
splash Goldschläger®
splash Apricot Brandy
splash Vanilla Liqueur
fill with Orange Juice
Collins Glass

Shake with ice and strain over ice

Golden Skyway

1 part Apricot Brandy
1/2 part Triple Sec
1/2 part Gin
dash Bitters
fill with Lemonade
Collins Glass

Shake with ice and pour

Golden Sunset

4 parts Grapefruit Juice
1 part Grenadine
dash Powdered Sugar
Collins Glass

Shake with ice and pour

Golden Years

1 part Crème de Banana
1 part Galliano®
1 part Milk
2 parts Orange Juice
2 parts Pineapple Juice
Collins Glass

Shake with ice and pour

The Gold, the Bad, and the Ugly

1 1/2 parts Coffee Liqueur
1 part Irish Cream Liqueur
fill with Milk
1 1/2 parts Goldschläger®
Collins Glass

Build over ice

Golfer's Passion

2 parts Gin
2 parts Passion Fruit Liqueur
2 parts Campari®
fill with Orange Juice
Collins Glass

Shake with ice and pour

Gombay Smash

1 part Light Rum
1 part Dark Rum
1 part Vodka
1/2 part Triple Sec
1 part Pineapple Juice
1 part Apricot Brandy
dash Powdered Sugar
Collins Glass

Shake with ice and strain over ice

Goober

1 1/2 parts Vodka
1 1/2 parts Blackberry Liqueur
1 1/2 parts Melon Liqueur
1 part Triple Sec
1 part Grenadine
1 part Pineapple Juice
1 part Orange Juice
Collins Glass

Shake with ice and strain over ice

Good Fortune

1 1/4 parts Citrus-Flavored Vodka
3/4 part Alizé® Gold Passion
fill with Lemonade
Hurricane Glass

Shake with ice and strain over ice

Good Time Charlie

1 part Light Rum
1 part Dark Rum
1 part Cranberry Juice Cocktail
1 part Pink Grapefruit Juice
1 part Pineapple Juice
1 part Sour Mix
Collins Glass

Build over ice and stir

Goodnight Joyce

2 parts Vodka
1 part Raspberry Liqueur
fill with Orange Juice
splash Cranberry Juice Cocktail
Collins Glass

Build over ice and stir

Google Juice

1 part Vodka
1 part Amaretto
1 part Cranberry-Flavored Vodka
fill with Cranberry Juice Cocktail
Collins Glass

Build over ice and stir

Gorilla Punch

1 part Vodka
1/2 part Blue Curaçao
2 parts Orange Juice
2 parts Pineapple Juice
1 Maraschino Cherry
Collins Glass

Shake with ice and strain over ice

Governor

1 part Rye Whiskey
2 parts Sweet Vermouth
fill with Apple Cider
Collins Glass

Build over ice and stir

Graffiti
$1^1/_2$ parts Pisang Ambon® Liqueur
$1^1/_2$ parts Passion Fruit Liqueur
splash Chartreuse®
3 parts Orange Juice
1 part Lime Juice
Collins Glass

Build over ice and stir

Grand Marshall
1 part Brandy
1 part Rum
1 part Root Beer Schnapps
fill with Cola
Collins Glass

Build over ice and stir

Grandma's Peach Fuzz
$1^1/_2$ parts Sour Apple Schnapps
1 part Southern Comfort®
$^1/_2$ part Peach Schnapps
splash Lemon-Lime Soda
fill with Cranberry Juice Cocktail
Hurricane Glass

Build over ice and stir

Granny's Rocker
$1^1/_2$ parts Melon Liqueur
$^1/_2$ part Citrus-Flavored Vodka
splash Blue Curaçao
$^1/_2$ part Lime Cordial
2 parts Margarita Mix
Collins Glass

Shake with ice and pour

Grape Gazpacho
1 part Vodka
1 part Apricot Brandy
1 part Ginger Ale
1 part Grape Juice (White)
Collins Glass

Build over ice and stir

Grape Margarita
1 part Tequila
1 part Grape-Flavored Schnapps
fill with Margarita Mix
Margarita Glass

Shake with ice and pour

Grape Soda
1 part Blueberry Schnapps
1 part Raspberry Liqueur
1 part Vodka
splash Lemon-Lime Soda
fill with Cranberry Juice Cocktail
Collins Glass

Build over ice and stir

Grapefruit Teaser
4 parts Coconut-Flavored Rum
splash Lime Juice
fill with Grapefruit Juice
Collins Glass

Build over ice and stir

Grapes of Wrath
$1^1/_2$ parts Grain Alcohol
1 part Grape Juice (Red)
1 part Club Soda
Collins Glass

Build over ice and stir

Grass Widower
1 part Light Rum
1 part Blue Curaçao
fill with Orange Juice
Collins Glass

Build over ice and stir

Green Anita
1 part Banana Liqueur
1 part Blue Curaçao
1 part Melon Liqueur
splash Lemon Juice
splash Lime Juice
fill with Lemon-Lime Soda
Collins Glass

Build over ice and stir

Green Banana
1 1/2 parts Pisang Ambon® Liqueur
fill with Orange Juice
Collins Glass

Build over ice and stir

Green Doodoo
1 part Coffee Liqueur
1 part Melon Liqueur
1/2 part Peppermint Schnapps
1/2 part Vodka
fill with Cream
Collins Glass

Build over ice and stir

Green Dream
1 part Crème de Banana
1 part Pisang Ambon® Liqueur
1 part Pineapple Juice
1 part Orange Juice
Collins Glass

Shake with ice and pour

Green Eyes
1 part Vodka
1 part Blue Curaçao
2 parts Orange Juice
Collins Glass

Build over ice and stir

Green Field
1 part Melon Liqueur
1/2 part Blue Curaçao
1/2 part Triple Sec
1/2 part Coconut-Flavored Liqueur
fill with Orange Juice
Collins Glass

Shake with ice and pour

Green Fjord
1 part Gin
1 part Melon Liqueur
1/2 part Triple Sec
2 parts Sour Mix
fill with Lemon-Lime Soda
Collins Glass

Build over ice and stir

Green Force Five
1 1/2 parts Rum
1/2 part Crème de Banana
1/2 part Melon Liqueur
1 1/2 parts Orange Juice
7 parts Lemon-Lime Soda
Collins Glass

Build over ice and stir

Green Gilli
2 parts Melon Liqueur
1 part Kiwi Liqueur
1 part Gin
1 Egg White
fill with Lemonade
Collins Glass

Shake with ice and strain over ice

Green Haze
1 part Light Rum
1 part Spiced Rum
1 part Pineapple Juice
1 part Orange Juice
splash Blue Curaçao
Collins Glass

Build over ice and stir

Green Hell

1 part Blue Curaçao
1 part Gin
1 part Vodka
1 part Rum
1 part Triple Sec
1 part Tequila Silver
fill with Orange Juice
Hurricane Glass

Shake with ice and pour

Green Lantern®

2 parts Melon Liqueur
1 part Orange Juice
1 part Lemon-Lime Soda
Collins Glass

Build over ice and stir

Green Lantern® #2

3 parts Hypnotiq®
fill with Red Bull® Energy Drink
Collins Glass

Build over ice and stir

Green Meanie

1 part Rum
1 part Blue Curaçao
fill with Orange Juice
Collins Glass

Build over ice and stir

Green Mexican

1 part Tequila
1 part Melon Liqueur
fill with Sour Mix
Collins Glass

Build over ice and stir

Green Peace

1 part Vodka
1 part Dry Vermouth
1 part Pisang Ambon® Liqueur
1 part Apricot Brandy
fill with Pineapple Juice
Collins Glass

Build over ice and stir

Green Scorpion

1 part Jack Daniel's®
1 part Vodka
2 splashes Blue Curaçao
fill with Lemon-Lime Soda
Collins Glass

Build over ice and stir

Green Tuberia

2 parts Vodka
1 part Melon Liqueur
1 part Lemon Juice
fill with Lemon-Lime Soda
Collins Glass

Build over ice and stir

Green Velvet

1 part Gin
1 part Blue Curaçao
1 part Coconut-Flavored Liqueur
fill with Pineapple Juice
1/2 part Cream
Hurricane Glass

Build over ice and stir

Green Wave

3/4 part Coconut-Flavored Rum
3/4 part Spiced Rum
3/4 part Blue Curaçao
1 part Pineapple Juice
1 part Orange Juice
1 part Sour Mix
Collins Glass

Shake with ice and pour

Green Whale
$1^1/_2$ parts Blue Curaçao
splash Vodka
dash Sugar
1 part Pineapple Juice
1 part Orange Juice
Collins Glass

Shake with ice and pour

Greeny
$1^1/_2$ parts Blue Curaçao
1 part Southern Comfort®
fill with Pineapple Juice
Collins Glass

Build over ice and stir

Gremlin
$1^1/_2$ parts Citrus-Flavored Rum
$1^1/_2$ parts Lemon-Lime Soda
1 part Melon Liqueur
1 part Sour Mix
fill with Pineapple Juice
Collins Glass

Build over ice and stir

Grendel
$^1/_2$ part Vodka
$^1/_2$ part Rum
$^1/_2$ part Cointreau®
$^1/_2$ part Blue Curaçao
$^1/_2$ part Crème de Menthe (White)
$^1/_2$ part Advocaat
1 part Cream
fill with Lemonade
Collins Glass

Shake with ice and pour

Grinch
$1^1/_2$ part Melon Liqueur
1 part Malibu® Rum
1 part Gin
1 part Vodka
1 part Lemon-Lime Soda
1 part Sour Mix
1 part Blue Curaçao
Hurricane Glass

Build over ice and stir

Grizzly Bear
1 part Amaretto
1 part Jägermeister®
1 part Coffee Liqueur
fill with Milk
Collins Glass

Shake with ice and pour

Gumby's® Ruby Red
1 part Light Rum
$1^1/_2$ parts Pink Grapefruit Juice
1 part Pineapple Juice
fill with Lemon-Lime Soda
Collins Glass

Build over ice and stir

The Gummy Bear
2 parts Vodka
1 part Lemon-Lime Soda
2 parts Fruit Punch
Beer Mug

Build over ice and stir

Gump
$1^1/_2$ parts Whiskey
$^1/_2$ part Pernod®
$^1/_2$ part Crème de Cacao (Dark)
1 part Cream
dash Ground Nutmeg
Collins Glass

Build over ice and stir

Hail Mary
2 parts Vodka
splash Grenadine
fill with Orange Juice
splash Tabasco® Sauce
1 Egg
Collins Glass

Shake with ice and pour

Hairy Lime
3 parts Gin
splash Grenadine
1/2 part Lemon Juice
1/2 part Lime Juice
fill with Cola
Collins Glass

Build over ice and stir

Hairy Sunrise
3/4 part Tequila
3/4 part Vodka
1/2 part Triple Sec
fill with Orange Juice
splash Grenadine
Collins Glass

Build over ice

Hala-Balloo
1 part Brandy
1 part Scotch
fill with Lemonade
Collins Glass

Build over ice and stir

Halaballoosa
2 parts Citrus-Flavored Vodka
1 part Jamaican Rum
2 parts Blue Curaçao
1 part Orange Juice
1 part Clamato®
Collins Glass

Shake with ice and pour

Hale & Hearty
1/2 part Vodka
1/2 part Blue Curaçao
1 1/2 parts Maple Syrup
splash Honey
fill with Grapefruit Juice
Collins Glass

Shake with ice and strain over ice

Half Moon
2 parts Coconut-Flavored Rum
1 1/2 parts Crème de Banana
1 1/2 parts Coconut Cream
1 part Fresh Lime Juice
Collins Glass

Shake with ice and pour

Halfway Special
1 part Citrus-Flavored Vodka
1 part Coconut-Flavored Rum
1 part Blackberry Liqueur
fill with Orange Juice
splash Grenadine
Hurricane Glass

Build over ice and stir

Hamlet
1 part Vodka
1/2 part Campari®
fill with Orange Juice
Collins Glass

Build over ice and stir

Hangover Cure
1 part Amaretto
2 parts Tequila Reposado
1 part Spiced Rum
1 part Coconut Cream
2 parts Raspberry Juice
Beer Mug

Build over ice and stir

Happy Daze

1 part Rye Whiskey
1 part Brandy
1 part Apricot Brandy
1 part Lemon-Lime Soda
1 part Orange Juice
splash Grenadine
Collins Glass

Build over ice and stir

Happy Morning

1 part Apricot Juice
2 parts Orange Juice
splash Grenadine
Collins Glass

Build over ice and stir

Harvey Wallbanger

1 part Vodka
1/2 parts Galliano®
fill with Orange Juice
Collins Glass

Build over ice and stir

Hasta la Vista

1 part Coconut-Flavored Liqueur
1 part Licor 43®
1/2 part Crème de Cacao (White)
fill with Cherry Juice
Collins Glass

Build over ice and stir

Hasta Luego

1 1/2 parts Spiced Rum
1 Egg Yolk
1/2 part Crème de Cacao (White)
1/2 part Simple Syrup
fill with Milk
Collins Glass

Shake with ice and pour

Havana 3 A.M.

1 part Passion Fruit Liqueur
1 part Tequila Reposado
1/2 part Mango Nectar
fill with Pineapple Juice
Collins Glass

Shake with ice and pour

Hawaiian Hurricane Volcano

1 part Amaretto
1 part Southern Comfort®
1 part Vodka
splash Grenadine
Collins Glass

Shake with ice and pour

Headcrack

3 parts Hennessy®
2 parts Coffee Liqueur
fill with Milk
Hurricane Glass

Build over ice and stir

Headway

1 part Triple Sec
1 part Peach Schnapps
1 part Light Rum
fill with Orange Juice
Collins Glass

Shake with ice and pour

Healing Garden

1 1/2 parts Vodka
2/3 part Galliano®
2/3 part Benedictine®
fill with Pineapple Juice
Collins Glass

Shake with ice and pour

Heartbreaker
1 part Dark Rum
1 part Cherry Brandy
1 part Pineapple Juice
1 part Orange Juice
Collins Glass

Shake with ice and pour

Heatwave
1 part Dark Rum
1/2 part Peach Schnapps
fill with Pineapple Juice
splash Grenadine
Collins Glass

Build over ice

Heavenly Days
2 parts Amaretto
1/2 part Grenadine
fill with Sparkling Water
Collins Glass

Build over ice and stir

Hector Special
1 1/2 parts Vodka
1 part Tequila Silver
1 part Grenadine
fill with Orange Juice
Collins Glass

Build over ice and stir

Hi Rise
1 part Vodka
splash Cointreau®
1 part Sour Mix
fill with Orange Juice
splash Grenadine
Collins Glass

Build over ice and stir

Hillinator
3 parts Spiced Rum
1 part Fire Water®
fill with Mountain Dew®
Collins Glass

Build over ice and stir

Hippity Dippity
1 1/2 parts Spiced Rum
1/2 part Triple Sec
1/2 part Lime Juice
fill with Orange Juice
splash Grenadine
Collins Glass

Build over ice and stir

Hitchhiker
1 part Vodka
1 part Mandarine Napoléon® Liqueur
1/2 part Crème de Banana
1/2 part Campari®
1/2 part Coconut-Flavored Liqueur
fill with Lemonade
Collins Glass

Build over ice and stir

A Hint of Mint
3 parts Lemonade
1 part Peppermint Schnapps
1 part Coconut-Flavored Liqueur
Collins Glass

Build over ice and stir

Hoarfrost Palace
2/3 part Apricot Brandy
1 1/2 parts Light Rum
2/3 part Galliano®
fill with Pineapple Juice
1/2 part Lemon Juice
Collins Glass

Shake with ice and strain over ice

Hokes Royal Flush

2 parts Crown Royal® Whiskey
1 part Peach Schnapps
fill with Cranberry Juice Cocktail
Collins Glass

Build over ice and stir

Hollywood & Vine

$1\frac{1}{2}$ parts Citrus-Flavored Vodka
$\frac{2}{3}$ part Orange Liqueur
$\frac{2}{3}$ part Lime Juice
fill with Grapefruit Juice
dash Powdered Sugar
Collins Glass

Shake with ice and strain over ice

Hollywood Tea

1 part Gin
1 part Light Rum
1 part Tequila
1 part Vodka
fill with Lemon-Lime Soda
Collins Glass

Build over ice and stir

Home Alone

$\frac{1}{2}$ part Blue Curaçao
$\frac{2}{3}$ part Plum Brandy
$\frac{2}{3}$ part Lemon Juice
fill with Pear Juice
Collins Glass

Shake with ice and strain over ice

Home by the Sea

1 part Blue Curaçao
1 part Pernod®
1 part Crème Liqueur
1 part Orange Juice
1 part Mango Juice
Collins Glass

Shake with ice and strain over ice

Homicidal Maniac

2 parts Peach Schnapps
2 parts Vodka
1 part Cranberry Juice Cocktail
1 part Apple Juice
Beer Mug

Shake with ice and pour

Honey Dew This

$1\frac{1}{2}$ parts Vodka
$\frac{1}{2}$ part Melon Liqueur
splash Crème de Banana
fill with Pineapple Juice
Collins Glass

Shake with ice and strain over ice

Honey Driver

$1\frac{1}{2}$ parts Vodka
1 part Melon Liqueur
fill with Orange Juice
splash Honey
Collins Glass

Shake with ice and strain over ice

Honey Getter

2 parts Gin
1 part Cranberry Juice Cocktail
1 part Orange Juice
Collins Glass

Build over ice and stir

Hong Kong Fuey

1 part Tequila Silver
1 part Vodka
1 part Light Rum
1 part Melon Liqueur
1 part Gin
1/2 part Lime Cordial
fill with Lemonade
Collins Glass

Shake with ice and pour

Honky Tonk

1 1/2 parts Light Rum
1 1/2 parts Pineapple Juice
1/2 part Triple Sec
fill with Cola
Collins Glass

Build over ice and stir

Honolulu Juicy Juicer

1 1/2 parts Pineapple Juice
1 1/2 parts Rum
1 1/2 parts Southern Comfort®
1 part Fresh Lime Juice
Collins Glass

Shake with ice and strain over ice

Hoochekoo

1 part Banana Liqueur
1 part Raspberry Liqueur
1 part Watermelon Schnapps
fill with Fruit Punch
Collins Glass

Build over ice and stir

Horny Juice

4 parts Peach Schnapps
fill with Cola
Collins Glass

Build over ice and stir

Horseshoe

2 parts Tequila
1 part Southern Comfort®
fill with Orange Juice
splash Grenadine
Collins Glass

Build over ice and stir

Hot Damn! Dew

1 part Hot Damn!® Cinnamon Schnapps
fill with Mountain Dew®
Collins Glass

Build over ice and stir

Hot Land

1 1/2 parts Absolut® Peppar Vodka
2 splashes Amaretto
3/4 part Peach Schnapps
fill with Orange Juice
Collins Glass

Build over ice and stir

Hot Young Lady

1 part Coffee Liqueur
1 part Irish Cream Liqueur
1 part Cinnamon Schnapps
1 part Rumple Minze®
Collins Glass

Shake with ice and strain over ice

Hotel Riviera

1 part Vodka
1 part Blackberry Liqueur
1/2 part Sour Mix
fill with Lemon-Lime Soda
Collins Glass

Build over ice and stir

Howling Dingo
2 parts Amaretto
1 part 151-Proof Rum
fill with Dr Pepper®
Collins Glass
Build over ice and stir

Hulk Smash!
1 part Vodka
1 part Gin
1 part Melon Liqueur
fill with Mountain Dew®
Collins Glass
Build over ice and stir

Humboldt Sunset
1 1/2 parts Orange-Flavored Vodka
1/2 part Lemon Juice
1 part Pineapple Juice
1 part Cranberry Juice Cocktail
Collins Glass
Build over ice and stir

Hurricane Carole
1 part Coconut-Flavored Rum
1 part Spiced Rum
1 part Light Rum
1 part Orange Juice
1 part Cranberry Juice Cocktail
splash 151-Proof Rum
Collins Glass
Shake with ice and pour

I Am Not Sure
2 parts Tequila
fill with Root Beer
Collins Glass
Build over ice and stir

IBO Cream
1 part Blackberry Liqueur
1 part Peach Schnapps
fill with Milk
Collins Glass
Build over ice and stir

Ice Palace
1 part Light Rum
1/2 part Galliano®
1/2 part Apricot Brandy
1/4 part Lemon Juice
fill with Pineapple Juice
1 Orange Slice
Collins Glass
Build over ice and stir

Iced Lemon
1 part Vodka
1 part Sour Mix
1/2 part Vanilla Liqueur
fill with Lemon-Lime Soda
Collins Glass
Build over ice and stir

Illusions
1 part Melon Liqueur
1 part Coconut-Flavored Rum
1 part Cointreau®
1/2 part Vodka
fill with Pineapple Juice
Collins Glass
Shake with ice and pour

The Incredible Hulk®
2 parts Spiced Rum
dash Sugar
fill with Mountain Dew®
Collins Glass
Build over ice and stir

In the Sack

3 parts Cream Sherry
2 parts Apricot Nectar
3 parts Orange Juice
1/2 part Lemon Juice
1 Orange Slice
Collins Glass

Build over ice and stir

Instant Karma

2 parts Spiced Rum
fill with Mountain Dew®
splash Cola
Collins Glass

Build over ice and stir

Intercourse

2 parts Vodka
1 part Orange Juice
1 part Hawaiian Punch®
1 part Mountain Dew®
Collins Glass

Build over ice and stir

Inverted Cherry

1 part Gin
1/2 part Grenadine
1/4 part Light Rum
1/4 part Cherry Brandy
fill with Apple Juice
Collins Glass

Build over ice and stir

Irish Bulldog

1 part Amaretto
3/4 part Coffee Liqueur
3/4 part Crème de Cacao (White)
1 part Irish Cream Liqueur
Collins Glass

Shake with ice and strain over ice

Irish Mudslide

1 part Irish Cream Liqueur
fill with Root Beer
Beer Mug

Build over ice and stir

Irish Spring

1 part Irish Whiskey
1/2 part Peach Brandy
1 part Orange Juice
1 part Sour Mix
1 Orange Slice
1 Maraschino Cherry
Collins Glass

Shake with ice and strain over ice

Irish Whip

1 part Vodka
1 part Pernod®
1 part 151-Proof Rum
1 part Crème de Menthe (White)
1 part Lemon-Lime Soda
1 part Orange Juice
Beer Mug

Build over ice and stir

Isle of the Blessed Coconut

2 parts Light Rum
1/2 part Orange Juice
1/2 part Fresh Lime Juice
1/2 part Amaretto
1/2 part Coconut Cream
Collins Glass

Shake with ice and pour

Isle of Tropics

2 parts Coconut-Flavored Rum
1 part Orange Juice
1 part Pineapple Juice
Collins Glass

Shake with ice and pour

Italian Beauty
1 part Sambuca
1/2 part Parfait Amour
1/2 part Grenadine
fill with Pineapple Juice
Collins Glass

Build over ice and stir

The Italian Job
2 parts Vodka
1 part Cointreau®
1 part Pineapple Juice
1 part Orange Juice
splash Cream
Mason Jar

Build over ice and stir

Italian Canary
1/2 part Vodka
1/2 part Amaretto
1/2 part Rum
1/2 part Vanilla Liqueur
2 parts Sour Mix
fill with Lemon-Lime Soda
Collins Glass

Build over ice and stir

Izcaragua
1 part Dark Rum
1/2 part Crème de Banana
1/2 part Dry Vermouth
fill with Orange Juice
Collins Glass

Build over ice and stir

J & P
2 parts Peach Schnapps
1 1/2 parts Dark Rum
1 part Lemon Juice
splash Simple Syrup
fill with Pineapple Juice
Collins Glass

Build over ice and stir

Jack & Coke
2 parts Jack Daniel's®
fill with Cola
Collins Glass

Build over ice and stir

Jack Frost
2 parts Jack Daniel's®
1 part Drambuie®
splash Grenadine
1 part Sour Mix
1 part Orange Juice
Collins Glass

Shake with ice and pour

Jack Hammer
2 parts Jack Daniel's®
fill with Orange Juice
Collins Glass

Build over ice and stir

Jack-O'-Lantern Juice
1 part Rum
1/2 part Crème de Banana
2 parts Lemonade
1 1/2 parts Pineapple Juice
1 1/2 parts Orange Juice
fill with Lemon-Lime Soda
Hurricane Glass

Build over ice and stir

Jack the Legend
1 part Jack Daniel's®
1 part Amaretto
fill with Pineapple Juice
Collins Glass

Shake with ice and pour

Jack Your Melon
2 parts Watermelon Schnapps
1 part Jack Daniel's®
fill with Mountain Dew®
Collins Glass

Build over ice and stir

Jade Isle
2 parts Melon Liqueur
1 part Blue Curaçao
1 part Currant Flavored Vodka
1 part Sour Mix
1 part Lemon-Lime Soda
1 Maraschino Cherry
Hurricane Glass

Build over ice and stir

Jäger Bomb
1 part Jägermeister®
fill with Red Bull® Energy Drink
Collins Glass

Build over ice and stir

Jamaharon
1 part Blue Curaçao
1 part Melon Liqueur
fill with Cola
Collins Glass

Build over ice and stir

Jamaican Jambaylaya
2 parts Spiced Rum
fill with Fruit Punch
Collins Glass

Build over ice and stir

Jamaican Me Crazy
1 part Dark Rum
1 part Tia Maria®
fill with Pineapple Juice
Collins Glass

Build over ice and stir

Jamaican Me Crazy #2
1 part Light Rum
1 part Coconut-Flavored Rum
1 part Banana Liqueur
splash Cranberry Juice Cocktail
splash Pineapple Juice
Collins Glass

Shake with ice and strain over ice

Jamaican Sunrise
2 parts Vodka
2 parts Peach Schnapps
fill with Orange Juice
1 part Cranberry Juice Cocktail
Collins Glass

Build over ice

Java's Punch
1 part Vodka
1 part Pisang Ambon® Liqueur
1 part Coconut-Flavored Liqueur
fill with Orange Juice
Collins Glass

Build over ice and stir

Jeannie's Dream
2 parts Malibu® Rum
1 part Sloe Gin
1 part Orange Juice
1 part Pineapple Juice
1 part Lemon-Lime Soda
Hurricane Glass

Build over ice and stir

Jet Ski®
1 part Coconut-Flavored Liqueur
splash Blue Curaçao
splash Crcam
fill with Pineapple Juice
Collins Glass

Shake with ice and strain over ice

Jinx
2 parts Vodka
1 part Blueberry Schnapps
1/2 part Irish Cream Liqueur
2 parts Lemon-Lime Soda
1 part Grape Juice (Red)
Collins Glass

Build over ice and stir

Joe Collins

1 part Scotch
2 parts Sour Mix
fill with Cola
1 Maraschino Cherry
Collins Glass

Build over ice and stir

Joe Falchetto

1 part Vodka
1/2 part Triple Sec
1/2 part Vanilla Liqueur
1/2 part Strawberry Syrup
fill with Pineapple Juice
Collins Glass

Shake with ice and strain over ice

John Cooper Deluxe

2 parts Vodka
1 part Orange Juice
1 part Root Beer
Collins Glass

Build over ice and stir

John Daly

1 1/4 part Citrus-Flavored Vodka
1/4 part Triple Sec
1 part Lemonade
1 part Iced Tea
Collins Glass

Build over ice and stir

Johnnie Red

1 part Vodka
1/2 part Parfait Amour
1/2 part Crème de Banana
fill with Orange Juice
splash Grenadine
Collins Glass

Build over ice and stir

Jolly Jumper

1 part Whiskey
1 part Vodka
1 part Gin
1 part Passion Fruit Liqueur
fill with Orange Juice
Collins Glass

Build over ice and stir

Juicy Lucy

1 part Vodka
1 part Gin
1 part Blue Curaçao
1 part Orange Juice
1 part Lemon-Lime Soda
Beer Mug

Build over ice and stir

Jump Up and Kiss Me

1 part Apricot Brandy
1 part Galliano®
1 part Rum
fill with Pineapple Juice
splash Grenadine
Beer Mug

Build over ice

June Bug

1 part Coconut-Flavored Rum
1/2 part Melon Liqueur
1/2 part Crème de Banana
1 part Pineapple Juice
1 part Sour Mix
Collins Glass

Build over ice and stir

Jungle Juice

1 part Vodka
1 part Rum
1/2 part Triple Sec
splash Sour Mix
1 part Cranberry Juice Cocktail
1 part Orange Juice
1 part Pineapple Juice
Collins Glass

Build over ice and stir

Jungle Rumble
1 part Crème de Banana
1/2 part Blue Curaçao
1/2 part Light Rum
1/2 part Lime Juice
fill with Pineapple Juice
Collins Glass

Shake with ice and strain over ice

Kamaniwanalaya
1 part Amaretto
1 part Light Rum
1 part Dark Rum
fill with Pineapple Juice
Collins Glass

Shake with ice and pour

Kamehameha Rum Punch
1 part Light Rum
1/2 part Dark Rum
1/2 part Blackberry Liqueur
1/2 part Amaretto
1 part Fresh Lime Juice
fill with Pineapple Juice
Collins Glass

Shake with ice and pour

Kanarie
2 parts Crème de Banana
fill with Pineapple Juice
Collins Glass

Build over ice and stir

Kansas Tornado
1 part Light Rum
1 part Dark Rum
1/2 part Gin
1/2 part Amaretto
1 part Pineapple Juice
1 part Grapefruit Juice
1 part Orange Juice
splash Grenadine
Hurricane Glass

Build over ice and stir

Karma Killer
1 part Dark Rum
1/2 part Triple Sec
1/2 part Peach Brandy
1 part Fruit Punch
1 part Orange Juice
1 part Pineapple Juice
1 part Grapefruit Juice
Collins Glass

Build over ice and stir

Kenny McCormick
1 part Rum
1 part Tequila
1 part Tia Maria®
fill with Cola
Collins Glass

Build over ice and stir

Kentucky Wildcat
1/2 part Jack Daniel's®
1/2 part Southern Comfort®
1/2 part Yukon Jack®
1/2 part Jim Beam®
1 part Sour Mix
1 part Cola
Hurricane Glass

Build over ice and stir

Kermit®
1/2 part Vodka
1/2 part Whiskey
1/2 part Gin
fill with Orange Juice
1 part Blue Curaçao
Collins Glass

Build over ice and stir

Kermit® Green
1 part Vodka
1 part Melon Liqueur
fill with Lemon-Lime Soda
Collins Glass

Build over ice and stir

Kermit's® Revenge
1 part Rum
1 part Tequila
1 part Vodka
1 part Gin
1 part Triple Sec
1 part Crème de Menthe (White)
fill with Lemonade
Hurricane Glass

Build over ice and stir

Kick in the Glass
2 parts Light Rum
splash Cranberry Juice Cocktail
fill with Orange Juice
1 scoop Vanilla Ice Cream
Beer Mug

Build over ice

Kingston Spritzer
splash Melon Liqueur
1 part Spiced Rum
fill with Pineapple Juice
Collins Glass

Shake with ice and strain over ice

Kinky Monday
1 part Vodka
1/2 part Blackberry Liqueur
1/2 part Crème de Cassis
1/2 part Raspberry Liqueur
1 part Fresh Lime Juice
fill with Lemon-Lime Soda
Collins Glass

Build over ice and stir

Kiss of Blue
1 part Citrus-Flavored Vodka
1 part Blue Curaçao
1 part Lime Cordial
fill with Orange Juice
Collins Glass

Shake with ice and pour

Kitchen Sink
1 part Blue Curaçao
1 part Gin
1 part Light Rum
1 part Sour Apple Schnapps
1 part Vodka
1 part Triple Sec
splash Lemon-Lime Soda
splash Sour Mix
splash Lemon Juice
splash Melon Liqueur
Collins Glass

Build over ice and stir

Kiwi Kicker
1 part Advocaat
1 part Kiwi Schnapps
1 part Melon Liqueur
fill with Pineapple Juice
Collins Glass

Build over ice and stir

Kiwi River
1 1/2 parts Kiwi Schnapps
fill with Lemonade
Collins Glass

Build over ice and stir

Kiwi Wee Wee
1 part Kiwi Schnapps
3/4 part Coconut-Flavored Liqueur
1/2 part Crème de Banana
1/2 part Lemon Juice
1/2 part Lime Cordial
fill with Pineapple Juice
Collins Glass

Shake with ice and pour

Klingon® Blood Wine

1 part Tequila
1 part Spiced Rum
splash Grenadine
splash Tabasco® Sauce
fill with Cranberry Juice Cocktail
Beer Mug

Build over ice and stir

KMart® Screwdriver

2 parts Vodka
fill with Orange Soda
Collins Glass

Build over ice and stir. Use the cheapest Vodka available and a store brand Soda.

Knoxville Lemonade

1 part Vodka
1 part Peach Schnapps
fill with Lemonade
splash Ginger Ale
Collins Glass

Build over ice and stir

Kodachrome

1 part Vodka
1 part Blue Curaçao
splash Lemonade
splash Orange Juice
splash Cranberry Juice Cocktail
Collins Glass

Shake with ice and pour

Kona

1 part Coconut-Flavored Liqueur
1 part Melon Liqueur
1 part Sour Mix
1 part Orange Juice
fill with Lemon-Lime Soda
Collins Glass

Build in the glass with no ice

Konloo

1 part Light Rum
1/2 part Blackberry Liqueur
1/2 part Crème de Banana
splash Coconut-Flavored Liqueur
fill with Pineapple Juice
Collins Glass

Build over ice and stir

Konoko

1 part Gin
1 part Coconut-Flavored Liqueur
1/2 part Kiwi Schnapps
1 part Pineapple Juice
1 part Orange Juice
Collins Glass

Build over ice and stir

Kosmo

1 1/2 parts Orange-Flavored Vodka
1/2 part Triple Sec
fill with Cranberry Juice Cocktail
splash Lime Juice
splash Lemon Juice
Collins Glass

Shake with ice and pour

Krazy Kool-Aid®

1 part Currant-Flavored Vodka
1 part Amaretto
1 part Melon Liqueur
fill with Pineapple Juice
Collins Glass

Shake with ice and pour

Kuaui King

2 parts Coconut-Flavored Liqueur
splash Grenadine
fill with Pineapple Juice
Collins Glass

Shake with ice and strain over ice

Kung Fu
1 part Jägermeister®
1 part Pisang Ambon® Liqueur
fill with Cola
Collins Glass

Build over ice and stir

Kurant Mellow
1 part Southern Comfort®
1 part Currant-Flavored Vodka
fill with Lemon-Lime Soda
Collins Glass

Build over ice and stir

L.A. Sunrise
1 part Vodka
1/2 part Crème de Banana
1 part Pineapple Juice
1 part Orange Juice
splash Dark Rum
Collins Glass

Build over ice

La Bomba
1 1/4 part Tequila Gold
3/4 part Cointreau®
1 part Pineapple Juice
1 part Orange Juice
splash Grenadine
Collins Glass

Build over ice and stir

La Musa
1 part Dark Rum
1/2 part Crème de Banana
1/2 part Sweet Vermouth
fill with Orange Juice
splash Grenadine
Collins Glass

Build over ice

Labyrinth
1 part Advocaat
1 part Whiskey
1 part Kiwi Liqueur
fill with Lemonade
Collins Glass

Build over ice and stir

Lady Killer
1 1/4 part Gin
3/4 part Sweet Vermouth
3/4 part Dry Vermouth
3 dashes Orange Bitters
Collins Glass

Shake with ice and strain

Lady Love Fizz
2 parts Gin
2 splashes Light Crème
dash Powdered Sugar
1/2 part Lemon Juice
1 Egg White
fill with Carbonated Water
Collins Glass

Shake all but Carbonated Water with ice and strain into the glass. Top with Carbonated

A Laid-Back Drink
1 part Vodka
1 part Lemon-Lime Soda
1 part Orange Juice
Collins Glass

Build over ice and stirWater.

Laid Back Limeade
1 1/2 parts Jack Daniel's®
1/2 part Triple Sec
1 part Lime Juice
fill with Lemon-Lime Soda
Collins Glass

Build over ice and stir

Lait Grenadine
1 part Grenadine
fill with Milk
Collins Glass

Build in the glass with no ice and stir

Lake Water
1/2 part Gin
1/2 part Jack Daniel's®
1/2 part Tequila
1/2 part Vodka
1 part Blueberry Schnapps
1 part Cola
1 part Lemon-Lime Soda
Collins Glass

Build over ice and stir

Lamoone
1 part Dry Vermouth
1 part Whiskey
1 part Crème de Banana
splash Fresh Lime Juice
fill with Sparkling Water
Collins Glass

Build over ice and stir

Land Shark
1 1/2 parts Rum
3/4 part Coconut-Flavored Rum
1/4 part Grenadine
fill with Pineapple Juice
Collins Glass

Shake with ice and pour

Latin Dream
1 part Light Rum
1 part Dry Sherry
splash Grenadine
1 part Pineapple Juice
1 part Ginger Ale
Collins Glass

Build over ice and stir

Leaving Las Vegas
1 part Triple Sec
1 part Vodka
1 part Light Rum
1 part Gin
fill with Lemonade
splash Lemon-Lime Soda
Hurricane Glass

Build over ice and stir

Leg Spreader
1 part Coconut-Flavored Rum
1 part Apricot Brandy
1 part Melon Liqueur
1 part Cranberry Juice Cocktail
1 part Pineapple Juice
Collins Glass

Shake with ice and pour

Lemon Fizz
1 1/2 parts Vodka
1 1/2 parts Triple Sec
2 parts Carbonated Water
fill with Lemonade
1 Lemon Wedge
Hurricane Glass

Build over ice and stir

Lennart
1 1/2 parts Pear Brandy
1 part Sweetened Lime Juice
fill with Lemon-Lime Soda
Collins Glass

Build over ice and stir

Lesbian Baseball Team
1 part Dark Rum
1 part Southern Comfort®
1 part Amaretto
1 part Banana Liqueur
1 part Blackberry Liqueur
fill with Pineapple Juice
Collins Glass

Shake with ice and pour

Lethal Injection
2 parts Light Rum
1 part Orange Juice
1 part Grapefruit Juice
splash Grenadine
Collins Glass

Shake with ice and pour

Light Bulb
1 1/2 parts Blue Curaçao
splash Lime Juice
fill with Lemon-Lime Soda
Collins Glass

Build over ice and stir

Lightning Bug
1 part Lychee Liqueur
1 part Blue Curaçao
1/2 part 151-Proof Rum
2 parts Sour Mix
1 part Orange Juice
Collins Glass

Shake with ice and strain over ice

Lights of Havana
1 part Coconut-Flavored Rum
1/2 part Melon Liqueur
1 part Pineapple Juice
1 part Orange Juice
splash Sparkling Water
Collins Glass

Build over ice and stir

Lime and Coke
1 part Lime Juice
fill with Cola
1 Lime Slice
Collins Glass

Build over ice and stir

Limelon
1 part Melon Liqueur
1 part Vodka
fill with Limeade
Collins Glass

Build over ice and stir

Linux®
1 1/2 parts Vodka
1/2 part Lime Juice
fill with Cola
Collins Glass

Build over ice and stir

Lipstick
1 part Vodka
1/2 part Apricot Brandy
1/2 part Grenadine
1 part Lemon Juice
fill with Orange Juice
Collins Glass

Shake with ice and pour

Liquid Bomb
1/2 part Vodka
1/2 part Citrus-Flavored Rum
1 part Alizé®
1 part Peach Schnapps
1 part Cranberry Juice Cocktail
1 part Orange Juice
Collins Glass

Build over ice and stir

Liquid Marijuana
1 part Blue Curaçao
1 part Coconut-Flavored Rum
1 part Spiced Rum
fill with Pineapple Juice
splash Sour Mix
1 part Melon Liqueur
Hurricane Glass

Shake with ice and pour

Lively Shamrock
1 part Whiskey
1 part Crème de Menthe (Green)
fill with Milk
Collins Glass

Shake with ice and pour

Loco in Acapulco
$1\frac{1}{2}$ parts Aperol™
$\frac{1}{2}$ part Tequila Silver
splash Crème de Banana
fill with Banana Juice
Collins Glass

Build over ice and stir

London Fever
1 part Dry Gin
1 part Light Rum
1 part Lime Juice
splash Grenadine
fill with Sparkling Water
Collins Glass

Build over ice and stir

Long Hot Night
2 parts Bourbon
1 part Cranberry Juice Cocktail
1 part Pineapple Juice
Collins Glass

Build over ice and stir

Long Pan
1 part Light Rum
1 part Gin
1 part Grenadine
fill with Cola
Collins Glass

Build over ice and stir

Long Suit
2 parts Southern Comfort®
1 part Grapefruit Juice
1 part Tonic Water
Collins Glass

Build over ice and stir

Long Vacation
1 part Dry Gin
1 part Amaretto
1 part Red Curaçao
$\frac{1}{2}$ part Triple Sec
fill with Pineapple Juice
Collins Glass

Build over ice and stir

Longaberger® Lemonade
1 part Cranberry-Flavored Vodka
1 part Triple Sec
1 part Sour Mix
fill with Lemon-Lime Soda
Collins Glass

Build over ice and stir

Loose Caboose
2 parts Vodka
1 part Cranberry Juice Cocktail
1 part Lemonade
splash Grenadine
1 Maraschino Cherry
Collins Glass

Build over ice and stir

Loretto Lemonade
$1\frac{1}{2}$ parts Bourbon
$\frac{1}{2}$ part Melon Liqueur
$\frac{1}{2}$ part Fresh Lime Juice
fill with Apple Juice
Collins Glass

Shake with ice and pour

Losing Your Cherry

1 1/2 parts Vodka
1/2 part Cherry Brandy
1 part Sour Mix
1 part Lemonade
Collins Glass

Build over ice and stir

Loudmouth

1 part Tequila
1 part Coffee Liqueur
fill with Cranberry Juice Cocktail
Collins Glass

Build over ice and stir

Lounge Lizard

1 part Dark Rum
1/2 part Amaretto
fill with Cola
Collins Glass

Build over ice and stir

Love Dream

1 part Blue Curaçao
1 part Peach Schnapps
2/3 part Coconut-Flavored Liqueur
fill with Pineapple Juice
splash Lemon Juice
Collins Glass

Shake with ice and pour

Love Juice

1/2 part Vodka
1/2 part Passion Fruit Liqueur
1/4 part Pisang Ambon® Liqueur
1 part Pineapple Juice
1 part Orange Juice
1/2 part Grenadine
Collins Glass

Build over ice and stir

Love on the Lawn

1 part Blue Curaçao
1 part Cranberry-Flavored Vodka
fill with Orange Juice
splash Grenadine
Collins Glass

Shake with ice and pour

Love Shack

1 1/2 parts Dark Rum
1 part Orange Juice
fill with Lemon-Lime Soda
splash Grenadine
Collins Glass

Build over ice and stir

Lucky Driver

1/2 part Coconut-Flavored Liqueur
1 part Lemon Juice
1 part Pineapple Juice
1 part Grapefruit Juice
1 part Orange Juice
splash Simple Syrup
Collins Glass

Shake with ice and strain over ice

Lucy

1 part Crème de Banana
1 part Blue Curaçao
1 part Coconut-Flavored Liqueur
fill with Pineapple Juice
Collins Glass

Shake with ice and pour

Luisita

1 1/2 parts Blue Curaçao
1/2 part Cream
fill with Sparkling Water
Collins Glass

Build over ice and stir

Lunapop
3/4 part Vodka
1/2 part Crème de Menthe (Green)
1/4 part Vanilla Liqueur
splash Amaretto
fill with Milk
Collins Glass

Build over ice and stir

M.V.P.
1 part Vodka
1/2 part Melon Liqueur
1/2 part Coconut-Flavored Rum
fill with Pineapple Juice
Hurricane Glass

Build over ice and stir

Macambo
2 parts Dark Rum
1 1/2 parts Orange-Flavored Gin
1 part Orange Juice
1 part Papaya Juice
splash Grenadine
Collins Glass

Build over ice and stir

Macarena
1 part Tequila
1/2 part Coconut-Flavored Rum
3 parts Sour Mix
1 part Orange Juice
1 part Pineapple Juice
splash Cranberry Juice Cocktail
Collins Glass

Build over ice and stir

Made in Heaven
1 part Cream
1 part Vodka
1 part Coconut-Flavored Liqueur
1 part Strawberry Liqueur
fill with Lemon-Lime Soda
Hurricane Glass

Build over ice and stir

Madeleine
1 part Passoa
1 part Gin
1 part Coconut-Flavored Liqueur
fill with Pineapple Juice
Collins Glass

Build over ice and stir

Magic Wonder
1 part Rum
1 part Strawberry Syrup
fill with Lemon-Lime Soda
Collins Glass

Build over ice and stir

Magnolia
2 parts Coconut-Flavored Rum
1 part Grenadine
fill with Dr Pepper®
Collins Glass

Build over ice and stir

Main Attraction
1/2 part Orange Juice
1 part Peach Schnapps
4 parts Orange/Pineapple Juice
1 part Cranberry Liqueur
1 part Wild Berry Schnapps
Collins Glass

Build over ice and stir

Maka Hua Hula
1 part Coconut-Flavored Liqueur
1/2 part Crème de Banana
1 part Light Rum
fill with Pineapple Juice
1/2 part Cranberry Juice Cocktail
Collins Glass

Build over ice and stir

Malibu Barbie®

1 part Peach Schnapps
1 part Coconut-Flavored Rum
2 parts Mango Juice
Collins Glass

Build over ice and stir

A Malibu Twist

1 part Rum
1 part Lime Juice
fill with Lemonade
Collins Glass

Build over ice and stir

Mama Jama

splash Triple Sec
splash Grenadine
1/2 part Spiced Rum
1 part Orange Juice
2 parts Apple Juice
splash Coconut Cream
Collins Glass

Shake with ice and pour

Mamacita

1 1/2 parts Malibu® Rum
1/2 part Passoã®
1/2 part Cointreau®
fill with Guava Juice
Hurricane Glass

Shake with ice and pour

Mambo

1 1/2 parts Sour Mix
1 part Lemonade
1 part Melon Liqueur
1/2 part Light Rum
Collins Glass

Shake with ice and strain over ice

Mandarin Sunrise

1 1/2 parts Orange-Flavored Vodka
1 part Peach Schnapps
2 parts Pineapple Juice
1 part Orange Juice
Collins Glass

Build over ice and stir

Mandy Sea

1 1/2 parts Amaretto
1/2 part Triple Sec
1 part Sour Mix
1 part Orange Juice
1 part Pineapple Juice
splash Grenadine
splash Lemon-Lime Soda
Collins Glass

Shake with ice and strain over ice

Mangorita

2 parts Tequila
1/2 part Triple Sec
1 1/2 parts Mango Nectar
Margarita Glass

Shake with ice and pour

Maple Queen

1 part Scotch
1 part Triple Sec
1/2 part Maple Syrup
dash Bitters
fill with Lemonade
Collins Glass

Shake with ice and pour

Maracas

1 1/2 parts Vodka
1/4 part Blackberry Liqueur
splash Parfait Amour
fill with Pineapple Juice
Collins Glass

Build over ice and stir

Margarita
$1^1/_2$ parts Tequila
$^1/_2$ part Triple Sec
1 part Lime Juice
Margarita Glass

Rub rim of the glass with Lime wedge and dip rim in Salt. Shake all ingredients with ice and strain into the salt-rimmed glass and serve.

Maria
1 part Crème de Banana
1 part Strega®
1 part Orange Juice
1 part Pineapple Juice
Collins Glass

Shake with ice and strain over ice

Marienne
1 part Crème de Menthe (Green)
1 part Crème de Cacao (Dark)
fill with Milk
Collins Glass

Shake with ice and pour

Marion Barry
$^1/_2$ part Blackberry Liqueur
$1^1/_2$ parts Currant-Flavored Vodka
fill with Cranberry Juice Cocktail
1 part Cola
Collins Glass

Shake with ice and pour

Marrakech Express
$1^1/_2$ parts Gin
splash Grenadine
splash Orange Flower Water
fill with Orange Juice
Collins Glass

Shake with ice and pour

Martian Urine Sample
1 part Banana Liqueur
1 part Blue Curaçao
1 part Melon Liqueur
1 part Pineapple Juice
1 part Club Soda
Collins Glass

Build over ice

Masroska
2 parts Vodka
1 part Orange Juice
2 parts Apple Juice
Collins Glass

Build over ice and stir

Mattapoo
1 part Vodka
$^1/_2$ part Melon Liqueur
1 part Grapefruit Juice
1 part Pineapple Juice
Collins Glass

Build over ice and stir

Maverick
$1^1/_2$ parts Vodka
$^1/_2$ part Amaretto
$^1/_2$ part Triple Sec
2 splashes Galliano®
fill with Pineapple Juice
Collins Glass

Shake with ice and strain over ice

Meema
1 part Amaretto
1 part Peach Schnapps
1 part Vodka
fill with Cranberry Juice Cocktail
Collins Glass

Build over ice and stir

Melon Highball

1½ parts Melon Liqueur
1 part Vodka
fill with Orange Juice
Collins Glass

Shake with ice and strain over ice

Melon Illusion

2 parts Melon Liqueur
½ part Vodka
½ part Triple Sec
1 part Lemon Juice
fill with Pineapple Juice
Collins Glass

Shake with ice and strain over ice

Melon Spritz

1 part Spiced Rum
¼ part Melon Liqueur
fill with Pineapple Juice
splash Club Soda
Collins Glass

Build over ice and stir

Mentholyzer

1 part Vodka
1 part Tia Maria®
¼ part Crème de Menthe (White)
2 parts Cream
fill with Cola
Collins Glass

Build over ice and stir

Merlin

1 part Peach Schnapps
splash Strawberry Syrup
fill with Pineapple Juice
Collins Glass

Shake with ice and strain over ice

Merlin's Monkey

1 part Irish Cream Liqueur
1 part 99-Proof Banana Liqueur
1 part Butterscotch Schnapps
½ part Crème de Cacao (Dark)
fill with Milk
Collins Glass

Shake with ice and strain over ice

Mexicali Rose

⅔ part Raspberry Liqueur
2 parts Tequila
1 part Margarita Mix
splash Lime Juice
Collins Glass

Shake with ice and pour

Mexican Mockingbird

1½ parts Tequila Silver
1 part Crème de Menthe (Green)
fill with Sparkling Water
Collins Glass

Build over ice and stir

Mexicola

2 parts Tequila
½ part Lime Juice
fill with Cola
Collins Glass

Build over ice and stir

Miami Ice

½ part Vodka
½ part Peach Schnapps
½ part Gin
½ part Rum
2 parts Sour Mix
fill with Orange Juice
Collins Glass

Shake with ice and pour

Midnight Lemonade
$1^1/_2$ parts Raspberry Liqueur
fill with Lemonade
splash Lemon-Lime Soda
Collins Glass

Build over ice and stir

Milk Punch
2 parts Whiskey
dash Powdered Sugar
dash Ground Nutmeg
fill with Milk
Collins Glass

Shake with ice and strain over ice

Mind Twist
$^2/_3$ part Blue Curaçao
$^2/_3$ part Absinthe
$^2/_3$ part Black Currant syrup
1 part Grapefruit Juice
1 part Pineapple Juice
Collins Glass

Shake with ice and pour

Minnesota Slammer
1 part Cherry Brandy
1 part Peach Schnapps
1 part Sour Apple Schnapps
2 parts Sour Mix
fill with Lemon-Lime Soda
Hurricane Glass

Build over ice and stir

Mint Chocolate Milk
2 parts Crème de Cacao (Dark)
$^1/_2$ part Light Rum
1 part Crème de Menthe (White)
fill with Milk
Collins Glass

Build over ice and stir

Mint Julep
3 Fresh Mint Leaves
dash Powdered Sugar
2 splashes Water
2 parts Bourbon
Collins Glass

Muddle the Mint Leaves, Powdered Sugar, and Water in the glass. Fill with crushed ice and add Bourbon. Garnish with a Mint leaf and serve with a straw.

Misty Ice
1 part Pernod®
$^1/_2$ part Crème de Menthe (White)
fill with Lemon-Lime Soda
Collins Glass

Build over ice and stir

Misty You
1 part Light Rum
$^1/_2$ part Peach Schnapps
splash Blue Curaçao
dash Sugar
fill with Sparkling Water
Collins Glass

Build over ice and stir

Mizzy
splash Melon Liqueur
splash Citrus-Flavored Vodka
$^1/_4$ part Pineapple Juice
splash Simple Syrup
fill with Orange Juice
Collins Glass

Shake with ice and pour

Mojito

1 Mint Sprig
1/2 part Lime Juice
1 1/4 part Dark Rum
dash Sugar
2 parts Club Soda
Collins Glass

Muddle 1 Mint Sprig with Lime Juice and Sugar in bottom of the glass. Fill with crushed ice. Add Rum, stir, and top with Club Soda. Garnish with a Mint Leaf.

Monkey Dance

1 part Rum
1 part Crème de Cacao (Dark)
1 part Crème de Banana
splash Cream
fill with Cola
Collins Glass

Build over ice and stir

Monkey Poop

3/4 part Vodka
3/4 part Crème de Banana
1/2 part Lime Cordial
1 part Pineapple Juice
1 part Orange Juice
Collins Glass

Shake with ice and strain over ice

Monk's Habit

1 part Light Rum
1 part Raspberry Liqueur
1/2 part Triple Sec
1/4 part Grenadine
fill with Pineapple Juice
Collins Glass

Shake with ice and pour

Monolith

1 1/2 parts Dark Rum
1/2 part Crème de Cacao (White)
1/2 part Lemon Juice
1 part Orange Juice
fill with Pineapple Juice
Collins Glass

Shake with ice and strain over ice

Moon Tea

1 part Gin
1 part Rum
1 part Triple Sec
1 part Vodka
fill with Orange Juice
Collins Glass

Shake with ice and pour

Mount Red

1 part Vodka
1 part Light Rum
1 part Gin
1 part Peach Schnapps
fill with Cranberry Juice Cocktail
splash Lime Juice
Collins Glass

Build over ice and stir

Mountaineer

1 1/2 parts Rum
1 part Orange Juice
1/2 part Ginger Ale
1/4 part Milk
1/4 part Lemon Juice
dash Pepper
Collins Glass

Build over ice and stir

Mouse Trap
2 parts Vodka
1 1/2 parts Triple Sec
2 parts Orange Juice
1 1/2 parts Grenadine
fill with Lemon-Lime Soda
Collins Glass

Build over ice and stir

Mr. Freeze
1 part Black Haus® Blackberry Schnapps
1 part Vodka
1 part Blue Curaçao
3 parts Sour Mix
1 part Lemon-Lime Soda
Collins Glass

Build over ice and stir

Mr. Wilson
1 part Apple Brandy
1 part Coconut-Flavored Rum
fill with Orange Juice
Collins Glass

Build over ice and stir

Muff Rider
2 parts Sake
1 part Light Rum
3 parts Pineapple Juice
fill with Lemon-Lime Sod
a
Collins Glass

Build over ice and stir

Mundo Fine
1 1/2 parts Whiskey
1 part Melon Liqueur
1 1/2 parts Cream
splash Lemon Juice
splash Grenadine
fill with Orange Juice
Collins Glass

Shake with ice and pour

A Mystery
1 part Coconut-Flavored Rum
fill with Milk
Collins Glass

Build over ice and stir

Nantucket
2 parts Brandy
1 part Cranberry Juice Cocktail
1 part Grapefruit Juice
Collins Glass

Shake with ice and pour

Nashville Egg Nog
2 parts Advocaat
1 part Brandy
1 part Dark Rum
1/2 part Bourbon
fill with Milk
Collins Glass

Shake with ice and strain over ice

Nashville Low Rider
1 part Triple Sec
1 part Southern Comfort®
1 part Simple Syrup
fill with Lemonade
Collins Glass

Shake with ice and strain over ice

Naval Lint
2 parts Amaretto
1 part Vodka
splash Lime Juice
fill with Cola
Collins Glass

Build over ice and stir

Navel Caribbean Love
2 parts Coconut-Flavored Rum
fill with Orange Juice
Collins Glass

Build over ice and stir

Nectar of the Gods
1/2 part Apricot Brandy
1/2 part Peach Schnapps
1/2 part Coconut-Flavored Rum
1/2 part 151-Proof Rum
1 part Pineapple Juice
1 part Cranberry Juice Cocktail
1 part Orange Juice
Collins Glass

Shake with ice and strain over ice

Needle in Your Eye
1 part Gin
1 part Vodka
splash Lemon Juice
splash Lime Juice
splash Orange Juice
fill Lemon-Lime Soda
Collins Glass

Build over ice and stir

Nell Gwynne
2 parts Apricot Brandy
fill with Orange Juice
Collins Glass

Shake with ice and pour

Neon Green
1 part Melon Liqueur
1 part Coconut-Flavored Liqueur
1/2 part Crème de Menthe (Green)
fill with Lemon-Lime Soda
Collins Glass

Build over ice and stir

Neon Nightmare
1 1/4 part Coconut-Flavored Rum
1/2 part Melon Liqueur
1/4 part Blue Curaçao
fill with Pineapple Juice
Hurricane Glass

Shake with ice and strain over ice

Neon Tea
1/2 part Gin
1/2 part Sour Apple Schnapps
1/2 part Vanilla-Flavored Vodka
1/2 part Light Rum
1/4 part Triple Sec
1 part Sour Mix
1/4 part Melon Liqueur
Collins Glass

Shake with ice and pour

New Madonna
1 part Sloe Gin
fill with Lemonade
splash Cherry Brandy
Collins Glass

Build over ice and stir

New Orleans Fizz
2 parts Gin
2 splashes Lime Juice
2 splashes Lemon Juice
dash Sugar
1 part Cream
1 Egg White
splash Seltzer Water
Collins Glass

Shake with ice and pour

Nickel
1 part Currant-Flavored Vodka
1 part Melon Liqueur
1 part Orange Juice
1 part Lemon-Lime Soda
Collins Glass
Build over ice and stir

Nickel Fever
1/2 parts Blue Curaçao
2/3 part Southern Comfort®
2/3 part Galliano®
1 part Cream
1 part Orange Juice
Collins Glass
Build over ice and stir

Nikko
1 1/2 parts Vodka
1/2 part Blue Curaçao
1/2 part Pineapple Juice
fill with Orange Juice
Collins Glass
Build over ice and stir

No Pressure
1 part 151-Proof Rum
1 part Blue Curaçao
1 part Strawberry Daiquiri Mix
1 part Piña Colada Mix
Hurricane Glass
Build over ice and stir

No Reason to Live
1 part Tequila
1 part Vodka
1 part Gin
1 part Sambuca
2 splashes Tabasco® Sauce
fill with Orange Juice
Collins Glass
Build over ice and stir

No. 7
1 part Amaretto
1 part Peach Schnapps
1 part Iced Tea
1 part Cola
Collins Glass
Build over ice and stir

North Dakota Summer
2 parts Cinnamon Schnapps
fill with Lemonade
Collins Glass
Build over ice and stir

Northern Lights
1 1/2 parts Yukon Jack®
1 part Cranberry Juice Cocktail
1 part Orange Juice
Collins Glass
Build over ice and stir

Norwegian Iceberg
2 parts Vodka
fill with Lemon-Lime Soda
1 part Blue Hawaiian Schnapps
Beer Mug
Build over ice and stir

Norwich Collins
2 parts Gin
1 part Lemon Juice
dash Sugar
fill with Cola
Collins Glass
Build over ice and stir

Nothing at All
1 part Peach Schnapps
1/2 part Blue Curaçao
1/2 part Raspberry Liqueur
1/2 part Orange Juice
fill with Sour Mix
Collins Glass
Shake with ice and pour

Nuclear Meltdown
1 part Gin
1 part Tequila Silver
1 part Vodka
1 part Light Rum
1 part Sour Mix
1 part Melon Liqueur
fill with Lemon-Lime Soda
Collins Glass

Build over ice and stir

Nuclear Sensation
1 part Dry Gin
1 part Vodka
1 part Rum
1 part Blue Curaçao
fill with Sour Mix
Collins Glass

Build over ice and stir

Nut Twister
1 part Banana Liqueur
1 part Coconut-Flavored Rum
fill with Orange Juice
Collins Glass

Build over ice and stir

Nutty Cola
2 parts Amaretto
1 part Fresh Lime Juice
fill with Cola
Collins Glass

Build over ice and stir

O&O
2 parts Orange-Flavored Vodka
fill with Orange Soda
Collins Glass

Build over ice and stir

Oak Tree
1 part Brandy
1 part Amaretto
1 part Tia Maria®
fill with Milk
Collins Glass

Shake with ice and pour

Ocho Rios
1 1/2 parts Dark Rum
1 part Cream
1 part Fresh Lime Juice
1 part Guava Juice
1/2 part Sugar
Collins Glass

Shake with ice and strain over ice

Odie
1 part Coffee Liqueur
1 part Frangelico®
1 part Irish Cream Liqueur
1 part Rye Whiskey
fill with Milk
Collins Glass

Build over ice and stir

Okennatt
1 part Blue Curaçao
1 part Parfait Amour
2 parts Bitter Lemon Soda
1 part Sparkling Water
Collins Glass

Build over ice and stir

Omnibus
1 part Kirschwasser
1 part Raspberry Syrup
fill with Sparkling Water
Collins Glass

Build over ice and stir

On the Deck

1 1/4 parts Spiced Rum
3/4 part Dark Rum
1/2 part Cointreau®
fill with Lemonade
splash Cranberry Juice Cocktail
Beer Mug

Build over ice and stir

OOO

1 part Orange-Flavored Vodka
1 part Orange Juice
1 part Orange Soda
Hurricane Glass

Build over ice and stir

Oral Invasion

1 part Spiced Rum
1 part Coconut-Flavored Rum
1/2 part Banana Liqueur
1/2 part Peach Schnapps
1 part Lemonade
1 part Sour Mix
Hurricane Glass

Build over ice and stir

Orange Delight

3 parts Maraschino Liqueur
fill with Orange Juice
Collins Glass

Shake with ice and pour

Orange Jolie

1 part Gin
1/2 part Triple Sec
1/2 part Coconut-Flavored Liqueur
fill with Orange Juice
Collins Glass

Shake with ice and pour

Orange Passion

1 part Vodka
2 parts Passion Fruit Liqueur
fill with Orange Juice
Collins Glass

Build over ice and stir

Orlando

1 part Vodka
1/2 part Crème de Banana
1 part Pineapple Juice
1 part Cream
fill with Orange Juice
Hurricane Glass

Shake with ice and pour

Orlando Quencher

1 1/2 parts Rum
1 part Orange Juice
1/2 part Fresh Lime Juice
1/2 part Simple Syrup
fill with Lemon-Lime Soda
Collins Glass

Build over ice and stir

Oslo Nights

1 part Citrus-Flavored Vodka
1 part Blue Curaçao
1 part Aquavit
1 part Cider
1 part Lime Juice
fill with Lemonade
Collins Glass

Build over ice and stir

Othello

1 part Southern Comfort®
1 part Parfait Amour
1/2 part Crème de Banana
fill with Lemonade
splash Pineapple Juice
splash Triple Sec
Collins Glass

Build over ice and stir

Over the Top

1 part Cachaça
1/2 part Blue Curaçao
1/2 part Crème de Banana
1/2 part Coconut-Flavored Liqueur
fill with Pineapple Juice
Collins Glass

Build over ice and stir

Oyster Bay

1 part Dark Rum
1 part Grapefruit Juice
1 part Pineapple Juice
1 part Papaya Juice
1 part Fresh Lime Juice
1/2 part Simple Syrup
splash Anisette
fill with Mango Juice
Collins Glass

Shake with ice and strain over ice

Paddy's Day Mooch

1 1/2 parts Whiskey
1/2 part Peach Schnapps
1 part Orange Juice
1 part Ginger Ale
Collins Glass

Build over ice and stir

Painkiller

1/4 part Rum
1/4 part Crème de Coconut
1 part Pineapple Juice
1 part Orange Juice
dash Ground Nutmeg
Collins Glass

Build over ice and stir

Painkiller #2

1 1/2 parts Rum
3 parts Orange Juice
3 parts Pineapple Juice
splash Coco Lopez®
dash Ground Nutmeg
Collins Glass

Shake with ice and pour

Palm Tree

1 part Passion Fruit Liqueur
splash Cream
1 part Mango Juice
1 part Orange Juice
Collins Glass

Shake with ice and pour

Paloma

2 parts Tequila Gold
fill with Grapefruit Juice
1/2 part Lime Juice
splash Club Soda
Collins Glass

Build over ice and stir

Pan Galactic Gargle Blaster

1 part Vodka
1 part Tia Maria®
1/2 part Cherry Brandy
splash Lime Juice
1 part Lemon-Lime Soda
1 part Apple Cider
Hurricane Glass

Build over ice and stir

Panama Jack

1 1/2 parts Spiced Rum
1 part Dark Rum
splash Strawberry Liqueur
fill with Orange Juice
Collins Glass

Build over ice and stir

Pancho Sanchez

1 part Peach Schnapps
1 part Sloe Gin
fill with Orange Juice
Collins Glass

Build over ice and stir

Panty Dropper

1 part Vodka
1 part Coconut-Flavored Rum
1 part Peach Schnapps
1 part Pineapple Juice
1 part Orange Juice
Collins Glass

Build over ice and stir

Papa Yaya

1 1/2 parts Gin
1/4 part Lime Juice
1/4 part Papaya Syrup
1/2 part Pineapple Juice
fill with Carbonated Water
Collins Glass

Shake all but Carbonated Water with ice and strain into the glass. Top with Carbonated Water.

Paradise Is Calling

1 part Rum
1 part Passion Fruit Liqueur
fill with Mango Juice
Collins Glass

Build over ice and stir

Paradise Quencher

1 part Spiced Rum
1/4 part Apricot Brandy
2 parts Pineapple Juice
1 part Orange Juice
1 part Cranberry Juice Cocktail
Collins Glass

Build over ice and stir

Parrot Head

1 part Spiced Rum
1 part Light Rum
1 part Blackberry Liqueur
fill with Pineapple Juice
Collins Glass

Shake with ice and pour

Part-Time Lover

1 1/2 parts Coconut-Flavored Rum
1/2 part Raspberry Liqueur
1/2 part Cranberry Juice Cocktail
fill with Cream
Collins Glass

Shake with ice and pour

Partymeister

1 part Gin
1 part Coconut-Flavored Rum
splash Lime Juice
fill with Lemonade
Collins Glass

Build over ice and stir

Passion

1 1/2 parts Coconut-Flavored Rum
1 1/2 parts Rum
dash Sugar
1 part Pineapple Juice
1 part Sour Mix
splash Lemon-Lime Soda
Collins Glass

Build over ice and stir

Passionate Cherry

1 1/2 parts Cherry Brandy
1/2 part Vodka
fill with Sour Mix
Collins Glass

Shake with ice and strain over ice

Passionate Dream

$1^1/_2$ parts Light Rum
1 part Passion Fruit Liqueur
1 part Strawberry Liqueur
1 part Grapefruit Juice
1 part Pineapple Juice
Collins Glass

Shake with ice and pour

Passover

1 part Vodka
2 parts Passion Fruit Juice
fill with Grapefruit Juice
Collins Glass

Build over ice and stir

Peaceful Treasure

1 part Dark Rum
$^3/_4$ part Lemon Juice
splash Simple Syrup
splash Grenadine
fill with Orange Juice
Collins Glass

Build over ice and stir

Peach Beseech

1 part Vodka
$1^1/_2$ parts Peach Schnapps
$^1/_2$ part Crème de Cacao (White)
fill with Milk
Collins Glass

Shake with ice and pour

Peach Bomber

$1^1/_2$ parts Peach Schnapps
1 part Vodka
$^1/_2$ part Blue Curaçao
1 part Pineapple Juice
1 part Orange Juice
Collins Glass

Shake with ice and pour

Peach Margarita

1 part Tequila
1 part Peach Schnapps
1 part Sour Mix
splash Grenadine
Margarita Glass

Shake with ice and pour

Peachberry Crush

1 part Peach Schnapps
1 part Orange Juice
1 part Black Currant Juice
1 part Sour Mix
$^1/_2$ part Strawberry Liqueur
Collins Glass

Build over ice and stir

Peachface

1 part Vodka
1 part Peach Schnapps
fill with Cranberry Juice Cocktail
Collins Glass

Build over ice and stir

Peach's Up

1 part Peach Schnapps
1 part Light Rum
1 part Apricot Brandy
1 part Lime Juice
1 part Strawberry Syrup
fill with Lemonade
Collins Glass

Build over ice and stir

Peachy

1 part Vodka
1 part Peach Schnapps
1 part Melon Liqueur
1 part Orange Juice
1 part Pear Juice
Collins Glass

Shake with ice and pour

Peachy Keen
2 parts Peach Schnapps
1 part Orange Juice
1 part Lemonade
Collins Glass

Build over ice and stir

Peanut Butter and Jelly
1 part Frangelico®
1 part Raspberry Liqueur
Collins Glass

Shake with ice and strain

Peariphery
2/3 part Triple Sec
1 1/2 parts Cachaça
1/2 part Lime Juice
fill with Pear Juice
Collins Glass

Shake with ice and strain over ice

Pedro Collins
1 1/2 parts Bacardi® Limón Rum
splash Sour Mix
1 part Lemon-Lime Soda
1 part Club Soda
Collins Glass

Build over ice and stir

Pegasus
1 part Vodka
1 part Peach Schnapps
1/2 part Lime Juice
1/2 part Lemon Juice
1/2 part Cherry Juice
fill with Red Bull® Energy Drink
Collins Glass

Build over ice and stir

Pepe Ramon
1 part Tequila Reposado
1 part Crème de Banana
1 part Melon Liqueur
1/2 part Grenadine
fill with Orange Juice
Collins Glass

Shake with ice and pour

Pepito Lolito
1 part Gin
1 part Blue Curaçao
1 part Tonic Water
1 part Club Soda
Collins Glass

Build over ice and stir

Pepper Eater
1 1/2 parts Tequila Silver
1/2 part Triple Sec
fill with Orange Juice
splash Cranberry Juice Cocktail
Collins Glass

Build over ice and stir

Peppermint Milk Punch
1 part Crème de Menthe (White)
1 part Dark Rum
1 part Cream
splash Simple Syrup
fill with Milk
Collins Glass

Shake with ice and pour

Pervert
1 part Orange-Flavored Rum
3/4 part Apricot Brandy
3/4 part Banana Liqueur
fill with Pineapple Juice
Collins Glass

Shake with ice and pour

Phantasm
1 1/2 parts Vodka
1/2 part Galliano®
1/2 part Cream
fill with Cola
Collins Glass

Build over ice and stir

Phillips Screwdriver
2 parts Vodka
fill with SunnyD® Orange Drink
Collins Glass

Shake with ice and pour

Piece of Cake
1 1/2 parts Rye Whiskey
splash Lime Juice
fill with Cola
Collins Glass

Build over ice and stir

Pimp Punch
1 part Raspberry Liqueur
1 part Currant-Flavored Vodka
fill with Lemon-Lime Soda
Collins Glass

Build over ice and stir

Piña Rita
2 parts Tequila
1/2 part Triple Sec
fill with Pineapple Juice
Margarita Glass

Shake with ice and pour

Piña Verde
1 part Rum
1/4 part Melon Liqueur
fill with Pineapple Juice
Collins Glass

Build over ice and stir

Pineapple Plantation
3/4 part Amaretto
3/4 part Southern Comfort®
1 1/2 parts Sour Mix
fill with Pineapple Juice
Collins Glass

Shake with ice and pour

Pineapple Splash
1 part Peach Schnapps
1 part Vodka
1 part Orange Juice
1 part Pineapple Juice
Collins Glass

Shake with ice and pour

Pink Banana
1 part Crème de Banana
fill with Pink Lemonade
Collins Glass

Build over ice and stir

Pink Cadillac Margarita
2 parts Tequila
1 part Triple Sec
2 parts Lime Juice
1 part Cranberry Juice Cocktail
1 part Powdered Sugar
Margarita Glass

Shake with ice and pour

Pink Cat
1 part Light Rum
1 part Crème de Cacao (White)
1 part Crème de Banana
1 part Passion Fruit Liqueur
1/2 part Grenadine
fill with Milk
Hurricane Glass

Shake with ice and strain over ice

Pink Cello

1 part Vodka
1/2 part Limoncello
fill with Cranberry Juice Cocktail
Collins Glass

Build over ice and stir

Pink Creamsicle®

1 part Vodka
1 part Orange Juice
fill with Cream Soda
Collins Glass

Build over ice and stir

Pink Flamingo

1 part Vodka
1 part Cointreau®
fill with Orange Juice
Collins Glass

Shake with ice and pour

Pink Paradise

1 1/2 parts Coconut-Flavored Rum
1 part Amaretto
1 part Pineapple Juice
1 part Cranberry Juice Cocktail
Hurricane Glass

Build over ice and stir

Pink Pillow

2 parts Vodka
splash Grenadine
1 part Sour Mix
1 part Ginger Ale
Collins Glass

Build over ice and stir

Pink Pussycat

1 1/2 parts Vodka
splash Grenadine
fill with Pineapple Juice
Collins Glass

Build over ice and stir

Pink Surprise

1 part Gin
1 part Cherry Brandy
fill with Lemonade
dash Bitters
Collins Glass

Shake with ice and pour

Pink Tutu

1 part Peach Schnapps
1/2 part Vodka
1/2 part Campari®
dash Powdered Sugar
fill with Grapefruit Juice
Collins Glass

Shake with ice and pour

Pirate's Revenge

1 part Cachaça
1/2 part Blue Curaçao
1/2 part Coconut-Flavored Rum
splash Vanilla Extract
1 part Pineapple Juice
1 part Orange Juice
Collins Glass

Shake with ice and pour

Pirate's Treasure

2 parts Spiced Rum
1 1/2 parts Crown Royal® Whiskey
fill with Cola
Collins Glass

Build over ice and stir

Piss in the Snow
1 part Vodka
1 part Peppermint Schnapps
fill with Mountain Dew®
Collins Glass

Build over ice and stir

Pixie-Hood
1 part Crème de Banana
1 part Cherry Brandy
1 part Coconut-Flavored Liqueur
fill with Lemon-Lime Soda
Collins Glass

Build over ice and stir

Pixy Stix®
1 part Vodka
1 part Apricot Brandy
1 part Blue Curaçao
1 part Grape Schnapps
fill with Lemonade
Collins Glass

Shake with ice and pour

Platinum Liver
1/2 part Gin
1/2 part Blue Curaçao
1/2 part Vodka
1/2 part Dark Rum
1/2 part Tequila Silver
1 part Sour Mix
1 part Lemon-Lime Soda
Collins Glass

Build over ice and stir

Play with Fire
1 1/2 parts Brandy
1 part Amaretto
1/2 parts Grenadine
1 part Orange Juice
Collins Glass

Shake with ice and pour

Playball
1 part Spiced Rum
1 part Vodka
1 part Peach Schnapps
fill with Orange Juice
Collins Glass

Shake with ice and pour

Plutonic
1 part Vodka
1 part Light Rum
1 part Gin
1 part Tequila Reposado
splash Grenadine
fill with Milk
Collins Glass

Shake with ice and pour

Polar Bear Collar
2 parts Dark Rum
1 part Sweet Vermouth
1 part Orange Juice
fill with Lemon-Lime Soda
Collins Glass

Build over ice and stir

Polkagris
1 part Vodka
1 part Crème de Menthe (White)
1/2 part Grenadine
fill with Lemon-Lime Soda
Collins Glass

Build over ice and stir

Pollenade
1 part Tequila
1 part Drambuie®
1 part Raspberry Liqueur
fill with Lemonade
Collins Glass

Shake with ice and pour

Pomme Rouge

1 1/2 parts Scotch
fill with Apple Cider
splash Grenadine
Collins Glass

Build over ice and stir

Ponche Tropical

1 part Dark Rum
1 part Apricot Brandy
1 part Cherry Brandy
1 part Triple Sec
fill with Orange Juice
splash Grenadine
Collins Glass

Build over ice and stir

Poop

1 part Raspberry Liqueur
1 part Citrus-Flavored Vodka
fill with Lemon-Lime Soda
Collins Glass

Build over ice and stir

Popo-Naval

3 parts Peach Schnapps
1 1/2 parts Vodka
fill with Orange Juice
Collins Glass

Build over ice and stir

Popped Cherry

1 part Vodka
1 part Cherry Liqueur
1 part Cranberry Juice Cocktail
1 part Orange Juice
Collins Glass

Build over ice and stir

Poppin's

1 part Dark Rum
1/2 part Triple Sec
1 part Pineapple Juice
1 part Orange Juice
dash Bitters
Collins Glass

Build over ice and stir

Port Milk Punch

2 parts Port
dash Powdered Sugar
fill with Milk
dash Ground Nutmeg
Collins Glass

Shake with ice and strain

Portland Poker

1 part Blackberry Liqueur
1 part Citrus-Flavored Vodka
1/2 part Vanilla Liqueur
1 part Mango Juice
1 part Peach Puree
1 part Club Soda
Hurricane Glass

Shake all but Club Soda with ice and strain over ice into the glass. Top with Club Soda.

The Power of Milk

3 dashes Sugar
1 part Vodka
fill with Milk
Collins Glass

Build over ice and stir

Power Play

1 1/2 parts Orange-Flavored Vodka
1 part Raspberry Liqueur
1/2 part Lemon Juice
fill with Orange Juice
Collins Glass

Shake with ice and pour

Prav Da
1/2 part Blue Curaçao
1/2 part Goldschläger®
1 part Sour Mix
fill with Apple Juice
Collins Glass

Shake with ice and strain over ice

Premium Herbal Blend
2 parts Citrus-Flavored Vodka
1/2 part Grenadine
fill with Sour Mix
top with Club Soda
Collins Glass

Build over ice and stir

Prom Night Virgin
2 parts Southern Comfort®
1/2 part Lemon Juice
1 part Zima®
2 parts Mountain Dew®
Collins Glass

Build over ice and stir

Psycho Citrus
1 part Vodka
1 part Tequila
1/2 part Crème de Menthe (White)
splash Lime Juice
splash Grand Marnier®
fill with Orange Juice
Collins Glass

Shake with ice and pour

Puckered Parrot
1 part Coconut-Flavored Rum
1 part Sour Apple Schnapps
fill with Mountain Dew®
Collins Glass

Build over ice and stir

Puerto Escondido
1 1/2 parts Tequila Silver
1/2 part Triple Sec
fill with Pineapple Juice
Collins Glass

Build over ice and stir

Pulp Friction
1 1/2 part Gold Tequila
1/2 part Cointreau®
1/2 part Lime Juice
1/2 part Margarita Mix
1/2 part Orange Juice
Margarita Glass

Shake with ice and pour

Punch in the Stomach
3 parts Tequila Reposado
fill with Lemon-Lime Soda
splash Fruit Punch
Collins Glass

Build over ice and stir

Punta Gorda
1 1/2 parts Dark Rum
1 part Fresh Lime Juice
1 part Sloe Gin
1/2 part Grenadine
fill with Pineapple Juice
Collins Glass

Shake with ice and pour

Purple Fairy Dream
1/2 part Currant-Flavored Vodka
1 part Blue Curaçao
1 part Raspberry Liqueur
2 parts Coconut Cream
fill with Lemon-Lime Soda
splash Cranberry Juice Cocktail
Hurricane Glass

Build over ice and stir

Purple Gecko
$1^1/_2$ parts Tequila
$^1/_2$ part Blue Curaçao
1 part Cranberry Juice Cocktail
1 part Sour Mix
$^1/_2$ part Lime Juice
Margarita Glass

Shake with ice and pour

Purple Margarita
2 parts Tequila
2 parts Raspberry Liqueur
2 parts Sour Mix
1 part Lime Juice
1 part Cranberry Juice Cocktail
Margarita Glass

Shake with ice and pour

Purple Pancho
1 part Tequila
$^1/_2$ part Blue Curaçao
$^1/_2$ part Sloe Gin
2 parts Lime Juice
2 parts Sour Mix
Margarita Glass

Shake with ice and pour

Purple Passion
$1^1/_2$ parts Vodka
dash Sugar
1 part Grape Juice (Red)
1 part Grapefruit Juice
Collins Glass

Shake with ice and pour

Purple Problem Solver
1 part Vodka
1 part Rum
1 part Melon Liqueur
1 part Blue Curaçao
1 part Sour Apple Schnapps
1 part Peach Schnapps
1 part Sour Mix
fill with Pineapple Juice
splash Grenadine
Hurricane Glass

Shake with ice and strain over ice

Purple Pussycat Juice
$^3/_4$ part Tequila Reposado
$^3/_4$ part Vodka
$^1/_2$ part Triple Sec
$^1/_2$ part Raspberry Liqueur
1 part Pineapple Juice
1 part Sour Mix
Hurricane Glass

Shake with ice and pour

Purple Rain
1 part Vodka
1 part Gin
1 part Rum
1 part Blue Curaçao
1 part Cranberry Juice Cocktail
fill with Lemon-Lime Soda
Collins Glass

Build over ice and stir

Pussycat
$1^1/_2$ parts Bourbon
splash Grenadine
1 part Sour Mix
1 part Orange Juice
Collins Glass

Build over ice and stir

Pussyfoot
1 part Pineapple Juice
1 part Orange Juice
1 part Grapefruit Juice
1/2 part Grenadine
Collins Glass
Build over ice

Quantum Theory
3/4 part Rum
1/2 part Strega®
1/4 part Grand Marnier®
2 parts Pineapple Juice
fill with Sour Mix
Collins Glass
Shake with ice and pour

Queen's Blossom
1 1/2 parts Dry Gin
1 part Crème de Banana
fill with Lemonade
Collins Glass
Build over ice and stir

Quikster's Delight
1 1/2 parts Bacardi® Limón Rum
1 part Orange Juice
1 part Pineapple Juice
1/2 part Grenadine
Collins Glass
Build over ice

Racer's Edge
1 part Sweetened Lime Juice
fill with Pineapple Juice
splash Crème de Menthe (Green)
Collins Glass
Build over ice

Rainbow
1 1/4 part Citrus-Flavored Vodka
1 part Grapefruit Juice
1 part Grape Juice (Red)
Collins Glass
Build over ice

Rainforest
1 part Blue Curaçao
1 part Coconut-Flavored Liqueur
1/2 part Crème de Menthe (White)
fill with Lemon-Lime Soda
Collins Glass
Build over ice

Raleigh Autumn
1 part Light Rum
1/2 part Galliano®
1/2 part Apricot Brandy
fill with Pineapple Juice
splash Lemon Juice
Collins Glass
Shake with ice and strain over ice

Ramsey
1 part Tequila
1 part Coffee Liqueur
1 part Irish Cream Liqueur
fill with Milk
Collins Glass
Shake with ice and pour

Raspava Berry
1 part Raspberry Liqueur
2 parts Lime Juice
fill with Guava Juice
Collins Glass
Shake with ice and pour

Raspberry Bulldozer
1 part Raspberry Liqueur
fill with Red Bull® Energy Drink
Collins Glass

Build over ice and stir

Raspberry Drop
1 part Raspberry Liqueur
1/2 part Amaretto
1 part Lemon-Lime Soda
3 parts Orange Juice
Collins Glass

Build over ice and stir

Rasta's Revenge
1 part Light Rum
1 part Spiced Rum
1/2 part Dark Rum
splash 151-Proof Rum
1/2 part Grenadine
1 part Pineapple Juice
1 part Mango Juice
Collins Glass

Build over ice and stir

Rattler
1 1/2 parts Tequila
splash Triple Sec
1/4 part Lime Juice
fill with Grapefruit Juice
Collins Glass

Build over ice and stir

Razzberry Ice
2 parts Raspberry Liqueur
fill with Lemonade
Collins Glass

Build over ice and stir

Razzerini
1 part Coconut-Flavored Rum
1/2 part Raspberry Liqueur
1 part Pineapple Juice
1 part Cranberry Juice Cocktail
Collins Glass

Build over ice and stir

Reason to Believe
1 part Gin
1/2 part Benedictine®
fill with Orange Juice
Collins Glass

Build over ice and stir

Recliner
1 part Vodka
1 part Whiskey
1 part Sour Mix
1 part Cranberry Juice Cocktail
2 parts Pineapple Juice
2 parts Orange Juice
1/2 part Grenadine
Collins Glass

Shake with ice and pour

Red Bessie
1 1/2 parts Gin
1 part Strawberry Liqueur
1 part Strawberry Puree
1 part Simple Syrup
fill with Passion Fruit Juice
Collins Glass

Shake with ice and strain over ice

Red Colada
1 part Light Rum
1 part Triple Sec
1/2 part Cream
2 parts Pineapple Juice
2 parts Coconut Cream
Hurricane Glass

Shake with ice and pour

Red Crusher
1 part Tequila Silver
1 part Vodka
1 part Strawberry Syrup
1 part Mango Juice
1 part Strawberry Juice
Hurricane Glass

Shake with ice and pour

Red Haze
1 part Rum
1 part Cherry Liqueur
1 part Cranberry Juice Cocktail
1 part Orange Juice
Collins Glass

Shake with ice and pour

Red Kawasaki®
1 part Gin
1 part Rum
1 part Sloe Gin
1 part Triple Sec
1 part Vodka
fill with Sour Mix
splash Club Soda
Collins Glass

Shake all but Club Soda with ice and strain into the glass. Top with Club Soda.

Red Ox
1 part Light Rum
1/2 part Coconut-Flavored Rum
1 part Pineapple Juice
1/2 part Cranberry Juice Cocktail
fill with Sour Mix
splash Grenadine
Beer Mug

Build over ice and stir

Red Point
1 part Vodka
1 part Sloe Gin
splash Kiwi Schnapps
fill with Cranberry Juice Cocktail
splash Lemon Juice
Collins Glass

Shake with ice and pour

Red Racer
1 part Vodka
1 part Amaretto
1 part Southern Comfort®
1 part Sloe Gin
fill with Orange Juice
Collins Glass

Shake with ice and pour

Red Rooster
1 1/4 parts Rum
1/2 part Crème de Noyaux
fill with Guava Juice
splash Grenadine
Collins Glass

Build over ice and stir

Red Royal
1 part Crown Royal® Whiskey
1 part Amaretto
fill with Cranberry Juice Cocktail
splash Lemon-Lime Soda
Collins Glass

Build over ice and stir

Red Sea
$1^1/_2$ parts Red Curacao
1 part Pineapple Juice
1 part Orange Juice
Collins Glass

Shake with ice and pour

Red Shock
2 parts Cinnamon Schnapps
fill with Red Bull® Energy Drink
Collins Glass

Build over ice and stir

Red Stinger Bunny
1 part Bacardi® Limón Rum
1 part Peach Schnapps
1 part Fresh Lime Juice
splash Grenadine
fill with Lemon-Lime Soda
Collins Glass

Build over ice and stir

Red Umbrella
1 part Campari®
1 part Maraschino Liqueur
$^1/_2$ part Crème de Banana
fill with Banana Juice
Collins Glass

Shake with ice and pour

Redneck
2 parts Southern Comfort®
fill with Mountain Dew®
Collins Glass

Build over ice and stir

Redstar
$^1/_2$ part Vodka
fill with Red Bull® Energy Drink
Collins Glass

Build over ice and stir

Reef Juice
$1^1/_2$ parts Dark Rum
1 part Crème de Banana
$^1/_2$ part Vodka
1 part Grenadine
$^1/_2$ part Fresh Lime Juice
fill with Pineapple Juice
Hurricane Glass

Shake with ice and pour

Reggae Summer
1 part Light Rum
$1^1/_2$ parts Strawberry Liqueur
fill with Sparkling Water
Collins Glass

Build over ice and stir

Reindeer's Tear
1 part Vodka
1 part Blue Curaçao
1 part Lemon Juice
Collins Glass

Build over ice and stir

Relaxer
1 part Cognac
fill with Cola
Collins Glass

Build over ice and stir

Rémy Cup
$1^1/_2$ parts Cognac
$^1/_2$ part Grenadine
fill with Passion Fruit Juice
Collins Glass

Shake with ice and strain over ice

Return to Bekah
1 part Vodka
1/2 part Blue Curaçao
1/2 part Grape Juice (Red)
fill with Sour Mix
1/2 part Cranberry Juice Cocktail
Collins Glass
Build over ice and stir

Rewstar
1 1/2 parts Spiced Rum
1 1/2 parts Coconut-Flavored Rum
1/2 part Frangelico®
1 part Pink Grapefruit Juice
1 part Orange Juice
Collins Glass
Shake with ice and pour

A Ride in a Bumpy Lowrider
1 part Melon Liqueur
1 part Tequila
1 part Vodka
splash Grenadine
Collins Glass
Build over ice and stir

Ride in the Desert
1 1/2 parts Tequila Silver
1 part Triple Sec
1 part Grapefruit Juice
fill with Orange Juice
Collins Glass
Build over ice and stir

Right Field Bleachers
2 parts Bacardi® Limón Rum
fill with Cherry Cola
Collins Glass
Build over ice and stir

Rising Sun
2 parts Sake
fill with Orange Juice
1/2 part Grenadine
Collins Glass
Build over ice

Riviera
1 part Dark Rum
1 part Passion Fruit Liqueur
1 part Coconut-Flavored Liqueur
fill with Lemonade
Collins Glass
Build over ice and stir

Robicheaux
1 1/2 parts Bourbon
1/2 part Lime Juice
splash Cherry Juice
fill with Cola
Collins Glass
Build over ice and stir

Rodeo Tea
1 part Citrus-Flavored Vodka
2 parts Blackberry Liqueur
1/2 part Powdered Sugar
1/2 part Lemon Juice
fill with Iced Tea
Collins Glass
Shake with ice and strain over ice

Roly Poley
2 parts Rum
fill with Dr Pepper®
Collins Glass
Build over ice and stir

Root Beer Fizz

2 parts Gin
1 part Lemon Juice
dash Sugar
fill with Root Beer
Collins Glass

Build over ice and stir

Root Canal

2 parts Root Beer Schnapps
1/4 part Peppermint Schnapps
fill with Dr Pepper®
Hurricane Glass

Build over ice and stir

Rosarita Margarita

1 1/2 parts Tequila Reposado
3/4 part Grand Marnier®
1/2 part Cranberry Juice Cocktail
1/2 part Sweetened Lime Juice
1 1/2 parts Sour Mix
Margarita Glass

Shake with ice and pour

Rosebud

2 parts Citrus-Flavored Vodka
1/2 part Triple Sec
1 part Lime Juice
fill with Grapefruit Juice
Collins Glass

Build over ice and stir

Rosette Merola

1 part Dry Gin
1 part Goldschläger®
1 part Kiwi Liqueur
1 part Aperol™
fill with Orange Juice
Collins Glass

Build over ice and stir

Rovert

1 1/2 parts Coconut-Flavored Rum
1/2 part 151-Proof Rum
2 parts Cranberry Juice Cocktail
1 part Orange Juice
Collins Glass

Build over ice and stir

Roy Rogers

splash Grenadine
fill with Cola
Collins Glass

Build over ice and stir

Royal Fizz

1 part Gin
2 parts Sour Mix
1 Whole Egg
fill with Cola
Collins Glass

Shake all but Cola with ice and strain into the glass. Top with Cola.

A Royal Sour Kiss

1/2 part Crown Royal® Whiskey
1 part Sour Apple Schnapps
splash Lime Juice
fill with Lemon-Lime Soda
Collins Glass

Build over ice and stir

Rudolph's Nose

1 1/4 parts Light Rum
1 1/2 parts Lemon Juice
1/2 part Grenadine
fill with Cranberry Juice Cocktail
Collins Glass

Build over ice and stir

Rum Butter Balls
2 parts Rum
1 part Butterscotch Schnapps
fill with Root Beer
Collins Glass

Build over ice and stir

Rum Collins
2 parts Light Rum
1/2 part Lime Juice
dash Powdered Sugar
fill with Club Soda
Collins Glass

Shake all but Club Soda with ice and strain into the glass. Top with Club Soda.

Rum Cow
1 1/4 parts Dark Rum
dash Sugar
2 dashes Bitters
fill with Milk
Collins Glass

Shake with ice and pour

Russian Elektric
1 part Vodka
1 part Strawberry Liqueur
fill with Red Bull® Energy Drink
Collins Glass

Build over ice and stir

Russian Sunset
1 part Vodka
1 part Triple Sec
fill with Sour Mix
splash Grenadine
Collins Glass

Build over ice

Russian Virgin Fizz
2 parts Vodka
1 part Lemon-Lime Soda
1 part Lemonade
Collins Glass

Build over ice and stir

Rusted Root
2 parts Gin
1/4 part Lemon Juice
dash Powdered Sugar
1 Egg White
fill with Root Beer
Collins Glass

Shake all but Root Beer with ice and strain into the glass. Top with Root Beer.

S and M
2 parts Southern Comfort®
fill with Mountain Dew®
Collins Glass

Build over ice and stir

Sabor Latino
1 part Light Rum
1 part Dark Rum
splash Raspberry Liqueur
1/2 part Mango Juice
1/2 part Fresh Lime Juice
1/2 part Papaya Juice
fill with Pineapple Juice
Collins Glass

Shake with ice and pour

Sake Sunshine
1 part Brandy
1 part Sake
fill with Grapefruit Juice
splash Grenadine
Collins Glass

Build over ice

Salem Witch

1/2 part Vodka
1/2 part Raspberry Liqueur
1/2 part Midori®
splash Lime Juice
splash Grenadine
1 part Sour Mix
1 part Club Soda
Collins Glass

Build over ice and stir

Salim

1 part Dry Gin
1/2 part Crème de Banana
1/2 part Southern Comfort®
1 part Pineapple Juice
fill with Orange Juice
Collins Glass

Build over ice and stir

Salty Balls

1 1/2 parts Vodka
1 part Midori®
2 parts Orange Juice
fill with Grapefruit Juice
pinch Salt
Collins Glass

Build over ice and stir

Samovar Sass

1 1/2 parts Raspberry Liqueur
3 parts Banana Puree
2/3 part Lemon Juice
fill with Orange Juice
Collins Glass

Shake with ice and strain over ice

San Francisco

1 part Vodka
1 part Triple Sec
1 part Crème de Banana
1 part Pineapple Juice
1 part Orange Juice
1/4 part Grenadine
Collins Glass

Shake with ice and pour

San Juan Tea

1 1/2 parts Bacardi® Limón Rum
1/2 part 151-Proof Rum
fill with Sour Mix
splash Cola
Collins Glass

Build over ice

Sanders' Special

1 part Vodka
1 part Sour Apple Schnapps
1 part Peach Schnapps
fill with Fruit Punch
Collins Glass

Shake with ice and pour

Sans Souci

1 1/2 parts Triple Sec
splash Vodka
splash Fresh Lime Juice
fill with Lemonade
Collins Glass

Shake with ice and pour

Santa Esmeralda

1 1/2 parts Vodka
1/4 part Kiwi Schnapps
fill with Grapefruit Juice
Collins Glass

Build over ice

Santa Fe Express

$1^1/_2$ parts Tequila Reposado
$^1/_2$ part Triple Sec
fill with Sour Mix
Collins Glass

Build over ice and stir

Santa's Pole

1 part Peppermint Schnapps
1 part Vodka
2 splashes Grenadine
fill with Lemon-Lime Soda
Collins Glass

Build over ice

Sapphire Blues

$1^1/_2$ parts Gin
$^1/_2$ part Blue Curaçao
$^1/_2$ part Lime Cordial
$^1/_2$ part Peach Schnapps
fill with Lemon-Lime Soda
Hurricane Glass

Build over ice and stir

Satin Sheet

2 parts Brandy
1 part Peach Schnapps
splash Grenadine
fill with Orange Juice
Collins Glass

Build over ice and stir

Schlägerfloat

2 parts Goldschläger®
2 scoops Vanilla Ice Cream
fill with Root Beer
Collins Glass

Build in the glass with no ice

Schnapp It Up

1 part Peach Schnapps
1 part Wild Berry Schnapps
1 part Vodka
fill with Cranberry Juice Cocktail
Collins Glass

Build over ice and stir

Schwartzy

1 part Peach Schnapps
1 part Southern Comfort®
fill with Orange Juice
splash Pineapple Juice
Collins Glass

Build over ice and stir

Scotch Milk Punch

2 parts Scotch
dash Powdered Sugar
dash Ground Nutmeg
fill with Milk
Collins Glass

Shake with ice and pour

Scottie's Popsicle®

1 part Crème de Cacao (Dark)
1 part Crème de Banana
1 part Raspberry Liqueur
splash Vodka
fill with Half and Half
Collins Glass

Shake with ice and pour

Screaming in the Dark

$1^1/_2$ parts Black Vodka
1 part Coffee Liqueur
$^1/_2$ part Brandy
$^1/_2$ part Bourbon
fill with Cola
Collins Glass

Build over ice and stir

Screaming Toilet
1½ parts Tequila Reposado
1 part Peach Schnapps
1 part Triple Sec
1 part Melon Liqueur
fill with Pineapple Juice
Collins Glass

Build over ice and stir

Screw Up
1 part Vodka
1 part Orange Juice
1 part Lemon-Lime Soda
Collins Glass

Build over ice and stir

Screwball
2 parts Whiskey
fill with Orange Juice
Collins Glass

Build over ice and stir

Screwdriver with a Twist
2 parts Vodka
1 part Lemon-Lime Soda
1 part Orange Juice
Collins Glass

Build over ice and stir

Seattle Smog
1 part Midori®
1 part Peach Schnapps
1 part Blue Curaçao
2 parts Cranberry Juice Cocktail
1 part Orange Juice
Collins Glass

Build over ice and stir

Secret
1½ parts Scotch
splash Crème de Menthe (White)
fill with Sparkling Water
Collins Glass

Build over ice and stir

Serrera
1 part Vodka
1 part Blue Curaçao
fill with Sparkling Water
Collins Glass

Build over ice and stir

Set the Juice Loose
1 part Apricot Brandy
1 part Cherry Brandy
1 part Crème de Banana
1 part Pineapple Juice
1 part Orange Juice
Collins Glass

Build over ice and stir

Seven Year Itch
2 parts Spiced Rum
splash Lemon Juice
fill with Lemon-Lime Soda
Collins Glass

Build over ice and stir

Sewer Rat
1 part Vodka
½ part Peach Schnapps
½ part Coffee Liqueur
fill with Orange Juice
Collins Glass

Build in the glass with no ice

Sgt. Pepper
2 parts Southern Comfort®
fill with Dr Pepper®
Collins Glass
Build over ice and stir

Shag by the Shore
1/2 part Melon Liqueur
1/2 part Peach Schnapps
1 part Cranberry Juice Cocktail
1 part Orange Juice
Collins Glass
Build over ice and stir

Shamrock Juice
1 part Gin
1 part Tequila
1 part Rum
1 part Vodka
1 part Blue Curaçao
fill with Orange Juice
Hurricane Glass
Build over ice and stir

Shark Tank
2 parts Vodka
1 part Grenadine
fill with Lemonade
Collins Glass
Build over ice and stir

Shattered Dreams
1 part Vodka
1 1/2 parts Blueberry Schnapps
splash Grenadine
splash Lemon-Lime Soda
fill with Grape Juice (Red)
Collins Glass
Build over ice and stir

Shipwreck
1 part Rum
1/4 part Triple Sec
1/4 part Crème de Banana
fill with Sour Mix
Collins Glass
Build over ice and stir

Shirley Temple Black
1 part Coffee Liqueur
fill with Lemon-Lime Soda
splash Grenadine
Collins Glass
Build over ice and stir

Shirley Temple of Doom
2 parts Vodka
splash Grenadine
fill with Lemon-Lime Soda
Collins Glass
Build over ice and stir

Shock-a-Bull
1 part Peppermint Schnapps
1 part Vodka
fill with Red Bull® Energy Drink
Beer Mug
Build over ice and stir

Shoo In
1/2 part Light Rum
1/2 part Dark Rum
1/2 part Brandy
1/2 part Maraschino Liqueur
1 part Grapefruit Juice
1 part Pineapple Juice
Collins Glass
Build over ice and stir

Shoot to the Moon

$2^1/_2$ parts Light Rum
1 part Club Soda
1 part Cranberry Juice Cocktail
splash Grenadine
Collins Glass

Build over ice and stir

Sierra Nevada

1 part Dark Rum
$^1/_2$ part Apricot Brandy
$^1/_2$ part Triple Sec
splash Grenadine
fill with Pineapple Juice
Collins Glass

Build over ice and stir

Silk Boxers

1 part Light Rum
$^1/_2$ part Cherry Brandy
$^1/_4$ part Crème de Cacao (White)
fill with Cream
Collins Glass

Shake with ice and pour

Silly Orange

1 part Hazelnut Liqueur
1 part Strawberry Liqueur
fill with Orange Juice
Collins Glass

Build over ice and stir

Silver Cloud

1 part Amaretto
1 part Coffee Liqueur
fill with Milk
Collins Glass

Shake with ice and pour. Top with Whipped Cream.

Silver Whisper

1 part Gin
$^1/_2$ part Sloe Gin
splash Blackberry Liqueur
$^1/_2$ part Lime Juice
splash Simple Syrup
fill with Grapefruit Juice
Collins Glass

Shake with ice and pour

Simple Pimms'®

1 part Pimm's® No. 1 CUP
1 part Ginger Ale
fill with Lemonade
Collins Glass

Build over ice and stir

Sirocco

1 part Gin
1 part Lychee Liqueur
1 part Cointreau®
splash Kirschwasser
fill with Lemon-Lime Soda
Collins Glass

Build over ice

Sister Havana

$1^1/_2$ parts Spiced Rum
$^1/_2$ part Passion Fruit Liqueur
$^1/_2$ part Lemon Juice
fill with Pineapple Juice
Collins Glass

Shake with ice and pour

Sit and Spin

$1^1/_2$ parts Dark Rum
$^1/_4$ part Lime Juice
2 splashes Lemon Juice
dash Sugar
fill with Grapefruit Juice
Collins Glass

Shake with ice and strain over ice

Ska Club
$1^1/_2$ parts Whiskey
$^1/_2$ part Light Rum
fill with Orange Juice
Collins Glass

Shake with ice and pour

Skeet Shooter Special
$1^1/_2$ parts Dark Rum
$^1/_2$ part Light Rum
1 part Lemon-Lime Soda
1 part Pineapple Juice
1 part Grapefruit Juice
1 part Orange Juice
dash Cinnamon
Collins Glass

Build over ice and stir

Skittle®
1 part Vodka
1 part 99-proof Banana Liqueur
fill with Fruit Punch
Collins Glass

Build over ice and stir

Sky Blue Fallout
$^1/_2$ part Blue Curaçao
$^1/_2$ part Gin
$^1/_2$ part Vodka
$^1/_2$ part Triple Sec
$^1/_2$ part Tequila
$^1/_2$ part 151-Proof Rum
1 part Sour Mix
1 part Lemon-Lime Soda
Hurricane Glass

Build over ice and stir

Sky Walker
1 part Spiced Rum
1 part Sloe Gin
$1^1/_2$ parts Triple Sec
1 part Grenadine
fill with Orange Juice
Collins Glass

Build over ice and stir

Slice O' Heaven
1 part Kiwi Liqueur
1 part Melon Liqueur
fill with Apple Juice
Collins Glass

Shake with ice and pour

Slimy Worm
1 part Blueberry Schnapps
$^1/_2$ part Brandy
fill with Apple Juice
Collins Glass

Build over ice and stir

Slippery Giraffe
1 part Light Rum
fill with Cream Soda
Collins Glass

Build over ice and stir

Sloe Ahead
$1^1/_2$ parts Light Rum
$^1/_2$ part Melon Liqueur
$^1/_4$ part Sloe Gin
1 part Pineapple Juice
1 part Orange Juice
Collins Glass

Build over ice and stir

Sloe Coach
1 part Vodka
1 part Southern Comfort®
1 part Sloe Gin
fill with Orange Juice
Hurricane Glass

Shake with ice and strain over ice

Sloe Smack in the Face

1 1/2 parts Southern Comfort®
1 1/2 parts Sloe Gin
1 part Red Curaçao
1 part Orange Juice
1 part Lemon-Lime Soda
Collins Glass

Build over ice and stir

Sludge

1 part Vodka
1 part Triple Sec
1/2 part Blue Curaçao
1/2 part Peach Schnapps
1 part Cranberry Juice Cocktail
1 part Orange Juice
splash Melon Liqueur
Collins Glass

Build over ice and stir

Smile Maker

1 part Amaretto
1 part Orange Juice
1 part Passion Fruit Liqueur
fill with Sour Mix
Collins Glass

Build over ice and stir

Smooch

1 part Coconut-Flavored Rum
1 part Midori®
1 part Sloe Gin
1 part Amaretto
1 part Peach Schnapps
fill Orange Juice
splash Pineapple Juice
Collins Glass

Shake with ice and pour

Smoove

1 part Vodka
1 part Peach Schnapps
fill with Lemon-Lime Soda
Collins Glass

Build over ice and stir

Sniper

1 part Tia Maria®
1 part Triple Sec
fill with Orange Juice
Collins Glass

Build over ice and stir

Sno Cone

1 1/2 parts Coconut-Flavored Rum
1/2 part Blue Curaçao
1/2 part Sour Mix
fill with Pineapple Juice
Collins Glass

Shake with ice and pour

Snowball

2 parts Advocaat
fill with Lemon-Lime Soda
Collins Glass

Build over ice and stir

Something Peachie

3/4 part Vodka
3/4 part Peach Schnapps
3/4 part Triple Sec
1 part Pineapple Juice
1 part Orange Juice
Collins Glass

Shake with ice and pour

Something to Lose

1 part Dark Rum
1 part Southern Comfort®
1/2 part Apricot Brandy
1 part Pineapple Juice
1 part Orange Juice
Collins Glass

Shake with ice and pour

Somewhere in Time
1 part Lychee Liqueur
1 part Passion Fruit Liqueur
1 1/2 parts Spiced Rum
fill with Papaya Juice
2/3 part Lemon Juice
Collins Glass

Build over ice and stir

Sonic Blaster
1/2 part Vodka
1/2 part Light Rum
1/2 part Banana Liqueur
1 part Pineapple Juice
1 part Orange Juice
1 part Cranberry Juice Cocktail
Collins Glass

Shake with ice and pour

Sonoma
1 part Vodka
1 part Grape Juice (Red)
fill with Mountain Dew®
Collins Glass

Build over ice and stir

Sophie's Choice
1 part Vodka
1 part Peach Schnapps
1 part Melon Liqueur
fill with Sour Mix
Collins Glass

Build over ice and stir

Sour Appleball
1 1/2 parts Sour Apple Schnapps
1/2 part Vodka
1/2 part Triple Sec
fill with Lemon-Lime Soda
Collins Glass

Build over ice and stir

Sour Squishy
1 part Light Rum
1/2 part Sour Apple Schnapps
2 parts Sour Mix
1/2 part Grenadine
fill with Lemon-Lime Soda
Collins Glass

Shake all but Lemon-Lime Soda with ice and strain into the glass. Top with Lemon-Lime Soda.

Sourkraut's Heaven
1 1/2 parts Apple Brandy
1 part Apple Juice
1 part Tonic Water
Collins Glass

Build over ice and stir

South End Lemonade
1 part Rum
1 part Triple Sec
1 part Vodka
1 part Raspberry Liqueur
fill with Lemon-Lime Soda
Collins Glass

Build over ice and stir

Southern Decadence
1 part Jack Daniel's®
1 part Southern Comfort®
fill with Lemon-Lime Soda
Collins Glass

Build over ice and stir

Southern Dew
2 parts Southern Comfort®
fill with Mountain Dew®
Collins Glass

Build over ice and stir

Southern Doctor
2 parts Southern Comfort®
fill with Dr Pepper®
Collins Glass

Build over ice and stir

Southern Isle
3/4 part Blue Curaçao
1/2 part Southern Comfort®
1/2 part Citrus-Flavored Vodka
fill with Orange Juice
Collins Glass

Build over ice and stir

Southern Raspberry Tart
1 part Southern Comfort®
1 part Jack Daniel's®
1 part Raspberry Liqueur
fill with Sour Mix
splash Lemon-Lime Soda
Hurricane Glass

Shake all but Lemon-Lime Soda with ice and strain into the glass filled with ice. Top with Lemon-Lime Soda.

Southern Stirrup
1 1/2 parts Southern Comfort®
1/2 part Lemon Juice
1 1/2 parts Cranberry Juice Cocktail
1 part Grapefruit Juice
1 part Club Soda
Collins Glass

Build over ice and stir

Space Orbiter
1 1/2 parts Crème de Menthe (Green)
1 part Maple Syrup
1/2 part Amaretto
fill with Grapefruit Juice
Hurricane Glass

Build over ice and stir

Spanish Love
1/2 part Melon Liqueur
1/2 part Peach Schnapps
1/2 part Damiana®
fill with Orange Juice
2/3 part Mango Juice
Collins Glass

Build over ice and stir

Sparkling Garden
1 1/2 parts Citrus-Flavored Vodka
2/3 part Parfait Amour
splash Lime Juice
splash Lemon Juice
fill with Sparkling Water
Collins Glass

Build over ice and stir

Sparkling Red Driver
1 part Vodka
1 part Grapefruit Juice
1 part Ginger Ale
Collins Glass

Build over ice and stir

Special Margarita
1 part Tequila
1 part Calvados Apple Brandy
1 part Grand Marnier®
1 part Grenadine
1 part Lemon Juice
Margarita Glass

Shake with ice and pour

Speedy Gonzales®
1 part Blue Curaçao
1 part Grapefruit Juice
1 part Passion Fruit Juice
1 part Banana Juice
Collins Glass

Shake with ice and strain over ice

Sperm Count

1 1/2 parts Scotch
1 part Crème de Cacao (Dark)
fill with Milk
Collins Glass

Shake with ice and pour

Spice Orgasm

1 part Spiced Rum
1 part Crème de Banana
1 part Banana Puree
fill with Milk
Collins Glass

Shake with ice and strain over ice

Spiced Cherry

1 1/2 parts Spiced Rum
fill with Cherry Cola
Collins Glass

Build over ice and stir

Splash and Crash

2 parts Amaretto
3 parts Cranberry Juice Cocktail
1 part Orange Juice
1/2 part 151-Proof Rum
Collins Glass

Build over ice

Splendid Brandy

1 part Brandy
splash Vanilla Liqueur
1/2 part Strawberry Liqueur
1/2 part Coconut-Flavored Liqueur
1/2 part Lemon Juice
fill with Raspberry-Flavored Seltzer
Collins Glass

Build over ice and stir

Spritsor

2 parts Canadian Whiskey
fill with Lemon-Lime Soda
Beer Mug

Build over ice and stir

Spunky Monkey

1/2 part Rum
1/2 part Crème de Banana
1/2 part Crème de Cacao (Dark)
1/2 part Triple Sec
1 part Sour Mix
1 part Orange Juice
1 part Cranberry Juice Cocktail
Collins Glass

Shake with ice and pour

Sputnik

1 1/4 parts Vodka
1 1/4 parts Peach Schnapps
1 part Orange Juice
1 part Light Cream
Collins Glass

Shake with ice and pour

Squeeze

1 1/2 parts Citrus-Flavored Vodka
1 part Pineapple Juice
1 part Orange Juice
Collins Glass

Build over ice and stir

St. Charles Punch

1 part Brandy
1/2 part Triple Sec
1/2 part Lemon Juice
dash Sugar
fill with Port
Collins Glass

Shake all but Port with ice and strain into the glass. Top with Port.

Staggering Squirrel
1 part Southern Comfort®
1/2 part Amaretto
fill with Cola
Collins Glass

Build over ice and stir

Stale Perfume
1 part Raspberry-Flavored Vodka
1 part Raspberry Liqueur
fill with Lemon-Lime Soda
Collins Glass

Build over ice and stir

Star Light
1 part Apricot Brandy
1 part Gin
1 part Dry Vermouth
fill with Grapefruit Juice
Collins Glass

Build over ice and stir

Steady Eddie
1 part Vodka
1 part Coconut-Flavored Rum
splash Passion Fruit Liqueur
fill with Orange Juice
Collins Glass

Shake with ice and pour

Stiffy
1 part Vodka
1 part Pink Lemonade
fill with Mountain Dew®
Collins Glass

Build over ice and stir

Stimulator
1 part Coffee Liqueur
1 part Irish Cream Liqueur
1 part Galliano®
1 part Frangelico®
1 part Tuacã®
fill with Milk
Collins Glass

Shake with ice and pour

Sting
1 part Vodka
1 part Crème de Banana
fill with Lemonade
Collins Glass

Shake with ice and pour

Stone Cold
1 part Vodka
1 part Peach Schnapps
2 parts Orange Juice
1/2 part Strawberry Syrup
fill with Lemon-Lime Soda
Collins Glass

Build over ice and stir

Strawberry Fruitcup
2/3 part Strawberry Liqueur
2/3 part Apricot Brandy
1/2 part Lemon Juice
2/3 part Cream
1 1/2 parts Apricot Juice
1 part Pineapple Juice
1 part Passion Fruit Juice
Collins Glass

Shake with ice and pour

Strawberry Heart

1 part Strawberry Liqueur
1 part Apricot Brandy
1 part Fresh Lime Juice
1 1/2 parts Pineapple Juice
1 1/2 parts Orange Juice
fill with Sparkling Water
Hurricane Glass

Build over ice and stir

Strawberry Margarita

1 part Tequila
1/2 part Strawberry Liqueur
1/2 part Triple Sec
1 part Lemon Juice
Margarita Glass

Shake with ice and pour

Strawberry Marsh

1 part Strawberry Liqueur
1 part Dark Rum
fill with Cranberry Juice Cocktail
Collins Glass

Shake with ice and pour

Strawberry Screwdriver

2 parts Vodka
1 part Strawberry Liqueur
fill with Orange Juice
Collins Glass

Shake with ice and pour

Strawberry Storm

1 part Coffee Liqueur
1 1/2 parts Strawberry Liqueur
1 1/2 parts Cream
fill with Pineapple Juice
Hurricane Glass

Shake with ice and pour

Stress Killer

splash Blue Curaçao
2 parts Pineapple Juice
2 parts Grapefruit Juice
1 1/2 parts Passion Fruit Juice
1 1/2 parts Orange Juice
Collins Glass

Shake with ice and strain over ice

Stretcher Bearer

1 part Myers's® Rum
1 part Malibu® Rum
1 part Cointreau®
1 part Crème de Banana
fill with Pineapple Juice
1 part 151-Proof Rum
Collins Glass

Build over ice and stir

String Bikini

1/2 part Rum
1/2 part Coconut-Flavored Rum
1/2 part Melon Liqueur
1/2 part Raspberry Liqueur
1 part Orange Juice
1 part Pineapple Juice
Collins Glass

Shake with ice and pour

Stroumf

1 part Apricot Brandy
1 part Gin
1/2 part Amaretto
splash Lemon Juice
fill with Orange Juice
Collins Glass

Build over ice and stir

Stumblebum

1/2 part Tequila Reposado
1/2 part Light Rum
1/2 part Triple Sec
fill with Sour Mix
splash Lemon-Lime Soda
1/2 part Melon Liqueur
Collins Glass

Build over ice and stir

Sugar High

1/2 part Crème de Cacao (White)
1/2 part Blue Curaçao
1/2 part Midori®
1/2 part Crème de Banana
2 parts Watermelon Schnapps
2 dashes Sugar
fill with Lemon-Lime Soda
Collins Glass

Shake all but Lemon-Lime Soda with ice and strain over ice into the glass. Top with Lemon-Lime Soda.

Summer Delight

1/2 part Orange-Flavored Vodka
1/4 part Peach Schnapps
1 part Cranberry Juice Cocktail
1 part Orange Juice
3/4 part Melon Liqueur
Collins Glass

Build over ice and stir

Summer Fun

1 part Cognac
3/4 part Crème de Banana
1 part Pineapple Juice
1 part Orange Juice
Collins Glass

Build over ice and stir

Summer Hummer

2 parts Citrus-Flavored Vodka
2 parts Lemonade
1 part Lemon-Lime Soda
Collins Glass

Build over ice and stir

Summer Slider

2 parts Dark Rum
1 part Peach Schnapps
fill with Orange Juice
Collins Glass

Build over ice and stir

Summer Smile

1 part Vodka
1 part Coconut-Flavored Liqueur
fill with Orange Juice
Collins Glass

Build over ice and stir

Summer Sunset

2 parts Light Rum
1 part Fruit Punch
1 part Ginger Ale
Collins Glass

Build over ice and stir

Summertime

1 part Gin
1 part Mandarine Napoléon® Liqueur
fill with Orange Juice
splash Grenadine
Collins Glass

Build over ice and stir

Sun Fire

2 parts Gin
1/2 part Blue Curaçao
splash Grenadine
fill with Pineapple Juice
Collins Glass

Build over ice and stir

Sun-Kissed Virgin
1/2 part Amaretto
1/2 part Sugar
1 part Fresh Lime Juice
1 part Pineapple Juice
1 part Orange Juice
Collins Glass

Build over ice and stir

Sunblock
1 1/2 parts Vodka
1 part Triple Sec
fill with Grapefruit Juice
Collins Glass

Build over ice and stir

Sundowner Delight
2 parts Dark Rum
1 part Mango Juice
1 part Pineapple Juice
1 part Orange Juice
Collins Glass

Build over ice and stir

Sunfire Bird
1 1/2 parts Coconut-Flavored Rum
1/2 part Crème de Noyaux
fill with Pineapple Juice
Collins Glass

Shake with ice and pour

Sunflowers
2 parts Gin
2/3 part Caramel Syrup
1 part Lemon Juice
1 part Pineapple Juice
1 part Passion Fruit Juice
Collins Glass

Shake with ice and pour

Sunny Day
1 1/2 parts Peach Schnapps
1 part Maraschino Liqueur
1/2 part Lime Juice
1 part Orange Juice
1 part Cranberry Juice Cocktail
Collins Glass

Shake with ice and strain over ice

Sunny Sam
1 part Vodka
1/2 part Sambuca
fill with Orange Juice
Collins Glass

Shake with ice and pour

Sunrise Surprise
2 parts Coconut-Flavored Rum
splash Grenadine
1 part Orange Juice
1 part Pineapple Juice
Collins Glass

Build over ice

Sunset
1 part Vodka
1 part Apricot Brandy
fill with Orange Juice
splash Grenadine
Collins Glass

Build over ice

Sunset Boulevard
1 1/2 parts Vodka
3/4 part Peach Schnapps
fill with Orange Juice
Collins Glass

Build over ice and stir

Sunset on the Coast
1 part Light Rum
1 part Melon Liqueur
1 part Sour Mix
fill with Lemon-Lime Soda
splash Sloe Gin
Collins Glass

Build over ice

Sunsplash
2 parts Orange-Flavored Vodka
1/2 part Cointreau®
1 part Lime Juice
1 part Cranberry Juice Cocktail
1 part Orange Juice
Collins Glass

Build over ice and stir

Sunstroke
2 parts Vodka
fill with Grapefruit Juice
splash Cointreau®
Collins Glass

Build over ice

Superjuice
1 part Vodka
1 part Gin
1/2 part Lime Juice
1 part Orange Juice
1 part Tonic Water
Collins Glass

Build over ice and stir

Survivor
1 1/2 parts Light Rum
1/4 part Crème de Cacao (White)
fill with Pineapple Juice
1/4 part Lime Juice
Collins Glass

Build over ice and stir

Swamp Juice
1 part Vodka
1 part Blue Curaçao
1 part Triple Sec
1 part Orange Juice
1 part Pineapple Juice
Collins Glass

Shake with ice and pour

Sweat Heat
1 part Crème de Banana
1 part Pisang Ambon® Liqueur
1 part Coconut-Flavored Liqueur
fill with Orange Juice
Collins Glass

Shake with ice and strain over ice

Swedish Apple Pie
1 1/2 parts Cream
1/2 part Goldschläger®
1/2 part Vanilla Liqueur
1/2 part Apple Liqueur
fill with Milk
Collins Glass

Shake with ice and pour

Swedish Blue
1 1/2 parts Vodka
1/2 part Blue Curaçao
fill with Pineapple Juice
splash Fresh Lime Juice
Collins Glass

Build over ice and stir

Sweet Creams
1 1/2 parts Blackberry Liqueur
1 1/2 parts Crème de Banana
1 part Orange Juice
1 part Milk
Collins Glass

Shake with ice and strain over ice

Sweet Dream
2 parts Coconut-Flavored Rum
1 part Strawberry Juice
1 part Banana Juice
1 part Orange Juice
Collins Glass

Shake with ice and pour

Sweet Escape
1 part Citrus-Flavored Vodka
1 part Peach Schnapps
1 part Aquavit
1 part Lime Cordial
fill with Pear Juice
Collins Glass

Build over ice and stir

Sweet Flamingo
1 part Gin
1 part Cherry Brandy
1 part Coconut Cream
1 part Pineapple Juice
1 part Orange Juice
Hurricane Glass

Shake with ice and strain over ice

Sweet Mary
1 1/2 parts Crème de Banana
1/2 part Gin
fill with Lemonade
splash Crème de Cassis
Collins Glass

Shake with ice and pour

Sweet Melissa
1 1/2 parts Coconut-Flavored Rum
1 1/2 parts Vanilla-Flavored Vodka
splash Cranberry Juice Cocktail
1 part Orange Juice
1 part Pineapple Juice
Hurricane Glass

Shake with ice and strain over ice

Sweet Passion
1 part Parfait Amour
1 part Strawberry Liqueur
1/2 part Amaretto
1/4 part Maraschino Liqueur
fill with Apple Juice
Collins Glass

Build over ice and stir

Sweet Passoã®
1 part Vodka
1 part Passoã®
1 part Tonic Water
fill with Pineapple Juice
splash Orange Juice
Collins Glass

Build over ice and stir

Sweet Pea
2 parts Citrus-Flavored Vodka
1 part Melon Liqueur
2 parts Cream
1 part Melon Puree
Hurricane Glass

Build over ice

Sweet Ranger
2 parts Coconut-Flavored Rum
1 part Orange Juice
1 part Lemon-Lime Soda
Hurricane Glass

Build over ice and stir

Sweet Smell of Success
1 part Passion Fruit Liqueur
1/2 part Campari®
fill with Apple Juice
Collins Glass

Build over ice and stir

Sweet Submission

2 parts Amaretto
fill with Apple Juice
Collins Glass
Build over ice and stir

Sweet Tooth

2 parts Godiva® Liqueur
fill with Milk
Collins Glass
Shake with ice and pour

Sweets for My Sweet

1 part Amaretto
1 part Whiskey
1/2 part Crème de Cacao (White)
1/2 part Strawberry Liqueur
fill with Milk
Collins Glass
Shake with ice and pour

Swift Kick in the Crotch

1 part Dark Rum
1 part Light Rum
1 part Orange Juice
fill with Cranberry Juice Cocktail
Collins Glass
Shake with ice and pour

Swimming Pool

1 part Vodka
1 part Gin
1 part Rum
1 part Blue Curaçao
fill with Lemon-Lime Soda
Collins Glass
Build over ice and stir

Take the A Train

1 1/2 parts Citrus-Flavored Vodka
1/2 part Vodka
1 part Grapefruit Juice
1 part Cranberry Juice Cocktail
Collins Glass
Shake with ice and pour

Takemoto Twister

1 part Vodka
1 part Sour Apple Schnapps
1 part Strawberry Liqueur
1 part Grapefruit Juice
2 parts Orange Juice
Collins Glass
Shake with ice and pour

Tall Blonde

1 part Aquavit
1/2 part Apricot Brandy
fill with Lemon-Lime Soda
Collins Glass
Build over ice and stir

Tall Sunrise

1 1/2 parts Tequila Silver
1/2 part Triple Sec
1/2 part Fresh Lime Juice
1/2 part Crème de Cassis
fill with Orange Juice
Collins Glass
Shake with ice and pour

Tangeri

1 1/2 parts Orange-Flavored Vodka
1/2 part Passion Fruit Liqueur
fill with Grape Juice (Red)
Collins Glass
Build over ice and stir

Tartan Sword

$1^1/_2$ parts Scotch
1 part Dry Vermouth
fill with Pineapple Juice
Collins Glass

Shake with ice and strain over ice

Teddy Bear

2 parts Pisang Ambon® Liqueur
splash Bacardi® Limón Rum
fill with Orange Soda
splash Lemon Juice
Collins Glass

Build over ice and stir

Telenovela

$^2/_3$ part Coconut-Flavored Liqueur
splash Dark Rum
1 part Cachaça
2 parts Passion Fruit Juice
splash Coconut Cream
Collins Glass

Shake with ice and strain over ice

Tell It to the Navy

1 part Coffee
1 part Whiskey
1 part Apricot Brandy
splash Light Rum
fill with Lemonade
Collins Glass

Build over ice and stir

Templar

1 part Vodka
$^1/_2$ part Kiwi Schnapps
$^1/_2$ part Triple Sec
splash Dry Vermouth
fill with Orange Juice
Collins Glass

Shake with ice and pour

Tenedor del Diablo

1 part Tequila Reposado
$^1/_2$ part Blue Curaçao
$^1/_2$ part Triple Sec
$^1/_2$ part Fresh Lime Juice
fill with Pineapple Juice
Collins Glass

Shake with ice and strain over ice

Teq and Tea

1 part Tequila
fill with Iced Tea
Collins Glass

Shake with ice and strain over ice

Tequila Caliente

$1^1/_2$ parts Tequila Silver
1 part Grenadine
1 part Crème de Cassis
fill with Sparkling Water
Collins Glass

Build over ice and stir

Tequila Canyon

$1^1/_2$ parts Tequila
splash Triple Sec
$^1/_4$ part Pineapple Juice
$^1/_4$ part Orange Juice
fill with Cranberry Juice Cocktail
Collins Glass

Build over ice and stir

Tequila Colagallo
$1^1/_2$ parts Tequila Gold
splash Lemon Juice
dash Salt
fill with Cola
Collins Glass

Build over ice and stir

Tequila Collins
2 parts Tequila
$^1/_2$ part Lemon Juice
dash Powdered Sugar
fill with Carbonated Water
Collins Glass

Shake all but Carbonated Water with ice and strain into the glass. Top with Carbonated Water.

Tequila Fever
$1^1/_2$ parts Tequila Reposado
$^1/_2$ part Triple Sec
1 part Mango Nectar
fill with Passion Fruit Juice
Collins Glass

Shake with ice and strain over ice

Tequila Sunset
1 part Tequila
fill with Orange Juice
splash Blackberry Brandy
Collins Glass

Build over ice

Texas Mud Slammer
2 parts Jack Daniel's®
1 part Cola
fill with Orange Juice
Collins Glass

Build over ice and stir

Thais
1 part Dark Rum
1 part Crème de Banana
1 part Pineapple Juice
1 part Frangelico®
Collins Glass

Shake with ice and strain over ice

Thaitian Tea
1 part Vodka
1 part Triple Sec
1 part Gin
1 part Rum
fill with Orange Juice
Hurricane Glass

Shake with ice and strain over ice

Thompson Tonic
1 part Peach Schnapps
1 part Spiced Rum
1 part Vodka
fill with Mountain Dew®
Collins Glass

Build over ice and stir

Tiajuana Taxi
2 parts Tequila Reposado
$^1/_2$ part Crème de Cassis
$^1/_2$ part Blackberry Liqueur
fill with Orange Juice
Collins Glass

Shake with ice and pour

Tie Die
2 parts Sour Apple Schnapps
splash Cranberry Juice Cocktail
fill with Lemonade
Collins Glass

Build over ice

Tiger's Tail
$1\frac{1}{2}$ parts Pernod®
fill with Orange Juice
Collins Glass

Build over ice and stir

Timberwolf
1 part Light Rum
1 part Tequila
1 part Gin
1 part Vodka
1 part Crème de Noyaux
fill with Orange Juice
Collins Glass

Shake with ice and pour

Timor
2 parts Light Rum
1 part Crème de Banana
1 part Cream
1 part Pineapple Juice
Collins Glass

Shake with ice and pour

To the Core
1 part Mandarine Napoléon® Liqueur
1 part Southern Comfort®
1/2 part Fresh Lime Juice
fill with Lemon-Lime Soda
Collins Glass

Build over ice and stir

Tolle
1 part Vodka
1 part Crème de Banana
fill with Hard Apple Cider
Collins Glass

Build over ice and stir

Tom Collins
2 parts Gin
1/2 part Lemon Juice
dash Powdered Sugar
fill with Carbonated Water
Collins Glass

Shake all but Carbonated Water with ice and strain into the glass. Top with Carbonated Water.

Tombstone Special
$1\frac{1}{2}$ parts Southern Comfort®
splash Lemon Juice
splash Lime Juice
fill with Mountain Dew®
Collins Glass

Build over ice and stir

Tongue Tangler
1 part Irish Cream Liqueur
1/2 part Brandy
fill with Heavy Cream
Collins Glass

Build over ice and stir

Top Gun
$1\frac{1}{2}$ parts Spiced Rum
1 part Orange Juice
1 part Pineapple Juice
1/2 part 151-Proof Rum
Collins Glass

Build over ice and stir

Torch
1 part Cream
1 part Raspberry Liqueur
fill with Lemon-Lime Soda
Collins Glass

Build over ice and stir

Toucan
1 part Coconut-Flavored Rum
1 part Peach Schnapps
1 part Lemon-Lime Soda
1 part Orange Juice
Collins Glass

Build over ice and stir

Toxic Antifreeze
1 part Vodka
1 part Triple Sec
1 part Midori®
fill with Lemonade
Collins Glass

Build over ice and stir

Toxic Blue-Green Algae
1 part Blue Curaçao
1 part Cointreau®
1 part Green Chartreuse®
1 part Vodka
1 part Light Rum
1 part Melon Liqueur
fill with Pineapple Juice
Collins Glass

Shake with ice and pour

Toxic Waste
1 part Vodka
1/2 part Southern Comfort®
1/4 part Blue Curaçao
1 part Orange Juice
1 part Pineapple Juice
Collins Glass

Shake with ice and pour

Trang Tricot
1 part Vodka
1 part Pineapple Juice
1/2 part Crème de Banana
fill with Grape Soda
Collins Glass

Build over ice and stir

Transfusion
1 1/4 part Vodka
fill with Grape Juice (Red)
Collins Glass

Build over ice and stir

Trevell
1 part Coconut-Flavored Rum
1 part Vodka
fill with Lemon-Lime Soda
Collins Glass

Build over ice and stir

Triple B
1 part Dark Rum
1/2 part Blue Curaçao
1/2 part Coconut-Flavored Liqueur
fill with Pineapple Juice
Collins Glass

Build over ice and stir

Triple Sec and Brandy
1 part Brandy
1 part Triple Sec
1 Sugar Cube
Collins Glass

Build over ice and stir

Triple XXX
1 part Red Curaçao
1 part Triple Sec
2 parts Passion Fruit Juice
fill with Apricot Juice
Collins Glass

Shake with ice and strain over ice

Triple XYZ
2 parts Coconut-Flavored Rum
1 part Raspberry Liqueur
1/4 part Triple Sec
fill with Pineapple Juice
Collins Glass

Build over ice and stir

Troia
1 part Vodka
1 part Coconut-Flavored Liqueur
1 part Strawberry Syrup
fill with Lemon-Lime Soda
Collins Glass

Build over ice and stir

Tropic Moon
1 part Dry Gin
1/2 part Crème de Banana
1/2 part Apricot Brandy
fill with Orange Juice
splash Grenadine
Collins Glass

Build over ice and stir

Tropic Purple Haze
1 1/2 parts Raspberry Liqueur
1/2 part Vodka
1/2 part Triple Sec
2 parts Cranberry Juice Cocktail
1 part Pineapple Juice
Collins Glass

Shake with ice and pour

Tropic Star
1 part Cognac
1/2 part Crème de Banana
1/2 part Apricot Brandy
splash Pastis
fill with Lemonade
Collins Glass

Build over ice and stir

Tropic Twister
3/4 part Southern Comfort®
3/4 part Melon Liqueur
3/4 part Passion Fruit Liqueur
1 part Pineapple Juice
1 part Orange Juice
Collins Glass

Build over ice and stir

Tropical Blue Moon
1 part Dark Rum
1 part Blue Curaçao
splash Lemonade
fill with Pineapple Juice
Collins Glass

Shake with ice and pour

Tropical Fruits
1 part Rum
1 part Apricot Brandy
1 part Melon Liqueur
1 part Coconut-Flavored Liqueur
fill with Orange Juice
Collins Glass

Shake with ice and strain over ice

Tropical Growlers
2 parts Blackberry Liqueur
2/3 part Coconut-Flavored Liqueur
fill with Pineapple Juice
Collins Glass

Shake with ice and pour

Tropical Hit
2 parts Triple Sec
1 part Mango Schnapps
1 part Simple Syrup
splash Blue Curaçao
fill with Pineapple Juice
Collins Glass

Build over ice and stir

Tropical Leprechaun
1 part Vodka
1/2 part Coconut-Flavored Rum
fill with Lemon-Lime Soda
splash Melon Liqueur
Collins Glass

Build over ice and stir

Tropical Melody
1/2 part Cognac
1/2 part Dark Rum
1/2 part Blackberry Liqueur
1 part Orange Juice
1 part Mango Juice
Collins Glass

Shake with ice and pour

Tropical Pear Fizz
2 parts Pear Liqueur
1 part RedRum®
1/2 part Apple Brandy
1/2 part Banana Liqueur
fill with Lemon-Lime Soda
Collins Glass

Build over ice and stir

Tropical Red
1 1/2 parts Blue Curaçao
1 part Gin
1 part Orange Juice
1 part Grapefruit Juice
Collins Glass

Shake with ice and pour

Tropical Storm
1 part Passion Fruit Liqueur
splash Amaretto
1 part Pineapple Juice
1 part Fresh Lime Juice
Collins Glass

Build over ice and stir

Tropical Sunrise
2 parts Spiced Rum
1 part Triple Sec
1 part Orange Juice
1 part Pineapple Juice
1/2 part Grenadine
Collins Glass

Build over ice and stir

Tropical Trance
1/2 part Crème de Cassis
1 part Crème de Banana
1 1/2 parts Dark Rum
1/2 part Passion Fruit Nectar
2 parts Grapefruit Juice
1 part Orange Juice
Collins Glass

Shake with ice and strain over ice

Tropicetto
2 parts Amaretto
1 part Coffee Liqueur
1 part Heavy Cream
fill with Orange Juice
Collins Glass

Shake with ice and pour

Truman State Mouthwash
1 part Peppermint Schnapps
1 part Mountain Dew®
1 part Fruit Punch
Collins Glass
Build over ice

Try Soft and Hard
1 part Light Rum
1 part Jamaican Rum
1 part Passion Fruit Nectar
1 1/2 parts Pineapple Juice
fill with Cherry Juice
Collins Glass
Shake with ice and pour

Tukky Tukky Wookiee
3 parts Irish Whiskey
fill with Mountain Dew®
Collins Glass
Build over ice and stir

Turbo
1 part Coconut-Flavored Rum
1/2 part Passoã®
1/2 part Pisang Ambon® Liqueur
1/2 part Piña Colada Mix
fill with Pineapple Juice
Collins Glass
Shake with ice and strain

Turbocharger
2 parts Spiced Rum
2 parts Sour Mix
fill with Orange Juice
1/2 part Grenadine
Collins Glass
Build over ice

Turbocharged
1 part Sambuca
1 part Vodka
1 part Blue Curaçao
2 parts Coconut Cream
fill with Pineapple Juice
Collins Glass
Build over ice and stir

Turkish Cola
2 parts Jack Daniel's®
fill with Cola
Collins Glass
Build over ice and stir

Turlock Bulldog
1 part Irish Cream Liqueur
1 part Coffee Liqueur
fill with Root Beer
Collins Glass
Build over ice and stir

Turn Off
1 part Gin
1 part Apricot Brandy
fill with Apple Juice
Collins Glass
Build over ice and stir

Turquoise Blue
1 1/2 parts Sour Mix
1 1/2 parts Rum
1/2 part Blue Curaçao
1/2 part Triple Sec
fill with Pineapple Juice
Collins Glass
Shake with ice and pour

Tutti Fruiti LifeSaver®

1½ parts Crème de Banana
1 part Pineapple Juice
1 part Orange Juice
Collins Glass

Shake with ice and pour

Twist and Shout

1 part Vodka
1 part Peach Schnapps
1½ parts Orange Juice
fill with Cola
Collins Glass

Build over ice and stir

Twisted Breeze

1½ parts Citrus-Flavored Vodka
1½ parts Kiwi Schnapps
1 part Grapefruit Juice
1 part Cranberry Juice Cocktail
Collins Glass

Shake with ice and pour

Twisted Pink Lemonade

1½ parts Smirnoff® Citrus Twist
¾ part Triple Sec
1 part Cranberry Juice Cocktail
1 part Sour Mix
Beer Mug

Shake with ice and pour

Two Seater

⅔ part Vodka
½ part Apricot Brandy
splash Triple Sec
1 part Orange Juice
1 part Grapefruit Juice
Collins Glass

Shake with ice and pour

Umbongo

1 part Vodka
2 parts Passion Fruit Liqueur
1 part Orange Juice
1 part Passion Fruit Juice
Collins Glass

Build over ice and stir

Uncle Art

2 parts Lime Juice
1 part Vodka
dash Sugar
1 part Ginger Ale
1 part Lemon-Lime Soda
Collins Glass

Build over ice and stir

Uncle John

1 part Gin
splash Triple Sec
1 part Lemon Juice
fill with Orange Juice
Collins Glass

Shake with ice and pour

Uncle Vanya

1½ parts Vodka
½ part Blackberry Liqueur
fill with Sour Mix
Collins Glass

Build over ice and stir

The Unforgettable Fire

1 part Vodka
½ part Apricot Brandy
½ part Orange Liqueur
1 part Orange Juice
1 part Red Bull® Energy Drink
Collins Glass

Build over ice and stir

Urine Sample

2 parts Vodka
fill with Malt Liquor
Collins Glass

Build in the glass with no ice

Valldemossa

1 part Triple Sec
1 part Crème de Banana
1 part Apricot Brandy
splash Fresh Lime Juice
fill with Sparkling Water
Collins Glass

Build over ice and stir

Valletta

1 part Scotch
1/2 part Amaretto
1/2 part Coffee-Flavored Brandy
1 part Pineapple Juice
1 part Apple Juice
Collins Glass

Shake with ice and pour

Vampire Juice

1 part Coconut-Flavored Rum
1 part Blue Curaçao
1 part Bacardi® Limón Rum
fill with Orange Juice
Collins Glass

Shake with ice and pour

Van Gogh's Ear

2 parts Absinthe
1 part Grenadine
fill with Grapefruit Soda
Collins Glass

Build over ice and stir

Vanilla Rose

1 1/2 parts Vanilla-Flavored Vodka
fill with Cola
splash Tuaca®
Collins Glass

Build over ice and stir

Vegan Milk

1 1/2 parts Irish Cream Liqueur
1 part Frangelico®
1 part Coffee Liqueur
fill with Milk
Collins Glass

Shake with ice and pour

Venus Flytrap

2 parts Tequila
1 part Melon Liqueur
1 part Triple Sec
1 part Lime Juice
Margarita Glass

Shake with ice and pour

Vertical Horizon

1 part Vodka
1 part Gin
1 1/2 parts Orange Liqueur
1/2 part Lemon Juice
fill with Cranberry Juice Cocktail
Collins Glass

Shake with ice and strain over ice

Very Screwy Driver

1 part Vodka
1/2 part Tequila Silver
1/2 part Gin
fill with Orange Juice
Collins Glass

Build over ice and stir

Vaya con Dios
2 parts Vodka
1 part Pineapple-Orange Juice
1 part Strawberry Daiquiri Mix
Pilsner Glass

Shake with ice and pour

Vietnam Acid Flashback
1 part Apple Liqueur
1 part 151-Proof Rum
1 part Jim Beam®
1 part Light Rum
1 part Vodka
1 part Yukon Jack®
1 part Triple Sec
splash Grenadine
fill with Orange Juice
Hurricane Glass

Shake with ice and pour

Vile Green Stuff
1 part Melon Liqueur
1 part Peach Schnapps
2 parts Carbonated Water
2 parts Orange Juice
Collins Glass

Build over ice and stir

Violet Symphony
1 part Parfait Amour
1 part Grenadine
fill with Sparkling Water
Collins Glass

Build over ice and stir

Virgin Bloody Mary
splash Tabasco® Sauce
dash Celery Salt
dash Pepper
2 splashes Worcestershire Sauce
fill with Tomato Juice
Collins Glass

Shake with ice and pour

Vitamin C
1 1/2 parts Orange-Flavored Vodka
1 part Sour Mix
1 part Orange Juice
Collins Glass

Shake with ice and pour

Viva Mexico
1/2 part Tequila
1/2 part Crème de Cacao (White)
1/2 part Melon Liqueur
1 part Pineapple Juice
1 part Orange Juice
Collins Glass

Build over ice and stir

Vlad the Impaler
2 parts Vodka
2/3 part Peach Schnapps
fill with Cranberry Juice Cocktail
Collins Glass

Shake with ice and pour

Vodka 7
2 parts Vodka
1/2 part Lime Juice
fill with Lemon-Lime Soda
Collins Glass

Build over ice and stir

Vodka Collins
2 parts Vodka
1/2 part Lemon Juice
dash Powdered Sugar
fill with Carbonated Water
Collins Glass

Shake all but Carbonated Water with ice and strain into the glass. Top with Carbonated Water.

Vodka Paralyzer

3/4 part Vodka
3/4 part Coffee Liqueur
2 parts Milk
fill with Cola
Collins Glass

Build over ice and stir

Vodka Smooth

1 1/2 parts Vodka
1/2 part Triple Sec
fill with Orange Juice
splash Grenadine
Collins Glass

Build over ice

Vodka Storm

1 part Vodka
1 part Raspberry Liqueur
fill with Cola
Collins Glass

Build over ice and stir

Vodka with Wings

1 1/2 parts Vodka
fill with Red Bull® Energy Drink
Collins Glass

Build over ice and stir

Vodka Yummy

2 parts Vodka
1 part Cinnamon Schnapps
fill with Apple Juice
Collins Glass

Build over ice and stir

Volcano

1/2 part Vodka
1/2 part Jim Beam®
1/2 part Gin
1/2 part Rum
1/2 part Tequila
1 part Orange Juice
1 part Pineapple Juice
splash Grenadine
splash Lemon-Lime Soda
Collins Glass

Build over ice and stir

Vomit Juice

1 part Cinnamon Schnapps
1/2 part Irish Whiskey
1/2 part Southern Comfort®
1/2 part Tequila Silver
1/2 part Vodka
fill with Red Bull® Energy Drink
Beer Mug

Build over ice and stir

Voodoo Dew

2 parts 151-Proof Rum
fill with Mountain Dew®
Collins Glass

Build over ice and stir

Voodoo Sunrise

1 part Vodka
1 part Rum
2 parts Grenadine
fill with Orange Juice
Collins Glass

Build over ice

Vulgar Virgin
2 parts Bacardi® Limón Rum
fill with Pink Lemonade
Collins Glass

Shake with ice and strain over ice

Wagon Burner
3 parts Yukon Jack®
1/2 part Lime Juice
1 part Lemon-Lime Soda
1 part Cranberry Juice Cocktail
splash Sour Mix
Collins Glass

Build over ice and stir

Waikiki
1 part Light Rum
1 part Passion Fruit Liqueur
1 part Campari®
fill with Orange Juice
Collins Glass

Build over ice and stir

Waikiki Tease
1 part Dark Rum
1 part Orange Juice
1 part Pineapple Juice
Collins Glass

Shake with ice and pour

Walking Home
1/2 part Vodka
1/2 part Rum
1/2 part Tequila
1/2 part Sloe Gin
1 part Lime Juice
splash Maraschino Cherry Juice
Collins Glass

Shake with ice and pour

Warrior Angel
1 1/2 parts Crème de Banana
2/3 part Gin
splash Apricot Brandy
splash Lemon Juice
fill with Orange Juice
Collins Glass

Shake with ice and pour

Water Buffalo
1 1/2 parts Vodka
1/2 part Grand Marnier®
fill with Orange Juice
Collins Glass

Build over ice and stir

Watermelon Slice
1/2 part Grenadine
1/2 part Rum
1/2 part Gin
1/2 part Triple Sec
1/2 part Vodka
1 part Orange Juice
1 part Cranberry Juice Cocktail
1 part Melon Liqueur
Hurricane Glass

Build over ice and stir

Wave Rider
1 1/2 parts Coconut-Flavored Rum
splash Cranberry Juice Cocktail
1 part Grapefruit Juice
1 part Pineapple Juice
Collins Glass

Build over ice and stir

Wave Runner
1 part Light Rum
1 part Cranberry Juice Cocktail
fill with Lemon-Lime Soda
Collins Glass
Build over ice and stir

Wayang Dream
1 part Cherry Brandy
1 part Pisang Ambon® Liqueur
fill with Lemonade
Collins Glass
Build over ice and stir

Wedding Anniversary
1 part Vodka
1 part Galliano®
1 part Campari®
fill with Orange Juice
Collins Glass
Shake with ice and strain over ice

Weekend Passion
1 1/2 parts Gin
1 part Sour Mix
1 part Passion Fruit Nectar
fill with Lemon-Lime Soda
Collins Glass
Build over ice and stir

Weightlessness
1 1/2 parts Vodka
1 part Peach Schnapps
1 part Sour Mix
1 part Coconut Cream
1 part Cranberry Juice Cocktail
Collins Glass
Shake with ice and strain over ice

A Wellidian
1 part Apple Liqueur
1 part Jamaican Rum
1 part Kiwi Juice
fill with Orange Fanta® Soda
Collins Glass
Build over ice and stir

West Indies Yellowbird
2 parts Dark Rum
1/2 part Crème de Banana
1/2 part Galliano®
1 part Pineapple Juice
1 part Orange Juice
Collins Glass
Shake with ice and strain over ice

West Salem Cider
1 part Peach Brandy
1 part Vodka
fill with Apple Cider
Collins Glass
Build over ice and stir

Whale Orgasm
1 part Vodka
1 part Crème de Menthe (White)
2 parts Piña Colada Mix
Collins Glass
Shake with ice and pour

Whambam
1/4 part Amaretto
1/4 part Peach Schnapps
1/4 part Coconut-Flavored Rum
1/4 part Butterscotch Schnapps
1/4 part Cherry Liqueur
1/4 part Irish Cream Liqueur
1 part Milk
1 part Orange Juice
Collins Glass
Shake with ice and pour

Whammy Kiss

1/2 part Crème de Banana
1/2 part Coconut-Flavored Liqueur
1/2 part Frangelico®
1/2 part Spiced Rum
fill with Cream
Collins Glass

Shake with ice and pour

Whiskey Collins

2 parts Whiskey
dash Powdered Sugar
1/2 part Lemon Juice
fill with Carbonated Water
Collins Glass

Build over ice and stir

White Plush

2 parts Blended Scotch Whiskey
fill with Milk
dash Powdered Sugar
Collins Glass

Shake with ice and strain over ice

White Puerto Rican

1 part Rum
1 part Coffee Liqueur
fill with Milk
Collins Glass

Shake with ice and strain over ice

White Widow

1 part Coffee Liqueur
1/2 part Coconut-Flavored Rum
fill with Cream
Collins Glass

Shake with ice and strain over ice

Whiting Sunset

2 parts Vodka
1 part Tequila
fill with Orange Juice
splash Grenadine
Collins Glass

Build over ice and stir

Why Santa Has a Naughty List

1 part Amaretto
1 part Banana Liqueur
1 part Gin
1/2 part Grenadine
fill with Lemon-Lime Soda
Collins Glass

Build over ice and stir

Wild Dog

1 part Dark Rum
1 part Southern Comfort®
fill with Pineapple Juice
Collins Glass

Build over ice and stir

Wild Fling

1 1/2 parts Wild Berry Schnapps
2 parts Pineapple Juice
1 part Cranberry Juice Cocktail
Collins Glass

Build over ice and stir

Wile E. Coyote®

3/4 part Dark Rum
3/4 part Banana Liqueur
3/4 part Blackberry Brandy
1 part Pineapple Juice
1 part Cranberry Juice Cocktail
Collins Glass

Build over ice and stir

Windward Isles

$1\frac{1}{2}$ parts Light Rum
$\frac{1}{2}$ part Kiwi Schnapps
splash Blue Curaçao
fill with Pineapple Juice
Collins Glass

Shake with ice and strain over ice

Winona Ryder

2 parts Gin
1 part Blue Curaçao
1 part Triple Sec
fill with Orange Juice
Collins Glass

Build over ice and stir

Winter Breeze

1 part Crème de Cacao (White)
1 part Vanilla Liqueur
1 part Irish Cream Liqueur
fill with Milk
Beer Mug

Build over ice and stir

Wobbly Knee

$1\frac{1}{2}$ parts Gin
1 part Blue Curaçao
1 part Orange Juice
1 part Lemon-Lime Soda
Collins Glass

Build over ice and stir

Wolf Blood

1 part Raspberry Liqueur
$1\frac{1}{2}$ parts Fresh Lime Juice
fill with Grape Soda
Collins Glass

Build over ice and stir

Wonder Woman®

1 part Melon Liqueur
1 part Peach Schnapps
1 part Pineapple Juice
2 parts Cranberry Juice Cocktail
3 parts Orange Juice
Hurricane Glass

Build over ice

Woody Woodpecker®

$1\frac{1}{2}$ parts Cachaça
$\frac{1}{2}$ part Galliano®
fill with Orange Juice
Collins Glass

Shake with ice and strain over ice

Wrath of Grapes

$1\frac{1}{4}$ part Dark Rum
1 part Sour Mix
fill with Grape Juice (Red)
Collins Glass

Build over ice and stir

Wrong Number

1 part Gin
1 part Rum
1 part Vodka
1 part Orange Juice
1 part Pineapple Juice
Collins Glass

Build over ice and stir

Xixu

$1\frac{1}{2}$ parts Vodka
$\frac{1}{2}$ Campari®
$\frac{1}{2}$ Melon Liqueur
splash Crème de Menthe (White)
fill with Cola
Collins Glass

Build over ice and stir

Yeah Dude

1 part Vodka
1 part Southern Comfort®
splash Tabasco® Sauce
fill with Cola
Collins Glass

Build over ice and stir

Yellow Bird

$1^1/_2$ parts Rum
$^1/_2$ part Banana Liqueur
$^1/_2$ part Galliano®
1 part Grapefruit Juice
1 part Orange Juice
Collins Glass

Shake with ice and pour

Yellow Fingers

1 part Southern Comfort®
1 part Vodka
$^1/_2$ part Galliano®
1 part Orange Juice
1 part Lemon-Lime Soda
Collins Glass

Build over ice and stir

Yellow Fun

1 part Peach Schnapps
1 part Passion Fruit Liqueur
2 parts Pear Juice
2 parts Passion Fruit Juice
1 part Lemon Juice
1 part Mango Juice
Collins Glass

Shake with ice and strain over ice

Yellow Screwdriver

2 parts Vodka
fill with Lemonade
Collins Glass

Build over ice and stir

Yellow Star

1 part Dry Gin
1 part Crème de Banana
1 part Pastis
$^1/_2$ part Passion Fruit Nectar
fill with Orange Juice
Collins Glass

Shake with ice and strain over ice

Yesterday Sun

1 part Pineapple Juice
1 part Mandarine Napoléon® Liqueur
$^1/_2$ part Melon Liqueur
$^1/_2$ part Bourbon
$^1/_2$ part Crème de Banana
$^1/_4$ part Grenadine
Collins Glass

Build over ice and stir

You Never Can Tell

$1^1/_2$ parts Rum
$^1/_2$ part Crème de Banana
fill with Orange Juice
Collins Glass

Build over ice and stir

Yukon Dew Me

2 parts Yukon Jack®
fill with Mountain Dew®
Collins Glass

Build over ice and stir

Zagoskin

$^{1}/_{2}$ part Sloe Gin
$^{2}/_{3}$ part Peach Schnapps
splash Guava Juice
splash Lychee Liqueur
fill with Pineapple Juice
Collins Glass

Shake with ice and pour

Zambeer

$1^{1}/_{2}$ parts Sambuca
fill with Root Beer
Collins Glass

Build over ice and stir

Zoot Liscious

1 part Rum
$^{1}/_{2}$ part Grenadine
fill with Cola
Collins Glass

Build over ice

Zula Lake Slammer

1 part Light Rum
1 part Sambuca
fill with Cola
Collins Glass

Build over ice and stir

Zyphar

2 parts Vodka
1 part Maraschino Cherry Juice
fill with Mountain Dew®
Collins Glass

Build over ice and stir

Short Drinks

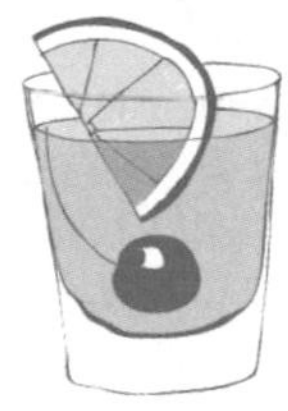

These altitudinally challenged drinks don't fit into any other marketable category.

1-800 Bite the Berry

1 1/4 parts Jose Cuervo® 1800 Tequila
1/2 part Triple Sec
1/4 part Raspberry Liqueur
2 1/2 parts Sour Mix
2 parts Cranberry Juice Cocktail
Whiskey Sour Glass

Shake with ice and strain over ice

1-800 Pink Cad

1 part Jose Cuervo® 1800 Tequila
1/2 part Triple Sec
2 1/2 parts Sour Mix
1/2 part Lime Juice
splash Cranberry Juice Cocktail
Highball Glass

Shake with ice and strain over ice

2 Gs and a Double R

1 1/2 parts Citrus-Flavored Rum
1 part Gin
splash 151-Proof Rum
fill with Grapefruit Juice
Old-Fashioned Glass

Build all but 151-Proof Rum over ice. Top with the Rum.

39 Steps

1 part Raspberry Liqueur
1 part Jim Beam®
1 part Lemon Juice
Highball Glass

Shake with ice and strain over ice

3rd Wheel

2 parts Alizé®
1 part Grand Marnier®
Coupette Glass

Shake with ice and strain over ice

43 Ole

1 part Brandy
1 part Licor 43®
2 parts Orange Juice
Old-Fashioned Glass

Mix with ice

'57 T-Bird

1/2 part Southern Comfort®
1/2 part Grand Marnier®
1/2 part Amaretto
splash Pineapple Juice
splash Orange Juice
splash Grenadine
Whiskey Sour Glass

Build over ice and stir

77 Sunset Strip

1/2 part Vodka
1/2 part Gin
1/2 part Spiced Rum
1/2 part Triple Sec
1 1/2 parts Pineapple Juice
1/2 part Grenadine
Highball Glass

Build over ice and stir

9 to 5

1 part Blackberry Liqueur
1 part Jim Beam®
1/2 part Lemon Juice
fill with Ginger Ale
Highball Glass

Build over ice and stir

A.B.C.

1 part Amaretto
1 part Irish Cream Liqueur
1 part Cointreau®
Highball Glass

Shake with ice and strain over ice

Abacaxi

2 parts Cachaca
1 part Simple Syrup
1 part Pineapple Juice
1 part Fresh Lime Juice
Old-Fashioned Glass

Build over ice and stir

Abilene

1 1/2 parts Dark Rum
2 parts Peach Nectar
3 parts Orange Juice
Highball Glass

Build over ice and stir

Absinthe Friends

2 parts Blackberry Liqueur
1 part Absinthe
Highball Glass

Build over ice and stir

Absolero Liqueur

3/4 part Melon Liqueur
3/4 part Absolut® Citron Vodka
3/4 part Absolut® Kurant Vodka
1 Egg White
1/4 part Fresh Lime Juice
Old-Fashioned Glass

Shake with ice and strain over ice

Absolut® Heaven

1 1/2 parts Orange-Flavored Vodka
fill with Pineapple Juice
splash Cranberry Juice Cocktail
Highball Glass

Build over ice and stir

Absolut® Mixer

1 part Absolut® Citron Vodka
1 part Absolut® Peppar Vodka
1 part Absolut® Kurant Vodka
1 part Absolut® Vodka
fill with Orange Juice
Highball Glass

Build over ice and stir

Absolut® Stress

1 part Vodka
1 part Coconut-Flavored Rum
1 part Peach Schnapps
splash Cranberry Juice Cocktail
splash Orange Juice
Highball Glass

Build over ice and stir

Absolut® Trouble

1 1/2 parts Citrus-Flavored Vodka
1 part Grand Marnier®
1 part Orange Juice
1/2 part Grenadine
Old-Fashioned Glass

Shake with ice and strain over ice

Absolut® Vacation
1 part Vodka
1 part Cranberry Juice Cocktail
1 part Orange Juice
1 part Pineapple Juice
Old-Fashioned Glass

Build over ice and stir

The Abyss
2/3 part Dark Rum
splash Blue Curaçao
splash Cherry Brandy
splash Vermouth
fill with Orange Juice
Highball Glass

Shake with ice and strain over ice

Acapulco
1 1/2 part Light Rum
2 splashes Triple Sec
2 splashes Lime Juice
dash Sugar
1 Egg White
1 Fresh Mint Leaf
Old-Fashioned Glass

Shake with ice and strain over ice

Acapulco Clamdigger
1 1/2 parts Tequila Silver
6 parts Clamato®
splash Lemon Juice
1 Lemon Wedge
splash Tabasco® Sauce
splash Worcestershire® Sauce
dash Horseradish
Old-Fashioned Glass

Shake with ice and strain over ice

Ademar
1 part Dark Rum
1 part Sweet Vermouth
1 part Triple Sec
splash Blue Curaçao
splash Strawberry Liqueur
Highball Glass

Shake with ice and strain over ice

Admiral
1 part Rye Whiskey
2 parts Dry Vermouth
splash Lemon Juice
Old-Fashioned Glass

Shake with ice and strain over ice

Adrian Wixcey
1 1/4 parts Rum
1 1/2 parts Passion-Grapefruit Juice
1 1/2 parts Sour Mix
1 part Orange Juice
splash Grenadine
White Wine Glass

Build over ice and stir

Aero Bar
1 part Irish Cream Liqueur
1 part Coffee Liqueur
1 1/2 part Crème de Menthe (White)
fill with Milk
Highball Glass

Shake with ice and strain over ice

Affirmative Action

2 parts Vodka
1 part Cognac
1 part Orange Juice
Highball Glass

Shake with ice and strain over ice

African Rumble

1 part Coffee Liqueur
1 part Cream
1 part Irish Cream Liqueur
1 part Tia Maria®
Highball Glass

Shake with ice and strain over ice

After Burner

1 part Rye Whiskey
1 part Tequila
2 parts Scotch
2 parts Tabasco® Sauce
2 parts Lemon Juice
Highball Glass

Shake with ice and strain over ice

After Eighteen

1 part Coffee Liqueur
1 part Crème de Menthe (White)
fill with Chocolate Milk
Old-Fashioned Glass

Shake with ice and strain over ice

Afternoon Pleasure

1 part Sweet Vermouth
1 part Amaretto
fill with Orange Juice
Old-Fashioned Glass

Build over ice

Afterwhile Crocodile

1 part Vodka
1 part Melon Liqueur
1 part Blue Curaçao
fill with Margarita Mix
Highball Glass

Shake with ice and strain over ice

Agent Orange

1 part Southern Comfort®
1 part Irish Cream Liqueur
Old-Fashioned Glass

Build over ice and stir

Aggie Slammer

1 part Southern Comfort®
1 part Hennessy®
splash Grenadine
splash Sour Mix
Highball Glass

Build over ice and stir

Aggravation

1 1/2 parts Scotch
1/2 part Coffee Liqueur
1/2 part Cream
Highball Glass

Build over ice and stir

Airborne Lemon Drop

1 1/4 parts Vodka
3/4 part Chambord®
3/4 part 151-Proof Rum
1 Lemon Wedge
dash Sugar
Highball Glass

Shake with ice and strain over ice

Akis Special
1 part Light Rum
$1^1/_2$ parts Banana Liqueur
1 part Lemon Juice
fill with Lemon-Lime Soda
Highball Glass

Build over ice and stir

Al Capone
$1^1/_2$ parts Brandy
$^3/_4$ part Marsala
splash Drambuie®
Red Wine Glass

Shake with ice and strain

Alabama
1 part Blue Curaçao
1 part Brandy
$^1/_2$ part Lime Juice
splash Simple Syrup
Old-Fashioned Glass

Shake with ice and strain over ice

Alabama Fizz
2 parts Gin
dash Powdered Sugar
$^1/_2$ part Lemon Juice
fill with Carbonated Water
2 Fresh Mint Leaves
Highball Glass

Shake with ice and strain over ice

Alabama Mamma
1 part Crème de Banana
1 part Raspberry Liqueur
$^1/_2$ part Southern Comfort®
fill with Orange Juice
Highball Glass

Shake with ice and strain over ice

The Alamo
1 part Tequila
$^3/_4$ part Coffee-Flavored Brandy
$^1/_4$ part Lime Juice
Whiskey Sour Glass

Shake with ice and strain over ice

Albatross
$^1/_2$ part Crème de Banana
$^2/_3$ part Tequila Silver
$^1/_2$ part Pineapple Juice
splash Cream
splash Lemon Juice
Highball Glass

Shake with ice and strain over ice

Albysjön
2 parts Vodka
1 part Orange Fanta® Soda
$^1/_2$ part Lemon-Lime Soda
$^1/_2$ part Kiwi Concentrate
Highball Glass

Build over ice and stir

The Alderman
1 part Citrus-Flavored Vodka
$^1/_2$ part Strawberry Liqueur
$^1/_2$ part Lemon Juice
$1^1/_2$ parts Apple Juice
$^2/_3$ part Sparkling Water
Old-Fashioned Glass

Shake with ice and strain over ice

Alex Chi-Chi
2 parts Vodka
1 part Cointreau®
1 part Coconut Cream
2 parts Pineapple Juice
White Wine Glass

Shake with ice and strain

Alexander the Great
$1^1/_2$ parts Vodka
$^1/_2$ part Crème de Cacao (White)
$^1/_2$ part Coffee Liqueur
$^1/_2$ part Cream
Highball Glass

Shake with ice and strain over ice

Alexander's Layers
1 part Apricot Brandy
1 part Crème de Cacao (Dark)
1 part Cream
Highball Glass

Build over ice and stir

Algae
$^1/_2$ part Vodka
$^1/_2$ part Melon Liqueur
$^1/_2$ part Raspberry Liqueur
$^1/_2$ part Blue Curaçao
2 parts Sour Mix
fill with Lemon-Lime Soda
Highball Glass

Shake with ice and strain over ice

Algonquin
$1^1/_2$ part Bourbon
1 part Dry Vermouth
1 part Pineapple Juice
dash Bitters
Old-Fashioned Glass

Shake with ice and strain over ice

Alice in Wonderland
1 part Amaretto
1 part Grand Marnier®
1 part Southern Comfort®
Old-Fashioned Glass

Shake with ice and strain over ice

Alien Secretion
1 part Coconut-Flavored Rum
1 part Melon Liqueur
fill with Pineapple Juice
Highball Glass

Build over ice and stir

Alien Slime
1 part Vodka
2 parts Blue Curaçao
3 parts Orange Juice
Highball Glass

Shake with ice and strain over ice

All-American
1 part Southern Comfort®
fill with Cola
Highball Glass

Build over ice and stir

All Puckered Out
$1^1/_2$ parts Sour Apple Schnapps
fill with Ginger Ale
Highball Glass

Build over ice and stir

Alligator Piss
1 part Melon Liqueur
1 part Peach Schnapps
1 part Southern Comfort®
1 part Amaretto
splash Sour Mix
Old-Fashioned Glass

Shake with ice and strain over ice

Alligator Tongue
1 part Vodka
$1^1/_2$ parts Melon Liqueur
2 parts Pineapple Juice
$^1/_2$ part Lemon-Lime Soda
$^1/_4$ part Fresh Lime Juice
Old-Fashioned Glass

Shake with ice and strain over ice

All-Star Summit

1 part Light Rum
1/2 part Triple Sec
1/2 part Gin
1/2 part Raspberry Syrup
Old-Fashioned Glass

Shake with ice and strain over ice

Alma Rosa

1 part Dark Rum
1/2 part Vanilla Ice Cream
1/4 part Triple Sec
1/4 part Crème de Banana
White Wine Glass

Shake with ice and strain over ice

Almeria

1 1/2 parts Rum
1 part Brandy
1 part Coffee
1 Egg
Old-Fashioned Glass

Shake with ice and strain over ice

Almond Joy®

1/2 part Coconut-Flavored Rum
1 part Amaretto
1 part Crème de Cacao (White)
2 parts Cream
Highball Glass

Shake with ice and strain over ice

Almond Passion

1 part Dark Rum
1/4 part Crème de Noyaux
splash Apricot Brandy
2 parts Orange Juice
Highball Glass

Shake with ice and strain over ice

Almond Punch

1 part Amaretto
1 part Passion Fruit Liqueur
splash Orange Juice
Highball Glass

Shake with ice and strain over ice

Almond Schwarzenegger

2 parts Blavod® Black Vodka
1 part Amaretto
Old-Fashioned Glass

Shake with ice and strain over ice

Almost a Virgin

2/3 part Raspberry Liqueur
2/3 part Amaretto
1 1/2 parts Currant-Flavored Vodka
splash Pineapple Juice
splash Cranberry Juice Cocktail
Highball Glass

Build over ice and stir

Aloha Screwdriver

1 part Vodka
1 part Orange Juice
2 parts Pineapple Juice
Highball Glass

Build over ice and stir

Alpine Lemon-Lime Soda

2 parts Peppermint Schnapps
fill with Lemon-Lime Soda
Highball Glass

Build over ice and stir

Alternate Root

1 part Root Beer Schnapps
2 parts Orange Juice
Highball Glass

Build over ice and stir

Altoids® in France
1 part Chambord®
1 part Peppermint Liqueur
Highball Glass
Build over ice and stir

Amaretto Alexander
1 part Amaretto
1 part Crème de Cacao (White)
fill with Cream
Brandy Snifter
Shake with ice and strain over ice

Amaretto Big Red
2 parts Amaretto
fill with Strawberry Soda
Highball Glass
Build over ice and stir

Amaretto Daiquiri
1 part Rum
1 part Amaretto
fill with Sour Mix
Highball Glass
Shake with ice and strain over ice

Amaretto '57 Chevy®
1 part Vodka
1 part Amaretto
1 part Cherry Juice
1 part Lemonade
1 part Orange Juice
Highball Glass
Build over ice and stir

Amaretto '57 T-Bird
1 part Vodka
1 part Amaretto
1 part Cherry Juice
1 part Sour Mix
1 part Pineapple Juice
Highball Glass
Build over ice and stir

Amaretto Hawaiian Fizz
2 parts Amaretto
1 part Sour Mix
1 part Pineapple Juice
fill with Lemon-Lime Soda
Highball Glass
Build over ice and stir

Amaretto Heartwarmer
2 parts Southern Comfort®
2 Almonds
1 Peach Kernel, Crushed
dash Sugar
1 part Dry Vermouth
1 part Amaretto
Old-Fashioned Glass
Warm the Southern Comfort® and add the Almonds, Peach Kernel, and Sugar. Stir. Allow to cool and add the Vermouth and Amaretto. Stir again and strain over ice into an Old-Fashioned glass.

Amaretto Margarita
1 part Tequila
1 part Amaretto
fill with Margarita Mix
Highball Glass
Build over ice and stir

Amaretto Piña Colada
1 part Rum
1 part Amaretto
1/2 part Piña Colada Mix
1/2 part Pineapple Juice
Highball Glass
Shake with ice and strain

Amaretto Pucker
1 part Vodka
1 part Amaretto
1 part Cherry Juice
fill with Grapefruit Juice
Highball Glass
Build over ice and stir

Amaretto Punch
2 parts Amaretto
1 part Cherry Juice
1 part Orange Juice
1 part Pineapple Juice
Highball Glass

Build over ice and stir

Amaretto Pussycat
1 part Vodka
1 part Amaretto
1 part Cherry Juice
fill with Pineapple Juice
Highball Glass

Build over ice and stir

Amaretto Rummy Tea
1 part Rum
1 part Amaretto
1 part Sour Mix
fill with Cola
Highball Glass

Build over ice and stir

Amaretto Russian Tea
1 part Vodka
1 part Amaretto
1 part Sour Mix
fill with Cola
Highball Glass

Build over ice and stir

Amaretto Slinger
1 part Vodka
1 part Amaretto
1 part Sour Mix
fill with Orange Juice
Highball Glass

Build over ice and stir

Amaretto Smooth Sailing
1 part Vodka
1 part Amaretto
1 part Sour Mix
1 part Cranberry Juice Cocktail
1 part Orange Juice
Highball Glass

Build over ice and stir

Amaretto Sombrero
1 part Amaretto
4 parts Cream
Old-Fashioned Glass

Build over ice and stir

Amaretto Sour
3 parts Amaretto
1 1/2 parts Lemon-Lime Soda
1 1/2 parts Lime Juice
1 1/2 parts Sour Mix
Old-Fashioned Glass

Shake with ice and strain over ice

Amaretto Stone Sour
1 part Amaretto
1 part Sour Mix
1 part Orange Juice
Highball Glass

Build over ice and stir

Amaretto Sunrise
1 part Amaretto
fill with Orange Juice
splash Grenadine
Old-Fashioned Glass

Build over ice and stir. Top with a splash of Grenadine.

Amaretto Sunset
3 parts Amaretto
1 part Triple Sec
fill with Apple Cider
Old-Fashioned Glass

Build over ice and stir

Amaretto Toasted Almond
1 part Amaretto
1 part Coffee Liqueur
1 1/2 parts Cream
Old-Fashioned Glass

Build over ice and stir

Amaretto Vodka Hawaiian
1 part Vodka
1 part Amaretto
1 part Sour Mix
1 part Lemon-Lime Soda
fill with Pineapple Juice
Highball Glass

Build over ice and stir

Amaretto Vodka Punch
1 part Vodka
1 part Amaretto
1 part Cherry Juice
1 part Orange Juice
1 part Pineapple Juice
Highball Glass

Build over ice and stir

Amaretto White Italian
1 part Vodka
1 part Amaretto
fill with Cream
Highball Glass

Build over ice and stir

Amazontic
2 parts Ginger Ale
1 part Rum
dash Sugar
Whiskey Sour Glass

Shake with ice and strain over ice

Ambijaxtrious
1 part Vodka
1 part Tequila
1 part Coffee Liqueur
fill with Milk
splash Grenadine
Old-Fashioned Glass

Build over ice and stir

American Cream Soda
1 part Butterscotch Schnapps
1 part Vanilla Liqueur
2 parts Sour Mix
1 part Lemonade
Highball Glass

Shake with ice and strain over ice

American Sweetheart
1 part Southern Comfort®
splash Dry Vermouth
fill with Sour Mix
Whiskey Sour Glass

Shake with ice and strain over ice

American Yakuza
1 part Lychee Liqueur
1 part Jim Beam®
1 part Lemon Juice
Highball Glass

Shake with ice and strain over ice

AmoreAde
1 1/2 parts Amaretto
3/4 part Triple Sec
3 parts Club Soda
Red Wine Glass

Build over ice and stir

Amsterdam Surprise
1/2 part Goldschläger®
1/2 part Amaretto
1/2 part Vodka
1/2 part Southern Comfort®
3 parts Pineapple Juice
Highball Glass

Build over ice and stir

Amy's Ambrosia
1/2 part Currant-Flavored Vodka
1 part Melon Liqueur
1 part Strawberry Liqueur
fill with Cranberry Juice Cocktail
Highball Glass

Build over ice and stir

Anchors Aweigh
1 part Bourbon
1 part Triple Sec
1 part Peach Schnapps
1 part Maraschino Liqueur
1 part Cream
Old-Fashioned Glass

Shake with ice and pour

Andorian Milk
1 part Blue Curaçao
fill with Milk
Old-Fashioned Glass

Build over ice and stir

Andy's Blend
2 parts Vodka
1 part Orange Juice
1 part Pineapple Juice
Highball Glass

Build over ice and stir

Anesthetic
3 parts Gin
1 part Vermouth
1 part Cognac
dash Orange Bitters
Highball Glass

Build over ice and stir

Angel & Co.
1 1/2 parts Frangelico®
1/4 part Crème de Banana
fill with Pineapple Juice
Old-Fashioned Glass

Shake with ice and strain over ice

Angel's Hug
1 1/2 parts Pisang Ambon® Liqueur
1 part Dark Rum
1 part Crème de Banana
Highball Glass

Shake with ice and pour

Angel's Poison
1 part Raspberry Liqueur
1/4 part Triple Sec
splash Lime Juice
fill with Lemon-Lime Soda
Old-Fashioned Glass

Build over ice and stir

Angie's Dildo
1 part Vodka
2 parts Triple Sec
dash Sugar
Old-Fashioned Glass

Shake with ice and pour

Angostura® Sour
3 parts Lemon-Lime Soda
1 1/2 parts Sour Mix
dash Bitters
Old-Fashioned Glass

Build over ice and stir

Angry Irishman
1 part Irish Cream Liqueur
1 part Irish Whiskey
Old-Fashioned Glass

Build over ice and stir

Angry Parakeet
3 parts Tequila
1 1/2 parts Green Chartreuse®
Old-Fashioned Glass

Shake with ice and pour

Animal in Man
1/2 part Pisang Ambon® Liqueur
1/2 part Melon Liqueur
1 1/2 parts Aquavit
1/2 part Lemon Juice
Highball Glass

Shake with ice and strain over ice

Ankle Breaker
2 parts 151-Proof Rum
1 part Cherry Brandy
1 part Lime Juice
splash Simple Syrup
Old-Fashioned Glass

Shake with ice and pour

Antifreeze
1 part Vodka
1/2 part Blue Curaçao
1/2 part Crème de Banana
fill with Orange Juice
Highball Glass

Shake with ice and pour

Antoine Special
1 part Dubonnet® Blonde
1 part Dry Vermouth
Red Wine Glass

Shake Dubonnet® with ice and strain into the glass. Top with Vermouth.

Anvil
2 parts Vodka
2 parts Coconut Cream
3 parts Pineapple Juice
Highball Glass

Build over ice and stir

Aperol™ Schuhmann
1 1/2 parts Aperol™
1 part Lemon Juice
1 part Lime Juice
fill with Orange Juice
Highball Glass

Shake with ice and strain over ice

Apfel Orange
1 part Apple Brandy
1/2 part Vodka
1 part Orange Juice
1 part Lemon-Lime Soda
Highball Glass

Build over ice and stir

Apfelkuchen
1 part Vodka
fill with Apple Juice
splash Grenadine
Highball Glass

Build over ice and stir

Apollo 13

2 parts Light Rum
2 parts Cream
1/2 part Grand Marnier®
1/2 part Galliano®
splash Grenadine
Old-Fashioned Glass

Shake with ice and strain over ice

Apple Blossom

1 1/2 parts Sour Apple Schnapps
1/2 part Cranberry Juice Cocktail
Old-Fashioned Glass

Shake with ice and pour

Apple Brandy Highball

2 parts Apple Brandy
fill with Carbonated Water
1 Lemon Twist
Highball Glass

Build over ice and stir

Apple Brandy Rickey

1 1/2 parts Apple Brandy
1/2 part Lime Juice
fill with Carbonated Water
Highball Glass

Build over ice and stir

Apple Brandy Sour

2 parts Apple Brandy
dash Powdered Sugar
1/2 part Lemon Juice
1 Lemon Slice
1 Maraschino Cherry
Whiskey Sour Glass

Shake with ice and strain over ice

Apple Chill

2 parts Sour Apple Schnapps
2 parts Lemonade
1 part Pineapple Juice
Highball Glass

Shake with ice and pour

Apple Daiquiri

1 part Rum
1 part Sour Apple Schnapps
fill with Sour Mix
Highball Glass

Shake with ice and pour

Apple Delight

1 part Vodka
1 part Peach Schnapps
1 part Melon Liqueur
1/2 part Crème de Banana
Old-Fashioned Glass

Shake with ice and pour

Apple Dew

2 parts Sour Apple Schnapps
fill with Mountain Dew®
Highball Glass

Build over ice and stir

Apple Dreamsicle®

2 parts Sour Apple Schnapps
1 part Cherry Juice
1 part Orange Juice
1 part Pineapple Juice
1 part Cream
Highball Glass

Shake with ice and pour

Apple Eden

1 1/2 part Vodka
3 parts Apple Juice
Highball Glass

Shake with ice and pour

Apple Fizz
2 parts Sour Apple Schnapps
1/2 part Sour Mix
splash Orange Juice
fill with Lemon-Lime Soda
Highball Glass

Build over ice and stir

Apple Jack®
1 1/2 part Sour Apple Schnapps
1 part Cinnamon Schnapps
Old-Fashioned Glass

Build over ice and stir

Apple Pie
3 parts Sour Apple Schnapps
1 part Cinnamon Schnapps
Old-Fashioned Glass

Build over ice and stir

Apple Pie with a Crust
1 part Coconut-Flavored Rum
3 parts Apple Juice
3 splashes Cinnamon Schnapps
Highball Glass

Shake with ice and pour

Apple Piña Colada
1 part Rum
1 part Sour Apple Schnapps
1 part Piña Colada Mix
1 part Pineapple Juice
Highball Glass

Shake with ice and pour

Apple Pucker
1 part Vodka
1 part Sour Apple Schnapps
1 part Cherry Juice
fill with Grapefruit Juice
Highball Glass

Shake with ice and pour

Apple Punch
2 parts Sour Apple Schnapps
1 part Cherry Juice
1 part Orange Juice
1 part Pineapple Juice
Highball Glass

Shake with ice and pour

Apple Pussycat
1 part Vodka
1 part Sour Apple Schnapps
1 part Cherry Juice
fill with Pineapple Juice
Highball Glass

Shake with ice and pour

Apple Rum Rickey
1 part Light Rum
1 part Applejack
splash Lime Juice
fill with Carbonated Water
Highball Glass

Build over ice and stir

Apple Screwdriver
1 part Vodka
1 part Sour Apple Schnapps
fill with Orange Juice
Highball Glass

Build over ice and stir

Apple Sour
2 parts Sour Apple Schnapps
fill with Sour Mix
Highball Glass

Shake with ice and pour

Apple Tequila Sunrise
1 part Tequila
1 part Sour Apple Schnapps
fill with Orange Juice
splash Grenadine
Highball Glass

Build over ice

Apres Ski
1 part Coffee Liqueur
1 part Crème de Cacao (White)
1 part Peppermint Schnapps
Highball Glass
Shake with ice and pour

Apricot and Tequila Sour
1 1/2 parts Tequila
1 part Amaretto
1/2 part Fresh Lime Juice
Old-Fashioned Glass
Shake with ice and pour

Apricot Hurricane
1 part Rum
1 part Apricot Brandy
1 part Cherry Juice
2 parts Orange Juice
1 part Pineapple Juice
Highball Glass
Shake with ice and pour

Apricot Lady
1 1/4 parts Light Rum
1 part Apricot Brandy
splash Triple Sec
splash Lime Juice
1 Egg White
1 Orange Slice
Old-Fashioned Glass
Shake all ingredients except Orange Slice with ice and strain into the glass over ice. Top with the Orange Slice.

Apricot Lemondrop
1 part Vodka
1 part Apricot Brandy
fill with Lemonade
Whiskey Sour Glass
Shake with ice and pour

Apricot Screwdriver
1 part Vodka
1 part Apricot Brandy
fill with Orange Juice
Highball Glass
Build over ice and stir

Apricot Twist
1 1/2 parts Rum
1 part Apricot Nectar
1/2 part Lime Cordial
splash Kirschwasser
1 Lemon Twist
Highball Glass
Shake with ice and pour

Aqua
1 part Vodka
1 part Irish Cream Liqueur
1 part Blue Curaçao
fill with Lemon-Lime Soda
Highball Glass
Build over ice and stir

Aqua Fodie
1 part Gin
1 part Blue Curaçao
fill with Orange Juice
Highball Glass
Shake with ice and pour

Arabian Sunset
1/2 part Pisang Ambon® Liqueur
1/2 part Sloe Gin
1 part Cream
splash Blue Curaçao
Champagne Flute
Shake all but Blue Curaçao with ice and strain into the glass. Top with a splash of Blue Curaçao for a sunset effect.

Arawak Cup
2 parts Dark Rum
1/2 part Amaretto
1/2 part Pineapple Juice
1/2 part Fresh Lime Juice
Old-Fashioned Glass

Build over ice and stir

Arc Welder
2 parts Blue Curaçao
1/2 part 151-Proof Rum
splash Light Rum
Highball Glass

Shake with ice and pour

Archers Slingback
1 1/2 parts Gin
1 1/2 parts Apple Juice
1 part Peach Puree
1/2 part Fresh Lime Juice
1/4 part Sugar
Champagne Flute

Shake with ice and strain

Arizona Evening
1 part Triple Sec
1 1/2 parts Limoncello
2 parts Cranberry Juice Cocktail
2 parts Club Soda
Highball Glass

Build over ice and stir

Arkansas Razorback
1 part Rum
1 part Vodka
1 part Amaretto
1 part Coffee Liqueur
Old-Fashioned Glass

Shake with ice and strain over ice

Arlequin
1 1/2 parts Tequila
splash Grenadine
splash Lemon Juice
1 part Orange Juice
1 part Grapefruit Juice
Highball Glass

Shake with ice and pour

Armadillo
1 part Southern Comfort®
1 part Amaretto
1/2 Sour Mix
fill with Orange Juice
Highball Glass

Build over ice and stir

Arturro's Death
1 part Rum
1 part Tequila
1 part Sweet Vermouth
1 part Vodka
1 part Blue Curaçao
splash Grenadine
Highball Glass

Shake with ice and strain

Aruba Ariba
3/4 part Rum
3/4 part Vodka
1/2 part Grand Marnier®
splash Grenadine
splash Orange Juice
splash Pineapple Juice
splash Grapefruit Juice
Highball Glass

Shake with ice and pour

Asthma Attack
1/2 part Grain Alcohol
1/2 part 151-Proof Rum
1/2 part Raspberry Liqueur
1 part Amaretto
Highball Glass

Shake with ice and pour

Astroturf®
1 part Crème de Menthe (Green)
1 part Crème de Cacao (Dark)
fill with Milk
splash Chocolate Syrup
Highball Glass

Build over ice and stir

A-Team
1 part Vodka
1 part Brandy
1 part Lime Juice
2 parts Sour Mix
fill with Fruit Punch
Highball Glass

Shake with ice and pour

Atlanta Belle
1 part Bourbon
3/4 part Crème de Cacao (White)
3/4 part Crème de Menthe (Green)
Old-Fashioned Glass

Shake with ice and pour

Atlantean Uprising
1 part Rum
1/2 part Banana Liqueur
1/2 part Raspberry Liqueur
1/2 part Blue Curaçao
splash Grenadine
Highball Glass

Build over ice and stir

Atlantic Sun
1 part Vodka
1 part Southern Comfort®
1 part Grenadine
2 parts Sour Mix
splash Club Soda
Highball Glass

Shake all but Club Soda with ice and strain into the glass. Top with Club Soda.

Atlas
2 parts Vodka
1 part Blue Curaçao
splash Orange Juice
fill with Cranberry Juice Cocktail
Highball Glass

Shake with ice and strain over ice

Atomic Body Slam
1 part Gin
1 part Vodka
1 part Blackberry Brandy
1 part Light Rum
2 parts Strawberry Fruit Drink
Highball Glass

Build over ice and stir

Aunt Jemima®
3 parts Light Rum
1 part Maple Syrup
1 part Lemon Juice
Highball Glass

Shake with ice and strain

Aurelia
1/2 part Blue Curaçao
1/2 part Grenadine
2/3 part Coconut Cream
Highball Glass

Build over ice and stir

Aussie Orgasm
1 part Cointreau®
1 part Irish Cream Liqueur
Highball Glass

Shake with ice and pour

Aussie Tea

1 part Kiwi Schnapps
1 part Strawberry Liqueur
fill with Iced Tea
Highball Glass

Build over ice and stir

Avalanche

1 part Crown Royal® Whiskey
1 part Coffee Liqueur
fill with Cream
Highball Glass

Shake with ice and pour

Aye Are So Dunk

1 part Apricot Brandy
1 part Blackberry Liqueur
1 part Piña Colada Mix
1 part Blueberry Schnapps
Highball Glass

Build over ice and stir

Aztec

1 part Gin
1/2 part Cherry Brandy
1 part Piña Colada Mix
1 part Orange Juice
1 Pineapple Slice
2 Maraschino Cherries
Old-Fashioned Glass

Shake all but Pineapple and Cherries with ice and strain into the glass. Top with Pineapple Slice and Maraschino Cherries.

Azur

2 parts Orange Juice
1 part Apricot Brandy
1/2 part Passion Fruit Nectar
1/2 part Blue Curaçao
White Wine Glass

Shake with ice and pour

B.S. on the Rocks

1 part Light Rum
1 part Peach Schnapps
Highball Glass

Build over ice and stir

B.W. Wrecker

1 part Amaretto
1 part Cranberry Juice Cocktail
1 part Coconut-Flavored Rum
1 part Southern Comfort®
Highball Glass

Shake with ice and strain over ice

B-53

1 part Coffee Liqueur
1 part Irish Cream Liqueur
1 part Grand Marnier®
1 part Vodka
Old-Fashioned Glass

Layer in the glass with no ice

B-69

1 part Grand Marnier®
1 part Coffee Liqueur
1 part Irish Cream Liqueur
1 part Amaretto
1 part Vodka
Whiskey Sour Glass

Shake with ice and strain

Baam Scream

1 part Cinnamon Schnapps
1 part Jim Beam®
Sherry Glass

Pour ingredients into glass neat (do not chill)

Baby Fioula
1/2 part Crème de Cacao (White)
1/2 part Triple Sec
1/2 part Banana Liqueur
1 part Strawberry Juice
Champagne Flute

Shake with ice and strain over ice

Baby's Milk
1/4 part Amaretto
1 part Irish Cream Liqueur
1/4 part Peppermint Schnapps
1/2 part Club Soda
Highball Glass

Build over ice and stir

Bacardi® Tu Tu Cherry
1 part Dark Rum
3 parts Cranberry Juice Cocktail
2 splashes Grenadine
2 parts Orange Juice
Old-Fashioned Glass

Shake with ice and pour

Backseat Boogie
1/2 part Gin
1/2 part Vodka
1 part Cranberry Juice Cocktail
1 part Ginger Ale
Highball Glass

Build over ice and stir

Baehr Chunky Monkey
1/2 part Apricot Brandy
1/2 part Blue Curaçao
1 part Vodka
2 parts Blueberry Schnapps
Highball Glass

Build over ice and stir

Bagpiper's Melody
1 part Crème de Menthe (Green)
1 part Scotch
Old-Fashioned Glass

Layer over ice

Bahama Blue
1/2 part Light Rum
1/2 part Dark Rum
1 part Blue Curaçao
1 1/2 parts Pineapple Juice
splash Coconut Cream
Whiskey Sour Glass

Shake with ice and pour

Bahama Margarita
1 part Tequila
1 part Triple Sec
1 part Cherry Juice
2 parts Margarita Mix
1 part Pineapple Juice
Highball Glass

Shake with ice and pour

Bahamut Gold
2/3 part Vodka
splash Peppermint Liqueur
1 part Goldschläger®
Highball Glass

Build over ice

Bairn
2 parts Scotch
1/2 part Triple Sec
2 dashes Bitters
Old-Fashioned Glass

Shake with ice and strain

Baitreau
1 part Irish Cream Liqueur
1 part Cointreau®
Old-Fashioned Glass

Layer over ice

Baja Coktail
2/3 part Melon Liqueur
2/3 part Kiwi Schnapps
2 parts Sparkling Water
Highball Glass

Build over ice and stir

Balalaika
2 parts Vodka
1 part Triple Sec
Old-Fashioned Glass

Shake with ice and strain

Ball Banger
1 1/2 parts Ouzo
fill with Orange Juice
Highball Glass

Build over ice and stir

Banana Apple Pie
1 part Vodka
1 part Banana Liqueur
fill with Apple Juice
Highball Glass

Build over ice and stir

Banana Banshee
1 part Banana Liqueur
1 part Crème de Cacao (White)
1 part Cream
Highball Glass

Shake with ice and strain over ice

Banana Berry Felch
1 part Irish Cream Liqueur
splash Banana Liqueur
1 part Crème de Cacao (Dark)
1 part Strawberry-Flavored Vodka
Old-Fashioned Glass

Build over ice and stir

Banana Breeze
1 part Vodka
1 part Banana Liqueur
1 part Pineapple Juice
1 part Cranberry Juice Cocktail
Highball Glass

Build over ice and stir

Banana Cream Soda
2 parts Banana Liqueur
fill with Cream Soda
Highball Glass

Build over ice and stir

Banana D.A.
1 part Rum
1 part Cherry Juice
1 part Banana Juice
fill with Piña Colada Mix
splash Pineapple Juice
Highball Glass

Build over ice and stir

Banana Irish Cream
1 part Crème de Cacao (Dark)
1/2 part Cream
1/2 part Banana Puree
Old-Fashioned Glass

Shake with ice and pour

Banana Jabs
1 part Banana Liqueur
1 part Malibu® Rum
fill with Mountain Dew®
Highball Glass

Build over ice and stir

Banana Lemonade
2 parts Banana Liqueur
fill with Lemonade
Highball Glass

Build over ice and stir

Banana LifeSaver®

1 part Coconut-Flavored Rum
1 part Melon Liqueur
1 part Banana Liqueur
1/2 part Sour Mix
fill with Pineapple Juice
Highball Glass

Shake with ice and pour

Banana Marble Drop

1 part Crème de Cacao (White)
1 part Crème de Cacao (Dark)
1 part Banana Syrup
Brandy Snifter

Shake with ice and strain. Top with Whipped Cream.

Banana Paraiso

1 part Rum
2 parts Banana Juice
fill with Orange Juice
splash Pineapple Juice
Highball Glass

Build over ice and stir

Banana Pop

1 part Vodka
1 part Cherry Juice
1 part Banana Juice
fill with Orange Juice
Highball Glass

Build over ice and stir

Banana Pudding

1 part Banana Liqueur
1 part Crème de Cacao (White)
3 parts Milk
1 part Tia Maria®
1 part Vodka
Highball Glass

Shake with ice and strain

Banana Rainstorm

1 part Vodka
1 part Blue Curaçao
2 parts Lemon-Lime Soda
1 part Pineapple Juice
Highball Glass

Build over ice and stir

Banana Rum Sour

1 part Rum
1 part Banana Liqueur
fill with Sour Mix
Highball Glass

Build over ice and stir

Banango

1 1/2 parts Light Rum
1/2 part MangoJuice
1/2 part Fresh Lime Juice
1/4 part Crème de Banana
Old-Fashioned Glass

Shake with ice and strain

Banangrove

1 part Vodka
1 part Crème de Banana
1 part Orange Juice
Highball Glass

Shake with ice and strain

Banshee

1 part Irish Whiskey
1 part Irish Mist®
Old-Fashioned Glass

Build over ice and stir

Barkeep Special

3/4 part Amaretto
1 1/2 part Jack Daniel's®
3 parts Pineapple Juice
Highball Glass

Shake with ice and strain over ice

Barnum & Baileys®
1 part Irish Cream Liqueur
1 part Banana Juice
fill with Cream
Highball Glass

Build over ice and stir

Barracuda Bite
1 1/2 parts Dark Rum
1/2 part Cherry Brandy
1 part Lemon Juice
Highball Glass

Build over ice and stir

Bartender's Delight
1 part Orange-Flavored Vodka
1 part Dry Vermouth
1 part Dubonnet® Blonde
1 part Dry Sherry
Highball Glass

Shake with ice and strain over ice

Bartender's Revenge
1 part Brandy
1 part Cognac
1 part Rum
1 part Tequila
splash Tabasco® Sauce
dash Horseradish
splash Lemon Juice
Highball Glass

Build over ice and stir

Bartender's Root Beer
1/2 part Coffee Liqueur
1/2 part Galliano®
3 parts Club Soda
1 part Cola
Highball Glass

Build over ice and stir

Basic Instinct
1 part Light Rum
1 part Gin
1/2 part Blue Curaçao
1/2 part Southern Comfort®
2 parts Pineapple Juice
2 parts Passion Fruit Juice
Old-Fashioned Glass

Shake with ice and strain over ice

Batman®
1 part Melon Liqueur
1 part Frangelico®
1 part Coconut-Flavored Rum
1 part Cream
Highball Glass

Shake with ice and pour

Battering Ram
1 part Vodka
1 part Tequila
fill with Red Bull® Energy Drink
Highball Glass

Build over ice and stir

Bavarian Alps
2 parts Blackberry Liqueur
1 part Chocolate Liqueur
1 part Milk
Highball Glass

Shake with ice and strain over ice

Bawdy Baboon
1 part Melon Liqueur
1/2 part Blue Curaçao
1/2 part Crème de Banana
1/2 part Coconut-Flavored Liqueur
splash Lemon Juice
Highball Glass

Shake with ice and strain over ice

Bay Breeze
$1^1/_2$ parts Vodka
fill with Grapefruit Juice
splash Cranberry Juice Cocktail
Old-Fashioned Glass

Shake with ice and pour

Bay Horse
$1^1/_2$ parts Whiskey
$^1/_2$ part Pernod®
$^1/_2$ part Crème de Cacao (Dark)
1 part Heavy Cream
dash Ground Nutmeg
Old-Fashioned Glass

Shake with ice and strain

Bay Spritzer
$1^1/_2$ parts Coconut-Flavored Rum
fill Lemon-Lime Soda
splash Grenadine
splash Lime Juice
Highball Glass

Build over ice and stir

Beam Me Up
1 part Vodka
1 part Peach Schnapps
1 part Cherry Juice
fill with Lemon-Lime Soda
Highball Glass

Build over ice and stir

Beam Me Up Scotty (Smooth 'n' Painless)
1 part Whiskey
$^1/_2$ part Vodka
$^1/_2$ part Amaretto
$^1/_2$ part Crème de Banana
splash Southern Comfort®
Old-Fashioned Glass

Build over ice and stir

Beautiful Day
1 part Apple Liqueur
1 part Irish Mist®
1 part Parfait Amour®
Old-Fashioned Glass

Shake with ice and strain over ice

Bec
2 parts Tequila
fill with Dr Pepper®
splash Lime Juice
Highball Glass

Build over ice and stir

Bed Spinner
1 part Tia Maria®
1 part Amaretto
splash Sour Mix
Old-Fashioned Glass

Shake with ice and strain

Beekman's Beeker
1 part Jim Beam®
1 part Sour Mix
$1^1/_2$ parts Passion Fruit Liqueur
Highball Glass

Build over ice and stir

Belfast Bomber
1 part Irish Cream Liqueur
1 part Cognac
Old-Fashioned Glass

Build over ice and stir

Belgian Blue
1 part Vodka
$^1/_2$ part Coconut-Flavored Liqueur
$^1/_2$ part Blue Curaçao
fill with Lemon-Lime Soda
Highball Glass

Build over ice and stir

Belgian Brownie
1 part Gin
1/2 part Cognac
1 part Chocolate Liqueur
fill with Heavy Cream
Old-Fashioned Glass

Build over ice and stir

Belinda's Fuzzy Melon
1 part Peach Schnapps
1 part Melon Liqueur
splash Lime Juice
splash Grenadine
Highball Glass

Shake with ice and strain

Bella Italia
2/3 part Blackberry Liqueur
splash Sambuca
splash Galliano®
fill with Mango Juice
Highball Glass

Shake with ice and pour

Bellas Noches De Mai
1 part Vodka
1/2 part Parfait Amour
1/2 part Maraschino Liqueur
Highball Glass

Shake with ice and strain over ice

Bend Me Over
1 part Amaretto
1 part Vodka
1 part Sour Mix
4 parts Orange Juice
Highball Glass

Build over ice and stir

Beneditine® Scaffe
1 part Benedictine®
1 part Jim Beam®
Highball Glass

Build over ice and stir

Bermuda Bouquet
1 1/2 parts Gin
1 part Apricot Brandy
splash Triple Sec
splash Grenadine
dash Powdered Sugar
1 part Orange Juice
1 part Lemon Juice
Highball Glass

Shake with ice and strain over ice

Bermuda Triangle
1 part Peach Schnapps
1/2 part Spiced Rum
fill with Orange Juice
Old-Fashioned Glass

Build over ice and stir

Berry Sour
1 part Raspberry Liqueur
1/2 part Kirschwasser
1/2 part Crème de Cassis
1/2 part Simple Syrup
Old-Fashioned Glass

Shake with ice and strain over ice

Bessemer
1/2 part Jack Daniel's®
1/2 part Jim Beam®
1/2 part Southern Comfort®
2 parts Sour Mix
Old-Fashioned Glass

Shake with ice and strain

Beth and Jen's Sleigh Ride
1 part Vodka
1 part Lemon-Lime Soda
1 part Cranberry Juice Cocktail
Highball Glass
Build over ice and stir

Betsy Clear
1 part Vodka
1 part Peach Schnapps
fill with Lemon-Lime Soda
Highball Glass
Build over ice and stir

Better Bachelor
1 part Sloe Gin
1 part Apricot Brandy
2/3 part Lemon Juice
splash Sour Mix
Highball Glass
Build over ice and stir

Bible Belt
2 parts Southern Comfort®
1/2 part Triple Sec
2 parts Sour Mix
Old-Fashioned Glass
Shake with ice and pour

Big Bad Voodoo Kooler
2 parts Malibu® Rum
1 part RedRum®
1 part Melon Liqueur
1 part Orange Juice
1 part Pineapple Juice
splash Club Soda
Highball Glass
Build over ice and stir

Big Bang Boom
1 part Vodka
1 part Crème de Banana
1 part Melon Liqueur
1 part Pineapple Juice
1 part Orange Juice
1/2 part Grenadine
Old-Fashioned Glass
Shake with ice and strain

Big Bird
1 part Banana Liqueur
1 part Pineapple Juice
1 part Orange Juice
Highball Glass
Build over ice and stir

The Big Booty
1 part Gin
2/3 part Lychee Liqueur
1/2 part Orange Liqueur
1/2 part Lemon Juice
1 part Papaya Juice
Highball Glass
Build over ice and stir

Big Bull
1 part Tequila
1 part Coffee Liqueur
Whiskey Sour Glass
Build over ice and stir

Big Dog
1 1/2 parts Vodka
1 part Coffee Liqueur
fill with Milk
splash Cola
Highball Glass
Build over ice and stir

Big Fat One
1 part Vodka
1 part Triple Sec
1 part Melon Liqueur
splash Orange Juice
Old-Fashioned Glass

Shake with ice and pour

Big Red Chevy
1 part Vodka
1 part Sour Mix
1 part Strawberry Soda
splash Orange Juice
Highball Glass

Build over ice and stir

Big Sammie
1 part Sambuca
1/2 part Coconut-Flavored Liqueur
splash Gin
Highball Glass

Build over ice and stir

Bijoux
1 part Vodka
1 part Melon Liqueur
splash Triple Sec
splash Lemon Juice
splash Pineapple Juice
Highball Glass

Shake with ice and pour

Bikini on the Rocks
1 part Cherry Brandy
1/2 part Blackberry Liqueur
2/3 part Frangelico®
1 part Milk
Highball Glass

Shake with ice and strain over ice

Bill Clinton Zipper Dropper
1 part Coffee Liqueur
1 part Crème de Cacao (White)
1 part Crème de Menthe (White)
Old-Fashioned Glass

Shake with ice and pour

Bill's Bongobay
1 part Coconut-Flavored Rum
1 part Melon Liqueur
fill with Pineapple Juice
splash Grenadine
Highball Glass

Build over ice and stir

Binky
1 part Coffee Liqueur
1 part Crème de Cacao (White)
1 part Irish Cream Liqueur
Highball Glass

Build over ice and stir

Bionda
2/3 part Triple Sec
splash Maraschino Liqueur
fill with Orange Juice
Highball Glass

Build over ice and stir

The Bionic Drink
2 parts Vodka
fill with Grapefruit Juice
splash Lemon Juice
Highball Glass

Build over ice and stir

Birth Control
1 part Whiskey
1 part Gin
Old-Fashioned Glass
Build over ice and stir

Bishop's Silk
1 1/2 parts Amaretto
1 1/2 parts Hazelnut Liqueur
1 part Butterscotch Schnapps
Old-Fashioned Glass
Build over ice and stir

Bison
1 part Vodka
splash Blue Curaçao
splash Campari®
splash Sweet Vermouth
Highball Glass
Shake with ice and strain

Bitch
1 part Cinnamon Schnapps
1 part Orange Juice
Highball Glass
Shake with ice and pour

Bitter Apple
1 1/2 parts Apple Brandy
1 part Club Soda
Old-Fashioned Glass
Build over ice and stir

Bitter End
2 parts Sweet Vermouth
3 dashes Angostura® Bitters
Old-Fashioned Glass
Build over ice and stir

Bitter Pill
1 part Vodka
1 part Jack Daniel's®
splash Lemon Juice
fill with Cola
Highball Glass
Build over ice and stir

Bittersweet Italian
1 1/2 parts Vodka
1 part Amaretto
1 part Grapefruit Juice
1/2 part Lemon Juice
dash Sugar
fill with Pineapple Juice
Old-Fashioned Glass
Shake with ice and strain

Bitty Orange
1 part Coffee Liqueur
1 part Cointreau®
Highball Glass
Build over ice and stir

Bizmark
1 part Jim Beam®
1 part Triple Sec
1 part Cherry Brandy
2 parts Sour Mix
2 parts Club Soda
Highball Glass
Build over ice and stir

Black Blonde
2 parts Amaretto
splash Crème de Menthe (White)
fill with Orange Juice
Highball Glass
Shake with ice and pour

Black Cactus
1 part Tequila
1 part Blackberry Brandy
1 part Club Soda
Old-Fashioned Glass
Build over ice and stir

Black Charro
2 parts Tequila
1 part Lemon Juice
fill with Cola
Highball Glass
Build over ice and stir

Black Cherry
1 part Vodka
1 part Raspberry Liqueur
1 part Irish Cream Liqueur
1 part Coffee Liqueur
1 part Half and Half
splash Cola
Highball Glass
Shake with ice and pour

Black Christmas
1 1/2 parts Black Sambuca
fill with Egg Nog
Highball Glass
Build over ice and stir

Black Death
2 parts Jack Daniel's®
splash Sambuca
fill with Cola
Highball Glass
Build over ice and stir

Black Dog
3 parts Bourbon
1 part Sweet Vermouth
1/2 part Blackberry Liqueur
Old-Fashioned Glass
Build over ice and stir

Black Fruit Tree
1 part Blue Curaçao
1 part Amaretto
1 part Triple Sec
1 part Blackberry Brandy
1 part Grenadine
Highball Glass
Build over ice and stir

Black Irish
3 parts Irish Whiskey
1 part Coffee Liqueur
Whiskey Sour Glass
Build over ice and stir

Black Lagoon
1 part Citrus-Flavored Vodka
1 part Blackberry Liqueur
fill with Orange Juice
splash Cranberry Juice Cocktail
Highball Glass
Build over ice and stir

Black Mexican
1 part Tequila
1 part Coffee Liqueur
Old-Fashioned Glass
Shake with ice and strain

Black of Night
1 part Vodka
1 part Wild Berry Schnapps
2 parts Lemonade
1 part Cola
Highball Glass
Build over ice and stir

Black Opal
1/2 part Gin
1/2 part Rum
1/2 part Vodka
1/2 part Triple Sec
2 parts Sour Mix
Highball Glass
Build over ice and stir

Black Orchid
2 parts Black Sambuca
1/2 part Cream
Old-Fashioned Glass
Layer over ice

Black River Boogie
1 part Peach Schnapps
1 part Raspberry Liqueur
2 1/2 parts Sour Mix
Highball Glass
Build over ice and stir

Black Russian
1 1/2 parts Vodka
1 part Coffee Liqueur
Old-Fashioned Glass
Build over ice and stir

Black Tartan
1 part Johnnie Walker® Black Label
1 part Irish Whiskey
1 part Drambuie®
1 1/2 parts Coffee Liqueur
Old-Fashioned Glass
Shake with ice and strain over ice

Black Watch
1 part Coffee Liqueur
1 part Scotch
splash Club Soda
Highball Glass
Build over ice and stir

Black Widow
1 part Dark Rum
1 part Coffee Liqueur
Old-Fashioned Glass
Shake with ice and strain

Blackbeard
1 part Spiced Rum
1 part Root Beer Schnapps
fill with Cola
Highball Glass
Build over ice and stir

Blackberry Breeze
1 part Vodka
1 part Blackberry Liqueur
1 part Pineapple Juice
1 part Cranberry Juice Cocktail
Highball Glass
Shake with ice and pour

Blackberry Chill
1 part Vodka
2 parts Blackberry Juice
2 parts Lemonade
1 part Pineapple Juice
Highball Glass
Shake with ice and pour

Blackberry Hill
1 1/2 parts Blackberry Liqueur
fill with Cola
Highball Glass
Build over ice and stir

Blackberry Jack
1 part Jack Daniel's®
1 part Blackberry Liqueur
2 parts Lemon-Lime Soda
splash Grenadine
Highball Glass
Build over ice and stir

Blackberry Lifesaver
1 1/2 parts Vodka
1 part Blackberry Liqueur
fill with Orange Juice
Highball Glass
Build over ice and stir

Blackberry Punch
2 parts Black Haus® Blackberry Schnapps
1 part Rum
splash Lemon Juice
dash Powdered Sugar
Highball Glass

Shake with ice and pour

Blackberry Pussycat
1 part Vodka
1 part Blackberry Liqueur
1 part Cherry Juice
fill with Pineapple Juice
Highball Glass

Shake with ice and pour

Blackberry Sour
2 parts Blackberry Liqueur
fill with Sour Mix
Highball Glass

Build over ice and stir

Blackberry Tequila
1 part Tequila
1 part Blackberry Liqueur
1 part Cherry Juice
fill with Orange Juice
Highball Glass

Build over ice and stir

Blackjack
1/2 part Brandy
1 part Kirschwasser
1 part Coffee Liqueur
Highball Glass

Shake with ice and strain

Blackjack #2
1 1/2 parts Scotch
1 part Coffee Liqueur
1/2 part Triple Sec
1/2 part Lemon Juice
Old-Fashioned Glass

Shake with ice and strain

Blackjack #3
1/2 part Brandy
1 part Kirschwasser
1 part Coffee Liqueur
Old-Fashioned Glass

Shake with ice and strain over ice

Blackula
1 1/2 parts Blavod® Black Vodka
fill with Bloody Mary Mix
Highball Glass

Shake with ice and pour

Blazing Probe
1 part 151-Proof Rum
1 part Honey
1 part Strawberry Juice
Highball Glass

Build over ice and stir

Bleeding Heart
2 parts Sloe Gin
1/4 part Lemon Juice
2 splashes Grenadine
dash Powdered Sugar
1 Egg White
Highball Glass

Shake with ice and pour

Blessed Event
2 parts Applejack
2 parts Benedictine®
splash Lime Juice
splash Blue Curaçao
Highball Glass

Shake with ice and pour

Blind Russian
3/4 part Irish Cream Liqueur
3/4 part Godiva® Liqueur
3/4 part Coffee Liqueur
1/2 part Butterscotch Schnapps
Highball Glass
Shake with ice and pour

Blindside
2 parts Vodka
2 parts Orange Juice
2 parts Grapefruit Juice
1 part Strawberry Syrup
Highball Glass
Build over ice and stir

Blonde Bombshell
1 part Vodka
1 part Brandy
1/2 part Sour Apple Schnapps
1/2 part Peach Schnapps
Highball Glass
Shake with ice and pour

Blonde Ron
1 part Light Rum
fill with Lemon-Lime Soda
Highball Glass
Build over ice and stir

Bloody Biker
2 parts Vodka
5 parts Spicy Vegetable Juice Blend
splash Worchestershire Sauce
splash Hot Sauce
1 Lime Wedge
splash Olive Brine
Old-Fashioned Glass
Shake with ice and pour

Bloody Bitch
2 parts Grapefruit Juice
1 part Vodka
1 part Grenadine
Highball Glass
Shake with ice and pour

Bloody Californian
1 part Raspberry Liqueur
1 part Orange Liqueur
2 parts Pineapple Juice
fill with Cranberry Juice Cocktail
Highball Glass
Build over ice and stir

Bloody Knuckle
1 part Irish Cream Liqueur
1 part Cherry Whiskey
Highball Glass
Build over ice and stir

Bloody Maria
1 1/2 parts Tequila
splash Tabasco® Sauce
splash Worchestershire Sauce
dash Horseradish
dash Celery Salt
dash Pepper
splash Lemon Juice
1 Celery Stalk
1 Lime Wedge
Highball Glass
Build over ice and stir.

Bloody Mary
1 part Vodka
1 part Sherry
splash Worchestershire Sauce
dash Salt
splash Tabasco® Sauce
dash Pepper
1 Celery Stalk
1 Lime Wedge
Highball Glass

Build over ice and stir. There are many different variations on the Bloody Mary. This is the basic recipe that you can adjust to your taste.

Bloody Passion
1 part Hennessy®
1 part Alizé® Red Passion
Highball Glass

Build over ice

Bloody Smurf®
1 1/2 parts Blueberry Schnapps
fill with Cranberry Juice Cocktail
Highball Glass

Build over ice and stir

Bloody Sunday
1 part Tropical Punch Schnapps
1 part Grenadine
1 part Piña Colada Mix
1 1/2 part Vodka
Highball Glass

Shake with ice and pour

Bloody Temple
2 parts Vodka
1 part Grenadine
1 part Lemon-Lime Soda
Highball Glass

Build over ice and stir

Blue Almond
2 parts Scotch
1 part Amaretto
1/2 part Kirschwasser
Champagne Flute

Shake with ice and strain

Blue Ball
1 part Blue Curaçao
1 part Coconut-Flavored Rum
1 part Raspberry-Flavored Vodka
Old-Fashioned Glass

Build over ice and stir

Blue Bermuda
1 part Blue Curaçao
1 part Light Rum
3 parts Pineapple Juice
Highball Glass

Shake with ice and pour

Blue Bike
1 part Vodka
1/2 part Light Rum
1 part Blue Curaçao
1/2 part Triple Sec
1/2 part Sour Mix
Highball Glass

Shake with ice and pour

Blue Blarney
1 1/4 parts Tequila
3/4 part Blue Curaçao
1 part Triple Sec
fill with Sour Mix
1 Lime Wedge
Old-Fashioned Glass

Build over ice and stir

Blue Denim
splash Blue Curaçao
1/2 part Dry Vermouth
2 dashes Angostura® Bitters
Highball Glass

Shake with ice and strain over ice

Blue Dolphin
2 parts Dry Vermouth
1/2 part Blue Curaçao
fill with Lemonade
splash Grenadine
1 Lemon Slice
Highball Glass

Shake with ice and pour

Blue Eye
1 1/2 parts Vodka
1 part Battery® Energy Drink
1 part Sour Mix
splash Blue Curaçao
Highball Glass

Shake with ice and strain over ice

Blue Flannel
1 part Blue Curaçao
1 part Peppermint Liqueur
1 part Cream
Highball Glass

Shake with ice and pour

A Blue Gold Banana
1 part Goldschläger®
1 part Blue Curaçao
splash Crème de Banana
Highball Glass

Build over ice and stir

Blue Hawaiian
1 part Rum
1 part Blue Curaçao
1 part Piña Colada Mix
1 part Pineapple Juice
Highball Glass

Build over ice and stir

Blue Hurricane Highball
1 part Rum
1 part Blue Curaçao
2 parts Orange Juice
1 part Pineapple Juice
Highball Glass

Build over ice and stir

Blue Ice
1 part Coconut-Flavored Rum
1 part Triple Sec
1 part Hypnotiq®
Highball Glass

Build over ice and stir

Blue Lagoon
1 part Vodka
1 part Blue Curaçao
fill with Lemonade
1 Maraschino Cherry
Highball Glass

Build over ice and stir

Blue Mango
1 part Blue Curaçao
1 part Vodka
1 part Mango Nectar
fill with Orange Juice
Highball Glass

Build over ice and stir

Blue Monkey

1 part Orange-Flavored Vodka
1 part Banana Liqueur
1 part Cream
splash Blue Curaçao
Highball Glass

Shake with ice and strain over ice

Blue Mountain

1½ parts Añejo Rum
½ part Tia Maria®
½ part Vodka
1 part Orange Juice
splash Lemon Juice
Old-Fashioned Glass

Shake with ice and strain over ice

Blue Note

1½ parts Gin
¼ part Blue Curaçao
splash Triple Sec
fill with Pineapple Juice
Old-Fashioned Glass

Build over ice and stir

Blue Poison

1 part Tequila Silver
1 part Vodka
1 part Blue Curaçao
fill with Lemonade
Highball Glass

Build over ice and stir

Blue Russian

1 part Blue Curaçao
1 part Vodka
fill with Cream
Old-Fashioned Glass

Shake with ice and pour

Blue Sunset

1 part Tequila
1 part Blue Curaçao
1 part Lemon-Lime Soda
1 part Sour Mix
2 parts Orange Juice
Highball Glass

Build over ice and stir

Blue Valium

½ part Canadian Whiskey
½ part 151-Proof Rum
½ part Blue Curaçao
1 part Lemonade
1 part Sour Mix
Old-Fashioned Glass

Build over ice and stir

Blueberry Pucker

1 part Vodka
1 part Blueberry Schnapps
1 part Cherry Juice
fill with Grapefruit Juice
Highball Glass

Build over ice and stir

Blue-Woo

1 part Vodka
1 part Blueberry Schnapps
fill with Cranberry Juice Cocktail
Highball Glass

Build over ice and stir

Blushing Bride

1 part Vodka
2 parts Cranberry Juice Cocktail
3 parts Orange Juice
2 parts Lemon-Lime Soda
Highball Glass

Build over ice and stir

BMW
1 part Irish Cream Liqueur
1 part Coconut-Flavored Rum
1 part Rye Whiskey
Highball Glass

Build over ice and stir

Boardwalk Breezer
1 part Rum
1 part Banana Liqueur
1 part Cherry Juice
1 part Margarita Mix
1 part Pineapple Juice
Highball Glass

Shake with ice and pour

Boat Drink
2 parts Rum
1 part Pineapple Juice
1 part Orange Juice
Highball Glass

Shake with ice and pour

Bocci Ball
1 part Amaretto
fill with Orange Juice
Cordial Glass

Build over ice and stir

Bocci Ball #2
1 part Amaretto
1 part Vodka
fill with Orange Juice
Highball Glass

Build over ice and stir

Bon Bini
1 part Dark Rum
1 part Blue Curaçao
fill with Pineapple Juice
Highball Glass

Shake with ice and pour

Bonfire
2/3 part Apricot Brandy
splash Sweet Vermouth
splash Benedictine®
splash Orange-Flavored Vodka
Highball Glass

Shake with ice and pour

Bongo Congo
1 part Crème de Cassis
fill with Orange Juice
Old-Fashioned Glass

Build over ice and stir

Bongobay
1 part Melon Liqueur
1 part Coconut-Flavored Rum
fill with Pineapple Juice
splash Grenadine
Old-Fashioned Glass

Build over ice and stir

Bonny Doon
1 1/2 parts Scotch
1/2 part Vermouth
2 splashes Benedictine®
Cordial Glass

Shake with ice and strain

Boogy Woogy
2 parts Blue Curaçao
2/3 part Orange-Flavored Vodka
fill with Lemon-Lime Soda
Highball Glass

Build over ice and stir

Boomerang
1 part Rye Whiskey
3/4 part French Vermouth
dash Powdered Sugar
splash Lemon Juice
dash Angostura® Bitters
White Wine Glass

Shake with ice and pour

Booster Blaster
1 part Jack Daniel's®
1 part Southern Comfort®
1 part Yukon Jack®
fill with Cola
Highball Glass

Build over ice and stir

Bootlegger
1 part Tequila
1 part Southern Comfort®
Old-Fashioned Glass

Build over ice and stir

Booty Juice
1 part Coconut-Flavored Rum
1 part Spiced Rum
1 part Melon Liqueur
1/2 part 151-Proof Rum
Old-Fashioned Glass

Shake with ice and pour

Border Crossing
1 1/2 parts Tequila
splash Lime Juice
splash Lemon Juice
fill with Cola
1 Lime Wedge
Highball Glass

Build over ice and stir

Borinquen
1 1/2 part Light Rum
splash 151-Proof Rum
splash Passion Fruit Nectar
1 part Orange Juice
1 part Lime Juice
Old-Fashioned Glass

Shake with ice and pour

Bosom's Caress
1 part Brandy
1/2 part Triple Sec
1 Egg White
splash Grenadine
Highball Glass

Shake with ice and strain

Boston Tea Party
1/2 part Vodka
1/2 part Scotch
1/2 part Dry Vermouth
1/2 part Triple Sec
1/2 part Rum
1/2 part Gin
1/2 part Tequila
1 part Orange Juice
1 part Cola
splash Sour Mix
Highball Glass

Build over ice and stir

Botany Bay
2 parts Gin
1 part Orange Juice
1 part Grapefruit Juice
splash Simple Syrup
Old-Fashioned Glass

Shake with ice and strain over ice

Bottom Rose
1 part Vodka
splash Apricot Brandy
splash Sweet Vermouth
Highball Glass

Build over ice and stir

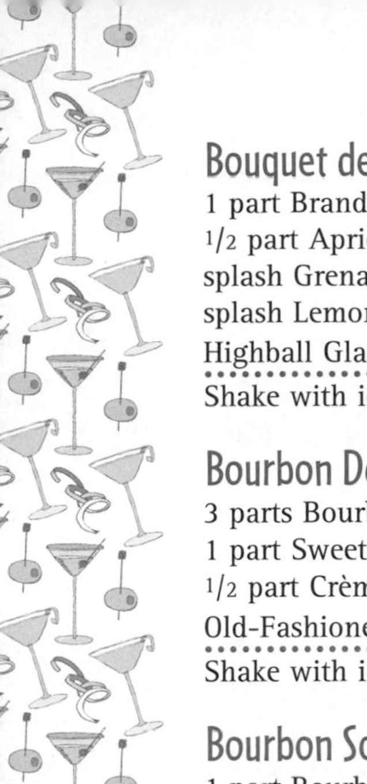

Bouquet de Paris
1 part Brandy
1/2 part Apricot Brandy
splash Grenadine
splash Lemon Juice
Highball Glass

Shake with ice and pour

Bourbon Delight
3 parts Bourbon
1 part Sweet Vermouth
1/2 part Crème de Cassis
Old-Fashioned Glass

Shake with ice and strain

Bourbon Sour
1 part Bourbon
1 part Lemon Juice
dash Sugar
1 Orange Slice
1 Maraschino Cherry
Whiskey Sour Glass

Shake with ice and strain over ice

Brain Booster
1 part Coffee Liqueur
1 part Irish Cream Liqueur
1/2 part Grappa
Highball Glass

Build over ice and stir

Brain Damager
1 part Jamaican Rum
1 part Triple Sec
splash Banana Juice
Highball Glass

Build over ice and stir

Bramble
2 parts Gin
1/2 part Blackberry Liqueur
dash Sugar
Old-Fashioned Glass

Shake with ice and strain over ice

Brandy Daisy
2 parts Brandy
1 part Lemon Juice
dash Sugar
splash Grenadine
1 Maraschino Cherry
1 Orange Slice
Old-Fashioned Glass

Build over ice and stir

Brandy Fino
1 1/2 parts Brandy
1/2 part Dry Sherry
Old-Fashioned Glass

Shake with ice and strain

Brass
1 part Tequila
1 part Passion Fruit Liqueur
Highball Glass

Build over ice and stir

Brass Monkey
1 part Vodka
1 part Light Rum
fill with Orange Juice
Highball Glass

Shake with ice and pour

Brave Bull
1 1/2 parts Tequila
1 part Coffee-Flavored Vodka
1 Lemon Twist
Old-Fashioned Glass

Layer over ice

Brazilian Beast

2 parts Rum
splash Lime Juice
2 dashes Sugar
Old-Fashioned Glass

Shake with ice and pour

Breeze

1 part Vodka
1/2 part Blue Curaçao
1/2 part Crème de Menthe (Green)
Old-Fashioned Glass

Shake with ice and pour

Brimstone

1 part Dark Rum
1 1/2 parts Cherry Brandy
1 part Light Rum
1/2 part Triple Sec
1/2 part Crème de Noyaux
1 1/2 parts Sour Mix
1 1/2 parts Orange Juice
Highball Glass

Shake with ice and pour

Broadway

1/2 part Vodka
1/2 part Apricot Brandy
1 part Mango Juice
Highball Glass

Shake with ice and strain

Broken Heart

1 part Vodka
1 part Raspberry Liqueur
fill with Orange Juice
splash Grenadine
Highball Glass

Shake with ice and pour

Broken Nose

1 part Tequila
1 1/2 parts Advocaat
2 parts Grenadine
fill with Lemonade
Highball Glass

Shake with ice and pour

Brooke Shields

2 parts Lemon-Lime Soda
1 part Ginger Ale
splash Grenadine
1 Orange Slice
Highball Glass

Build over ice and stir for a Shirley Temple without the cherry.

Brown

1 1/2 parts Dry Vermouth
2 dashes Orange Bitters
Highball Glass

Shake with ice and strain

Brown Russian

1 part Chocolate Liqueur
2 parts Vodka
Old-Fashioned Glass

Layer over ice

Bruja Cubana

3 Fresh Mint Leaves
dash Sugar
splash Lime Juice1 part Whiskey
1/2 part Coffee Liqueur
fill with Lemon-Lime Soda
Highball Glass

Muddle the Mint, Sugar, and Lime Juice in the Glass. Add the Whiskey and Coffee Liqueur and fill with Lemon-Lime Soda.

Bubblegum Smash

1½ parts Light Rum
1 part Sour Mix
½ part Triple Sec
¼ part Lemonade
splash Grenadine
Old-Fashioned Glass

Shake with ice and pour

Bubbly Irish Nut

1 part Irish Cream Liqueur
1 part Amaretto
4 parts Club Soda
Highball Glass

Build over ice and stir

Bull Rider

1 part Malibu® Rum
1 part Coffee Liqueur
½ part Crème de Banana
½ part Jägermeister®
Highball Glass

Shake with ice and pour

Bull Shot

1½ parts Vodka
fill with Chilled Beef Bouillion
splash Worcestershire Sauce
dash Salt
dash Pepper
Old-Fashioned Glass

Shake with ice and pour

Bull Stuff

1½ parts Brandy
1 part Light Rum
fill with Milk
splash Cinnamon Schnapps
Highball Glass

Shake with ice and pour

Bullfrog

1 part Vodka
1 part Margarita Mix
fill with Lemon-Lime Soda
Highball Glass

Build over ice and stir

Bun Warmer Jack

1 part Yukon Jack®
fill with Cola
Highball Glass

Build over ice and stir

Bunny Hop

1 part Jim Beam®
½ part Peach Schnapps
1 part Cranberry Juice Cocktail
1 part Pineapple Juice
Highball Glass

Build over ice and stir

Bunny Killer

1 part Rum
2 parts Coconut-Flavored Rum
1 part Pineapple Juice
1 part Orange Juice
Highball Glass

Build over ice and stir

Burlesque

1 part Jim Beam®
½ part Triple Sec
½ part Parfait Amour
splash Lemon Juice
Highball Glass

Shake with ice and pour

Burning Sun

$1^1/_2$ parts Strawberry Liqueur
fill with Pineapple Juice
Highball Glass

Build over ice

Bushwacker

1 part Light Rum
1 part Amaretto
1 part Coffee Liqueur
1 part Grand Marnier®
1 part Irish Cream Liqueur
Highball Glass

Shake with ice and strain over ice

Buster

2 parts Goldschläger®
1 part Anisette
$^1/_2$ part Amer Picon®
Old-Fashioned Glass

Shake with ice and strain

Butterfinger®

$1^1/_2$ parts Butterscotch Schnapps
$1^1/_2$ parts Irish Cream Liqueur
fill with Milk
Highball Glass

Build over ice and stir

Butternut Scotch

1 part Scotch
1 part Butterscotch Schnapps
1 part Amaretto
Old-Fashioned Glass

Build over ice

Buttered Toffee

1 part Coffee Liqueur
1 part Irish Cream Liqueur
1 part Amaretto
fill with Half and Half
Old-Fashioned Glass

Build over ice and stir

By the Pool

1 part Melon Liqueur
1 part Peach Schnapps
1 part Orange Juice
fill with Lemon-Lime Soda
Highball Glass

Build over ice and stir

Cacatoes

1 part Cognac
$^1/_2$ part Mandarine Napoléon® Liqueur
$^1/_4$ part Crème de Banana
$^1/_2$ part Orange Juice
splash Grenadine
Old-Fashioned Glass

Shake with ice and pour

Cadillac Margarita

1 part Jose Cuervo® 1800 Tequila
$^1/_2$ part Grand Marnier®
$^1/_2$ part Cointreau®
fill with Margarita Mix
Highball Glass

Shake with ice and pour

Cadiz

1 part Blackberry Brandy
1 part Dry Sherry
$^1/_2$ part Triple Sec
splash Light Cream
Old-Fashioned Glass

Shake with ice and pour

Caipirissima
1 Lime
2 dashes Sugar
2 parts Light Rum
Whiskey Sour Glass

Cut the Lime into wedges and put into a mixing glass with the Sugar. Muddle the Lime until the Lime Juice and Sugar develop a rich froth. Add ice and the Rum and shake vigorously.

Caipiroska
2 parts Vodka
1 Lime
2 dashes Sugar
Old-Fashioned Glass

Cut the lime into wedges and put into a mixing glass with the Sugar. Muddle the Lime until the Lime Juice and Sugar develop a rich froth. Add ice and the Vodka and shake vigorously.

Cajun Comforter
1 1/2 parts Southern Comfort®
1/2 part Old Grand-Dad®
splash Tabasco® Sauce
Old-Fashioned Glass

Build over ice

Caledonia
1 part Brandy
1 part Crème de Cacao (Dark)
1 part Milk
1 Egg Yolk
dash Cinnamon
Old-Fashioned Glass

Shake with ice and pour

Calico Cat
1 part Rum
1 part Orange Juice
1 part Cola
Highball Glass

Build over ice

California Kool-Aid®
1 part Rum
1 part Raspberry Liqueur
1 part Cherry Juice
1 part Lemonade
1 part Orange Juice
Highball Glass

Build over ice and stir

Californian
1 part Vodka
1 part Orange Juice
1 part Grapefruit Juice
Highball Glass

Build over ice and stir

Calimero
1 part Brandy
1 part Orange Juice
1 Egg White
splash Coffee Liqueur
White Wine Glass

Shake with ice and strain

Calypso Kool-Aid®
1 part Vodka
1 part Raspberry Liqueur
1 part Cherry Juice
2 parts Lemonade
1 part Pineapple Juice
Highball Glass

Build over ice and stir

Campobello
$1^1/_2$ parts Gin
1 part Campari®
1 part Sweet Vermouth
Highball Glass

Shake with ice and strain over ice

Canada Dream
1 part Apricot Brandy
1 part Amaretto
3 parts Orange Juice
Whiskey Sour Glass

Shake with ice and strain over ice

Canado Saludo
$1^1/_2$ parts Light Rum
1 part Orange Juice
1 part Pineapple Juice
$^1/_2$ part Lemon Juice
$^1/_2$ part Grenadine
dash Bitters
Highball Glass

Build over ice and stir

Candy Apple
1 part Butterscotch Schnapps
fill with Apple Cider
Highball Glass

Build over ice and stir

Candy Bar
1 part Coffee Liqueur
1 part Cream
$^1/_2$ part Crème de Cacao (White)
$^1/_2$ part Frangelico®
Highball Glass

Shake with ice and strain over ice

Canyon de Chelly
$1^1/_2$ parts Tequila
splash Triple Sec
fill with Cranberry Juice Cocktail
splash Pineapple Juice
splash Orange Juice
Highball Glass

Build over ice and stir

Cape Grape
$1^1/_2$ parts Vodka
1 part Cranberry Liqueur
fill with Grapefruit Juice
Highball Glass

Build over ice and stir

Capri
1 part Crème de Cacao (White)
1 part Crème de Banana
1 part Light Cream
Old-Fashioned Glass

Shake with ice and strain over ice

Captain Caribbean
1 part Spiced Rum
1 part Coconut-Flavored Rum
1 part Strawberry Liqueur
fill with Orange Juice
Highball Glass

Build over ice and stir

Captain Climer
$1^1/_2$ parts Spiced Rum
$^3/_4$ part Irish Cream Liqueur
fill with Root Beer
Highball Glass

Build over ice and stir

Captain Crunch

1 part Tequila Rose®
1 part Vanilla Liqueur
1 part Coffee Liqueur
1 part Cream
splash Grenadine
Old-Fashioned Glass

Shake with ice and strain over ice

Captain Hamilton

$1^1/_2$ parts Spiced Rum
2 parts Coconut-Flavored Rum
$^1/_2$ part Lime Juice
Highball Glass

Shake with ice and strain over ice

Caramel

2 parts Coffee Liqueur
fill with Pineapple Juice
Highball Glass

Shake with ice and pour

Caribbean Bliss

1 part Vodka
1 part Tequila
fill with Orange Juice
Highball Glass

Build over ice and stir

Caribbean Chat

1 part Spiced Rum
$^1/_4$ part Crème de Cacao (White)
1 part Orange Juice
1 part Club Soda
Highball Glass

Build over ice and stir

Caribbean Romance

$1^1/_2$ parts Light Rum
1 part Amaretto
1 part Orange Juice
1 part Pineapple Juice
splash Grenadine
Highball Glass

Build over ice and stir

Carilia

1 part Dark Rum
1 part Crème de Banana
1 part Cherry Brandy
1 part Lemon Juice
Highball Glass

Shake with ice and pour

Carmalita

1 part Vodka
1 part Coffee
1 part Frangelico®
Old-Fashioned Glass

Shake with ice and pour

Carmen

1 part Gin
splash Apricot Brandy
splash Triple Sec
$^1/_2$ part Dry Vermouth
Highball Glass

Shake with ice and strain over ice

Carrot Cake

1 part Butterscotch Schnapps
1 part Cinnamon Schnapps
1 part Irish Cream Liqueur
Highball Glass

Build over ice and stir

Casa Vieja
1 part Gin
splash Apricot Brandy
splash Grenadine
1 part Apricot Juice
Highball Glass

Shake with ice and pour

Casablanca
1 part Vodka
1/2 part Southern Comfort®
1/2 part Amaretto
3/4 part Orange Juice
splash Grenadine
Highball Glass

Shake with ice and pour

Cascade Special
2/3 part Gin
1/2 part Triple Sec
splash Dry Vermouth
1 part Pineapple Juice
Highball Glass

Shake with ice and pour

Casino d'Amsterdam
1 part Gin
1 part Triple Sec
splash Kirschwasser
1 part Dry Vermouth
splash Pineapple Juice
Highball Glass

Shake with ice and pour

Casino Royale
1 part Gin
1 part Apricot Brandy
1 part Pineapple Juice
Old-Fashioned Glass

Shake with ice and pour

Castaway
1 1/2 parts Light Rum
1 part Dark Rum
1/2 part Blue Curaçao
splash Apricot Brandy
splash Grenadine
1/2 part Lemon Juice
2 parts Pineapple Juice
Highball Glass

Shake with ice and pour

Cato
1 part Dark Rum
1 part Sweet Vermouth
splash Blue Curaçao
splash Campari®
1 part Lemon Juice
Highball Glass

Shake with ice and strain

Cat's Eye
2 parts Dry Vermouth
1/2 part Chartreuse®
2 dashes Orange Bitters
Highball Glass

Shake with ice and strain over ice

Caucasian
2 parts Vodka
1 1/2 parts Coffee Liqueur
splash Cream
Old-Fashioned Glass

Shake with ice and strain

Cayman Sunset
1 1/2 parts Light Rum
1/2 part Piña Colada Mix
fill with Pineapple Juice
1/2 part Grenadine
Highball Glass

Build over ice and stir

Celtic Comrade

1 part Coffee Liqueur
1 part Drambuie®
1 part Irish Cream Liqueur
1 part Vodka
Highball Glass

Shake with ice and strain over ice

Chapala

1 1/2 parts Tequila
splash Triple Sec
2 splashes Grenadine
2 splashes Orange Juice
2 splashes Lemon Juice
1 Orange Slice
Old-Fashioned Glass

Shake with ice and strain

Charlie Chaplin

1 part Apricot Brandy
1 part Sloe Gin
1 part Lemon Juice
Old-Fashioned Glass

Shake with ice and strain

Charlie's Angel

1 1/2 parts Mezcal
1 part Grand Marnier®
dash Orange Bitters
1 part Orange Juice
1 part Grapefruit Juice
1 part Club Soda
Highball Glass

Build over ice and stir

The Cheap Date

1 part Light Rum
1 part Peach Schnapps
1 part Melon Liqueur
1/2 part Triple Sec
fill with Apple Juice
Highball Glass

Build over ice and stir

Chattanooga

1 1/2 parts Vodka
1/2 part Apricot Brandy
1/2 part Fresh Lime Juice
fill with Pineapple Juice
Old-Fashioned Glass

Shake with ice and strain over ice

Cheap Sunglasses

1 part Vodka
1 part Cranberry Juice Cocktail
1 part Lemon-Lime Soda
Old-Fashioned Glass

Build over ice and stir

Cheerio

1 part Jim Beam®
1/2 part Cherry Brandy
1/2 part Lemon Juice
splash Grenadine
Highball Glass

Shake with ice and strain over ice

Cherry Breeze

1 part Vodka
1 part Cherry Liqueur
1 part Pineapple Juice
1 part Cranberry Juice Cocktail
Highball Glass

Shake with ice and strain over ice

Cherry Malibu

1 part Coconut-Flavored Rum
1/2 part Cherry Brandy
2 parts Lime Juice
Old-Fashioned Glass

Build over ice and stir

Cherry Pucker
1 part Vodka
1 part Cherry Liqueur
1 part Cherry Juice
fill with Grapefruit Juice
Highball Glass

Build over ice and stir

Cheshire Cat
1 part Spiced Rum
1 part Peach Schnapps
1 part Orange Juice
White Wine Glass

Shake with ice and strain

Chi Chi
1 1/2 parts Light Rum
1/2 part Blackberry Liqueur
fill with Pineapple Juice
Highball Glass

Build over ice and stir

Chocoholic
1 part Chocolate Syrup
2 parts Coffee Liqueur
1 part Irish Cream Liqueur
1 part Rum
Highball Glass

Shake with ice and strain over ice

Chocolate-Covered Banana
1 part Vodka
1 part Crème de Cacao (Dark)
1 part Crème de Banana
1 part Cream
Highball Glass

Shake with ice and pour

Chocolate-Covered Cherry
1/2 part Crème de Cacao (Dark)
1/2 part Amaretto
2 parts Milk
splash Grenadine
Highball Glass

Shake with ice and strain over ice

Chocolate-Covered Strawberries
1 part Godiva® Liqueur
1 part Tequila Rose®
Old-Fashioned Glass

Shake with ice and strain

Chocolate Milwaukee
1 part Coffee Liqueur
1 part Tia Maria®
1 part Crème de Cacao (White)
1 part Half and Half
Whiskey Sour Glass

Shake with ice and pour

Christmas Rum Punch
1 part Rum
1 part Cherry Juice
1 part Cranberry Juice Cocktail
1 part Pineapple Juice
Highball Glass

Build over ice and stir

Cinnamon Pussycat
1 part Vodka
1 part Cinnamon Schnapps
1 part Cherry Juice
fill with Pineapple Juice
Highball Glass

Build over ice and stir

Cinniberry Crasher
1 part Goldschläger®
fill with Cranberry Juice Cocktail
Highball Glass

Build over ice and stir

Citrus Twist on Fire
1 part Goldschläger®
1 part Citrus-Flavored Vodka
Highball Glass
Build over ice and stir

City Lights
1 part Vodka
1 part Raspberry Liqueur
1 part Cherry Juice
fill with Lemonade
Highball Glass
Build over ice and stir

Clamdigger
1 part Vodka
1/2 part Clamato®
splash Worchestershire Sauce
dash Salt
dash Pepper
1 Lime Wedge
Highball Glass
Shake with ice and pour

Class
1 part Scotch
3/4 part Sambuca
fill with Iced Coffee
Highball Glass
Shake with ice and pour

Class Act
1 part Advocaat
1/2 part Coconut-Flavored Rum
splash Southern Comfort®
fill with Pineapple Juice
Old-Fashioned Glass
Shake with ice and pour

Classic
1 1/2 parts Brandy
1/4 part Cherry Liqueur
1/4 part Cointreau®
splash Lemon Juice
Highball Glass
Shake with ice and pour

Clear Blue Sky
2 parts Blue Curaçao
1/2 part Grain Alcohol
fill with Milk
Highball Glass
Shake with ice and pour

Clockwork Orange
2 parts Vodka
2 parts Orange Juice
1 1/2 part Peach Schnapps
splash Campari®
Highball Glass
Shake with ice and strain over ice

Cloudy Sunset
1 part Peach Brandy
2 parts Orange Juice
2 parts Cranberry Juice Cocktail
Highball Glass
Build over ice and stir

Clueless
2 parts Vodka
1 part Orange Juice
1 part Strawberry Juice
fill with Lemon-Lime Soda
Highball Glass
Build over ice and stir

Coastline
1 part Blue Curaçao
1 part Vodka
fill with Pineapple Juice
splash Lemon-Lime Soda
Highball Glass
Build over ice and stir

Cobbler

2 parts Gin
splash Blue Curaçao
splash Simple Syrup
Highball Glass

Build over ice and stir

Cobra Venom

1 part Sambuca
1 part Rumple Minze®
Old-Fashioned Glass

Shake with ice and strain

Cocaine Lady

1/2 part Vodka
1/2 part Amaretto
1/2 part Coffee Liqueur
1 part Cream
fill with Cola
Highball Glass

Build over ice and stir

Cocaine Shooter

1 1/2 part Vodka
3/4 part Raspberry Liqueur
1/2 part Southern Comfort®
1 part Orange Juice
1 part Cranberry Juice Cocktail
Old-Fashioned Glass

Shake with ice and strain

Coco Butter

1 1/2 part Butterscotch Schnapps
1 part Coffee Liqueur
fill with Milk
Highball Glass

Shake with ice and pour

Coco Colada

1 part Dark Rum
1 part Crème de Cacao (Dark)
1 part Coconut Cream
fill with Pineapple Juice
Old-Fashioned Glass

Build over ice and stir

Coco Miami

1 part Coconut-Flavored Liqueur
1 part Orange Juice
1 part Grapefruit Juice
Highball Glass

Build over ice and stir

Coconut Apple Pie

1 part Vodka
1 part Coconut-Flavored Rum
fill with Apple Juice
Highball Glass

Shake with ice and pour

Coconut Dream

2 parts Coconut-Flavored Liqueur
1 part Vanilla Liqueur
1/2 part Crème de Cacao (Dark)
2 parts Pineapple Juice
1 part Coconut Cream
Old-Fashioned Glass

Shake with ice and pour

Coffee Alexander

1 part Coffee-Flavored Brandy
1 part Crème de Cacao (White)
1 part Cream
Highball Glass

Shake with ice and strain over ice

Coffee Fantasy
1 part Irish Cream Liqueur
1 part Coffee Liqueur
1 part Milk
Highball Glass

Build over ice and stir

Coffin Nail
1 1/2 parts Whiskey
1/2 part Amaretto
1/2 part Drambuie®
Old-Fashioned Glass

Build over ice and stir

Cold Fusion
1 part Vodka
1 part Triple Sec
1/2 part Melon Liqueur
1 1/2 parts Sour Mix
1/2 part Fresh Lime Juice
Highball Glass

Shake with ice and strain over ice

Cold Lips
1 1/2 parts Gin
2/3 part Lemon Juice
1 part Ginger Ale
1 part Grape Juice (Red)
Highball Glass

Build over ice and stir

Cold Shoulder
1 part Southern Comfort®
1 part Cherry Brandy
splash Orange Juice
1 part Sour Mix
2 parts Pineapple Juice
2 parts Ginger Ale
Highball Glass

Build over ice and stir

Colorado Kool-Aid®
1 part Vodka
1 part Southern Comfort®
1/2 part Sloe Gin
1 part Amaretto
1 part Orange Juice
2 parts Cranberry Juice Cocktail
splash Lemon-Lime Soda
Highball Glass

Build over ice and stir

Combo
2 1/2 part Dry Vermouth
1 splash Brandy
1/2 splash Triple Sec
1/2 dash Powdered Sugar
dash Bitters
Old-Fashioned Glass

Shake with ice and strain over ice

Comfortable Fuzz
1 part Peach Schnapps
1 part Southern Comfort®
1 part Cranberry Juice Cocktail
1 part Orange Juice
Old-Fashioned Glass

Build over ice and stir

Communicator
1 1/2 parts Dark Rum
1/2 part Galliano®
2 splashes Crème de Cacao (Dark)
Old-Fashioned Glass

Build over ice and stir

Confidence Booster
1 part Dark Rum
1 part Peach Schnapps
1 1/2 parts Pineapple Juice
Highball Glass

Build over ice and stir

Continential Sour
1 1/2 parts Rye Whiskey
1/2 part Simple Syrup
1 Egg White
Old-Fashioned Glass

Shake with ice and strain

Cool Jerk
1 part Vodka
1 part Amaretto
2 parts Orange Juice
1 part Lemon-Lime Soda
Highball Glass

Build over ice and stir

Cool of the Evening
1 part Rum
1 part Peach Schnapps
1 part Cranberry Juice Cocktail
1 part Pineapple Juice
Highball Glass

Build over ice and stir

Cool Running
1 part Vodka
1 part Blue Curaçao
fill with Lemonade
splash Cola
Highball Glass

Build over ice and stir

Cool Summer
1 part Vodka
1 part Peach Schnapps
1 part Cherry Juice
1 part Lemonade
1 part Orange Juice
Highball Glass

Build over ice and stir

Cordial Daisy
1 part Vodka
1 part Cherry Liqueur
1 part Lemonade
1 part Club Soda
Highball Glass

Build over ice and stir

The Cornell
1 part Vodka
1/2 part Watermelon Schnapps
1/2 part Sour Mix
Highball Glass

Shake with ice and strain over ice

Cowboy Killer
1 1/4 parts Tequila
3/4 part Irish Cream Liqueur
1/2 part Butterscotch Schnapps
fill with Half and Half
Highball Glass

Build over ice and stir

Cowpoke
1 part Whiskey
1 part Southern Comfort®
1 part Orange Juice
splash Lemon Juice
dash Sugar
Highball Glass

Shake with ice and pour

Crack Whore
1 part Vodka
1 part Triple Sec
fill with Orange Soda
Highball Glass

Build over ice and stir

Cracklin' Rosie

1 part Light Rum
1/2 part Passion Fruit Juice
splash Pineapple Juice
splash Lime Juice
splash Crème de Banana
Highball Glass

Shake with ice and strain over ice

Cranberry Lemondrop

1 part Vodka
1 part Triple Sec
1 part Lemonade
1 part Cranberry Juice Cocktail
Highball Glass

Shake with ice and pour

Cran-Collins

1 1/2 parts Vodka
2 parts Cranberry Juice Cocktail
2 parts Collins Mix
Old-Fashioned Glass

Shake with ice and strain over ice

Cranial Meltdown

1 part Rum
1 part Raspberry Liqueur
1 part Coconut-Flavored Rum
Highball Glass

Shake with ice and strain over ice

Cranilla Dew

1 part Vanilla-Flavored Vodka
1 part Cranberry Juice Cocktail
1 part Mountain Dew®
Highball Glass

Build over ice and stir

Crazy Caribbean Gentleman

1 part 151-Proof Rum
1 part Frangelico®
fill with Sour Mix
Highball Glass

Build over ice and stir

Crazy Man

1 part Gin
1 part Orange Liqueur
1/2 part Lemon Juice
splash Apple Juice
Highball Glass

Shake with ice and pour

Crazy Orgasm

1 part Vodka
1 part Triple Sec
1 part Cranberry Juice Cocktail
1 part Orange Juice
Highball Glass

Shake with ice and pour

Creamsicle®

2 parts Amaretto
1 part Triple Sec
2 parts Sour Mix
4 parts Orange Juice
splash Club Soda
Highball Glass

Build over ice and stir

Creamy Kiss

1 part Amaretto
1 part Irish Cream Liqueur
1 part Peach Schnapps
1 part Cream
Highball Glass

Shake with ice and pour

Creamy Mimi
1 part Vodka
1 part Sweet Vermouth
2 splashes Crème de Cacao (White)
2 splashes Triple Sec
Highball Glass

Shake with ice and pour

Creamydreams
1 part Irish Cream Liqueur
splash Advocaat
1/2 part Cream
2 parts Banana Juice
Highball Glass

Shake with ice and pour

Creeping Death
1 part Vodka
1 part Extra Dry Vermouth
dash Salt
fill with Orange Juice
Highball Glass

Shake with ice and pour

Crème d'Amour
1 part Vodka
1 part Crème de Banana
splash Cherry Brandy
1 part Pineapple Juice
splash Cream
Highball Glass

Shake with ice and pour

Crème de Café
1 part Coffee-Flavored Brandy
1/2 part Rum
1/2 part Anisette
1 part Light Cream
Old-Fashioned Glass

Shake with ice and pour

Creole
1 1/2 parts Light Rum
splash Lemon Juice
splash Tabasco® Sauce
splash Beef Bouillion
dash Salt
dash Pepper
Old-Fashioned Glass

Shake with ice and pour

Crillon
1 1/2 parts Dry Vermouth
1/2 part Campari®
1/2 part Kirschwasser
Old-Fashioned Glass

Shake with ice and strain over ice

Crime of Passion
1/2 part Sweet Vermouth
1/2 part Cherry Brandy
1 part Passion Fruit Liqueur
Old-Fashioned Glass

Shake with ice and strain over ice

Critical Mass
1 part Vodka
1 part Blue Curaçao
1 part Cherry Juice
fill with Lemonade
Highball Glass

Build over ice and stir

The Crown Cherry
1 1/2 parts Crown Royal® Whiskey
1 part Cherry Brandy
1/2 part Cherry Vodka
fill with Cherry Cola
Highball Glass

Build over ice and stir

Crowned Bull
1 part Crown Royal® Whiskey
fill with Red Bull® Energy Drink
Highball Glass
Build over ice and stir

Cruise
1 part Gin
1 part Dry Vermouth
splash Peach Schnapps
Highball Glass
Shake with ice and strain

Cry No More
1 part Vodka
1 part Cherry Brandy
1 1/2 parts Orange Juice
fill with Lemon-Lime Soda
Highball Glass
Build over ice and stir

Crypto Nugget
3/4 part Sour Apple Schnapps
1/2 part Vodka
1/4 part Blue Curaçao
1/4 part Sweetened Lime Juice
Whiskey Sour Glass
Shake with ice and pour

Crystal de Amour
1 1/2 parts Vodka
1/2 part Parfait Amour
Highball Glass
Build over ice and stir

C-Team
1 part Grand Marnier®
1 part Crème de Menthe (White)
1 part Melon Liqueur
1 part Licor 43®
fill with Cranberry Juice Cocktail
Highball Glass
Shake with ice and pour

Cuba Libre
2 parts Light Rum
splash Lime Juice
fill with Cola
Highball Glass
Build over ice and stir

Cuban Kirschwasser
1 1/2 parts Kirschwasser
fill with Cola
splash Lime Juice
Highball Glass
Build over ice and stir

Cuff and Buttons
2 parts Southern Comfort®
1/2 part Lime Juice
4 splashes Sweet Vermouth
Old-Fashioned Glass
Shake with ice and strain

Cumulous
1 part Drambuie®
1 part Tia Maria®
1/2 part Cream
1 Egg Yolk
2 dashes Sugar
Highball Glass
Shake with ice and strain

Curious Comfort
1 part Southern Comfort®
2 parts Blue Curaçao
3 parts Pineapple Juice
Highball Glass
Shake with ice and pour

Curled Satan's Whiskers
1 part Gin
1 part Sweet Vermouth
1 part Dry Vermouth
1 part Orange Juice
splash Orange Bitters
1 part Blue Curaçao
Highball Glass

Shake with ice and strain

D.A.
1 part Rum
1 part Cherry Juice
1 part Piña Colada Mix
1 part Orange Juice
Highball Glass

Build over ice and stir

Da Rasta Slamma
2 parts Coconut-Flavored Rum
1 part Blue Curaçao
1/2 part Pineapple Juice
Highball Glass

Build over ice and stir

Dambuster
1 part Rum
1 part Coffee Liqueur
1 part Ginger Ale
fill with Milk
Highball Glass

Shake with ice and pour

Dances with Wenches
2 parts Spiced Rum
1/3 part Margarita Mix
fill with Cranberry Juice Cocktail
Highball Glass

Shake with ice and pour

Dancing Dawn
1/2 part Strawberry Liqueur
splash Crème de Banana
1/2 part Kiwi Schnapps
Highball Glass

Shake with ice and pour

Dangerous Liaisons
1 part Tia Maria®
1 part Cointreau®
1/2 part Sour Mix
Sherry Glass

Shake with ice and strain

Danini
2 parts Vodka
1 part Lime Cordial
fill with Cola
Highball Glass

Build over ice and stir

Danish Gin Fizz
2 parts Gin
1/2 part Cherry Brandy
1/2 part Powdered Sugar
1/2 part Fresh Lime Juice
1/2 part Kirschwasser
Highball Glass

Shake with ice and strain over ice

Danish Kiss
1 1/2 parts Vanilla-Flavored Vodka
1/2 part Amaretto
2 parts Orange Juice
fill with Red Bull® Energy Drink
Old-Fashioned Glass

Build over ice and stir

Danish Slammer
1 1/2 parts Vodka
1 1/2 parts Kirschwasser
1 part Aquavit
Old-Fashioned Glass

Shake with ice and strain

Darien Librarian
1 part Whiskey
1 part Cola
1 part Ginger Ale
Highball Glass

Build over ice and stir

Dark Eyes
1 part Vodka
1/4 part Blackberry Brandy
splash Sweetened Lime Juice
Brandy Snifter

Shake with ice and strain

Dark Morning
1 part Rum
1 part Coffee Liqueur
3 splashes Chocolate Syrup
2 dashes Sugar
fill with Milk
Highball Glass

Shake with ice and pour

Daytona 501
1 1/2 parts Dark Rum
1/2 part Vodka
1/2 part Triple Sec
2 parts Orange Juice
Highball Glass

Shake with ice and pour

Daytona Daydream
1 1/4 parts Spiced Rum
3 parts Pink Grapefruit Juice
2 parts Crème de Coconut
1/2 part Grenadine
Highball Glass

Shake with ice and pour

Dead Bitches
1 part Vodka
1 part Canadian Mist®
1 part Jack Daniel's®
1 part Coffee Liqueur
Highball Glass

Shake with ice and pour

Death Kiss
1 part Crème de Cacao (White)
1 part Crème de Menthe (Green)
fill with Cream
Champagne Flute

Shake with ice and strain

Deceiver
1 part Tequila
1/2 part Galliano®
Highball Glass

Build over ice

Deep Freeze
1 part Blue Curaçao
1 part Raspberry Liqueur
fill with Lemon-Lime Soda
Highball Glass

Build over ice and stir

Deep in the Forest
1 1/2 parts Gin
1 part Blue Curaçao
1 part Grapefruit Juice
1 part Pineapple Juice
1 part Orange Juice
1 part Passion Fruit Nectar
Old-Fashioned Glass

Shake with ice and pour

Deep Pearl Diver
1 part Vodka
1 part Melon Liqueur
1 part Coconut-Flavored Rum
fill with Cream
Highball Glass

Shake with ice and pour

Deerslayer
$1^1/_2$ parts Whiskey
$^1/_2$ part Jägermeister®
Highball Glass

Shake with ice and strain

Delta
$1^1/_2$ parts Whiskey
1 part Fresh Lime Juice
$^1/_2$ part Powdered Sugar
$^1/_2$ part Southern Comfort®
Old-Fashioned Glass

Shake with ice and strain

Denver Bulldog
1 part Vodka
1 part Coffee Liqueur
$^2/_3$ part Cream
$^1/_3$ part Lemon-Lime Soda
Highball Glass

Shake with ice and pour

Desert Shield
$1^1/_2$ parts Vodka
$^1/_2$ part Cranberry Liqueur
fill with Cranberry Juice Cocktail
Highball Glass

Shake with ice and pour

Devil's Advocate
1 part Citrus-Flavored Rum
1 part Triple Sec
$^3/_4$ part Sour Mix
$^1/_2$ part Grenadine
fill with Cranberry Juice Cocktail
Old-Fashioned Glass

Shake with ice and pour

Devotion
1 part Watermelon Schnapps
1 part Apple-Flavored Vodka
fill with Lemon-Lime Soda
Highball Glass

Build over ice and stir

Dewpond
1 part Blue Curaçao
1 part Coconut-Flavored Liqueur
1 part Fresh Lime Juice
2 parts Orange Juice
Champagne Flute

Shake with ice and strain

Diamond Romeo
$1^1/_2$ parts Coconut-Flavored Rum
$1^1/_2$ parts Sour Apple Schnapps
fill with Lemon-Lime Soda
splash Cherry Juice
Old-Fashioned Glass

Shake with ice and strain over ice

Dictator
1 part Vodka
$^2/_3$ part Cherry Brandy
splash Apricot Brandy
Highball Glass

Build over ice and stir

Dingo
$^1/_2$ part Light Rum
$^1/_2$ part Amaretto
$^1/_2$ part Southern Comfort®
2 parts Sour Mix
2 parts Orange Juice
splash Grenadine
Highball Glass

Shake with ice and pour

Dirty Ashtray
1/2 part Gin
1/2 part Vodka
1/2 part Light Rum
1/2 part Tequila
1/2 part Blue Curaçao
1/2 part Grenadine
1 1/2 parts Pineapple Juice
2 parts Sour Mix
Highball Glass

Shake with ice and pour

Dirty Bastard
1 1/2 parts Vodka
1/2 part Blackberry Brandy
splash Lime Juice
Highball Glass

Shake with ice and pour

Dirty Dimebag
2 parts Rum
splash Tabasco® Sauce
dash Black Pepper
Highball Glass

Pour ingredients into glass neat (do not chill)

Dirty Girl Scout
1 part Irish Cream Liqueur
1 part Coffee Liqueur
1 part Vodka
splash Crème de Menthe (Green)
Highball Glass

Shake with ice and strain

Dirty Grasshopper
1 part Crème de Menthe (White)
1 part Coffee Liqueur
fill with Milk
Highball Glass

Build over ice and stir

Dirty Irishman
1 part Irish Cream Liqueur
1 part Irish Whiskey
Highball Glass

Build over ice and stir

Dirty Mexican
2 parts Tequila
1 part Lime Juice
fill with Cola
Highball Glass

Build over ice and stir

Dirty Momma
1 part Coffee Liqueur
1 part Brandy
1 part Vodka
fill with Milk
Highball Glass

Build over ice and stir

Dirty Sock
1 part Scotch
1 part Pineapple Juice
Old-Fashioned Glass

Build over ice and stir

Dirty Virgin
1 1/2 parts Gin
1/2 part Crème de Cacao (Dark)
Highball Glass

Build over ice and stir

Disappointed Lady
1 part Brandy
1 part Tia Maria®
1 part Orange Juice
1 part Crème de Noyaux
splash Grenadine
Highball Glass

Shake with ice and strain over ice

Dizzy Blue

1 part Vodka
1 part Lemon-Lime Soda
1/2 part Blue Curaçao
1/2 part Kiwi Schnapps
1/2 part Lychee Liqueur
Highball Glass

Build over ice and stir

Doctor Dawson

2 parts Tequila
1/2 part Lemon Juice
dash Sugar
dash Bitters
1 Egg
3 parts Club Soda
Highball Glass

Shake all but Club Soda with ice and strain into the glass. Top with Club Soda.

Dog House Dew

3 parts Vodka
fill with Mountain Dew®
3 splashes Lemon Juice
Highball Glass

Build over ice and stir

Dog Nuts

1 1/2 parts Bourbon
1 1/2 parts Crown Royal® Whiskey
1 1/2 parts Jamaican Rum
1 part Dr Pepper®
1 part Red Bull® Energy Drink
Highball Glass

Build over ice and stir

Dolce Vita

1 part Jim Beam®
1/2 part Apricot Brandy
2/3 part Sweet Vermouth
Highball Glass

Shake with ice and pour

Dollar Bill

1 part Vodka
1 part Melon Liqueur
1/2 part Lime Cordial
Old-Fashioned Glass

Shake with ice and pour

Double Standard Sour

1 part Whiskey
1 part Gin
splash Grenadine
1/2 part Lemon Juice
dash Powdered Sugar
Whiskey Sour Glass

Shake with ice and strain over ice

Downhill Racer

1 part Rum
1 part Orange Juice
1 part Pineapple Juice
Highball Glass

Shake with ice and pour

Dr. Nut

2 parts Amaretto
fill with Dr Pepper®
Highball Glass

Build over ice and stir

Drag Queen

1/2 part Triple Sec
1 part Vodka
dash Angostura® Bitters
dash Salt
Highball Glass

Shake with ice and pour

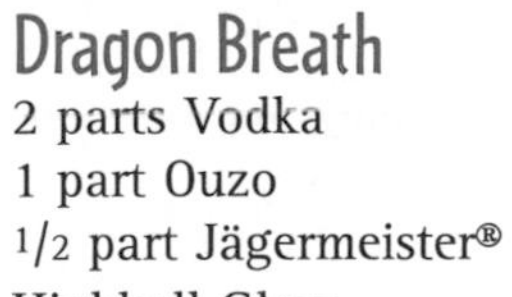

Dragon Breath
2 parts Vodka
1 part Ouzo
1/2 part Jägermeister®
Highball Glass

Shake with ice and pour

Dragon Slayer
1/2 part Vodka
1/2 part Coconut-Flavored Rum
3/4 part Blueberry Schnapps
1/4 part Blue Curaçao
1 part Pineapple Juice
1 part Orange Juice
fill with Lemon-Lime Soda
splash Grenadine
Whiskey Sour Glass

Build over ice and stir

Drainpipe
1 part Irish Cream Liqueur
1 part Blue Curaçao
fill with Cola
Highball Glass

Build over ice and stir

Dreamsicle®
1 part Vodka
1 part Cherry Juice
1 part Orange Juice
1 part Pineapple Juice
splash Cream
Highball Glass

Shake with ice and pour

Drink
3/4 part Sour Apple Schnapps
1 part Melon Liqueur
1 part Cranberry Juice Cocktail
1 part Orange Juice
Highball Glass

Shake with ice and pour

Drink of the Gods
2 parts Vodka
1 part Blueberry Schnapps
1 part Pineapple Juice
Highball Glass

Shake with ice and pour

Drunk Monkey
3/4 part Banana Liqueur
3/4 part Coconut-Flavored Rum
3/4 part Watermelon Schnapps
2 parts Cranberry Juice Cocktail
3 parts Pineapple Juice
Highball Glass

Build over ice and stir

Drunk on Christmas
3 parts Melon Liqueur
2 parts Irish Whiskey
1 part Sour Apple Schnapps
4 parts Sour Mix
Whiskey Sour Glass

Build over ice and stir

Drunken Monkey's Lunch
1 part Banana Liqueur
1 part Coffee Liqueur
1 part Vodka
fill with Milk
Old-Fashioned Glass

Build over ice and stir

Dry Hump
1 part Vodka
1 part Coffee Liqueur
1 part Amaretto
Highball Glass

Shake with ice and pour

Dublin Driver
1 part Irish Mist®
fill with Orange Juice
Highball Glass

Shake with ice and strain over ice

Dulcet
1 part Blue Curaçao
1 part Coconut-Flavored Liqueur
2 parts Grapefruit Juice
1 1/2 parts Passion Fruit Juice
1 part Amaretto
White Wine Glass

Shake with ice and pour

Dunlop
2 parts Light Rum
1 1/2 parts Sherry
2 dashes Bitters
Highball Glass

Shake with ice and strain over ice

Durango
1 part Tequila
1 part Grapefruit Juice
splash Amaretto
fill with Spring Water
Old-Fashioned Glass

Build over ice and stir

Easter Bunny
1 1/2 parts Crème de Cacao (Dark)
1/2 part Vodka
splash Chocolate Syrup
splash Cherry Brandy
Old-Fashioned Glass

Shake with ice and strain over ice

Eastern Night
1 part Gin
1 part Crème de Banana
1 part Parfait Amour
Highball Glass

Shake with ice and strain over ice

Ecstasy
1 part Peach Schnapps
1 part Cherry Brandy
1 part Pear Liqueur
fill with Cranberry Juice Cocktail
Old-Fashioned Glass

Shake with ice and strain over ice

Edison
1 part Strawberry Liqueur
1 part Vodka
1 part Grand Marnier®
splash Grapefruit Juice
fill with Lemon-Lime Soda
Highball Glass

Build over ice and stir

The Eel Skin
1 part Coconut-Flavored Rum
1/2 part Citrus-Flavored Vodka
2 parts Pineapple Juice
1/2 part Smirnoff® Citrus Twist
1 part Midori®
Old-Fashioned Glass

Shake with ice and strain

The Egret
2 parts Vodka
2 parts Apple Juice
1 part Cola
Highball Glass

Build over ice and stir

Eight-Inch Tongue
1 part Southern Comfort®
1 part Vodka
1 part Peach Schnapps
1 part Brandy
1 part Amaretto
fill with Cranberry Juice Cocktail
Highball Glass

Shake with ice and pour

El Morocco

1 part Gin
1 part Crème de Banana
1 part Campari®
Old-Fashioned Glass

Shake with ice and strain over ice

Electric Dreams

1 part Vodka
1 part Amaretto
1 part Lemonade
1 part Orange Juice
Highball Glass

Shake with ice and pour

Electric Jam

1 1/4 parts Vodka
1/2 part Blue Curaçao
2 parts Sour Mix
2 parts Lemon-Lime Soda
Highball Glass

Shake with ice and pour

Electric Kool-Aid®

1 part Amaretto
1 part Triple Sec
1 part Cherry Brandy
1 part Melon Liqueur
1 part Southern Comfort®
1 part Sour Mix
splash Grenadine
Old-Fashioned Glass

Shake with ice and strain over ice

Elf Tea

1 part Peppermint Liqueur
fill with Iced Tea
splash Lemon Juice
Highball Glass

Build over ice and stir

Elmer Fud® Pucker

2 parts Apricot Brandy
1 part Orange Juice
1 part Pineapple Juice
1 part Cranberry Juice Cocktail
Highball Glass

Shake with ice and strain over ice

Elmo

1 part Southern Comfort®
1 part Amaretto
1 part Vodka
Highball Glass

Shake with ice and pour

Emerald

4 parts Brandy
2 parts Crème de Menthe (White)
1 part Lemon Juice
Highball Glass

Shake with ice and strain over ice

Endless Summer

1 part Vodka
1 part Peach Schnapps
1 part Strawberry Daiquiri Mix
2 parts Lemonade
1 part Orange Juice
Highball Glass

Shake with ice and pour

English Water

1 part Extra Dry Gin
fill with Lemonade
Highball Glass

Build over ice and stir

Entrust Your Heart

1/2 part Blue Curaçao
1/2 part Apricot Brandy
1 1/2 parts Dark Rum
1/2 part Lemon Juice
fill with Orange Juice
Highball Glass

Shake with ice and strain over ice

Estrella del Caribe

1 part Light Rum
1/2 part Melon Liqueur
1/4 part Strawberry Liqueur
1 part Orange Juice
1 part Passion Fruit Juice
Old-Fashioned Glass

Shake with ice and pour

Evil Blue Thing

1 1/2 parts Crème de Cacao (White)
1 part Blue Curaçao
/2 part Coconut Cream
1/2 part Light Rum
Highball Glass

Shake with ice and strain over ice

Evil Blue Thing #2

1 1/2 parts Crème de Cacao (White)
1 part Blue Curaçao
1/2 part Light Rum
Old-Fashioned Glass

Shake with ice and pour

Evil Tongue

1 1/2 parts Gin
1 part Melon Liqueur
splash Sour Mix
splash Lemon-Lime Soda
White Wine Glass

Build over ice and stir

Exit the Brain

1 1/2 parts 151-Proof Rum
1 1/2 parts Coconut-Flavored Rum
1 part Grenadine
3 parts Passion Fruit Juice
1 part Red Bull® Energy Drink
Highball Glass

Build over ice and stir

Exotic

1 part Gin
1/2 part Crème de Cacao (Dark)
1/2 part Crème de Banana
Highball Glass

Build over ice and stir

Eyes of a Stranger

1 part Gin
splash Lime Juice
1 part Apple Juice
Highball Glass

Shake with ice and strain over ice

Fairy Godmother

1 part Amaretto
1 part Vodka
Highball Glass

Build over ice and stir

Falling Star

1 1/4 parts Spiced Rum
1/4 part Lime Juice
2 parts Orange Juice
2 parts Tonic Water
Highball Glass

Shake with ice and strain over ice

Family Jewels

2 parts Goldschläger®
1 part Raspberry Liqueur
1 part Chocolate Mint Liqueur
Highball Glass

Build over ice and stir

Fantasia

$1^1/4$ parts Orange-Flavored Vodka
$^3/4$ part Peach Schnapps
1 Lemon Twist
fill with Orange Soda
Highball Glass

Build over ice and stir

Fat Face

$1^1/2$ parts Gin
$^1/2$ part Apricot Brandy
splash Grenadine
1 Egg White
Whiskey Sour Glass

Shake with ice and strain over ice

Fat Hooker

1 part Vodka
$^1/2$ part Peach Schnapps
$^1/2$ part Coconut-Flavored Rum
fill with Orange Juice
Highball Glass

Build over ice and stir

Fatkid on the Rocks

1 part Goldschläger®
1 part Tequila
1 part Vodka
1 part Water
Highball Glass

Shake with ice and pour

Federation

1 part Vodka
$1^1/2$ parts Peach Schnapps
2 parts Cranberry Juice Cocktail
fill with Lemon-Lime Soda
Highball Glass

Build over ice and stir

Fern Gully

1 part Dark Rum
1 part Light Rum
$^1/2$ part Crème de Noyaux
$^1/2$ part Coconut Cream
splash Lime Juice
1 part Orange Juice
Highball Glass

Shake with ice and strain over ice

Ferndale Road

$^1/2$ part Vanilla Liqueur
1 part Brandy
$^1/2$ part Grenadine
fill with Apple Juice
splash Lemon Juice
Highball Glass

Shake with ice and strain over ice

Ferrari®

2 parts Dry Vermouth
1 part Amaretto
1 Lemon Twist
Old-Fashioned Glass

Shake with ice and strain over ice

Fickle Pickle

$^3/4$ part Vodka
$^3/4$ part Melon Liqueur
$^1/4$ part Crown Royal® Whiskey
$^1/2$ part Triple Sec
splash Sour Mix
Highball Glass

Shake with ice and strain over ice

Fidel Castro Special
1 part Dark Rum
1/2 part Melon Liqueur
1/2 part Blue Curaçao
1 part Pear Juice
1/2 part Coconut Cream
Highball Glass

Shake with ice and strain over ice

Figaro
1 part Crème de Cacao (White)
1 part Crème de Menthe (White)
1 part Triple Sec
Highball Glass

Build over ice and stir

Fiji Fizz
1 1/2 parts Dark Rum
3 dashes Orange Bitters
splash Cherry Liqueur
fill with Cola
Highball Glass

Build over ice and stir

Fiorenza
1 part Dark Rum
1/4 part Amaretto
fill with Cola
Highball Glass

Build over ice and stir

Fireball
1 part Coffee Liqueur
1 part Ouzo
Old-Fashioned Glass

Shake with ice and pour

Fireball Glory
1 part Cinnamon Schnapps
1 part Vodka
3 parts Cranberry Juice Cocktail
Highball Glass

Shake with ice and pour

Firebomb
1 part Tequila
1 part Jack Daniel's®
1 part Vodka
splash Tabasco® Sauce
Highball Glass

Shake with ice and pour

Firecracker
1 part Cinnamon Schnapps
1 part Cherry Brandy
splash Tabasco® Sauce
Whiskey Sour Glass

Shake with ice and strain over ice

Firefighter
1 part Triple Sec
1 part Raspberry Liqueur
1 part Kirschwasser
Highball Glass

Build over ice and stir

Firefly
1 1/4 parts Vodka
2 parts Grapefruit Juice
splash Grenadine
Highball Glass

Build over ice and stir

Firestorm
1 part Cinnamon Schnapps
1 part Peppermint Schnapps
1 part Rum
Whiskey Sour Glass

Build over ice and stir

Fishbone
1 part Coconut-Flavored Rum
1 part Blue Curaçao
1 part Melon Liqueur
2 parts Orange Juice
2 parts Sour Mix
splash Lemon-Lime Soda
Highball Glass

Build over ice and stir

Fizzetti
1 part Triple Sec
1/2 part Cherry Brandy
2 parts Cream Sherry
1 part Club Soda
Highball Glass

Build over ice and stir

Flaming Iceberg
splash Blue Curaçao
2 parts Sambuca
Highball Glass

Build over ice and stir

Flamingo
4 parts Cranberry Juice Cocktail
2 parts Pineapple Juice
1/2 part Lemon Juice
2 parts Club Soda
1 Lime Wedge
Highball Glass

Shake all but Club Soda and Lime with ice and strain into the glass. Top with Club Soda. Garnish with Lime.

Flapper
1 part Rum
1 part Sweet Vermouth
dash Angostura® Bitters
Highball Glass

Shake with ice and pour

Flash Gordon®
2 parts Gin
splash Melon Liqueur
fill with Lemon-Lime Soda
Highball Glass

Build over ice and stir

Flim Flam
1 1/2 parts Light Rum
3/4 part Triple Sec
1/2 part Lemon Juice
1/2 part Orange Juice
Highball Glass

Shake with ice and strain over ice

Flor de Mayo
1 part Crème de Banana
1/2 part Dark Rum
1/2 part Dry Vermouth
Highball Glass

Build over ice and stir

Florida Gold
1 part Tequila Gold
fill with Orange Juice
Highball Glass

Build over ice and stir

Fly Away
1 part Vanilla Liqueur
1 part Licor 43®
2 parts Banana Juice
Highball Glass

Build over ice and stir

Flyin' Hawaiian
1 part Melon Liqueur
1 part Light Rum
2 parts Lemon-Lime Soda
3 parts Pineapple Juice
Highball Glass

Build over ice and stir

Flying Dutchman
2 parts Gin
splash Triple Sec
Old-Fashioned Glass

Shake with ice and strain over ice

Flying Fortress
1 part Brandy
3/4 part Vodka
1/2 part Absinthe
1/2 part Triple Sec
White Wine Glass

Shake with ice and pour

Flying Squirrel
1 1/2 parts Tequila
1 part Triple Sec
splash Sour Mix
splash Sweetened Lime Juice
fill with Orange Juice
Highball Glass

Build over ice and stir

Flying Swan
1 part Coconut-Flavored Rum
1 part Sour Apple Schnapps
fill with Orange Juice
Highball Glass

Build over ice and stir

Fonso
1/2 part Amaretto
1 1/2 parts Whiskey
3 parts Club Soda
Highball Glass

Build over ice and stir

Foolish Pleasure
2 parts Parfait Amour
1/2 part Coffee Liqueur
1/2 part Peppermint Liqueur
1/2 part Irish Cream Liqueur
Highball Glass

Build over ice and stir

Fort Lauderdale
1 1/2 parts Light Rum
1/2 part Sweet Vermouth
1/2 part Orange Juice
splash Lime Juice
Old-Fashioned Glass

Shake with ice and strain over ice

Foxhaven Suprise
1 1/2 parts Vodka
1 part Gin
1/4 part Grenadine
2 parts Orange Juice
Highball Glass

Shake with ice and strain

Foxhound
1 1/2 parts Brandy
1/2 part Cranberry Juice Cocktail
splash Lemon Juice
splash Kümmel
Highball Glass

Shake with ice and strain over ice

Freak Me
1/2 part Cherry Brandy
2/3 part Apricot Brandy
2/3 part Campari®
Highball Glass

Build over ice and stir

Freddie Fudpucker
1 part Tequila
fill with Orange Juice
1/2 part Galliano®
1/2 part Coffee Liqueur
Highball Glass

Build over ice and stir

French Afternoon
1 part Coffee Liqueur
1 part Pernod®
Highball Glass

Shake with ice and strain over ice

French Alps
1 1/2 parts Passion Fruit Liqueur
1/4 part Crème de Cacao (Dark)
2 parts Pineapple Juice
3 parts Cream
White Wine Glass

Shake all but Cream with ice and strain into the glass. Top with Cream.

French Bubbles
1 1/2 parts Amaretto
2/3 part Grand Marnier®
1 part Simple Syrup
1 part Lemon Juice
Highball Glass

Shake with ice and strain over ice

French Connection
1 1/2 parts Cognac
3/4 part Amaretto
Old-Fashioned Glass

Build over ice and stir

French Fantasy
1 part Blackberry Liqueur
1 part Grand Marnier®
2 parts Cranberry Juice Cocktail
2 parts Orange Juice
Highball Glass

Build over ice and stir

French Orgasm
2 1/2 parts Cognac
1 1/2 parts Irish Cream Liqueur
Brandy Snifter

Pour ingredients into glass neat (do not chill)

French Sailor
1 part Cointreau®
1 part Vodka
1 Sugar Cube
Highball Glass

Build over ice and stir

Friday Harbor
1 part Vodka
1 part Peach Schnapps
1 part Cranberry Juice Cocktail
1 part Grapefruit Juice
Highball Glass

Build over ice and stir

Friendly Foe
1 part Canadian Whiskey
1/2 part Passion Fruit Liqueur
1/2 part Tequila Silver
1 part Lime Juice
Highball Glass

Build over ice and stir

Frisco Sour
2 parts Whiskey
1/2 part Benedictine®
1/4 part Lemon Juice
1/2 part Lime Juice
Whiskey Sour Glass

Shake with ice and pour

Frisky Whiskey
1 part Whiskey
1 part Gin
splash Lemon Juice
Highball Glass

Shake with ice and strain over ice

Frogster
1 1/2 parts Blue Curaçao
1 part Tequila
Highball Glass

Shake with ice and strain over ice

Froot Loop®

1/2 part Vodka
1/2 part Cherry Brandy
1 part Apple Brandy
1 part Orange Juice
Old-Fashioned Glass

Shake with ice and pour

Fruit Grenade

1 part Blackberry Liqueur
1/2 part Light Rum
1 part Orange-Flavored Vodka
1/2 part Sour Mix
fill with Cranberry Juice Cocktail
Highball Glass

Build over ice and stir

Fruit of the Loons

1 part Blackberry Liqueur
1 part Orange Juice
1 part Grape Juice (Red)
Old-Fashioned Glass

Shake with ice and strain over ice

The Full Monty

1 part Vodka
1/2 part Pisang Ambon® Liqueur
1/2 part Passoa®
fill with Orange Juice
splash Grenadine
Highball Glass

Build over ice

Full Moon Fever

1/2 part Spiced Rum
1 part Light Rum
2 parts Coconut-Flavored Rum
1 part Melon Liqueur
splash Sour Mix
fill with Pineapple Juice
Highball Glass

Build over ice and stir

Full Nelson

1/2 part Crème de Menthe (Green)
1 part Lime Juice
dash Sugar
fill with Carbonated Water
Highball Glass

Build over ice and stir

Fun Squeeze

1/2 part 151-Proof Rum
1 part Blue Curaçao
fill with Orange Juice
Highball Glass

Build over ice and stir

Fury

1 part Vodka
1 part Spiced Rum
splash Sour Mix
2 parts Orange Juice
Whiskey Sour Glass

Build over ice and stir

Fuzzy Balls

1/2 part Peach Schnapps
1/2 part Vodka
1/2 part Melon Liqueur
1 1/2 parts Grapefruit Juice
1 1/2 parts Cranberry Juice Cocktail
Old-Fashioned Glass

Build over ice and stir

Fuzzy Banana

2 parts Orange Juice
1 part 99-Proof Banana Liqueur
1 part Peach Schnapps
Highball Glass

Build over ice and stir

Fuzzy Comfort
1 1/2 parts Rum
1/2 part Sloe Gin
1/2 part Southern Comfort®
1/2 part Peach Schnapps
fill with Orange Juice
Highball Glass
Shake with ice and pour

Fuzzy Navel
2 parts Peach Schnapps
fill with Orange Juice
1 Orange Slice
Highball Glass
Build over ice and stir

Fuzzy Navel #2
1 part Vodka
1 part Peach Schnapps
fill with Orange Juice
Highball Glass
Build over ice and stir

Fuzzy Peach
1 part Vodka
1 part Peach Schnapps
fill with Grapefruit Juice
splash Grenadine
Old-Fashioned Glass
Shake with ice and pour

Fuzzy Rita
1 1/2 parts Tequila
1/2 part Peach Schnapps
1/2 part Cointreau®
1 1/2 parts Lime Juice
Highball Glass
Shake with ice and pour

Gadzooks
1 part Vodka
1 part Raspberry Liqueur
1 part Cherry Juice
2 parts Lemonade
1 part Cola
Highball Glass
Build over ice and stir

Gallina
2/3 part Gin
splash Blue Curaçao
splash Apricot Brandy
splash Dry Vermouth
Highball Glass
Build over ice and stir

Gangbuster Punch
1 1/2 parts Vodka
1 1/2 parts Peach Schnapps
1 part Cranberry Juice Cocktail
splash Lemon-Lime Soda
Highball Glass
Shake with ice and pour

Gangrene
1 part Spiced Rum
1 part Johnnie Walker® Red Label
fill with Mountain Dew®
Highball Glass
Build over ice and stir

Gator Milk
1 part KeKe Beach® Key Lime-Cream Liqueur
1 part Coconut-Flavored Rum
1 part Piña Colada Mix
fill with Mountain Dew®
Highball Glass
Build over ice and stir

Gattaca

1 part Gin
1 part Blue Curaçao
1 part Peach Schnapps
1 part Lemon Juice
Highball Glass

Build over ice and stir

Gay Pirate

1 part Apricot Brandy
1 part 151-Proof Rum
1 part Coconut-Flavored Rum
splash Lemon Juice
fill with Pineapple Juice
Highball Glass

Shake with ice and strain over ice

Geezer!

1 part Citrus-Flavored Vodka
1 part Triple Sec
1/2 part Lime Juice
Whiskey Sour Glass

Shake with ice and strain over ice

Gemini Dream

1 1/2 parts Citrus-Flavored Vodka
splash Blue Curaçao
2 1/2 parts Passoã®
3 parts Orange Juice
splash Lime Juice
Highball Glass

Shake with ice and strain

Gene Splice

1 part Vodka
1/2 part Triple Sec
1/2 part Raspberry Liqueur
2 parts Pineapple Juice
1/4 part Lime Juice
Highball Glass

Shake with ice and pour

Gentle Bull

1 1/2 parts Tequila
1 part Heavy Cream
3/4 part Coffee Liqueur
Highball Glass

Shake with ice and pour

Gentleman's Club

1 1/2 parts Gin
1 part Brandy
1 part Sweet Vermouth
1 part Club Soda
Old-Fashioned Glass

Build over ice and stir

Georgia Peach

3/4 part Southern Comfort®
1 part Peach Schnapps
4 parts Orange Juice
splash Grenadine
Highball Glass

Shake with ice and pour

Georgia Pie

1/2 part Peach Schnapps
1/2 part Southern Comfort®
1/2 part Malibu® Rum
1 1/2 parts Orange Juice
Highball Glass

Shake with ice and pour

Get Laid

1 part Vodka
3/4 part Raspberry Liqueur
fill with Pineapple Juice
splash Cranberry Juice Cocktail
Highball Glass

Build over ice and stir

Ghost

2 parts Vanilla-Flavored Vodka
1 part Jack Daniel's®
fill with Cream Soda
Highball Glass

Build over ice and stir

Gin and Juice

2 parts Gin
1 part Orange Juice
1 part Grapefruit Juice
Highball Glass

Shake with ice and pour

Gin Blossom

1 1/2 parts Peach Schnapps
1 part Gin
fill with Lemon-Lime Soda
Old-Fashioned Glass

Build over ice and stir

The Ginfather

1 part Amaretto
1 part Gin
Old-Fashioned Glass

Shake with ice and strain over ice

Gin Mint Fix

1 1/2 parts Gin
1/2 part Crème de Menthe (White)
1/2 part Simple Syrup
Old-Fashioned Glass

Shake with ice and strain over ice

Gin Smash

1 Sugar Cube
1 part Carbonated Water
4 Fresh Mint Leaves
2 parts Gin
1 Orange Slice
1 Maraschino Cherry
Old-Fashioned Glass

Muddle Sugar with Carbonated Water and Mint leaves in the glass. Add Gin and 1 ice cube. Stir, add the Orange Slice and the Maraschino Cherry, and serve.

Gingersnap

1 part Coffee Liqueur
1 part Irish Cream Liqueur
1 part Frangelico®
1 part Jägermeister®
fill with Cola
Highball Glass

Build over ice and stir

Gladiator

1/2 part Amaretto
1/2 part Southern Comfort®
2 parts Orange Juice
fill with Lemon-Lime Soda
Highball Glass

Build over ice and stir

Glitch

2 parts Vodka
fill with Mango Juice
1 part Lemon Juice
2 parts Blue Curaçao
Whiskey Sour Glass

Build over ice and stir

Gloom Lifter
1 part Whiskey
1/2 part Brandy
splash Raspberry Syrup
1/2 part Lemon Juice
dash Sugar
1/2 Egg White
Highball Glass

Shake with ice and strain over ice

Glowworm
1 1/2 parts Melon Liqueur
1 1/2 parts Southern Comfort®
3 parts Orange Juice
3 parts Pineapple Juice
1 1/2 parts Blue Curaçao
Highball Glass

Build over ice and stir

Goblin Bowl
1 part Dubonnet® Blonde
1 part Applejack
1/2 part Raspberry Liqueur
fill with Apple Cider
dash Bitters
Brandy Snifter

Shake with ice and strain over ice

Godfather
1 1/2 parts Scotch
3/4 part Amaretto
Old-Fashioned Glass

Shake with ice and strain over ice

Godmother
3 parts Vodka
1 part Amaretto
Old-Fashioned Glass

Shake with ice and pour

God's Great Creation
2 1/2 parts Whiskey
1 part Peach Schnapps
2 parts Fruit Punch
1/2 part Lemon Juice
fill with Cola
Highball Glass

Build over ice and stir

Going Blue
1 1/2 parts Grenadine
3/4 part Blue Curaçao
3/4 part Light Rum
1/2 part Crème de Banana
Brandy Snifter

Shake with ice and strain

Gold Carp
1 part Apricot Brandy
1 part Jim Beam®
1 part Dry Vermouth
1 part Tequila Silver
Highball Glass

Build over ice and stir

Golden Beauty
1 part Apricot Brandy
1 part Peach Schnapps
splash Remy Martin VS®
splash Pineapple Juice
Old-Fashioned Glass

Build over ice and stir

Golden Bronx
2 parts Gin
splash Dry Vermouth
splash Sweet Vermouth
1/2 part Orange Juice
1 Egg Yolk
Whiskey Sour Glass

Shake with ice and strain over ice

Golden Comet

1 part Gin
1/2 part Blue Curaçao
1/2 part Lime Juice
Highball Glass

Shake with ice and pour

Golden Dreamer

1 part Triple Sec
splash Brandy
splash Dry Vermouth
1 part Light Rum
Highball Glass

Shake with ice and strain over ice

Golden Hornet

2 parts Gin
1/2 part Cream Sherry
1/2 part Scotch
Old-Fashioned Glass

Shake with ice and strain over ice

Golden Lilly

1 part Brandy
1 part Gin
1 part Triple Sec
1 splash Pernod®
Highball Glass

Shake with ice and strain over ice

Golden Miller

1 part Amaretto
1 part Grand Marnier®
1 part Crème de Cacao (White)
1 part Orange Juice
Old-Fashioned Glass

Shake with ice and strain over ice

Golden Panther

2/3 part Gin
2/3 part Brandy
2/3 part Whiskey
1/2 part Dry Vermouth
1 part Orange Juice
Highball Glass

Shake with ice and strain over ice

Golden Rooster

2 parts Gin
1/2 part Dry Vermouth
1/2 part Apricot Brandy
Old-Fashioned Glass

Shake with ice and strain over ice

Golden Sunrise

1/4 part Amaretto
1/4 part Spiced Rum
1/4 part Wild Berry Schnapps
1/4 part Key Largo® Schnapps
1/4 part Raspberry Liqueur
1 part Orange Juice
1 part Pineapple Juice
Highball Glass

Shake with ice and pour

Golden Volcano

1/2 part Galliano®
1/2 part Tequila Silver
splash Triple Sec
splash Cream
splash Lemon Juice
splash Orange Juice
Highball Glass

Shake with ice and pour

Goldfinger
1 part Goldschläger®
1 part Amaretto
fill with Lemonade
Highball Glass

Shake with ice and pour

Good Morning Sunshine
1 part Vodka
fill with Cranberry Juice Cocktail
Highball Glass

Build over ice and stir

Good Vibrations
2 parts Tequila
fill with Orange Soda
Highball Glass

Build over ice and stir

Gooseberry Jam
1 part Vodka
1 part Southern Comfort®
2 parts Blue Curaçao
fill with Orange Juice
Highball Glass

Build over ice and stir

Grace of Monaco
1 part Apricot Brandy
1 part Mandarine Napoléon Liqueur
1 part Tequila Silver
Highball Glass

Shake with ice and strain over ice

Grainne
1 part Vodka
1 part Maraschino Liqueur
1 part Crème de Banana
splash Lemon Juice
splash Orange Juice
Highball Glass

Shake with ice and strain over ice

Grand Blue
1 part Coconut-Flavored Rum
1 part Peach Schnapps
1 part Blue Curaçao
1 part Sour Mix
Old-Fashioned Glass

Shake with ice and strain over ice

Grand Canard
1/2 part Grand Marnier®
1 part Southern Comfort®
1 part Tia Maria®
fill with Milk
Highball Glass

Build over ice and stir

Grand Midori®
splash Crème de Banana
splash Melon Liqueur
splash Dry Vermouth
1 part Remy Martin® VSOP
Highball Glass

Shake with ice and strain over ice

Grandma in a Wheelchair
2 parts Grand Marnier®
1 part Tequila
1 part Lemon-Lime Soda
splash Lime Juice
Whiskey Sour Glass

Build over ice and stir

Grandpa's Ol' Cough Syrup

1 part Old Grand-Dad®
fill with Orange Juice
Highball Glass

Build over ice and stir

Grape Expectations

1 part Melon Liqueur
1 part Vodka
1 part Grape Juice (Red)
1 part Lemon-Lime Soda
Highball Glass

Build over ice and stir

Grape Lifesaver

1 part Coconut-Flavored Rum
1 part Melon Liqueur
1 part Sour Mix
1 part Pineapple Juice
1 part Grape Juice (Red)
Highball Glass

Build over ice and stir

Grape Rainstorm

1 part Vodka
1 part Blue Curaçao
1 part Pineapple Juice
1 part Lemon-Lime Soda
Highball Glass

Build over ice and stir

Grappa Gimlet

2 parts Gin
2 parts Sweetened Lime Juice
1 part Grappa
Highball Glass

Shake with ice and pour

Grass Skirt

1 1/2 part Gin
1 part Triple Sec
1 part Pineapple Juice
splash Grenadine
1 Pineapple Slice
Old-Fashioned Glass

Shake with ice and strain over ice

Grateful Dead

1/2 part Gin
1/2 part Vodka
1/2 part Triple Sec
1/2 part Rum
2 parts Sour Mix
1 part Raspberry Liqueur
Highball Glass

Shake with ice and pour

Great Head

1 1/2 parts Whiskey
1/2 part Applejack
Highball Glass

Shake with ice and pour

Greek Passion

2 parts Vodka
2/3 part Vanilla Liqueur
2/3 part Passion Fruit Liqueur
splash Triple Sec
fill with Orange Juice
Highball Glass

Build over ice and stir

Green Alien

2 parts Melon Liqueur
1 part Lemon Juice
1 part Lime Cordial
Highball Glass

Shake with ice and strain over ice

Green and Sour

1 part Pisang Ambon® Liqueur
1 part Melon Liqueur
1 part Kibowi
splash Lemon Juice
Highball Glass

Shake with ice and strain over ice

Green Arrow

1 part Blue Curaçao
1 part Tequila Gold
1 part Lemon Juice
1/2 part Lime Juice
Old-Fashioned Glass

Shake with ice and pour

Green Babe

1 1/2 parts Citrus-Flavored Rum
1 1/2 parts Vodka
1 part Melon Liqueur
fill with Cranberry Juice Cocktail
splash Sour Mix
Highball Glass

Build over ice and stir

Green Cow

1 part Vodka
1 part Pisang Ambon® Liqueur
1/2 part Milk
fill with Lemon-Lime Soda
Old-Fashioned Glass

Build over ice and stir

Green Delight

1 part Vodka
1 part Pisang Ambon® Liqueur
1 part Lemon-Lime Soda
1 part Orange Juice
Highball Glass

Build over ice and stir

Green Demon

1 part Vodka
1 part Rum
1 part Melon Liqueur
fill with Lemonade
1 Maraschino Cherry
Highball Glass

Build over ice and stir

Green Devil

1 1/2 parts Gin
1 1/2 parts Crème de Menthe (Green)
splash Lime Juice
3 Mint Leaves
Old-Fashioned Glass

Shake with ice and strain

Green Eggs and Ham

2 parts Melon Liqueur
1/2 part Sour Mix
fill with Cranberry Juice Cocktail
splash Cola
Highball Glass

Build over ice and stir

Green-Eyed Lady

1 part Vodka
1 part Melon Liqueur
1 part Lemonade
1 part Lemon-Lime Soda
Highball Glass

Build over ice and stir

Green Hornet

1 1/2 parts Vodka
1/2 part Sweetened Lime Juice
splash Crème de Menthe (Green)
Highball Glass

Shake with ice and strain

Green Killer
1 part Vodka
1 part Crème de Banana
1 part Blue Curaçao
fill with Orange Juice
Red Wine Glass

Shake with ice and pour

Green Sea
1 part Crème de Menthe (Green)
1 part Vodka
1 part Dry Vermouth
Old-Fashioned Glass

Shake with ice and strain over ice

Green Slime
2 parts Vodka
1 part Limeade
1 part Orange Juice
Highball Glass

Build over ice and stir

Green Stinger
1 part Crème de Menthe (White)
1 part Brandy
Old-Fashioned Glass

Shake with ice and pour

Green Sunset
1 1/2 parts Coconut-Flavored Rum
splash Lemon-Lime Soda
splash Cranberry Juice Cocktail
fill with Pineapple Juice
1 part Melon Liqueur
Highball Glass

Build over ice

Green Swamps
2 parts Light Rum
1 part Blue Curaçao
2 splashes Cherry Juice
fill with Pineapple Juice
Red Wine Glass

Build over ice and stir

Greenback
1 1/2 parts Gin
1 part Crème de Menthe (Green)
1 part Lemon Juice
Old-Fashioned Glass

Shake with ice and strain over ice

Greenham's Grotto
2 parts Gin
1 part Brandy
2 splashes Amaretto
2 splashes Lemon Juice
Old-Fashioned Glass

Shake with ice and strain over ice

Gremlin Fixer
1 part Vodka
1 part Dry Vermouth
1 part Apricot Brandy
1 part Pisang Ambon® Liqueur
fill with Pineapple Juice
Old-Fashioned Glass

Build over ice and stir

Grinch
1 part Melon Liqueur
1 part Banana Liqueur
1 part Malibu® Rum
splash Lemon-Lime Soda
Highball Glass

Build over ice and stir

G-Strings

1 part 151-Proof Rum
1 part Vodka
1 part Grenadine
1 part Pineapple Juice
Highball Glass

Shake with ice and strain over ice

GTV

1 part Gin
1 part Tequila
1 part Vodka
Whiskey Sour Glass

Shake with ice and strain over ice

Guatacarazo

1 part Dark Rum
1/2 part Vodka
1/4 part Crème de Banana
1/4 part Pineapple Juice
splash Lemon Juice
Old-Fashioned Glass

Shake with ice and strain over ice

Gulf Air

1 part Light Rum
1 part Triple Sec
1 part Melon
1 part Pernod®
Old-Fashioned Glass

Shake with ice and strain over ice

Gull's Wing

2 parts Tequila
1/2 part Crème de Banana
1/2 part Lemon Juice
Old-Fashioned Glass

Shake with ice and strain over ice

Gumby®

1 part Melon Liqueur
fill with Apple Cider
Highball Glass

Build over ice and stir

Gummiberry Juice

1 1/2 parts Peach Schnapps
1 1/2 parts Strawberry Liqueur
1/2 part Triple Sec
fill with Fruit Punch
splash Lemon Juice
Highball Glass

Build over ice and stir

Gummy Bears

1 part Gin
1 part RedRum®
fill with Pink Lemonade
1 Maraschino Cherry
Highball Glass

Build over ice and stir

Hairy Happy Trail

1 part Vodka
1 part RedRum®
1/2 part Limoncello
1/2 part Lime Juice
fill with Orange Juice
Highball Glass

Build over ice and stir

Hairy Navel

1 part Vodka
1 part Peach Schnapps
fill with Orange Juice
Highball Glass

Build over ice and stir

Halloween
2 parts Vodka
1 part Scotch
fill with Orange Juice
Highball Glass

Shake with ice and strain over ice

Halloween Spiced Cider
3/4 part Spiced Rum
1/2 part Tequila Reposado
fill with Apple Cider
Old-Fashioned Glass

Shake with ice and pour

Hammer
1 part Orange Juice
1 part Sloe Gin
Highball Glass

Build over ice and stir

Hammerhead
2 parts Scotch
1/2 part Gin
fill with Orange Juice
Highball Glass

Build over ice and stir

Hang Ten
1 part Black Sambuca
1 part Light Rum
1/2 part Crème de Banana
1 part Cranberry Juice Cocktail
1 part Pineapple Juice
Highball Glass

Build over ice and stir

Happy Captain's Ball
1 part Blue Curaçao
1 part Peach Liqueur
1 part Coconut-Flavored Liqueur
fill with Pineapple Juice
Old-Fashioned Glass

Shake with ice and strain over ice

Happy Hawaiian
1 1/2 part Coffee Liqueur
1 1/2 part Irish Cream Liqueur
fill with Pineapple Juice
Old-Fashioned Glass

Shake with ice and pour

Happy Mascot
1 part Apricot Brandy
1 part Light Rum
1 1/2 parts Sour Mix
fill with Orange Juice
Highball Glass

Build over ice and stir

Harbor Lights
1 part Vodka
2 parts Peach Nectar
2 parts Lemonade
1 part Cranberry Juice Cocktail
Highball Glass

Shake with ice and pour

Hari Kari
1 part Brandy
1 part Cointreau®
1 Orange Juice
Highball Glass

Shake with ice and strain over ice

Harlequin Frappé
1 part Vodka
1 part Crème de Cacao (Dark)
1 part Triple Sec
Old-Fashioned Glass

Build over ice and stir

Harry Boy
1 part Cointreau®
1 part Coffee Liqueur
1 part Whiskey
fill with Milk
Whiskey Sour Glass

Shake with ice and pour

Harvey Cowpuncher
1 part Vodka
1/2 part Galliano®
fill with Milk
Highball Glass

Build over ice and stir

Haus Special
2 parts 100-Proof Blackberry Schnapps
fill with Cranberry Juice Cocktail
Highball Glass

Build over ice and stir

Hawaiian Volcano
1 part Amaretto
1 part Southern Comfort®
1/2 part Vodka
2 parts Orange Juice
1 part Pineapple Juice
1 Maraschino Cherry
Highball Glass

Build over ice and stir

Headkick
1 part Cognac
2 parts Rum
fill with Red Bull® Energy Drink
Highball Glass

Build over ice and stir

Headspin
1 part Vodka
1 part Crème de Banana
1 part Apricot Brandy
fill with Orange Juice
Old-Fashioned Glass

Shake with ice and pour

Heartbeat
1 part Triple Sec
1 part Jamaican Rum
splash Mango Juice
Highball Glass

Build over ice and stir

Heatseeker
1 part Crème de Cacao (White)
2/3 part Butterscotch Schnapps
1 part Irish Cream Liqueur
fill with Coffee
Highball Glass

Build over ice and stir

Hell Raiser
1 part Jack Daniel's®
1 part Tequila
1 part Vodka
Highball Glass

Shake with ice and strain over ice

Hell's Kitchen
1 part Bushmills® Irish Whiskey
1 1/2 parts Irish Cream Liqueur
Old-Fashioned Glass

Build over ice and stir

Her Name Was Lola
1½ parts Tequila Silver
1 part Lime Juice
splash Honey
splash Orange Liqueur
Highball Glass

Shake with ice and pour

High Roller
1½ parts Vodka
¾ part Grand Marnier®
fill with Orange Juice
splash Grenadine
Highball Glass

Build over ice

Highland Margarita
1½ parts Tequila
½ part Grand Marnier®
½ part Drambuie®
fill with Sour Mix
Highball Glass

Shake with ice and pour

Hispaniola
1 part Dark Rum
1 part Blue Curaçao
2 splashes Sour Mix
Highball Glass

Shake with ice and pour

Hit in the Face
2 parts Coconut-Flavored Rum
1 part Southern Comfort®
1 part Jägermeister®
fill with Dr Pepper®
Highball Glass

Build over ice and stir

Hollywood
1½ parts Vodka
1½ parts Raspberry Liqueur
1 part Triple Sec
splash Sweetened Lime Juice
Highball Glass

Shake with ice and strain over ice

Holy Cow
2 parts Irish Cream Liqueur
½ part Irish Whiskey
1 part Coffee Liqueur
fill with Root Beer
Highball Glass

Build over ice and stir

Homewrecker
1 part Melon Liqueur
1 part Tequila
1 part Jägermeister®
fill with Cranberry Juice Cocktail
Highball Glass

Shake with ice and pour

Honey Drop
½ part Blue Curaçao
½ part Melon Liqueur
1 part Margarita Mix
fill with Lemonade
Old-Fashioned Glass

Build over ice and stir

Honeymoon Sunrise
1 part Light Rum
1 part Passion Fruit Nectar
½ part Coconut-Flavored Liqueur
fill with Orange Juice
White Wine Glass

Shake with ice and strain over ice

Hoo Doo
1 part Southern Comfort®
1 part Vodka
1/2 part Orange Juice
1/2 part Lime Juice
splash Peppermint Schnapps
splash Lemon-Lime Soda
Old-Fashioned Glass

Shake with ice and strain over ice

Hop Frog
2 parts Vodka
1 part Crème de Menthe (Green)
1 part Dry Vermouth
Old-Fashioned Glass

Shake with ice and strain over ice

Horny Toad
2 parts Vodka
1/2 part Triple Sec
fill with Lemonade
Highball Glass

Shake with ice and strain over ice

Hose Wallbanger
1 1/2 parts Tequila
fill with Orange Juice
1/2 part Galliano®
Highball Glass

Build over ice and stir

Hot and Spicy Men
1 part Cinnamon Schnapps
1 part Jack Daniel's®
1 part Jim Beam®
1 part Spiced Rum
fill with Dr Pepper®
Highball Glass

Build over ice and stir

Hot Night
1 part Crème de Cacao (Dark)
splash Sambuca
splash Absinthe
Highball Glass

Shake with ice and strain over ice

Hot Summer Breeze
1 part Vodka
1 part Orange Juice
1 part Ginger Ale
Highball Glass

Build over ice and stir

Hula Hoop
1 part Vodka
1 part Peach Schnapps
1 part Lemonade
1 part Orange Juice
1 part Cranberry Juice Cocktail
Highball Glass

Shake with ice and pour

Hulkster
1 part Vodka
1 part Melon Liqueur
1 part Kiwi Schnapps
fill with Lemon-Lime Soda
Highball Glass

Build over ice and stir

Las Special
1 part Banana Liqueur
1 part Aquavit
1 1/2 parts Lime Juice
fill with Lemon-Lime Soda
Highball Glass

Build over ice and stir

Iblis
2 parts Campari®
1 part Gin
splash Lemon Juice
Highball Glass

Build over ice and stir

Ice Blue Aqua Velva®

3/4 part Vodka
3/4 part Gin
1/2 part Blue Curaçao
fill with Lemon-Lime Soda
Old-Fashioned Glass

Build over ice and stir

Ice Breaker

1 part Peppermint Schnapps
1 part Vodka
Highball Glass

Shake with ice and pour

Iceberg

1 part Crème de Menthe (White)
1/2 part Peppermint Schnapps
1/2 part Goldschläger®
fill with Milk
Highball Glass

Build over ice and stir

Iced Latte

1 part Crème de Cacao (Dark)
1/2 part Coffee Liqueur
1/2 part Cherry Brandy
fill with Cream
Highball Glass

Shake with ice and pour

Illiad

1 part Amaretto
2 parts Ouzo
splash Strawberry Liqueur
Highball Glass

Shake with ice and strain

Incredible Hulk®

2 parts Melon Liqueur
1 part Vodka
fill with Mountain Dew®
Highball Glass

Build over ice and stir

Indian Summer

1 part Vodka
1 part Coffee Liqueur
fill with Pineapple Juice
Highball Glass

Shake with ice and strain over ice

Indigo

1 1/2 parts Gin
1 part Triple Sec
2 splashes Blue Curaçao
Old-Fashioned Glass

Build over ice

Infernal Love

1/2 part Scotch
1 part Apricot Brandy
1/4 part Grenadine
3 parts Orange Juice
Highball Glass

Shake with ice and strain over ice

International Airport

splash Grenadine
1 part Citrus-Flavored Rum
2 parts Passion Fruit Juice
2 parts Mango Juice
Highball Glass

Shake with ice and strain over ice

Irish Canadian Sangee

2 parts Whiskey
1 part Orange Juice
1 part Irish Mist®®
Old-Fashioned Glass

Shake with ice and strain over ice

Irish Coconut
1 part Irish Cream Liqueur
1 part Coconut-Flavored Rum
fill with Cream
Highball Glass

Shake with ice and pour

Irish Curdling Cow
1 part Irish Cream Liqueur
1 part Vodka
1 part Irish Whiskey
fill with Orange Juice
Highball Glass

Build over ice and stir

Irish Fix
2 parts Whiskey
1 part Irish Mist®®
1/2 part Pineapple Juice
Old-Fashioned Glass

Shake with ice and strain over ice

Irish Hooker
1 part Irish Whiskey
splash Irish Cream Liqueur
splash Irish Mist®®
splash Coffee Liqueur
splash Frangelico®
Old-Fashioned Glass

Shake with ice and strain over ice

Irish Russian
1 part Vodka
1 part Coffee Liqueur
splash Cola
fill with Guinness® Stout
Highball Glass

Build in the glass with no ice

Irish Shillelagh
1 1/2 parts Whiskey
1/2 part Light Rum
1/2 part Powdered Sugar
1/2 part Sloe Gin
Old-Fashioned Glass

Shake with ice and strain over ice

Irish Whiskey Highball
2 parts Irish Whiskey
fill with Carbonated Water
1 Lemon Twist
Highball Glass

Build over ice and stir

Irish Winter Coffee
2 parts Irish Cream Liqueur
1 part Coffee Liqueur
fill with Coffee
Old-Fashioned Glass

Build in a heat-proof cup or mug. Top with Whipped Cream.

Iron Butterfly
1 part Vodka
1 part Coffee Liqueur
1 part Irish Cream Liqueur
Highball Glass

Shake with ice and strain

Iron Curtain
2 parts Vodka
1/2 part Apricot Brandy
Highball Glass

Shake with ice and strain over ice

Isle of Blue
1 part Gin
1 part Blue Curaçao
splash Lemon Juice
splash Lime Juice
Highball Glass

Build over ice and stir

Italian Heather
1 1/2 parts Scotch
1 part Galliano®
1 Lime Wedge
Old-Fashioned Glass
Build over ice and stir

Italian Ice
1 part Vodka
1 part Blue Curaçao
1 part Raspberry Liqueur
1 part Sour Mix
fill with Lemon-Lime Soda
Whiskey Sour Glass
Build over ice

Italian Nut
1 part Coconut-Flavored Rum
1 part Amaretto
fill with Orange Juice
splash Grenadine
Highball Glass
Shake with ice and pour

Jack Be Nimble
1 part Jack Daniel's®
1/2 part Triple Sec
splash 151-Proof Rum
1/2 part Cranberry Juice Cocktail
Highball Glass
Build over ice and stir

Jack Dempsey
1 part Dry Gin
1 part Triple Sec
splash Grenadine
splash Pastis
Old-Fashioned Glass
Shake with ice and strain

Jack Lemmon, M.D.
2 parts Jack Daniel's®
1/2 part Lemon Juice
fill with Dr Pepper®
Highball Glass
Build over ice and stir

Jack-O'-Lantern
1 part Amaretto
1 part Pineapple Juice
1 part Orange Juice
1 part Southern Comfort®
splash Grenadine
Old-Fashioned Glass
Shake with ice and pour

Jack the Ripper
2 1/2 parts Crown Royal® Whiskey
3/4 part Butterscotch Schnapps
Brandy Snifter
Shake with ice and strain

Jackhammer
1 1/2 parts Vodka
fill with Pineapple Juice
Highball Glass
Build over ice and stir

Jacobs Haze
1 part Jägermeister®
1 part Currant-Flavored Vodka
fill with Red Bull® Energy Drink
Highball Glass
Build over ice and stir

Jade Lady
1 part Dark Rum
1 part Gin
1/2 part Crème de Menthe (Green)
1/2 part Simple Syrup
Champagne Flute
Shake with ice and strain over ice

Jaffa Frost
1 part Vodka
1 part Crème de Cacao (Dark)
1 part Triple Sec
Highball Glass
Shake with ice and strain over ice

Jagasm

1 part Advocaat
1 part Sweet Vermouth
1 part Coconut-Flavored Liqueur
splash Grenadine
Old-Fashioned Glass

Shake with ice and strain over ice

Jager Monster

1 1/2 parts Jägermeister®
1/2 part Amaretto
fill with Orange Juice
splash Grenadine
Highball Glass

Build over ice and stir

Jaguar

1 part Vodka
1 part Crème de Banana
fill with Lemon-Lime Soda
Highball Glass

Build over ice and stir

Jailbait

1 part Spiced Rum
1 part Orange Juice
1 part Passion Fruit Liqueur
Highball Glass

Shake with ice and pour

Jamaican

1 part Rum
1 part Coffee Liqueur
1 part Lime Juice
dash Angostura® Bitters
fill with Lemon-Lime Soda
Highball Glass

Build over ice and stir

Jamaican Gravel

1 part Coffee Liqueur
1 part Rum
1 part Canadian Mist®
1 part Cream
Highball Glass

Shake with ice and strain over ice

Jamaican Honeymoon

1 part Crème de Banana
2 parts Lemon-Lime Soda
2 parts Pear Juice
2 parts Orange Juice
splash Lemon Juice
Highball Glass

Build over ice and stir

Jamaican Mountain Bike

1 part Vodka
1 part Melon Liqueur
1 part Crème de Banana
1 part Coconut-Flavored Rum
fill with Cream
Highball Glass

Shake with ice and strain over ice

Jamaican Sourball

1 part Dark Rum
1 part Triple Sec
1 part Lemonade
1 part Orange Juice
Highball Glass

Build over ice and stir

Jamaican Tea

1 part Dark Rum
1 part Triple Sec
2 parts Sour Mix
1 part Cola
Highball Glass

Build over ice and stir

Jamaican Vacation
1 1/2 parts Light Rum
1/3 part Sour Mix
splash Sweetened Lime Juice
splash Cherry Juice
1 part Pineapple Juice
1 part Lemon-Lime Soda
Highball Glass

Build over ice and stir

Jamaican Yo Yo
1 part Rum
1 part Tia Maria®
Highball Glass

Shake with ice and strain over ice

Javahopper
1 part Coffee-Flavored Brandy
1 part Crème de Menthe (White)
1 part Light Cream
Old-Fashioned Glass

Shake with ice and strain over ice

Jazzy Green
1 part Citrus-Flavored Vodka
1 part Blue Curaçao
1 part Peach Schnapps
1 part Orange Juice
1 part Pineapple Juice
Highball Glass

Shake with ice and pour

Jeremiah
1 part Crème de Cacao (White)
1 part Crème de Menthe (White)
1 part Coffee Liqueur
Highball Glass

Shake with ice and strain over ice

Jericho's Breeze
1 part Vodka
3/4 part Blue Curaçao
2 1/2 parts Sour Mix
splash Lemon-Lime Soda
splash Orange Juice
Highball Glass

Build over ice and stir

Jersey Shore Cherry Lemonade
1 1/2 parts Vodka
1 1/4 parts Sour Mix
dash Sugar
fill with Lemon-Lime Soda
splash Grenadine
Highball Glass

Build over ice and stir

Jesus
1 part Southern Comfort®
splash Grenadine
splash Lemon Juice
fill with Orange Juice
Highball Glass

Build over ice

Jewel
1 part Gin
1 tbs. Green Chartreuse®
1 part Sweet Vermouth
2 dashes Orange Bitters
Highball Glass

Shake with ice and strain over ice

Jitterbug
2 parts Gin
$1^1/_2$ parts Vodka
3 splashes Grenadine
splash Lime Juice
dash Sugar
3 splashes Simple Syrup
fill with Seltzer Water
Highball Glass

Build over ice and stir

Jo Jo Original
1 part Myers's® Rum
$^1/_2$ part Amaretto
fill with Cola
splash 151-Proof Rum
Old-Fashioned Glass

Build over ice

Jock-in-a-Box
$1^1/_2$ parts Scotch
$^1/_2$ part Sweet Vermouth
$^1/_2$ part Lemon Juice
1 Egg White
Old-Fashioned Glass

Shake with ice and strain

Joker
1 part Scotch
1 part Triple Sec
Old-Fashioned Glass

Shake with ice and strain over ice

Jolly Rancher®
$1^1/_2$ parts Melon Liqueur
$^1/_2$ part Peach Schnapps
fill with Sour Mix
splash Grenadine
1 Maraschino Cherry
Old-Fashioned Glass

Shake with ice and pour

John Lee Hooker
1 part Spiced Rum
1 part Triple Sec
1 part Peach Schnapps
splash Strawberry Syrup
fill with Lemon-Lime Soda
Highball Glass

Build over ice and stir

A Joy of Almond
1 part Coffee Liqueur
$^1/_2$ part Amaretto
$^1/_2$ part Crème de Almond
Whiskey Sour Glass

Build over ice

Juan Blue
$1^1/_2$ parts Tequila
$^1/_2$ part Lemon Juice
2 parts Orange Juice
1 part Grapefruit Juice
dash Bitters
splash Blue Curaçao
Highball Glass

Shake with ice and strain over ice

Juice Juice
1 part Vodka
1 part Triple Sec
1 part Grape Juice (Red)
1 part Orange Juice
1 part Cranberry Juice Cocktail
Highball Glass

Build over ice and stir

Juicy Fruit Remix
$^1/_2$ part Banana Liqueur
$^1/_2$ part Peach Schnapps
$^1/_2$ part Vodka
$^1/_2$ part Cranberry Juice Cocktail
1 part Lemonade
$1^1/_2$ parts Orange Juice
Highball Glass

Shake with ice and pour

Juicy Melon
$1^1/_2$ parts Peach Schnapps
$1^1/_2$ parts Melon Liqueur
1 part Orange Juice
1 part Grapefruit Juice
1 part Cranberry Juice Cocktail
splash Melon Liqueur
splash Grenadine
Highball Glass

Build over ice and stir

Juicy Red Lips
1 part Rum
1 part Advocaat
$^1/_2$ part Triple Sec
$^1/_2$ part Red Curacao
1 part Cream
1 part Orange Juice
Champagne Flute

Shake with ice and strain

Jumpin' Jack Flash
1 part Brandy
1 part Blackberry Liqueur
1 part Orange Juice
dash Sugar
Old-Fashioned Glass

Shake with ice and strain

Jungle Lust
$^1/_2$ part Vodka
1 part Melon Liqueur
1 part Peach Schnapps
1 part Orange Juice
1 part Pineapple Juice
Highball Glass

Build over ice and stir

Just Like Romeo
1 part Vodka
1 part Raspberry Liqueur
1 part Strawberry Daiquiri Mix
2 parts Lemonade
1 part Orange Juice
Highball Glass

Build over ice and stir

Just Married
1 part Dark Rum
1 part Melon Liqueur
fill with Orange Juice
Highball Glass

Shake with ice and pour

Ka-Boom
$1^1/_2$ parts Coconut-Flavored Rum
1 part Banana Liqueur
1 part Grenadine
fill with Pineapple Juice
$^1/_2$ part Lime Juice
Highball Glass

Shake with ice and pour

Kansas City Ice Water
$^3/_4$ part Gin
$^3/_4$ part Vodka
$^1/_2$ part Lime Juice
fill with Lemon-Lime Soda
Highball Glass

Build over ice and stir

Kappa Colada
1 part Brandy
1 part Coconut Cream
fill with Pineapple Juice
Highball Glass

Shake with ice and strain over ice

Karen's Melons
$1^1/_2$ parts Melon Liqueur
1 part Vodka
fill with Lemon-Lime Soda
Highball Glass

Build over ice and stir

Karma Chameleon

1 part Vodka
1 part Peach Schnapps
fill with Lemon-Lime Soda
splash Grenadine
Highball Glass

Build over ice and stir

Kevorkian

1/2 part Spiced Rum
1/2 part Dark Rum
1/2 part Coconut-Flavored Rum
1/2 part Crème de Noyaux
1 part Orange Juice
1 part Cranberry Juice Cocktail
Highball Glass

Shake with ice and strain over ice

Kenai Campfire

1 part Canadian Whiskey
1 part Irish Cream Liqueur
1 part Butterscotch Schnapps
Old-Fashioned Glass

Shake with ice and strain over ice

Kentucky B & B

1 1/2 parts Bourbon
1/2 part Benedictine®
Brandy Snifter

Build in the glass with no ice

Kentucky Orange Blossom

2 parts Bourbon
1 part Orange Juice
Old-Fashioned Glass

Shake with ice and strain over ice

Kermit the Frog® Piss

1 part Melon Liqueur
1/2 part Coconut-Flavored Rum
2 parts Sour Mix
fill with Lemon-Lime Soda
Highball Glass

Build over ice and stir

Key West Lemonade

1 part Vodka
1 part Sour Mix
splash Lemon-Lime Soda
splash Cranberry Juice Cocktail
Old-Fashioned Glass

Build over ice and stir

Kialoa

1/2 part Rum
1 part Coffee Liqueur
1 part Cream
Highball Glass

Shake with ice and strain over ice

Kid Creole

1 1/2 parts Light Rum
1 part Mango Juice
1 part Papaya Juice
1/4 part Passion Fruit Juice
splash Strawberry Syrup
Old-Fashioned Glass

Shake with ice and strain over ice

Kilt Lifter

1 part Drambuie®
1 part Butterscotch Schnapps
Old-Fashioned Glass

Shake with ice and strain

Kingdom Come
1 1/2 parts Dry Vermouth
3/4 part Gin
splash Crème de Menthe (White)
splash Grapefruit Juice
Highball Glass

Shake with ice and strain over ice

Kings Crown
2 parts Crown Royal® Whiskey
splash Lime Juice
fill with Lemon-Lime Soda
Highball Glass

Build over ice and stir

Kinky Orgasm
1 part Irish Cream Liqueur
1 part Amaretto
1 part Coffee Liqueur
fill with Milk
Highball Glass

Build over ice and stir

Kirchoff's Law
1 part Coffee Liqueur
1/2 part Godiva® Liqueur
fill with Chocolate Milk
Highball Glass

Build over ice and stir

Kirios
1 part Dark Rum
1 part Blue Curaçao
splash Maraschino Liqueur
Highball Glass

Build over ice and stir

Kiss 'n' Tell
1 part Calvados Apple Brandy
1 part Sloe Gin
splash Lemon Juice
1 Egg White
Highball Glass

Shake with ice and strain over ice

Kiss Off
1 part Gin
1 part Cherry Liqueur
splash Dry Vermouth
Highball Glass

Shake with ice and strain over ice

Kiwi Pussycat
1 part Vodka
1 part Kiwi Schnapps
1 part Cherry Juice
fill with Pineapple Juice
Highball Glass

Build over ice and stir

Kiwi Screwdriver
1 part Vodka
1 part Kiwi Schnapps
fill with Orange Juice
Highball Glass

Build over ice and stir

Klingon Battlejuice
2 parts Vodka
1 part Lemon Juice
splash Orange Juice
Old-Fashioned Glass

Build over ice and stir

Knockout

1 part Southern Comfort®
1 part Apricot Brandy
1 part Sloe Gin
splash Orange Juice
Old-Fashioned Glass

Shake with ice and strain

Kokomo

1 part Vodka
1 part Triple Sec
1 part Margarita Mix
1 part Orange Juice
1 part Cranberry Juice Cocktail
Highball Glass

Shake with ice and pour

Kos Kos Ponch

1 part Dark Rum
1/2 part Pineapple Juice
1/4 part Crème de Banana
1/4 part Coconut Cream
2 dashes Bitters
Old-Fashioned Glass

Shake with ice and strain over ice

Kosak's Milk

1 part Vodka
1 part Coffee Liqueur
fill with Milk
Highball Glass

Shake with ice and pour

K-Otic

1 1/2 parts Vodka
1 1/2 parts Grand Marnier®
1 part Lemon Juice
Highball Glass

Shake with ice and strain over ice

Krypto Kami

1 part Currant-Flavored Vodka
1 part Melon Liqueur
1 part Peach Schnapps
1 part Pineapple Juice
1 part Sour Mix
Highball Glass

Shake with ice and pour

Kryptonite

1 part Vodka
1/2 part Melon Liqueur
fill with Pineapple
Highball Glass

Shake with ice and pour

Kurant Affair

1 part Currant-Flavored Vodka
1 part Orange Juice
1 part Cranberry Juice Cocktail
Whiskey Sour Glass

Shake with ice and strain over ice

La Bamba

1 part Vodka
1 part Frangelico®
fill with Orange Juice
Highball Glass

Shake with ice and pour

La Ligne Maginot

1/2 part Peach Schnapps
1 part Armagnac
1/2 part Pear Brandy
1/2 part Lemon Juice
fill with Apple Juice
Highball Glass

Shake with ice and strain over ice

Lacy Blue

1 part Vodka
1 part Blue Curaçao
1 part Cream
1 part Orange Juice
1 part Pineapple Juice
Highball Glass

Shake with ice and pour

Ladder

1 part Gin
1 part Pisang Ambon® Liqueur
1 part Crème de Banana
1 part Blue Curaçao
fill with Lemon-Lime Soda
Highball Glass

Build over ice and stir

Lady-Killer

1 part Gin
1/2 part Cointreau®
1/2 part Apricot Brandy
fill with Pineapple Juice
Champagne Flute

Shake with ice and strain

Lafayette

2 parts Bourbon
1/2 part Dry Vermouth
1 Egg White
dash Powdered Sugar
Old-Fashioned Glass

Shake with ice and strain

Lake Louise

1 part Crème de Cassis
1 part Southern Comfort®
1 part Orange Juice
1 part Grapefruit Juice
Highball Glass

Shake with ice and pour

Lara Croft®

1 1/2 parts Jim Beam®
1 part Crème de Menthe (White)
splash Lime Juice
splash Triple Sec
Old-Fashioned Glass

Shake with ice and strain over ice

Laser Beam

1 part Amaretto
1 part Galliano®
1 part Peppermint Schnapps
Highball Glass

Shake with ice and strain over ice

Latino Americano

1 part Tequila Silver
splash Grenadine
splash Cream
fill with Orange Juice
Highball Glass

Shake with ice and pour

Lawn Bowler

1/2 part Blue Curaçao
1 part Jägermeister®
fill with Orange Juice
fill with Sour Mix
1 Lime Wedge
1/2 part Melon Liqueur
Brandy Snifter

Build over ice and stir

Lazy Sunday

1 1/2 parts Tequila
1 part Ginger Ale
fill with Cranberry Juice Cocktail
Highball Glass

Build over ice and stir

Le Blue Dream
2/3 part Gin
1/2 part Blue Curaçao
splash Crème de Banana
1/2 part Pineapple Juice
Highball Glass

Shake with ice and strain over ice

Leche de Pantera
1/2 part Gin
splash Crème de Banana
1/2 part Crème de Cassis
splash Cream
splash Mango Juice
Highball Glass

Shake with ice and strain over ice

LeFreak
1 1/2 parts Butterscotch Schnapps
1 1/2 parts Amaretto
fill with Milk
Highball Glass

Shake with ice and pour

Legspreader
1 part Melon Liqueur
1 part Coconut-Flavored Rum
fill with Pineapple Juice
splash Lemon-Lime Soda
Highball Glass

Build over ice and stir

Lemon Beat
2 parts Cachaca
1 part Fresh Lime Juice
1 part Honey
Old-Fashioned Glass

Shake with ice and strain over ice

Lemon Highlander
1/2 part Limoncello
1 part Scotch
1/2 part Drambuie®
Old-Fashioned Glass

Shake with ice and strain over ice

Lemon Loop
2 parts Citrus-Flavored Vodka
1/2 part Melon Liqueur
1/2 part Kiwi Schnapps
2 parts Sour Mix
2 parts Lemon-Lime Soda
splash Lemon Juice
dash Sugar
Highball Glass

Build over ice and stir

Lemon PineSol®
1 part Gin
1 part Lemon Juice
1 part Water
Highball Glass

Shake with ice and pour

Lemon Tree
1 part Wild Berry Schnapps
1 part Melon Liqueur
fill with Lemonade
Highball Glass

Shake with ice and pour

Lemon Zip
1 part Gin
1 part Jack Daniel's®
1/2 part Brandy
1/2 part Grenadine
Highball Glass

Shake with ice and strain over ice

Lemonade Lush
1 part Tequila
1 part Triple Sec
1 part Lemon Juice
1 part Sour Mix
Highball Glass

Shake with ice and pour

Lemonado Denado
1 part Citrus-Flavored Vodka
1 part Bacardi® Limón Rum
splash Grenadine
fill with Lemon-Lime Soda
splash Sour Mix
Highball Glass

Build over ice and stir

Lethal Weapon
1/2 part 151-Proof Rum
1 part Vodka
fill with Mountain Dew®
splash Triple Sec
Highball Glass

Build over ice and stir

Lethal Weapon Shooter
1 part Vodka
1/2 part Peach Schnapps
splash Lime Cordial
Old-Fashioned Glass

Build over ice and stir

Lick Me Silly
1 part Blue Curaçao
1 part Cointreau®
1 part Gin
1 part Vodka
1 part Melon Liqueur
fill with Lemonade
Highball Glass

Shake with ice and pour

Licorice Twist
1 part Black Currant Cordial
1 part Pernod®
2 parts Lemonade
Highball Glass

Build over ice and stir

Liebestraum
1 part Peach Schnapps
1 part Blue Curaçao
1 part Coconut-Flavored Liqueur
splash Lemon Juice
fill with Pineapple Juice
Highball Glass

Shake with ice and pour

Lifesaver
1 part Melon Liqueur
1 part Light Rum
fill with Pineapple Juice
Whiskey Sour Glass

Shake with ice and pour

Lightning Lemonade
1 part Citrus-Flavored Vodka
1 part Triple Sec
fill with Lemonade
splash Sour Mix
Highball Glass

Build over ice and stir

Limbo Calypso
1 1/2 parts Light Rum
splash Fresh Lime Juice
splash Crème de Banana
fill with Passion Fruit Juice
Old-Fashioned Glass

Shake with ice and strain over ice

Limo Driver

2 parts Cherry Brandy
splash Lemon Juice
fill with Cola
splash Ginger Ale
Highball Glass

Build over ice and stir

Liquid Big Red

1 part Goldschläger®
1 part Jägermeister®
fill with Dr Pepper®
Highball Glass

Build over ice and stir

Liquid Candy

1 part Peach Schnapps
1 part Apple Liqueur
fill with Cranberry Juice Cocktail
Highball Glass

Build over ice and stir

Liquid Grass

1 part Blue Curaçao
1 part Gin
1 part Orange Juice
splash Grapefruit Juice
splash Apple Juice
splash Melon Liqueur
Highball Glass

Shake with ice and strain over ice

Liquid Snickers®

1 part Crème de Cacao (Dark)
1/2 part Irish Cream Liqueur
1/2 part Frangelico®
1/2 part Light Cream
Old-Fashioned Glass

Build over ice and stir

Little Bigman

1 part Dark Rum
2 splashes Galliano®
2 parts Orange Juice
Highball Glass

Shake with ice and strain over ice

A Little Dinghy

2 parts Coconut-Flavored Rum
splash Orange Juice
splash Cranberry Juice Cocktail
splash Pineapple Juice
Highball Glass

Build over ice and stir

Little Dix Mix

2 parts Dark Rum
1/2 part Triple Sec
1/2 part Crème de Banana
1/2 part Fresh Lime Juice
Old-Fashioned Glass

Shake with ice and strain over ice

Little Venus

2 parts Gin
2/3 part Passion Fruit Liqueur
1/2 part Cranberry Juice Cocktail
fill with Guava Juice
Highball Glass

Shake with ice and strain over ice

Loco Lemonade

1 1/2 parts Tequila
1 part Grenadine
fill with Lemonade
1/2 part Lemon Juice
Highball Glass

Build over ice and stir

Log Cabin
$1^1/_2$ parts Canadian Whiskey
$^1/_2$ parts Triple Sec
$^1/_2$ part Cream
fill with Orange Juice
Highball Glass

Shake with ice and strain over ice

Lollapalooza
1 part Vodka
1 part Triple Sec
1 part Lemonade
1 part Cola
Highball Glass

Build over ice and stir

Lollipop
1 part Cointreau®
1 part Kirschwasser
splash Green Chartreuse®
splash Cherry Liqueur
Highball Glass

Shake with ice and strain over ice

London Trio
1 part Pineapple Juice
1 part Gin
$^1/_2$ part Triple Sec
Old-Fashioned Glass

Shake with ice and strain over ice

Lone Marshall
1 part Jim Beam®
1 part Peach Schnapps
$^1/_2$ part Southern Comfort®
$^1/_2$ part Sour Mix
2 parts Orange Juice
Highball Glass

Shake with ice and strain over ice

Long John Silver
2 parts Spiced Rum
$^1/_2$ part Crème de Cacao (White)
fill with Orange Juice
Highball Glass

Shake with ice and pour

Long Summer Night
1 part Southern Comfort®
1 part Triple Sec
1 part Sour Mix
fill with Mountain Dew®
Highball Glass

Build over ice and stir

Looking for Love
$1^1/_2$ parts Gin
1 part Parfait Amour
splash Lime Juice
Highball Glass

Shake with ice and strain over ice

Loosie Goosie
2 parts Rum
1 part Amaretto
1 part Coconut Cream
Old-Fashioned Glass

Shake with ice and pour

Lorelee
1 part Peach Schnapps
1 part Cherry Brandy
1 part Sour Mix
fill with Cranberry Juice Cocktail
Highball Glass

Shake with ice and pour

Lost Wallet
$^2/_3$ part Melon Liqueur
$^1/_2$ part Grenadine
$1^1/_2$ parts Cointreau®
fill with White Port
Highball Glass

Build over ice and stir

Lotus Elixir

2/3 part Passion Fruit Liqueur
1 1/2 parts Sake
1 part Raspberry-Flavored Seltzer
2/3 part Lemon Juice
fill with Orange Juice
Highball Glass

Shake with ice and strain over ice

Louisiana Bayou

1 part Irish Cream Liqueur
1/2 part Coffee Liqueur
1/2 part Crème de Cacao (White)
fill with Cream
Highball Glass

Shake with ice and strain over ice

Love

2 parts Sloe Gin
splash Raspberry Syrup
splash Lemon Juice
1 Egg
Old-Fashioned Glass

Shake with ice and strain over ice

Love Junk

1 part Vodka
3/4 part Peach Schnapps
3/4 part Melon Liqueur
fill with Apple Juice
Old-Fashioned Glass

Build over ice and stir

Love Potion Number 9

1 part Vodka
1 part Raspberry Liqueur
1 part Lemonade
1 part Orange Juice
1 part Cranberry Juice Cocktail
Highball Glass

Shake with ice and pour

Lovely

1 part Jim Beam®
1/2 part Cherry Brandy
1/2 part Apricot Brandy
1/2 part Cream
Highball Glass

Shake with ice and strain over ice

Lucky Lemon

1 part Vodka
fill with Lemon-Lime Soda
splash Lemonade
Old-Fashioned Glass

Build over ice and stir

Lucky Night

2/3 part Peach Schnapps
2/3 part Orange Liqueur
1 part Lemon Juice
Highball Glass

Shake with ice and strain over ice

Ludwig and the Gang

1 part Añejo Rum
1 part Vodka
1/2 part Amaretto
1/2 part Southern Comfort®
dash Bitters
Old-Fashioned Glass

Shake with ice and strain

Lulu

1 part Vodka
1 part Light Rum
1 part Peach Schnapps
1 part Triple Sec
1 part Sour Mix
Highball Glass

Shake with ice and strain over ice. Garnish with a Maraschino Cherry.

Lumberjack

1 1/2 part Vermouth
2 parts Club Soda
1/2 part Sugar
2 Maraschino Cherries
White Wine Glass

Blend Vermouth with crushed ice, pour over ice, and top with Club Soda

Lynchburg Lemonade®

1 part Jack Daniel's®
1 part Sour Mix
1 part Triple Sec
1 part Lemon Juice
fill with Lemon-Lime Soda
Highball Glass

Build over ice and stir

Macorix

2/3 part Cherry Brandy
1/2 part Jim Beam®
dash Orange Bitters
2 parts Lemon-Lime Soda
Highball Glass

Build over ice and stir

Mad Hatter

1 part Vodka
1 part Peach Schnapps
2 parts Lemonade
1 part Cola
Highball Glass

Shake with ice and pour

Madras

1 1/2 parts Vodka
4 parts Cranberry Juice Cocktail
1 part Orange Juice
Highball Glass

Shake with ice and pour

Maeek

1 part Whiskey
1 part Campari®
fill with Orange Juice
Highball Glass

Shake with ice and pour

Mafia's Kiss

1 part Amaretto
1 part Sour Mix
1 part Southern Comfort®
Highball Glass

Shake with ice and strain over ice

Magic Cider

1/2 part Goldschläger®
1 part Cherry Brandy
fill with Apple Juice
Highball Glass

Build over ice and stir

Magpie

1 part Cream
1/2 part Crème de Cacao (White)
1 part Melon Liqueur
1 part Vodka
Highball Glass

Shake with ice and strain

Maipo

splash Gin
1 part Cherry Brandy
1/2 part Grand Marnier®
2 parts Black Currant Juice
Old-Fashioned Glass

Shake with ice and strain over ice

Major Bailey

2 splashes Lime Juice
2 splashes Lemon Juice
dash Sugar
4 Fresh Mint Leaves
2 parts Gin
Old-Fashioned Glass

Muddle all ingredients except the Gin and pour into a glass over ice. Add Gin and stir until glass is frosted. Decorate with a Mint Leaf and serve with a straw.

Malawi

1 part Vodka
1/2 part Coconut-Flavored Liqueur
1/2 part Passoã®
fill with Pineapple Juice
Highball Glass

Build over ice and stir

Malibu Bay Breeze

1 1/2 parts Coconut-Flavored Rum
1 part Cranberry Juice Cocktail
1 part Pineapple Juice
Highball Glass

Build over ice and stir

Malibu Coral Reef

1 part Rum
1 part Coconut-Flavored Rum
1 part Cherry Juice
fill with Pineapple Juice
Highball Glass

Build over ice and stir

Malibu Cove

2 parts Coconut-Flavored Rum
1 part Lemonade
1 part Cranberry Juice Cocktail
Highball Glass

Build over ice and stir

Malibu Sea Breeze

2 parts Coconut-Flavored Rum
1 part Cranberry Juice Cocktail
1 part Grapefruit Juice
Highball Glass

Build over ice and stir

Malizia

1 part Gin
1 part Triple Sec
1/2 part Blue Curaçao
fill with Grapefruit Juice
Highball Glass

Shake with ice and pour

Man

2/3 part Vodka
splash Grenadine
1 1/2 part Mandarine Napoléon® Liqueur
2/3 part Lemon Juice
Highball Glass

Build over ice and stir

Man Overboard

2 parts Vodka
1/2 part Melon Liqueur
1 part Raspberry Liqueur
fill with Pineapple Juice
Highball Glass

Shake with ice and strain over ice

Mandevile

1 1/2 parts Light Rum
1 part Dark Rum
splash Galliano®
splash Sweetened Lime Juice
splash Cola
splash Grenadine
Old-Fashioned Glass

Shake with ice and strain over ice

Maracaibo
2 parts Pineapple Juice
1 1/2 parts Spiced Rum
1/2 part Fresh Lime Juice
1/4 part Apricot Brandy
Old-Fashioned Glass

Shake with ice and strain over ice

March Hare
1 part Vodka
1 part Wild Berry Schnapps
2 parts Lemonade
1 part Cola
Highball Glass

Build over ice and stir

March Madness
1 part Peach Schnapps
1 1/2 parts Vodka
1 part Triple Sec
fill with Gatorade®
Highball Glass

Build over ice and stir

Mario Driver
1 part Myers's® Rum
1 part Grand Marnier®
fill with Orange Juice
Old-Fashioned Glass

Shake with ice and pour

Marionette
1 part Light Rum
1 part Cherry Heering®
1 part Apricot Brandy
1 part Dry Sake
Highball Glass

Shake with ice and pour

Marlboro®
1 part Sour Apple Schnapps
1 part Peach Schnapps
splash Orange Juice
splash Grenadine
Highball Glass

Shake with ice and pour

Marlon Brando
1 1/2 parts Scotch
1/2 part Amaretto
1 part Cream
Old-Fashioned Glass

Shake with ice and strain

Maserati®
1 part Citrus-Flavored Vodka
1 part Cranberry Juice Cocktail
fill with Lemon-Lime Soda
Highball Glass

Build over ice and stir

Masked Mirror
1 part Citrus-Flavored Vodka
1 part Blackberry Liqueur
2 parts Cranberry Juice Cocktail
2 parts Sour Mix
fill with Lemon-Lime Soda
Highball Glass

Build over ice and stir

Masturbation
1 part Pernod®
1 part Crème de Banana
fill with Cola
Old-Fashioned Glass

Build over ice and stir

Matador
1 1/2 parts Tequila
2 parts Pineapple Juice
1/2 part Lime Juice
Highball Glass

Shake with ice and strain over ice

Matinee
1 part Gin
1 part Sambuca
3/4 part Cream
1 Egg White
1 part Fresh Lime Juice
Old-Fashioned Glass

Shake with ice and strain over ice

Matisse
2 1/2 parts Orange-Flavored Vodka
splash Raspberry Liqueur
Highball Glass

Shake with ice and strain over ice

Mattapoo Shooter
2 parts Vodka
1 part Melon Liqueur
1 part Grapefruit Juice
1 part Pineapple Juice
Old-Fashioned Glass

Shake with ice and strain

Mayan
1 1/2 parts Tequila Silver
1/2 part Coffee
fill with Pineapple Juice
Old-Fashioned Glass

Build over ice and stir

Mean Green Lovemaking Machine
1 part Vodka
1 part Melon Liqueur
1 part Blue Curaçao
fill with Orange Juice
Highball Glass

Shake with ice and pour

Meet Joe Black
1 part Whiskey
2/3 part Amaretto
2/3 part Lemon Juice
fill with Cola
Highball Glass

Build over ice and stir

Mega Mixer
2 parts Vodka
1 part Cranberry Juice Cocktail
2 parts Lemonade
Highball Glass

Build over ice and stir

Megalomaniac
1 1/2 parts Jim Beam®
1/2 part Vanilla Liqueur
splash Honey
splash Lemon Juice
fill with Apple Juice
Highball Glass

Shake with ice and strain over ice

Mellow Hiker
1 part Melon Liqueur
1/2 part Watermelon Schnapps
1/2 part Banana Liqueur
1/2 part Coconut-Flavored Rum
fill with Mountain Dew®
Highball Glass

Build over ice and stir

Melon Ball
1 part Vodka
1 part Melon Liqueur
fill with Pineapple Juice
Highball Glass

Shake with ice and strain over ice

Melon Citron

1 part Citrus-Flavored Vodka
3/4 part Melon Liqueur
splash Raspberry Liqueur
1 part Grapefruit Juice
Old-Fashioned Glass

Shake with ice and strain over ice

Melon Madness

1 1/2 parts Dark Rum
2/3 part Melon Liqueur
1/2 part Grenadine
1 part Pineapple Juice
1 part Orange Juice
Highball Glass

Shake with ice and pour

Melon Snowball

3/4 part Melon Liqueur
3/4 part Citrus-Flavored Vodka
1/2 part Pineapple Juice
1/4 part Cream
Old-Fashioned Glass

Shake with ice and strain over ice

The Melville

1 part Rum
1 part Sambuca
Old-Fashioned Glass

Shake with ice and strain over ice

Memories

1 part Amaretto
1 part Melon Liqueur
fill with Cream
Highball Glass

Shake with ice and pour

Mental Enema

1 part Melon Liqueur
1 part Peach Schnapps
1 part 151-Proof Rum
1 part Coconut-Flavored Rum
fill with Pineapple Juice
Highball Glass

Shake with ice and strain over ice

Mental Hopscotch

2 parts Spiced Rum
1/2 part Crème de Banana
1/2 part Frangelico®
Old-Fashioned Glass

Shake with ice and strain over ice

Menthe Breeze

1 1/2 parts Crème de Menthe (Green)
fill with Orange Juice
Old-Fashioned Glass

Shake with ice and strain over ice

Merry Mule

1 part Maraschino Liqueur
1 1/2 parts Peach Schnapps
1 part Anisette
1 part Club Soda
Highball Glass

Build over ice and stir

Mexican Gold

1 1/2 parts Tequila
3/4 part Galliano®
Old-Fashioned Glass

Shake with ice and strain over ice

Mexican Grasshopper
1 part Crème de Menthe (White)
1 part Coffee Liqueur
1 part Cream
Highball Glass

Shake with ice and strain over ice

Mexican Madras
1 part Tequila Gold
3 parts Cranberry Juice Cocktail
1 part Orange Juice
splash Lime Juice
Old-Fashioned Glass

Shake with ice and strain over ice

Mexican Rose
1 part Tequila
1 part Strawberry Liqueur
1 part Cherry Juice
fill with Milk
Highball Glass

Shake with ice and strain over ice

Mexicano
2 parts Light Rum
2 splashes Kümmel
2 splashes Orange Juice
4 dashes Angostura® Bitters
Highball Glass

Shake with ice and strain over ice

Midwinter
splash Triple Sec
1 part Dark Rum
1/2 part Lemon Juice
splash Passion Fruit Nectar
1/2 part Honey
Highball Glass

Build over ice and stir

Midnight
1 part Black Sambuca
1 part Vodka
Brandy Snifter

Build over ice

Midnight Express
1 1/2 parts Dark Rum
1/2 part Cointreau®
3/4 part Lime Juice
splash Sour Mix
Old-Fashioned Glass

Shake with ice and strain over ice

Midnight Manx
1 part Coffee Liqueur
1 part Irish Cream Liqueur
splash Goldschläger®
1 part Heavy Cream
1 part Hazlenut Coffee
Whiskey Sour Glass

Shake with ice and strain over ice

Midnight Train to Georgia
1 1/2 parts Whiskey
1 part Peach Schnapps
1 part Orange Juice
1 part Cranberry Juice Cocktail
Highball Glass

Build over ice and stir

A Midsummer Night's Dream
2 parts Vodka
1 part Kirschwasser
1/2 part Strawberry Liqueur
2 parts Strawberry Puree
Highball Glass

Shake with ice and strain over ice

Mikado
$1^1/_2$ parts Brandy
$^1/_2$ part Triple Sec
splash Crème de Noyaux
splash Grenadine
dash Bitters
Old-Fashioned Glass

Shake with ice and strain over ice

Mike Tyson
1 part Tia Maria®
1 part Jägermeister®
1 part Pernod®
Highball Glass

Shake with ice and strain over ice

Milky Way®
1 part Irish Cream Liqueur
1 part Butterscotch Schnapps
fill with Milk
Highball Glass

Shake with ice and pour

Millennium
1 part Cinnamon Schnapps
1 part Blue Curaçao
fill with Lemon-Lime Soda
Highball Glass

Build over ice and stir

Mimi
1 part Cherry Brandy
1 part Crème de Banana
1 part Dark Rum
Highball Glass

Shake with ice and strain over ice

The Mind Bender
1 part Jack Daniel's®
1 part Jim Beam®
1 part Wild Turkey 101®
fill with Orange Juice
Old-Fashioned Glass

Shake with ice and strain over ice

Mint Chip
1 part Peppermint Schnapps
1 part Coffee Liqueur
Old-Fashioned Glass

Shake with ice and pour

Mir
1 part Vodka
1 part Jack Daniel's®
fill with Cola
Highball Glass

Build over ice and stir

Missing Fortune
1 part Peach Schnapps
1 part Southern Comfort®
1 part Cranberry Juice Cocktail
1 part Orange Juice
3 parts Club Soda
Highball Glass

Build over ice and stir

Mission Accomplished
2 parts Vodka
1 part Triple Sec
splash Lime Juice
splash Grenadine
Old-Fashioned Glass

Shake with ice and strain over ice

Mississippi Rum Punch
1 part Rum
1 part Cherry Juice
1 part Orange Juice
1 part Pineapple Juice
1 part Cola
Highball Glass

Build over ice and stir

Misty Dew
1 part Whiskey
1 part Irish Mist®
Old-Fashioned Glass

Shake with ice and strain over ice

Mix-O
3/4 part Southern Comfort®
3/4 part Strawberry Syrup
1/4 part Grenadine
Brandy Snifter

Shake with ice and strain

Moat Float
1 part Vodka
1 part Amaretto
fill with Cola
White Wine Glass

Build over ice and stir

Mockingbird
1 part Tequila Silver
1 part Triple Sec
1/2 part Grapefruit Juice
1/2 part Sour Mix
Old-Fashioned Glass

Shake with ice and strain over ice

Mocos
1 part Melon Liqueur
1 part Crème de Banana
splash Irish Cream Liqueur
1 part Coconut-Flavored Rum
Highball Glass

Shake with ice and strain over ice

Molly Brown
1/2 part Blue Curaçao
1 part Aquavit
1/2 part Lime Juice
Highball Glass

Shake with ice and strain over ice

Mombasa
1 part Light Rum
1 part Sweet Vermouth
1/2 part Crème de Cassis
1 1/2 parts Grapefruit Juice
1 1/2 parts Pineapple Juice
Champagne Flute

Shake with ice and strain

Mona Lisa
2 parts Amaretto
fill with Pineapple Juice
1 part Cream
Highball Glass

Shake with ice and pour

Monkey Doo
3 parts Banana Liqueur
fill with Mountain Dew®
Highball Glass

Build over ice and stir

Monkey See, Monkey Doo
1 1/2 parts Orange Juice
1/2 part Crème de Banana
1/2 part Dark Rum
Old-Fashioned Glass

Shake with ice and strain over ice

Monkey Wrench

1 part Light Rum
1/2 part Orange Juice
1/4 part Sour Mix
splash Grenadine
Old-Fashioned Glass

Shake with ice and strain over ice

Monkey Wrench #2

1 1/2 parts Light Rum
3 parts Grapefruit Juice
dash Bitters
Old-Fashioned Glass

Shake with ice and strain over ice

Monk's Man

1 part Tequila Silver
1 part Frangelico®
Old-Fashioned Glass

Shake with ice and pour

Montana Fire

2 parts Cinnamon Schnapps
2 parts Peppermint Schnapps
1/2 part Tabasco® Sauce
1 part Tequila
Highball Glass

Shake with ice and pour

Montana Smoothie

1 part Butterscotch Schnapps
1 part Canadian Whiskey
Old-Fashioned Glass

Pour ingredients into glass neat (do not chill)

Monte Carlo

1 1/2 parts Rye Whiskey
1/2 part Benedictine®
4 dashes Angostura® Bitters
Highball Glass

Shake with ice and pour

Monterey Bay

1 part Vodka
1 part Melon Liqueur
1 part Cherry Juice
1 part Banana Juice
fill with Orange Juice
Highball Glass

Shake with ice and pour

Montreal Gin Sour

1 part Gin
1 part Lemon Juice
dash Powdered Sugar
1/2 Egg White
1 Lemon Slice
Whiskey Sour Glass

Shake with ice and strain over ice

Moo Moo

1 part Irish Cream Liqueur
1 part Crème de Cacao (White)
fill with Cream
Highball Glass

Shake with ice and pour

Moonlight

2 parts Apple Brandy
1/2 part Lemon Juice
dash Powdered Sugar
Old-Fashioned Glass

Shake with ice and strain over ice

Moonraker

1 part Rum
1 part Blue Curaçao
fill with Pineapple Juice
Highball Glass

Build over ice

Moon River
1 part Vodka
1 part Blue Curaçao
2/3 part Lemon Juice
fill with Grape Juice (White)
Highball Glass

Shake with ice and pour

Moose Gooser
1 part Crème de Banana
1 part Blue Curaçao
splash 151-Proof Rum
Highball Glass

Build over ice and stir

Morango
1 part Vodka
1 part Strawberry Daiquiri Mix
1 part Lemonade
1 part Orange Juice
1 part Cranberry Juice Cocktail
1 part Wild Berry Schnapps
Highball Glass

Build over ice

More Orgasms
1 part Irish Cream Liqueur
1 part Vodka
1 part Coconut-Flavored Rum
Highball Glass

Shake with ice and pour

Morgan Madras
1 1/4 parts Spiced Rum
fill with Orange Juice
splash Cranberry Juice Cocktail
Highball Glass

Shake with ice and pour

Morgan's Booty
1/2 part Goldschläger®
1 part Spiced Rum
2/3 part Lime Juice
fill with Grapefruit Juice
Highball Glass

Shake with ice and strain over ice

Morning Glory Fizz
2 parts Scotch
splash Anisette
1 Lemon Wedge
dash Powdered Sugar
1 Egg White
fill with Carbonated Water
Highball Glass

Shake all but carbonated water with ice and strain into the glass. Top with carbonated water.

Morning Macintyre
1/2 part Blackberry Liqueur
1/2 part Raspberry Liqueur
2/3 part Frangelico®
2/3 part Irish Cream Liqueur
fill with Milk
Highball Glass

Shake with ice and strain over ice

Moscow Dawn
2 parts Vodka
1 part Crème de Menthe (White)
1/4 part Triple Sec
White Wine Glass

Shake with ice and strain

Mother
1 part Vodka
1 part Gin
1 part Sour Mix
1 part Grenadine
Highball Glass

Shake with ice and strain over ice

Motor Oil
1 part Jägermeister®
$1/2$ part Peppermint Schnapps
$1/2$ part Goldschläger®
$1/2$ part Coconut-Flavored Rum
Whiskey Sour Glass

Shake with ice and pour

Motown Smash
1 part Spiced Rum
1 part Raspberry Liqueur
1 part Pineapple Juice
1 part Lemon-Lime Soda
Highball Glass

Build over ice and stir

Mountain Cider High
1 part Vodka
1 part Apple Cider
1 part Mountain Dew®
Beer Mug

Build over ice and stir

Mountain Sunset
2 parts Wild Berry Schnapps
1 part Grenadine
fill with Mountain Dew®
Highball Glass

Build over ice and stir

Mountaineer on Acid
1 part Jägermeister®
1 part Coconut-Flavored Rum
1 part Pineapple Juice
Highball Glass

Shake with ice and strain over ice

Mousse
2 parts Apricot Brandy
splash Blue Curaçao
Highball Glass

Build over ice and stir

Mud Puddle
1 part Vanilla-Flavored Vodka
$2/3$ part Coffee Liqueur
$1/2$ part Irish Cream Liqueur
1 part Cream
Highball Glass

Shake with ice and strain over ice

Muddy Jake
$1\frac{1}{2}$ parts Amaretto
1 part Jägermeister®
fill with Lemon-Lime Soda
Highball Glass

Build over ice and stir

Mud Slide
2 parts Vodka
2 parts Coffee Liqueur
2 parts Irish Cream Liqueur
Highball Glass

Shake with ice and pour

Muff Diver
$1\frac{1}{4}$ parts Crème de Cacao (White)
$1\frac{1}{4}$ parts Cream
1 part Lime Juice
1 part Lemon Juice
Highball Glass

Shake with ice and strain over ice

Mulligan Stew
1 part Irish Cream Liqueur
$1/2$ part Crème de Cacao (Dark)
$1/2$ part Amaretto
splash 151-Proof Rum
Highball Glass

Build over ice and stir

Mumbo Jumbo
1 1/2 parts Dark Rum
1/2 part Applejack
1/2 part Lemon Juice
dash Sugar
dash Cinnamon
dash Ground Nutmeg
Old-Fashioned Glass

Shake with ice and strain over ice

Mummy Dust
2 parts Goldschläger®
2 parts Lemonade
1 part Cola
Highball Glass

Build over ice and stir

Muppet®
2 parts Tequila
1 1/2 parts Lemon-Lime Soda
Highball Glass

Build over ice and stir

Mustang Sally
1 part Vodka
1 part Strawberry Liqueur
1 part Raspberry Liqueur
fill with Lemonade
Highball Glass

Shake with ice and pour

Mutual Orgasm
2 parts Amaretto
1 part Crème de Cacao (White)
1 part Vodka
fill with Half and Half
Highball Glass

Shake with ice and pour

MVP
1 part Melon Liqueur
1 part Coconut-Flavored Rum
1 part Vodka
1 part Pineapple Juice
Highball Glass

Shake with ice and strain

Mystical Marquee
1 part Jack Daniel's®
1 part Peach Schnapps
1 part Vodka
fill with Lemon Juice
Highball Glass

Shake with ice and strain over ice

Nail Puller
2 parts Coffee Liqueur
1 part Vodka
fill with Dr Pepper®
Highball Glass

Build over ice and stir

Napoleon on the Back
1 part Dark Rum
1 part Cognac
Old-Fashioned Glass

Shake with ice and strain over ice

Napoli Citric Flip
1 part Tequila Silver
1/2 part Triple Sec
2/3 part Galliano®
fill with Orange Juice
Highball Glass

Shake with ice and strain over ice

Narcissist
1$^{1}/_{2}$ parts Raspberry Liqueur
$^{1}/_{2}$ part Vanilla Liqueur
fill with Apple Juice
Highball Glass

Shake with ice and strain over ice

National Aquarium
$^{1}/_{2}$ part Rum
$^{1}/_{2}$ part Vodka
$^{1}/_{2}$ part Gin
$^{1}/_{2}$ part Blue Curaçao
2 parts Sour Mix
fill with Lemon-Lime Soda
Highball Glass

Build over ice and stir

Navsky at Noon
1 part Vodka
1 part Blackberry Liqueur
1 part Orange Juice
$^{1}/_{2}$ part Lime Juice
splash Grenadine
fill with Sour Mix
Highball Glass

Shake with ice and strain over ice

Nazzy Baby
1 part Coconut-Flavored Rum
1 part Peach Schnapps
1 part Vodka
splash Lemon Juice
fill with Orange Juice
Highball Glass

Shake with ice and pour

Neck Roll
2 parts Jack Daniel's®
fill with Lemonade
Highball Glass

Build over ice and stir

Neckbrace
2 parts Light Rum
$^{1}/_{2}$ part Triple Sec
fill with Orange Juice
Highball Glass

Build over ice and stir

Neiler
1 part Banana Liqueur
1 part Melon Liqueur
fill with Milk
Highball Glass

Shake with ice and pour

Nelson Special
1$^{1}/_{2}$ parts Gin
1 part Cranberry Juice Cocktail
1 part Tonic Water
Highball Glass

Build over ice and stir

Neon
1 part Gin
1 part Raspberry Liqueur
1 part Lemon Juice
Highball Glass

Shake with ice and strain over ice

Neon Iguana
1 part Spiced Rum
1 part Coconut-Flavored Rum
1 part Blue Curaçao
1$^{1}/_{2}$ parts Lime Juice
fill with Orange Juice
Highball Glass

Shake with ice and strain over ice

Neon Nights
$1^1/_2$ parts Coconut-Flavored Rum
1 part Melon Liqueur
1 part Orange Juice
1 part Pineapple Juice
1 part Cranberry Juice Cocktail
Highball Glass

Shake with ice and pour

Neon Smurf®
$^3/_4$ part Blue Curaçao
$^3/_4$ part Blueberry Schnapps
2 parts Lemon-Lime Soda
1 part Sour Mix
Highball Glass

Build over ice and stir

Netherland
1 part Triple Sec
1 part Brandy
dash Bitters
Old-Fashioned Glass

Shake with ice and strain over ice

New Orleans Fizz
1 part Rum
1 part Simple Syrup
1 part Sour Mix
1 part Orange Juice
1 part Lemon-Lime Soda
Highball Glass

Build over ice and stir

New World
$1^1/_2$ parts Rye Whiskey
$^1/_2$ part Lime Juice
splash Grenadine
Highball Glass

Shake with ice and strain over ice

New York
1 part Rye Whiskey
$^1/_2$ part Simple Syrup
splash Grenadine
Old-Fashioned Glass

Shake with ice and strain over ice

New York Sour
2 parts Whiskey
$^1/_2$ part Lemon Juice
dash Sugar
splash Claret
1 Lemon Slice
1 Maraschino Cherry
Whiskey Sour Glass

Shake with ice and pour

Newman
1 part Gin
1 part Ginger Ale
1 part Lemon Juice
splash Orange Juice
Highball Glass

Build over ice and stir

Newport Punch
1 part Amaretto
1 part Peach Schnapps
1 part Southern Comfort®
1 part Ketel One® Vodka
splash Cranberry Juice Cocktail
splash Orange Juice
Highball Glass

Build over ice and stir

Night Bird
1 part Coconut-Flavored Liqueur
$^1/_2$ part Coffee Liqueur
$^1/_2$ part Butterscotch Schnapps
fill with Cream
Highball Glass

Shake with ice and strain over ice

Night Vampire
$1^{1}/_{2}$ parts Sweet Vermouth
$1^{1}/_{2}$ parts Scotch
1 part Orange Juice
1 part Cherry Brandy
Highball Glass

Shake with ice and strain over ice

Nightingale
1 part Banana Liqueur
$^{1}/_{2}$ part Blue Curaçao
1 part Cream
$^{1}/_{2}$ Egg White
Highball Glass

Shake with ice and strain over ice

A Night in Old Mandalay
1 part Light Rum
1 part Añejo Rum
1 part Orange Juice
$^{1}/_{2}$ part Lemon Juice
3 parts Ginger Ale
1 Lemon Twist
Highball Glass

Shake with ice and strain over ice

Nightmare Shooter
1 part Gin
1 part Cherry Brandy
1 part Orange Juice
Old-Fashioned Glass

Shake with ice and strain over ice

Nilla® Wafer
2 parts Vodka
2 parts Cream
$^{1}/_{2}$ part Vanilla Liqueur
$^{1}/_{2}$ dash Brown Sugar
Highball Glass

Shake with ice and strain over ice

Ninety-Nine Palms
1 part Vodka
1 part Peach Schnapps
1 part Piña Colada Mix
1 part Lemonade
1 part Pineapple Juice
Highball Glass

Shake with ice and pour

Ninja Turtle
$1^{1}/_{2}$ parts Gin
$^{1}/_{2}$ part Blue Curaçao
fill with Orange Juice
Highball Glass

Shake with ice and pour

No Way
$^{1}/_{2}$ part Gin
$^{1}/_{2}$ part Grand Marnier®
$^{1}/_{2}$ part Light Rum
$^{1}/_{2}$ part Peach Schnapps
$^{1}/_{2}$ part Vodka
1 part Cranberry Juice Cocktail
1 part Sour Mix
Highball Glass

Shake with ice and pour

Noche de Amor
1 part Brandy
1 part Crème de Banana
1 part Blue Curaçao
Highball Glass

Build over ice and stir

Noche de Phoof
1 part Vodka
$^{1}/_{2}$ part Light Rum
$^{1}/_{2}$ part Crown Royal® Whiskey
1 part Pineapple Juice
1 part Cranberry Juice Cocktail
splash Melon Liqueur
Highball Glass

Shake with ice and strain over ice

Nokia
1 part Blackberry Liqueur
1/2 part Vodka
1 1/2 parts Milk
1 Egg Yolk
Champagne Flute

Shake with ice and strain

North Dakota Special
1 part Wild Turkey® Bourbon
1 part Black Velvet® Whiskey
1 part Canadian Whiskey
1 part Southern Comfort®
1 part Jack Daniel's®
fill with Cola
Highball Glass

Build over ice and stir

North Polar
1 part Gin
1 part Cointreau®
1 part Campari®
Highball Glass

Build over ice and stir

Nothing Is Eternal
1 1/2 parts Orange-Flavored Vodka
1/2 part Apricot Brandy
1/2 part Lemon Juice
fill with Orange Juice
dash Bitters
Highball Glass

Build over ice and stir

Notre Dame Pick-Me-Up
1 part Vodka
1 part Light Rum
1 part Triple Sec
fill with Orange Juice
dash Powdered Sugar
Highball Glass

Build over ice and stir

Notte a Mosca
1 1/2 parts Vodka
1/2 part Campari®
splash Blue Curaçao
Highball Glass

Shake with ice and strain over ice

Nouvelle Vague
1/2 part Peach Schnapps
2 parts Calvados Apple Brandy
Highball Glass

Shake with ice and strain over ice

Nuclear Kool-Aid®
1 1/2 parts Southern Comfort®
3/4 part Amaretto
1 part Lemon-Lime Soda
1 part Cranberry Juice Cocktail
Highball Glass

Shake with ice and pour

Nuclear Screwdriver
1 part Vodka
1 part Grand Marnier®
fill with Orange Juice
Highball Glass

Build over ice and stir

Null and Void
1 part Vodka
1/2 part Wild Berry Schnapps
1/2 part Peach Schnapps
splash Southern Comfort®
fill with Fruit Punch
Highball Glass

Shake with ice and pour

Numbnut

$1^1/_2$ parts Dark Rum
$^1/_2$ part Galliano®
2 splashes Crème de Cacao (Dark)
Old-Fashioned Glass

Shake with ice and strain over ice

Nutcracker

1 part Vodka
1 part Coffee Liqueur
1 part Irish Cream Liqueur
1 part Amaretto
Highball Glass

Shake with ice and strain over ice

Nutty Belgian

1 part Chocolate Liqueur
1 part Frangelico®
$^1/_2$ part Vodka
Old-Fashioned Glass

Shake with ice and strain over ice

Nutty Russian

1 part Vodka
1 part Frangelico®
1 part Coffee Liqueur
Highball Glass

Shake with ice and strain over ice

Nyquil®

2 parts Triple Sec
1 part Sambuca
1 part Grenadine
Old-Fashioned Glass

Shake with ice and strain over ice

Oaxaca

2 parts Gin
1 part Grapefruit Juice
1 part Orange Juice
2 dashes Orange Bitters
Old-Fashioned Glass

Shake with ice and strain over ice

Ocean Water

$^3/_4$ part Blue Curaçao
1 part Coconut-Flavored Rum
fill with Lemon-Lime Soda
Highball Glass

Shake with ice and strain over ice

October Sky

1 part Vodka
$^1/_2$ part Wild Berry Schnapps
2 parts Lemonade
1 part Orange Juice
Highball Glass

Shake with ice and pour

Octopus in the Water

1 part Vodka
1 part Blue Curaçao
1 part Lemonade
1 part Margarita Mix
1 part Wild Berry Schnapps
Highball Glass

Build over ice and stir

Odwits

$1^1/_2$ parts Mescal
$1^1/_2$ parts Vodka
1 part Southern Comfort®
splash Galliano®
fill with Orange Juice
Highball Glass

Shake with ice and pour

Oh Oh

1 part Light Rum
1 part Blue Curaçao
1 part Limeade
1 part Orange Juice
1/2 part Passion Fruit Nectar
Highball Glass

Shake with ice and strain over ice

Oil Spill

1 part Vodka
1 part Blue Curaçao
1 part Irish Cream Liqueur
fill with Cola
Highball Glass

Build over ice and stir

Okinawa Special

1 part Coconut-Flavored Rum
1 part Light Rum
1 part Vodka
1 part Orange Juice
1 part Pineapple Juice
Highball Glass

Shake with ice and pour

Oklahoma Bulldog

1 part Tequila
1 part Coffee Liqueur
2 parts Cream
1 part Cola
Highball Glass

Build over ice and stir

Old Dirty Surprise

1 part Vodka
1/2 part Bacardi® Limón Rum
1/2 part Melon Liqueur
fill with Pineapple Juice
Highball Glass

Shake with ice and strain over ice

Old Green and Gold

1 part Galliano®
1 part Tequila
splash Blue Curaçao
Champagne Flute

Build over ice

Old Hag's Cackle

1 part Vodka
1 part Raspberry Liqueur
1 part Lemonade
1 part Cola
Highball Glass

Build over ice and stir

Old James

1 1/2 parts Triple Sec
1 part Light Rum
fill with Banana Juice
Old-Fashioned Glass

Shake with ice and strain over ice

Old Nick

1 part Rye Whiskey
1/4 part Orange Juice
Old-Fashioned Glass

Shake with ice and strain over ice

Old Pal

1 part Dry Vermouth
1 part Whiskey
1 part Campari®
Old-Fashioned Glass

Shake with ice and strain over ice

Old Pirate

$1^1/_2$ parts Vodka
1 part Coconut-Flavored Rum
1 part Irish Cream Liqueur
$^1/_2$ part Orange Juice
$^1/_2$ part Pineapple Juice
$^1/_2$ part Mango Juice
Old-Fashioned Glass

Shake with ice and pour

Old Spice®

1 part Gin
1 part Vodka
1 part Applejack
Whiskey Sour Glass

Shake with ice and strain over ice

Old Yellow Pages

$1^1/_2$ parts Gin
splash Pernod®
2 parts Pineapple Juice
Old-Fashioned Glass

Shake with ice and strain over ice

On Deck

1 part Light Rum
1 part Melon Liqueur
$^1/_2$ part Sloe Gin
1 part Orange Juice
1 part Pineapple Juice
Highball Glass

Shake with ice and strain over ice

One Bad Mutha

2 parts Whiskey
1 part Cranberry Juice Cocktail
fill with Cola
Highball Glass

Build over ice and stir

One Exciting Night

1 part Gin
1 part Dry Vermouth
1 part Sweet Vermouth
1 part Orange Juice
White Wine Glass

Shake with ice and pour

Ooh-La-La

1 part Vodka
1 part Cherry Juice
1 part Piña Colada Mix
2 parts Lemonade
1 part Cola
Highball Glass

Build over ice and stir

Opaline

1 part Gin
splash Blue Curaçao
splash Pear Liqueur
Highball Glass

Shake with ice and strain over ice

Orange Bliss

$1^1/_2$ parts Orange-Flavored Vodka
1 part Grand Marnier®
fill with Orange Juice
Old-Fashioned Glass

Shake with ice and strain over ice

Orange Clockwork

$1^1/_2$ parts Orange-Flavored Vodka
$^1/_2$ part Triple Sec
$^1/_2$ part Orange Juice
$^1/_4$ part Fresh Lime Juice
Old-Fashioned Glass

Shake with ice and strain over ice

Orange Crush

3 parts Triple Sec
1 part Cranberry Juice Cocktail
Old-Fashioned Glass

Shake with ice and strain over ice

Orange Freestyle

1 part Gin
1 part Dry Vermouth
fill with Orange Juice
Highball Glass

Shake with ice and pour

Orange Glow

1/2 part Blue Curaçao
1/2 part Triple Sec
1 part Remy Martin® VSOP
fill with Orange Juice
Highball Glass

Shake with ice and pour

Orange Outrage

1 1/2 parts Dark Rum
1/2 part Triple Sec
1/2 part Vanilla Liqueur
fill with Orange Juice
Highball Glass

Build over ice and stir

Orange Rum Daiquiri

1 part Rum
1 part Triple Sec
2 parts Sour Mix
1 part Orange Juice
Highball Glass

Shake with ice and pour

Orange Smartie®

1 part Vodka
1 part Coffee Liqueur
1 part Triple Sec
fill with Orange Juice
Highball Glass

Shake with ice and pour

Orange Spew

2 parts Rum
1 part Cranberry Juice Cocktail
1 part Orange Juice
Highball Glass

Shake with ice and pour

Orange Surprise

1 part Vodka
1 part Peach Schnapps
2 parts Sour Mix
fill with Lemon-Lime Soda
Highball Glass

Build over ice and stir

Orange Whip

1 part Rum
1 part Vodka
1 part Cream
fill with Orange Juice
Highball Glass

Shake with ice and strain over ice

Orchard

2 parts Raspberry Liqueur
1 part Apple Brandy
1 part Cherry Brandy
1 part Orange Juice
Highball Glass

Shake with ice and strain over ice

Orchard Punch
1 part Rum
1 part Cherry Juice
1 part Peach Nectar
1 part Orange Juice
1 part Pineapple Juice
1 part Cranberry Juice Cocktail
Highball Glass

Shake with ice and pour

Orchid
1 part Vodka
1 part Peach Schnapps
1 part Cherry Juice
1 part Lemonade
1 part Orange Juice
1 part Cranberry Juice Cocktail
Highball Glass

Shake with ice and pour

Orlando Amethyst
1 part Gin
1/2 part Chambord®
fill with Pineapple Juice
Old-Fashioned Glass

Shake with ice and pour

Orlando Sun
1 part Light Rum
1/2 part Vodka
1/2 part Grand Marnier®
1 part Orange Juice
1/4 part Lemon Juice
Highball Glass

Shake with ice and strain over ice

Oscar's Flame
1 1/2 parts Amaretto
1/2 part Crème de Banana
splash Strawberry Liqueur
Old-Fashioned Glass

Shake with ice and strain over ice

Out of the Blue
1/2 part Vodka
1/2 part Blueberry Schnapps
1/2 part Blue Curaçao
1 part Club Soda
splash Sour Mix
Highball Glass

Build over ice and stir

Outrigger
1 part Peach Brandy
1 part Vodka
1 part Pineapple Juice
splash Lime Juice
Old-Fashioned Glass

Shake with ice and strain over ice

Overdose
1 1/2 parts Gin
splash Crème de Banana
splash Kiwi Schnapps
splash Raspberry Liqueur
splash Campari®
Highball Glass

Build over ice and stir

Oxygen Mask
2 parts Melon Liqueur
1 part Amaretto
3 parts Orange Juice
2 parts Pineapple Juice
Highball Glass

Shake with ice and strain over ice

Oxymoron
1 part Vodka
1/2 part Lemon Juice
splash Honey
Old-Fashioned Glass

Shake with ice and strain over ice

P.T.O.

$1^1/_2$ parts Dark Rum
$^1/_2$ part Vodka
$^1/_2$ part Triple Sec
fill with Orange Juice
Highball Glass

Shake with ice and strain over ice

Pacific Blue

1 part Crème de Banana
1 part Blue Curaçao
splash Vodka
splash Coconut-Flavored Liqueur
Highball Glass

Build over ice and stir

Pacific Pacifier

1 part Triple Sec
$^1/_2$ part Crème de Banana
$^1/_2$ part Light Cream
Old-Fashioned Glass

Shake with ice and strain over ice

Paducah Punch

$^1/_2$ part Light Rum
1 part Amaretto
1 part Maraschino Liqueur
2 parts Pineapple Juice
2 parts Orange Juice
2 parts Grapefruit Juice
Highball Glass

Shake with ice and strain over ice

Paisano

1 part Vodka
1 part Frangelico®
fill with Milk
Highball Glass

Shake with ice and pour

Pajama Jackhammer

1 part Vodka
1 part Blue Curaçao
1 part Peach Schnapps
fill with Pineapple Juice
Highball Glass

Shake with ice and strain over ice

Palisades Park

1 part Vodka
1 part Peach Schnapps
1 part Banana Juice
2 parts Lemonade
1 part Orange Juice
Highball Glass

Shake with ice and pour

Palmetto

$1^1/_2$ parts Light Rum
$^1/_2$ part Sweet Vermouth
2 dashes Orange Bitters
Highball Glass

Shake with ice and strain over ice

Pamplemousse

1 part Whiskey
1 part Southern Comfort®
1 part Pineapple Juice
2 parts Grapefruit Juice
Old-Fashioned Glass

Shake with ice and strain over ice

Panama Jack

2 parts Coconut-Flavored Rum
1 part Banana Juice
1 part Orange Juice
1 part Pineapple Juice
Highball Glass

Build over ice and stir

Panama Red

1 part Tequila Reposado
1/4 part Grenadine
1/4 part Sour Mix
Old-Fashioned Glass

Shake with ice and strain over ice

Panda King

1/2 part Crème de Cacao (White)
1 1/2 parts Amaretto
1 1/2 parts Milk
1 1/2 parts Club Soda
Highball Glass

Shake with ice and strain over ice

Panic on Board

1 1/2 parts Plum Brandy
2/3 part Apricot Brandy
splash Goldschläger®
fill with Raspberry-Flavored Seltzer
Highball Glass

Build over ice and stir

Panty Ripper

1 part Coconut-Flavored Rum
splash Cherry Juice
2 parts Pineapple Juice
Old-Fashioned Glass

Shake with ice and strain over ice

Paradise Bliss

1 1/2 parts Vodka
1 1/2 parts Coconut-Flavored Rum
1 part Cranberry Juice Cocktail
1 part Pineapple Juice
Highball Glass

Shake with ice and pour

Paradise Punch

1 part Coconut-Flavored Rum
2 parts Cranberry Juice Cocktail
1 part Pineapple Juice
Highball Glass

Build over ice and stir

Parfait Punch

1 part Parfait Amour
2 1/2 parts Light Rum
dash Powdered Sugar
fill with Milk
Highball Glass

Shake with ice and strain

Paris Burning

1 part Raspberry Liqueur
1 part Hennessy®
Brandy Snifter

Build in the glass with no ice

Parisian Blond

1 part Light Rum
1 part Dark Rum
1 part Triple Sec
Old-Fashioned Glass

Shake with ice and strain over ice

Park West

1 1/2 parts Gin
2 parts Grapefruit Juice
2 parts Pineapple Juice
Old-Fashioned Glass

Shake with ice and strain over ice

Parrot

1 part Vodka
1 part Gin
3 splashes Tabasco® Sauce
Old-Fashioned Glass

Shake with ice and strain over ice

Partly Cloudy
1 part Vodka
1 part Blue Curaçao
1 part Piña Colada Mix
fill with Lemonade
Highball Glass

Shake with ice and pour

Pascal's Passion
1 part Amaretto
1 part Irish Cream Liqueur
1/2 part Blue Curaçao
fill with Milk
White Wine Glass

Shake with ice and pour

Passion Cup
2 parts Vodka
2 parts Orange Juice
1 part Passion Fruit Juice
1/2 part Pineapple Juice
1/2 part Coconut Cream
White Wine Glass

Shake with ice and strain over ice

Passionate Slopes
1 1/2 parts Southern Comfort®
1 1/2 parts Dark Rum
2 parts Passion Fruit Liqueur
fill with Iced Tea
splash Lemon Juice
Highball Glass

Build over ice and stir

Pastis Rouge
splash Grenadine
2/3 part Pastis
fill with Water
Highball Glass

Build over ice and stir

Pavlova
1 part Vodka
1/2 part Crème de Cacao (White)
1/2 part Cream
Old-Fashioned Glass

Shake with ice and strain over ice

Peach Blossom
2 parts Gin
splash Lemon Juice
dash Powdered Sugar
1/2 part Peach Schnapps
fill with Carbonated Water
Highball Glass

Shake all but Carbonated Water with ice and strain into the glass. Top with Carbonated Water.

Peach Crush
1 part Vodka
1 part Peach Schnapps
1 1/2 parts Sour Mix
Old-Fashioned Glass

Shake with ice and strain over ice

Peach Fuzz
1 part Peach Schnapps
1 part Cranberry Juice Cocktail
Highball Glass

Shake with ice and pour

Peach Pit
1 part Peach Schnapps
1 part Apple Brandy
Old-Fashioned Glass

Shake with ice and strain over ice

Peacher

2/3 part Peach Schnapps
2/3 part Citrus-Flavored Vodka
1 part Lemon-Lime Soda
1 part Club Soda
Highball Glass

Build over ice and stir

Peacock

1 part Crème de Cacao (White)
1 part Parfait Amour
1 part Triple Sec
1/2 part Cream
Champagne Flute

Layer in a champagne flute

Peanut Butter-Chocolate Chip Cookie

1 part Frangelico®
1 part Tia Maria®
1 part Coffee Liqueur
Highball Glass

Shake with ice and strain over ice

Pee Wee's Beamer

3/4 part Vodka
3/4 part Coconut-Flavored Rum
1/2 part Orange Juice
Old-Fashioned Glass

Shake with ice and strain over ice

Peep Show

1 part Dubonnet® Blonde
1 part Brandy
1 part Pernod®
splash Lime Juice
Old-Fashioned Glass

Shake with ice and strain over ice

Pelican

1 part Bourbon
1/2 part Triple Sec
1/2 part Sugar
fill with Orange Juice
Highball Glass

Shake with ice and strain over ice

Pensacola

1 part Rum
1 part Lemonade
1 part Orange Juice
1 part Guava Nectar
Highball Glass

Shake with ice and pour

Pentecostal

1 part Vodka
1 part Bourbon
fill with Lemon-Lime Soda
Whiskey Sour Glass

Build over ice and stir

Peppermint Crisp

1 part Crème de Menthe (White)
1 part Coffee Liqueur
fill with Milk
Highball Glass

Shake with ice and pour

Peppermint Stick

1 part Peach Schnapps
1 1/2 parts Crème de Cacao (White)
1 part Light Cream
Champagne Flute

Shake with ice and strain

Perestroika
$1^1/_2$ parts Vodka
1 part Vanilla Liqueur
1 part Crème de Cacao (White)
Old-Fashioned Glass

Shake with ice and strain over ice

Pernod® Riviera
1 part Pernod®
$^1/_2$ part Gin
2 parts Lemonade
Old-Fashioned Glass

Shake with ice and strain over ice

Perpetual Depth
$^2/_3$ part Blackberry Liqueur
$^2/_3$ part Raspberry Liqueur
1 part Orange-Flavored Vodka
1 part Pineapple Juice
Highball Glass

Shake with ice and strain over ice

Perroquet
$1^1/_2$ parts Pernod®
splash Peppermint Schnapps
Old-Fashioned Glass

Shake with ice and strain over ice

Persian Prince
1 part Vodka
1 part Citrus-Flavored Rum
1 part Sour Mix
1 part Orange Juice
1 part Lemon-Lime Soda
Highball Glass

Shake with ice and strain over ice

Petit Caprice
1 part Vodka
$^1/_2$ part Melon Liqueur
$^1/_2$ part Limoncello
$^1/_2$ part Lemon Juice
$1^1/_2$ parts Apple Juice
Highball Glass

Shake with ice and strain over ice

Philishake
1 part Sloe Gin
1 part Triple Sec
splash Cherry Brandy
splash Strawberry Juice
Highball Glass

Shake with ice and strain over ice

Phillips Head Screwdriver
2 parts Vodka
1 part Orange Juice
1 part Pineapple Juice
Highball Glass

Shake with ice and pour

Philofan
1 part Root Beer Schnapps
1 part Amaretto
1 part Cola
Highball Glass

Build over ice and stir

Pier 66
1 part Vodka
1 part Wild Berry Schnapps
1 part Piña Colada Mix
2 parts Lemonade
1 part Orange Juice
Highball Glass

Shake with ice and pour

Pierced Navel
1 part Vodka
1 part Peach Schnapps
1 part Orange Juice
1 part Cranberry Juice Cocktail
Highball Glass

Shake with ice and strain over ice

Pillow Mint
2 parts Irish Whiskey
1/2 part Coffee Liqueur
splash Crème de Menthe (White)
Old-Fashioned Glass

Shake with ice and strain over ice

Pimm's® Cup
1 1/2 parts Pimm's Cup No. 1®
splash Lemon Juice
splash Lime Juice
1 part Lemon-Lime Soda
1 part Ginger Ale
White Wine Glass

Build over ice and stir

Pimp Juice
1 part Alizé®
1 part Hypnotiq®
Old-Fashioned Glass

Build over ice and stir

Pina
1 1/2 parts Tequila
1 part Lime Juice
1 splash Simple Syrup
fill with Pineapple Juice
Highball Glass

Build over ice and stir

Piñata
1 part Tequila
splash Banana Liqueur
1 part Lime Juice
Highball Glass

Shake with ice and strain over ice

Pineapple Princess
1 1/2 parts Melon Liqueur
1 part Passion Fruit Liqueur
1 part Lime Juice
2 parts Orange Juice
fill with Pineapple Juice
Highball Glass

Build over ice and stir

Pineapple Slapper
1 part Coconut-Flavored Liqueur
1/2 part Lemon Juice
1/2 part Lime Juice
2 parts Sour Mix
fill with Pineapple Juice
Highball Glass

Shake with ice and strain over ice

Pinetree Martyr
1 part Vodka
1/2 part Peach Schnapps
fill with Pineapple Juice
Highball Glass

Shake with ice and strain over ice

Pink
1 part Vodka
1 part Grenadine
fill with Milk
Highball Glass

Shake with ice and pour

Pink Almond
1 part Rye Whiskey
1/2 part Amaretto
1/2 part Crème de Noyaux
1/2 part Kirschwasser
1/2 part Lemon Juice
Highball Glass

Shake with ice and strain over ice

Pink Cloud
1 part Vodka
1 part Crème de Almond
2 parts Piña Colada Mix
fill with Lemonade
Highball Glass

Shake with ice and pour

Pink Drink
2 parts Vodka
fill with Lemon-Lime Soda
splash Cranberry Juice Cocktail
Highball Glass

Build over ice and stir

Pink Elephants on Parade
2 parts Vodka
1/2 part Melon Liqueur
dash Sugar
fill with Pink Lemonade
Highball Glass

Shake with ice and strain over ice

Pink Explosion
1 1/2 parts Cream
3/4 part Dry Vermouth
1/2 part Pernod®
splash Grenadine
White Wine Glass

Shake with ice and strain over ice

Pink Fix
2 parts Gin
2 parts Lemon Juice
3/4 part Grenadine
Old-Fashioned Glass

Shake with ice and strain over ice

Pink Forest
1 part Gin
1/2 part Cream
1/2 part Triple Sec
fill with Strawberry Juice
Highball Glass

Shake with ice and pour

Pink Goody
1 part Gin
1 part Dark Rum
1 part Lime Juice
splash Cherry Juice
splash Club Soda
Highball Glass

Build over ice and stir

Pink Jinx
1 part Gin
1 part Lemon Juice
splash Grenadine
Old-Fashioned Glass

Shake with ice and pour

Pink Lemonade
1 1/2 parts Citrus-Flavored Vodka
1/2 part Raspberry Liqueur
fill with Sour Mix
Highball Glass

Shake with ice and pour

Pink Missile
2 parts Vodka
1 part Raspberry Liqueur
1 part Cranberry Juice Cocktail
1 part Ginger Ale
1 part Grapefruit Juice
Highball Glass

Build over ice and stir

Pink Panty Pulldown
1 1/2 parts Vodka
1 part Sour Mix
splash Lemon-Lime Soda
splash Grenadine
Highball Glass

Build over ice

Pink Russian
1 part Tequila Rose®
1 part Coffee Liqueur
1 part Vodka
Highball Glass

Shake with ice and pour

Pink Top
1 1/2 parts Gin
3/4 part Grand Marnier®
1/4 part Lemon Juice
splash Grenadine
Highball Glass

Shake with ice and strain over ice

Pink Veranda
1 part Gold Rum
1 1/2 parts Cranberry Juice Cocktail
1 part Lime Juice
1 1/2 parts Simple Syrup
Highball Glass

Shake with ice and strain over ice

Pinocchio
1 1/2 parts Gin
1/2 part Blackberry Liqueur
2/3 part Dubonnet® Blonde
fill with Raspberry-Flavored Seltzer
Highball Glass

Build over ice and stir

Piper at the Gates of Dawn
1 1/2 parts Scotch
1 part Coffee Liqueur
1/2 part Maraschino Liqueur
1 part Heavy Cream
Old-Fashioned Glass

Shake with ice and strain over ice

Pirate Float
1 part Spiced Rum
1 part Root Beer Schnapps
1 part Vanilla-Flavored Vodka
1 part Cream
Highball Glass

Shake with ice and pour

Pirate Jenny
1 1/2 parts Light Rum
1 part Orange Liqueur
splash Lime Juice
splash Simple Syrup
fill with Pineapple Juice
Highball Glass

Shake with ice and pour

Pisa
1 part Dry Vermouth
1 part Amaretto
1 part Scotch
1 part Crème de Banana
1 part Lime Cordial
Old-Fashioned Glass

Shake with ice and strain over ice

Pisco Kid

$1^1/_2$ parts Pineapple Juice
$1^1/_2$ parts Pisco
$^3/_4$ part Dark Rum
Old-Fashioned Glass

Shake with ice and strain over ice

Planet of the Apes

1 part Dark Rum
$^1/_2$ part Crème de Banana
$^1/_2$ part Coconut Cream
fill with Pineapple Juice
Highball Glass

Shake with ice and strain over ice

Plastic Gangster

1 part Blue Curaçao
1 part Tequila Silver
1 part Lemonade
1 part Sour Mix
White Wine Glass

Shake with ice and strain over ice

Plum

$^1/_2$ part Amaretto
$^1/_2$ part Peach Schnapps
1 part Cranberry Juice Cocktail
1 part Sour Mix
Highball Glass

Shake with ice and pour

Pluto

1 part Vodka
1 part Peach Schnapps
1 part Lime Cordial
$^1/_2$ part Blue Curaçao
Old-Fashioned Glass

Shake with ice and strain over ice

Plutonium Q 26 Space Modulator

1 part Vodka
1 part Cherry Juice
1 part Lemonade
1 part Orange Juice
1 part Cola
Highball Glass

Build over ice and stir

Pocket Ball

1 part Apricot Brandy
1 part Orange Juice
1 part Sour Mix
Whiskey Sour Glass

Shake with ice and strain over ice

Poison Sumac

2 parts Vodka
1 part Blue Curaçao
1 part Orange Juice
Highball Glass

Shake with ice and strain over ice

Poker Face

$1^1/_2$ parts Tequila
$^1/_2$ part Triple Sec
fill with Pineapple Juice
Highball Glass

Build over ice and stir

Polar Bear

1 part Vodka
1 part Triple Sec
1 part Maraschino Liqueur
1 scoop Vanilla Ice Cream
1 Egg White
Highball Glass

Shake with ice and pour

Polish Red Hair
1 part Vodka
$1/2$ part Amaretto
$1/2$ part Lime Cordial
splash Grenadine
fill with Cola
Old-Fashioned Glass

Build over ice and stir

Polly's Special
$1\,1/2$ parts Scotch
$1/2$ part Triple Sec
$1/2$ part Grapefruit Juice
Highball Glass

Shake with ice and strain

Polonaise
$1\,1/2$ parts Brandy
$1/2$ part Dry Sherry
splash Blackberry Brandy
splash Lemon Juice
Old-Fashioned Glass

Shake with ice and strain over ice

Polynesian
1 part Rum
1 part Banana Juice
1 part Piña Colada Mix
1 part Lemonade
1 part Pineapple Juice
Highball Glass

Shake with ice and pour

Pompier Highball
1 part Triple Sec
1 part Crème de Cassis
fill with Sparkling Water
Collins Glass

Build over ice and stir

Pontiac
1 part Coconut-Flavored Liqueur
1 part Parfait Amour
1 part Cranberry Juice Cocktail
1 part Lemon-Lime Soda
Highball Glass

Build over ice and stir

Poolside Tropical
$1\,1/2$ parts Tequila Reposado
$1/2$ part Blue Curaçao
$1/2$ part Coconut-Flavored Liqueur
fill with Orange Juice
Old-Fashioned Glass

Shake with ice and strain over ice

Popsicle®
1 part Amaretto
1 part Orange Juice
1 part Cream
Highball Glass

Shake with ice and pour

Porcupine
1 part Scotch
1 part Cointreau®
$1/2$ part Amaretto
$1\,1/2$ parts Grapefruit Juice
$1\,1/2$ parts Pineapple Juice
Highball Glass

Shake with ice and strain over ice

Porky Bone
1 part Vodka
$1/2$ part Maple Syrup
1 part Cinnamon Schnapps
2 parts Coffee Liqueur
Highball Glass

Stir gently with ice

Porn Star
1 part Blue Curaçao
1 part Raspberry Liqueur
fill with Lemon-Lime Soda
Highball Glass

Build over ice and stir

Port Light
1 part Bourbon
1 part Honey
1 Egg White
Old-Fashioned Glass

Shake with ice and strain over ice

Portuguese in Love
1 part Raspberry Liqueur
2 parts White Port
1 part Apple Juice
Old-Fashioned Glass

Shake with ice and strain over ice

Prado
1 1/2 parts Tequila
3/4 part Lemon Juice
splash Grenadine
splash Maraschino Cherry
1 Egg White
Whiskey Sour Glass

Shake with ice and strain over ice

Prairie Pearl
1 part Amaretto
1/2 part Limoncello
1/2 part Galliano®
fill with Milk
Highball Glass

Shake with ice and strain over ice

Praline & Cream
2 parts Praline Liqueur
fill with Cream
Highball Glass

Shake with ice and strain over ice

Praying for Liberty
1 part Currant-Flavored Vodka
1/2 part Triple Sec
1/2 part Plum Brandy
1/2 part Lemon Juice
fill with Pineapple Juice
Highball Glass

Shake with ice and strain over ice

Praying Mantis
1 1/2 parts Tequila
2 splashes Lime Juice
splash Lemon Juice
fill with Cola
Highball Glass

Build over ice and stir

Predator
1 part Brandy
1 part Light Rum
1/2 part Apricot Brandy
1/2 part Benedictine®
1 part Lemon Juice
1/2 part Simple Syrup
Highball Glass

Shake with ice and strain over ice

Presbyterian
1 part Whiskey
1 part Club Soda
1 part Ginger Ale
Highball Glass

Build over ice and stir

Pretty in Pink
2 parts Dark Rum
1 part Cream
Old-Fashioned Glass

Shake with ice and strain over ice

Prima Donna
1/2 part Galliano®
2 parts Passion Fruit Liqueur
2 parts Orange Juice
splash Lemon Juice
Highball Glass

Shake with ice and strain over ice

Primavera
1 part Dry Gin
1 part Grapefruit Juice
1/2 part Blue Curaçao
1/2 part Triple Sec
Highball Glass

Shake with ice and strain over ice

Prince of Darkness
1 1/2 parts Scotch
1 part Coffee Liqueur
splash Club Soda
Old-Fashioned Glass

Build over ice and stir

Prince of Norway
3/4 part Vodka
3/4 part Apricot Brandy
1/4 part Lime Juice
fill with Lemon-Lime Soda
Highball Glass

Build over ice and stir

Princess
1 part Crème de Banana
1 part Dark Rum
1 part Lemon Juice
Highball Glass

Shake with ice and strain over ice

Professor and Mary Ann
1 1/2 parts Vodka
1/2 part Apricot Brandy
1/4 part Lime Juice
fill with Carbonated Water
Highball Glass

Build over ice and stir

Prussian Winter
1 part Vanilla Liqueur
1/2 part Goldschläger®
splash Lemon Juice
fill with Cranberry Juice Cocktail
splash Honey
Highball Glass

Shake with ice and strain

Psycho
1 part Light Rum
1 part Galliano®
1 part Orange Juice
1 part Pineapple Juice
splash Grenadine
Highball Glass

Shake with ice and pour

Public Library
1 part Sambuca
1 part Black Currant Syrup
fill with Piña Colada Mix
Brandy Snifter

Shake with ice and pour

Pucker Up
1 part Apple Liqueur
2 parts Sour Apple Schnapps
3 parts Lemon-Lime Soda
splash Lemon Juice
Highball Glass

Build over ice and stir

Puerto Plata

2 parts Light Rum
$1/2$ part Blue Curaçao
$1/2$ part Dark Rum
2 parts Pineapple Juice
$1 1/2$ parts Orange Juice
Highball Glass

Shake with ice and strain over ice

Puerto Rican Sky Rocket

1 part Vodka
1 part Tequila Reposado
$1/2$ part Galliano®
fill with Orange Juice
Highball Glass

Shake with ice and strain over ice

Punch Drunk

1 part Spiced Rum
1 part Light Rum
splash Blackberry Liqueur
fill with Pineapple Juice
$1/2$ part Lemon Juice
dash Powdered Sugar
Highball Glass

Shake with ice and strain over ice

Purple

1 part Southern Comfort®
1 part Blue Curaçao
1 part Blueberry Schnapps
1 part Sloe Gin
splash Lime Juice
splash Sour Mix
splash Lemon-Lime Soda
Old-Fashioned Glass

Shake with ice and strain over ice

Purple Chevy

1 part Vodka
1 part Cherry Juice
1 part Wild Berry Schnapps
1 part Sour Mix
2 parts Orange Juice
Highball Glass

Shake with ice and pour

Purple Death

1 part Blue Curaçao
2 parts Wild Berry Schnapps
splash Grenadine
fill with Red Bull® Energy Drink
Highball Glass

Build over ice and stir

Purple Devil

1 part Triple Sec
1 part Cointreau®
1 part Amaretto
fill with Cranberry Juice Cocktail
splash Lemon-Lime Soda
Highball Glass

Shake with ice and strain over ice

Purple Dinosaur

1 part Vodka
1 part Blue Curaçao
1 part Wild Berry Schnapps
1 part Orange Juice
1 part Cranberry Juice Cocktail
Highball Glass

Shake with ice and strain over ice

Purple Hard-on

1 part Cherry Liqueur
1 part Southern Comfort®
fill with Sour Mix
splash Lemon-Lime Soda
Highball Glass

Build over ice and stir

Purple Jesus
2 parts Vodka
1 part Ginger Ale
1 part Grape Juice (Red)
Highball Glass
Build over ice and stir

Purple Lobster
1 1/2 parts Crown Royal® Whiskey
1 1/2 parts Raspberry Liqueur
1 part Cranberry Juice Cocktail
1 part Lemon-Lime Soda
Highball Glass
Build over ice and stir

Purple Moon
1 part Vodka
1 part Blue Curaçao
1 part Cherry Juice
1 part Lemonade
1 part Cranberry Juice Cocktail
Highball Glass
Shake with ice and pour

Purple Nurple
1 part Vodka
1 part Grape Juice (Red)
2 parts Wild Berry Schnapps
Highball Glass
Shake with ice and pour

Purple Passion Tea
1/4 part Vodka
1/4 part Rum
1/4 part Gin
1/2 part Blackberry Liqueur
1 part Sour Mix
1 part Lemon-Lime Soda
Highball Glass
Build over ice and stir

Purple Pussycat
1 part Vodka
1 part Cherry Juice
1 part Wild Berry Schnapps
fill with Pineapple Juice
Highball Glass
Shake with ice and strain over ice

Purple Rose of Cairo
1 part Citrus-Flavored Vodka
1 part Raspberry Liqueur
fill with Cranberry Juice Cocktail
Highball Glass
Shake with ice and strain over ice

Purple Russian
2 parts Vodka
2 parts Raspberry Liqueur
1 part Cream
Highball Glass
Shake with ice and pour

Push Up
2 parts Vodka
splash Grenadine
1 part Lemon-Lime Soda
1 part Orange Juice
Highball Glass
Build over ice and stir

Pushkin
1 part Crème de Cacao (White)
1 part Vodka
1 part Gin
Old-Fashioned Glass
Shake with ice and strain over ice

Putting Green
$1^1/_2$ parts Melon Liqueur
$^3/_4$ part Gin
$1^1/_2$ parts Lemon Juice
$1^1/_2$ parts Orange Juice
Highball Glass
Shake with ice and pour

Quarter Deck
$1^1/_2$ parts Light Rum
splash Sherry
splash Lime Juice
Highball Glass
Shake with ice and strain over ice

Quashbuckler
2 parts Vodka
1 part Gin
1 part Orange Juice
1 part Strawberry Juice
Highball Glass
Shake with ice and strain over ice

Queen of Hearts
1 part Amaretto
1 part Melon Liqueur
1 part Blue Curaçao
fill with Cranberry Juice Cocktail
Highball Glass
Shake with ice and pour

Qui Oui
$^2/_3$ part Kiwi Schnapps
$1^1/_2$ part Orange Juice
Highball Glass
Shake with ice and strain over ice

Quick Slammer
1 part Whiskey
1 part Sloe Gin
$^1/_2$ part Sour Apple Schnapps
fill with Cola
Old-Fashioned Glass
Build over ice and stir

Quickset
$1^1/_2$ parts Gin
1 part Blackberry Liqueur
1 part Cranberry Juice Cocktail
1 part Pineapple Juice
Highball Glass
Shake with ice and strain over ice

Quicksilver
1 part Anisette
1 part Triple Sec
1 part Tequila
Highball Glass
Shake with ice and strain over ice

R&B
$1^1/_2$ parts Spiced Rum
1 part Orange Juice
1 part Pineapple Juice
splash Grenadine
Highball Glass
Build over ice and stir

Race Day Tea
1 part Light Rum
$^2/_3$ part Crème de Cacao (Dark)
$^1/_2$ part Lemon Juice
dash Powdered Sugar
fill with Iced Tea
Highball Glass
Build over ice and stir

Radical Sabatical
1 part Amaretto
1 part Blackberry Liqueur
2 parts Sour Mix
3 parts Pineapple Juice
Highball Glass

Shake with ice and strain over ice

Radioactive Lemonade
1 part Vodka
1 part Amaretto
fill with Lemonade
splash Wild Berry Schnapps
Highball Glass

Build over ice

Raggae Sunsplash
2 parts Gin
2 splashes Strawberry Syrup
2 splashes Melon Liqueur
fill with Pineapple Juice
Highball Glass

Shake with ice and strain over ice

Raggedy Andy®
1 part Cranberry-Flavored Vodka
1 part Cream
1 part Crème de Cacao (Dark)
1/2 part Crème de Banana
Old-Fashioned Glass

Shake with ice and strain over ice

Ragin' Cajun
1 part Tequila Silver
1 part Vodka
dash Cayenne Pepper
dash Salt
Old-Fashioned Glass

Shake with ice and strain over ice

Raging Ratoga
1 part Melon Liqueur
1 part Amaretto
1 part Cranberry-Flavored Vodka
fill with Pineapple Juice
Highball Glass

Build over ice and stir

Rainbow Brite®
1 part Gin
2 parts Tonic Water
1 scoop Rainbow Sherbert
Old-Fashioned Glass

Build in the glass with no ice

Rainstorm
1 part Vodka
1 part Blue Curaçao
2 parts Lemonade
1 part Cola
Highball Glass

Shake with ice and strain over ice

Rainy Day Marley
1 part Vodka
1 part Triple Sec
1 part Coconut-Flavored Rum
fill with Orange Juice
Highball Glass

Build over ice and stir

Rampancy
2 parts Tequila Silver
2/3 part Coconut-Flavored Liqueur
fill with Pineapple Juice
Highball Glass

Shake with ice and strain over ice

Raspberry Breeze
1 part Vodka
2 parts Raspberry Liqueur
1 part Pineapple Juice
1 part Cranberry Juice Cocktail
Highball Glass
Shake with ice and pour

Raspberry Lynchburg
1 1/2 parts Whiskey
2/3 part Raspberry Liqueur
1 part Lemon Juice
1/2 part Simple Syrup
Old-Fashioned Glass
Shake with ice and pour

Raspberry Romance
3/4 part Coffee Liqueur
3/4 part Blackberry Liqueur
1 1/4 parts Irish Cream Liqueur
Old-Fashioned Glass
Build over ice and stir

Rastafari
1 part Crème de Banana
1 part Spiced Rum
fill with Cream
Old-Fashioned Glass
Shake with ice and strain over ice

Rattlesnake Shake
1 part Kiwi Schnapps
1 part Light Rum
1 part Cranberry Juice Cocktail
fill with Orange Juice
Highball Glass
Shake with ice and strain over ice

Rauhreif
1 part Gin
1 part Blue Curaçao
2 splashes Grenadine
3 splashes Lemon Juice
Highball Glass
Shake with ice and pour

Real World
1 part Calvados Apple Brandy
1/2 part Frangelico®
1/2 part Hazelnut Liqueur
splash Amaretto
2 parts Cream
Highball Glass
Shake with ice and strain over ice

Rebel Charge
1/2 part Triple Sec
splash Lemon Juice
splash Orange Juice
1 Egg White
Old-Fashioned Glass
Shake with ice and strain over ice

Rebel Russian
1 part Southern Comfort®
1 part Coffee Liqueur
fill with Half and Half
Highball Glass
Shake with ice and pour

Rebel Yell
2 parts Bourbon
1/2 part Triple Sec
1 part Lemon Juice
1 Egg White
Old-Fashioned Glass
Shake with ice and strain over ice

Recrimination
1/2 part Crème de Cassis
1 part Calvados Apple Brandy
1/2 part Armagnac
2/3 part Lemon Juice
2 parts Raspberry-Flavored Seltzer
Highball Glass
Build over ice and stir

Red Alert
1/2 part Tequila Silver
1/2 part Banana Liqueur
1 part Sloe Gin
fill with Sour Mix
Highball Glass
Shake with ice and pour

Red Baby
1 part Southern Comfort®
1 part Vodka
1 part Amaretto
1/2 part Grenadine
1 part Orange Juice
1 part Lemon Juice
Highball Glass
Shake with ice and pour

Red Baron
1 1/2 parts Vodka
fill with Orange Juice
splash Grenadine
Highball Glass
Build over ice

Red Devil
1 part Vodka
1 part Southern Comfort®
1 part Triple Sec
1 part Banana Liqueur
1 part Sloe Gin
splash Lime Juice
fill with Orange Juice
Highball Glass
Shake with ice and pour

Red Dwarf
2 parts Light Rum
1 part Peach Schnapps
1/2 part Crème de Cassis
1/2 part Lemon Juice
fill with Orange Juice
Highball Glass
Shake with ice and pour

Redhead on the Moon
1/2 part Vodka
1/2 part Melon Liqueur
1/2 part Sour Apple Schnapps
1 part Sour Mix
splash Cranberry Juice Cocktail
fill with Lemon-Lime Soda
Highball Glass
Build over ice and stir

Red Hope
2 parts Gin
1 part Crème de Banana
1/2 part Apricot Brandy
splash Strawberry Syrup
Old-Fashioned Glass
Shake with ice and strain over ice

Red Hot Mama
1 1/2 parts Light Rum
2 parts Cranberry Juice Cocktail
1 part Club Soda
Highball Glass
Build over ice and stir

Red Hurricane
1 part Bacardi® Limón Rum
1 part Tequila
fill with Cranberry Juice Cocktail
Highball Glass
Build over ice and stir

Red Jewel

splash Cinnamon Schnapps
1 part Amaretto
1 part Bourbon
Highball Glass

Shake with ice and strain over ice

Red Rage

1 part Jägermeister®
1 part Vodka
fill with Red Bull® Energy Drink
Highball Glass

Build over ice and stir

Red Rasputin

2 parts Vodka
1 part Grenadine
fill with Cola
Highball Glass

Build over ice and stir

Red Snapper

1 part Crown Royal® Whiskey
1 part Amaretto
fill with Cranberry Juice Cocktail
Highball Glass

Shake with ice and pour

Red Tea Stinger

2 parts Cinnamon Schnapps
fill with Iced Tea
Highball Glass

Build over ice and stir

Red Velvet

1 part Gin
1/2 part Pisang Ambon® Liqueur
1/2 part Lime Juice
fill with Lemon-Lime Soda
splash Grenadine
Highball Glass

Build over ice

Redheads and Blondes

1 part Strawberry Liqueur
1 part Peach Schnapps
1 part Coconut-Flavored Rum
1 part Strawberry Juice
1 part Pineapple Juice
Highball Glass

Build over ice and stir

Reggata the Blank

1 part Dry Gin
1 part Light Rum
1 part Amaretto
1 part Pineapple Juice
1 part Orange Juice
dash Orange Bitters
Old-Fashioned Glass

Shake with ice and pour

Rest in Peace

1 part Jack Daniel's®
1/2 part Vodka
1/2 part Tequila
1/2 part Jim Beam®
Highball Glass

Shake with ice and strain over ice

Richelieu

1 part Bourbon
1/2 part Vanilla Liqueur
1/4 part Lillet®
Old-Fashioned Glass

Shake with ice and strain over ice

Riedinger
$1\frac{1}{2}$ parts Light Rum
1 part Midori®
1 part Lime Juice
fill with Cola
Highball Glass

Build over ice and stir

Rigor Mortis
$1\frac{1}{2}$ parts Vodka
$\frac{3}{4}$ part Amaretto
1 part Pineapple Juice
1 part Orange Juice
Old-Fashioned Glass

Shake with ice and strain over ice

Rio Blanco
1 part Dark Rum
$\frac{1}{2}$ part Crème de Cacao (Dark)
$\frac{1}{2}$ part Triple Sec
splash Fresh Lime Juice
Old-Fashioned Glass

Shake with ice and strain over ice

Rio's Carnival
$1\frac{1}{2}$ parts Cachaça®
$\frac{1}{2}$ part Vanilla Liqueur
splash Lemon Juice
$\frac{1}{2}$ part Sweetened Lime Juice
$1\frac{1}{2}$ parts Orange Juice
Highball Glass

Shake with ice and strain over ice

Ritz Bellboy
$\frac{2}{3}$ part Crème de Banana
$\frac{1}{2}$ part Dry Vermouth
1 part Jim Beam®
1 part Orange Juice
Old-Fashioned Glass

Shake with ice and strain over ice

Rivaldinho
2 parts Cachaça®
splash Coconut-Flavored Liqueur
Highball Glass

Build over ice and stir

Roadkill
3 parts Amaretto
1 part Grenadine
fill with Dr Pepper®
Old-Fashioned Glass

Build over ice and stir

Roadrunner
1 part Tia Maria®
1 part Grand Marnier®
Old-Fashioned Glass

Shake with ice and strain over ice

Roadrunner #2
1 part Vodka
$\frac{1}{2}$ part Amaretto
$\frac{1}{2}$ part Coconut Cream
Champagne Flute

Shake with ice and strain over ice

Robert Paulsen
2 parts Southern Comfort®
2 parts Cola
1 part Cranberry Juice Cocktail
Highball Glass

Build over ice and stir

Robitussin®
1 part Cherry Liqueur
1 part Root Beer Schnapps
Highball Glass

Shake with ice and strain over ice

Robson
$1^1/_2$ parts Rum
splash Grenadine
splash Lemon Juice
splash Orange Juice
Old-Fashioned Glass

Shake with ice and strain over ice

Rocking Root Beer
$1^1/_2$ parts Root Beer Schnapps
$^2/_3$ part Crème de Cacao (Dark)
3 parts Cream
1 part Cola
Highball Glass

Shake with ice and strain over ice

Rocky Dane
1 part Gin
1 part Cherry Brandy
1 part Kirschwasser
$^1/_2$ part Dry Vermouth
Old-Fashioned Glass

Shake with ice and strain over ice

Rocky Mountain High
1 part Southern Comfort®
1 part Amaretto
fill with Cranberry Juice Cocktail
Highball Glass

Build over ice and stir

Roller
$1^1/_2$ parts Vodka
splash Amaretto
splash Melon Liqueur
fill with Cranberry Juice Cocktail
Highball Glass

Shake with ice and pour

Rolling Green Elixer
$1^1/_2$ parts Peach Schnapps
1 part Blue Curaçao
$^1/_2$ part Vodka
fill with Cranberry Juice Cocktail
Highball Glass

Build over ice and stir

Roman Riot
1 part Sambuca
1 part Galliano®
1 part Amaretto
Old-Fashioned Glass

Shake with ice and strain

Romantica
1 part Bacardi® Limón Rum
1 part Sweet Vermouth
Highball Glass

Shake with ice and strain over ice

Romulan Ale
$1^1/_2$ parts Light Rum
1 part Blue Curaçao
fill with Lemon-Lime Soda
splash Tabasco® Sauce
Highball Glass

Build over ice

Romulan Dream
1 part Grand Marnier®
1 part Blue Curaçao
1 part Lemon Juice
Highball Glass

Shake with ice and strain over ice

Root Beer
1 part Coffee Liqueur
1 part Galliano®
1 part Lemon Juice
dash Powdered Sugar
fill with Cola
Highball Glass

Build over ice and stir

Rooty Tooty
2 parts Root Beer Schnapps
fill with Orange Juice
Highball Glass

Shake with ice and pour

Rosalita
1 1/2 parts Tequila
1 part Campari®
1/2 part Sweet Vermouth
1/2 part Dry Vermouth
Highball Glass

Shake with ice and pour

Roscoe
1 part Jack Daniel's®
1 part Melon Liqueur
Highball Glass

Shake with ice and pour

Rose Hall Nightcap
2 parts Cognac
1 part Pernod®
1/2 part Crème de Cacao (Dark)
Old-Fashioned Glass

Shake with ice and strain over ice

Rosemary
1 part Jim Beam®
1 part Apricot Brandy
splash Crème de Banana
splash Lemon Juice
Highball Glass

Shake with ice and strain over ice

Round Robin
1 part Absinthe
1 part Brandy
1 Egg White
dash Sugar
White Wine Glass

Shake with ice and strain

Rowdy German
1 part Coffee Liqueur
1 part Bacardi® Limón Rum
1 part Jägermeister®
Highball Glass

Shake with ice and strain over ice

Roxanne
3/4 part Vodka
3/4 part Peach Schnapps
1/2 part Amaretto
1/2 part Orange Juice
1/2 part Cranberry Juice Cocktail
Old-Fashioned Glass

Shake with ice and strain over ice

Royal Gin Fizz
2 parts Gin
1/2 part Lemon Juice
dash Powdered Sugar
1 Whole Egg
fill with Carbonated Water
Highball Glass

Shake all but Carbonated Water with ice and strain into the glass. Top with Carbonated Water.

Royal Lemon
1 part Crown Royal® Whiskey
fill with Pink Lemonade
Highball Glass

Shake with ice and pour

Royal Nightcap

2 parts Goldschläger®
dash Powdered Sugar
fill with Milk
Highball Glass

Shake with ice and pour

Rub-a-Dub-Dub

1 part Dark Rum
1/2 part Apricot Brandy
1/2 part Galliano®
1/2 part Lime Juice
fill with Pineapple Juice
Highball Glass

Shake with ice and strain over ice

Rubber Chicken

3 parts Rye Whiskey
1 part Limeade
1 part Ginger Ale
Highball Glass

Build over ice and stir

Rubenstein's Revenge

1 part Vodka
1 part Cranberry Juice Cocktail
1 part Gin
1 part Orange Juice
1 part Tonic Water
Highball Glass

Shake with ice and strain over ice

Ruby Fizz

2 parts Sloe Gin
splash Grenadine
1/2 part Lemon Juice
dash Powdered Sugar
1 Egg White
fill with Carbonated Water
Highball Glass

Shake all but Carbonated Water with ice and strain into the glass. Top with Carbonated Water.

Ruby Tuesday

2 parts Gin
2 splashes Grenadine
fill with Cranberry Juice Cocktail
Highball Glass

Build over ice and stir

Rudolph the Red-Nosed Reindeer®

1 1/4 parts Light Rum
1 1/2 parts Lemon Juice
1/2 part Grenadine
Highball Glass

Shake with ice and strain over ice

Rum Boogie

1 part Dark Rum
1/2 part Amaretto
splash Lime Juice
fill with Cola
Highball Glass

Build over ice and stir

Rum Cure

1 part 151-Proof Rum
1 part Brandy
splash Blue Curaçao
1 part Pineapple Juice
1 part Orange Juice
1 part Lemon Juice
splash Grenadine
Highball Glass

Shake with ice and strain over ice

Rum Runner
1/2 part Light Rum
1/2 part Spiced Rum
1/2 part Crème de Banana
1/2 part Blackberry Brandy
1 part Sour Mix
1 part Orange Juice
Old-Fashioned Glass

Shake with ice and pour

Rum Scoundrel
1 part Light Rum
1/2 part Lime Juice
dash Sugar
Old-Fashioned Glass

Shake with ice and pour

Rum Sour
2 parts Light Rum
1/2 part Lemon Juice
dash Powdered Sugar
Whiskey Sour Glass

Shake with ice and strain over ice

Rum Spice Whacker
1 part Spiced Rum
1 part Coffee Liqueur
2 parts Coconut Cream
Old-Fashioned Glass

Shake with ice and strain over ice

Rum Ta Tum
1 part Rum
1 part Cherry Juice
1 part Lemonade
1 part Pineapple Juice
Highball Glass

Shake with ice and pour

Rumple
1 part Light Rum
1 part Coconut-Flavored Rum
1 part Bacardi® Limón Rum
fill with Orange Juice
Highball Glass

Build over ice and stir

Runaway
1 part Triple Sec
1 part Tequila Gold
fill with Grape Juice (Red)
Highball Glass

Build over ice and stir

Runaway Train
1 part Rum
1 part Triple Sec
1 part Sour Mix
1 part Grapefruit Juice
1 part Cola
Highball Glass

Build over ice and stir

Ruptured Duck
1 part Crème de Noyaux
1 part Banana Liqueur
1 part Cream
Highball Glass

Shake with ice and strain over ice

Russian Banana
1 part Vodka
1 part Crème de Cacao (White)
1 part Banana Liqueur
fill with Cream
Highball Glass

Shake with ice and strain over ice

Russian Chameleon
1 part Blue Curaçao
2 parts Vodka
fill with Orange Juice
Highball Glass
Build over ice and stir

Russian Cream
2 parts Vodka
1 part Coffee Liqueur
1 part Irish Cream Liqueur
Old-Fashioned Glass
Shake with ice and pour

Russian Jack
1 part Vodka
1 part Jack Daniel's®
fill with Sour Mix
Highball Glass
Shake with ice and pour

Russian Quaalude
1 part Vodka
1 part Irish Cream Liqueur
1 part Frangelico®
Highball Glass
Shake with ice and strain over ice

Russian Quartet
1 part Vodka
1 part Peppermint Schnapps
1 part Coffee Liqueur
1 part Irish Cream Liqueur
1 part Amaretto
1 part Half and Half
Old-Fashioned Glass
Shake with ice and strain over ice

Russian Turkey
1 part Vodka
1 part Cranberry Juice Cocktail
Old-Fashioned Glass
Shake with ice and strain over ice

Rusty Mist
1 part Drambuie®
1 part Irish Mist®
Old-Fashioned Glass
Build over ice

Rusty Nail
1 1/2 parts Scotch
1/2 part Drambuie®
Old-Fashioned Glass
Build over ice and stir

Rye and Dry
1 part Dry Vermouth
1/2 part Whiskey
Old-Fashioned Glass
Shake with ice and strain over ice

Safari Juice
1 part Cointreau®
1 part Midori®
fill with Orange Juice
splash Grenadine
Highball Glass
Build over ice

Saint Paul
1 part Gin
1 part Light Rum
dash Angostura® Bitters
Highball Glass
Shake with ice and strain over ice

Salisbury Special
1 part Vodka
1 part Raspberry Liqueur
1 part Cola
1 part Orange Juice
Cordial Glass

Build over ice and stir

Salty Dog
1 1/2 parts Gin
dash Salt
fill with Grapefruit Juice
Highball Glass

Shake with ice and pour

Samba
1 1/2 parts Light Rum
1/2 part Triple Sec
1/4 part Grenadine
1 part Pineapple Juice
1 part Orange Juice
Highball Glass

Shake with ice and pour

Samba de Janeiro
1 1/2 parts Gin
1/2 part Apricot Brandy
1/2 part Lime Juice
Old-Fashioned Glass

Shake with ice and strain over ice

Sambario
1 part Vodka
1/2 part Apricot Brandy
1/2 part Dry Vermouth
Highball Glass

Build over ice and stir

Sambrazinha
2 parts Cachaca®
1/2 part Fresh Lime Juice
fill with Cola
Old-Fashioned Glass

Build over ice and stir

San Diego Silver Bullet
1 part Vodka
1 part Sambuca
Old-Fashioned Glass

Shake with ice and strain over ice

San Fransisco Driver
1 part Vodka
1 part Sour Mix
1 part Orange Juice
Highball Glass

Shake with ice and pour

Sancho Panza
2 parts Cream Sherry
3/4 part Campari®
dash Angostura® Bitters
Sherry Glass

Build in the glass with no ice

Sanctuary
1 1/2 parts Dubonnet® Blonde
3/4 part Cointreau®
3/4 part Amer Picon®
Old-Fashioned Glass

Shake with ice and strain over ice

Sandra Buys a Dog
1 part Dark Rum
1 part Añejo Rum
3 parts Cranberry Juice Cocktail
1 part Orange Juice
dash Bitters
Highball Glass

Shake with ice and strain over ice

Santa Fe
1 1/4 parts Tequila
1/2 part Triple Sec
fill with Lemon-Lime Soda
Highball Glass

Build over ice and stir

Saratoga Swim
1 part Citrus-Flavored Vodka
1 part Peach Schnapps
1/2 part Passion Fruit Liqueur
1 part Sour Mix
fill with Orange Juice
Highball Glass

Build over ice and stir

Saronnada
1 1/2 parts Vodka
1 1/2 parts Pineapple Juice
3/4 part Amaretto
3/4 part Coconut Cream
White Wine Glass

Shake with ice and strain

Satin Angel
1 part Frangelico®
fill with Cream
splash Cola
Highball Glass

Build over ice and stir

Saturn's Rings
1 part Vodka
1 part Raspberry Liqueur
1 part Lemon-Lime Soda
1 part Orange Juice
1 part Cranberry Juice Cocktail
Highball Glass

Shake with ice and pour

Scarecrow
1 1/2 parts Light Rum
1 part Peach Schnapps
splash Crème de Cassis
splash Lemon Juice
fill with Orange Juice
Highball Glass

Shake with ice and strain over ice

Scarlet O'Hara
2 parts Southern Comfort®
fill with Cranberry Juice Cocktail
Highball Glass

Build over ice and stir

Schmegma
1 1/2 parts 151-Proof Rum
1 part Pineapple Juice
1 part Cranberry Juice Cocktail
splash Triple Sec
splash Grenadine
splash Orange Juice
splash Lemon-Lime Soda
Highball Glass

Shake with ice and strain over ice

Schnorkel
2 parts Dark Rum
1/2 part Pernod®
1 part Lime Juice
dash Sugar
Highball Glass

Shake with ice and strain over ice

Scooby Snack®
1 part Melon Liqueur
1 part Rum
1 part Milk
Highball Glass

Shake with ice and pour

Scooley Slammer
1 part Triple Sec
1 part Peach Schnapps
2 parts Sour Mix
fill with Lemon-Lime Soda
Old-Fashioned Glass

Stir gently with ice

Scotch Bird Flyer
$1^1/_2$ parts Scotch
$^1/_2$ part Triple Sec
1 part Light Cream
dash Powdered Sugar
1 Egg Yolk
Champagne Flute

Shake with ice and strain

Scotch Cobbler
2 parts Scotch
1 part Brandy
1 part Blue Curaçao
Old-Fashioned Glass

Shake with ice and strain over ice

Scotch Dream
1 part Scotch
splash Orange Liqueur
splash Crème de Banana
Highball Glass

Shake with ice and strain over ice

Scotch Explorer
$1^1/_2$ parts Scotch
$^1/_2$ part Amaretto
$^1/_2$ part Sherry
Old-Fashioned Glass

Shake with ice and strain over ice

Scotch Rickey
$1^1/_2$ parts Scotch
$^1/_2$ part Lime Juice
fill with Carbonated Water
Highball Glass

Build over ice and stir

Scotch Sour
$1^1/_2$ parts Scotch
$^1/_2$ part Lime Juice
dash Powdered Sugar
1 Lemon Slice
Whiskey Sour Glass

Shake with ice and strain over ice

Scottish Surprise
2 parts Scotch
2 parts Passion Fruit Juice
$^1/_2$ part Grenadine
dash Bitters
Old-Fashioned Glass

Shake with ice and strain over ice

Scratch and Sniff
$1^1/_2$ parts Tequila
$^1/_2$ part Raspberry Liqueur
1 part Pineapple Juice
1 part Orange Juice
Highball Glass

Shake with ice and pour

Screamin' Blue
1 part Gin
1 part Vodka
1 part Light Rum
1 part Triple Sec
1 part Banana Liqueur
1 part Blue Curaçao
1 part Pineapple Juice
1 part Sour Mix
Highball Glass

Shake with ice and strain over ice

Screamin' Coyote
1 part Crème de Menthe (White)
1 part Goldschläger®
1 part Absolut® Peppar Vodka
splash Tabasco® Sauce
Old-Fashioned Glass

Shake with ice and strain over ice

Screaming Blue Monkey
3/4 part Vodka
1 part Blue Curaçao
1 part Banana Liqueur
fill with Sour Mix
Highball Glass

Shake with ice and strain over ice

Screaming Mimi
3 parts Irish Cream Liqueur
3 parts Crème de Cacao (White)
1 part Grenadine
Highball Glass

Shake with ice and strain over ice

Screaming White Orgasm
1 part Irish Cream Liqueur
1 part Coffee Liqueur
1 part Rum
splash Cointreau®
splash Milk
Highball Glass

Shake with ice and strain over ice

Screwdriver
2 parts Vodka
fill with Orange Juice
Highball Glass

Build over ice and stir

Screwdriver Boricua
2 parts Vodka
1 part Orange Juice
1 part Cranberry Juice Cocktail
Highball Glass

Build over ice and stir

Screwlimer
2 parts Vodka
splash Lime Juice
fill with Orange Juice
Highball Glass

Build over ice and stir

Sea Breeze
1 1/2 parts Vodka
3 parts Cranberry Juice Cocktail
1 part Grapefruit Juice
Highball Glass

Build over ice and stir

Sea Horses
2/3 part Blue Curaçao
splash Irish Cream Liqueur
1 part Orange-Flavored Vodka
Highball Glass

Shake with ice and strain over ice

Sea Siren
1 part Light Rum
1 part Pineapple Juice
1 part Guava Juice
splash Grenadine
Old-Fashioned Glass

Shake with ice and strain over ice

Sea Turtle
1 part Melon Liqueur
1 part Vodka
2 parts Pineapple Juice
splash Grenadine
Old-Fashioned Glass

Shake with ice and strain over ice

Seaboard
1 part Whiskey
1 part Gin
splash Lemon Juice
dash Powdered Sugar
Old-Fashioned Glass

Shake with ice and strain over ice

Seagle
1 part Crème de Cacao (White)
splash Blue Curaçao
splash Scotch
2/3 part Cream
splash Strawberry Syrup
Old-Fashioned Glass

Shake with ice and strain over ice

Seamen Special
1 part Gin
1 part Sour Apple Schnapps
1 part Lemon Juice
2 parts Apple Cider
Old-Fashioned Glass

Shake with ice and strain over ice

Secret Blue
1 1/2 parts Vodka
1/2 part Lime
dash Sugar
splash Blue Curaçao
Highball Glass

Shake with ice and strain over ice

Seduction on the Rocks
1/2 part Butterscotch Schnapps
1/2 part Lemon-Lime Soda
fill with Orange Juice
Old-Fashioned Glass

Build over ice and stir

Seesaw
1 part Vodka
1 part Light Rum
1/2 part Dark Rum
2 parts Cranberry Juice Cocktail
2 parts Orange Juice
dash Bitters
Highball Glass

Build over ice and stir

Señor Frog
1 part Melon Liqueur
1/2 part Blue Curaçao
fill with Apple Juice
Old-Fashioned Glass

Shake with ice and strain over ice

Serena
1 part Vodka
1/2 part Strawberry-Flavored Vodka
1/2 part Dry Vermouth
1/2 part Pineapple Juice
1/2 part Blue Curaçao
splash Lemon Juice
Highball Glass

Shake with ice and pour

Serendipity
1 part Vodka
1/2 part Grand Marnier®
1/2 part Amaretto
1/2 part Triple Sec
1/4 part Grenadine
fill with Orange Juice
Highball Glass

Shake with ice and pour

Serpent's Tooth
2 parts Whiskey
1 part Sweet Vermouth
Old-Fashioned Glass

Shake with ice and strain over ice

Seven & Seven
2 parts Canadian Whiskey
fill with Lemon-Lime Soda
Highball Glass

Build over ice and stir

Seven Deadly Sins
1 part Vodka
1/2 part Sour Apple Schnapps
1/2 part Raspberry Liqueur
1/2 part Watermelon Schnapps
1 part Orange Juice
1 part Sour Mix
1 part Papaya Juice
Old-Fashioned Glass

Shake with ice and pour

Seville
2 parts Gin
1/2 part Simple Syrup
1/2 part Lemon Juice
1/2 part Orange Juice
1/2 part Sherry
Old-Fashioned Glass

Shake with ice and strain over ice

Shadowstorm
1 part Pisco
splash Triple Sec
splash Black Currant Juice
Old-Fashioned Glass

Shake with ice and strain over ice

Shady Lady
1 part Melon Liqueur
1 part Tequila
fill with Grapefruit Juice
Highball Glass

Build over ice and stir

Shalom
1 1/2 parts Vodka
1 part Madeira
splash Orange Juice
Old-Fashioned Glass

Shake with ice and strain over ice

Shark Bite
1 part Rum
fill with Orange Juice
splash Grenadine
Highball Glass

Build over ice

Shark in the Water
1 part Vodka
1 part Blue Curaçao
fill with Lemonade
splash Strawberry Daiquiri Mix
Highball Glass

Shake with ice and pour

Shavetail
1 1/2 parts Peppermint Schnapps
1 part Pineapple Juice
1 part Light Cream
Highball Glass

Shake with ice and strain over ice

Shogun

1 part Citrus-Flavored Vodka
1 part Grand Marnier®
1 part Sweetened Lime Juice
Brandy Snifter

Build in the glass with no ice

Shoot

1 part Sherry
1 part Scotch
splash Lemon Juice
splash Orange Juice
dash Powdered Sugar
Highball Glass

Shake with ice and strain over ice

Short-Sighted

1 part Vodka
1 1/2 parts Dry Vermouth
2/3 part Calvados Apple Brandy
1/2 part Triple Sec
Highball Glass

Shake with ice and strain over ice

Shotgun

1 part Citrus-Flavored Vodka
1 part Grand Marnier®
1 part Lime Juice
Brandy Snifter

Shake with ice and strain over ice

Shuddering Orgasm

1 part Amaretto
1 part Coffee Liqueur
1 part Irish Cream Liqueur
Highball Glass

Shake with ice and pour

Siberian Sleighride

1 1/4 parts Vodka
3/4 part Crème de Cacao (White)
1/2 part Crème de Cacao (Dark)
3 parts Light Cream
Highball Glass

Shake with ice and strain over ice

Siberian Slider

1 part Crème de Menthe (White)
1 part Vodka
1 part Light Rum
Old-Fashioned Glass

Shake with ice and strain over ice

Sid Vicious

1 part Whiskey
1 part Gin
1/2 part Sweet Vermouth
dash Bitters
splash Worcestershire Sauce
Old-Fashioned Glass

Build over ice and stir

Silver Bronx

2 parts Gin
splash Orange Juice
1/2 part Dry Vermouth
1/2 part Sweet Vermouth
1 Egg White
Whiskey Sour Glass

Shake with ice and strain over ice

Silver Fox

1 part Triple Sec
1 part Crème de Cacao (Dark)
1 part Cream
Highball Glass

Shake with ice and strain over ice

Silverado
1 1/2 parts Vodka
1 1/2 parts Campari®
1 part Orange Juice
Old-Fashioned Glass

Shake with ice and strain over ice

Sing Sing
2 parts Scotch
1 part Triple Sec
1 part Sweet Vermouth
Champagne Flute

Shake with ice and strain

Sink or Swim
1 1/2 parts Brandy
2 splashes Vermouth
dash Bitters
Old-Fashioned Glass

Shake with ice and strain over ice

Sino Soviet Split
2 parts Vodka
1 part Amaretto
fill with Milk
Old-Fashioned Glass

Build over ice and stir

Sir Francis
1 part Raspberry-Flavored Vodka
1 part Peach-Flavored Vodka
1 part Vanilla-Flavored Vodka
fill with Lemonade
1 part Grenadine
Highball Glass

Build over ice and stir

Skedattle
1 1/2 parts Scotch
1 part Amaretto
1 part Triple Sec
splash Maraschino Liqueur
2/3 part Lemon Juice
1 1/2 parts Orange Juice
Highball Glass

Shake with ice and strain over ice

Skeleton
1/2 part Tequila Silver
2/3 part Lemon-Lime Soda
2/3 part Blackberry Juice
Highball Glass

Build over ice and stir

Ski Slope
1 part Vodka
1 part Amaretto
1/2 part Jack Daniel's®
1/2 part Southern Comfort®
1/2 part Sloe Gin
Highball Glass

Shake with ice and pour

Skinny Dipper
2 parts Midori®
fill with Cranberry Juice Cocktail
Old-Fashioned Glass

Build over ice and stir

Skinny Pirate
3 parts Spiced Rum
splash Lemon Juice
fill with Diet Cola
Highball Glass

Build over ice and stir

Sky Symphony
1 part Blue Curaçao
$1^1/_2$ parts Grapefruit Juice
$1^1/_2$ parts Pineapple Juice
Champagne Flute

Layer over ice

Skylab
1 part Vodka
$^1/_2$ part Peach Schnapps
splash Blue Curaçao
1 part Pineapple Juice
1 part Orange Juice
1 part Lemon-Lime Soda
Highball Glass

Build over ice and stir

Slacker's Slammer
1 part Vodka
1 part Root Beer Schnapps
fill with Root Beer
1 scoop Ice Cream
Highball Glass

Build over ice

Slapshot
1 part Vodka
splash Banana Liqueur
splash Pineapple Juice
fill with Orange Juice
Highball Glass

Build over ice and stir

Sled Ride
$1^1/_2$ parts Vodka
$1^1/_2$ parts Sloe Gin
$^1/_2$ part Sour Apple Schnapps
fill with Lemon-Lime Soda
Highball Glass

Build over ice and stir

Sleepy Lemon Glegg
$^1/_2$ part Crème de Banana
$1^1/_2$ parts Dark Rum
$^1/_2$ part Lemon Juice
1 part Orange Juice
1 part Pineapple Juice
Highball Glass

Build over ice and stir

Sleezy Bitch
3 parts Strawberry Liqueur
fill with Orange Juice
Highball Glass

Build over ice and stir

Slime
2 parts Vodka
1 part Cream
1 part Melon Liqueur
Old-Fashioned Glass

Shake with ice and strain over ice

Slippery Golden Egg
1 part Goldschläger®
1 part Chartreuse®
1 Egg Yolk
Highball Glass

Shake with ice and pour

Slippery Lips
1 part Sweet Vermouth
$^1/_2$ part Triple Sec
$^1/_2$ part Orange Juice
$^1/_2$ part Sour Mix
Old-Fashioned Glass

Shake with ice and pour

Sloe Brandy
2 parts Brandy
2 splashes Sloe Gin
splash Lemon Juice
Old-Fashioned Glass

Shake with ice and strain over ice

Sloe Gin Fizz
2 parts Sloe Gin
1/2 part Lemon Juice
dash Powdered Sugar
fill with Carbonated Water
Highball Glass

Build over ice and stir

Sloehand
1 1/2 parts Sloe Gin
1 part Vodka
1 1/2 parts Orange Juice
1/2 part Lemon Juice
2 splashes Grenadine
Highball Glass

Shake with ice and strain over ice

Slow Tequila
1 part Tequila Silver
1 part Sloe Gin
1/2 part Lime Cordial
Old-Fashioned Glass

Build over ice and stir

Small Sand
1 part Gin
1 part Midori®
1/2 part Strawberry Liqueur
fill with Sour Mix
Highball Glass

Shake with ice and strain over ice

Smashed Pumpkin
1 part Vodka
1 part Orange Juice
1 part Cranberry Ginger Ale
Highball Glass

Shake with ice and pour

Smiling Irish
2 parts Irish Cream Liqueur
1 part Cognac
1 part Cream
Highball Glass

Shake with ice and pour

Smith & Kerns
1 part Coffee Liqueur
fill with Cola
Highball Glass

Build over ice and stir. Top with Cream.

Smith & Wesson®
1/2 part Coffee Liqueur
1/2 part Vodka
fill with Cola
Highball Glass

Build over ice and stir. Top with Cream.

Smooth Sailing
1 1/2 parts Vodka
1 1/2 parts Triple Sec
1/2 part Cherry Brandy
1 part Orange Juice
1 part Cranberry Juice Cocktail
Highball Glass

Build over ice and stir

Smoothberry
1 part Vodka
1 part Strawberry Liqueur
fill with Lemonade
1 part Pear Juice
Highball Glass

Build over ice and stir

Smurf®
1 part Vodka
1 parts Orange Juice
2 splashes Grenadine
splash Strawberry Daiquiri Mix
fill with Lemon-Lime Soda
Highball Glass

Build over ice and stir

Smurf® Piss
1 part Light Rum
1 part Blueberry Schnapps
1 part Blue Curaçao
1 part Sour Mix
1 part Lemon-Lime Soda
Old-Fashioned Glass

Shake with ice and strain

Sneaky Pete
1 part Coffee Liqueur
1 part Rye Whiskey
fill with Milk
Highball Glass

Build over ice and stir

Sno-Cone
2 parts Raspberry Liqueur
fill Lemon-Lime Soda
1 part Grenadine
1 part Blue Curaçao
Highball Glass

Build over ice

Snooker
1 part Gin
1 part Sloe Gin
1/2 part Orange Liqueur
fill with Orange Juice
Highball Glass

Shake with ice and strain over ice

Snoopy®
1 part Vodka
splash Crème de Banana
splash Amaretto
Highball Glass

Shake with ice and strain over ice

Snowflake
1 part Frangelico®
1 part Crème de Cacao (White)
fill with Cream
Highball Glass

Shake with ice and pour

Snow White
2 parts Southern Comfort®
1 part Vodka
1 part Pineapple Juice
1/2 part Orange Juice
Highball Glass

Shake with ice and strain over ice

Socket Wrench
2 1/2 parts Vodka
fill with Apple Juice
Highball Glass

Shake with ice and pour

Soda Cracker
2 parts Vodka
1 part Frangelico®
Old-Fashioned Glass

Build over ice and stir

Soft Love
1 part Crème de Banana
1 part Cherry Brandy
1 part Cream
splash Grenadine
Highball Glass

Shake with ice and strain over ice

Soho

$1^1/_2$ parts Crème de Cassis
$^2/_3$ part Triple Sec
1 part Grapefruit Juice
1 part Orange Juice
Highball Glass

Build over ice and stir

Sombrero

$1^1/_2$ parts Coffee-Flavored Brandy
1 part Light Cream
Old-Fashioned Glass

Build over ice

Sonora Sunset

1 part Melon Liqueur
1 part Amaretto
1 part Vodka
4 parts Orange Juice
2 parts Cranberry Juice Cocktail
Highball Glass

Build over ice

Soprano Sour

2 parts Whiskey
1 part Amaretto
$^1/_2$ part Simple Syrup
splash Campari®
Old-Fashioned Glass

Shake with ice and strain over ice

Soup

1 part Vodka
1 part Coconut-Flavored Rum
1 part Cointreau®
1 part Peach Schnapps
fill with Red Bull® Energy Drink
Highball Glass

Build over ice and stir

Sour Bee

2 parts Whiskey
$^1/_2$ part Benedictine®
$^1/_4$ part Lemon Juice
$^1/_4$ part Lime Juice
Old-Fashioned Glass

Shake with ice and strain over ice

Sour Kiss

1 part Vodka
1 part Sour Apple Schnapps
fill with Sour Mix
Highball Glass

Build over ice and stir

South of the Border

1 part Tequila
$^3/_4$ part Coffee-Flavored Brandy
$^1/_2$ part Lime Juice
1 Lime Slice
Whiskey Sour Glass

Shake with ice and strain over ice

South Pacific

1 part Vodka
2 parts Brandy
3 parts Pineapple Juice
splash Grenadine
Highball Glass

Shake with ice and strain over ice

South Side Fizz

$^1/_2$ part Gin
$^1/_2$ part Lemon Juice
dash Sugar
fill with Carbonated Water
Highball Glass

Shake all but Carbonated Water with ice and strain into the glass. Top with Carbonated Water.

Southern Cross

1 part Advocaat
1 part Southern Comfort®
1 part Cranberry Juice Cocktail
1 part Pineapple Juice
Highball Glass

Shake with ice and strain over ice

Southern Harmony

1 1/4 parts Jack Daniel's®
3/4 part Southern Comfort®
fill with Sour Mix
splash Lemon-Lime Soda
Whiskey Sour Glass

Build over ice and stir

Southern Lady

1 part Southern Comfort®
1 part Amaretto
fill with Lemon-Lime Soda
Old-Fashioned Glass

Build over ice and stir

Southern Salutation

2 parts Southern Comfort®
1 part Peach Schnapps
fill with Lemonade
Highball Glass

Build over ice and stir

Soviet Holiday

2 parts Vodka
1/2 part Coconut-Flavored Rum
1/4 part Tequila Rose®
fill with Fruit Punch
Highball Glass

Build over ice and stir

Sparkling Iceberg

1 part Peppermint Liqueur
1 part Coffee Liqueur
2 parts Cream
2 parts Ginger Ale
Highball Glass

Build over ice and stir

Special K®

1 part Vodka
1/2 part Blue Curaçao
1/2 part Triple Sec
dash Sugar
fill with Lemonade
Highball Glass

Shake with ice and pour

Special Reserve

1 part Goldschläger®
1 1/2 part Apple Brandy
fill with Cranberry Juice Cocktail
Highball Glass

Shake with ice and pour

Spice and Ice

1 part Citrus-Flavored Vodka
1 part Goldschläger®
fill with Dr Pepper®
Highball Glass

Build over ice and stir

Spice Whip

1 part Peppermint Liqueur
splash Goldschläger®
1/2 part Crème de Cacao (Dark)
fill with Hot Cocoa
Highball Glass

Build in a heat-proof cup or mug

Spicy Tiger
$1^1/_2$ parts Peach Schnapps
$1^1/_2$ parts Vodka
2 parts Lemon-Lime Soda
1 part Cranberry Juice Cocktail
1 part Orange Juice
Highball Glass

Build over ice and stir

Spiky Cactus
1 part Blue Curaçao
1 part Vodka
1 part Triple Sec
fill with Mountain Dew®
Highball Glass

Build over ice and stir

Spinster's Delight
1 part Vodka
1 part Brandy
1 part Crème de Cacao (White)
1 part Cream
Highball Glass

Shake with ice and strain over ice

A Splash of Nash
$^1/_2$ part Crème de Banana
$^1/_2$ part Melon Liqueur
2 parts Cranberry Juice Cocktail
2 parts Club Soda
Shot Glass, Highball Glass

Fill shot glass with Crème de Banana and Melon Liqueur, and drop it into a highball glass containing Cranberry Juice and Club Soda. Drink quickly.

Spoodie Oodie
1 part Scotch
2 parts Port
Highball Glass

Stir gently with ice

Spooky Juice
1 part Vodka
2 splashes Blue Curaçao
splash Grenadine
fill with Orange Juice
Highball Glass

Build over ice and stir

Spymaster
$1^1/_2$ parts Vodka
$^1/_2$ part Crème de Banana
$^1/_2$ part Lemon Juice
1 Egg White
Old-Fashioned Glass

Shake with ice and strain over ice

Squashed Frog
1 part Melon Liqueur
1 part Strawberry Liqueur
splash Crème de Menthe (White)
splash Crème de Cacao (White)
splash Irish Cream Liqueur
Old-Fashioned Glass

Build in the glass with no ice

St. John
1 part Coffee Liqueur
1 part Gin
Old-Fashioned Glass

Shake with ice and strain over ice

St. Louis Blues
1 part Vodka
1 part Blue Curaçao
1 part Lemonade
1 part Lemon-Lime Soda
Highball Glass

Build over ice and stir

St. Lucian Delight

1 part Rum
2 parts Blue Curaçao
1 part Lime Juice
fill with Pineapple Juice
Highball Glass

Build over ice and stir

St. Paul Punch

2 parts Melon Liqueur
1 part Vodka
1 part Lime Juice
fill with Lemonade
Highball Glass

Build over ice and stir

St. Peter

1 part Vodka
1 part Coffee Liqueur
Old-Fashioned Glass

Shake with ice and strain over ice

St. Valentine's Day

2/3 part Peach Schnapps
2/3 part Citrus-Flavored Vodka
1 part Cream
Highball Glass

Shake with ice and strain over ice

A Star Is Shining

1 part Gin
1 part Pernod®
1 part Crème de Banana
3 parts Orange Juice
2 parts Passion Fruit Nectar
Old-Fashioned Glass

Shake with ice and strain over ice

Star Kiss

2 parts Strawberry Liqueur
splash Grenadine
splash Cream
fill with Lemon-Lime Soda
Highball Glass

Build over ice and stir

Star Wars

1 part Southern Comfort®
1 part Amaretto
1 part Sour Mix
1 part Lemon-Lime Soda
Highball Glass

Build over ice and stir

Starry Starry Night

1 part Vodka
1 part Wild Berry Schnapps
fill with Lemon-Lime Soda
Highball Glass

Build over ice and stir

Stay Up Late

2 parts Gin
1/2 part Brandy
1/2 part Lemon Juice
1/2 part Club Soda
Highball Glass

Build over ice and stir

Stiletto

1 1/2 parts Whiskey
1 1/2 parts Amaretto
1/2 part Lemon Juice
Old-Fashioned Glass

Shake with ice and strain over ice

Stock Market Crash
1 part Jack Daniel's®
1 part Yukon Jack®
1 part Southern Comfort®
1 part Wild Turkey® Bourbon
1 part Dark Rum
fill with Cola
Highball Glass

Build over ice and stir

Stomach Reviver
2 parts Brandy
1/2 part Fernet-Branca®
Old-Fashioned Glass

Shake with ice and strain over ice

Stop & Go
1 part Apricot Brandy
1 part Campari®
fill with Orange Juice
Old-Fashioned Glass

Shake with ice and pour

Storm at Sea
1 part Vodka
1 part Apricot Brandy
1/2 part Melon Liqueur
1 part Sour Mix
1 part Orange Juice
Highball Glass

Build over ice and stir

Stormtrooper
1 part Vodka
1 part Coconut-Flavored Rum
fill with Milk
Highball Glass

Build over ice and stir

Storybook Ending
1 part Light Rum
1 part Apricot Brandy
splash Grenadine
1 part Sour Mix
1 part Orange Juice
Highball Glass

Shake with ice and strain over ice

Strawberry Assassin
1 part Vodka
fill with Cranberry Juice Cocktail
1 scoop Ice Cream
Highball Glass

Shake with ice and pour

Strawberry Fair
1 part Tequila Silver
1/2 part Cream
1/2 part Strawberry Puree
Old-Fashioned Glass

Shake with ice and pour

Strawberry Fields Forever
2 parts Strawberry Liqueur
1/2 part Brandy
fill with Carbonated Water
Highball Glass

Build over ice and stir

Strawberry Pussycat
1 part Vodka
1 part Strawberry Liqueur
1 part Cherry Juice
fill with Pineapple Juice
Highball Glass

Shake with ice and pour

Strawberry Starburst®
1 part Strawberry Liqueur
1 part Watermelon Schnapps
fill with Lemonade
Highball Glass

Build over ice and stir

Strawgasm
1 part Cointreau®
1 part Strawberry Liqueur
1 part Galliano®
1 part Coconut-Flavored Rum
fill with Cream
Old-Fashioned Glass

Shake with ice and pour

Stress Ball
1 part Vodka
1/2 part Rum
1/4 part Galliano®
1/4 part Irish Cream Liqueur
fill with Orange Juice
Highball Glass

Shake with ice and pour

Stubbly Beaver
1 part Vodka
1 part Irish Cream Liqueur
splash Butterscotch Schnapps
fill with Milk
Highball Glass

Build over ice and stir

Stumplifter
1 part Blackberry Brandy
1 part Amaretto
1 part Southern Comfort®
1 part Sloe Gin
fill with Orange Juice
splash Lemon-Lime Soda
Old-Fashioned Glass

Build over ice and stir

Sucker Punch
2 parts Vodka
1 part Sour Apple Schnapps
splash Cranberry Juice Cocktail
fill with Lemon-Lime Soda
Highball Glass

Build over ice and stir

Sugar and Spice
1 part Gin
1 1/2 parts Coffee Liqueur
1 part Tequila Rose®
1 part Tropical Punch Schnapps
fill with Lemon-Lime Soda
Highball Glass

Build over ice and stir

Sugar Reef
1 1/2 parts Orange-Flavored Vodka
1/2 part Triple Sec
1 part Pineapple Juice
1 part Cranberry Juice Cocktail
1 part Orange Juice
splash Lime Juice
Highball Glass

Shake with ice and strain over ice

Sukiaki
1 part Amaretto
1 part Butterscotch Schnapps
1 part Irish Cream Liqueur
1 part Triple Sec
1 part Lemon-Lime Soda
Highball Glass

Shake with ice and pour

Summer Bahia Baby
1 part Vodka
1 part Pisang Ambon® Liqueur
1/2 part Triple Sec
fill with Pineapple Juice
Old-Fashioned Glass

Shake with ice and strain over ice

Summer in the City

1 part Vodka
1 part Cherry Juice
1 part Lemonade
1 part Iced Tea
Highball Glass

Build over ice and stir

Summer of 69

1 part Vodka
1 part Strawberry Liqueur
1 part Lemonade
1 part Cola
Highball Glass

Build over ice and stir

Summer Sensation

1 part Banana Liqueur
fill with Orange Juice
splash Grenadine
Highball Glass

Build over ice and stir

Summer Share

1 part Light Rum
1 part Vodka
1/2 part Tequila
splash Apricot Brandy
1 part Cranberry Juice Cocktail
1 part Orange Juice
fill with Lemon-Lime Soda
Highball Glass

Build over ice and stir

Summer Splash

1 1/2 parts Gin
splash Lemon-Lime Soda
fill with Lemonade
Highball Glass

Build over ice and stir

Sun Burn

2 parts Cinnamon Schnapps
1 part Cherry Juice
fill with Pineapple Juice
Highball Glass

Shake with ice and pour

Sun on the Rocks

2 parts Tequila
dash Sugar
fill with Orange
splash Lemon Juice
Highball Glass

Shake with ice and pour

Sunblock 42

1 part Peach Schnapps
1 part Amaretto
fill with Cranberry Juice Cocktail
Highball Glass

Build over ice and stir

Sundance

1 part Apricot Brandy
1 part Vodka
splash Passion Fruit Nectar
splash Lemon Juice
fill with Pineapple Juice
Highball Glass

Shake with ice and pour

Sundown

1 part Vodka
1 part Apricot Brandy
fill with Pineapple Juice
Old-Fashioned Glass

Build over ice and stir

Sunniest Sour

1 1/4 parts Dark Rum
1/2 part Lemon Juice
dash Powdered Sugar
1 part Orange Juice
1 part Club Soda
Highball Glass

Shake all but Club Soda with ice and strain into the glass. Top with Club Soda.

Sunny Campari®

1/2 part Campari®
1 1/2 parts Orange Juice
Highball Glass

Shake with ice and strain over ice

Sunrise

1 part Gin
splash Sweet Vermouth
1 part Orange Juice
splash Grenadine
Highball Glass

Shake with ice and strain over ice

Sunset Sour

1 1/2 parts Whiskey
3 parts Sour Mix
splash Grenadine
Whiskey Sour Glass

Shake with ice and strain over ice

Sunset Strip

2 parts Dark Rum
1/4 part Grenadine
2 parts Orange Juice
2 parts Pineapple Juice
Highball Glass

Shake with ice and pour

Superman

1 part Scotch
1 part Vodka
1 part Gin
1 part Grenadine
splash Orange Juice
Old-Fashioned Glass

Shake with ice and strain over ice

Supersonic Sunshine

1 part Coconut-Flavored Rum
1 part Vodka
fill Chocolate Milk
1 Orange Slice
Highball Glass

Shake with ice and pour

Surrey Slider

1 1/2 parts Añejo Rum
1/2 part Peach Schnapps
fill with Orange Juice
Highball Glass

Build over ice and stir

Sweaty Belly

1 1/2 parts Amaretto
1 part Orange Juice
1 part Cranberry Juice Cocktail
Highball Glass

Build over ice and stir

Swedish Bear

3/4 part Vodka
1/2 part Crème de Cacao (Dark)
fill with Heavy Cream
Old-Fashioned Glass

Shake with ice and pour

Swedish Pinkie

1 part Currant-Flavored Vodka
1 part Cranberry Juice Cocktail
1 part Sour Mix
Champagne Flute

Shake with ice and pour

Sweet and Sour Rum
1 part Light Rum
1 part Dark Rum
1 part Orange Juice
1/2 part Lemon Juice
1/2 part Lime Juice
Highball Glass

Shake with ice and strain over ice

Sweet Candy Apple
3/4 part Southern Comfort®
3/4 part Amaretto
3/4 part Melon Liqueur
1/2 part Grenadine
2 splashes Sour Mix
Highball Glass

Shake with ice and strain over ice

Sweet Caroline
1 part Vodka
1 part Strawberry Liqueur
1 part Peach Schnapps
1 part Lemonade
2 parts Lemon-Lime Soda
Highball Glass

Build over ice and stir

Sweet City
1 part Vodka
1 part Apricot Brandy
1 part Sweet Vermouth
Highball Glass

Build over ice and stir

Sweet Death
1 part Coconut-Flavored Rum
1 part 151-Proof Rum
1 part Vodka
1 part Sour Mix
1 part Cranberry Juice Cocktail
Highball Glass

Shake with ice and pour

Sweet Jane
2 parts Fresh Lime Juice
2 parts Orange Juice
1 part Amaretto
1 part Coconut Cream
White Wine Glass

Shake with ice and pour

Sweet Kiss
1 part Amaretto
fill with Pineapple Juice
splash Grenadine
Highball Glass

Shake with ice and pour

Sweet Patootie
2 parts Gin
1 part Triple Sec
1 part Orange Juice
Old-Fashioned Glass

Shake with ice and strain over ice

Sweet Revenge
1 part Cointreau®
1 part Melon Liqueur
fill with Orange Juice
Highball Glass

Build over ice and stir

Sweet Satisfaction
1 part Coconut-Flavored Rum
1 part Irish Cream Liqueur
1 part Amaretto
1 part Butterscotch Schnapps
Highball Glass

Shake with ice and strain over ice

Sweet Scotch
1½ parts Scotch
½ part Benedictine®
splash Honey
fill with Peach Nectar
Highball Glass

Shake with ice and pour

Sweet Sensation
1½ parts Southern Comfort®
fill with Lemon-Lime Soda
Highball Glass

Build over ice and stir

Sweet Surrender
1 part Coconut-Flavored Rum
1 part Amaretto
1 part Orange Juice
1 part Pineapple Juice
1 part Lemon-Lime Soda
Highball Glass

Build over ice and stir

Sweet Temptation
2 parts Triple Sec
1 part Peach Schnapps
fill with Lemon-Lime Soda
splash Sour Mix
Highball Glass

Build over ice and stir

Sweet Water
1 part Extra Dry Gin
1 part Butterscotch Schnapps
2 parts Triple Sec
2 parts Vodka
Highball Glass

Shake with ice and strain over ice

Sweetie Pie
1½ parts Apricot Brandy
½ part Gin
¾ part Orange Juice
Old-Fashioned Glass

Shake with ice and strain over ice

Sword of Damocles
1 part Rum
1 part Melon Liqueur
1 part Fresh Lime Juice
Old-Fashioned Glass

Shake with ice and strain

T-Bird
1 part Canadian Whiskey
¾ part Amaretto
2 parts Pineapple Juice
1 part Orange Juice
2 splashes Grenadine
Highball Glass

Shake with ice and strain

T.K.O.
1 part Tequila
1 part Coffee Liqueur
1 part Ouzo
Old-Fashioned Glass

Shake with ice and strain over ice

Tachyon
1 part Pernod®
1 part Tequila
splash Lemon Juice
Highball Glass

Shake with ice and strain over ice

Tahiti Rainstorm
1 part Rum
1 part Blue Curaçao
1 part Margarita Mix
1 part Lemon-Lime Soda
Highball Glass

Build over ice and stir

Tahiti Vacation
1 part Rum
1 part Wild Berry Schnapps
1 part Cherry Juice
1 part Margarita Mix
2 parts Pineapple Juice
Highball Glass

Shake with ice and pour

Tainted Cherry
1 part Vodka
1 part Cherry Brandy
fill with Orange Juice
Highball Glass

Shake with ice and strain over ice

Tanahgoyang
1 part Vodka
1/2 part Pisang Ambon® Liqueur
1/2 part Coconut-Flavored Liqueur
1 part Lemon Juice
fill with Orange Juice
Highball Glass

Shake with ice and strain over ice

Tango & Cash
1/2 part Crème de Cassis
1 part Vanilla-Flavored Vodka
2/3 part Lemon Juice
2 parts Raspberry-Flavored Seltzer
Highball Glass

Stir gently with ice

Tart and Tangy
1 part Sour Mix
1 part Bacardi® Limon Rum
splash Grenadine
Old-Fashioned Glass

Shake with ice and strain over ice

Tattooed Smurf®
2 parts Blueberry Schnapps
fill with Lemon-Lime Soda
Highball Glass

Build over ice and stir

Tawny Russian
1 part Amaretto
1 part Vodka
Highball Glass

Build over ice and stir

Tea Bag
1 1/2 parts Dark Rum
1/2 part Crème de Cacao (Dark)
1/4 part Lemon Juice
2 dashes Sugar
fill with Iced Tea
Highball Glass

Shake with ice and strain over ice

Tea Spike
1 1/2 parts Rum
1/2 part Crème de Cacao (Dark)
fill with Iced Tea
Highball Glass

Shake with ice and strain over ice

Technicolor®
1/2 part Melon Liqueur
1/2 part Blue Curaçao
1 part Cointreau®
2 parts Orange Juice
Highball Glass

Shake with ice and strain over ice

Tee Off
1 part Brandy
1 part Crème de Menthe (White)
1 part Pineapple Juice
1 part Orange Juice
Old-Fashioned Glass

Shake with ice and pour

Temptress
1 part Vodka
1 part Grenadine
Highball Glass

Shake with ice and strain over ice

Ten Quidder
1 1/2 parts Gin
1 part Triple Sec
dash Bitters
splash Blue Curaçao
Old-Fashioned Glass

Shake with ice and strain over ice

Tennessee
2 parts Rye Whiskey
1/2 part Cherry Liqueur
1/2 part Lemon Juice
Highball Glass

Shake with ice and strain

Tennessee Lemonade
1 part Jack Daniel's®
1 part Triple Sec
fill with Lemonade
Highball Glass

Build over ice and stir

Tennessee Tea
1 part Vodka
1 part Rum
1 part Gin
1 part Triple Sec
1 part Jack Daniel's®
fill with Sour Mix
splash Orange Juice
splash Cola
Highball Glass

Shake with ice and strain over ice

Tequila Aloha
1/2 part Blue Curaçao
1 part Tequila Reposado
1/2 part Triple Sec
fill with Pineapple Juice
Highball Glass

Build over ice and stir

Tequila Ghost
1/2 part Lemon Juice
2 parts Tequila
1 part Pernod®
Old-Fashioned Glass

Shake with ice and strain over ice

Tequila Manhattan
2 parts Tequila
1 part Sweet Vermouth
splash Lime Juice
Old-Fashioned Glass

Shake with ice and strain over ice

Tequila Matador
1 1/2 parts Tequila
3 parts Pineapple Juice
1/2 part Lime Juice
Champagne Flute

Shake with ice and strain

Tequila Mirage
1 part Tequila
1 part Raspberry Liqueur
1 part Orange Juice
1 part Lemon-Lime Soda
Highball Glass

Build over ice and stir

Tequila Old-Fashioned
1½ parts Gold Tequila
splash Simple Syrup
2 dashes Angostura® Bitters
splash Club Soda
Old-Fashioned Glass

Build over ice and stir

Tequila Paralyzer
1 part Tequila
1 part Coffee Liqueur
splash Milk
fill with Cola
Highball Glass

Build over ice and stir

Tequila Razz
1½ parts Tequila
½ part Raspberry Liqueur
1 part Orange Juice
1 part Pineapple Juice
Highball Glass

Build over ice and stir

Tequila Sour
2 parts Tequila
½ part Lemon Juice
dash Powdered Sugar
Whiskey Sour Glass

Shake with ice and strain over ice

Tequila Sunrise
2 parts Tequila
fill with Orange Juice
splash Grenadine
Highball Glass

Build over ice

Tequila Vertigo
1 part Tequila
1 part Triple Sec
½ Sour Mix
fill with Cranberry Juice Cocktail
Highball Glass

Shake with ice and pour

Tequiria
2 parts Tequila Silver
1 part Raspberry Liqueur
1 part Ginger Ale
1 part Lime Juice
1 part Simple Syrup
Highball Glass

Build over ice and stir

Ter
1 part Peach Schnapps
2 parts Sake
Highball Glass

Shake with ice and strain over ice

Texas Cool-Aid
1 part Vodka
1 part Midori®
1 part Crème de Noyaux
splash Cranberry Juice Cocktail
Highball Glass

Shake with ice and pour

Texas Ice Pick
1 part Tequila
1 part Lemonade
2 parts Iced Tea
Highball Glass

Shake with ice and pour

Texas Sundowner

1 part Light Rum
1/2 part Grenadine
1/2 part Sambuca
Old-Fashioned Glass

Build over ice

Texas Tea

1 part Gin
1 part Tequila
1 part Rum
1 part Sour Mix
fill with Cola
Highball Glass

Build over ice and stir

They Killed Kenny!

2 parts Jack Daniel's®
1 1/2 parts Sour Apple Schnapps
2 parts Apple Juice
fill with Lemon-Lime Soda
Highball Glass

Build over ice and stir

Think Tank

1/2 part Vodka
1 part Coffee Liqueur
1 part Cream
fill with Carbonated Water
Highball Glass

Build over ice and stir

Three Fifths

2 parts Vodka
1 1/2 parts Grape Soda
1 1/2 parts Club Soda
Old-Fashioned Glass

Build over ice and stir

Three Wise Men Go Hunting

1 part Jack Daniel's®
1 part Jim Beam®
1 part Johnnie Walker® Black Label
1 part Wild Turkey® Bourbon
Highball Glass

Pour ingredients into glass neat (do not chill)

Threesome

1 1/2 parts Vodka
1 part Amaretto
splash Sour Mix
splash Blue Curaçao
splash Grenadine
Highball Glass

Shake all but Blue Curaçao and Grenadine with ice. Place the Blue Curaçao in the glass, fill the glass with ice, and strain the shaken mixture into the glass. Top with Grenadine.

Thunder King

1 part Citrus-Flavored Vodka
1 part Whiskey
1/2 part Coffee Liqueur
fill with Milk
Whiskey Sour Glass

Shake with ice and pour

Thunder Road

1 1/2 parts Applejack
3/4 part Light Rum
1/4 part Amaretto
1/4 part Lime Juice
Highball Glass

Shake with ice and pour

Thursday Night Juice Break

1 1/2 parts Peach Schnapps
1 1/2 parts Grape Fruit Juice
3 parts Lemonade
3 parts Orange Juice
splash Maraschino Cherry Juice
Highball Glass

Build over ice and stir

Tickle Me Elmo®

1 part Strawberry Liqueur
fill with Pineapple Juice
Highball Glass

Build over ice and stir

Tidal Wave

1 part Vodka
1 part Blue Curaçao
2 parts Margarita Mix
1 part Lemon-Lime Soda
Highball Glass

Shake with ice and pour

Tie-Dyed

1 part Blueberry Schnapps
1 part Raspberry-Flavored Vodka
1 part Cranberry Juice Cocktail
1 part Orange Juice
1 part Lemon-Lime Soda
Highball Glass

Build over ice and stir

Tiffany's

1 1/2 parts Vodka
2/3 part Crème de Cassis
Highball Glass

Build over ice and stir

Tiger's Milk

2 parts Dark Rum
1 1/2 parts Cognac
1/2 part Simple Syrup
fill with Milk
White Wine Glass

Shake with ice and pour

Tijuana Bulldog

1 part Tequila
1 part Coffee Liqueur
1 part Cola
1 part Cream
Highball Glass

Build over ice and stir

Tijuana Taxi

2 parts Tequila Gold
1 part Blue Curaçao
1 part Tropical Punch Schnapps
fill with Lemon-Lime Soda
Highball Glass

Build over ice and stir

Tijuana Tea

3/4 part Tequila
1/2 part Triple Sec
1 part Sour Mix
fill with Cola
Highball Glass

Build over ice and stir

Tiny Tim

1 part Brandy
1 part Dry Vermouth
1/2 part Triple Sec
dash Sugar
Highball Glass

Shake with ice and strain over ice

Tiptoe

2 parts Light Rum
2 parts Pineapple Juice
1 part Triple Sec
Old-Fashioned Glass

Build over ice and stir

Titan

1 part Crème de Cacao (Dark)
1 part Amaretto
1 part Light Rum
1 part Cream
Highball Glass

Shake with ice and strain over ice

Tivoli Cola

1 part Light Rum
1 part Triple Sec
1/2 part Raspberry Liqueur
1/2 part Sour Mix
fill with Cola
Highball Glass

Build over ice and stir

Toast the Ghost

1 part Vodka
1 part Coconut-Flavored Liqueur
1 part Amaretto
1 part Irish Cream Liqueur
fill with Milk
Highball Glass

Shake with ice and strain over ice

Toasted Almond

1 part Amaretto
1 1/2 parts Coffee Liqueur
fill with Light Cream
Highball Glass

Shake with ice and pour

Tokyo at Dawn

1 part Mango Schnapps
1 part Coconut-Flavored Rum
1 part Orange Juice
1/2 part Pineapple Juice
Old-Fashioned Glass

Shake with ice and strain over ice

Tokyo Tea

1/2 part Vodka
1/2 part Rum
1/2 part Triple Sec
1/2 part Gin
1 part Melon Liqueur
fill with Sour Mix
Highball Glass

Shake with ice and pour

Tomahawk

1 part Vodka
1/2 part Crème de Cacao (White)
1/2 part Triple Sec
2 splashes Lime Juice
1 part Cream
Highball Glass

Shake with ice and strain over ice

Tomakazi

3/4 part Vodka
3/4 part Gin
1/2 part Lime Cordial
splash Sour Mix
splash Cola
Old-Fashioned Glass

Build over ice and stir

Tom-Tom

1 part Coffee Liqueur
1 part Whiskey
fill with Cold Coffee
Highball Glass

Shake with ice and pour

Top o' the Morning

1 part Vodka
1 part Triple Sec
1/4 part Tequila
1 part Orange Juice
1 part Cranberry Juice Cocktail
Highball Glass

Shake with ice and strain over ice

Top Spinner
1 part Cognac
1 part Lime Juice
1 part Pineapple Juice
1 part Orange Juice
White Wine Glass

Shake with ice and pour

Topshelf
1 part Gin
1/2 part Orange Juice
1/2 part Sloe Gin
Old-Fashioned Glass

Shake with ice and strain over ice

Topsy-Turvy
1 1/2 parts Coconut Liqueur
1/2 part Vanilla Liqueur
1/2 part Jägermeister®
2 parts Pineapple Juice
Highball Glass

Shake with ice and strain over ice

Toreador
1 1/2 parts Tequila
1/2 part Crème de Cacao (White)
dash Cocoa Powder
Old-Fashioned Glass

Shake with ice and strain. Top with Whipped Cream and Cocoa Powder.

Torombolo
2 parts Chocolate Milk
1 part Licor 43®
Highball Glass

Build over ice and stir

Touchdown Tea
2 parts Peach Schnapps
1 part Lemon Juice
fill with Iced Tea
Highball Glass

Build over ice and stir

Traffic
1 part Apricot Brandy
1 part Peach Schnapps
splash Angostura® Bitters
1 part Lemon Juice
fill with Passion Fruit Juice
Highball Glass

Shake with ice and strain over ice

Transmission
1 part Apricot Brandy
2/3 part Orange Liqueur
3 parts Passion Fruit Liqueur
2 parts Orange Juice
splash Lemon Juice
Highball Glass

Shake with ice and pour

Treasure Hunt
1 part Crème de Menthe (Green)
1 part Whiskey
1/2 part Sugar
Old-Fashioned Glass

Shake with ice and strain over ice

Tremor
1 part Midori®
1 part Spiced Rum
1 part Vodka
1 part Crème de Noyaux
fill with Orange Juice
Highball Glass

Shake with ice and pour

Trinidad Punch
3 parts Rum
1 part Simple Syrup
1 part Lime Juice
4 dashes Bitters
Highball Glass

Shake with ice and strain over ice

Triple Jump
1 1/2 parts Vodka
1/2 part Triple Sec
1/2 part Apricot Brandy
1/2 part Strawberry Liqueur
fill with Orange Juice
Old-Fashioned Glass

Build over ice and stir

Triple Pleasure
1 part Vodka
1 part Tequila
1 part Yukon Jack®
1 part Cranberry Juice Cocktail
1 part Orange Juice
1 part Pineapple Juice
Highball Glass

Build over ice and stir

Trois Rivières
1 1/2 parts Canadian Whiskey
1/2 part Dubonnet® Blonde
splash Triple Sec
Old-Fashioned Glass

Shake with ice and strain over ice

Trojan Horse
1 part Triple Sec
1 part Dry Vermouth
1 part Gin
1 part Kirschwasser
1 part Pineapple Syrup
Old-Fashioned Glass

Shake with ice and strain over ice

Tropical 2x4
1 part Light Rum
1 part Triple Sec
1 part Pineapple Juice
1 part Orange Juice
Highball Glass

Build over ice and stir

Tropical Blue
1/2 part Gin
1/2 part Dark Rum
1/2 part Blue Curaçao
1/2 part Apricot Brandy
1/2 part Coconut-Flavored Liqueur
1 part Grapefruit Juice
1 part Pineapple Juice
1 part Orange Juice
Old-Fashioned Glass

Shake with ice and strain over ice

Tropical Daydream
1 part Vodka
1 part Peach Schnapps
1/2 part Amaretto
1 part Cranberry Juice Cocktail
1 part Orange Juice
Highball Glass

Build over ice and stir

Tropical Itch
1 part Light Rum
1 part Dark Rum
1 part Vodka
1 part Grand Marnier®
1 part Lemon Juice
fill with Mango Nectar
Highball Glass

Shake with ice and pour

Tropical LifeSaver®

3/4 part Midori®
3/4 part Coconut-Flavored Rum
1/2 part Citrus-Flavored Vodka
2 parts Pineapple Juice
1 part Sour Mix
splash Lemon-Lime Soda
Highball Glass

Build over ice and stir

Tropical Rainstorm

1 part Vodka
1 part Blue Curaçao
2 parts Lemon-Lime Soda
1 part Pineapple Juice
Highball Glass

Build over ice and stir

Tropical Sunset

1 part Vodka
1 part Cherry Juice
1 part Wild Berry Schnapps
fill with Orange Juice
Highball Glass

Build over ice and stir

Tropical Torpedo

3/4 part Spiced Rum
3/4 part Melon Liqueur
3/4 part Peach Schnapps
1 part Piña Colada Mix
1 part Pineapple Juice
Highball Glass

Build over ice and stir

Tsunami

1 part Spiced Rum
1/2 part Coconut-Flavored Rum
1/2 part Meyers's® Rum
fill with Pineapple Juice
splash Grenadine
Highball Glass

Build over ice and stir

Tu Tu Can Can

1 part Gin
1 part Blue Curaçao
1/2 part Dry Vermouth
1/2 part Lime Juice
fill with Orange Juice
Highball Glass

Shake with ice and strain over ice

Tuaca® Nutter

1 part Tuaca®
1 part Frangelico®
1 part Coffee Liqueur
2 parts Cream
Highball Glass

Shake with ice and strain over ice

Tumbled Marble

1 part Apricot Brandy
1 part Port
1 part Remy Martin® VSOP
1 Egg Yolk
splash Simple Syrup
Old-Fashioned Glass

Shake with ice and strain over ice

Tumbleweed

1 part Vodka
1 part Peach Schnapps
1 part Raspberry Liqueur
2 parts Lemonade
1 part Cola
Highball Glass

Build over ice and stir

Turkey on Fire

1 part Jim Beam®
1 part Blue Curaçao
1 part Coffee Liqueur
splash Triple Sec
Highball Glass

Build over ice and stir

Twat in the Hat
$1^1/_2$ parts Rum
1 part Lemon Juice
3 parts Orange Juice
fill with Lemon-Lime Soda
Highball Glass
Build over ice and stir

Twilight Zone
1 part Vodka
1 part Blue Curaçao
splash Lemon Juice
Highball Glass
Shake with ice and strain over ice

Twin Hills
$1^1/_2$ parts Whiskey
$1^1/_2$ splashes Lemon Juice
$1^1/_2$ splashes Lime Juice
2 splashes Benedictine®
dash Sugar
Old-Fashioned Glass
Shake with ice and strain over ice

Twinkle My Lights
1 part Amaretto
1 part Raspberry Liqueur
1 part Lemon-Lime Soda
Highball Glass
Shake with ice and strain over ice

Twisted Delight
2 parts Gin
1 part Lemon-Lime Soda
1 part Orange Juice
Highball Glass
Build over ice and stir

Twister
1 part Triple Sec
1 part Vodka
fill with Orange Juice
splash Grenadine
Highball Glass
Build over ice

Two Wheeler
$1^1/_4$ parts Dark Rum
fill with Orange Juice
Highball Glass
Build over ice and stir

Ultra Z
2 parts Brandy
1 part Crème de Banana
2 parts Pear Juice
1 part Lemon Juice
Old-Fashioned Glass
Shake with ice and strain over ice

Umbrella Man Special
1 part Vodka
1 part Coffee Liqueur
1 part Irish Cream Liqueur
1 part Grand Marnier®
1 part Drambuie®
Highball Glass
Shake with ice and strain over ice

Uncle Wiggley
$^1/_2$ part Crown Royal® Whiskey
$^1/_2$ part Amaretto
1 part Cranberry Juice Cocktail
1 part Sour Mix
Highball Glass
Shake with ice and strain over ice

Unconventional Bloody Mary

$1^1/_2$ parts Citrus-Flavored Vodka
splash Lime Juice
fill with Tomato Juice
splash Tabasco® Sauce
splash Worcestershire Sauce
dash Salt
dash White Pepper
Highball Glass

Shake with ice and pour

Under the Sea

1 part Light Rum
1 part Crème de Banana
$^3/_4$ part Blue Curaçao
1 part Simple Syrup
splash Lemon Juice
Old-Fashioned Glass

Shake with ice and strain

Underdog

2 parts Coffee Liqueur
fill with Apple Juice
Highball Glass

Build over ice and stir

Union League

2 parts Gin
1 part Port
2 dashes Orange Bitters
Highball Glass

Stir gently with ice

Up on the Roof

1 part Vodka
1 part Cherry Juice
1 part Lemonade
1 part Cola
Highball Glass

Build over ice and stir

Upper-Class

1 part Amaretto
2 parts Southern Comfort®
Old-Fashioned Glass

Shake with ice and strain over ice

Upside Down Pineapple

1 part Southern Comfort®
1 part Coconut-Flavored Rum
splash Pineapple Juice
fill with Orange Juice
Old-Fashioned Glass

Build over ice and stir

Usual Suspect

1 part Cream
splash Vodka
splash Crème de Banana
Old-Fashioned Glass

Shake with ice and strain over ice

Utter Butter

2 parts Coffee Liqueur
1 part Butterscotch Schnapps
2 parts Cream
Highball Glass

Build over ice and stir

V8® Ceasar's

1 part Vodka
1 part V8® Vegetable Juice Blend
1 part Clamato® Juice
$^1/_4$ part Worcestershire® Sauce
dash Salt
dash Pepper
splash Lime Juice
Highball Glass

Shake with ice and pour

V8® Mary
1 part Vodka
fill with V8® Vegetable Juice Blend
$1/4$ part Worcestershire® Sauce
dash Salt
dash Pepper
splash Lime Juice
Highball Glass

Shake with ice and pour

Valentine
2 parts Banana Liqueur
1 part Vodka
fill with Cranberry Juice Cocktail
Red Wine Glass

Shake with ice and strain

Vampire's Kiss
2 parts Vodka
$1/2$ part Dry Gin
$1/2$ part Dry Vermouth
$1/2$ part Tequila
dash Salt
Old-Fashioned Glass

Shake with ice and strain over ice

Vaughn Purple Haze
2 parts Vodka
$1 1/2$ parts Raspberry Liqueur
fill with Cranberry Juice Cocktail
Highball Glass

Build over ice and stir

VCG
1 part Vodka
fill with Cranberry Juice Cocktail
splash Grenadine
Old-Fashioned Glass

Build over ice and stir

Velociraptor
$1 1/2$ parts Vodka
splash Chicken Broth
3 splashes Tabasco® Sauce
Highball Glass

Shake with ice and strain over ice

Velvet Tu-Tu
$1 1/2$ parts Black Velvet® Whiskey
1 part Amaretto
1 part Orange Juice
1 part Pineapple Juice
Highball Glass

Shake with ice and pour

Venetian Peach
1 part Spiced Rum
1 part Peach Schnapps
fill with Lemonade
splash Strawberry Daiquiri Mix
Highball Glass

Shake with ice and pour

Ventura Highway
1 part Vodka
2 parts Raspberry Liqueur
1 part Lemonade
1 part Orange Juice
Highball Glass

Shake with ice and strain over ice

Vermont Maple Blaster
1 part Rum
1 part Maple Syrup
1 part Water
Highball Glass

Shake with ice and strain over ice

Vermouth Cassis
$1^1/_2$ parts Dry Vermouth
$^3/_4$ part Crème de Cassis
fill with Carbonated Water
Highball Glass

Build over ice and stir

Vernal Equinox
2 parts Port
1 part Grand Marnier®
$^1/_2$ part Triple Sec
Old-Fashioned Glass

Stir gently with ice

Vesuvio
1 part Light Rum
$^1/_2$ part Sweet Vermouth
$^1/_2$ part Lemon Juice
dash Powdered Sugar
1 Egg White
Old-Fashioned Glass

Shake with ice and strain over ice

Veteran
2 parts Dark Rum
$^1/_2$ part Cherry Brandy
Old-Fashioned Glass

Shake with ice and strain over ice

Victoria's Secret®
1 part Currant-Flavored Vodka
$1^1/_2$ parts Sweet Vermouth
$^1/_4$ part Sour Mix
Old-Fashioned Glass

Shake with ice and strain

Viking Blood
1 part Aquavit
1 part Tia Maria®
fill with Lemon-Lime Soda
Highball Glass

Build over ice and stir

Villa Park
1 part Bourbon
1 part Pineapple Juice
1 part Orange Juice
Highball Glass

Build over ice and stir

Vincow Somba
1 part Vodka
1 part Triple Sec
1 part Pineapple Juice
Highball Glass

Build over ice and stir

Vinyl Sunset
1 part Absinthe
$^1/_2$ part Crème de Cassis
$^1/_2$ part Lime Juice
fill with Lemonade
Highball Glass

Build over ice and stir

Viper Venom
$1^1/_2$ parts Yukon Jack®
$^1/_2$ part Triple Sec
1 part Sweetened Lime Juice
1 part Lemon Juice
Old-Fashioned Glass

Shake with ice and strain over ice

Virgin Maiden
1 part Blue Curaçao
1 part Grenadine
1 part Benedictine®
1 part Chartreuse®
1 part Crème de Noyaux
Highball Glass

Build over ice and stir

Virgo
1 part Vodka
1 part Wild Berry Schnapps
2 parts Lemonade
1 part Cola
Highball Glass

Build over ice and stir

Vodka Boatman
1 part Vodka
1 part Cherry Brandy
fill with Orange Juice
Highball Glass

Build over ice and stir

Vodka Dog
1 part Vodka
fill with Grapefruit Juice
Highball Glass

Build over ice and stir

Vodka Red Bull®
2 1/2 parts Vodka
fill with Red Bull® Energy Drink
Highball Glass

Build over ice and stir

Vodka Salty Dog
1 1/2 parts Vodka
fill with Grapefruit Juice
dash Salt
Highball Glass

Shake with ice and pour

Vodka Screw-Up
1 part Vodka
1 part Lemon-Lime Soda
1 part Orange Juice
Highball Glass

Build over ice and stir

Vodka Sour
2 parts Vodka
1/2 part Lemon Juice
dash Sugar
Old-Fashioned Glass

Shake with ice and strain over ice

Vodka Sourball
1 1/2 parts Lemon-Flavored Vodka
1/2 part Triple Sec
1/2 part Pineapple Juice
Old-Fashioned Glass

Shake with ice and strain over ice

Vodka Sunrise
1 part Vodka
fill with Orange Juice
splash Grenadine
Highball Glass

Build over ice

Vodka Sunset
1 1/2 parts Vodka
fill with Grapefruit Juice
2 splashes Grenadine
Highball Glass

Build over ice

Vodka Volcano
2 parts Vodka
1 part Grapefruit Juice
splash Grenadine
Highball Glass

Build over ice

Waffle Dripper
1 $1/2$ parts Vodka
1 part Butterscotch Schnapps
fill with Orange Juice
Highball Glass

Shake with ice and strain

Wake-Up Call
1 part Jack Daniel's®
1 part Vodka
$1/2$ part Lemon Juice
Old-Fashioned Glass

Shake with ice and strain

A Walk on the Moon
2 parts Blackberry Liqueur
1 part Vodka
3 parts Cola
3 parts Milk
Highball Glass

Shake with ice and strain over ice. Serve with a straw.

Walkover
1 $1/2$ parts Frangelico®
1 part Coffee-Flavored Brandy
$1/2$ part Coconut Cream
fill with Pineapple Juice
Highball Glass

Shake with ice and strain over ice

Walterbury
1 part Kiwi Schnapps
1 part Dark Rum
fill with Lemon-Lime Soda
Highball Glass

Build over ice and stir

Waltzing Matilda
1 part Dry Sherry
1 part Dry Gin
1 part Passion Fruit Liqueur
$1/2$ part Triple Sec
Old-Fashioned Glass

Shake with ice and strain over ice

Warm Summer Rain
1 $1/2$ parts Vodka
$1/2$ part Coconut-Flavored Liqueur
fill with Pineapple Juice
splash Orange Juice
Highball Glass

Shake with ice and strain over ice

Warrior's Cup
1 part Amaretto
$1/2$ part Scotch
1 part Tequila
Old-Fashioned Glass

Build over ice and stir

Washington Apple
1 part Canadian Whiskey
1 part Sour Apple Schnapps
fill with Apple-Cranberry Juice
Highball Glass

Shake with ice and pour

Wasp Sting
1 part Brandy
1 part Crème de Cacao (White)
fill with Cola
Highball Glass

Build over ice and stir

Waterslide
1 part Amaretto
1/2 part Light Rum
1/2 part Lime Juice
fill with Pineapple Juice
Highball Glass

Build over ice and stir

Wave Breaker
1 part Vodka
1 part Coconut Cream
splash Fresh Lime Juice
Old-Fashioned Glass

Shake with ice and strain over ice

Wedding Day
1 part Gin
1/2 part Vodka
1 part Jägermeister®
fill with Apple Cider
Highball Glass

Build over ice and stir

Weeping Willow
1 1/2 parts Gin
1/2 part Pisang Ambon® Liqueur
splash Coconut-Flavored Liqueur
fill with Orange Juice
Highball Glass

Shake with ice and strain over ice

West Indies Russian
1 part Vodka
1 part Rum
1 part Coffee Liqueur
fill with Cola
Highball Glass

Build over ice and stir

Wet & Wild
1 1/2 parts Tequila Silver
1/2 part Triple Sec
fill with Grapefruit Juice
White Wine Glass

Shake with ice and strain

Wet T-Shirt
1 part Light Rum
1/2 part Orange Liqueur
2 parts Orange Juice
1 part Pineapple Juice
1/2 part Lemon Juice
Highball Glass

Shake with ice and strain over ice

Whammy
1 part Rum
1 part Peach Schnapps
1 part Cherry Juice
2 parts Orange Juice
1 part Cola
Highball Glass

Build over ice and stir

Wheelbarrow
2 parts Rum
1 part Drambuie®
Highball Glass

Shake with ice and strain over ice

Where's My Kilt
1 part Scotch
2/3 part Crème de Cacao (White)
1/2 part Coconut Cream
splash Lemon Juice
3 parts Orange Juice
Highball Glass

Shake with ice and strain over ice

Whippet
1 part Vodka
fill with Orange Juice
splash Raspberry Liqueur
Highball Glass

Build over ice

Whirly Bird
1 part Pineapple Juice
1 part Melon Liqueur
1 part Southern Comfort®
1 part Citrus-Flavored Vodka
Old-Fashioned Glass

Shake with ice and strain over ice

Whiskey Cobbler
2 1/2 parts Whiskey
1/2 part Lemon Juice
1/2 part Grapefruit Juice
1/2 part Amaretto
Old-Fashioned Glass

Shake with ice and strain over ice

Whiskey Lover
1 part Scotch
1 part Amaretto
Old-Fashioned Glass

Shake with ice and strain over ice

Whispering Shadow
1 part Amaretto
1/2 part Lemon Juice
1 1/2 parts Pineapple Juice
1 Egg White
Old-Fashioned Glass

Shake with ice and strain over ice

White Bull
1 part Tequila
1 part Coffee Liqueur
fill with Cream
Highball Glass

Shake with ice and pour

White Chocolate
1 part Vanilla-Flavored Vodka
2 parts Crème de Cacao (White)
Brandy Snifter

Shake with ice and strain over ice

White Christmas
1 part Gin
1 part Milk
Highball Glass

Shake with ice and strain over ice

White Heat
1 part Gin
1/2 part Triple Sec
1/2 part Dry Vermouth
1 part Pineapple Juice
Highball Glass

Shake with ice and strain over ice

White Lily
1 part Gin
1 part Light Rum
1 part Triple Sec
splash Pernod®
Old-Fashioned Glass

Shake with ice and strain over ice

White Mint and Brandy Frappe´

1 part Brandy
2 parts Crème de Menthe (White)
Highball Glass

Build over ice and stir

White Out

2 parts Crème de Menthe (White)
1 part Cointreau®
1 part Cognac
Highball Glass

Build over ice and stir

White Rabbit

1 part Light Rum
1/2 part Irish Cream Liqueur
1/2 part Amaretto
1/2 part Coffee Liqueur
fill with Cream
Old-Fashioned Glass

Shake with ice and pour

White Russian

1 part Vodka
1 part Coffee Liqueur
fill with Light Cream
Old-Fashioned Glass

Build over ice and stir

White Stinger

2 parts Vodka
3/4 part Crème de Cacao (White)
Old-Fashioned Glass

Shake with ice and strain over ice

White Wedding

1 1/2 parts Gin
2/3 part Peppermint Liqueur
Old-Fashioned Glass

Shake with ice and strain over ice

Wicked Manhattan

2 parts Jim Beam®
1 part Sweet Vermouth
dash Bitters
Old-Fashioned Glass

Shake with ice and strain

Wicked Witch

1 1/2 parts Whiskey
1/4 part Maraschino Liqueur
1/4 part Pineapple Juice
splash Lemon Juice
Old-Fashioned Glass

Shake with ice and strain over ice

Wild Thing

1 1/2 parts Tequila
1 part Cranberry Juice Cocktail
1 part Club Soda
1/2 part Lime Juice
Old-Fashioned Glass

Build over ice and stir

Wild Wild West

1 1/2 parts Jack Daniel's®
1 part Peach Schnapps
fill with Cranberry Juice Cocktail
Highball Glass

Build over ice and stir

Windex®

2 parts Vodka
1 part Light Rum
1/2 part Blue Curaçao
1/2 part Lime Juice
Highball Glass

Shake with ice and strain over ice

Wisconsin Dells

1 part Southern Comfort®
1/2 part Sloe Gin
1/2 part Crème de Banana
fill with Pineapple Juice
splash Orange Juice
Highball Glass

Shake with ice and strain over ice

Wishing Well

1 part Apricot Brandy
1 part Crème de Cassis
1 part Sour Mix
splash Simple Syrup
1 part Club Soda
1 part Cranberry Juice Cocktail
Highball Glass

Build over ice and stir

Witch's Brew

1 part Vodka
1 part Raspberry Liqueur
1 part Cranberry Juice Cocktail
1 part Sour Mix
Highball Glass

Build over ice and stir

Wolf

1 part Blue Curaçao
1/2 part Crème de Menthe (White)
1/2 part Vodka
fill with Lemon-Lime Soda
Old-Fashioned Glass

Build over ice and stir

Wolfsbane

2 parts Vodka
1 1/2 parts Cherry Brandy
1/2 part Cream
1 Egg White
Highball Glass

Shake with ice and strain over ice

Woman in Blue

1 part Vodka
1 part Crème de Cacao (White)
1 part Frangelico®
splash Blue Curaçao
Highball Glass

Shake with ice and strain over ice

Wombat

2 parts Dark Rum
1/2 part Strawberry Liqueur
1 part Pineapple Juice
1 part Orange Juice
Old-Fashioned Glass

Shake with ice and pour

Woo Woo

1 part Vodka
1 part Peach Schnapps
fill with Cranberry Juice Cocktail
Highball Glass

Shake with ice and strain over ice

Wookiee

1 part Rum
1/2 part Vodka
1/2 part Tequila
1/2 part Vermouth
1 part Orange Juice
1 part Cola
Highball Glass

Build over ice and stir

Woolly Navel
$3/4$ part Peach Schnapps
$1 1/2$ parts Vodka
fill with Orange Juice
Highball Glass

Build over ice and stir

Working Man's Zinfandel
1 part Tequila
1 part Scotch
$1/2$ part Cinnamon Schnapps
$1/2$ part Peach Schnapps
fill with Lemon-Lime Soda
White Wine Glass

Build over ice and stir

Wrightsville Sunset
1 part Rum
1 part Tequila
$1/2$ part Lime Juice
$1/2$ part Grenadine
dash Bitters
fill with Orange Juice
White Wine Glass

Shake with ice and strain over ice

X Marks the Spot
1 part Rum
1 part Amaretto
1 part Lemonade
1 part Cola
Highball Glass

Build over ice and stir

X-Wing
1 part Scotch
1 part Coffee Liqueur
1 part Crème de Cacao (White)
splash Irish Cream Liqueur
Highball Glass

Shake with ice and strain over ice

Yabba Dabba Doo
1 part Rum
1 part Strawberry Liqueur
1 part Wild Berry Schnapps
1 part Sour Mix
1 part Orange Juice
Highball Glass

Shake with ice and pour

Yankee Dutch
1 part Cherry Brandy
1 part Triple Sec
1 part Vodka
1 part Jim Beam®
Highball Glass

Shake with ice and strain over ice

Yellow Bird
1 part Coconut-Flavored Rum
1 part Crème de Banana
1 part Apricot Brandy
fill with Orange Juice
Highball Glass

Shake with ice and pour

Yellow Dog
1 part Vodka
1 part Coconut-Flavored Rum
1 part Mountain Dew®
1 part Pineapple Juice
Highball Glass

Build over ice and stir

Yellow Pages
1½ parts Gin
fill with Pineapple Juice
splash Pernod®
splash Lemon Juice
dash Bitters
Old-Fashioned Glass

Shake with ice and strain over ice

Yellow Sock
1 part Vodka
1 part Pisang Ambon® Liqueur
fill with Orange Juice
Highball Glass

Build over ice and stir

Yellow Sunset
1 part Vodka
1 part Grand Marnier®
fill with Pineapple Juice
1 part Cherry Juice
Highball Glass

Build over ice

Yeoman's Passion
½ part Pisang Ambon® Liqueur
½ part Gin
¼ part Dry Vermouth
1 part Passion Fruit Juice
Old-Fashioned Glass

Shake with ice and strain over ice

Yorktown Yell
1 part Whiskey
1 part Raspberry Liqueur
1 part Cranberry Juice Cocktail
1 part Lemon-Lime Soda
Highball Glass

Build over ice and stir

Young Nobleman
1 part Grand Marnier®
1 part Southern Comfort®
⅔ part Crème de Cacao (White)
splash Galliano®
Highball Glass

Build over ice and stir

Yuppidoo
1 part Irish Cream Liqueur
1 part Coffee Liqueur
1 part Galliano®
1 part Vanilla Liqueur
splash Half and Half
Highball Glass

Shake with ice and strain over ice

Yup-Yupie
1½ parts Vodka
½ part Melon Liqueur
½ part Maraschino Liqueur
½ part Crème de Cassis
Highball Glass

Shake with ice and strain over ice

Za Za
1 part Gin
1 part Dubonnet® Rouge
dash Angostura® Bitters
Highball Glass

Shake with ice and strain over ice

Zebra Fizz
1 part Vodka
1 part Lemonade
1 part Lemon-Lime Soda
Highball Glass

Build over ice and stir

Zocolo

1 part Rum
1 part Cherry Juice
1 part Lemonade
1 part Cola
Highball Glass

Build over ice and stir

Zoom Bang Boom

1 part Vodka
1 part Wild Berry Schnapps
1 part Lemonade
2 parts Lemon-Lime Soda
Highball Glass

Build over ice and stir

Zoom Shooter

1 part Vodka
1 part Grand Marnier®
1 part Cherry Juicc
fill with Orange Juice
Highball Glass

Build over ice and stir

Iced Teas

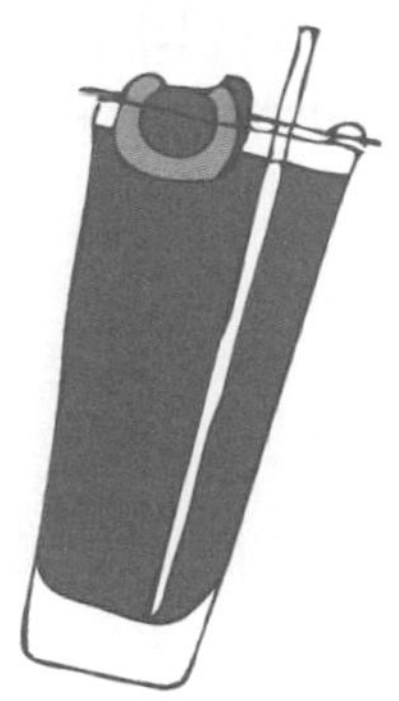

It started with the Long Island Iced Tea in the 70's and rapidly grew into a collection of potent drinks that combined various ingredients to make a muddy brown color. These drinks don't necessarily contain any actual tea (although some do).

3-Mile Long Island Iced Tea

1 part Gin
1 part Light Rum
1 part Tequila
1 part Vodka
1 part Triple Sec
1 part Melon Liqueur
splash Sour Mix
splash Cola
Collins Glass

Mix with ice

Apple Iced Tea

2 parts Sour Apple Schnapps
fill with Iced Tea
Highball Glass

Build over ice and stir

Apricot Iced Tea

2 parts Apricot Brandy
fill with Iced Tea
Highball Glass

Build over ice and stir

Bacardi® South Beach Iced Tea

3/4 part Spiced Rum
3/4 part Citrus-Flavored Rum
3/4 part Light Rum
3 parts Sour Mix
1 part Cola
Collins Glass

Build over ice and stir

Bambi's Iced Tea

1 part Vodka
splash Sour Mix
1 part Cola
1 part Lemon-Lime Soda
Collins Glass

Build over ice and stir

Binghampton Iced Tea

1 part Coconut-Flavored Rum
1 part Vanilla-Flavored Vodka
1 part Gin
1 part Tequila
1/2 part Rum
fill with Sour Mix
splash Cola
Collins Glass

Build over ice and stir

BJ's Long Island Iced Tea

1 part Amaretto
1 part Rum
1 part Triple Sec
1 part Vodka
splash Lime Juice
fill with Cola
Highball Glass

Build over ice and stir

Blue Long Island Iced Tea

1 part Vodka
1 part Tequila
1 part Rum
1 part Gin
1 part Blue Curaçao
Collins Glass

Build over ice and stir

Boston Iced Tea

1 part Vodka
1 part Gin
1 part Rum
1 part Tia Maria®
1 part Grand Marnier®
fill with Sour Mix
splash Cola
Collins Glass

Build over ice and stir

California Iced Tea

1/2 part Gin
1/2 part Light Rum
1/2 part Tequila
1/2 part Vodka
1/2 part Triple Sec
1/2 part Sour Mix
1 part Orange Juice
1 part Pineapple Juice
Highball Glass

Build over ice and stir

Caribbean Iced Tea

1 part Gin
1 part Light Rum
1 part Tequila
1 part Vodka
1 part Blue Curaçao
fill with Sour Mix
Hurricane Glass

Build over ice and stir

Caribbean Iced Tea #2

2 parts Coconut-Flavored Rum
1 part Light Rum
fill with Iced Tea
splash Lemon Juice
Highball Glass

Build over ice and stir

Carolina Iced Tea

1 1/2 parts Southern Comfort®
1 part Spiced Rum
1 part Peach Schnapps
1/2 part Vodka
fill with Iced Tea
Highball Glass

Build over ice and stir

Dead Grasshopper

1 part Crème de Menthe (White)
1 part Crème de Cacao (White)
1 part Milk
fill with Iced Tea
splash Grenadine
Collins Glass

Shake all but Grenadine with ice and strain into the glass. Place a few drops of Grenadine in the center of the drink.

Dignified Iced Tea

2 parts Citrus-Flavored Vodka
fill with Iced Tea
Highball Glass

Build over ice and stir

Electric Iced Tea

1 1/2 parts Rum
1 1/2 parts Vodka
1 1/2 parts Gin
1 part Tequila
1 part Triple Sec
splash Blue Curaçao
fill with Lemon-Lime Soda
Collins Glass

Build over ice and stir

Embassy Iced Tea

1 part Blue Curaçao
1 part Vodka
1 part Light Rum
1 part Cachaça®
fill with Lemon-Lime Soda
Collins Glass

Build over ice and stir

Ewa Beach Iced Tea

1/2 part Gin
1/2 part Tequila
1/2 part Spiced Rum
1/2 part Vodka
1/2 part Triple Sec
1 part Fruit Punch
1 part Pineapple Juice
Collins Glass

Build over ice and stir

Georgia Peach Iced Tea

1 part Vodka
1 part Gin
1 part Rum
fill with Sour Mix
1 part Peach Schnapps
Collins Glass

Shake with ice and pour

Iced Tea

1 part Vodka
1 part Gin
1/2 part Triple Sec
2 parts Sour Mix
splash Cola
1 Lemon Wedge
Collins Glass

Build over ice and stir

Iced Tea Limoni

1 part Limoncello
fill with Iced Tea
Collins Glass

Build over ice and stir

Iced Teaspoon

1 part Tequila Silver
1 part Vodka
1 part Triple Sec
1 part Light Rum
1 part Gin
2 parts Sour Mix
fill with Iced Tea
Collins Glass

Shake with ice and pour

Lake George Iced Tea

1/2 part Tequila
1/2 part Rum
1/2 part Vodka
1/2 part Gin
1/2 part Triple Sec
1 part Pineapple Juice
fill with Cola
Highball Glass

Shake all but Cola with ice and strain into the glass. Top with Cola.

Long Austin Iced Tea

1/2 part Vodka
1/2 part Gin
1/2 part Rum
1/2 part Triple Sec
1 part Ginger Ale
1 part Iced Tea
Highball Glass

Build over ice and stir

Long Beach Ice Tea

1 part Vodka
1 part Rum
1 part Gin
1 part Triple Sec
1 part Melon Liqueur
fill with Cranberry Juice Cocktail
Highball Glass

Build over ice and stir

Long Island Beach

1 part Vodka
1 part Rum
1 part Triple Sec
2 parts Sour Mix
1 part Cranberry Juice Cocktail
Highball Glass

Build over ice and stir

Long Island Blue

1/2 part Tequila Silver
1/2 part Vodka
1/2 part Light Rum
1/2 part Gin
1 part Blue Curaçao
2 parts Pineapple Juice
fill with Lemonade
Collins Glass

Build over ice and stir

Long Island Iced Berry Tea

1 part Blackberry Brandy
1 part Amaretto
1 part Sloe Gin
1/2 part 151-Proof Rum
fill with Pineapple Juice
Highball Glass

Shake with ice and pour

Long Island Iced Tea

1 part Vodka
1 part Tequila
1 part Rum
1 part Gin
1 part Triple Sec
1 1/2 parts Sour Mix
splash Cola
1 Lemon Wedge
Collins Glass

Mix ingredients together over ice. Pour into shaker and give one brisk shake. Pour back into glass and make sure there is a touch of fizz at the top. Garnish with Lemon Wedge.

Long Island Iced Tea Boston Style

1 part Sour Mix
1 part Gin
1 part Rum
1 part Grand Marnier®
1 part Tia Maria®
1 part Orange Juice
fill with Cola
Collins Glass

Build over ice and stir

Long Island Spiced Tea

3/4 part Spiced Rum
1/2 part Vodka
1/2 part Fresh Lime Juice
1/2 part Gin
1/4 part Triple Sec
fill with Cola
Collins Glass

Build over ice and stir

Long Iver Iced Tea

1 part Coconut-Flavored Rum
1 part Vodka
1 part Gin
1 part Tequila
1 part Triple Sec
fill with Sour Mix
splash Cola
Collins Glass

Build over ice and stir

Mahwah Iced Tea

1 part Jim Beam®
1 part Southern Comfort®
fill with Iced Tea
Highball Glass

Build over ice and stir

Nuclear Iced Tea

1/2 part Vodka
1/2 part Gin
1/2 part Rum
1/2 part Triple Sec
1 part Melon Liqueur
fill with Sour Mix
splash Lemon-Lime Soda
Collins Glass

Build over ice and stir

Radioactive Long Island Iced Tea

1 part Rum
1 part Vodka
1 part Tequila
1 part Gin
1 part Triple Sec
1 part Raspberry Liqueur
1 part Melon Liqueur
fill with Pineapple Juice
splash Cola
Collins Glass

Build over ice and stir

Raspberry Long Island Iced Tea

1/2 part Gin
1/2 part Vodka
1/2 part Light Rum
1/2 part Tequila
2 parts Sour Mix
2 parts Cola
1/2 part Raspberry Liqueur
1 Lemon Wedge
Highball Glass

Build over ice and stir. Float Raspberry Liqueur on top and garnish with Lemon Wedge.

Raspberry Long Island Iced Tea #2
1 part Vodka
1 part Rum
1 part Tequila
1 part Gin
1 part Triple Sec
1 part Chambord®
fill with Sour Mix
splash Cola
Collins Glass

Shake with ice and pour

A Real Iced Tea
3/4 part Vodka
3/4 part Gin
3/4 part Rum
3/4 part Tequila
1/2 part Triple Sec
splash Cranberry Juice Cocktail
splash Sour Mix
splash Cola
Highball Glass

Build over ice and stir

Russian Iced Tea
1 part Vodka
fill with Iced Tea
Highball Glass

Build over ice and stir

Short Island Iced Tea
1 part Southern Comfort®
1 part Spiced Rum
splash Sour Mix
Highball Glass

Shake with ice and strain over ice

Sidney Iced Tea
1/2 part Cointreau®
1/2 part Gin
1/2 part Rum
1/2 part Vodka
1 part Peach Schnapps
fill with Cola
Collins Glass

Build over ice and stir

South Beach Iced Tea
2/3 part Spiced Rum
2/3 part Light Rum
2/3 part Bacardi® Limón Rum
1 part Simple Syrup
2 parts Lemon Juice
fill with Cola
Collins Glass

Build over ice and stir

Southern Long Island Tea
1 part Gin
1 part Tequila Silver
1 part Vodka
1 part Light Rum
1 part Triple Sec
fill with Orange Juice
splash Cola
Highball Glass

Shake with ice and pour

Texas Iced Tea
1 part Tequila
fill with Iced Tea
Highball Glass

Build over ice and stir

Three Mile Island Iced Tea
1 part Gin
1 part Rye Whiskey
1 part Tequila
1 part Triple Sec
1 part Vodka
fill with Cola
Collins Glass

Build over ice and stir

Tokyo Iced Tea
1/2 part Gin
1/2 part Rum
1/2 part Vodka
1/2 part Tequila Silver
1/2 part Triple Sec
1/2 part Melon Liqueur
1 part Fresh Lime Juice
fill with Lemonade
Collins Glass

Shake with ice and pour

Tropical Iced Tea
1/2 part Vodka
1/2 part Rum
1/2 part Gin
1/2 part Triple Sec
1 part Sour Mix
1 part Pineapple Juice
1 part Cranberry Juice Cocktail
1/2 part Grenadine
Collins Glass

Shake with ice and pour

Tropical Spiced Tea
1 1/4 parts Spiced Rum
fill with Iced Tea
splash Lemon Juice
Highball Glass

Build over ice and stir

Westwood Iced Tea
1 part Vanilla Flavored Vodka
1/2 part Tequila
1/2 part Gin
1/2 part Light Rum
1/2 part Goldschläger®
1/2 part 151-Proof Rum
fill with Sour Mix
splash Cola
Beer Mug

Build over ice and stir

Zurich Iced Tea
1 1/2 parts Scotch
1 part Apricot Brandy
1 part Gin
fill with Iced Tea
Collins Glass

Build over ice and stir

Blended and Frozen Drinks

Where would bartending be without the invention of the electric blender? From a frozen Margarita to a Cherry Repair Kit, the collection of drinks below pay tribute to the power of the blender.

As a general guide, drinks that contain ice cream are made in the blender without adding additional ice. Those without ice cream will need ice to achieve the desired consistency.

151 Florida Bushwacker

1/2 part 151-Proof Rum
1/2 part Coconut-Flavored Rum
1/2 part Light Rum
1 part Crème de Cacao (Dark)
1 part Cointreau®
1 part Coconut-Flavored Liqueur
3 parts Milk
1 scoop Vanilla Ice Cream
Beer Mug

Combine all ingredients in a blender. Blend until smooth. Garnish with Chocolate Shavings.

155 Belmont

1 part Dark Rum
2 parts Light Rum
1 part Vodka
1 part Orange Juice
White Wine Glass

Combine all ingredients in a blender. Blend until smooth.

3rd Street Promenade

1 1/2 parts Vanilla-Flavored Vodka
1 part Gin
1 part Tequila
1 part Triple Sec
1/2 part Goldschläger®
6 parts Orange Juice
Hurricane Glass

Combine all ingredients in a blender with icc. Blend until smooth.

98 Beatle

1 part Vodka
1 part Peach Schnapps
1 part Grenadine
2 parts Cranberry Juice Cocktail
1 Banana
Collins Glass

Combine all ingredients in a blender with ice. Blend until smooth.

Abbot's Dream

2 parts Irish Cream Liqueur
1 part Frangelico®
1/2 Banana
1/2 part Cream
Coupette Glass

Combine all ingredients in a blender with ice. Blend until smooth.

Absinthe Frappé

1 1/2 parts Absinthe
1 Egg White
dash Sugar
Coupette Glass

Combine all ingredients in a blender with ice. Blend until smooth.

African Lullaby

1 1/2 parts Amarula® Crème Liqueur
1/2 part Coconut Cream
3 parts Milk
dash Ground Nutmeg
Coupette Glass

Combine all ingredients in a blender with ice. Blend until smooth.

After Sunset

1 part Coffee Liqueur
1/2 part Triple Sec
2 parts Vanilla Ice Cream
1 part Chocolate Syrup
3 parts Cola
2 parts Cream
Collins Glass

Combine all ingredients in a blender with ice. Blend until smooth.

Afternoon Balloon

1 1/2 parts Light Rum
1 part Crème de Banana
1 part Blackberry Liqueur
splash Coconut Cream
splash Lime Juice
4 parts Pineapple Juice
Coupette Glass

Combine all ingredients in a blender with ice. Blend until smooth.

Agent Orange

1 part Vodka
1 part Gin
1 part Yukon Jack®
1 part Sour Apple Schnapps
1 part Melon Liqueur
2 parts Grenadine
6 parts Orange Juice
Hurricane Glass

Combine all ingredients in a blender with ice. Blend until smooth.

Alaskan Monk

1 part Frangelico®
1 part Irish Cream Liqueur
1 part Coffee Liqueur
1 part Vodka
1 part White Chocolate Liqueur
splash Half and Half
Coupette Glass

Combine all ingredients in a blender with ice. Blend until smooth.

Alaskan Suntan

1 part Gin
1 part Rum
1 part Vodka
3 parts Orange Juice
3 parts Pineapple Juice
Coupette Glass

Combine all ingredients in a blender with ice. Blend until smooth.

Albino Baby Snowpiglet

1 part Vodka
1 part Butterscotch Schnapps
1 part Crème de Menthe (White)
2 parts Cream
Coupette Glass

Combine all ingredients in a blender with ice. Blend until smooth.

Albuquerque Real

1 1/2 parts Tequila
1/2 part Triple Sec
1/2 part Sour Mix
1/4 part Cranberry Juice Cocktail
splash Grand Marnier®
Coupette Glass

Combine all ingredients in a blender with ice. Blend until smooth.

Alien Abduction

2 parts Cointreau®
1 part Melon Liqueur
1 part Peach Schnapps
Coupette Glass

Combine all ingredients in a blender with ice. Blend until smooth.

Almond Joey

1 1/2 parts Amaretto
1 part Coconut Cream
1 part Chocolate Syrup
2 scoops Vanilla Ice Cream
Coupette Glass

Combine all ingredients in a blender. Blend until smooth.

Almond Velvet Hammer

2 parts Coffee Liqueur
1/2 part Chocolate Syrup
2 dashes Chopped Almonds
2 scoops Ice Cream
fill with Cream
Coupette Glass

Combine all ingredients in a blender. Blend until smooth.

Al's Frozen Amaretto Mudslide

2 parts Irish Cream Liqueur
1 part Amaretto
2 parts Coffee Liqueur
2 scoops Ice Cream
Coupette Glass

Combine all ingredients in a blender with ice. Blend until smooth.

Amaretto Big Red Float

2 parts Amaretto
fill with Strawberry Soda
2 scoops Ice Cream
splash Strawberry Syrup
Collins Glass

Combine all but Ice Cream in a pint glass. Top with Ice Cream followed by Strawberry Syrup.

Amaretto Chi Chi

1 part Vodka
1 part Amaretto
1/2 part Orange Juice
2 parts Pineapple Juice
2 parts Coconut Cream
Collins Glass

Combine all ingredients in a blender with ice. Blend until smooth.

Amaretto Choco-Cream

1 part Amaretto
1 part Crème de Cacao (Dark)
1 part Chocolate Syrup
2 scoops Ice Cream
Coupette Glass

Combine all ingredients in a blender with ice. Blend until smooth.

Amaretto Colada

1 part Amaretto
1/2 part Rum
2 parts Pineapple Juice
2 parts Coconut Cream
1 part Orange Juice
Hurricane Glass

Combine all ingredients in a blender with ice. Blend until smooth.

Amaretto Cruise

1/2 part Amaretto
1/2 part Peach Schnapps
1/2 part Light Rum
2 parts Orange Juice
2 parts Cranberry Juice Cocktail
1 part Sour Mix
1 part Half and Half
Coupette Glass

Combine all ingredients in a blender with ice. Blend until smooth.

Ameretto Cruise #2

1/2 part Amaretto
1/2 part Banana Schnapps
1/2 part Light Rum
2 parts Orange Juice
2 parts Cherry Juice
1 part Sour Mix
1 part Half and Half
Coupette Glass

Combine all ingredients in a blender with ice. Blend until smooth.

Amaretto Dreamsicle®

1 part Cream
1 part Vodka
1 part Amaretto
1 part Orange Juice
1 part Pineapple Juice
Hurricane Glass

Combine all ingredients in a blender with ice. Blend until smooth.

Amaretto Hurricane

1 part Rum
1 part Amaretto
1 part Cherry Juice
2 parts Orange Juice
1 part Pineapple Juice
Hurricane Glass

Combine all ingredients in a blender with ice. Blend until smooth.

Amaretto Mud Pie

1 part Amaretto
1 part Crème de Cacao (Dark)
fill with Cream
1 Candy Bar
2 scoops Ice Cream
Coupette Glass

Combine all ingredients in a blender. Blend until smooth. Works with almost any Candy Bar.

Amaretto Mud Slide

1 part Amaretto
1 part Crème de Cacao (Dark)
fill with Cream
4 Oreo® Cookies
2 scoops Ice Cream
Coupette Glass

Combine all ingredients in a blender. Blend until smooth.

Ambrosia Pudding

1 part Vanilla Liqueur
2 parts Crème de Banana
2 parts Milk
fill with Yogurt
Collins Glass

Combine all ingredients in a blender. Blend until smooth.

American Leroy

1 part Coffee Liqueur
1 part Vodka
1 part Irish Cream Liqueur
1 part Crème de Cacao (White)
Highball Glass

Combine all ingredients in a blender with ice. Blend until smooth.

Amore

1 part Amaretto
1 part Coffee Liqueur
1 part Cream
Coupette Glass

Combine all ingredients in a blender with ice. Blend until smooth.

Amsterdam Iced Coffee

2/3 part Crème de Cacao (Dark)
2/3 part Frangelico®
2/3 part Dark Rum
2 parts Coffee
splash Cream
Collins Glass

Combine all ingredients in a blender with ice. Blend until smooth.

Andrea's Colada Collision

1 1/2 parts Light Rum
3 parts Coconut Cream
6 parts Pineapple Juice
1 Banana
Hurricane Glass

Combine all ingredients in a blender with ice. Blend until smooth.

Angel in Harlem

1 1/2 parts Vodka
1 part Peach Schnapps
splash Cranberry Juice Cocktail
3 parts Lemonade
Coupette Glass

Combine all ingredients in a blender with ice. Blend until smooth.

Angel's Hug

2 parts Pisang Ambon® Liqueur
1 part Crème de Banana
1 part Dark Rum
2 parts Passion Fruit Juice
1 Banana
Hurricane Glass

Combine all ingredients in a blender with ice. Blend until smooth.

Anthracite

1 part Coffee Liqueur
1 part Vodka
1 scoop Coffee Ice Cream
Coupette Glass

Combine all ingredients in a blender with ice. Blend until smooth.

Any Given Sunday

1 part Peach Schnapps
1 part Orange Juice
1 part Grape Juice (Red)
Collins Glass

Combine all ingredients in a blender with ice. Blend until smooth.

Aphrodisiac Dessert

2 parts Light Rum
1 part Crème de Cacao (White)
2 scoops Ice Cream
1 Banana
Hurricane Glass

Combine all ingredients in a blender with ice. Blend until smooth.

Apple Colada

1 part Sour Apple Schnapps
1 part Peach Schnapps
1 part Coconut Cream
1 part Half and Half
Collins Glass

Combine all ingredients in a blender with ice. Blend until smooth.

Apple Creamsicle®

1 part Cherry Brandy
1 part Cream
1/2 part Pineapple Juice
1/2 part Apple Juice
White Wine Glass

Combine all ingredients in a blender with ice. Blend until smooth.

Apple Daiquiri Sour

1 1/2 parts Rum
1 1/2 parts Sour Apple Schnapps
1 part Lime Juice
dash Sugar
splash Triple Sec
Collins Glass

Combine all ingredients in a blender with ice. Blend until smooth.

Apple Granny Crisp

1 part Sour Apple Schnapps
1/2 part Brandy
1/2 part Irish Cream Liqueur
2 scoops Vanilla Ice Cream
1 Graham Cracker
Coupette Glass

Combine all ingredients in a blender. Blend until smooth.

Apple Pie à la Mode

3/4 part Spiced Rum
1/2 part Sour Apple Schnapps
2 parts Apple Juice
1 part Coconut Cream
1 part Heavy Cream
dash Cinnamon Powder
Coupette Glass

Combine all ingredients in a blender with ice. Blend until smooth.

Apple Sauce

1 part Spiced Rum
3 parts Apple Sauce
4 parts Sour Mix
splash Triple Sec
Hurricane Glass

Combine all ingredients in a blender with ice. Blend until smooth.

Apple Slush Puppy

2 parts Sour Apple Schnapps
fill with Lemonade
Coupette Glass

Combine all ingredients in a blender with ice. Blend until smooth.

Apricot Freeze

2 parts Apricot Brandy
2 scoops Ice Cream
Coupette Glass

Combine all ingredients in a blender. Blend until smooth.

A-Rang-a-Tang

1 part 99-Proof Banana Liqueur
1 part Coconut-Flavored Rum
1 part Light Rum
3 parts Orange Juice
2 parts Pineapple Juice
3 splashes Tang®
3 dashes Powdered Sugar
Coupette Glass

Combine all ingredients in a blender with ice. Blend until smooth.

Archduchess

1 1/2 parts Brandy
1/2 part Raspberry Liqueur
1 scoop Vanilla Ice Cream
Coupette Glass

Combine all ingredients in a blender. Blend until smooth.

Arctic Mouthwash

1 part Tropical Punch Schnapps
1 part Mountain Dew®
Collins Glass

Combine all ingredients in a blender with ice. Blend until smooth.

Arctic Mud Slide

1 part Coffee Liqueur
1 part Irish Cream Liqueur
1 part Vodka
1 part Crème de Menthe (White)
2 scoops Ice Cream
Coupette Glass

Combine all ingredients in a blender with ice. Blend until smooth. Top with Whipped Cream.

Atlantic Dolphin Shit

1 part Rum
1 part Crème de Cacao (White)
1 part Coffee Liqueur
1 part Cream
2 Oreo® Cookies
2 parts Milk
Coupette Glass

Combine all ingredients in a blender with ice. Blend until smooth.

Atomic Smoothie

2 parts Vodka
1/2 part Peach Schnapps
2 scoops Ice Cream
1 part Lemon Juice
6 parts Orange Juice
Coupette Glass

Combine all ingredients in a blender with ice. Blend until smooth.

Aurora

3 parts Vodka
3 scoops Rainbow Sherbert
1 part Orange Juice
2 parts Cranberry Juice Cocktail
Collins Glass

Combine all ingredients in a blender with ice. Blend until smooth.

Avalanche

$1^1/_2$ parts Crème de Banana
$^3/_4$ part Crème de Cacao (White)
$^1/_2$ part Amaretto
2 parts Cream
$^1/_2$ Banana
Collins Glass

Combine all ingredients in a blender with ice. Blend until smooth.

B3

1 part Blue Curaçao
$^1/_2$ part Crème de Banana
$^1/_2$ part Lime Cordial
1 part Passion Fruit Juice
2 parts Pineapple Juice
2 parts Orange Juice
Collins Glass

Combine all ingredients in a blender with ice. Blend until smooth.

Baby Eskimo

2 parts Coffee Liqueur
fill with Milk
2 scoops Vanilla Ice Cream
Coupette Glass

Combine all ingredients in a blender. Blend until smooth.

Baby Jane

1 part Vodka
1 part Butterscotch Schnapps
1 part Irish Cream Liqueur
1 part Grenadine
2 scoops Ice Cream
Coupette Glass

Combine all ingredients in a blender with ice. Blend until smooth.

Bahama Breeze

1 part Dark Rum
$^1/_2$ part Coconut-Flavored Rum
$^1/_2$ part Apricot Brandy
$^1/_2$ part Banana Liqueur
$^1/_4$ part Grenadine
$^1/_4$ part Honey
$^1/_2$ part Lemon Juice
1 part Orange Juice
1 part Pineapple Juice
Collins Glass

Combine all ingredients in a blender with ice. Blend until smooth.

Baileys® Banana Colada

2 parts Irish Cream Liqueur
1 part Dark Rum
1 part Banana Liqueur
4 parts Piña Colada Mix
1 Banana
Coupette Glass

Combine all ingredients in a blender with ice. Blend until smooth.

Baileys® Blizzard

1 part Irish Cream Liqueur
1 part Peppermint Schnapps
$^1/_2$ part Brandy
1 scoop Vanilla Ice Cream
Coupette Glass

Combine all ingredients in a blender. Blend until smooth.

Baileys® Mud Pie

1 part Irish Cream Liqueur
1 part Crème de Cacao (Dark)
fill with Cream
1 Candy Bar
2 scoops Ice Cream
Coupette Glass

Combine all ingredients in a blender. Blend until smooth. Works with almost any candy bar.

Baileys® Mud Slide

1 part Irish Cream Liqueur
1 part Crème de Cacao (Dark)
fill with Cream
2 Oreo® Cookies
2 scoops Ice Cream
Coupette Glass

Combine all ingredients in a blender. Blend until smooth.

Baleares under Snow

2/3 part Grenadine
2 parts Light Rum
1 1/2 parts Strawberry Puree
2 parts Cream
Coupette Glass

Combine all ingredients in a blender with ice. Blend until smooth.

Banana Bender

1 part Coffee Liqueur
1 part Crème de Banana
1 part Irish Cream Liqueur
1 part Banana Puree
2 parts Cream
Collins Glass

Combine all ingredients in a blender with ice. Blend until smooth.

Banana Brilliance

1 part Crème de Banana
1 part Vanilla Liqueur
1 part Banana Puree
1/4 part Caramel Syrup
Hurricane Glass

Combine all ingredients in a blender with ice. Blend until smooth.

Banana di Amore

1 part Amaretto
1 part Crème de Banana
2 parts Orange Juice
1 part Sour Mix
Red Wine Glass

Combine all ingredients in a blender with ice. Blend until smooth.

Banana Dream

1 part Vodka
1 part Banana Liqueur
3 parts Orange Juice
1 part Cream
Coupette Glass

Combine all ingredients in a blender with ice. Blend until smooth.

Banana Dreamsicle®

1 part Vodka
1 part Banana Liqueur
1 part Cherry Juice
1 part Orange Juice
1 part Pineapple Juice
1 part Cream
Highball Glass

Combine all ingredients in a blender with ice. Blend until smooth.

Banana Flip

2 parts Banana Liqueur
1 part Cream
2 parts Orange Juice
splash Cherry Liqueur
splash Sour Apple Schnapps
1 scoop Ice Cream
Coupette Glass

Combine all ingredients in a blender with ice. Blend until smooth. Top with Whipped Cream.

Banana Foster

2 scoops Vanilla Ice Cream
$1^1/_2$ parts Spiced Rum
$^1/_2$ part Banana Liqueur
1 Banana
Highball Glass

Combine all ingredients in a blender with ice. Blend until smooth.

Banana Hurricane

1 part Rum
1 part Banana Liqueur
2 parts Orange Juice
1 part Pineapple Juice
Highball Glass

Combine all ingredients in a blender with ice. Blend until smooth.

Banana Ivanov

$1^1/_2$ parts Dry Vermouth
1 part Lime Cordial
$^1/_2$ part Banana Juice
$^1/_2$ Banana
Hurricane Glass

Combine all ingredients in a blender with ice. Blend until smooth.

Banana Mama Bumpin

2 parts Rum
1 part Vanilla Ice Cream
1 part Banana Puree
$^1/_2$ part Coconut-Flavored Liqueur
$^1/_2$ part Banana Syrup
Old-Fashioned Glass

Combine all ingredients in a blender with ice. Blend until smooth.

Banana Man

2 parts Coconut-Flavored Rum
2 parts Banana Juice
fill with Lemonade
splash Orange Juice
Highball Glass

Combine all ingredients in a blender with ice. Blend until smooth.

Banana Margarita

$1^1/_2$ parts Tequila Silver
1 part Fresh Lime Juice
$^1/_2$ part Crème de Banana
Coupette Glass

Combine all ingredients in a blender with ice. Blend until smooth.

Banana Nutbread

1 scoop Vanilla Ice Cream
1 part Crème de Banana
1 part Frangelico®
White Wine Glass

Combine all ingredients in a blender. Blend until smooth.

Banana Queen

2 parts Dark Rum
$1^1/_2$ parts Coconut Cream
1 part Banana Puree
1 part Cream
2 parts Pineapple Juice
Collins Glass

Combine all ingredients in a blender with ice. Blend until smooth.

Banana Split

2 parts Irish Cream Liqueur
1 part Banana Liqueur
2 parts Coffee Liqueur
fill with Cream
Hurricane Glass

Combine all ingredients in a blender with ice. Blend until smooth.

Banana Tree

1 part Banana Liqueur
1/2 part Crème de Cacao (White)
1/2 part Galliano®
1 scoop Vanilla Ice Cream
1/2 Banana
splash Vanilla Extract
Collins Glass

Combine all ingredients in a blender with ice. Blend until smooth.

Banana's Milk

1 part Vodka
1 1/2 parts Banana Puree
3 parts Milk
Coupette Glass

Combine all ingredients in a blender with ice. Blend until smooth.

Banoffie Dream

1 part Crème de Banana
1 part Irish Cream Liqueur
1 part Cream
2 parts Milk
Collins Glass

Combine all ingredients in a blender with ice. Blend until smooth.

Banshee

3/4 part Banana Liqueur
3/4 part Crème de Cacao (White)
1/2 part Amaretto
3/4 part Half and Half
Coupette Glass

Combine all ingredients in a blender with ice. Blend until smooth.

Barnaby's Buffalo Blizzard

3/4 part Vodka
1 part Crème de Cacao (White)
1 part Galliano®
1 scoop Vanilla Ice Cream
splash Grenadine
Coupette Glass

Combine all ingredients in a blender. Blend until smooth.

Barnamint Baileys®

1 part Crème de Menthe (White)
1 part Irish Cream Liqueur
3 scoops Ice Cream
2 Oreo® Cookies
2 parts Milk
Collins Glass

Combine all ingredients in a blender. Blend until smooth.

Barney® Fizz

1 part Raspberry Liqueur
1 part Amaretto
1/2 part Vodka
3 parts Grape Juice (Red)
1 Egg White
1 part Sugar
Collins Glass

Combine all ingredients in a blender with ice. Blend until smooth.

Barranquillero

2 parts Light Rum
1/2 part Coconut-Flavored Liqueur
2 parts Cream
1 part Melon Liqueur
Hurricane Glass

Combine all ingredients in a blender with ice. Blend until smooth.

Batida Abaci

1 part Cachaça®
2 parts Pineapple Juice
dash Sugar
White Wine Glass

Combine all ingredients in a blender with ice. Blend until smooth.

Batida de Piña

3 parts Rum
6 parts Pineapple Juice
1/4 part Powdered Sugar
Old-Fashioned Glass

Combine all ingredients in a blender with ice. Blend until smooth.

Batida Mango

1 part Cachaça®
2 parts Mango Juice
2 dashes Sugar
White Wine Glass

Combine all ingredients in a blender with ice. Blend until smooth.

Bay City Bomber

1/2 part Vodka
1/2 part Rum
1/2 part Tequila
1/2 part Gin
1/2 part Triple Sec
1 part Orange Juice
1 part Pineapple Juice
1 part Cranberry Juice Cocktail
1 part Sour Mix
splash 151-Proof Rum
Parfait Glass

Combine all ingredients in a blender with ice. Blend until smooth.

Beaconizer

1 part Irish Cream Liqueur
1 part Crème de Cacao (Dark)
2 scoops Ice Cream
splash Cream
Coupette Glass

Combine all ingredients in a blender. Blend until smooth.

Belly-Button Fluff

1 part Light Rum
1 1/2 parts Coconut Liqueur
3 parts Pineapple Juice
1/2 Banana
Coupette Glass

Combine all ingredients in a blender with ice. Blend until smooth.

Berries 'n' Cream

1/2 part Spiced Rum
3/4 part Wild Berry Schnapps
3 parts Strawberry Daiquiri Mix
5 Raspberries
2 parts Heavy Cream
Hurricane Glass

Combine all ingredients in a blender with ice. Blend until smooth.

Betty Swallocks

1 1/2 parts Butterscotch Schnapps
1 1/2 parts Coffee Liqueur
1 part Brandy
fill with Milk
Hurricane Glass

Combine all ingredients in a blender with ice. Blend until smooth.

Big Blue Sky

1/2 part Light Rum
1/2 part Blue Curaçao
1/2 part Coconut Cream
2 parts Pineapple Juice
Coupette Glass

Combine all ingredients in a blender with ice. Blend until smooth.

Big Booty Shake

1 1/2 parts Southern Comfort®
8 parts Milk
splash Vanilla Extract
2 scoops Chocolate Ice Cream
Beer Mug

Combine all ingredients in a blender. Blend until smooth.

Big Chill

1 1/2 parts Dark Rum
1 part Pineapple Juice
1 part Orange Juice
1 part Cranberry Juice Cocktail
1 part Coconut Cream
Pilsner Glass

Combine all ingredients in a blender with ice. Blend until smooth.

Big John's Special

1 part Vodka
1/2 part Gin
3 parts Grapefruit Juice
3 dashes Orange Bitters
3 dashes Maraschino Cherry Juice
Coupette Glass

Combine all ingredients in a blender with ice. Blend until smooth.

Bitch Monkey Lost Its Lunch

3 parts Crème de Cacao (White)
2 parts Peppermint Schnapps
1 Banana
Coupette Glass

Combine all ingredients in a blender with ice. Blend until smooth.

Black Bear in the Wood

1 part Amaretto
1/2 part Crème de Cacao (White)
1/2 part Crème de Cacao (Dark)
splash Vanilla Extract
splash Chocolate Syrup
1 scoop Vanilla Ice Cream
Coupette Glass

Combine all ingredients in a blender. Blend until smooth.

Black Cherry Margarita

1/2 part Tequila Reposado
1/2 part Triple Sec
3/4 part Cherry Liqueur
2 parts Orange Juice
2 parts Sour Mix
Coupette Glass

Combine all ingredients in a blender with ice. Blend until smooth.

Black Forest

1 part Vodka
1 part Coffee Liqueur
1 part Blackberry Liqueur
1 scoop Chocolate Ice Cream
Coupette Glass

Combine all ingredients in a blender. Blend until smooth.

Blaster Bates

1 Banana
5 Blueberries
5 Raspberries
1 part Milk
2 parts Orange Juice
Collins Glass

Combine all ingredients in a blender with ice. Blend until smooth.

Blended Comfort

1 part Southern Comfort®
1/2 part Dry Vermouth
1 part Orange Juice
1 part Lemon Juice
splash Peach Schnapps
Collins Glass

Combine all ingredients in a blender with ice. Blend until smooth.

Blended Georgia Peach

3/4 part Vodka
3/4 part Peach Schnapps
3 parts Orange Juice
2 parts Peach Puree
Hurricane Glass

Combine all ingredients in a blender with ice. Blend until smooth.

Blended Puppy Guts

2 parts Strawberry Puree
2 parts Lemon-Lime Soda
1 part Strawberry Liqueur
1 Strawberry
Collins Glass

Combine all ingredients in a blender with ice. Blend until smooth.

Blizzard

1 part Gin
1 scoop Vanilla Ice Cream
1/4 part Dry Sherry
Highball Glass

Combine all ingredients in a blender. Blend until smooth.

Blue Hurricane

1/2 part Blue Curaçao
1/2 part Light Rum
4 parts Pineapple Juice
2 parts Blueberries
Coupette Glass

Combine all ingredients in a blender with ice. Blend until smooth.

Blue Max

1 part Vodka
1 part Blue Curaçao
1/2 part Coconut Cream
3 parts Pineapple Juice
2 parts Cream
Hurricane Glass

Combine all ingredients in a blender with ice. Blend until smooth.

Blue Night Shadow

1 part Blue Curaçao
1 part Crème de Cacao (White)
1 1/2 parts Cream
1 part Coconut Cream
fill with Pineapple Juice
Hurricane Glass

Combine all ingredients in a blender with ice. Blend until smooth.

Blue Popsicle®

1 part Blue Curaçao
1 1/2 parts Sour Mix
1 part Triple Sec
1 1/2 parts Blueberry Schnapps
Coupette Glass

Combine all ingredients in a blender with ice. Blend until smooth.

Blue Velvet

1 part Blackberry Liqueur
1 part Melon Liqueur
1 scoop Vanilla Ice Cream
splash Blue Curaçao
Parfait Glass

Combine all ingredients in a blender with ice. Blend until smooth.

Blue Whale

1 part Vodka
1 part Blue Curaçao
2 parts Sour Mix
Coupette Glass

Combine all ingredients in a blender with ice. Blend until smooth.

Blueberry Tango

1 part Peach Schnapps
1 part Blue Curaçao
fill with Blueberries
2 parts Grapefruit Juice
1/2 part Lemon Juice
Collins Glass

Combine all ingredients in a blender with ice. Blend until smooth.

Blushin' Russian

1 part Coffee Liqueur
1 part Vodka
1 scoop Vanilla Ice Cream
4 Strawberries
Parfait Glass

Combine all ingredients in a blender. Blend until smooth.

Bonzai Berries

1/2 part Strawberry Liqueur
1/2 part Amaretto
1/2 part Blackberry Liqueur
2 scoops Vanilla Ice Cream
1 part Cream
1 part Blueberries
2 parts Strawberry Puree
Coupette Glass

Combine all ingredients in a blender with ice. Blend until smooth.

Booty Drink

2 parts Coconut-Flavored Rum
1 part Grenadine
2 parts Orange Juice
2 parts Pineapple Juice
1/2 Banana
Collins Glass

Combine all ingredients in a blender with ice. Blend until smooth.

Border Thrill

1 part Southern Comfort®
1/2 part Tequila
1/4 part Triple Sec
1 part Sour Mix
fill with Orange Juice
splash Grenadine
Coupette Glass

Combine all ingredients in a blender with ice. Blend until smooth.

Bosco 42DD

2 parts Crème de Cacao (Dark)
2 parts Coffee Liqueur
1/2 part Brandy
1/2 part Gin
2 scoops Chocolate Ice Cream
Highball Glass

Combine all ingredients in a blender. Blend until smooth.

Boston Freeze

1 1/4 part Dark Rum
3 parts Cranberry Juice Cocktail
1 part Coconut Cream
White Wine Glass

Combine all ingredients in a blender with ice. Blend until smooth.

Bourbon Dessert

1 1/2 parts Jim Beam®
2/3 part Strawberry Liqueur
1/2 part Hazelnut Liqueur
2 parts Cream
Coupette Glass

Combine all ingredients in a blender with ice. Blend until smooth.

Bourbon Rouge

1 part Peach Schnapps
1 part Jim Beam®
1 part Espresso
1 scoop Vanilla Ice Cream
Coupette Glass

Combine all ingredients in a blender. Blend until smooth.

Brass Fiddle

2 parts Peach Schnapps
3/4 part Jack Daniel's®
2 parts Pineapple Juice
1 part Orange Juice
1 part Grenadine
Parfait Glass

Combine all ingredients in a blender with ice. Blend until smooth.

Brazilian Monk

1 part Crème de Cacao (Dark)
1 part Coffee
1 part Frangelico®
2 scoops Vanilla Ice Cream
White Wine Glass

Combine all ingredients in a blender. Blend until smooth.

Brown Cow

1 part Light Rum
1/2 part Crème de Cacao (White)
1/4 part Crème de Menthe (White)
1 scoop Chocolate Ice Cream
Champagne Flute

Combine all ingredients in a blender. Blend until smooth.

Brown Squirrel

1 part Amaretto
1 part Crème de Cacao (Dark)
1 scoop Vanilla Ice Cream
White Wine Glass

Combine all ingredients in a blender. Blend until smooth.

Bunky Punch

$1^1/_2$ parts Vodka
1 part Melon Liqueur
1 part Peach Schnapps
$1^1/_2$ parts Cranberry Juice Cocktail
2 parts Orange Juice
$^1/_2$ part Grape Juice (Red)
Parfait Glass

Combine all ingredients in a blender with ice. Blend until smooth.

Burnt Almond

1 part Amaretto
1 part Coffee Liqueur
2 scoops Vanilla Ice Cream
White Wine Glass

Combine all ingredients in a blender. Blend until smooth.

Bushwacker

1 part Dark Rum
1 part Crème de Cacao (Dark)
2 parts Coffee Liqueur
1 part Coconut Cream
1 part Milk
White Wine Glass

Combine all ingredients in a blender with ice. Blend until smooth.

Cabana Club

1 part Rum
$^1/_2$ part Coconut Cream
1 part Pineapple Juice
1 part Cranberry Juice Cocktail
splash Grenadine
Hurricane Glass

Combine all ingredients in a blender with ice. Blend until smooth.

Cactus

$1^1/_2$ parts Vodka
1 part Melon Liqueur
1 part Coconut Cream
fill with Pineapple Juice
Coupette Glass

Combine all ingredients in a blender with ice. Blend until smooth.

Cactus Colada

$1^1/_2$ parts Tequila Silver
$^2/_3$ part Melon Liqueur
$^1/_2$ part Grenadine
2 parts Coconut Cream
1 part Orange Juice
1 part Pineapple Juice
Collins Glass

Combine all ingredients in a blender with ice. Blend until smooth.

Cactus Love

1 part Crème de Banana
1 part Jim Beam®
splash Triple Sec
splash Lemon Juice
2 parts Pineapple Juice
Coupette Glass

Combine all ingredients in a blender with ice. Blend until smooth.

Cadillac®

$1^1/_2$ parts Tequila Silver
$^1/_2$ part Triple Sec
3 parts Sour Mix
Hurricane Glass

Combine all ingredients in a blender with ice. Blend until smooth.

Calm Voyage

1/2 part Light Rum
1/2 part Strega®
splash Passion Fruit Nectar
2 splashes Lemon Juice
1/2 Egg White
Champagne Flute

Combine all ingredients in a blender with ice. Blend until smooth.

Camino Real

1 1/2 parts Tequila
1/2 part Banana Liqueur
1 part Orange Juice
splash Lime Juice
splash Coconut Cream
Coupette Glass

Combine all ingredients in a blender with ice. Blend until smooth.

Candy Store

2 parts Raspberry Liqueur
2 parts Amaretto
1 part Crème de Noyaux
2 scoops Cookies and Cream Ice Cream
Coupette Glass

Combine all ingredients in a blender. Blend until smooth.

Canyon Quake

1 part Irish Cream Liqueur
1 part Brandy
1 part Amaretto
2 parts Light Cream
Coupette Glass

Combine all ingredients in a blender with ice. Blend until smooth.

Caribbean Threesome

1/2 part Citrus-Flavored Rum
1/2 part Coconut-Flavored Rum
1 part Spiced Rum
fill with Pineapple Juice
1 Banana
3 Strawberries
Hurricane Glass

Combine all ingredients in a blender with ice. Blend until smooth.

Carol Ann

1 part Vodka
1 part Amaretto
fill with Skim Milk
Hurricane Glass

Combine all ingredients in a blender with ice. Blend until smooth.

The Catalina Margarita

1 1/4 parts Tequila
1 part Peach Schnapps
1 part Blue Curaçao
4 parts Sour Mix
Margarita Glass

Combine all ingredients in a blender with ice. Blend until smooth.

Cavanaugh's Special

1 part Coffee Liqueur
1 part Crème de Cacao (White)
1 part Amaretto
2 scoops Vanilla Ice Cream
Hurricane Glass

Combine all ingredients in a blender. Blend until smooth.

Chamborlada

1 part Dark Rum
2 parts Light Rum
2 parts Coconut Cream
3 parts Pineapple Juice
White Wine Glass

Combine all ingredients in a blender with ice. Blend until smooth.

Cherry Repair Kit

1 part Amaretto
1 part Crème de Cacao (White)
1 part Half and Half
1 part Maraschino Cherry Juice
6 Maraschino Cherries
Coupette Glass

Combine all ingredients in a blender with ice. Blend until smooth.

Chi Chi

1 1/2 parts Vodka
1 part Coconut Cream
3 parts Pineapple Juice
Coupette Glass

Combine all ingredients in a blender with ice. Blend until smooth.

China Doll

1 part Tequila
1 part Brandy
fill with Milk
Coupette Glass

Combine all ingredients in a blender with ice. Blend until smooth.

Chiquita® Punch

1 part Banana Liqueur
1 part Orange Juice
1 part Heavy Cream
splash Grenadine
Hurricane Glass

Combine all ingredients in a blender with ice. Blend until smooth.

Chocolate Almond Cream

2 parts Amaretto
2 parts Crème de Cacao (White)
1 scoop Vanilla Ice Cream
Parfait Glass

Combine all ingredients in a blender. Blend until smooth.

Chocolate Almond Kiss

1 part Crème de Cacao (Dark)
1 part Frangelico®
1 part Vodka
2 scoops Vanilla Ice Cream
Coupette Glass

Combine all ingredients in a blender. Blend until smooth.

Chocolate Orgasm

1/2 part Crème de Cacao (Dark)
1 part Chocolate Mint Liqueur
1/2 part Irish Cream Liqueur
1 scoop Vanilla Ice Cream
Coupette Glass

Combine all ingredients in a blender. Blend until smooth.

Chocolate Snow Bear

1 part Amaretto
1 part Crème de Cacao (White)
1/4 part Chocolate Syrup
2 splashes Vanilla Extract
1 scoop French Vanilla Ice Cream
Champagne Flute

Combine all ingredients in a blender. Blend until smooth.

Chocolate Snowman

3 parts Coconut-Flavored Liqueur
2 parts Almond Syrup
1 part Maple Syrup
1/2 part Crème de Cacao (White)
1/2 part Cream
1/2 part Crème de Cacao (Dark)
1/2 part Crème Liqueur
1/2 part Milk
Coupette Glass

Combine all ingredients in a blender with ice. Blend until smooth.

Cloud 9

1 part Irish Cream Liqueur
1 part Amaretto
1/2 part Raspberry Liqueur
2 scoops Vanilla Ice Cream
Parfait Glass

Combine all ingredients in a blender. Blend until smooth.

Cocoa Colada

1 1/2 parts Light Rum
1/4 part Coffee Liqueur
1/2 part Coconut Cream
1/2 part Chocolate Syrup
1 1/2 parts Milk
Collins Glass

Combine all ingredients in a blender with ice. Blend until smooth.

Coco-Mocha Alexander

1 part Spiced Rum
1/2 part Coffee-Flavored Brandy
1 part Coffee
1 part Coconut Cream
1 part Cream
Coupette Glass

Combine all ingredients in a blender with ice. Blend until smooth.

Coconut Delight

1 part Coconut-Flavored Liqueur
1 part Vanilla Ice Cream
1 part Coconut Cream
fill with Milk
Coupette Glass

Combine all ingredients in a blender with ice. Blend until smooth.

Coconut Kisses

1 part Light Rum
1 part Coconut-Flavored Liqueur
1 part Apricot Brandy
1 part Coconut Cream
1 part Apricot Juice
1 part Pineapple Juice
Hurricane Glass

Combine all ingredients in a blender with ice. Blend until smooth.

Colorado Avalanche

3 parts Blackberry Brandy
1 part Vanilla Liqueur
1 scoop Vanilla Ice Cream
Hurricane Glass

Combine all ingredients in a blender. Blend until smooth.

Columbia Gold

$1^1/_4$ parts Yukon Jack®
$^3/_4$ part Strawberry Liqueur
fill with Orange Juice
White Wine Glass

Combine all ingredients in a blender with ice. Blend until smooth.

Comfortably Numb

1 part Spiced Rum
1 part Vanilla-Flavored Vodka
1 part Coconut-Flavored Liqueur
$^2/_3$ part Coconut Cream
2 parts Pineapple Juice
1 part Orange Juice
Coupette Glass

Combine all ingredients in a blender with ice. Blend until smooth.

Coo Coo

$1^1/_2$ parts Rum
$1^1/_2$ parts Melon Liqueur
3 parts Piña Colada Mix
3 parts Sour Mix
Coupette Glass

Combine all ingredients in a blender with ice. Blend until smooth.

Cookie Dough

1 part Gin
1 part Crème de Cacao (White)
2 dashes Angostura® Bitters
$1^1/_2$ parts Coconut Cream
$^1/_2$ part Cream
Coupette Glass

Combine all ingredients in a blender with ice. Blend until smooth.

Country & Western

$1^1/_4$ parts Dark Rum
1 part Coconut Cream
1 part Pineapple Juice
1 part Orange Juice
Coupette Glass

Combine all ingredients in a blender with ice. Blend until smooth.

Crazy Banana Mama

1 part Cream
1 part Amaretto
1 part Rum
1 part Banana Puree
Old-Fashioned Glass

Combine all ingredients in a blender with ice. Blend until smooth.

Crazy Monkey

1 part Banana Liqueur
2 parts Strawberry Daiquiri Mix
2 parts Orange Juice
Hurricane Glass

Combine all ingredients in a blender with ice. Blend until smooth.

Creamsicle® Dream

$1^1/_2$ parts Coconut-Flavored Rum
1 scoop Vanilla Ice Cream
fill with Orange Juice
Highball Glass

Combine all ingredients in a blender with ice. Blend until smooth.

Creamy Champ

1 1/2 parts Melon Liqueur
1 part Light Rum
1 part Coconut Cream
4 parts Pineapple Juice
2 parts Vanilla Ice Cream
Coupette Glass

Combine all ingredients in a blender. Blend until smooth.

Creamy Imperial

2 parts Crème de Cacao (White)
1 part Blackberry Liqueur
1 scoop Vanilla Ice Cream
2 parts Milk
Coupette Glass

Combine all ingredients in a blender with ice. Blend until smooth.

Crème de Menthe Parfait

1/2 part Spiced Rum
1/4 part Crème de Cacao (White)
1/2 part Crème de Menthe (Green)
1 part Coconut Cream
2 parts Heavy Cream
Coupette Glass

Combine all ingredients in a blender with ice. Blend until smooth.

Crickets

1 1/2 parts Peach Brandy
2 parts Crème de Cacao (White)
2 scoops Ice Cream
Coupette Glass

Combine all ingredients in a blender. Blend until smooth.

Dark Indulgence

1/2 part Tia Maria®
3 parts Cola
1 scoop Vanilla Ice Cream
Coupette Glass

Combine all ingredients in a blender. Blend until smooth.

The Dark Side

1 part Amaretto
1 part 151-Proof Rum
1 part Crème de Cacao (Dark)
1 part Coffee Liqueur
1 part Triple Sec
3 scoops Vanilla Ice Cream
Highball Glass

Combine all ingredients in a blender with ice. Blend until smooth.

Delightful Mistery

1 part Gin
2/3 part Peach Schnapps
2/3 part Pisang Ambon® Liqueur
4 parts Orange Juice
Coupette Glass

Combine all ingredients in a blender with ice. Blend until smooth.

Derby Special

1 1/2 parts Light Rum
1/2 part Cointreau®
1/2 part Lime Juice
1 part Orange Juice
Coupette Glass

Combine all ingredients in a blender with ice. Blend until smooth.

Devil's Gun

$1^1/_2$ parts Dark Rum
1 part Light Rum
1 part Pineapple Juice
$^1/_4$ part Apricot Brandy
$^1/_4$ part Fresh Lime Juice
splash Grenadine
Coupette Glass

Combine all ingredients in a blender with ice. Blend until smooth.

Devil's Tail

$1^1/_2$ parts Light Rum
1 part Vodka
2 splashes Grenadine
2 splashes Apricot Brandy
1 part Lime Juice
1 Lemon Twist
Champagne Flute

Combine all ingredients in a blender with ice. Blend until smooth.

Di Amore Dream

$1^1/_2$ parts Amaretto
$^3/_4$ part Crème de Cacao (White)
2 parts Orange Juice
2 scoops Vanilla Ice Cream
Parfait Glass

Combine all ingredients in a blender. Blend until smooth.

Dirty Banana

1 part Light Rum
2 parts Coffee Liqueur
2 parts Half and Half
dash Powdered Sugar
1 Banana
Champagne Flute

Combine all ingredients in a blender with ice. Blend until smooth.

Dirty Dog

1 part Hennessy®
$1^1/_2$ parts Vodka
fill with Orange Juice
1 part Cranberry Juice Cocktail
Coupette Glass

Combine all ingredients in a blender with ice. Blend until smooth.

Dominican Coco Loco

$^1/_2$ part Amaretto
1 part Coconut Cream
splash Grenadine
1 part Milk
$^1/_2$ part Pineapple Juice
$1^1/_2$ parts Light Rum
Coupette Glass

Combine all ingredients in a blender with ice. Blend until smooth.

Don Pedro

1 part Whiskey
1 part Coffee Liqueur
2 scoops Vanilla Ice Cream
Coupette Glass

Combine all ingredients in a blender. Blend until smooth.

Donna Reed

1 part Absolut® Vodka
2 parts Cranberry Juice Cocktail
2 parts Sour Mix
Coupette Glass

Combine all ingredients in a blender with ice. Blend until smooth.

Down Under Snowball

1 part Light Rum
1 part Peach Schnapps
1/2 part Grenadine
3 parts Orange Juice
Coupette Glass

Combine all ingredients in a blender with ice. Blend until smooth.

Dreamy Monkey

1 part Vodka
1/2 part Crème de Banana
1/2 part Crème de Cacao (Dark)
1 Banana
2 scoops Vanilla Ice Cream
1 part Light Cream
Parfait Glass

Combine all ingredients in a blender. Blend until smooth.

E Pluribus Unum

1 part Frangelico®
1 part Raspberry Liqueur
1 part Coffee Liqueur
2 scoops Chocolate Ice Cream
Coupette Glass

Combine all ingredients in a blender. Blend until smooth.

The Event Horizon

1 part Peppermint Schnapps
1 part Vodka
1 part Milk
1 scoop Chocolate Ice Cream
Highball Glass

Combine all ingredients in a blender. Blend until smooth.

Feeler

1 1/2 parts Light Rum
1/2 part Galliano®
1/4 part Passion Fruit Nectar
1/4 part Pineapple Juice
2 splashes Lemon Juice
Champagne Flute

Combine all ingredients in a blender with ice. Blend until smooth.

Finnish Flash

1 part Cranberry-Flavored Vodka
1/2 part Crème de Menthe (White)
1/2 part Tequila Silver
Coupette Glass

Combine all ingredients in a blender with ice. Blend until smooth.

Flicker

2 parts Light Rum
1/4 part Passion Fruit Nectar
2 splashes Lemon Juice
2 splashes Lime Juice
Collins Glass

Combine all ingredients in a blender with ice. Blend until smooth.

Florida Freeze

1 1/4 parts Dark Rum
1 1/4 parts Coconut Cream
1 part Orange Juice
2 parts Pineapple Juice
Coupette Glass

Combine all ingredients in a blender with ice. Blend until smooth.

Florida Rum Runner
1 1/2 parts Rum
1 part Blackberry Brandy
1 part Banana Liqueur
1 part Lime Juice
1/2 part Grenadine
Coupette Glass

Combine all ingredients in a blender with ice. Blend until smooth.

Flying Bikini
1 part Brandy
1 part Triple Sec
1 part Strawberry Liqueur
1 part Spiced Rum
1 part Amaretto
fill with Orange Juice
Hurricane Glass

Combine all ingredients in a blender with ice. Blend until smooth.

Flying Bliss
1 part Crème de Banana
1 part Cognac
2 parts Vanilla Liqueur
Coupette Glass

Combine all ingredients in a blender with ice. Blend until smooth.

Flying Carpet
1 part Vodka
1 part Advocaat
1 part Crème de Banana
Highball Glass

Combine all ingredients in a blender with ice. Blend until smooth.

Flying Gorilla
1 part Vodka
1 part Banana Liqueur
1 part Crème de Cacao (White)
2 scoops Vanilla Ice Cream
Coupette Glass

Combine all ingredients in a blender. Blend until smooth.

Freezy Melonkiny
1 1/2 parts Vodka
2/3 part Kiwi Schnapps
2/3 part Melon Liqueur
2 parts Cream
Coupette Glass

Combine all ingredients in a blender with ice. Blend until smooth.

Fresa
1/2 part Parfait Amour
2 parts Cachaça®
1 1/2 parts Strawberry Puree
dash Sugar
Coupette Glass

Combine all ingredients in a blender with ice. Blend until smooth.

Frisket City
1 1/2 parts Southern Comfort®
2/3 part Apricot Brandy
1/2 part Pear Brandy
2 parts Cream
Coupette Glass

Combine all ingredients in a blender with ice. Blend until smooth.

Frozen Arctic Cream

2 parts Vodka
2 parts Vanilla Liqueur
1 part Blue Curaçao
2 parts Cream
1 scoop Vanilla Ice Cream
Collins Glass

Combine all ingredients in a blender. Blend until smooth.

Frozen Banana Smoothie

1 part Rum
1 1/2 parts Banana Liqueur
1/2 part Sour Mix
1/2 Banana
Collins Glass

Combine all ingredients in a blender with ice. Blend until smooth.

Frozen Berkeley

1 1/2 parts Light Rum
1/2 part Brandy
1 part Passion Fruit Nectar
1 part Lemon Juice
Champagne Flute

Combine all ingredients in a blender with ice. Blend until smooth.

Frozen Black Irish

1 part Coffee Liqueur
1 part Irish Cream Liqueur
1 part Vodka
1 scoop Chocolate Ice Cream
Coupette Glass

Combine all ingredients in a blender. Blend until smooth.

Frozen Blue Daiquiri

2 parts Light Rum
1/2 part Blue Curaçao
1/2 part Lime Juice
Old-Fashioned Glass

Combine all ingredients in a blender with ice. Blend until smooth.

Frozen Brandy and Rum

1 1/2 parts Brandy
1 part Light Rum
splash Lemon Juice
dash Powdered Sugar
1 Egg White
Old-Fashioned Glass

Combine all ingredients in a blender with ice. Blend until smooth.

Frozen Cappuccino

1 part Irish Cream Liqueur
1 part Coffee Liqueur
1 part Frangelico®
1 scoop Vanilla Ice Cream
splash Light Cream
Parfait Glass

Combine all ingredients in a blender with ice. Blend until smooth.

Frozen Citron Neon

1 1/2 parts Citrus-Flavored Vodka
1 part Melon Liqueur
1/2 part Blue Curaçao
1/2 part Lime Juice
1 part Sour Mix
Parfait Glass

Combine all ingredients in a blender. Blend until smooth.

Frozen Citrus Banana

1½ parts Dark Rum
1½ parts Fresh Lime Juice
2 parts Orange Juice
2 parts Milk
2 parts Club Soda
dash Brown Sugar
1 Banana
Collins Glass

Combine all ingredients in a blender with ice. Blend until smooth.

Frozen Daiquiri

1 part Light Rum
1 part Lime Juice
splash Triple Sec
dash Sugar
Champagne Flute

Combine all ingredients in a blender with ice. Blend until smooth.

Frozen Danube

2 parts Vodka
2 parts Melon Liqueur
1 part Blue Curaçao
3 parts Grapefruit Juice
3 parts Melon Puree
Hurricane Glass

Combine all ingredients in a blender with ice. Blend until smooth.

Frozen Domingo

1½ parts Spiced Rum
2 parts Piña Colada Mix
2 parts Orange Juice
2 parts Cranberry Juice Cocktail
Coupette Glass

Combine all ingredients in a blender with ice. Blend until smooth.

Frozen Girl Scout

1½ parts Crème de Menthe (Green)
3 scoops Chocolate Ice Cream
splash Milk
Coupette Glass

Combine all ingredients in a blender. Blend until smooth.

Frozen Grasshopper

1 part Crème de Menthe (Green)
1 part Crème de Cacao (White)
2 cups Vanilla Ice Cream
Coupette Glass

Combine all ingredients in a blender. Blend until smooth.

Frozen Irish Mint

1 part Crème de Menthe (Green)
1 part Irish Cream Liqueur
2 scoops Vanilla Ice Cream
White Wine Glass

Combine all ingredients in a blender. Blend until smooth.

Frozen Mandarin Sour

2 parts Mandarine Napoléon® Liqueur
1 part Cream
1 scoop Vanilla Ice Cream
White Wine Glass

Combine all ingredients in a blender. Blend until smooth.

Frozen Margarita

1½ parts Tequila
½ part Triple Sec
1 part Lemon Juice
Coupette Glass

Combine all ingredients in a blender with ice. Blend until smooth.

Frozen Monk

1 part Frangelico®
1 part Coffee Liqueur
1 part Crème de Cacao (White)
2 parts Cream
2 scoops Ice Cream
Coupette Glass

Combine all ingredients in a blender. Blend until smooth.

Frozen Mud Slide

1 part Vodka
1 part Coffee Liqueur
1 part Irish Cream Liqueur
2 scoops Vanilla Ice Cream
Coupette Glass

Combine all ingredients in a blender. Blend until smooth.

Frozen Rum Runner

3 parts Dark Rum
3 parts Light Rum
2 parts Crème de Banana
1 part Pineapple Juice
1 part Orange Juice
2 parts Grenadine
Coupette Glass

Combine all ingredients in a blender with ice. Blend until smooth.

Frozen Strawberry Daiquiri

1 part Rum
1 part Lemon Juice
4 Strawberries
dash Sugar
Champagne Flute

Combine all ingredients in a blender with ice. Blend until smooth.

Frozen Strawberry Margarita

3 parts Tequila
1 part Triple Sec
1 part Sweetened Lime Juice
1/2 part Lemon Juice
1 part Strawberry Liqueur
Coupette Glass

Combine all ingredients in a blender with ice. Blend until smooth.

Frozen Tahiti

2 parts Dark Rum
1 part Pineapple Juice
1/2 part Passion Fruit Nectar
splash Grenadine
White Wine Glass

Combine all ingredients in a blender with ice. Blend until smooth.

Frozen Vomit

2 parts Gin
1 part Grain Alcohol
1 part Banana Liqueur
2 parts Beef Bouillion
Coupette Glass

Combine all ingredients in a blender with ice. Blend until smooth.

Fruit Booty

2 parts 151-Proof Rum
1 part Blue Curaçao
1 part Cranberry Liqueur
1 part Cranberry-Flavored Vodka
3 parts Apple-Cranberry Juice
3 parts Pineapple Juice
splash Grenadine
Highball Glass

Combine all ingredients in a blender with ice. Blend until smooth.

Fruit Frosty

1 part Sour Apple Schnapps
1 part Peach Schnapps
1 part Orange Liqueur
1 part Cranberry Juice Cocktail
1 part Cream
Coupette Glass

Combine all ingredients in a blender with ice. Blend until smooth.

Fruit Loop®

1 part Midori®
1 part Blue Curaçao
1/2 part Granadine
3 parts Pineapple Juice
1 part Cream
1 Strawberry
Parfait Glass

Combine all ingredients in a blender with ice. Blend until smooth.

Fruit Margarita

2 parts Tequila
1 part Triple Sec
4 parts Sour Mix
Fresh Fruit
Coupette Glass with Salted Rim

Combine all ingredients in a blender with ice. Blend until smooth. This basic recipe works with almost any fruit.

Fubuki-So-San

1 part Coconut-Flavored Liqueur
1 part Sake
1/2 part Blue Curaçao
1/2 part Cream
1/2 part Coconut Cream
2 parts Pineapple Juice
Old-Fashioned Glass

Combine all ingredients in a blender with ice. Blend until smooth.

Funky Freezer

1 1/2 parts Tequila Gold
1/2 part Peach Schnapps
splash Apricot Brandy
splash Blue Curaçao
1/2 part Lime Juice
Coupette Glass

Combine all ingredients in a blender with ice. Blend until smooth.

Funky Monkey

2 parts Brandy
2 parts Coffee Liqueur
1 part Milk
1 scoop Ice Cream
1 Banana
Coupette Glass

Combine all ingredients in a blender. Blend until smooth.

Gauguin

1 1/4 parts Dark Rum
1/2 part Passion Fruit Nectar
1/2 part Lemon Juice
1/2 part Lime Juice
Old-Fashioned Glass

Combine all ingredients in a blender with ice. Blend until smooth.

Geisha Girl

1 part Gin
1 part Melon Liqueur
2 parts Passion Fruit Juice
1/2 Pear
White Wine Glass

Combine all ingredients in a blender with ice. Blend until smooth.

General's Salute

1½ parts Tequila Silver
½ part Blue Curaçao
dash Sugar
Coupette Glass

Combine all ingredients in a blender with ice. Blend until smooth.

Glaciermeister

1½ part Jägermeister®
3 scoops Vanilla Ice Cream
1 part Milk
Coupette Glass

Combine all ingredients in a blender. Blend until smooth.

Glass Slipper

1 part Dry Vermouth
1 part Cream
2 scoops Vanilla Ice Cream
White Wine Glass

Combine all ingredients in a blender. Blend until smooth.

Golden Cadillac® with White-Walled Tires

1½ parts Vanilla-Flavored Vodka
1½ parts Chocolate Liqueur
½ part Galliano®
1½ parts Crème de Cacao (White)
1 part Cream
splash Simple Syrup
Champagne Flute

Combine all ingredients in a blender with ice. Blend until smooth.

Golden Star

1 part Vanilla Liqueur
¾ part Amaretto
2 scoops Ice Cream
Parfait Glass

Combine all ingredients in a blender. Blend until smooth.

Great Idea

1 part Tequila Gold
1 part Triple Sec
2 parts Strawberry Puree
3 parts Pineapple Juice
1 part Sour Mix
1 part Vanilla Ice Cream
Coupette Glass

Combine all ingredients in a blender with ice. Blend until smooth.

Green Angel

1 part Pisang Ambon® Liqueur
1 part Peach Schnapps
1 part Coconut-Flavored Rum
splash Lemon Juice
Coupette Glass

Combine all ingredients in a blender with ice. Blend until smooth.

Green Eyes

1 part Rum
¾ part Melon Liqueur
½ part Coconut Cream
½ part Sweetened Lime Juice
1½ parts Pineapple Juice
Coupette Glass

Combine all ingredients in a blender with ice. Blend until smooth.

Green Goddess
4 parts Melon Liqueur
1 part Milk
1 Banana
Coupette Glass

Combine all ingredients in a blender with ice. Blend until smooth.

Green Ocean
1 part Gin
1 part Pisang Ambon® Liqueur
1 part Sour Mix
1 part Passion Fruit Juice
$1/2$ part Orange Juice
Highball Glass

Combine all ingredients in a blender with ice. Blend until smooth.

Green Weenie
1 part Jack Daniel's®
1 part Rum
1 part Tequila
1 part Vodka
fill with Margarita Mix
Coupette Glass

Combine all ingredients in a blender with ice. Blend until smooth.

Grinch
2 parts Tequila Reposado
4 parts Margarita Mix
$1/2$ Apple
1 Banana
Margarita Glass

Peel the Apple and cut it into chunks. Combine all ingredients in a blender with ice. Blend until smooth.

G-Spot
2 parts Advocaat
1 part Cream
1 part Amaretto
1 part Chocolate Mint Liqueur
White Wine Glass

Combine all ingredients in a blender with ice. Blend until smooth.

Guava Colada
$1 1/4$ parts Dark Rum
3 parts Guava Juice
1 part Coconut Cream
Coupette Glass

Combine all ingredients in a blender with ice. Blend until smooth.

Habit Rogue
$1 1/2$ parts Gin
2 parts Cranberry Juice Cocktail
1 part Grapefruit Juice
splash Honey
Coupette Glass

Combine all ingredients in a blender with ice. Blend until smooth.

Hana Lei Bay
2 parts Dark Rum
1 part Raspberry Liqueur
1 part Pineapple Juice
1 part Coconut Cream
Hurricane Glass

Combine all ingredients in a blender with ice. Blend until smooth.

Happy Banana Mama

1 1/2 parts Light Rum
1 part Dark Rum
1 part Coconut Cream
1 part Strawberry Puree
1/4 part Crème de Banana
2 parts Pineapple Juice
Hurricane Glass

Combine all ingredients in a blender with ice. Blend until smooth.

Havana Banana Fizz

2 parts Dark Rum
1 1/2 parts Fresh Lime Juice
dash Bitters
3 parts Pineapple Juice
Collins Glass

Combine all ingredients in a blender with ice. Blend until smooth.

Hawaiian Eye

1/2 part Banana Liqueur
1 part Coffee Liqueur
1 part Heavy Cream
1 Egg White
1/2 part Vodka
splash Pernod®
Coupette Glass

Combine all ingredients in a blender with ice. Blend until smooth.

Hibiscus

3/4 part Dark Rum
1/4 part Raspberry Liqueur
1/4 part Crème de Cacao (White)
1/2 part Grenadine
2 parts Collins Mix
Coupette Glass

Combine all ingredients in a blender with ice. Blend until smooth.

High Flier

1 part Blue Curaçao
1 part Triple Sec
1 part Melon Liqueur
1 part Coconut Cream
1 part Orange Juice
1 part Mango Juice
Hurricane Glass

Combine all ingredients in a blender with ice. Blend until smooth.

Highland Winter

1 1/2 parts Scotch
splash Cherry Brandy
splash Drambuie®
1/2 part Cream
Coupette Glass

Combine all ingredients in a blender with ice. Blend until smooth.

Hi-Rise

1 part Vodka
1/4 part Cointreau®
2 parts Orange Juice
1 part Sour Mix
1/4 part Grenadine
Old-Fashioned Glass

Combine all ingredients in a blender with ice. Blend until smooth.

Hocus Pocus

1 part Gin
1 part Cointreau®
1 part Lemon Juice
Champagne Flute

Combine all ingredients in a blender with ice. Blend until smooth.

Holiday Isle

$1^1/_2$ parts Pineapple Juice
$1^1/_2$ parts Piña Colada Mix
1 part Peach Puree
1 scoop Vanilla Ice Cream
1 scoop Orange Sorbet
White Wine Glass

Combine all ingredients in a blender. Blend until smooth.

Honey Boombastic

$1^1/_2$ parts Vodka
1 part Crème de Cacao (Dark)
1 part Frangelico®
$1^1/_2$ parts Honey
1 Egg
$^1/_2$ part Vanilla Extract
Hurricane Glass

Combine all ingredients in a blender with ice. Blend until smooth.

Hop in the Space

$^1/_2$ part Crème de Cacao (White)
$^1/_2$ part Hazelnut Liqueur
2 parts Cream
$^2/_3$ part Honey
Coupette Glass

Combine all ingredients in a blender with ice. Blend until smooth.

Horny Bull

$1^1/_2$ parts Tequila
3 parts Orange Juice
1 part Lemonade
$^1/_2$ part Grenadine
Coupette Glass

Combine all ingredients in a blender with ice. Blend until smooth.

Horny Leprechaun

1 part Melon Liqueur
1 part Peach Schnapps
1 part Vodka
2 parts Orange Juice
Coupette Glass

Combine all ingredients in a blender with ice. Blend until smooth.

Humdinger

$1^1/_2$ parts Melon Liqueur
$^1/_2$ part Tequila Silver
3 parts Fresh Lime Juice
dash Sugar
Coupette Glass

Combine all ingredients in a blender with ice. Blend until smooth.

Hummer

1 part Coffee-Flavored Vodka
1 part Light Rum
2 scoops Vanilla Ice Cream
Highball Glass

Combine all ingredients in a blender. Blend until smooth.

Hummingbird

1 part Rum Crème Liqueur
1 part Amaretto
1 part Milk
$^1/_2$ part Strawberry Syrup
$^1/_2$ Banana
Coupette Glass

Combine all ingredients in a blender with ice. Blend until smooth.

Hydraulic Screwdriver

1 can Frozen Orange Juice Concentrate
1 part Vodka
1 part Triple Sec
1 part Water
Coupette Glass

Make the Orange Juice but instead of refilling container with water 3 times, fill with Vodka once and Triple Sec once. Mix well and serve on the rocks or blend it with ice for a frozen drink.

I Scream the Blues

splash Blue Curaçao
splash Lychee Liqueur
1 part Dark Rum
3 parts Pear Juice
1 part Cream
Collins Glass

Combine all ingredients in a blender with ice. Blend until smooth.

Ice Storm

1/2 part 151-Proof Rum
2 parts Strawberry Liqueur
1/2 Banana
5 Strawberries
3 scoops Vanilla Ice Cream
Highball Glass

Combine all ingredients in a blender. Blend until smooth.

Iceball

1 1/2 parts Gin
3/4 part Crème de Menthe (White)
3/4 part Sambuca
splash Cream
Coupette Glass

Combine all ingredients in a blender with ice. Blend until smooth.

Iceberg in Radioactive Water

3 parts Melon Liqueur
1 part Coconut-Flavored Rum
1 part Banana Liqueur
fill with Pineapple Juice
1 scoop Vanilla Ice Cream
Coupette Glass

Combine all ingredients in a blender. Blend until smooth.

Icebreaker

2 parts Tequila
2 parts Grapefruit Juice
splash Grenadine
2 splashes Cointreau®
Coupette Glass

Combine all ingredients in a blender with ice. Blend until smooth.

Icemeister

2 parts Jägermeister®
2 scoops Ice Cream
Coupette Glass

Combine all ingredients in a blender. Blend until smooth.

Igloo Sue

2 parts Vodka
1 part Grenadine
fill with Lemonade
Hurricane Glass

Combine all ingredients in a blender with ice. Blend until smooth.

Illegal Cuban

2 parts Blue Curaçao

1 part Coconut Cream

1/2 part Amaretto

1 part Lemon Juice

1 part Lime Juice

Coupette Glass

Combine all ingredients in a blender with ice. Blend until smooth.

Inertia Creeps

1 1/2 parts Vodka

2 parts Strega®®

2/3 part Pineapple Juice

1/2 part Cream

Collins Glass

Combine all ingredients in a blender with ice. Blend until smooth.

Irish Dream

1/2 part Frangelico®

1/2 part Irish Cream Liqueur

3/4 part Crème de Cacao (Dark)

1 scoop Vanilla Ice Cream

Pilsner Glass

Combine all ingredients in a blender with ice. Blend until smooth.

Italian Margarita

1 part Amaretto

1/2 part Tequila Gold

1/2 part Triple Sec

2 parts Sour Mix

Coupette Glass

Combine all ingredients in a blender with ice. Blend until smooth.

Italian Stallion

3/4 part Galliano®

3/4 part Crème de Banana

1 1/2 parts Heavy Cream

White Wine Glass

Combine all ingredients in a blender with ice. Blend until smooth.

Italian Sunrise

1 part Galliano®

1 part Banana Liqueur

1 part Triple Sec

fill with Cream

Collins Glass

Combine all ingredients in a blender with ice. Blend until smooth.

Jäger Vacation

1 part Jägermeister®

2 parts Piña Colada Mix

2 parts Pineapple Juice

Coupette Glass

Combine all ingredients in a blender with ice. Blend until smooth.

Jamafezzca

1 1/2 parts Jamaican Rum

1 1/2 parts Cream

2/3 part Passion Fruit Liqueur

2 parts Guava Juice

Coupette Glass

Combine all ingredients in a blender with ice. Blend until smooth.

Jamaica Safari

1/2 part Peach Schnapps
2/3 part Dark Rum
1/2 part Safari®
1 1/2 parts Banana Juice
splash Lime Juice
splash Coconut Cream
2 parts Passion Fruit Juice
Coupette Glass

Combine all ingredients in a blender with ice. Blend until smooth.

Jamaican Blues

1 part Dark Rum
1/4 part Blue Curaçao
2 parts Coconut Cream
2 parts Pineapple Juice
Coupette Glass

Combine all ingredients in a blender with ice. Blend until smooth.

Jamaican Toothbrush

1/2 part Peppermint Liqueur
1/2 part Spiced Rum
splash Crème de Cacao (White)
1 part Coconut Cream
2 parts Cream
Collins Glass

Combine all ingredients in a blender with ice. Blend until smooth.

Jen & Berry's

1 1/2 parts Blue Curaçao
1 part Coconut-Flavored Liqueur
1/2 part Coffee Liqueur
2 scoops Vanilla Ice Cream
Coupette Glass

Combine all ingredients in a blender. Blend until smooth.

Jersey Girl

1 part Currant-Flavored Vodka
1 part Strawberry Liqueur
2 parts Pineapple Juice
1 1/2 parts Orange Juice
1 part Strawberry Syrup
Hurricane Glass

Combine all ingredients in a blender with ice. Blend until smooth.

Johnny Banana

2/3 part Crème de Banana
2/3 part Citrus-Flavored Rum
1 part Banana Puree
3 parts Mango Juice
1 1/2 parts Vanilla Ice Cream
Coupette Glass

Combine all ingredients in a blender with ice. Blend until smooth.

Julia and Romeo

1 part Rum
1 part Amaretto
1 part Strawberry Puree
2 parts Cream
Coupette Glass

Combine all ingredients in a blender with ice. Blend until smooth.

Kaunakakai

1 part Light Rum
1 part Coconut-Flavored Liqueur
2 parts Strawberry Juice
1 part Banana Puree
2 parts Pineapple Juice
2 parts Coconut Cream
Coupette Glass

Combine all ingredients in a blender with ice. Blend until smooth.

Key Lime Quencher

1$^1/_4$ parts Dark Rum
1$^1/_2$ parts Lime Juice
3 parts Heavy Cream
1 part Coconut Cream
dash Powdered Sugar
Hurricane Glass

Combine all ingredients in a blender with ice. Blend until smooth.

Key West Margarita

1 part Tequila
1 part Cherry Juice
1 part Piña Colada Mix
1 part Margarita Mix
1 part Orange Juice
Coupette Glass

Combine all ingredients in a blender with ice. Blend until smooth.

Killer Colada

1$^1/_2$ parts Vanilla-Flavored Vodka
1 part Coconut-Flavored Rum
1 part Crème de Banana
fill with Cream
Hurricane Glass

Combine all ingredients in a blender with ice. Blend until smooth.

Kiwiquiri

$^1/_2$ part Crème de Cacao (White)
1$^1/_2$ parts Kiwi Schnapps
2 parts Spiced Rum
Coupette Glass

Combine all ingredients in a blender with ice. Blend until smooth.

Knuckleduster

1 part Blue Curaçao
1 part Coconut-Flavored Liqueur
fill with Pineapple Juice
White Wine Glass

Combine all ingredients in a blender with ice. Blend until smooth.

Kodiak Sled Dog

1 part Irish Cream Liqueur
1 part Crown Royal® Whiskey
1 part Frangelico®
1 part Coffee Liqueur
2 parts Milk
Hurricane Glass

Combine all ingredients in a blender with ice. Blend until smooth.

Kokomo Joe

1 part Light Rum
1 part Banana Liqueur
1 part Orange Juice
1 part Piña Colada Mix
$^1/_2$ Banana
Coupette Glass

Combine all ingredients in a blender with ice. Blend until smooth.

Latin Beat

1$^1/_2$ parts Light Rum
1 part Coconut-Flavored Liqueur
$^1/_2$ part Crème de Banana
3 parts Pineapple Juice
1 part Coconut Cream
1 part Raspberry Juice
Coupette Glass

Combine all ingredients in a blender with ice. Blend until smooth.

Lazy Luau

2 parts Coconut-Flavored Rum
1 part Peach Schnapps
1 part Vodka
1 part Cranberry Juice Cocktail
2 parts Orange Juice
1 part Pineapple Juice
1 can Pineapple Chunks
Old-Fashioned Glass

Combine all ingredients in a blender with ice. Blend until smooth.

Lebanese Snow

1 1/2 parts Strawberry Liqueur
1 part Crème de Banana
1 part Light Cream
Red Wine Glass

Combine all ingredients in a blender with ice. Blend until smooth.

Lechery

1 part Vodka
1/2 part Apricot Brandy
1/2 part Mandarine Napoleon Liqueur
2 parts Lemon Sherbet
2 1/2 parts Orange Juice
Coupette Glass

Combine all ingredients in a blender with ice. Blend until smooth.

Left of Center

1 1/2 parts Dark Rum
2/3 part Peach Schnapps
1/2 part Coconut-Flavored Liqueur
2 parts Orange Juice
1 1/2 parts Pineapple Juice
1 1/2 parts Coconut Cream
Coupette Glass

Combine all ingredients in a blender with ice. Blend until smooth.

Licorice Mist

1 1/4 parts Sambuca
1/2 part Coconut-Flavored Liqueur
2 parts Light Cream
Parfait Glass

Combine all ingredients in a blender with ice. Blend until smooth.

Lil Lolita

1 part Blue Curaçao
2 parts Triple Sec
2 parts Blackberry Liqueur
2 parts Orange Juice
Coupette Glass

Combine all ingredients in a blender with ice. Blend until smooth.

Limelight

1/2 part Blue Curaçao
1/4 part Banana Liqueur
1/4 part Vodka
2 parts Orange Juice
2 parts Pineapple Juice
Coupette Glass

Combine all ingredients in a blender with ice. Blend until smooth.

Liquid Temptation

1 1/2 parts Light Rum
1/2 part Crème de Banana
1 part Sour Mix
5 Strawberries
Red Wine Glass

Combine all ingredients in a blender with ice. Blend until smooth.

Little Brother

2 parts Coffee Liqueur
1 part Vodka
1 scoop Ice Cream
splash Vanilla Extract
Old-Fashioned Glass

Combine all ingredients in a blender. Blend until smooth.

Little Darlin'

1 part Crème de Cacao (White)
1 part Crème de Menthe (Green)
1 scoop Vanilla Ice Cream
Coupette Glass

Combine all ingredients in a blender. Blend until smooth.

Lonely Night

1 1/4 parts Irish Cream Liqueur
1 1/4 parts Frangelico®
3/4 part Coffee Liqueur
1 scoop Vanilla Ice Cream
Parfait Glass

Combine all ingredients in a blender with ice. Blend until smooth.

Loomdog

1 part Rum
3 parts Orange Juice
2 parts Pineapple Juice
Collins Glass

Combine all ingredients in a blender with ice. Blend until smooth.

Loose Moose

1 part Crème de Cacao (White)
1 part Frangelico®
1 part Strawberry Liqueur
2 parts Cream
Coupette Glass

Combine all ingredients in a blender with ice. Blend until smooth.

Love Birds

1 1/2 parts Vodka
2 parts Lemon Juice
splash Dark Rum
1/2 part Grenadine
Old-Fashioned Glass

Combine all ingredients in a blender with ice. Blend until smooth.

Luna

1 part Passion Fruit Liqueur
2/3 part Blue Curaçao
splash Crème de Banana
1 part Orange Juice
1 part Pineapple Juice
splash Lime Juice
Collins Glass

Combine all ingredients in a blender with ice. Blend until smooth.

Malibu Wipeout

1 part Coconut-Flavored Rum
1 part Citrus-Flavored Vodka
1 part Cranberry Juice Cocktail
1 part Pineapple Juice
Parfait Glass

Combine all ingredients in a blender with ice. Blend until smooth.

Mambo's Dream

1 part Dark Rum
1/2 part Banana Liqueur
1 part Pineapple Juice
1/2 part Lemon Juice
1/2 part Triple Sec
Coupette Glass

Combine all ingredients in a blender with ice. Blend until smooth.

Mango Tango

2 parts Orange Juice
1 part Mango Nectar
1 part Dark Rum
1/2 part Coconut-Flavored Liqueur
1/2 part Passion Fruit Juice
1/2 part Guava Juice
Collins Glass

Combine all ingredients in a blender with ice. Blend until smooth.

Margarita (Frozen)

1 1/2 parts Tequila
1/2 part Triple Sec
1 part Lime Juice
dash Salt
Coupette Glass

Rub rim of the glass with Lime Juice and dip rim in Salt. Combine all ingredients in a blender with ice. Blend until smooth.

Margarita Imperial

2 parts Tequila Reposado
1 part Mandarine Napoléon® Liqueur
1 part Fresh Lime Juice
Coupette Glass

Combine all ingredients in a blender with ice. Blend until smooth.

Margarita Madres

1 1/4 parts Tequila
1/2 part Cointreau®
1 1/2 parts Sour Mix
1 1/2 parts Orange Juice
1 1/2 parts Cranberry Juice Cocktail
Coupette Glass

Combine all ingredients in a blender with ice. Blend until smooth.

Marlin

1 part Vodka
2 parts Orange Juice
1 part Grapefruit Juice
Collins Glass

Combine all ingredients in a blender with ice. Blend until smooth.

Marshmallow Blue Hawaiian

1 part Rum
1 part Blue Curaçao
1/3 part Pineapple Juice
2/3 part Piña Colada Mix
4 Marshmallows
Coupette Glass

Combine all ingredients in a blender with ice. Blend until smooth.

Marshmallow Piña Colada

1 part Rum
1 part Pineapple Juice
2 parts Piña Colada Mix
4 Marshmallows
Coupette Glass

Combine all ingredients in a blender with ice. Blend until smooth.

Mary-Huana

1 1/2 parts Absinthe
2/3 part Blue Curaçao
2/3 part Lime Juice
2/3 part Passion Fruit Nectar
fill with Orange Juice
splash Simple Syrup
Collins Glass

Combine all ingredients in a blender with ice. Blend until smooth.

Maui Breeze

1/2 part Amaretto
1/2 part Triple Sec
1/2 part Brandy
1 part Sour Mix
2 parts Orange Juice
1 part Guava Juice
Parfait Glass

Combine all ingredients in a blender with ice. Blend until smooth.

McMalted

1 part Vanilla Liqueur
2 parts Irish Cream Liqueur
2 scoops Vanilla Ice Cream
dash Ground Nutmeg
Highball Glass

Combine all ingredients in a blender. Blend until smooth.

Mello Yello

1 part Melon Liqueur
1 part Grapefruit Juice
Coupette Glass

Combine all ingredients in a blender with ice. Blend until smooth.

Melon Colada

1 1/2 parts Light Rum
1/2 part Dark Rum
1/2 part Melon Liqueur
fill with Pineapple Juice
1 part Coconut Cream
splash Cream
Coupette Glass

Combine all ingredients in a blender with ice. Blend until smooth.

Melon Margarita

1 part Tequila
1 part Melon Liqueur
1 part Triple Sec
Coupette Glass

Combine all ingredients in a blender with ice. Blend until smooth.

Melon Suprise

1 1/2 parts Melon Liqueur
1 part Light Rum
fill with Pineapple Juice
Hurricane Glass

Combine all ingredients in a blender with ice. Blend until smooth.

Mexican Dream

1 part Coffee Liqueur
1 part Milk
2 scoops Vanilla Ice Cream
Coupette Glass

Combine all ingredients in a blender. Blend until smooth.

Mexican Mud Slide

1 part Coffee Liqueur
1 part Amaretto
2 scoops Ice Cream
Highball Glass

Combine all ingredients in a blender. Blend until smooth.

Midnight Lace

1 1/2 parts Light Rum
1 part Cream
3/4 part Chocolate Mint Liqueur
2 scoops Vanilla Ice Cream
White Wine Glass

Combine all ingredients in a blender. Blend until smooth.

Millenium Eclipse

1 part Southern Comfort®
1 part Pineapple Syrup
1 part Blue Curaçao
Coupette Glass

Combine all ingredients in a blender with ice. Blend until smooth.

Mississippi Mud

1 part Southern Comfort®
1 part Coffee Liqueur
2 scoops Ice Cream
Beer Mug

Combine all ingredients in a blender. Blend until smooth.

Mont Blanc

1 part Blackberry Liqueur
1 part Vodka
1 part Light Cream
3 parts Vanilla Ice Cream
Red Wine Glass

Combine all ingredients in a blender. Blend until smooth.

Montezuma

1 1/2 parts Tequila
1 part Madeira®
1 Egg Yolk
Champagne Flute

Combine all ingredients in a blender with ice. Blend until smooth.

Moose Milk

1 part Light Rum
1 part Spiced Rum
1/2 part Coffee Liqueur
2 scoops Ice Cream
2 Strawberries
Coupette Glass

Combine all ingredients in a blender. Blend until smooth.

Morgan Melon

2 parts Spiced Rum
1 part Lemon-Lime Soda
1 part Watermelon Schnapps
splash Lime Juice
splash Sour Mix
Parfait Glass

Combine all ingredients in a blender with ice. Blend until smooth.

Morning Milk

1 part Milk
3 parts Gin
10 Strawberries
1 Kiwi, peeled and sliced
Coupette Glass

Combine all ingredients in a blender with ice. Blend until smooth.

Mountain Brook

1 part Citrus-Flavored Vodka
1/2 part Blue Curaçao
1/2 part Lime Syrup
1/2 part Hard Cider
Collins Glass

Combine all ingredients in a blender with ice. Blend until smooth.

Mud Pie

2 parts Crème de Cacao (Dark)
fill with Cream
1 Candy Bar
2 scoops Ice Cream
Coupette Glass

Combine all ingredients in a blender. Blend until smooth. Works with almost any candy bar.

Mud Slide (Mud Boy Recipe)

1 part Coffee Liqueur
1 part Irish Cream Liqueur
1 part Vodka
1/2 part Chocolate Syrup
Coupette Glass

Combine all ingredients in a blender with ice. Blend until smooth.

Multiple Orgasm Cajun Style

2 parts Dark Rum
2 parts Coffee Liqueur
1 part Amaretto
1 part Crème de Cacao (White)
1 part Rum Crème Liqueur
Coupette Glass

Combine all ingredients in a blender with ice. Blend until smooth.

My Blue Heaven

1 part Cinnamon Schnapps
1 part Tropical Punch Schnapps
1 1/2 parts Blueberry Schnapps
fill with Blueberries
Highball Glass

Combine all ingredients in a blender. Blend until smooth.

Nappy Rash

1 1/2 parts Rye Whiskey
1 1/2 parts Spiced Rum
3/4 part Peach Schnapps
2 dashes Iced Tea Mix
fill with Grapefruit Juice
Hurricane Glass

Combine all ingredients in a blender with ice. Blend until smooth.

Negril Bay

1 1/2 parts Dark Rum
1 part Guava Juice
1/2 part Cream
1/2 part Fresh Lime Juice
1/4 part Blackberry Liqueur
Old-Fashioned Glass

Combine all ingredients in a blender with ice. Blend until smooth.

Neon Voodoo

1 part Vodka
1 part Apple Juice
3 parts Mountain Dew®
Coupette Glass

Combine all ingredients in a blender with ice. Blend until smooth.

Nuclear Slush

3/4 part CitrusFlavored Vodka
3/4 part Bacardi® Limon Rum
1/2 part Melon Liqueur
1/2 part Blue Curaçao
fill with Sour Mix
Coupette Glass

Combine all ingredients in a blender with ice. Blend until smooth.

Nutella®

1 part Crème de Cacao (Dark)
1 part Irish Cream Liqueur
1 part Hazelnut Liqueur
1 scoop Vanilla Ice Cream
Coupette Glass

Combine all ingredients in a blender with ice. Blend until smooth.

Nutty Colada

1 part Amaretto
1 part Coconut Cream
1 part Fresh Pineapple
Collins Glass

Combine all ingredients in a blender with ice. Blend until smooth.

Ogre Drink

3 parts Coconut-Flavored Rum
2 scoops Vanilla Ice Cream
4 parts Cola
Beer Mug

Combine all ingredients in a blender. Blend until smooth.

Old Bailey

1 part Light Rum
2 parts Cream
1 part Coconut Cream
Coupette Glass

Combine all ingredients in a blender with ice. Blend until smooth.

Orange Bonbon

1 part Crème de Cacao (White)
1 part Vodka
1 part Orange Juice
2 scoops Orange Sorbet
White Wine Glass

Combine all ingredients in a blender. Blend until smooth.

Orange Daiquiri

2 parts Light Rum
1/2 part Triple Sec
1 part Orange Juice
1/2 part Lime Juice
splash Grenadine
Collins Glass

Combine all ingredients in a blender with ice. Blend until smooth.

Orange Julius

1 part Vodka
1 part Milk
1 part Orange Juice
dash Sugar
splash Vanilla Extract
Coupette Glass

Combine all ingredients in a blender with ice. Blend until smooth.

Orange Margarita

1 part Tequila
1/2 part Triple Sec
fill with Orange Juice
splash Lime Juice
Coupette Glass

Combine all ingredients in a blender with ice. Blend until smooth.

Orange Tree

1 1/2 part Amaretto
3/4 part Crème de Noyaux
1 1/2 parts Orange Juice
3/4 part Vanilla Ice Cream
Parfait Glass

Combine all ingredients in a blender with ice. Blend until smooth.

Organ Grinder

1 part Dark Rum
1 part Light Rum
1 part Whiskey
splash Crème de Cacao (White)
2 parts Coconut Cream
Highball Glass

Combine all ingredients in a blender with ice. Blend until smooth.

Orgasmatron

$1^1/_2$ parts Crème de Cacao (White)
$1^1/_2$ parts Coconut-Flavored Liqueur
$^1/_2$ part Advocaat
4 parts Strawberry Puree
2 parts Cream
Hurricane Glass

Combine all ingredients in a blender with ice. Blend until smooth.

Orient Express

1 part Grand Marnier®
1 part Melon Liqueur
1 part Coconut Cream
1 part Pineapple Juice
Hurricane Glass

Combine all ingredients in a blender with ice. Blend until smooth.

Out of Africa

$2^1/_2$ parts Vodka
$2^1/_2$ parts Safari®
1 part Pineapple Juice
1 part Grapefruit
2 splashes Grenadine
Hurricane Glass

Combine all ingredients in a blender with ice. Blend until smooth.

Pacific Sunset

$1^1/_2$ parts Light Rum
1 part Coconut-Flavored Liqueur
3 parts Pineapple Juice
2 parts Papaya Juice
2 parts Strawberry Puree
Hurricane Glass

Combine all ingredients in a blender with ice. Blend until smooth.

Papakea

1 part Coconut-Flavored Liqueur
1 part Vodka
fill with Pineapple Juice
Collins Glass

Combine all ingredients in a blender with ice. Blend until smooth.

Parrot Perch

$1^1/_2$ parts Coconut-Flavored Rum
$^1/_2$ part Triple Sec
1 Banana
3 parts Orange Juice
1 part Banana Liqueur
Hurricane Glass

Combine all ingredients in a blender with ice. Blend until smooth.

Passion Mama

1 part Pineapple-Flavored Rum
$^1/_2$ part Passion Fruit Liqueur
$1^1/_2$ parts Pineapple Juice
1 part Orange Juice
$^1/_2$ part Cream
Coupette Glass

Combine all ingredients in a blender with ice. Blend until smooth.

Passion on the Nile

2 parts Passion Fruit Liqueur
1 part Maraschino Liqueur
2 parts Lime Juice
2 parts Orange Juice
2 parts Pineapple Juice
Coupette Glass

Combine all ingredients in a blender with ice. Blend until smooth.

Patria Colada

1 part Light Rum
1 part Spiced Rum
1 part Passion Fruit Juice
1 part Coconut Cream
Collins Glass

Combine all ingredients in a blender with ice. Blend until smooth.

Peach Tree

1 1/2 parts Vodka
3/4 part Peach Schnapps
1 part Cranberry Juice Cocktail
1 part Orange Juice
Collins Glass

Combine all ingredients in a blender with ice. Blend until smooth.

Peach Velvet

1 1/2 parts Peach Brandy
1 part Crème de Cacao (White)
1 part Heavy Cream
Coupette Glass

Combine all ingredients in a blender with ice. Blend until smooth.

Peaches and Cream

1/2 part Vodka
1 part Peach Schnapps
2 parts Cream
3 Peach Slices
Red Wine Glass

Combine all ingredients in a blender with ice. Blend until smooth.

Peanut Butter Sundae

1/2 part Amaretto
2 scoops Vanilla Ice Cream
1 Chocolate Syrup
1 part Milk
1 part Rum
Coupette Glass

Combine all ingredients in a blender. Blend until smooth.

Pebbles

1 part Amaretto
1 part Triple Sec
1 part Milk
1 part Coconut-Flavored Rum
White Wine Glass

Combine all ingredients in a blender with ice. Blend until smooth.

Pensacola Bushwacker

1 part Dark Rum
1/2 part Coconut Cream
1/2 part Coffee Liqueur
1/2 part Crème de Cacao (White)
fill with Half and Half
Coupette Glass

Combine all ingredients in a blender with ice. Blend until smooth.

Peppermint Penguin

1/2 part Crème de Menthe (Green)
1/2 part Crème de Cacao (Dark)
3 parts Cream
3 Oreo® Cookies
White Wine Glass

Combine all ingredients in a blender. Blend until smooth.

Pest Control Nightmare

1 part Light Rum
1 part Orange Juice
1 part Apricot Brandy
1/2 part Triple Sec
1/2 part Simple Syrup
1/2 part Raspberry Syrup
Coupette Glass

Combine all ingredients in a blender with ice. Blend until smooth.

Phish-Phood

1 part Bourbon
1/2 part Crème de Cacao (Dark)
1/2 part Butterscotch Schnapps
1/4 part Vanilla Liqueur
2 scoops Vanilla Ice Cream
Hurricane Glass

Combine all ingredients in a blender with ice. Blend until smooth.

Picker's Peach

1 part Light Rum
1 part Peach Schnapps
1 part Orange Juice
1 part Peach Puree
1/2 part Dark Rum
splash Simple Syrup
dash Orange Bitters
Collins Glass

Combine all ingredients in a blender with ice. Blend until smooth.

Pickled Parrot

1 part Melon Liqueur
1 part Dark Rum
1/2 part Lime Juice
2 parts Grapefruit Juice
fill with Orange Juice
Collins Glass

Combine all ingredients in a blender with ice. Blend until smooth.

Piña Colada

3 parts Light Rum
2 parts Coconut Cream
2 parts Crushed Pineapple
Coupette Glass

Combine all ingredients in a blender with ice. Blend until smooth.

Pino Frio

1 1/4 parts Spiced Rum
2 Pineapple Slices
dash Sugar
Coupette Glass

Combine all ingredients in a blender with ice. Blend until smooth.

Piritta

1 part Crème de Banana
1 part Pisang Ambon® Liqueur
1 part Citrus-Flavored Vodka
2 scoops Vanilla Ice Cream
Hurricane Glass

Combine all ingredients in a blender. Blend until smooth.

Plainfield Sleeper

1 part Vodka
1 part Coffee Liqueur
3 scoops Vanilla Ice Cream
Coupette Glass

Combine all ingredients in a blender. Blend until smooth.

Polyester Velvet Hammer

1 part Vodka
1 part Bourbon
1 part Raspberry Liqueur
1 scoop Ice Cream
fill with Cream
Hurricane Glass

Combine all ingredients in a blender with ice. Blend until smooth.

Poolside Margarita

2 parts Tequila
$1^1/_2$ parts Triple Sec
splash Blue Curaçao
$^1/_2$ part Lime Juice
dash Powdered Sugar
Coupette Glass

Combine all ingredients in a blender with ice. Blend until smooth.

Population Killer

1 part Crème de Cacao (White)
1 part Crème de Menthe (Green)
1 Egg White
fill with Cream
Hurricane Glass

Combine all ingredients in a blender with ice. Blend until smooth.

Port of Call

2 parts Coconut-Flavored Liqueur
1 part Lime Juice
2 parts Orange Juice
fill with Pineapple Juice
Collins Glass

Combine all ingredients in a blender with ice. Blend until smooth.

Princess' Pleasure

1 part Peach Schnapps
2 parts Coconut Cream
2 parts Pineapple Juice
$^1/_4$ Banana
Collins Glass

Combine all ingredients in a blender with ice. Blend until smooth.

Puerto Banana

$1^1/_2$ parts Vodka
$^1/_2$ part Cream
$^1/_4$ part Crème de Banana
$^1/_4$ part Fresh Lime Juice
$^1/_2$ Banana
Coupette Glass

Combine all ingredients in a blender with ice. Blend until smooth.

Pumpkin Eater

$1^1/_2$ parts Light Rum
1 part Triple Sec
1 part Orange Juice
$^1/_2$ part Cream
Parfait Glass

Combine all ingredients in a blender with ice. Blend until smooth.

Pure Ecstasy

1 part Coffee Liqueur
2 parts Irish Cream Liqueur
1 part Vodka
Coupette Glass

Combine all ingredients in a blender with ice. Blend until smooth.

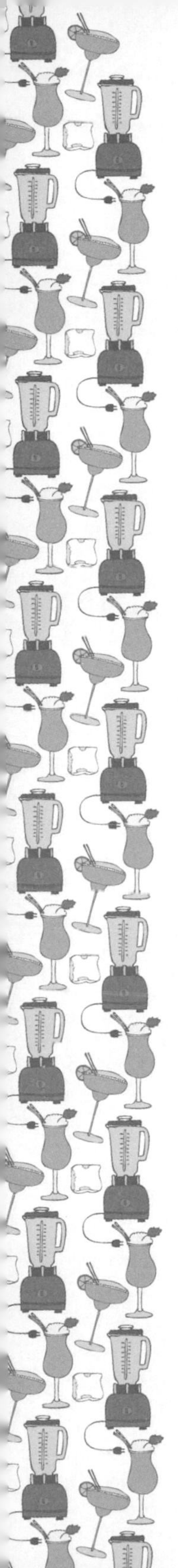

Ragnampiza
1 part Coffee Liqueur
1 part Jamaican Rum
1 part Amaretto
1 part Crème de Cacao (Dark)
2 scoops Vanilla Ice Cream
Hurricane Glass

Combine all ingredients in a blender. Blend until smooth.

Rainbow Dream
2 parts Melon Liqueur
1/2 part Grenadine
2 scoops Vanilla Ice Cream
White Wine Glass

Combine all ingredients in a blender. Blend until smooth.

Rainbow Sherbet
1/2 part Crème de Banana
1/2 part Melon Liqueur
1/2 part Strawberry Juice
1 part Grenadine
2 parts Orange Juice
2 scoops Orange Sorbet
White Wine Glass

Combine all ingredients in a blender. Blend until smooth.

Rama Lama Ding Dong
1 part Scotch
1 part Triple Sec
fill with Passion Fruit Juice
Old-Fashioned Glass

Combine all ingredients in a blender with ice. Blend until smooth.

Razzbaretto
1 part Raspberry Liqueur
1 part Amaretto
2 scoops Ice Cream
Coupette Glass

Combine all ingredients in a blender. Blend until smooth.

Red Cactus
1 part Tequila
4 parts Raspberry Juice
1 1/2 parts Sour Mix
Coupette Glass

Combine all ingredients in a blender with ice. Blend until smooth.

Reese's Revenge
1 part Crème de Cacao (Dark)
1 part Frangelico®
2 parts Chocolate Syrup
1 part Peanut Butter
2 scoops Vanilla Ice Cream
splash Cream
Coupette Glass

Combine all ingredients in a blender with ice. Blend until smooth.

Release Valve
1 part Rum
2 parts Vodka
1 part Grenadine
fill with Pineapple Juice
Coupette Glass

Combine all ingredients in a blender with ice. Blend until smooth.

Roasted Dog

2 parts Whiskey
1 part Advocaat
1 part Amaretto
fill with Milk
Hurricane Glass

Combine all ingredients in a blender with ice. Blend until smooth.

Robin Hood

1 part Tequila Reposado
1 part Vodka
2 splashes Pisang Ambon® Liqueur
3 parts Orange Juice
2 parts Pineapple Juice
Coupette Glass

Combine all ingredients in a blender with ice. Blend until smooth.

Rocky Road

1 part Frangelico®
1 part Crème de Cacao (Dark)
fill with Cream
Coupette Glass

Combine all ingredients in a blender with ice. Blend until smooth.

Roll in the Fruit Field

1 part Strawberry Liqueur
1 part Triple Sec
1 part Coconut-Flavored Liqueur
3 parts Cream
2 scoops Lemon Sherbet
Coupette Glass

Combine all ingredients in a blender with ice. Blend until smooth.

Rootin' Tootin' Varmint

1 part Root Beer Schnapps
1/2 part Coffee
splash Amaretto
1 scoop Vanilla Ice Cream
Collins Glass

Combine all ingredients in a blender. Blend until smooth.

Rose Runner

1 part Tequila Rose®
1 part Coconut-Flavored Rum
splash Lime Juice
splash Lemon-Lime Soda
splash Grenadine
splash 151-Proof Rum
Collins Glass

Combine all ingredients execpt the 151-Proof Rum in a blender with ice. Blend until smooth. Top with the 151-Proof Rum.

Roses in Blue

1 1/2 parts Vanilla Ice Cream
1 part Coconut-Flavored Liqueur
splash Blue Curaçao
splash Coconut Cream
Coupette Glass

Combine all ingredients in a blender with ice. Blend until smooth.

Royal Peaches and Cream

1/2 parts Peach Schnapps
1/2 part Crown Royal® Whiskey
1/2 part Cointreau®
1 1/2 parts Heavy Cream
2 scoops Vanilla Ice Cream
Coupette Glass

Combine all ingredients in a blender with ice. Blend until smooth.

Royal Temptation

4 parts Amaretto
3 parts Coffee Liqueur
2 parts Melon Liqueur
1 part Cream
Coupette Glass

Combine all ingredients in a blender with ice. Blend until smooth.

Rummy Sour

1 1/2 parts Spiced Rum
2 parts Lemonade
Coupette Glass

Combine all ingredients in a blender with ice. Blend until smooth.

Russian Coffee

1 part Vodka
1 part Coffee Liqueur
1 part Heavy Cream
Coupette Glass

Combine all ingredients in a blender with ice. Blend until smooth.

Russian in Exile

1 part Irish Cream Liqueur
1 part Coffee Liqueur
1 part Vodka
2 splashes Chocolate Syrup
2 scoops Vanilla Ice Cream
Coupette Glass

Combine all ingredients in a blender with ice. Blend until smooth.

Sabuzzo

1 part Irish Cream Liqueur
1 part Frangelico®
1/2 part Banana Liqueur
1/2 part Coffee Liqueur
1/2 Banana
1 part Espresso
1 part Chocolate Syrup
Hurricane Glass

Combine all ingredients in a blender with ice. Blend until smooth.

Sambuca Whirl

1 part Cream
1 part Light Rum
1 part Sambuca
1 part Lime Cordial
Champagne Flute

Combine all ingredients in a blender with ice. Blend until smooth.

San Juan

1 1/2 parts Rum
1/2 part Coconut Cream
1 part Grapefruit Juice
1 part Lime Juice
splash 151-Proof Rum
Coupette Glass

Combine all ingredients in a blender with ice. Blend until smooth.

Sandman

1 part Pineapple Juice
1/2 part Light Rum
splash Amaretto
splash Strawberry Liqueur
splash Fresh Lime Juice
Hurricane Glass

Combine all ingredients in a blender with ice. Blend until smooth.

Sandstorm

1 part Cream
1 part Coffee
1 part Triple Sec
White Wine Glass

Combine all ingredients in a blender with ice. Blend until smooth.

Saturday Night Fever

$1\frac{1}{2}$ parts Tequila Reposado
1 part Passion Fruit Liqueur
$\frac{2}{3}$ part Kiwi Schnapps
2 parts Cream
2 parts Melon Puree
Collins Glass

Combine all ingredients in a blender with ice. Blend until smooth.

Sauzarily

2 parts Tequila Reposado
splash Fresh Lime Juice
fill with Orange Juice
$\frac{1}{2}$ Banana
White Wine Glass

Combine all ingredients in a blender with ice. Blend until smooth.

Scarlet Ibis

$\frac{3}{4}$ part Rum
$1\frac{1}{2}$ parts Sweet Vermouth
fill with Cranberry Juice Cocktail
2 parts Ginger Ale
Coupette Glass

Combine all ingredients in a blender with ice. Blend until smooth.

Scat Man

$\frac{1}{2}$ part Tequila Gold
2 parts Passion Fruit Liqueur
3 parts Pineapple Juice
2 parts Orange Juice
Coupette Glass

Combine all ingredients in a blender with ice. Blend until smooth.

Seaside Liberty

$\frac{3}{4}$ part Coffee Liqueur
2 splashes Half and Half
1 part Coconut Cream
3 parts Pineapple Juice
Coupette Glass

Combine all ingredients in a blender with ice. Blend until smooth.

Segne

1 part Light Rum
1 part Coffee Liqueur
2 scoops Vanilla Ice Cream
Collins Glass

Combine all ingredients in a blender with ice. Blend until smooth.

Sherbert Pervert

1 part Vodka
2 parts Lemon-Lime Soda
$\frac{1}{2}$ part Grenadine
1 scoop Orange Sorbet
Coupette Glass

Combine all ingredients in a blender with ice. Blend until smooth.

Shipper's Clipper

2 parts Blue Curaçao
2 parts Coconut Cream
2 parts Grapefruit Juice
1 part Lime Juice
Coupette Glass

Combine all ingredients in a blender with ice. Blend until smooth.

Shit on a Hot Tin Roof

2 parts Vodka
3 parts Irish Cream Liqueur
1 Banana
Collins Glass

Combine all ingredients in a blender with ice. Blend until smooth.

Sin Industries

1 1/2 parts Blue Curaçao
1 1/2 parts Triple Sec
1 part Vodka
1 part Grapefruit Juice
Coupette Glass

Combine all ingredients in a blender with ice. Blend until smooth.

Singing Orchard

1 1/4 parts Dark Rum
1 part Coconut Cream
1/2 part Raspberry Liqueur
3 splashes Grenadine
fill with Pineapple Juice
Hurricane Glass

Combine all ingredients in a blender with ice. Blend until smooth.

Skinny Tart

1 1/4 parts Dark Rum
2 parts Grapefruit Juice
2 parts Pineapple Juice
1 packet Artificial Sweetener
Coupette Glass

Combine all ingredients in a blender with ice. Blend until smooth.

Slalom

1 part Vodka
1 part Crème de Cacao (White)
1 part Sambuca
1 part Heavy Cream
Coupette Glass

Combine all ingredients in a blender with ice. Blend until smooth.

Slapstick

3/4 part Spiced Rum
1/2 part Strawberry Liqueur
1 part Coconut Cream
1 part Strawberry Syrup
2 parts Pineapple Juice
Coupette Glass

Combine all ingredients in a blender with ice. Blend until smooth.

Sleeping Panda

1 part Amaretto
1 part Butterscotch Schnapps
1 part Milk
fill with Vanilla Ice Cream
Coupette Glass

Combine all ingredients in a blender. Blend until smooth.

Sloe Melting Iceberg

2/3 part Sloe Gin
2/3 part Crème de Cassis
1 part Light Rum
1 part Club Soda
fill with Pineapple
Coupette Glass

Combine all ingredients in a blender with ice. Blend until smooth.

Sloppy Kiss

1 part Raspberry Liqueur
1 part Apple Brandy
1 part Sour Mix
Coupette Glass

Combine all ingredients in a blender with ice. Blend until smooth.

Slushy

2 parts Light Rum
1 1/2 parts Blue Curaçao
1 part Raspberry Liqueur
4 parts Pineapple Juice
Coupette Glass

Combine all ingredients in a blender with ice. Blend until smooth.

Slushy Hanky

1 part Godiva® Liqueur
1 part Irish Cream Liqueur
1 part Coconut-Flavored Rum
Coupette Glass

Combine all ingredients in a blender with ice. Blend until smooth.

Smooth Banana

1 part Rum
1 part Coconut Cream
1 part Banana Puree
fill with Pineapple Juice
Hurricane Glass

Combine all ingredients in a blender with ice. Blend until smooth.

Smooth Operator

1 part Frangelico®
1/2 part Coffee Liqueur
1/2 part Irish Cream Liqueur
1/2 Banana
3 parts Cream
Coupette Glass

Combine all ingredients in a blender with ice. Blend until smooth.

Smooth Prospect

1 1/2 parts Raspberry Liqueur
1 1/2 parts Cranberry Juice Cocktail
1 part Club Soda
1 scoop Vanilla Ice Cream
Coupette Glass

Combine all ingredients in a blender. Blend until smooth.

Snow Way

1 1/2 parts Vodka
1 1/2 parts Pineapple Juice
2 scoops Vanilla Ice Cream
White Wine Glass

Combine all ingredients in a blender. Blend until smooth.

Snowshot

3 parts Citrus-Flavored Vodka
1 scoop Lemon Sherbet
splash Lemon Juice
dash Sugar
Highball Glass

Combine all ingredients in a blender with ice. Blend until smooth.

Soft Touch

3/4 part Peach Schnapps
1/2 part Banana Syrup
3 parts Piña Colada Mix
Hurricane Glass

Combine all ingredients in a blender with ice. Blend until smooth.

Sorbettino

1 1/2 parts Vodka
1 part Triple Sec
1/2 part Cream
splash Grenadine
2 scoops Lemon Sherbet
Coupette Glass

Combine all ingredients in a blender. Blend until smooth.

Spice Me Up Nice

1 part Light Rum
1 part Orange Juice
1 part Sour Mix
1/2 part Spiced Rum
dash Orange Bitters
fill with Pineapple Juice
Coupette Glass

Combine all ingredients in a blender with ice. Blend until smooth.

Spiced Banana Daiquiri

1 part Spiced Rum
1/2 part Crème de Banana
2 parts Sour Mix
1/2 Banana
Hurricane Glass

Combine all ingredients in a blender with ice. Blend until smooth.

Spider Monkey

1 part Crème de Banana
1 part Coffee Liqueur
1 scoop Ice Cream
Highball Glass

Combine all ingredients in a blender. Blend until smooth.

Spookie Juice

1 1/2 parts Dark Rum
1 part Crème de Banana
2 parts Coconut Cream
1 part Banana Juice
1 part Mango Juice
Hurricane Glass

Combine all ingredients in a blender with ice. Blend until smooth.

Spotted Chocolate Monkey

2 parts Coconut-Flavored Rum
1 part Banana Liqueur
1/2 part Chocolate Syrup
2 scoops Vanilla Ice Cream
2 Chocolate Chip Cookies
Coupette Glass

Combine all ingredients in a blender with ice. Blend until smooth.

Squinting Daedelus

1 1/2 parts Tequila Silver
1/2 part Triple Sec
fill with Sour Mix
dash Salt
Collins Glass

Combine all ingredients in a blender with ice. Blend until smooth.

Straw Hat

1 part Vodka
1 part Coconut-Flavored Rum
1/4 cup Strawberries
Coupette Glass

Combine all ingredients in a blender with ice. Blend until smooth.

Strawberries & Cream

1 part Strawberry Liqueur
2 dashes Sugar
2 parts Half and Half
2 Strawberries
Coupette Glass

Combine all ingredients in a blender with ice. Blend until smooth.

Strawberry Blush

2 parts Vodka
2 parts Strawberry Liqueur
1 part Strawberries
2 scoops Vanilla Ice Cream
White Wine Glass

Combine all ingredients in a blender. Blend until smooth.

Strawberry Colada

1 part Dark Rum
1 part Light Rum
1 1/2 part Coconut Cream
4 parts Pineapple Juice
6 Strawberries
Collins Glass

Combine all ingredients in a blender with ice. Blend until smooth.

Strawberry Patch

1 1/2 parts Southern Comfort®
3 parts Frozen Strawberries
2 parts Orange Juice
Coupette Glass

Combine all ingredients in a blender with ice. Blend until smooth.

Strawberry Piña Colada

1 part Rum
1 part Strawberry Liqueur
1 part Piña Colada Mix
1 part Pineapple Juice
Highball Glass

Combine all ingredients in a blender with ice. Blend until smooth.

Strawberry Shortcake

1 part Amaretto
1 part Crème de Cacao (Dark)
3 parts Strawberries
2 scoops Ice Cream
Coupette Glass

Combine all ingredients in a blender with ice. Blend until smooth.

Strawberry Smash

1 part Light Rum
1 part Wild Berry Schnapps
1/2 part 151-Proof Rum
1 part Sour Mix
6 Strawberries
1 Banana
Coupette Glass

Combine all ingredients in a blender with ice. Blend until smooth.

Sudberry Blast

1 part Amaretto
1 part Coconut-Flavored Rum
1 part Spiced Rum
1 part Whipping Cream
2 parts Strawberry Daiquiri Mix
splash Pineapple Juice
1 1/2 parts Piña Colada Mix
Whipped Cream
Hurricane Glass

Combine all ingredients in a blender with ice. Blend until smooth. Top with Whipped Cream.

Summer Breeze

1 1/2 parts Rum
1 part Papaya Juice
2 parts Orange Juice
1/2 Banana
White Wine Glass

Combine all ingredients in a blender with ice. Blend until smooth.

Summer Dream

1 part Crème de Cacao (White)
1 part Light Rum
1 part Red Curacao
1 scoop Vanilla Ice Cream
Collins Glass

Combine all ingredients in a blender with ice. Blend until smooth.

A Sundae on Sunday

2/3 part Light Rum
2/3 part Amaretto
1 part Coconut Cream
1 part Cherry Syrup
splash Milk
Coupette Glass

Combine all ingredients in a blender with ice. Blend until smooth.

Sunny Dream

1 1/2 parts Apricot Brandy
3/4 part Triple Sec
4 parts Orange Juice
2 scoops Vanilla Ice Cream
White Wine Glass

Combine all ingredients in a blender. Blend until smooth.

Surf's Up

1/2 part Crème de Banana
1/2 part Crème de Cacao (White)
1 part Light Cream
fill with Pineapple Juice
Parfait Glass

Combine all ingredients in a blender with ice. Blend until smooth.

Surfside Swinger

1 part Light Rum
1 part Gin
1 part Passion Fruit Juice
1/4 part Grenadine
White Wine Glass

Combine all ingredients in a blender with ice. Blend until smooth.

Sweet Love

2/3 part Crème de Cacao (Dark)
2/3 part Galliano®
2/3 part Vanilla-Flavored Vodka
2 parts Milk
1 scoop Vanilla Ice Cream
Collins Glass

Combine all ingredients in a blender. Blend until smooth.

Sweet Sunset

1 1/2 parts Light Rum
2 1/2 parts Passion Fruit Nectar
2 parts Sour Mix
1 part Strawberries
Hurricane Glass

Combine all ingredients in a blender with ice. Blend until smooth.

Taipan

2 parts Brandy
1 part Apricot Brandy
1 part Mango Juice
1/2 part Fresh Papaya
White Wine Glass

Combine all ingredients in a blender with ice. Blend until smooth.

Tan Russian

8 parts Coffee Liqueur
3 scoops Vanilla Ice Cream
fill with Milk
Coupette Glass

Combine all ingredients in a blender with ice. Blend until smooth.

Teal Squeal

1 part Vodka
1 part Blue Curaçao
2 parts Pineapple Juice
Highball Glass

Combine all ingredients in a blender with ice. Blend until smooth.

Tennessee Waltz

1 1/4 parts Peach Schnapps
2 parts Pineapple Juice
2 scoops Vanilla Ice Cream
Parfait Glass

Combine all ingredients in a blender. Blend until smooth.

Tequila Bay Breeze

1 part Tequila Rose®
1/2 part Midori®
1/2 part Blue Curaçao
1/4 part 151-Proof Rum
1 part Orange Juice
1 part Pineapple Juice
Hurricane Glass

Combine all ingredients in a blender with ice. Blend until smooth.

Terrazo

1 1/2 parts Vodka
1/2 part Crème de Banana
fill with Orange Juice
Coupette Glass

Combine all ingredients in a blender with ice. Blend until smooth.

Terry

2 parts Tequila
2 parts Coconut Cream
3 parts Orange Juice
3 parts Pineapple Juice
Hurricane Glass

Combine all ingredients in a blender with ice. Blend until smooth.

Thompson

2 parts Jägermeister®
1 part Coconut-Flavored Rum
1 part Triple Sec
3 parts Sour Mix
3 parts Pineapple Juice
Collins Glass

Combine all ingredients in a blender with ice. Blend until smooth.

Thurston Howell

3/4 part Spiced Rum
1/2 part Crème de Banana
2 parts Orange Juice
1 part Sour Mix
1/2 part Simple Syrup
1/2 part Grenadine
Hurricane Glass

Combine all ingredients in a blender with ice. Blend until smooth.

Tidbit

1 part Gin
1 scoop Vanilla Ice Cream
splash Dry Sherry
Highball Glass

Combine all ingredients in a blender with ice. Blend until smooth.

Tire Swing

1 part Rum
3 parts Amaretto
fill with Orange Juice
Coupette Glass

Combine all ingredients in a blender with ice. Blend until smooth.

Titanic Monkey

1/2 part Light Rum
1/2 part Vodka
1 1/2 parts Banana Liqueur
2 parts Coconut Cream
2 parts Pineapple Juice
Coupette Glass

Combine all ingredients in a blender with ice. Blend until smooth.

Toblerone®

1 part Frangelico®
1 part Coffee Liqueur
1 part Irish Cream Liqueur
2 parts Cream
1 part Honey
Highball Glass

Combine all ingredients in a blender with ice. Blend until smooth.

Touchie Feelie

1 1/2 parts Light Rum
1/2 part Brandy
1/4 part Passion Fruit Nectar
2 splashes Lemon Juice
Champagne Flute

Combine all ingredients in a blender with ice. Blend until smooth.

Tropic Freeze

1 1/4 parts Spiced Rum
1 1/2 parts Coconut Cream
2 parts Orange Juice
2 parts Pineapple Juice
1/2 part Grenadine
Coupette Glass

Combine all ingredients in a blender with ice. Blend until smooth.

Tropical Coffee
1 part Coconut-Flavored Liqueur
2/3 part Vanilla Liqueur
2 parts Coffee
2/3 part Cream
Collins Glass

Combine all ingredients in a blender with ice. Blend until smooth.

Tumbleweed
1 part Amaretto
1 part Crème de Cacao (White)
2 parts Cream
Coupette Glass

Combine all ingredients in a blender with ice. Blend until smooth.

Turtledove
1 part Dark Rum
1/4 part Amaretto
fill with Orange Juice
Coupette Glass

Combine all ingredients in a blender with ice. Blend until smooth.

Tutti-Frutti
1 1/2 parts Rum
1 part Papaya Juice
1 part Strawberry Puree
1 part Peach Puree
1/4 Banana
1/2 part Simple Syrup
White Wine Glass

Combine all ingredients in a blender with ice. Blend until smooth.

Up the Duff
1 part Coffee Liqueur
1 part Crème de Cacao (White)
1 part Brandy
1 scoop Vanilla Ice Cream
Highball Glass

Combine all ingredients in a blender. Blend until smooth.

Vanilla Jesus
2 parts Peach Schnapps
1 part Vodka
1 part Coconut-Flavored Rum
splash Vanilla Extract
Coupette Glass

Combine all ingredients in a blender with ice. Blend until smooth.

Very Berry Colada
1/2 part Dark Rum
3/4 part Wild Berry Schnapps
2 parts Coconut Cream
2 parts Pineapple Juice
White Wine Glass

Combine all ingredients in a blender with ice. Blend until smooth.

Very Merry Berry
3/4 part Blackberry Liqueur
3/4 part Raspberry Liqueur
3/4 part Strawberry Liqueur
1/2 part Amaretto
1 scoop Vanilla Ice Cream
White Wine Glass

Combine all ingredients in a blender with ice. Blend until smooth.

Vulgar Witch

$1^1/_2$ parts Passion Fruit Liqueur
1 part Sloe Gin
2 parts Grapefruit Juice
1 part Lime Juice
3 parts Orange Juice
Coupette Glass

Combine all ingredients in a blender with ice. Blend until smooth.

Wedding Cake

2 parts Light Rum
1 part Amaretto
1 part Cream
1 part Milk
1 part Coconut Cream
3 parts Pineapple Juice
Hurricane Glass

Combine all ingredients in a blender with ice. Blend until smooth.

A Weekend in Pleasantville

2 parts Dark Rum
1 part Coconut-Flavored Liqueur
2 parts Strawberry Puree
$^1/_2$ part Vanilla Syrup
1 part Cream
Coupette Glass

Combine all ingredients in a blender with ice. Blend until smooth.

Wet Blanket

1 part Crème de Cacao (Dark)
1 part Crème de Banana
Collins Glass

Combine all ingredients in a blender with ice. Blend until smooth.

White Dove

1 part Amaretto
1 part Crème de Cacao (White)
3 scoops Ice Cream
Coupette Glass

Combine all ingredients in a blender. Blend until smooth.

White Monkey

$1^1/_2$ parts Light Rum
$1^1/_2$ parts Dark Rum
$^1/_2$ part Crème de Banana
1 part Coconut Cream
4 parts Pineapple Juice
Hurricane Glass

Combine all ingredients in a blender with ice. Blend until smooth.

White Mountain

1 part Sake
1 part Piña Colada Mix
1 part Half and Half
Coupette Glass

Combine all ingredients in a blender with ice. Blend until smooth.

White Witch

1 part Vodka
1 part Crème de Cacao (White)
2 scoops Vanilla Ice Cream
Coupette Glass

Combine all ingredients in a blender. Blend until smooth.

Whitecap Margarita

2 parts Tequila
$1^1/_2$ parts Lime Juice
fill with Coconut Cream
Coupette Glass

Combine all ingredients in a blender with ice. Blend until smooth.

Wigwam

1 part Melon Liqueur

1 part Strawberry Liqueur

1 part Lemon Juice

Coupette Glass

Combine all ingredients in a blender with ice. Blend until smooth.

Wild Banshee

1 part Spiced Rum

1/4 part Amaretto

1 1/2 parts Half and Half

1/2 Banana

Coupette Glass

Combine all ingredients in a blender with ice. Blend until smooth.

Wild Tusker

1 part Light Rum

1 part Irish Cream Liqueur

1/2 part Amaretto

splash Crème de Cacao (Dark)

1 scoop Vanilla Ice Cream

Coupette Glass

Combine all ingredients in a blender. Blend until smooth.

Winter Sunshine

2 parts Rum

2 parts Vodka

fill with Orange Juice

1 Banana

Hurricane Glass

Combine all ingredients in a blender with ice. Blend until smooth.

World News

2 parts Dark Rum

1 part Crème de Banana

1 part Cream

1 1/2 parts Coconut Cream

1 part Pineapple Juice

1 part Strawberry Juice

1 part Blue Curaçao

Hurricane Glass

Combine all ingredients except the Blue Curaçao in a blender with ice. Blend until smooth. Top with Blue Curaçao.

Wow-Monkey

1 1/2 parts Crème de Banana

2 parts Orange Juice

1 scoop Vanilla Ice Cream

1/2 Banana

Highball Glass

Combine all ingredients in a blender with ice. Blend until smooth.

Xylophone

1 part Tequila

1/2 part Crème de Cacao (White)

1 part Crème

1/2 part Simple Syrup

Coupette Glass

Combine all ingredients in a blender with ice. Blend until smooth.

Yahoo

1 part Vodka

1 part Triple Sec

fill with Fruit Punch

Hurricane Glass

Combine all ingredients in a blender with ice. Blend until smooth.

Yellow Tiger

$1^1/_2$ part Vodka
2 scoops Ice Cream
2 parts Lemonade
Highball Glass

Combine all ingredients in a blender with ice. Blend until smooth.

Yo-Yo

1 part Banana Juice
1 part Cherry Juice
fill with Milk
Collins Glass

Combine all ingredients in a blender with ice. Blend until smooth.

Yucatán

$1^1/_2$ parts Tequila Reposado
1 part Crème de Banana
fill with Passion Fruit Juice
splash Galliano®
Collins Glass

Combine all ingredients in a blender with ice. Blend until smooth.

Yum Yum

1 part Melon Liqueur
1 part Banana Liqueur
fill with Cream
2 scoops Ice Cream
Coupette Glass

Combine all ingredients in a blender. Blend until smooth.

Zodiac

$1^1/_2$ parts Light Rum
1 part Triple Sec
$^1/_2$ part Banana Liqueur
2 parts Lemon Juice
2 parts Orange Juice
Coupette Glass

Combine all ingredients in a blender with ice. Blend until smooth.

Nonalcoholic Drinks

This section is for the two of you who bought this book but don't drink alcohol. More likely, these are for those whose turn it is to gestate, drive, or otherwise be a responsible adult. Here is a collection of drinks that allow you to watch your friends make fools of themselves (don't forget your camera) while you remain composed.

Note that some of these drinks contain grenadine. Most grenadine brands do not contain alcohol, but there arc some that do. Those that do contain alcohol have only a small amount, mainly to keep it from going bad as quickly. If your perusal of this section is part of a twelve-step program, you might want to steer clear of the grenadine, just in case.

451 Gone Sour

1 part Lemon Juice
1 part Orange Juice
fill with Club Soda
Collins Glass

Mix with ice

Ab Fab Cocktail

1/2 part Fresh Lime Juice
4 parts Lemonade
Old-Fashioned Glass

Build over ice and stir

Acapulco Glow

3 parts Pineapple Juice
1 part Cream
1 part Grapefruit Juice
1 part Coconut Cream
Collins Glass

Shake with ice and strain over ice

Afterglow

1 part Orange Juice
1 part Pineapple Juice
splash Grenadine
Highball Glass

Build over ice

Alice

1/2 part Grenadine
1/2 part Orange Juice
1/2 part Pineapple Juice
1 1/2 parts Cream
Cocktail Glass

Shake with ice and strain

Alice (Modern Long Drink)

2 parts Orange Juice
1 1/2 parts Pineapple Juice
1 part Cream
1 part Grenadine
1 part Passion Fruit Nectar
Collins Glass

Shake with ice and strain over ice

Amazing Grape

5 parts Grapefruit Juice
3 parts Grape Juice (White)
1 part Fresh Lime Juice
1/2 part Grenadine
Collins Glass

Shake with ice and strain over ice

Andre the Peachlifter

2 parts Peach Puree
1 1/2 parts Fresh Lime Juice
1 part Coconut Cream
1/2 part Vanilla Extract
Hurricane Glass

Combine all ingredients in a blender with ice. Blend until smooth.

Angel Paradise

2 parts Orange Juice
2 parts Apricot Brandy
1 1/2 parts Grapefruit Juice
splash Passion Fruit Juice
Collins Glass

Build over ice and stir

Annabelle

2 parts Pineapple Juice
2 parts Orange Juice
1 part Cream
1 part Grenadine
Collins Glass

Shake with ice and pour

Apello

2 parts Orange Juice
1 part Grapefruit Juice
1 part Apple Juice
1 Maraschino Cherry
Highball Glass

Build over ice and stir.

Apple Berry Smoothie

2 Apples, Cored and sliced
1 pint Mixed Berries
2 parts Milk
Pitcher

Combine all ingredients in a blender. Blend until smooth.

Apple Spritzer

1 part Apple Juice
1 part Club Soda
Collins Glass

Build over ice and stir

Applesinth

2 parts Apple Juice
1 part Fresh Lime Juice
splash Grapefruit Juice
Old-Fashioned Glass

Shake with ice and pour

Apricot Sparkler

1 part Apricot Juice
2 parts Club Soda
Collins Glass

Build over ice and stir

Arnold Palmer

1 part Lemonade
1 part Iced Tea
Collins Glass

Build over ice and stir

Atomic Cat
1 part Orange Juice
1 part Tonic Water
Highball Glass

Build over ice and stir.

Baan Cocktail
splash Grenadine
fill with Orange Juice
1 Orange Slice
Collins Glass

Build over ice and stir

Baby Cocktail
1 part Pineapple Juice
1 part Cream
Highball Glass

Shake with ice and pour

Bahamas
fill with Apple Juice
splash Grenadine
Collins Glass

Build over ice and stir

Banana Boat
1 Banana
3 parts Milk
1 part Coconut Cream
1 part Pineapple Juice
Collins Glass

Combine all ingredients in a blender with ice. Blend until smooth.

Banana Kong
1 part Milk
1 part Chocolate Syrup
1 part Strawberry Puree
splash Vanilla Extract
1 scoop Vanilla Ice Cream
1 scoop Orange Sorbet
Collins Glass

Combine all ingredients in a blender. Blend until smooth.

Bandita
1 Banana
8 parts Milk
Collins Glass

Combine all ingredients in a blender with ice. Blend until smooth.

Bite of the Apple
1 part Fresh Lime Juice
1/2 part Amaretto
fill with Apple Juice
Collins Glass

Build over ice and stir

Bloody Driver
3/4 parts Lime Juice
1 part Orange Juice
2 parts Tomato Juice
fill with Club Soda
Collins Glass

Build over ice and stir

Bloody OJ
splash Club Soda
splash Grenadine
fill with Orange Juice
Highball Glass

Build over ice

Bloody PJ
1 1/2 parts Banana Juice
1 1/2 parts Cherry Juice
1/2 part Mango Nectar
fill with Orange Juice
Collins Glass

Build over ice and stir

Bloody Shame
splash Tabasco® Sauce
fill with Vegetable Juice Blend
dash Salt
dash Pepper
1 Celery Stick
Old-Fashioned Glass

Build over ice and stir

Bobby Cocktail
2 splashes Orange Juice
2 splashes Lemon Juice
splash Simple Syrup
fill with Cream
Cocktail Glass

Shake with ice and strain

Bora Bora
2 parts Pineapple Juice
1/2 part Lemon Juice
splash Grenadine
Cocktail Glass

Shake with ice and strain

Bora Bora #2
1 part Pineapple Juice
1 part Ginger Ale
splash Grenadine
Collins Glass

Build over ice and stir

Cherry Bing
4 parts Cherry Juice
1 part Orange Juice
1 part Club Soda
Collins Glass

Build over ice and stir

Coconapple
1 part Coconut Cream
4 parts Pineapple Juice
Collins Glass

Combine all ingredients in a blender with ice. Blend until smooth.

Cranberry Bomber
4 parts Cranberry Juice Cocktail
1/2 parts Orange Juice
1 part Grenadine
splash Honey
Cocktail Glass

Shake with ice and strain

The Cooler
1 part Apple Juice
1 part Pineapple Juice
1 part Tonic Water
Collins Glass

Buiid over ice and stir

Cranberry Cooler
2 parts Cranberry Juice Cocktail
1 part Grape Juice (Red)
1 part Lemon-Lime Soda
Highball Glass

Build over ice and stir

Cranberry Frog
1 part Orange Juice
1 part Cranberry Juice Cocktail
fill with Club Soda
Cocktail Glass

Shake with ice and strain

Cranberry Toad
1 part Orange Juice
1 part Cranberry Juice Cocktail
Cocktail Glass

Shake with ice and strain

Crazy Cooler
1/2 part Lemon Juice
fill with Lemon-Lime Soda
splash Grenadine
Collins Glass

Build over ice and stir

Creamsicle® Shot

1 part Cream
1 part Orange Juice
Shot Glass

Shake with ice and strain.

Daydream Believer

$1\frac{1}{2}$ parts Passion Fruit Nectar
fill with Orange Juice
Collins Glass

Build over ice and stir

Designated Driver

1 part Cranberry Juice Cocktail
1 part Grapefruit Juice
1 part Orange Juice
1 part Pineapple Juice
Collins Glass

Shake with ice and pour

Ding-a-Ling

3 parts Pineapple Juice
3 parts Orange Juice
1 part Cream
Collins Glass

Shake with ice and strain over ice

Driver Cooler

2 parts Pineapple Juice
$1\frac{1}{2}$ parts Orange Juice
1 part Lemon Juice
1 part Cranberry Juice Cocktail
$\frac{1}{2}$ parts Grenadine
Collins Glass

Shake with ice and pour

Driver's Delight

$\frac{1}{2}$ parts Strawberry Syrup
fill with Iced Tea
splash Grenadine
Highball Glass

Build over ice and stir

Driver's Dream

1 part Grapefruit Juice
1 part Pineapple Juice
1 part Orange Juice
1 part Lemon Juice
1 part Grenadine
1 part Egg White
Hurricane Glass

Shake with ice and pour

Elephant Charger

2 parts Orange Juice
2 parts Milk
1 Peach, Diced
1 Banana
6 Raspberries
2 scoops Vanilla Ice Cream
Collins Glass

Combine all ingredients in a blender with ice. Blend until smooth.

Flying Fairbrother

2 parts Grapefruit Juice
1 part Orange Juice
1 part Cranberry Juice Cocktail
splash Honey
3 parts Ginger Ale
Collins Glass

Build over ice and stir

For Kids 'n' Granma's

1 part Grenadine
3 parts Banana Juice
3 parts Pear Juice
1 part Lemon Juice
Collins Glass

Shake with ice and strain over ice

Fruit Juice Cooler
1 part Cranberry Juice Cocktail
1 part Grapefruit Juice
1 part Orange Juice
1 part Pineapple Juice
fill with Ginger Ale
Collins Glass

Build over ice and stir

Fuzzless Navel
2 parts Peach Nectar
fill with Orange Juice
Highball Glass

Shake with ice and pour

Fuzzy Lemon Fizz
2 parts Peach Nectar
fill with Lemon-Lime Soda
Highball Glass

Build over ice and stir

Grapeberry
1 part Cranberry Juice Cocktail
1 part Grapefruit Juice
splash Lime Juice
Highball Glass

Shake with ice and pour

Grapefruit and Orange Cocktail
1 part Orange Juice
1 part Grapefruit Juice
Cocktail Glass

Shake with ice and strain

Grapple
1 part Grape Juice (Red)
1 part Apple Cider
splash Lemon Juice
dash Cinnamon
Coupette Glass

Combine all ingredients in a blender with ice. Blend until smooth.

Horse's Ass
1 part Ginger Ale
1 part Club Soda
Highball Glass

Build over ice and stir

Innocent Passion
splash Cranberry Juice Cocktail
splash Lemon Juice
fill with Club Soda
Highball Glass

Build over ice and stir

Keep Fit
1 part Orange Juice
1 part Mango Juice
splash Grenadine
Collins Glass

Shake with ice and pour

Keep Sober
1 part Cola
1 part Tonic Water
Collins Glass

Build over ice and stir

Kiddie Cocktail
splash Grenadine
fill with Lemon-Lime Soda
Highball Glass

Build over ice and stir

La Hoya

2 parts Orange Juice
1 part Grapefruit Juice
1/2 Banana
Collins Glass

Combine all ingredients in a blender with ice. Blend until smooth.

Lemon Cocktail

1 part Orange Juice
2 parts Lemon Juice
Cocktail Glass

Shake with ice and strain

Lime Rickey

1 part Fresh Lime Juice
splash Grenadine
fill with Sparkling Water
Collins Glass

Build over ice and stir

A Little Bit of Everything

2 parts Pineapple Juice
2 parts Orange Juice
1 part Grapefruit Juice
1 part Cola
1 part Fresh Lime Juice
1 part Lemon-Lime Soda
1/2 part Grenadine
Hurricane Glass

Build over ice and stir

Little Prince

2 parts Apple Juice
1 part Apricot Juice
Old-Fashioned Glass

Shake with ice and strain over ice

Mandy's Cure

4 parts Grapefruit Juice
1 part Fresh Lime Juice
Collins Glass

Shake with ice and pour

Mermaid's Song

2 parts Orange Juice
1 part Pineapple Juice
1 part Coconut Cream
1 part Passion Fruit Juice
1/2 part Fresh Lime Juice
White Wine Glass

Shake with ice and strain over ice

Midnight Mocktail

1 part Apricot Juice
1 part Orange Juice
Cocktail Glass

Shake with ice and strain

Morning Call

4 parts Pineapple Juice
1 part Peach Puree
1 part Lime Cordial
1/2 parts Grenadine
Collins Glass

Combine all ingredients in a blender with ice. Blend until smooth.

No Gin Fizz

4 parts Lemon Juice
1 part Lime Juice
dash Powdered Sugar
fill with Club Soda
Highball Glass

Shake all but Club Soda with ice and strain into the glass. Top with Club Soda.

No No

1 part Grenadine
1 part Apricot Nectar
1 part Red Bull® Energy Drink
Hurricane Glass

Build over ice and stir

No Rum Rickey
1 part Lime Juice
dash Bitters
splash Grenadine
fill with Club Soda
Old-Fashioned Glass

Build over ice and stir

November Cider
1 part Orange Juice
1 part Apple Juice
1 part Cold Coffee
Collins Glass

Build over ice and stir

Nursery Fizz
1 part Orange Juice
1 part Ginger Ale
Collins Glass

Build over ice and stir

Orange and Tonic
1 part Orange Juice
1 part Tonic Water
Collins Glass

Build over ice and stir

Orange Cocktail
1 part Lemon Juice
2 parts Orange Juice
Cocktail Glass

Shake with ice and strain

Orange Cream
2 splash Grenadine
1 scoop Vanilla Ice Cream
fill with Orange Juice
Collins Glass

Combine all ingredients in a blender. Blend until smooth.

Orange Velvet
1 part Cream
1 part Pineapple Juice
1 part Orange Juice
Cocktail Glass

Shake with ice and strain

Pac-Man®
2 splashes Lemon Juice
splash Grenadine
dash Bitters
fill with Ginger Ale
Highball Glass

Build over ice and stir

Passion Fruit Spritzer
2 parts Passion Fruit Juice
fill with Club Soda
Champagne Flute

Build in Flute

Passion Perfect
3 parts Passion Fruit Juice
1/2 part Grenadine
1/2 part Fresh Lime Juice
fill with Ginger Ale
Collins Glass

Build over ice and stir

Peach Creamy
2 parts Peach Juice
1 part Cream
Old-Fashioned Glass

Shake with ice and strain over ice

Piña Non Colada
2 parts Pineapple Juice
2 parts Coconut Cream
splash Lime Juice
Collins Glass

Combine all ingredients in a blender with ice. Blend until smooth.

Poco Rios

1 part Cream
1 part Fresh Lime Juice
dash Sugar
fill with Guava Juice
Collins Glass

Shake with ice and pour

Punch and Judy

3 parts Pineapple Juice
3 parts Orange Juice
1/2 part Grenadine
Collins Glass

Build over ice

Punchless Pina Colada

1 part Coconut Cream
1 part Pineapple Juice
splash Lime Juice
Highball Glass

Combine all ingredients in a blender with ice. Blend until smooth.

Pussyfoot

1 part Lemon Juice
2 parts Orange Juice
splash Grenadine
1 Maraschino Cherry
White Wine Glass

Shake with ice and pour

Quiet Passion

4 parts Grapefruit Juice
4 parts Grape Juice (White)
1 part Passion Fruit Juice
Collins Glass

Build over ice and stir

Razzle Dazzle Lemonade

1 part Passion Fruit Juice
1 part Raspberry Juice
fill with Lemonade
Collins Glass

Build over ice and stir

Rebirth

2/3 part Grenadine
2 parts Bitter Lemon Soda
2 parts Grape Juice (White)
3 parts Pineapple Juice
2/3 part Simple Syrup
Collins Glass

Build over ice and stir

Red Apple Sunset

1 part Grapefruit Juice
1 part Apple Juice
Cocktail Glass

Shake with ice and strain

Rose De Mai

2 splashes Raspberry Syrup
2 parts Cream
1 part Pineapple Juice
Cocktail Glass

Shake with ice and strain

Rumless Rickey

1 part Lime Juice
splash Grenadine
dash Bitters
fill with Club Soda
Old-Fashioned Glass

Build over ice and stir

Runner,s Mark

splash Tabasco® Sauce
splash Lemon Juice
splash Worcestershire Sauce
fill with Vegetable Juice Blend
Old-Fashioned Glass

Build over ice and stir

Safe Sex on the Beach
1 part Peach Nectar
3 parts Pineapple Juice
3 parts Orange Juice
1/4 part Grenadine
Highball Glass

Shake with ice and pour

Safety Belt
1/2 part Grenadine
1 part Pineapple Juice
1 part Lemon Juice
Cocktail Glass

Shake with ice and strain

Saint Clements
1 part Orange Juice
1 part Bitter Lemon Soda
Highball Glass

Build over ice and stir

Saint Matthew
1 part Cranberry Juice Cocktail
1 part Grapefruit Juice
1 part Orange Juice
1 part Strawberry Juice
Coupette Glass

Combine all ingredients in a blender with ice. Blend until smooth.

San Juan Capistrano
2 parts Grapefruit Juice
1 part Fresh Lime Juice
1 part Coconut Cream
White Wine Glass

Shake with ice and pour

Schmooze
1 part Orange Juice
1 part Lemon-Lime Soda
Collins Glass

Build over ice and stir

Shirley Temple
2 parts Lemon-Lime Soda
1 part Ginger Ale
splash Grenadine
1 Maraschino Cherry
Highball Glass

Build over ice and stir

Shot in the Pot
1 part Ginger Ale
1 part Tabasco® Sauce
Shot Glass

Pour ingredients into glass neat (do not chill)

Spiky Hedgehog
1 part Grenadine
1 part Cranberry Juice Cocktail
splash Lime Juice
fill with Club Soda
Highball Glass

Build over ice and stir

Stanley Spritzer
2 parts Fresh Lime Juice
1 part Ginger Ale
1 part Orange Juice
Collins Glass

Build over ice and stir

Subway Cooler
1 part Cherry Juice
2 parts Orange Juice
fill with Ginger Ale
Collins Glass

Build over ice and stir

Summer Cyclist
2 parts Strawberry Puree
2 parts Grapefruit Juice
1 part Pineapple Juice
1 scoop Orange Sorbet
White Wine Glass

Combine all ingredients in a blender. Blend until smooth.

Summer Soul Shake
1 part Strawberry Syrup
1 part Lemonade
1 part Apple Juice
splash Grenadine
Old-Fashioned Glass

Build over ice and stir

Sunset Island
$1^1/_2$ parts Pineapple Juice
1 part Grape Juice (Red)
$1^1/_2$ parts Lemon-Lime Soda
splash Simple Syrup
Collins Glass

Shake with ice and strain over ice

Tropical Fantasy
2 parts Sweetened Lime Juice
1 part Grenadine
fill with Tonic Water
Collins Glass

Build over ice and stir

Tropical Island
2 scoops Vanilla Ice Cream
2 parts Orange Juice
1 part Coconut Cream
$^1/_2$ Banana
Collins Glass

Combine all ingredients in a blender with ice. Blend until smooth.

Unfuzzy Navel
1 part Orange Juice
1 part Peach Nectar
2 splashes Lemon Juice
2 splashes Grenadine
Collins Glass

Shake with ice and pour

Vice President
$^1/_2$ part Grenadine
$^1/_2$ part Simple Syrup
2 parts Pineapple Juice
Cocktail Glass

Shake with ice and strain

Virgin Banana Colada
1 Banana
$1^1/_2$ parts Coconut Cream
fill with Pineapple Juice
Collins Glass

Combine all ingredients in a blender with ice. Blend until smooth.

Virgin Lime Rickey
1 part Lime Juice
splash Grenadine
fill with Club Soda
Highball Glass

Build over ice and stir

Virgin Margarita
1 part Lime Juice
1 part Orange Juice
fill with Sour Mix
Margarita Glass

Shake with ice and pour

Virgin Martini
1 Olive
Cocktail Glass

Place an olive in a cocktail glass

Virgin Sea Breeze
1 part Cranberry Juice Cocktail
1 part Grapefruit Juice
Highball Glass

Build over ice and stir

Wheeler Dealer

$1\frac{1}{2}$ parts Grapefruit Juice

$1\frac{1}{2}$ parts Orange Juice

$1\frac{1}{2}$ parts Grape Juice (White)

$\frac{1}{2}$ part Grenadine

fill with Tonic Water

Collins Glass

Shake all but Tonic Water with ice and strain into the glass. Top with Tonic Water.

White Splash

1 part Piña Colada Mix

3 parts Cola

Hurricane Glass

Build over ice and stir

Wholy Holy

3 parts Pineapple Juice

3 parts Orange Juice

$\frac{1}{2}$ part Lemon Juice

Highball Glass

Shake with ice and strain over ice

Xanadu

2 parts Fresh Lime Juice

2 parts Guava Juice

1 part Passion Fruit Juice

1 part Grapefruit Juice

Champagne Flute

Shake with ice and strain.

Yellow-Bellied Sap Sucker

1 part Tonic Water

1 part Lime Juice

splash Grapefruit Juice

Shot Glass

Build in the glass with no ice

Yellow Jacket

1 part Pineapple Juice

1 part Orange Juice

Old-Fashioned Glass

Shake with ice and pour

Yellow Jacket Cocktail

1 part Pineapple Juice

1 part Orange Juice

1 part Lemon Juice

Cocktail Glass

Shake with ice and strain

Yellow Orchid

1 part Grenadine

1 part Sweetened Lime Juice

1 part Orange Juice

1 part Grapefruit Juice

Collins Glass

Shake with ice and strain over ice

Index

A

Coconut-Flavored Rum

Coffee Liqueur

Coffee-Flavored Brandy

Crème de Cacao (Dark), XIX

Crème de Cassis, XIX

Crème de Coconut, XIX

Crème de Menthe (Green), XIX

R

Raspberry Liqueur

Rum, Spiced, XXII

Index

Index